The ANDREW MURRAY Devotional Reader

HIS BEST on the HIGHER LIFE

275 Chapters from 31 of Rev. Murray's Classics

Chronologically Ordered, Lightly Edited/Abridged

Set in 365 Longer Devotional Readings

REV. ANDREW MURRAY, DD

David Belt, PhD

The Reverend Andrew Murray Devotional Reader

ISBN 978-0-9989578-2-1

First published in the United States by

David Belt
Productions

Annapolis, Maryland

www.DavidBeltProductions.com

Paperback Edition Special Offer

Quantity discounts for Christian organizations and bookstores.
Free copies for Church leadership.
Contact DavidBeltProductions@gmail.com

REV. ANDREW MURRAY

A Christian mystic and evangelical of South Africa's Dutch Reformed (Presbyterian) Church, and a leading voice in the broader worldwide Higher Life and Holiness movements, Reverend Andrew Murray, D.D., wrote over two hundred books and tracts on what he called the higher, deeper, or more Spirit-filled Christian life. Although he died in 1918, over thirty of Rev. Murray's devotional-quality classics are still in print in dozens of the world's languages, and widely read across the Christian spectrum. Tens of thousands of reviews of these classics—found posted on the websites of various internet booksellers—consistently produce five-star ratings, and are typically accompanied by statements that express the profound effect of spiritual force or anointed quality of Rev. Murray's insights. Mature Christians who read Rev. Murray for the first time often express gratitude to God for having used this humble late minister to make a key difference in their spiritual life, with many even describing a more marked transformation into a much higher, richer life in Christ.

About this Devotional and Reader

The Reverend Andrew Murray Devotional Reader presents longer devotional and reader quality readings from more than 275 of the most insightful chapters in 31 of this anointed late South African minister's best loved classics on the "higher life" in Christ. Longer chapters are divided in two, producing 365 substantive daily readings, averaging two pages or so in length. The readings proceed chronologically across the span of more than fifty-five years of Rev. Murray's ministry, and capture the very best of his best spiritual insights, systematically, across the full range of his topical emphasis areas. Selected chapters are lightly abridged, and lightly edited—replacing some antiquated words—but never paraphrased, thereby faithfully presenting *only* Andrew Murray's words and voice. The resulting year with this profoundly distinctive and beloved man of God promises to powerfully help us grasp the "full salvation" that he discovered and then evangelized within the Church to such broad acclaim.

About the Editor and Author of the Introduction

Dr. David Belt, since 2008, has served as Professor, Regional Security and Intelligence Studies, in the College of Strategic Intelligence, at National Intelligence University, Washington DC—the graduate institution for the seventeen U.S. intelligence agencies. He develops and leads courses, and supervises graduate-level research, in the social analysis of strategic-level security issues in the Broader Middle East and North Africa region, including Turkey and Iran. Previously, David served as Assistant Professor, National Security Studies, National Defense University, Washington DC. In a former naval career, Captain Belt served twenty-six years on active-duty in high-risk operational, combat, and executive leadership positions in the U.S. Navy's Special Operations Officer community.

A personal note: I was—in the words of Jesus—"born again" at the U.S. Naval Academy in 1981. In the subsequent three decades of frequent military moves, I studied God's Word, studied theology at seminary, and volunteered in over a dozen churches and eight local and international ministries across the Christian spectrum. Along the way, the Lord blessed my feeble obedience with many memorable faith-building experiences. Yet, throughout, I remained under the conviction that my inner life was somehow lacking—that I was not progressing in the way that God had intended. After 33 years in this strangely unfulfilled spiritual state, our loving Father in Heaven used both a moment of crisis, and Rev. Andrew Murray, to lead me to first believe in, and then to continually experience, the markedly higher, more Spirit-filled Christian life. My aim here is to share it with you.

How to Hold This Book While Reading to Protect the Spine

To protect the thick spine of this large book and prevent creases, try and hold the book by the spine when reading, and spread open the book about three-quarters of the way. This is enough to still see part of the inside margin. You'll find that this has a nice feel.

Rev. Andrew Murray—from his book, *The Spiritual Life: A Series of Lectures Given Before the Students of the Moody Bible Institute*, the summer of 1895, on his first trip to America.

Credit: Philadelphia: George W. Jacobs & Co, 1897 (Public Domain).

CONTENTS

To Our First Love

"I know your works ….
You have tested those who say they are apostles,
but are not, and have found them to be liars.
You have endured, and have been patient,
and for My name's sake have labored and have not grown weary.

But I have something against you:
You have abandoned your first love."

—Jesus
REVELATION 2: 2–4

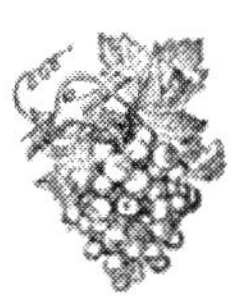

PREFACE

Our main need—Reverend Andrew Murray often said—is *more of God.* And, this was the paradigm that governed my early walk as Christian. My new life in Christ began in 1981, at the U.S. Naval Academy. It was there, at the start of my fourth year, and after having actually read the New Testament for the first time, that I knelt beside my bed in the middle of the night and gave my heart to Christ. Instantly, I was "born again"; much of the old was gone; everything—it seemed—was new. I began to experience God's discernable presence, and my new life in Christ progressed tangibly and wonderfully in those first few years. As I struggled for God, He struggled for me; He increasingly revealed Himself through His Word and other revelations, and through many memorable faith-building experiences, both privately, and while serving and leading others.

But, although I was visibly growing and experiencing God's obvious providence in my life—even having some success in building God's Kingdom in others—there remained this gnawing sense of lack. In a constant witness from God's Word and His Spirit, I sensed that both I and the Church around me were *still missing something*; I sensed that I was not progressing as I should in the realms of God's abiding presence, His holy likeness, and His power, both in prayer, and over remaining sins of omission and commission.

Of course, I did not just sit idly and allow this spiritual dissonance to fester without a fight. In every one of my thirteen military and post-military moves crisscrossing the continent and ocean, I sought feebly the presence, likeness, and power of God that I knew was lacking. I seriously pursued an advanced knowledge of God's Word, and even devoted five years of distance learning toward a master's of theology in Christian philosophy and apologetics. And, I joined and served across the full diverse gamut of Christian churches and other well-known U.S. and in international Christian ministries. Yet, no one from this wide range of Evangelical and charismatic churches or ministries, and none of the authors of the hundred or so more popular Christian books that I had read, spoke to my gnawing sense of spiritual lack in any meaningful way. So, in spite of that earnest activity, I remained camped on the desert side of the Jordan, as it were—spying into the Promised Land, but ever waiting for someone to lead me in. The fullness of God's salvation, it seemed, was not intended to be experienced in this life; that, evidently, would have to wait until after my own passing from this life, when Christ returned.

That also was something of Reverend Andrew Murray's story. He began with a great head start. His father was a minister in the Dutch Reformed (Presbyterian) Church of South Africa, and his leadership was such that Andrew at a young age had learned all of

God's Word, had embraced fully the Christian worldview, had pledged his life to serving God, and had taken the first step of more formal training for that profession, entering seminary in Holland. It was there, in seminary, that Andrew was—in his words—"born again." And, for the next fifteen years, he zealously served God as a minister of a vast frontier and mission-like parish, leading many of South Africa's toughest souls to Christ.

Yet, Rev. Murray described that early phase in his own spiritual life in the same terms that I just described more than three decades of my own—as repeated spiritual failure, marked more by struggling after a deep spiritual need that seemed impossible to satisfy. He even referred to this early stage of his spiritual life as "the time of darkness."

But, in Rev. Murray's case, a couple of profound spiritual experiences, along with mentorship by some of God's most faithful, obedient, and anointed souls, led him out of that place of desert wandering, and into the Canaan life—into a second, deeper, more Spirit-filled stage of Christian life, whereupon he began the kind of spiritual progress or sanctification that had for so long eluded him. Over the next fifty-seven years, as his experience continued to deepen, Murray faithfully evangelized within the Church this "higher life" in Christ, into which he had finally entered.

I discovered this higher life during a moment of crisis, in my mid-fifties. I had been diagnosed with an incurable heart disease that, according to several consistent studies in the medical literature, typically kills within two to five years after the onset of symptoms. It was God's grace. In that diagnosis, all of the many layers of "me"—my independent Self-reliance, my remaining worldliness, my well-developed plan for a major, innovative green energy business, my future plans for Self-pleasing, and even my major plans for serving God with the skills I had been acquiring—were stripped away. In a word, I died.

The effect was remarkable: A wave of perfect freedom and godly singlemindedness swept over me. It was then that I first realized how shackled I had been *to my Self*. And, with those shackles broken, I was finally able to do what I somehow always knew God expected; I was free to be *obedient*. So, some thirty-three years after I had knelt beside my "rack" at the Naval Academy and accepted Christ as my Savior, I once again fell to my knees in Annapolis—this time in an old colonial attic—and gave our Father the parts of me and my life that I had not yet fully surrendered. "Lord, for the time that I have left," I prayed, "here—finally—is *all* of me. In return, I want *only You*, and *all of You*."

That earnest prayer of consecration, evidently, triggered some kind of spiritual law. To my great surprise, God began to answer that prayer by giving me precisely what I had asked for. But, He did this in a way that I had never conceptualized; He began to fill me with the *only* and *all* of Himself. Several times a day from then on, God's enrapturing presence has graced many of the moments of my long, busy days as a national security professional in Washington DC. That "presence" was palpable; I was just as much aware of Him in me as I was of anything around me that I could grasp with my physical senses. Without the lexicon for this second seminal experience of God's grace, I could only describe it to my family and closest brothers as "like being born again—*again*."

This far greater and abiding presence of God's Holy Spirit had a surprising effect—doing for me what I had been powerless to do for so many years. By making room for

God's Holy Spirit to fill and rule all of my life, the Spirit of Christ could finally markedly sanctify me—replacing much of my old Self-life with so much more of Christ's likeness. I immediately experienced a triumph over remaining worldliness, unbecoming habits, and my rather worldly, carnal thought-life that had still plagued my conscience all those years since my initial salvation. Those that stubbornly remained, steadily diminished.

While I was still growing in, and trying to make theological sense of, this unexpected higher, deeper, more spiritual life, it seemed that another spiritual law had been triggered: I began to discern the Holy Spirit's leading in a more palpable way. This first emerged with the sense that God wanted to extend this new life into the realm of my physical body. It was in this leading, one day at lunch, that I typed the words, "Divine healing" into YouTube. From my charismatic and Pentecostal church experiences, I thought that I would not hear anything new about what God's Word said or implied about healing. After an unmoving experience watching two popular preachers on that topic, I scrolled down and landed on an audiobook with the words, "Divine Healing" and the picture of an old man on the cover. It was then that I discovered Andrew Murray.

God's anointing on this late South African minister was evident from the start. The book's title, *Divine Healing*, I thought, would be about the prospect of God healing my body. Yet, every sentence was more about healing my spirit. Rev. Murray spoke a new, and far more spiritual language; it was quite unlike that of other Christian writers and leaders. There was a revelational quality to it. I heard myself saying things like "I sort of knew that; but I didn't know it like that," or "I've *never* heard that!" Although my spiritual paradigm already had begun to rupture, Murray provided the doctrinal understanding of what I was experiencing, along with a new lexicon to adequately describe it.

After re-listening to *Divine Healing*, I listened to two other books by Murray—*Absolute Surrender and Other Addresses*, and *The Spiritual Life—A Series of Lectures Delivered Before the Students of the Moody Bible Institute, Chicago, 1895.* Despite their focus on different topics, the impact was identical: A decades-old Christian, I was profoundly moved in new ways.

Of course, I wanted to know more about Andrew Murray. A celebrated leader in the evangelical and holiness movements of his day, I learned that he had somehow managed to publish an astounding number of works by the time of his passing in 1917—many still in print in dozens of languages, and read across the global Church spectrum. With each of them that I could find and read, there were new revelations from God.

Another blessing still, was when I began reading the reviews of his works that were posted to the websites of various internet booksellers. It was clear that Murray's insights on what he called the higher, more Spirit-filled, victorious life in Christ were transforming these readers—reproducing in many something of my own recent experience.

Why had I never heard of him? Of the hundreds of pastors, leaders, authors, and fellow believers around the world, whom I had known, read their works, or listened to on the radio or television, why had none of them ever mentioned this anointed evangelist and shepherd of the Spirit-filled life? His obscurity seemed a great loss for the Church.

So, I wondered: How could I share Andrew Murray's insights into this higher Christian life with my family and friends? Giving them even three books would not suffice.

Why? Because, Murray's spiritual insights grew as he grew; each of his works along his ministry years contained unique and indispensable treasures that his other books did not capture nearly as well. Although I might reread several of his books each year, I knew that others read little, and only then during their devotional time. What we need, it seemed, is an anthology of Murray's better insights set into a devotional format. We needed one that more substantively and systematically shares the very best of his best, across his lifetime of writing, and across all of the key emphasis areas in his higher Christian life paradigm. Finding nothing like that, I set out to create this "devotional-reader."

How This Devotional Reader Was Produced

To begin, I obtained thirty-five of Dr. Murray's most-important and popular books, spanning the fifty-seven years of his writing. For the next three years, I immersed myself in them—reading, rereading, and listening to them. This process produced over 275 of Murray's best chapters across the full range of his topical emphasis areas.

Second, I lightly edited these chapters. Since Rev. Murray wrote in the 1800s, this step corrected some of the antiquated and British spellings and removed the Elizabethan variants, so as not to be a continual stumbling block for modern readers. As another light editing function, I usually made the subject and object personal pronouns consistent, and changed about half of them to the gender-neutral.

Third, I abridged the majority of these chapters by simply omitting sentences or paragraphs that were redundant. Here, I followed Murray's own practice. He produced "a series of abstracts" from the longer mid-1700s works of the English mystic, William Law, published, and abridged the post-Reformation theologian Walter Marshall's classic 1692 work *The Gospel Mystery of Sanctification.* Murray defended his abridgements as always retaining "the author's own words," and only "leaving out what was not essential to his argument, and shortening when he appeared diffuse." Similarly, never in a single sentence did I summarize or paraphrase Murray. To show where unessential, less anointed sentences or paragraphs were omitted, I inserted the symbol for such ellipses— "…".

Lastly, I divided longer chapters or addresses into two and sometimes three longer sections, until I had 365 devotional quality selections, under two pages of reading length.

As the result of this painstaking process—by far, the best three years of my life—you are now holding what I hope you will agree is a highly readable compendium of the best of Andrew Murray's lifetime of insights into the higher Christian life.

David Belt, September 2017

Post Script

As a sequel and companion to this devotional reader, I have written the forthcoming *Reverend Andrew Murray's Spiritual Biography.* That 400-page "spiritual biography" blends the more important spiritual events from Rev. Murray's life, with a systematic theology or map of the key belief-strands regarding the higher life in Christ that he acquired and then championed. Greatly, expanding upon the following introduction, it proceeds chronologically and hermeneutically by setting his key belief-forming experiences and the beliefs themselves in the historical and interpersonal contexts that shaped them.

REVEREND

ANDREW MURRAY

INTRODUCTION

by David Belt, PhD

In 1978, South Africa issued a postage stamp to commemorate the 150th anniversary of the birth of the man whose statue (right) stands in front of Cape Town's *Groote Kerk* (Great Church): The Reverend Andrew Murray (1828–1917).

People gain such stature not from performance that is common, but from that which is uncommon. Often, such distinction arises from performance of something *more*, or *uniquely produced*, or *better* than the others in the field. In other instances, such distinction arises from performance of something remarkably *different*, or *new*—even revolutionary.

Clearly, Andrew Murray stands out in the performance categories of "more" and "uniquely produced." In an active writing ministry of over five-and-a-have decades, he published more than 240 books and tracts. Even more remarkably, was the unique way in which they were produced. Most of these books—many of which are now classics and increasingly consumed—were unpremeditated, or written extemporaneously, without notes and without a series of editing. Due to a problem with his hand, he dictated most of them to his daughter, in a few settings, amidst the rush of his busy days as an evangelical leader. In other words, he simply spoke these remarkable books into existence. They simply flowed out of him!

Still more profound was the rate at which he produced them. Murray often completed several chapters in a single day. One day, for instance, Murray began and completed *eighteen* chapters of his book *Joy*, or—in his native Dutch—*De Blijdschap.*[1]

But, for those Christians worldwide who have discovered Andrew Murray's books, his stature has stemmed from their *qualitative* content. These books gained such a following during his life for two main reasons: first, because of the unique insights they contain into what Rev. Murray began to call the "higher life" in Christ; and, second, due to their transformational power to help us believe in that life, and to obtain it. For many even long-time students of God's Word, Murray's books have what they describe as a revelational or anointed quality—as if the author had been carried along by the Holy Spirit.

From this, Rev. Murray gained an international following. People wanted to meet this humble South African minister whose books had so improved their spiritual life. One of them was evangelist Rev. Dwight L. Moody. Moody gained renown for having led England through its first post-Wesleyan revival—what some have described as "one of the most remarkable religious movements of the nineteenth century, or indeed of any century of the Christian era."[2] Moody saw Murray as a latter-day prophet, and so he zealously promoted dozens of his books through his Moody Press and Revell publishing house. In 1895, he pleaded with Murray to participate in the 13th General Bible Conference in Northfield Massachusetts. Even Moody's biography lauded Murray, describing the impact that he had on the Christian leaders at that landmark Bible conference:

> Each morning … in the August conference of 1895, we enjoyed an hour which was spent as nearly within the holy of holies as is possible this side of heaven, while Andrew Murray, that true mystic, yet faithful worker, who exemplified in such remarkable degree the humility, purity, and love which he urged upon his eager auditors, with the authority of a veritable prophet of God, and yet with the yearning of a spiritual father pleading with his own children that they might be willing to be blessed in soul as they were in body. Holiness is the supreme aim and passion of Andrew Murray's life, and his mind and soul seemed consumed with the longing that every child of God should become like Christ in purity and beauty of character.[3]

Some four-hundred ministers and evangelists attending this conference collectively wrote this letter of gratitude to Andrew Murray for helping them gain an a "*new insight*" into a fuller prospect for their salvation. Never, the said, "have we heard such teaching":

> We, the ministers of the gospel and evangelists assembled at the Northfield Conference, desire to put on record for the glory of God, our grateful thanksgiving for the *new insight* into the word of God, the *new apprehension* of our standing, privileges, and possibilities in Christ Jesus, and the *new advance* toward the *fuller* acceptance and enjoyment of the exceeding great and glorious promises which are in Him, which have *come to us* as the blessed fruit of these weeks of communion with each other and the

Lord. … And we desire to express to our beloved brethren, Rev. Andrew Murray and Rev. Prebendary H.W. Webb-Peploe, who have led us in our studies in the word, and deep sense of indebtedness for their *clear, searching, candid, scriptural, and spiritual expositions and applications of God's truth*. In their words, *we have heard God speaking to us*, calling us to holiness, to separation from the world unto himself, and inviting us *to a new life* of the rest of faith. *Never have we heard teaching* that has more magnified and glorified the all-sufficiency of the power and grace of God. And we unitedly pray God to pour into their hearts rich recompense, long to spare their lives and greatly to multiply their seed sown, that thousands may, through them, become *partakers of the fullness* [*emphasis added*].[4]

The signifiers of their letter—"new insight," "new apprehension," "new advance," and "fuller"—are those of discovery, and are typical of many seasoned Christians who stumble onto Andrew Murray for the first time. Writing one year after his death, for instance, Rev. Murray's earliest biographer—after inspecting over one hundred and fifty letters from total strangers—concluded:

> Unknown persons in every quarter of the globe hail him as their spiritual father, and ascribe whatever growth their Christian life has undergone to the influence of his priceless devotional works. "What I owe to you eternity alone will reveal," is the language of a lady in New South Wales; and her testimony can be paralleled by that of correspondents from the United States and Canada, Great Britain and the Continent, Holland and South Africa, India, China and Australasia.[5]

This kind of acclaim continues today. At the moment when I began to research this introduction, in November 2016, for example, the following review had just been posted to the internet bookseller Amazon.com, for Andrew Murray's *first* classic, *Abide in Christ*:

> Most impactful book ever. Broke so many chains in my life as I used this book as a daily devotional. I love Andrew Murray works. Floored by the giftedness that God gave to him to explain scripture.

Another reader at this same instance posted this about Murray's fifth classic, *The Spirit of Christ*: "This book *had to be inspired*. I've read it twice and intend to read it again. It is one of my lifetime favorites" (Amazon.com). Similarly, at his same juncture, the last three readers who Rev. Murray's classic, *Absolute Surrender*, had this to say:

> *Five Stars: Life changing!*—Excellent material for Spiritual Enrichment!!! The author breaks down areas of a Christian's life that might be hidden to the individual, which need to be surrender if they want the Holy Spirit to have total access to his or her life. ….
>
> *Five Stars: Excellent book on developing an intimate relationship with the Lord Jesus Christ*—Excellent: Absolute Surrender challenges us to become more than complacent Christians, going through the motions and not really connecting with Christ moment to moment. It's a book that I read and reread, drawing something fresh and challenging each time. A true blessing.
>
> *Five Stars: Surely one of the great books of history*—Wonderful news of Surrender: This book is wonderfully described. I am so thankful for Andrew's inspired writings from God. Each book seems to unveil more of what it means to have a continuous walk

with God. I am so thankful for Andrew's struggles towards total surrender and for his willingness to share that struggle with us. … Thank you God for these inspiring books.

The Holy Spirit, the Presence of God, and Holiness: Full Salvation

That last reviewer's notion that Rev. Murray's inspiration evidently stemmed from his own "struggles towards total surrender," is something that Murray candidly admitted. But, it was only two times in fifty-seven years of writing ministry that he grudgingly relented and shared his personal testimony with fellow ministers. Speaking at the urging of an assembly of ministers at Chicago's Moody Bible Institute during his much-anticipated trip to America in 1895, for instance, Murray began telling of his struggle-filled spiritual journey. "I could divide my Christian life into three periods," he said: "The time of darkness, the time of the vision of the light, and then the time of the richer experience."[6]

The first of these periods, "the time of darkness," began in the wake of his own remarkable salvation. That landmark event did not occur in his home, under the leadership of his father who was a prominent Dutch Reformed minister; it occurred at seminary in Holland, as a result of an extracurricular Christian club. Murray recorded that first spiritual leap in his 1945 letter home. "My dear Parents," he began, "I am sure, will be your delight when I tell you that I can communicate to you far gladder tidings, over which angels have rejoiced, that your son has been born again."[7]

For the next "fifteen years after my conversion," Murray went on, "I was, as a young minister, most earnest," and "I was counted a most faithful gospel preacher … diligent in the enormous parish that was entrusted to me." At this point, he was ministering in rugged missionary conditions—in colonial hinterlands, among fiercely independent farmers, the Boers, and even spent his vacations on new evangelistic thrusts into this wild.

Yet, while his outward Christian activity seemed to be exceeding the prevailing norm of a surrendered Christian life, Murray then told the ministers assembled that his inner spiritual life was still marked more by lack than any fullness. "I loved my work," he said, "and yet all the time my spiritual life was one of deep unhappiness."

At the "Higher Life" movement's annual convention that same year, in Keswick, England, stenographers captured the only other instance where Murray, when asked by several of the ministers, again reluctantly and briefly shared that basic testimony:

> Some of you have heard how I have pressed upon you the two stages of the Christian life, and the step from the one to the other. The first ten years of my spiritual life were manifestly spent on the lower stage. I was a minister, I may say, as zealous and as earnest and as happy in my work as anyone, as far as love of the work was concerned. Yet, all the time, there was burning my heart a dissatisfaction and restlessness inexpressible.[8]

He added that although he knew he was saved, there was something out of sorts—a kind of dissonance between his experience and the promised life God's Word calls us to.

> I remember in my little room in Bloemfontein how I used to sit and think, "What is the matter?" Here I am knowing that God has justified me in the blood of Christ,

but I have no power for service. My thoughts, my words, my actions, my unfaithfulness—everything troubled me. Though all around thought me one of the most earnest of men, my life was one of deep dissatisfaction.[9]

Part of Andrew Murray's deep dissatisfaction during that lower stage of his spiritual life seemed to be a function of his increasing awareness of the low, lukewarm condition of the Church. As he expressed this in an 1852 letter to his brother John, "I begin to fear that the state of the great majority of members is much sadder than I at first realized."[10]

An Outpouring of the Holy Spirit

Eight years after penning that letter, something happened that would finally begin to lead both Rev. Murray and the South African Church out of that sad spiritual state. It was then that a remarkable outpouring of the Holy Spirit—what has become known as South Africa's great revival—took place in the small parish to which Rev. Murray had just been posted. As he put it at Keswick:

> So the Lord led me till in His great mercy I had been eleven or twelve years in Bloemfontein. Then He brought me to another congregation in Worcester, about the time when God's Holy Spirit was being poured out in America, Scotland and Ireland. In 1860 when I had been six months in the congregation, God poured out His Spirit there in connection with my preaching, especially as I was moving about in the country, and *a very unspeakable blessing came to me.*[11]

Of this "very unspeakable blessing," Andrew was then careful to clarify that he was *not* speaking of his first born-again experience, which had occurred fifteen years earlier, in 1845. Of that much earlier spiritual experience, he told the ministers gathered: "My justification was clear as the noonday; I knew the hour in which I received from God the joy of pardon."[12] Then, *what was he referring to*? In the ensuring fifty-seven years of ministry until his passing, this was the only instance in which he even mentioned anything that God had done for him in the revival. A cursory analysis of his discourse in the immediate wake of the revival quickly answers our question; it is filled with highly unorthodox references to this one subjective, experiential blessing: *the palpable and continual presence of God.*

Although such discourse was unorthodox, it was not entirely new. Despite having been relegated to obscurity by the prevailing Church orthodoxy, the transformational experience of the palpable, abiding, indwelling presence of God in this life had been a key theme of Christian mysticism for centuries; it was popularized in the classic *The Practice of the Presence of God*—the account of 17th century French mystic, Brother Lawrence.

And, in spite of the Church's typical silence on this subjective part of God's salvation, it was the chief miraculous experience that Murray empirically observed in fellow parishioners during the revival. According to historian Olea Nel, the key mark of this outpouring of the Spirit in South Africa was the actual experience of God's presence, and how it remained nearly continually in people. In one instance, she recorded in her *South Africa's Forgotten Revival*, "The presence of the Spirit was so powerful" that a meeting that began on Sunday "lasted non-stop until Tuesday midday," and "only then did the farmers and their families return home."[13] Recounting a similar experience during the revival, Rev. J.C.

De Vries, wrote of the impact of this infilling of God's Spirit:

> A feeling which I cannot describe took possession of me. Even now, forty-three years after these occurrences, the events of that never-to-be-forgotten night pass before my mind's eye like a soul-stirring panorama. I feel again as I then felt, and I cannot refrain from pushing my chair backwards, and thanking the Lord fervently for His mighty deeds.[14]

That Murray himself experienced for the first time this transformational abiding presence of Christ, is corroborated by the title and major theme of his first post-revival book, *Abide in Christ.* Every page of that book was permeated with a strange, new discourse about our Lord's call and provision for this subjective, mystical experience of his palpable presence in our everyday lives, via the fuller infilling of His Holy Spirit. It begins this way:

> During the life of Jesus on earth, the word He chiefly used when speaking of the relations of the disciples to Himself was: "Follow me." When about to leave for Heaven, He gave them a new word, in which their more *intimate and spiritual union* with Himself in glory should be expressed. That chosen word was: "*Abide in Me*."
>
> If, in our orthodox Churches, the abiding in Christ, the living union with Him, the *experience of His daily and hourly presence* and keeping, were preached with the same distinctness and urgency as His atonement and pardon through His blood, I am confident that many would be found to accept with gladness the invitation to such a life, and that its influence would be manifest in their experience of the purity and the power, the love and the joy, the fruit-bearing, and all the blessedness which the Savior connected with the abiding in Him.

Filling a deep spiritual need or gap in the prevailing orthodox Church paradigm, the book quickly attained international acclaim; as the testimony of its readers above suggest, it transformed the lives of so many similarly struggling Christians on several continents.

Holiness, "Full Salvation"

In addition to the bringing the presence of Christ, Murray also observed during the revival how the Spirit's fuller indwelling led his parishioners to the conviction of their *remaining* sin, and remarkable progress in their sanctification. The revival's historian, Olea Nel, recorded believers' typical "experience when the Holy Spirit sweeps over them":

> The first thing that happens is that they became achingly aware of their sinfulness in the presence of God's glorious holiness. They weep and moan in agony over their sin. And it is only after a protracted inner wrestling (which can last for days) that joy and love finally floods their souls.[15]

On April 18, 1861, for instance, the revival that had begun in Murray's parish had moved to his birthplace—the small village of Graaff-Reinet. At prayer meeting after a communion service one Sunday evening, "Scoffers, who had come to the meeting out of blatant curiosity, were soon overcome by the Holy Spirit and convicted of sin."[16]

Murray's first biographer, reading letters from those present, similarly described this powerful experience of God's holiness when they were overcome with his Holy Spirit:

In the Breede River ward of the Worcester congregation, several months previously,

> a weekly prayer-meeting had been instituted, in which, however, so little interest was displayed that the usual attendance was but three or four. But when the influences of God's Spirit began to be felt, young and old, parents and children, white and coloured, flocked to the gathering, driven by a common impulse to cast themselves before God and utter their souls in cries of penitence.[17]

From his observation in others and personal experience of this remarkable abiding presence of God and deep conviction and power of holiness, Rev. Murray's paradigm on redemption gradually *expanded.* Our salvation, he increasingly believed, was meant to include so much "*more of God*"—as he put it—than the prevailing Reformed and evangelical Church orthodoxy had allowed. The first and more objective blessing of salvation of the New Covenant—the central focus of the Evangelical movement—is for the *unbeliever*; it imparts by faith *legal righteousness*, or the removal of the *guilt* of sin. The second and more subjective blessing of our salvation—the one much less widely believed and experienced—is for the *believer*; it offers—by still more faith and surrender—*intimate holiness.* It does this through the mystical imparting of His complete and continual abiding presence—an "intimate and spiritual union"—with Christ.

Such talk about an expanded concept of redemption, Murray knew, was threatening to the established Reformed paradigm. Yet, he was certain about what he had witnessed and experienced. And, so, even that first post-revival book had a reformationist edge: "If we ask the reason why those who have indeed accepted the Savior, and been made partakers of the renewing of the Holy Spirit, thus come short of the *full salvation* prepared for them," he wrote; "I am sure the answer will in very many cases be, that ignorance is the cause of the unbelief that fails of the inheritance." He added: "We have become so accustomed to a low life of continual stumbling that we hardly desire, and still less expect, deliverance." "Holiness," he further added, "perfect conformity to Jesus, unbroken fellowship with His love, can scarcely be counted distinct articles of our creed."

The Church's unbelief about this fuller salvation that God had promised had an internal source, and Murray named it: the doctrine of "free grace." As with all paradigms, this prevailing doctrine had veiled the pervasive scriptural discourse on holiness; it obscured God's will, His command, and His provision for the *believer who had been saved by grace* to then go on to perfection, as Paul said, or perfect obedience to "be holy," or "be perfect," as Jesus commanded, and as so many of the apostles instructed and expected in their epistles. In his Chicago testimony, Murray noted that, even as a young minister, his spiritual life was hindered by this doctrine of free grace:

> I was, as a young minister, most earnest. I was counted a most faithful gospel preacher, and I was diligent in the enormous parish that was entrusted to me. I loved my work and yet all the time my spiritual life was one of deep unhappiness. …
>
> One thing that I thought was that a Christian must go on sinning every day. I really thought that this was a must. As a result of that, I had no definite expectation that God would keep me from it. I am sorry to say that that was my belief, and then along with that I had no conception that obedience was a possible thing. I look back with shame when, in later years, I began to see the place that obedience ought to take in a Christian life. I remember how little I understood that—that Christianity is to

give up yourself to entire obedience to God. I never saw it.

This distorted doctrine of free grace, Murray added, was so strong that it took him several years after the revival before he finally grasped the importance that God intended a "perfect heart"—a heart surrendered to full obedience to occupy in the believer's life:

> It was at that time, now thirty years ago, in a time of revival in my Dutch parish in South Africa, that I wrote "Abide in Christ" in Dutch. It was not, perhaps, exactly the same as now, but the substance. It was at that time that my heart was feeling after the truth and beginning to find it, beginning to get hold of something—a little of the blessed experience of better knowledge of God and of more trust in Him. And yet I have to confess with shame that, at that time, I often stumbled. One thing was, I had never been taught the absolute necessity, the supreme importance of literal, immediate, actual obedience to God.

The doctrine of free grace, when misapplied to the believer, instead of the *un*believer, Murray realized, had stunted the spiritual growth of the Church; it had the effect of keeping us as babe-like or "carnal" Christians, whose outwardly observable lives were not all that different from the masses of socially-concerned, compassionate unbelievers. Here is Murray expressing this point in *Abide in Christ*, using Paul's distinction between the "righteousness and sanctification" aspects of Christ's "redemption" (1 Corinthians 1: 30):

> The word *redemption*, though sometimes applied to our deliverance from the guilt of sin, here refers to our complete and final deliverance from all its consequences, when the Redeemer's work shall become fully manifest, even to the redemption of the body itself (Romans 8: 21–23; Ephesians 1: 14; 4: 30). … As a Priest, He is our righteousness, restoring us to right relations to God, and securing us His favor and friendship. As a King, He is our sanctification, forming and guiding us into the obedience to the Father's holy will. As these three offices work out God's one purpose, the grand consummation will be reached, the complete deliverance from sin and all its effects be accomplished, and ransomed humanity regain all that it had ever lost.

In *Abide in Christ's* preface, Murray lamented that this second, more subjective New Covenant provision was little known:

> It is to be feared that there are many earnest followers of Jesus from whom the meaning of this word, with the blessed experience it promises, is very much hidden. While trusting in their Savior for pardon and for help, and seeking to some extent to obey Him, they have hardly realized to what closeness of union, to what intimacy of fellowship, to what wondrous oneness of life and interest, He invited them when He said, "*Abide in Me.*" This is not only an unspeakable loss to themselves, but the Church and the world suffer in what they lose.

Despite his early, post-revival confidence in this new spiritual paradigm, Murray, later at Keswick, admitted that he was then only beginning to grasp and experience it all:

> The first Dutch edition of my book *Abide in Christ* was written at that time. I would like you to understand that a minister or Christian author may often be led to say more than he has experienced. I had not then experienced all that I wrote of: I cannot say that I experience it all perfectly, even now.[18]

The Higher Life and Broader Holiness Movements

Andrew Murray's discovery of God's second and more subjective part of redemption, he later shared at Keswick, began to accelerate a decade after South Africa's revival:

> God helped me, and for seven or eight years I went on, always enquiring and seeking and always getting. Then came, about 1870, the great Holiness Movement. The letters that appeared in *The Revival* touched my heart; and I was in close fellowship with what took place at Oxford and Brighton and it all helped me.[19]

England's holiness movement was already changing lives by 1873. Anglican Church leader, Canon Battersby, recounted how it was at that year's Oxford Convention that he witnessed to having "received a new and distinct blessing to which he had been a stranger before." For the previous 25 years, Canon Battersby had been a most diligent minister of the gospel, and, judging from his journals, most faithful in seeking to maintain a close walk with God. But, as a result of these early meetings, he began to read what was being published of the "Higher Life"—a term and movement derived from the book, *The Higher Christian Life*, by the Presbyterian businessman-turned-minister, William E. Boardman, who popularized holiness in non-Methodist terms. The effect was to render Battersby utterly dissatisfied with his spiritual state. That conviction, in turn, led to what he described as a kind of second conversion into an entirely new life in Christ.

The Higher Life Movement grew more prominent by 1874, when Philadelphia Quakers, Hannah Whitall Smith and Robert Pearsall Smith, capably advanced this imperative of holiness in these British cities. The next June, Canon Battersby—inspired by his new Spirit-filled life—began organizing the Higher Life Movement's annual convention in Keswick, England. He announced this first "Keswick Convention" this way:

> Many are everywhere thirsting that they may be brought to enjoy more of the Divine presence in their daily life, and a fuller manifestation of the Holy Spirit's power, whether in subduing the lusts of the flesh, or in enabling them to offer more effective service to God. It is certainly God's will that His children should be satisfied in regard to these longings, and there are those who can testify that He has satisfied them, and does satisfy them with daily fresh manifestations of His grace and power.[20]

After the convention, Battersby wrote "There is a very remarkable resemblance in the testimonies I have since received as to the nature of the blessing obtained, viz., the ability given to make a full surrender to the Lord, and the consequent experience of an abiding peace, far exceeding anything previously experienced."[21] Andrew Murray would later describe the Higher Life or Keswick Movement this way: "Through all the chief thought, was Christ, first drawing and enabling the soul to rest in Him, and then meeting it with the fulfillment of its desire, the abiding experience of His power to keep it in victory over sin, and communion with God."[22]

By 1877, Rev. Murray had begun to converse with many of the leaders of the broader holiness trend in America. Their testimonies about discovering a much more victorious Christian life than they had expected, aligned with what Murray had witnessed in South Africa's revival, and what he himself had begun to experience. From this cloud of many witnesses, he gained sufficiently more confidence about this new spiritual paradigm to set down his sequel to *Abide in Christ.* That second post-revival book, *Like Christ*, was a clarion call to (and a manual for) entering Christ-like holiness. Murray began that book explaining his purpose, to show "that likeness to Christ is no mere ideal, but—through the power of the Holy Spirit—a most blessed reality." He added:

> *Abiding in Christ and walking like Christ*: these are the two blessings of the new life which are here set before us in their essential unity. The fruit of a life *in Christ* is a life *like Christ.* … The second expression, walking like Christ, is not less significant than the first. It is the promise of the wonderful power which the abiding in Him will exert. As the fruit of our surrender to live wholly in Him, His life works so mightily in us, that our walk, the outward expression of the inner life, becomes like His. The two are inseparably connected. The abiding in always precedes the walking like Him. And yet the aim to walk like Him must equally precede any large measure of abiding. Only then is the need for a close union fully realized, or is the Heavenly Giver free to bestow the fullness of His grace, because He sees that the soul is prepared to use it according to His design. When the Savior said, "If you keep my commandments, you shall abide in my love," He meant just this: the surrender to walk like Me is the path to the full abiding in Me. Many a one will discover that just here is the secret of his failure in abiding in Christ; he did not seek it with the view of walking like Christ.

In the spirit of a reformationist, Murray filled the book with gentle chastisements that recentered our God's greater commission to abide in and walk like Christ:

> Every believer is *in* Christ; but not everyone *abides* in Him, in the consciously joyful and *trustful surrender of the whole being* to His influence. You know what abiding in Him is. It is to consent with our whole soul to His being our life, to reckon upon Him to inspire us in all that goes to make up life, and then to *give up everything most absolutely for Him to rule and work in us*. It is the rest of the full assurance that He does, each moment, work in us what we are to be, and so Himself enables us to maintain that *perfect surrender*, in which He is free to do all His will. Let all who do indeed long to walk like Christ take courage at the thought of what He is and will prove Himself to be if they trust Him. He is the *True Vine.* … We have only to consent to be branches. Honor Him by a joyful trust that He is, beyond all conception, the *True Vine*, holding you by His almighty strength, supplying you from His infinite fullness.

Full salvation, or holiness—Christlike obedience—begins with the abiding, or continual presence of God. "The Indwelling Presence alone makes us holy," he wrote in *Like Christ.* Here is how he expressed this in his third work of the series, *Holy in Christ*:

> The Holy One is the holy-making One: He redeems and saves that He may win our confidence for Himself, that He may draw us to Himself as the Holy One, that in the personal attachment to Himself we may learn to obey, to become of one mind with Him, to be holy as He is holy. … It is that energy of the Divine life in the power of which God not only keeps Himself free from all creature weakness or sin, but unceasingly seeks to lift the creature into union with Himself and the full participation of His own purity and perfection. … It is in the adoring contemplation of His holiness, in the trustful surrender to it, in the loving fellowship with Himself, the Holy One, that we can be made holy.

The degree of God's presence is synonymous with the degree of the fullness of the Holy Spirit. Murray's concept of full salvation, therefore, was reformationist in its firmer concept of the Trinity; it entailed a much-expanded role for the heretofore scarcely mentioned or understood Holy Spirit. We see this in Murray's first post-revival book, where he mentioned the Holy Spirit nearly *three hundred* times—each reference in the context of God's indwelling Spirit who makes us Holy. Its sequel, *Like Christ*, similarly, was just as unorthodox in its more developed concept of the Trinity and its emphasis on the present ministry of the Holy Spirit—whom Murray referred to at least once on nearly every one of the book's hundred pages. In comparison, the most popular Christian book other than the Bible itself, and the foundational text for the Holiness movement—Thomas à Kempis's *The Imitation of Christ* (ca 1418–1427)—mentions the Holy Spirit only *seven* times, and then only as customary, such that its omission would not affect sentence meaning. Why this huge disparity? Again, because, in Murray's higher life paradigm, all real imitation of Christ depends on being filled with the Spirit. In his words, from *Like Christ*:

> To be like Christ we must be led by the same Spirit, and to be led by the Spirit as He was, we must be filled with the Spirit. Nothing less than the fullness of the Spirit is absolutely necessary to live a truly Christian, Christ-like life.
>
> The way to arrive at it is simple. It is Jesus who baptizes with the Spirit: we who come to Him desiring it will get it. All that He requires of us is, the surrender of faith to receive what He gives. What He asks is whether we are indeed in earnest to follow in His footsteps, and for this to be baptized of the Spirit. … Acknowledge the sacred right of ownership Christ has in you, His blood-bought ones: and let nothing prevent your answering: "Yes, dear Lord, as far as is allowed to a child of dust, I will be like You. I am entirely Yours; I must, I will, in all things bear Your image. It is for this I ask to be filled with the Spirit."

This more balanced Trinity, or increased importance of the Holy Spirit in God's great plan for us in this life, would be a mark of all Murray's subsequent works as well. His next classic, *Holy in Christ*, for instance, has nearly *five-hundred* references to the fruit of holiness that flows from the Holy Spirit's fuller indwelling. His fifth classic, *The Spirit of Christ*—the Church's most-important, seminal treatise on the Holy Spirit—has more than a thousand references to "the Spirit who makes the spiritual man." Here is one of them:

> It is generally admitted in the Church that the Holy Spirit has not the recognition which becomes Him as being the equal of the Father and the Son, the Divine Person through whom alone the Father and the Son can be truly possessed and known, in whom alone the Church has her beauty and her blessedness. In the Reformation, of blessed memory, the Gospel of Christ had to be vindicated from the terrible misapprehension which makes man's righteousness the ground of his acceptance, and the freeness of Divine grace had to be maintained. To the ages that followed was committed the trust of building on that foundation, and developing what the riches of grace would do for the believer through the indwelling of the Spirit of Jesus. The Church rested too content in what it had received, and the teaching of all that the Holy Spirit will be to each believer in His guiding, sanctifying, strengthening power, has never yet taken the place it ought to have in our evangelical teaching and living.

For Murray, recapturing the Church's misplaced center of the Holy Spirit was an evangelical imperative. In *The Key to the Missionary Problem*—his response to the *Report of the Ecumenical Missions Conference*, held in New York in 1900, for instance, he dealt with the low state of the Church with regard to world missions by forcefully pointing evangelicals back to Pentecost. Over two hundred times in that text, Murray interchangeably used the words "Holy Spirit" and its symbol, "Pentecost," to pinpoint the key to the Church's poor performance in the Lord's last great commission. For Murray, it was simply a matter of first principles, or Christ's first commands. Murray told the Church that, in its zeal to go forth and make disciples of others, it had neglected our Lord's first and weightier great commissions for ourselves—to "be perfect," "be holy," to "be filled with the Spirit."

The world would not believe the gospel, Murray said, if the Spirit of the living and glorified Christ was not first living in and overflowing from His saints, as it was in the first Christian generation. As he said in *Like Christ*: "Only by a life of serving and suffering love, in which the Christian distinctly confesses that the glory of God is the aim of our existence, and in which, full of the Holy Spirit, we bring others into direct contact with the warmth and love of the heavenly life, can we be a blessing to the world."

Together, and over time, both the *presence* of Christ and the *likeness* of Christ impart the *power* of a perfect obedient heart, and victory over remaining sin. Christ's presence and His likeness is also the chief power in fruit-bearing. As Murray said in one of his addresses before the students at Chicago's Moody Bible Institute in 1895: "The Holy Spirit," he said, "brings the presence of Christ; He gives the likeness of Christ, and the Holy Spirit works the power of Christ." That, he added, is "the full blessing of Pentecost."

Murray's focus throughout all of his many later books, similarly, sought to return the Church to its birthplace, Pentecost, to regain the more subjective part of the New Covenant's redemption had largely misplaced or decentered in its Dark Age. His more fully worked-out doctrine on the Father's intended role for His Holy Spirit in the life of the Church, represented a kind of second or neo-reformation; it sought to "make room" for the more prominent role of Christ's chief gift to His Church.

Divine Healing

In 1879, about the time that Rev. Murray was beginning *Like Christ*, the second South African revival broke out, and demand for his insightful leadership pushed his public speaking to its career zenith. Yet, it was at this crucial juncture that he lost his voice. The sickness persisted—proving itself intractable under the care of many doctors and their remedies, rending him unable to preach or carry out his leadership duties for two years.

At this early point, Murray's paradigm on bodily sickness did not emphasize Divine heling; he simply did not believe that it was God's will to heal *virtually all* sickness, or to heal as a general rule. There were likely two reasons for this. First, Divine healing was not mentioned in the Holiness movement's more popular foundational texts, such as Rev. Boardman's *The Higher Christian Life*. Many of the early holiness texts reflected the same element of unbelief or silence on the matter of healing, viewing bodily sickness through the holiness paradigm—a tool in our heavenly Father's kit of afflictions by which He graciously becomes ever nearer in love and forms us in a short life into His image and likeness. Think of David in the Psalm 119: "*Before I was afflicted I went astray, but now I obey Your word,*" and "*It was good for me to be afflicted so that I might learn Your decrees.*" Second, Divine healing of sickness as a general rule for believers ran counter to both Church and Holiness Movement experience. Even during South Africa's Revival in 1860, among the many unexpected manifestations of the Spirit, there was no mention of miraculous bodily healing. Thus, it is not surprising that he and his wife, Emma, had since South Africa's revival, unflinchingly endured the death of three of their young children—two in 1866, and the three-year-old Fanny in 1873.

Later, under the holiness movement influence, Murray would also view sickness as a chastisement for remaining sin. This view could be seen in a letter to his wife in 1880 from Murraysburg, where he had gone to place his voice under the care of a doctor:

> You know what I have said about the two views of affliction; the one always seeing it as chastisement for sin, and the other regarding it in the light of kindness and love. And you know what very great kindness I have felt it, to have such a time for the renewal of bodily strength, and for mental refreshment and quiet, for the work before me. The thought has come whether I might not be in danger of overlooking the former aspect. ... I have been asking the Lord to show me what specially He wants changed. The general answer is a very easy one, and yet it is difficult to realize at once distinctly where and how the change is to come. What is needed is a more spiritual life, more of the power of the Holy Ghost, in the life first and then in the preaching. And yet it looks as if one's life is very much of a settled thing, and as if there is not much prospect of one's being lifted to a different platform. If the Holy Spirit were to come in great power to search out and expose either individual failings or the general low state of devotion in the soul, this would be the first step towards forsaking what is behind. Let us pray earnestly that our gracious God would search and try us and see whether there be any evil way in us.[23]

Two years later, in 1882, after only some improvement, Murray's sickness underwent a serious relapse during South Africa's winter. Unable to speak or preach, his congregation arranged passage for him and Mrs. Murray to England, where it was summer, in the hope that both the warmer climate and rest might prove beneficial, and also that he might consult another specialist. But, by this juncture, Murray's view of sickness as suffering had begun to change in an impactful way, having come under the influence of the broader holiness trend's early ideologues and practitioners of faith healing. This milestone could be seen in this letter from Holland in September to his congregation:

> At the Cape I had already frequently given thought to James 5: 14–16—"*the prayer of faith shall heal the sick*"—and, in union with others, I had already made this matter of faith healing a subject of intercession. What I had read concerning the work of Dorothea Trudel and Dr. Cullis had removed from my mind all doubts but that the Lord, even yet, bestows healing in answer to the prayer of faith. And yet I felt that it would be a serious question for me whether I should place myself under the treatment of a physician, or should turn to those who appear to have received this gift of healing from the Lord. I thought that I would have time on board [the ship] to think over this question and come to a decision.[24]

Apparently, he had read *Dorothea Trudel: On The Prayer of Faith*, published in 1865, which describes how hundreds had been miraculously healed of God in her own home in Zurich,[25] as well as the aforementioned Rev. William Boardman's 1874 book on healing by faith, *Faith Work Under Dr. Cullis in Boston*, which is filled with accounts of healing by faith in medical doctor Charles Cullis' home in Boston.[26] By his arrival to London, it seems that Murray had also read Boardman's recently published *"The Lord that Healeth Thee" (Jehovah-Rophi)*.[27] And, then, in London, Murray providentially met the Swiss Pastor Otto Stockmeyer, who—like Trudel and Cullis—ran a faith healing establishment at Hauptwal in Switzerland. It was Stockmeyer who persuaded Murray to enter Bethshan—Boardman's own home in London for Divine healing. There, under intense scriptural exegesis, Murray's paradigm on sickness and its healing fully ruptured; he became convinced that the fullness of God's redemption in Christ included not just deliverance from present sin, but also sickness. Specifically, he began to see that God's *general* will—as part of the broader provision in the New Covenant—was *not* that we remain sick, but that we be restored to health just as soon as we addressed the deeper, more eternally-important spiritual matter, of which He was convicting us.

And, what was that God was wanting changed in Murray's life? An analysis of his discourse after this event readily yields the answer: Our Father was convicting him of his remaining unbelief—that is, unbelief regarding the unequivocal will, promises, and provision of God, that He explicitly declares or clearly implies in His Word. Murray doubted, for example, whether God's will and power that was expressed literally and exemplified historically by Jesus, Paul, the rest of the apostles, and the first generation of Christians, was a trustworthy guide for the rest of the Church moving forward. Or, was that merely an ideal, for which God had not made provision beyond this time, for some reason? After all, it was nowhere experienced today; nor had such acts been recorded at any point since the great persecution of the Church during the first century.

Under the illumination of Scripture by a more faithful narrative in Bethshan, Murray became convicted of the reason that he had not yet fully entered into all of God's promised New Covenant blessing. He had failed for the same reason that most of Israel had not entered Canaan, but wandered and perished in the desert wilderness: their *disobedience*, or *sin of unbelief*. All such remaining unwillingness to fully trust and surrender to God's will—all disobedience in conformity to Christ and live only to do all of the will of God in our life—Murray became convinced, was due to our failure to completely surrender our life. He wrote this to his congregation, telling of how he overcame this sin:

> Morning by morning the sixteen or eighteen inmates were assembled around the Word of God, and instructed as to what there still remained in themselves to prevent them from appropriating the promise, and what there was in Scripture to encourage them to faith and to complete surrender. I cannot remember that I have ever listened to expositions of the Word of God in which greater simplicity and a more glorious spirit of faith were revealed, combined with heart-searching application of God's demand to surrender everything to Him.[28]

At the moment that he was led to this more complete faith and was able to *completely surrender both his life and his disbelief*, the sickness of being unable to speak for over two years ended instantly. He was, in his words, finally "delivered from the chastisement."

After the miraculous healing of His voice, Murray—in another letter home to his congregation—reflected on what had just happened: "The disease was designed to bring us to complete severance from what God disapproved of in our life, and when the Lord has attained this purpose, the disease itself may be removed." What he wrote next seems to reveal what he sensed that God had disapproved of his life: "lack of complete consecration, the assertion of one's own will, confidence in one's own strength in performing the Lord's work, a forsaking of the first love and tenderness in the walk with God, or the absence of that gentleness which desires to follow only the leading of the Spirit of God."

He then wrote how sickness and its healing fit into God's plan for full salvation:

> It is difficult to express what a sight we sometimes obtain of the unutterable tenderness and sanctity of the surrender to which we are called when we beseech the Lord for healing by faith. It fills the soul with holy fear and reverence when we ask the Lord truly to impart to the body the eternal youth of His heavenly life, and when we express our readiness to receive the Holy Spirit in order to infuse health into the body which He inhabits, and our readiness to live every day in complete dependence upon the Lord for our bodily welfare. We learn to understand how complete the surrender of the body to the Lord must be, down to the very smallest particulars, and how the Lord, in thus giving and preserving health by faith, is really effecting the most intimate union with Himself.
>
> When faith healing is regarded from this point of view, one of the chief objections against it is removed. We are so apt to think that the disease and the chastisement bring us the blessing, that the thought hardly finds an entrance that the recovery from disease may bring even greater blessing. And if the recovery consists in nothing but the removal of the disease, our view of the matter would be justified. But if the disease is only removable after its cause has been discovered and removed, and after a closer contact with the living Lord, and a more complete union of the body with Him, then we can understand that such a recovery brings infinitely greater blessing to the soul than the disease could convey.[29]

After his miraculous healing, in 1884, Murray published in Dutch, *Jezus de Geneesheer der Kranken*, or *Jesus, the Physician of the Sick*. The book was then translated into English with more clarity as *Divine Healing*. On the surface, the book delivered what it promised; it was the consummate scripture-based argument for the continuationist doctrine on this topic of bodily healing. Murray began the book's Preface with this humble testimony:

> The publication of this work may be regarded as a testimony of my faith in divine healing. After being stopped for more than two years in the exercise of my ministry, I was healed by the mercy of God in answer to the prayer of those who see in Him "*the Lord that heals you*" (Exodus 15: 26). This healing, granted to faith, has been the source of rich spiritual blessing to me. I have clearly seen that the Church possesses in Jesus, our Divine Healer, an inestimable treasure, which she does not yet know how to appreciate. I have been convinced anew of that which the Word of God teaches us in this matter, and of what the Lord expects of us; and I am sure that if Christians learned to realize practically the presence of the Lord that heals, their spiritual life would thereby be developed and sanctified. I can therefore no longer keep

> silence, and I publish here a series of meditations, with the view of showing, according to the Word of God, that "*the prayer of faith*" (James 5:15) is the means appointed by God for the cure of the sick, that this truth is in perfect accord with Holy Scripture, and that the study of this truth is essential for everyone who would see the Lord manifest His power and His glory in the midst of His children.

But, far more than bodily healing, the book was profoundly transformative in the spiritual dimension; it was more a manifesto and a manual on entering the higher, Spirit-filled life, by way of a completely surrendering, fully trustful kind of faith. The book, in this sense, was part of the early genealogy of the contemporary faith movement, albeit without the associated controversies. It amounted to a one-man campaign against the unbelief that still remained in what he began to call the *only partially* Reformed Church. He bluntly stated: "It is the Church's unbelief which has lost the gift of healing."

The rest of the text had wide-ranging implications for a Church that—by its worldliness and unfaithfulness—had reasoned away its only power to remain healthy and transform the world; it had lost the weightier elements of faith, hope and love, which are entire surrender to belief in, or full trust in, God's explicit and implicit promises regarding the higher life in Christ, including Divine healing. He wrote:

> Does not the history of the Church show us the necessity of these warnings? Does it not furnish us with numerous examples of backward steps, of world pleasing, in which faith grew weak in the exact measure in which the spirit of the world took the upper hand? For such faith is only possible to him who lives in the world invisible. Until the third century the healings by faith in Christ were numerous, but in the centuries following they became more infrequent. Do we not know from the Bible that it is always unbelief which hinders the mighty working of God?

The Second Conversion—Via Absolute Surrender

The obvious implication of Andrew Murray's writing on the concept of the higher life is that God expects the believers who have been cleansed by Christ's blood to go onto spiritual maturity; His chief will for us is to be filled with His Spirit, and thereby to become like Christ in all respects. Spiritual progress, of course, means *measurable change over time*; we are to be able to look back at our path and always see remarkable difference from our lower, babe-like stage of Christ's salvation, to the higher, spiritually mature one.

But, as Murray observed in others and personally experienced, most of us do not progress along this ideal path of sanctification. *Why*? Again, *because of our disobedience*, particularly, our sin of remaining unbelief. Most unbelief that Murray spoke about stemmed from doctrinal error; the Church's paradigm of free grace has so obscured the command to be perfect, or be holy—to be filled with the Spirit of Christ and thus walk as He did—that most view God's will for us mainly in terms of righteousness, not holiness. We narrowly construct the New Covenant's salvation as righteousness alone—a function of what Jesus did long ago on the cross, and view their fuller salvation in terms of His future second coming. We also limit holiness to obedience, which is also narrowly viewed as glorifying God in service, which—for evangelicals—is centered almost exclusively on Christ's *last* great command. This prevailing paradigm, therefore, obscures the higher life in Christ that God's Word suggests should be our experience; it limits God by believing, expecting, and obeying only the lower part of what He said, promised, and commanded. It is in this paradigm, that so many of us tend to serve the Lord *in place*, like marching in place—failing to progress in the *presence*, *likeness*, and *power* of Christ in our lives.

Since so many of us go for so long after our initial conversion without grasping, believing in, and prayerfully yearning for this more mature, deeper Christian life, then—if and when we do—we typically undergo a more rapid conversion into it. Most often, Murray observed, this more rapid, eventful, baptism-like process is catalyzed by a crisis, such as a severe trial, a life-changing ailment, or a major spiritual epiphany.

For Murray, again, the crisis was his debilitating illness that had brought his ministry to a standstill. It was during this intense soul-searching time that Murray began to see the need for a kind of second conversion. He conceptualized it in various scriptural terms. In an 1881 letter to his brother, Professor John Murray, for instance, he wrote: "Mahan's *Baptism of the Spirit* I have read with profit."[30] And, after his experience of Divine healing, in his *The Spirit of Christ*, we find an explosion of discourse on the vast importance of such an event at some later point in the believer's life. The text is replete with terms like being "filled with His fullness," or experiencing God's promise entailed in the command to "be filled with the Spirit"—a phrase that appears 139 times in the text. "This baptism of the Holy Spirit is the crown and glory of Jesus' work," he said in that book; "We need it; the Holy Jesus needed it; Christ's loving, obedient disciples needed it." Therefore, he added, "it is something more than the working of the Spirit in regeneration."

He began to see *God's will* for our second conversion, along with *our unbelief* that hinders it, everywhere in Scripture. These segments of his *The Deeper Christian Life* are typical:

> In our text, we have these words: "God brought us out [from Egypt], that He might bring us in" to Canaan. There are two steps: one was bringing them out; and the other was bringing them in. So in the life of the believer, there are ordinarily two steps quite separate from each other—the bringing him out of sin and the world; and the bringing him into a state of complete rest afterward. It was the intention of God that Israel should enter the land of Canaan from Kadesh-Barnea, immediately after He had made His covenant with them at Sinai. But they were not ready to enter at once, on account of their sin and unbelief, and disobedience. They had to wander after that for forty years in the wilderness.
>
> Now, look how God led the people. In Egypt, there was a great crisis, where they had first to pass through the Red Sea, which is a figure of conversion; and when they went into Canaan, there was, as it were, a second conversion in passing through the Jordan. At our conversion, we get into liberty, out of the bondage of Egypt; but, when we fail to use our liberty through unbelief and disobedience, we wander in the wilderness for a longer or shorter period before we enter into the Canaan of victory, and rest, and abundance. Thus God does for His Israel two things: He brings them out of Egypt; and He leads them into Canaan.

Despite this unorthodox notion that the baptism in the Spirit was something more than what the unbeliever experiences at his or her point of conversion—something more than our having been born again—Murray avoided much criticism by agreeing with the orthodox position, that God *gives* His Holy Spirit to the unbeliever entirely at our point of conversion. But, as he also observed, this does not mean that the new believer is "filled" with the Spirit. Rather, since God will not overpower us against our will, He allows us to determine how much God fills and rules our lives. "In the gift of God, the Spirit of Christ in all His fullness is bestowed once for all as an Indwelling Spirit," he wrote; "but He is received and possessed only as far as the faith of the believer reaches." In other words, the Father gives us all of His Holy Spirit, but we—for reasons of both ignorance and Self-centeredness—do not let Him rule over all of our lives. Instead, most new believers, after their conversion, never surrender the remaining realms of their sovereign Self-life.

In his 1908 work, *The Full Blessing of Pentecost*, Murray deals with many of the more doctrinal questions around the Spirit's infilling. He wrote:

> The first is: whence must this blessing come, from within or from above? Some earnest Christians will say at once that "it must come from within." The Holy Spirit descended upon the earth on the day of Pentecost and was given to the Christian community. At the moment of conversion He comes into our heart. We have therefore no longer to pray that He may be given to us: we have simply to recognize and use what we already have. It is not as if we had to seek to have more of the Spirit: we have Him in the fullness of the gift as it is. It is rather the Holy Spirit who must have more of us. As we yield ourselves entirely to Him He will entirely fill us. It is from within that the blessing must come: the fountain of living water is already there; the fountain has only to be opened and every obstruction cleared out of the way and the water shall stream forth. It must spring from within.

On the other hand, Murray added, there are not a few that say, "No; it must come from above." He noted too many cases after Pentecost, beginning with Cesarea and Samaria, where God's new and greater manifestation of the Spirit was a not function of something coming from within believers, but something far more miraculous and Heaven sent, as a result of fasting and prayer, and entire consecration.

Murray then dismissed this controversy, pointing out how God has blessed people in *both* ways. An unbiased examination of testimonies, he observed, establishes the point.

But, Murray then opened the related controversy: "Does this blessing come gradually or at once? Will it manifest itself in the shape of a silent, unobserved increase of the grace of the Spirit or as a momentary, immediate outpouring of His power?" He added:

> It must suffice for me to say here again that God has already sent this blessing in both modes, and will continue to do so still. What must take place at once is this: there must be a definite resolve to place the whole life unreservedly under the control of the Spirit, and a conviction of faith that God has accepted this surrender. In the majority of cases this is done at once. It must at last come to this, perhaps after a long course of seeking and praying, that the soul shall present itself to God for this blessing in one definite, irrevocable act, and shall believe that the offering is then sanctified and accepted upon the altar. Thenceforth, whether the experience of the blessing comes at once and with power, or comes quietly and gradually, the soul must maintain its act of Self-dedication and simply look to God to do His own work.

Although he knew from testimonies that the baptism in the Spirit was typically more eventful than gradual, Murray's two brief testimonies, including this segment from Keswick, reveal that his own transformation was not at all dramatic:

> Later on, my mind became much exercised about the baptism of the Holy Spirit, and I gave myself to God as perfectly as I could to receive the baptism of the Spirit. Yet there was failure; God forgive it. It was somehow as if I could not get what I wanted. Through all these stumblings God led me, without any very special experience that I can point to; but as I look back I do believe now that He was giving me more and more of His blessed Spirit, had I but known it better. ... Perhaps if I were to talk of consecration I might tell you of an evening there in my own study in Cape Town. Yet I cannot say that that was my deliverance, for I was still struggling.[31]

In neither of his two known testimonies about what God had done for him, did Murray explicitly describe his experience of this baptism-like event. Yet, within a couple years after his Divine healing, his discourse was marked by a new *positionality*; he spoke not only more forcefully and confidently of the higher life in Christ, but also more from the perspective of someone who was experiencing what he was talking about. That authoritative writing perspective would persist for the next four decades. In his 1895 *The Deeper Christian Life*, in a chapter titled "A Word to Workers," for example, Murray chastised other ministers for not yet putting away their remaining unbelief about the higher, Spirit-filled life, and entering into it:

> Beloved, "The first duty of every clergyman is to humbly ask God that all that he wants done in his hearers may be first fully and truly done in himself." And the second thing is his duty towards those who are awakened and brought to Christ, to lead them on to the full knowledge of the presence and indwelling of the Holy Spirit. And yet, if we understand our calling aright, every one of us will have to say, That is the one thing on which everything depends. What profit is it to tell men that they may be filled with the Spirit of God, if, when they ask us, "Has God done it for you?" we have to answer, "No, He has not done it"?

In continuing implicit reference to his own first-hand, personal experience, he said "If the life of God dwell in me, and I am filled with His power, then I can hope that the life that goes out from me may be infused into my hearers too," and "brethren, the message must come from us as a witness of our personal experience."

Although that notion of such an eventful second conversion into a more Spirit-filled life was unorthodox in Murray's day, it was, nevertheless, for some, the crucial event in which they finally began experience the kind of spiritual progress which had to that point eluded them. It had first emerged in doctrinal form with the early Holiness movement ideologue and founder of Methodism, John Wesley. It was established more empirically, before and after, by the testimonies of scores of the Church's best-loved saints. Murray's second biographer noted how some "passed into" this "new state and experience":

> In a remarkable book which relates truthfully the "*Deeper Experience of Famous Christians*," such as Madame Guyon, Fenelon, George Foxe, [John] Wesley, Whitfield, Fletcher, Christmas Evans, Bramwell, General Booth, [D.L]Moody, Dr. Gordon, A. B. Earle, [Frances] Havergal, and others, it is made abundantly clear from their own testimony and the fruits that followed this experience that they, after their conversion

> sooner or later by *a definite crisis*, as marked as a birth, or a death, or a marriage, passed into a new state and experience, a new relation to Christ and the Holy Spirit.[32]

Recall Rev. William Boardman, author of *The Higher Christian Life*, the seminal text or manifesto for the Holiness trend. Boardman described his second conversion this way:

> *Ten years after my conversion*, the Lord Jesus graciously revealed Himself to me as always with me, my Savior from my sins, and brought me to accept Him and rest in Him each moment for *present deliverance* and *constant keeping in perfect peace*, as truly has He before had revealed Himself to me and brought me to accept Him, as my sin-bearing and pardoning Savior. The *new light* that then opened my soul in the Scriptures was marvelous. Old favorite passages were *made new* in the effulgence of fresh significance, and others, meaningless to me before, were now radiant with divine glory, all through the Bible. The book became *new* within, old in the letter, but new in spirit and power.[33]

Absolute Surrender

What spiritual secret did these better-known pillars of the Church discover that enabled them to enter into this higher, deeper, more Spirit-filled life? For most, it was higher-level act of faith that they variously called *full surrender*, or *entire consecration*. The man who lived by faith more than anyone in history, George Müller of Bristol, described this higher-level faith-act of full surrender and his ensuing second conversion this way:

> That leads to another thought—the *full surrender* of the heart to God. I was converted in November 1825, but I only came, into the *full surrender* of the heart four years later, in July 1829. The love of money was gone, the love of place was gone, the love of position was gone, the love of worldly pleasures and engagements was gone. God, God, God alone became my portion. I found my all in Him; I wanted nothing else. And by the grace of God this has remained, and has made me a happy man, an exceedingly happy man, and it led me to care only about the things of God.[34]

"The change was so great," Müller added, "that it was like a second conversion."

And, in the case of Frances Havergal, the Church's celebrated hymnist, Murray's friend and biographer gives this account of her "second experience of grace":

> Before Miss Havergal passed into this deeper experience, she had had an unmistakable conversion, leading to a life of *entire devotion* to her Saviour and continual service for Him unchecked by any deviation from the path of righteousness, or backsliding into sloth, worldliness or sin. … And by a crisis, as distinct as her conversion, she passed into this second experience of grace, and her *Journals and Letters*, a rich heritage for the Church of God, show us what intimate communion she enjoyed with the Triune God, whom she adoringly loved, until her very body was overwhelmed with "that speechless awe which dares not move." At length the long looked for experience came, and lifted her whole life into perpetual sunshine. She saw it as a flash of electric light. She remembered the place, Winterdine, in the Midland Counties, and the day, December 2nd, 1873. She saw that there must be a *full and true consecration* before blessing—*absolute surrender*, as Andrew Murray insists.[35]

We had already seen how Keswick's founder, the Anglican Canon Battersby, at the Oxford Convention—in Murray's words—"received a new and distinct blessing to which he had been a stranger before." Recall Battersby's own words: "There is a very remarkable resemblance in the testimonies I have since received as to the nature of the blessing obtained, viz., the ability given to make a *full surrender* to the Lord, and the consequent experience of an abiding peace, far exceeding anything previously experienced."[36]

Note that all three—Müller, Havergal, and Boardman—all attributed their higher Christian life experience to the prerequisite faith-act of full surrender or full consecration. As Frances Havergal put it, "Full and true consecration *before* blessing."

Murray also had glimpsed and mentioned this spiritual law in South Africa's revival. As he put it in his first post-revival text, "The path of entire consecration is the path of full salvation." And, he had later again seen the importance of full surrender in the next big spiritual event in his life. Recall from his letter from Bethshan—Boardman's home for healing—how he attributed God's restoration of his voice to his discovery of "complete surrender," and his obedience to "God's demand to surrender everything to Him."

After that event, Murray not only placed much greater emphasis on this notion of a second conversion, but he increasingly seemed to realize how it depended on this higher-level faith-act of—in the terms of his classic address on the subject—"absolute surrender." And, as he grew, Rev. Murray's conception of this all-important faith-act also grew—eventually entailing three constituent parts: The first part—as Murray learned in Bethshan—is repenting of our sin of *remaining* disobedience and unbelief, and of fully, restfully trusting God to fulfill His will and promise as reflected so literally and unequivocally in His Word. Again, it is always unbelief that is the chief hindrance to our enjoying what God promises, just as it kept the larger part of Israel wandering and perishing in the desert. The second part is *dying to Self*, or wholeheartedly crucifying the rest of the world in us, and all of the aspects of the Self-life that remains. This means humbling ourselves, so that God might fill our consecrated heart-temples, and truly be all in us. And, the third part is *living to God*, or living in the spirit of complete obedience, love, and humility, to do *all* of His will, or to not neglect any of His commands. Here is how Murray expressed this in the Preface to his ensuing classic holiness text, *The Spirit of Christ*:

> As we first yield ourselves to be led by the Spirit, to confess His presence in us—as believers rise to realize and accept His guidance in all their daily life—will our God be willing to entrust to us larger measures of His mighty workings. If we give ourselves entirely into His power, as our life, ruling within us, He will give Himself to us in taking a more complete possession, to work through us.
>
> If there is one thing I desire, it is that the Lord may use what I have written to make clear and impress this one truth: It is as an indwelling life that the Holy Spirit must be known. In a living, adoring faith, the indwelling must be accepted and treasured, until it becomes part of the consciousness of the new man: The Holy Spirit possesses me. In this faith the whole life, even to the least things, must be surrendered to His leading, while all that is of the flesh or Self is crucified and put to death. ...The Holy Spirit only demands vessels entirely set apart to Him.

The spirit of absolute surrender, he added, is the spirit of *full obedience*, to only and all of God's will: "We do not understand that the obedience of love must precede the fullness of the Spirit;" "Obedience," he added, "must precede the baptism of the Spirit." He made a life surrendered to full obedience a beautiful, mystical element of salvation."

He then noted how part of the Church was awakening to the necessity of "full surrender":

> It is this truth which has in these latter years come home with power to the hearts of many in the use of the words *full surrender and entire consecration.* As they understood that the Lord Jesus did indeed claim *implicit obedience*, that *the giving up all to Him and His will was absolutely necessary*, and in the power of His grace truly possible, and in the faith of His power did it, they found the entrance to a life of peace and strength *formerly unknown* [*emphasis added*].

This three-part faith-act of "full surrender and entire consecration," Murray became convinced, is of such advanced spiritual nature that it cannot be even understood by new Christians, after our initial conversion. Rather, he saw, it can be sufficiently conceptualized and enacted only by more experienced believers, who are in a state of dissonance and deep conviction over their persistent feebleness and failures to both fully believe in, and unselfishly act upon, all of God's explicit and implicit will. When we become convicted that it is our own remaining unbelief and Self-life that have prevented us from being able to experience all that God's Word commands, promises, and implies is our intended inheritance—to be filled with His Spirit, and truly walk as Jesus did—then, and only then, are we are primed for this faith-act of absolute surrender.

His earlier interest in the baptism of the Spirit notwithstanding, Murray believed that this faith-act by which we enter the higher life is, ideally, less of an eventful leap or leaps onto a plateau that we might point back to, and more of a gradual, everyday process of salvation. It is something that God works out in hearts who abide in Christ in the spirit of full surrender or entire consecration. But, again, as he observed in his life and others, the spiritual life of the more typical prodigal sons and daughters, for various reasons, do not follow the ideal path of sanctification after their conversion, but become stalled—both by our remaining unbelief, and by our remaining Self-life.

For this reason, Murray increasingly stressed that the contemporary Church—especially his own Evangelical segment—had lost its first love; it had centered our Lord's last great commission, with its focus on unbelievers, to the point that it decentered our Lord's earlier great commands for believers—to "abide in Me," to "be perfect," or holy, and to "be filled with the Spirit." The Church's first duty—the necessary prerequisite to the last great command leading *un*believers to the point of conviction and saving faith in Christ—Murray became convinced, is to lead believers to the point of a second conviction over remaining unbelief regarding the higher life, and our remaining worldliness or Self-life, and then onto this all-important faith-act of full surrender. Only this way, he said, can we enter the higher life and bear the kinds and quantities of fruit that God intended in His other promises and commands.

Progressive Surrender, and Progressive Salvation, or Sanctification

Murray also discovered that it is *not* our typically more eventful conversion, or our *entrance into* this higher life, that is our Father's ultimate blessing and ideal for us. Rather, His chief purpose or focus in this New Covenant provision is what occurs after such entrance: even more remarkable *spiritual progress.* The higher life, in other words, is *progressive*; it advances; it is not a life of being, but of becoming.

It is only after our transition *out of* the first, more carnal, worldly, or Selfish stage and *into* this second, more consecrated, spiritual stage, that that we have the spirit of continual or *progressive surrender.* It is the spirit of ever-increasing faith, marked by ever-increasing trust in God's literal Word, death to remaining Self-life, and living to God in full obedience, which always translates into acts of selfless love, and placing ourselves in the path of suffering for others. Thus, although the grace of our initial salvation is free; it is not the result of work; the grace of our fuller salvation is a harmonious blend of *faith and faith-based works.* Our part, as Murray said, is a "progressive work by which we are personally to accept and voluntarily to appropriate this Divine holiness."

And, it is only in this everyday spirit of progressive faith and progressive surrender, that we can experience the markedly greater spiritual progress for which He created us. It is only then, in the everyday habitus of continual surrender of what Self-life remains, that we realize the New Covenant's full potential in our sanctification—becoming remarkably like Christ in His self-sacrificing love, humility, and power over remaining sin. Again, the higher life is a progressive stage, marked by continual surrender, which leads to real spiritual progress, or sanctification, is a kind of progressive salvation.

Murray expressed this in thousands of ways, beginning in the wake of South Africa's Revival. He wrote in *Abide in Christ*, for instance: "The measure of sanctification will depend on the measure of abiding in Him; as the soul learns wholly to abide in Christ, the promise is increasingly fulfilled: *'The very God of peace sanctify you wholly.'*"

This theme of spiritual progress in Murray's writing increased after his experience of Divine healing. In his fourth book of his early series, *Holy in Christ*, for example, he wrote:

> It is as we are led to see what God sees, as our faith grasps that the holy life of Christ is ours in actual possession, to be accepted and appropriated for daily use, that we shall really be able to live the life God calls us to, the life of holy ones in Christ Jesus. We shall then be in the right position in which what is called our progressive sanctification can be worked out. It will be, the acceptance and application in daily life of the power of a holy life which has been prepared in Jesus, which has in the union with Him become our present and permanent possession, and which works in us according to the measure of our faith.

The progressive nature of the New Covenant's second blessing remained a constant and central theme in Murray's writing. As he wrote in his classic Holiness text, *Be Perfect*:

> The perfection of the perfect heart, a heart wholly yielded to seek God with all its strength, is again a seed, with infinite power of growth and increase. … Perfection is a growth. As we awaken to the consciousness of what God asks and gives, and maintains the vow of a wholehearted surrender, we grow in sense of need and trust in the promise of a Divine life and strength, until all the promises of grace come to a focus in the one assurance: "*The God of all grace will Himself perfect you.*" That faith which was the fruit of previous growth, becomes the new seed of further growth.

He even alluded to it in his testimony before the gathered ministers and evangelists in Chicago to describe the higher stage of his Christian life: "So it went on, year after year," he said; "I enjoyed more of God, I enjoyed more rest, I enjoyed more peace, I got more victory, and I learned to trust God more." At Keswick also, we find that joyous expectation of an ever-increasing, ever-progressive redemption:

> You will ask me. Are you satisfied? Have you got all you want? God forbid. With the deepest feeling of my soul I can say that I am satisfied with Jesus now; but there is also the consciousness of how much fuller the revelation can be of the exceeding abundance of His grace. Let us never hesitate to say: This is only the beginning; when we are brought into the holiest of all, we are only beginning to take our right position with the Father.

Absolute Dependence or Waiting on God

In addition to absolute surrender—the act of faith by which we first *enter* and then *remain* in the Spirit-filled life—Andrew Murray also increasingly emphasized the subsequent and still higher-level faith-act by which we *progress* in the higher life. Lacking an established lexicon, as was always the case, Rev. Murray signified this faith-act in various new terms, such as "patient waiting," "absolute dependence" upon God, or—as he put it in Chicago—giving ourselves "to the leading of the Spirit."

Although Murray had become sensitive to this consummate faith-act after the revival, it became much more prominent in his discourse at the point of his Divine healing. We find this emphasis of absolute dependence in his classic text, *Divine Healing*, for instance, commenting on Jesus' "*I am the vine; You are the branches*":

> Now, just a few thoughts about this blessed branch-life. In the first place it is a life of absolute dependence. The branch has nothing: it just depends upon the vine for everything. That word, absolute dependence, is one of the most solemn and large and precious of words. A great German theologian wrote two large volumes some years ago, to show that the whole of Calvin's theology is summed up in that one principle of absolute dependence upon God; and he was right. If you can learn every moment of the day to depend upon God, everything will come right.

"You will get the higher life if you depend absolutely upon God," Murray said, adding:

> From moment to moment the sap flows from the vine to the branches. And just so, my Lord Jesus wants me to take that blessed position as a worker, and, morning by morning and day by day and hour by hour and step by step, in every work I have to go out to, just to abide before Him in the simple, utter helplessness. … Absolute dependence upon God is the secret of all power in work. The branch has nothing but what it gets from the vine, and you and I can have nothing but what we get from Jesus. Secondly, the life of the branch is not only a life of entire dependence, but of deep restfulness. … If there was anything in the grapes not good, the owner never blamed the branch; the blame was always on the vine. And if you would be a true branch of Christ, the living Vine, just rest on Him. Let Christ bear the responsibility. … Rest in Christ, who can give wisdom and strength, and you do not know how that restfulness will often prove to be the very best part of your message.

What caused Murray's increased emphasis on this notion of patient waiting or entire dependence on God? Plainly, Christian mysticism. As his biographer put it, he had "come under the potent spell" of William Law, the famous English Christian mystic, whose writings had caused such a stir a century earlier.[37] Murray was so inspired by this late mystic and holiness leader that, in 1893, he published a series of extracts from Law's writings, titled *Wholly for God: The True Christian Life*. Law corroborated Murray's sense that it was God's highest will for us is to progress into this stage of completely trustful, patient waiting, or dependence—allowing Him to do all. As he put it in that book's introduction, "I know of no writer who equals Law in the clearness and the force with which the claims of God on man are asserted. God is all; God must have all; God alone must work all: round these central truths all his teaching gathers." He added:

> One of the great reasons that our religion is so powerless, is that it is too much a thing of reason and sense. We place our dependence on the intellectual apprehensions of truth, and the influence these exert in stirring the feelings, the desires, and the will. But they cannot reach to the life, to the reality of God, both because they are in their nature unfitted for receiving God, and are darkened under the power of sin. Mysticism insists upon this—and presses unceasingly the cultivation of the spiritual faculty which retires within itself, and seeks in *patient waiting for God* by faith to open the deepest recesses of its being to His presence.

Murray would increasingly use this phrase, *waiting on God*, and used it for the title of his 1896 book on the topic. Introducing that Christian classic, he wrote:

> At a "welcome" breakfast in Exeter Hall, I gave very simple expression to this thought in connection with all our religious work. I have already said elsewhere that I was surprised at the response the sentiment met with. I saw that God's Spirit had been working the same desire in many hearts. The experiences of the past year, both personal and public, have greatly deepened the conviction. It is as if I myself am only beginning to see the deepest truth concerning God, and our relation to Him, center in this: *waiting on God*. Yet, how very little, in our life and work, we have been surrounded by its spirit. The following pages are the outcome of my conviction, and of the desire to direct the attention of all God's people to this one great remedy for all our needs. ...I do not know if it will be possible for me to put into a few words what are the chief things we need to learn. In a note at the close of the book on William Law I have mentioned some. But what I want to say here is this: *The great lack of our religion is, we do not know God.*
>
> The answer to every complaint of feebleness and failure, the message to every congregation or convention seeking instruction on holiness, ought to be simply, What is the matter: Have you not God? If you really believe in God, He will put all right. God is willing and able by His Holy Spirit. Cease from expecting the least good from yourself, or the least help from anything there is in man, and just yield yourself unreservedly to God to work in you: He will do all for you. How simple this looks! And yet this is the gospel we so little know. ... Would God that we might get some right conception of what the influence would be of a life given, not in thought, or imagination, or effort, but in the power of the Holy Spirit, wholly to *waiting upon God.*

Yet, most Christians, he lamented, "have no sense of the need of absolute and unceasing dependence, or of the unspeakable blessedness of continual waiting on God." He added:

> But when once a believer begins to see it, and consent to it, that we by the Holy

Spirit must each moment receive what God each moment works, waiting on God becomes his brightest hope and joy. As we apprehend how God, as God, as Infinite Love, delights to impart His own nature to His child as fully as He can, how God is not weary of each moment keeping charge of our life and strength, we wonder that we ever thought otherwise of God than as a God to be waited on all the day. God unceasingly giving and working; His child unceasingly waiting and receiving: this is the blessed life.

The notion of waiting as working is antithetical to human reason and nature, so the question arises: "how does this spirit of waiting or absolute dependence on God jive with the Evangelical imperative, or to walk in Jesus' steps?" How, practically, do we wait and let God do everything and still obey the last great commission of evangelizing the good news of God's redemption in Christ Jesus? This was the great paradox that Christian mystics like Law had addressed. Through their writings, Murray—the consummate evangelical, who was leading major Christian undertakings to build the Kingdom of God—discovered that the most obedient, faithful, and effective form of *working for God* is patiently *waiting on God.* This is the nature of faith; it is God's design for our spiritual growth.

And, that seemingly paradoxical spiritual law was the foundation of Murray's sequel, *Working for God.* "Waiting on God," he wrote in that book, "has its value in this: it makes us strong in work for God." Why? Quite simply, Murray answered; because, "God works for Him who wait for Him." He went on:

> The waiting on God secures the working of God for us and in us, out of which our work must spring. The two passages teach the great lesson, that as waiting on God lies at the root of all true working for God, so working for God must be the fruit of all true waiting on Him. Our great need is to hold the two sides of the truth in perfect conjunction and harmony.

He added these comments in his testimony at Keswick and in an address at Chicago:

> I have learned to place myself before God every day, as a vessel to be filled with His Holy Spirit. He has filled me with the blessed assurance that He, as the everlasting God, has guaranteed His own work in me. If there is one lesson that I am learning day by day, it is this: that it is God who works all in all.

> The great mark of Christ is that He lived in the deepest humility and dependence upon the Father. He said, *"I can do nothing of Myself."* In everything He had His life from God. That is why we want Christ to come into us—to breathe in us that very disposition. … The very highest virtue of any Christian life is only to let God have His way. Only to give God the opportunity of doing His work in us, and coming day by day, hour by hour, to the place of *absolute dependence* upon God, and to learn one lesson: "Oh! God, I have nothing. I do not know anything, I am nothing, nothing, and I can only do what God makes me." …The great reason why our Christian life does not advance more, is: we try to do too much ourselves. We are far too Self-active and Self-confident. We, perhaps, never learned the simple lesson that the only place for me before God is just to be nothing—and God will work in me.
>
> And why was Christ so perfect, and why did Christ gain such victory, and why did Christ please God so? It is this one reason. He allowed God to work in Him from

morning until night, and every step was just in dependence upon God. He said, "Father, guide me," "Father, *I wait upon You*," "Father, work in me," and when Christ comes to live in us, do believe me and God's word, the first and chief thing He wants to work in you, is an *absolute dependence* upon your God [*emphases added*].

Murray practiced this spirit of complete dependence, refusing to limit God's promises. In one instance, in 1907, he contracted a potentially lethal influenza, and seemed to his family to be at the point of death. His daughter asked, "Will you have the doctor or will you have someone to anoint you and pray with you?" He said "neither my child, I will have neither. You can hold as many prayer meetings as you like but I will trust in God." The next Sunday, Murray was well and preached a most remarkable sermon on the Church's unbelief, using the text, "*They limited the Holy One of Israel*" (Psalm 128: 41).[38]

This more faithful and complete dependence—the kind that removes the limits that our unbelief places on God—Murray acknowledged, is not for everyone. It is, in the words of his first biographer, "only for those choice spirits who are so simple and steadfast in faith, and so completely detached from the world, as to be able sincerely and unreservedly to place themselves in God's hands."[39]

Conclusion

"More of God," "abiding in Christ," "the full indwelling of the Holy Spirit," "like Christ," "Divine healing," "holy in Christ," "full salvation," "the Spirit of Christ," "absolute surrender," "the full blessing of Pentecost," "the second blessing," "second conversion," "absolute dependence," "waiting on God," "the leading of the Holy Spirit."

It was in new terms like these that Andrew Murray tried to express the higher Christian life that he increasingly discovered over six decades. His distinctive holiness discourse—however unorthodox it was in his day—gained authority during his lifetime. *Why*? Because of Murray's classic Reformed, scripturally-grounded epistemology, and his distinctive voice, which, in the spirit of humility and love carried his constant reformationist and jeremiad themes. Grounded in Scripture, humility, and love, his message was both an exuberant call to the higher life of holiness, and a loving chastisement of a Protestant Church that is still in a very low state. We see this in *Holy in Christ*, for example:

> There are not a few who can praise God that during the past twenty years the watchword, "Be holy," has been taken up in many a church and Christian circle with greater earnestness than before. In books and magazines, in conventions and conferences, in the testimonies and the lives of believers, we have abundant tokens that what is called the Holiness movement is a reality. And yet how much is still wanting! What multitudes of believing Christians there are who have none but the very vaguest thoughts of what holiness is!

His only intentional jeremiad, *The State of the Church*, Murray wrote in his eighties. It was a book that his friend and biographer, Rev. Douglas, described as "too faithful to be popular." His chief lamentation in that book was this: "There are many Christians in our churches who never come farther than the initial faith of conversion." People say they know God has saved them, he adds, yet "they rest content" with that, as if that was all that our Lord willed for them, promised them, and made provision for. Consequently, he continues, "there is no hearty desire, no earnest purpose to press on to a life of holiness, no readiness at any sacrifice to go up into the promised land of rest and of victory."

In that late-life jeremiad, we find Murray in his comfortable reformationist role, urging the Church to recapture its misplaced center—its first love—that it had gained in birth at Pentecost, and had lost in its Dark Age:

> The revival we need is the revival of holiness, in which the consecration of the whole being to the service of Christ, and that for the whole life, shall be counted possible. And for this there will be needed a new style of preaching, in which the promises of God to dwell in His people, and to sanctify them for Himself, will take a place which they do not now have. … A revival of holiness is what we need. Such a preaching of the claim that Christ has on us as shall lead us to live entirely for Him and His Kingdom; such an attachment of love to Him as shall make His fellowship our highest joy; such a faith in His freeing us from the dominion of sin as shall enable us in all things to obey His commandments; such a yielding to the Holy Spirit as to be led by Him in all our daily walk—these will be some of the elements of the revival of true holiness for which the Church must learn to seek as for the Pearl of great price.

There is still another reason why Rev. Murray's higher life paradigm gained a vast number of admirers across the broad Christian spectrum. It is because they found in the messenger a walking testimony to—an authentic reflection of—the higher, Spirit-filled life that his writing led us to expect. In the *British Weekly*, of December 6th1894, for instance, Rev. H. V. Taylor introduced Rev. Murray to British Christians this way:

> He desires to be known as a Christian, as a follower of Jesus simply, and he seems to examine every one he meets for the Christian element in him. That is the impression left on the mind when one is in conversation with him. His keen, yearning look appears to scan the face of his interlocutor for the witness of the Christ-life there, and to plead above all things for loyalty to the one Master. You cannot help saying to yourself, "This man wants me to belong to Jesus Christ." No one who has talked with him, even on casual themes, can forget that wistful glance. He is, I suppose, well known to most readers of religious literature by his devotional books, notably *Abide in Christ.* His nature is profoundly devotional; he carries with him the atmosphere of prayer. He seems always wrapped about with a mantle of adoration. When preaching or conducting a service, his whole being is thrown into the task, and he glows with a fervency of spirit which it seems impossible for human flesh to sustain. At times he startles and overwhelms the listeners. Earnestness and power of the electric sort stream from him, and affect alike the large audience or the quiet circle gathered round him. In his slight, spent frame, of middle height, he carries in repose a volcanic energy which, when he is roused, bursts its barriers and sweeps all before it. Then his form quivers and dilates, the lips tremble, the features work, the eyes spasmodically open and close, as from the white-hot furnace of his spirit he pours the molten torrent of his unstudied eloquence. The thin face and almost emaciated body are transfigured and illumined. The staid, venerable minister of the nineteenth century, with the sober, clerical garb and stiff white tie, which is de rigueur among the Dutch clergy, disappears, and an old Hebrew prophet stands before us—another Isaiah with his glowing imagery, a second Hosea with his plaintive, yearning appeals. Audiences bend before the sweeping rain of his words like willows before a gale. The heart within the hearer is bowed, and the intellect awed. Andrew Murray's oratory is of that kind for which

> men willingly go into captivity. His disposition is mystical, with, as in the best of mystics, the religious thought clothing a strong and fearless nature. No man can study his face without being struck by the inwardness of the deep-set grey eyes. Even when one gets to hand-grips with him in closeness of intercourse, one is conscious of the great part that remains unexpressed, the spiritual Hinterland which extends far beyond the visible shore. There is ever and anon the suggestion of great strength held in reserve. A student of character cannot help the conviction that if the old days of persecution were to return, Andrew Murray would go to the stake as cheerfully as he steps up to the Moderator's chair.[40]

A few months later, in the holiness periodical, *The Life of Faith*, its editor, Rev. Evan H. Hopkins, gave this review of Rev. Murray's addresses at Keswick's 21st convention:

> The main feature of this Convention has been the presence of our beloved brother, the Rev. Andrew Murray of South Africa, whose addresses have come home to so many with peculiar power. … As message after message was enforced by one who has evidently been the marked minister of God this time, it seemed as if none could escape … but let Christ Himself, in the power of His living Spirit, be the One to live, although the cost was our taking the place of death. ... As this was dwelt on more and more deeply as the days went on, especially at the solemn evening meetings, there came over some of us a memory of Keswick in 1879, when an awe of God fell upon the whole assembly in a way the writer has never seen equaled.[41]

Dr. Alexander Whyte, the renowned Scottish divine, and one of the most prominent pastors in Scotland, was profoundly moved by Murray's insights on prayer. He pleaded for Andrew to give an autobiography of his spiritual experiences, especially his experiences in connection with prayer. That was the one piece of the world's literature, Whyte said, that he wished to read before he passed away. He added this in his letter to Murray: "Happy man! You have been chosen and ordained by God to go to the heart of things."[42]

Even in China, Rev. Murray's books had vast influence. Rev. Donald McGillivray, of the Christian Literature Society for China, wrote:

> A good many years ago I was travelling in the interior, and came to a missionary's home. She very soon informed me that she had made a discovery. She said that for some years she had had some of Andrew Murray's books on her bookshelf, but had not read them. Lately, however, she was moved to take one down, and it revealed to her the blessedness of being filled with the Spirit. From that time I also began to read his books. *The Spirit of Christ* in particular brought great blessing to myself and to the Chinese, to whom I passed on its message. Some years afterwards I was called to Shanghai to do literary work in connexion with the Christian Literature Society. One of the first books which I translated was Andrew Murray's *Spirit of Christ*. The book passed through many editions, and we often heard of the good it was doing. In one city a revival broke out through the book.[43]

Murray profoundly influenced China's most influential Christian, Watchman Nee—author of the renowned three-volume 1928 classic, *The Spiritual Man*, and founder of China's home church movement. Nee acknowledged Murray in that classic's preface.

After his evangelistic tour to South Africa in 1908, the famous British Baptist Dr. F. B. Meyer, in his *A Winter in South Africa*, wrote this of "the venerable Dr. Andrew Murray":

I can never forget or repay his kindness. On a future page I hope to allude at length to the influence of this saintly man upon his Church. It is enough to say here that, notwithstanding his eighty years, his intellect is as bright and his natural force almost as vigorous as when he visited England fifteen years ago. He is honoured and loved throughout the Church, of which he is the recognized father and leader....[44]

This higher life in Christ permeated the entire spirit of Murray home—the place where any feigned public façade is typically unsustainable. One visitor, Mr. Walton, described his longer stay at Wellington in Andrew's home this way:

> This is a Bethany indeed, just fragrant with the Master's presence. Mr. Murray seems to live in heaven, and certainly heaven is in him, and with it all there is such perfect simplicity and humility, and a joyful willingness to be the servant of all. It has been a privilege to work with him, and our talks have been most searching to my own heart. He has led me to see and realize more of the blessed life. We talked much about Christ in us, and he thinks there is much more to be realized than many at present teach. This visit has been a season of untold blessing to my soul.[45]

At the time of Murray's death, there was still much animosity between the Catholic and Reformed Churches—everywhere, except in South Africa, that is. Rev. Dr. Kolbe, of St. Mary's Roman Catholic Cathedral, wrote this in a longer tribute in *The Cape*:

> The name of Andrew Murray is graven with an iron pen and lead on the rock of South African history, and there it will stand for ever. But it is also written in softer characters on the hearts of many, and in that gentler form of survival it will endure far beyond the ordinary lot of human names.[46]

This wide acclaim from so many segments of the worldwide Christian continuum, reveals that Andrew Murray—in all of his higher life insights—was exegetically faithful to the broader spirit, context, and the specific text of God's Word. As a result, his first biographer, Dr. Johannes Du Plessis, Professor of New Testament Exegesis at South Africa's Stellenbosch Theological Seminary, could conclude his biography with this:

> And being dead, he speaketh yet. For we cannot imagine a time when Andrew Murray's words will have spent their force, and will be consigned to that oblivion which has overtaken the writings of so many authors who were famous in their day and generation. The issues with which he deals are eternal issues: the manner in which he deals with these issues is characterized by a sane and sanctified common sense: the spirit which breathes through all is that of a tender and yearning love. Is it too much to prophesy that Andrew Murray's works ...will continue to establish the faith and kindle the love and reinforce the purposes of unborn generations...?[47]

And, with that introduction, let us begin our walk with Andrew Murray into the progressively higher life in Christ.

1

ABIDE IN CHRIST

Thoughts on the Blessed Life of Fellowship with the Son of God

Chicago; London: Fleming H. Revell Co., 1895
From the 1864 Dutch version

Preface

January 1st

"Abide in Me, and I in you. As the branch cannot bear fruit of itself, except it abides in the vine; no more can you, except you abide in Me. I am the vine; you are the branches: he that abides in Me, and I in him, the same brings forth much fruit: for without me you can do nothing. ...If you abide in Me, and My words abide in you, you shall ask what you will, and it shall be done unto you."

JOHN 15: 3–8

During the life of Jesus on earth, the word He chiefly used when speaking of the relations of the disciples to Himself was: "Follow me." When about to leave for Heaven, He gave them a new word, in which their more intimate and spiritual union with Himself in glory should be expressed. That chosen word was: "*Abide in Me.*"

It is to be feared that there are many earnest followers of Jesus from whom the meaning of this word, with the blessed experience it promises, is very much hidden. While trusting in their Savior for pardon and for help, and seeking to some extent to obey Him, they have hardly realized to what closeness of union, to what intimacy of fellowship, to what wondrous oneness of life and interest, He invited them when He said, "*Abide in Me.*" This is not only an unspeakable loss to themselves, but the Church and the world suffer in what they lose.

If we ask the reason why those who have indeed accepted the Savior, and been made partakers of the renewing of the Holy Spirit, thus come short of the full salvation prepared for them, I am sure the answer will in very many cases be, that ignorance is the cause of the unbelief that fails of the inheritance. If, in our orthodox Churches, the abiding in Christ, the living union with Him, the experience of His daily and hourly presence and keeping, were preached with the same distinctness and urgency as His atonement and pardon through His blood, I am confident that many would be found to accept with gladness the invitation to such a life, and that its influence would be manifest in their experience of the purity and the power, the love and the joy, the fruit-bearing, and all the blessedness which the Savior connected with the *abiding in Him.*

Abide in Christ: As Christ in the Father

"As the Father has loved me, so I have loved you. Abide in my love, even as I abide in my Father's love" (John 15: 9–10). Think then of the mode of that abiding in the Father and His love which is to be the law of your life. *"I kept my Father's commandments and abide in His love."* His was a life of subjection and dependence and yet most blessed. To our proud Self-seeking nature, the thought of dependence and subjection suggests the idea of humiliation and servitude; but, in the life of love which the Son of God lived, and to which He invites us, they are the secret of blessedness. …

Hence when He had said, *"The Son can do nothing of Himself, except He see the Father do it,"* He adds at once, *"Whatsoever things the Father does, them also does the Son likewise: for the Father loves the Son, and shows Him all things that Himself does."* … [we learn] to glory in infirmities, to take pleasure in necessities and distresses for Christ's sake; for *"when I am weak, then am I strong."*

We rise above the ordinary tone in which so many Christians speak of their weakness, while they are content to abide there, because we have learned from Christ that in the life of Divine love, the emptying of Self and the sacrifice of our will, is the surest way to have all we can wish or will. Dependence, subjection, Self-sacrifice, are for the Christian as they were for Christ: the blessed path of life. As Christ lived through and in the Father, even so the believer lives through and in Christ. …

Believer! Abide in the love of Christ. Take and study His relation to the Father as pledge of what your own can become. … In the light of His life in the Father, let it henceforth be to you a blessed rest in the union with Him, an overflowing fountain of joy and strength. … We need to have our souls still unto God, gazing upon that life of Christ in the Father until the light from Heaven falls on it, and we hear the living voice of our Beloved whispering gently to us personally the teaching He gave to the disciples. Soul, be still and listen; let every thought be hushed until the Word has entered your heart too: *"Child! I love you, even as the Father loved me. Abide in my love, even as I abide in the Father's love. Your life on earth in me is to be the perfect counterpart of mine in the Father."*

All You Who Have Come to Him

"Come unto Me" (Matthew 11: 28); *"Abide in Me"* (John 15: 4). It is to you who have heard and hearkened to the call, *"Come unto me,"* that this new invitation comes, *"Abide in Me."* The message comes from the same loving Savior. You doubtless have never regretted having come at His call. You experienced that His word was truth; all His promises He

fulfilled; He made you partakers of the blessings and the joy of His love. Was not His welcome most hearty, His pardon full and free, His love most sweet and precious? You, more than once, at your first coming to Him, had reason to say, "The half was not told me."

And yet you have had to complain of disappointment: as time went on, your expectations were not realized. The blessings you once enjoyed were lost; the love and joy of your first meeting with your Savior, instead of deepening, have become faint and feeble. And often you have wondered what the reason could be, that with such a Savior, so mighty and so loving, your experience of salvation should not have been a fuller one.

The answer is very simple: you wandered from Him. The blessings He bestows are all connected with His *"Come to Me,"* and are only to be enjoyed in close fellowship with Himself. You either did not fully understand, or did not rightly remember, that the call meant, "Come to Me to *stay* with Me." And yet this was in very deed His object and purpose when first He called you to Himself. It was not to refresh you for a few short hours after your conversion with the joy of His love and deliverance, and then to send you forth to wander in sadness and sin.

He had destined you to something better than a short-lived blessedness, to be enjoyed only in times of special earnestness and prayer, and then to pass away, as you had to return to those duties in which far the greater part of life has to be spent. No, indeed; He had prepared for you an abiding dwelling with Himself, where your whole life and every moment of it might be spent, where the work of your daily life might be done, and where all the while you might be enjoying unbroken communion with Himself.

It was this He meant when to that first word, *"Come to Me,"* He added this, *"Abide in Me."* As earnest and faithful, as loving and tender, as the compassion that breathed in that blessed "Come," was the grace that added this no less blessed "Abide." As mighty as the attraction with which that first word drew you, were the bonds with which this second, had you but listened to it, would have kept you. And as great as were the blessings with which that coming was rewarded, so large, yea, and much greater, were the treasures to which that abiding would have given you access.

And observe especially, it was not that He said, "Come to me and abide *with* Me," but, "Abide *in* Me." The intercourse was not only to be unbroken, but most intimate and complete. He opened His arms, to press you to His bosom; He opened His heart, to welcome you there; He opened up all His Divine fullness of life and love, and offered to take you up into its fellowship, to make you wholly one with Himself. There was a depth of meaning you cannot yet realize in His words: *"Abide in Me."*...

In very truth, there is nothing that moved you to come, that does not plead with thousandfold greater force: "Abide in Him." You did well to come; you do better to abide. Who would, after seeking the King's palace, be content to stand in the door, when he is invited in to dwell in the King's presence, and share with Him in all the glory of His royal life? Oh, let us enter in and abide, and enjoy to the full all the rich supply His wondrous love has prepared for us!

And yet I fear that there are many who have indeed come to Jesus, and who yet have mournfully to confess that they know but little of this blessed abiding in Him. With some the reason is, that they never fully understood that this was the meaning of the Savior's call. With others, that though they heard the word, they did not know that such a life of abiding fellowship was possible, and indeed within their reach.

Others will say that, though they did believe that such a life was possible, and seek after it, they have never yet succeeded discovering the secret of its attainment. And others, again, alas! will confess that it is their own unfaithfulness that has kept them from the enjoyment of the blessing. When the Savior would have kept them, they were not found ready to stay; they were not prepared to give up everything, and always, only, wholly to abide in Jesus. …

Come, let us day by day set ourselves at His feet, and meditate on this word of His, with an eye fixed on Him alone. Let us set ourselves quiet trust before Him, waiting to hear His holy voice—the still small voice that is mightier than the storm that rends the rocks—breathing its quickening spirit within us, as He speaks: "*Abide in Me.*"

As the Branch in the Vine

January 2nd

"I am the Vine, you are the branches."

—JOHN 15: 5

It was in connection with the parable of the Vine that our Lord first used the expression, *"Abide in Me."* That parable, so simple, and yet so rich in its teaching, gives us the best and most complete illustration of the meaning of our Lord's command, and the union to which He invites us.

The parable teaches us the nature of that union. The connection between the vine and the branch is a living one. … No work of man can effect it: the branch, whether an original or an engrafted one, is such only by the Creator's own work, in virtue of which the life, the sap, the fatness, and the fruitfulness of the vine communicate themselves to the branch. And just so it is with we believers, too; our union with our Lord is no work of human wisdom or human will, but an act of God, by which the closest and most complete life-union is effected between the Son of God and the sinner.

"God has sent forth the Spirit of His Son into your hearts." The same Spirit which dwelled and still dwells in the Son, becomes the life of the believer. In the unity of that one Spirit, and the fellowship of the same life which is in Christ, we are one with Him. As between the vine and branch, it is a life-union that makes them one.

The parable teaches us the completeness of the union. So close is the union between the vine and the branch, that each is nothing without the other, that each is wholly and only for the other.

Without the vine the branch can do nothing. To the vine it owes its right of place in the vineyard, its life and its fruitfulness. And so the Lord says, *"Without me you can do nothing."* The believer can each day be pleasing to God only in that which we do through the power of Christ dwelling in us. The daily inflowing of the life-sap of the Holy Spirit is our only power to bring forth fruit. We live alone in Him and are for each moment dependent on Him alone.

Without the branch the vine can also do nothing. A vine without branches can bear no fruit. No less indispensable than the vine to the branch, is the branch to the vine. Such is the wonderful condescension of the grace of Jesus—that just as His people are dependent on Him, He has made Himself dependent on them. Without His disciples, He cannot dispense His blessing to the world; He cannot offer sinners the grapes of the heavenly Canaan. Marvel not! It is His own appointment; and this is the high honor to which He has called His redeemed ones, that as indispensable as He is to them in Heaven, that from Him their fruit may be found, so indispensable are they to Him on earth, that through them His fruit may be found.

Believers, meditate on this, until your soul bows to worship in presence of the mystery of the perfect union between Christ and the believer. There is more: as neither vine nor branch is anything without the other, so is neither anything except *for* the other. All the vine possesses belongs to the branches. The vine does not gather from the soil its fatness and its sweetness for itself; all it has is at the disposal of the branches. As it is the parent, so it is the servant of the branches. And Jesus, to whom we owe our life, how completely does He give Himself for us and to us: *"The glory You gave me, I have given them"*; *"He that believes in me, the works that I do shall he do also; and greater works shall he do."* All His fullness and all His riches are for you, O believer; for the vine does not live for itself, keeps nothing for itself, but exists only for the branches. All that Jesus is in Heaven, He is for us: He has no interest there separate from ours; as our representative, He stands before the Father.

And all the branch possesses belongs to the vine. The branch does not exist for itself, but to bear fruit that can proclaim the excellence of the vine: it has no reason of existence except to be of service to the vine—a glorious image of the calling of the believer, and the entireness of his consecration to the service of his Lord. As Jesus gives Himself so wholly over to us, we feel the urge to be wholly our Lord's. Every power of our being, every moment of our life, every thought and feeling, belong to Jesus, that from Him and for Him we may bring forth fruit. As we realize what the vine is to the branch, and what the branch is meant to be to the vine, we feel that we have but one thing to think of and to live for, and that is, the will, the glory, the work, the kingdom of his blessed Lord—the bringing forth of fruit to the glory of His name.

The parable teaches us the object of the union. The branches are for fruit and fruit alone. *"Every branch that bears not fruit He takes away."* The branch needs its leaves for the maintenance of its own life, and the perfection of its fruit: the fruit itself it bears to give away to those around. As the believer enters into his calling as a branch, we see that we have to forget our Self, and to live entirely for our fellow men—to love them, to seek for them, and to save them. Jesus came for this. ... It is for fruit, much fruit, that the Father has made us one with Jesus.

Wondrous parable of the vine—unveiling the mysteries of the Divine love, of the heavenly life, of the world of Spirit—how little have I understood you! Jesus the living vine in Heaven, and I the living branch on earth! How little have I understood how great my need, but also how perfect my claim, to all His fullness! How little understood, how great His need, but also how perfect His claim, to my emptiness!

Let me, in its beautiful light, study the wondrous union between Jesus and His people, until it becomes to me the guide into full communion with my beloved Lord. Let me listen and believe, until my whole being cries out, "Jesus is indeed to me the True Vine, bearing me, nourishing me, supplying me, using me, and filling me to the full to make me bring forth fruit abundantly." Then shall I not fear to say, "I am indeed a branch to Jesus, the True Vine, abiding in Him, resting in Him, waiting in Him, serving Him, and living only that, through me, too, He may show forth the riches of His grace, and give His fruit to a perishing world."

It is when we try thus to understand the meaning of the parable, that the blessed command spoken in connection with it will come home to us in its true power. The thought of what the vine is to the branch, and Jesus to the believer, will give new force to the words, *"Abide in Me!"*

The Crucified One

January 3rd

"I am crucified with Christ. Nevertheless, I live; yet not I, but Christ lives in me."

—GALATIANS 2: 20

I am *"crucified with Christ."* Thus the apostle expresses his assurance of his fellowship with Christ in His sufferings and death, and his full participation in all the power and the blessing of that death. And so really did he mean what he said, and know that he was now indeed dead, that he adds: *"It is no longer I that live, but Christ that lives in me."*

How blessed must be the experience of such a union with the Lord Jesus! To be able to look upon His death as mine, just as really as it was His—upon His perfect obedience to God, His victory over sin, and complete deliverance from its power, as mine; and to realize that the power of that death does by faith work daily with a Divine energy in mortifying the flesh, and renewing the whole life into the perfect conformity to the resurrection life of Jesus!

Abiding in Jesus, the Crucified One, is the secret of the growth of that new life which is ever begotten of the death of nature. Let us try to understand this. The suggestive expression, "*Planted into the likeness of His death,*" will teach us what the abiding in the Crucified One means. When a graft is united with the stock on which it is to grow, we know that it must be kept fixed, it must abide in the place where the stock has been cut, been wounded, to make an opening to receive the graft. No graft without wounding—the laying bare and opening up of the inner life of the tree to receive the stranger branch. It is only through such wounding that access can be obtained to the fellowship of the sap and the growth and the life of the stronger stem. Even so with Jesus and the sinner. Only when we are planted into the likeness of His death shall we also be in the likeness of His resurrection, partakers of the life and the power there are in Him. In the death of the Cross Christ was wounded, and in His opened wounds a place prepared where we might be grafted in.

And just as one might say to a graft, and does practically say as it is fixed in its place, "Abide here in the wound of the stem, that is now to bear you"; so to the believing soul the message comes, "Abide in the wounds of Jesus; there is the place of union, and life, and growth. There you shall see how His heart was opened to receive you; how His flesh was rent that the way might be opened for your being made one with Him, and having access to all the blessings flowing from His divine nature." You have also noticed how the graft has to be torn away from the tree where it by nature grew, and to be cut into conformity to the place prepared for it in the wounded stem. Even so the believer has to be made conformable to Christ's death—to be crucified and to die with Him. …

There is a fellowship between Christ's sufferings and your sufferings. His experiences must become yours. The disposition He manifested in choosing and bearing the cross must be yours. Like Him, you will have to give full assent to the righteous judgment and curse of a holy God against sin. Like Him, you have to consent to yield your life, as laden with sin and curse, to death, and through it to pass to the new life. Like Him, you shall experience that it is only through the Self-sacrifice of Gethsemane and Calvary that the path is to be found to the joy and the fruit-bearing of the resurrection life. …

It is in Jesus, the Crucified One, I must abide. I must learn to look upon the cross as not only an atonement to God, but also a victory over the devil—not only a deliverance from the guilt, but also from the power of sin. I must gaze on Him on the cross as wholly mine, offering Himself to receive me into the closest union and fellowship, and to make me partaker of the full power of His death to sin, and the new life of victory to which it is but the gateway. I must yield myself to Him in an undivided surrender, with much prayer and strong desire, imploring to be admitted into the ever closer fellowship and conformity of His death, of the spirit in which He died that death. …

The life He imparts is a life *from the dead*; each new experience of the power of that life depends upon the fellowship of the death. The death and the life are inseparable. All the grace which Jesus the Saving One gives is given only in the path of fellowship with Jesus the Crucified One. Christ came and took my place; I must put myself in His place, and abide there. And there is but one place which is both His and mine: that place is the cross—His in virtue of His free choice; mine by reason of the curse of sin. He came there to seek me; there alone I can find Him. When He found me there, it was the place of cursing; this He experienced, for "*cursed is every one that hangs on a tree.*" He made it a place of blessing; this I experienced, for Christ has delivered us from the curse, being made a curse for us. … When I stand in His place, which is still always mine, I am still what I was by nature, the accursed one, who deserves to die; but as united to Him, I share His blessing, and receive His life.

Beloved believer! It is a deep mystery, this of the cross of Christ. I fear there are many Christians who are content to look upon the cross, with Christ on it dying for their sins, who have little heart for *fellowship with* the Crucified One. They hardly know that He invites them to it. ... They have no conception of what it is to be crucified with Christ that bearing the cross means likeness to Christ in the principles which animated Him in His path of obedience. The entire surrender of all Self-will, the complete denial to the flesh of its every desire and pleasure, the perfect separation from the world in all its ways of thinking and acting, the losing and hating of one's life, the giving up of Self and its interests for the sake of others-this is the disposition which marks him who has taken up Christ's cross, who seeks to say, *"I am crucified with Christ; I abide in Christ, the Crucified One."*

... O Jesus, our crucified Redeemer, teach us not only to believe on You, but to abide in You, to take Your cross not only as the ground of our pardon, but also as the law of our life. Oh, teach us to love it not only because on it You did bear our curse, but because on it we enter into the closest fellowship with Yourself, and are crucified with You. And teach us, that as we yield ourselves wholly to be possessed of the Spirit in which You did bear the cross, we shall be made partakers of the power and the blessing to which the cross alone gives access.

And in His Love

January 4th

"As the Father has loved Me, so have I loved you: abide in My love"

—JOHN 15: 9

As the Father has loved Me." How shall we be able to form right conceptions of this love? Lord, teach us. God is love. Love is His very being. Love is not an attribute, but the very essence of His nature, the center round which all His glorious attributes gather. It was because He was love that He was the Father, and that there was a Son. Love needs an object to whom it can give itself away, in whom it can lose itself, with whom it can make itself one. Because God is love, there must be a Father and a Son. The love of the Father to the Son is that Divine passion with which He delights in the Son, and speaks, *"My beloved Son, in whom I am well pleased."* The Divine love is as a burning fire; in all its intensity and infinity it has but one object and but one joy, and that is the only begotten Son.

When we gather together all the attributes of God—His infinity, His perfection, His immensity, His majesty, His omnipotence—and consider them but as the rays of the glory of His love, we still fail in forming any conception of what that love must be. It is a love that passes knowledge.

And yet this love of God to His Son must serve...as the [lens through] which you are to learn how Jesus loves you. As one of His redeemed ones, you are His delight, and all His desire is to you, with the longing of a love which is stronger than death, and which many waters cannot quench. His heart yearns after you, seeking your fellowship and your love. Were it needed, He could die again to possess you. As the Father loved the Son, and could not live without Him— could not be God the blessed without Him—so Jesus loves you. His life is bound up in yours; you are to Him inexpressibly more indispensable and precious than you ever can know. You are one with Himself. *"As the Father has loved me, so have I loved you."* What a love! It is an eternal love.

From before the foundation of the world, God's Word teaches us this: the purpose had been formed that Christ should be the Head of His Church, that He should have a body in which His glory could be set forth. In that eternity He loved and longed for those who had been given Him by the Father; and when He came and told His disciples that He loved them, it was indeed not with a love of earth and of time, but with the love of eternity. And it is with that same infinite love that His eye still rests upon each of us here seeking to abide in Him, and in each breathing of that love there is indeed the power of eternity. *"I have loved you with an everlasting love."*

It is a perfect love. It gives all, and holds nothing back. *"The Father loves the Son, and has given all things into His hand."* And just so Jesus loves His own: all He has is theirs. When it was needed, He sacrificed His throne and crown for you: He did not count His own life and blood too dear to give for you. His righteousness, His Spirit, His glory, even His throne, all are yours. This love holds nothing, nothing back, but, in a manner which no human mind can fathom, makes you one with itself. O wondrous love! To love us even as the Father loved Him, and to offer us this love as our everyday dwelling.

It is a gentle and most tender love. As we think of the love of the Father to the Son, we see in the Son everything so infinitely worthy of that love. When we think of Christ's love to us, there is nothing but sin and unworthiness to meet the eye. And the question comes: How can that love within the bosom of the divine life and its perfections be compared to the love that rests on sinners? Can it indeed be the same love? Blessed be God, we know it is so.

The nature of love is always one, however different the objects. Christ knows of no other law of love but that with which His Father loved Him. Our wretchedness only serves to call out more distinctly the beauty of love, such as could not be seen even in Heaven. With the tenderest compassion He bows to our weakness, with patience inconceivable He bears with our slowness, with the gentlest lovingkindness He meets our fears and our follies. It is the love of the Father to the Son, beautified, glorified, in its condescension, in its exquisite adaptation to our needs.

And it is an unchangeable love. *"Having loved His own which were in the world, He loved them to the end." "The mountains shall depart, and the hills be removed, but My kindness shall not depart from you."* The promise with which it begins its work in the soul is this: *"I shall not leave you, until I have done that which I have spoken to you of."* And just as our wretchedness was what first drew it to us, so the sin, with which it is so often grieved, and which may well cause us to fear and doubt, is but a new motive for it to hold to us all the more. And why? We can give no reason but this: *"As the Father has loved Me, so I have loved you."*

And now, does not this love suggest the motive, the measure, and the means of that surrender by which we yield ourselves wholly to abide in Him? This love surely supplies a motive. Only look and see how this love stands and pleads and prays. Gaze, oh, gaze on the Divine form, the eternal glory, the heavenly beauty, the tenderly pleading gentleness of the crucified love, as it stretches out its pierced hands and says, "Oh, will you not abide with Me? Will you not come and abide in Me?" …

"Soul, as the Father has loved Me, so I have loved you: abide in My love." … That love is not only the motive, but also the measure, of our surrender to abide in it. Love gives all, but asks all. It does so, not because it grudges us aught, but because without this it cannot get possession of us to fill us with itself. In the love of the Father and the Son, it was so. In the love of Jesus to us, it was so. In our entering into His love to abide there, it must be so too; our surrender to it must have no other measure than its surrender to us.

As Your Redemption

January 5th

"Of God are you in Christ Jesus, who was made for us … righteousness and sanctification, and redemption."
—1 CORINTHIANS 1: 30

Here we have the top of the ladder, reaching into heaven—the blessed end to which Christ and life in Him is to lead. The word *redemption*, though sometimes applied to our deliverance from the guilt of sin, here refers to our complete and final deliverance from all its consequences, when the Redeemer's work shall become fully manifest, even to the redemption of the body itself (Romans 8: 21–23; Ephesians 1: 14; 4: 30).

The expression points us to the highest glory to be hoped for in the future, and therefore also to the highest blessing to be enjoyed in the present in Christ. We have seen how, as a Prophet, Christ is our wisdom, revealing to us God and His love, with the nature and conditions of the salvation that love has prepared. As a Priest, He is our righteousness, restoring us to right relations to God, and securing us His favor and friendship. As a King, He is our sanctification, forming and guiding us into the obedience to the Father's holy will. As these three offices work out God's one purpose, the grand consummation will be reached, the complete deliverance from sin and all its effects be accomplished, and ransomed humanity regain all that it had ever lost.

Christ is made of God unto us redemption. The word invites us to look upon Jesus, not only as He lived on earth, teaching us by word and example, as He died, to reconcile us with God, as He lives again, a victorious King, rising to receive His crown, but as, sitting at the right hand of God, He takes again the glory which He had with the Father, before the world began, and holds it there for us. It consists in this, that there His human nature, yea, His human body, freed from all the consequences of sin to which He once had been exposed, is now admitted to share the divine glory. As Son of Man, He dwells on the throne and in the bosom of the Father: the deliverance from what He had to suffer from sin is complete and eternal. The complete redemption is found embodied in His own Person: what He as man is and has in Heaven is the complete redemption. He is made of God to us redemption. We are in Him as such. And the more intelligently and believingly we abide in Him as our redemption, the more shall we experience, even here, of "*the powers of the world to come.*"

As our communion with Him becomes more intimate and intense, and we let the Holy Spirit reveal Him to us in His heavenly glory, the more we realize how the life in us is the life of One who sits upon the throne of Heaven. We feel the power of an endless life working in us. We taste the eternal life. We have the foretaste of the eternal glory. … The believer who abides in Christ as his full redemption, realizes even now his spiritual victory over death. It becomes to him the servant that removes the last rags of the old carnal vesture, ere he be clothed upon with the new body of glory. … This faith exercises its sanctifying influence in the willing surrender of the sinful members of the body to be mortified and completely subjected to the dominion of the Spirit, as preparation for the time when the frail body shall be changed and fashioned like to His glorious body.

This full redemption of Christ as extending to the body, has a depth of meaning not easily expressed. It was of man as a whole—soul and body—that it is said that he was made in the image and likeness of God. In the angels, God had created spirits without material bodies; in the creation of the world, there was matter without spirit. Man was to be the highest specimen of divine art: the combination in one being, of matter and spirit in perfect harmony, as type of the most perfect union between God and His own creation. Sin entered in, and appeared to thwart the divine plan: the material obtained a fearful supremacy over the spiritual. The Word was made flesh, the divine fullness received an embodiment in the humanity of Christ, that the redemption might be a complete and perfect one; that the whole creation, which now groans and travails in pain together, might be delivered from the bondage of corruption into the liberty of the glory of the children of God. God's purpose will not be accomplished, and Christ's glory will not be manifested fully, until the body, with that whole of nature of which it is part and head, has been transfigured by the power of the spiritual life, and made the transparent vesture for showing forth the glory of the Infinite Spirit. Then only shall we understand: "*Christ Jesus is made unto us (complete) redemption.*" Meantime we are taught to believe: "*Of God are you in Christ, as your redemption.*"

This is not meant as a revelation, to be left to the future; for the full development of the Christian life, our present abiding in Christ must seek to enter into and appropriate it. We do this as we learn to triumph over death. We do it as we learn to look upon Christ as the Lord of our body, claiming its entire consecration, securing even here, if faith will claim it (Mark 16:17-18), victory over the terrible dominion sin hath had in the body. We do this as we learn to look on all nature as part of the Kingdom of Christ, destined, even though it be through a baptism of fire, to partake in His redemption. We do it as we allow the powers of the coming world to possess us, and to lift us up into a life in the heavenly places, to enlarge our hearts and our views, to anticipate, even here, the things which have never entered into the heart of man to conceive.

Believer, abide in Christ as your redemption. Let this be the crown of your Christian life. Seek it not first or only, apart from the knowledge of Christ in His other relations. But seek it truly as that to which they are meant to lead you up. Abide in Christ as your redemption. Nothing will fit you for this but faithfulness in the previous steps of the Christian life. Abide in Him as your wisdom, the perfect revelation of all that God is and has for you. Follow, in the daily ordering of the inner and the outer life, with meek docility His teaching, and you shall be counted worthy to have secrets revealed to you which to most disciples are a sealed book. The wisdom will lead you into the mysteries of complete redemption. Abide in Him as your righteousness, and dwell clothed upon with Him in that inner sanctuary of the Father's favor and presence to which His righteousness gives you access. As you rejoice in your reconciliation, you shall understand how it includes all things, and how they too wait the full redemption; *"for it pleased the Father by Him to reconcile all things unto Himself; by Him, I say, whether they be things on earth or things in Heaven."*

And abide in Him as your sanctification; the experience of His power to make you holy, spirit and soul and body, will quicken your faith in a holiness that shall not cease its work until the bells of the horses and every pot in Jerusalem shall be holiness to the Lord. Abide in Him as your redemption, and live, even here, as the heir of the future glory. And as you seek to experience in yourself to the full, the power of His saving grace, your heart shall be enlarged to realize the position man has been destined to occupy in the universe, as having all things made subject to him, and you shall for your part be fitted to live worthy of that high and heavenly calling.

As Your Righteousness

January 6th

"Of God are you in Christ Jesus, who was made for us … righteousness and sanctification, and redemption."
—1 CORINTHIANS 1: 30.

The first of the great blessings which Christ our wisdom reveals to us as prepared in Himself, is—*righteousness*. It is not difficult to see why this must be first. There can be no real prosperity or progress in a nation, a home, or a soul, unless there be peace. As not even a machine can do its work unless it be in rest, secured on a good foundation, quietness and assurance are indispensable to our moral and spiritual wellbeing. Sin had disturbed all our relations; we were out of harmony with ourselves, with men, and with God.

The first requirement of a salvation that should really bring blessedness to us was peace. And peace can only come with right. Where everything is as God would have it, in God's order and in harmony with His will, there alone can peace reign. Jesus Christ came to restore peace on earth, and peace in the soul, by restoring righteousness.

Because He is Melchizedek, King of righteousness, He reigns as King of Salem, King of peace (Hebrews 7: 2). He so fulfills the promise the prophets held out: *"A king shall reign in righteousness," and "the work of righteousness shall be peace, and the effect of righteousness, quietness and assurance forever"* (Isaiah 32: 1, 17). Christ is our righteousness; of God we are *in Him* as our righteousness; we are made the righteousness of God *in Him.* Let us try to understand what this means. When first as sinners were led to trust in Christ for salvation, we, as a rule, looked more to His work than His person. As we look at the cross, and Christ suffering there, the Righteous One for the unrighteous, we see in that atoning death the only but sufficient foundation for our faith in God's pardoning mercy. The substitution, and the curse-bearing, and the atonement of Christ dying in the stead of sinners, are what gives us peace.

And as we understand how the righteousness which Christ brings becomes our very own, and how, in the strength of that, we are counted righteous before God, we feel that we have what we need to restore us to God's favor: *"Being justified by faith, we have peace with God."* We seek to wear this robe of righteousness in the ever-renewed faith in the glorious gift of righteousness which has been bestowed upon us. But as time goes on, and we seek to *grow* in the Christian life, new needs arise. We want to understand more fully how it is that God can thus justify the ungodly on the strength of the righteousness of another. We find the answer in the wonderful teaching of Scripture as to the true union of the believer *with Christ*.... He sees that it is because Christ had made Himself one with His people, and they were one with Him; that it was in perfect accordance with all law in the kingdom of nature and of Heaven, that each member of the body should have the full benefit of the doing and the suffering as of the life of the head. And so we are led to feel that it can only be in fully realizing our *personal union with Christ* as the Head, that we can fully experience the power of His righteousness to bring the soul into the full favor and fellowship of the Holy One. The *work of Christ* does not become less precious, but the *Person of Christ* more so....

And this experience sheds its light again upon Scripture. It leads us to notice... how distinctly the righteousness of God, as it becomes ours, is connected with the Person of the Redeemer. "This is His name whereby *He* shall be called, *Jehovah our righteousness.*" *"In Jehovah* have I righteousness and strength." "Of God is *He* made unto us righteousness." "That we might be made the righteousness of God *in Him.*" "That I may be found *in Him*, having the righteousness of God."

We see how inseparable righteousness and life in Christ are from each other: *"The righteousness of one comes upon all unto justification of life." "They which receive the gift of righteousness shall reign in life by one, Jesus Christ."* And he understands what deep meaning there is in the key-word of the Epistle to the Romans: *"The righteous shall live by faith."* We are not now content with only thinking of the imputed righteousness as our robe. But, by *putting on Jesus Christ,* and seeking to be wrapped up in, to be clothed ... with Himself and His life, we feel how completely the righteousness of God is ours, because the Lord our righteousness is ours. ... The living Christ Himself is our righteousness—that Christ who watches over, and keeps and loves us as His own. It is no longer an impossibility to walk all the day enrobed in the loving presence with which He covers His people.

Such an experience leads still further. The life and the righteousness [of Christ] are inseparably linked, and the believer becomes more conscious than before of a righteous nature planted within us. The new person created in Christ Jesus, is *"created in righteousness and true holiness."* ... The union to Jesus has effected a change not only in the relation to God, but in the personal state before God. And as the intimate fellowship to which the union has opened up the way is maintained, the growing renewal of the whole being makes righteousness to be our very nature.

To a Christian who begins to see the deep meaning of the truth, "*He is made to us righteousness*," it is hardly necessary to say, "Abide in Him." As long as he only thought of the righteousness of the substitute, and our being counted judicially righteous for His sake, the absolute necessity of abiding in Him was not apparent. But as the glory of "*Jehovah our righteousness*" unfolds to the view, he sees that abiding in Him personally is the only way to stand, at all times, complete and accepted before God, as it is the only way to realize how the new and righteous nature can be strengthened from Jesus our Head.

To the penitent sinner, the chief thought was the righteousness which comes through Jesus dying for sin; to the intelligent and advancing believer, Jesus, the Living One, through whom the righteousness comes, is everything, because having Him we have the righteousness too.

Believer, abide in Christ as your righteousness. You bear about with you a nature altogether corrupt and vile, ever seeking to rise up and darken your sense of acceptance, and of access to unbroken fellowship with the Father. Nothing can enable you to dwell and walk in the light of God, without even the shadow of a cloud between, but the habitual abiding in Christ as your righteousness.

As Your Sanctification

January 7th

"Of God are you in Christ Jesus, who was made for us ... righteousness and sanctification, and redemption."
—1 CORINTHIANS 1: 30

P*aul unto the Church of God which is at Corinth to them that are sanctified in Christ Jesus, called to be saints";* thus the chapter opens in which we are taught that in Christ is our sanctification. In the Old Testament, believers were called the righteous; in the New Testament they are called saints, the holy ones, sanctified *in* Christ Jesus.

Holy is higher than righteous. Holy in God has reference to His inmost being; righteous, to His dealings with His creatures. In man, righteousness is but a stepping stone to holiness. It is in this he can approach most near to the perfection of God (compare Matthew 5: 48; 1 Peter 1: 16). In the Old Testament righteousness was found, while holiness was only typified; *in* Jesus Christ, the Holy One, and in His people, His saints or holy ones, it is first realized.

As in Scripture—as in our text—so in personal experience, righteousness precedes holiness. When first we found Christ as our righteousness, we had such joy in the new-made discovery that the study of holiness hardly had a place. But as we grow, the desire for holiness makes itself felt, and we seek to know what provision God has made for supplying that need.

A superficial acquaintance with God's plan leads to the view that while justification is God's work, by faith in Christ, sanctification is our work, to be performed under the influence of the gratitude we feel for the deliverance we have experienced, and by the aid of the Holy Spirit. But the earnest Christian soon finds how little gratitude can supply the power. When we think that more prayer will bring it, we find that, indispensable as prayer is, it is not enough. Often we struggle hopelessly for years, until we listen to the teaching of the Spirit, as He glorifies Christ again, and reveals Christ, our sanctification, to be appropriated by faith alone. ...

Holiness is the very nature of God, and that alone is holy which God takes possession of and fills with Himself. God's answer to the question, "How could sinful man become holy?" is: "*Christ, the Holy One of God*"; in Him, whom the Father sanctified and sent into the world, God's holiness was revealed incarnate, and brought within reach of man. "*I sanctify myself for them, that they also may be sanctified in truth.*" There is no other way of our becoming holy, but by becoming partakers of the holiness of Christ. And there is no other way of this taking place than by our personal spiritual union with Him, so that through His Holy Spirit—His holy life—flows into us. ...

Abiding by faith *in* Christ our sanctification is the simple secret of a holy life. The measure of sanctification will depend on the measure of abiding in Him; as the soul learns wholly to abide in Christ, the promise is increasingly fulfilled: "*The very God of peace sanctify you wholly.*"

... Christian, fear not to claim God's promises to make you holy. Listen not to the suggestion that the corruption of your old nature would render holiness an impossibility. In your flesh dwells no good thing, and that flesh, though crucified with Christ, is not yet dead, but will continually seek to rise and lead you to evil. But the Father is the Husbandman. He has grafted the life of Christ on your life. That holy life is mightier than your evil life; under the watchful care of the Husbandman, that new life can keep down the workings of the evil life within you. The evil nature is there, with its unchanged tendency to rise up and show itself. But the new nature is there too—the living Christ, your sanctification, is there; and through Him all your powers can be sanctified as they rise into life, and be made to bear fruit to the glory of the Father.

And now, if you would live a holy life, abide in Christ your sanctification. Look upon Him as the Holy One of God, made man that He might communicate to us the holiness of God. Listen when Scripture teaches that there is within you a new nature, a new man, created in Christ Jesus in righteousness and true holiness. Remember that this holy nature which is in you is singularly fitted for living a holy life, and performing all holy duties, as much so as the old nature is for doing evil. Understand that this holy nature within you has its root and life in Christ in Heaven, and can only grow and become strong as the intercourse between it and its source is uninterrupted.

And above all, believe most confidently that Jesus Christ Himself delights in maintaining that new nature within you, and imparting to it His own strength and wisdom for its work. Let that faith lead you daily to the surrender of all Self-confidence, and the confession of the utter corruption of all there is in you by nature. Let it fill you with a quiet and assured confidence that you are indeed able to do what the Father expects of you as His child, under the covenant of His grace, because you have Christ strengthening you. Let it teach you to lay yourself and your services on the altar as spiritual sacrifices, holy and acceptable in His sight, a sweet-smelling savor. Look not upon a life of holiness as a strain and an effort, but as the natural outgrowth of *the life of Christ within you.* The evil nature is there, with its unchanged tendency to rise up and show itself. But the new nature is there too—the living Christ, your sanctification, is there—and through Him all your powers can be sanctified as they rise into life, and be made to bear fruit to the glory of the Father.

And now, if you would live a holy life, abide in Christ your sanctification. Look upon Him as the Holy One of God, made man that He might communicate to us the holiness of God. Listen when Scripture teaches that there is within you a new nature, a new man, created in Christ Jesus in righteousness and true holiness. Remember that this holy nature which is in you is singularly fitted for living a holy life, and performing all holy duties, as much so as the old nature is for doing evil. Understand that this holy nature within you has its root and life in Christ in heaven, and can only grow and become strong as the intercourse between it and its source is uninterrupted.

And above all, believe most confidently that Jesus Christ Himself delights in maintaining that new nature within you, and imparting to it His own strength and wisdom for its work. Let that faith lead you daily to the surrender of all Self-confidence, and the confession of the utter corruption of all there is in you by nature. Let it fill you with a quiet and assured confidence that you are indeed able to do what the Father expects of you as His child, under the covenant of His grace, because you have Christ strengthening you. Let it teach you to lay yourself and your services on the altar as spiritual sacrifices, holy and acceptable in His sight, a sweet-smelling savor. Look not upon a life of holiness as a strain and an effort, but as the natural outgrowth of the life of Christ within you. And let ever again a quiet, hopeful, gladsome faith hold itself assured that all you need for a holy life will most assuredly be given you out of the holiness of Jesus. …

As Your Strength

January 8th

"Be strong in the Lord and in the power of his might."

—EPHESIANS 6: 10

There is no truth more generally admitted among earnest Christians than that of their utter weakness. There is no truth more generally misunderstood and abused. Here, as elsewhere, God's thoughts are heaven-high above man's thoughts. We often try to forget our weakness; God wants us to remember it, to feel it deeply. We want to conquer our weakness and to be freed from it: God wants us to rest and even rejoice in it. We mourn over our weakness: Christ teaches His servant to say, "*I take pleasure in infirmities; most gladly will I glory in my infirmities.*" We think of our weakness as our greatest hindrance in the life and service of God: God tells us that it is the secret of strength and success. It is our weakness, heartily accepted and continually realized, that gives us our claim and access to the strength of Him who has said, "*My strength is made perfect in weakness.*"

When our Lord was about to take His seat upon the throne, one of His last words was: "*All power is given unto me in Heaven and on earth.*" ... Hence He connected with this revelation of what He was to receive, the promise of the share that His disciples would have in it: "*When I am ascended, you shall receive power from on high*" (Luke 24:49; Acts 1:8). It is in the power of the omnipotent Savior that the believer must find strength for life and for work. It was thus with the disciples. During ten days they worshipped and waited at the footstool of His throne. They gave expression to their faith in Him as their Savior, to their adoration of Him as their Lord, to their love to Him as their Friend, to their devotion and readiness to work for Him as their Master. Jesus Christ was the one object of thought, of love, of delight. In such worship of faith and devotion their souls grew up into intense communion with Him upon the throne, and when they were prepared, the baptism of power came. It was power within and power around.

The power came to qualify for the work to which they had yielded themselves—of testifying by life and word to their unseen Lord. With some the chief testimony was to be that of a holy life, revealing the Heaven and the Christ from whom it came. The power came to set up the Kingdom within them, to give them the victory over sin and Self, to fit them by living experience to testify to the power of Jesus on the throne, to make us live in the world as saints. Others were to give themselves up entirely to the speaking in the name of Jesus. But all needed and all received the gift of power, to prove that now Jesus had received the Kingdom of the Father, all power in Heaven and earth was indeed given to Him, and by Him imparted to His people just as they needed it, whether for a holy life or effective service. They received the gift of power, to prove to the world that the Kingdom of God, to which they professed to belong, was not in word but in power. By having power within, they had power without and around. The power of God was felt even by those who would not yield themselves to it (Acts 2:43; 4:13; 5:13).

And what Jesus was to these first disciples, He is to us too. Our whole life and calling as disciples find their origin and their guarantee in the words: "*All power is given to me in Heaven and on earth.*" What He does in and through us, He does with almighty power. What He claims or demands, He works Himself by that same power. All He gives, He gives with power. Every blessing He bestows, every promise He fulfills, every grace He works—all, all is to be with power. Everything that comes from this Jesus on the throne of power is to bear the stamp of power. The weakest believer may be confident that in asking to be kept from sin, to grow in holiness, to bring forth much fruit, he or she may count upon these ... petitions being fulfilled with Divine power. The power is in Jesus; Jesus is ours with all His fullness; it is in us His members that the power is to work and be made manifest.

And if we want to know how the power is bestowed, the answer is simple: Christ gives His power in us by giving His life in us. He does not, as so many believers imagine, take the feeble life He finds in them, and impart a little strength to aid them in their feeble efforts. No; it is in giving His own life in us that He gives us His power. The Holy Spirit came down to the disciples direct from the heart of their exalted Lord, bringing down into them the glorious life of Heaven into which He had entered.

And so His people are still taught to be strong in the Lord and in the power of His might. When He strengthens them, it is not by taking away the sense of feebleness, and giving in its place the feeling of strength. By no means. But in a very wonderful way leaving and even increasing the sense of utter impotence, He gives them along with it the consciousness of strength in Him. *"We have this treasure in earthen vessels, that the excellency of the power may be of God and not of us."* The feebleness and the strength are side by side; as the one grows, the other too, until they understand the saying, *"When I am weak, then am I strong; I glory in my infirmities, that the power of Christ may rest on me."*

As believing disciples, we learn to look upon Christ on the throne, Christ the Omnipotent, as our life. We study that life in its infinite perfection and purity, in its strength and glory; it is the eternal life dwelling in a glorified soul. And when we think of our own inner life, and long for holiness, to live well-pleasing unto God, or for power to do the Father's work, we look up, and, rejoicing that Christ is our life, we confidently reckon that that life will work mightily in us all we need.

In things little and things great, in the being kept from sin from moment to moment for which we have learned to look, or in the struggle with some special difficulty or temptation, the power of Christ is the measure of our expectation. We live a most joyous and blessed life, not because we are no longer feeble, but because, being utterly helpless, we consent and expect to have the mighty Savior work in us.

God Himself Will Establish You

January 9th

"He which establishes us with you in Christ, is God."

—2 CORINTHIANS 1: 21

These words of Paul teach us a much needed and most blessed truth—that just as our first being united with Christ was the work of Divine omnipotence, so we may look to the Father, too, for being kept and being fixed more firmly in Him. *"The Lord will perfect that which concerns me"*—this expression of confidence should ever accompany the prayer, *"Forsake not the work of Your own hands."* In all our longings and prayers to attain to a deeper and more perfect abiding in Christ, we must hold fast our confidence: *"He which has begun a good work in you, will perform it until the day of Jesus Christ."* There is nothing that will so help to root and ground us in Christ as this faith: *"He which establishes us in Christ is God."*

How many there are who can witness that this faith is just what they need! They continually mourn over the variableness of their spiritual life. Sometimes there are hours and days of deep earnestness, and even of blessed experience of the grace of God. But how little is needed to mar their peace, to bring a cloud over the soul! And then, how their faith is shaken! All efforts to regain their standing appear utterly fruitless; and neither solemn vows, nor watching and prayer, avail to restore to them the peace they for a while had tasted. Could they but understand how just their own efforts are the cause of their failure, because it is God alone who can establish us in Christ Jesus. They would see that just as in justification they had to cease from their own working, and to accept in faith the promise that God would give them life in Christ, so now, in the matter of their sanctification, their first need is to cease from striving themselves to establish the connection with Christ more firmly, and to allow God to do it.

"God is faithful; by whom you were called unto the fellowship of His Son Jesus Christ." What we need is the simple faith that the establishing in Christ, day by day, is God's work—a work that He delights to do, in spite of all our weakness and unfaithfulness, if we will but trust Him for it. To the blessedness of such a faith, and the experience it brings, many can testify. What peace and rest, to know that there is a Husbandman who cares for the branch, to see that it grows stronger, and that its union with the Vine becomes more perfect, who watches over every hindrance and danger, who supplies every needed aid! What peace and rest, fully and finally to give up our abiding into the care of God, and never have a wish or thought—never to offer a prayer or engage in an exercise connected with it—without first having the glad remembrance that what we do is only the manifestation of what God is doing in us!

The establishing in Christ is His work: He accomplishes it by stirring us to watch, and wait, and work. But this He can do with power only as we cease interrupting Him by our Self-working—as we accept in faith the dependent posture which honors Him and opens the heart to let Him work. How such a faith frees the soul from care and responsibility! In the midst of the rush and bustle of the world's stirring life, amid the subtle and ceaseless temptations of sin, amid all the daily cares and trials that so easily distract and lead to failure, how blessed it would be to be an established Christian—always abiding in Christ!

You know how Scripture teaches us that in all God's leadings of His people faith has everywhere been the one condition of the manifestation of His power. Faith is the ceasing from all nature's efforts, and all other dependence; faith is confessed helplessness casting itself upon God's promise, and claiming its fulfillment; faith is the putting ourselves quietly into God's hands for Him to do His work. What you and I need now is to take time, until this truth stands out before us in all its spiritual brightness: It is God Almighty, God the Faithful and Gracious One, who has undertaken to establish us in Christ Jesus.

Listen to what the Word teaches you: *"The Lord shall establish you an holy people unto Himself"; "O Lord God, establish their heart unto You"; "Your God loved Israel, to establish them forever"; "You will establish the heart of the humble"; "Now to Him that is of power to establish you, be glory forever"; "To the end He may establish your hearts unblameable in holiness"; "The Lord is faithful, who shall establish you and keep you from all evil"; "The God of all grace, who has called us in Christ*

Jesus, make you perfect, establish, strengthen, settle you."

Can you take these words to mean anything less than that you too—however fitful your spiritual life has hitherto been, however unfavorable your natural character or your circumstances may appear—can be established in Christ Jesus—can become an established Christian? Let us but take time to listen, in simple childlike teachableness, to these words as the truth of God, and the confidence will come: As surely as I am in Christ, I shall also, day by day, be established in Him. …

Believer, you cannot but admit that such a life of trust must be a most blessed one. You say, perhaps, that there are times when you do, with your whole heart, consent to this way of living, and do wholly abandon the care of your inner life to your Father. But somehow it does not last. You forget again; and instead of beginning each morning with the joyous transference of all the needs and cares of your spiritual life to the Father's charge, you again feel anxious, and burdened, and helpless. Is it not, perhaps, my brother, because you have not committed to the Father's care this matter of daily remembering to renew your entire surrender? …

Through the Holy Spirit

January 10th

"The anointing which you received of him, abides in you; and as it has taught you, you shall abide in Him."

—1 JOHN 2: 27

How beautiful the thought of a life always abiding in Christ! The longer we think of it, the more attractive it becomes. And yet how often it is that the precious words, *"Abide in Me,"* are heard by the young disciple with a sigh! It is as if he understands so little what they really mean, and can realize so little how this full enjoyment can be attained. … If such a one would but listen to the word we have from John this day, what hope and joy it would bring! It gives us the Divine assurance that we have the anointing of the Holy Spirit to teach us all things, also to teach us how to abide in Christ. …

[Here is] an error which is very common among believers. They imagine that the Spirit, in teaching them, must reveal the mysteries of the spiritual life first to their intellect, and afterwards in their experience. And God's way is just the contrary of this. What holds true of all spiritual truth is specially true of the abiding in Christ: We must live and experience truth in order to know it. Life-fellowship with Jesus is the only school for the science of heavenly things. *"What I do, you know not now, but you shall know hereafter,"* is a law of the Kingdom, specially true of the daily cleansing of which it first was spoken, and the daily keeping. Receive what you do not comprehend, submit to what you cannot understand, accept and expect what to reason appears a mystery, believe what looks impossible, walk in a way which you know not—such are the first lessons in the school of God.

"If you abide in My word, you shall understand the truth." In these and other words of God we are taught that there is a habit of mind and life which precedes the understanding of

the truth. True discipleship consists in first following, and then knowing the Lord. The believing surrender to Christ, and the submission to His word to expect what appears most improbable, is the only way to the full blessedness of knowing Him.

These principles hold specially good in regard to the teaching of the Spirit. That teaching consists in His guiding the spiritual life within us to that which God has prepared for us, without our always knowing how. On the strength of God's promise, and trusting in His faithfulness, we yield our Self to the leading of the Holy Spirit, without claiming to have it first made clear to the intellect what He is to do, but consenting to let Him do His work in the soul, and afterwards to know what He has wrought there.

Faith trusts the working of the Spirit unseen in the deep recesses of the inner life. And so the word of Christ and the gift of the Spirit are to the believer sufficient guarantee that we will be taught of the Spirit to abide in Christ. By faith we rejoice in what we do not see or feel: we know, and are confident that the blessed Spirit within is doing His work silently but surely, guiding us into the life of full abiding and unbroken communion. The Holy Spirit is the Spirit of life in Christ Jesus; it is His work, not only to breathe, but ever to foster and strengthen, and so to perfect the new life within. And just in proportion as we yield our Self in simple trust to the unseen, but most certain law of the Spirit of life working within us, our faith will pass into knowledge. It will be rewarded by the Spirit's light revealing in the Word what has already been wrought by the Spirit's power in the life.

Apply this now to the promise of the Spirit's teaching us to abide in Christ. The Holy Spirit is indeed the mighty power of God. And He comes to us from the heart of Christ, the bearer of Christ's life, the revealer and communicator of Christ Himself within us. In the expression, *"the fellowship of the Spirit,"* we are taught what His highest work is. He is the bond of fellowship between the Father and the Son: by Him they are one. He is the bond of fellowship between all believers: by Him we are one. Above all, He is the bond of fellowship between Christ and believers; He is the life-sap through which Vine and branch grow into real and living oneness: by Him we are one. And we can be assured of it, that if we do but believe in His presence and working, if we do but watch not to grieve Him, because we know that He is in us, if we wait and pray to be filled with Him, He will teach us how to abide. First guiding our will to a whole-hearted cleaving to Christ, then quickening our faith into ever larger confidence and expectation, then breathing into our hearts a peace and joy that pass understanding, He teaches us to abide, we scarce know how. Then coming through the heart and life into the understanding, He makes us know the truth-not as mere thought-truth, but as the truth which is in Christ Jesus, the reflection into the mind of the light of what He has already made a reality in the life. *"The life was the light of men."*

In view of such teaching, it is clear how, if we would have the Spirit to guide us into the abiding life, our first need is quiet restful faith. Amid all the questions and difficulties that may come up in connection with our striving to abide in Christ—amid all the longing we may sometimes feel to have a Christian of experience to aid us—amid the frequent painful consciousness of failure, of ignorance, of helplessness—do let us holdfast the blessed confidence: We have the unction of the Holy One to teach us to abide in Him. *"The anointing which you have received of Him, abides in you; and even as it has taught you, you shall abide in Him."* Make this teaching of His in connection with the abiding a matter of special exercise of faith. Believe that assuredly as you have part in Christ, you have His Spirit too. Believe that He will do His work with power, if only you do not hinder Him. Believe that He is working, even when you cannot discern it. Believe that He will work mightily if you ask this from the Father.

It is impossible to live the life of full abiding without being full of the Holy Spirit; believe that the fullness of the Spirit is indeed your daily portion. Be sure and take time in prayer to dwell at the footstool of the throne of God and the Lamb, whence flows the river of the water of life. It is there, and only there, that you can be filled with the Spirit. Cultivate carefully the habit of daily, yea, continually honoring Him by the quiet, restful confidence that He is doing His work within. Let faith in His indwelling make you jealous of whatever could grieve Him—the spirit of the world or the actings of Self and the flesh. Let that faith seek its nourishment in the Word and all it says of the Spirit, His power, His comfort, and His work.

Above all, let that faith in the Spirit's indwelling lead you specially, to look away to Jesus; as we have received the anointing of Him, it comes in ever stronger flow from Him as we are occupied with Him alone. Christ is the Anointed One. As we look up to Him, the holy anointing comes....

In Stillness of Soul

January 11th

"In returning and rest shall you be saved; in quietness and confidence shall be your strength"
— ISAIAH 30: 15

"Be still before the Lord, and wait patiently for him."
—PSALM 37: 7

There is a view of the Christian life that regards it as a sort of partnership, in which God and man have each to do their part. It admits that it is but little that man can do, and that little defiled with sin; still he must do his utmost--then only can he expect God to do His part. To those who think thus, it is extremely difficult to understand what Scripture means when it speaks of our being still and doing nothing, of our resting and waiting to see the salvation of God. It appears to them a perfect contradiction, when we speak of this quietness and ceasing from all effort as the secret of the highest activity of man and all his powers.

And yet this is just what Scripture does teach. The explanation of the apparent mystery is to be found in this, that when God and man are spoken of as working together, there is nothing of the idea of a partnership between two partners who each contribute their share to a work. The relation is a very different one. The true idea is that of cooperation founded on subordination. As Jesus was entirely dependent on the Father for all His words and all His works, so the believer can do nothing of himself. What he can do of himself is altogether sinful.

We must therefore cease entirely from our own doing, and wait for the working of God in us. As we cease from Self-effort, faith assures us that God does what He has undertaken, and works in us. And what God does is to renew, to sanctify, and waken all our energies to their highest power. So that just in proportion as we yield ourself a truly passive instrument in the hand of God, will we be wielded of God as the active instrument of His almighty power. The soul in which the wondrous combination of perfect passivity with the highest activity is most completely realized, has the deepest experience of what the Christian life is.

Among the lessons to be learned of those who are studying the blessed art of abiding in Christ, there is none more needful and more profitable than this one of stillness of soul. In it alone can we cultivate that teachableness of spirit, to which the Lord will reveal His secrets--that meekness to which He shows His ways. ... It is a soul silent unto God that is the best preparation for knowing Jesus, and for holding fast the blessings He bestows. It is when the soul is hushed in silent awe and worship before the Holy Presence that reveals itself within, that the still small voice of the blessed Spirit will be heard.

Therefore, beloved Christian, as often as you seek to understand better the blessed mystery of abiding in Christ, let this be your first thought: "*My soul, only be silent unto God; for my expectation is from Him*" (Psalm 62: 5).

Do you in very deed hope to realize the wondrous union with the Heavenly Vine? Know that flesh and blood cannot reveal it unto you, but only the Father in Heaven. "Cease from your own wisdom." You have but to bow in the confession of your own ignorance and impotence; the Father will delight to give you the teaching of the Holy Spirit. If but your ear be open, and your thoughts brought into subjection, and your heart prepared in silence to wait upon God, and to hear what He speaks, He will reveal to you His secrets. And one of the first secrets will be the deeper insight into the truth, that as you sink low before Him in nothingness and helplessness, in a silence and a stillness of soul that seeks to catch the faintest whisper of His love, teachings will come to you which you had never heard before for the rush and noise of your own thoughts and efforts.

You shall learn how your great work is to listen, and hear, and believe what He promises; to watch and wait and see what He does; and then, in faith, and worship, and obedience, to yield yourself to His working who works in you mightily. One would think that no message could be more beautiful or welcome than this, that we may rest and be quiet, and that our God will work for us and in us. And yet how far this is from being the case!

And how slow many are to learn that quietness is blessedness, that quietness is strength, that quietness is the source of the highest activity—the secret of all true abiding in Christ! Let us try to learn it, and to watch against whatever interferes with it. The dangers that threaten the soul's rest are not a few. There is the dissipation of soul which comes from entering needlessly and too deeply into the interests of this world.

Every one of us has his divine calling; and within the circle pointed out by God Himself, interest in our work and its surroundings is a duty. But even here the Christian needs to exercise watchfulness and sobriety. And still more do we need a holy temperance in regard to things not absolutely imposed upon us by God. If abiding in Christ really be our first aim, let us beware of all needless excitement.

Let us watch even in lawful and necessary things against the wondrous power these have to keep the soul so occupied, that there remains but little power or zest for fellowship with God. Then there is the restlessness and worry that come of care and anxiety about earthly things; these eat away the life of trust, and keep the soul like a troubled sea. There the gentle whispers of the Holy Comforter cannot be heard. No less hurtful is the spirit of fear and distrust in spiritual things; with its apprehensions and its efforts, it never comes really to hear what God has to say.

Above all, there is the unrest that comes of seeking in our own way and in our own strength the spiritual blessing which comes alone from above. The heart occupied with its own plans and efforts for doing God's will, and securing the blessing of abiding in Jesus, must fail continually. God's work is hindered by our interference. He can do His work perfectly only when the soul ceases from its work. He will do His work mightily in the soul that honors Him by expecting Him to work both to will and to do.

And, last of all, even when the soul seeks truly to enter the way of faith, there is the impatience of the flesh, which forms its judgment of the life and progress of the soul not after the divine but the human standard. In dealing with all this, and so much more, blessed the man who learns the lesson of stillness, and fully accepts God's word: "In quietness and confidence shall be your strength." Each time he listens to the word of the Father, or asks the Father to listen to his words, he dares not begin his Bible reading or prayer without first pausing and waiting, until the soul be hushed in the presence of the Eternal Majesty.

Under a sense of the divine nearness, the soul, feeling how Self is always ready to assert itself, and intrude even into the holiest of all with its thoughts and efforts, yields itself in a quiet act of Self-surrender to the teaching and working of the divine Spirit. It is still and waits in holy silence, until all is calm and ready to receive the revelation of the divine will and presence. Its reading and prayer then indeed become a waiting on God with ear and heart opened and purged to receive fully only what He says. "Abide in Christ!"

Let no one think that he can do this if he has not daily his quiet time, his seasons of meditation and waiting on God. In these a habit of soul must be cultivated, in which the believer goes out into the world and its distractions, the peace of God, that passes all understanding, keeping the heart and mind. It is in such a calm and restful soul that the life of faith can strike deep root, that the Holy Spirit can give His blessed teaching, that the Holy Father can accomplish His glorious work. May each one of us learn every day to say, "*Truly my soul is silent unto God.*" And may every feeling of the difficulty of attaining this only lead us simply to look and trust to Him whose presence makes even the storm a calm. Cultivate the quietness as a means to the abiding in Christ; expect the ever-deepening quietness and calm of Heaven in the soul as the fruit of abiding in Him.

By Obeying His Commandment

January 12th

"If you keep My commandments, you shall abide in My love; even as I kept My Father's commandments, and abide in His love"

—JOHN 15: 10

How clearly we are taught here the place which good works are to occupy in the life of the believer! Christ as the beloved Son was in the Father's love. He kept His commandments, and so He abode in the love. So the believer, without works, receives Christ and is in Him; we keep the commandments, and so abide in the love. When the sinner, in coming to Christ, seeks to prepare himself by works, the voice of the Gospel sounds, *"Not of works."* When once in Christ, lest the flesh should abuse the word, "Not of works," the Gospel lifts its voice as loud: *"Created in Christ Jesus for good works"* (Ephesians 2: 9–10). To the sinner *out of* Christ, works may be his greatest hindrance, keeping him from the union with the Savior. To the believer *in* Christ, works are strength and blessing, for by them faith is made perfect (James 2: 22), the union with Christ is cemented, and the soul established and more deeply rooted in the love of God. *"If someone loves Me, they will keep my words, and My Father will love them"; "If you keep my commandments, you shall abide in my love."*

The connection between this keeping the commandments and the abiding in Christ's love is easily understood. Our union with Jesus Christ is not a thing of the intellect or sentiment, but a real vital union in heart and life. The holy life of Jesus, with His feelings and disposition is breathed into us by the Holy Spirit. Our calling is to think and feel and will just what Jesus thought and felt and willed. We desire to be partaker not only of the grace but also of the holiness of His Lord; or rather, we see that holiness is the chief beauty of grace. To live the life of Christ means to be delivered from the life of Self; the will of Christ is to us the only path of liberty from the slavery of our evil Self-will.

To the ignorant or slothful believer there is a great difference between the promises and commands of Scripture. The former he counts his comfort and his food; but to us who are really seeking to abide in Christ's love, the commands become no less precious. As much as the promises, they are the revelation of the Divine love, guiding into the deeper experience of the Divine life, blessed helpers in the path to a closer union with the Lord. We see how the harmony of our will with His will is one of the chief elements of our fellowship with Him.

The will is the central faculty in the Divine as in the human being. The will of God is the power that rules the whole moral as well as the natural world. How could there be fellowship with Him without delight in His will? It is only as long as salvation is nothing but a personal safety, we can be careless or afraid of the doing of God's will. No sooner is what Scripture and the Holy Spirit reveal it to be—the restoration to communion with

God and conformity to Him—than we feel that there is no law more natural or more beautiful than this: keeping Christ's commandments as the way to abide in Christ's love. Our inmost soul approves when we hear the beloved Lord make the larger measure of the Spirit, with the manifestation of the Father and the Son in the believer, entirely dependent upon the keeping of His commandments (John 14: 15, 16, 21, 23).

In no other way did Christ Himself abide in the Father's love. In the life which Christ led upon earth, obedience was a solemn reality. The dark and awful power that led man to revolt from his God, came upon Him too, to tempt Him. To Him as man its offers of Self-gratification were not matters of indifference; to refuse them, He had to fast and pray. He suffered, being tempted. He spoke very distinctly of not seeking to do His own will, as a surrender He had continually to make. He made the keeping of the Father's commandments the distinct object of His life, and so abode in His love. Does He not tell us, "*I do nothing of myself, but as the Father taught me, I speak these things. And He that sent me is with me; He has not left me alone; for I do always the things that are pleasing to Him.*"

Believer! Would you abide in Jesus, be very careful to keep His commandments? Keep them in the love of your heart. Be not content to have them in the Bible for reference, but have them transferred by careful study, by meditation and by prayer, by a loving acceptance, by the Spirit's teaching.... Be not content with the knowledge of some of the commands, those most commonly received among Christians, while others lie unknown and neglected. ... Be assured that there is still much of your Lord's will that you do not yet understand. Make Paul's prayer for the Colossians yours for yourself and all believers, *"that you might be filled with the knowledge of His will in all wisdom and spiritual understanding"*; and that of wrestling Epaphras, *"that you may stand perfect and complete in all the will of God."* Remember that this is one of the great elements of spiritual growth—a deeper insight into the will of God concerning you.

Imagine not that entire consecration is the end—it is only the beginning—of the truly holy life. See how Paul, after having (Romans 12:1) taught believers to lay themselves upon the altar, whole and holy burnt-offerings to their God, at once proceeds (ver. 2) to tell them what the true altar-life is: being ever more and more "*renewed in their mind to prove what is the good and perfect and acceptable will of God.*"

The progressive renewal of the Holy Spirit leads to growing like-mindedness to Christ; then comes a delicate power of spiritual perception—a holy instinct—by which the soul "quick of understanding ... in the fear of the Lord," knows to fullness the meaning and the application of the Lord's commands to daily life in a way that remains hidden to the ordinary Christian. Keep them dwelling richly within you, hide them within your heart, and you shall taste the blessedness of the one whose *"delight is in the law of the Lord, and in His law does he meditate day and night."* Love will assimilate into your inmost being the commands as food from Heaven. They will no longer come to you as a law standing outside and against you, but as the living power which has transformed your will into perfect harmony with all your Lord requires.

Labor earnestly in prayer to stand perfect and complete in all the will of God. Ask earnestly for the discovery of every secret sin—of anything that is not in perfect harmony with the will of God. … Be careful of disobedience even in little things. Disobedience dulls the conscience, darkens the soul, deadens our spiritual energies—therefore keep the commandments of Christ with implicit obedience. Be a soldier that asks for nothing but the orders of the Commander. And if even for a moment the commandments appear grievous, just remember whose they are.

They are the commandments of Him who loves you. They are all love, they come from His love; they lead to His love. Each new surrender to keep the commandments, each new sacrifice in keeping them, leads to deeper union with the will, the spirit, and the love of the Savior. The double recompense of reward shall be yours—a fuller entrance into the mystery of His love—a fuller conformity to His own blessed life.

And you shall learn to prize these words as among your choicest treasures: *"If you keep My commandments, you shall abide in My love, even as I have kept My Father's commandments and abide in His love."*

By Forsaking All for Him

January 13th

"I have suffered the loss of all things, and count them but dung, that I may win Christ, and be found in Him."

—PHILEMON 3: 8–9

There are Christians who look on [the faith's] blessedness as consisting all in the privilege of ever receiving; they know not how the capacity for receiving is only kept up and enlarged by continual giving up and giving out—how it is only in the emptiness that comes from the parting with what we have, that the Divine fullness can flow in. It was a truth our Savior continually insisted on. When He spoke of selling all to secure the treasure, of losing our life to find it, of the hundred-fold to those who forsake all, He was expounding the need of Self-sacrifice as the law of the Kingdom for Himself as well as for His disciples. If we are really to abide in Christ, and to be found in Him-to have our life always and wholly in Him-we must each in our measure say with Paul, *"I count all things but loss for the excellency of the knowledge of Christ Jesus my Lord, that I may win Christ, and be found in Him."*

Let us try and see what there is to be forsaken and given up. First of all, there is sin. There can be no true conversion without the giving up of sin. And yet, owing to the ignorance of the young convert of what really is sin, of what the claims of God's holiness are, and what the extent to which the power of Jesus can enable us to conquer sin, the giving up of sin is but partial and superficial.

With the growth of the Christian life there comes the want of a deeper and more entire purging out of everything that is unholy. And it is specially when the desire to abide in Christ uninterruptedly, to be always found in Him, becomes strong, that the soul is led to see the need of a new act of surrender, in which it afresh accepts and ratifies its death to sin in Christ, and parts indeed with everything that is sin. Availing ourselves, in the strength of God's Spirit, of that wonderful power of our nature by which the whole of future life can be gathered up and disposed of in one act of the will, we yield to sin no more—to be only and wholly a servant of righteousness. We do it in the joyful assurance that every sin surrendered is gain indeed—room for the inflowing of the presence and the love of Christ.

Next to the parting with unrighteousness is the giving up of Self-righteousness. Though contending most earnestly against our own works or merits, it is often long before we come really to understand what it is to refuse Self the least place or right in the service of God. Unconsciously we allow the acting of our own mind and heart and will free scope in God's presence. In prayer and worship, in Bible reading and working for God, instead of absolute dependence on the Holy Spirit's leading, Self is expected to do a work it never can do. We are slow to learn the lesson, "*In me, that is, in my flesh, dwells no good thing.*" As it is learned, and we see how corruption extends to everything that is of nature, we see that there can be no entire abiding in Christ without the giving up of all that is of Self in religion—without giving it up to the death, and waiting for the breathings of the Holy Spirit as alone able to work in us what is acceptable in God's sight.

Then, again, there is our whole natural life, with all the powers and endowments bestowed upon us by the Creator, with all the occupations and interests with which Providence has surrounded us. It is not enough that, when once you are truly converted, you have the earnest desire to have all these devoted to the service of the Lord. The desire is good, but can neither teach the way nor give the strength to do it acceptably. Incalculable harm has been done to the deeper spirituality of the Church, by the idea that when once we are God's children the using of our gifts in His service follows as a matter of course. No; for this there is indeed needed very special grace. And the way in which the grace comes is again that of sacrifice and surrender.

I must see how all my gifts and powers are, even though I be a child of God, still defiled by sin, and under the power of the flesh. I must feel that I cannot at once proceed to use them for God's glory. I must first lay them at Christ's feet, to be accepted and cleansed by Him. I must feel myself utterly powerless to use them aright. I must see that they are most dangerous to me, because through them the flesh, the old nature, Self, will so easily exert its power. In this conviction I must part with them, giving them entirely up to the Lord. When He has accepted them, and set His stamp upon them, I receive them back, to hold them as His property, to wait on Him for the grace to use them aright day by day, and to have them act only under His influence.

And so experience proves it true here too, that the path of entire consecration is the path of full salvation. Not only is what is thus given up received back again to become doubly our own, but the forsaking all is followed by the receiving all. We abide in Christ more fully as we forsake all and follow Him. As I count all things loss for His sake, I am found in Him.

The same principle holds good of all the lawful occupations and possessions with which we are entrusted of God. Such were the fish nets on the Sea of Galilee, and the household duties of Martha of Bethany—the home and the friends of many a one among

Jesus' disciples. Jesus taught them in very deed to forsake all for Him. It was no arbitrary command, but the simple application of a law in nature to the Kingdom of His grace, that the more perfectly the old occupant is cast out, the more complete can be the possession of the new....

No sooner does the believer begin to rejoice in the possession of what we have than the inflow of new grace is retarded, and stagnation threatens. It is only into the thirst of an empty soul that the streams of living waters flow. Ever thirsting is the secret of never thirsting.

Each blessed experience we receive as a gift of God, must at once be returned back to Him from whom it came, in praise and love, in Self-sacrifice and service; so only can it be restored to us again, fresh and beautiful with the bloom of Heaven. Is not this the wonderful lesson Isaac on Moriah teaches us? Was he not the son of promise, the God-given life—the wonder-gift of the omnipotence of Him who quickens the dead? (Romans 4:17). And yet even he had to be given up, and sacrificed, that he might be received back again a thousandfold more precious than before—a type of the Only-begotten of the Father, whose pure and holy life had to be given up ere He could receive it again in resurrection power, and could make His people partakers of it. A type, too, of what takes place in the life of each believer, as, instead of resting content with past experiences or present grace, we press on, forgetting and giving up all that is behind, and reach out to the fullest possible apprehension of Christ. ...

Believer, would you abide in Christ, see here the blessed path. Nature shrinks back from such Self-denial and crucifixion in its rigid application to our life in its whole extent. But what nature does not love and cannot perform, grace will accomplish, and make to you a life of joy and glory. Do you but yield up yourself to Christ your Lord; the conquering power of His incoming presence will make it joy to cast out all that before was most precious. ... And the secret of a life of close abiding will be seen to be simply this: As I give myself wholly to Christ, I find the power to take Him wholly for myself; and as I lose myself and all I have for Him, He takes me wholly for Himself, and gives Himself wholly to me.

That You May Not Sin

January 14th

"In Him is no sin. Whosoever abides in Him sins not."

—1 JOHN 3: 5, 6

You know, the apostle had said, *"that He was manifested to take away our sin,"* and had thus indicated salvation from sin as the great object for which the Son was made man. The connection shows clearly that the taking away has reference not only to the atonement and *freedom from guilt*, but to deliverance from *the power of sin*, so that the believer no longer does it.

It is Christ's personal holiness that constitutes His power to effect this purpose. He admits sinners into life union with Himself; the result is, that their life becomes like His. *"In Him is no sin. Whosoever abides in Him sins not."* As long as we abide, and as far as we abide, we do not sin. Our holiness of life has its roots in the personal holiness of Jesus. *"If the root be holy, so also are the branches."*

The question at once arises: How is this consistent with what the Bible teaches of the abiding corruption of our human nature, or with what John himself tells of the utter falsehood of our profession, if we say that we have no sin, that we have not sinned? (1 John 1: 8, 10). … Having sin is having a sinful nature. The holiest believer must each moment confess that sin is within, the flesh, namely, in which dwells no good thing.

Sinning or doing sin is something very different: it is yielding to indwelling sinful nature, and falling into actual transgression. And so we have two admissions that every true believer must make. The one is that he has still sin within him (verse 8); the second that that sin has in former times broken out into sinful actions (verse 10). …

But how is it possible that a believer, having sin—sin of such intense vitality, and such terrible power as we know the flesh to have—that a believer having sin should yet not be doing sin? The answer is: "*In Him is no sin. He that abides in Him sins not.*" When the abiding in Christ becomes close and unbroken, so that the soul lives from moment to moment in the perfect union with the Lord its keeper; He does, indeed, keep down the power of the old nature, so that it does not regain dominion over the soul.

We have seen that there are degrees in the abiding. With most Christians the abiding is so feeble and intermittent, that sin continually obtains the ascendency, and brings the soul into subjection. The Divine promise given to faith is: "*Sin shall not have dominion over you.*" But with the promise is the command: "*Let not sin reign in your mortal body.*" The believer who claims the promise in full faith has the power to obey the command, and sin is kept from asserting its supremacy. Ignorance of the promise, or unbelief, or unwatchfulness, opens the door for sin to reign. And so the life of many believers is a course of continual stumbling and sinning. But when the believer seeks full admission into, and a permanent abode in Jesus, the Sinless One, then the life of Christ keeps from actual transgression. "*In Him is no sin. He that abides in Him sins not.*" Jesus does indeed save us from sin—not by the removal of our sinful nature, but by keeping us from yielding to it.

I have read of a young lion whom nothing could awe or keep down but the eye of his keeper. … To approach him without the keeper would be instant death. And so it is that the believer can have sin and yet not do sin. The evil nature, the flesh, is unchanged in its enmity against God, but the abiding presence of Jesus keeps it down.

In faith, we entrust ourselves to the keeping, to the indwelling, of the Son of God; we abide in Him, and count on Jesus to abide in us too. This union and fellowship is the secret of a holy life: *"In Him is no sin; he that abides in Him sins not."* …

Oh, let us believe that when Jesus said, *"Abide in Me, and I in you,"* He did indeed mean that, while we were not to be freed from the world and its tribulation, from the sinful nature and its temptations, we were at least to have this blessing fully secured to us—grace to abide wholly, only, even in our Lord. The abiding in Jesus makes it possible to keep from actual sinning; and Jesus Himself makes it possible to abide in Him.

Beloved Christian! I do not wonder if the promise of the text appears almost too high. Do not, I pray, let your attention be diverted by the question as to whether it would be possible to be kept for your whole life, or for so many years, without sinning. Faith has ever only to deal with the present moment. Ask this: Can Jesus at the present moment, as I abide in Him, keep me from those actual transgressions which have been the stain and the weariness of my daily life? You cannot but say: Surely He can. Take Him then at this present moment, and say, "Jesus keeps me now, Jesus saves me now." Yield yourself to Him in the earnest and believing prayer to be kept abiding, by His own abiding in you—and go into the next moment, and the succeeding hours, with this trust continually renewed. As often as the opportunity occurs in the moments between your occupations, renew your faith in an act of devotion: Jesus keeps me now, Jesus saves me now. Let failure and sin, instead of discouraging you, only urge you still more to seek your safety in abiding in the Sinless One.

Abiding is a grace in which you can grow wonderfully, if you will but make at once the complete surrender, and then persevere with ever larger expectations. Regard it as His work to keep you abiding in Him, and His work to keep you from sinning. It is indeed your work to abide in Him; but it is that, only because it is His work as Vine to bear and hold the branch.

Gaze upon His holy human nature as what He prepared for you to be partaker of with Himself, and you will see that there is something even higher and better than being kept from sin—that is but the restraining from evil: there is the positive and larger blessing of being now a vessel purified and cleansed, of being filled with His fullness, and made the channel of showing forth His power, His blessing, and His glory.

That You May Bear Much Fruit

January 15th

"He that abides in Me, and I in him, the same brings forth much fruit";
"Herein is my Father glorified, that you bear much fruit."
—JOHN 15: 5, 8

We all know what fruit is. The produce of the branch, by which men are refreshed and nourished. The fruit is not for the branch, but for those who come to carry it away. ... And so the branch exists only and entirely for the sake of the fruit. To make glad the heart of the husbandman is its object, its safety, and its glory.

Beautiful image of the believer, abiding in Christ! We not only grow in strength, the union with the Vine becoming ever surer and firmer, we also bear fruit, yea, much fruit. We have the power to offer that to others of which they can eat and live. Amid all who surround us, we become like a tree of life, of which they can taste and be refreshed. We are in our circle a center of life and of blessing, and that simply because we abide in Christ, and receives from Him the Spirit and the life of which we can impart to others.

Learn thus, if you would bless others, to abide in Christ, and that if you do abide, you shall surely bless. As surely as the branch abiding in a fruitful vine bears fruit, so surely, yea, much more surely, will a soul abiding in Christ with His fullness of blessing be made a blessing. The reason of this is easily understood. If Christ, the heavenly Vine, has taken the believer as a branch, then He has pledged Himself, in the very nature of things, to supply the sap and spirit and nourishment to make it bring forth fruit. … The soul need but have one care—to abide closely, fully, wholly. He will give the fruit. He works all that is needed to make the believer a blessing.

Abiding in Him, you receive of Him His Spirit of love and compassion towards sinners, making you desirous to seek their good. By nature the heart is full of Selfishness. Even in the believer, his own salvation and happiness are often too much his only object. But abiding in Jesus, you come into contact with His infinite love; its fire begins to burn within your heart; you see the beauty of love; you learn to look upon loving and serving and saving others as the highest privilege a disciple of Jesus can have.

Abiding in Christ, your heart learns to feel the wretchedness of the sinner still in darkness, and the fearfulness of the dishonor done to your God. With Christ you begin to bear the burden of souls, the burden of sins not your own. As you are more closely united to Him, somewhat of that passion for souls which urged Him to Calvary begins to breathe within you, and you are ready to follow His footsteps, to forsake the Heaven of your own happiness, and devote your life to win the souls Christ has taught you to love. The very spirit of the Vine is love; the spirit of love streams into the branch that abides in Him.

The desire to be a blessing is but the beginning. As you undertake to work, you speedily become conscious of your own weakness and the difficulties in your way. … Believing what Christ teaches—that it is He who through you will give His blessing to the world—you understand that you are but the feeble instrument through which the hidden power of Christ does its work, that His strength may be perfected and made glorious in your weakness.

It is a great step when the believer fully consents to his or her own weakness, and the abiding consciousness of it, and so works faithfully on, fully assured that his Lord is working through them. We rejoice that the excellence of the power is of God, and not of us. Realizing this oneness with the Lord, we consider no longer our own weakness, but count on the power of Him of whose hidden working within we are assured. It is this secret assurance that gives a brightness to our look, and a gentle firmness to our tone, and a perseverance to all our efforts.

We claim and expect a blessing, because it is not us, but Christ in us, that works. The great secret of abiding in Christ is the deep conviction that we are nothing, and He is everything. As this is learned, it no longer seems strange to believe that our weakness need be no hindrance to His saving power. Those who yield ourselves wholly up to Christ for service in the spirit of a simple, childlike trust, will assuredly bring forth much fruit. We will not fear even to claim our share in the wonderful promise: *"He that believes in Me, the works that I do shall he do also; and greater works than these shall he do, because I go to the Father."*

... Let us learn two lessons. If we are abiding in Jesus, let us begin to work. Let us first seek to influence those around us in daily life. Let us accept distinctly and joyfully our holy calling, that we are even now to live as the servants of the love of Jesus to our fellowmen. Our daily life must have for its object the making of an impression favorable to Jesus. When you look at the branch, you see at once the likeness to the Vine. We must live so that somewhat of the holiness and the gentleness of Jesus may shine out in us. We must live to represent Him. As was the case with Him when on earth, the life must prepare the way for the teaching. What the Church and the world both need is this: men and women full of the Holy Spirit and of love, who, as the living embodiments of the grace and power of Christ, witness for Him, and for His power on behalf of those who believe in Him.

Living so, with our hearts longing to have Jesus glorified in the souls He is seeking after, let us offer ourselves to Him for direct work. There is work in our own home. There is work among the sick, the poor, and the outcast. There is work in a hundred different paths which the Spirit of Christ opens up through those who allow themselves to be led by Him. ... Let us work, not like those who are content if they now follow the fashion, and take some share in religious work. No; let us work as those who are growing more like Christ, because they are abiding in Him, and who, like Him, count the work of winning souls to the Father the very joy and glory of Heaven begun on earth.

And the second lesson is: If you work, abide in Christ. This is one of the blessings of work if done in the right spirit, it will deepen your union with your blessed Lord. It will discover your weakness, and throw you back on His strength. It will stir you to much prayer; and in prayer for others is the time when the soul, forgetful of itself, unconsciously grows deeper into Christ. It will make clearer to you the true nature of branch-life; its absolute dependence, and at the same time its glorious sufficiency—independent of all else, because dependent on Jesus.

If you work, abide in Christ. There are temptations and dangers. Work for Christ has sometimes drawn away from Christ, and taken the place of fellowship with Him. Work can sometimes give a form of godliness without the power. As you work, abide in Christ. Let a living faith in Christ working in you be the secret spring of all your work; this will inspire at once humility and courage. Let the Holy Spirit of Jesus dwell in you as the Spirit of His tender compassion and His divine power.

Abide in Christ, and offer every faculty of your nature freely and unreservedly to Him, to sanctify it for Himself. If Jesus Christ is really to work through us, He needs an entire consecration of ourselves to Him, daily renewed. But we understand now, just this is abiding in Christ; just this it is that constitutes our highest privilege and happiness. To be a branch bearing much fruit—nothing less, nothing more—be this our only joy.

So Will You Have Power in Prayer

January 16th

"If you abide in Me, and My words abide in you, you shall ask what you will, and it shall be done for you."
—JOHN 15: 7

Prayer is both one of the means and one of the fruits of union to Christ. As a means it is of unspeakable importance. All the things of faith, all the pleadings of desire, all the yearnings after a fuller surrender, all the confessions of shortcoming and of sin, all the exercises in which the soul gives up Self and clings to Christ, find their utterance in prayer.

In each meditation on abiding in Christ, as some new feature of what Scripture teaches concerning this blessed life is apprehended, the first impulse of the believer is at once to look up to the Father and pour out our heart into His, and ask from Him the full understanding and the full possession of what we have been shown in the Word. And it is we who are not content with this spontaneous expression of our hope, but who take time in secret prayer to wait until we have received and laid hold of what we have seen, who will really grow strong in Christ. However feeble the soul's first abiding, its prayer will be heard, and it will find prayer one of the great means of abiding more abundantly.

But it is not so much as a means, but as a fruit of the abiding, that the Savior mentions it in the parable of the Vine. He does not think so much of prayer—as we, alas! too exclusively do—as a means of getting blessing for ourselves, but as one of the chief channels of influence by which, through us as fellow-workers with God, the blessings of Christ's redemption are to be dispensed to the world.

He sets before Himself and us the glory of the Father, in the extension of His Kingdom, as the object for which we have been made branches; and He assures us that if we but abide in Him, we shall be Israels, having power with God and man. Ours shall be the effectual, fervent prayer of the righteous man, availing much, like Elijah's for ungodly Israel. Such prayer will be the fruit of our abiding in Him, and the means of bringing forth much fruit.

To Christians who are not abiding wholly in Jesus, the difficulties connected with prayer are often so great as to rob us of the comfort and the strength it could bring. Under the guise of humility, we ask how one so unworthy could expect to have influence with the Holy One. We think of God's sovereignty, His perfect wisdom and love, and cannot see how our prayer can really have any distinct effect. We pray, but it is more because we cannot rest without prayer, than from a loving faith that the prayer will be heard. But what a blessed release from such questions and perplexities is given to the soul who is truly abiding in Christ! We realize increasingly how it is in the real spiritual unity with Christ that we are accepted and heard. The union with the Son of God is a life union: we are in very deed one with Him; our prayer ascends as His prayer.

It is because we abide in Him that we can ask what we will, and it is given to us. There are many reasons why this must be so. One is, that abiding in Christ, and having His words abiding in us, teach us to pray in accordance with the will of God. With the abiding in Christ, our Self-will is kept down, the thoughts and wishes of nature are brought into captivity to the thoughts and wishes of Christ; likemindedness to Christ grows upon us—all our working and willing become transformed into harmony with His.

There is deep and oft-renewed heart-searching to see whether the surrender has indeed been entire; fervent prayer to the heart-searching Spirit that nothing may be kept back. Everything is yielded to the power of *His life in us*, that it may exercise its sanctifying influence even on ordinary wishes and desires. His Holy Spirit breathes through our whole being; and without our being conscious how, our desires, as the breathings of the Divine life, are in conformity with the Divine will, and are fulfilled. Abiding in Christ renews and sanctifies the will: we ask what we will, and it is given to us.

In close connection with this is the thought that the abiding in Christ teaches the believer in prayer only to seek the glory of God. In promising to answer prayer, Christ's one thought is this, *"that the Father may be glorified in the Son"* (John 14: 13). In His intercession on earth (John I7), this was His one desire and plea; in His intercession in Heaven, it is still His great object. As the believer abides in Christ, the Savior breathes this desire into him. The thought, "only the glory of God," becomes more and more the keynote of the life hid in Christ.

Abiding in Christ, the soul learns not only to desire, but spiritually to discern what will be for God's glory; and one of the first conditions of acceptable prayer is fulfilled in it when, as the fruit of its union with Christ, the whole mind is brought into harmony with that of the Son as He said: *"Father, glorify Your name."*

Once more: Abiding in Christ, we can fully avail ourselves of the name of Christ. ... The promise *"Whatsoever you ask in my name,"* may not be severed from the command, *"Whatsoever you do, do all in the name of the Lord Jesus."* If the name of Christ is to be wholly at my disposal, so that I may have the full command of it for all I will, it must be because I first put myself wholly at His disposal, so that He has free and full command of me. It is the abiding in Christ that gives the right and power to use His name with confidence. To Christ the Father refuses nothing. Abiding in Christ, I come to the Father as one with Him. His righteousness is in me, His Spirit is in me; the Father sees the Son in me, and gives me my petition.

It is not—as so many think--by a sort of imputation that the Father looks upon us as if we were in Christ, though we are not in Him. No; the Father wants to see us living in Him: thus shall our prayer really have power to prevail. Abiding in Christ not only renews the will to pray aright, but secures the full power of His merits to us.

Again: Abiding in Christ also works in us the faith that alone can obtain an answer. "*According to your faith be it unto you*": this is one of the laws of the kingdom. "*Believe that you receive, and you shall have.*" This faith rests upon, and is rooted in the Word, but is something infinitely higher than the mere logical conclusion: God has promised, I shall obtain.

No; Faith, as a spiritual act, depends upon the words abiding in us as living powers, and so upon the state of the whole inner life. Without fasting and prayer (Mark 9: 29), without humility and a spiritual mind (John 5: 44), without a wholehearted obedience (1 John 3: 22), there cannot be this living faith. But as the soul abides in Christ, and grows into the consciousness of its union with Him, and sees how entirely it is He who makes it and its petition acceptable, it dares to claim an answer because it knows itself one with Him. It was by faith it learned to abide in Him; as the fruit of that faith, it rises to a larger faith in all that God has promised to be and to do. It learns to breathe its prayers in the deep, quiet, confident assurance: *"We know we have the petition we ask of Him."*

Made Perfect in Weakness

January 17th

"My power is made perfect in weakness."

—2 CORINTHIANS 12: 9

There is no truth more generally admitted among earnest Christians than that of their utter weakness. There is no truth more generally misunderstood and abused. Here, as elsewhere, God's thoughts are Heaven-high above our thoughts. We often try to forget our weakness: God wants us to remember it, to feel it deeply. We want to conquer our weakness and to be freed from it: God wants us to rest and even rejoice in it. We mourn over our weakness: Christ teaches His servant to say, *"I take pleasure in infirmities; most gladly will I glory in my infirmities."* We think our weakness is our greatest hindrance in the life and service of God. God tells us that it is the secret of strength and success. It is our weakness, heartily accepted and continually realized, that gives us our claim and access to the strength of Him who has said, *"My strength is made perfect in weakness."*

When our Lord was about to take His seat upon the throne, one of His last words was: "*All power is given unto me in Heaven and on earth.*" Just as His taking His place at the right hand of the power of God was something new and true—a real advance in the history of the God-man—so was this clothing with all power. Omnipotence was now entrusted to the man Christ Jesus, that from henceforth through the channels of human nature it might put forth its mighty energies. Hence He connected with this revelation of what He was to receive, the promise of the share that His disciples would have in it: *"When I am ascended, you shall receive power from on high"* (Luke 24: 49; Acts 1: 8).

And what Jesus was to these first disciples, He is to us too. Our whole life and calling as disciples find their origin and their guarantee in the words: "*All power is given to me in heaven and on earth.*" What He does in and through us, He does with almighty power. What He claims or demands, He works Himself by that same power. All He gives, He gives with power. Every blessing He bestows, every promise He fulfills, every grace He works—all, all is to be with power. Everything that comes from this Jesus on the throne of power is to bear the stamp of power. The weakest believer may be confident that in asking to be kept from sin, to grow in holiness, to bring forth much fruit, be may count upon these his petitions being fulfilled with divine power. The power is in Jesus; Jesus is ours with all His fullness; it is in us His members that the power is to work and be made manifest.

And if we want to know how the power is bestowed, the answer is simple: Christ gives His power in us by giving *His life in us.* He does not, as so many believers imagine, take the feeble life He finds in them, and impart a little strength to aid them in their feeble efforts. No; it is in giving His own life in us that He gives us His power. The Holy Spirit came down to the disciples direct from the heart of their exalted Lord, bringing down into them the glorious life of Heaven into which He had entered. And so His people are still taught to be strong in the Lord and in the power of His might. When He strengthens us, it is not by taking away the sense of feebleness, and giving in its place the feeling of strength. By no means. But in a very wonderful way leaving and even increasing the sense of utter impotence, He gives us along with it the consciousness of strength in Him. *"We have this treasure in earthen vessels, that the excellency of the power may be of God and not of us."* The feebleness and the strength are side by side; as the one grows, the other too, until we understand the saying, *"When I am weak, then am I strong; I glory in my infirmities that the power of Christ may rest on me."*

Believing disciples learn to look upon Christ on the throne, Christ the Omnipotent, as our life. We study that life in its infinite perfection and purity, in its strength and glory; it is the eternal life dwelling in a glorified man. And when we think of our inner life, and long for holiness, to live well-pleasing unto God, or for power to do the Father's work, we look up, and, rejoicing that Christ is our life, we confidently reckon that that life will work mightily in us all that we need. In things little and things great, in the being kept from sin from moment to moment for which we have learned to look, or in the struggle with some special difficulty or temptation, the power of Christ is the measure of our expectation. We live a most joyous and blessed life, not because we are no longer feeble, but because, being utterly helpless, we consent and expect to have the mighty Savior work in us.

The lessons these thoughts teach us for practical life are simple, but very precious. The first is, that all our strength is in Christ, laid up and waiting for use. It is there as an almighty life, which is in Him for us, ready to flow in according to the measure in which it finds the channels open. But whether its flow is strong or feeble, whatever our experience of it be, there it is in Christ: All power in heaven and earth. Let us take time to study this. Let us get our minds filled with the thought: That Jesus might be to us a perfect Savior, the Father gave Him all power. That is the qualification that fits Him for our needs: All the power of heaven over all the powers of earth, over every power of earth in our heart and life too.

The second lesson is: This power flows into us as we abide in close union with Him. When the union is feeble, little valued or cultivated, the inflow of strength will be feeble. When the union with Christ is rejoiced in as our highest good, and everything sacrificed for the sake of maintaining it, the power will work: *"His strength will be made perfect in our weakness."* Our one care must therefore be to abide in Christ as our strength. Our one duty is to *"be strong in the Lord, and in the power of His might."* Let our faith cultivate large and clear apprehensions of the exceeding greatness of God's power in them that believe, even that power of the risen and exalted Christ by which He triumphed over every enemy (Ephesians 1: 19–21).

Let our faith daily go out of Self and its life into the life of Christ, placing our whole being at His disposal for Him to work in us. Let our faith, above all, confidently rejoice in the assurance that He will in very deed, with His almighty power, perfect His work in us. As we thus abide in Christ, the Holy Spirit, the Spirit of His power, will work mightily in us, and we too shall sing… *"I can do all things through Christ, who strengthens me."*

Trusting Him to Keep You

January 18th

"I follow after, that I may apprehend that for which I also am apprehended, Christ Jesus."
—PHILIPPIANS 3: 12

More than one admits that it is a sacred duty and a blessed privilege to abide in Christ, but shrinks back continually before the question: Is it possible, a life of unbroken fellowship with the Savior?

Abiding in Christ is just meant for the weak, and so beautifully suited to their feebleness. It is not the doing of some great thing, and does not demand that we first lead a very holy and devoted life. No, it is simply weakness entrusting itself to a Mighty One to be kept-the unfaithful one casting Self on One who is altogether trustworthy and true. Abiding in Him is not a work that we have to do as the condition for enjoying His salvation, but a consenting to let Him do all for us, and in us, and through us. It is a work He does *for us*—the fruit and the power of His redeeming love. Our part is simply to yield, to trust, and to wait for He has engaged to perform.

It is this quiet expectation and confidence, resting on the word of Christ that in Him there is an abiding place prepared, which is so sadly wanting among Christians. They scarce take the time or the trouble to realize that when He says *"Abide in Me,"* He offers Himself, the Keeper of Israel that slumbers not nor sleeps, with all His power and love, as the living home of the soul, where the mighty influences of His grace will be stronger to keep than all their feebleness to lead astray. The idea they have of grace is this: that their conversion and pardon are God's work, but that now, in gratitude to God, it is their work to live as Christians, and follow Jesus. There is always the thought of a work that has to be done, and even though they pray for help, still the work is theirs. They fail continually, and become hopeless; and the despondency only increases the helplessness.

No, wandering one; as it was Jesus who drew you when He spoke "Come," so it is Jesus who keeps you when He says "Abide." The grace to come and the grace to abide are alike from Him alone. That word, "Come"—heard, meditated on, accepted—was the cord of love that drew you nigh; that word, "Abide," is even so the band with which He holds you fast and binds you to Himself. Let the soul but take time to listen to the voice of Jesus. *"In Me,"* He says, "is your place, in My almighty arms; it is I who loves you so, who speaks "Abide in Me"; surely you can trust Me." The voice of Jesus entering and dwelling in the soul cannot but call for the response: "Yes, Savior, in You I can, I will abide."

Abide in Me: These words are no law of Moses, demanding from the sinful what they cannot perform. They are the command of love, which is ever only a promise in a different shape. Think of this until all feeling of burden and fear and despair pass away, and the first thought that comes as you hear of abiding in Jesus be one of bright and joyous hope: it is for me, I know I shall enjoy it. You are not under the law, with its inexorable Do, but under grace, with its blessed Believe what Christ will do for you.

And if the question be asked, "But surely there is something for us to do?" the answer is, "Our doing and working are but the fruit of Christ's work in us." It is when the soul becomes utterly passive, looking and resting on what Christ is to do, that its energies are stirred to their highest activity, and that we work most effectually because we know that He works in us. It is as we see in that word "in Me"—the mighty energies of love reaching out after us to have us and to hold us—that all the strength of our will is roused to abide in Him.

This connection between Christ's work and our work is beautifully expressed in the words of Paul: *"I follow after, so that I may apprehend that for which I also am apprehended of Christ Jesus."* It was because he knew that the mighty and the faithful One had grasped him with the glorious purpose *of making him one with Himself,* that he did his utmost to grasp the glorious prize. The faith, the experience, the full assurance, *"Christ has apprehended me,"* gave him the courage and the strength to press on and apprehend that for which he was apprehended. …

Fix first your eyes on the whereunto for which He has apprehended you. It is nothing less than a life of abiding, unbroken fellowship with Himself to which He is seeking to lift you up. All that you have already received-pardon and peace, the Spirit and His grace are but preliminary to this. And all that you see promised to you in the future—holiness and fruitfulness and glory everlasting—are but its natural outcome. Union with Himself, and so with the Father, is His highest object. Fix your eyes on this, and gaze until it stands out before you clear and unmistakable: Christ's aim is to have me abiding in Him.

And then let the second thought enter your heart: Unto this I am apprehended by Christ. His almighty power has laid hold on me, and offers now to lift me up to where He would have me. Fix your eyes on Christ. Gaze on the love that beams in those eyes, and that asks whether you cannot trust Him, who sought and found and brought you nigh, now to keep you. Gaze on that arm of power, and say whether you have reason to be assured that He is indeed able to keep you abiding in Him.

And as you think of the spot whither He points-the blessed whereunto for which He apprehended you—and keep your gaze fixed on Himself, holding you and waiting to lift you up, O say, could you not this very day take the upward step, and rise to enter upon this blessed life of abiding in Christ? Yes, begin at once, and say, "O my Jesus, if You bid me, and if You engage to lift and keep me there, I will venture. Trembling, but trusting, I will say: Jesus, I do abide in You."

My beloved fellow-believer, go, and take time alone with Jesus, and say this to Him. I dare not speak to you about abiding in Him for the mere sake of calling forth a pleasing religious sentiment. God's truth must at once be acted on. O yield yourself this very day to the blessed Savior in the surrender of the one thing He asks of you: give up yourself to abide in Him. He Himself will work it in you. You can trust Him to keep you trusting and abiding.

And Not Trusting in Self

January 19th

"In me, that is, in my flesh, dwells no good thing."

—ROMANS 7: 18 …

To seek life, not in itself, but in God, is the highest honor of the creature. To live in and to himself is the folly and guilt of sinful man; to live to God in Christ is the blessedness of the believer. To deny, to hate, to forsake, to lose his own life, such is the secret of the life of faith. *"I live, yet not I, but Christ lives in me"; "not I, but the grace of God which is with me";* this is the testimony of each one who has found out what it is to give up their life, and to receive instead the blessed life of Christ within. There is no path to true life, to abiding in Christ, other than that which our Lord took—the path of death.

At the first commencement of the Christian life, few see this. In the joy of pardon, they feel constrained to live for Christ, and trust with the help of God to be enabled to do so. They are as yet ignorant of the terrible enmity of the flesh against God, and its absolute refusal in the believer to be subject to the law of God. They do not yet know that nothing but death—the absolute surrender to death of all that is of Self or their nature—will suffice if the life of God is to be manifested in them with power.

But bitter experience of failure soon teaches them the insufficiency of what they have yet known of Christ's power to save, and deep heart-longings are awakened to know Him better. He lovingly points them to His cross. He tells them that as there, in the faith of His death as their substitute, they found their title to life, so there they shall enter into its fuller experience too. He asks them if they are indeed willing to drink of the cup of which He drank—to be crucified and to die with Him. He teaches them that in Him they are indeed already crucified and dead—all unknowing, at conversion they became partakers of His death. But what they need now is to give a full and intelligent consent to what they received ere they understood it, by an act of their own choice to will to die with Christ.

This demand of Christ's is one of unspeakable solemnity. Many a believer shrinks back from it. We can hardly understand it. We have become so accustomed to a low life of continual stumbling, that we hardly desire, and still less expect, deliverance. Holiness, perfect conformity to Jesus, unbroken fellowship with His love, can scarcely be counted distinct articles of our creed.

How different the light in which the believer who is really seeking to abide fully in Christ looks upon it. Bitter experience has taught him how, both in the matter of entire surrender and simple trust, his greatest enemy in the abiding life, is Self. Now it refuses to give up its will; then again, by its working, it hinders God's work. Unless this life of Self, with its willing and working, be displaced by the life of Christ, with His willing and working, any abiding in Him will be impossible.

It is in the mortifying, the slaying of Self, that the wonderful powers with which God has fitted you to serve Him, can be set free for a complete surrender to God, and offered to Him to be accepted, and sanctified, and used. And though, as long as you are in the flesh, there is no thought of being able to say that Self is dead, yet when the life of Christ is allowed to take full possession, Self can be so kept in its crucifixion place, and under its sentence of death, that it shall have ho dominion over you, not for a single moment. Jesus Christ becomes your second Self.

Believer! Would you truly and fully abide in Christ, prepare yourself to part forever from Self, and not to allow it, even for a single moment, to have aught to say in your inner life. If you are willing to come entirely away out of Self, and to allow Jesus Christ to become your life within you, inspiring all your thinking, feeling, acting, in things temporal and spiritual, He is ready to undertake the charge. In the fullest and widest sense the word "life" ever can have, He will be your life, extending His interest and influence to each one—even the minutest—of the thousand things that make up your daily life. To do this He asks but one thing: Come away out of Self and its life, abide in Christ and the Christ life, and Christ will be your life. The power of His holy presence will cast out the old life.

To this end give up Self at once and for ever. If you have never yet dared to do it, for fear you might fail of your engagement, do it now, in view of the promise Christ gives you that His life will take the place of the old life. Try and realize that though Self is not dead, you are indeed dead to Self. Self is still strong and living, but it has no power over you. You, your renewed nature—you, your new Self, begotten again in Jesus Christ from the dead-are indeed dead to sin and alive to God. Your death in Christ has freed you completely from the control of Self: it has no power over you, except as you, in ignorance, or unwatchfulness, or unbelief, consent to yield to its usurped authority.

Come and accept by faith simply and heartily the glorious position you have in Christ. As one who, in Christ, has a life dead to Self, as one who is freed from the dominion of Self, and has received His divine life to take the place of Self, to be the animating and inspiring principle of your life, venture boldly to plant the foot upon the neck of this enemy of yours and your Lord's. Be of good courage, only believe; fear not to take the irrevocable step, and to say that you have once for all given up Self to the death for which it has been crucified in Christ (Romans 6: 6). And trust Jesus the Crucified One to hold Self to the cross, and to fill its place in you with His own blessed resurrection life. In this faith, abide in Christ! Cling to Him; rest on Him; hope on Him. Daily renew your consecration; daily accept afresh your position as ransomed from your tyrant, and now in turn made a conqueror.

Daily look with holy fear on the enemy, Self, struggling to get free from the cross, seeking to allure you into giving it some little liberty, or else ready to deceive you by its profession of willingness now to do service to Christ. Remember, the Self's seeking to serve God is more dangerous than the Self's refusing obedience. Look upon it with holy fear, and hide yourself in Christ: in Him alone is your safety.

Bring every interest of your life, every power of your nature, all the unceasing flow of thought, and will, and feeling that makes up life, and trust Him to take the place that Self once filled so easily and so naturally. Jesus Christ will indeed take possession of you and dwell in you; and in the restfulness and peace and grace of the new life you shall have unceasing joy at the wondrous exchange that has been made—the coming out of Self to abide in Christ alone.

In Affliction and Trial

January 20th

"Every branch that bears fruit, He purges it, that it may bring forth more."
—JOHN 15: 2

What treasures of teaching and comfort to the bleeding branch in its hour of trial: *"Every branch that bears fruit, He purges it, that it may bring forth more fruit."* ...

Abide in Christ! This is indeed the Father's object in sending the trial. In the storm the tree strikes deeper roots in the soil.... So by suffering the Father would lead us to enter more deeply into the love of Christ. Our hearts are continually prone to wander from Him; prosperity and enjoyment all too easily satisfy us, dull our spiritual perception, and unfit us for full communion with Himself. It is an unspeakable mercy that the Father comes with His chastisement, makes the world round us all dark and unattractive, leads us to feel more deeply our sinfulness, and for a time lose our joy in what was becoming so dangerous. He does it in the hope that, when we have found our rest in Christ in time of trouble, we shall learn to choose abiding in Him as our only portion; and when the affliction is removed, have so grown more firmly into Him, that in prosperity He still shall be our only joy. So much has He set His heart on this, that though He has indeed no pleasure in afflicting us, He will not keep back even the most painful chastisement if He can but thereby guide His beloved child to come home and abide in the beloved Son.

Christian! Pray for grace to see in every trouble, small or great, as the Father's finger pointing to Jesus, and saying, "Abide in Him. Abide in Christ: so will you become partaker of all the rich blessings God designed for you in the affliction." The purposes of God's wisdom will become clear to you, your assurance of the unchangeable love become stronger, and the power of His Spirit fulfill in you the promise: *"He chastens us for our profit, that we might be partakers of His holiness."*

Abide in Christ: In the fiery oven, one like the Son of Man will be seen as never before; the purging away of the dross and the refining of the gold will be accomplished, and Christ's own likeness reflected in you. Oh, abide in Christ: the power of the flesh will be mortified, the impatience and Self-will of the old nature be humbled, to make place for the meekness and gentleness of Christ. A believer may pass through much affliction, and yet secure but little blessing from it all. Abiding in Christ is the secret of securing all that the Father meant the chastisement to bring us. …

Believer! Abide in Christ in times of affliction, and you shall bring forth more fruit. The deeper experience of Christ's tenderness and the Father's love will urge you to live to His glory. The surrender of Self and Self-will in suffering will prepare you to sympathize with the misery of others, while the softening that comes of chastisement will fit you for becoming, as Jesus was, the servant of all. … You shall learn the blessed are of forgetting Self, and, even in affliction, availing yourself of your separation from ordinary life to plead for the welfare of others.

Dear Christian, in affliction, abide in Christ. When you see it coming, meet it in Christ; when it comes, feel that you are more in Christ than in it, for He is nearer you than affliction ever can be….

And let the one thought of the Savior, as He speaks of the pruning, and the one desire of the Father, as He does the pruning, be yours too: *"Every branch that bears fruit, He purges, that it may bring forth more fruit."* So shall your times of affliction become your times of choicest blessing—preparation for richest fruitfulness, led into closer fellowship with the Son of God, and deeper experience of His love and grace—established in the blessed confidence that He and you entirely belong to each other, more completely satisfied with Him, and more wholly given up to Him than ever before. With your own will crucified afresh, and the heart brought into deeper harmony with God's will, you shall be a vessel cleansed, *"meet for the Master's use, prepared for every good work."*

Every Moment

January 21st

"In that day sing you unto her, A vineyard of red wine. I the Lord do keep it; I will water it every moment: lest any hurt it, I will keep it night and day."

—ISAIAH 27: 2, 3

What an answer from the mouth of God Himself to the question so often asked: Is it possible for the believer always to abide in Jesus? Is a life of unbroken fellowship with the Son of God indeed attainable here in this earthly life? Truly not, if the abiding is our work, to be done in our strength. But the things that are impossible with men are possible with God. If the Lord Himself will keep the soul night and day, yea, will watch and water it every moment, then surely the uninterrupted communion with Jesus becomes a blessed possibility to those who can trust God to mean and to do what He says. Then surely the abiding of the branch of the vine day and night, summer and winter, in a never-ceasing life-fellowship, is nothing less than the simple but certain promise of your abiding in your Lord.

In one sense, it is true, there is no believer who does not always abide in Jesus; without this there could not be true life. *"If anyone abide not in Me, they are cast forth."* But when the Savior gives the command, *"Abide in Me,"* with the promise, *"They that abide in Me bring forth much fruit,"* He speaks of that willing, intelligent, and wholehearted surrender by which we accept His offer, and consent to the abiding in Him *as the only life we choose or seek*. The objections raised against our right to expect that we shall always be able thus voluntarily and consciously to abide in Jesus are chiefly two.

The one is derived from the nature of man. It is said that our limited powers prevent our being occupied with two things at the same moment. God's providence places many Christians in business, where for hours at a time the closest attention is required to the work they have to do. How can such a one, it is asked, with their whole mind in the work they have to do, be at the same time occupied with Christ, and keeping up fellowship with Him? The consciousness of abiding in Jesus is regarded as requiring such a strain, and such a direct occupation of the mind with heavenly thoughts, that to enjoy the blessing would imply a withdrawing of oneself from all the ordinary avocations of life. This is the same error as drove the first monks into the wilderness. Blessed be God, there is no necessity for such a going out of the world.

Abiding in Jesus is not a work that needs each moment the mind to be engaged, or the affections to be directly and actively occupied with it. It is an entrusting of oneself to the keeping of the Eternal Love, in the faith that it will abide near us, and with its holy presence watch over us and ward off the evil, even when we have to be most intently occupied with other things. And so the heart has rest and peace and joy in the consciousness of being kept when it cannot keep itself.

In ordinary life, we have abundant illustration of the influence of a supreme affection reigning in and guarding the soul, while the mind concentrates itself on work that requires its whole attention. ... A loving wife and mother never for one moment loses the sense of her relation to the husband and children: the consciousness and the love are there, amid all her engagements.

And shall it be thought impossible for the Everlasting Love so to take and keep possession of our spirits, that we too shall never for a moment lose the secret consciousness: We are in Christ, kept in Him by His almighty power. Oh, it is possible; we can be sure it is. Our abiding in Jesus is even more than a fellowship of love—it is a fellowship of life. ... Christ, who is our life, Himself dwells within us, and by His presence maintains our consciousness that we are in Him.

The second objection has reference to our sinfulness. Christians are so accustomed to look upon sinning daily as something absolutely inevitable, that they regard it as a matter of course that no one can keep up abiding fellowship with the Savior: we must sometimes be unfaithful and fail.

As if it was not just because we have a nature which is naught but a very fountain of sin, that the abiding in Christ has been ordained for us as our only but our sufficient deliverance! As if it were not the Heavenly Vine, the living, loving Christ, in whom we have to abide, and whose almighty power to hold us fast is to be the measure of our expectations! As if He would give us the command, "*Abide in Me*," without securing the grace and the power to enable us to perform it! As if, above all, we had not the Father as the Husbandman to keep us from falling, and that not in a large and general sense, but according to His own precious promise: "Night and day, every moment!"

Oh, if we will but look to our God as the Keeper of Israel, of whom it is said, "*Jehovah shall keep you from all evil; He shall keep your soul*," we shall learn to believe that conscious abiding in Christ every moment, night and day, is indeed what God has prepared for them that love Him.

My beloved fellow Christians, let nothing less than this be your aim. I know well that you may not find it easy of attainment; that there may come more than one hour of weary struggle and bitter failure. Were the Church of Christ what it should be—were older believers to younger converts what they should be, witnesses to God's faithfulness, like Caleb and Joshua, encouraging their brethren to go up and possess the land with their, "*We are well able to overcome; if the Lord delight in us, then He will bring us into this land*"—were the atmosphere which the young believer breathes as he enters the fellowship of the saints that of a healthy, trustful, joyful consecration—abiding in Christ would come as the natural outgrowth of being in Him.

But in the sickly state in which such a great part of the body is, souls that are pressing after this blessing are sorely hindered by the depressing influence of the thought and the life around them. It is not to discourage that I say this, but to warn, and to urge to a more entire casting of ourselves upon the Word of God Himself. There may come more than our hour in which you are ready to yield to despair; but be of good courage. Only believe. He who has put the blessing within your reach will assuredly lead to its possession.

The way in which souls enter into the possession may differ. To some it may come as the gift of a moment. In times of revival, in the fellowship with other believers in whom the Spirit is working effectually, under the leading of some servant of God who can guide, and sometimes in solitude too, it is as if all at once a new revelation comes upon the soul. It sees, as in the light of Heaven, the strong Vine holding and bearing the feeble branches so securely, that doubt becomes impossible. It can only wonder how it ever could have understood the words to mean aught else than this: To abide unceasingly in Christ is the portion of every believer. …

To others it comes by a slower and more difficult path. Day by day, amid discouragement and difficulty, the soul has to press forward. Be of good cheer; this way, too, leads to the rest. Seek but to keep your heart set upon the promise: "*I the Lord do keep it, night and day.*" Take from His own lips the watchword: "*Every moment.*" In that you have the law of His love, and the law of your hope. Be content with nothing less. …

And be assured that, if Jehovah keep the branch night and day, and water it every moment, a life of continuous and unbroken fellowship with Christ is indeed our privilege.

2

LIKE CHRIST

Thoughts on the Blessed Life of Conformity to The Son of God

Toronto: S.R. Briggs, 1886
From the 1880 Dutch version

Preface

January 22nd

In sending forth this little book on the image of our blessed Lord, and the likeness to Him to which we are called … there were two things I had to do. The one was to draw such a portrait of the Son of God, as *"in all things made like unto His brethren,"* as to show how, in the reality of His human life, we have indeed an exact pattern of what the Father wants us to be. What was wanted was such a portrait as should make likeness to Him infinitely and mightily attractive, should rouse desire, awaken love, inspire hope, and strengthen faith in all who are seeking to imitate Jesus Christ. And then I had to sketch another portrait—that of the believer who, with some degree of spiritual exactness, reflects this Image, who amid the trials and duties of daily life proves that likeness to Christ is no mere ideal, but—through the power of the Holy Spirit—a most blessed reality. …

The second remark I wish to make is a suggestion as to what I think is needed really to behold the glory of the blessed Image into which we are to be changed. … We are too easily content with the thoughts suggested by the words of the Bible, though these are but forms of truth, without giving time for the substantial spiritual reality, which the Word as the truth of God contains, to get lodged and rooted in the heart. Let us, in meditating on the image of God in Christ, to which we are to be conformed, remember this: When some special trait [of Christ] has occupied our thoughts, let us shut our eyes, and open our hearts; let us think, and pray, and believe in the working of the Holy Spirit, until we really see the blessed Master in that special light in which the Word has been setting Him before us, and can carry away for that day the deep and abiding impression of that heavenly beauty in Him which we know is to be reproduced in us. Let us gaze, and gaze again, let us worship and adore; the more we see Him as He is, the more like Him we must become.

To study the image of God in the man Christ Jesus, to yield and set open our inmost being for that image to take possession and live in us, and then to go forth and let the heavenly likeness reflect itself and shine out in our life among our fellow men—this is what we have been redeemed for; let this be what we live for. …

May God help us to see that there is no beauty or blessedness like that of a Christ-like life. May He teach us to believe that in union with Him the Christ-like life is indeed for us. And as each day we listen to what His Word tells us of His image, may each one of us have grace to say, "O my Father! Even as Your beloved Son lived in You, with You, for You on earth, even so would I also live."

Like Christ: He Himself Calls Us to It

"I have given you an example, that you also should do even as I have done to you" (John 13: 15). All that [the disciples] had seen in Him, and experienced from Him, is thus made the rule of their life: *"you also should do even as I have done to you."* The word of the blessed Savior is for us too. … Jesus Christ does indeed ask every one of us in everything to act just as we have seen Him do. What He has done to us, and still does each day, we are to do over again to others. In His condescending, pardoning, saving love, He is our example; each of us is to be the copy and image of the Master. … What can I do but open my heart to His word, and fix my gaze on His example, until it exercises its Divine power upon me, and draws me with irresistible force to cry: Lord, even as You have done, so will I do also.

… In Him we see God. In Him we see how God would act were He here in our place on earth. In Him all that is beautiful and lovely and perfect in the heavenly world is revealed to us in the form of an earthly life. If we want to see what is really counted noble and glorious in the heavenly world, if we would see what is really Divine, we have only to look at Jesus; in all He does the glory of God is shown forth.

But oh, the blindness of God's children: this heavenly beauty has to many of them no attraction; there is no form or comeliness that they should desire it. The manners and the way of living, in the court of an earthly king exercise influence throughout the empire. The example it gives is imitated by all who belong to the nobility or the higher classes. But the example of the King of Heaven, who came and dwelled in the flesh, that we might see how we might here on earth live a God-like life, alas! with how few of His followers does it really find imitation. When we look upon Jesus, His obedience to the will of the Father, His humiliation to be a servant of the most unworthy, His love as manifested in the entire giving up and sacrifice of Himself, we see the most wondrous and glorious thing Heaven has to show; in Heaven itself we shall see nothing greater or brighter. Surely such an example, given of God on very purpose to make the imitation attractive and possible, ought to win us. Is it not enough to stir all that is within us with a holy jealousy and with joy unutterable as we hear the message, "*I have given you an example, that even as I have done, you should also do*"?

This is not all. The power of an example consists not only in its own intrinsic excellence, but also in the personal relation to him who gives it. Jesus had not washed the feet of others in presence of His disciples; it was when He had washed *their feet* that He said: *"Even as I have done to you, you should also do."* It is the consciousness of a personal relationship to Christ that enforces the command. Do as I have done. It is the experience of what Jesus has done to me that is the strength in which I can go and do the same to others. He does not ask that I shall do more than has been done to me. But not less either: EVEN AS I have done to you. He does not ask that I shall humble myself as servant deeper than He has done. It would not have been strange if He had asked this of such a worm. But this is not His wish: He only demands that I shall just do and be what He, the King, has done and been. He humbled Himself as low as humiliation could go, to love and to bless me. He counted this *His highest honor and blessedness.* And now He invites me to partake of the same honor and blessedness, in loving and serving as He did. Truly, if I indeed know the love that rests on me, and the humiliation through which alone that love could reach me, and the power of the cleansing which has washed me, nothing can keep me back from saying: "Yes, blessed Lord, even as You have done to me, I will also do." The heavenly loveliness of the great Example, and the Divine lovingness of the great Exemplar, combine to make the example above everything attractive.

Only there is one thing I must not forget. It is not the remembrance of what Jesus has once done to me, but the living experience of what He is now to me, that will give me the power to act like Him. His love must be a present reality, the inflowing of a life and a power in which I can love like Him. It is only as by the Holy Spirit I realize *what* Jesus is doing for me, and *how* He does it, and that it is *He* who does it, that it is possible for me to do to others what He is doing to me.

"*Even as I have done to you, you should also do.*" What a precious word! What a glorious prospect! Jesus is going to show forth in me the Divine power of His love, that I may show it forth to others. He blesses me, that I may bless others. He loves me that I may love others. He becomes servant to me that I may become a servant to others. He saves and cleanses me that I may save and cleanse others. He gives Himself wholly for and to me, that I may wholly give myself for and to others. I have only to be doing over to others what He is doing to me—nothing more. I can do it, just because He is doing it to me. What I do is nothing but the repeating, the showing forth of what I am receiving from Him.

Wondrous grace! which thus calls us to be like our Lord in that which constitutes His highest glory. Wondrous grace! which fits us for this calling by Himself first being to us and in us what we are to be to others. Shall not our whole heart joyously respond to His command? Yes, blessed Lord I even as You do to me will I also do to others.

Gracious Lord! what can I now do but praise and pray? My heart feels overwhelmed with this wondrous offer, that You will reveal all Your love and power in me, if I will yield myself to let it flow through me to others. Though with fear and trembling, yet in deep and grateful adoration, with joy and confidence, I would accept the offer and say: Here I am; show me how much You love me, and I will show it to others by loving them even so.

And that I may be able to do this, blessed Lord, grant me these two things. Grant me, by Your Holy Spirit, a clear insight into Your love to me, that I may know how You love me, how Your love to me is Your delight and blessedness, how in that love You give Yourself so completely to me, that You are indeed mine to do for me all I need. Grant this, Lord, and I shall know how to love and how to live for others, even as You love and live for me. And then grant me to see, as often as I feel how little love I have, that it is not with the love of my little heart, but with Your love shed abroad in me, that I have to fulfill the command of loving like You. …

Like Christ: Our Head

January 23rd

"For this were you called; because Christ also suffered for us, leaving us an example, that we should follow in His steps."
—1 PETER 2: 21

The call to follow Christ's example, and to walk in His footsteps, is so high that there is every reason to ask with wonder, "How can it be expected of sinful men that they should walk like the Son of God?" The answer that most people give is practical—that it cannot really be expected; the command sets before us an ideal—beautiful, but unattainable. The answer Scripture gives is different. It points us to the wonderful relationship in which we stand to Christ. Because our union to Him sets in operation within us a heavenly life with all its powers, therefore the claim may be made … that we should live as Christ did. The realization of this relationship between Christ and His people is necessary for everyone who is earnest in following Christ's example.

In one sense His work is unique; in another we have to follow Him in it; we must do as He did, live and suffer like Him. "Christ *suffered for us, leaving us an example*" that we should follow in His footsteps. As a believer I am spiritually one with Him. In this union He lives in me, and imparts to me the power of His finished work, the power of His sufferings and death and resurrection. It is on this ground that we are taught in Romans 6 and elsewhere that the Christian is indeed dead to sin and alive to God. The very life that Christ lives, the life that passed through death, and the power of that death, work in believers, so that we are dead, and has risen again with Christ. It is this thought Peter gives utterance to when he says: *"Who His own Self bore our sins upon the tree,"* not alone that we through His death might receive forgiveness, but *"that we, being dead to sins, should live unto righteousness."*

His very life lives in me. He lives Himself in me, whom He bought with His blood.

To follow His footsteps is a duty, because it is a possibility, the natural result of the wonderful union between the Head and members. It is only when this is understood aright that the blessed truth of Christ's example will take its right place. If Jesus Himself through his life union will work in me the life likeness, then my duty becomes plain, but glorious. I have, on the one side, to gaze on His example so as to know and follow it. On the other, to abide in Him, and open my heart to the blessed workings of His life in me. As surely as He conquered sin and its curse for me, will He conquer it in its power in me. What He began by His death for me, He will perfect by His life in me. Because my Surety is also my Head, His Example must and will be the rule of my life.

There is a saying of Augustine that is often quoted: "Lord I give what You command, and command what You will." This holds good here. If the Lord, who lives in me, *gives* what He requires of me, then no requirement can be too high. Then I have the courage to gaze upon His holy example in all its height and breadth, and to accept of it as the law of my conduct. It is no longer merely a command telling what I must be, but a promise of what I shall be.

There is nothing that weakens the power of Christ's Example so much as the thought that we cannot really walk like Him. Do not listen to such thoughts. The perfect likeness in Heaven is begun on earth, can grow with each day, and become more visible as life goes on. As certain and mighty as the work of surety which Christ, your Head, completed once for all, is the renewal after His own Image, which He is still working out. Let this double blessing make the cross doubly precious: Our Head suffered as a Surety, that in union with us he might bear sin for us. Our Head offered as an Example, that He might show us what the path is in which, in union with Himself, He would lead us to victory and to glory. The suffering Christ is our Head, our Surety, and our Example.

And so the great lesson I have to learn is the wonderful truth that it is just in that mysterious path of suffering, in which He wrought out our atonement and redemption, that we are to follow His footsteps, and that the full experience of that redemption depends upon the personal fellowship in that suffering. "*Christ suffered for us, leaving us an Example.*" May the Holy Spirit reveal to me what this means.

Precious Savior! how shall I thank You for the work that You have done as Surety? Standing in the place of me a guilty sinner, You have borne my sins in Your body on the cross. That cross was my due. You did take it, and was made like unto me, that thus the cross might be changed into a place of blessing and life.

And now You call me to the place of crucifixion as the place of blessing and life, where I may be made like You, and may find in You power to suffer and to cease from sin. As my Head, You were my Surety to suffer and die with me; as my Head, You are my Example that I might suffer and die with You.

Precious Savior! I confess that I have too little understood this. Your Suretyship was more to me than Your Example. I rejoiced much that You had borne the cross for me, but too little that I like You and with You might also bear the cross. The atonement of the cross was more precious to me than the fellowship of the cross; the hope in Your redemption more precious than the personal fellowship with Yourself.

Forgive me this, dear Lord, and teach me to find my happiness in union with You, my Head, not more in Your Suretyship than in Your Example. And grant, that in my meditations as to how I am to follow You, my faith may become stronger and brighter: Jesus is my Example because He is my life. I must and can be like Him, because I am one with Him. Grant this, my blessed Lord, for Your love's sake. Amen.

Note*—from M. Diemer, A new book on the imitation of Jesus Christ*:

Thomas à Kempis has said, "All men wish to be with Christ, and to belong to His people; but few are really willing to follow the life of Christ." There are many who imagine that to imitate Jesus Christ is a specially advanced state in the Christian life, to which only a few elect can attain: they think that one can be a real Christian if he only confesses his weakness and sin, and holds fast to the Word and Sacrament, *without attaining any real conformity to the life of Christ*; they even count it pride and fanaticism if one venture to say *that conformity to the likeness of Jesus Christ is an indispensable sign of the true Christian.* And yet our Lord says to all without exception: "*He that doth not take his cross, and follow after me, is not worthy of me;*" He mentions expressly the most difficult thing in His life—the cross, that which includes all else. And Peter writes not to some, but to the whole Church: "*Christ has left us an Example that ye should follow His footsteps.*"

It is a sad sign that these unmistakable commands have been so darkened in our modern Christianity, that our leading ministers and church members have quietly, as by common consent, agreed to rob these words of their sting. A false dogmatic must bear no small share of the blame. … For, of a truth, if Christ's suffering and cross be only and altogether something supernatural, we must cease to speak of the imitation of Christ in any true or real sense of the word.

Oh, the gulf of separation which comes between the life of Christ and the life of Christians …. And how slow and slothful the Church of our day is to apply the great and distinct rule so clearly laid down in the life of Christ, to the filling of these gulfs and the correcting of the disorders of our modern life. The Church of Christ will not be brought again out of its confusions until the faithful actual imitation of her Lord and Head again become the banner round which she rallies His disciples.

Like Christ: As the Elect of God

January 24th

"Predestined to be conformed to the image of His Son"

—ROMANS 8: 29

Scripture teaches us a personal election. … The more I believe not only in general that I am elected of God, but see how this election has reference to every part of my calling, the more shall I be strengthened in the conviction that God Himself will perfect His work in me, and that therefore it is possible for me to be all that God really expects. With every duty Scripture lays upon me, with every promise for whose fulfilment I long, I will go to find in God's purposes the firm footing upon which my expectations may rest, and the true measure by which they are to be guided. I shall understand that my life on earth is to be a copy of the heavenly life-plan, that the Father has drawn out, of what I am to be on earth. Christian! make your calling and election sure; let it become clear to you that you are elected, and to what: "*If you do these things, you shall never stumble.*" Quiet communion with God on the ground of His unchangeable purpose imparts to the soul an immoveable firmness that keeps from stumbling.

One of the most blessed expressions in regard to God's purpose concerning us in Christ is this word: "*Predestinated to be conformed to the image of His Son.*" The man Christ Jesus is the elect of God; in Him election has its beginning and ending. "*In Him we are chosen*"; for the sake of our union with Him and to His glory our election took place. The believer who seeks in election merely the certainty of his own salvation, or relief from fear and doubt, knows very little of its real glory. …

"*Chosen in Him that we should be holy and blameless before Him in love.*" It is only when the connection between election and sanctification is rightly apprehended in the Church that the doctrine of election will bring its full blessing (2 Thessalonians 2:13; 1 Peter 1: 2). It teaches the believer how it is God who must work all in him, who will work all in him, and how he may rely even in the smallest matters upon the unchangeable purpose of God to work out itself in the accomplishment of everything that He expects of His people. In this light the word "*Predestined to be conformed to the image of His Son.*" gives new strength to everyone who has begun to take what Christ is as the rule of what he himself is to be.

Christian! would you in very deed be like Christ? Fix your mind upon the thought of how certainly this is God's will concerning you; how the whole of redemption has been planned with the view of your becoming so; how God's purpose is the guarantee that your desires must be fulfilled. There, where your name is written in the Book of Life, there stands also, "*Predestined to be conformed to the image of His Son.*" All the powers of the Deity which have already wrought together in the accomplishment of the first part of the eternal purpose, the revealing of the Father's perfect likeness in the man Christ Jesus, are equally engaged to accomplish the second part, and work that likeness in each of God's children.

In the work of Christ there is the most perfect provision possible for the carrying out of God's purposes in this. Our union to Christ, held fast in a living faith, will be an all-prevailing power. We can depend upon it as something ordained with a Divine certainty, and that must come if we yield ourselves to it. Has not God elected us to be conformed to the image of His Son? It can easily be understood what a powerful influence the living consciousness of this truth will have. It teaches us to give up ourselves to the Eternal Will, that it may, with Divine power, effect its purpose in us. It shows us how useless and impotent our own efforts are to accomplish this work: all that is *of* God must also be *through* Him. He who is the beginning, must be the middle and the end. In a very wonderful manner it strengthens our faith with a holy boldness to glory in God alone, and to expect from God Himself the fulfillment of every promise and every command, of every part of the purpose of His blessed will.

And where does this likeness to Christ consist? In Sonship. It is to the image of *His Son* we are to be conformed. All the different traits of a Christ-like life resolve themselves into this one as their spring and end. We are "*predestined for the adoption of children by Jesus*

Christ." It was *as the Son* Christ lived and served and pleased the Father. It is only *as a son* with the Spirit of His own Son in my heart, that I can live and serve and please the Father. I must each day walk in the full and clear consciousness: like Christ, I am a son of the Most High God, born from above, the beloved of the Father. As a son the Father is engaged to provide my every need. As a son I live in dependence and trust, in love and obedience, in joy and hope. It is when I live with the Father as a son, that it becomes possible to make any sacrifice and to obey every command.

Believer! Take time and prayer to take in this truth, and let it exercise its full power in your soul Let the Holy Spirit write it into your inmost being, that you are predestined to be conformed to the image of His Son. The Father's object was the honor of His Son, *"that He might be the firstborn among many brethren."* Let this be your object, too, in all your life, so to show forth the image of your Elder Brother, that other Christians may be pointed to Him alone, may praise Him alone, and seek to follow Him more closely too. Let it be the fixed and only purpose of your life, the great object of your believing prayer, that *"Christ be magnified in my body."* This will give you new confidence to ask and expect all that is necessary to live like Christ.

Your conformity to Christ will be one of the links connecting the eternal purpose of the Father with the eternal fulfillment of it in the glorifying of the Son. Your conformity to Christ becomes then such a holy, heavenly, Divine work, that you realize that it can come only from the Father, but that from Him you can and shall most certainly receive it. What God's purpose has decreed, God's power will perform. What God's love has ordained and commanded, God's love will most certainly accomplish. A living faith in His eternal purpose will become one of the mightiest powers in urging and helping us to live like Christ.

Like Christ: Because We Abide in Him

January 25th

"He that says he abides in Him, ought also so to walk even as He walked"

—1 JOHN 2: 6

Abiding in Christ and walking like Christ: these are the two blessings of the new life which are here set before us in their essential unity. The fruit of a life *in Christ* is a life *like Christ.* To the first of these expressions, *abiding in Christ*, we are no strangers. The wondrous parable of the Vine and the branches, with the accompanying command, *"Abide in Me, and I in you,"* has often been to us a source of rich instruction and comfort. …

The second expression, *walking like Christ*, is not less significant than the first. It is the promise of the wonderful power which the abiding in Him will exert. As the fruit of our surrender to live wholly in Him, His life works so mightily in us, that our walk—the outward expression of the inner life—becomes like His. The two are inseparably connected.

The abiding in always precedes the walking like Him. And yet the aim to walk like

Him must equally precede any large measure of abiding. Only then is the need for a close union fully realized, or is the Heavenly Giver free to bestow the fullness of His grace, because He sees that the soul is prepared to use it according to His design.

When the Savior said, *"If you keep my commandments, you shall abide in My love,"* He meant just this: the surrender to walk like Me is the path to the full abiding in Me. Many of us will discover that just here is the secret of our failure in abiding in Christ; we did not seek it with the view of walking like Christ.

The words of St. John invite us to look at the two truths in their vital connection and dependence on each other. The first lesson they teach is: We that seek to abide in Christ must *walk even as He walked.* We all know that it is a matter of course that a branch bears fruit of the same sort as the vine to which it belongs. The life of the vine and the branch is so completely identical, that the manifestation of that life must be identical too. When the Lord Jesus redeemed us with His blood, and presented us to the Father in His righteousness, He did not leave us in our old nature to serve God as best we could. No; in Him dwelled the eternal life, the holy Divine life of Heaven, and everyone who is in Him receives from Him that same eternal life in its holy heavenly power. Hence nothing can be more natural than the claim that we that abide in Him, continually receiving life from Him, must *also so* walk *even as He* walked.

This mighty life of God in the soul does not, however, work as a blind force, compelling us ignorantly or involuntarily to act like Christ. On the contrary, the walking like Him must come as the result of a deliberate choice, sought in strong desire, accepted of a living will. With this view, the Father in Heaven showed us in Jesus' earthly life what the life of heaven would be when it came down into the conditions and circumstances of our human life. And with the same object the Lord Jesus, when we receive the new life from Him, and when He calls us to abide in Him, that we may receive that life more abundantly, ever points us to His own life on earth, and tells us that it is to walk even as He walked that the new life has been bestowed. "*Even as I, so you also*:" that word of the Master takes His whole earthly life, and very simply makes it the rule and guide of all our conduct. If we abide in Jesus, we may not act otherwise than He did. "Like Christ" gives in one short all-inclusive word the blessed law of the Christian life. We are to think, to speak, to act as Jesus did; as Jesus was, *even so* are we to be.

The second lesson is the complement of the first: We that seek to walk like Christ, must *abide in Him.* … With some there is the earnest desire and effort to follow Christ's example, without any sense of the impossibility of doing so, except by deep, real abiding in Him. They fail because they seek to obey the high command to live like Christ, without the only power that can do so—the living in Christ. With others there is the opposite error; they know their own weakness, and count the walking like Christ an impossibility. As much as those who seek to do it and who fail, do those who do not seek because they expect to fail, need the lesson we are enforcing. To walk like Christ one must abide in Him; he that abides in Him has the power to walk like Him; not indeed in himself or his own efforts, but in Jesus, who perfects His strength in our weakness.

It is just when I feel my utter impotence most deeply, and fully accept Jesus in His wondrous union to myself as my life, that His power works in me, and I am able to lead a life completely beyond what my power could obtain. I begin to see that abiding in Him is not a matter of moments or special seasons, but the deep life process in which, by His keeping grace, I continue without a moment's intermission, and from which I act out all my Christian life. …

Every believer is *in* Christ; but not everyone *abides* in Him, in the consciously joyful and trustful surrender of the whole being to His influence. You know what abiding in Him is. It is to consent with our whole soul to His being our life, to reckon upon Him to inspire us in all that goes to make up life, and then to give up everything most absolutely for Him to rule and work in us. It is the rest of the full assurance that He does, each moment, work in us what we are to be, and so Himself enables us to maintain that perfect surrender, in which He is free to do all His will. Let all who do indeed long to walk like Christ take courage at the thought of what He is and will prove Himself to be if they trust Him. He is the *True Vine*. … We have only to consent to be branches. Honor Him by a joyful trust that He is, beyond all conception, the *True Vine*, holding you by His almighty strength, supplying you from His infinite fullness.

And as your faith thus looks to Him, instead of sighing and failure, the voice of praise will be heard repeating the language of faith: Thanks be to God! We that abide in Him walk even as He walked. Thanks be to God! I abide in Him, and I walk as He walked. Yes, thanks be to God! In the blessed life of God's redeemed these two are inseparably one: abiding in Christ and walking like Christ.

Like Christ: Crucified with Him

January 26th

"I am crucified with Christ: nevertheless I live; yet not I, but Christ lives in me."

—GALATIANS 2: 20

Taking up the cross was always spoken of by Christ as the test of discipleship. On three different occasions (Matthew 10: 38; 16: 24; Luke 14: 27) we find the words repeated, *"If any man will come after Me, let him take up his cross and follow Me."* While the Lord was still on His way to the cross, this expression—taking up the cross, was the most appropriate to indicate that conformity to Him to which the disciple is called.

Christians entirely miss the point of the Lord's command when they refer to the taking up of the cross only to the crosses or trials of life. It means much more. The cross means death. Taking up the cross means going out to die. It is just in the time of prosperity that we most need to bear the cross. Taking up the cross and following Him is nothing less than living every day with our own life and will, given up to death. …

One of the chief elements of likeness to Christ consists in being crucified with Him. Whoever wishes to be like Him must seek to understand the secret of fellowship with His cross. At first sight the Christian who seeks conformity to Jesus is afraid of this truth: we shrink from the painful suffering and death with which the thought of the cross is connected. As our spiritual discernment becomes clearer, however, this word becomes all our hope and joy, and we glory in the cross, because it makes us a partner in a death and victory that has already been accomplished, and in which the deliverance from the powers of the flesh and of the world has been secured to us. To understand this, we must notice carefully the language of Scripture: *"I am crucified with Christ,"* Paul says; *"nevertheless I live; yet not I, but Christ lives in me"! ...*

If I am crucified and dead with Him, then I am a partner in His life and victory. I learn to understand the position I must take to allow the power of that cross and that death to manifest itself in mortifying or making dead the old man and the flesh, in destroying the body of sin (Romans 6: 6). ... It is my duty to glory in the cross, and with my whole heart to maintain the dominion of the cross, and to set my seal to the sentence that has been pronounced, to make dead every uprising of sin, as already crucified, and so not to suffer it to have dominion. This is what Scripture means when it says, "*If you through the Spirit do make to die the deeds of the body, you shall live*" (Romans 8: 13). "*Make dead therefore your members which are upon the earth*" (Colossians 3: 5). Thus, I continually and voluntarily acknowledge that in my flesh dwells no good thing; that my Lord is Christ the Crucified One; that I have been crucified and am dead in Him; that the flesh has been crucified and, though not yet dead, has been for ever given over to the death of the cross. And so I live like Christ, in very deed crucified with Him.

In order to enter fully into the meaning and the power of this fellowship of the crucifixion of our Lord, two things are specially necessary to those who are Christ's followers. The first is the clear consciousness of this their fellowship with the Crucified One through faith. At conversion they became partakers of it without fully understanding it. Many remain in ignorance all their life long through a want of spiritual knowledge. Pray that the Holy Spirit may reveal to you your union to the Crucified One. "*I have been crucified with Christ*"; "*I glory in the cross of Christ, through which I have been crucified to the world.*" Take such words of Holy Scripture, and by prayer and meditation make them your own, with a heart that expects and asks the Holy Spirit to make them living and effectual within you. Look upon yourself in the light of God as what you really are, "*crucified with Christ.*" Then you will find the grace for the second thing you need to enable you to live as a crucified one, in whom Christ lives. You will be able always to look upon and to treat the flesh and the world as nailed to the cross.

The old nature seeks continually to assert itself, and to make you feel as if it is expecting too much that you should always live this crucifixion life. Your only safety is in fellowship with Christ. "Through Him and His cross," says Paul, "*I have been crucified to the world.*" In Him the crucifixion is an accomplished reality; in Him you have died, but also have been made alive: Christ lives in you. With this fellowship of His cross let it be with you, the deeper the better: it brings you into deeper communion with His life and His love.

To be crucified with Christ means freed from the power of sin: a redeemed one, a conqueror. Remember that the Holy Spirit has been specially provided to glorify Christ in you, to reveal within you, and make your very own, all that is in Christ for you. Do not be satisfied, with so many others, only to know the cross in its power to atone: the glory of the cross is, that it was not only to Jesus, but is to us too, the path to life, but that each moment it can become to us the power that destroys sin and death, and keeps us in the power of the eternal life.

Learn from your Savior the holy art of using it for this. Faith in the power of the cross and its victory will day by day make dead the deeds of the body, the lusts of the flesh. This faith will teach you to count the cross, with its continual death to Self. all your glory. Because you regard the cross, not as one who is still on the way to crucifixion, with the prospect of a painful death, but as one to whom the crucifixion is past, who already lives in Christ, and now only bears the cross as the blessed instrument through which the body of sin is done away (Romans 6: 6). …

Above all, remember what still remains the chief thing: It is Jesus, the living loving Savior, who Himself enables you to be like Him in all things. His sweet fellowship, His tender love, His heavenly power, make it a blessedness and joy to be like Him, the Crucified One, make the crucifixion life a life of resurrection—joy and power. ...

Like Christ: In His Self-Denial

January 27th

"We that we strong ought to bear the weak, and not to please ourselves. …For even Christ pleased not Himself"

—ROMANS 15: 1–3

"If anyone will come after me, let him deny himself, and take up his cross, and follow me".

—MATTHEW 16: 24

Christ pleased not Himself: with reference both to God and man, this word is the key of His life. In this, too, His life is our rule and example: we who are strong ought not to please ourselves. To deny Self—this is the opposite of pleasing Self. … Through the cross of Christ, I am crucified to the world, and the flesh, and Self…. The Christian who only thinks of our salvation from curse and condemnation cannot understand this; we find it impossible to deny Self. Although we may sometimes try to do so, our life mainly consists in pleasing ourselves. The Christian who has taken Christ as our pattern cannot be content with this. We have surrendered ourselves to seek the most complete fellowship with the cross of Christ. The Holy Spirit has taught us to say, "*I have been crucified with Christ, and so am dead to sin and Self.*" In fellowship with Christ we see the old man crucified, a condemned malefactor; … and we have received the power for it too, no longer to please the old nature, but to deny it. Because the crucified Christ is our life, Self-denial is the law of our life.

This Self-denial extends itself over the whole domain of life. It was so with the Lord Jesus, and is so with everyone who longs to follow Him perfectly. This Self-denial has not so much to do with what is sinful, and unlawful, and contrary to the laws of God, as with what is lawful, or apparently indifferent. To the Self-denying spirit the will and glory of God and the salvation of man are always more than our own interests or pleasure.

Before we can know how to please our neighbor, Self-denial must first exercise itself in our own personal life. It must rule the body. The holy fasting of Him who said, *"Man shall not live by bread alone, but by every word that proceeds out of the mouth of God"*; and who would not eat until His Father gave Him food, and His Father's work was done, teaches the believer a holy temperance in eating and drinking. The holy poverty of Him who had not where to lay His head, teaches him so to regulate the possession, and use, and enjoyment of earthly things that we may always possess as not possessing. After the example of the holy suffering of Him who bore all our sins in His own body on the tree, we learn to bear all suffering patiently: even in the body as the temple of the Holy Spirit, we desire to bear about the dying of the Lord Jesus; with Paul he keeps under the body and brings it into subjection; all its desires and appetites he would have ruled by the Self-denial of Jesus. He does not please himself.

This Self-denial keeps watch over the spirit too. His own wisdom and judgment the believer brings into subjection to God's word: he gives up his own thoughts to the teaching of the Word and the Spirit. Towards man he manifests the same Self-denial of his own wisdom in a readiness to hear and learn, in the meekness and humility with which, even when he knows he is in the right, he gives his opinion, in the desire ever to find and to acknowledge what is good in others.

And then Self-denial has special reference to the heart. All the affections and desires are placed under it. The will, the kingly power of the soul is specially under its control. As little as Self-pleasing could be a part of Christ's life, may Christ's follower allow it ever to influence his conduct. *"We ought not to please ourselves. For even Christ pleased not Himself."* Self-denial is the law of our life.

Nor do we find it hard when once we have truly surrendered ourselves to it. To those who, with a divided heart, seek to force ourselves to a life of Self-denial, it is hard indeed; but to those who have yielded ourselves to it unreservedly, because we have with our whole heart accepted the cross to destroy the power of sin and Self, the blessing it brings more than compensates for apparent sacrifice or loss. We hardly dare any longer speak of Self-denial; there is such blessedness in becoming conformed to the image of Jesus.

Self-denial has not its value with God, as some think, from the measure of pain it causes. No, for this pain is very much caused by the remaining reluctance to fullness it. But it has its highest worth in that meek or even joyful acquiescence which counts nothing a sacrifice for Jesus' sake, and feels surprised when others speak of Self-denial.

There have been ages when men thought they must fly to the wilderness or cloister to deny themselves. The Lord Jesus has shown us that the best place to fullness Self-denial is in our ordinary intercourse with men. So, Paul also says here, *"We ought not to please ourselves .... For even Christ pleased not Himself. ...* Nothing less than the Self-denial of our Lord, who pleased not Himself, is our law. What He was we must be. What He did we must do. What a glorious life will it be in the Church of Christ when this law prevails!

each one considers it the object of existence to make others happy. Each one denies himself, seeks not his own, esteems others better than himself. All thought of taking offence, of wounded pride, of being slighted or passed by, would pass away. As a follower of Christ, each would seek to bear the weak and to please his neighbor. The true Self-denial would be seen in this, that no one would think of himself, but live in and for others.

"If any man will come after me, let him deny himself, take up his cross, and follow me." This word not only gives us the will, but also the power for Self-denial. He who does not simply wish to reach Heaven through Christ, but comes after Him for His own sake, will follow Him. And in his heart Jesus speedily takes the place that Self had. Jesus only becomes the center and object of such a life. The undivided surrender to follow Him is crowned with this wonderful blessing, that Christ by His Spirit Himself becomes his life. Christ's spirit of Self-denying love is poured out upon him, and to deny Self is the greatest joy of his heart, and the means of the deepest communion with God. Self-denial is no longer a work he simply does as a means of attaining perfection for himself.

Nor is it merely a negative victory, of which the main feature is the keeping Self in check. Christ has taken the place of Self, and His love and gentleness and kindness flow out to others, now that Self is parted with. No command becomes more blessed or more natural than this: "*We ought not to please ourselves, for even Christ pleased not Himself.*" "*If any man come after me, let him deny himself, and FOLLOW ME.*"

Like Christ: In His Heavenly Mission

January 28th

"As my Father has sent me, even so send I you."

—JOHN 20: 21

The Lord Jesus lived here on earth under a deep consciousness of having a mission from His Father to fulfill. He continually used the expression, *"The Father has sent me."* It will repay the trouble to compare carefully the following passages: John 5:24, 30, 37, 38; 6: 38, 39, 40, 44; 7: 16, 28, 29, 3; 8:16, 18, 26, 29, 42; 9: 4; 11: 42; 12: 44, 45, 49; 13: 20; 14: 24; 15: 21; 16: 25; 17: 8, 18, 21, 23, 25; 20: 21.

Christ wanted us to know that He did not act independently, but on behalf of Another who had sent Him. The consciousness of a mission never left Him for a moment. He knew what this mission was. He knew the Father had chosen Him, and sent Him into the world with the one purpose of fulfilling that mission, and He knew the Father would give Him all that He needed for it. Faith in the Father having sent Him was the motive and power for all that He did.

Our heavenly mission is one of the most glorious parts of our conformity to our Lord. He says it plainly in the most solemn moments of His life; *"that even as the Father sent Him,"* so He sends His disciples. He says it to the Father in His high-priestly prayer, as the ground upon which He asks for their keeping and sanctification. He says it to the disciples after His resurrection, as the ground on which they are to receive the Holy Spirit. Nothing will help us more to know and fulfill our mission than to realize how perfectly it corresponds to the mission of Christ, how they are, in fact, identical.

Our mission is like His *in its object.* Why did the Father send His Son? To make known His love and His will in the salvation of sinners. He was to do this, not alone by word and precept, but in His own person, disposition, and conduct to exhibit the Father's holy love. He was so to represent the unseen Father in Heaven that men on earth might know what the Father was like. ...

And now He has given His mission to His disciples, after having shown them how to fulfill it. They must so represent Him ... that from seeing us men can judge who and what He is. Every Christian must so be the image of Jesus—must so exhibit in person and conduct the same love to sinners...so that the world may know what "like Christ" is.

"*You have not chosen Me, but I have chosen you and ordained you, that you should go and bring forth fruit.*" Believer! Whoever you are, and wherever you dwell, the Lord, who knows you and your surroundings, has need of you, and has chosen you to be His representative in the circle in which you move. Fix your heart on this. He has fixed His heart on you and saved you, in order that you should bear and exhibit to those who surround you the very image of His unseen glory. Oh, think of this origin of your heavenly mission in His everlasting love, as His had its origin in the love of the Father. Your mission is in very truth just like His.

Like it, too, *in the fitting for it.* Every ambassador expects to be supplied with all that he needs for his embassy. "*He who has sent Me is with Me. The Father has not left Me alone*"; that word tells us how, when the Father sent the Son, He was always with Him, His strength and comfort. Even so the Church of Christ in her mission: "*Go and teach all nations,*" has the promise: "*Lo, I am with you.*" The Christian need never hold back because of unfitness. The Lord does not demand anything which He does not give the power to perform. Every believer may depend on it—that as the Father gave His Holy Spirit to the Son to fit Him for His work, so the Lord Jesus will give His people too all the preparation they need. The grace to show forth Christ evermore, to exhibit the lovely light of His example and likeness, and like Christ Himself to be a fountain of love and life and blessing to all around, is given to everyone who only heartily and believingly takes up this heavenly calling.

The Lord Jesus gave Himself entirely and undividedly over to accomplish His work; He lived for it alone. "*I must work the work of Him that sent Me while it is day: the night comes when no one can work.*" The Father's mission was the only reason of His being on earth; for that alone He would live; to reveal to mankind what a glorious blessed God the Father in Heaven was.

As with Jesus, so with us. Christ's mission is *the only reason for our being on earth*; were it not for that, He would take us away. Most believers do not believe this. To fulfill Christ's mission is with them at best something to be done along with other things, for which it is difficult to find time and strength.

And yet it is so certainly true: to accomplish Christ's mission is the only reason of our being upon earth. Then first when we believe this, and like our Lord in His mission consecrate our Self undividedly to it, shall we indeed live well-pleasing to Him. This heavenly mission is so great and glorious, that without an entire consecration to it we cannot accomplish it. Without this, the powers which fit us for it cannot take possession of us. Without this, we have no liberty to expect the Lord's wonderful help and the fulfillment of all His blessed promises. Just as with Jesus, our heavenly mission demands nothing less than entire consecration. Am I prepared for this? Then I have indeed the key through which the holy hidden glories of this word of Jesus will be revealed to my experience: "*As the Father sent me, even so I send you.*"

O Christians! This heavenly mission is indeed worthy that we devote ourselves entirely to it as the only thing we live for.

Like Christ: Not of the World

January 29th

"The world has hated them because they are not of the world, even as I am not of the world."

—JOHN 17:14

In *"In the world," "Not of the world,"* we find the whole secret of His work as Savior, of His glory as the God-man.

"In the world"; in fellowship with men, to enter into loving relationship with them, to be seen and known of them, and thus to win them back to the Father. *"In the world";* in the struggle with the powers which rule the world, to learn obedience, and so to perfect and sanctify human nature.

"Not of the world"; but of Heaven, to manifest and bring nigh the life that is in God, and which man had lost, that men might see and long for it. *"Not of the world";* witnessing against its sin and departure from God, its impotence to know and please God. *"Not of the world";* ... of a kingdom entirely heavenly in origin and nature, entirely independent of all that the world holds desirable or necessary, with principles and laws the very opposite of those that rule in the world. *"Not of the world";* in order to redeem all who belong to Him, and bring them into that new and heavenly kingdom which He had revealed.

"In the world"; "Not of the world." In these two expressions we have revealed to us the great mystery of the person and work of the Savior. "Not *of* the world," in the power of His Divine holiness judging and overcoming it; still in the world, and through His humanity and love seeking and saving all that can be saved. The most entire separation from the world, with the closest fellowship with those in the world; these two extremes meet in Jesus, in His own person He has reconciled them. And it is the calling of each Christian—to prove that these two dispositions however much they may seem at variance, can in our life, too, be united in perfect harmony. In each believer there must be seen a heavenly life shining out through earthly forms.

To take one of these two truths and exclusively cultivate it, is not so difficult. So you have those who have taken "Not of the world" as their motto. From the earliest ages, when people thought they must fly to cloisters and deserts to serve God, to our own days, when some seek to show the earnestness of their piety by severity in judging all that is in the world, there have been those who counted this the only true religion. There was separation from sin, but then there was also no fellowship with sinners. The sinner could not feel surrounded with the atmosphere of a tender heavenly love. It was a one-sided and therefore a defective religion.

Then there are those who, on the other side, lay stress on "In the world," and very specially appeal to the words of the apostle, "*For then you must go out of the world.*" They think that, by showing that religion does not make us unfriendly or unfit to enjoy all that there is to enjoy, they will induce the world to serve God. It has often happened that they have indeed succeeded in making the world very religious, but at too high a price; religion became very worldly.

"In the world"; "Not of the world." The true follower of Jesus must combine both. If we do not clearly show that we are not of the world, and prove the greater blessedness of a heavenly life, how will we convince the world of sin, or prove that there is a higher life, or lead others to desire what they do not yet possess? Earnestness, and holiness, and separation from the spirit of the world must characterize our life. Our heavenly spirit must manifest that we belong to a kingdom not of this world. An unworldly, an other-worldly, a heavenly spirit must breathe in us.

And still we must live as ones who are "in the world"—expressly placed here of God, among those who are of the world, to win their hearts, to acquire influence over them, and to communicate to them of the Spirit which is in us. It must be the great study of our life how we can fulfill this mission. Not, as the wisdom of the world would teach, by yielding, and complying, and softening down the solemn realities of religion, will we succeed. No, but only by walking in the footsteps of Him who alone can teach how to be in the world and yet not of it. Only by a life of serving and suffering love, in which the Christian distinctly confesses that the glory of God is the aim of his existence, and in which, full of the Holy Spirit, we bring others into direct contact with the warmth and love of the heavenly life, can we be a blessing to the world.

Oh, who will teach us the heavenly secret, of uniting every day in our lives what is so difficult to unite—to be in the world, and not of the world? He can do it who has said: "They are not of the, world, *even as* I am not of the world." That "even as" has a deeper meaning and power than we know. If we suffer the Holy Spirit to unfold that word to us, we shall understand what it is to be in the world as He was in the world. That "even as" has its root and strength in a life union. In it we shall discover the divine secret, that the more entirely one is not of the world, the more fit he is to be in the world. The freer the Church is of the spirit and principles of the world, the more influence she will exert in it. The life of the world is Self-pleasing and Self-exaltation. The life of Heaven is holy, Self-denying love.

The weakness of the life of many Christians who seek to separate themselves from the world, is that they have too much of the spirit of the world. They seek their own happiness and perfection more than ought else. Jesus Christ was not of the world, and had nothing of its spirit; this is why He could love sinners, could win them and save them. ... The disciple who believes fully in the Christ-likeness of his inner life, will experience the truth of it. We cultivate and give utterance to the assurance: "Even as Christ, so am I not of the world, because I am in Christ." We understand that alone in close union with Christ can our separation from the world be maintained; in as far as Christ lives in us can we lead a heavenly life. We see that the only way to answer to our calling is, on the one side, as crucified to the world to withdraw ourselves from its power; and, on the other, as living in Christ to go into it and bless it. We live in Heaven and walk on earth.

Christians! See here the true imitation of Jesus Christ. *"Wherefore come out from among them, and be you separate, says the Lord."* Then the promise is fulfilled, "I will dwell in them and walk in them." Then Christ sends you, as the Father sent Him, to be in the world as the place ordained of your Father to glorify Him, and to make known His love. Not so much in the desire to leave earth for Heaven, as in the willingness to live the life of Heaven here on earth, does a truly unworldly, a heavenly Spirit, manifest itself.

"*Not of the world*" is not only separation from and testimony against the world, but is the living manifestation of the spirit, and the love, and the power of the other world, of the Heaven to which we long, in its divine work of making this world partaker of its blessedness. ...

The world has still entrance to our hearts, its Selfish spirit is still too much within us. Through unbelief the new nature has not always full power. Lord, we beseech of You, as fruit of Your all-powerful intercession, let that word be fully realized in us: "*Not of the world, even as I am not of the world.*" In our likeness to You is our only power against the world.

Like Christ: In His Self-Sacrifice

January 30th

"Hereby we know the love of God: because He laid down His life for us; and we ought to lay down our lives for the brethren."

—1 JOHN 3:16

Self-sacrifice is of the very essence of true love. The very nature and blessedness of love consist in forgetting Self, and seeking its happiness in the loved one. Where in the beloved there is a want or need, love is impelled by its very nature to offer up its own happiness for that of the other....

Who can say whether this is not one of the secrets which eternity will reveal, that sin was permitted because otherwise God's love could never so fully have been revealed? The highest glory of God's love was manifested in the Self-sacrifice of Christ. It is the highest glory of the Christian to be like his Lord in this. Without entire Self-sacrifice the new command, the command of love, cannot be fulfilled. Without entire Self-sacrifice, we cannot love as Jesus loved. "*Be imitators of God,*" says the apostle, *"and walk in love, even as Christ has loved us, and has given Himself a sacrifice for us."* …

Let all your walk and conversation be, according to Christ's example, in love. It was this love that made His sacrifice acceptable in God's sight, a sweet-smelling savor. As His love exhibited itself in Self-sacrifice, let your love prove itself to be conformable to His in the daily Self-sacrifice for the welfare of others, so will it also be acceptable in the sight of God. *"We ought to lay down our lives for the brethren."*

Down even into the daily affairs of home life … Christ's Self-sacrifice must be the rule of our walk. *"Likewise, you husbands, love your wives, even as Christ loved the Church, and gave Himself for it."*

And mark specially the words, *"Has given Himself for us an offering to God."* We see that Self-sacrifice has here two sides. Christ's Self-sacrifice had a Godward as well as a man-ward aspect. It was *for us*, but it was *to God* that He offered Himself as a sacrifice. In all our Self-sacrifice there must be these two sides in union, though now the one and then again the other may be more prominent. It is only when we sacrifice ourselves *to God* that there will be the power for an entire Self-sacrifice.

The Holy Spirit reveals to the believer the right of God's claim on us, how we are not our own, but His. The realization of how absolutely we are God's property, bought and paid for with blood, of how we are loved with such a wonderful love, and of what blessedness there is in the full surrender to Him, leads us to yield ourselves.... We lay our Self on the altar of consecration, and find it our highest joy to be a sweet-smelling savor to God—God-devoted and God-accepted. And then it becomes our first and most earnest desire to know how God would have us show this entire Self-sacrifice in life and walk.

God points him to Christ's example. He was a sweet-smelling savor to God when He gave Himself a sacrifice for us. For every Christian who gives himself entirely to His service, God has given the same honor as He had for His Son, He uses him as an instrument of blessing to others. Therefore, John says, "*He who loves not his brother whom he has seen, how can he love God whom he has not seen?*" The Self-sacrifice in which you have devoted yourself to God's service, binds you also to serve your fellow-man; the same act which makes you entirely God's, makes you entirely theirs.

It is just this surrender to God that gives the power for Self-sacrifice towards others, and even makes it a joy. When faith has first appropriated the promise, *"Inasmuch as you have done it to the least of these my brethren, you have done it unto me,"* I understand the glorious harmony between sacrifice *to God* and sacrifice for men. My intercourse with my fellow-man, instead of being, as many complain, a hindrance to unbroken communion with God, becomes an opportunity of offering myself unceasingly to Him.

Blessed calling! To walk in love even as Christ loved us, and gave Himself for us a sacrifice … Only thus can the Church fulfill its destiny, and prove to the world that she is set apart to continue Christ's work of Self-sacrificing love ….

But does God really expect us to deny ourselves so entirely for others? Is it not asking too much? Can anyone really sacrifice himself so entirely? Christian! God does expect it; nothing less than this is the conformity to the image of His Son.... This is the path by which Jesus entered into His glory and blessedness and by no other way can the disciple enter into the joy of the Lord. It is in very deed our calling to become exactly like Jesus in His love and Self-sacrifice. *"Walk in love, even as Christ loved."* It is a great thing when a believer sees and acknowledges this. That God's people and even God's servants understand it so little, is one great cause of the impotence of the Church.

In this matter the Church indeed needs a second reformation. In the great Reformation three centuries ago, the power of Christ's atoning death and righteousness were brought to light, to the great comfort and joy of anxious souls. But we need a second reformation to lift on high the banner of Christ's example as our law, to restore the truth of the power of Christ's resurrection as it makes us partakers of the life and the likeness of our Lord. ...

Like Christ: In Doing God's Will

January 31st

"For I came down from Heaven, not to do my own will, but the will of Him who sent Me"

—JOHN 6: 38; 5: 30

In the will of God we have the highest expression of His Divine perfection, and at the same time the highest energy of His Divine power. Creation owes its being and its beauty to it; it is the manifestation of God's will. In all nature the will of God is done. In Heaven the angels find their highest blessedness in doing God's will. For this man was created with a free will, in order that we might have the power to choose, and of our own accord do God's will. And, lo! deceived by the devil, man committed the great sin of rather doing his own than God's will. Yes, rather his own than God's will! in this is the root and the wretchedness of sin.

Jesus Christ became man to bring us back to the blessedness of *doing God's will.* The great object of redemption was to make us and our will free from the power of sin, and to lead us again to live and do the will of God. In His life on earth He showed us what it is to live only for the will of God; in His death and resurrection He won for us the power to live and do the will of God as He had done.

"*Lo, I come to do Your will, O God.*" These words, uttered through the Holy Spirit by the mouth of one of His prophets long ages before Christ's birth, are the key to His life on earth. ... Let us not think that this cost Him nothing. He says repeatedly, "*Not my will, but the will of the Father,*" to let us understand that there was in very deed a denial of His own will. In Gethsemane the sacrifice of His own will reached its height, but what took place there was only the perfect expression of what had rendered His whole life acceptable to the Father. ...

And the believer who knows the power of Jesus' death and resurrection, has the power to consecrate himself entirely to God's will. He knows that the call to follow Christ means nothing less than to take and speak the words of the Master as his own solemn vow, *"I seek not my own will, but the will of the Father."*

To attain this we must begin by taking the same stand that our Lord did. Take God's will as *one great whole*, as the only thing for which you live on earth. Look at the Sun and moon, the grass and flowers, what glory each of them has, only because it is just doing God's will. Let your heart be filled with the thought of the glory of God's will concerning His children, and concerning you, and say that it is your one purpose that that will should be done in you. Yield yourself to the Father frequently and distinctly, with the declaration that with you, as with Jesus, it is a settled thing that His beautiful and blessed will must and shall be done. Say it frequently in your quiet meditations, with a joyful and trusting heart: Praise God! I may live only to do the will of God.

Let no fear keep us back from this. Think not that this will be too hard for us to do; God's will only seems hard as long as we look at it from a distance, and are unwilling to submit to it. Just look again how beautiful the will of God makes everything in nature. Ask yourself, now that He loves and blesses you as a child, if it is right to distrust Him. The will of God is the will of His love, how can you fear to surrender yourself to it?

Nor let the fear that you will not be able to obey that will, keep you back. The Son of God came on earth to show what the life of man must and may become. His resurrection life gives us power to live as He lived. Jesus Christ enables us, through His Spirit, to walk not after the flesh, but according to the will of God.

"*I come to do Your will, O God*": before ever the Lord Jesus was come down to earth, a believer in the Old Testament was able, through the Spirit, to speak that word of himself as well as for Christ. Christ took it up and filled it with new life-power. And now He expects of His redeemed ones that, since He has been on earth, they will even more heartily and entirely make it their choice. Let us do so. We must not first try and see whether, in single instances, we succeed in doing God's will, in the hope of afterwards attaining to the entire consecration that can say: "*I come to do Your will.*" No, this is not the right way. Let us first recognize God's will *as a whole*, and the claims it has upon us, as well as its blessedness and glory.

Let us surrender ourselves to it as to God Himself, and consider it as one of the first articles of our creed: I am in the world, like Christ, only to do the Father's will. This surrender will teach us with joy to accept every command and every providence as part of the will we have already yielded ourselves to. …There is nothing that will bring us closer to God and union to Christians than loving and keeping and doing the will of God.

Child of God! One of the first marks of conformity to Christ is obedience, simple and implicit obedience to all the will of God. Let it be the most marked thing in your life. Begin by a willing and wholehearted keeping of every one of the commands of God's holy Word. Go on to a very tender yielding to everything that conscience tells you to be right, even when the Word does not directly command it. So shall you rise higher: a hearty obedience to the commandments, as far as you know them, and a ready obedience to conscience wherever it speaks, are the preparation for that Divine teaching of the Spirit which will lead you deeper into the meaning and application of the Word, and into a more direct and spiritual insight into God's will with regard to yourself personally. It is to those *who obey* Him God gives the Holy Spirit, through whom the blessed will of God becomes the light that shines ever more brightly on our path.

And if ever it appears too hard to live only for God's will, let us remember wherein Christ found His strength: it was because it was *the Father's* will that the Son rejoiced to do it. "This commandment have I received *of my Father*." This made even the laying down of His life possible. Our union to Jesus, and our calling to live like Him, ever point us to *His Sonship* as the secret of His life and strength. Let it be our chief desire to say each day: I am the Father's beloved child, and to think of each commandment as *the Father's* will; a Christ-like sense of sonship will lead to a Christ-like obedience.

Like Christ: In His Compassion

February 1st

"Should not you also have had compassion on your fellow servant, even as I have had compassion on you?"
—MATTHEW 18: 32

On three different occasions Matthew tells us that our Lord was moved with compassion on the multitude. His whole life was a manifestation of the compassion with which He had looked on the sinner from everlasting, and of the tenderness with which He was moved at the sight of misery and sorrow. He was in this the true reflection of our compassionate God—of the father who, moved with compassion towards his prodigal son, fell on his neck and kissed him.

In this compassion of the Lord Jesus we can see how He did not look upon the will of God He came to do as a duty or an obligation, but had that Divine will dwelling within Him as His own, inspiring and ruling all His sentiments and motives.

After He had said, '*I came from Heaven not to do my own will, but the will of Him that sent me,*" He at once added, "*And this is the will of the Father, that of all He has given me, I should lose nothing, but should raise it up again at the last day.*" "*And this is the will of Him that sent me, that everyone who believes on the Son may have everlasting life.*"

For the Lord Jesus the will of God consisted not in certain things which were forbidden or commanded. No, He had entered into that which truly forms the very heart of God's will, and that is, that to lost sinners He should give eternal life. Because God Himself is love, His will is that love should have full scope in the salvation of sinners. The Lord Jesus came down to earth in order to manifest and accomplish this will of God. He did not do this as a servant obeying the will of a stranger. In His personal life and all His dispositions He proved that the loving will of His Father to save sinners was His own.

Beloved followers of Christ, who have offered yourselves to imitate Him, let the will of the Father be to you what it was to your Lord. The will of the Father in the mission of

His Son was the manifestation and the triumph of Divine compassion in the salvation of lost sinners. Jesus could not possibly accomplish this will in any other way than by having and showing this compassion. *God's will is for us what it was for Jesus: the salvation of the perishing.* It is impossible for us to fulfill that will otherwise than by having, and bearing about, and showing in our lives, the compassion of our God.

The seeking of God's will must not be only denying ourselves certain things which God forbids, and doing certain works which God commands, but must consist specially in this: that we surrender ourselves to have the same mind and disposition towards sinners as God has, and that we find our pleasure and joy alone in living for this. By the most personal devotion to each poor perishing sinner around us, and by our helping them in compassionate love, we can show that the will of God is become our will. With the compassionate God as our Father, with Christ who was so often moved with compassion as our life, nothing can be more just than the command that the life of every Christian should be one of compassionate love.

Compassion is the spirit of love which is awakened by the sight of need or wretchedness. What abundant occasion is there every day for the practice of this heavenly virtue, and what a need of it in a world so full of misery and sin! Every Christian ought therefore by prayer and practice to cultivate a compassionate heart, as one of the most precious marks of likeness to the blessed Master. …

Like Christ *in His compassion:* let this now be our motto. After uttering the parable of the compassionate Samaritan, who, "*moved with compassion,*" helped the wounded stranger, the Lord said, "*Go and do likewise.*" He is Himself the compassionate Samaritan, who speaks to every one of us whom He has saved, "*Go and do likewise.*" Even as I have done to you, do you likewise. We, who owe everything to His compassion, who profess ourselves His followers, who walk in His footsteps and bear His image, oh let us exhibit His compassion to the world. We can do it. He lives in us; His Spirit works in us. Let us with much prayer and firm faith look to *His example* as the sure promise of what we can be. …

Like Christ: In His Love

February 2nd

"A new commandment I give unto you: Love one another; even as I have loved you, you also love one another."

—JOHN 13: 34

Even *as I have loved you*: that word gives us the measure of the love wherewith we must love each other. True love knows no measure: it gives itself entirely. … This is the greatest glory of Divine Love that we have, in the Father and Son, two persons, who in love remain One Being, each losing Himself in the other. This is the glory of the love of Jesus, who is the image of God, that He loves us even as the Father loves Him. And this is the glory of brotherly love—that it will know of no other law than to love even as God and Christ.

We who would be like Christ must unhesitatingly accept this as our rule of life. We know how difficult, how impossible it often is thus to love others in whom there is so much that is offensive or unamiable. Before going out to meet them in circumstances where his love may be tried, we go in secret to the Lord, and with our eye fixed on our own sin and unworthiness ask: How much do you owe your Lord?

We go to the cross and seek there to fathom the love wherewith the Lord has loved us. We let the light of the immeasurable love of Him who is in Heaven, our Head and our Brother, shine in upon our soul, until we learn to feel Divine Love has but one law: love seeks not its own, love gives itself wholly.

And we lay ourselves upon the altar before our Lord: even as You have loved me, so will I love the brethren. In virtue of my union with Jesus, and in Jesus with them, there can be no question of anything less: I love them as Christ did. Oh that Christians would close their ears to all the reasoning of their own hearts, and fix their eyes only on the law which He who loves them has promulgated in His own example; they would realize that there is nothing for them to do but this—to accept His commands and to obey them.

Our love may recognize no other measure than His, because His love is the strength of ours. The love of Christ is no mere idea or sentiment: it is a real Divine life power. As long as the Christian does not understand this, it cannot exert its full power in us. But when our faith rises to realize that Christ's love is nothing less than the imparting of Himself and His love to the beloved, and we become rooted in this love as the source whence his life derives its sustenance, then we see that his Lord simply asks that we should allow His love to flow through us. We must live in a Christ-given strength: the love of Christ constrains us, and enables us to love as He did.

From this love of Christ, the Christian also learns what *the work* of his love to the brethren must be. We have already had occasion to speak of many manifestations of love: its loving service, its Self-denial, its meekness. Love is the root of all these. It teaches the disciple to look upon ourselves as really called upon to be, in our little circle, just like Jesus—the one who lives solely to love and help others. Paul prays for the Philippians: *"That your love may abound more and more in knowledge, and in all judgment"* (1: 9).

Love does not comprehend at once what the work is that it can do. We who pray that our love may abound in knowledge, and really take Christ's example as our rule of life, will be taught what a great and glorious work there is for us to do. The Church of God, and every child of God, as well as the world, has an unspeakable need of love, of the manifestation of Christ's love. The Christian who really takes the Lords word, *"Love one another, even as I have loved you,"* as a command that must be obeyed, carries about a power for blessing and life for all with whom we come in contact. Love is the explanation of the whole wonderful life of Christ, and of the wonder of His death: Divine Love in God's children will still work its mighty wonders.

"*Behold what manner of love*!" "*Behold how He loved*!" These words are the superscription over the love of the Father and of the Son. They must yet become the keywords to the life of every Christian. They will be so where in living faith and true consecration the command of Christ to love, even as He loved, is accepted as the law of life. As early as the call of Abraham this principle was deposited as a living seed in God's kingdom, that what God is for us, we must be for others. "I will bless you," "*and you shall be a blessing.*" If "*I have loved you*" is the highest manifestation of what God is for us, then "*Even so love one another*" must be the first and highest expression of what the child of God must be. In preaching, as in the life, of the Church, it must be understood: The love which loves like Christ is the sign of true discipleship.

Beloved Christians! Christ Jesus longs for you in order to make you, amid those who surround you, a very fountain of love. The love of Heaven would fain take possession of you, in order that, in and through you, it may work its blessed work on earth. Yield to its rule. Offer yourself unreservedly to its indwelling. Honor it by the confident assurance that it can teach you to love as Jesus loved. As conformity to the Lord Jesus must be the chief mark of your Christian walk, so love must be the chief mark of that conformity.

Be not disheartened if you do not attain it at once. Only keep fast hold of the command, "*Love, even as I have loved you.*" It takes time to grow into it. Take time in secret to gaze on that image of love. Take time in prayer and meditation, to fan the desire for it into a burning flame. Take time to survey all around you, whoever they be, and whatever may happen, with this one thought, "I must love them." Take time to become conscious of your union with your Lord, that every fear as to the possibility of thus loving, may be met with the word: 'Have not I commanded you: Love as I have loved"? Christian, take time in loving communion with Jesus your loving example, and you will joyfully fulfil this command, too, to love even as He did.

Like Christ: In His Praying

February 3rd

"In the morning, rising up a great while before day, He departed into a desert place, and there prayed"
—MARK 1: 35

In His life of secret prayer, too, my Savior is my example. He could not maintain the heavenly life in His soul without continually separating Himself from the world, and communing with His Father. With the heavenly life in me it is not otherwise: it has the same need of entire separation from the world, the need not only of single moments, but of time enough for intercourse with the Fountain of Life, the Father in Heaven.

It was at the commencement of His public ministry that the event happened which so attracted the attention of His disciples that they wrote it down. After a day full of wonders and of work at Capernaum (Mark 1: 21–35), the press in the evening became still greater. The whole town is before the door; sick are healed, and devils are cast out. It is late before they get to sleep: in the throng there is little time for quiet or for secret prayer. And, lo, as they rise early in the morning, they find Him gone. In the silence of the night He has gone out to seek a place of solitude in the wilderness. When they find Him there,

He is still praying.

And why did my Savior need these hours of prayer? Did He not know the blessedness of silently lifting up His soul to God in the midst of the most pressing business? Did not the Father dwell in Him? And did He not in the depth of His heart enjoy unbroken communion with Him? Yes, that hidden life was indeed His portion. But that life, as subject to the law of humanity, had need of continual refreshing and renewing from the fountain. It was a life of dependence; just because it was strong and true, it could not bear the loss of direct and constant intercourse with the Father, with whom and in whom it had its being and its blessedness.

What a lesson for every Christian! Much intercourse with others is dissipating and dangerous to our spiritual life: it brings us under the influence of the visible and temporal. Nothing can atone for the loss of secret and direct intercourse with God. Even work in the service of God and of love is exhausting: we cannot bless others without power going out from us; this must be renewed from above. The law of the manna, that what is heavenly cannot remain good long upon earth, but must day by day be renewed afresh from Heaven, still holds good.

Jesus Christ teaches it us: we need every day time to have communion with our Father in secret. Our life is like His is a life hid in Heaven, in God; it needs time day by day to be fed from Heaven. It is *from Heaven* alone that the power to lead a heavenly life on earth can come. … This was to Him the greatest need and greatest blessing of prayer, to enter into the full enjoyment of the Father's love. …

He speaks: *"I have glorified You; glorify Your Son, that Your Son also may glorify You."* That will assuredly have been the spirit of every prayer; the entire surrender of Himself only to live for the Father's will and glory. All that He asked had but one object, "That God might be glorified." In this too He is my example. I must seek to have the spirit of each prayer I offer: Father! Bless Your child, and glorify Your grace in me, only that Your child may glorify You. Everything in the universe must show forth God's glory. The Christian who is inspired with this thought, and avails himself of prayer to express it, until we are thoroughly imbued with it, will have power in prayer. Even of His work in Heaven our Lord says: *"Whatsoever you shall ask in my name, that will I do, that the Father may be glorified in the Son."*

O my soul, learn from your Savior, ere ever you pour out your desires in prayer, first to yield yourself as a whole burnt-offering, with the one object that God may be glorified in you. Then you have sure ground on which to pray. You will feel the strong desire, as well as the full liberty, to ask the Father that in each part of Christ's example, in each feature of Christ's image, you may be made like Him, that so God may be glorified. You will understand how, only in continually renewed prayer, the soul can surrender itself to wait that God may from Heaven work in it what will be to His glory.

Because Jesus surrendered Himself so entirely to the glory of His Father, He was worthy to be our Mediator, and could in His high-priestly prayer ask such great blessings for His people. Learn like Jesus only to seek God's glory in prayer, and you shall become a true intercessor, who can not only approach the throne of grace with our own needs, but can also pray for others—*the effectual fervent prayer of a righteous man that avails much.* …

And he who in every prayer makes God's glory the chief object will also, if God calls him to it, have strength for the prayer of Gethsemane. Every prayer of Christ was intercession, because He had given Himself for us; all He asked and received was in our interest: every prayer He prayed was in the spirit of Self-sacrifice. Give yourself too wholly to God for man, and as with Jesus so with us, the entire sacrifice of ourselves to God in every prayer of daily life is the only preparation for those single hours of soul-struggle in which we may be called to some special act of the surrender of the will that costs us tears and anguish. …

O my brother, my sister! If you and I would be like Jesus, we must especially contemplate Jesus praying alone in the wilderness. There is the secret of His wonderful life. What He did and spoke to us, was first spoken and lived through with the Father. In communion with Him, the anointing with the Holy Spirit was each day renewed. We who would be like Him in His walk and conversation, must simply begin here—that we follow Jesus into solitude.

Like Christ: In His Use of Scripture

February 4th

"All must be fulfilled that was written in the law of Moses, and the Prophets, and in the Psalms, about me."
—LUKE 24: 44

What the Lord Jesus accomplished here on earth as man He owed greatly to His use of the Scriptures. He found in them the way marked in which He had to walk, the food and the strength on which He could work, the weapon by which He could overcome every enemy.

It is scarcely necessary to adduce proofs of this. In the temptation in the wilderness it was by His "*It is written*" that He conquered Satan. In His conflicts with the Pharisees, He continually appealed to the Word "*What says the Scripture*?" "*Have you not read*?" "*Is it not written*?" In His intercourse with His disciples it was always from the Scriptures that He proved the certainty and necessity of His sufferings and resurrection: "*How otherwise can the Scriptures be fulfilled*?" And in His intercourse with His Father in His last sufferings, it is in the words of Scripture that He pours out the complaint of being forsaken, and then again commends His spirit into the Father's hands.

All this has a very deep meaning. He was Himself the living Word. He had the Spirit without measure. If ever any one, He could have done without the written Word. And yet we see that it is everything to Him. More than anyone else, He thus shows us that the life of God in human flesh and the word of God in human speech are inseparably connected. Jesus would not have been what He was, could not have done what He did, had He not yielded Himself step by step to be led and sustained by the Word of God. …

True life is found only in God. But that life cannot be imparted to us unless set before us in some shape in which we know and apprehend it. It is in the Word of God that the

Invisible Divine life takes shape, and brings itself within our reach, and becomes communicable. The life, the thoughts, the sentiments, the power of God are embodied in His words. And it is only through His Word that the life of God can really enter into us. His Word is the seed of the Heavenly life.

As the bread of life we eat it, we feed upon it. In eating our daily bread, the body takes in the nourishment which visible nature, the sun and the earth, prepared for us in the seed-corn. We assimilate it, and it becomes our very own, part of ourselves, it is our life. In feeding upon the Word of God, the powers of the Heavenly life enter into us, and become our very own; we assimilate them, they become a part of ourselves, the life of our life.

In feeding upon the Word of God, the powers of the Heavenly life enter into us, and become our very own; we assimilate them, they become a part of ourselves, the life of our life. ... The words of God are sown in our heart. They have a Divine power of reproduction and multiplication. The very life that is in them, the Divine thought, or disposition, or powers that each of them contains, takes root in the believing heart and grows up; and the very thing of which the word was the expression, is produced within us. ...

When the Lord Jesus was made man, He became entirely dependent upon the Word of God, He submitted Himself wholly to it. His mother taught it Him. The teachers of Nazareth instructed Him in it. In meditation and prayer, in the exercise of obedience and faith, He was led, during His silent years of preparation, to understand and appropriate it. The Word of the Father was to the Son the life of His soul. What He said in the wilderness was spoken from His inmost personal experience: *"Man shall not live by bread alone, but by every word that proceeds out of the mouth of God."* He felt He could not live but as the Word brought Him the life of the Father. His whole life was a life of faith, a depending on the Word of the Father.

The Word was to Him not instead of the Father, but the vehicle for the living fellowship with the living God. And He had His whole mind and heart so filled with it that the Holy Spirit could at each moment find within Him, all ready for use, the right word to suggest just as He needed it.

Child of God! Would you become a man of God, strong in faith, full of blessing, rich in fruit to the glory of God? Then, be full of the Word of God. Like Christ, make the Word your bread; let it dwell richly in you; have your heart full of it; feed on it; believe it; obey it. It is only by believing and obeying that the Word can enter into our inward parts, into our very being.

Take it day by day as the Word that proceeds—not *has* proceeded, but proceeds, is proceeding—out of the mouth of God, as the Word of the living God, who in it holds living fellowship with His children, and speaks to them in living power. Take your thoughts of God's will, and God's work, and God's purpose with you, and the world, not from the Church, not from Christians around you, but from the Word taught you by the Father, and like Christ, you will be able to fulfill all that is written in the Scripture concerning you. ... It is especially in *Him and His* example that we must find our own image in the Scriptures. *"To be changed into the same image, from glory to glory, by the Spirit of the Lord,"* we must in the Scripture-glass gaze on that image as our own. In order to accomplish His work in us, the Spirit teaches us to take Christ as in very deed our example, and to gaze on every feature as the promise of what we can be.

Blessed are the Christians who have truly done this; who have not only found Jesus in the Scriptures, but also in His image the promise and example of what we are to become. Blessed are the Christians who yield themselves to be taught by the Holy Spirit not to indulge in human thoughts as to the Scriptures and what it says of believers, but in simplicity to accept what it reveals of God's thoughts about His children.

Child of God! It was "according to the Scriptures" that Jesus Christ lived and died; it was "according to the Scriptures" that He was raised again: all that the Scriptures said He must do or suffer He was able to accomplish, because He knew and obeyed them. All that the Scriptures had promised that the Father should do for Him, the Father did. Oh, give yourself up with an undivided heart to learn in the Scriptures what God says and seeks of you. Let the Scriptures in which Jesus found every day the food of His life, be your daily food and meditation. Go to God's Word each day with the joyful and confident expectation, that through the blessed Spirit who dwells in us, the Word will indeed accomplish its Divine purpose in you. Every word of God is full of a Divine life and power. Be assured that when you seek to use the Scriptures as Christ used them, they will do for you what they did for Him.

God has marked out the plan of your life in His Word; each day you will find some portion of it there. Nothing makes us more strong and courageous than the assurance that we are just living out the will of God. God Himself, who had your image portrayed in the Scriptures, will see to it that the Scriptures are fulfilled in you, if like His Son you will but surrender yourself to this as the highest object of your life.

Like Christ: In Beholding Him

February 5th

"But we all, with open face beholding as in a glass the glory of the Lord, are changed into the same image; from glory to glory, by the Spirit of the Lord"

—2 CORINTHIANS 3: 18

Moses had been forty days on the mount in communion with God. When he came down, his face shone with Divine glory. He did not know it himself, but Aaron and the people saw it (Exodus 34: 30). It was so evidently God's glory that Aaron and the people feared to approach him. In this we have an image of what takes place in the New Testament. The privilege Moses there alone enjoyed is now the portion of every believer. When we behold the glory of God in Christ, in the glass of the Holy Scriptures, His glory shines upon us, and into us, and fills us, until it shines out from us again. By gazing on His glory the believer is changed through the Spirit into the same image. *Beholding Jesus makes us like Him.*

It is a law of nature that the eye exercises a mighty influence on mind and character. The education of a child is carried on greatly through the eye; he is molded very much by the manners and habits of those he sees continually. To form and mold our character the heavenly Father shows us His Divine glory in the face of Jesus. He does it in the expectation that it will give us great joy to gaze upon it, and because He knows that, gazing on it, we shall be conformed to the same image. Let everyone who desires to be like Jesus note how we can attain to it.

Look continually to the Divine glory as seen in Christ. What is the special characteristic of that glory? It is the manifestation of Divine perfection in human form. The chief marks of the image of the Divine glory in Christ are these two: His humiliation and His love.

There is the glory of His humiliation. When you see how the eternal Son emptied Himself and became man, and how as man He humbled Himself as a servant and was obedient even unto the death of the cross, you have seen the highest glory of God. The glory of God's omnipotence as Creator, and the glory of God's holiness as King, is not so wonderful as this: the glory of grace which humbled itself as a servant to serve God and man. We must learn to look upon this humiliation as really glory.

To be humbled like Christ must be to us the only thing worthy the name of glory on earth. It must become in our eyes the most beautiful, the most wonderful, the most desirable thing that can be imagined; a very joy to look upon or to think of. The effect of thus gazing upon it and admiring it will be that we will not be able to conceive of any glory greater than to be and act like Jesus, and will long to humble ourself even as He did. Gazing on Jesus, admiring, and adoring Him, will work in us the same mind that there was in Him, and so we shall be changed into His image.

Inseparable from this is the glory of His love. The humiliation leads you back to the love as its origin and power. It is from love that the humiliation has its beauty. Love is the highest glory of God. But this love was a hidden mystery, until it was manifest in Christ Jesus. It is only in His humanity, in His gentle, compassionate, and loving intercourse with men—with foolish, sinful, hostile men—that the glory of Divine love was first really seen. The soul that gets a glimpse of this glory, and that understands that to love like Christ is alone worthy the name of glory, will long to become like Christ in this. Beholding this glory of the love of God in Christ, we are changed to the same image.

You would be like Christ? Here is the path: Gaze on the glory of God in Him; that is to say: do not look only to the words and the thoughts and the graces in which His glory is seen, but look to Himself, the living, loving, Christ. Behold Him, look into His very eye; look into His face, as a loving friend, as the living God.

Look to Him in adoration. Bow before Him as God, His glory has an almighty living power to impart itself to us, to pass over into us and to fill us. Look to Him in faith. Exercise the blessed trust that He is yours, that He has given Himself to you, and that you have a claim to all that is in Him. It is His purpose to work out His image in you. Behold Him with the joyful and certain expectation: "The glory that I behold in Him is destined for me. He will give it to me. As I gaze and wonder and trust, I will become like Christ.

Look to Him with strong desire. Do not yield to the slothfulness of the flesh that is satisfied without the full blessing of conformity to the Lord. Pray God to free you from all carnal resting content with present attainments, and to fill you with the deep unquenchable longing for His glory. Pray most fervently the prayer of Moses, "*show me Your glory.*" Let nothing discourage you, not even the apparently slow progress you make, but press onwards with ever growing desire after the blessed prospect that God's Word holds out to you: "*We are changed into the same image, from glory to glory.*"

And as you behold Him, above all, let the look of love not be wanting. Tell Him continually how He has won your heart, how you do love Him, how entirely you belong to Him. Tell Him that to please Him, the beloved One, is your highest, your only joy. Let the bond of love between you and Him be drawn continually closer. Love unites and makes like.

Like Christ! we can be it, we shall be it, each in our measure. The Holy Spirit is the pledge that it shall be. God's Holy Word has said, "*We are changed into the same image, from glory to glory, even as by the Spirit of the Lord.*" This is the Spirit that was in Jesus, and through Whom the Divine glory lived and shone on Him. This Spirit is called "*The Spirit of Glory.*" This Spirit is in us as in the Lord Jesus, and it is His work, in our silent adoring, contemplation, to bring over into us and work within us, what we see in our Lord Jesus. Through this Spirit we have already Christ's life in us, with all the gifts of His grace. But that life must be stirred up and developed: it must grow up, pass into our whole being, take possession of our entire nature, penetrate and pervade it all.

We can count on the Spirit to work this in us, if we but yield ourselves to Him and obey Him. As we gaze on Jesus in the Word, He opens our eyes to see the glory of all that Jesus does and is. He makes us willing to be like Him. He strengthens our faith, that what we behold in Jesus can be in us, because Jesus Himself is ours. He works in us unceasingly the life of abiding in Christ, a wholehearted union and communion with Him. He does according to the promise: "*The Spirit shall glorify me: for He shall take of mine and shall show it unto you.*"

We are changed into the image on which we gaze, from glory to glory, as by the Spirit of the Lord. Let us only understand, that the fullness of the Spirit is given to us, and that he who believingly surrenders himself to be filled with Him, will experience how gloriously He accomplishes His work of stamping on our souls and lives the image and likeness of Christ.

Brother! Sister! beholding Jesus and His glory, you can confidently expect to become like Him: only trust yourself in quietness and restfulness of soul to the leading of the Spirit. "*The Spirit of glory rests upon you.*" Gaze on and adore the glory of God in Christ; you will be changed with Divine power from glory to glory; in the power of the Holy Spirit the mighty transformation will be wrought by which your desires will be fulfilled, and like Christ will be the blessed God-given experience of your life.

Like Christ: In His Humility

February 6th

"In lowliness of mind each counting other better than himself. Have this mind in you, which was also in Christ Jesus, who, being in the form of God, emptied Himself, taking the form of a servant, being made in the likeness of men … He humbled Himself, becoming obedient unto death, even the death of the cross."

—PHILIPPIANS 2: 3–8

In this wonderful passage we have a summary of all the most precious truths that cluster round the person of the blessed Son of God. There is first, His adorable Divinity: *"in the form of God," "equal with God."* Then comes the mystery of His incarnation, in that word of deep and inexhaustible meaning: *"He emptied Himself."* The atonement follows, with the humiliation, and obedience, and suffering, and death, whence it derives its worth: *"He humbled Himself, becoming obedient unto death, even the death of the cross."* And all is crowned by his glorious exaltation: *"God has highly exalted Him."* Christ as God, Christ becoming man, Christ as man in humiliation working out our redemption, and Christ in glory as Lord of all: such are the treasures of wisdom this passage contains.

Among the Philippians there was still pride and want of love: it is with the distinct view of setting Christ's example before them, and teaching them to humble themselves as He did, that this portion of inspiration was given: "*In lowliness of mind each counting other better than himself Have this mind in you which was also in Christ Jesus.*" Those of us who do not study this portion of God's Word with the wish to become lowly as Christ was, have never used it for the one great purpose for which God gave it. Christ descending from the throne of God, and seeking His way back there as man through the humiliation of the cross, reveals the only way by which we ever can reach that throne. The faith which, with His atonement, accepts His example too, is alone true faith.

Each soul that would truly belong to Him must in union with Him have His Spirit, His disposition, and His image. *"Have this mind in you which was also in Christ Jesus, who being in the form of God emptied Self, and as a man humbled himself."* We must be like Christ in His Self-emptying and Self-humiliation. The first great act of Self-abnegation in which as God He emptied Himself of His Divine glory and power and laid it aside, was followed up by the no less wondrous humbling of Himself as man, to the death of the cross. And in this amazing twofold humiliation, the astonishment of the universe and the delight of the Father, Holy Scripture with the utmost simplicity tells us we must, as a matter of course, be like Christ.

And does Paul, and do the Scriptures, and does God really expect this of us? Why not? or rather, how can they expect anything else? They know indeed the fearful power of pride and the old Adam in our nature. But they know also that Christ has redeemed us not only from the curse but from the power of sin, and that He gives us His resurrection life and power to enable us to live as He did on earth. They say that He is not only our Surety, but our Example also; so that we not only live through Him, but like Him. And further, not only our Example but also our Head, who lives in us, and continues in us the life He once led on earth. With such a Christ, and such a plan of redemption, can it be otherwise? The follower of Christ must have the same mind as was in Christ; we must especially be like Him in His humility.

The nearer the soul comes to God, the more His majestic presence makes it feel its littleness. It is this alone that makes it possible for each to count others better than ourself. Jesus Christ, the Holy One of God, is our example of humility: it was, knowing that the Father had given all things into His hands, and that He was come from God and went to God that He washed the disciples' feet. It is the Divine presence, the consciousness of the Divine life and the Divine love in us that will make us humble.

It appears to many Christians an impossibility to say: I will not think of Self, I will esteem others better than myself. They ask grace to overcome the worst ebullitions of pride and vain glory, but an entire Self-renunciation, such as Christ's, is too difficult and too high for them. If we only understood the deep truth and blessedness of the word, *"He who humbles himself still be exalted," "He who loses his life shall find it,"* we would not be satisfied with anything less than entire conformity to our Lord in this. And we would find that there is a way to overcome Self and Self-exaltation: to see it nailed to Christ's cross, and there keep it crucified continually through the Spirit (Galatians 5: 24; Romans 8: 13). We only can grow to such humility, if we heartily yield ourselves to live in the fellowship of Christ's death.

To attain this, two things are necessary. The first is a fixed purpose and surrender to be nothing and seek nothing for oneself; but to live only for God and our neighbor. The other is the faith that appropriates the power of Christ's death in this also, as our death to sin and our deliverance from its power. This fellowship of Christ's death brings an end to the life, where sin is too strong for us; it is the commencement of a life in us where Christ is too strong for sin. It is only under the teaching and powerful working of the Holy Spirit that we can realize, accept, and keep hold of this truth. But, thank God, we have the Holy Spirit. Oh that we may trust ourselves fully to His guidance. He will guide us; it is His work; He will glorify Christ in us. He will teach us to understand that we are dead to sin and the old Self, that Christ's life and humility are ours.

Thus Christ's humility is appropriated in faith; this may take place at once. But the appropriation in experience is gradual. Our thoughts and feelings, our very manners and conversation, have been so long under the dominion of the old Self, that it takes time to imbue and permeate and transfigure them with the heavenly light of Christ's humility. At first the conscience is not perfectly enlightened, the spiritual taste and the power of discernment have not yet been exercised. But with each believing renewal of the consecration in the depth of the soul: "I have surrendered myself to be humble like Jesus," power will go out from Him, to fill the whole being, until in face, and voice, and action the sanctification of the Spirit will be observable, and the Christian will truly be clothed with humility.

The blessedness of a Christ-like humility is unspeakable. It is of great worth in the sight of God: "*He gives grace to the humble.*" In the spiritual life it is the source of rest and joy. To the humble all God does is right and good. Humility is always ready to praise God for the least of His mercies. Humility does not find it difficult to trust. It submits unconditionally to all that God says. The two whom Jesus praises for their great faith are just those who thought least of themselves. The centurion had said, "*I am not worthy that You should come under my roof*"; the Syrophoenician woman was content to be numbered with the dogs. In intercourse with men it is the secret of blessing and love. The humble believer does not take offence, and is very careful not to give it. We are ever ready to serve our neighbor, because we have learned from Jesus the Divine beauty of being a servant: "*He finds favor with God and man.*" Oh what a glorious calling for the followers of Christ! To be sent into the world by God to prove that there is nothing more Divine than Self-humiliation.

In the Likeness of His Death

February 7th

"If we have been planted together in the likeness of His death, we shall be also in the likeness of resurrection."
—ROMANS 6: 5

Let everyone who truly longs to be like Christ in His life, seek to understand aright what the likeness of His death means. Christ had a double work to accomplish in His death. … *Christ died for our sin:* He took sin upon Himself, bore its punishment; so He made atonement, and brought in a righteousness in which we could stand before God. When Scripture speaks of the second part of this work, it uses the expression: *He died to sin.* Dying *for sin* has reference to the judicial relation between Him and sin: God laid our sin upon Him: through His death atonement is made for in before God. *Dying to sin* has reference to a personal relation: through His death the connection in which He stood to sin was entirely dissolved. During His life had great power to cause Him conflict and suffering: His death made an end of this. Sin had now no more power to tempt or to hurt Him. He was beyond its reach. …

Most believers are in their conversion so occupied with Christ's death *for* sin as their justification that they do not seek to know what it means, that in Him they are dead *to* sin. When they first learn to feel their need of Him as their sanctification, then the desire is awakened to understand this likeness of His death. They find the secret of holiness in it: that as Christ, so they also have died to sin.

The Christian who does not understand this always imagines that sin is too strong that sin has still power over us, and that we must sometimes obey it. But we think this because we do not know that we, like Christ, are dead to sin. If we but believed and understood what this means, our language would be: "Christ has died to sin. … In His life and death sin had power over Him: it was sin that caused Him the sufferings of the cross, and the humiliation of the grave. But He is dead to sin: it has lost all claim over Him, He is entirely and forever freed from its power. Even so am I as a believer: the new life that is in me, is the life of Christ from the dead, a life that has been begotten through death—a life that is entirely dead to sin.

The believer as a new creature in Christ Jesus can glory and say: "like Christ I am dead to sin. Sin has no right or power over me whatever. I am freed from it; therefore, I need not sin." And if the believer still sins, it is because we do not use our privilege to live as one who is dead to sin. Through ignorance or unwatchfulness or unbelief, we forget the meaning and the power of this likeness of Christ's death.... But if we hold fast what our participation with Christ's death signifies: we have the power to overcome sin. …

Sin is not dead; sin lives and works still in the flesh. But we are dead to sin, and alive to God; and so sin cannot for a single moment, without our consent, have dominion over us. If we sin, it is because we allow it to reign, and submit our Self to obey it.

Beloved Christian, who seeks to be like Christ, take the likeness of His death as one of the most glorious parts of the life you covet. Appropriate it first of all in faith. Reckon that you are indeed dead to sin. Let it be a settled thing; God says it to every one of His children, even the weakest; say it before Him too: "Like Christ I am dead to sin."

Fear not to say it; it is the truth. Ask the Holy Spirit earnestly to enlighten you with regard to this part of your union with Christ, so that it may not only be a doctrine, but power and truth. Endeavor to understand more deeply what it says to live as dead to sin, as one who, in dying, has been freed from its dominion, and who can now reign in life through Jesus Christ over it. …

The likeness of Christ's death in Romans 6 precedes the likeness of His resurrection; no one can be made alive in Him who has not given himself up to die with Him. The conformity to Christ's death in Philippians 3 is spoken of as coming after the knowing Him in the power of His resurrection: the growth of the resurrection life within us leads to a deeper experience of the death. The two continually act and react—something that is gradually and increasingly appropriated, as Christ's death manifests its full power in all the faculties and powers of your life.

And in order to have the full benefit of this likeness of Christ's death, notice particularly two things. The one is the obligation under which it brings you, *"How shall we who are dead to sin live any longer therein?"* (Romans 6: 2). Endeavor to enter more deeply into the meaning of this death of Christ into which you have been baptized. His death meant: Rather die than sin: willing to die in order to overcome sin: dead, and therefore released from the power of sin. Let this also be your position: *"that as many of us as were baptized into Jesus Christ were baptized into His death?"* (Romans 6: 3). Let the Holy Spirit baptize you continually deeper into His death, until the power of God's Word—dead to sin until the conformity to Christ's death—is discernible in all your walk and conversation.

Being Made Conformable to His Death

"That I may know Him, and the power of His resurrection, and the fellowship of His sufferings, being made conformable to His death" (Philippians 3: 10). Of all the articles of conformity, this must necessarily be the chief and most glorious one—conformity to His death. This is what made it so attractive to Paul. What were Christ's glory and blessedness must be his glory too: he knew that the most intimate likeness to Christ was conformity to His death.

… Conformity to Christ's death is the power to keep us from the power of sin. As I by the grace of the Holy Spirit am kept in my position as crucified with Christ, and live out my crucifixion life as the Crucified One lives it in me, I am kept from sinning. …

Above all, it was Christ's death on the cross that made Him the life of the world, gave Him the power to bless and to save (John 12: 24). In the conformity to Christ's death there is an end of Self: we give up ourselves to live and die for others: we are full of the faith that our surrender of ourselves to bear the sin of others is accepted of the Father. Out of this death we rise, with the power to love and to bless. …

The cross means entire Self-abnegation. The cross means the death of Self—the utter surrender of our own will and our life to be lost in the will of God, to let God's will do with us what it pleases. This was what the cross meant to Jesus. It cost Him a terrible struggle before He could give Himself up to it. When He was sore amazed and very heavy, and His soul exceeding sorrowful unto death, it was because His whole being shrank back from that cross and its curse. Three times He had to pray before He could fully say, *"yet not my will, but Yours be done."* But He *did* say it. … And this is being made conformable to Christ's death, that we so give away ourselves and our whole life, with its power of willing and acting, to God, that we learn to be and work, and do nothing but what God reveals to us as His will.

In the power of the Holy Spirit, as the Spirit of the crucified Jesus, the believer knows that the blessed resurrection life has its power and its glory from its being a crucifixion life, begotten from the cross. We yield ourselves to it; we believe that it has possession of us. Realizing that we have not the power to think or do anything that is good or holy—that the power of the flesh asserts itself and defiles everything that is in us—we yield and hold every power of our being as far as his disposal of them goes in the place of crucifixion and condemnation. And so we yield and hold every power of our being, every faculty of body, soul, and spirit, at the disposal of Jesus. The distrust and denial of Self in everything, the trust of Jesus in everything, mark our life. The very spirit of the cross breathes through our whole being.

And so far is it from being, as might appear, a matter of painful strain and weary effort thus to maintain the crucifixion position, to one who knows Christ in the power of His resurrection…and so is made conformed to His death, it is rest and strength and victory. …

And how is this blessed conformity to be attained? Paul will give us the answer. *"What things were gain to me, these I counted loss for Christ. Yes, doubtless, I count all things but loss for the excellency of the knowledge of Jesus Christ my Lord, that I may know Him, being made conformed to His death."* The pearl is of great price; but, oh, it is worth the purchase. Let us give up all, yes, all, to be admitted by Jesus to a place with Him on the cross. And if it appears hard to give up all, and then as our reward only have a whole lifetime on the cross, oh let us listen again to Paul as he tells us what made him so willingly give up all, and so intently choose the cross. It was Christ Jesus, my Lord. The cross was the place where he could get into fullest union with his Lord. To know Him, to win Him, to be found in Him, to be made like to Him—this was the burning passion that made it easy to cast away all, that gave the cross such mighty attractive power. Anything to come nearer to Jesus. All for Jesus, was his motto.

Like Christ: As One Who Serves

February 8th

"I am among you as He who serves."
—LUKE 22: 27

For the hands into which God had given all things, nothing is common or unclean. The meanness of a work never lowers the person; the person honors and elevates the work, and imparts his own worth even to the meanest service. In such deep humiliation, as we call it, our Lord finds Divine glory, and is in this the Leader of His Church in the path of true blessedness. It is as the Son that He is the servant. Just because He is the beloved of His Father, in whose hands all things are given, it is not difficult for Him to stoop so low.

In thus taking the form of a servant, Jesus proclaims the law of rank in the Church of Christ. The higher we wish to stand in grace, the more it must be our joy to be servant of all. *"Whosoever will be chief among you, let him be your servant"* (Matthew 20: 27); *"He that is greatest among you shall be your servant"* (Matthew 23:11). The higher we rise in the consciousness of being like Christ, God's beloved child, the deeper shall we stoop to serve all around us. A servant is one who is always caring for the work and interest of his master, is ever ready to let his master see that he only seeks to do what will please or profit him.

Thus Jesus lived: *"For even the Son of man came not to be ministered unto, but to minister, and to give His life a ransom for many"* (Mark 10: 45): *"I am among you as He who serves."* Thus I must live, moving about among God's children as the servant of all. If I seek to bless others, it must be in the humble, loving readiness with which I serve them, not caring for my own honor or interest, if I can but be a blessing to them. I must follow Christ's example in washing the disciples' feet.

A servant counts it no humiliation, and is not ashamed of being counted an inferior: it is his or her place and work to serve others. The reason why we so often do not bless others is that we wish to address them as if we were their superiors in grace or gifts, or at least their equals. If we first learned from our Lord to associate with others in the blessed spirit of a servant, what a blessing we should become to the world! When once this example is admitted to the place it ought to have in the Church of Christ, the power of His presence would soon make itself felt.

And what is now the work the disciple has to perform in this spirit of lowly service? The foot-washing speaks of a double work—the one, for the cleansing and refreshing of the body; the other, the cleansing and saving of the soul. During the whole of our Lord's life upon earth these two things were ever united: the sick were healed; the gospel was preached. … It is love alone will make the servant's place and work such blessedness to us, that we shall persevere in it at all costs. … Only love, a heavenly unquenchable love, gives the patience, the courage, and the wisdom for this great work the Lord has set before us in His holy example: *"Wash one another's feet."* …

O my soul, your love cannot attain to this; therefore, listen to Him who says, *"Abide in my love."* Our one desire must be that He may show us how He loves us, and that He Himself may keep us abiding in *"His love."* Live every day, as the beloved of the Lord, in the experience that His love washes and cleanses, bears and blesses you all the day long. This love of His flowing into you, will flow out again from you, and make it your greatest joy to follow His example in washing the feet of others. Do not complain much of the want of love and humility in others, but pray much that the Lord would awaken His people to their calling, truly so to follow in His footsteps that the world may see that they have taken Him for their example. …

Like Christ: In His Meekness

February 9th

"Learn of me, for I am meek and lowly of heart, and you shall find rest for your soul."
—MATTHEW 11: 29

It is on His way to the cross that we find the first of these two words written of our Lord Jesus. It is in His sufferings that the meekness of Jesus is specially manifested. … Is it not a precious thought, that there is one part of His work, as the suffering Lamb of God, in which you may bear His image and be like Him every day? You can be meek and gentle even as He was.

Meekness is the opposite of all that is hard or bitter or sharp. It has reference to the disposition which animates us towards our inferiors. "With meekness" ministers must instruct those that oppose themselves, teach and bring back the erring (Galatians 6:1; 2 Timothy 2: 25). It expresses our disposition towards superiors: we must *"receive the word with meekness"* (James 1: 21); if the wife is to be in subjection to her husband, it must be in a meek and quiet spirit, which is in the sight of God of great worth (1 Peter 3: 1–4). As one of the fruits of the Spirit, meekness ought to characterize all our daily intercourse with fellow Christians, and extend to all with whom we have to do (Ephesians 4: 2; Galatians 5: 22; Colossians 3: 12; Titus 3: 2). It is mentioned in Scripture along with humility, because that is the inward disposition concerning oneself, out of which meekness towards others springs.

There is perhaps none of the lovely virtues which adorn the image of God's Son, which is more seldom seen in those who ought to be examples. There are many servants of Jesus, in whom much love to souls, much service for the salvation of others, and much zeal for God's will, are visible, and yet who continually come short in this.

How often, when offence comes unexpectedly, whether at home or abroad, they are carried away by temper and anger, and have to confess that they have lost the perfect rest of soul in God! There is no virtue, perhaps, for which some have prayed more earnestly: they feel they would give anything, if in their intercourse with partner, or children, or servants, in company or in business, they could always keep their temper perfectly, and exhibit the meekness and gentleness of Christ. Unspeakable is the grief and disappointment experienced by those who have learnt to long for it, and yet have not discovered where the secret of meekness lies.

The Self-command needed for this seems to some so impossible, that they seek comfort in the belief that this blessing belongs to a certain natural temperament, and is too contrary to their character for them ever to expect it. To satisfy themselves they find all sorts of excuses. They do not mean it so ill: though the tongue or the temper be sharp, there is still love in their hearts: it would not be good to be too gentle: evil would be strengthened by it.

And thus the call to entire conformity to the holy gentleness of the Lamb of God is robbed of all its power. And the world is strengthened in its belief, that Christians are after all not very much different from other people, because, though they do indeed say, they do not show, that Christ changes the heart and life after His own image. And the soul suffers itself, and causes unspeakable harm in Christ's Church, through its unfaithfulness in appropriating this blessing of salvation: the bearing the image and likeness of God.

This grace is of great price in the sight of God. In the Old Testament there are many glorious promises for the meek, which were by Jesus gathered up into this one, "*Blessed are the meek, for they shall inherit the earth*" (see Psalm 25:9; 76:9; Proverbs 3:34; Jeremiah 2:3). In the, New Testament, its praise consists in this, that it is His meekness that gives its supernatural incomparable beauty to the image of our Lord. A meek spirit is of great price in God's sight; it is the choicest ornament of the Beloved Son. The Father could surely offer no higher inducement to His children, to seek it above all things.

For every one who longs to possess this spirit, Christ's word is full of comfort and encouragement: "*Learn of me that I am meek.*" And what will it profit us to learn that He is meek? Will not just the experience of His meekness make the discovery of our want of it all the more painful? What we ask, Lord, is that You should teach us how we may be meek. The answer is again: "*Learn of me, that I AM MEEK.*"

When we begin to realize this, we next fix our hearts upon the truth: This meek One is Jesus the Savior. All He is, all He has, is for His redeemed ones; His meekness is to be communicated to us. But He does not impart it, by giving, as it were from Himself, something of it away to us. No I we must learn that He alone is meek, and that only when He enters and takes possession of heart and life, He brings His meekness with Him. It is with the meekness of Jesus that we can be meek.

We know how little He succeeded in making His disciples meek and lowly while on earth. It was because He had not yet obtained the new life, and could not yet bestow, through His resurrection, the Holy Spirit. But now He can do it. He has been exalted to the power of God from thence to reign in our hearts, to conquer every enemy, and continue in us His own holy life. Jesus was our visible example on earth, that we might see in Him what like the hidden life is that He would give us from Heaven, that He Himself would be within us. …Therefore, only believe! Believe that Jesus is able to fill your heart with His own spirit of meekness. Believe that Jesus Himself will, through His Spirit, accomplish in you the work that you have in vain endeavored to do. *"Behold! Your King comes to you, meek."* Welcome Him to dwell in your heart. Expect Him to reveal Himself to you. Everything depends on this. *"Learn of Him that He is meek and lowly of heart, and you shall find rest to your soul."*

Like Christ: Giving His Life for Others

February 10th

"Hereby we know the love of God; because He laid down His life for us: and we ought to lay down our lives for the brethren."

—1 JOHN 3: 16

In speaking of the likeness of Christ's death, and of being made conformable to it, of bearing the cross and being crucified with Him, there is one danger to which even the earnest believer is exposed, and that is of seeking after these blessings for our own sake, or, as we think, for the glory of God in our own personal perfection. The error would be a fatal one; we would never attain the close conformity to Jesus' death we hoped for; for we would be leaving out just that which is the essential element in the death of Jesus, and in the Self-sacrifice it inculcates; that characteristic is its absolute unselfishness—its reference to others. To be made conformable to Christ's death implies a dying to Self, a losing sight of Self altogether in giving up and laying down our life for others.

To the question, how far we are to go in living for, in loving, in serving, in saving men, the Scriptures do not hesitate to give the unequivocal answer: We are to go as far as Jesus, even to the laying down of our life. We are to consider this so entirely as the object for which we are redeemed, and are left in the world, the one object for which we live, that the laying down of the life in death follows as a matter of course. Like Christ, the only thing that keeps us in this world is to be the glory of God in the salvation of sinners. Scripture does not hesitate to say that it is in His path of suffering, as He goes to work out atonement and redemption, that we are to follow Him.

Compare Matthew 20: 28 with Ephesians 5: 2, 25, 26; Philippians 2: 5–8; 1 Peter 2: 21–23, and note how distinctly it is in connection with His redemptive work that Christ is set before us as our example: the giving His life away for others is its special significance.

How clearly this comes out in the words of the Master Himself: *"Whoever will be chief among, you, let him be your bond-servant"; "As the Son of man came not to be ministered unto, but to minister, and to give His life a ransom for many."* The highest in glory will be those who were lowest in service, and like the Master in His giving His life a ransom. And so again, a few days later, after having spoken of His own death in the words: *"The hour is come that the Son of man should be glorified. Verily, verily, I say unto you, Except a kernel of wheat fall into the ground and die, it abides alone; but if it die, it brings forth much fruit";* He at once applied to His disciples what He had said by repeating what they had already heard spoken to themselves, *"He that loves his life shall lose it; and he that hates his life in this world shall keep it unto life eternal."*

The kernel of wheat dying to rise again, losing its life to regain it multiplied manifold, is clearly set forth as the emblem not only of the Master but of each one of His followers. Loving life, refusing to die, means remaining alone in Selfishness: losing life to bring forth much fruit in others is the only way to keep it for ourselves. There is no way to find our life but as Jesus did, in giving it up for the salvation of others. Herein is the Father, herein shall we be glorified. The deepest underlying thought of conformity to Christ's death is, giving our life to God for saving others. Without this, the longing, for conformity to that death is in danger of being a refined Selfishness.

How remarkable the exhibition we have in the Apostle Paul of this spirit, and how instructive the words in which the Holy Spirit in him expressed to us its meaning! To the Corinthians he says: "*Always bearing about the dying of the Lord Jesus, that the life also of Jesus might be made manifest in our body. For we which live are always delivered to death for Jesus' sake, that the life also of Jesus might be made manifest in our mortal flesh. So, then death works in us, but life in you,*" [and] "we shall live with Him by the power of God toward you" (2 Corinthians 4:10–12; 13: 4). "*I now rejoice in my sufferings for you, and fill up that which is behind of the afflictions of Christ in my flesh for His body's sake, which is the Church*" (Colossians 1:24).

These passages teach us how the vicarious element of the suffering that Christ bore in His body on the tree, to a certain extent still characterizes the sufferings of His body the Church. Believers who give themselves up to bear the burden of the sins of men before the Lord, who suffer reproach and shame, weariness and pain, in the effort to win souls, are filling up that which is lacking of the afflictions of Christ in their flesh. The power and the fellowship of His suffering and death work in them, the power of Christ's life through them in those for whom they labor in love.

There is no doubt that in the fellowship of His sufferings, and the conformity to His death in his epistle to the Philippians (chapter 3), Paul had in view not only the inner spiritual, but also the external bodily participations in the suffering of Christ. And so it must be with each of us in some measure. Self-sacrifice not merely for the sake of our own sanctification, but for the salvation of our fellow-men, is what brings us into true fellowship with the Christ who gave Himself for us.

The practical application of these thoughts is very simple. … As the most essential thing in likeness to Christ is likeness to His death, so the most essential thing in likeness to His death is the giving up our life to win others to God. It is a death in which all thought of saving Self is lost in that of saving others. Let us pray for the light of the Holy Spirit to show us this, until we learn to feel that we are in the world just as Christ was, to give up Self, to love and serve, to live and die, "*Even as the Son of man came not to be ministered unto, but to minister, and to give His life a ransom for many.*" Oh that God would give His people to know their calling; that they do not belong to themselves, but to God and to their fellow-men; that, even as Christ, they are only to live to be a blessing to the world.

Then let us believe in the grace that is waiting to make our experience of this truth a reality. Let us believe that God accepts of our giving up of our whole life for His glory in the saving of others. Let us believe that conformity to the death of Jesus in this, its very life-principle, is what the Holy Spirit will work out in us.

Let us above all believe in Jesus: it is He Himself who will take up every soul that in full surrender yields itself to Him, into the full fellowship of His death, of His dying, in love to bring forth much fruit. Yes, let us believe, and believing seek from above, as the work end the gift of Jesus, likeness to Jesus in this too.

And let us at once begin and act this faith. let us put it into practice. Looking upon ourselves now as wholly given up, just like Christ, to live and die for God in our fellow-men, let us with new zeal exercise the ministry of love in winning souls. As we wait for Christ to work out His likeness, as we trust the Holy Spirit to give His mind in us more perfectly, let us, in faith begin at once to act as followers of Him who only lived and died to be a blessing to others. Let our love open the way to the work it has to do by the kindness, and gentleness, and helpfulness, with which it shines out on all whom we meet in daily life. Let it give itself to the work of intercession, and look up to God to use us as one of His instruments in the answering of those prayers.

Let us speak and work for Jesus as those who have a mission and a power from on high which make us sure of a blessing.

Let us make soul-winning our object. Let us band ourselves with the great army of reapers the Lord is sending out into His harvest. And ere we thought of it, we shall find that giving our life to win others for God is the most blessed way of dying to Self, of being even as the Son of man was, a servant and a Savior of the lost.

O most wonderful and inconceivably blessed likeness to Christ! He gave Himself to men, but could not really reach them, until, giving Himself a sacrifice to God for them, the seed-corn died, the life was poured out; then the blessing flowed forth in mighty power. I may seek to love and serve men; I can only really influence and bless them as I yield myself unto God and give up my life into His hands for them; as I lose myself as an offering on the altar, I become in His spirit and power in very deed a blessing. My spirit given into His hands, He can use and bless me.

In His Life Through the Father

February 11th

"Even as I live by the Father, so the one who feeds upon me shall live by me."

—JOHN 6: 57

Like Christ: the longer we meditate on the word, the more we realize how impossible it is without that other: *In Christ.* The outward likeness can only be the manifestation of a living inward union. To do the same works as Christ, we must have the same life. The more earnestly we take Him for my example, the more we are driven to Him as our Head. Only an inner life essentially like His, can lead us to a visible walk like His.

What a blessed word we have here, to assure us that His life on earth and ours are really like each other: "*Even as I live by the Father, so he who feeds on me shall live like me.*" If you desire to understand your life in Christ, what He will be for you and how He will work in you, you have only to contemplate what the Father was for, and how He worked in Him. Christ's life in and through the Father is the image and the measure of what our life in and through the Son may be. Let us meditate on this.

As Christ's life was a life hidden in God in Heaven, so must ours be. When He emptied Himself of His Divine glory, He laid aside the free use of His Divine attributes. He needed thus as a man to live by faith; He needed to wait on the Father for such communications of wisdom and power, as it pleased the Father to impart to Him. He was entirely dependent on the Father; His life was hid in God. Not in virtue of His own independent Godhead, but through the operations of the Holy Spirit, He spoke and acted as the Father from time to time taught Him.

Exactly so, believer, must your life be hid with Christ in God. Let this encourage you. Christ calls you to a life of faith and dependence, because it is the life He Himself led. He has tried it and proved its blessedness; He is willing now to live over again His life in you, to teach you also to live in no other way. He knew that the Father was His life, and that He lived through the Father, and that the Father supplied His need moment by moment. And now He assures you that as He lived through the Father, even so you shall live through Him. Take this assurance in faith. Let your heart be filled with the thought of the blessedness of this fullness of life, which is prepared for you in Christ, and will be abundantly supplied as you need it. Do not think any more of your spiritual life, as something that you must watch over and nourish with care and anxiety. Rejoice every day that you need not live on your own strength, but in your Lord Jesus, even as He lived through His Father.

Even as Christ's life was a life of Divine power, although a life of dependence, so ours will *also be*. He never repented having laid aside His glory, to live before God as a man upon earth. The Father never disappointed His confidence, He gave Him all He needed to accomplish His work. Christ experienced that, blessed as it was to be like God in Heaven, and to dwell in the enjoyment of Divine perfection, it was no less blessed to live in the relation of entire dependence on earth, and to receive everything day by day from His hands.

Believer, if you will have it so, your life can be the same. The Divine power of the Lord Jesus will work in and through us. Do not think that your earthly circumstances make a holy life to God's glory impossible. It was just to manifest, in the midst of earthly surroundings which were even more difficult, the Divine life, that Christ came and lived on earth. As He lived so blessed an earthly life through the Father, so may ye also live your earthly life through Him. Only cultivate large expectations of what the Lord will do for you. Let it be your sole desire to attain to an entire union with Him. It is impossible to say what the Lord Jesus would do for a soul who is truly willing to live as entirely through Him as He through the Father. Because just as He lived through the Father, and the Father made that life with all its work so glorious, so will you experience in all your work how entirely He has undertaken to work all in you.

As the life of Christ was the manifestation of His real union with the Father, so ours also. … To attain this, seek continually to have your heart filled with a believing and lively assurance that all Christ's fullness of life is truly yours. Rejoice in the contemplation of His humanity in Heaven, and the wonderful provision God has made through the Holy Spirit for the communication of this life of your Head in Heaven, to flow unbroken and unhindered down upon you.

Thank God unceasingly for the redemption in which He opened the way to the life of God, and for the wonderful life now provided for you in the Son. Offer yourself unreservedly to Him with an open heart and consecrated life that seeks His service alone. In such trust and consecration of faith, in the outpouring of love and cultivation of communion, with His words abiding in you, let Jesus be your daily food. "*He who feeds upon me shall live by Me, even as the Father has sent Me, and I live by the Father.*"

Beloved Christian! what think you? Does not the imitation of Christ begin to seem possible in the light of this promise? He who lives through Christ can also live like Him. Therefore let this wonderful life of Christ on earth through the Father be the object of our adoring contemplation, until our whole heart understands and accepts the word, "*Even so, He who feeds upon Me shall live through Me.*" Then we shall dismiss all care and anxiety, because the same Christ who set us the example works in us from Heaven that life which can live out the example.

And our life will become a continual song: To Him who lives in us, in order that we may live like Him, be the love and praise of our hearts.

Like Christ: Led by the Spirit

February 12th

"And Jesus being full of the Holy Spirit, returned from Jordan, and was led by the Spirit into the wilderness."

—LUKE 4: 1

Even as Jesus was filled with the Spirit, and then led by the Spirit, so must we be also filled with the Spirit and be led by the Spirit. More than once, in our meditations on the different traits of Christ's character, it has seemed to us almost impossible to be like Him. We have lived so little for it: we feel so little able to live thus. Let us take courage in the thought: Jesus Himself could only live thus through the Spirit. It was after He was filled with the Spirit that He was led forth by that Spirit to the place of conflict and of victory.

And this blessing is ours as surely as it was His: we may be filled with the Spirit; we may be led by the Spirit. Jesus, who was Himself baptized with the Spirit, to set us an example how to live, has ascended into Heaven to baptize us into the likeness with Himself. He who would live like Jesus must begin here: He must be baptized with the Spirit. What God demands from His children, He first gives. He demands entire likeness to Christ because He will give us, as He did Jesus, the fullness of the Spirit. We must be filled with the Spirit.

We have here the reason why the teaching of the imitation and likeness to Christ has so little prominence in the Church of Christ. Believers sought it in their own strength, with the help of some workings of the Holy Spirit: they did not understand that nothing less was needed than being *filled with the Spirit.* No wonder that they thought that real conformity to Christ could not be expected, because they had mistaken thoughts about being *filled with the Spirit:* It was thought to be the privilege of a few, and not the calling and duty of every child of God. It was not sufficiently realized that *"Be filled with the Spirit,"* is a command to every Christian.

Only when the Church first gives the baptism of the Spirit, and Jesus, as the Savior who baptizes with the Spirit each one who believes in Him, their right place, only then will likeness to Christ be sought after and attained. People will then understand and acknowledge: To be like Christ we must be led by the same Spirit, and to be led by the Spirit as He was, we must be filled with the Spirit. Nothing less than the fullness of the Spirit is absolutely necessary to live a truly Christian, Christ-like life.

The way to arrive at it is simple. It is Jesus who baptizes with the Spirit: we who come to Him desiring it will get it. All that He requires of us is, the surrender of faith to receive what He gives.

What He asks is whether we are indeed in earnest to follow in His footsteps, and for this to be baptized of the Spirit. Do not let there be any hesitation as to our answer. First, look back on all the glorious promises of His love and of His Spirit, in which the blessed privilege is set forth: *Even as I ... You also.* Remember that it was of this likeness to Himself in everything He said to the Father: "*The glory which You gave me have I given them.*"

Think how the love of Christ and the true desire to please Him, how the glory of God and the needs of the world, plead with us not through our sloth to despise this heavenly birthright of being Christ-like. Acknowledge the sacred right of ownership Christ has in you, His blood-bought ones: and let nothing prevent your answering: "Yes, dear Lord, as far as is allowed to a child of dust, I will be like You. I am entirely Yours; I must, I will, in all things bear Your image. It is for this I ask to be filled with the Spirit."

The surrender of faith: only this; but nothing less than this He demands. Let us give what He asks. If we yield ourselves to be like Him, in all things, let it be in the quiet trust that He accepts, and at once begins in secret to make the Spirit work more mightily in us. Let us believe it although we do not at once experience it. To be filled with the Holy Spirit, we must wait on our Lord in faith. We can depend upon it that His love desires to give us more than we know. Let our surrender be made in this assurance.

And let this surrender of faith be entire. The fundamental law of following Christ is this: *"He who loses his life shall find it."* The Holy Spirit comes to take away the old life, and to give in its place the life of Christ in you. Renounce the old life of Self-working and Self-watching, and believe that, as the air you breathe renews your life every moment, so naturally and continually the Holy Spirit will renew your life. In the work of the Holy Spirit in you there are no breaks or interruptions: you are in the Spirit as your vital air: the Spirit is in you as your life-breath: "*through the Spirit God works in you both to will and to do according to His good pleasure.*"

O Christian, have a deep reverence for the work of the Spirit who dwells within you. Believe in God's power, which works in you through the Spirit, to conform you to Christ's life and image moment by moment. Be occupied with Jesus and His life, that life which is at the same time your example and your strength, in the full assurance that the Holy Spirit knows in deep quiet to fulfill His office of communicating Jesus to you.

Remember that the fullness of the Spirit is yours in Jesus, a real gift which you accept and hold in faith, even when there is not such feeling as you could wish, and on which you count to work in you all you need. The feeling may be weakness and fear and much trembling, and yet the speaking, and working, and living *in demonstration of the Spirit and of power* (1 Corinthians 2: 3, 4). … Thus, with the loving presence of Jesus in you, the living likeness to Jesus will be seen on you; the Spirit of life in Christ Jesus dwelling within, the likeness of the life of Christ Jesus will shine around.

Christ was filled with the Spirit that He might be fitted to work and live and die for us. Give yourself to such a Christ-like living and dying for men, and you may depend upon it; a Christ-like baptism of the Spirit, a Christ-like fullness of the Spirit, will be your portion.

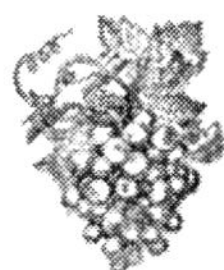

Like Christ: In His Glory

February 13th

"We know that, when He appears, we shall be like Him …
And everyone who has this hope purifies themselves, even as He is pure."
—1 JOHN 3: 2–3

God's glory is His holiness. To glorify God is to yield ourselves that God in us may show forth His glory. It is only by yielding ourselves to be holy, to let His holiness fill our life that His glory can shine forth from us. The one work of Christ was to glorify the Father—to reveal what a glorious, holy God He is. Our one work is, like Christ's, so by our obedience, and testimony, and life, to make known our God as "glorious in holiness," that He may be glorified in heaven and earth.

When the Lord Jesus had glorified the Father on earth, the Father glorified Him with Himself in heaven. This was not only His just reward; it was a necessity in the very nature of things. There is no other place for a life given up to the glory of God, as Christ's was, than in that glory. The law holds good for us too: a heart that yearns and thirsts for the glory of God, that is ready to live and die for it, becomes prepared and fitted to live in it.

Living to God's glory on earth is the gate to living in Gods glory in heaven. If with Christ we glorify the Father, the Father will with Christ glorify us too. Yes, we shall be like Him in His glory.

We shall be like Him in His spiritual glory, the glory of His holiness. In the union of the two words in the name of the Holy Spirit, we see that what is holy and what is spiritual stand in the closest connection with each other. When Jesus as man had glorified God by revealing, and honoring, and giving Himself up to His holiness, he was as man taken up into and made partaker of the Divine glory.

And so it will be with us. If here on earth we have given ourselves to have God's glory take possession of us, and God's holiness, God's Holy Spirit, dwell and shine in us, then our human nature with all our faculties, created in the likeness of God, shall have poured into and transfused through it, in a way that passes all conception, the purity and the holiness and the life, the very brightness of the glory of God.

We shall be like Him in His glorified body. It has been well said: Embodiment is the end of the ways of God. The creation of man was to be God's masterpiece. There had previously been spirits without bodies, and animated bodies without spirits, but in man there was to be a spirit in a body lifting up and spiritualizing the body into its own heavenly purity and perfection. Man as a whole is God's image, his body as much as his spirit. In Jesus a human body—O mystery of mysteries!—is set upon the throne of God, is found a worthy partner and container of the Divine glory. Our bodies are going to be the objects of the most astonishing miracle of Divine transforming power: "*He will fashion our vile body like unto His glorious body, according to the working whereby He is able even to subdue all things unto Himself.*" The glory of God as seen in our bodies, made like Christ's glorious body, will be something almost more wonderful than in our spirits. We are "waiting for the adoption, to wit, the redemption of our body.

Such Divine God-given glimpses into the future reveal to us, more than all our thinking, what intense truth, what Divine meaning there is in God's creative word: "*Let us make man in Our image, after Our likeness.*" To show forth the likeness of the Invisible, to be partaker of the Divine Nature, to share with God His rule of the universe, is man's destiny. His place is indeed one of unspeakable glory. Standing between two eternities, the eternal purpose in which we were predestinated to be conformed to the image of the first-born Son, and the eternal realization of that purpose when we shall be like Him in His glory, we hear the voice from every side: Oh, image-bearers of God! on the way to share the glory of God and of Christ: Live a God-like life; live a Christ-like life!

"I shall be satisfied when I awake with Your likeness," so the Psalmist sung of old. Nothing can satisfy the soul but God's image, because for that it was created. And this not as something external to it, only seen but not possessed; it is as partaker of that likeness that we shall be satisfied. Blessed are they who long for it with insatiable hunger; they shall be filled. This, the very likeness of God, will be the glory, streaming down on them from God Himself, streaming through their whole being, streaming, out from them through the universe: *"When Christ who is our life appears, we also shall appear with Him in glory."*

Beloved fellow Christians! nothing can be made manifest in that day that has not a real existence here in this life. If the glory of God is not our life here, it cannot be hereafter. It is impossible; him alone who glorifies God here, can God glorify hereafter. "*Man is the image and glory of God.*" It is as you bear the image of God here, as you live in the likeness of Jesus, who is the brightness of His glory, and the express image of His person, that you will be fitted for the glory to come. If we are to be as the image of the heavenly, the Christ in glory, we must first bear the image of the earthly, the Christ in humiliation.

Child of God! Christ is the uncreated image of God. Man is created image. On the throne, in the glory, the two will be eternally one. You know what Christ did—how He drew near, how He sacrificed all, to restore us to the possession of that image. Oh, shall we not at length yield ourselves to this wonderful love, to this glory inconceivable, and give our life wholly to manifest the likeness and the glory of Christ? Shall we not, like Him, make the Father's glory our aim and hope, living to His glory here, as the way to live in His glory there?

The Father's glory: It is in this—that Christ's glory and ours have their common origin. Let *the Father* be to us what He was to Him, and the Father's glory will be ours as it is His. All the traits of the life of Christ converge to this as their center. He was Son; He lived as Son; God was to Him "Father." As the Son, He sought the Father's glory; as Son He found it. Oh! Let this be our conformity to the image of the Son, that the Father is the all in all our life; the Father's glory must be our everlasting home. …

Like Christ: In Glorifying the Father

February 14th

"Herein is My Father glorified, that you bear much fruit."

—JOHN 15: 8

To glorify is to remove every hindrance, and so to reveal the full worth and perfection of the object, that its glory is seen and acknowledged by all. The highest perfection of God, and the deepest mystery of Godhead, is His holiness. In it righteousness and love are united. As the Holy One He hates and condemns sin. As the Holy One He also frees the sinner from its power, and raises him to communion with Himself. His name is, "*The Holy One of Israel, your Redeemer.*" The song of redemption is: "*Great is the Holy One of Israel in the midst of you.*" To the blessed Spirit, whose special work it is to maintain the fellowship of God with man, is given the title of Holy ….

When Jesus came to earth, it was that He might glorify the Father, that He might again show forth in its true light and beauty that glory which sin had so entirely hid from man. Man himself had been created in the image of God, so that God might lay of His glory upon him, to be shown forth in him—so that God might be glorified in him. The Holy Spirit says, "*Man is the image and glory of God.*" Jesus came to restore us to our high destiny: He laid aside the glory which He had with the Father, and came in our weakness and humiliation that He might teach us how to glorify the Father on earth. God's glory is perfect and infinite: we cannot contribute any new glory to God, above what He has: we can only serve as a glass in which the glory of God is reflected. God's holiness is His glory: as the holiness of God is seen in him, God is glorified; His glory as God is shown forth.

Jesus glorified God by obeying Him. In giving His commandments to Israel, God continually said, "*Be holy, for I am holy*"; in keeping them they would be transformed into a life of harmony with Him, they would enter into fellowship with Him as the Holy One. In His conflict with sin and Satan, in His sacrifice of His will, in His waiting for the Father's teaching, in His unquestioning obedience to the Word, Christ showed that He counted nothing worth living for, but that we might understand what a blessed thing it is to let this holy God really be God—His will alone acknowledged and obeyed. Because He alone is holy, His will alone should be done, and so His glory be shown in us.

Jesus … not only in His teaching made known the message God had given Him, and showed us who the Father is. There is something far more striking. He continually spoke of His own personal relation to the Father. He did not trust to the silent influence of His holy life; He wanted us distinctly to understand what the root and aim of that life was. Time after time He told us that He came as a servant sent from the Father, that He depended upon Him and owed everything to Him, that He only sought the Fathers honor, and that all His happiness was to please the Father, to secure His love and favor.

Jesus glorified God *by giving Himself for the work of His redeeming love.* … He gave Himself, His whole life and being, Himself wholly, to show how the Father loved, and longed to bless, how the Father must condemn the sin, and yet would save the sinner. He counted nothing too great a sacrifice, He lived and died only for this—that the glory of the Father, the glory of His holiness, of His redeeming love, might break through the dark veil of sin and flesh, and shine into our hearts. … It was thus Jesus as man was prepared to have part in the glory of God. … And so He is become our forerunner, leading many children to glory: He shows us that the sure way to the glory of God in Heaven is to live only for the glory of God on the earth. Yes, this is the glory of a life on earth: glorifying God here, we are prepared to be glorified with Him forever.

Beloved Christian! is it not a wonderful calling, blessed beyond all conception, like Christ to live only to glorify God, to let God's glory shine out in every part of our life? Let us take time to take in the wondrous thought: our daily life, down to its most ordinary acts, may be transparent with the glory of God. Oh! Let us study this trait as one that makes the wondrous image of our Jesus especially attractive to us: He glorified the Father. Let us listen to Him as He points us to the high aim, *that your Father in Heaven may be glorified,* and as He shows us the way, *Herein is my Father glorified.*

Let us remember how He told us that, when in Heaven He answers our prayer, this would still be His object, and let in every breathing of prayer and faith it be our object too: *"That the Father may be glorified in the Son."* Let our whole life, like Christ's, be animated by this as its ruling principle, growing stronger until in a holy enthusiasm our watchword has become: All, all to the glory of God.

And let our faith hold fast the confidence that in the fullness of the Spirit there is the sure provision for our desire being fulfilled: *"Do you not know that your body is the temple of the Holy Spirit, who is in you? Therefore glorify God in your body and in your spirit."*

If we want to know the way, let us again study Jesus. He obeyed the Father. Let simple downright obedience mark our whole life. Let a humble, childlike waiting for direction, a soldier-like looking for orders, a Christ-like dependence on the Father's showing us His way, be our daily attitude. Let everything be done to the Lord—according to His will, for His glory, in direct relationship to Himself. Let God's glory shine out in the holiness of our life. He confessed the Father: He did not hesitate to speak often of His personal relationship and intercourse, just as a little child would do of an earthly parent. It is not enough that we live right before others: *"how can they understand, if there be no interpreter?"* They need, not as a matter of preaching, but as a personal testimony, to hear that who we are and what we do is because we love the Father, and are living for Him. The witness of the life and the words must go together.

On Preaching Christ Our Example

February 15th

"Let as make mankind in Our image, after Our likeness."

—GENESIS 1: 26

In these words of the Council of Creation, with which the Bible history of man opens, we have the revelation of the eternal purpose to which we owe our existence, of the glorious eternal future to which we are destined. God proposes to make a Godlike creature, a being who shall be His very image and likeness, the visible manifestation of the glory of the Invisible One. To have a being, at once created and yet Godlike, was indeed a task worthy of Infinite Wisdom. It is the nature and glory of God that He is absolutely independent of all else, having life in Himself, owing His existence to none but Himself alone. If we are to be Godlike, we must bear His image and likeness in this too…

It is the nature and glory of the creature to be dependent, to owe everything to the Blessed Creator. How can the contradiction be reconciled—a being at once dependent and yet Self-determined, created and yet Godlike? In mankind the mystery is solved. As a creature God gives us life, but endows us with the wonderful power of a free will; it is only in the process of a personal and voluntary appropriation that anything so high and holy as likeness to God can really become our very own. …

Of His revelation in Israel the central thought was: *"Be holy, as I am holy."* Likeness to God in that which constitutes His highest perfection is to be Israel's hope. Redemption had no higher ideal than Creation had revealed; it could only take up and work out the Father's eternal purpose.

It was with this in view that the Father sent to the earth the Son who was the express image of His person. In Him the God-likeness to which we had been created, and which we had personally to appropriate and make our own, was revealed in human form: He came to show to us at once the image of God and our own image. In looking upon Him, the desire after our long-lost likeness to God was to be awakened, and that hope and faith begotten which gave us courage to yield ourselves to be renewed after that image.

To accomplish this, there was a twofold work He had to do. The one was *to reveal in His life the likeness of God,* so that we might know what a life in that likeness was, and understand what it was we had to expect and accept from Him as our Redeemer. When He had done this, and shown us the likeness of the life of God in human form, He died that He might win for us, and impart to us, His own life as the life of the likeness of God, that in its power we might live in the likeness of what we had seen in Him. And when He ascended to Heaven, it was to give us in the Holy Spirit the power of that life He had first set before us and then won to impart to us.

It is easy to see how close the connection between these two parts of the work of our Lord, and how the one depends upon the other. For what as our example He had in His life revealed, He as our redeemer by His death purchased the power. His earthly life showed the path, His heavenly life gives the power, in which we are to walk. … Christ lived on earth that He might show forth *the image of God in His life:* He lives in Heaven that we may show forth *the image of God in our lives.*

The Church of Christ has not always maintained the due relation of these two truths. In the Catholic Church the former of the two was placed in the foreground, and the following of Christ's example pressed with great earnestness. As the fruit of this, she can point to no small number of saints who, notwithstanding many errors, with admirable devotion sought literally and entirely to bear the Master's image. But to the great loss of earnest souls, the other half of the truth was neglected, that only they who in the power of Christ's death receive His life within them, are able to imitate His life as set before them.

The Protestant Churches owe their origin to the revival of the second truth. … The doctrine that Christ lived on earth, not only to die for our redemption, but to show us how we were to live, did not receive sufficient prominence. While no orthodox Church will deny that Christ is our example, *the absolute necessity* of following the example of His life is not preached with the same distinctness as that of trusting the atonement of His death. Great pains are taken, and that most justly, to lead men to accept the merits of His death. But, great pains are not taken—and this is what is not right—to lead men to accept the imitation of His life as the one mark and test of true discipleship.

It is hardly necessary to point out what influence the mode of presenting this truth will exercise in the life of the Church. If atonement and pardon be everything, and the life in His likeness something secondary … then the chief attention will be directed to the former; pardon and peace will be the great objects of desire. And, with these attained, there will be a tendency to rest content. If, on the other hand, conformity to the image of God's Son be the chief object, and the atonement the means to secure this end, as the fulfillment of God's purpose in creation, then in all the preaching of repentance and pardon, the true aim will ever be kept in the foreground; faith in Jesus and conformity to character will be regarded as inseparable. Such a Church will produce real followers of the Lord. …

"In all He suffered for us, He left us an example that we should follow in His footsteps." As the banner of the cross is lifted high, the *atonement of the cross* and *the fellowship of the cross* must equally be preached as the condition of true discipleship. … The disciple must be as the Master. He spoke of it as the instrument of Self-sacrifice, the mark and the means of giving up our own life to the death, the only path for the entrance upon the new Divine life He came to bring. It is not only I who must die, He said, but you too; the cross, the spirit of daily Self-sacrifice, is to be the badge of your allegiance to me. …

Like Christ: Abiding in the Love of God

February 16th

"Even as the Father has loved Me, so have I loved you: abide in My love. If you keep My commandments, you shall abide in My love; even as I have kept My Father's commandments, and abide in His love."

—JOHN 15: 9–10

Our blessed Lord not only said, "*Abide in Me*," but also, "*Abide in my love*." Of the abiding in Him, the principal part is the entering into and dwelling and being rooted in that wonderful love with which He loves us and gives Himself to us. … Christ's love longs to possess us. The abiding in Christ is an intensely personal relationship, the losing ourselves in the fellowship of an Infinite Love; it is finding our life in the experience of being loved by Him, and being nowhere at home but in His love.

To reveal this life in His love to us in all its Divine beauty and blessedness, Jesus tells us that this love of His for us in which we are to abide is just the same as the Fathers love for Him in which He abides. Surely, if anything were needed to make the abiding in His love more wonderful and attractive, this ought to do so. *"Even as the Father loved Me, so have I loved you: abide in My love."* …

We know how this was the secret of Christ's wonderful life, and His strength in prospect of death. At His baptism the voice was heard, the Divine message which the Spirit brought and unceasingly maintained in living power, *"This is my beloved Son, in whom I am well pleased."* More than once we read: *"The Father loves the Son"* (John 3: 35; 5: 20). Christ speaks of it as His highest blessedness: *"That the world may know that You have loved them, even as You had loved Me"* … "That *the love wherewith You loved Me may be in them.*" Just as we day by day walk and live in the light of the sun shining around us, so Jesus just lived in the light of the glory of the Father's love shining on Him all the day. It was as the beloved of God that He was able to do God's will, and finish His work. He dwelled in the love of the Father.

And just so we are the beloved of Jesus. Even as the Father loved Him, He loves us. And what we need is just to take time, and, shutting our eyes to all around us, to worship and to wait until we see the Infinite Love of God in all its power and glory streaming forth upon us through the heart of Jesus, seeking to make itself known, and to get complete possession of us, offering itself to us as our home and resting-place. Oh, if the Christian would but take time to let the wondrous thought fill him: "I am the beloved of the Lord; Jesus loves me every moment, just as the Father loved Him," how the faith would grow.

The one who is loved as Christ was, must walk as He walked! … Not only is the love we are to abide in like that in which He abode, but the way to our abiding is the same as His. … It was in giving up His own will, and learning obedience by what He suffered, in becoming obedient unto the death, even the death of the cross, that He kept the Father's commandments and abode in His love. "*Therefore does My Father love me, because I lay down My life*"; "*This commandment have I received of My Father*"; "*The Father has not left me alone; for I do always those things that please Him.*" And having thus given us His example, and proved how surely the path of obedience takes us up into the presence and love and glory of God, He invites us to follow Him. "*If you keep my commandments, you shall abide in my love, even as I kept my Father's commandments, and abide in His love.*"

Christ-like obedience is the way to a Christ-like enjoyment of Love Divine. How it secures our boldness of access into God's presence! "*Let us love in deed and in truth, hereby shall we assure our hearts before Him.*" "*Beloved! If our heart condemns us not, then have we confidence towards God; and whatsoever we ask, we receive of Him, because we keep His commandments, and do those things that are pleasing in His sight.*" … The heart filled with the thought of direct and entire obedience to God alone, rises above the world into the will of God, into the place where God's love rests on us: like Christ, we have our abode in the love of God.

3

DIVINE HEALING

1884

Pardon and Healing

February 17th

"That you may know that the Son of man has power on earth to forgive sins, Arise, take up your bed and go unto your house."

—MATTHEW 9: 6

In man two natures are combined. He is at the same time spirit and matter, Heaven and earth, soul and body. For this reason, on one side he is the son of God, and on the other he is doomed to destruction because of the Fall; sin in his soul and sickness in his body bear witness to the right which death has over him. It is the twofold nature which has been redeemed by Divine grace. When the Psalmist calls upon all that is within him to bless the Lord for His benefits, he cries, *"Bless the Lord, oh, my soul, Who ... forgives all your iniquities, Who heals all your diseases"* (Psalm 103:2–3). When Isaiah foretells the deliverance of his people, he adds, "*The inhabitant shall not say, I am sick; the people that dwell therein shall be forgiven their iniquity*" (Isaiah 33: 24).

This prediction was accomplished beyond all anticipation when Jesus the Redeemer came down to this earth. How numerous were the healings wrought by Him who was come to establish upon earth the Kingdom of Heaven! Whether by His own acts or whether afterwards by the commands which He left for His disciples, does He not show us clearly that the preaching of the Gospel and the healing of the sick went together in the salvation which He came to bring? Both are given as evident proof of His mission as the Messiah: "*The blind receive their sight and the lame walk .., and the poor have the Gospel preached to them*" (Matthew 11: 5). Jesus, who took upon Him the soul and body of man, delivers both in equal measure from the consequences of sin.

This truth is nowhere more evident or better demonstrated than in the history of the paralytic. The Lord Jesus begins by saying to him, "*Your sins are forgiven*" (Matthew 9: 5) after which He adds, "*Arise, take up your bed and go.*" The pardon of sin and the healing of sickness complete one the other, for in the eyes of God, who sees our entire nature, sin and sickness are as closely united as the body and the soul. In accordance with the Scriptures, our Lord Jesus has regarded sin and sickness in another light than we have. With us sin belongs to the spiritual domain; we recognize that it is under God's just displeasure, justly condemned by Him, while sickness, on the contrary, seems only a part of the present condition of our nature, and to have nothing to do with God's condemnation and His righteousness.

Some go so far as to say that sickness is a proof of the love and grace of God. But neither the Scripture nor yet Jesus Christ Himself ever spoke of sickness in this light, nor do they ever present sickness as a blessing, as a proof of God's love which should be borne with patience. The Lord spoke to the disciples of divers sufferings which they should have to bear, but when He speaks of sickness, it is always as of an evil caused by sin and Satan, and from which we should be delivered.

Very solemnly Jesus declared that every disciple of His would have to bear his cross (Matthew 16: 24), but He never taught one sick person to resign himself to be sick. Everywhere Jesus healed the sick, everywhere He dealt with healing as one of the graces belonging to the Kingdom of Heaven. Sin in the soul and sickness in the body both bear witness to the power of Satan, and "*the Son of God was manifested that He might destroy the works of the Devil*" (1 John 3: 8). Jesus came to deliver men from sin and sickness that He might make known the love of the Father.

In His actions, in His teaching of the disciples, in the work of the apostles, pardon and healing are always to be found together. Either the one or the other may doubtless appear more in relief, according to the development or the faith of those to whom they spoke. Sometimes it was healing which prepared the way for the acceptance of forgiveness, sometimes it was forgiveness which preceded the healing, which, coming afterwards, became a seal to it. In the early part of His ministry, Jesus cured many of the sick, finding them ready to believe in the possibility of their healing. In this way He sought to influence hearts to receive Himself as He who is able to pardon sin. When He saw that the paralytic could receive pardon at once, He began by that which was of the greatest importance; after which came the healing which put a seal on the pardon which had been accorded to him. …

It is true that healing is not given in this day as in those times, to the multitudes whom Christ healed without any previous conversion. In order to receive it, it is necessary to begin by confession of sin and the purpose to live a holy life. This is without doubt the reason why people find more difficulty to believe in healing than in forgiveness; and this is also why those who receive healing receive at the same time new spiritual blessing, feel more closely united to the Lord Jesus, and learn to love and serve Him better. Unbelief may attempt to separate these two gifts, but they are always united in Christ. He is always the same Savior both of the soul and of the body, equally ready to grant pardon and healing. The redeemed may always cry: "*Bless the Lord, oh, my soul … Who forgives all your iniquities, Who heals all your diseases*" (Psalm 103: 2–3).

"The prayer of faith shall save the sick, and the Lord shall raise them up; and if they have committed sins, they shall be forgiven. Confess your faults one to another, and pray one for another that you may be healed" (James 5: 15, 16). Here, as in other Scriptures, the pardon of sins and the healing of sickness are closely united. James declares that pardon of sins will be granted with the healing; and for this reason he desires to see confession of sin accompany the prayer which claims healing. We know that confession of sin is indispensable to obtain from God the pardon of sin: it is not less so to obtain healing. Unconfessed sin presents an obstacle to the prayer of faith; in any case, the sickness may soon reappear, and for this reason.

The first care of a physician, when he is called to treat a patient, is to diagnose the cause of the disease. If he succeeds he stands a better chance to combat it. Our God also goes back to the primary cause of all sickness that is, sin. It is our part to confess and God's to grant the pardon which removes this first cause, so that healing can take place. In seeking for healing by means of earthly remedies, the first thing to do is to find a clever physician, and then to follow his prescriptions exactly; but in having recourse to the prayer of faith, it is needful to fix our eyes, above all, upon the Lord, and to ascertain how we stand with Him. James therefore points out to us a condition which is essential to the recovery of our health; namely, that we confess and forsake sin.

Sickness is a consequence of sin. It is because of sin that God permits it; it is in order to show us our faults, to chasten us, and purify us from them. Sickness is therefore a visible sign of God's judgment upon sin. It is not that the one who is sick is necessarily a greater sinner than another who is in health. On the contrary, it is often the most holy among the children of God, whom He chastens, as we see from the example of Job. Neither is it always to check some fault which we can easily determine: it is specially to draw the attention of the sick one to that which remains the egotism of the old Self and of all which hinders from a life entirely consecrated to God. The first step which the sick one has to take in the path of Divine healing will be therefore to let the Holy Spirit of God probe the heart and convince of sin. After which will come, also, humiliation, decision to break with sin, and confession. To confess our sins is to lay them down before God and to subject them to His judgment, with the fixed purpose to fall into them no more. A sincere confession will be followed by a new assurance of pardon.

"*If he has committed sins they shall be forgiven him.*" When we have confessed our sins, we must receive also the promised pardon, believing that God gives it in very deed. Faith in God's pardon is often vague in the child of God. Either he is uncertain, or he returns to old impressions, to the time when he first received pardon; but the pardon which he now receives with confidence, in answer to the prayer of faith, will bring him new life and strength. The soul then rests under the efficacy of the blood of Christ, receives from the Holy Spirit the certainty of the pardon of sin, and that therefore nothing remains to hinder the Savior from filling him with His love and with His grace.

God's pardon brings with it a divine life which acts powerfully upon him who receives it. When the soul has consented to make a sincere confession and has obtained pardon, it is ready to lay hold of the promise of God; it is no longer difficult to believe that the Lord will raise up His sick one. It is when we keep far from God that it is difficult to believe; confession and pardon bring us quite near to Him. As soon as the cause of the sickness has been removed, the sickness itself can be arrested. …

The Will of God

February 18th

"Your Kingdom come; Your will be done."
—MATTHEW 6: 10

In days of sickness, when doctors and medicines fail, recourse is generally had to the words we have here quoted, and they may easily become a stumbling-block in the way of Divine healing. … It is a great mistake to think that the child of God cannot know the heavenly Father's will about healing.

In order to know His Divine will, we must be guided by the Word of God. It is His Word which promises us healing. The promise of James 5 is so absolute that it is impossible to deny it. This promise only confirms other passages, equally strong, which tell us that Jesus Christ has obtained for us the healing of our diseases, because He has borne our sicknesses. According to this promise, we have right to healing, because it is a part of the salvation which we have in Christ, and therefore we may expect it with certainty. Scripture tells us that sickness is, in God's hands, the means of chastening His children for their sins, but that this discipline ceases to be exercised as soon as His suffering child acknowledges and turns from the sin. Is it not as much as to say clearly that God desires only to make use of sickness to bring back His children when they are straying?

Sick Christian, open your Bible, study it and see in its pages that sickness is a warning to renounce sin; but that whoever acknowledges and forsakes his sins finds in Jesus pardon and healing. Such is God's promise in His Word. If the Lord had in view some other dispensation for such of His children whom He was about to call home to Him, He would make known to them His will, giving them by the Holy Spirit a desire to depart; in other special cases, He would awaken some special conviction; but as a general rule, the Word of God promises us healing in answer to the prayer of faith.

"Nevertheless," some might say, "is it not better in all things to leave it to the will of God?" And they quote the instance of such and such Christians who would have, so to speak, forced the hand of God by their praying without adding, "*Your will be done*," (Matthew 6:10) and who would not have experienced blessing in the answer to their prayers. And these would say, "How do we know whether sickness would not be better for us than health?" Notice here that this is no case of forcing the hand of God, since it is His Word which tells us that it is His will to heal us. "*The prayer of faith shall save the sick*" (James 5:15).

God wills that the health of the soul should have a blessed reflex influence on the health of the body, that the presence of Jesus in the soul should have its confirmation in the good condition of the body. And when you know that such is His will you cannot, when speaking in such a way, say truthfully that you are in all things leaving it to Him. It is not leaving it to Him when you make use of all possible remedies to get healing, instead of laying hold of His promise. Your submission is nothing else than spiritual sloth in view of that which God commands you to do.

As to knowing whether sickness is not better than health, we do not hesitate to reply that the return to health which is the fruit of giving up sin, of consecration to God, and of an ultimate communion with God, is infinitely better than sickness. "*This is the will of God, even your sanctification*" (1 Thessalonians 4: 3), and it is by healing that God confirms the reality of this.

When Jesus comes to take possession of our body, and cures it miraculously, and when it follows that the health received must be maintained from day to day by an uninterrupted communion with Him, then the experience which we thus gain of the Savior's power and of His love is a result very superior to any which sickness has to offer. Doubtless sickness may teach us submission, but healing received direct from God makes us better acquainted with our Lord, and teaches us to confide in Him better. Besides, it prepares the believer to accomplish better the service of God.

Christians who are sick, if you will really seek to know what is the will of God in this thing, do not let yourself be influenced by the opinions of others, nor by your own former prejudices, but listen to and study what the Word of God has to say. Examine whether it does not tell you that Divine healing is a part of the redemption of Jesus, and that God wills that every believer should have the right to claim it; see whether it does not promise that the prayer of every child of God for this thing shall be heard, and whether health restored by the power of the Holy Spirit does not manifest the glory of God in the eyes of the Church and of the world. Inquire of it; it will answer you, that, according to the will of God, sickness is a discipline [most often] occasioned by sin (or shortcoming), and that healing, granted to the prayer of faith, bears witness to His grace which pardons, which sanctifies, and which takes away sin.

The Lord Who Heals You

"*I will put none of these diseases upon you which I have brought upon the Egyptians, for I am the Lord that heals you*" (Exodus 15: 26). There is nothing in the Bible to make the Church believe that the promise made to Israel has been since retracted, and she hears from the mouth of the Apostle James this new promise: "*The prayer of faith shall heal the sick*" (James 5: 15). She [the Church] knows that at all times it has been unbelief which has limited the Holy One of Israel (Psalm 78: 41), and she asks herself if it is not unbelief which hinders in these days this manifestation of the power of God. Who can doubt it? It is not God or His Word which are to blame here; it is our unbelief which prevents the miraculous power of the Lord, and which holds Him back from healing as in past times.

Let our faith awake, let it recognize and adore in Christ the all-power of Him who says, "*I am the Lord that heals you.*" It is by the works of God that we can best understand what His Word tells us, the healings which again are responding to the prayer of faith confirm, by gloriously illustrating, the truth of His promise.

Let us learn to see in the risen Jesus the Divine Healer, and let us receive Him as such. In order that I may recognize in Jesus my justification, my strength, and my wisdom, I must grasp by faith that He is really all this to me; and equally when the Bible tells me that Jesus is the sovereign Healer, I must myself appropriate this truth, and say, "Yes, Lord, it is You who are my Healer." And why may I hold Him as such? It is because He gives Himself to me, that I am "*one plant with Him*" (Romans 6: 5), and that, inseparably united to Him, I thus possess His healing power; it is because His love is pleased to load His beloved with His favors, to communicate Himself with all His heart to all who desire to receive Him. Let us believe that He is ready to extend the treasure of blessing, contained in the name, "*The Lord that heals you,*" to all who know and who can trust in this Divine name.

This is the treatment for the sick indicated by the law of His kingdom. When I bring my sickness to the Lord, I do not depend on what I see, on what I feel or what I think, but on what He says. Even when everything appears contrary to the expected healing, even if it should not take place at the time or in the way that I had thought I should receive it, even when the symptoms seem only to be aggravated, my faith, strengthened by the very waiting, should cling immovably to this Word which has gone out of the mouth of God, "*I am the Lord that heals you.*"

God is ever seeking to make us true believers. Healing and health are of little value if they do not glorify God, and serve to unite us more closely with Him; thus in the matter of healing our faith must always be put to the proof. He who counts on the name of God, who can hear Jesus saying to him, "*Said I not unto you that if you would believe that you would see the glory of God?*" (John 11: 40), will have the joy of receiving from God Himself the healing of the body, and of seeing it take place in a manner worthy of God, and conformably to His promises. …

Jesus and the Doctors

February 19th

"*A woman had an issue of blood twelve years … When she heard of Jesus, she came in among the crowd from behind and touched His garment; for she said, 'If I may touch but His clothes, I shall be whole.' … And straightway her bleeding stopped ….* "

—MARK 5: 25–29

Jesus heals diseases in which earthly physicians can do nothing, for the Father gave Him this power when He charged Him with the work of our redemption. Jesus, in taking upon Him our human body, delivered it from the dominion of sin and Satan; He has made our bodies temples of the Holy Spirit and members of His own body (1 Corinthians 6:15, 19), and even in our day how many have been given up by the doctors as incurable, how many cases of tuberculosis, of gangrene, of paralysis, of dropsy, of blindness and of deafness, have been healed by Him! Is it not then astonishing that so small a number of the sick apply to Him?

The method of Jesus is quite another than that of earthly physicians. They seek to serve God in making use of remedies which are found in the natural world, and God makes use of these remedies according to natural law, according to the natural properties of each, while the healing which proceeds from Jesus is of a totally different order; it is by divine power, the power of the Holy Spirit, that Jesus heals. Thus, the difference between these two modes of healing is very marked. That we may understand it better, let us take an example; here is a physician who is an unbeliever, but extremely clever in his profession; many sick people owe their healing to him. God gives this result by means of the prescribed remedies, and the physicians knowledge of them.

Here is another physician who is a believer, and who prays God's blessing on the remedies which he employs. In this case also, a large number are healed, but neither in the one case nor the other does the healing bring with it any spiritual blessing. They will be preoccupied, even the believing among them, with the remedies which they use, much more than with what the Lord may be doing with them, and in such a case their healing will be more hurtful than beneficial.

On the contrary, when it is Jesus only to whom the sick person applies for healing, he learns to reckon no longer upon remedies, but to put himself into direct relation with His love and His almightiness. In order to obtain such healing, he must commence by confessing and renouncing his sins, and exercising a living faith. Then healing will come directly from the Lord, who takes possession of the sick body, and it thus becomes a blessing for the soul as well as for the body.

But is it not God who has given remedies to man? it is asked. Does not their power come from Him? Without doubt; but on the other hand, is it not God who has given us His Son with all power to heal? Shall we follow the way of natural law with all those who do not yet know Christ, and also with those of His children whose faith is still too weak to abandon themselves to His almightiness; or rather do we choose the way of faith, receiving healing from the Lord and from the Holy Spirit, seeing therein the result and the proof of our redemption?

The healing which is wrought by our Lord Jesus brings with it and leaves behind it more real blessing than the healing which is obtained through physicians. Healing has been a misfortune to more persons than one. On a bed of sickness serious thoughts had taken possession, but from the time of his healing how often has a sick man been found anew far from the Lord! It is not thus when it is Jesus who heals. Healing is granted after confession of sin; therefore, it brings the sufferer nearer to Jesus, and establishes a new link between him and the Lord, it causes him to experience His love and power, it begins within him a new life of faith and holiness. When the woman who had touched the hem of Christ's garment felt that she was healed, she learned something of what divine love means. She went away with the words: "*Daughter, your faith has saved you: go in peace.*"

O you who are suffering from some sickness, know that Jesus the sovereign Healer is yet in our midst. He is close to us, and He is giving anew to His Church manifest proofs of His presence. Are you ready to break with the world, to abandon yourself to Him with faith and confidence? Then fear not, remember that Divine healing is a part of the life of faith. If nobody around you can help you in prayer, if no elder is at hand to pray the prayer of faith, fear not to go yourself to the Lord in the silence of solitude, like the woman who touched the hem of His garment. Commit to Him the care of your body. Get quiet before Him and like the poor woman say, I will be healed. Perhaps it may take some time to break the chains of your unbelief, but assuredly none that wait on Him shall be ashamed. "*Yea, let none that wait on You be ashamed*" (Psalm 25: 3).

The Holy Spirit—The Spirit of Healing

"*Now there are diversities of gifts, but the same Spirit... To another faith by the same Spirit; to another the gifts of healing by the same Spirit*" (1 Corinthians 12: 4, 9). What is it that distinguishes the children of God? What is their glory? It is that God dwells in the midst of them and reveals Himself to them in power (Exodus 33:16; 34: 9–10). Under the New Covenant this dwelling of God in the believer is still more manifest than in former times. God sends the Holy Spirit to His Church, which is the Body of Christ, to act in her with power, and her life and her prosperity depend on Him. The Spirit must find in her unreserved, full liberty, that she may be recognized as the Church of Christ, the Lord's Body. In every age the Church may look for manifestations of the Spirit, for they form our indissoluble unity; "*one body and one Spirit*" (Ephesians 4: 4).

The gift of healing is one of the most beautiful manifestations of the Spirit. It is recorded how God anointed Jesus ... "*Who went about doing good, and healing all ...*" (Acts 10: 38). The Holy Spirit in Him was a healing Spirit, and He was the same in the disciples after Pentecost. Thus the words of our text express what was the continuous experience of the early Church (Acts 3:7; 4:30; 5:12,15-16; 6:8; 8:7; 9:41; 14:9-10; 16:18-19; 19:12; 28: 8-9). The abundant pouring out of the Spirit produced abundant healings. What a lesson for the Church in our days!

Divine healing is the work of the Holy Spirit. Christ's redemption extends its powerful working to the body, and the Holy Spirit is responsible both to transmit it to and maintain it in us. Our body shares in the benefit of the redemption, and even now it can receive the pledge of it by divine healing. It is Jesus who heals, Jesus who anoints and baptizes with the Holy Spirit. Jesus, who baptized His disciples with the same Spirit, is He who sends us the Holy Spirit here on earth either to keep sickness away from us, or to restore us to health when sickness has taken hold upon us.

Divine healing accompanies the sanctification by the Spirit. It is to make us holy that the Holy Spirit makes us partakers of Christ's redemption. Hence His name "Holy." Therefore, the healing which He works is an intrinsic part of His Divine mission, and He bestows it either to lead the sick one to be converted and to believe (Acts 4: 29–30; 5:12,14; 6: 7–8; 8:6, 8; 9: 42), or to confirm the faith of the one already converted. He constrains him thus to renounce sin, and to consecrate himself entirely to God and to His service (I Corinthians 10: 31; James 5: 15, 16; Hebrews 12: 10).

Divine healing tends to glorify Jesus. It is God's will that His Son should be glorified, and the Holy Spirit does this when He comes to show us what the redemption of Christ does for us. The redemption of the mortal body appears almost more marvelous than that of the immortal soul. In these two ways God wills to dwell in us through Christ, and thus to triumph over the flesh. …

Divine healing takes place wherever the Spirit of God works in power. Proofs of this are to be found in the lives of the Reformers, and in those of certain Moravians in their best times. But there are yet other promises touching the pouring out of the Holy Spirit which have not been fulfilled up to this time. Let us live in a holy expectation, praying the Lord to accomplish them in us.

God's Prescription for the Sick

February 20th

"Is any sick among you? Let him call for the elders of the church, and let them pray over him, anointing him with oil in the Name of the Lord; and the prayer of faith shall save the sick, and the Lord shall raise him up.

—JAMES 5:14–15

This text, above all others, is that which most clearly declares to the sick what they have to do in order to be healed. Sickness and its consequences abound in the world. What joy, then, for the believer to learn from the Word of God the way of healing for the sick!

The Bible teaches us that it is the will of God to see His children in good health. The Apostle James has no hesitation in saying that "*the prayer of faith shall save the sick, and the Lord shall raise him up.*" May the Lord teach us to hearken and to receive with simplicity what His Word tells us!

Notice, first, that James here makes a distinction between affliction (or suffering) and sickness. He says (verse 13): "*Is any among you afflicted? Let him pray.*" He does not specify what shall be requested in such a case; still less does he say that deliverance from suffering shall be asked. No; suffering which may arise from various exterior causes is the portion of every Christian. Let us therefore understand that the object of James is to lead the tried believer to ask for deliverance only with a spirit of submission to the will of God, and, above all, to ask the patience which he considers to be the privilege of the believer (James 1: 2–4,12; 5: 7–8).

But in dealing with the words, "*Is any sick among you?*" James replies in quite another manner. Now he says with assurance that the sick may ask for healing with confidence that they shall obtain it, and the Lord will hear them. There is therefore a great difference between suffering and sickness. The Lord Jesus spoke of suffering as being necessary, as being willed and blessed of God; while He says of sickness that it ought to be cured. All other suffering comes to us from without, and will only cease when Jesus shall triumph over the sin and evil which are in the world; while sickness is an evil in the body itself, in this body saved by Christ that it may become the temple of the Holy Spirit, and which, consequently, ought to be healed as soon as the sick believer receives by faith the working of the Holy Spirit, the very life of Jesus.

What is the direction here given to the sick? Let them call for the elders of the church, and let the elders pray for them. In the time of James there were physicians, but it is not to them the sick believer must turn. The elders then were the pastors and leaders of the churches, called to the ministry not because they had passed through schools of theology, but because they were filled with the Holy Spirit, and well known for their piety and for their faith. Why should their presence be needed by the sick one? Could not friends have prayed? Yes; but it is not so easy for everybody to exercise the faith which obtains healing, and, doubtless, that is one reason why James desired that those should be called whose faith was firm and sure. Besides this, they were representatives to the sick one of the Church, the collective body of Christ, for it is the communion of believers which invites the Spirit to act with power.

In short, the elders should, after the pattern of the great Shepherd of the sheep, care for the flock as He does, identify themselves with the sick, understand their trouble, receive from God the necessary discernment to instruct them and encourage them to persevere in faith. It is, then, to the elders of the Church that the healing of the sick is committed, and it is they, the servants of the God who pardons iniquities and heals diseases (Psalm 103), who are called to transmit to others the Lord's graces for soul and body.

"*The prayer of faith shall save the sick, and the Lord shall raise him up.*" This promise ought to stimulate in every believer the desire and expectation of healing. Receiving these words with simplicity and as they are written, ought we not to see in them an unlimited promise, offering healing to whomsoever shall pray in faith? The Lord teach us to study His Word with the faith of a truly believing heart!

Sickness and Death

February 21st

"With long life will I satisfy him, and show him My salvation."

—PSALM 91:16

How can a sick person know whether God, who fixes the time of our life, has not decided that we shall die by such a sickness? In such a case, would not prayer be useless … to ask for healing?

Before replying, we would remark that this objection touches not such as believe in Jesus as the Healer of the sick, but the Word of God itself, and the promise so clearly declared in the epistle of James and elsewhere.

We are not at liberty to change or to limit the promises of God whenever they present some difficulty to us; neither can we insist that they shall be clearly explained to us before we can bring ourselves to believe what they state. It is for us to begin by receiving them without resistance; then only can the Spirit of God find us in the state of mind in which we can be taught and enlightened.

Furthermore, we would remark that in considering a divine truth which has been for a long time neglected in the Church, it can hardly be understood at the outset. It is only little by little that its importance and bearing are discerned. In measure as it revives, after it has been accepted by faith, the Holy Spirit will accompany it with new light. Let us remember that it is by the unbelief of the Church that divine healing has left her. It is not on the answers of such or such a one that faith in Bible truths should be made to depend. "*There arises light in the darkness*" (Psalm 112: 4) for the "upright" who are ready to submit themselves to the Word of God. …

Scripture fixes seventy or eighty years as the ordinary measure of human life. "*The days of our years are threescore years and ten; and if by reason of strength they be fourscore years, yet is their strength labor and sorrow; for it is soon cut off, and we fly away*" (Psalm 90: 10). The believer who receives Jesus as the Healer of the sick will rest satisfied then with the declaration of the Word of God. He will feel at liberty to expect a life of seventy years, but not longer. The believer who receives Jesus as the Healer of the sick will rest satisfied then with the declaration of the Word of God. We will feel at liberty to expect a life of seventy years, but not longer. Besides, as people of faith, we place ourselves under the direction of the Spirit, which will enable us to discern the will of God if something should prevent our attaining the age of seventy.

Every rule has its exceptions, in the things of heaven as in the things of earth. Of this, therefore, we are sure according to the Word of God, whether by the words of Jesus or by those of James, that our heavenly Father wills, as a rule, to see His children in good health that they may labor in His service.

For the same reason, the Father wills to set us free from sickness as soon as we have made confession of sin and prayed with faith for our healing. For believers who have walked with our Savior, strong with the strength which proceeds from Divine healing, and whose bodies are consequently under the influence of the Holy Spirit, it is not necessary that when our time comes to die, we should die of sickness. To fall asleep in Jesus Christ, such is the death of believers when the end of our life is come. …

The promise, "*That it may be well with you, and you may live long on the earth*" (Ephesians 6: 3), is addressed to us who live under the New Covenant. The more we have learned to see in the Savior Him who "*took our infirmities*" (Matthew 8:17), the more we have the liberty to claim the literal fulfillment of the promises: "*With long life will I satisfy him*" (Psalm 91:16); "*They shall bring forth fruit in old age* (Psalm 92:14).

The sick one sees in God's Word that it is His will to heal His children after the confession of their sins, and in answer to the prayer of faith. It does not follow that they shall be exempt from other trials; but as for sickness, they are healed of it because it attacks the body, which is become the dwelling place of the Holy Spirit. The sick one should then desire healing that the power of God may be made manifest in them, and that they may serve Him in accomplishing His will. …

We would insist here that faith is not a logical reasoning which ought in some way to oblige God to act according to His promises. It is rather the confiding attitude of the child who honors his Father, who counts upon His love to see Him fulfilling His promises, and who knows that He is faithful to communicate to the body as well as to the soul the new strength which flows from the redemption, until the moment of departure is come.

Your Body is the Temple of the Holy Spirit

February 22nd

"Know you not that your bodies are the members of Christ? ...Know you not that your body is the temple of the Holy Spirit which is in you, which you have of God, and you are not your own? For you are bought with a price; therefore, glorify God in your body, and in your spirit, which are God's."

—1 CORINTHIANS 6:15, 19–20

When the Church understands that the body also has part in the redemption which is by Christ, by which it ought to be brought back to its original destiny, to be the dwelling place of the Holy Spirit, to serve as His instrument, to be sanctified by His presence, she will also recognize all the place which Divine healing has in the Bible and in the counsels of God.

The account of the creation tells us that man is composed of three parts. God first formed the body from the dust of the earth, after which He breathed into it "*the breath of life*" (Genesis 2: 7). He caused His own life, His Spirit, to enter into it. By this union of Spirit with matter, the man became a "*living soul*" (2: 7). The soul, which is essentially the man, finds its place between the body and the spirit; it is the link which binds them together. ... The soul, subject to the solicitations of both spirit and body, is in a position to choose between the voice of God, speaking by the Spirit, or the voice of the world, speaking through the senses.

This union of spirit and body forms a combination which is unique in the creation; it makes man to be the jewel of God's work. Other creatures had existed already; some, like angels, were all spirit, without any material body, and others, like the animals, were only flesh, possessing a body animated with a living soul, but devoid of spirit. Man was destined to show that the material body, governed by the spirit, was capable of being transformed by the power of the Spirit of God, and of being thus led to participate of heavenly glory.

We know what sin and Satan have done with this possibility of gradual transformation. By means of the body, the spirit was tempted, seduced, and became a slave of sense. We know also what God has done to destroy the work of Satan and to accomplish the purpose of creation. "*The Son of God was manifested that he might destroy the works of the Devil*" (1 John 3:8). God prepared a body for His Son (Hebrews 10:5). Wherefore when He cometh into the world, He said, "*Sacrifice and offering You would not, but a body You prepared for Me.*" "*The Word was made flesh*" (John 1: 14). "*In Him dwells all the fullness of the Godhead bodily*" (Colossians 2: 9). "*Who His Own Self bare our sins in His Own Body on the tree*" (1 Peter

2: 24). And now Jesus, raised up from the dead with a body as free from sin as His spirit and His soul, communicates to our body the virtue of His glorified body. The Lord's Supper is "*the communion of the body of Christ*"; and our bodies are "*the members of Christ*" (1 Corinthians 10: 16; 6: 15; 12: 27).

Faith puts us in possession of all that the death of Christ and His resurrection have procured for us, and it is not only in our spirit and our soul that the life of the risen Jesus manifests its presence here below; it is in the body also that it would act according to the measure of our faith. "*Do you not know that your body is the temple of the Holy Spirit?*"

Many believers represent to themselves that the Holy Spirit comes to dwell in our body as we dwell in a house. Nothing of the kind. I can dwell in a house without its becoming part of my being. I may leave it without suffering; no vital union exists between my house and me. It is not thus with the presence of our soul and spirit in our body. The life of a plant lives in and pervades every part of it; and our soul is not limited to dwell in such or such part of the body, the heart or the head, for instance, but penetrates throughout, even to the end of the lowest members. The life of the soul pervades the whole body; the life throughout proves the presence of the soul. It is in like manner that the Holy Spirit comes to dwell in our body. He penetrates its entirety. He animates and possesses us infinitely more than we can imagine. In the same way in which the Holy Spirit brings to our soul and spirit the life of Jesus, His holiness, His joy, His strength, He comes also to impart to the sick body all the vigorous vitality of Christ as soon as the hand of faith is stretched out to receive it.

When the body is fully subject to Christ, crucified with Him, renouncing all Self-will and independence, desiring nothing but to be the Lord's temple, it is then that the Holy Spirit manifests the power of the risen Savior in the body. Then only can we glorify God in our body, leaving Him full freedom to manifest therein His power, to show that He knows how to set His temple free from the domination of sickness, sin, and Satan.

The Body for the Lord

"*Now the body is ... for the Lord; and the Lord for the body*" (1 Corinthians 6: 13). Many believers fail to watch over their bodies fail to observe a holy sobriety so as to avoid rendering their bodies unfit for the service of God. Eating and drinking should never impede communion with God; their purpose is, rather, to facilitate communion by maintaining the body in its normal condition.

The apostle speaks also of fornication, this sin which defiles the body, and which is in direct opposition to the words, "*The body is... for the Lord.*" It is not simply incontinence outside the married state, but in that state also, which is meant here; all voluptuousness, all want of sobriety of whatsoever kind is condemned in these words: "*Your body is the temple of the Holy Spirit*" (1 Corinthians 6: 19). In the same way, all what goes to maintain the body to clothe it, strengthen it, rest it in sleep, or afford it enjoyment should be placed under the control of the Holy Spirit. As under the Old Covenant, the temple was constructed solely for God, and for His service, even so our body has been created for the Lord and for Him alone.

One of the chief benefits then of Divine healing will be to teach us that our body ought to be set free from the yoke of our own will to become the Lord's property. God does not grant healing to our prayers until He has attained the end for which He has permitted the sickness. He wills that this discipline should bring us into a more intimate communion with Him; He would make us understand that we have regarded our body as our own property, while it belonged to the Lord; and that the Holy Spirit seeks to sanctify all its actions. He leads us to understand that if we yield our body unreservedly to the influence of the Holy Spirit, we shall experience His power in us, and He will heal us by bringing into our body the very life of Jesus; He leads us, in short, to say with full conviction, "*The body is... for the Lord.*" ...

Oh, what a renewing takes place in us when, by His own touch, the Lord heals our bodies, when He takes possession of them, and when by His Spirit He becomes life and health to them! It is with an indescribable consciousness of holiness, of fear and of joy that the believer can then offer his body a living sacrifice to receive healing, and to have for his motto these words: "*The body is... for the Lord.*"

Jesus Heals the Sick

February 23rd

"He healed all who were sick, that it might be fulfilled which was spoken by Esaias the prophet, saying: He took our infirmities and bore our sicknesses."

—MATTHEW 8:16–17

It is expressly said regarding all the sick ones whom Jesus healed, "*That it might be fulfilled which was spoken by Esaias the prophet.*" It was because Jesus had taken on Him our sicknesses that He could—that He ought to—heal them. If He had not done so, one part of His work of redemption would have remained powerless and fruitless.

This text of the Word of God is not generally understood in this way. It is the generally accepted view that the miraculous healings done by the Lord Jesus are to be looked upon only as the proof of His mercy, or as being the symbol of spiritual graces. They are not seen to be a necessary consequence of redemption, although that is what the Bible declares. The body and the soul have been created to serve together as a habitation of God; the sickly condition of the body is, as well as that of the soul, a consequence of sin, and that is what Jesus came to bear, to expiate and to conquer.

When the Lord Jesus was on earth, it was not in the character of the Son of God that He cured the sick, but as the Mediator who had borne sickness. This enables us to understand why Jesus gave so much time to His healing work, and why also the evangelists speak of it in a manner so detailed.

Read for example what Matthew says about it: When the disciples of John the Baptist came to ask Jesus if He were the Messiah, that He might prove it to them, He replied,

"*The blind receive their sight, and the lame walk, the lepers are cleansed, and the deaf hear, the dead are raised up, and the poor have the Gospel preached to them*" (11: 5). After the cure of the withered hand, and the opposition of the Pharisees who sought to destroy Him, we read that "*great multitudes followed Him, and He healed them all*" (12: 15). When later, the multitude had followed Him into a desert place, it is said, "*And Jesus went forth and saw a great multitude, and was moved with compassion toward them, and He healed their sick*" (14:14). Farther on: "*They sent out into all that country round about, and brought unto Him all that were diseased; and besought Him that they might only touch the hem of His garment; and as many as touched were made perfectly whole*" (14: 35–36). It is said also of the sick which were among the multitudes that they "*cast them down at Jesus feet and He healed them,*" and Matthew adds: "*insomuch that the multitude wondered when they saw the dumb to speak, the maimed to be whole, the lame to walk, and the blind to see; and they glorified the God of Israel*" (15: 30–31). And finally, when He came into the coasts of Judea beyond Jordan, "*Great multitudes followed Him, and He healed them there*" (19: 2).

Let us add to these many texts those which give us in detail the account of healings wrought by Jesus, and let us ask ourselves if these healings afford us only the proof of His power during His life here on earth, or if they are not much rather the undoubted and continual result of His work of mercy and of love, the manifestation of His power of redemption which delivers the soul and body from the dominion of sin? Yes; that was in very deed the purpose of God.

If, then, Jesus bore our sicknesses as an integral part of the redemption, if He has healed the sick "*that it might be fulfilled which was spoken by Esaias,*" and if His Savior-heart is always full of mercy and of love, we can believe with certainty that to this very day it is the will of Jesus to heal the sick in answer to the prayer of faith.

According to the Measure of Faith

"*And Jesus said unto the centurion, Go your way; and as you have believed, so be it done unto you. And his servant was healed in the same hour*" (Matthew 8: 13). This passage of Scripture brings before us one of the principal laws of the kingdom of Heaven. In order to understand God's ways with His people, and our relations with the Lord, it is needful to understand this law thoroughly and not to deviate from it. Not only does God give or withhold His gifts according to the faith or unbelief of each, but they are granted in greater or lesser measure, only in proportion to the faith which receives them.

God respects the right to decide which He has conferred on man. Therefore, He can only bless us in the measure in which each yields to His Divine working, and opens all the heart to Him. Faith in God is nothing else than the full opening of the heart to receive everything from God; therefore, we can only receive Divine grace according to our faith; and this applies as much to Divine healing as to any other grace of God.

This truth is confirmed by the spiritual blessings which may result from sickness. Two questions are often asked: First, is it not God's will that His children should sometimes remain in a prolonged state of sickness? Second, since it is a recognized thing that Divine healing brings with it greater spiritual blessing than the sickness itself, why does God allow certain of His children to continue sick through many years, and while in this condition give them blessing in sanctification, and in communion with Himself?

The answer to these two questions is that God gives to His children according to their faith. We have already had occasion to remark that in the same degree in which the Church has become worldly, her faith in Divine healing has diminished until at last it has disappeared. Believers do not seem to be aware that they may ask God for the healing of their sickness, and that thereby they may be sanctified and fitted for His service. They have come to seek only submission to His will and to regard sickness as a means to be separate from the world. In such conditions the Lord gives them what they ask. He would have been ready to give them yet more, to grant them healing in answer to the prayer of faith, but they lacked the faith to receive it. God always meets His children where they are, howsoever weak they may be. …

Many sick people, having witnessed the healing of others, gained confidence in Jesus just far enough to be healed, and Jesus granted them their request, without adding other blessings for their souls. Before His ascension the Lord had not as free an entrance as He now has into our hearts, because "*the Holy Spirit was not yet given*" (John 7: 39). The healing of the sick was then hardly more than a blessing for the body. It was only later, in the dispensation of the Spirit, that the conviction and confession of sin have become for the believer the first grace to be received, the essential condition for obtaining healing, as St. Paul tells us in his Epistle to the Corinthians, and James in his: "*For if we would judge ourselves, we should not be judged; But when we are judged, we are chastened of the Lord, that we should not be condemned with the world*" (1 Corinthians 11: 31, 32); "*Confess your faults one to another, and pray one for another, that you may be healed*" (James 5: 16).

Health and Salvation by the Name of Jesus

February 24th

By the Name of Jesus Christ of Nazareth, whom you crucified, whom God raised from the dead, even by Him does this man stand here before you whole. … Neither is there salvation in any other: for there is none other name under Heaven given among men, whereby we must be saved."

—ACTS 4:10, 12

When after Pentecost, the paralytic was healed through Peter and John at the gate of the temple, it was in "*the Name of Jesus Christ of Nazareth*" that they said to him, "*Rise up and walk*," and as soon as the people in their amazement ran together to them, Peter declared that it was the name of Jesus which had so completely healed the man. As the result of this miracle and of Peter's discourse, many people who had heard the Word believed (Acts 4: 4). On the morrow Peter repeated these words before the Sanhedrin, "*By the Name of Jesus Christ of Nazareth... does this man stand here before you whole*"; and then he added, "*There is none other name under Heaven. ... whereby we must be saved.*" This statement of Peter's declares to us that the name of Jesus both heals and saves. We have here a teaching of the highest import for Divine healing.

We see that healing and health form part of Christ's salvation. Does not Peter clearly state this in his discourse to the Sanhedrin where, having spoken of healing, he immediately goes on to speak of salvation by Christ? (Acts 4: 10,12). In Heaven, even our bodies will have their part in salvation; salvation will not be complete for us until our bodies shall enjoy the full redemption of Christ. Why then should we not believe in this work of redemption here below? Even already here on earth, the health of our bodies is a fruit of the salvation which Jesus has acquired for us.

We see also that health as well as salvation is to be obtained by faith. The tendency of mankind by nature is to bring about our salvation by our works, and it is only with difficulty that we come to receive it by faith; but when it is a question of the healing of the body, we have still more difficulty in seizing it. As to salvation, we end it by accepting it because by no other means can we open the door of Heaven; while for the body, we make use of well-known remedies. Why then should we seek for Divine healing?

Happy is the one who comes to understand that it is the will of God; that God wills to manifest the power of Jesus, and also to reveal to us His Fatherly love; to exercise and to confirm our faith, and to make us prove the power of redemption in the body as well as in the soul. The body is part of our being; even the body has been saved by Christ; therefore, it is in our body that our Father wills to manifest the power of redemption, and to let others see that Jesus lives. Oh, let us believe in the name of Jesus! Was it not in the name of Jesus that perfect health was given to the impotent man? And were not these words: Your faith has saved you, pronounced when the body was healed? Let us seek then to obtain Divine healing.

Wherever the Spirit acts with power, there He works Divine healings. Would it not seem that if ever miracles were superfluous, it was at Pentecost, for then the word of the apostles worked mightily, and the pouring out of the Holy Spirit was abundant? ... If Divine healing is seen but rarely in our day, we can attribute it to no other cause than that the Spirit does not act with power. The unbelief of worldlings and the want of zeal among believers stop His working. The healings which God is giving here and there are the precursory signs of all the spiritual graces which are promised to us, and it is only the Holy Spirit who reveals the almightiness of the name of Jesus to operate such healings. Let us pray earnestly for the Holy Spirit, let us place ourselves unreservedly under His direction, and let us seek to be firm in our faith in the name of Jesus, whether for preaching salvation or for the work of healing.

God grants healing to glorify the name of Jesus. Let us seek to be healed by Jesus that His name may be glorified. It is sad to see how little the power of His name is recognized, how little it is the end of preaching and of prayer. Treasures of Divine grace, of which Christians deprive themselves by their lack of faith and zeal, are hidden in the name of Jesus. It is the will of God to glorify His Son in the Church; and He will do it wherever He finds faith. Whether among believers, or whether among the heathen, He is ready with virtue from on high to awaken consciences, and to bring hearts to obedience. God is ready to manifest the all-power of His Son, and to do it in a striking way in body as well as in soul. Let us believe it for ourselves, let us believe it for others, for the circle of believers around us, and also for the Church in the whole world. Let us give ourselves to believe with firm faith in the power of the name of Jesus, let us ask great things in His name, counting on His promise, and we shall see God still do wonders by the name of His holy Son.

Do Not Consider Your Body

February 25th

"Yield your members as servants to righteousness unto holiness."
—ROMANS 6: 20

There is a difference between] the healing which is expected from earthly remedies and the healing which is looked for from God only. When we have recourse to remedies for healing, all the attention of the sick one is upon the body, considering the body, while Divine healing calls us to turn away our attention from the body, and to abandon ourselves, soul and body, to the Lord's care, occupying ourselves with Him alone. …

It is true that in the case of healing obtained by earthly remedies, many people would be more blessed in remaining ill than in recovering health, but it is quite otherwise when healing comes directly from the hand of God. In order to receive Divine healing, sin must be so truly confessed and renounced, one must be so completely surrendered to the Lord, Self must be so really yielded up to be wholly in His hands, and the will of Jesus to take charge of the body must be so firmly counted on that the healing becomes the commencement of a new life of intimate communion with the Lord.

Thus we learn to give up to Him entirely the care of the health, and the smallest indication of the return of the evil is regarded as a warning not to consider our body, but to be occupied with the Lord only.

What a contrast this is from the greater number of sick people who look for healing from remedies. If some few of them have been sanctified by the sickness, having learned to lose sight of themselves, how many more are there who are drawn by the sickness itself to be constantly occupied with themselves and with the condition of their body. What infinite care they exercise in observing the least symptom, favorable or unfavorable! What a constant preoccupation to them is their eating and drinking, the anxiety to avoid this or that! How much they are taken up with what they consider due to them from others, whether they are sufficiently thought of, whether well enough nursed, whether visited often enough! How much time is thus devoted to considering the body and what it exacts, rather than the Lord and the relations which He seeks to establish with their souls! Oh, how many are they who, through sickness, are occupied almost exclusively with themselves!

All this is totally different when healing is looked for in faith from the loving God. Then the first thing to learn is to cease to be anxious about the state of your body, you have trusted it to the Lord and He has taken the responsibility. If you do not see a rapid improvement immediately, but on the contrary the symptoms appear to be more serious, remember that you have entered on a path of faith, and therefore you ought not to consider the body, but cling only to the living God.

The commandment of Christ, "*Be not anxious for your... body*" (Matthew 6: 25), appears here in a new light. When God called Abraham not to consider his own body, it was that He might call him to the greatest exercise of faith which could be, that he might learn to see only God and His promise. Sustained by his faith, he gave glory to God, convinced that God would do what He had promised.

Divine healing is a marvelous tie to bind us to the Lord. At first one may fear to believe that the Lord will stretch forth His mighty hand and touch the body; but in studying the Word of God the soul takes courage and confidence. At last one decides, saying, "I yield up my body into the hands of God; and I leave the care of it to Him." Then the body and its sensations are lost sight of, and only the Lord and His promise are in view.

Will you also enter upon this way of faith …? Walk in the steps of Abraham. Learn from him not to consider your own body, and not to doubt through unbelief. To consider the body gives birth to doubts, while clinging to the promise of God and being occupied with Him alone gives entrance into the way of faith, the way of Divine healing, which glorifies God.

Because of Your Unbelief

February 26th

"Then the disciples came to Jesus privately, and said, Why could not we cast him out? And Jesus said unto them, Because of your unbelief: for I say unto you, If you have faith as a grain of mustard seed, you shall say unto this mountain, Remove hence to yonder place; and it shall remove; and nothing shall be impossible to you."

—MATTHEW 17:19–20

When the Lord Jesus sent His disciples into different parts of Palestine, He endued them with a double power—that of casting out unclean spirits and that of healing all sickness and all infirmity (Matthew 10: 1). He did the same for the seventy who came back to Him with joy, saying, "*Lord, even the spirits are subject unto us through Your Name*" (Luke 10:17). On the day of the Transfiguration, while the Lord was still upon the mountain, a father brought his son who was possessed with a demon, to His disciples, beseeching them to cast out the evil spirit, but they could not. When, after Jesus had cured the child, the disciples asked Him why they had been unable to do it themselves as in other cases. He answered them, "*Because of your unbelief.*" It was, then, their unbelief, and not the will of God which had been the cause of their defeat.

In our days Divine healing is very little believed in, because it has almost entirely disappeared from the Christian Church. One may ask the reason, and here are the two answers which have been given. The greater number think that miracles, the gift of healing included, should be limited to the time of the primitive Church, that their object was to establish the first foundation of Christianity, but that from that time circumstances have altered.

Other believers say unhesitatingly that if the Church has lost these gifts, it is by her own fault; it is because she has become worldly that the Spirit acts but feebly in her; it is because she has not remained in direct and habitual relation with the full power of the unseen world; but that if she were to see anew springing up within her men and women who live the life of faith and of the Holy Spirit, entirely consecrated to their God, she would see again the manifestation of the same gifts as in former times.

Which of these two opinions coincides the most with the Word of God? Is it by the will of God that the "gifts of healing" have been suppressed, or is it rather we who are responsible for it? Is it the will of God that miracles should not take place? Will He in consequence of this no longer give the faith which produces them? Or again, is it the Church which has been guilty of lacking faith?

What does the Scripture say? The Bible does not authorize us, either by the words of the Lord or His apostles, to believe that the gifts of healing were granted only to the early times of the Church. On the contrary, the promises which Jesus made to the apostles when He gave them instructions concerning their mission, shortly before His ascension, appear to us applicable to all times (Mark 16: 15–18). Paul places the gift of healing among the operations of the Holy Spirit. James gives a precise command on this matter without any restriction of time. The entire Scriptures declare that these graces will be granted according to the measure of the Spirit and of faith.

It is also alleged that, at the outset of each new dispensation, God works miracles, that it is His ordinary course of action; but it is nothing of the kind. Think of the people of God in the former dispensation, in the time of Abraham, all through the life of Moses, in the exodus from Egypt, under Joshua, in the time of the Judges and of Samuel, under the reign of David and other godly kings up to Daniel's time; during more than a thousand-years miracles took place. But, it is said, miracles were much more necessary in the early days of Christianity than later. But what about the power of heathenism even in this day, wherever the Gospel seeks to combat it? It is impossible to admit that miracles should have been more needful for the heathen in Ephesus (Acts 19: 11–12) than for the heathen of Africa in the present day.

And if we think of the ignorance and unbelief which reign even in the midst of the Christian nations, are we not driven to conclude that there is a need for manifest acts of the power of God to sustain the testimony of believers and to prove that God is with them? Besides, among believers themselves, how much of doubt, how much of weakness there is! How their faith needs to be awakened and stimulated by some evident proof of the presence of the Lord in their midst. One part of our being consists of flesh and blood; it is therefore in flesh and blood that God wills to manifest His presence.

In order to prove that it is the Church's unbelief which has lost the gift of healing, let us see what the Bible says about it. Does not the history of the Church show us the necessity of these warnings? Does it not furnish us with numerous examples of backward steps, of world pleasing, in which faith grew weak in the exact measure in which the spirit of the world took the upper hand? For such faith is only possible to him who lives in the world invisible. Until the third century the healings by faith in Christ were numerous, but in the centuries following they became more infrequent. Do we not know from the Bible that it is always unbelief which hinders the mighty working of God?

Oh, that we could learn to believe in the promises of God! God has not gone back from His promises; Jesus is still He who heals both soul and body; salvation offers us even now healing and holiness, and the Holy Spirit is always ready to give us some manifestations of His power. Even when we ask why this Divine power is not more often seen, He answers us: "*Because of your unbelief.*"

The more we give ourselves to experience personally sanctification by faith, the more we shall also experience healing by faith. These two doctrines walk abreast. The more the Spirit of God lives and acts in the soul of believers, the more will the miracles multiply by which He works in the body. Thereby the world can recognize what redemption means.

Discipline and Sanctification

February 27th

"If you endure chastening, God deals with you as with sons; for what son is he whom the Father chastens not?... God chastens us for our profit, that we may be partakers of His holiness."

—HEBREWS 12: 7, 10

To sanctify anything is to set apart—to consecrate to God and to His service. The temple at Jerusalem was holy; that is to say, it was consecrated—dedicated to God that it might serve Him as a dwelling place. The vessels of the temple were holy, because they were devoted to the service of the temple. The priests were holy, chosen to serve God and ready to work for Him. In the same way the Christian ought also to be sanctified, at the Lord's disposal, ready to do every good work.

When the people of Israel went out of Egypt, the Lord reclaimed them for His service as a holy people: "*Let my people go that they may serve Me*" (Exodus 7:16), He said to Pharaoh. Set free from their hard bondage, the children of Israel were debtors to enter at once upon the service of God, and to become His happy servants. Their deliverance was the road which led to their sanctification.

Again in this day, God is forming for Himself a holy people.... [Jesus] "*gave Himself for us that He might redeem us from all iniquity, and purify unto Himself a people for His own possession, zealous of good works*" (Titus 2:14). It is the Lord who breaks the chains by which Satan would hold us in bondage. He would have us free, wholly free to serve Him. He wills to save us, to deliver both the soul and the body, that each of the members of the body may be consecrated to Him and placed unreservedly at His disposal.

A large number of Christians do not yet understand all this, they do not know how to take in that the purpose of their deliverance is that they may be sanctified, prepared to serve their God. They make use of their life and their members to procure their own satisfaction; consequently, they do not feel at liberty to ask for healing with faith. It is therefore to chasten them that they may be brought to desire sanctification that the Lord permits Satan to inflict sickness upon them and by it keep them chained and prisoners (Luke 13:11,16). God chastens us "*for our profit, that we may be partakers of His holiness*" (Hebrews 12:10), and that we may be sanctified, "*meet for the Master's use*" (2 Timothy 2: 21).

The discipline which inflicts the sickness brings great blessings with it. It is a call to the sick one to reflect; it leads him to see that God is occupied with him, and seeks to show him what there is which still separates him from Himself. God speaks to him, He calls him to examine his ways, to acknowledge that he has lacked holiness, and that the purpose of the chastisement is to make him partaker of His holiness. He awakens within him the desire to be enlightened by the Holy Spirit down into the inmost recesses of his heart, that he may be enabled to get a clear idea of what his life has been up to the present time, a life of Self-will, very unlike the holy life which God requires of him. He leads him to confess his sins, to entrust them to the Lord Jesus, to believe that the Savior can deliver him from them. He urges him to yield to Him, to consecrate his life to Him, to die to himself that he may be able to live unto God.

Sanctification is not something which you can accomplish yourself; it cannot even be produced by God in you as something which you can possess and contemplate in yourself. No, it is the Holy Spirit, the Spirit of holiness alone who can communicate His holiness to you and renew it continually. Therefore it is by faith you can become partakers of his holiness.

Having understood that Jesus has been made unto you of God sanctification (1 Corinthians 1: 30), and that it is the Holy Spirits work to impart to you His holiness which was manifested in His life on earth, surrender yourself to Him by faith that He may enable you to live that life from hour to hour. Believe that the Lord will by His Spirit lead you into, and keep you in this life of holiness and of consecration to God's service. Live thus in the obedience of faith, always attentive to His voice, and the guidance of His Spirit.

From the time that this Fatherly discipline has led the sick one to a life of holiness, God has attained His purpose, and He will heal him who asks it in faith. Our earthly parents "*for a few days chastened us... All chastening seems for the present to be not joyous, but grievous: yet afterward it yields peaceable fruit unto them that have been exercised thereby, even the fruit of righteousness*" (Hebrews 12: 10–11). Yes, it is when the believer realizes this "*peaceable fruit... of righteousness*," that he is in a condition to be delivered from the chastisement.

Oh, it is because believers still understand so little that sanctification means an entire consecration to God that they cannot really believe that healing will quickly follow the sanctification of the sick one. Good health is too often for them only a matter of personal comfort and enjoyment which they may dispose of at their will, but God cannot thus minister to their Selfishness. If they understood better that God requires of His children that they should be "*sanctified and meet for the Master's use*," they would not be surprised to see Him giving healing and renewed strength to those who have learned to place all their members at His disposal, willing to be sanctified and employed in His service by the Holy

Spirit. The Spirit of healing is also the Spirit of sanctification.

Is Sickness a Chastisement?

"For this cause many among you are weak and sickly, and not a few sleep. For if we discerned ourselves, we should not be judged. But when we are judged, we are chastened of the Lord, that we may not be condemned with the world" (1 Corinthians 11: 30–32). Sickness is, more often than we believe it, a judgment, a chastisement for sin. ... It is not without a cause that He deprives us of health. Perhaps it may be to render us attentive to some sin which we can recognize: *"Sin no more, lest a worse thing come unto you"* (John 5:14); perhaps because God's child has become entangled in pride and worldliness; or it may be that Self-confidence or caprice have been mixed with service for God. ... Thus, in many a case, sickness is a discipline which ought to awaken our attention to sin, and turn us from it.

Therefore, a sick person should begin by condemning, or discerning himself (1 Corinthians 11:31), by placing himself before his heavenly Father with a sincere desire to see anything which could have grieved Him, or could have rendered the chastisement necessary. ... Let us be ready at once to renounce what we may discern, and to place our Self at the Lord's disposal to serve Him with perfect obedience, but let us not imagine that we can conquer sin by our own efforts. No, that is impossible to him. But let us, with all power of will, be on God's side in renouncing what is sin in His sight, and let us believe that we are accepted of Him. So doing, we will be yielding our Self, consecrating our Self anew to God, willing to do only His holy will in all things.

Scripture assures us that if we thus examine ourselves the Lord will not judge us. Our Father only chastens His child as far as needful. God seeks to deliver us from sin and Self; as soon as we understand Him and break with these, sickness may cease; it has done its work. We must come to see what the sickness means, and recognize in it the discipline of God. One may recognize vaguely that he commits sins while scarcely attempting to define what they are; or if he does, he may not believe it is possible to give them up; and if he decides to renounce them, he may fail to count on God that He will put an end to the chastisement. And yet, how glorious is the assurance which Paul's words here give us!

Dear sick one, do you understand that your heavenly Father has something to reprove in you? He would have your sickness help you to discover it, and the Holy Spirit will guide you in the search. Then renounce at once what He may point out to you.... It is His will to pardon our sin and to heal our sickness. In Jesus we have both pardon and healing; they are two sides of His redemptive work. He calls us to live a life of dependence upon Him in a greater degree than hitherto. Abandon yourself, then, to Him in a complete obedience, and walk henceforth as a little child in following His steps. It is with joy that your heavenly Father will deliver you from chastisement, that He will reveal Himself to you as your Healer, that He will bring you nearer to Him by this new tie of His love, that He will make you obedient and faithful in serving Him. If, as a wise and faithful Father, He has been obliged to chasten you, it is also as a Father that He wills your healing, and that He desires to bless and keep you henceforth.

The Holy Spirit: The Spirit of Healing

February 28th

"Now there are diversities of gifts, but the same Spirit... To another faith by the same Spirit; to another the gifts of healing by the same Spirit... But all these works that one and the Selfsame Spirit..."

—1 CORINTHIANS 12: 4, 9, 11)

What is it that distinguishes the children of God? What is their glory? It is that God dwells in the midst of them and reveals Himself to them in power. ... Under the New Covenant this dwelling of God in the believer is still more manifest than in former times. God sends the Holy Spirit to His Church, which is the Body of Christ, to act in her with power, and her life and her prosperity depend on Him. The Spirit must find in her unreserved, full liberty, that she may be recognized as the Church of Christ, the Lord's Body. In every age the Church may look for manifestations of the Spirit, for they form our indissoluble unity; "*one body and one Spirit*" (Ephesians 4: 4).

The Spirit operates variously in such or such a member of the Church. It is possible to be filled with the Spirit for one special work and not for another. There are also times in the history of the Church when certain gifts of the Spirit are given with power, while at the same time ignorance or unbelief may hinder other gifts. Wherever the life more abundant of the Spirit is to be found, we may expect Him to manifest all His gifts.

The gift of healing is one of the most beautiful manifestations of the Spirit. It is recorded of Jesus, "*how God anointed Jesus of Nazareth... Who went about doing good, and healing all that were oppressed of the Devil*" (Acts 10: 38). The Holy Spirit in Him was a healing Spirit, and He was the same in the disciples after Pentecost.

Thus, the words of our text express what was the continuous experience of the early Church (compare attentively Acts 3:7; 4:30; 5:12,15-16; 6:8; 8:7; 9:41; 14:9-10; 16:18-19; 19:12; 28: 8-9). For example: "*And by the hands of the apostles were many signs and wonders wrought among the people; (and they were all with one accord in Solomon's porch* (Acts 5: 12); "*Insomuch that they brought forth the sick into the streets, and laid them on beds and couches, that at the least the shadow of Peter passing by might overshadow some of them. There came also a multitude out of the cities round about unto Jerusalem, bringing sick folks, and them which were vexed with unclean spirits: and they were healed every one*" (Acts 5: 15 –16); "*So that from Paul's body were brought unto the sick handkerchiefs or aprons, and the diseases departed from them, and the evil spirits went out of them*" (Acts 19: 12).

The abundant pouring out of the Spirit produced abundant healings. What a lesson for the Church in our days! Divine healing is the work of the Holy Spirit. Christ's redemption extends its powerful working to the body, and the Holy Spirit is responsible both to transmit it to and maintain it in us. Our body shares in the benefit of the redemption, and even now it can receive the pledge of it by divine healing.

It is Jesus who heals, Jesus who anoints and baptizes with the Holy Spirit. Jesus, who baptized His disciples with the same Spirit, is He who sends us the Holy Spirit here on earth either to keep sickness away from us, or to restore us to health when sickness has taken hold upon us.

Divine healing accompanies the sanctification by the Spirit. It is to make us holy that the Holy Spirit makes us partakers of Christ's redemption. Hence His name "Holy." Therefore, the healing which He works is an intrinsic part of His Divine mission, and He bestows it either to lead the sick one to be converted and to believe (Acts 4: 29-30; 5: 12, 14; 6: 7–8; 8: 6, 8; 9: 42) or to confirm his faith if he is already converted.

Divine healing tends to glorify Jesus. It is God's will that His Son should be glorified, and the Holy Spirit does this when He comes to show us what the redemption of Christ does for us. The redemption of the mortal body appears almost more marvelous than that of the immortal soul. In these two ways God wills to dwell in us through Christ, and thus to triumph over the flesh. As soon as our body becomes the temple of God through the Spirit, Jesus is glorified.

Divine healing takes place wherever the Spirit of God works in power. Proofs of this are to be found in the lives of the Reformers, and in those of certain Moravians in their best times. But there are yet other promises touching the pouring out of the Holy Spirit which have not been fulfilled up to this time. Let us live in a holy expectation, praying the Lord to accomplish them in us.

Obedience and Health

March 1st

"If you will diligently hearken to the voice of the Lord your God, and will do that which is right in His sight, and will give ear to His Commandments, and keep all His Statutes, I will put none of these diseases upon you which I have brought upon the Egyptians; for I am the Lord that heals you."

—EXODUS 15: 25–26

It was at Marah that the Lord gave to His people this ordinance. Israel was just released from the yoke of Egypt when their faith was put to the proof in the desert by the waters of Marah. It was after He had sweetened the bitter waters that the Lord promised He would not put upon the children of Israel any of the diseases which He had brought upon the Egyptians so long as they would obey Him. They would be exposed to other trials; they might sometimes suffer the need of bread and of water, and encounter great dangers; all these things might come upon them in spite of their obedience, but sickness might not touch them. In a world still under the power of Satan, they might be a butt for attacks coming from without, but their bodies would not be oppressed with sickness, for God had delivered them from it.

Had He not said, *"If you will diligently hearken to the voice of the Lord your God... I will put none of these diseases upon you which I have brought upon the Egyptians, for I am the Lord that heals you?"* Again elsewhere, *"You shall serve the Lord your God... and I will take sickness away from the midst of you"* (Exodus 23:25; read also Leviticus 26:14–16; Deuteronomy 7:12–16; 28:15–61). This calls our attention to a truth of the greatest importance: the intimate relations which exist between obedience and health, between sanctification which is the health of the soul, and the Divine healing which ensures the health of the body both are comprised in the salvation that comes from God. It is noteworthy that in several languages these three words, salvation, healing, and sanctification, are derived from the same root and present the same fundamental thought: for instance, the German *heil*, salvation; *heilung*, healing; *heilichung*, sanctification.

Salvation is the redemption which the Savior has obtained for us, health is the salvation of the body which also comes to us from the Divine Healer, and lastly, sanctification reminds us that true salvation and true health consist in being holy as God is holy. Thus it is in giving health to the body and sanctification to the soul that Jesus is really the Savior of His people. Our text clearly declares the relation which exists between holiness of life and the healing of the body. The expressions which bear this out seem to be purposely multiplied: *"If you will diligently hearken... if you will do that which is right... if you will give ear... if you will keep all His Statutes, I will not send any sickness upon you."*

... The call to holiness sounds daily stronger and more clearly in the Church. More and more believers are coming to understand that God wants them to be like Christ; and the Lord is beginning again to make use of His healing virtue, seeking thereby to show us that still in our own days the Holy One of Israel is "*the Lord that heals you*," and that it is His will to keep His people both in health of body and in obedience. ...

Full Salvation; Our High Privilege

March 2nd

"Son, you are ever with me, and all that I have is yours."

—LUKE 15: 31

We may talk a great deal, and write a great deal, about the father's love to the prodigal, but when we think of the way he treated the elder brother, it brings to our hearts a truer sense of the wonderful love of the Father. ... The elder son, being ever with his father, had, if he liked, the privilege of two things: unceasing fellowship and unlimited partnership. But he was worse than the prodigal, for, although always at home, yet he had never known, nor enjoyed, nor understood the privileges that were his. All this fullness of fellowship had been waiting for and offered to him, but not received. While the prodigal was away from home in the far country, his elder brother was far from the enjoyment of home, while he was at home. ...

"All I have is yours." The elder son complained of the father's gracious reception of the prodigal, of all the feasting and rejoicing over his return, while to him had never been given a kid that he might make merry with his friends. The father, in the tenderness of his love, answers him, "Son, you were always in my house; you had only to ask and you would have got all you desired and required." And that is what our Father says to all His children.

… Why are you so poor? God's Word is sure, and does He not promise all this? See in John, chapters 14 to 16, how He tells us that we may have wonderful answers to prayer if we come in Jesus' name and abide in Him.

Now, we have looked at this high privilege which is for all, so we pass on to consider our second point: The low experience of many of God's dear children. What is it? Just living in poverty and starvation. The elder son—the child of a rich man, yet living in utter poverty!—never had a kid, while all that was his father's was his. Just exactly is the state of many a child of God. The way He wants us to live is in the fullest fellowship of all His blessings, yet what a contrast! …

These two sons represent two classes of Christians: the prodigal away backslidden; the elder son out of full fellowship with God. They were alike poor, and the elder son needed as great a change as did the prodigal; he needed to repent and confess and claim his full privileges; and so ought all low-level Christians to repent, confess, and claim full salvation. Oh, both of you, come today and say, "*Father, I have sinned*" (Luke 15:18).

Now, we ask, "What is the cause of this terrible discrepancy? Why the great difference in the experience?" Ask yourself, "What is the reason I am not enjoying this full blessing? God's Word speaks of it, others speak of it, and I see some who are living in it." Oh, do ask the reason; come to God and ask: "Why is it I never live the life You want me to live?" You will find the answer in our story. The elder son had an un-childlike spirit, and entertained wrong thoughts about his father; and, if you had known the real character of your Father, your life would have been all right. You have, as it were, said, "I never got a kid to make merry; my Father is rich, but He never gives. I have prayed quite enough, but God does not answer me. I hear other people say that God fills and satisfies them, but He never does that for me." …

Friends, there is no doubt as to God's sovereignty. He dispenses His gifts as He will; we are not all Pauls or Peters; places at the right and left hand of God are prepared for whomsoever He will. But this is not a matter of Divine sovereignty; it is a question of a child's heritage. The Father's love offers to give to every child in actual experience His full salvation. Now look at an earthly father. His children are of various ages, but all have equal right to the joy of their father's countenance. True, he gives to his son of twenty years more money than to the son of five, and he has more to speak of to the boy of fifteen than to the child of three; but, as regards his love toward them, it is all the same, and in their privileges as children they are all alike. And God's love to His dear children is all the same. Oh, do not try to throw the blame on God, but say, "I have had hard thoughts of You, O God, and I have sinned. As a father I have done for my children what I did not believe God was able and willing to do for me, and I have been lacking in childlike faith." Oh, do believe in the love, the willingness and power of God to give you full salvation, and a change must surely come.

Now let us consider the way of restoration: how to get out of this poor experience. The prodigal repented and so must those children of God who have been living within sight of, but not enjoying, His promises. … By God's grace give yourself up to Him. … Put yourself, as you are in sin and weakness, into the bosom of your Father. God will deliver you, and you will find that it is only one step out of the darkness into the light. Say, "Father, what a wretch I have been, in being with You and yet not believing Your love to me!"

Yes, I come today with a call to "repent;" addressed, not to the unsaved, but to those who know what it is to be pardoned. For have you not sinned in the hard thoughts you have had of God, and is there not a longing, a thirsting and hungering after something better? Come, then, repent, and just believe that God does blot out the sin of your unbelief. Do you believe it? Oh, do not dishonor God by unbelief, but come today and confidently claim full salvation. Then trust in Him to keep you.

This seems difficult to some; but there is no difficulty about it. God will shine His light upon you always, saying, "*Son, you are ever with me*"; and all you have to do is to dwell in and walk in that light.

The Way of Faith

March 3rd

"And straightway the father of the child cried out and said with tears, Lord, I believe; help my unbelief."
—MARK 9: 24

In one and the same soul there can arise a struggle between faith and unbelief, and that it is not without a struggle that we come to believe in Jesus and in His all-power to heal the sick. In this we find the needful encouragement for realizing the Savior's power. I speak here especially to sufferers who do not doubt the power or the will of the Lord Jesus to heal in this day without the use of earthly remedies, but who lack the boldness to accept healing for themselves. They believe in the Divine power of Christ, they believe in a general manner His good will to heal; they have acquired, either by the Scriptures, or by facts of healings by the Lord alone which have taken place in our days, the intellectual persuasion that the Lord can help even them, but they shrink back from accepting healing, and from saying with faith, "The Lord has heard me; I know that He is healing me."

Take notice first that without faith no one can be healed. When the father of the afflicted child said to Jesus, "If you can do anything, have compassion on us, and help us," Jesus replied: "*If you can believe*" (Mark 9: 23). Jesus had the power to heal and He was ready to do it, but He casts responsibility on the man. "*If you can believe, all things are possible to those who believe.*" In order to obtain your healing from Jesus, it is not enough to pray. Prayer without faith is powerless. It is "*the prayer of faith*" which saves the sick (James 5:15). If you have already asked for healing from the Lord, or if others have asked it for you, you must, before you are conscious of any change, be able to say with faith, On the authority of God's Word I have the assurance that He hears me and that I shall be healed.

To have faith means in your case to surrender your body absolutely into the Lord's hands, and to leave yourself entirely to Him. Faith receives healing as a spiritual grace which proceeds from the Lord even while there is no conscious change in the body. Faith can glorify God and say, "*Bless the Lord, O my soul... Who heals all [my] diseases*" (Psalm 103:1–3). The Lord requires this faith that He may heal.

But how is such faith to be obtained? Tell your God the unbelief which you find in your heart, and count on Him for deliverance from it. Faith is not money by which your healing can be purchased from the Lord. It is He who desires to awaken and develop in you the necessary faith. "*Help my unbelief*," cried the father of the child. It was his ardent desire that his faith should not come short.

Confess to the Lord all the difficulty you have to believe Him on the ground of His Word; tell Him you want to be rid of this unbelief, that you bring it to Him with a will to hearken only to His Word. Do not lose time in deploring your unbelief, but look to Jesus. ... He calls on you to trust in Him; listen to Him, and by His grace faith will triumph in you. Say to Him, "Lord, I am still aware of the unbelief which is in me. I find it difficult to believe that I am sure of my healing because I possess Him who works it. And, nevertheless, I want to conquer this unbelief. You, Lord, will give me the victory. I desire to believe, I will believe, by Your grace I dare to say I can believe. Yes, Lord, I believe, for You come to the help of my unbelief."

It is when we are in intimate communion with the Lord, and when our heart responds to His, that unbelief is overcome and conquered.

It is needful also to testify to the faith one has. Be resolved to believe that which the Lord says to you, to believe, above all, that which He is. Lean wholly upon His promises. "*The prayer of faith shall save the sick.*" "*I am the Lord that heals you*" (Exodus 15:26). Look to Jesus, who "*bare our sicknesses*" (Matthew 8:17), and who "*healed all who came to Him*"; count on the Holy Spirit to manifest in your heart the presence of Jesus who is also now in Heaven, and to work also in your body the power of His grace. Praise the Lord without waiting to feel better, or to have more faith. Praise Him, and say with David, "*O Lord, my God, I cried unto You, and You have healed me*" (Psalm 30:2).

Divine healing is a spiritual grace which can only be received spiritually and by faith, before feeling its effect on the body. Accept it, then, and give glory to God. ...If, therefore, your sickness does not yield at once, if Satan and your own unbelief attempt to get the upper hand, do not heed them, cling closely to Jesus your Healer, and He will surely heal you.

You Are the Branches

March 4th

"You are the branches."

—JOHN 15: 5

What a simple thing it is to be a branch the branch of a tree, or the branch of a vine! The branch grows out of the vine, or out of the tree, and there it lives and in due time bears fruit. … Now, just a few thoughts about this blessed branch-life. In the first place it is a life of absolute dependence. The branch has nothing: it just depends upon the vine for everything. That word, absolute dependence, is one of the most solemn and large and precious of words. A great German theologian wrote two large volumes some years ago, to show that the whole of Calvin's theology is summed up in that one principle of absolute dependence upon God; and he was right. If you can learn every moment of the day to depend upon God, everything will come right. You will get the higher life if you depend absolutely upon God. …

From moment to moment the sap flows from the vine to the branches. And just so, my Lord Jesus wants me to take that blessed position as a worker, and, morning by morning and day by day and hour by hour and step by step, in every work I have to go out to, just to abide before Him in the simple, utter helplessness. … Absolute dependence upon God is the secret of all power in work. The branch has nothing but what it gets from the vine, and you and I can have nothing but what we get from Jesus.

Secondly, the life of the branch is not only a life of entire dependence, but of deep restfulness. … If there was anything in the grapes not good, the owner never blamed the branch; the blame was always on the vine. And if you would be a true branch of Christ, the living Vine, just rest on Him. Let Christ bear the responsibility. … Rest in Christ, who can give wisdom and strength, and you do not know how that restfulness will often prove to be the very best part of your message. …

The branch teaches a lesson of much fruitfulness. You know the Lord Jesus repeated that word fruit often in that parable; He spoke first of fruit, and then of more fruit, and then of much fruit. Yes, you are ordained not only to bear fruit, but to bear much fruit. "*Herein is My Father glorified, that you bear much fruit*" [John 15: 8]. In the first place, Christ said: "'*I am the True Vine, and My Father is the Husbandman' who has charge of Me and you.*" He who will watch over the connection between Christ and the branches is God; and it is in the power of God, through Christ, that we are to bear fruit. … "*You are the branches,*" and you cannot bear heavenly fruit unless you are in close connection with Jesus Christ. …

The life of the branch is a life of close communion. Let us again ask: "What has the branch to do?" You know that precious, inexhaustible word that Christ used: "Abide." "*Abide in Me, and I in you. As the branch cannot bear fruit of itself, except it abide in the vine; no more can you, except you abide in Me*" (John 15: 4). Your life is to be an abiding life. And how is the abiding to be? It is to be just like the branch in the vine, abiding every minute of the day. … You may have ten hours hard work daily, during which your brain has to be occupied with temporal things; God orders it so. But the abiding work is the work of the heart, not of the brain, the work of the heart clinging to and resting in Jesus, a work in which the Holy Spirit links us to Christ Jesus. Oh, do believe that deeper down than the brain, deep down in the inner life, you can abide in Christ, so that every moment you are free the consciousness will come: Blessed Jesus, I am still in You. …

Take time to be alone with Christ. Nothing in Heaven or earth can free you from the necessity for that, if you are to be happy and holy Christians. Oh, how many Christians look upon it as a burden, and a tax, and a duty, and a difficulty to get much alone with

God! That is the great hindrance to our Christian life everywhere. We need more quiet fellowship with God, and I tell you in the name of the heavenly Vine that you cannot be healthy branches, branches into which the heavenly sap can flow, unless you take plenty of time for communion with God. If you are not willing to sacrifice time to get alone with Him, and give Him time every day to work in you, and to keep up the link of connection between you and Himself, He cannot give you that blessing of His unbroken fellowship. Jesus Christ asks you to live in close communion with Him. Let every heart say: "O Christ, it is this I long for, it is this I choose." And He will gladly give it to you.

And then my last thought. The life of the branch is a life of entire surrender. … Oh, we need this entire surrender to the Lord Jesus Christ. … But the one question I ought to study quietly is: "What is meant by entire surrender?" It means that just as literally as Christ was given up entirely to God, I am given up entirely to Christ. Is that too strong? Some of you think so. Some think that never can be; that just as entirely and absolutely as Christ gave up His life to do nothing but seek the Father's pleasure, and depend on the Father absolutely and entirely, I am to do nothing but to seek the pleasure of Christ. But that is actually true. Christ Jesus came to breathe His Spirit into us, to make us find our very highest happiness in living entirely for God, just as He did. …

Oh, we find the Christian life so difficult because we seek for God's blessing while we live in our own will. We would be glad to live the Christian life according to our own liking. We make our own plans and choose our own work, and then we ask the Lord Jesus to come in and take care that sin shall not conquer us too much, and that we shall not go too far wrong; we ask Him to come in and give us so much of His blessing. But our relation to Jesus ought to be such that we are entirely at His disposal, and every day come to Him humbly and straightforwardly, and say: "Lord, is there anything in me that is not according to Your will, that has not been ordered by You, or that is not entirely given up to You?" Oh, if we would wait and wait patiently, there would spring up a relationship between us and Christ so close and so tender that we should afterwards be amazed how far distant our intercourse with Him had previously been.

The Prayer of Faith

March 5th

"The prayer of faith shall save the sick, and the Lord shall raise them up."

—JAMES 5: 15

The prayer of faith! Only once does this expression occur in the Bible, and it relates to the healing of the sick. The Church has adopted this expression, but she hardly ever has recourse to the prayer of faith except for the sake of obtaining other graces; while according to Scripture it is especially intended for the healing of the sick.

Does the Apostle expect healing through the prayer of faith alone, or should it be accompanied by the use of remedies? This is generally the question which is raised. It is easily decided, if we take into consideration the power of the Church's spiritual life in the early ages: the gifts of healing bestowed on the Apostles by the Lord, augmented by the subsequent pouring out of the Holy Spirit (Acts 4: 30; 5:15–16), what Paul says of "*the gifts of healing by the same Spirit*" (1 Corinthians 12:9), what James here insists upon when, in order to strengthen the reader in the expectation of faith, he recalls Elijah's prayer and God's wonderful answer (James 5:17–18). Does not all this clearly show that the believer is to look for healing in response to the prayer of faith alone, and without the addition of remedies?

Another question will arise: Does the use of remedies exclude the prayer of faith? To this we believe our reply should be: "No," for the experience of a large number of believers testifies that in answer to their prayers God has often blessed the use of remedies, and made them a means of healing.

We come here to a third question: Which is then the line to follow, that we may prove with the greatest certainty, and according to the will of God, the efficacy of the prayer of faith? Is it, according to James, in setting aside all remedies or in using remedies as believers do for the most part? Is it with or without remedies that the prayer of faith best obtains the grace of God?

Which of these two methods will be most directly to the glory of God and for blessing to the sick one? Is it not perfectly simple to reply that if the prescription and the promise in James apply to believers of our time, they will find blessing in receiving them just as they were given to believers then, conforming to them on all points, expecting healing only from the Lord Himself, without having any recourse to remedies besides? It is, in fact, in this sense that Scripture always speaks of effectual faith and of the prayer of faith.

Both the laws of nature and the witness of Scripture show us that God often makes use of intermediary agencies to manifest His glory, but whether by experience or by Scripture, we know also that under the power of the fall, and the empire of our senses, our tendency is to attach more importance to the remedies than to the direct action of God. It often happens that remedies so occupy us as to intercept the presence of our God and turn us away from Him.

God would form for Himself a people of faith, living more in the unseen than in the things visible; and in order to lead them into this life it was necessary to take away their confidence in ordinary means. We see therefore that it was not by the ordinary ways which He has traced in nature that God led Abraham, Moses, Joshua, Gideon, the Judges, David and many other kings of Israel. His object was to teach them by this to confide only in Him, to know Him as He is: "*You are the God that does wonders*" (Psalm 77: 14). God wills to act in a similar way with us. It is when we seek to walk according to His prescription in James 5, abandoning the things which are seen (2 Corinthians 4: 18), to lay hold of the promise of God, and so receive directly from Him the desired healing, that we discover how much importance we have attached to earthly remedies.

Doubtless there are Christians who can make use of remedies without damage to their spiritual life, but the larger number of them are apt to count much more on the remedies than on the power of God. Now the purpose of God is to lead His children into a more intimate communion with Christ, and this is just what does happen when by faith we commit ourselves to Him as our sovereign Healer, counting solely on His invisible presence. Renouncing remedies strengthens faith in an extraordinary manner. Healing becomes, then, far more than sickness, a source of numberless spiritual blessings. It makes real to us what faith can accomplish, it establishes a new tie between God and the believer, and commences in him a life of confidence and dependence. The body equally with the soul is placed under the power of the Holy Spirit, and the prayer of faith, which saves the sick, thus leads us to a life of faith, strengthened by the assurance that God manifests His presence in our earthly life.

Let the One Who is Healed Glorify God

March 6th

"Jesus answered, Neither has this man sinned, nor his parents: but that the works of God should be made manifest in him."

—JOHN 9: 3

It is a prevalent idea that piety is easier in sickness than in health; that silence and suffering incline the soul to seek the Lord and enter into communion with Him better than the distractions of active life; that, in fact, sickness throws us more upon God. For these reasons sick people hesitate to ask for healing from the Lord; for they say to themselves, "How can we know whether sickness may not be better for us than health?" To think thus is to ignore that the healing and its fruits are Divine.

Let us try to understand that though a healing through ordinary means may at times run the risk of making God relax His hand, Divine healing, on the contrary, binds us more closely to Him. Thus it comes to pass that in our day, as in the time of the early ministry of Jesus Christ, the believer who has been healed by Him can glorify Him far better than the one who remains sick.

Sickness can only glorify God in the measure in which it gives occasion to manifest His power (John 9: 3; 11: 4). ... Healing by means of remedies shows us the power of God in nature; but it does not bring us into living and direct contact with Him; while Divine healing is an act proceeding from God, without anything but the Holy Spirit. In this latter, contact with God is the thing which is essential, and it is for this reason that examination of the conscience and the confession of sins should be the preparation for it (James 5: 15–16).

One who is so healed is called to consecrate himself quite anew and entirely to the Lord (1 Corinthians 6: 13,19). All this depends upon the act of faith which lays hold of the Lord's promise, which yields to Him, and which does not doubt that the Lord at once takes possession of what is consecrated to Him. This is why the continuance of health received depends on the holiness of the life, and the obedience in seeking always the good pleasure of the Divine Healer. *"And said, If you will diligently hearken to the voice of the Lord your God, and will do that which is right in His sight, and will give ear to His Commandments, and keep all His Statutes, I will put none of these diseases upon you, which I have brought upon the Egyptians: for I am the Lord who heals you"* (Exodus 15: 26).

Health obtained under such conditions ensures spiritual blessings. The mere restoration to health by ordinary means does not. When the Lord heals the body it is that He may take possession of it and make it a temple that He may dwell in. The joy which then fills the soul is indescribable. It is not only the joy of being healed; it is joy mingled with humility, and a holy enthusiasm which recognizes the touch of the Lord and receives a new life from Him. In exuberant joy the healed one exalts the Lord, and glorifies Him by word and deed, and all is consecrated to God. …

Oh, what may not the Church become when she lives in this faith, when every sick person shall recognize in sickness a call to be holy, and to expect from the Lord a manifestation of His presence, when healings shall be multiplied, producing in each a witness of the power of God, all ready to cry with the Psalmist, *"Bless the Lord, O my soul... Who heals all your diseases"* (Psalm 103: 2–3).

Fervent and Effectual Prayer

March 7th

"Confess your faults one to another, and pray one for another, that you may be healed. The effectual fervent prayer of a righteous man avails much. Elias was a man subject to like passions as we are, and he prayed earnestly that it might not rain: and it rained not on the earth by the space of three years and six months. And he prayed again, and the Heaven gave rain, and the earth brought forth her fruit."

—JAMES 5:16–18

James knew that a faith which obtains healing is not the fruit of human nature; therefore, he adds that the prayer must be "fervent." Only such can be efficacious. In this he stands upon the example of Elijah, a man of the same nature ("*subject to like passions*") as we are, drawing therefore the inference that our prayer can be and ought to be of the same nature as his.

How then did Elijah pray? This will throw some light upon what the prayer of faith should be. … He knows, he believes that God's will is to send rain, and nevertheless he must pray, or the rain will not come. His prayer is no empty form; it is a real power, the efficacy of which is about to make itself felt in Heaven. God wills that it shall rain, but the rain will only come at Elijah's request, a request repeated with faith and perseverance until the appearance of the first cloud in the sky. In order that the will of God shall be accomplished, this will must on one side be expressed by a promise, and on the other it must be received and laid hold of by the believer who prays. We, therefore, must persevere in prayer that we may show God that our faith expects an answer, and will not grow weary until it is obtained.

This is how prayer must be made for the sick. The promise of God, "*The Lord will raise him up*," must be rested on, and His will to heal recognized. Jesus Himself teaches us to pray with faith which counts on the answer of God; He says to us: "*All things whatsoever you pray for, and ask for, believe that you have received them and you shall have them*" (Mark 11: 24). After the prayer of faith which receives beforehand that which God has promised, comes the prayer of perseverance, which does not lose sight of that which has been asked until God has fulfilled His promise (1 Kings 18: 43).

There may be some obstacle which hinders the fulfillment of the promise; whether on the side of God and His righteousness (Deuteronomy 9:18), or on the side of Satan, and his constant opposition to the plans of God, something which may still impede the answer to the prayer (Daniel 10:12–13). It may be also that our faith needs to be purified (Matthew 15:22–28). Whatever it may be, our faith is called to persevere until the answer comes. The one who prays six times fervently and stops there, when he ought to have prayed seven times (2 Kings 13:18–19), deprives themself of the answer to prayer.

Perseverance in prayer, a perseverance which strengthens the faith of the believer against all which may seem opposed to the answer, is a real miracle; it is one of the impenetrable mysteries of the life of faith. Does it not say to us that the Savior's redeemed one is in very deed His friend, a member of His body, and that the government of the world and the gifts of Divine grace depend in some sense upon his prayers? Prayer, therefore, is no vain form. It is the work of the Holy Spirit, who intercedes here on earth in us and by us, and as such, it is as efficacious, as indispensable as the work of the Son interceding for us before the throne of God. It might seem strange that after having prayed with the certainty of being heard, and having seen therein the will of God, we should still need to continue in prayer. Nevertheless, it is so. In Gethsemane, Jesus prayed three times in succession. On Carmel Elijah prayed seven times; and we, if we believe the promise of God without doubting, shall pray until we receive the answer. Both the importunate friend at midnight and the widow who besieged the unjust judge are examples of perseverance in seeking the end in view.

Let us learn from Elijah's prayer to humble ourselves, to recognize why the power of God cannot be more manifested in the Church, whether in the healing of the sick, or in conversion, or sanctification. "*You have not because you ask not*" (James 4: 2). Let it also teach us patience. In the cases where healing is delayed, let us remember that obstacles may exist over which only perseverance in prayer can triumph. Faith which ceases to pray, or which is allowed to relax in its fervor, cannot appropriate that which God has nevertheless given. Let not our faith in the promises of Scripture be shaken by those things which are as yet beyond our reach. God's promise remains the same: "*The prayer of faith shall save the sick*." May the prayer of Elijah strengthen our faith. Let us remember that we have to imitate them "*who through faith and patience inherit the promises*" (Hebrews 6:12). If we learn to persevere in prayer, its fruit will be always more abundant, always more evident, and we shall obtain, as Jesus obtained when He was on earth, healing of the sick, often immediate healing, which shall bring glory to God.

Persevering Prayer

March 8th

"Shall not God avenge His own elect, which cry day and night unto Him, though He bear long with them? He will avenge them speedily. Nevertheless, when the Son of man comes, shall He find faith on the earth?"

—LUKE 18:1–8

The necessity of praying with perseverance is the secret of all spiritual life. What a blessing to be able to ask the Lord for such and such a grace until He gives it, knowing with certainty that it is His will to answer prayer. But, what a mystery for us is the call to persevere in prayer, to knock in faith at His door, to remind Him of His promises, and to do so without wearying until He arises and grants us our petition! Is not the assurance that our prayer can obtain from the Lord that which He would not otherwise give the evident proof that we have been created in the image of God, that we are His friends, that we are His fellow workers, and that the believers who together form the body of Christ participate in this manner in His intercessory work? It is to Christ's intercession that the Father responds, and to which He grants His Divine favors.

More than once the Bible explains to us the need for persevering prayer. There are many grounds, the chief of which is the justice of God. God has declared that sin must bear its consequences; sin therefore has rights over a world which welcomes and remains enslaved by it. When the child of God seeks to quit this order of things, it is necessary that the justice of God should consent to this; time therefore is needed that the privileges which Christ has procured for the believers should weigh before God's tribunal. Besides this, the opposition of Satan, who always seeks to prevent the answer to prayer, is a reason for it (Daniel 10:12–13). The only means by which this unseen enemy can be conquered is faith. Standing firmly on the promises of God, faith refuses to yield, and continues to pray and wait for the answer, even when it is delayed, knowing that the victory is sure (Ephesians 6: 12–13).

Finally, perseverance in prayer is needful for ourselves. Delay in the answer is intended to prove and strengthen our faith; it ought to develop in us the steadfast will which will no longer let go the promises of God, but which renounces its own side of things to trust in God alone. It is then that God, seeing our faith, finds us ready to receive His favor and grants it to us. …

This perseverance in prayer will become easy to us as soon as we fully understand what faith is. Jesus teaches us in these words, "*All things whatsoever you shall ask in prayer, believing, you shall receive*" (Matthew 21: 22). When the Word of God authorizes us to ask anything, we ought at once to believe that we receive it. God gives it to us; this we know by faith, and we can say between God and us that we have received it, although it might be only later that we are permitted to realize the effects here on earth. It is before having seen or experienced anything whatsoever that faith rejoices in having received, perseveres in praying, and waits until the answer is manifest.

This is of great importance in obtaining Divine healing. Sometimes, it is true, the healing is immediate and complete; but it may happen that we have to wait, even when a sick person has been able to ask for it in faith. Sometimes also the first symptoms of healing are immediately manifest; but afterwards the progress is slow, and interrupted by times when it is arrested or when the evil returns. In such cases it is important for both the sick person and those who pray with him to believe in the efficacy of persevering prayer, even though they may not understand the mystery of it. That which God appears at first to refuse, He grants later to the prayer of the Canaanite woman, to the [persistent] prayer of the widow, to that of the importune friend who knocks at midnight (Matthew 15: 22–28; Luke 18: 3–8; 11: 5–8).

Let us lay hold with a holy promptitude of the grace which is promised us, as if we had already received it; let us await with untiring patience the answer which is slow to come. Such faith belongs to living in Him. It is to produce in us this faith that sickness is sent to us, and that the healing is granted to us, for such faith glorifies God.

4

THE POWER OF THE BLOOD OF JESUS

The Kerkbade, 1882

Preface

March 9th

An appropriate preface for this book on the power of the blood of Jesus—power to sanctify us and make us holy in this life—is found in the second biography of Andrew Murray, written by his friend, Rev. W.M. Douglas (1925). It is of such devotional quality and help that an abridged version is reproduced here:

In a remarkable book which relates truthfully the "*Deeper Experience of Famous Christians*," such as Madame Guyon, Fenelon, George Foxe, Wesley, Whitfield, Fletcher, Christmas Evans, Bramwell, General Booth, Moody, Dr. Gordon, A. B. Earle, Havergal, and others, it is made abundantly clear from their own testimony and the fruits that followed this experience that they, after their conversion sooner or later by a definite crisis, as marked as a birth, or a death, or a marriage, passed into a new state and experience, a new relation to Christ and the Holy Spirit, and a new apprehension and application of the all-cleansing power of the Blood to cleanse and to keep clean.

From all these witnesses, so illustrious and reliable, we call up one, whose name is a household word, whose *Sacred Songs* have been sung in the Church of God everywhere in rapturous strains. We mean Frances Ridley Havergal. Her deeper experience is selected because it furnishes a concrete example of the wondrous power of the blood of the Lamb, which Andrew Murray considers to be the special teaching of the Epistle to the Hebrews: "*How much more shall the blood of Christ cleanse.*"

Before asking Frances Ridley Havergal to relate her vivid experience of the purifying, transforming effect of the Redeemer's blood on her heart, life and service, the reader ought to be introduced to one more book by Andrew Murray on the subject of Holiness, namely: *De Kracht Van Jezus Bloed* (*The Power of the Blood of Jesus*) which contains twenty addresses on this transporting theme.

As we learn from his introduction, it was on his voyage to Europe, 1882, that he meditated much on the expression "There is power in the blood" .... The more he meditated, the more he enquired in the spirit of prayer: What is this power, and why has it this power? And the following year, on his return, he decided to give the answer to the question in a series of fifteen addresses delivered in the Dutch Church during the season of preparation for Easter, corresponding to what is otherwise called Lent. Five other addresses were subsequently added, and the whole published in the *Kerkbade*, the magazine of the Dutch Church. ...

Before Miss Havergal passed into this deeper experience, she had had an unmistakable conversion, leading to a life of entire devotion to her Saviour and continual service for Him unchecked by any deviation from the path of righteousness, or backsliding into sloth, worldliness or sin. Still, she longed for a deeper, richer, fuller experience. In her *Gleams and Glimpses* she wrote "Oh to be filled with the Holy Spirit." Once she wrote: "Oh that He would indeed purify me, and make me white at any cost," and again: "I wait for the hour when He will reveal Himself to me more directly, according to John 14: 21." And by a crisis, as distinct as her conversion, she passed into this second experience of grace, and her *Journals and Letters*, a rich heritage for the Church of God, show us what intimate communion she enjoyed with the Triune God, whom she adoringly loved, until her very body was overwhelmed with "that speechless awe which dares not move."

At length, the long looked-for experience came, and lifted her whole life into perpetual sunshine. The "Sunless ravines" were forever passed. She could now sing: "Like a river glorious is God's perfect peace." What was it brought this transformation? It was a little booklet, setting forth the fullness in Jesus. She read its contents and the letter of her correspondent explaining the power of the Blood to cleanse from all sin. To this she sent a joyous reply: "I see it all, and I have the blessing."

She saw it as a flash of electric light. She remembered the place, Winterdine, in the Midland Counties, and the day, December 2nd, 1873. She saw that there must be a full and true consecration before blessing—absolute surrender, as Andrew Murray insists. Then trust in the Blood to cleanse from all sin, all means and all power to keep clean because of the present tense, "cleanses": "It goes on cleansing, and I have no words to tell how my heart rejoices in it. Not a coming to be cleansed in the fountain only, but a remaining in the fountain, so that it may and can go on cleansing."

"One of the intensest moments of my life was when I saw the force of that word, "cleanses." The utterly unexpected and altogether unimagined sense of its fulfilment to me, on simply believing in its fullness, was just indescribable. I expected nothing like it short of Heaven.""

What more shall we say, what further need have we of witnesses? There is enough to confirm Andrew Murray's luminous exposition of this most glorious epistle, that one can enter into the Holiest now through the blood, "and Heaven comes down our souls to meet," even while we are on the way to heaven. Need we be surprised that when at length, after a life of holiness and still more fruitful service that when she came to die, suffering could not prevent her saying: "God's will is delicious. It is so beautiful to go. It is all perfect peace. I only wait for Jesus to take me in. When I am gone, let my favorite text be put on my tomb, "the blood of Jesus Christ His Son cleanses from all sin.""

Oh, that like her, all the saints of God would seek to have the blood on the heart and to testify to its power. The danger is in thinking such an experience as hers and others like it are exceptional, and holiness is optional. But the possibility argues its necessity; that it is attainable shows it is indispensable. But if there are allurements to incite us to progress heavenward, there are temptations to turn back, and in the Epistle five solemn warnings are sounded to prevent our going back to perdition. Holiness is our only safety, "To be sure of being kept from willful sin, let us keep from all sin. The only sure sign that the perseverance of the saints will be ours is perseverance in sainthood, in sanctification and obedience."

Sanctification Through the Blood 1

March 10th

"Therefore, Jesus also suffered that he might sanctify his people with his own blood."

—HEBREWS 13: 12

To a superficial observer it might seem that there is little difference between cleansing and sanctification, that the two words mean about the same thing; but the difference is great and important.

Cleansing has to do chiefly with the old life, and the stain of sin which must be removed, and is only preparatory. Sanctification concerns the new life and that characteristic of it which must be imparted to it by God. Sanctification, which means union with God, is the peculiar fullness of blessing purchased for us by the blood. The distinction between these two things is clearly marked in Scripture. Paul reminds us that "*Christ gave himself for the Church, that he might sanctify it, having cleansed it*" (Ephesians 5: 25). Having first cleansed it, then He sanctifies it. Writing to Timothy he says, "*If a man therefore purge himself from these, he shall be a vessel unto honor, sanctified, and meet for the master's use*" (2 Timothy 2: 21). Sanctification is a blessing which follows after and surpasses cleansing.

It is also strikingly illustrated by the ordinances connected with the consecration of the priests, compared with that of the Levites. In the case of the latter, who took a lower position than the Priests in the service of the Sanctuary, no mention is made of sanctification; but the word cleansing is used five times (Numbers 8). In the consecration of the priests, on the other hand, the word "to sanctify" is often used; for the priests stood in a closer relationship to God than the Levites (Exodus 29; Leviticus 8).

This record at the same time emphasizes the close connection between the sacrificial blood, and sanctification. In the case of the consecration of the *Levites, reconciliation* for sin was made, and they were sprinkled with the water of purification for *cleansing*, but they were not sprinkled with blood. But in the consecration of the *Priests*, blood had to be sprinkled upon them. They were sanctified by a more personal and intimate application of the blood.

All this was typical of sanctification through the blood of Jesus, and this is what we now seek to understand, that we may obtain a share in it. Let us then consider: (1) What sanctification is; (2) That it was the great object of the sufferings of Christ; and (3) That it can be obtained by the blood of Christ.

What Sanctification Is

To understand what the sanctification of the redeemed is, we must first learn what the holiness of God is. He alone is the holy one. Holiness in the creature must be received from Him. God's holiness is often spoken of as though it consisted in His hatred of, and hostility to sin; but this gives no explanation of what holiness actually is. It is a merely negative statement that God's holiness cannot bear sin. Holiness is that attribute of God because of which He always is, and wills, and doer what is supremely good; because of which also He desires what is supremely good in His creatures, and bestows it upon them.

God is called "The Holy One" in Scripture, not only because He punishes sin, but also because He is the Redeemer of His people. It is His holiness, which ever wills what is good for all, that moved Him to redeem sinners. Both the wrath of God which punishes sin, and love of God which redeems the sinner, spring from the same source: His holiness. Holiness is the perfection of God's nature.

Holiness in man is a disposition in entire agreement with that of God; which chooses in all things to will as God wills: as it is written: "*As he is holy, so be you holy*" (1 Peter 1:15). Holiness in us is nothing else than oneness with God. The sanctification of God's people is effected by the communication to them of the holiness of God. There is no other way of obtaining sanctification, save by the Holy God bestowing what He alone possesses. He alone is the Holy One. He is the Lord who sanctifies.

By the different meanings which Scripture attaches to the words sanctification, and "to sanctify"—a certain relationship with God, into which we are brought, is pointed out.

The first and simplest meaning of the word sanctification is "separation." That which is taken out of its surroundings, by God's command, and is set aside or separated as His own possession and for his service—that is holy. This does not mean separation from sin only, but from all that is in the world, even from what may be permissible. Thus, God sanctified the seventh day. The other days were not unclean, for God saw all that He had made and "*behold; it was very good*." But that day alone was holy, which God had taken possession of by His own special act. In the same way, God had separated Israel from other nations, and in Israel, had separated the priests, to be holy unto Him.

This separation unto sanctification is always God's own work, and so the electing grace of God is often closely connected with sanctification. "*You shall be holy unto me … I have separated you … that you should be mine*" (Leviticus 20: 26); "*The man whom the Lord shall choose shall be holy*" (Numbers 26: 7); "*You are a holy people unto the Lord, the Lord your God has chosen you"* (Deuteronomy 7: 6).

God cannot take part with other lords. He must be the sole possessor, and ruler, of those to whom He reveals and imparts His holiness. But this separation is not all that is included in the word sanctification. It is only the indispensable condition of what must follow. When separated, man stands before God in no respect differing from an object without life that has been sanctified to the service of God. If the separation is to be of value, something more must take place. Man must surrender himself willingly, and heartily, to this separation. Sanctification includes personal consecration to the Lord to be His.

Sanctification can become ours only when it sends down its roots into, and takes up its abode in the depths of our personal life; in our will, and in our love. God sanctifies no man against his will, therefore the personal, hearty, surrender to God is an indispensable part of sanctification. It is for this reason that the Scriptures not only speak of God sanctifying us, but they say often, that we must sanctify ourselves.

But even by consecration, true sanctification is not yet complete. Separation and consecration are together only the preparation for the glorious work that God will do, as He imparts His own holiness to the soul. "Partaking of the Divine nature" is the blessing which is promised to believers in sanctification. "*That we might be partakers of his holiness*" (Hebrews 12: 10)—that is the glorious aim of God's work in those whom He separates for Himself. But this impartation of His holiness is not a gift of something that is apart from God Himself; no! it is in personal fellowship with Him, and partaking of His Divine life, that sanctification can be obtained.

As the Holy One, God dwelled among the people of Israel to sanctify his people (Exodus 29: 45–46). As the Holy One, He dwells in us. It is the presence of God alone that can sanctify.

But so surely is this our portion, that Scripture does not shrink from speaking of God dwelling in our hearts in such power that we may be *"filled unto all the fullness of God."* True sanctification is fellowship with God and His dwelling in us. So, it was necessary that God in Christ should take up His abode in the flesh, and that the Holy Spirit should come to dwell in us. This is what sanctification means.

Sanctification Through the Blood 2

March 11th

"For their sakes I sanctify myself, that they also may be sanctified through the truth."

—JOHN 17: 19

This sanctification was the object for which Christ suffered. This is plainly stated in Hebrews 13: 12: *"Jesus suffered that He might sanctify his people."* In the wisdom of God, participation in His holiness is the highest destiny of man. Therefore, also, this was the central object of the coming of our Lord Jesus to earth; and above all, of His sufferings and death. It was *"that He might sanctify his people"* and *"that they might be holy and without blame"* (Ephesians 1: 4).

How the sufferings of Christ attained this end, and became our sanctification, is made plain to us by the words which He spoke to His Father, when He was about to allow Himself to be bound as a sacrifice. *"For their sakes I sanctify myself, that they also may be sanctified through the truth"* (John 17: 19). It was because His sufferings and death were a sanctification of Himself, that they can become sanctification for us.

What does that mean? Jesus was the holy one of God, *"The Son whom the Father had sanctified and sent into the world,"* and must He sanctify Himself? He must do so; it was indispensable. The sanctification which He possessed was not beyond the reach of temptation. In His temptation, He must maintain it, and show how perfectly His will was surrendered to the holiness of God. We have seen that true holiness in man is the perfect oneness of His will with that of God. Through all our Lord's life, from the temptation in the wilderness onwards, He had subjected His will to the will of His Father, and had consecrated Himself as a sacrifice to God. But it was chiefly in Gethsemane He did this. There was the hour, and the power of darkness; the temptation to put away the terrible cup of wrath from His lips, and to do His own will came with almost irresistible power, but He rejected the temptation.

He offered up Himself, and His will, to the will and holiness of God. He sanctified Himself, by a perfect oneness of will, with that of God. This sanctification of Himself has become the power by which we also may be sanctified through the truth. This is in perfect accord with what we learn from the epistle to the Hebrews, where, speaking of the words used by Christ, we read, *"I come to do your will, O God,"* and then it is added, *"Because of this, we are sanctified—made holy—by the offering of the body of Jesus Christ once for all"* (Hebrews 10: 9–10).

It was because the offering of His body was His surrender of Himself to do the will of God, that we become sanctified by that will. He sanctified Himself there, for us, that we might be sanctified through the truth. The perfect obedience in which He surrendered Himself, that God's holy will might be accomplished in Him, was not only the meritorious cause of our salvation, but is at the same time the power by which sin was forever conquered, and by which the same disposition, and the same sanctification, may be created in our hearts.

Elsewhere in this epistle to the Hebrews, the true relationship of our Lord to His own people is even more clearly recognized as having sanctification for its chief end. After speaking of how becoming it was, that our Lord should suffer as He did, we read: *"For both he that sanctifies, and they who are sanctified, are all one"* (Hebrews 2: 11). The unity between the Lord Jesus and His people consists in the fact, that they both receive their life from one Father, and both have a share in one and the same sanctification. Jesus is the sanctifier, they become the sanctified. Sanctification is the bond that unites them. *"Therefore Jesus also suffered that he might sanctify his people with his own blood"* (Hebrews 13:12).

If we are willing to really understand, and experience what sanctification by the blood means, then it is of the utmost importance for us, to first lay fast hold of the fact that sanctification is the characteristic, and purpose of the entire sufferings of our Lord, of which sufferings the blood was the fruit, and means of blessing. His sanctification of Himself has the characteristic of those sufferings, and therein lay its value and power. Our sanctification is the purpose of those sufferings, and only to attain that purpose do they work out the perfect blessing. In proportion as this is clear to us, we shall press forward into the true meaning and blessing of His sufferings.

It was as the Holy One that God foreordained redemption. It was His will to glorify His holiness in victory over sin, by the sanctification of man after His own image. It was with the same object that our Lord Jesus endured, and accomplished His sufferings; we must be consecrated to God. And if the Holy Spirit, the holy God as Spirit, comes into us to reveal in us the redemption that is in Jesus, this continues to be with Him, also, the main object. As the Holy Spirit, He is the Spirit of holiness.

Reconciliation, pardon and cleansing from sin, have all an unspeakable value; they all, however, point onwards to sanctification. It is God's will that each one who has been marked by the precious blood, should know that it is a Divine mark, recognizing our entire separation to God; that this blood calls us to an undivided consecration to a life, wholly for God, and that this blood is the promise, and the power of a participation in God's holiness, through which God Himself will make His abiding place in us, and be our God. Oh, that we might understand, and believe that: "*Jesus also suffered, that he might sanctify his people, with his own blood.*"

Sanctification Through the Blood 3

March 12th

"That He might sanctify his people, that they might be holy and without blame"

—EPHESIANS 1: 4

How Sanctification by the Blood is to be Obtained. … An answer to this question, in general, is that everyone who is a partaker of the virtue of the blood, is also a partaker of sanctification, and is in God's sight a sanctified person. In proportion as he lives in close and abiding contact with the blood, he continues to experience, increasingly, its sanctifying effects; even though he still understands but little of how those effects are produced. … It is the Lord Jesus Himself who sanctifies His people "*by His own blood.*" We who heartily give our Self up to believing worship of, and intercourse with, the Lamb, who has bought us with His blood, will experience through that blood a sanctification beyond conception. The Lord Jesus will do this for us.

But the believer ought to grow in knowledge also; thus only can we enter into the full blessing which is prepared for us. We have not only the right, but it is our duty to inquire earnestly what the essential connection is between the blessed effect of the blood, and our sanctification, and in what way the Lord Jesus will work out in us, by His blood, those things which we have ascertained to be the chief qualities of sanctification.

We have seen that the beginning of all sanctification is separation to God, as His entire possession, to be at His disposal. And is not this just what the blood proclaims? that the power of sin is broken; that we are loosed from its bonds; that we are no longer its bond-servants; but belong to Him who purchased our freedom with His blood? "*You are not your own; you are bought with a price*"—this is the language in which the blood tells us that we are God's possession.

Because He desires to have us entirely for Himself, He has chosen and bought us, and set upon us the distinguishing mark of the blood, as those who are separated from all around them, to live only for His service. This idea of separation is clearly expressed in the words we so often repeat, "*Jesus, that he might sanctify his people with his own blood, suffered without the gate. Let us go forth therefore to him without the camp bearing his reproach.*" "Going out" from all that is of this world, was the characteristic of Him who was holy, undefiled, separate from sinners; and it must be the characteristic of all His followers.

Believer, the Lord Jesus has sanctified you through His own blood, and He desires to make you experience, through that blood, the full power of this sanctification. Endeavor to gain a clear impression of what has taken place in you through the sprinkling of that blood. The holy God desires to have you entirely for Himself. No one, nothing, may any longer have the least right over you, nor have you any right over yourself. God has separated you unto Himself, and that you might feel this He set His mark upon you. That mark is the most wonderful thing that is to be found on earth or in Heaven.

The blood in which the life of the eternal Son of God is; the blood that on the throne of grace is ever before God's face; the blood that assures you of full redemption from the power of sin; that blood is sprinkled upon you, as a sign that you belong to God. Believer, I pray you, let every thought about the blood awaken in you the glorious confession, "By his own blood, the Lord Jesus has sanctified me, he has taken complete possession of me for God, and I belong entirely to God."

We have seen that sanctification is more than separation. That is only the beginning. We have seen also that personal consecration and hearty and willing surrender to live only for, and in God's holy will, is part of sanctification. In what way can the blood of Christ work out this surrender in us, and sanctify us in that surrender? The answer is not difficult. It is not enough to believe in the power of the blood to redeem us, and to free us from sin, but we must, above all, notice the source of this power.

We know that it has this power, because of the willingness with which the Lord Jesus surrenders Himself. In the shedding of His blood He sanctifies: Himself, offered Himself entirely to God and His holiness. It is because of this that the blood is so holy, and possesses such sanctifying power. In the blood we have an impressive representation of the Self-surrender of Christ. The blood ever speaks of the consecration of Jesus to the Father, as the opening of the way, and supplying the power for victor: over sin. And the closer we come into contact with the blood, and the more we live under the deep impression of having been sprinkled by the blood, we shall hear more clearly the voice of the blood, declare that "Entire surrender to God is the way to full redemption from sin."

The voice of the blood will not speak simply teach us or to awaken thought; the blood speaks with a divine and life giving power. What it commands, that it bestows. It works out in us the same disposition that was in our Lord Jesus. By His own blood Jesus sanctifies us, that we, holding nothing back, might surrender ourselves with all our hearts to the holy will of God.

But consecration itself even along with any; following separation is still only a preparation, Entire sanctification takes place when God takes possession of and falls with His glory the temple that is consecrated to Him.

"*There will I meet with the children of Israel, and they shall be sanctified by my glory*" (Exodus 29: 43). Actual, complete sanctification consists in God's impartation of His own holiness—of Himself.

Here also the blood speaks: It tells us that Heaven is opened, that the powers of the heavenly life have come down to earth, that every hindrance has been removed, and God can make His abode with man.

Immediate nearness and fellowship with God, are made possible by the blood. The believer who surrenders unreservedly to the blood, obtains the full assurance that God will bestow Himself wholly, and will reveal His holiness in him.

How glorious are the results of such a sanctification! Through the Holy Spirit, the soul's intercourse is in the living experience of God's abiding nearness; accompanied by the awakening of the tenderest carefulness against sin; guarded by caution and the fear of God.

But to live in watchfulness against sin does not satisfy the soul. The temple must not only be cleansed but it must be filled with God's glory. All the virtues of Divine holiness, as manifested in the Lord Jesus, are to be sought for and found, in fellowship with God. Sanctification means union with God; fellowship in His will; sharing His life; conformity to His image.

Christians, "*Wherefore Jesus also … suffered without the gate that He might sanctify his people with his own blood. Let us go forth unto Him without the camp.*" Yes; it is He who sanctifies His people. "*Let us go forth unto Him.*" Let us trust Him to make known to us the power of the blood. Let us yield ourselves wholly to its blessed efficacy. That blood, through which He sanctified Himself, has entered heaven to open it for us. It can make our hearts also a throne of God, that the grace and glory of God may dwell in us. Yes; "*let us go forth unto Him outside the camp.*" He who is willing to lose, and say farewell to everything, in order that Jesus may sanctify him, will not fail to obtain the blessing. He who is willing at any cost to experience the full power of the precious blood, can confidently reckon that he will be sanctified by Jesus Himself, through that blood.

"*The very God of peace sanctify you wholly.*" Amen.

5

HOLY IN CHRIST

Thoughts on the Calling of God's Children to be Holy as He is Holy

Chicago; London: Fleming H. Revell Co., 1887

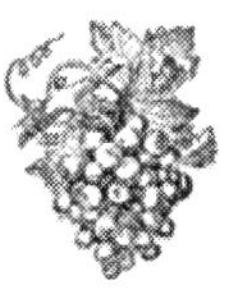

Preface

March 13th

"Consecrate yourselves and be holy, because I am holy."
—LEVITICUS 11: 44

There is not in Scripture a word more distinctly Divine in its origin and meaning than the word holy. There is not a word that leads us higher into the mystery of Deity, nor deeper into the privilege and the blessedness of God's children. And yet it is a word that many a Christian has never studied or understood.

There are not a few who can praise God that during the past twenty years the watchword, "*Be holy*," has been taken up in many a church and Christian circle with greater earnestness than before. In books and magazines, in conventions and conferences, in the testimonies and the lives of believers, we have abundant tokens that what is called the Holiness movement is a reality. And yet how much is still wanting! What multitudes of believing Christians there are who have none but the very vaguest thoughts of what holiness is! And of those who are seeking after it how many who have hardly learn what it is to come to God's Word and to God Himself for the teaching that can alone reveal this part of the mystery of Christ and of God! To many, holiness has simply been a general expression for the Christian life in its more earnest form, without much thought of what the term really means.

In writing this little book, my object has been to discover in what sense God uses the word, "holy," so it may mean to us what it means to Him. I have sought to trace the word through some of the most important passages of Holy Scripture where it occurs, there to learn what God's holiness is, what ours is to be, and what the way by which we attain it. I have been especially anxious to point out how many and various the elements are that go to make up true holiness as the Divine expression of the Christian life in all its fullness and perfection. I have at the same time striven continually to keep in mind the wonderful unity and simplicity there is in it, as centered in the person of Jesus.

... I fear there are some to whom the book may be a disappointment. They have heard that the entrance to the life of holiness is often but a step. They have heard of or seen believers who could tell of the blessed change that has come over their lives since they found the wonderful secret of holiness by faith. And now they are seeking for this secret. They cannot understand that the secret comes to those who seek it not, but only seek Jesus. ...

There is such a thing as a Pentecost still to the disciples of Jesus; but it comes to those who have forsaken all to follow Jesus only, and in following fully has allowed the Master to reprove and instruct them. There are often very blessed revelations of Christ, as a Savior from sin, both in the secret chamber and in the meetings of the saints; but these are given to those for whom they have been prepared, and who have been prepared to receive. Let all learn to trust in Jesus, and rejoice in Him, even though their experience be not what they would wish. He will make us holy. But whether we have entered the blessed life of faith in Jesus as our sanctification, or are still longing for it from afar, we all need one thing: the simple, believing, and obedient acceptance of each word that our God has spoken. ...

And may He stir us all to cry day and night to Him for a visitation of the Spirit and the power of holiness upon all His people, that the name of Christian and of saint may be synonymous, and every believer be a vessel made holy and meet for the Master's use.
—A.M. Wellington, 10th November 1887.

The Holy Spirit

"I the Lord am holy—I who make you holy" (Leviticus 21: 8). The unseen and unapproachable holiness of God had been revealed and brought near in the life of Christ Jesus; all that hindered our participation in it had been removed by His death. The name of Holy Spirit teaches us that it is specially the Spirit's work to impart it to us and make it our own.

Try and realize the meaning of this; the epithet that through the whole Old Testament has belonged to the Holy God, is now appropriated to that Spirit which is within you. The holiness of God in Christ becomes holiness in you, because this Spirit is in you. The words, and the Divine realities the words express, Holy and Spirit, are now inseparably and eternally united. You can only have as much of the Spirit as you are willing to have of holiness. You can only have as much holiness as you have of the indwelling Spirit.

There are some who pray for the Spirit because they long to have His light and joy and strength. And yet their prayers bring little increase of blessing or power. It is because they do not rightly know or desire Him as the Holy Spirit. His burning purity, His searching and convicting light, His making dead of the deeds of the body, of Self with its will and its power, His leading into the fellowship of Jesus as He gave up His will and His life to the Father—of all this they have not thought. The Spirit cannot work in power in them because they receive Him not as the Holy Spirit, in sanctification of the Spirit. At times, in seasons of revival, as among the Corinthians and Galatians, He may indeed come with His gifts and mighty workings, while His sanctifying power is but little manifest (1 Corinthians 14: 4, 13: 8, 3: 1–3; Galatians 3: 3, 15–26). ... *"Be full of the Spirit,"* must mean to us, "Be fully holy." ... "*Be holy*" means, "*Be filled with the Spirit*."

If we inquire more closely how it is that this Holy Spirit makes holy, the answer is, He reveals and imparts the holiness of Christ. Scripture tells us: Christ is made unto us sanctification. He sanctified Himself for us, that we ourselves might also be sanctified in truth. We have been sanctified through the offering of the body of Jesus Christ once for all. We are sanctified in Christ Jesus. The whole living Christ is just a treasury of holiness for man. In His life on earth He exchanged the Divine Holiness He possessed into the current coin needed for this human earthly life: obedience to the Father, and humility, and love, and zeal. As God, He has a sufficiency of it for every moment of the life of every believer. And yet, it is all beyond our reach, except as the Holy Spirit brings it to us and inwardly, communicates it. But this is the very work for which He bears the Divine Name, the Holy Spirit—to glorify Jesus, the Holy One of God, within us, and so make us partakers of His Holiness.

He does it by revealing Christ, so that we begin to see what is in Him. He does it by discovering the deep unholiness of our nature (Romans 7: 14–23). He does it by mightily strengthening us to believe, to receive Jesus Himself as our life. He does it by leading us to utter despair of Self, to absolute surrender of obedience to Jesus as Lord, to the assured confidence of faith in the power of an indwelling Christ. He does it by, in the secret silent depths of the heart and life, imparting the dispositions and graces of Christ, so that from the inner center of our life, which has been renewed and sanctified in Christ, holiness should flow out and pervade all to the utmost circumference.

Where the desire has once been awakened, and the delight in the law of God after the inward man been created, there, as the Spirit of this life in Christ Jesus, He makes free from the law of sin and death in the members, he leads into the glorious liberty of the sons of God. As God within us, He communicates what God in Christ has prepared.

And if we ask once more how the working of this Holy Spirit, who thus makes holy, is to be secured, the answer is very simple and clear. He is the Spirit of the Holy Father, and of Christ, the Holy One of God: from them He must be received. *"He showed me a river of water of life proceeding out of the throne of God and the Lamb."* Jesus speaks of *"the Holy Spirit, whom the Father will send in my Name."* ... He told us to believe in Himself. *"Whosoever believes in Me, rivers of living water shall flow out of them."*

The Holy One of Israel

March 14th

"I the Lord who makes you holy, am holy."
—LEVITICUS 21: 8

"I am the Lord your God; you shall therefore make yourselves holy; be holy, for I am holy."
—LEVITICUS 11: 44

In the book of Exodus we found God making provision for the holiness of His people. In the holy times and holy places, holy persons, holy things, and holy services, He had taught His people that everything around Him, that all that would come near Him, must be holy. He would only dwell in the midst of holiness; His people must be a holy people. But there is no direct mention of God Himself as holy. In the book of Leviticus, we are led on a step further. Here first we have God speaking of His own holiness, and making it the plea for the holiness of His people, as well as its pledge and power.

Without this the revelation of holiness was incomplete, and the call to holiness powerless. True holiness will come to us as we learn that God alone is holy. It is He alone makes holy; it is as we come to Himself, and in obedience and love are linked to Him, that His holiness can rest on us.

From the books of Moses onwards we shall find that the name of God as holy is found but seldom in the inspired writings, until we come to Isaiah, the evangelist prophet. There it occurs twenty-six times, and has its true meaning opened up in the way in which it is linked with the name of Savior and Redeemer. The sentiments of joy and trust and praise, with which a redeemed people would look upon their Deliverer, are all mentioned in connection with the name of the Holy One.

"*I am the Lord your God; you shall therefore make yourselves holy and be holy, for I am holy*" (Leviticus 11: 44); "*I am the Lord that brings you up out of the land of Egypt to be your God: You shall therefore be holy, for I am holy*" (Leviticus 11: 45); "*You shall be holy, for I the Lord your God am holy*" (Leviticus 19: 2); "*Consecrate yourselves therefore, and be holy, for I am the Lord your God* (Leviticus 20: 7, 8); "*And you shall be holy to Me, for I the Lord am holy, and have separated you from the peoples, that you should be Mine*" (Leviticus 20: 26). …

In Israel we saw that God the Redeemer was ever God the Sanctifier, making holy the people He had chosen for Himself. Here in Isaiah we see how it is God the Sanctifier, the Holy One, who is to bring about the great redemption of the New Testament: as the Holy One, He is the Redeemer. God redeems because He is holy, and loves to make holy. Holiness will be redemption perfected. Redemption and holiness together are to be found in the personal relation to God. The key to the secret of holiness is offered to each believer in that word: *"Thus says the Lord, your Redeemer, the Holy One of Israel: I am the Lord, your Holy One."* To come near, to know, to possess the Holy One, and be possessed of Him, is holiness.

If God's Holiness is thus the only hope for ours, it is right that we seek to know what that Holiness is. And though we may find it indeed to be something that passes knowledge, it will not be in vain to gather up what has been revealed in the Word concerning it. Let us do so in the spirit of holy fear and worship, trusting to the Holy Spirit to be our teacher.

And let us first notice how this Holiness of God, though it is often mentioned as one of the Divine attributes, can hardly be counted such, on a level with the others. The other attributes all refer to some special aspect or characteristic of the Divine Nature; Holiness appears to express what is the very essence or perfection of the Divine Being Himself. None of the attributes can be predicated of all that belongs to God; but Scripture speaks of His Holy Name, His Holy Day, His Holy Habitation, His Holy Word. In the word Holy, we have the nearest possible approach to a summary of all the Divine perfections, the description of what Divinity is. We speak of the other attributes as Divine perfections, but in this we have the only human expression for the Divine Perfection itself. It is for this reason that theologians have found such difficulty in framing a definition that can express all the word means.

The original Hebrew word, whether derived from a root signifying to separate, or another with the idea of shining, expressed the idea of something distinguished from others, separate from them by superior excellence. God is Separate and different from all that is created, keeps Himself separate from all that is not God; as the Holy One, He maintains His Divine glory and perfection against whatever might interfere with it: *"There is none holy, but the Lord"; "To whom will you liken me? Or shall I be equal? says the Holy One."* As Holy, God is indeed the Incomparable One; holiness is His alone; there is nothing like it in Heaven or earth, except when He gives it. And so our holiness will consist, not in a human separation in which we attempt to imitate God's, no, but in entering into His separateness; belonging entirely to Him; set apart by Him and for Himself.

If we inquire more closely wherein the infinite excellence of this separateness ... consists, we are led to think of the Divine Purity, and that not only in its negative aspect as hatred of sin but with the more positive element of perfect beauty. Because we are sinners, and the revelation of God's holiness is in a world of sin, it is natural, it is right and meet, that the first, that the abiding impression of God's holiness should be that of an Infinite Purity that cannot look upon sin, in whose presence it becomes the sinner to hide his face and tremble. ... If the holiness of God is to become ours, to rest upon us, and enter into us, there must be, without ceasing, the holy fear that trembles at the thought of grieving the infinite sensitiveness of this Holy One by our sins, and yet side by side, and in perfect harmony with it, the deep longing to behold the beauty of the Lord, an admiration of its Divine glory, and a joyful surrender to be His alone.

We must go one step further. When God says, *"I am holy; I make holy,"* we see that one of the chief elements of His holiness is this: that it seeks to communicate itself, to make partaker of its own perfection and blessedness. ... We are taught that as the Holy One—just because He is the Holy One, who delights to make holy—He will be the Deliverer of His people (See Hosea 11: 9). It is holiness above everything else that we are invited to look to, to trust in, to rejoice in.

The Holy One is the holy-making One: He redeems and saves that He may win our confidence for Himself, that He may draw us to Himself as the Holy One, that in the personal attachment to Himself we may learn to obey, to become of one mind with Him, to be holy as He is holy. … It is that energy of the Divine life in the power of which God not only keeps Himself free from all creature weakness or sin, but unceasingly seeks to lift the creature into union with Himself and the full participation of His own purity and perfection. … It is in the adoring contemplation of His holiness, in the trustful surrender to it, in the loving fellowship with Himself, the Holy One, that we can be made holy.

Would you be holy? listen again, and in the deep silence of trust, let God's words sink into your heart…. Come to Him and claim Him as your God, and claim all that He, as the Holy One who makes holy, can do for you. Just remember that holiness is God Himself. … Seek not, even from Him, holiness in yourself; let Self be abased, and be content that the Holiness is His. As His presence fills your heart, as His holiness and glory are your one desire, as His holy will and love are your delight, as the Holy One becomes all in all to you, you will be holy with the holiness He loves to see. … BE HOLY, AS I AM HOLY.

A Call to Holiness

March 15th

"As He who called you is holy, be also holy in all manner of living; because it is written: You shall be holy, for I am holy."

—1 PETER 1: 15–16

Holy Scripture uses more than one word to indicate the object or aim of our calling, but none more frequently than what Peter speaks of here: God has called us to be holy as He is holy. Paul addresses believers twice as *"called to be holy"* (Romans 1: 7; 1 Corinthians 1: 2). *"God called us,"* he says, *"not for uncleanness, but in sanctification"* (1 Thessalonians 4: 7). When he writes, *"The God of peace sanctify you wholly,"* he adds, *"Faithful is He which calls you, who also will do it"* (1 Thessalonians 5: 24). The calling itself is spoken of as *"a holy calling."* … The call is the unveiling of the purpose that the Father from eternity had set His heart upon: *that we should be holy. …*

Let us ask God to show us how, as He who has called us is Himself holy, so we are to be holy too; our calling is a holy calling, a calling before and above everything, to Holiness. … to show us how He has set His heart upon it as the one thing He wants to see in us, as being His own image and likeness; to show us, too, the unutterable blessedness and glory of sharing with Christ in His Holiness. Oh! That God by His Spirit would teach us what it means that we are called to be holy as He is holy. We can easily conceive what a mighty influence it would exert.

"Like He who called you is holy, be also holy." How this call God shows us the true motive to Holiness. *"Be holy, for I am holy."* … Shall we not cry earnestly to God to show us the

glory of His holiness, that our souls may be made willing to give everything in response to this wondrous call? As we listen to the call, it shows also the nature of true Holiness. *"As He is holy, so you also be holy."*

To be holy is to be Godlike, to have a disposition, a will, a character like God. The thought almost looks like blasphemy, until we listen again, *"He has chosen us in Christ to be holy."* In Christ the holiness of God appeared in a human life: in Christ's example, in His mind and Spirit, we have the Holiness of the Invisible One translated into the forms of human life and conduct. To be Christlike is to be Godlike; to be Christlike is to be holy as God is holy.

The call equally reveals the power of holiness. "*There is none holy but the Lord*"; there is no Holiness but what He has, or rather what He is, and gives. Holiness is not something we do or attain: it is the communication of the Divine life, the inbreathing of the Divine nature, the power of the Divine Presence resting on us. And our power to become holy is to be found in the call God.

The Holy One calls us to Himself, that He may make us holy in possessing Himself. He not only says, *"I am holy,"* but "*I am the Lord, who makes you holy.*" It is because the call to holiness comes from the God of infinite Power and Love that we may have the confidence: we can be holy.

The call no less reveals the standard of Holiness. *"As He is holy…be also holy."* There is not one standard of holiness for God and another for man. The nature of light is the same, whether we see it in the Sun or in a candle: the nature of holiness remains unchanged, whether it be God or man in whom it dwells. The Lord Jesus could say nothing less than, "*Be perfect, even as your Father in Heaven is perfect.*" When God calls us to holiness, He calls us to Himself and His own life: the more carefully we listen to the voice, and let it sink into our hearts, the more will all human standards fall away, and only the words be heard, *Holy, as I am holy.*

And the call [to be holy] shows us the path to holiness. The calling of God is one of mighty efficacy, an effectual calling. Oh! Let us but listen to it, let us but listen to Him, and the call will with Divine power work what it offers. He calls the things that are not as though they were: His call gives life to the dead, and holiness to those whom He has made alive. He calls us to listen as He speaks of His holiness, and of our holiness like His. He calls us to Himself, to study, to fear, to love, to claim His holiness. He calls us to Christ, in whom Divine holiness became human holiness, to see and admire, to desire and accept what is all for us. He calls us to the indwelling and the teaching of the Spirit of Holiness, to yield ourselves that He may bring home to us and breathe within us what is ours in Christ. Christian! listen to God calling you to holiness.

Come and learn what His holiness is, and what yours is and must be. Yes, be very silent and listen. When God called Abraham, he answered, "Here am I." When God called Moses from the bush, he answered, "Here am I," and he hid his face, for he was afraid to look upon God. God is calling you to holiness, to Himself the Holy One, that He may make you holy. Let your whole soul answer, "Here am I, Lord! Speak, Lord! Show yourself, Lord! Here am I." As you listen, the voice will sound ever deeper and ever stiller: *Be holy, as I am holy.*

You will hear a voice coming out of the great eternity, from the council-chamber of redemption, and as you catch its distant whisper, it will be, *Be holy, I am holy.* You will hear a voice from Paradise, the Creator making the seventh day holy for man whom He had created, and saying, *Be holy.* You will hear the voice from Sinai, amid thunderings and lightnings, and still it is, *Be holy, as I am holy.* You will hear a voice from Calvary, and there above all it is, *Be holy, for I am holy.*

Child of God, have you ever realized it, our Father is calling us to Himself, to be holy as He is holy? Must we not confess that happiness has been to us more than holiness, salvation than sanctification? Oh! It is not too late to redeem the error. Let us now band ourselves together to listen to the voice that calls, to draw nigh, and find out and know what Holiness is, or rather, find out and know Himself the Holy One.

And if the first approach to Him fill us with shame and confusion, make us fear and shrink back, let us still listen to the Voice and the Call, *"Be holy, as I am holy." "Faithful is He which calls, who also will do it."* All our fears and questions will be met by the Holy One who has revealed His Holiness, with this one purpose in view, that we might share it with Him. As we yield ourselves in deep stillness of soul to listen to the Holy Voice that calls us, it will waken within us new desire and strong faith, and the most precious of all promises will be to us this word of Divine command: BE HOLY, FOR I AM HOLY.

God's Provision for Holiness

March 16th

"To those that are made holy in Christ Jesus, called to be holy."

—1 CORINTHIANS 1: 2

Holy! In Christ! In these two expressions we have perhaps the most wonderful words of all the Bible. Holy! The word of unfathomable meaning, which the Seraphs utter with veiled faces. HOLY! The word in which all God's perfections center, and of which His glory is but the streaming forth. HOLY! The word which reveals the purpose with which God from eternity thought of man, and tells what man's highest glory in the coming eternity is to be; to be partaker of His Holiness! …

What wealth of meaning and blessing in the two words combined: Holy in Christ! Here is God's provision for our holiness, God's response to our question, "How to be holy?" Often and often as we hear the call, *Be holy, even as I am holy*, it is as if there is and ever must be a great gulf between the holiness of God and man. In Christ! Is the bridge that crosses the gulf; nay rather, His fullness has filled it up. In Christ! God and man meet; in Christ! The holiness of God has found us, and made us its own—has become human, and can indeed become our very own. To the anxious cries and the heart-yearnings of thousands of thirsty souls who have believed in Jesus and yet know not how to be holy, here is God's answer: you are holy in Christ Jesus. Would they but hearken, and believe; would they but take these Divine words, and say them over, if need be, a thousand times, how God's light would shine, and fill their hearts with joy and love as they echo them back: Yes, now I see it. Holy in Christ! Made holy in Christ Jesus! The being in Him, the abiding in Him, the being rooted in Him, the growing up in Him and into Him in all things, are the Divine expressions in which the wonderful and complete oneness between us and our Savior are brought as near us as human language can do.

As the Old Testament had no higher word than "holy," the New has none deeper than this, "in Christ." The being in Him, the abiding in Him, the being rooted in Him, the growing up in Him and into Him in all things, are the Divine expressions in which the wonderful and complete oneness between us and our Savior are brought as near us as human language can do.

And when Old and New Testament have each given their message, the one in teaching us what Holy, the other what in Christ means, we have in the word of God, that unites the two, the most complete summary of the great redemption that God's love has provided. The everlasting certainty, the wonderful sufficiency, the infinite efficacy of the holiness that God has prepared for us in His Son, are all revealed in this blessed, *holy in Christ.*

"The Holy Ones in Christ Jesus!" Such is the name, beloved fellow-believers, which we bear in Holy Scripture, in the language of the Holy Spirit. It is no mere statement of doctrine, that we are holy in Christ: it is no deep theological discussion to which we are invited; but out of the depths of God's loving heart, there comes a voice thus addressing His beloved children. It is the name by which the Father calls His children. That name tells us of God's provision for our being holy. It is the revelation of what God has given us, and what we already are; of what God waits to work in us, and what can be ours in personal practical possession. That name, gratefully accepted, joyfully confessed, trustfully pleaded, will be the pledge and the power of our attainment of the holiness to which we have been called.

And so we shall find that as we go along, all our study and all God's teaching will be comprised in three great lessons. The first a revelation, *"I am holy"*; the second a command, *"Be holy"*; the third a gift—the link between the two, *"You are holy in Christ."*

First comes the revelation, *"I am holy."* Our study must be on bended knee, in the spirit of worship and deep humility. God must reveal Himself to us, if we are to know what Holy is. The deep unholiness of our nature and all that is of nature must be shown us; with Moses and Isaiah, when the Holy One revealed Himself to them, we must fear and tremble, and confess how utterly unfit we are for the revelation or the fellowship, without the cleansing of fire.

In the consciousness of the utter impotence of our own wisdom or understanding to know God, our souls must in contrition, brokenness from ourselves and our power or efforts, yield to God's Spirit, the Spirit of Holiness, to reveal God as the Holy One. And as we begin to know Him in His infinite righteousness, in His fiery burning zeal against all that is sin, and His infinite Self-sacrificing love to free the sinner from his sin, and to bring him to His own perfection, we shall learn to wonder at and worship this glorious

God, to feel and deplore our terrible unlikeness to Him, to long and cry for some share in the Divine beauty and blessedness of this holiness. And then will come with new meaning the command, *"Be holy, as I am holy."*

O, my brethren! You who profess to obey the commands of your God, do give this all-surpassing and all-including command that first place in your heart and life which it claims. Do be holy with the likeness of God's holiness. Do be holy as He is holy. And if you find that the more you meditate and study, the less you can grasp this infinite holiness; that the more you at moments grasp of it, the more you despair of a holiness so Divine; remember that such breaking down and such despair is just what the command was meant to work. Learn to cease from your own wisdom as well as your own goodness; draw near in poverty of spirit to let the Holy One show you how utterly above human knowledge or human power is the holiness He demands; to the soul that ceases from Self, and has no confidence in the flesh, He will show and give the holiness He calls us to.

It is to such that the great gift of holiness in Christ becomes intelligible and acceptable. Christ brings the holiness of God nigh by showing it in human conduct and intercourse. He brings it nigh by removing the barrier between it and us, between God and us. He brings it nigh, because He makes us one with Himself—"*Holy in Christ.*"

Our holiness is a Divine bestowment, held for us, communicated to us, working mightily in us because we are in Him. "*In* Christ!" Oh, that wonderful *in*! Our very life rooted *in* the life of Christ. That holy Son and Servant of the Father, beautiful in His life of love and obedience on earth, sanctifying Himself for us that life of Christ, the ground in which I am planted and rooted, the soil from which I draw as my nourishment its every quality and its very nature. How that word sheds its light both on the revelation, "*I am holy*" and on the command, "*Be holy, as I am*," and binds them in one! In Christ I see what God's Holiness is, and what my holiness is. In Him both are one, and both are mine. In Him I am holy; abiding and growing up in Him, I can be holy in all manner of living, as God is holy.

Holiness and Indwelling

March 17th

"And let them make me a holy place, that I may dwell among them."
—EXODUS 25: 8

The presence of God makes holy, even when it descends but for a little while, as at Horeb, in the burning bush. How much more must that presence make holy the place where it dwells, where it fixes its permanent abode! So much is this the case, that the place where God dwells came to be called the holy place, *"the holy place of the habitation of the Most High."* All around where God dwelled was holy: the holy city, the mountain of God's holiness, His holy house, till we come within the veil, to the most holy place, the holy of holies. It is as the indwelling God that He sanctifies His house, that He reveals

Himself as the Holy One in Israel, that He makes us holy too.

Because God is holy, the house, in which He dwells is holy too. This is the only attribute of God, which He can communicate to His house; but this one He can and does communicate. Among men there is a very close link between the character of a house and its occupants. When there is no obstacle to prevent it, the house unintentionally reflects the master's likeness. Holiness expresses not so much an attribute as the very being of God in His infinite perfection, and His house testifies to this one truth, that He is holy, that where He dwells He must have holiness, that His indwelling makes holy.

In His first command to His people to build Him a holy place, God distinctly said that it was that He might dwell among them: the dwelling in the house was to be the shadowing forth of His dwelling in the midst of His people. The house with its holiness thus leads us on to the holiness of His dwelling among His redeemed ones.

The holy place, the habitation of God's Holiness, was the center of all God's work in making Israel holy. Everything connected with it was holy. The altar, the priests, the sacrifices, the oil, the bread, the vessels, all were holy, because they belonged to God. From the house there issued the twofold voice God's call to be holy, God's promise to make holy. God's claim was manifested in the demand for cleansing, for atonement, for holiness, in all who were to draw near, whether as priests or worshippers. And God's promise shone forth from His house in the provision for making holy, in the sanctifying power of the altar, of the blood and the oil. The house embodied the two sides that are united in holiness, the repelling and the attracting, the condemning and the saving. Now by keeping the people at a distance, then by inviting and bringing them nigh, God's house was the great symbol of His own Holiness. He had come nigh even to dwell among them; and yet they might not come nigh, they might never enter the secret place of His presence.

All these things are written on our behalf. It is as the Indwelling One that God is the sanctifier of His people still; the Indwelling Presence alone makes us holy. This comes out with special clearness if we note how, the nearer the presence was, the greater the degree of holiness. Because God dwelled among them, the camp was holy: all uncleanness was to be removed from it. But the holiness of the court of the tabernacle was greater: uncleanness which did not exclude from the camp would not be tolerated there. Then the holy place was still holier, because still nearer God. And the inner sanctuary, where the Presence dwelled on the mercy seat, was the Holiest of All, was most holy. The principle still holds good: holiness is measured by nearness to God; the more of His presence, the more of true holiness; perfect indwelling will be perfect holiness.

There is none holy but the Lord; there is no holiness but in Him. He cannot part with somewhat of His holiness, and give it to us apart from Himself; we have only so much of holiness as we have of God Himself. And to have Himself truly and fully, we must have Him as the Indwelling One. And His indwelling in a house or locality, without life or spirit, is only a faint shadow of the true indwelling as the Living One, when He enters into and penetrates our very being, and fills us, our very selves, with His own life.

There is no union so intimate, so real, so perfect, as that of an indwelling life. Think of the life that circulates through a large and fruitful tree. How it penetrates and fills every portion; how inseparably it unites the whole as long as it really is to exist! In wood and leaf, in flower and fruit, everywhere the indwelling life flows and tills. This life is the life of nature, the life of the Spirit of God which dwells in nature. It is the same life that animates our bodies, the spirit of nature pervading every portion of them with the power of sensibility and action. Not less intimate, yea rather, far more wonderful and real, is the indwelling of the Spirit of the New Life, through whom God dwells in the heart of the believer. And it is as this indwelling becomes a matter of conscious longing and faith, that the soul obeys the command, *"Let them make Me a holy place, that I may dwell among them,"* and experiences the truth of the promise, *"The tent shall be sanctified by My glory, and I will dwell among the children of Israel, and will be their God"* (Exodus 29: 43, 45).

It was as the Indwelling One that God revealed Himself in the Son, whom He sanctified and sent into the world. More than once our Lord insisted upon it, *"Believe Me, that I am in the Father and the Father in Me; the Father abiding in Me does the works."* It is specially as the temple of God that believers are more than once called holy in the New Testament: *"The temple of God is holy"* ... *"Your body is a temple of the Holy Spirit."* ...

It is we shall later on learn to understand this better just because it is through the Spirit that the heart is prepared for the indwelling, and the indwelling effected and maintained, that the Spirit so peculiarly takes the attribute of holy. The Indwelling Spirit is the Holy Spirit. The measure of His indwelling, or rather of His revealing the Indwelling Christ, is the measure of holiness.

We have seen what the various degrees of nearness to God's Presence in Israel were. They are still to be found. You have Christians who dwell in the camp, but know little of drawing nigh to the Holy One. Then you have outer court Christians: they long for pardon and peace; they come ever again to the altar of atonement; but they know little of true nearness or holiness; of their privilege as priests to enter the holy place.

... Blessed they to whom this, the secret of the Lord, has been revealed. They know what the rent veil means, and the access into the immediate Presence. The veil has been taken away from their hearts: they have found the secret of true holiness in the indwelling of the Holy One, the God who is holy and makes holy.

Believer! The God who calls you to holiness is the God of the Indwelling Life. The tabernacle typifies it, the Son reveals it, the Spirit communicates it, the eternal glory will fully manifest it. And you may experience it. It is your calling as a believer to be God's Holy Temple. Oh, do but yield yourself to His full indwelling!

Seek not holiness in the first place in what you are or do; seek it in God. Seek it not even as a gift from God, seek it in God Himself, in His indwelling Presence. Worship Him in the beauty of holiness, as He dwells in the high and holy place. And as you worship, listen to His voice: *"Thus says the high and lofty One, that inhabits eternity, whose name is Holy: I dwell in the high and holy place, with him also that is of a contrite and humble spirit."*

It is as the Spirit strengthens us mightily in the inward man, so that Christ dwells in our heart by faith, and the Father comes and makes with Him His abode in us, that we are truly holy. Oh, let us but, in true, true-hearted consecration, yield ourselves to be, as distinctly as was the tabernacle or the temple, given up entirely to be the dwelling of the

Most High, the habitation of His Holiness. A house filled with the glory of God, a heart filled with all the fullness of God, is God's promise, is our portion. Let us in faith claim and accept and hold fast the blessing: Christ, the Holy One of God, will in His Father's Name, enter and take possession. Then faith will bring the solution of all our difficulties, the victory over all our failures, the fulfilment of all our desires: "*The tent, the heart, shall be sanctified by My glory; and I will dwell among them.*" The open secret of true holiness, the secret of the joy unspeakable, is Christ dwelling in the heart by faith. BE HOLY, AS I AM HOLY.

Holiness and the Will of God

March 18th

"This is the will of God, even your sanctification."

—1 THESSALONIANS 4: 3 …

God very distinctly and definitely has willed your sanctification: your sanctification has its source and certainty in its being God's will. We are *"elect in sanctification of the Spirit," "chosen to be holy";* the purpose of God's will from eternity, and His will now, is our sanctification. There is, however, another most precious thought suggested. If our sanctification be God's will, its central thought and its contents, every part of that will must bear upon it, and the sure entrance to sanctification will be the hearty acceptance of the will of God in all things. To be one with God's will is to be holy. Let us who would be holy take our place here and *"stand in all the will of God."* We will there meet God Himself, and be made partaker of His holiness, because His will works out its purpose in power to each one who yields to it.

Everything in a life of holiness depends upon our being in the right relation to the will of God. There are many Christians to whom it appears impossible to think of their accepting all the will of God, or of their being one with it. They look upon the will of God in its thousand commands.... They have sometimes found it so hard to obey one single command, or to give up willingly to some light disappointment. They imagine that they would need to be a thousand-fold holier and stronger in grace, before venturing to say that they do accept all God's will, whether to do or to bear.

They cannot understand that all the difficulty comes from their not occupying the right standpoint. They are looking at God's will as at variance with their natural will, and they feel that that natural will will never delight in all God's will. They forget that the new man has a renewed will. This new will delights in the will of God, because it is born of it. This new will sees the beauty and the glory of God's will, and is in harmony with it. If they are indeed God's children, the very first impulse of the spirit of a child is surely to do the will of the Father in heaven. And they have but to yield themselves heartily and wholly to this spirit of sonship, and they need not fear to accept God's will as theirs.

The mistake they make is a very serious one. Instead of living by faith they judge by feeling, in which the old nature speaks and rules. It tells them that God's will is often a burden too hard to be borne, and that they never can have the strength to do it. Faith speaks differently. It reminds us that God is Love, and that His will is nothing but Love revealed. It asks if we do not know that there is nothing more perfect or beautiful in heaven or earth than the will of God. It shows us how in our conversion we have already professed to accept God as Father and Lord. It assures us, above all, that if we will but definitely and trustingly give ourselves to that will which is Love, it will as Love fill our hearts and make us delight in it, and so become the power that enables us joyfully to do and to bear.

Faith reveals to us that the will of God is the power of His love, working out its plan in Divine beauty in each one who wholly yields to it. And which shall we now choose? And where shall we take our place? Shall we attempt to accept Christ as a Savior without accepting His will? Shall we profess to be the Father's children, and yet spend our life in debating how much of His will we shall perform? Shall we be content to go on from day to day with the painful consciousness that our will is not in harmony with God's will? Or shall we not at once and for ever give up our will as sinful to His, to that will which He has already written on our heart?

This is a thing that is possible. It can be done. In a simple, definite transaction with God, we can say that we do accept His holy will to be ours. Faith knows that God will not pass such a surrender unnoticed, but accept it. In the trust that He now takes us up into His will, and undertakes to breathe it into us, with the love and the power to perform it in this faith let us enter into God's will, and begin a new life; standing in, abiding in the very center of this most holy will. Such an acceptance of God's will prepares the believer, through the Holy Spirit, to recognize and know that will in whatever form it comes.

The great difference between the carnal and the spiritual Christian is that the latter acknowledges God, under whatever low and poor [circumstances] He manifests Himself. When God comes in trials which can be traced to no hand but His, we say, *"Your will be done."* When trials come through the weakness of others or our own folly, when circumstances appear unfavorable to our religious progress, and temptations threaten to be too much for us and to overcome us, we learn first of all to see God in everything, and still to say, *"Your will be done."* ...

Seeing and honoring God's will thus in everything, we learn always to abide in that will, and also by doing that will. As our spiritual discernment grows to say of whatever happens, "All things are of God," so we grow too in wisdom and spiritual understanding to know the will of God as it is to be done. In the indications of conscience and of Providence, in the teaching of the Word and the Spirit, we learn to see how God's will has reference to every part and duty of life, and it becomes our joy, in all things, to live, *"doing the will of God from the heart, as unto the Lord and not unto men."* Laboring fervently in prayer to stand complete and fully assured in all the will of God, we find how blessedly the Father has accepted our surrender, and supplies all the light and strength that is needed that—as Jesus taught us to pray—His "*will be done*" by us, "*on earth as it is in Heaven.*"

Holiness and Redemption

March 19th

"For I am the Lord your God that brings you up out of the land of Egypt to be your God: you shall therefore be holy, for I am holy."

—LEVITICUS 11: 45

At Horeb we saw how the first mention of the word holy in the history of fallen man was connected with the inauguration of a new period in the revelation of God: *that of redemption.* In the Passover we have the first manifestation of what redemption is; and here the more frequent use of the word holy begins. In the Feast of Unleavened Bread we have the symbol of the putting off of the old and the putting on of the new, to which redemption through blood is to lead. …

As soon as the people had been redeemed from Egypt, God's very first word to them was, *"Sanctify—make holy unto me—all the first-born: it is mine"* (Exodus 13: 2). The Word reveals how proprietorship is one of the central thoughts both in redemption and in sanctification, the link that binds them together. And though the word is here only used of the first born, they are regarded as the type of the whole people … as the type of what the whole people is to be as God's first-born among the nations, His peculiar treasure— *"a holy nation."*

This idea of proprietor ship as related to redemption and sanctification comes out with especial clearness when God speaks of the exchange of the priests for the firstborn: *"The Levites are wholly given unto m; instead of the first-born have I taken them unto me; for all the first-born are mine; in the day that I smote every first-born in the land of Egypt, I sanctified them for myself"* (Numbers 3: 12, 13; 8: 16, 17). Let us try and realize the relation existing between redemption and holiness. In Paradise, we saw what God's sanctifying the seventh day was: He took possession of it, He blessed it, He rested in it and refreshed Himself. Where God enters and rests, there is holiness; the more perfectly the object is fitted for Him to enter and dwell, the more perfect the holiness. …

Having thus redeemed [Israel from bondage], He tells them that they are now His own. During their stay at Sinai and in the wilderness, the thought is continually pressed upon them that they are now the Lord's people, whom He has made His own by the strength of His arm, that He may make them holy for Himself, even as He is holy. The purpose of redemption is possession, and the purpose of possession is likeness to Him who is Redeemer and Owner, is holiness.

In regard to this Holiness, and the way it is to be attained as the result of redemption, there is more than one lesson the sanctifying of the first born will teach us. First of all, we want to realize how inseparable redemption and holiness are. Neither can exist without the other. Only redemption leads to holiness. If I am seeking holiness, I must abide in the clear and full experience of being a redeemed one, and as such of being owned and possessed by God. Redemption is too often looked at from its negative side as *deliverance from*; its real glory is the positive element of being *redeemed unto* Himself. …

God has redeemed me and made me His own with the view of getting complete possession of me. He says of my soul, "It is mine," and seeks to have His right of ownership acknowledged and made fully manifest. That will be perfect holiness, where God has entered in and taken complete and entire possession. It is redemption that gives God His right and power over me; it is redemption that sets me free for God now to possess and bless: it is redemption realized and filling my soul, that will bring me the assurance and experience of all His power will work in me. In God, redemption and sanctification are one: the more redemption as a Divine reality possesses me, the closer am I linked to the Redeemer-God, the Holy One.

And just so, only holiness brings the assurance and enjoyment of redemption. If I am seeking to hold fast redemption on lower ground, I may be deceived. If I have become unwatchful or careless, I should tremble at the very idea of trusting in redemption apart from holiness as its object. To Israel God spoke, *"I brought you up out of the land of Egypt: therefore, you shall be holy, for I am holy."* It is God the Redeemer who made us His own, who calls us too to be holy: let Holiness be to us the most essential, the most precious part of redemption: the yielding of ourselves to Him who has taken us as His own, and has undertaken to make us His own entirely.

A second lesson suggested is the connection between God's and man's working in sanctification. To Moses the Lord speaks, "*Sanctify unto me all the first-born.*" He afterwards says, "*I sanctified all the first-born for myself.*" What God does He does to be carried out and appropriated through us. When He tells us that we are made holy in Christ Jesus, that we are His holy ones, He speaks not only of His purpose, but of what He has really done; we have been sanctified in the one offering of Christ, and in our being created anew in Him. But this work has a human side. To us comes the call to be holy, to follow after holiness, to perfect holiness. God has made us His own, and allows us to say that we are His: but He waits for us now to yield Him an enlarged entrance into the secret places of our inner being, for Him to fill it all with His fullness.

Holiness is not something we bring to God or do for Him. Holiness is what there is of God in us. God has made us His own in redemption, that He might make Himself our own in sanctification. And our work in becoming holy is the bringing our whole life, and every part of it, into subjection to the rule of this holy God, putting every member and every power upon His altar.

And this teaches us the answer to the question as to the connection between the sudden and the gradual in sanctification: between its being a thing once for all complete, and yet imperfect and needing to be perfected. What God sanctifies is holy with a Divine and perfect holiness as His gift: man has to sanctify by acknowledging and maintaining and carrying out that holiness in relation to what God has made holy. God sanctified the Sabbath day: man has to sanctify it, that is, to keep it holy. God sanctified the first-born as His own: Israel had to sanctify them, to treat them and give them up to God as holy.

… God has sanctified us in Christ Jesus: we are to be holy by yielding ourselves to the power of that holiness, by acting it out, and manifesting it in all our life and walk. The objective Divine gift, bestowed once for all and completely, must be appropriated as a subjective personal possession; we must cleanse ourselves, perfecting holiness. Redeemed unto holiness: as the two thoughts are linked in the mind and work of God, they must be linked in our heart and life. …

Holiness and Cleansing

March 20th

"Having therefore these promises, beloved, let us cleanse ourselves from all defilement of flesh and spirit, perfecting holiness in the fear of God."

—2 CORINTHIANS 7: 1

That holiness is more than cleansing, and must be preceded by it, is taught us in more than one passage of the New Testament. … The cleansing is the negative side, the being separate, and not touching the unclean thing, the removal of impurity; the sanctifying is the positive union and fellowship with God, and the participation of the graces of the Divine life and holiness (2 Corinthians 6: 17–18). … Cleansing must ever prepare the way, and ought always to lead on to holiness.

Paul speaks of a twofold defilement, of flesh and spirit, from which we must cleanse ourselves. The connection between the two is so close, that in every sin both are partakers. The lowest and most carnal form of sin will enter the spirit, and, dragging it down into partnership in crime, will defile and degrade it. …

From all this, Christians, who would be holy, must most determinedly cleanse ourselves. We must yield ourselves to the searching of God's Spirit, to be taught what there is in the flesh that is not in harmony with the temperance and Self-control demanded both by the law of nature and the law of the Spirit. We must believe, what Paul felt that the Corinthians so emphatically needed to be taught, that the Holy Spirit dwells in the body, making its members the members of Christ, and in this faith, we must put off the works of the flesh; we must cleanse ourselves from all defilement of flesh.

As the source of all defilement of the flesh is Self-gratification, so Self-seeking is at the root of all defilement of the spirit. In relation to God, it manifests itself in idolatry, be it in the worship of other gods after our own heart, the love of the world more than God, or the doing our will rather than His. In relation to our fellow-men it shows itself in envy, hatred, and want of love, cold neglect or harsh judging of others. In relation to ourselves it is seen as pride, ambition, or envy, the disposition that makes Self the center round which all must move, and by which all must be judged. For the discovery of such defilement of spirit, no less than of the sins of the flesh, the believer needs the light of the Holy Spirit; that the uncleanness may indeed be cleansed out and cast away forever. Even unconscious sin, if we are not earnestly willing to have it shown to us, will most effectually prevent our progress in the path of holiness.

"*Beloved! let us cleanse ourselves*" (2 Corinthians 7: 1). The cleansing is sometimes spoken of as the work of God (Acts 15: 9; 1 John 1: 9); sometimes as that of Christ (John 15: 3; Ephesians 5: 26; Titus 2: 14). Here we are commanded to cleanse ourselves. God does His work in us by the Holy Spirit; the Holy Spirit does His work by stirring us up and enabling us to do. The Spirit is the strength of the new life; in that strength, we must set ourselves determinedly to cast out whatever is unclean. "*Come out from them, and be separate, says the Lord. And touch no unclean thing, and I will receive you. I will be a Father to you*" (2 Corinthians 2: 17). It is not only the doing what is sinful, it is not only the willing of it, that the Christian must avoid, but even the touching it: the involuntary contact with it must be so unbearable as to force the cry with Paul, "*O wretched man that I am*!" and to lead on to the deliverance which the Spirit of the life of Christ does bring.

And how is this cleansing to be done? When Hezekiah called the priests to sanctify the temple that had been defiled, we read, "*The priests went in unto the inner part of the house of the Lord to cleanse it, and brought out all the uncleanness that they found*" (2 Chronicles 29). Only then could the sin-offering of atonement and the burnt-offering of consecration, with the thank-offerings, be brought, and God's service be restored. Even thus must all that is unclean be looked out, and brought out, and utterly cast out.

However deeply rooted the sin may appear, rooted in constitution and habit, we must cleanse ourselves of it if we would be holy. "*If we walk in the light, as He is in the light, the blood of Jesus Christ cleanses from all sin.*" As we bring out every sin from the inner part of the house into the light of God and walk in the light, the precious blood that justifies will work mightily to cleanse too: the blood brings into living contact with the life and the love of God. Let us come into the light with the sin: the blood will prove its mighty power. Let us cleanse ourselves in yielding ourselves to the light to reveal and condemn, to the blood to cleanse and sanctify.

"*Let us cleanse ourselves, perfecting holiness in the fear of the Lord!*" We read in Hebrews (10: 14). … We must perfect holiness: holiness must be carried out into the whole of life, and carried on even to its end. As God's holy ones, we must go on to perfection, perfecting holiness. Do not let us be afraid of the word, "perfect." Our Blessed Lord used it when He gave us the command, "*Be perfect, even as your Father in Heaven is perfect.*"

A child striving after the perfection in knowledge of his profession, which he hopes to attain when he has finished school, is told by his teacher that the way to the perfection he hopes for at the end of his course is to seek to be perfect in the lessons of each day. To be perfect in the small portion of the work that each hour brings, is the path to the perfection that will crown the whole.

The Master calls us to a perfection like that of the Father: He has already perfected us in Himself: He holds out the prospect of perfection ever growing. His word here calls us day by day to be perfecting holiness. Let us seek in each duty to be whole-hearted and entire. Let us, as teachable scholars, in every act of worship or obedience, in every temptation and trial, do the very best which God's Spirit can enable us to do.

"*Let patience have its perfect work, that you may be perfect and entire, lacking in nothing.*" "*The*

God of peace make you perfect in every good work to do His will." "*Having therefore these promises, beloved, let us cleanse ourselves from all defilement of flesh and spirit, perfecting holiness in the fear of God.*" It is faith that gives the courage and the power to cleanse from all defilement, perfecting holiness in the fear of God. It is as the promises of the Divine love and indwelling (2 Corinthians 6: 16–18) are made ours by the Holy spirit, that we shall share the victory which overcomes the world, even our faith. In the path along which we have already come, from the rest in Paradise down through Holy Scripture, we have seen the wondrous revelation of these promises in ever-growing splendor.

That God the Holy One will make us holy; that God the Holy One will dwell with the lowly; that God in His Holy One has come to be our holiness; that God has planted us in Christ that He may be our sanctification; that God, who chose us in sanctification of the Spirit, has given us the Holy Spirit in our hearts, and now watches over us in His love to work out through Him His purposes and to perfect our holiness: such are the promises that have been set before us.

"*Having therefore these promises, beloved, let us cleanse ourselves from all filthiness of flesh and spirit, perfecting holiness in the fear of God.*" Beloved! See here again God's way of holiness. Arise and step on to it in the faith of the promise, fully persuaded that what He has promised He is mighty to perform. Bring out of the inner part of the house all uncleanness; bring it into the light of God; confess it and cast it at His feet, who takes it away, and cleanses you in His blood. Yield yourself in faith to perfect, in Christ your Strength, the Holiness to which you are called. As your Father in Heaven is perfect, give yourself to Him as a little child to be perfect too in your daily lessons and your daily walk. Believe that your surrender is accepted: that the charge committed to Him is undertaken. And give glory to Him who is able to do above what you can ask or think. BE HOLY AS I AM HOLY.

Holiness in Christ Our Sanctification

March 21st

"Of God are you in Christ Jesus, who was made unto us wisdom from God, both righteousness and sanctification and redemption."

—1 CORINTHIANS 1: 30

These words lead us on now to the very center of God's revelation of the way of holiness. We know the steps of the road leading hither. He is holy, and holiness is His. He makes holy by coming near. His presence is holiness. In Christ's life, the holiness that had only been revealed in symbol, and as a promise of good things to come, had really taken possession of a human will, and been made one with true human nature. In His death every obstacle had been removed that could prevent the transmission of that holy nature to us: Christ had truly become our sanctification. In the Holy Spirit the actual communication of that holiness took place.

And now we want to understand what the work is the Holy Spirit does, and how He communicates this holy nature to us: what our relation is to Christ as our sanctification, and what the position we have to take up toward Him, that in its fullness and its power it may do its work for us. …

In the Holy Spirit the Lord Jesus is with His people here on earth. Though unseen, and not in the flesh, His Personal Presence is as real on earth as when He walked with His disciples. In regeneration the believer is taken out of his old place *"in the flesh";* he is no longer in the flesh, but *"in the spirit"* (Romans 8: 9); he is really and actually in Christ. … By an act of Divine and omnipotent grace, he has been planted into Christ, encircled on every side by the Power and the Love of Him who fills all things, whose fullness specially dwells in His body here below, the Church. …

The promise of the indwelling and the quickening of the Holy One is to the humble and contrite. Just when I feel most deeply that I am not holy, and can do nothing to make myself holy, when I feel ashamed of myself, just then is the time to turn from Self and very quietly to say: I am in Christ. Here He is all around me. Like the air that surrounds me, like the light that shines on me, here is my Lord Jesus with me in His hidden but Divine and most real presence. My faith must in quiet rest and trust bow before the Father, of whom and by whose Mighty Grace I am in Christ: He will reveal it to me with ever-growing clearness and power. He does it as I believe, and in believing open my whole soul to receive what is implied in it: the sense of sinfulness and unholiness must become the strength of my trust and dependence. In such faith I abide in Christ. …

As the Spirit reveals to us where we are dwelling—in Christ and His love— and that this Christ is a living Lord and Savior, there wakens within us the enthusiasm of a personal attachment, and the devotion of a loving allegiance, that make us wholly His. And it becomes possible for us to believe that we can be holy: we feel sure that in the path of holiness we can go from strength to strength.

Such believing insight into our relation to Christ as being in Him, and such personal attachment to Him who has received us into His love and keeps us abiding there, becomes the spring of a new obedience. The will of God comes to us in the light of Christ's life and His love—each command first fulfilled by Him, and then passed on to us as the sure and most blessed help to more perfect fellowship with the Father and His holiness. Christ becomes Lord and King in the soul, in the power of the Holy Spirit, guiding the will into all the perfect will of God, and proving Himself to be its sanctification, as He crowns its obedience with ever larger inflow of the presence and the Holiness of God.

Christ, as He lived and died on earth, is our sanctification. His life, the Spirit of His life, is what constitutes our holiness. To be in perfect harmony with Christ, to have His mind, is to be holy.

Christ's holiness had two sides. God sanctified Him by His Spirit: Christ sanctified Himself by following the leading of the Spirit, by giving up His will to God in everything. So God has made us holy in Christ; and so we follow after and perfect holiness by yielding ourselves to God's Spirit, by giving up our will and living in the will of God.

Is there any dear child of God at all disposed to lose heart as he thinks of what manner of man he ought to be in all holy living, let me call him to take courage. Could God have devised anything more wonderful or beautiful for such sinful, impotent creatures? Just think, Christ, God's own Son, made to be sanctification to you. The Mighty, Loving, Holy Christ, sanctified through suffering that He might have sympathy with you, given to make you holy. What more could you desire?

Yes, there is more: *"Of God you are in Him."* … You are in Christ, by an act of God's own Mighty Power. And there, in Christ, God Himself longs to establish and confirm you to the end. And you have, greatest wonder of all, the Holy Spirit within you to teach you to know, and believe, and receive, all that there is in Christ for you. And if you will but confess that there is in you no wisdom or power for holiness, none at all, and allow Christ, *"the Wisdom of God and the Power of God"* by the Holy Spirit within you, to lead you on, and prove how completely, how faithfully, how mightily, He can be your sanctification, He will do it most gloriously. …

Holiness and Humility

March 22nd

"Thus says the High and Lofty One who inhabits eternity, whose name is Holy: I dwell in the High and Holy place, with him that is of a contrite and humble spirit…."

—ISAIAH 57: 15

Our text is perhaps the only one in the Old Testament in which this indwelling of the Holy One, not among the people only, but in the heart of the individual believer, is clearly brought out. In this the two aspects of the Divine Holiness would reach their full manifestation: *"I dwell in the High and Holy place," "with him also that is of a contrite and humble spirit."* In His Heaven above, the high and lofty place, and in the heart contrite and humble, God has His home. God's holiness is His glory that separates Him by an infinite distance, not only from sin, but even from the creature, lifting Him high above it. God's holiness is His love, drawing Him down to the sinner, that He may lift him into His fellowship and likeness, and make him holy as He is holy. …

There is no law in the natural and the spiritual world more simple, than that two bodies cannot at the same moment occupy the same space. Only so much as the new occupant can expel of what the space was filled with can it really possess. In man, Self has possession, and Self-will the mastery, and there is no room for God. It is simply impossible for God to dwell or rule when Self is on the throne. As long as, through the blinding influence of sin and Self-love, even the believer is not truly conscious of the extent to which this Self-will reigns, there can be no true contrition or humility. But as it is discovered by God's Spirit, and the soul sees how it has just been Self that has been secretly keeping out God, with what shame it is broken down, and how it longs to break utterly away from Self, that God may have His place! It is this brokenness and continued breaking down, that is expressed by the word *contrition.*

And as the soul sees what folly and guilt it has been, by its secret honoring of Self, to keep the Holy One from the place which He alone has a right to, and which He would so blessedly have filled, it casts itself down in utter Self-abasement, with the one desire to be nothing, and to give God the place and the praise that is His due.

Such breaking down and humiliation is painful. Its intense reality consists in this, that the soul can see nothing in itself to trust or hope in. And least of all can it imagine that it should be an object of Divine complacency, or a fit vessel for the Divine blessing. And yet just this is the message which the Word of the Lord brings to our faith. It tells us that the Holy One, who dwells in the High and Lofty place, is seeking and preparing for Himself a dwelling here on this earth. It tells us, just what the truly contrite and humble never could imagine, and even now can hardly believe, that it is even, that it is only, with such that He will dwell.

These are they in whom God can be glorified, in whom there is room for Him to take the place of Self and to fill the emptied place with Himself. The Holy One seeks the humble. Just when we see that there is nothing in us to admire or rest in, God sees in us everything to admire and to rest in, because there is room for Himself. The lowly one is the home of the Holy One.

When Paul says of himself, *"as dying, and behold we live; as sorrowful, yet always rejoicing; as having nothing, yet possessing all things,"* he only gives expression to the law of the Kingdom—that as Self is displaced and man becomes nothing, God will become all. Side by side with deepest sense of nothingness and weakness, the sense of infinite riches and the joy unspeakable can fill the heart. However deep and blessed the experience becomes of the nearness, the blessing, the love, the actual indwelling of the Holy One, it is never an indwelling in the old Self; it is ever a Divine presence humbling Self to make place for God alone to be exalted.

The power of Christ's death, the fellowship of His cross, works each moment side by side with the power and the joy of His resurrection. "*He that humbles himself shall be exalted*"; in the blessed life of faith the humiliation and the exaltation are simultaneous, each dependent on the other. The humble find the Holy One; and when they have found, the possession only humbles all the more. Not that there is no danger or temptation of the flesh exalting itself in the possession, but, once knowing the danger, the humble soul seeks for grace to fear continually, with a fear that only clings more firmly to God alone.

Never for a moment imagine that you attain a state in which Self or the flesh are absolutely dead. No; by faith you enter into and abide in a fellowship with Jesus, in whom they are crucified; abiding in Him, you are free from their power, but only as you believe, and, in believing, have gone out of Self and dwell in Jesus. Therefore, the more abundant God's grace becomes, and the more blessed the indwelling of the Holy One, keep so much the lower. Your danger is greater, but your Help is now nearer: be content in trembling to confess the danger, it will make you bold in faith to claim the victory.

Believers, who profess to be nothing, and to trust in grace alone, I pray you, do listen to the wondrous message. The High and Lofty One, whose name is Holy, and who dwells in the Holy Place, and who can dwell nowhere but in a Holy Place, seeks a dwelling here on earth. Will you give it Him? Will you not fall down in the dust, that He may find in you the humble heart He loves to dwell in? Will you not now believe that even in you, however low and broken you feel, He does delight to make His dwelling? *"Blessed are the poor in spirit: for theirs is the Kingdom";* with them the King dwells. Oh, this is the path to holiness! Be humble, and the holy nearness and presence of God in you will be your holiness.

Holiness and Obedience

March 23rd

"If you will obey my voice, and keep my covenant, you shall be a peculiar treasure unto me above all people, you shall be unto me a holy nation."

—EXODUS 19: 5–6

Israel has reached Horeb. The law is to be given and the covenant made. Here are God's first words to the people; He speaks of redemption and its blessing, fellowship with Himself: *"You have seen how I brought you unto myself."* He speaks of holiness as His purpose in redemption… and as the link between the two He places obedience: *"If you will indeed obey my voice, you shall be unto me a holy nation."*

God's will is the expression of His holiness; as we do His will, we come into contact with His holiness. The link between redemption and holiness is obedience. This takes us back to what we saw in Paradise. God sanctified the seventh day as the time for sanctifying man. And what was the first thing He did with this purpose? He gave him a commandment. Obedience to that commandment would have opened the door, would have been the entrance, into the holiness of God.

Holiness is a moral attribute [not a legal one, as is righteousness]; and moral is that which a free will chooses and determines for itself. What God creates and gives is only naturally good; what man wills to have of God and His will, and really appropriates, has moral worth, and leads to holiness. In creation God manifested His wise and good will. His holy will He speaks in His commands. As that holy will enters man's will, as man's will accepts and unites itself with God's will, he becomes holy. …

Obedience is the path to holiness, because it is the path to union with God's holy will. … It is not itself holiness; but as the will opens itself to accept and to do the will of God, God communicates Himself and His holiness. To obey His voice is to follow Him as He leads in the way to the full revelation and communication of Himself and His blessed nature as the Holy One.

Obedience. Not knowledge of the will of God, not even approval, not even the will to do it, but *the doing of it*! Knowledge, and approval, and will must lead to action; the will of God *must be done*. *"If you indeed obey my voice, you shall be unto me a holy nation."*

It is not faith, and not worship, and not profession, that God here asks in the first place from His people when He speaks of holiness; *it is obedience.* God's will must be *"done on earth, as in Heaven." "Remember and do all my commandments, that you may be holy to your God"* (Numbers 15: 40). *"Sanctify yourselves therefore, and be holy; and you shall keep my statutes and do them. I am the Lord which sanctify you"* (Leviticus 20: 7–8). *"Therefore shall you keep my commandments and do them: I am the Lord: I will be hallowed among the children of Israel: I am the Lord which hallow you…"* (22: 21, 33). …

Thinking is easier than willing, and willing is easier than doing. Action alone proves whether the object of my interest has complete mastery over me. God wants His will done. This alone is obedience. In this alone it is seen whether the whole heart, with all its strength and will, has given itself over to the will of God; whether we live it, and are ready at any sacrifice to make it our own by doing it. God has no other way for making us holy. *"You shall keep my statutes and do them: I am the Lord who makes you holy."*

To all seekers after holiness this is a lesson of deep importance. Obedience is not holiness; holiness is something far higher, something that comes from God to us, or rather, something of God coming into us. But obedience is indispensable to holiness: it cannot exist without it. While, therefore, your heart seeks to follow the teaching of God's word, and looks in faith to what God has done, as He has made you holy in Christ. …

Begin by doing at once whatever appears right to do. Give up at once whatever conscience tells that you dare not say is according to the will of God. Not only pray for light and strength, but act; do what God says. *"He that does the will of God is My brother,"* Jesus says. Every son of God has been begotten of the will of God; in it he has his life. To do the Father's will is the meat, the strength, the mark, of every son of God.

It is nothing less than the surrender to such a life of simple and entire obedience that is implied in becoming a Christian. There are, alas! too many Christians who, from the want either of proper instruction, or of proper attention to the teaching of God's word, have never realized the place of supreme importance that obedience takes in the Christian life. They know not that Christ, and redemption, and faith all lead to it, because through it alone is the way to the fellowship of the love, and the likeness, and the glory of God.

We have all, possibly, suffered from it ourselves: in our prayers and efforts after the perfect peace and the rest of faith, after the abiding joy and the increasing power of the Christian life, there has been a secret something hindering the blessing, or causing the speedy loss of what had been apprehended. A wrong impression as to the absolute necessity of obedience was probably the cause. … It is in obedience that the will is molded, and the character fashioned, and an inner man built up which God can clothe and adorn with the beauty of holiness. …

We have already seen how holiness in its very nature supposes the personal relation to God, His personal presence. *"I have brought you unto Myself; if you obey, you shall be unto Me a holy nation."* It is as we understand and hold fast this personal element that obedience will become possible, and will lead to holiness. Mark well God's words: *"If you will obey My voice, and keep My covenant."* The voice is more than a law or a book; it always implies a living person and intercourse with him. It is this that is the secret of gospel obedience:

hearing the voice and following the lead of Jesus as a personal friend, a living Savior.

Such obedience is the pathway of holiness. Its every act is a link to the living God, a surrender of the being for God's will, for God Himself to take possession. It is being led by the Spirit of God, having Him to reveal the Presence, and the Will, and the Love of the Father, that will work in us that personal relation which the New Testament means when it speaks of doing everything unto the Lord, as pleasing God.

Let every believer study to realize this. When God sanctified the seventh day as His period of making holy, He taught us that He could not do it at once. The revelation and communication of holiness must be gradual, as man is prepared to receive it. God's sanctifying work with each of us, as with the race, needs time. The time it needs and seeks is the life of daily, hourly obedience. All that is spent in Self-will, and not in the living relation to the Lord, is lost.

But when the heart seeks day by day to hearken to the voice and to obey it, the Holy One Himself watches over His words to fulfil them: "*You shall be unto me n holy nation.*" In a way of which the soul beforehand can have but little conception, God will overshadow and make His abode in the obedient heart. The habit of always listening for the voice and obeying it will only be the building of the temple: The Living God Himself, the Holy One, will come to take up His abode. The glory of the Lord will fill the house, and the promise be made true, "*I will sanctify it by my glory*"; "*I brought you unto myself; if you will obey my voice in deed, you shall be unto me a holy nation.*"

Seekers after holiness! God has brought you to Himself. And now His voice speaks to you. All the thoughts of His heart, that as you take them in, and make them your own, and make His will your own by living and doing it, you may enter into the most complete union with Himself, the union of will as well as of life, and so become a holy people unto Him. Let obedience, the listening to and the doing the will of God, be the joy and the glory of your life; it will give you access unto the Holiness of God. BE HOLY, AS I AM HOLY.

The Way "Into the Holiest"

March 24th

"Having therefore, brethren, boldness to enter into the Holiest by the blood of Jesus, by the way which He dedicated, a new and living way, through the veil, that is to say, His flesh, and having a great Priest over the house of God, let us draw near with a true heart, in fullness of faith."

—HEBREWS 10: 19–22

When the High Priest once a year entered into the second tabernacle behind the veil, it was, we are told in the epistle to the Hebrews, *"the Holy Spirit signifying that the way into the Holiest of all was not yet made manifest."* When Christ died, the veil was torn; and all who were serving in the holy place had free access at once into the Most Holy place; the way into the Holiest of all was opened up. When the epistle passes over to its practical application (Hebrews 10: 19), all its teaching is summed up in the words: *"Having therefore, brethren, boldness to enter into the Holiest, let us draw near."* Christ's redemption has opened the way to the Holiest of all; our acceptance of it must lead to nothing less than our drawing near and entering in.

The words of our text suggest to us four very precious thoughts in regard to the place of access, the right of access, the way of access, the power of access.

The place of access. Whither are we invited to draw nigh? "*Having boldness to enter into the Holiest.*" The priests in Israel might enter the holy place, but were always kept excluded from the Holiest—God's immediate presence. The torn veil proclaimed liberty of access into that Presence. It is there that believers as a royal priesthood are now to live and walk. Within the veil, in the very Holiest of all, in the same place … in which God dwells, in God's very Presence, is to be our abode, our home.

Some speak as if the *"Let us draw near"* meant prayer, and that in our special approach to God in acts of worship we enter the Holiest. No; great as this privilege is, God has meant something for us infinitely greater. We are to draw near, and dwell always, to live our life and do our work within the sphere, the atmosphere, of the inner sanctuary. It is God's Presence makes holy ground; God's immediate Presence in Christ makes any place the Holiest of all: and this is it into which we are to draw nigh, and in which we are to abide. There is not a single moment of the day, there is not a circumstance or surrounding, in which the believer may not be kept dwelling in the secret place of the Most High. As by faith we enter into the completeness of our reconciliation with God, and the reality of our oneness with Christ, as we thus, abiding in Christ, yield to the Holy Spirit to reveal within the Presence of the Holy One, the Holiest of all is around us, and we are indeed in it. With an uninterrupted access we draw near.

The right of access. The thought comes up, and the question is asked: Is this not simply an ideal? Can it be a reality, an experience in daily life to those who know how sinful their nature is? Blessed be God! it is meant to be. It is possible, because our right of access rests not in what we are, but in the blood of Jesus. "*Having boldness to enter into the Holiest by the blood of Jesus, let us draw near.*" In the Passover we saw how redemption, and the holiness it aimed at, were dependent on the blood. In the sanctuary, God's dwelling, we know how in each part, the court, the holy place, the Most Holy, the sprinkling of blood was what alone secured access to God. And now that the blood of Jesus has been shed, oh! in what Divine power, what intense reality, what everlasting efficacy, we now have access into the Holiest of all, the Most Holy of God's heart and His love! We are indeed brought nigh by the blood. We have boldness to enter by the blood. …

The way of access. It is often thought that what is said of the new and living way, dedicated for us by Jesus, means nothing different from the boldness through His blood. This is not the case. The words mean a great deal more. "*Having boldness—by the blood of Jesus, let us draw near—by the way which He dedicated for us.*" That is, He opened for us a way to walk in, as He walked in it, "*a new and living way, through the veil, that is to say, His flesh.*" The way in which Christ walked when He gave His blood, is the very same in which we must walk too. That way is the way of the Cross. There must not only be faith in Christ's sacrifice, but fellowship with Him *in* it. That way led to the rending of the veil of the flesh, and so through the rent veil of the flesh, in to God. And was the veil of Christ's holy flesh rent that the veil of our sinful flesh might be spared? Verily, no. He meant us to walk in the very same way in which He did, following closely after Himself. He dedicated for us a new and living way through the veil, that is, His flesh. As we go in through the rent veil of His flesh, we find in it at once the need and the power for our flesh being rent too: following Jesus ever means conformity to Jesus.

It is Jesus with the rent flesh, in whom we are, in whom we walk. There is no way to God but through the rending of the flesh. In acceptance of Christ's life and death by faith as the power that works in us, in the power of the Spirit which makes us truly one with Christ, we all follow Christ as He passes on through the rent veil, that is, His flesh, and become partakers with Him of His crucifixion and death. The way of the cross, "*by which I have been crucified*," is the way through the rent veil. Man's destiny, fellowship with God in the power of the Holy Spirit, is only reached through the sacrifice of the flesh.

And here we find now the solution of a great mystery why so many Christians remain standing afar off, and never enter this Holiest of all; why the holiness of God's Presence is so little seen on them. They thought that it was only in Christ that the flesh needed to be rent, not in themselves. They thought that the liberty they had in the blood was the new and living way. They knew not that the way into true and full holiness, into the Holiest of all, that the full entrance into the fellowship of the holiness of the Great High Priest, was only to be reached through the rent veil of the flesh, through conformity to the death of Jesus. This is in very deed the way He dedicated for us. He is Himself the way; into His Self-denial, His Self-sacrifice, His crucifixion, He takes up all who long to be holy with His Holiness, holy as He is holy.

The power of access. Does anyone shrink back from entering the very Holiest for fear of this rending of the flesh, because he doubts whether he could bear it, whether he could indeed walk in such a path? ...Hear what follows: "*And having a Great Priest over the House of God, let us draw near.*" We have not only the Holiest of all inviting us, and the blood giving us boldness, and the way through the rent veil consecrated for us, but the Great Priest over the House of God, the Blessed Living Savior, to draw, to help, and to welcome us. He is our Aaron. On His heart we see our name, because He only lives to think of us, and pray for us. On His forehead we see God's name, "*Holy to the Lord*," because in His Holiness the sins of our holy things are covered.

In Him we are accepted and sanctified; God receives us as holy ones. In the power of His love and His Spirit, in the power of Him the Holy One, in the joy of drawing nearer to Him and being drawn by Him, we gladly accept the way He has dedicated, and walk in His holy footsteps of Self-denial and Self-sacrifice. We see how the flesh is the thick veil that separates from the Holy One who is a Spirit, and it becomes an unceasing and most fervent prayer, that the crucifixion of the flesh may, in the power of the Holy Spirit, be in us a blessed reality.

With the glory of the Holiest of all shining out on us through the opened veil, and the Precious Blood speaking so loudly of boldness of access, and the Great Priest beckoning us with His loving Presence to draw near and be blessed, with all this, we dare no longer fear, but choose the way of the rent veil as the path we love to tread, and give ourselves to enter in and dwell within the veil, in the very Holiest of all. … As the Holy Spirit reveals our union to Christ more clearly, and our hearts and wills lose themselves in Him, we dwell in the Holy Presence, which is the Holiest of all. We are "*holy in Christ*"; draw near, enter in with boldness, and take possession have no home but in the Holiest of all. … This entrance into the Holiest of all—an ever fresh and ever deeper entrance—is, at the same time, an ever blessed resting in the Father's Presence.

Faith in the blood, following in the way of the rent flesh, and fellowship with the living Jesus, are the three chief steps. Enter into the Holiest of all, and dwell there. It will enter into you, and transform you, and dwell in you.

The Unction from the Holy One 1

March 25th

"*And you have an anointing from the Holy One, and you know all things.*"

—1 JOHN 2: 20

In the revelation by Moses of God's Holiness and His way of making holy, the priests, and specially the high priests, were the chief expression of God's Holiness in man. In the priests themselves, the holy anointing oil was the one great symbol of the grace that made holy. Moses was to make a holy anointing oil: "*And you shall take of the anointing oil, and sprinkle it upon Aaron and upon his sons, and he shall be hallowed, and his sons with him.*" "*This shall be a holy anointing oil unto me. Upon man's flesh shall it not be poured; neither shall ye make any other like it; it is holy, it shall be holy unto you*" (Exodus 29: 21, 30: 25-32). With this the priests, and especially the high priests, were to be anointed and consecrated: "*He that is the high priest among you, upon whose head the anointing oil was poured, shall not go out of the holy place, nor profane the holy place of his God; for the crown of the anointing oil of his God is upon him*" (Leviticus 21: 10, 12). And even so it is said of David, as type of the Messiah, "*Our king is of the Holy One of Israel. I have found David, my servant; with my holy oil have I anointed him.*"

We know how the Hebrew name, Messiah, and the Greek, Christ, has reference to this [anointing]. So, in the passage just quoted, the Hebrew is, "*with my holy oil I have messiahed him.*" And so in a passage like Acts 10: 38: "*Concerning Jesus of Nazareth, whom God christed with the Holy Spirit and with power.*" Or Psalm 45: "*God has messiahed you with the oil of gladness above thy fellows;*" and in Hebrews 1: 9, "*Your God has christed you with the oil of gladness.*"

And so—as one of our Reformed Catechisms, the Heidelberg, has it, in answer to the question, Why are you called a Christian?—we are called Christians, because we are fellow-partakers with Him of His christing, His anointing. This is the anointing of which John speaks, the *chrisma* or christing of the Holy One. The Holy Spirit is the holy anointing which every believer receives: what God did to His Son to make Him the Christ, He does to me to make me a Christian: "*You have the anointing of the Holy One.*"

1. "*You have an anointing from the Holy One.*" It is as the Holy One that the Father gives the anointing: that [instrument] by which He anoints is called the oil of holiness, the Holy Spirit. Holiness is indeed a Divine ointment. Just as there is nothing so subtle and penetrating as the odor with which the ointment fills a house, so holiness is an indescribable, all-pervading breath of heavenliness which pervades the one on whom the anointing rests. Holiness does not consist in certain actions: this is righteousness.

Holiness is the unseen and yet manifest presence of the Holy One resting on His anointed. Direct from the Holy One, the anointing is alone received, or rather, only in the abiding fellowship with Him in Christ, who is the Holy One of God. And who receives it? Only the one who has given Self entirely to be holy, as God is holy. It was the priest, who was separated to be holy to the Lord, who received the anointing; upon other men's flesh it was not to be poured.

How many want the precious ointment for the sake of its perfume to themselves! No, only the one who is wholly consecrated to the service of the Holy One, to the work of the sanctuary, may receive it. If anyone had said: I want the anointing, but not be made a priest; I am not ready to go and always be at the call sinners seeking their God, that one could have no share in it. Holiness is the energy that only lives to make holy, and to bless in so doing; the anointing of the Holy One is for the priest, the servant of God Most High. It is only in the intensity of a soul truly roused and given up to God's glory, God's kingdom, God's work, that holiness becomes a reality. The holy garments were only prepared for priests and their service. In all our seeking after holiness, let us remember this. As we beware of the error of thinking that work for Christ will make holy, let us also watch against the other, the straining after holiness without work. It is the priest who is set apart for the service of the holy place and the Holy One, it is the believer who is ready to live and die that the Holiness of God may triumph among those around us, who will receive the anointing.

2. "*The anointing teaches you.*" The new man is created in knowledge, as well as in righteousness and holiness. Christ is made to us wisdom, as well as righteousness and sanctification. God's service and our holiness are above all to be a free and full, an intelligent and most willing, approval of His blessed will. And so the anointing, to fit us for the service of the sanctuary, teaches us to know all things. Just as the perfume of the ointment is the most subtle essence, something that has never yet been found or felt, except as it is smelt, so the spiritual faculty which the anointing gives is the most subtle there can be. It makes "quick of scent in the fear of the Lord"; it teaches us by a Divine instinct, by which the anointed one recognizes what has the heavenly fragrance in it, and what is of earth. It is the anointing that makes the Word and the name of Jesus in the Word to be indeed as ointment poured forth.

The great mark of the anointing is thus teachableness. It is the great mark of Christ, the Holy One of God, the Anointed One, that He listens: "*I speak not of myself; as I hear, so I speak.*" And so it is of the Holy Spirit too: "*He shall not speak out of Himself: whatsoever He shall hear, that shall He speak.*" It cannot be otherwise; one anointed with the anointing of this Christ, with this Holy Spirit, will be teachable, will listen to be taught. "*The anointing teaches.*" "*And you need not that anyone teach you, but the anointing teaches you concerning all things.*" "*They shall be all taught of God,*" includes every believer.

The Unction from the Holy One 2

March 26th

"*The anointing which you received of Him abides in you…*"

—1 JOHN 2: 27

The secret of true holiness is a very direct and personal relation to the Holy One; all the teaching through the Word or men made entirely dependent on and subordinate to the personal teaching of the Holy Spirit. *The teaching comes through the anointing*—not, in the first place, in the thoughts or feelings, but in that all-pervading fragrance which comes from the fresh oil having penetrated the whole inner life.

And "*the anointing abides in you.*" "*In you.*" In the spiritual life it is of deep importance ever to maintain the harmony between the objective and the subjective: God in Christ above me, God in the Spirit within me. In us—not as in a locality, but in us as one with us, entering into the most secret part of our being, and pervading all, dwelling in our very body—the anointing abides in us, forming part of our very selves. And this just in proportion as we know it and yield ourselves to it, as we wait and are still to let the secret fragrance permeate our whole being. And this, again, not interruptedly, but as a continuous and unvarying experience. Above circumstances and feelings, "*the anointing abides.*" Not, indeed, as a fixed state or as something in our own possession; but, according to the law of the new life, in the dependence of faith on the Holy One, and in the fellowship of Jesus. "I am anointed with fresh oil," this is the objective side; every new morning the believer waits for the renewal of the Divine gift from the Father. "*The anointing abides in you,*" this is the subjective side; the holy life, the life of faith and fellowship, the anointing, is always, from moment to moment, a spiritual reality. The holy anointing oil, always fresh, the anointing abiding always, is the secret of holiness.

4. "*And even as it taught you, ye abide in Him.*" Here we have again the Holy Trinity: the Holy One, from whom the holy anointing comes; the Holy Spirit, who is Himself the anointing; and Christ, the Holy One of God, in whom the anointing teaches us to abide. In Christ the unseen holiness of God was set before us, and brought nigh; it became human, vested in a human nature, that it might be communicated to us. Within us dwells and works the Holy Spirit, drawing us out to the Christ of God, uniting us in heart and will to Him, revealing Him, forming Him within us, so that His likeness and mind are embodied in us. It is thus we abide in Christ: the holy anointing of the Holy One teaches it to us. It is this that is the test of the true anointing: abiding in Christ, as He meant it, becomes truth in us. Here is the life of holiness as the Thrice Holy gives it: The Father, the first, the Holy One, making holy; the Son, the second, His Holy One, in whom we

are; the Spirit, the third, who dwells in us, and through whom we abide in Christ, and Christ in us. Thus, it is that the Thrice Holy makes us holy.

Let us study the Divine anointing. It comes from the Holy One. There is no other like it. It is God's way of making us holy—His holy priests. It is God's way of making us partakers of holiness in Christ. The anointing, received of Him day by day, abiding in us, teaching us all things, especially teaching us to abide in Christ, must be on us every day. Its subtle, all-pervading power must go through our whole life; the odor of the ointment must fill the house. Blessed be God, it can do so! The anointing that abides makes the abiding in Christ a reality and a certainty; and God Himself, the Holy One, makes the abiding anointing a reality and a certainty too. To His Holy Name be the praise! BE HOLY, FOR I AM HOLY.

Holy One, I come to You now for the renewed anointing. Father! This is the one gift Your child may most surely count on: the gift of Your Holy Spirit. … I desire to confess with deep shame that Your Spirit has been sorely grieved and dishonored. How often the fleshly mind has usurped His place in Your worship! How much the fleshly will has sought to do His work! My Father! Let Your light shine through me to convince me very deeply of this. Let Your judgment come on all that there is of human willing and running. Blessed Father! Grant me, according to the riches of Your glory, even now to be strengthened with might by Your Spirit in the inner life. Strengthen my faith to believe in Christ for a full share in His anointing. Oh, teach me day by day to wait for and receive the anointing with fresh oil! …

1. I think I know now the reason why at times we fall in the abiding. We think and read, we listen and pray, we try to believe and strive to look to Jesus only, and yet we fail. What was wanting was this: … you abide in him; so far, and no farther.

2. The washing always precedes the anointing: we cannot have the anointing if we fail in the cleansing. When cleansed and anointed, we are fit for use.

3. Would you have the abiding anointing? Yield yourself wholly to be sanctified and made meet for the Master's use: dwell in the Holiest of all, In God's presence: accept every chastisement as a fellowship. In the way of the rent flesh, be sure the anointing will flow in union with Jesus. "*It is like the precious ointment upon the head of Aaron, that went down to the skirts of his garments.*"

4. The anointing is the Divine eye-salve, opening the eyes of the heart to know Jesus. So it teaches to abide in Him. I am sure most Christians have no conception of the danger and deceitfulness of a thought religion, with sweet and precious thoughts coming to us in books and preaching, and little power. The teaching of the Holy Spirit is in the heart first; man's teaching in the mind. Let all our thinking ever lead us to cease from thought, and to open the heart and will to the Spirit to teach there in His own Divine way, deeper than thought and feeling. …

5. Oh that God would visit His Church, and teach His children what it is to wait for, and receive, and walk in the full anointing, the anointing that abides and teaches to abide! Oh that the truth of the personal leading of the Holy Spirit in every believer were restored in the Church! He is doing it; He will do it.

Holiness and Faith

March 27th

"That they may receive remission of sins,
and an inheritance among those who are sanctified by faith in Me."
—ACTS 26: 18

Because God is a spiritual and invisible Being, every revelation of Himself, whether in His works, His Word, or His Son, calls for faith. Faith is the spiritual sense of the soul, being to it what the senses are to the body; by it alone we enter into communication and contact with God. Faith is that meekness of soul which waits in stillness to hear, to understand, to accept what God says; to receive, to retain, to possess what God gives or works. By faith we allow, we welcome God Himself, the Living Person, to enter in to make His abode with us, to become our very life.

However well we think we know it, we always have to learn the truth afresh, for a deeper and fuller application of it, that in the Christian life faith is the first thing, the one thing that pleases God, and brings blessing to us. And because Holiness is God's highest glory, and the highest blessing He has for us, it is especially in the life of holiness that we need to live by faith alone.

Our Lord speaks here of "*those who are sanctified by faith in Me.*" He Himself is our Sanctification as He is our Justification: for the one as for the other it is faith that God asks, and both are equally given at once. The participle used here is not the present, denoting a process or work that is being carried on, but the aorist, indicating an act done once for all. When we believe in Christ, we receive the whole Christ, our justification and our sanctification: we are at once accepted by God as righteous in Him, and as holy in Him. God counts and calls us, what we really are, sanctified ones in Christ.

It is as we are led to see what God sees, as our faith grasps that the holy life of Christ is ours in actual possession, to be accepted and appropriated for daily use, that we shall really be able to live the life God calls us to, the life of holy ones in Christ Jesus. We shall then be in the right position in which what is called our progressive sanctification can be worked out. It will be, the acceptance and application in daily life of the power of a holy life which has been prepared in Jesus, which has in the union with Him become our present and permanent possession, and which works in us according to the measure of our faith.

From this point of view, it is evident that faith has a twofold operation. Faith is the evidence of things not seen, though now actually existing, the substance of things hoped for, but not yet present. It deals with the unseen present, as well as with the unseen future. As the evidence of things not seen, it rejoices in our complete sanctification as a present possession.

Through faith I simply look to what Christ is, as revealed in the Word by the Holy Spirit. Claiming all He is as my own, I know that His holiness, His holy nature and life, are mine; I am a holy one. By faith in Him I have been sanctified. This is the first aspect of sanctification: it looks to what is a complete and finished thing, an absolute reality. As the substance of things hoped for, this faith reaches out in the assurance of hope to the future, to things I do not yet see or experience, and claims, day by day, out of Christ my sanctification, what it needs for practical holiness, *"to be holy in all manner of living."*

This is the second aspect of sanctification: I depend upon Jesus to supply, in personal experience, gradually and unceasingly, for the need of each moment, what has been treasured up in His fullness. *"Of God are you in Christ Jesus, who of God is made for our wisdom and righteousness and sanctification and redemption"* (1 Corinthians 1: 30). Under its first aspect faith says, I know I am in Him, and all His holiness is mine; in its second aspect it speaks, I trust in Him for the grace and the strength I need each moment to live a holy life. … Faith in Jesus is the secret of a holy life: all holy conduct, all really holy deeds, are the fruit of faith in Jesus as our holiness.

Faith in God stands opposed to trust in Self. … Faith is hindered by every effort to do something ourselves. Faith looks to God working, and yields itself to His strength, as revealed in Christ through the Spirit; it allows God to work.… The true life of holiness, the life of them who are sanctified in Christ, has its root and its strength in an abiding sense of utter impotence, in the deep restfulness which trusts to the working of a Divine power and life, in the entire personal surrender to the loving Savior, in that faith which consents to be nothing, that He may be all. …

And as by effort, so faith is also hindered by the desire to see and feel. "*If you believe, you shall see;*" the Holy Spirit will seal our faith with a Divine experience; we shall see the glory of God. But this is His work: ours is, when all appears dark and cold, in the face of all that nature or experience testifies, still each moment to believe in Jesus as our all-sufficient sanctification, in whom we are perfected before God.

Complaints as to want of feeling, as to weakness or deadness, seldom profit: it is the soul that refuses to occupy itself with itself, either with its own weakness or the strength of the enemy, but only looks to what Jesus is, and has promised to do, to whom progress in holiness will be a joyful march from victory to victory. "*The Lord Himself fights for you*"; this thought, so often repeated in connection with Israel's possession of the promised land, is the food of faith: in conscious weakness, in presence of mighty enemies, it sings the conqueror's song. When God appears to be not doing what we trusted Him for, then is just the time for faith to glory in Him. …

"Sanctified by faith in me." Yes, "by faith in Me:" it is the personal living Jesus who offers Himself, Himself in all the riches of His Power and Love, as the object, the strength, the life of our faith. He tells us that if we would be holy, always and in everything holy, we must just see to one thing: to be always and altogether full of faith in Him. Faith is the eye of the soul: the power by which we discern the presence of the Unseen One, as He comes to give Himself to us. Faith not only sees, but appropriates and assimilates: let us set our souls very still for the Holy Spirit who dwells in us, to quicken and strengthen that faith, for which He has been given us.

Faith is surrender: yielding ourselves to Jesus to allow Him to do His work in us, giving up ourselves to Him to live out His life and work out His will in us, we shall find Him giving Himself entirely to us, and taking complete possession. So faith will be power—the power of obedience to do God's will: "*our most holy faith*"; "the faith delivered to the holy ones." And we shall understand how simple, to the single-hearted, is the secret of holiness: *just Jesus.* We are in Him, our sanctification: He personally is our Holiness; and the life of faith in Him, that receives and possesses Him, must necessarily be a life of holiness. Jesus says, "Sanctified by faith in me."

Holiness and Chastisement

March 28th

"He chastens us for our profit, that we may be partakers of His holiness";
"Follow after sanctification, without which no one shall see the Lord."
—HEBREWS 12: 10, 14

There is perhaps no part of God's word which sheds such Divine light upon suffering as the Epistle to the Hebrews. It does this because it teaches us what suffering was to the Son of God. It perfected His humanity. It so fitted Him for His work as the Compassionate High Priest. It proved that He, who had fulfilled God's will in suffering obedience, was indeed worthy to be its executor in glory, and "to sit down on the right hand of the Majesty on high." It was His will, in bringing many sons unto glory, "*to make the Author of their salvation perfect through suffering*" (Hebrews 2: 10). *"Though He was a Son, yet learned He obedience by the things which He suffered, and having been made perfect, became the Author of eternal salvation to all them that obey Him"* (Hebrews 5: 9). As He said Himself of His suffering, *"I sanctify myself."* So we see here that His sufferings were indeed to Him the pathway to perfection and holiness. …

The power which suffering was proved to have in Him to work out perfection—the power which He imparted to it in sanctifying Himself through suffering—is the power of the new life that comes from Him to us. In the light of His example we can see, in the faith of His power, we too can prove that suffering is to God's child the token of the Father's love, and the channel of His richest blessing. … We agree not only to what is written, *"It was His will to make the Author of salvation perfect through suffering,"* but understand somewhat how Divinely becoming and meet it is that we too should be sanctified by suffering.

"He chastens us for our profit, that we should be made partakers of His holiness." Of all the precious words Holy Scripture has for the sorrowful, there is hardly one that leads us more directly and more deeply into the fullness of blessing that suffering is meant to bring. It is His holiness, God's own holiness, we are to be made partakers of.

The epistle had spoken very clearly of our sanctification from its Divine side, as wrought out for us, and to be wrought in us, by Jesus Himself. *"He which sanctifies and they which are sanctified are all one." "We have been sanctified by the one offering of Christ."* In our text we have the other side, the progressive work by which we are personally to accept and voluntarily to appropriate this Divine holiness.

In view of all there is in us that is at variance with God's will, and that must be discovered and broken down, before we understand what it is to give up our will and delight in God's; in view of the personal fellowship of suffering which alone can lead to the full appreciation of what Jesus bore and did for us; in view, too, of the full personal entrance into and satisfaction with the love of God as our sufficient portion; chastisement and suffering are indispensable elements in God's work of making holy.

Chastisement leads to the acceptance of God's will. We have seen how God's will is our sanctification; how it is in the will of God Christ has sanctified us; yea more, how He found the power to sanctify us in sanctifying Himself by the entire surrender of His will to God. His *"I delight to do Your will"* derived its worth from His continual *"Not my will."*

And wherever God comes with chastisement or suffering, the very first object He has in view is, to ask and to work in us union with His own blessed will, that through it we may have union with Himself and His love. He comes in some one single point in which His will crosses our most cherished affection or desire, and asks the surrender of what we will to what He wills. When this is done willingly and lovingly, He leads the soul on to see how the claim for the sacrifice in the individual matter is the assertion of a principle that in everything His will is to be our one desire. …

It has sometimes appeared, even to God's children, as if affliction were not a blessing: it so rouses the evil nature, and calls forth all the opposition of the heart against God's will, that it has brought the loss of the peace and the piety that once appeared to reign. Even in such cases it is working out God's purpose. "*That He might humble you, to prove you, to know what was in your heart,*" is still His object in leading into the wilderness. To an extent we are not aware of, our religion is often Selfish and superficial. But, when we accept the teaching of chastisement in discovering the Self-will and love of the world which still prevails, we have learned one of its first and most needful lessons.

It is God's will that we should be in that position of difficulty to be tried and tested. Let our first thought be: "this position of difficulty is my Father's will for me: I accept that will as my place now where He sees it fit to try me." Such acceptance of the trial is the way to turn it into blessing. It will lead on to an ever clearer abiding in all the will of God all the day. …

"Though He was a Son, yet learned He obedience by the things which He suffered, and having been made perfect, became the Author of eternal salvation to all them that obey Him" (Hebrews 5: 9).

You suffering ones! All you whom the Father is chastening! Come and see Jesus suffering, giving up His will, being made perfect, sanctifying Himself. His suffering is the secret of His holiness, of His Glory, of His life. Will you not thank God for anything that can admit you into the nearer fellowship of your blessed Lord? Shall we not accept every trial, great or small, as the call His love to be one with Himself in living only for God's will. This is holiness, to be one with Jesus as He does the will of God, to abide in Jesus who was made perfect through suffering.

Chastisement leads to the enjoyment of God's love. Many a father has been surprised as he made his first experience of how a child, after being punished in love, began to cling to him more tenderly than before. Even so, while to those who live at a distance from their Father, the misery in this world appears to be the one thing that shakes their faith in God's love, it is just through suffering that His children learn to know the reality of that love. The chastening is so distinctly a father's prerogative; it leads so directly to the confession of its needfulness and its lovingness; it wakens so powerfully the longing for pardon and comfort and deliverance that it does indeed become, strange though this may seem, one of the surest guides into the deeper experience of the Divine love. Chastening is the school in which the blessed lesson is learned that the will of God is all love, and that holiness is the fire of love, consuming that it may purify, destroying the dross only, so that it may assimilate into its own perfect purity all that yields itself to the wondrous change.

"We know and have believed the love which God has in us. God is love: and he that abides in love abides in God, and God in Him." Man's destiny is fellowship with God, the fellowship, the mutual indwelling of love. It is only by faith that this love of God can be known. And faith can only grow by exercise, can only thrive in trial: when visible things fail, its energy is roused to yield itself to be possessed by the Invisible, by the Divine. Chastisement is the nurse of faith; one of its chosen attendants, to lead deeper into the Love of God. This is the new and living way, the way of the rent flesh in fellowship with Jesus leading up into the Holiest of All. There it is seen how the justice that will not spare the child, and the love that sustains and sanctifies it, are both one in the holiness of God. …

Holiness and Separation

March 29th

"I am the Lord your God, who has separated you from other people. And you shall be holy unto Me."
—LEVITICUS 20: 24

Separation is not holiness, but is the way to it. Though there can be no holiness without separation, there can be separation that does not lead to holiness. It is of deep importance to understand both the difference and the connection, that we may be kept from the right-hand error of counting separation alone as holiness, as well as the left-hand error of seeking holiness without separation.

The Hebrew word for holiness possibly comes from a root that means to separate. But where we have in our translation "separate" or "sever" or "set apart," we have quite different words. The word for holy is used exclusively to express that special idea. And though the idea of holy always includes that of separation, it is itself something infinitely higher. It is of great importance to understand this well, because the being set apart to

God, the surrender to His claim, the devotion or consecration to His service, is often spoken of as if this constituted holiness. We cannot too earnestly press the thought that this is only the beginning, the presupposition: holiness itself is infinitely more. It is not what I am, or do, or give, that is holiness, but what God is, and gives, and does to me. It is God's taking possession of me that makes me holy; it is the presence and the glory of God that really makes holy.

A careful study of God's words to Israel will make this clear to us. Eight times we find the expression in Leviticus, *"You shall be holy, for I am holy."* Holiness is the highest attribute of God, expressive not only of His relation to Israel, but of His very being and nature, His infinite moral perfection. And though it is by very slow and gradual steps that He can teach the carnal darkened mind of man what this means, yet from the very commencement He tells His people that His purpose is that they should be like Himself holy because and as He is holy.

To tell us that God separates us for Himself to be His, even as He gives Himself to be ours, tells us of a relation that exists, but tells us nothing of the real nature of this Holy Being, or of the essential worth of the holiness He will communicate to us. Separation is only the setting apart and taking possession of the vessel to be cleansed and used; it is the filling of it with the precious contents we entrust to it that gives it its real value. Holiness is the Divine filling without which the separation leaves us empty. Separation is not holiness.

But separation is essential to holiness. *"I have separated you from other people, and you shall be holy."* Until I have chosen out and separated a vessel from those around it, and, if need be, cleansed it, I cannot fill or use it. I must have it in my hand, full and exclusive command of it for the time being, or I will not pour into it the precious milk or wine. And just so God separated His people when He brought them up out of Egypt, separated them unto Himself when He gave them His covenant and His law, that He might have them under His control and power, to work out His purpose of making them holy. This He could not do until He had them apart, and had wakened in them the consciousness that they were His peculiar people, wholly and only His, until He had so taught them also to separate themselves to Him. Separation is essential to holiness. …

In the power of the Holy Spirit, the Spirit of Holiness, it seals the separation by the presence of the Indwelling God. This is indeed the power of separation. The separating power of the presence of God; this it is we need to know. *"Wherein now shall it be known that I have found grace in Your sight, I and Your people," said Moses: "is it not in that You go with us? So shall we be separated, I and Your people, from all the people that are upon the face of the earth."* It is the consciousness of God's Indwelling Presence, making and keeping us His very own, that works the true separateness from the world and its spirit, from ourselves and our own will. And it is as this separation is accepted and prized and persevered in by us, that the holiness of God will enter in and take possession.

And we shall realize that to be the Lord's property, a people of His own, is infinitely more than merely to be accounted or acknowledged as His, that it means nothing less than that God, in the power and indwelling of the Holy Spirit, fills our being, our affections, and our will with His own life and holiness. He separates us for Himself, and sanctifies us to be His dwelling. He comes Himself to take personal possession by the indwelling of Christ in the heart. And we are then truly separate, and kept separate, by the presence of God within us.

Holiness and Happiness

March 30th

"The Kingdom of God is joy in the Holy Spirit."
—ROMANS 14: 17

Are not suffering and sorrow among God's chosen means of sanctification? Are not the promises to the broken in heart, the poor in spirit, and the mourner? Are not Self-denial and the forsaking of all we have, the crucifixion with Christ and the dying daily, the path to holiness? And is not all this more matter of sorrow and pain than of joy and gladness? The answer will be found in the right apprehension of the life of faith.

Faith lifts above, and gives possession of, what is the very opposite of what we feel or experience. In the Christian life, there is always a paradox: what appear irreconcilable opposites are found side by side at the same moment. Paul expresses it in the words, *"As dying, and, behold, we live; as sorrowful, yet always rejoicing; as poor, yet making many rich; as having nothing, yet possessing all things."* And elsewhere thus, *"When I am weak, then am I strong."* The apparent contradiction has its reconciliation, not only in the union of the two lives, the human and the Divine, in the person of each believer, but specially in our being, at one and the same moment, partakers of [both] the death *and* the resurrection of Christ.

Christ's death was one of pain and suffering—a real and terrible death, a rending asunder of the bonds that united soul and body, spirit and flesh. The power of that death works in us: we must let it work mightily if we are to live holy; for in that death He sanctified Himself, that we ourselves might be sanctified in truth. Our holiness is, like His, in the death to our own will, and to all our own life. But this we must seek to grasp we do not approach death from the side from which Christ met it, as an enemy to be conquered, as a suffering to be borne, before the new life can be entered on.

No, the believer who knows what Christ is as the Risen One, approaches death, the crucifixion of Self and the flesh and the world, from the resurrection side, the place of victory, in the power of the Living Christ. When we were baptized into Christ, we were baptized into His death and resurrection as ours; and Christ Himself, the risen living Lord, leads us triumphantly into the experience of the power of His death. And so, to the believer who truly lives by faith, and seeks not in his own strugglings to crucify and mortify the flesh, but knows the living Lord, the deep resurrection joy never for a moment forsakes Him, but is his strength for what may appear to others to be only painful sacrifice and cross-bearing. He says with Paul, *"I glory in the cross through which I have been crucified."* . . .

It is the joy of a present Savior, of the experience of a perfect salvation, the joy of a resurrection life, which alone gives the power to enter deeply and fully into the death that Christ died, and yield our will and our life to be wholly sanctified to God. In the joy of that life, from which the power of the death is never absent, it is possible to say with the Apostle each moment, *"As dying, and, behold, we live; as sorrowful, yet always rejoicing."* …

If we lose our joy, it must be sin. It may be an actual transgression, or an unconscious following of Self or the world; it may be the stain on conscience of something doubtful, or it may be unbelief that would live by sight, and thinks more of itself and its joy than of the Lord alone: whatever it be, nothing can take away our joy but sin. …

The Spirit of holiness is the Spirit of joy, because He is the Spirit of God. It is the saints, God's holy ones, who will shout for joy. … Jesus was anointed by God with *"the oil of gladness,"* that He might give us *"the oil of joy."* … It is the evidence of your being in the Father's presence, and dwelling in His love. It is the proof of your being consciously free from the law and the strain of the spirit of bondage. It is the token of your freedom from care and responsibility, because you are rejoicing in Christ Jesus as your Sanctification, your Keeper, and your Strength.

Holiness and the Body

"Know you not that your body is the temple of the Holy Spirit who is in you"; "the temple of God is holy, and you are that temple" (1 Corinthians 3: 16, 17). Coming into the world, our blessed Lord spoke: *"A body You prepared for me; lo, I come to do Your will, God."* Leaving this world again, it was in His own body that He bore our sins upon the tree. So it was in the body, no less than in soul and spirit, that He did the will of God. And therefore it is said, *"By which will we have been sanctified through the offering of the body of Jesus Christ once for all."* When praying for the Thessalonians and their sanctification, Paul says, *"And the God of peace Himself sanctify you wholly; and may your spirit and soul and body be preserved entire, without blame, at the coming of our Lord Jesus Christ."* Of himself he had spoken as *"always bearing about in the body the dying of Jesus, that the life also of Jesus may be manifested in our body. For we which live are always delivered unto death for Jesus' sake, that the life also of Jesus may be manifested in our mortal flesh."* His earnest expectation and hope was, *"that Christ be magnified in my body, whether by life or by death."*

The relation between body and spirit is so intimate, the power of sin in the spirit comes so much through the body, the body is so distinctly the object both of Christ's redemption and the Holy Spirit's renewal, that our study of holiness will be seriously defective if we do not take in the teaching of Scripture on holiness in the body. …

To have every appetite of the body under the rule and regulation of the Holy Spirit appears to some needless, to others too difficult. And yet it must be, if the body is to be holy, as God's temple, and we are to glorify Him in our body and our spirit. … Sin must be combated not only in the region of the spirit: if we are to perfect holiness, we must cleanse ourselves from all defilement of flesh and spirit. *"If through the Spirit you do make dead the deeds of the body, you shall live."* …

"Know you not that your body is the temple of the Holy Spirit: glorify God therefore, in the power

of the Holy Spirit, in your body." … It is only in a body that is full of the holy life, very entirely possessed of God's Spirit, that this will be the case. …

When to be holy as God is holy indeed becomes the great desire and aim of life, everything will be cherished or given up as it promotes the chief end. The actual and active presence of the Holy Spirit in the life of the body will be the fire that is kept burning continually on the altar. …

Holiness and Service

March 31st

"If we cleanse ourselves from these, we shall be vessels of honor, sanctified, ready for the Master's use, prepared for every good work."

—2 TIMOTHY 2: 21

In the whole of Scripture we have seen that whatever God sanctifies is to be used in the service of His holiness. His holiness is an infinite energy that only finds its rest in making holy. To the revelation of what He is in Himself, *"I the Lord am holy,"* God continually adds the declaration of what He does, *"I am the Lord who makes holy."* Holiness is a burning fire that extends itself, that seeks to consume what is unholy, and to communicate its own blessedness to all that will receive it. Holiness and Selfishness, holiness and inactivity, holiness and sloth, holiness and helplessness, are utterly irreconcilable.

Whatever we read of as holy, was taken into the service of the holiness of God. … Of Israel, whom God redeemed from Egypt that they might be a holy nation, God said, *"Let my people go, that they may serve me."* The holy angels, the holy prophets and apostles, the holy Scriptures, all bore the title as having been sanctified for the service of God.

Our Lord speaks of Himself *"as the Son, whom the Father sanctified and sent into the world."* And when He says, "I sanctify myself," He adds at once the purpose: it is in the service of the Father and His redeemed ones, *"that they themselves may be sanctified in truth."* And can it be thought possible, now that God, in Christ the Holy One, and in the Holy Spirit, is accomplishing His purpose, and gathering a people of saints, "*holy ones*," "*made holy in Christ*," that now holiness and service would be put asunder? Impossible! Here first we shall fully realize how essential they are to each other. Let us try and grasp their mutual relation. We are only made holy that we may serve. We can only serve as we are holy.

Holiness is essential to effectual service. In the Old Testament, we see degrees of holiness, not only in the holy places, but as much in the holy persons. … It is even so in this more spiritual dispensation: the more of holiness, the greater the fitness for service; the more there is of true holiness; the more there is of God; and the more true and deep is the entrance He has had into the soul. The hold He has on the soul to use it in His service is more complete.

In the Church of Christ there is a vast amount of work done which yields very little fruit. Many throw themselves into work in whom there is but little true holiness, little of the Holy Spirit. They often work most diligently, and, as far as human influence is concerned, most successfully. And yet true spiritual results in the building up of a holy temple in the Lord are but few. The Lord cannot work in them, because He has not the mastery of their inner life. His personal indwelling and fellowship, the rest of His Holy Presence, His Holiness reigning and ruling in the heart and life, to all these they are comparative strangers.

It has been rightly said that work is the cure for spiritual poverty and disease; to some believers who had been seeking holiness apart from service, the call to work has been an unspeakable blessing. But to many it has only been an additional blind to cover up the terrible want of heart-holiness and heart-fellowship with the living God. They have thrown themselves into work more earnestly than ever, and yet have not in their heart the rest-giving and refreshing witness that their work is acceptable and accepted.

Listen to the message. "*If a man cleanse himself, he shall be a vessel unto honor, sanctified, meet for the Master's use, prepared unto every good work.*" You cannot have the law of service more clearly or beautifully laid down. A vessel of honor, one whom the King will delight to honor, must be a vessel cleansed from all defilement of flesh and spirit. Then only can it be a sanctified vessel, possessed and indwelt by God's Holy Spirit. So, it becomes meet for the Master's use. He can use it, and work in it, and wield it. And so, clean and holy, and yielded into the Master's hands, we are Divinely prepared for every good work.

Holiness is essential to service. If service is to be acceptable to God, and effectual for its work on souls, and to be a joy and a strength to ourselves, we must be holy. The will of God must first live in us, if it is to be done by us. How many faithful workers there are, mourning the want of power; longing and praying for it, and yet not obtaining it! They have spent their strength more in the outer court of work and service, than in the inner life of fellowship and faith. They truly have never understood that only as the Master gets possession of them, as the Holy Spirit has them at His disposal, can He use them, can they have true power. They often long and cry for what they call a baptism of power. They forget that the way to have God's power is to be in His power.

Put yourself into the power of God; let His holy will live in you; live in it and in obedience to it, as one who has no power to dispose of himself; let the Holy Spirit dwell within His Holy Temple, revealing the Holy One on the throne, ruling all; He will without fail use you as a vessel of honor, sanctified and ready for the Master's use.
Holiness is essential to effectual service.

And service is no less essential to true holiness. We have repeated it so often: Holiness is an energy, an intense energy of desire and Self-sacrifice, to make others partakers of its own purity and perfection. Christ sacrificed Himself wherein did that sacrifice consist, and what was its aim? He sanctified Himself that we might be sanctified too. A holiness that is Selfish is a delusion. True holiness, God's holiness in us, works itself out in love, in seeking and loving the unholy, that they may become holy too.

Self-sacrificing love is of the very essence of holiness. The Holy One of Israel is its Redeemer. The Holy One of God is the dying Savior. The Holy Spirit of God makes holy. There is no holiness in God but what is most actively engaged in loving and saving and blessing. It must be so in us too. Let every thought of holiness, every act of faith or prayer, every effort in pursuit of it, be animated by the desire and the surrender to the holiness of God for use in the attaining of its object. Let your whole life be one distinctly and definitely given up to God for His use and service.

Your circumstances may appear to be unfavorable. God may appear to keep the door closed against your working for Him in the way you would wish … Still, let it be a matter settled between God and the soul, that your longing for holiness is that you may be fitter for Him to use, and that what He has given you of His holiness in Christ and the Spirit is all at His disposal, waiting to be used. Be ready for Him to use you; live out, in a daily life of humble, Self-denying, loving service of others, what grace you have received. You will find that in the union and interchange of worship and work, God's Holiness will rest upon you.

"*The Father sanctified the Son, and sent Him into the world.*" The world is the place for the sanctified one, to be its light, its salt, its life. "*We are sanctified in Christ Jesus,*" and sent into the world too. Oh, let us not fear to accept our position our double position; in the world, and in Christ! In the world, with its sin and sorrow, with its thousands of needs touching us at every point, and its millions of souls all waiting for us. And in Christ too. For the sake of that world "*we have been sanctified in Christ*": we are "*holy in Christ,*" we have "*the spirit of sanctification*" dwelling in us. As a holy salt in a sinful world, let us give ourselves to our holy calling. …

Holiness and Truth

April 1st

"Make them holy in the Truth: Your word is Truth."

—JOHN 17: 17

The chief means of sanctification that God uses is His Word. And yet how much there is of reading and studying, of teaching and preaching the Word, that has almost no effect in making us holy. It is not the word that sanctifies; it is God Himself who alone can sanctify. Nor is it simply through the Word that God does it, but through the Truth which is in the Word. As a means the Word is of unspeakable value, as the vessel which contains the truth, if God use it; as a means it is of no value, if God does not use it. Let us strive to connect God's Holy Word with the Holy God Himself. God sanctifies in the Truth through His Word. …

Just as in the words of a man on earth we expect to find all the wisdom or all the goodness there is in him, so the Word of the Thrice Holy One is all alive with the Holiness of God. All the holy fire, alike of His burning zeal and His burning love, dwells in His words. And yet men can handle these words, and study them, and speak them, and be entire strangers to their holiness, or their power to make holy. It is God Himself, the Holy

One, who must make holy through the Word.

Every seed, in which the life of a tree is contained, has around it a husk or shell, which protects and hides the inner life. Only where the seed finds a place in congenial soil, and the husk is burst and removed, can the seed germinate and grow up. And it is only where there is a heart in harmony with God's Holiness, longing for it, yielding itself to it, that the Word will really make holy.

It is the heart that is not content *with* the Word, but seeks the Living, Holy One *in* the Word, to which He will reveal the Truth, and in it Himself. It is the Word given to us by Christ as God gave it Him, and received by us as it was by Him, to rule and fill our life, which has power to make holy.

But we must notice very specially how our Savior says, Sanctify them, not in the Word, but in the Truth. Just as in man there is body, soul, and spirit, so in truth too. There is first *word-truth*; we may have the correct form of words while we do not really apprehend the truth they contain. Then there is *thought-truth*; there may be a clear intellectual apprehension of truth without the experience of its power. The Bible speaks of truth as a living reality: this is the *life-truth*, in which the very Spirit of the truth we profess has entered and possessed our inner being.

Christ calls Himself the Truth: He is said to be full of grace and truth. The Divine life and grace are in Him as an actually substantial existence and reality. He not only acts upon us by thoughts and motives, but communicates, as a reality, the eternal life He brought for us from the Father. The Holy Spirit is called the Spirit of Truth; what He imparts is all real and actual, the very substance of unseen things; He guides into the Truth, not thought-truth or doctrine only, but life-truth, the personal possession of the Truth as it is in Jesus. As the Spirit of Truth He is the Spirit of Holiness; the life of God, which is His Holiness, He brings to us as an actual possession. It is now of this living Truth, which dwells in the word, as the seed-life dwells in the husk, that Jesus says, "*Make them holy in the Truth: Your word is Truth.*" He would have us mark the intimate connection, as well as the wide difference, between the Word and the Truth. The connection is one willed by God and meant to be inseparable.

"*Your word is truth*"; with God they are one. But not with carnal man. Just as there were men in close contact and continual intercourse with Jesus, to whom He was only a man, and nothing more, so there are Christians who know and understand the Word, and yet are strangers to its true spiritual power. They have the letter but not the spirit; the Truth comes to them in word but not in power. The Word does not make them holy, because they hold it not in Spirit and in Truth. To others, on the contrary, who know what it is to receive the truth in the love of it, who yield themselves, in all their dealings with the Word, to the Spirit of Truth who dwells in it and in them too, the word comes indeed as Truth, as a Divine reality, communicating and working what it speaks of.

And it is of such a use of the Word that the Savior says, "*Make them holy in the truth: Your Word is truth.*" As the words, which God gave Him, were all in the power of the eternal Life and Love and Will of God, the revelation and communication of the Father's purpose, as God's Word was Truth to Him and in Him, so it can be in us. And as we thus receive it, we are made holy in the Truth.

And what now are the lessons we have to learn here for the path of Holiness? The first is: Let us see to it that in all our intercourse with God's Blessed Word we rest content with nothing short of the experience of it, as truth of God, as spirit and as power.

Jesus said, "*If you abide in My Word, you shall know the truth.*" No analysis can ever find or prove the life of a seed: plant it in its proper soil, and the growth will testify to the life. It is only as the word of God is received in the love of it, as it grows and works in us, that we can know its truth, can know that it is the Truth of God. It is as we live in the words of Jesus, in love and obedience, keeping and doing them, that the Truth from Heaven, the Power of the Divine Life which there is in them, will unfold itself to us. Christ is the Truth; in Him the love and grace, the very life of God, has come to earth as a substantial existence, a Living, Mighty Power, something new that was never on earth before (John 1:17); let us yield ourselves to the Living Christ to possess us and to rule us as the Living Truth, then will God's word be Truth to us and in us.

The Spirit of Christ is the Spirit of Truth; that actual heavenly reality of Divine life and love in Christ, the Truth, has a Spirit, who comes to communicate and impart it. Let us beware of trying to study or understand or take possession of God's word without that Spirit through whom the Word was spoken of old; we shall find only the husk, the truth or thought and sentiment, very beautiful perhaps, but with no power to make us holy. We must have the Spirit of the Truth within us. He will lead us into the Truth; when we are in the Truth, God makes us holy in it and by it. The Truth must be in us, and we in it. …

Holiness and Blamelessness

April 2nd

"The Lord make you to increase and abound in love one toward another, and toward all men, to the end He may establish your hearts unblameable in holiness before our God and Father at the coming of our Lord Jesus."

—1 THESSALONIANS 3: 12–13

There are two Greek words, signifying nearly the same, used frequently along with the word holy, and following it, to express what the result and effect of holiness will be as manifested in the visible life. The one is translated "*without blemish, spotless,*" and is that also used of our Lord and His sacrifice, "*the Lamb without blemish*" (Hebrews 9: 14; 1 Peter 1: 19). It is then used of God's children, "*holy and without blemish*" (Ephesians 1: 4, 5, 27; Colossians 1: 22; Philippians 2: 15; Jude 24; 2 Peter 3: 14). The other is "*without blame, faultless,*" (Luke 1: 6; Philippians 2: 15, 3: 6), which is also found in conjunction with "holy" (1 Thessalonians 2: 10, 3: 13, 5: 23).

In answer to the question as to whether this blamelessness has reference to God's estimate of the saints or men's, Scripture clearly connects it with both. In some passages (Ephesians 1: 4, 5: 27; Colossians 1: 22; 1 Thessalonians 3: 1, 5; 2 Peter 3: 14) the words "*before Him*" "*to Himself*," "*before our God and Father*," indicate that the first thought is of the spotlessness and faultlessness in the presence of a Holy God, which is held out to us as His purpose and our privilege. In others (such as Philippians 2: 15; 1 Thessalonians 2: 10), the blamelessness in the sight of men stands in the foreground. In each case the word may be considered to include both aspects: without blemish and without blame must stand the double test of the judgment of God and man too.

And so, while most intent on trying to discover the secret of true and full holiness from the Divine side, we may be tolerating faults which all around us can notice, … ignorant of graces and beauties of holiness with which the Father would have had us adorn. Without such a doctrine of holiness before men, we may seek to live a very holy life, and yet think little of a perfectly *blameless* life. There have been such saints—holy but hard, holy but distant, holy but sharp in their judgments of others; holy, but to men around them unloving and Selfish ….

If this be true, it is not the teaching of Holy Scripture that is to blame. In linking holy and without blemish (or without blame) so closely, the Holy Spirit would have led us to seek for the embodiment of holiness as a spiritual power in the blamelessness of practice and of daily life. Let every believer who rejoices in God's declaration that he is holy in Christ seek also to perfect holiness, reach out after nothing less than to be "*unblameable in holiness.*"

The Lord make you to increase and abound in love one toward another, and toward all men, to the end He may establish your hearts unblameable in holiness before our God and Father at the coming of our Lord Jesus with all His holy ones (1 Thessalonians 3: 12–13). That this blamelessness has very special reference to our intercourse with our fellow-men we see from the way in which it is linked with love. Also in Ephesians 1: 4, "*That we should be holy and without blemish before Him in love.*" … The holiness and the blamelessness—the positive hidden Divine life-principle, and the external and human life-practice—both are to find their strength, by which we are to be established in them, in our abounding and ever-flowing love.

Holiness and lovingness: It is of deep importance that these words should be inseparably linked in our minds, and in our lives True holiness … is the expulsion and the death of Selfishness, taking possession of heart and life to be the ministers of that fire of love that consumes itself, to reach and purify and save others. Holiness is love. Abounding love is what Paul prays for as the condition of unblameable holiness. It is as the Lord [His presence, His Spirit indwelling us] makes us to increase and abound in love, that He can establish our hearts unblameable in holiness.

The Apostle speaks of a twofold love: "*love toward each other, and toward all men.*" Love to the brethren was what our Lord Himself enjoined as the chief mark of discipleship. And He prayed the Father for it as the chief proof to the world of the truth of His Divine mission. It is in the holiness of love, in a loving holiness, that the unity of the body will be proved and promoted, and prepared for the fuller workings of the Holy Spirit. In the Epistles to the Corinthians and Galatians, division and distance among believers are named as the sure proof of the life of Self and the flesh.

Oh, let us, if we would be holy, begin by being very gentle, and patient, and forgiving, and kind, and generous in our intercourse with all the Father's children. Let us study the Divine image of the love that seeks not its own, and pray unceasingly that the Lord may make us to abound in love to each other. The holiest will be the humblest and most Self-forgetting, the gentlest and most Self-denying, the kindest and most thoughtful of others for Jesus' sake. *"Put on therefore, as God's elect, holy and beloved, a heart of compassion, kindness, humility, meekness, long-suffering"* (Colossians 3: 12–13). …

A love proved in the conduct and intercourse of daily life. A love that not only avoids anger and evil temper and harsh judgments, but exhibits the more positive virtue of active devotion to the welfare and interests of all. A charitable love that cares for the bodies as well as the souls. A love that not only is ready to help when it is called, but that really gives itself up to Self-denial and Self-sacrifice to seek out and relieve the needs of the most wretched and unworthy. A love that does indeed take Christ's love, that brought Him from Heaven and led Him to choose the cross, as the only law and measure for its conduct, and makes everything subordinate to the Godlike blessedness of giving, of doing good, of embracing and saving the needy and lost. Thus abounding in love, we shall be *"unblameable in holiness."*

6

THE SPIRIT OF CHRIST

Thoughts on the Indwelling of the Holy Spirit in the Believer and the Church

London: James Nisbet & Co., 1888

Preface

April 3rd

In olden times, Israel knew God, walked with Him, had the clear and full consciousness that they had dealings with the God of heaven, and had, too, through faith, the assurance that they and their lives were well pleasing to Him. When the Son of God came to earth, and revealed the Father, it was that such intercourse with God, and the assurance of His favor, might become clearer, and be the abiding portion of every child of God. When He was exalted to the throne of glory, it was that He might send down into our hearts the Holy Spirit, in whom the Father and the Son have their own blessed life in Heaven, to maintain in us, in Divine power, the blessed life of fellowship with God.

It was to be one of the marks of the New Covenant that each member of it should walk in personal communion with God. "*They shall teach no more … Know the Lord; for they shall all know me, from the least to the greatest of them, says the Lord; for I will forgive their iniquity!*" The personal fellowship and knowledge of God in the Holy Spirit was to be the fruit of the pardon of sin.

The Spirit of God's own Son, sent into our hearts to do each moment a work as Divine as the work of the Son in redeeming us, to displace our life and replace it by the life of Christ in power, to make the Son of God Divinely and consciously present with us always—This was what the Father had promised as the distinctive blessing of the New

Testament. The fellowship of God as the Three-One was now to be within us; the Spirit revealing the Son in us, and through Him the Father.

That there are but few believers who realize this walk with God, this life in God, such as their Father has prepared for them, no one will deny. Nor will it admit of dispute what the cause of this failure is. It is acknowledged on all hands that the Holy Spirit, through whose Divine omnipotence this inner revelation of the Son and the Father in the life and the likeness of the believer is to take place, is not known or acknowledged in the Church as He should be. In our preaching and in our practice, He does not hold that place of prominence which He has in God's plan and in His promises. While our creed on the Holy Spirit is orthodox and scriptural, His presence and power in the life of believers, in the ministry of the word, in the witness of the Church to the world, is not what the word promises or God's plan requires. …

Some feel that their own life is not what it should and might be. Many of them can look back to some special season of spiritual revival, when their whole life was apparently lifted to a higher level. The experience of the joy and strength of the Savior's presence, as they learned that He would keep them trusting, was, for a time, most real and blessed. But it did not last: there was a very gradual decline to a lower stage, with much of vain effort and sad failure. They would fain know where the evil lies. There can be little doubt that the answer must be this: they did not know or honor the Indwelling Spirit as the strength of their life, as the power of their faith, to keep them always looking to Jesus and trusting in Him. They knew not what it was, day by day, to wait in lowly reverence for the Holy Spirit to deliver from the power of the flesh, and to maintain the wonderful presence of the Father and the Son within them. …

I have strong fears—I desire to say it in deep humility—that in the theology of our Churches the teaching and leading of the Spirit of Truth, the anointing which alone teaches all things, has not practical recognition which a Holy God demands, which our Savior meant Him to have. In everything that concerns the Word of God, and the Church of Christ, and the work of saving love to be done on the earth in the name of Christ, it was meant that the Holy Spirit should have the same and supreme place of honor that He had in the Church of the Acts of the Apostles. If the leaders of our church-thought and church-councils, our professors of theology and our commentators, if our ministers and students, our religious writers and workers, were all fully conscious of this fact, surely the signs of that honor given and accepted, marks of His Holy Presence would be clearer, His mighty works more manifest. I trust it has not been presumptuous in me to hope that what has been written may help to remind even our Masters … of what is so easily overlooked—that the first, the indispensable requirement for what is really to bear fruit for eternity is, that we be full of the power of the Eternal Spirit. …

There is a deep feeling abroad that the Scripture ideal, that Christ's own promise of what the Church should be, and its actual state, do not correspond. Of all questions in theology there is none that leads us more deeply into the glory of God, or that is of more intense vital and practical importance for daily life, than that which deals with what is the consummation and culmination of the revelation of God and the work of redemption: in what way and to what extent God's Holy Spirit can dwell in, can fill, can make into a holy and beautiful temple of God, the heart of His child, with Christ reigning there, as an Ever-present and Almighty Savior. It is the question in theology of which the solution, if it were sought and found in the presence and teaching of the Spirit Himself, would transform all our theology into that knowledge of God which is eternal life.

Of theology, in every possible shape, we have no lack. But it is as if, with all our writing, and preaching, and working, there is something wanting. Is not the power from on high the one thing we lack? May it not be that, with all our love for Christ and labor for His cause, we have not made the chief object of our desire what was the chief object of His heart when He ascended the throne … that in that power of the felt presence of their Lord they might testify of Him. May God raise from among our theologians many who shall give their lives to secure for God's Holy Spirit His recognition in the lives of believers, in the ministry try of the word by tongue and pen, in all the work done in His Church. … As we first yield ourselves to be led by the Spirit, to confess His presence in us—as believers rise to realize and accept His guidance in all their daily life—will our God be willing to entrust to us larger measures of His mighty workings. If we give ourselves entirely into His power, as our life, ruling within us, He will give Himself to us in taking a more complete possession, to work through us.

If there is one thing I desire, it is that the Lord may use what I have written to make clear and impress this one truth: It is as an indwelling life that the Holy Spirit must be known. In a living, adoring faith, the indwelling must be accepted and treasured, until it becomes part of the consciousness of the new man: The Holy Spirit possesses me. In this faith the whole life, even to the least things, must be surrendered to His leading, while all that is of the flesh or Self is crucified and put to death. …The Holy Spirit only demands vessels entirely set apart to Him. He will delight to manifest the glory of Christ our Lord.
—*ANDREW MURRAY,* Wellington, Cape of Good Hope, 1888.

A New Spirit, and God's Spirit

April 4th

"A new spirit will I put within you. And I will put my Spirit within you."
—EZEKIEL 36: 26–27

In the words of Ezekiel, we find in the one promise this twofold blessing that God bestows through His Spirit. The first is, *"I will put within you a new spirit,"* that is, our own spirit is to be renewed and quickened by the work of God's Spirit. When this has been done, then there is the second blessing, *"I will put my Spirit within you,"* to dwell in that new spirit.

Where God is to dwell, He must have a habitation. With Adam He had to create a body before He could breathe the spirit of life into him. In Israel the tabernacle and the temple had to be built and completed before God could come down and take possession. And just so a new heart is given, and a new spirit put within us, as the indispensable condition of God's own Spirit being given to dwell within us. … The importance of recognizing this distinction can easily be perceived. We shall then be able to understand the true relation between regeneration and the indwelling of the Spirit. The former is that work of the Holy Spirit, by which He convinces us of sin, leads to repentance and faith in Christ, and imparts a new nature. Through the Spirit God thus fulfills the promise, *"I will put a new spirit within you."* The believer is now a child of God, a temple ready for the Spirit to dwell in.

Where faith claims it, the second half of the promise is fulfilled as surely as the first. As long now as the believer only looks at regeneration, and the renewal wrought in his spirit, he will not come to the life of joy and strength which is meant for him. But when he accepts God's promise that there is something better than even the new nature, than the inner temple, that there is the Spirit of the Father and the Son to dwell within him, there opens up a wonderful prospect of holiness and blessedness. It becomes his one great desire to know this Holy Spirit aright, how He works and what He asks, to know how he may to the full experience His indwelling, and that revelation of the Son of God within us which it is His work to bestow.

The question will be asked, How these two parts of the Divine promise are fulfilled? simultaneously or successively? The answer is very simple: From God's side the twofold gift is simultaneous. The Spirit is not divided: in giving the Spirit, God gives Himself and all He is. So it was on the day of Pentecost. The three thousand received the new spirit, with repentance and faith, and then, when they had been baptized, the Indwelling Spirit, as God's seal to their faith, on one day.

Through the word of disciples, the Spirit, which had come upon them, wrought mightily on the multitude, changing disposition and heart and spirit. When, in the power of this new spirit working in them, they had believed and confessed, they received the baptism of Holy Spirit to abide in them.

And so still in times when the Spirit of God moves mightily, and the Church is living in the power of the Spirit, the children which are begotten of her receive from the first beginnings of their Christian life the distinct conscious sealing and indwelling of the Spirit. And yet we have indications in Scripture that there may be circumstances, dependent either on the enduement of the preacher or the faith of the bears in which the two halves of the promise are not so closely linked.

So it was with the believers in Samaria converted under Philip's preaching; and so too with the converts Paul met at Ephesus. In their case was repeated the experience of the apostles themselves. We regard them as regenerate men before our Lord's death; it was only at Pentecost that the promise was fulfilled, "*He shall be in you*!" What was seen in them, just as in the Old and New Testaments—the grace of the Spirit divided into two separate manifestations—may still take place in our day.

When, the standard of spiritual life in a Church is sickly and low, when neither in the preaching of the word nor in the testimony of believers, the glorious truth of an Indwelling

Spirit is distinctly proclaimed, we must not wonder if, even where God gives His Spirit, He be known and experienced only as the Spirit of regeneration. His Indwelling Presence will remain a mystery.

In the gift of God, the Spirit of Christ in all His fullness is bestowed once for all as an Indwelling Spirit; but He is received and possessed only as far as the faith of the believer reaches.

It is generally admitted in the Church that the Holy Spirit has not the recognition which becomes Him as being the equal of the Father and the Son, the Divine Person through whom alone the Father and the Son can be truly possessed and known, in whom alone the Church has her beauty and her blessedness. In the Reformation, of blessed memory, the Gospel of Christ had to be vindicated from the terrible misapprehension which makes man's righteousness the ground of his acceptance, and the freeness of Divine grace had to be maintained. To the ages that followed was committed the trust of building on that foundation, and developing what the riches of grace would do for the believer through the indwelling of the Spirit of Jesus. The Church rested too content in what it had received, and the teaching of all that the Holy Spirit will be to each believer in His guiding, sanctifying, strengthening power, has never yet taken the place it ought to have in our evangelical teaching and living.

Let us unite with all who are pleading that God in power may grant mighty Spirit workings in His Church, that each child of God may prove that in him the double promise is fulfilled: I will give a new spirit within you, and I will give my Spirit within you. Let us pray that we may so apprehend the wonderful blessing of the Indwelling Spirit, as to turn inward and have our whole inmost being opened up for this, the full revelation of the Father's love and the grace of Jesus.

"*Within you!*" Within you! This twice-repeated word of our text is one of the keywords of the 'New Covenant. "*I will put my law in their inward parts, and in their heart will I write it.*" "*I will put my fear in their hearts, that they shall not depart from me.*" God created man's heart for His dwelling. Sin entered, and defiled it. Four thousand years God's Spirit strove and wrought to regain possession. In the Incarnation and Atonement of Christ the Redemption was accomplished, and the Kingdom of God established. Jesus could say, "*The kingdom of God is come unto you;*" "*the kingdom of God is within you.*"

It is *within* we must look for the fulfilment of the New Covenant—the Covenant not of ordinances but of life: in the power of an endless life the law and the fear of God are to be given in our heart: The Spirit of Christ Himself is to be within us as the power of our life. Not only on Calvary, or in the resurrection, or on the throne, is the glory of Christ the Conqueror to be seen, but in our heart: within us, within us is to be the true display of the reality and the glory of His Redemption. Within us, in our inmost parts, is the hidden sanctuary where is the ark of the Covenant, sprinkled with the Blood, and containing the Law written in an ever-living writing by the Indwelling Spirit, and where, through the Spirit, the Father and the Son now come to dwell.

O my God! I do thank You for this double blessing. I thank You for that wonderful holy temple You have built up in me for Yourself—a new spirit given within me. And I thank You for that still more wonderful Holy Presence, Your Own Spirit, to dwell within me, and there reveal the Father and the Son. … I do pray for You to open mine eyes for this the mystery of Your love. Let Your words, "*within you*," bow me low in trembling fear before Your condescension, and may my one desire be to have my spirit indeed the worthy dwelling of Your Spirit. Let them lift me up in holy trust and expectation, to look for and claim all that Your promise means. O my Father! I thank You that Your Spirit dwells in me. I pray, let His indwelling be in power, in the living fellowship with Yourself, in the growing experience of His renewing power, in the ever-fresh anointing that witnesses to His Presence, and the indwelling of my Glorified Lord Jesus. May my daily walk be in the deep reverence of His Holy Presence within me, and the glad experience of all He works.

The Indwelling Spirit

April 5th

"I will pray to the Father, and He shall give you another Comforter, that He may be with you forever; this is the Spirit of truth; whom the world cannot receive; for it beholds Him not, neither knows Him. You know Him, for He abides with you, and shall be in you."

—JOHN 14:16–17

He *"shall be in you."* In these simple words our Lord announces that wonderful mystery of the Spirit's indwelling which was to be the fruit and the crown of His redeeming work. It was for this man had been created. It was for this, God's mastery within the heart, the Spirit had striven in vain with men through the past ages. It was for this Jesus had lived and was about to die. Without this the Father's purpose and His own work would fail of their accomplishment. For want of this the intercourse of the Blessed Master with the disciples had effected so little. He had hardly ever ventured to mention it to them, because He knew they would not understand it. But now, on the last night, when it was but a little time, He discloses the Divine Secret that, when He left them, their loss would be compensated by a greater blessing than His bodily presence. Another would come in His stead, to abide with them forever, and to dwell in them. Dwelling in them, He would prepare them to receive Himself their Lord, and the Father, within them too. "*He shall be in you.*"

Our Father has given us a twofold revelation of Himself. In His Son He reveals His Holy image, and setting him before men invites them to become like Him by receiving Him into their heart and life. In His Spirit He sends forth His Divine power, to enter into us, and from within prepare us for receiving the Son and the Father. The dispensation of the Spirit is the dispensation of the inner life. In the dispensation of the Word, or the Son, beginning as it did with the creation of man in God's image, continued as it was through all the preparatory stages down to Christ's appearing, in the flesh, all was more external and preparatory. There were at times special and mighty workings of the Spirit; but the indwelling was unknown; man had not yet become a habitation of God in the Spirit. Now first, this was to be attained. The eternal life was to become the very life of man, hiding itself within his very being and consciousness, and clothing itself in the forms of a human will and life.

Just as it is through the Spirit that God is what He is; just as in the Father and the Son, the Spirit is the principle in which their personality has its root and consciousness, so this Spirit of the Divine life is now to be in us, in the deepest sense of the word, the principle of our life, the root of our personality too, the very life of our being and consciousness. He is to be one with us in the absoluteness of a Divine immanence, dwelling in us, even as the Father in the Son, and the Son in the Father. Let us bow in holy reverence to worship and adore, and to receive the mighty blessing.

If we would enter into the full understanding and experience of what our Blessed Lord here promises, we must above everything remember that what He speaks of is a Divine indwelling. Wherever God dwells He hides Himself. In nature He hides Himself; most men see Him not there. In meeting His saints of old He mostly hid Himself under some manifestation in human weakness, so that it was often only after He was gone that they said, "*Surely the Lord is in this place, and I knew it not.*" The Blessed Son came to reveal God, and yet He came as a root out of a dry ground, without form or comeliness; even His own disciples were at times offended at Him. People always expect the Kingdom of God to come with observation; they know not that it is a hidden mystery, to be received only as, in His own Self-revealing power, God makes Himself known in hearts surrendered and prepared for Him.

Christians are always ready, when the promise of the Spirit occupies them, to form some conception as to how His leading can be known in their thoughts; how His quickening will affect their feelings; how His sanctifying can be recognized in their will and conduct. They need to be reminded that deeper than mind and feeling and will, deeper than the soul, where these have their seat, in the depths of the spirit that came from God, there comes the Holy Spirit to dwell. …

The deep importance of a right apprehension of the indwelling of the Spirit is evident from the place it occupies in our Lord's farewell discourse. In this and the two following chapters, He speaks of the Spirit more directly as teacher, as witness, as representing and glorifying Himself, as convincing the world. At the same time, He connects this, and He says of His and the Father's indwelling, of the union of the Vine and the branches, of the peace and joy and power in prayer which His disciples would have, with "that day," the time of the Spirit's coming. But, before all this, as its one condition and only source, He places the promise, "*the Spirit shall be in, you.*" It avails little that we know all that the Spirit can do for us, or that we confess our entire dependence on Him, unless we clearly realize, and place first, what the Master gave the first place; that it is as the indwelling Spirit alone that He can be our teacher or our strength. As the Church, as the believer, accepts our Lord's, "*He shall be in you,*" and lives under the control of this faith, our true relation to the blessed Spirit will be restored. He will take charge and inspire; He will mightily fill and bless the being given up to Him as His abode.

A careful study of the epistles will confirm this, In writing to the Corinthians, Paul had to reprove them for sad and terrible sins, and yet he says to all, including the feeblest and most unfaithful believer, 'Know you not that the Spirit of God dwelleth in you?' Know you not that your body is the temple of the Holy Spirit?' He is sure that if this were believed, if to this truth were given the place God meant it to have, it would not only be the motive, but the power of a new and holy life. To the backsliding Galatians, he has no mightier plea to address than this : they had received the Spirit by the preaching of faith; God had sent forth the Spirit of His Son into their hearts ; they had their life by the Spirit in them ; if they could but understand and believe this, they would also walk in the Spirit.

It is this teaching the Church of Christ needs in our days. I am deeply persuaded that very few of us realize aright to what extent believers are ignorant of this aspect of the truth concerning the Holy Spirit, or to what an extent this is the cause of their feebleness in holy walk and work. There may be a great deal of praying for the Holy Spirit's working, there may be great correctness in our confession, both in preaching and prayer, of entire and absolute dependence on Him; but unless His personal, continual, Divine indwelling be acknowledged and experienced, we must not be surprised if there be continual failure. The Holy Dove wants his resting place free from all intrusion and disturbance.

God wants entire possession of His temple. Jesus wants His home all to Himself. He cannot do His work there, He cannot rule and reveal Himself and His love as He would, unless the whole home, the whole inner being, be possessed and filled by the Holy Spirit. Let us consent to this. …

The Spirit of the Glorified Jesus

April 6th

"He spoke of the Spirit, whom they that believe on Him were to receive, for the Spirit was not yet given; because Jesus was not yet glorified."

—JOHN 7: 38–30

Our Lord promises here, that those who come unto Him and drink, who believe in Him, will not only never thirst, but will themselves become fountains, whence streams of living water, of life and blessing, will flow forth. In recording the words, John explains that the promise was a prospective one that would have to wait for its fulfillment till the Spirit should have been poured out. He also gave the double reason for this delay: "*The Holy Spirit was not yet given, because Jesus was not yet glorified.*" …

We have seen that God has given a twofold revelation of Himself, first as, God in the Old Testament, then as Father in the New. We know how the Son, who had from eternity been with the Father, entered upon a new stage of existence when He became flesh. When He returned to Heaven, He was still the same only—begotten Son of God, and yet not altogether the same. For He was now also, as Son of Man, the first—begotten from the dead, clothed with that glorified humanity which He had perfected and sanctified for Himself. And just so the Spirit of God as poured out on Pentecost was indeed something new. Through the Old Testament He was always called the Spirit of God or the Spirit of the Lord; the name of Holy Spirit He did not yet bear as His own proper name. It is only in connection with the work He has to do in preparing the way for Christ, and a body for Him, that the proper name comes into use (Luke 1: 15, 35). When poured out at Pentecost, He came as the Spirit of the glorified Jesus, the Spirit of the Incarnate, crucified, and exalted Christ, the bearer and communicator to us, not of the life of God as such, but of that life as it had been interwoven into human nature in the person of Christ Jesus. It is in this capacity specially that He bears the name of Holy Spirit, it is as the Indwelling One that God is Holy.

But now, Blessed be God! Jesus has been glorified; there is now the Spirit of the glorified Jesus; the promise can now be fulfilled: He that believes on me, out of him shall flow rivers of living waters. The great transaction which took place when Jesus was glorified is now an eternal reality. When Christ had entered with our human nature, in our flesh, into the Holiest of all, there took place that of which Peter speaks, "*Being by the right hand of God exalted, He received of the Father the promise of the Holy Spirit.*" ... He could come down as the Spirit of the glorified Jesus to be in each one who believes in Jesus, the Spirit of His personal life and His personal presence.... There is now the Spirit of the glorified Jesus: He has poured Him forth; we have received Him to stream into us, to stream through us, and to stream forth from us in rivers of blessing. ...

This is the mystery which was hid from ages and generations, but is now made known by the Holy Spirit, Christ in us; how He really can live His Divine life in us who are in the flesh. We have the most intense personal interest in knowing and understanding what it means that Jesus is glorified, that human nature shares the life and glory of God, that the Spirit was not yet, as long as Jesus was not glorified. And that not only because we are one day to see Him in His glory, and to be with Him in it. No, but even now, day by day, we are to live in it. The Holy Spirit is able to be to us just as much as we are willing to have of Him, and of the life of the glorified Lord.

"*This said Jesus of the Spirit, which they that believed on Him were to receive; for the Spirit was not yet; because Jesus was not yet glorified.*" God be praised! Jesus has been glorified: there is now the Spirit of the glorified Jesus; we have received Him. In the Old Testament, only the unity of God was revealed; when the Spirit was mentioned, it was always as His Spirit, the power by which God was working. ... With Pentecost, the Holy Spirit descended as a Person to dwell in us.

This is the fruit of Jesus' work that we now have the personal presence of the Holy Spirit on earth. Just as in Christ Jesus, the second person, the Son, came to reveal the Father, and the Father dwelled and spoke in Him, even so the Spirit, the third person, comes to reveal the Son, and in Him the Son dwells and works in us. This is the glory wherewith the Father glorified the Son of man, because the Son had glorified Him, that in His name and through Him, the Holy Spirit descends as a person to dwell in believers, and to make the glorified Jesus a present reality within them. This is it of which Jesus says, that whoever believes in Him shall never thirst, but shall have rivers of waters flowing out of him. This alone it is that satisfies the soul's thirst, and makes it a fountain to quicken others; the personal indwelling of the Holy Spirit, revealing the presence of the glorified Jesus.

The Expediency of the Spirit's Coming

April 7th

"I tell you the truth; it is expedient for you that I go away; for if I go not away, the Comforter will not come; but, if I go, I will send Him to you."

—JOHN 16: 7

As our Lord is leaving this world, He promises the disciples here that His departure will be their gain; the Comforter will take His place, and be to them far better than He ever had been or could be in His bodily presence. This very specially in two aspects. His intercourse with them had never been unbroken, but liable to interruption; now it would even be broken off by death, and they would see Him no more. The Spirit would *abide with them forever*. His own intercourse had been very much external, and, in consequence of this, had not resulted in what might have been expected. The Spirit would be *in* them; His coming would be as an indwelling presence, in the power of which they should have Jesus too in them as their life and their strength. …

All that Christ had been to them, the Spirit was to restore in greater power, and in a blessedness that should know no break. They were to be far happier and safer and stronger with Jesus in heaven, than they ever could have been with Him on earth. This, the chief beauty and blessedness of their discipleship of such a Master, that He was so wise and patient to give to each one just what he needed and to make each one feel that he had in Him his best friend, could never be left out. The indwelling of the Spirit was meant to restore Christ's most personal intercourse and guidance, His direct personal friendship.

It is to many a matter of great difficulty to conceive of this or to believe it; much less do they experience it. The thought of Christ walking with men on earth, living and guiding them, is so clear; the thought of a Spirit hiding Himself within us, and speaking, not in distinct thoughts, but only in the secret depths of the life, makes His guidance so much more difficult. …

God wants to educate us, indeed, to a perfect manhood, not ruled by an outward law, but by the inner life. As long as Jesus was with the disciples on earth, He had to work from without inward, and yet could never effectually reach or master the inmost parts. When He went away He sent the Spirit to be in them, that now their growth might be from within outward. Taking possession first by His Spirit of the inmost secret recesses of their being, He would have them, in the voluntary consent and surrender to His inspiration and guidance, personally become what He Himself is, through His Spirit in them.

… To have the Holy Spirit of God coming through the human nature of our Lord, entering, into our spirits, identifying Himself with us, and becoming our very own, just as

He was the Spirit of Christ Jesus on earth, surely this is a blessedness worth any sacrifice, for it is the beginning of the indwelling of God Himself. …

And so the question comes again: the intercourse of Jesus with His disciples on earth, so condescending in its tenderness, so particular and minute in its interest, so consciously personal in its love, how can this be ours in the same degree now that He is absent, and the Spirit is to be our guide? The first answer here, is, as through the whole Christian life: *by faith*. With Jesus on earth, the disciples, when once they had believed, walked by sight; we walk by faith. In faith, we must accept and rejoice in the word of Jesus: "*It is expedient for you that I go away*." We must take time distinctly to believe it, to approve of it, to rejoice that He is gone to the Father. We must learn to thank and praise Him that He has called us to this life in the Spirit.

We must believe that in this gift of the Spirit the presence and intercourse of our Lord are fully secured to us most certainly and effectually. It may indeed be in a way we do not yet understand, because we have so little believed and rejoiced in the gift of the Holy Spirit. But faith must believe and praise for what it does not yet understand; let us believe assuredly and joyfully that the Holy Spirit, and Jesus Himself through Him, will teach us how the intercourse and guidance are to be enjoyed. …

Knowledge, thought, feeling, action—all this is a part of that external religion which the external presence of Jesus had also wrought in the disciples. The Spirit was now to come, and, deeper down than all these, He was to be the Hidden Presence of Jesus within the depths of their personality. The Divine Life was in a newness of power to become their life. And the teaching of the Spirit would begin, not in word or thought, but in power. In the power of a Life working in them secretly, but with Divine energy; in the Power of a Faith that rejoiced that Jesus was really near, was really taking charge of the whole life and every circumstance of it; the Spirit would inspire them with the faith of the Indwelling Jesus. This would be the beginning and the blessedness of His teaching. They would have the Life of Jesus within them, and they would by faith know that it was Jesus: their faith would be at once cause and effect of the Presence of the Lord in the Spirit.

It is by such a faith—a faith which the Spirit breathes, which comes from His being and living in us—that the Presence of Jesus is to be as real and all-sufficient as when He was on earth. But why then is it that believers who have the Spirit do not experience it more consciously and fully!? The answer is very simple: they know and honor the Spirit who is in them so little. They have much faith in Jesus who died, or who reigns in Heaven, but little faith in Jesus who dwells in them by His Spirit. It is this we need: faith in Jesus as the fulfiller of the promise, "*He that believes in me, rivers of living water shall flow out of him.*" We must believe that the Holy Spirit is within us as the Presence of our Lord Jesus. And we must not only believe this with the faith of the understanding as it seeks to persuade itself of the truth of what Christ says. We must believe with the heart, a heart in which the Holy Spirit dwells. The whole gift of the Spirit, the whole teaching of Jesus concerning the Spirit, is to enforce the word: "*The Kingdom of God is within you.*" If we would have the true faith of the heart, let us turn inward, and very gently and humbly yield to the Holy Spirit to do His work in us. …

Filled with the Spirit

April 8th

"Be filled with the Spirit."

—EPHESIANS 5: 18

These words are a command. They enjoin upon us, not what the state of apostles or ministers ought to be, but what should be the ordinary consistent experience of every true-hearted believer. It is the privilege every child of God may claim from his Father, to be filled with the Spirit. Nothing less will enable him to live the life he has been redeemed for, abiding in Christ, keeping His commandments, and bearing much fruit. And yet, how little this command has been counted among those which all ought to keep! How little it has been thought possible or reasonable that all should be expected to keep it!

One reason of this is undoubtedly that the words have been wrongly understood. Because with the day of Pentecost, and on more than one subsequent occasion, the being filled with the Spirit was accompanied with the manifest enthusiasm of a supernatural joy and power, such a state has been looked on as one of excitement and strain, quite inconsistent with the quiet course of ordinary life. The suddenness and the strength and the outward manifestation of the Divine impulse were so linked with the idea of being filled with the Spirit, that it was thought to be something for special occasions, a blessing only possible to a very few. …

In a country like South Africa, where we often suffer from drought, we find two sorts of dams or reservoirs made for catching up and storing water. On some farms you have a fountain, but with a stream too weak to irrigate with. There a reservoir is made for collecting the water, and the filling of the reservoir is the result of the gentle, quiet inflow from the fountain day and night. In other cases, again, the farm has no fountain at all; the reservoir is built in the bed of a stream or in a hollow where, when rain falls, the water can be collected. In such a place, the filling of the reservoir, with a heavy fall rain, is often the work of a very few hours, and is accompanied with a rush and violence not free from danger. The noiseless supply of the former farm is, at the same time, the surer, because the supply, though apparently feeble, is permanent; in tracts where the rainfall is uncertain, a reservoir may stand empty for months or years.

There is no difference in the way in which the fullness of the Spirit comes. On the day of Pentecost, at times when new beginnings are made, in the outpouring of the Spirit of conversion in heathen lands, or of revival among Christian people, suddenly, mightily, manifestly, men are filled with the Holy Spirit. In the enthusiasm and the joy of the newly found salvation, the power of the Spirit is undeniably present. And yet, for those who receive it thus, there are special dangers. The blessing is often too much dependent on the fellowship with others, or extends only to the upper and more easily reached currents of the soul's life: the sudden is often the superficial; the depths of the will and the inner life have not been reached. Other Christians there are who have never been partakers of any such marked experience, and in whom, nevertheless, the fullness of the Spirit is no less distinctly seen in the deep and intense devotion to Jesus, in a walk in the light of His countenance and the consciousness of His Holy presence, in the blamelessness of a life of simple trust and obedience, and in the humility of a Self-sacrificing love to all around. …

And which of these is now the true way of being filled with the Spirit? The answer is easy. There are farms on which both the above-named reservoirs are to be found, auxiliary to each other. There are even reservoirs, where the situation is favorable, in which both the modes of filling are made use of. The regular, quiet, daily inflowing keeps them supplied in time of great drought; in time of rain they are ready to receive and store up large supplies. There are Christians who are not content but with special mighty visitations: the rushing mighty wind, floods outpoured, and the baptism of fire; these are their symbols. There are others to whom the fountain springing up from within, and quietly streaming forth, appears the true type of the Spirit's work. Happy they who can recognize God in both, and hold themselves always ready to be blessed in whichever way He comes.

And what are now the conditions of this fullness of the Spirit? God's Word has one answer: *faith.* It is faith alone that sees and receives the invisible—that sees and receives God Himself. The cleansing from sin and the loving surrender to obedience, which were the conditions of the first reception of the Spirit, are the fruit of the faith that saw what sin was, and what the blood, and what the will and the love of God is. …

All filling needs emptying. I do not here speak of the cleansing out of sin, and the surrender to full obedience. This is always the first essential. But I speak of believers who in this think they have done what God demands, and yet fail of the blessing. The first condition of all filling is emptiness. What is a reservoir but a great hollow, a great emptiness prepared, waiting, thirsting, crying for the water to come?

Any true abiding fullness of the Spirit is preceded by emptying. … In such emptying out there are various elements. A deep dissatisfaction with the religion we have hitherto had. A deep consciousness of how much there has been of the wisdom and the work of the flesh in it. A discovery, and confession, and giving up of all in life that had been kept in our own hands and management, in which Self had hitherto reigned, of all in which we had not thought it necessary or possible that Jesus should directly be consulted and pleased. A deep conviction of impotence and utter helplessness to grasp or seize what is offered. A surrender, in poverty of spirit to wait on the Lord in His great mercy and power, *"according to the riches of His glory, to strengthen us mightily by His Spirit in the inner man."* A great longing, thirsting, waiting, crying—a praying without ceasing for the Father to fulfill His promise in us and take full possession of us within. Such an emptying is on the way to the filling.

With this is needed the believing which accepts, which receives, which holds the gift. It is through faith in Christ and in the Father that the Divine fullness will flow into us. Of the same Ephesians, to whom the command is given, "*Be filled with the Spirit,*" Paul had said, "*In Christ, having believed, you were sealed with the Holy Spirit of promise.*" The command refers to what they had already received: the fountain was within them; it had to be opened up, and way made for it; it would spring up and fill their being. And yet not as if this was in their own power: Jesus had said, "*He that believes, and who keeps believing in me, rivers of living water shall flow out of him.*" The fullness of the Spirit is so truly in Jesus, the receiving out of Him must so really be in the unbroken continuity of a real life-fellowship—the ceaseless inflow of the sap from Him the living Vine must so distinctly be met by the ceaseless … simple faith—that the up-springing of the fountain within can only be in the dependence on Jesus above. It is by the faith of Jesus, whose baptism with the Spirit has as distinct a commencement as His cleansing with the blood, but is also maintained by, as continuous a renewal, that the inflow will grow ever stronger until it comes to the overflowing.

And yet the faith in Jesus, and the hourly and ever growing up-springing of the Spirit, will not dispense with faith in the Father's special gift and the prayer for His special renewed fulfillment of His promise. For these same Ephesians, who had thus the Spirit within them as the earnest of their inheritance, Paul prays to the Father "*that He would grant you, according to the riches of His glory, that you may be strengthened with power through His Spirit in the inner man.*" The verbs both denote not a gradual work, but an act, something done at once. The expression, "*according to the riches of His glory,*" indicates something which is to be a great exhibition of the Divine love and power, something very special and Divine. They had the Spirit indwelling. He prayed for them that the direct interposition of the Father might give them such mighty workings of the Spirit, such a fullness of the Spirit, that the indwelling of Christ, and a life in the love that passes knowledge, and a being filled with the fullness of God, might be their blessed personal experience. When the flood came of old, the windows of Heaven above, and the fountains of the great deep beneath, were together opened. It is still so in the fulfillment of the promise of the Spirit: "*I will pour floods upon the dry ground.*" The deeper and clearer the faith in the indwelling Spirit, and the simpler the waiting on Him, the more abundant will be the renewed down-coming of the Spirit from the heart of the Father direct into the heart of His waiting child. …

The Baptism of the Spirit

April 9th

"John bore witness, saying, He that sent me to baptize with water, He said unto me, Upon Whomsoever you shall see the, Spirit descending, and abiding on Him the same is He that baptizes with the Holy Spirit."

—JOHN 1:33

There were two things that John the Baptist preached concerning the person of Christ: the one was, that He was the Lamb of God that takes away the sin of the world. The other: that He would baptize His disciples with the Holy Spirit and with fire. The blood of the Lamb, and the Baptism of the Spirit were the two central truths of his creed and his preaching. They are, indeed, inseparable; the Church cannot do her work in power, nor can her exalted Lord be glorified in her, except as the blood as the foundation stone, and the Spirit as the cornerstone, are fully preached.

This has not at all times been done even among those who heartily accept Scripture as their guide. The preaching of the Lamb of God, of His suffering and atonement, of pardon and peace through Him, is more easily apprehended… and can more speedily influence our feelings, than the more inward spiritual truth of the baptism, and indwelling, and guidance of the Holy Spirit. …

And yet God would not have it so. The Old Testament promise had spoken of God's Spirit within us. The forerunner at once took up the strain, and did not preach the Atoning Lamb without telling whereunto it was that we were to be redeemed, and how God's high purpose was to be fulfilled in us. Sin was not only guilt and condemnation; it was defilement and death. It had incurred not only the loss of God's favor it had made us unfit for the Divine fellowship. And without this the wonderful love that had created us could not be content. God wanted really to have us for Himself—our hearts and affections, yea, our inmost personality, our very Self, a home for His love to rest in, a temple for His worship. The preaching of John included both the beginning and the end of redemption: the blood of the Lamb was to cleanse God's temple and restore His throne within the heart; nothing less than the baptism and indwelling of the Spirit could satisfy the heart of either God or man.

Of what that Baptism of the Spirit meant, Jesus Himself was to be the type: He would only give what He Himself had received: because the Spirit abode on Him, He could baptize with the Spirit. And what did the Spirit descending and abiding on Him mean? He had been begotten of the Holy Spirit; in the power of the Spirit He had grown up a holy child and youth, had entered manhood free from sin, and had now come to John to give Himself to fulfil all righteousness in submitting to the baptism of repentance. And now, as the reward of His obedience, as the Father's seal of approval on His having thus far yielded to the control of the Spirit, He receives a new communication of the Power of the Heavenly Life. Beyond what He had yet experienced, the Father's conscious indwelling presence and power takes possession of Him, and fits Him for His work. The leading and the power of the Spirit become His more consciously (Luke 4: 1, 14, 22) than before; He is now anointed with the Holy Ghost and with power.

What we see in Jesus teaches us what the baptism of the Spirit is. It is not that grace by which we turn to God, become regenerate, and seek to live as God's children. When Jesus reminded His disciples (Acts 1: 4) of John's prophecy, they were already partakers of this grace. Their baptism with the Spirit meant something more. It was to be to them the conscious presence of their glorified Lord, come back from Heaven to dwell in their hearts, their participation in the power of His new life. …

All that they were further to receive of wisdom, and courage, and holiness, had its root in this: what the Spirit had been to Jesus, when He was baptized, as the living bond with the Father's power and presence, He was to be to them. Through Him, the Son was to manifest Himself, and Father and Son were to make their abode with them.

"Upon whom you shall see the Spirit descending, and abiding upon Him, the same is He that

baptizes with the Holy Spirit." Was the outpouring of the Spirit at Pentecost the complete fulfillment of the promise, and is that the only baptism of the Spirit, given once for all to the newborn Church? Or is not the coming of the Holy Spirit on the disciples in the fourth of Acts, on the Samaritans (Acts 8), on the heathen in the house of Cornelius (Acts 10), and on the twelve disciples at Ephesus (Acts 19), also to be regarded as separate fulfillments of the words, "*He shall baptize with the Holy Spirit*"?

Is the sealing of the Spirit given to each believer in regeneration to be counted by him as his baptism of the Spirit? Or is it, as some say, a distinct, definite blessing to be received later on? Is it a blessing given only once, or can it be repeated and renewed? In the course of our study we shall find light in God's word that may help us to a solution of difficulties like these. …

The baptism of the Holy Spirit is the crown and glory of Jesus' work; we need it, and must know that we have it, if we are to live the true Christian life. We need it. The Holy Jesus needed it. Christ's loving, obedient disciples needed it. It is something more than the working of the Spirit in regeneration.

It is the Personal Spirit of Christ making Him present within us, always abiding in the heart in the power of His glorified nature, as He is exalted above every enemy. It is the Spirit of the Life of Christ Jesus making us free from the law of sin and death, and bringing us, as a personal experience, into the liberty from sin to which Christ redeemed us, but which to so many regenerate is only a blessing registered, on their behalf, but not possessed or enjoyed. It is the enduement with power to fill us with boldness in presence of every danger, and give the victory over the world and every enemy. It is the fulfilment of what God meant in His promise—"*I will dwell in them, and walk in them.*" Let us ask the Father to reveal to us all that His love meant for us, until our souls are filled with the glory of the thought: He baptizes with the Holy Spirit.

And then there is the other lesson: It is Jesus who thus baptizes. Whether we look upon this baptism as something we already have, and of which we only want a fuller apprehension, or something we still must receive, in this all agree: it is only in the fellowship of Jesus, in faithful attachment and obedience to Him, that a baptized life can be received or maintained or renewed. "*Those who believe in me,*" Jesus, said, "*out of their belly shall flow rivers of living water.*" The one thing we need is living faith in the indwelling Jesus: the living water will surely and freely flow. Faith is the instinct of the new nature, by which it recognizes and receives its Divine food and drink. In the power of the Spirit who dwells in every believer, let us trust Jesus, who fills with the Spirit, and cling to Him in love and obedience. It is He who baptizes: in contact with Him, in devotion to Him, in the confidence that He has given and will give Himself wholly to us, let us look to Him for nothing less than all that the baptism of the Spirit can imply.

In doing so let us specially remember one thing: only he that is faithful in the least will be made ruler over much. Be very faithful to what you already have and know of the Spirit's working. Regard yourself with deep reverence as God's holy temple. Wait for and listen to the gentlest whispering of God's Spirit within you. Listen especially to the conscience…. Keep that conscience very clean by simple childlike obedience. … Yield to the reproofs of conscience when you fail; but come again, have hope in God, and renew the vow: "What I know God wants me to do, I will do." Ask humbly every morning, and wait, for guidance in your path; the Spirit's voice will become better known, and His strength will be felt. … Be His loving, obedient disciple, and believe in Him on whom the Spirit abode, and who is full of the Spirit, and you too shall be prepared for the fullness of the blessing of the baptism of the Spirit.

Blessed Lord Jesus! with my whole heart I worship You, as exalted on the Throne to baptize with the Holy Spirit. Oh! reveal Yourself to me in this Your glory, that I may rightly know what I may expect from You. … O my Lord, the Spirit was always in You. And yet when You had surrendered Yourself to fulfill all righteousness, and to enter into fellowship with the sinners You came to save, in partaking of their baptism, You received from the Father a new inflowing of His Holy Spirit. It was to You the seal of His love, the revelation of His indwelling, the power for His service. And now You, on whom we see the Spirit descend and abide, do for us what the Father did for You. … I beseech You, give me yet the full, the overflowing measure You have promised. Let Him be to me the full unceasing revelation of Your presence in my heart, as glorious and as mighty as on the Throne of Heaven. O my Lord Jesus! baptize me, fill me with the Holy Spirit. Amen.

The Outpouring of the Spirit

April 10th

"And when the day of Pentecost finally came… they were all filled with the Holy Spirit."

—ACTS 2: 1–2

In the outpouring of the Holy Spirit, the work of Christ culminates. The adorable mystery of the Incarnation in Bethlehem, the great Redemption accomplished on Calvary, the revelation of Christ as the Son of God in the power of the Eternal Life by the Resurrection, His entrance into glory in the Ascension—these are all preliminary stages; their goal and their crown was the coming down of the Holy Spirit. As Pentecost is the last, it is the greatest of the Christian feasts; in it the others find their realization and their fulfillment. It is because the Church has hardly acknowledged this, and has not seen that the glory of Pentecost is the highest glory of the Father and the Son, that the Holy Spirit has not yet been able to reveal and glorify the Son in her as He fain would.

God made us in His own image, and for His likeness, with the distinct object that we should become like Himself. We were to be a temple for God to dwell in; we were to become the home in which God could rest. The closest and most intimate union, the indwelling of Love in love: this was what the Holy One longed for, and looked forward to. What was very feebly set forth in type in the temple in Israel became a Divine reality in Jesus of Nazareth: God had found a man in whom He could rest, whose whole being was opened to the rule of His will and the fellowship of His love. In Him there was a human nature, possessed by the Divine Spirit; and such God would have had all us to be.

And such all would be, who accepted of this Jesus and His Spirit as their life. His death was to remove the curse and power of sin, and make it possible for them to receive His Spirit. His resurrection was the entrance of human nature, free from all the weakness of the flesh, into the life of Deity, the Divine Spirit-life. His ascension was admittance as man into the very glory of God; the participation by human nature of perfect fellowship with God in glory in the unity of the Spirit. And yet, with all this, the work was not yet complete. Something, the chief thing, was still wanting. How could the Father dwell in us even as He had dwelled in Christ? This was the great question to which Pentecost gives the answer.

Out of the depths of Godhead, the Holy Spirit is sent forth in a new character and a new power, such as He never had before. In creation and nature, He came forth from God as the Spirit of Life. In the creation of man specially He acted as the power in which his god-likeness was grounded, and which, even after his fall, still testified for God. In Israel, He appeared as the Spirit of the theocracy, distinctly inspiring and fitting certain men for their work. In Jesus Christ He came as the Spirit of the Father, given to Him without measure, and abiding in Him. All these are manifestations, in different degrees, of one and the same Spirit. But now there comes the last, the long-promised, an entirely new manifestation of the Divine Spirit. The Spirit that has dwelled in Jesus Christ, and, in His life of obedience, has taken up His human spirit into perfect fellowship and unity with Himself, is now the Spirit of the exalted God-man.

As the Man-Christ, Jesus enters the glory of God and the full fellowship of that Spirit-life in which God dwells, He receives from the Father the right to send forth this Spirit into His disciples, yea, in the Spirit to descend Himself, and dwell in them. In a new power, which hitherto had not been possible, because Jesus had not been crucified or glorified, as the very Spirit of the crucified and now glorified Jesus, the Spirit comes. The work of the Son, the longing of the Father, receives its fulfilment. Man's heart is now indeed the home of his God. That a pure, holy body should be formed for the Son of God by the power of the Holy Spirit, and that in that body the Spirit should dwell, is indeed a miracle of Divine Power. But that the same Spirit should now come and dwell in the bodies of sinful men, that in them too the Father should take up His abode, this is a mystery of grace that passes all understanding. But this, glory be to God! is the blessing Pentecost brings and secures. …

The word now begins to be fulfilled: "*Behold! the tabernacle of God is with men, and He shall dwell with them.*" It is only in the light of all that preceded Pentecost, of all the mighty sacrifice which God thought not too great if He might dwell with sinful men, that the narrative of the outpouring of the Spirit can be understood. It is the earthly reflection of Christ's exaltation in Heaven; the participation He gives to His friends of the glory He now has with the Father. To be apprehended aright, it needs a spiritual vision; in the story that is so simply told the deepest mysteries of the Kingdom are unfolded, and the title-deeds given to the Church of her holy heritage until her Lord's return. …

Christ had promised to His disciples that in the Comforter He Himself would again come to them. During his life on earth, His personal manifested Presence, as revealing the unseen Father, was the Father's great gift to men, was the one thing the disciples wished and needed. This was to be their portion now in greater power than before. Christ had entered the glory with this very purpose, that now, in a Divine way, "*He might fill all things*," He might specially fill the members of His body with Himself and His glory-life.

When the Holy Spirit came down, He brought as a personal Life within them what had previously only been a Life near them, but yet outside their own. The very Spirit of God's own Son, as He had lived and loved, had obeyed and died, had been raised and glorified by Almighty power, was now to become their personal life. …

Such was the birth of the Church of Christ; such must be its growth and strength. The first and essential element of the true succession of the Pentecostal Church is a membership baptized with the Holy Spirit and with fire, every heart filled with: the experience of the Presence of the glorified Lord, every tongue and life witnessing to the wonderful work God had done, in raising Jesus to the glory of His Throne, and then filling His disciples with that glory too. It is not so much the baptism of power for our preachers we must seek; it is that every individual member of Christ's body may know, and possess, and witness to, the Presence of an indwelling Christ through the Holy Spirit. It is this will draw the attention of the world, and compel the confession to the power of Jesus. …

Pentecost is the glorious sunrise of "that day," the first of "those days" of which the prophets and our Lord had so often spoken, the promise and the pledge of what the history of the Church was meant to be. It is universally admitted that the Church has but ill fulfilled her destiny, that even now, after eighteen centuries, she has not risen to the height of her glorious privilege. Even when she strives to accept her calling, to witness for her Lord unto the ends of the earth, she does it too little in the faith of the Pentecostal Spirit, and the possession of His mighty power. …

Let the Church return to Pentecost, and Pentecost will return to her. The Spirit of God cannot take possession of believers beyond their capacity of receiving Him. The promise is waiting; the Spirit is now in all His fullness. Our capacity of reception needs enlargement. It is at the footstool of the throne, while believers continue with one accord in praise and love and prayer, while delay only intensifies the spirit of waiting and expectation, while faith holds fast the promise, and gazes up on the exalted Lord, in the confidence that He will make Himself known in power in the midst of His people; it is at the footstool of the throne that Pentecost comes.

Jesus Christ is still Lord of all, crowned with power and glory. His longing to reveal His presence in His disciples, and to make them share the glory life in which He dwells, is as fresh and full as when He first ascended the throne. Let us take our place at the footstool. Let us yield ourselves in strong, expectant faith, to be filled with the Holy Spirit, and to testify for Jesus. Let the indwelling Christ be our life, and our strength, and our testimony. Out of such a Church Spirit-filled preachers will rise, and the power go forth that will make Christ's enemies bow at His feet. …

We beseech Thee, O our Father, to reveal to Your Church how our Blessed Head counts us as His own body, sharing with Him in His life, His power, and His glory, and how the Holy Spirit, is the bearer of that life and power and glory, is waiting to reveal it within us. Oh, that Thy people might awake to know what the Holy Spirit means, as the real Presence within them of the glorified Lord, and as the clothing with Power from on high for their work on earth. Oh, that all Your people might learn to gaze on their exalted King until their whole being were opened up for His reception, and His Spirit fill them to their, utmost capacity!

Our Father, we plead with You, in the name of Jesus, revive Your Church. Make every believer to be indeed a temple full of the Holy Spirit: Make every church, in its believing members, a consecrated company ever testifying of a present Christ, ever waiting for the fullness of the power from on high. Make every preacher of the Word a minister of the Spirit. And let throughout the earth Pentecost be the sign that Jesus reigns, that His redeemed are His body, that His Spirit works, and that every knee shall bow to Him.

Waiting for The Spirit

April 11th

"He charged them to wait for the promise of the Father...."

—ACTS 1: 4

In the life of the Old Testament saints, waiting was one of the loved words in which they expressed the posture of their souls towards God. They waited for God, and waited upon God. Sometimes we find it in Holy Scripture as the language of an experience: *"Truly my soul waits upon God"; "I wait for the Lord, my soul does wait."* At others it is a plea in prayer: *"Lead me; on You do I wait all the day"; "Be gracious unto us; we have waited for You."* Frequently it is an injunction, encouraging to perseverance in a work that is not without its difficulty: *"Wait on the Lord; wait, I say, on the Lord"; "Rest in the Lord, and wait patiently for Him."* And then again there is the testimony to the blessedness of the exercise: *"Blessed are they that wait upon Him"; "They that wait upon the Lord shall renew their strength."*

All this blessed teaching and experience of the saints who have gone before, our Lord gathers up and connects specially, in His use of the word, with the promise of the Father: *The Holy Spirit.* [The notion of waiting that] had been so deeply woven into the very substance of the religious life and language of God's people was now to receive a new and a higher application. As they had waited for the manifestation of God, either in the light of His countenance on their own souls, or in special interposition for their deliverance, or in His coming to fulfil His promises to His people; so we too have to wait.

But now that the Father has been revealed in the Son, and that the Son has perfected the great redemption, now the waiting is specially to be occupied with the fulfillment of the great promise in which the love of the Father and the grace of the Son are revealed and made ours—the gift; the indwelling, the fullness of the Holy Spirit. We wait on the Father and the Son for ever-increasing inflowings and workings of the blessed Spirit; we wait for the blessed Spirit—His moving, and leading, and mighty strengthening—to reveal the Father and the Son within, and to work in us all the holiness and service to which the Father and the Son are calling us.

The Holy Spirit is not given to us as a possession of which we have the charge and mastery, and which we can use at our discretion. No. The Holy Spirit is given to us to be our Master, and to have charge of us. It is not we who are to use Him; He must use us. He is indeed ours; but ours as God, and our position towards Him is that of deep and entire dependence.

And all that the disciples did and felt during those ten days of waiting, and all that they got as its blessed fruit and reward, becomes to us the path and the pledge of the life of the Spirit in which we can live. The fullness of the Spirit, for such is the Father's Promise, and our waiting, are inseparably and forever linked together.

And have we not here now an answer to the question why so many believers know so little of the joy and the power of the Holy Spirit? They never knew to wait for it; they never listened carefully to the Master's parting words: "*He charged them to wait for the Promise of the Father, which ye have heard of me.*" The Promise they have heard. For its fulfillment they have longed. In earnest prayer they have pleaded for it. They have gone burdened and mourning under the felt want. They have tried to believe, and tried to lay hold, and tried to be filled with the Spirit. But they have never known what it was with it all to *wait.* They have never here said, or even truly heard, "*Blessed are all they that wait for Him.*" "*They that wait on the Lord shall renew their strength.*"

When God gives His Spirit, He gives His inmost Self. He gives with a Divine giving, that is, in the power of the eternal life, continuous, uninterrupted, and never-ceasing. When Jesus gave to those who believe in Him the promise of an ever-springing fountain of ever-flowing streams, He spoke not of a single act of faith that was once for all to make them the independent possessors of the blessing, but of a life of faith that, in never ceasing receptivity, would always and only possess His gifts in living union with Himself. And so this precious word wait…—with all its blessed meaning from the experience of the past—is woven into the very web of the new Spirit dispensation. …

As a believer, what you are to wait for is the fuller manifestation of the power of the Spirit within you. On the resurrection morn Jesus had breathed on His disciples, and said, "*Receive the Holy Spirit*"; yet, they had yet to wait for the full baptism of fire and of power. As God's child you have the Holy Spirit. Study the passages in the Epistles addressed to believers full of failings and sins (1 Corinthians 3: 1–3, 16, 6: 19, 2 0; Galatians 3: 2, 3, 4: 6). Begin in simple faith in God's Word to cultivate the quiet assurance: The Holy Spirit is dwelling within me. If you are not faithful in the less, you cannot expect the greater.

Acknowledge in faith and thanksgiving that the Holy Spirit is in you. Each time you enter your closet to speak to God, sit first still to remember and believe that the Spirit is within you as the Spirit of prayer who cries Father! Within you. Appear before God and confess to Him distinctly, until you become fully conscious of it yourself, that you are a temple of the Holy Spirit.

Now you are in the right posture for taking the second step, that is, asking God very simply and quietly, there and then, to grant you the workings of His Holy Spirit. The Spirit is in God and is in you. You ask the Father who is in Heaven that His Almighty Spirit may come forth from Him in greater life and power, and as the indwelling Spirit may work more mightily in you. As you ask this on the ground of the promises, or of some special promise you lay before Him, you believe that He hears and that He does it. …

And then comes the waiting. Wait on the Lord; wait for the Spirit. In great quietness set your soul still, silent unto God, and give the Holy Spirit time to quicken and deepen in you the assurance that God will grant Him to work mightily. …

As you wait before God in holy silence, He sees in it the confession that you have nothing—no wisdom to pray aright, no strength to work aright. Waiting is the expression of need, of emptiness. All along through the Christian life these go together: the sense of poverty and weakness, and the joy of all sufficient riches and strength. It is in waiting before God that the soul sinks down into its own nothingness, and is lifted up into the Divine assurance that God has accepted its sacrifice and will fulfil its desires. …

You have become so accustomed to the worship in the power of the understanding and the carnal mind, that truly spiritual worship does not come at once. But wait on: "*He charged them to wait.*" Keep up the waiting disposition in daily life and duty. "*On You do I wait all the day*"; it is to the Three One God I thus speak; the Holy Spirit brings nigh and unites to Him. Renew each day and, as you are able to do it, also extend, your exercise of waiting upon God. … Wait for the promise in all its fullness. Count not the time lost you thus give to this blessed expression of ignorance and emptiness, of faith and expectation, of full and real surrender to the dominion of the Spirit. Pentecost is meant to be for all times the proof of what the exalted Jesus does for His Church from His Throne. The ten days' waiting is meant to be for all time the posture before the Throne, which secures in continuity the Pentecostal blessing, Brother! Sister! the Promise of the Father is sure. It is from whom you have it. The Spirit is Himself already working in you. His full indwelling and guidance is your child's-portion. Oh, keep the charge of your Lord! Wait on God: wait for the Spirit. "*Wait, I say, on the Lord*"; "*Blessed are all they that wait for Him.*"

The Spirit Given to the Obedient

April 12th

"If you love Me, you will keep My commandments:
and I will pray the Father, and He shall give you another Comforter, even the Spirit of truth."
—JOHN 14: 15–16 …

Where there is not much knowledge of the Spirit's work, or where His workings in a Church or an individual are but feeble, there even believers will not get beyond the experience of His preparatory workings; though He be in them, they know Him not in

His power as the Spirit of the glorified Lord. They have Him in them to make them obedient; but, it is only as they yield obedience to this His more elementary work, the keeping of Christ's commandments, that they will be promoted to the higher experience of His conscious indwelling, as the representative and revealer of Jesus in His glory. *"If you love me, keep my commandments: and I will pray the Father, and He will send you another Comforter."*

The lesson is one we cannot study too attentively. In Paradise, in the angels of heaven, in God's own Son, by obedience and obedience alone, could the relationship with the Divine being be maintained, and admission secured to closer experience of His love and His life. God's will revealed is the expression of His hidden perfection and being; only in accepting and doing the will, in the entire giving up for the will to possess and use as He pleases, are we fitted for entering the Divine Presence. Was it not thus even with the Son of God? It was when, after a life in holy humility and obedience for thirty years, He had spoken that word of entire consecration, *"It becomes us to fulfill all righteousness,"* and given Himself to a baptism for the sins of His people, that He was baptized with the Spirit. The Spirit came because of His obedience. And again, it was after He had learned obedience in suffering, and became obedient to the death of the cross, that He again received the Spirit from the Father (Acts 2: 33) to pour out on His disciples. The fullness of the Spirit for His body the Church was the reward of obedience. And this law of the Spirit's coming, as revealed in the Head, holds for every member of the body: obedience is the indispensable condition of the Spirit's indwelling. *"If you love me, keep my commandments: and the Father will send you the Spirit."* ...

Christ Jesus had come to prepare the way for the Spirit's coming. Or rather, His outward coming in the flesh was the preparation for His inward coming in the Spirit to fulfil the promise of a Divine indwelling. The outward coming appealed to the soul, with its mind and feeling, and affected these. It was only as Christ in His outward coming was accepted, as He was loved and obeyed, that the inward and more intimate revelation would be given. Personal attachment to Jesus, the personal acceptance of Him as Lord and Master to love and obey, was the disciples' preparation for the baptism of the Spirit. And so now it is as in a tender listening to the voice of conscience, and a faithful effort to keep the commands of Jesus, we prove our love to Him, that the heart will be prepared for the fullness of the Spirit. Our attainments may fall short of our aims, we may have to mourn that what we want to do we do not do—if the Master sees the wholehearted surrender to His will, and the faithful obedience to what we already have of the leadings of His Spirit, we may be sure that the full gift will not be withheld.

Do not these words suggest to us the two great reasons why the presence and the power of the Spirit in the Church is so feebly realized? We do not understand that the obedience of love must precede the fullness of the Spirit.... Obedience must precede the baptism of the Spirit. John had preached Jesus as the true Baptist—baptizing with the Holy Spirit and with fire. Jesus took His disciples as candidates for this Baptism into a three years' course of training. First of all, attached them to Himself personally. He taught them to forsake all for Him. He called Himself their Master and Lord, and taught them to do what He said. And then in His farewell discourse He time after time spoke of obedience to His commands as the one condition of all further spiritual blessing.

It is to be feared that the Church has not given this word, Obedience, the prominence Christ gave it. Wrong views of the danger of Self-righteousness, of the way in which free grace is to be exalted, of the power of sin and the necessity of sinning, with the natural reluctance of the flesh to accept a high standard of holiness, have been the causes. While the [doctrine of free grace] and the simplicity of faith have been preached, the absolute necessity of obedience and holiness has not been equally insisted on. It has been thought that only those who had the fullness of the Spirit could be obedient. It was not seen that obedience was the lower platform—that the baptism of the Spirit, the full revelation of the glorified Lord as the Indwelling One, in His power to work in us and through us His mighty works, was something higher—the Presence that the obedient should inherit. It was not seen that simple and full allegiance to every dictate of conscience, and every precept of the word, that a "*walk worthy of the Lord to all well-pleasing*," was to be the passport to that full life in the Spirit in which He would witness to the abiding Presence of the Lord in the heart.

As the natural consequence of the neglect of this truth, the companion truth was also forgotten: The obedient must and may look for the fullness of the Spirit. The promise of the special, conscious, active indwelling of the Spirit to the obedient is a thing to many Christians unknown. The great part of life is spent in mourning over disobedience, over the want of the Spirit's power, and praying for the Spirit to help them to obey, instead of rising in the strength of the Spirit already in them to obedience, as indeed possible and necessary. The thought of the Holy Spirit being specially sent to the obedient to give in them the Presence of Jesus as a continuous reality, that He might do in them the greater works, even as the Father had worked in Him, was hardly thought of. The meaning of the life of Jesus as our example is not understood. How distinctly there was with Him the outward lowly life of trial and obedience in preparation for the hidden spiritual one of power and glory!

It is this inner life that we are made partakers of in the gift of the Spirit of the glorified Jesus. But in our inner personal participation of that gift we must walk in the way He dedicated for us; as in the crucifixion of the flesh we yield ourselves to God's will, for Him to do in us what He wills, and for us also to do what He wills, we shall experience that God is to be found nowhere but in His will. His will in Christ, accepted and done by us, with the heart in which it is done, is the home of the Holy Spirit. The revelation of the Son in His perfect obedience was the condition of the giving of the Spirit; the acceptance of the Son in love and obedience is the path to the indwelling of the Spirit.

It is this truth which has in these latter years come home with power to the hearts of many in the use of the words full surrender and entire consecration. As they understood that the Lord Jesus did indeed claim implicit obedience, that the giving up all to Him and His will was absolutely necessary, and in the power of His grace truly possible, and in the faith of His power did it, they found the entrance to a life of peace and strength formerly unknown. Many are learning, or have to learn, that they do not yet fully know the lesson.

They will find that there are applications of this principle beyond what we have conceived.

As we see how in the all-pervading power of the Spirit, as we already possess Him, every movement of our life must be brought into allegiance to Jesus, and give ourselves to it in faith, we shall also see that the Spirit of the glorified Lord can make Him present and work His mighty works in us and through us, in a way far beyond what we can ask or think. The indwelling of the Holy Spirit was intended by God and Christ to be to the Church more, oh! so much more, than we have yet known. Oh! Shall we not yield ourselves, in a love and obedience that will sacrifice anything for Jesus, that our hearts may be enlarged for the fullness of His blessing prepared for us.

Let us cry to God … that He may waken His Church and people to take in this double lesson: A living obedience is indispensable to the full experience of the indwelling; the full experience of the indwelling is what a loving obedience may certainly claim. Let each of us even now say to our Lord that we do love Him, and keep His commandments. In however much feebleness and failure it be, still let us speak it out to Him as the one purpose of our souls; this He will accept. Let us believe in the indwelling of the Spirit as already given to us, when in the obedience of faith that we gave ourselves to Him. Let us believe that the full indwelling, with the revelation of Christ within, can be ours. And let us be content with nothing less than the loving, reverent, trembling, but blessed consciousness that we are the temples of the Living God, because the Spirit of God dwells in us.

The Holy Spirit and Conscience

April 13th

"I say the truth in Christ, I lie not, my conscience also bearing me witness in the Holy Spirit."

—ROMANS 9: 1 …

God's highest glory is His Holiness in virtue of which He hates and destroys the evil, loves and works the good. In man, conscience has the same work: it condemns sin and approves the right.

Conscience is the remains of God's image in man, the nearest approach to the Divine in us, the guardian of God's honor amid the ruin of the fall. As a consequence, God's work of redemption must always begin with conscience. The Spirit of God is the Spirit of His holiness; conscience is a spark of the Divine holiness; harmony between the work of the Holy Spirit in, renewing and sanctifying man, and the work of conscience, is most intimate and essential. The believer who would be filled with the Holy Spirit, and experience to the full the blessings He has to give, must in the first place see to it that he yields to conscience the place and the honor which belong to it.

Faithfulness to conscience is the first step in the path of restoration to the holiness of God. Intense conscientiousness will be the groundwork and characteristic of true spirituality. As it is the work of conscience to witness to our being right towards our sense of duty and towards God, and the work of the Spirit to witness to God's acceptance of our faith in Christ and our obedience to Him, the testimony of the Spirit and of conscience will, as the Christian life progresses, become increasingly identical. We shall feel the need and the blessedness of saying with Paul, in regard to all our conduct: *"My conscience also bearing me witness in the Holy Spirit."* ...

The cause of the feebleness of our faith is owing to nothing so much as the want of a clean conscience. Mark well how closely Paul connects them in 1st Timothy: *"Love out of a pure heart, and a good conscience, and faith unfeigned"* (1: 5); *"Holding faith and a good conscience, which some having thrust from them, have made shipwreck of the faith"* (1: 19); and especially, *"Holding the mystery of the faith in a pure conscience"* (3: 9).

The conscience is the seat of faith. He that would grow strong in faith, and have boldness with God, must know that he is pleasing Him (1 John 3: 21–22). Jesus said most distinctly that it is for those who love Him and keep His commandments, that the promise of the Spirit, with the indwelling of the Father and the Son, the abiding in His love, and power in prayer, is meant. ...

And how is this blessed life to be attained, in which we can daily appeal to God and men with Paul: *"I say the truth in Christ, my conscience bearing me witness in the Holy Spirit"*? The first step is: Bow very low under the reproofs of conscience. Be not content with the general confession that there is a great deal wrong. Beware of confounding actual transgression with the involuntary workings of the sinful nature. If the latter are to be conquered and made dead by the indwelling Spirit (Romans 8: 13), you must first deal with the former.

Begin with some single sin, and give conscience time in silent submission and humiliation to reprove and condemn. Say to your Father, that in this one thing you are, by His grace, going to obey. Accept anew Christ's wonderful offer to take entire possession of your heart, to dwell in you as Lord and keeper. Trust Him by His Holy Spirit to do this, even when you feel weak and helpless.

Remember that obedience, the taking and keeping Christ's words in your will and life, is the only way to prove the reality of your surrender to Him, or your interest in His work and grace. And vow in faith, that by God's Grace you will exercise yourself herein, *"always to have a conscience void of offense toward God and toward man."*

When you have begun this with one sin, proceed with others, step by step. As you are faithful in keeping conscience pure, the light will shine more brightly from Heaven into the heart, discovering sin you had not noticed before, bringing out distinctly the law written by the Spirit you had not been able to read. Be willing to be taught; be trustfully sure that the Spirit will teach. Every honest effort to keep the blood-cleansed conscience clean, in the light of God, will be met with the aid of the Spirit.

As you thus bow to the reproofs of conscience, and give yourself wholly to do God's will, your courage will grow strong that it is possible to have a conscience void of offence. The witness of conscience, as to what you are doing, and will do by grace, will be met by the witness of the Spirit as to what Christ is doing and will do. In childlike simplicity you will seek to begin each day with the simple prayer: "Father! There is nothing now between

You and Your child. My conscience Divinely cleansed in the blood, bears me witness, Father! Let not even the shadow of a cloud intervene this day. In everything would I do Your will: Your Spirit dwells in me, and leads me, and makes me strong in Christ." …

The Temple of Holy Spirit

April 14th

"Know you not that you are the temple of God, and that the Spirit of God dwells in you?"
—1 CORINTHIANS 3:16

Because man was created in the image of God, the temple is not only the setting forth of the mystery of man's approach into the presence of God, but equally of God's way of entering into man, to take up His abode with him. We are familiar with the division of the Temple into three parts. There was its exterior, seen by all men, with the outer court, in to which every Israelite might enter, and where all the external religious service was performed. There was the Holy Place, into which alone the priests might enter, to present to God the blood or the incense, the bread or the oil, they had brought from without. But though near, they were still not within the veil; into the immediate presence of God they might not come. God dwells in the holiest of all, in a light inaccessible, where none might venture nigh. The momentary entering of the High Priest once a year was but to bring into full consciousness the truth that there was no place for man there, until the veil should have been rent and taken away.

Man is God's temple. In us, too, there are the three parts. In the body we have the outer court, the external visible life, where all the conduct has to be regulated by God's law, and where all the service consists in looking to that which is done without us and for us to bring us nigh to God. Then there is the soul, with its inner life, its power of mind and feeling and will. In the regenerate man this is the Holy Place, where thoughts and affections and desires move to and fro as the priests of the sanctuary, rendering God their service in the full light of consciousness. And then comes within the veil, hidden from all human sight and light, the hidden inmost sanctuary, "*the secret place of the Most High*," where God dwells, and where man may not enter, until the veil is rent at God's own bidding.

Man has not only body and soul, but also spirit. Deeper down than where the soul with its consciousness can enter, there is a spirit-nature linking man with God. So fearful is sin's power, that in some this power is given up to death: they are sensual, not having the Spirit. In others, it is nothing more than a dormant power, a possibility waiting for the quickening of the Holy Spirit. In the believer it is the inner chamber of the heart, of which the Spirit has taken possession, and from out of which He waits to do His glorious work, making soul and body holy to the Lord.

And yet this indwelling, unless where it is recognized, and yielded to, and humbly maintained in adoration and love, often brings comparatively little blessing. And the one great lesson which the truth that we are God's temple, because His Spirit dwells in us, must teach us, is this, to, acknowledge the Holy Presence that dwells within us. This alone will enable us to regard the whole temple, even to the outmost court, as sacred to His service, and to yield every power of our nature to His leading and will.

The most sacred part of the Temple, that for which all the rest existed and on which all depended, was the Holiest of all. Even though the priests might never enter there, and might never see the glory that dwelt there, all their conduct was regulated, and all their faith animated, by the thought of the unseen Presence there. It was this that gave the sprinkling of the blood and the burning of the incense their value. It was this made it a privilege to draw nigh, and gave confidence to go out and bless. It was the Most Holy, the Holiest of all, that made the place of their serving to them a Holy Place. Their whole life was controlled and inspired by the faith of the unseen indwelling glory within the veil.

It is not otherwise with the believer. Until we learn by faith to tremble in the presence of the wondrous mystery that we are God's temple, because God's Spirit dwells in us, we never will yield to this high vocation with the holy reverence or the joyful confidence that we should. … Each of us must learn to know that there is a Holiest of all in that temple which he himself is; the secret place of the Most High within us must become the central truth in our temple worship. This must be to us the meaning of our confession: "I believe in the Holy Spirit."

And how is this deep faith in the hidden indwelling to become ours? Taking our stand, upon God's blessed Word, we must accept and appropriate its teaching. We must take trouble to believe that God means what it says. I am a temple; just such a temple as God commanded to be built of old; He meant me to see in it what I am to be. There the Holiest of all was the central point, the essential thing. It was all dark, secret, hidden, till the time of unveiling came. It demanded and received the faith of priest and people. The Holiest of all within me, too, is unseen and hidden, a thing for faith alone to know and deal with. Let me, as I approach to the Holy One, bow before Him in deep and lowly reverence. Let me there say that I believe what He says, that His Holy Spirit— God, one with the Father and the Son—even now has His abode within me. I will meditate, and be still, until something of the overwhelming glory of the truth fall upon me, and faith begin to realize it: I am His temple, and in the secret place He sits upon His throne. As I yield myself in silent meditation and worship day by day, surrendering and setting open my whole being to Him, He will in His divine, loving, living power, shine into my consciousness the light of His presence.

As this thought fills the heart, the faith of the indwelling though hidden presence will influence; the Holy Place will be ruled from the Most Holy. The world of consciousness in the soul, with all its thoughts and feelings, its affections and purposes, will come and surrender themselves to the Holy Power that sits within on the throne. Amid the terrible experience of failure and sin a new hope will dawn. Though long I most earnestly strove, I could not keep the Holy Place for God, because I knew not that He kept the Most Holy for Himself. If I give Him there the glory due to His name, in the holy worship of the inner temple, He will send forth His light and His truth through my whole being, and through mind and will reveal His power to sanctify and to bless.

And through the soul, thus coming ever more mightily under His rule, His power will work out even into the body. With passions and appetites within, yea, with every thought brought into subjection, the hidden Holy Spirit will through the soul penetrate ever deeper into the body. Through the Spirit the deeds of the body will be made dead, and the river of water, that flows from under 'the throne of God and the Lamb, will go through all the outer nature, with its cleansing and quickening power.

O Christian, do believe that you are the temple of the living God, and that the Spirit of God dwelleth in you! You have been sealed with the Holy Spirit; He is the mark, the living assurance of your sonship and your Father's love. If this have hitherto been a thought that has brought you but little comfort, see if the reason is not here. You sought for Him in the Holy Place, amid the powers and services of your inner life which come within your vision, And you could hardly discern Him there. And so you could not appropriate the comfort and strength the Comforter was meant to bring.

No, my brother, my sister, not there, not there. Deeper down, in the secret place of the Most High, there you will find Him. Within you! in your inmost part! there faith will find Him. And as faith worships in holy reverence before the Father, and the heart trembles at the thought of what it has found, wait in holy stillness on God to grant you the mighty working of His Spirit; wait in holy stillness for the Spirit, and be assured He will, as God, arise and fill His temple with His glory …

Most Holy God! In adoring wonder I bow before You in the presence of this wondrous mystery of grace: my spirit, soul, and body, Your temple. In deep silence and worship, I accept the blessed revelation: that in me too there is a holiest of all, and that there Your hidden glory has its abode. O my God, forgive me that I have so little known it. I do now tremblingly accept the blessed truth: God the Spirit, the Holy Spirit, who is God Almighty, dwells in me. … Blessed Jesus! to You, who sits upon the throne, I yield my whole being. In You I trust to rise up in power and have dominion within me. In You I believe for the full streaming forth of the living waters. Blessed Spirit! Holy Teacher! Mighty Sanctifier! You are within me. On You do I wait all the day.

The Spirit, Convincer of Sin

April 15th

"If I go, I will send the Comforter unto you; and He, when He comes, will convince the world of sin."

—JOHN 16: 7–8 …

The disciples were to realize that the great work of the Holy Spirit, striving with us, convincing the world of sin, could only be done as He had a firm footing on earth in them. They were to be baptized with the Holy Spirit and with fire, to receive the power from on high, with the one purpose of being the instruments through whom the Holy

Spirit could reach the world. The mighty, sin-convicting power of the Spirit to dwell in them and work through them: it was for this our blessed Lord sought to prepare them and us by these words. The lessons they teach are very solemn.

1. The Holy Spirit comes to us, that through us He may reach others. The Spirit is the Spirit of the Holy One, of the redeeming God: when He enters us, He does not change His nature or lose His Divine character. He is still the Spirit of God striving with man, and seeking his deliverance. Wherever He is not hindered by ignorance or Selfishness, He looks out from the heart as His temple for the work He has to do on the world around, and makes it willing and bold to do that work; to testify against sin, and for Jesus the Savior from sin, He does this very specially as being the Spirit of the crucified and exalted Christ. For what purpose was it that He received the Spirit without measure? "*The Spirit of the Lord is upon me, because He anointed me to preach good tidings to the poor. He hath sent me to proclaim release to the captives*!"

It was this same Spirit—after Christ through Him had offered Himself unto God, and through Him as the Spirit of Holiness had been raised from the dead—whom He sent down on His Church, that now the Spirit might have a home in them, as He had had it in Himself. And no otherwise and no less than in Himself would the Divine Spirit in them pursue His Divine work, and as a Light shining in, and revealing, and condemning, and conquering the darkness, as "*the Spirit of burning and the Spirit of judgment*," be to the world the power of a Divine conviction and conversion. Not from Heaven direct so much, as the Spirit of God, but as the Holy Spirit dwelling in the Church, would He convince the world. "*I will send Him to you, and when He comes, He will convince the world of sin*" (John 16: 8). It is in and through us that the Spirit can reach the world.

2. The Spirit can only reach others through us by first bringing ourselves into perfect sympathy with Himself. He enters into us to become so one with us that He becomes as a disposition and a life within us; and His work in us, and through us in others, becomes identical with our work. The application of this truth to the conviction of sin in the world is one of great solemnity. The words of our Lord are frequently applied to believers in reference to the continued conviction of sin which He will ever have to work within them. In this sense they are, indeed, most true. This first work of the Spirit remains to the end the undertone of all His Comforting and Sanctifying work. It is only as He keeps alive the tender sense of the danger and shame of again sinning, that the soul will be kept in its low place before God—hiding in Jesus as alone its safety and its strength. As the Holy Spirit reveals and communicates the holy life of Christ within, the sure result will be a deeper sense of the sinfulness of sin. But the words mean more. If the Spirit through us, through our testimony, whether by word or walk, is to convince the world, He must first convince us, of its sin. He must give us personally such a sight and sense of the guilt of its unbelief and rejection of our Savior, such a sight and sense of each of its sins, as being at once the cause, the proof, the fruit of that rejection, that we shall in some measure think and feel in regard to the sin as He does. There will be then that inner fitness in us for the Spirit to work through us, that inner unity between our witness and His witness against sin and for God, which will reach the conscience and carry conviction with a power that is from

above. …

3. To obtain this conviction of sin, the believer needs not only to pray for it, but to have his whole life under the leading of the Holy Spirit. We cannot too earnestly insist upon it, that the many different gifts of the Spirit all depend upon His personal indwelling and supremacy in the inner life, and the revelation in us of the Christ that gave His life to have sin destroyed. When our Lord spoke that word of inexhaustible meaning, "*He shall be in you*," he opened up the secret of all the Spirit's teaching, and sanctifying, and strengthening. The Spirit is the Life of God; He enters in, and becomes our Life; it is as He can sway and inspire the life that He will be able to work in us all He wills. …

As your life in the Spirit becomes healthy and strong, as your spiritual constitution gets invigorated, your eye will see more clearly, your heart feel more keenly, what the sin around you is. Your thoughts and feelings will be those of the Holy Spirit breathing in you; your deep horror of sin, your deep faith in the redemption from it, your deep love to the souls who are in it, your willingness like your Lord to die if men can be freed from sin, will make you the fit instrument for the Spirit to convince the world of its sin.

4. There is one more lesson. We are seeking in this little book to find the way by which we all can be filled with the Spirit. Here is one condition: He must dwell in us as the world's Convincer of sin, "*I will send Him unto you, and He will convince the world of sin*" (John 16: 8). Offer yourself to Him to consider, and feel, and bear the sins of those around you. Let the sins of the world be your concern, as much as your own sin. Do they not dishonor God as much as yours? Are they not equally provided for in the great redemption? And does not the Spirit dwelling in you long to convince them too?

Just as the Holy Spirit dwelt in the body and nature of Jesus, and was the source of what He felt, and said, and did, and just as God through Him worked out the will of His holy love; so the Spirit now dwells in believers: they are His abode. The one purpose for which there has been a Christ in the world, for which there is now a Holy Spirit, was that sin may be conquered and made an end of. This is the great object for which the baptism of the Spirit and of fire was given, that in and through believers He might convince of sin, and deliver from it.

Put yourself into contact with the world's sin. Meet it in the love and faith of Jesus Christ, as the servant and helper of the needy and the wretched. Give yourself to prove the reality of your faith in Christ by your likeness to Him: so will the Spirit convince the world of its unbelief.

Seek the full experience of the indwelling Spirit, not for your own Selfish enjoyment, but for this one end, that He can do the Father's work through you as He did through Christ. Live, in unity of love with other believers, to work and pray, that others may be saved out of sin: "*then will the world believe that God has sent Him.*" It is the life of believers in Self-sacrificing love that will prove to the world that Christ is a reality, and so convince it of its sin of unbelief.

The comfort and success with which a man lives and carries on his business depends much upon his having a suitable building for it. When the Holy Spirit, in a believer, finds the whole heart free and given up to Him as His home, to fill it with God's thoughts of sin and God's power of redemption, He can through such a one do His work. Be assured that there is no surer way to receive a full measure of the Spirit than to be wholly yielded to Him, to let the very mind of Christ in regard to sin work in us. "*He took away sin by the sacrifice of Himself*," through the Eternal Spirit. What the Spirit was in Him, He seeks to be in us. What was true of Him, must in its measure be true of us.

Christians! would you be filled with the Holy Spirit, seek to have a clear impression of this: The Holy Spirit is in you to convince the world of sin. If you sympathize thoroughly with Him in this, if He sees that He can use you for this, if you make His work in this matter your work too, you may be sure He will dwell in you richly, and work in you mightily. The one object for which Christ came was to put away sin; the one work for which the Holy Spirit comes to men is to persuade them to give up sin. The one object for which the believer lives is to join in the battle against sin; to seek the will and the honor of God. Do let us be at one with Christ and His Spirit in their testimony against sin.

An exhibition of the life and Spirit of Christ will have its effect: the holiness, and the joy, and the love, and the obedience to Christ will convince the world of its sin of unbelief. The Presence of Christ in us through the Spirit will carry its own conviction. And just as Christ's death, as His sacrifice for sin, was the entrance to His glory in the power of the Spirit, so our experience of the Spirit's indwelling will become the fuller just as our whole life is more given up to Him for His holy work of convincing the world of sin.

The Leading of The Spirit

April 16th

"As many as are led by the Spirit of God, these are sons of God."

—ROMANS 8:14

As the conformity to this world spirit is crucified and dies, as we deliberate: and keep down the life of nature and the flesh, we are renewed in the spirit of our mind and so the mind becomes able to "*prove and know the good and perfect and acceptable will of God*" (Romans 12: 2). … This connection between the practical sanctifying work of the Spirit in our inner life, and His leading comes out very clearly in our context. "*If by the Spirit you make to die the deeds of the body, you shall live*," we read in 8: 13. Then follows immediately, *"For as many as are led by the Spirit of God are sons of God."* That is, as many as allow they to be led by Him in this mortifying of the body, these are the sons of God. The Spirit is the Spirit of the holy life which there was and is in Christ Jesus, and which works in us in a Divine life-power. He is the Spirit of Holiness, and only as such will He lead. Through Him God works in us both to will and to do of His good pleasure through Him God makes us perfect in every good work to do His will, working in us that which is well-pleasing in His sight. To be led of the Spirit implies in the first place the surrender to His work as He convinces of sin and cleanses soul and body for His temple. It is as the indwelling Spirit, filling, sanctifying, and ruling the heart and life, that He enlightens and leads.

In the study of what the leading of the Spirit means, it is of the first importance to grasp this thought in all its bearings. It is only the spiritual mind that can discern spiritual things, and can receive the leadings of the Spirit. The mind must grow spiritual to become capable of spiritual guidance. Paul said to the Corinthians, that because, though born again, they were still carnal, as babes in Christ, he had not been able to teach them spiritual truth. ...

The deepest mysteries of Scripture, as far as they are apprehended by human thought, can be studied and accepted and even taught by the unsanctified mind. But the leading of the Spirit, we cannot repeat it too often, does not begin in the region of thought or feeling. Deeper down, in the life itself, in the hidden laboratory of the inner life, whence issues the power that molds the will and fashions the character in our spirits, there the Holy Spirit takes up His abode, there He breathes and moves and impels. He leads by inspiring us with a disposition out of which right purposes and come forth. *"That you may be filled with the knowledge of His will in all wisdom and understanding";* that prayer teaches us that it is only to a spiritual understanding that the knowledge of God's will can be given. And the spiritual understanding only comes with the growth of the spiritual man, and the faithfulness to the spiritual life. He that would have the leading of Spirit must yield himself to have his life wholly possessed and filled of the Spirit. ...

All leading implies following. It is easily understood that to enjoy the leading of the Spirit demands a very teachable, followsome mind. The Spirit is not only hindered by the flesh as the power that commits sin, but still more by the flesh power that seeks to serve God. To be able to discern the Spirit's teaching, Scripture tells us that the ear must be circumcised, in a circumcision not made with hands, in the putting off of the body of the flesh, in the circumcision of Christ. The will and wisdom of the flesh must be feared and crucified, and denied. The ear must be closed to all that the flesh and its wisdom, whether in Self or in men around us, has to say. In all our thoughts of God or our study of His Word, in all our drawings nigh to worship, and all our goings out to work for Him, there must be a continued distrust and abnegation of Self, and a very definite waiting on God by the Holy Spirit to teach and lead us. A soul that thus daily and hourly waits for a Divine leading, for the light of knowledge and of duty, will assuredly receive it. Would you be led of the Spirit? Give up, day by day, not only your will and wisdom, but your whole life and being! The Fire will descend and consume the sacrifice.

This leading of the Spirit must very specially be a thing of faith, and that in two senses. The beginning of the leading will come when we learn in holy fear to cultivate and act upon the confidence the Holy Spirit is in me, and is doing His work.

The Spirit's indwelling is the crowning piece of God's redemption: the most spiritual and mysterious part of the mystery of godliness. Here, if anywhere, faith is needed. Faith is the faculty of the soul which recognizes the unseen, the Divine; which receives the impression of the Divine Presence when God draws near; which in its measure accepts of what the Divine Being brings and gives to us. In the Holy Spirit is the most intimate communication of the Divine Life; here faith may not judge by what it feels or understands, but simply submits to God to let Him do what He has said. It meditates and worships, it prays and trusts ever afresh, it yields the whole soul in adoring acceptance and thanksgiving to the Savior's word, "*He shall be in you.*"

But are we not in danger of being led away by the imaginings of our own hearts, and counting as leading of the Spirit what proves to be a delusion of the flesh? And if so, where is our safeguard against such error? The answer ordinarily given to this last question is: The Word of God. And yet that answer is but half the truth. Far too many have opposed to the danger of fanaticism the word of God, as interpreted by human reason, or by the Church, and have erred no less than those they sought to oppose.

The answer is: The word of God as taught by the Spirit of God. It is in the perfect harmony of the two that our safety is to be found. Let us on the one hand remember, that as all the Word of God is given by the Spirit of God, so each word must be interpreted to us by that same Spirit. That this interpretation comes not from the Spirit above us or around us, suggesting thoughts to us, but from the indwelling Spirit, we need hardly repeat. It is only the spiritual man whose inner life is under the dominion of the Spirit who can discern the spiritual meaning of the Word.

This brings us back to the lesson we urged at the commencement: the leading of the Spirit is inseparable from the sanctifying of the Spirit. Let each one who would be led of the Spirit begin by giving himself to be led of the Word as far as he knows it. Begin at the beginning: obey the commandments. He that will do, shall know, said Jesus. *"Keep my commandments, and the Father will send you the Spirit."* Give up every sin. Give up in everything to the voice of conscience. Give up in everything to God, and let Him have His way. Through the Spirit mortify the deeds the body. As a son of God place yourself at the entire disposal of the Spirit, to follow where He leads.

The Spirit and the Flesh

April 17th

"Are you so foolish? Having begun in the Spirit, are you now perfected in the flesh?"
—GALATIANS 3: 3

The flesh is the name by which Scripture designates our fallen nature, both soul and body. The soul at creation was placed between the spiritual or Divine and the sensible or worldly to guide them into that union which would result in man attaining his destiny, a spiritual body. When the soul yielded to the temptation of the sensible, it broke away from the rule of the Spirit and came under the power of the body—it became flesh. And now the flesh is not only without the Spirit, but even hostile to it: *"the flesh lusts against the Spirit."*

In this antagonism of the flesh to the Spirit there are two sides. On the one hand, the flesh lusts against the Spirit in its committing sin and transgressing God's law. On the other hand … even when the soul learns to serve God, the flesh still asserts its power, refuses to let the Spirit alone lead, and, in its efforts to be religious, is still the great enemy that ever hinders and quenches the Spirit.

It is owing to this deceitfulness of the flesh that there often takes place what Paul speaks of to the Galatians: *"Having begun in the Spirit, are you now perfected in the flesh?"* Unless the surrender to the Spirit be very entire, and the holy waiting on Him be kept up in great dependence and humility, what has been begun in the Spirit, very easily and very speedily passes over into confidence in the flesh. And the remarkable thing is, what at first sight might appear a paradox, that just where the flesh seeks to serve God, there it becomes the strength of sin.

Do we not know, how the Pharisees, with "self-righteousness" and carnal religion, fell into pride and Selfishness, and became the servants of sin? Was it not just so among the Galatians, of whom Paul asks the question about perfecting in flesh what was begun in the Spirit, and whom he has so to warn against the righteousness of works, that the works of the flesh were so manifest, and that they were in danger of devouring one another? Satan has no more crafty device for keeping souls in bondage than inciting them to a religion in the flesh. He knows that the power of flesh can never please God or conquer sin, and in due time the flesh that has gained supremacy over the Spirit in the service of God, will assert and maintain that same supremacy in the service of sin. It is only where the Spirit truly and unceasingly has the entire lead and rule in the life of worship, that it will have the power to lead and rule in the life of practical obedience. If I am to deny Self in intercourse with men, to conquer Selfishness and temper and want of love, I must first learn to deny Self in the intercourse with God. There the soul, seat of Self, must learn to bow to the Spirit, where God dwells.

The contrast between the worship in the Spirit and the trusting in the flesh is very beautifully expressed in Paul's description of the true circumcision—the circumcision of the heart—whose praise is not of men, but of God: *"Who worship the Spirit of God, and glory in Christ Jesus, and put no confidence in the flesh."*

Placing the glorying in Christ Jesus in the center, as the very essence of the Christian faith and life, he marks on the one hand the great danger by which it is beset, on the other the safeguard by which its full enjoyment is secured. Confidence in the flesh is the one thing above all others that renders the glorying in Christ Jesus of none effect; worship by the Spirit the one thing that alone can make it indeed life and truth. May the Spirit reveal to us what it is thus to glory in Christ Jesus!

That there is a glorying in Christ Jesus that is accompanied by much confidence in the flesh, all history and experience teach us. Among the Galatians it was so. The teachers whom Paul used so earnestly were all preachers of Christ His cross. But they preached it, not as men taught by the Spirit to know what the infinite and pervading influence of that cross must be, but those who; having had the beginnings of God's Spirit, had yet allowed their own wisdom and their thoughts to say what that cross meant, and so reconciled it with a religion which to a very extent was legal and carnal.

And the story of the Galatian Church is repeated to this day even in the Churches that are most confidently assured that they are free from the Galatian error. Just notice how often the doctrine of justification by faith is spoken of as if that were the only teaching of the epistle, while the doctrine of the Spirit's indwelling as received by faith, and walking by the Spirit, is hardly mentioned. …

Scripture is studied, and preached, and heard, and believed in, very much in the power of the natural mind with little insistence upon the absolute need the Spirit's personal teaching. It is seen in the absolute confidence with which men know that they have the truth, though they have it far more from human than Divine teaching, and in the absence of that teachableness that waits for God to reveal His truth in His own light. …

Listen, my brother, my sister, to the blessed teaching of God's word today. It was the confidence in the flesh that spoilt thy glorying in Christ Jesus. It was Self doing what the Spirit alone can do; it was Soul taking the lead, in the hope that the Spirit would second its efforts, instead of trusting the Holy Spirit to lead and do all, and then waiting Him. It was following Jesus, without the denial of Self. It was this was the secret trouble.

Come and listen to Paul as he tells of the only safeguard against this danger: "*We are the circumcision, who worship by the Spirit of God, and glory in Christ Jesus, and have no confidence in the flesh.*" Here are the two elements of spiritual worship, The Spirit exalts Jesus, and abases the flesh. And if we would truly glory in Jesus, and have Him glorified in us, if we would know the glory of Jesus in personal and unchanging experience, free from the impotence which always marks the efforts of the flesh, we must simply learn what this worship of God by the Spirit is.

I can only repeat, once again, what it is the purpose of this whole book to set forth as God's truth from His blessed word: Glory in Christ Jesus. Glory in Him as the Glorified One who baptizes with the Holy Spirit. In great simplicity and trustfulness believe in Him as having given His own Spirit within you. Believe in that gift; believe in the Holy Spirit dwelling within you. Accept this the secret of the life of Christ in you: The Holy Spirit is dwelling in the hidden recesses of your Spirit. Meditate on it, believe Jesus and His Word concerning it, until your soul bows with holy fear and awe before God under the glory of the truth: The Holy Spirit of God is indeed dwelling in me.

Yield yourself to His leading. We have seen that leading is not first in the mind or thoughts, but in the life and disposition. Yield yourself to God, to be guided by the Holy Spirit in all your conduct. He is promised to those who love Jesus and obey Him: fear not to say that He knows you love and do obey Him with your whole heart.

Remember, then, what the one central object of His coming was: to restore the departed Lord Jesus to His disciples. "*I will not leave you orphans,*" said Jesus; "*I will come again to you.*" I cannot glory a distant Jesus, from whom I am separated. When I try to do it, it is a thing of effort; I must have the help of the flesh to do it. I can only truly glory in a present Savior, whom the Holy Spirit glorifies, reveals in His glory, within me. As He does this, the flesh is abased, and kept in its place of crucifixion as an accursed thing: as He does it, the deeds of the flesh are made to die. And my sole religion will be: no confidence in the flesh, glorying in Christ Jesus, worship by the Spirit of God. …

Spiritual or Carnal

April 18th

"And I, brethren, could not speak unto you as spiritual, but as carnal—as babes in Christ. ... Whereas there is among you jealousy and strife, are you not carnal, and walk after the manner of unbelievers?"

—1 CORINTHIANS 3: 1–3

Here, the Apostle Paul tells the Corinthians that, though they have the Spirit, he cannot call them spiritual; that epithet belongs to those who have not only received the Spirit, but have yielded themselves to Him to possess and rule their whole life. Those who have not done this, in whom the power of the flesh is still more manifest than that of the Spirit, must be called not spiritual, but fleshly or carnal. There are thus three states in which a man may be found:

First, the unregenerate is the "natural"—not having the Spirit of God. Second, the regenerate one—who is still babe in Christ, whether because of being only lately converted, or because of having stood still and not advanced— is "carnal," giving way to the power of the flesh. The believer in whom the Spirit has obtained full supremacy, is "spiritual." …

The young Christian is still carnal. Regeneration is a birth: the center and root of the personality, the spirit, has been renewed and taken possession of by the Spirit of God. But time is needed for its power from that center to extend through all the circumference of our being. The Kingdom of God is like a seed; the life in Christ is a growth; and it would be against the laws of nature and grace alike if we expected from the babe in Christ the strength that can only be found in the young men, or the rich experience of the fathers. Even where in the young convert there is great singleness of heart and faith, with true love and devotion to the Savior, time is needed for a deeper knowledge of Self and sin, for a spiritual insight into what God's will and grace are. … We need not wonder if the babe in Christ is still carnal.

But, many Christians remain carnal. God has not only called us to grow, but has provided all the conditions and powers needful for growth. And yet it is true, sadly, that there are many Christians who, like the Corinthians, remain babes in Christ when they ought to be going on to perfection….

In some cases, the blame is almost more with the Church and its teaching, than with the individuals themselves. When the preaching makes salvation chiefly to consist in pardon and peace and the hope of Heaven, or when, if a holy life be preached, the truth of Christ our sanctification, our sufficient strength to be holy, and the Holy Spirit's indwelling, are not taught clearly and in the power of the Spirit, growth can hardly be expected. …

In other cases, the root of the evil is to be found in the unwillingness of the Christian to deny Self and crucify the flesh. The call Jesus to every disciple is, "*If any man will come after Me, let him deny himself.*" The Spirit is only given to the obedient; He can only do His work in those who are willing absolutely to give up Self to the death.

The sin that proved that the Corinthians were carnal was their jealousy and strife. When Christians are not willing to give up the sin of Selfishness and temper; when, whether in the home relationship or in the wider circle of church and public life, they want to retain the liberty of giving way to, or excusing evil feelings, of pronouncing their own judgments, and speaking words that are not in perfect love, then they remain carnal. With all their knowledge, and their enjoyment of religious ordinances, and their work for God's kingdom, they are carnal and not spiritual. They grieve the Holy Spirit of God; they cannot have the testimony that they are pleasing to God. God is Love: if we would not be carnal, let us love. "*Above all things, put on love, which is the bond of perfectness.*"

The carnal Christian cannot apprehend spiritual truth. Paul writes to these Corinthians: "*I fed you with milk, and not with meat; for you were not able to bear it….*" The Corinthians prided themselves on their wisdom; Paul thanked God that they were "*enriched in all knowledge.*" There was nothing in His teaching that they would not have been able to comprehend with the understanding. But the real spiritual entering into the truth in power, so as to possess it and be possessed by it—so as to have not only the thoughts but the very thing the words speak of—this the Holy Spirit only can give. And He gives it only in the spiritually-minded man. The teaching and leading of the Spirit is given to the obedient, is preceded by the dominion of the Spirit in mortifying the deeds of the body (Romans 8: 13–14).

Spiritual knowledge is not deep thought, but living contact, entering into and being united to the truth as it is in Jesus, a spiritual reality, a substantial existence. "*The Spirit teaches….*" It is not the power of intellect; it is not even the earnest desire to know the truth; that fits a man for the Spirit's teaching; it is a life yielded to Him in waiting dependence and full obedience to be made spiritual, that receives the spiritual wisdom and understanding. …

As far as we are giving way to the flesh, we are incapable of receiving spiritual insight into truth. We may "*know all mysteries, and have all knowledge,*" [but] without love—the love which the Spirit works in the inner life—it is only a knowledge that puffs up; it profits nothing. The carnal life makes the knowledge carnal. And this knowledge again, being thus held in the fleshly mind, strengthens the religion of the flesh, of Self—trust and Self-effort; the truth so received has no power to renew and make free. No wonder that there is so much Bible teaching and Bible knowledge, with so little of real spiritual result in a life of holiness. …

Unless we be living spiritual lives—full of humility, and love, and Self-sacrifice—spiritual truth, the truth of God, cannot enter or profit us. Love alone is light: want of love is darkness (1 John 2: 9). …

It is the Holy Spirit who makes the spiritual man. He alone can do it. He does it most certainly where the whole man is yielded up to Him. To have the whole being pervaded, influenced, sanctified by the Holy Spirit; to have first our spirit, then the soul, with the will, the feelings, the mind, and so even the body, under His control, moved and guided by Him—this makes and marks the spiritual man. The first step on the way to this is faith. We must seek the deep, living, absorbing conviction that there is a Holy Spirit in us; that He is the Mighty Power of God dwelling and working within; that He is the representative of Jesus, making Him present within us as our Redeemer King, mighty to save.

We find that there is an opposing power, the flesh. From Scripture we learn how the flesh has its twofold action: from the flesh springs not only unrighteousness, but Self-righteousness. Both must be confessed and surrendered to Him whom the Spirit would reveal and enthrone as Lord, our Mighty Savior. All that is carnal and sinful, all the works of the flesh, must be given up and cast out. But no less must all that is carnal, however religious it appears, all confidence in the flesh, all Self-effort and Self-struggling be rooted out. The soul, with its power, must be brought into the captivity and subjection of Jesus Christ. In deep and daily dependence on God must the Holy Spirit be accepted, waited for, and followed. …

The Spirit of Love

April 19th

"The fruit of the Spirit is love."

—GALATIANS 5: 22

Our subject today leads us up into the very center of the inner sanctuary. We are to think of the love of the Spirit. We shall have to learn that love is not only one, among others, of the graces of the Spirit, is not only the chief among them, but that the Spirit is indeed nothing less than the Divine Love itself come down to dwell in us, and that we have only so much of the Spirit as we have of love.

God is Spirit; *God is love*. In these two words, we have the only attempt that Scripture makes to give us, in human language, what may be called a definition of God. As a Spirit, He has life in Himself, is independent of all around Him, and has power over all to enter into it, to penetrate it with His own life, to communicate Himself to it. It is through the Spirit that God is the Father of Christ, the Father of spirits, that He is the God of creation, that He is the God and Redeemer of man. All life is owing to the Spirit of God.

And it is so because God is Love. Within Himself He is Love, as seen in the Father giving all He hath to the Son, and the Son seeking all He has in the Father. In this life of Love between the Father and the Son' the Spirit is the bond of fellowship. The Father is the Loving One, the Fountain; the Son the Beloved One, the great Reservoir of Love, ever receiving and ever giving back; the Spirit the Living Love that makes them one. In Him the Divine Life of Love hath its ceaseless flow and overflowing.

It is that same love with which the Father loves the Son that rests on us and seeks to fill us too, and it is through the Spirit that this love of God is revealed and communicated to us. In Jesus, it was the Spirit that led Him to the work of love for which He was anointed, to preach glad tidings to the poor and deliverance to the captives; through that same Spirit He offered Himself a sacrifice for us. The Spirit comes to us freighted with all the love of God and of Jesus: The Spirit is the love of God.

And when that Spirit enters us, His first work is: "*The love of God hath been shed abroad in our hearts by the Holy Spirit which was given unto us.*" What He gives is not only the faith or the experience of how greatly God loves, but something infinitely more glorious. The Love of God, as a spiritual existence, as a Living Power, enters our hearts. It cannot be otherwise, for the Love of God exists in the Spirit; the outpouring of the Spirit is the inpouring of Love. This Love now possesses the heart: that one same Love with which God loves Jesus, and ourselves, and all His children, and which overflows to all the world, is within us, and is, if we know it, and trust it, and give up to it, the power for us to live in too.

The Spirit in us is the love of God taking up abode within us. … As the renewed spirit becomes the abode of the Spirit of God and His love, and as the regenerate man yields himself to let the Spirit have sole sway that love will again become our life and our joy. To every disciple the Master says here again, "*Let him deny Self and follow me.*" Many a one has sought in vain to follow Jesus in His life of love, and could not, because he neglected what was so indispensable denying Self. Self following Jesus always fails because it cannot love as He loves.

If we understand this, we are prepared to admit the claim that Jesus makes, and that the world makes too, that our proof of discipleship is to be Love. The change we profess to have undergone is so Divine, the deliverance from the power of Self and sin so complete, the indwelling of the Spirit of God's love is so real and true, and the provision made to enable us thus to live so sufficient, that love, or the new commandment, as the fulfilling of the law, ought to be the natural overflow of the new life in every believer. That it is not so is simply another proof of how little believers understand their calling to walk after the Spirit, really to be spiritual men.

All the complaints that are continually being made by ourselves, or those around us, of tempers unconquered and of Selfishness prevailing, of harsh judgments and unkind words, of the want of a Christ-like meekness and patience and gentleness, of the little that is really being done by the majority of Christians in the way of Self-sacrifice for the social and religious needs of the perishing around them—all this is simply the proof that it has not yet been understood that to be a Christian just means to have the Spirit of Christ; just means to have His love, to have been made by Him a fountain of love springing up and flowing out in streams of living water.

We know not what the Spirit is meant to be in us, because we have not accepted Him for what the Master gave. We are more carnal than spiritual. It was thus with the Corinthians. In them we see the remarkable phenomenon of a Church, "*in everything enriched in Christ, in all utterance, and all knowledge, coming behind in no gift, abounding in everything in faith, and utterance, and knowledge,*" and yet so sadly wanting in love. "*Whereas there is among you jealousy and strife, are you not carnal?*" (1 Corinthians 3: 3).

The sad spectacle teaches us how—under the first movings of the Holy Spirit—the natural powers of the soul, knowledge, faith, utterance, may be mightily affected, without Self yet being entirely surrendered; and how thus many of the gifts of the Spirit may be seen, while the chief of all, love, is sadly wanting.

Not very different was the state of the Galatians, to whom the words, *"The fruit of the Spirit is love,"* were addressed. Though their error was not that of the Corinthians, boasting of gifts and knowledge, but a seeking after and trusting in carnal observances and ordinances, the result was in both the same—the Spirit's full dominion was not accepted in the inner life of love, and so the flesh ruled in them, causing bitterness and envy and enmity (Galatians 5:15, 16, 25, 26).

And even so it is still in much of what bears the name of the Christian Church. On the one hand the trust in gifts and knowledge, in soundness of creed and earnestness of work, on the other the satisfaction in forms and services, leaves the flesh in full vigor, not crucified with Christ, and so the Spirit is not free to work out true holiness or a life in the power of Christ's love. Oh, do let us learn the lesson, and pray God very fervently to teach it to His people, that a Church or a Christian professing to have the Holy Spirit must prove it in the first place by the exhibition of a Christ-like love. Both in its gentleness in bearing wrong, and in its life of Self-sacrifice to overcome the wrong, and to save all who are under its power, the life of Christ must be repeated in His members. The Spirit is indeed the Love of God come down to us. …

Walking by The Spirit

April 20th

"Walk by the Spirit and you shall not fulfill the lust of the flesh";
"They that are of Christ Jesus have crucified the flesh, with its passions and lusts."
—GALATIANS 5: 16, 24

If we live by the Spirit, by the Spirit let us walk. These words suggest to us very clearly the -difference, between the sickly and the healthy Christian life. In the former the Christian is content to "live by the Spirit;" we are satisfied with knowing that we have the new life; but we do not "walk by the Spirit." True believers, on the contrary, are not content without having our whole walk and conversation in the power of the Spirit. We walk by the Spirit, and so do not fulfill the lusts of the flesh. …

One of the deepest secrets of the Christian life is the knowledge that the one great power that keeps the Spirit of God from ruling, that the last enemy that must yield to Him, is the flesh. We that know what the flesh is, how it works and how it must be dealt with, will be conquerors.

We know how it was on account of their ignorance of this that the Galatians so sadly failed. It was this led them to attempt to perfect in the flesh what was begun in the Spirit

(Galatians 3: 3). It was this made them a prey to those who desired "*to make a fair show in the flesh*" that they might "*glory in the flesh*" (Galatians 6: 12–13). They knew not how incorrigibly corrupt the flesh was. They knew not that, as sinful as our nature is when fulfilling its own lusts … it apparently yields itself to the service of God, and undertakes to perfect what the Spirit had begun. Because they did not know this, they were unable to check the flesh in its passions and lusts; these obtained the victory over them, so that they did what they did not wish. They knew not that, as long as the flesh, Self-effort, and Self-will had any influence in serving God, it would remain strong to serve sin, and that the only way to render it impotent to do evil was to render it impotent in its attempts to do good.

… When Paul in the midst of his teaching about the walk in the Spirit (16–26) tells us, *"They that are Christ's have crucified the flesh with its passions and lusts,"* he tells us what the only way is in which deliverance from the flesh is to be found. To understand this word, "*crucified the flesh*," and abide in it, is the secret of walking not after the flesh but after the Spirit. Let each one who longs to walk by the Spirit try to enter into its meaning.

"The flesh": In Scripture, this expression means the whole of our human nature in its present condition under the power of sin. It includes our whole being, spirit, soul, and body. After the fall, God said, "man is flesh" (Genesis 6: 3). All his powers, intellect, emotions, will—all are under the power of the flesh.

Scripture speaks of the will of the flesh of the mind of the flesh (fleshly mind), of the passions and lusts of the flesh. It tells us that in our flesh dwells no good: the mind of the flesh is at enmity against God. … It warns us that our greatest danger in religion, the cause of our feebleness and failure, is our having confidence in the flesh, its wisdom and its work. It tells us that, to be pleasing to God, this flesh, with its Self-will and Self-effort, must entirely be dispossessed to make way for the willing and the working of Another, even the Spirit of God. And that the only way to be made free from the power of the flesh, and have it put out of the way, is to have it crucified and given over to the death.

… The one thing I need is: to look upon the flesh as God does; to accept of the death warrant the cross brings to everything in me that is of the flesh; to look upon it, and all that comes from it, as an accursed thing. As this habit of soul grows on me, I learn to fear nothing so much as myself. I tremble at the thought of allowing the flesh, my natural mind and will, to usurp the place of the Holy Spirit. My whole posture towards Christ is that of lowly fear, in the consciousness of having within me that accursed thing that is ever ready, as an angel of light, to intrude itself in the Holiest of all, and lead me astray to serve God, not in the Spirit of Christ, but in the power that is of nature. It is in such a lowly fear that the believer is taught to believe fully the need, but also the provision, of the Holy Spirit to take entirely the place which the flesh once had, and day by day to glory in the cross, of which he can say, *"By it I have been crucified to the world."*

Oh, that we knew to what an extent we have allowed the flesh to work in our religion! Let us pray God for grace to know it as our bitterest enemy, and the enemy of Christ. … Let us consent to what God says of the flesh, and all that comes of it: that it is sinful, condemned, accursed. Let us fear nothing so much as the secret workings of our flesh.

Let us accept the teaching of God's word: *"In my flesh dwells no good thing"*; *"The carnal mind is enmity against God."* Let us ask God to show us how entirely the Spirit must possess us, if we are to be pleasing to Him in all things. Let us believe that as we daily glory in the cross, and, in prayer and obedience, yield the flesh to the death on the cross, Christ will accept our surrender, and will, by His Divine Power, maintain mightily in us the Life of the Spirit. And we shall learn not only to live by the Spirit, but, as those who are made free from the power of the flesh, by its crucifixion, maintained by faith, in very deed to walk by the Spirit. …

7

WHOLLY FOR GOD

The True Christian Life

A Series of Extracts from the Writings of William Law

Selected and with an Introduction by the

REV. ANDREW MURRAY

New York: Ansen D.F. Randolf, 1893

Introduction 1

April 21st

A few words, first of all, to let my reader know what has given rise to the publication of this volume. Last winter Dr. Whyte of Edinburgh gave a lecture on William Law, in which he directed attention to the treasures to be found in the writings of this almost forgotten, though, as he styles him, "quite incomparable author." With many others, I owe Dr. Whyte a debt of gratitude for this introduction to one of the most powerful and suggestive writers on the Christian life it has been my privilege to become acquainted with. The present volume is a proof of my high appreciation of his teaching, and my desire to let others share with me in the profit to be derived from it.

Not long after the delivery of the lecture, a volume of selections was published, with the title *Character and Characteristics of William Law, Nonjuror and Mystic. Selected and Arranged, with an Introduction by Alexander Whyte, D.D.* (Hodder & Stoughton.) I would not have thought of now publishing this volume, were it not that I hoped that the special point of view from which these extracts have been made would prove an attraction to some, and introduce Law to readers to whom the larger volume would never find its way.

That point of view I have expressed in the title as the *True Christian Life*. I know of no writer who equals Law in the clearness and the force with which the claims of God on man are asserted. God is all; God must have all; God alone must work all: round these central truths all his teaching gathers. In their light he convicts the religious world of the hollowness and terrible Self-deception of the Christianity it professes. He proves to the believer no less how little he has lived as one who is wholly devoted to God in every action of common life, how little he has made exalted and eminent piety, and devotion to God, his one study, in the same way that a man of the world does with his business.

And what is more, in his later works Law lays bare the root and source of all this evil in the unconquerable power of Self, and shows how nothing but the mighty, immediate, and perpetual operation of God on the soul can give deliverance, and how nothing but the having the very spirit and humility, and love of the Lamb of God within can ever satisfy either God or our own heart. I feel confident that the teaching will be a stimulus and a strength to many.

William Law was born in 1686, and died in 1761, at the age of seventy-five. After completing his studies, he entered Holy Orders, and for five years held a Fellowship in Cambridge. At the end of that time, in 1716, he lost his Fellowship, owing to his refusal to take the oath of allegiance to George I. His loss of all hope of preferment in the Church has been its great gain. The closing of the door to active work set him free for that life of contemplation and prayer of which we reap the fruit. His forsaking all for what he deemed faithfulness to conscience helped to intensify that separation from the world, and that wholehearted allegiance to God and His will for which he was to be such a witness and advocate.

His earliest books were controversial . . . and at once gave him a name as an author. His first practical works were—*A Practical Treatise upon Christian Perfection* (1726) and *A Serious Gall to a Devout and Holy Life* (1729). It is by the latter of these works that Law is best known. The first short paragraph of the book contains the text into the exposition and application of which the writer throws his whole soul: "Devotion is neither private nor public prayer; but prayers, whether private or public, are particular parts of devotion. Devotion signifies a life given, or devoted, to God!" Throughout the volume he never wearies of illustrating and applying the two statements of his text. He sees Christians deceiving themselves with the thought that prayer is devotion: he proves to them, that as words are less than actions, prayer is the least part of devotion: devotion consists in a life given up to God.

And what this means, he puts in such a light, both from Scripture and the very nature of things, that every serious reader must confess that he has but little realized how wholly God expects us to live for Him, and how nothing less than a life with the spirit of Christ's commands and example animating us at all times and in every action is what God asks and accepts. The word "wholly unto God," which recurs unceasingly, is the keynote of the book.

As I have read and re-read the first ten chapters of the book, and felt how difficult it is to realize, even intellectually, this absolute devotion to God, I have more than once thought that if a minister were to try and reproduce in his preaching their substance, the result would in more than one way be a surprise to him. He would be surprised to find how difficult it is to get a clear and full grasp of that high standard of living, which he cannot but admit is nothing more than what Christ demands.

He would be surprised at his own want of success in conveying to his hearers the same impression of intense and entire devotion to God's will and pleasure as the one object of life. He would probably be surprised at discovering how, while he thought he had preached holiness and the imitation of Jesus Christ, he had given but a very faint impression of the unworldly, the heavenly life, which it is the duty of every Christian to lead. He would possibly be most of all surprised at finding how little his own life had really aimed at, not to say had attained, the true ideal, set before us in Christ Jesus.

It was not many years after the publication of this book that an event took place which exercised an unexpected influence on the life of Law. This was his becoming acquainted with the works of the German mystic, Jacob Boehme or Behmen. Though at first he found much in the writings of Behmen that appeared unintelligible, he came so completely under his influence that he gave himself up entirely to the study and the exposition of his teaching. The mystic element had always been strong in Law's nature.

One of the chief marks of the mystic is, that he seeks to pierce through all the appearances of nature to the Great Being who lives and moves in it all. *The Serious Call* is proof of how Law had learnt to see God in everything, and how he sought to bring men to let God in very deed be their All. Behmen taught Law what he had only faintly seen before, that God not only is All, and must have All, but that He alone must do All. In different works written after this time, between 1737 and 1740, the influence of Behmen was distinctly visible, and the substance of his teaching given.

Then there follows an interval of nine years (1740-1749), during which he published nothing. He appears to have given himself to that intense contemplation and fellowship of the Unseen, which is the only way in which eternal things can come with their full power into the spirit, and can so impart themselves as real existences, that in what is spoken and written, the weight and the fire of the Eternal makes itself felt. One cannot but observe this in the works written by Law after this season of silence.

They were — *The Spirit of Prayer* (Part I in 1749; Part II, 1750); *The Way to Divine Knowledge*, preparatory to a new edition of the works of Behmen, 1752; *The Spirit of Love* (Part I, 1752; Part II, 1754). In all these books, though some of them are quite small, one feels that a man is speaking who does not deal with thoughts and conceptions of the truth, but in whom the vision of the spiritual world has been opened, and through whom the fire of the sanctuary sheds its light and warmth. One feels impelled to pause and read again, and to confess that, though the meaning be clear and plain, there is a something behind that draws us on to long for the full possession and experience.

Of these later works. *The Spirit of Prayer* and *The Spirit of Love*, Dr. Whyte says: "Christopher Walton does not exaggerate one iota when he says that Law's readers will rise up from these books, saying, These are the two best books in the world! ... I have laid down these books again and again, saying with Walton, In their way, and on their subjects, show me another two books like them in all the world."

And yet I fear that, with many who might be induced to begin reading them, it might happen as it did to me, when *The Spirit of Prayer* came into my hands some years ago, in regard to prayer, as it is ordinarily taught, I found absolutely nothing. Discussion in regard to the origin of nature and matter and sin, that were not at once easily apprehended, and that appeared to have no direct bearing on the subject of the book, deterred an unprepared reader, and the book was laid aside. And so I have thought it might be a help to give such extracts from these books, as would bring his more direct teaching on the spiritual life within the reach of all. It will, I am sure, be the means of leading some to get the original works, and study Law's teaching on the Kingdom of Grace in its deep and wondrous unity with the Kingdom of Nature.

The spiritual insight into the truth of God acquired by Law, under Behmen's guidance, made its influence very marked and felt on his practical teaching. The difference between *The Serious Call* and *The Spirit of Prayer* or *The Spirit of Love* is very great. The former is from beginning to end a plea for God, in which every duty of the Christian life is exhibited and insisted upon with the voice of authority, and the motives to obedience are urged with all-convincing argument. But there is one thing wanting. To the question of the struggling soul who feels its impotence, and asks for strength to cast aside its bonds, and fulfil what is demanded of it, he gives no answer. Of the power that comes to faith, nothing is directly said; of the grace which the Holy Spirit works, mention is scarce made.

In the later works the tone is entirely different. The utter corruption and impotence of our nature, the absolute necessity of a new birth as an operation of God's mighty power in the soul, the indwelling of Christ in us, are preached in demonstration of the Spirit and in power. And these are passages in which the nature, the simplicity, the necessity, the alone efficacy of faith as making us partakers of the life and power of Christ, are set forth with singular beauty.

How deeply it was felt by some in Law's own day that there was something wanting in *The Serious Call*, is evident from what took place with John Wesley. His biography tells us that he had been some twelve years a minister before he found that salvation by faith of which he afterwards became such a preacher. During the years preceding what he counted his conversion, Wesley had frequent intercourse with Law, and looked up to him as a teacher. When brought to see how salvation is by faith alone, he wrote Law a letter, reproaching him for never having taught him this precious truth. Wesley tells him that for two years he had been preaching after the model of *The Serious Call and Christian Perfection*, and that the result had been to convince the people that the law of God was holy, but that when they attempted to fulfil it, they found themselves without power. And he asks Law, "Why did I scarce ever hear you name the name of Christ? Never so as to ground anything upon faith in His blood."

Law answers: "You have had a great many conversations with me, and you never were with me for half an hour without my being large upon that very doctrine which you make me totally silent and ignorant of. ... I have been governed through all that I have written and done by these two common, unchangeable maxims of our Lord: '*Without Me ye can do nothing*!' '*If any man will come after Me, or be My disciple, let him take up his cross and follow Me*.'"

These two texts were without doubt the spirit of all Law taught. *Christian Perfection* and *The Serious Call* are little else than an extended exposition of the second of the two. And as to the former, he did indeed insist upon the necessity of Divine aid. And yet we can quite understand how Wesley, when once he came to the light, could complain that Law had never pointed out to him the unique place that faith holds in God's plan of salvation. If we are to judge by his writings, Law, while holding that we are saved by faith, had not yet himself learnt what Self is, and what the vanity is of all Self-effort, and what the wondrous power of Christ is in him that believes. I have already alluded to the striking passages in his later works so infinitely beyond what he had ever written before.

These statements in regard to the difference between the earlier and the later works of our author will account for my not having, in these selections, adhered to the chronological order. I thought that, in beginning with *The Spirit of Love*, and setting before my readers some of the ripest, richest fruit first, I would tempt them on to search for the tree on which that fruit grew. That tree they will find in *The Spirit of Prayer*, and its teaching on Regeneration and the Birth from Heaven. In the strength of the faith of what God will do, we may then go on to *The Serious Call*, with its solemn, heart-searching exposition of true Christianity. That book will teach us what the tending and pruning, the digging and dressing, is that is needed to enable the tree to grow and bring forth fruit to perfection.

This order is that which is found in more than one of the New Testament Epistles. The high state and calling of the Christian in Christ is first expounded; then the reader is led on into everyday life, and shown what are the conditions of the maintenance and enjoyment of the grace bestowed in Christ. Or, as we have it in Ephesians, the first half lifts us into the heavenly places with the life in the Holy Spirit; the second brings us down to the practical duties of life on earth, with its cares and duties.

I am in hopes that even so, after the reader has been encouraged and quickened in the heavenly atmosphere of *The Spirit of Love* and *Prayer*, he will go down at the hand of *The Serious Call* into the valley of humiliation, to see what is still wanting in his life, spirit, and conduct, and to prove that the previous teaching of what God and faith can do indeed enable a man to live and love as God would have him do.

Introduction 2

April 22nd

Law is known as a mystic. Dr. Whyte calls him the greatest of English mystics. The deeper insight into spiritual truth which his later works reveal, and the higher life of which they testify, he all attributes to the teaching of the great German mystic, as Law calls him, "The heavenly illuminated and blessed man, Jacob Behmen."

That we be not, on the one hand, led unaware into error, nor, on the other, be prejudiced against truth by undue apprehension, it may be well for us to consider what this word "mystic" means.

In mysticism, as in everything human, there is an admixture of good and evil. Some writers give prominence to what they consider its errors and dangers, and count mysticism in principle to be untrue and unhealthy.

In the Preface to Vaughan's *Hours with the Mystics*, the author writes: "Mysticism, though an error, has been associated, for the most part, with a measure of truth so considerable, that its good has greatly outweighed its evil." The statement that what is at heart an error should effect so much more good than evil, cannot but strike one as somewhat strange. It would be surely more correct to say: Mysticism, because it is at root a truth, its good has, notwithstanding a considerable amount of error, greatly outweighed its evil. The writer of *Hours with the Mystics* would wish the word applied to the error in mysticism alone, and thinks that St. John ought not to be called a mystic.

In this case we should need another word to express that special element which is so marked a characteristic of the apostle.

> "Others, looking at its good, which even, according to Vaughan, so greatly outweighs the evil, noticing how many of the noblest and holiest of us have breathed its spirit, and remembering what the wonderful attraction its teaching often has for the most earnest and thoughtful minds, maintain that there must be truth in its root-principle, and that its errors must be put to the account of human weakness, and the difficulties of the high problem with which it deals. Lange says—
>
> "Mysticism has been defined as belief in an immediate and continuous communication between God and the soul, which may be established by means of certain peculiar religious exercises; as belief in an inner light, which may almost dispense with the written revelation. This definition identifies mysticism too closely with its extravagances, its more or less unsound developments, and overlooks that there is a mystical element in all true religion, both objectively in the revelation and subjectively in the faith. According to common acceptation, mysticism is simply a one-sided development of that element" (Herzog-Schaf Cyclopedia).

It is evident from what has just been said, that it is not easy to define what mysticism is. It is not a system of doctrine. It is found in all religious systems; in heathenism and pantheism, as well as in Christianity. With the Church of Christ it is not a sect or party;

every Church has its representatives. In every complete Christian character there is an element of mysticism. It is the outgrowth of a certain disposition or temperament, which ever seeks for the deepest ground or root of spiritual things.

The close connection between the words mystic and mystery will help us to understand what it means. In all religion, in all existence, there are hidden mysteries: for these the mystic has a natural affinity. In all the mysteries of revelation there is a human side, which the mind of man can master and reduce to a system. There is another, the Divine side, which human reason cannot grasp or express, but which opens itself to the faith that, in contemplation and worship, lives in the Invisible.

The mystic believes in a Divine light and power that comes on the soul that makes these its special object. The moment we attempt to formulate what the spiritual faculty is that receives this communication, in how far it may be counted a real revelation of God's Spirit, and what its relation to the inspired word, we come upon controverted ground. What we have said is enough to indicate very generally what distinguishes the mystic from the ordinary Christian.

It may help to prepare the way for reading these extracts from Law with profit, to mention some of the chief characteristics of his teaching, as they mark the true and healthy mysticism, from which the Church has nothing to fear, and a measure of which is necessary to a full and all-sided development of the gifts of the Spirit. As long as mysticism is regarded as a system which aims at making all whom it can reach into nothing but mystics, it is no wonder it should be looked on with apprehension.

But if once it be understood that mystics have a special gift and calling in the body of Christ, that, like all specialists, their value consists in their devoting themselves to one side or sphere of the Divine life, thereby to benefit those who have not the same gift or calling, and that the result of what they attain must become the common property of those members of Christ's body whose talents point them to other parts of the great field of Christian life and duty, prejudice will be lessened, and the immense benefit acknowledged which the Church has from the presence and life of those who so intensely witness for the Unseen and Incomprehensible.

1. The great mystery of the universe is God. The mystic seeks for God. To know God, to realize God, to live here on earth in conscious fellowship with Him, to love God, is his highest aim. "That God may be all," is the truth to which all others are subordinate. The words of Scripture, "*For whom are all things, and through whom are all things,*" stand in the very forefront of its theology.

"For whom all." Whether it be in nature or grace, in time or eternity, all things exist only for God, as the medium through which He can show forth His power and goodness, and so be glorified in the beauty and happiness of His creatures.

"And through whom all." All things glorify God only, because He alone works in them whatever is good and right. Just as these two truths hold in nature, so it is the one aim of religion to make them true in our lives. Man can have all for God as by faith he yields himself to expect all through God.

To know and enjoy and honor God thus, must be the one object of existence; to aim at it and increasingly to attain to it, is true religion and true happiness. Law will wonderfully help us to realize this. His *Serious Call* will teach us what all for God means. His later books, what all through God can be to us.

2. The mystic insists especially on the truth that the organ by which God is to be known, is not the understanding but the heart; that only love can know God in truth. Man was made in the image of God. We know God first in His works. From these we rise to His attributes, and form our conceptions of how these constitute the perfection of Him we seek to know.

But behind and beyond these attributes there is the Infinite and Incomprehensible Being, who hides Himself in a light that is inaccessible. Even so there is in man, who was made in the image of God, an outer life of thoughts and feelings, of words and actions.

From these we go inward to the powers from whence they come—the understanding, the affection, the will.

But then behind these, there is the deep center of the soul, what Scripture speaks of as the spirit, and at times as the heart, in which life has its secret roots, where its hidden character is found, and from whence all the issues of life proceed. This is that inner hidden sanctuary of man's nature which corresponds to the mystery of the Divine Being, whose likeness he bears, and which God created specially for Himself to dwell in. This is that hidden depth which none but He who searches the hearts can fathom or know. This is the seat of that renewing of the Holy Spirit, in which the birth of the Divine life creates a man anew.

Reason can form its conceptions, and frame its image of what God must be; but the Hidden, the Incomprehensible One Himself, reason cannot touch. As He is in Himself, so His working in man: His dwelling and His dwelling-place in the heart are a mystery too.

One of the great reasons that our religion is so powerless, is that it is too much a thing of reason and sense. We place our dependence on the intellectual apprehensions of truth, and the influence these exert in stirring the feelings, the desires, and the will. But they cannot reach to the life, to the reality of God, both because they are in their nature unfitted for receiving God, and are darkened under the power of sin. Mysticism insists upon this—and presses unceasingly the cultivation of the spiritual faculty which retires within itself, and seeks in patient waiting for God by faith to open the deepest recesses of its being to His presence.

How true and yet how little understood what Law says: "Man's intellectual faculties are by the fall in a much worse state than his natural animal appetites, and want a much greater Self-denial" (*Character*, p. 57).

> "When the call of God to repentance first rises in thy soul, thou are to be retired, silent, passive, and humbly attentive to this new risen Light within thee, by wholly stopping, or disregarding the workings of thy own will, reason, and judgment. It is because all these are false counsellors, the sworn servants, bribed slaves of thy fallen nature, they are all born and bred in the kingdom of Self; and therefore if a new kingdom is to be set up in thee, if the operation of God is to have its effect in thee, all these natural powers of Self are to be silenced and suppressed, till they have learned obedience and subjection to the Spirit of God" (*Spirit of Prayer*, p. 28).

> "If nothing can do any good, be any happiness or blessing but only God Himself in His holy Being, and if God cannot communicate Himself to you under a notion, or an idea of reason, but only as a degree of life, good, and blessing, born or brought to life in your soul, then you see that to give yourself up to reasoning and notional conceptions is to turn from God, and wander out of the way of all Divine communication" (*Character*, p. 224; see also pp. 185, 197).

We can now understand why such high value is attached to the contemplative life, to stillness of soul, and to the practice of the presence of God. It is as the insufficiency of our own powers of thought is deeply felt, and their activity is restrained, that the deeper the hidden powers of our nature can take their place, and faith can exercise its highest function as a faith of the operation of God, who raised Christ from the dead. The door is opened for God to become our inward life as truly as Self has been our very inmost life.

Introduction 3

April 23rd

Another point in which the mystic seeks to enter into the hidden mystery of God, is the nature of redemption. There are two views we find in Scripture, each the complement of the other. In the one, the simpler, more outward and objective, Christ as our representative did a certain work for us which He now in Heaven applies to us. In the other, the knowledge of Him as an outward person and of His outward work is considered as but the means to an end, a preparation leading up to the inward experience to His indwelling in us. Law says, "A Christ not in us is the same as a Christ not ours;" and opens up with wonderful clearness and power what this Christ in us and faith in Him means. He shows how, in the very nature of things, nothing less can restore that life of God which we lost in Adam, than a Christ whose life and disposition live in us as truly as that of Adam does.

If we ask what Christ in us means? his answer is, that that which constituted Him the Christ, made Him acceptable to God, and enabled Him to restore within us the perfection we lost, that that is what He must be in us. What constitutes Him the Lamb of God is His meekness, His humility, His resignation to God's will. And no faith in an outward Lamb of God, on the cross or on the throne, can possibly save us, except as it restores us to that humility before God, that resignation to His will, which is, whether in heaven or earth, the only possible way of entrance into God's presence.

> "Our salvation consists wholly in being saved from ourselves, or from that which we are by nature. In the whole nature of things, nothing could be this salvation or Saviour to us, but such an Humility of God as is beyond all expression."

> "Every man has within him a redeeming power, the making of the heavenly life, called the Lamb of God. This is the great trial of human life, whether a man will give himself

up to the meekness, the patience, the sweetness, the simplicity, the humility of the Lamb of God. This is the whole of the matter between God and the creature" (*Character*, pp. 57, 66).

"Death to Self is a man's only entrance into the Church of Life, and nothing but God can give death to Self. Self is an inward life, and God is an Inward Spirit of Life; therefore, nothing kills that which must be killed in us, or quickens that which must come to life in us, but the inward work of God in the soul, and the inward work of the soul in God. This is that mystic religion, which, though it has nothing in it but that same spirit, that same truth, and that same life, which always was and always must be the religion of all God's holy angels and saints in heaven, is by the wisdom of this world accounted to be madness" (*Character*, etc., p. 60; see also the very beautiful passage on the only way of dying to Self being by receiving the patience, meekness, humility, and resignation to God's will which was in Christ Jesus into our hearts—*Spirit of Love*, Part II).

It is just this element of mysticism that has formed its great attraction to those who truly thirst for God. Sin would be nothing if it were not sin in us, inspiring and ruling our inmost life. And Christ cannot be a complete Savior until His indwelling and inworking be as real and full as that of sin. I am confident that there will be no thoughtful reader of Law, who really hungers for the bread of heaven, but will lay down the book with the grateful acknowledgment that he has a deeper insight into the real nature of Christ's work and indwelling, and a stronger hope of the attainment of what so often appeared to be beyond his reach.

4. Just one more of the special teachings of mysticism. It is summed up in the expression that we must come away out of the manifold to the simple, out of multiplicity to unity, from the circumference to the center. The thought runs through its whole system, and is the key to the right apprehension of much of its teaching.

This truth holds in reference to God. Until a soul learns to see how entirely God is the center of all, how God is to be met and found and enjoyed in everything, so that nothing in heaven or earth can for one moment separate from Him, never can have perfect rest. And rest in God is the first duty and the true bliss of the creature. You have Christians who devote themselves most diligently to the study of God's word, who are delighted with every new truth they discover, or every new light in which an old truth is set before them, and who yet scarce ever meet the one Divine Word, who speaks in power within them. You have others who are consumed with zeal and labor, and yet know not what it is through all to have their rest in God. We need to be brought from the circumference to the living center; there we shall be rested and refreshed, and endued with the power of a Divine strength to do our work in the power of the eternal world.

This truth holds in reference to sin In Law's books we have a remarkable illustration of this, in the distinct advance to be seen in his teaching. In *The Serious Call*, individual sins, whether of life or heart, are uncovered and exposed with convincing power. Nothing less than entire conformity to God's requirement and Christ's example is held up as our only standard, or hope of being found meet for admission to Heaven. But there is nothing like the laying the axe to the root of the tree, the tracking of sin to its one source and beginning, as we have it in the later books. Behmen's teaching had opened up to him the meaning of the fall, and the entire corruption of human nature, and had shown him that there is but one deliverance from sin, and that is the deliverance from Self.

From all the manifold sins he had learned to look to the one sin—incarnate Self. He points out how the four elements of Self or fallen nature—covetousness, envy, pride, wrath—"are tied together in one inseparable band; they mutually generate and are generated by each other; they have but one common life, and must all of them live, or all die together" (*The Spirit of Love*, Part I). "Self is the whole evil of fallen nature." "Self is the root, the tree, and the branches of all the evils of our fallen state." "Self is not only the seat and habitation, but the very life of sin; the works of the devil are all wrought in Self; it is his peculiar workhouse; and therefore Christ is not come as a Savior from sin, but so far as Self is beaten down, and overcome in us" (*Spirit of Prayer*, § 32).

It is as the soul in this light is led to turn from the hopeless multiplicity of its sins, by which it has been distracted, to the one source of all, that it will learn how hopeless its efforts are, and see its need of a death to Self in the death of Christ as its only hope. This truth holds especially also in regard to faith. Law says:

> "I would have you believe that the reason why you, or anyone else, are for a long time vainly endeavoring after, and hardly ever attaining these first-rate virtues, is because you seek them in the way they are not to be found, in a multiplicity of human rules, methods, and contrivances, and not in that simplicity of faith in which those who applied to Christ immediately obtained that which they asked of Him" (*Spirit of Love*, Part II).

It is as the soul is led to see that in God is the unity and center of the universe and of our life, and thus that sin is nothing but our having turned from this God to Self, and that therefore our one need is the deliverance from Self, that it will discover in Christ a new meaning, and will understand how in the very nature of things nothing can save us but the simplicity of faith. Christ becomes to us the man who lived the life of God for us in human nature, and who brings salvation from Self by Himself being born into us, and giving us a life of God in which Self is swallowed up as darkness is swallowed up in light. This life must be received; and to receive it nothing avails but a true desire and a simple faith.

Law makes clear that in the Christian life there are two stages—that of babes, and that of men; that in the earlier stage our great duty is to remove hindrances, and to prepare the way for God to set up His Kingdom; and that it is only as we are faithful in the earlier stage that we shall be fitted for attaining the full outbirth of the Divine life within us. "Now, this way of attaining goodness (by rules and precepts), though thus imperfect, is yet absolutely necessary in the nature of the thing, and must first have its time, work, and place in us. Yet it is only for a time, as the law was a schoolmaster to the gospel."

All this effort is only to bring a man to such a total despair of all help, from human means, as to make him turn to God from whom alone life can come. Faith becomes the one thing needful. When the Virgin Mary conceived the birth of the Holy Jesus, all that she did toward it herself was only this single act of faith and resignation to God: "*Behold the handmaid of the Lord; be it unto me according to Your Word.*"

This is all that we can do toward the conception of that new man that is to be born in ourselves. The truth is easily consented to. But this is not enough: it is to be apprehended in a deep, full, practical assurance, in such a manner as a man knows and believes that he did not create the stars, or cause life to rise up in himself. Then it is a belief that puts the soul into a right state, and that makes room for the operation of God upon it."

Oh, blessed simplicity of the Christian life! May we all learn its blessed secret. Let God be all to us. Let Christ be all, as our way to God, as God working and dwelling in us. Let faith be all to us, the simple and unceasing turning of our souls to Christ Jesus; and out of the multiplicity of our strugglings and wanderings we shall by faith enter into the rest of God.

Just one word more in conclusion. There is a great deal in our modern habits of reading, and in our religious literature, that is not favorable to the cultivation of that habit of mind which is needed to read Law with pleasure or profit. Let me advise all those who hope by a cursory perusal to master his thoughts, to lay the book aside. But if we are prepared in quiet meditation to give time to the words of a man, who had, more than most, the powers of the invisible opened up to him and resting on him, to do their work in us, we shall, I am confident, be richly rewarded. And I am much mistaken if there will not be many of the readers of this volume who turn back time after time to dwell again on words, which, though they appear so simple and plain, yet will be increasingly felt to be full of the power of God and of eternity.

—ANDREW MURRAY, Wellington, 1893.

8

JESUS HIMSELF

How to Know God

New York: Fleming H. Revell Co., 1893

This brief message is a revision of two addresses, which originally appeared in the *South African Pioneer*, the organ of the "Cape General Mission" (Rev. Andrew Murray, President).

Jesus Himself 1

April 24th

"Their eyes were opened, and they knew Him."

—LUKE 24: 31

The words, from which I want to present a simple message, will be found in the Gospel according to St. Luke, the 24th chapter and the 31st verse: "*And their eyes were opened, and they knew Him.*" … I preached a sermon with the words "Jesus Himself" as the text; and as I went home I said to those who were walking with me: "How possible it is to have Jesus Himself with us and never to know it, and how possible to preach of, and to listen to, all the truth about Jesus Himself and yet not to know Him." Now these disciples had spent a most blessed time with Jesus, but if they had gone away before He revealed Himself that evening, they would never have been sure that it was Jesus, for their eyes were holden that they should not know Him. That is, alas, the condition of a great multitude in the Church of Christ. They know that Christ has risen from the dead. They believe, and they very often have blessed experiences that come from the risen Christ.

And now if you ask me what is to be the great blessing to be sought, my answer is this: Not only should we think about Jesus Himself and speak about Him and believe in Him, but we should come to the point that the disciples in the text arrived at, "*and they knew Him.*" Everything is to be found in that.

If I read that story of the disciples on the way to Emmaus, I get from it four stages in the Christian life.

1. Just think! How did they begin the morning that day? With "*hearts sad and troubled.*" They thought Jesus was dead; they did not know that He was alive. And that is the state of very many Christians. They look to the cross, and they struggle to trust Christ, but they have never yet learned the blessedness of believing that there is a living Christ to do everything for them. Oh! That word of the angel to the women! "*Why seek you the living among the dead?*" What is the difference between a dead Christ, whom the women went to anoint, and a living Christ? A dead Christ, I must do everything for; a living Christ does everything for me. …

2. Then there is the second stage. What is that? The stage of which Christ speaks: "*Slow of heart to believe.*" [The disciples] had the message from the women. They told the stranger [the unrecognized resurrected Lord] who walked with them: "*Certain women have astonished us, telling us they have seen an angel, who says He is alive.*" And Christ replied to them: "*Oh! Fools, and slow of heart to believe.*"

Yes! there are many Christians today who have heard and who know that they must not only believe in a crucified Christ, but in a living Christ, and they try to grasp it and take it in, but it does not bring them a blessing, and why? … They want to work for it, and with efforts get hold of it, instead of just quietly sinking down and believing, "Christ, the living Jesus, He will do everything for us."

That is the second stage. The first stage is that of ignorance, the second stage is that of unbelief—the doubting heart that cannot take in the wonderful truth that Jesus lives.

3. Then comes the third stage—"*The burning heart.*" Jesus came to the two disciples, and after He had reproved them and said: "*Oh! Fools, and slow of heart to believe,*" He began to open the Scriptures to them, and to tell them of all the wonderful things the prophets had taught. Then their eyes were opened, and they began to understand the Scriptures. They saw that it was true that it was prophesied that Christ must rise. As He talked, there came out from Him—the living risen One—a mighty influence, and it rested upon them, and they began to feel their hearts burn within them with joy and gladness. …

You may get in that third stage—the burning heart—and yet something is still wanting—*the revelation of Christ.* The disciples had had a blessed experience of His divine powers, but He had not revealed Himself, and oh! how often it is that at conventions and in churches, and in meetings and in blessed fellowship with God's saints, our hearts burn within us. These are precious experiences of the working of God's grace and Spirit, and yet there is something wanting. What is that? Jesus Himself has been working upon us, and the power of his risen life has touched us, but we cannot say, "I have met Him. He has made Himself known to me."

4. Oh, the difference between a burning heart, which becomes cold after a time, which comes by fits and starts, and the blessed revelation of Jesus Himself as my Savior, taking charge of me and blessing me and keeping me every day! This is the stage of—*the satisfied heart.*

O my brother, my sister! It is what I ask for you, and it is what I am sure you ask for yourself. I ask it for myself. Lord Jesus! may we know You in Your Divine glory as the Risen One, our Jesus, our Beloved and our Mighty One. Oh! If there are any sad ones who cannot take this in, and who say, "I have never known the joy of religion yet"—listen, we are going to tell you how you can. All will center round this one thing, that just as a little child lives day by day in the arms of its mother, and grows up year by year under a mother's eye, it is a possibility that you can live every day and hour of your life in fellowship with the Holy Jesus.

He will do it for you. Come, and let your sad heart begin to hope. Will He reveal Himself? He did it to the disciples and He will do it to you. Perhaps there are some who have got beyond the sad heart and who yet feel, "I have not got what I want." If you throw open your heart and give up everything but just believing and allowing Him to do what He wants, it will come.

Perhaps you have arrived at the stage of the burning heart, and can tell of many blessed experiences, but somehow there is a worm at the root. The experiences do not last, and the heart is so changeable.

Oh come, my beloved! Follow Christ. Say, "Jesus, reveal Yourself that we may know You. We ask not only to drink of the living water, we want the fountain. We ask not only to bathe ourselves in the light, we want the Sun of Righteousness within our hearts. We ask not only to know You, who has touched us and warmed our hearts and blessed us, but we want to know that we have the unchangeable Jesus dwelling within our hearts and abiding with us forevermore." …

Jesus Himself 2

April 25th

"I will come and dwell with you, and I will never leave you."

—DEUTERONOMY 31: 6; HEBREWS 13: 5 …

What are the conditions under which our blessed Lord reveals Himself? Or, put it this way: To whom is it that Jesus will reveal Himself? We have only to see how He dealt with these disciples, and we get the answer. …

First of all, I think I find here that Christ revealed Himself to those disciples who had given up everything for Him. He had said to them, "*Forsake all and follow Me*," and they had done it. With all their feebleness and all their unfaithfulness, they followed Christ to the end. … They were not perfect men, but they would have died for Him. They loved Him, they obeyed Him, they followed Him. They had left all, and for three years they had been following hard after Christ.

You say "Tell me what Christ wants of me, if I am to have his wonderful presence. Tell me what is the character of the man to whom Christ will reveal himself in this highest and fullest way?" I answer: "It is the one who is ready to forsake all and to follow Him." If Christ is to give Himself wholly to me, He must know that He has me wholly for Himself. …

The motto of the Cape General Mission is, "God first." In one sense that is a beautiful motto, and yet I am not always satisfied with it, because it is a motto that is often misunderstood. "God first" may mean "I" second, something else third, and something else fourth. God is thus first in order, but still God becomes one of a series of powers, and that is not the place God wants. The meaning of the words, "God first" is really "God all; God everything"; and that is what Christ wants. To be willing to give up everything, to submit to Christ to teach him what to say and what to do, is the first mark of the man to whom Christ will come. Are you not ready to take this step and say: "Jesus! I do give up everything; I have given up everything; reveal yourself"? Oh, brother! Oh, sister! Do not hesitate. Speak it out in your heart, and let this be the time in which a new sacrifice shall be laid at the feet of the blessed Lamb of God. …

But there is a second thing needed in the one who is to have this full revelation of Christ. We must be convicted of our unbelief. "*Oh! Fools,"* Jesus said, *"slow of heart to believe what the prophets have said.*" Oh! Brother, sister, if we could have a sight of the amount of unbelief in the hearts of God's children, barring the door and closing the heart against Christ, how we should stand astonished and ashamed!

When there is not unbelief but where there is faith, Christ cannot help coming in. He cannot help coming where there is a living faith, a full faith. The heart is opened, the heart is prepared; and as naturally as water runs into a hollow place, so naturally Christ must come into a heart that is full of faith. What is the hindrance with some earnest souls, who say: "I have given myself up to the Lord Jesus. I have done it often, and by His grace I am doing it every day, and God knows how earnestly and really I am doing it, and I have the sanction of God upon it, I know God has blessed me"? They have not been convicted of their unbelief. "*Oh! fools, and slow of heart to believe.*" …

Oh! May God convict us of unbelief. Do let us believe, because "*all things are possible to those who believe.*" That is God's Word, and this blessing, receiving the revelation of Jesus, can come only to those who learn to believe and to trust Him.

There is another mark of those to whom this special revelation of Christ will come, and that is: they do not rest until they obtain it. … It always reminds me of the story of Jacob, "*I will not let You go, except You bless me.*" That is the spirit that prepares us for the revelation of Jesus. Oh! My dear friend, has this been the spirit in which we have looked upon the wonderful blessing that we have sometimes heard of? "Oh! My Lord Jesus, though I do not understand it, though I cannot grasp it, though my struggles avail nothing, I am not going to let You go. If it is possible for a sinner on earth to have Jesus every day, every hour, and every moment in resurrection power dwelling in his heart, shining within him, filling him with love and joy—if that is possible, I want it."

Is that your language? Oh! Come then and say: "Lord Jesus, I cannot let You go except You bless me." The question is asked so often: "What is the cause of the feeble life of so many Christians?" What is really the matter? What is actually the want? How little the

Church responds to Christ's call! How little the Church is what Christ would have her to be! …

Oh! Christian, do you want peace and rest? You must have Jesus Himself. You talk of purity, you talk of cleansing, you talk of deliverance from sin. Praise God, here is the deliverance and the cleansing: when the living Jesus comes and gives power. Then we have this resurrection of Christ [in us], this heavenly Christ upon the throne [of our lives], making Himself known to us. Surely that will be the secret of purity and the secret of strength.

Where does the strength of so many come from? From the joy of a personal friendship with Jesus. … When we have Jesus with us, and when we go every footstep with the thought that it is Jesus wants us to go, it is Jesus who sends us and is helping us, then there will be brightness in our testimony, and it will help other believers, and they will begin to understand; "I see why I have failed. I took the word, I took the blessing, and I took, as I thought, the life, but I was without the living Jesus." …

Let us enter into the Holy Presence and begin, if you have never yet sought it before, begin to plead: "Oh! Savior, that I might have this blessedness every moment present with me—Jesus Himself, my portion forever."

You ask, "Is it really possible for a man in business, for a woman in the midst of a large and difficult household, for a poor man full of care; is it possible?" Can I always be thinking of Jesus? Thank God, you need not always be thinking of Him. You may be the manager of a bank, and your whole attention may be required to carry out the business that you have to do. But thank God, while I have to think of my business, Jesus will think of me, and He will come in and will take charge of me.

That little child, three months old, as it sleeps in its mother's arms, lies helplessly there; it hardly knows its mother, it does not think of her, but the mother thinks of the child. And this is the blessed mystery of love, that Jesus the God-man waits to come in to me in the greatness of His love; and as He gets possession of my heart, He embraces me in those Divine arms and tells me, "My child, I the Faithful One, I the Mighty One will abide in you, will watch over you and keep you all the days."

What a promise! And just as really as Christ was with Peter in the boat, just as Christ sat with John at the table, as really can I have Christ with me. And more really, for they had their Christ in the body and He was to them a man, an individual separate from them… But, … that same Christ glorified into the glory of God, can be *in* me ….

And now just think a moment what a blessed life that must be—the presence of Jesus always abiding. Is not that the secret of peace and happiness? If I could just attain to that blessed state in which every day and all the day I felt Jesus to be watching and ever keeping me, oh, what peace I would have in the thought, "I have no care if He cares for me, and I have no fear if He provides for me." Your heart says that this is too good to be true, and that it is too glorious to be for you. Still you acknowledge it must be most blessed. Fearful one, erring one, anxious one, I bring you God's promise—it is for me and for you: Jesus will do it; as God, He is able, and Jesus is willing and longing as the Crucified One to keep you in perfect peace. This is a wonderful fact, and it is the secret of joy unspeakable.

This is the secret of holiness: Instead of indwelling sin, an indwelling Christ conquering it; instead of indwelling sin, the indwelling life and light and love of the blessed Son of God. He is the secret of holiness. "*Christ is made unto us sanctification.*" Remember that it is Christ Himself who is made unto us sanctification. Christ coming into me, taking charge of my whole being; my nature and my thoughts and my affections and my will; ruling all things. It is this that will make me holy. We talk about holiness, but do you know what holiness is? You have as much holiness as you have of Christ, for it is written, "*Both he that sanctifies and they who are sanctified are all one*"; and Christ sanctifies by bringing God's life into me.

We read in Judges, "*The Spirit of the Lord clothed Gideon.*" But you know that there is in the New Testament an equally wonderful text, where we read, "*Put on the Lord Jesus Christ*"; that is, clothe yourself with Christ Jesus. And what does that mean? It does not only mean, by imputation of righteousness outside of me, but to clothe myself with the living character of the living Christ, with the living love of the living Christ.

Put on the Lord Jesus. Oh! What a work; I cannot do it unless I believe and understand that He whom I have to put on is as a garment covering my whole being. I have to put on a living Christ who has said, "*Lo, I am with you all the days.*" Just draw the folds closer round you, of that robe of light with which Christ would array you. Just come and acknowledge that Christ is with you, on you, in you. Oh, put Him on!

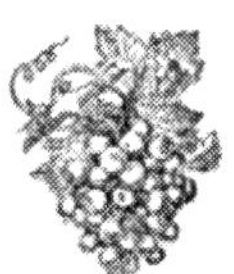

Jesus Himself 3

April 26th

"*Let this mind be in you which was also in Jesus Christ.*"
—PHILIPPIANS 2: 5

When you look at one characteristic of His after another, you hear God's Word: "*Let this mind be in you which was also in Jesus Christ,*" and that "*He was obedient even to death.*" And then you answer, Christ the obedient one, Christ whose whole life was obedience, it is that Christ whom I have received and put on. He becomes my life and His obedience rests upon me, until I learn to whisper as Jesus did, "*My Father, Your will be done; lo, I come to do Your will.*" …

Why is so difficult to be obedient, and why do I so often sin? … It is because I am trying to obey a distant Christ, and thus His commands do not come with power. Look what I find in God's Word. When God wanted to send any man upon His service, He first met him and talked with him and cheered him time after time. God appeared to Abraham seven or eight times, and gave to him one command after another; and so Abraham learned to obey Him perfectly. God appeared to Joshua and to Gideon, and they obeyed.

And why are we not obedient? Because we have so little of this near intercourse with Jesus. But, oh, if we knew this blessed, heavenly secret of having the presence of Christ with us every day, every hour, every minute, what a joy it would be to obey! We could not walk in this consciousness—My Lord Jesus is with me and around me—and not obey Him! Oh, do you not begin to long and say, "This is what I must have, the ever-abiding presence of Jesus!"

There are some Christians who try not to be disobedient, who come to their Sunday and week-day duties most faithfully, and pray for grace and a blessing, and they complain of so little blessing and power, so little power! And why? Because there is not enough of the living Jesus in their hearts. I sometimes think of this as a most solemn truth. There is a great diversity of gifts amongst ministers and others who speak; but I am sure of this, that our gifts are not the measure of our real power. I am sure of this … in proportion that we have in reality—not as a sentiment or an aspiration, or a thought, but in reality—the very Spirit and Presence of Jesus upon us, there comes out from us an unseen silent influence. That secret influence is the holy Presence of Jesus. …

I can hear someone say, "Tell me how I can get this blessed abiding presence of Jesus; and when I have got it, how I can ever keep it. I think if I have this, I have all. The Lord Jesus has come very near to me. I have tried to turn away from everything that can hinder, and have had my Lord very near. But how can I know that He will be with me always?" If you were to ask the Lord, "Oh, my blessed Lord Christ, what must I do, how can I enjoy Your never-failing presence?" His first answer would be, "Only believe. I have said it often, and you only partly understood it, but I will say it again—My child, only believe." …

You ask, "Where ought I to begin?" You ought to begin with first believing; with presenting yourself before this God in the attitude of silent worship, and asking Him to let a sense of His greatness and His Presence come upon you. You must ask Him to let your heart be covered over with His holy Presence. You must seek to realize in your heart the Presence of an Almighty and all-loving God, an unspeakably loving God. Take time to worship Him as the omnipotent God, to feel that the very power that created the world, the very power that raised Jesus from the dead, is at this moment working in your heart. We do not experience it because we do not believe. We must take time to believe. Jesus says, "Oh, my child, shut your eyes to the world, and shut out of your heart all these thoughts about religion, and begin to believe in God Himself." That is the first article of the Creed—"I believe in God."

By believing I open my heart to receive this glorious God, and I bow and worship. … Cultivate the habit of faith. "Jesus, I believe in Your glory; I believe in Your omnipotence; I believe in Your power working within me. I believe in Your living, loving Presence with me, revealing itself in Divine power."

Do not be occupied with feelings or experiences. You will find it far simpler and easier just to trust and say, "I am sure He is all for me." Get rid of yourself for the time; don't think or speak about yourself; but think what Jesus is. And then remember …

believe always.

I sometimes feel that I cannot find words to tell how God wants His people to believe from morning till night. Every breath ought to be just believing. Yes, it is indeed true; the Lord Jesus loves us to be just believing from morning to evening, and you must begin to make that the chief thing in life. … Oh, trust Jesus to fulfill His own promises.

There is a second answer that I think Christ would give if we come to Him believing, and say, "Is there anything more, my blessed Master?" I think I can hear His answer: "My child, always obey."

Do not fail to understand the lesson contained in this one word. You must distinctly and definitely take that word, "obey" and "obedience," and learn to say for yourselves: "Now I have to obey, and by the grace of God I am going to obey in everything." …

Oh! To have that thought in our hearts—"Jesus, I love to obey You." There must be personal intercourse with the Savior, and then comes the joy of personal service and allegiance. Are you ready to obey in all feebleness and weakness and fear? Can you say, "Yes, Lord Jesus, I will obey?" If so, then give yourself up absolutely. Then your feeling will be, "I am not going to speak one word if I think that Jesus would not like to hear it. I am not going to have an opinion of my own, but my whole life is to be covered with the purity of His obedience to the Father and His Self-sacrificing love to me. I want Christ to have my whole life, my whole heart, my whole character. I want to be like Christ and to obey." Give yourself up to this loving obedience.

The third thought is this: If I say, "My Master, blessed Savior, tell me all, I will believe, I do obey, and I will obey. Is there anything more I need to secure the enjoyment of Your abiding presence?" And I catch this answer: "My child, close intercourse with me every day." Ah, there is the fault of many who try to obey and try to believe; they do it in their own strength, and they do not know that if the Lord Jesus is to reign in their hearts, they must have close communion with Him every day. …

There are many Christians who fail here, and on that account do not understand what it is to have fellowship with Jesus. Do let me try and impress this upon you: God has given you a loving, living Savior, and how can He bless if you do not meet Him? The joy of friendship is found in intercourse; and Jesus asks for this, every day, that he may have time to influence me, to tell me of Himself, to teach me, to breathe His Spirit unto me, to give me new life and joy and strength.

And remember, intercourse with Jesus, does not mean half-an-hour or an hour in your closet. We may study our Bible or our commentary carefully; we may look up all the parallel passages in the chapter; when we come out of our closet we may be able to tell all about it, and yet we have never met Jesus that morning at all. We have prayed for five or ten minutes, and we have never met Jesus. And so we must remember that though the Bible is most precious, and the reading of it most blessed and needful; yet prayer and Bible reading are not fellowship with Jesus. What we need every morning is to meet Jesus, and to say, "Lord, here is the day again, and I am just as weak in myself as ever I was; do You come and feed me this morning with Yourself and speak to my soul."

Oh, friends, it is not your faith that will keep you standing, but it is a living Jesus, met every day in fellowship and worship and love. Wait in His presence, however cold and faithless you feel. Wait before Him and say: "Lord, helpless as I am, I believe and rest in the blessed assurance that what You have promised You will do for me."

I ask my Master once again, "Lord Jesus, is that all?" And his answer is: "No, my child; I have one thing more." "And what is that? You have told me to believe, and to obey, and to abide near to You: what wouldst You have more?" "Work for me my child. Remember, I have redeemed you for My service; I have redeemed you to have a witness to go out into the world confessing Me before others."

Oh, do not hide your treasure, or think that if Jesus is with you, you can hide it. One of two things will happen—either you must give all up, or it must come out. … Remember, it is not only our duty to confess Him; it is that, but it is something more. If you do not do it, it is just an indication that you have not given yourself up to Jesus; your character, your reputation, your all. You are holding back from Him. You must confess Jesus in the world, in your home; and in fact everywhere. You know the Lord's command, "*Go into all the world, and preach the Gospel to every creature*;" and, "*lo, I am with you*," meaning, "Any one may work for Me, and I will be with him." It is true of the minister, the missionary, and every believer who works for Jesus. The presence of Jesus is intimately connected with work for Him. … I do not believe that you could have the Presence of Jesus all the week and yet do nothing for Him. Therefore, my advice is: work for Him who is worthy. His blessing and His presence will be found in the work. It is a blessed privilege to work for Christ in this perishing world. …

To each of those who have come to Him, Christ says, "I give Myself to you, to be absolutely and wholly yours every hour of every day; to be with you and in you every moment, to bless you and sustain you, and to give you each moment the consciousness of My Presence; I will be wholly, wholly, wholly yours." And now, what is the other side? He wants me to be wholly His. Are you ready to take this as your motto now: "Wholly for God"?

O God, breathe Your presence in my heart that You may shine forth from my life. "Wholly for God," let this be our motto. Come let us cast ourselves on our faces before His feet. Our missionary from Nyassaland says he has often been touched by seeing how the native Christians, when they are brought to Jesus, do not stand in prayer; they do not kneel; but they cast themselves upon the earth with their foreheads to the ground, and there they lie, and with loud voices cry unto God. I sometimes feel that I wish we could do that ourselves. … Let us do it in spirit, for the everlasting Son of God has come into our hearts. Are you going to take Him and to keep Him there, to give Him glory and let Him have His way? Come now and say, "I will seek You with my whole heart; I am wholly Yours."

9

BE PERFECT

1893

Preface

April 27th

"Be perfect, therefore, even as your Father in Heaven is perfect."

—MATTHEW 5: 48

What I have wished to do is to go with my reader through the Word of God, noting the principal passages in which the word "Perfect" occurs, and seeking in each case from the context to find what the impression is the word was meant to convey. It is only when we have yielded ourselves simply and prayerfully to allow the words of Scripture to have their full force, that we are on the right track for combining the different aspects of truth into one harmonious whole.

Among the thoughts which have specially been brought home to me in these meditations, and in which I trust I may secure the assent of my reader, the following are the chief:

1. There is a perfection of which Scripture speaks as possible and attainable. There may be, there is, great diversity of opinion as to how the term is to be defined. But there can be only one opinion as to the fact that God asks and expects His children to be perfect with Him; that He promises it as His own work; and that Scripture speaks of some as having been perfect before Him, and having served Him with a perfect heart. Scripture speaks of a perfection that is at once our duty and our hope.

2. To know what this perfection is we must begin by accepting the command, and obeying it with our whole heart. Our natural tendency is the very opposite. We want to discuss and define what perfection is, to understand how the command can be reconciled with our assured conviction that no man is perfect, to provide for all the dangers we are sure are to be found in the path of Perfection.

This is not God's way. Jesus said, "*If any man will do … he will know.*" The same principle holds good in all human attainment. It is only those who have accepted the command, "*Be perfect,*" in adoring submission and obedience, who can hope to know what the Perfection is that God asks and gives. Until the Church is seen prostrate before God, seeking this blessing as her highest good, it will be no wonder if the very word, "perfection," instead of being an attraction and a joy, is a cause of apprehension and anxiety, of division and offence. May God increase the number of those who, in childlike humility, take the word from His own lips, as a living seed, in the assurance that it will bring forth much fruit.

3. Perfection is no arbitrary demand; in the very nature of things God can ask nothing less. And this is true whether we think of Him or of ourselves. If we think of Him, who as God has created the universe for Himself and for His glory, who seeks and alone is able to fill it with His happiness and love, we see how impossible it is for God to allow anything else to share man's heart with Himself. God must be all and have all. As Lawgiver and Judge; He dare not be content with anything less than absolute legal perfection. As Redeemer and Father it equally becomes Him to claim nothing less than a real childlike perfection. God must have it all.

If we think of ourselves, the call to perfection is no less imperative. God is such an Infinite, Spiritual Good, and the soul is so incapable of receiving or knowing or enjoying Him except as it gives itself wholly to Him, that for our own sakes God's love can demand of us nothing less than a perfect heart.

4. Perfection, as the highest aim of what God in His great power would do for us, is something so Divine, spiritual, and heavenly, that it is only the soul that yields itself very tenderly to the leading of the Holy Spirit that can hope to know its blessedness.

God has worked into every human heart a deep desire for perfection. That desire is manifested in the admiration which all men have for excellence in the different objects or pursuits to which they attach value. In the believer who yields himself wholly to God, this desire fastens itself upon God's wonderful promises, and inspires a prayer like that of M'Cheyne: "Lord, make me as holy as a pardoned sinner can be made."

The more we learn to desire this full conformity to God's will, for the consciousness that we are always pleasing to Him, we will see that all this must come as a gift direct from Heaven. This gift is the full outbirth in us of the life of God, the inbreathing of the Holy Spirit of Jesus in those who are wholly yielded to His indwelling and rule. Trusting ever less to men's thoughts and teachings, we will retire often into the secret of God's presence, in the assurance that the more we see God's face, and hear the secret voice that comes direct from Him, "*Be perfect,*" the more will the Holy Spirit dwelling within us unfold the heavenly fullness and power of the words, and make them, as God's words, bring and give and create the very thing He speaks. …

—ANDREW MURRAY

Walk Before Me and Be Perfect

April 28th

"And when Abram was ninety-nine years old, the Lord appeared to Abram, and said to him, I am Almighty God: walk before Me, and be perfect."

—GENESIS 17: 1–2

It was now twenty-four years since God had called Abram to go out from his father's home, and that he had obeyed. All that time he had been a learner in the school of faith. The time was approaching for him to inherit the promise, and God comes to establish His covenant with him. In view of this, God meets him with this threefold word: "*I am Almighty God: walk before Me: be perfect.*"

Be perfect. The connection in which we find the word will help us to understand its meaning. God reveals Himself as God Almighty. Abram's faith had long been tried: it was about to achieve one of its greatest triumphs: faith was to be changed to vision in the birth of Isaac. God invites Abram more than ever to remember, and to rest upon, His omnipotence. He is Almighty God: all things are possible to Him: He holds rule over all. All His power is working for those who trust Him. And all He asks of His servant is that he be perfect with Him: give Him his whole heart, his perfect confidence.

God Almighty with all His power is wholly for us; be wholly for God. The knowledge and faith of what God is lies at the root of what we are to be: *"I am Almighty God: be perfect."* As we know Him whose power fills Heaven and earth, we see that this is the one thing needed: to be perfect with Him, wholly and entirely given up to Him. Wholly for God is the keynote of perfection.

Walk before Me, and be perfect. It is in the life fellowship with God, in His realized presence and favor, that it becomes possible to be perfect with Him.

Walk before Me. Abraham had been doing this; God's word calls him to a clearer and more conscious apprehension of this as his life calling. It is easy for us to study what Scripture says of perfection, to form our ideas of it, and argue for them. But let us remember that it is only as we are walking closely with God, seeking and in some measure attaining, uninterrupted communion with Him, that the Divine command will come to us in its Divine Power, and unfold to us its Divine meaning.

Walk before Me, and be perfect. God's realized presence is the school, is the secret, of perfection. It is only he who studies what perfection is in the full light of God's presence to whom its hidden glory will be opened up. That realized presence is the great blessing of the redemption in Jesus Christ. The veil has been rent, the way into the true sanctuary, the Presence of God, has been opened; we have access with boldness into the Holiest of All. God, who has proved Himself God Almighty in raising Jesus from the dead and setting Him, and us in Him, at His right hand, speaks now to us: "*I am God Almighty: walk before Me, and be perfect.*" That command came not only to Abraham. Moses gave it to the whole people of Israel; "*You shall be perfect with the Lord your God.*" It is for all Abraham's children; for all the Israel of God; for every believer.

Oh! Think not that, ere you can obey, you must first understand and define what perfection means. No, God's way is the very opposite of this. Abraham went out, not knowing where he went. You are called to go on to perfection: go out, not knowing where you are going. It is a land that God will show you.

Let your heart be filled with His glory: *"I am God Almighty."* Let your life be spent in His presence: *"walk before Me."* As His power and His Presence rest upon you and fill you, your heart will, before you know, be drawn up, and strengthened to accept and rejoice in and fulfill the command: *"be perfect."* …

Perfect with the Lord Your God

April 29th

"*You shall be perfect with the Lord your God.*"

—DEUTERONOMY 18: 13

To be perfect before God is not only the calling and the privilege of a man like Abraham, it is equally the duty of all His children. The command is given to all Israel, for each man of God's people to receive and obey: "*You shall be perfect with the Lord your God.*" It comes to each child of God; no one professing to be a Christian may turn aside from it, or refuse it obedience, without endangering his salvation. It is not a command like, "You shall not kill," or, "You shall not steal," having reference to a limited sphere in our life, but is a principle that lies at the very root of all true religion. If our service of God is to be acceptable, it must not be with a divided, but a whole, a perfect heart.

The chief hindrance in the way of obedience to this command lies in our misapprehension of what religion is. Man was created simply to live for God, to show forth His glory, by allowing God to show how completely He could reveal His likeness and blessedness in man. God lives for man; longing in the greatness of His love to communicate His goodness and His love. It was to this life, lost by sin, Christ came to redeem us back. The Selfishness of the human heart looks upon salvation … with so much of holiness as is needed to make our happiness secure. Christ meant us to be restored to the state from which we had fallen—the whole heart, the whole will, the whole life given up to the glory and service of God. To be wholly given up to God, to be perfect with the Lord our God, lies at the very root, is the very essence of true religion. The enthusiastic devotion of the whole heart to God is what is asked of us.

When once this misconception has been removed, and the truth begins to dawn upon the soul, a second hindrance is generally met with in the question of unbelief: "How can these things be?" Instead of first accepting God's command, and then waiting in the path of obedience for the teaching of the Spirit, men are at once ready with their own interpretation of the Word, and confidently affirm, "it cannot be." They forget that the whole object of the gospel and the glory of Christ's redemption is that it makes possible what is beyond man's thoughts or powers; and that it reveals God, not as a Lawgiver and Judge, exacting the last penny, but as a Father, who in grace deals with each one according to his capacity, and accepts the devotion and the intention of the heart.

We understand this of an earthly father. A child of ten is doing some little service for the father, or helping him in his work. The work of the child is very defective, and yet the cause of joy and hope to the father, because he sees in it the proof of the child's attachment and obedience, as well as the pledge of what that spirit will do for the child when his intelligence and his strength have been increased. The child has served the father with a perfect heart, though the perfect heart does not at once imply perfect work. Even so the Father in Heaven accepts as a perfect heart the simple childlike purpose that makes His fear and service its one object.

The Christian may be deeply humbled at the involuntary uprisings of the evil nature; but God's Spirit teaches us to say, *"It is no more I that sin, but sin that dwells in me"* (Romans 7: 7). We may be sorely grieved by the consciousness of shortcoming and failure, but we hear the voice of Jesus, *"The spirit is willing, but the flesh is weak."* Even as Christ counted the love and obedience of His faithless disciples as such, and accepted it as the condition on which He had promised them the Spirit, the Christian can receive the witness of the Spirit that the Father sees and accepts the perfect heart, even where there is not yet the perfect performance.

"You shall be perfect with the Lord your God." Oh! Let us beware of making the Word of God of no effect by our traditions. Let us believe the message, *"You are not under the law, but under grace."* Let us realize what grace is in its pitying tenderness: *"As a father pities his children, so the Lord pities them that fear Him."* And what, in its mighty power working in both to will and to do: *"The God of all grace shall Himself perfect you."* If we hold fast our integrity, our confidence, and the rejoicing of hope steadfast unto the end, being perfect in heart will lead us on to be perfect in the way, and we will realize that Christ fulfills this too in us: *"You shall be perfect with the Lord your God."*

Lord, Give a Perfect Heart

April 30th

"Give to Solomon my son a perfect heart, to keep Your commandments."
—1 CHRONICLES 29: 19

In his parting commission to Solomon, David had laid it upon him to serve God with a perfect heart, because He is God, who searches the hearts. It is nothing less than the heart, the whole heart, a perfect heart, that God wants. Very shortly afterwards, in his dedication prayer after the giving of all the material for the temple, he turns again to this as the one thing needful, and asks it for his son as a gift from God: *"Give my son Solomon a perfect heart."* The perfect heart is a gift from God, given and received under the laws which rule all His giving, as a hidden seed to be accepted and acted on in faith.

The command, "*Be perfect*," comes and claims immediate and full submission. Where this submission is yielded, the need of a Divine power to make the heart fit for perfection becomes the motive for urgent and earnest prayer. The word of command, received and hid in a good and honest heart, becomes itself the seed of a Divine power. God works His grace in us by stirring us to work.

So the desire to listen to God's command, and to serve Him with a perfect heart, is a beginning that God looks to, and that He will Himself strengthen and perfect. The gift of a perfect heart is thus obtained in the way of the obedience of faith. Begin at once to serve God with a perfect heart, and the perfect heart will be given to you.

The perfect heart is a gift from God, to be asked for, to be obtained by prayer. No one will pray for it earnestly, perseveringly, believingly, until he accepts God's Word fully that it is a positive command and an immediate duty to be perfect. Where this has been done, the consciousness will soon grow strong of the utter impossibility of attempting obedience in human strength. And the faith will grow that the word of command was simply meant to draw the soul to Him who gives what He asks.

The perfect heart is a gift to be obtained in prayer. David asked the Lord to give it to his son Solomon, even as he had prayed for himself long before, *"Let my heart be perfect in Your testimonies."* Let all us who desire for this blessing follow his example: let us make it a matter of definite, earnest prayer. Let each son and daughter of God say to the Father: *"Give Your child a perfect heart."* Let us in the course of our meditations … turn each word of command, or teaching, or promise into prayer—pointed, personal prayer—that asks and claims, that accepts and proves the gift of a perfect heart.

And when the seed begins to strike root, and the spirit gives the consciousness that the first beginnings of the perfect heart have been bestowed in the wholehearted purpose to live for God alone, let us hold on in prayer for the perfect heart in all its completeness. A heart perfect in its purpose towards God—this is only the initial stage.

Then there comes the putting on of one grace after another—the going, from strength to strength, on to perfection— the putting on, in ever-growing distinctness of likeness, the Lord Jesus, with every trait of His holy image. All this is to be sought and found in prayer too. It is just he who knows most of what it is to be perfect in purpose who will pray most to be perfect in practice too.

In the words of Hezekiah, we see that there are two elements in the perfect heart: [first,] the relation to God, and, [second,]to His commandments: "*I have walked before You with a perfect heart, and have done that which is good in Your sight.*"

David speaks of the second of these in his prayer, "*a perfect heart to keep Your commandments.*" The two always go together: walking before God, in the awareness of His presence, will ensure walking in His commandments.

"Every good gift and every perfect gift is from above, and comes from the Father of lights," the gift of a perfect heart too. *"But let us ask in faith, nothing wavering."* Let us be sure that in the believing, adoring worship of God there will be given to the soul that is set upon having

it, nothing less than what God Himself means with a perfect heart. Let us pray the prayer boldly, *"Lord, give Your child a perfect heart. Let my heart be perfect in Your testimonies."*

I Have Walked Before You with a Perfect Heart

May 1st

"Then Hezekiah prayed unto the Lord, saying, I beg You, O Lord, remember now how I have walked before You in truth, and with a perfect heart, and have done that which is good in Your sight. And the word of the Lord came to Isaiah, saying, 'Tell Hezekiah, this is what the Lord says, I have heard your prayer, and seen your tears; I will heal you."

—2 KINGS 20: 2–5).

When the Son was about to die, He spoke, *"I have glorified You on earth, I have finished the work which You gave Me to do. And now, O Father, You glorify Me."* He pleaded His life and work as the ground for expecting an answer to His prayer. And so Hezekiah, the servant of God, also pleaded, not as a matter of merit, but in the confidence that *"God is not unrighteous to forget our work of faith and labor of love,"* that God should remember how he had walked before Him with a perfect heart.

The words first of all suggest to us this thought—that the man who walks before God with a perfect heart can know it; it may be a matter of consciousness. Let us look at the testimony Scripture gives of him (2 Kings 18: 3–6): *"He did that which was right in the sight of the Lord, according to all that David his father did."* Then follow the different elements of this life that was right in God's sight. "*He trusted in the Lord God of Israel. He held to the Lord. He departed not from following Him. He kept His commandments, which the Lord commanded Moses. And the Lord was with Him.*" His life was one of trust and love, of steadfastness and obedience. And the Lord was with him. He was one of the saints of whom we read, *"By faith they obtained a good report."* They had the witness that they were righteous, that they were pleasing to God.

Let us seek to have this blessed consciousness. Paul had it, he wrote, *"Our glorying is the testimony of our conscience, that in holiness and sincerity of God, not in fleshly wisdom, but in the grace of God, we behaved ourselves…"* (2 Corinthians 1: 12). John had it when he said, *"Beloved, if our heart condemns us not, we have boldness toward God; and whatever we ask we receive, because we keep His commandments, and do the things that are pleasing in His sight"* (1 John 3: 21–22). If we are to have perfect peace and confidence, if we are to walk in the holy boldness and the blessed glorying of which Scripture speaks, we must know that our heart is perfect with God.

Hezekiah's prayer suggests a second lesson—that the consciousness of a perfect heart gives wonderful power in prayer. Read over again the words of his prayer, and notice how distinctly this walk with a perfect heart is his plea. Read over again the words just quoted from John, and see how clearly he says that *"because we keep His commandments we receive what we ask."* It is a heart that does not condemn us, that knows that it is perfect toward God, that gives us boldness.

There is most probably not a single reader of these lines who cannot testify how painfully at some time or other the consciousness of the heart not being perfect with God has hindered confidence and prayer. And mistaken views as to what the perfect heart means, and as to the danger of Self-righteousness in praying Hezekiah's prayer, have in very many cases banished all idea of its ever being possible to attain to that boldness and confident assurance of an answer to prayer which John connects with a heart that does not condemn us.

Oh! That we would give up all our prejudices, and learn to take God's Word as it stands as the only rule of our faith, the only measure of our expectations. Our daily prayers would be a new reminder that God asks the perfect heart; a new occasion of childlike confession as to our walking or not walking with a perfect heart before God; a new motive to make nothing less the standard of our intercourse with our Father in Heaven. How our boldness in God's presence would be ever clearer; how our consciousness of His acceptance would be brighter; how the humbling thought of our nothingness would be quickened, and our assurance of His strength in our weakness, and His answer to our prayer, become the joy of our life.

Oh! The comfort, amid all consciousness of imperfection of attainment, of being able to say, in childlike simplicity, *"Remember, O Lord, how I have walked before You with a perfect heart."*

Perfect in Heart Leads to Perfect in Way

May 2nd

"Blessed are they that are perfect in the way, who walk in the law of the Lord … who keep His testimonies, who seek Him with the whole heart."

—PSALM 119: 1–2

We have seen what Scripture says of the perfect heart: here it speaks of the perfect walk. *"Blessed are the perfect in the way, who walk in the law of the Lord."* These are the opening words of the beautiful psalm, in which there is given to us the picture, from the witness of personal experience, of the wonderful blessedness of a life in the law and the will of God. As he looks back upon the past, the Psalmist does not hesitate to claim that he has kept that law: *"I have kept Your testimonies"; "I have conformed to Your law"; "I did not desert Your standards"; "I have not strayed from Your judgments"; "I have done judgment and justice"; "I have not swerved from Your testimonies"; "I have done Your commandments"; "My soul has conformed to Your declarations."* Of a truth may the man who can look up to God and, in simplicity of soul, speak thus, say, *"How blessed are the perfect in the way!"*

What is meant by this being "*perfect in the way*" becomes plain as we study the psalm. Perfection includes two elements. The one is the perfection of heart, the earnestness of purpose, with which we give ourselves up to seek God and His will. The other, the perfection of obedience, in which we seek, not only to do some, but all the commandments of God, and rests content with nothing less than the New Testament privilege of, *"standing perfect in all the will of God."*

Of both, the Psalmist speaks with great confidence. Hear how he testifies of the former in words such as these: *"Blessed are they that seek Him with the whole heart"; "With my whole heart I have sought You"; "With my whole heart, I will conform to Your law"; "I will keep Your standards with my whole heart"; "Your standards are my delight"; "O, how I love Your standards!" "Consider how I love Your standards"; "I love them exceedingly."* This is indeed the perfect heart of which we have already heard. The whole psalm is a prayer, and an appeal to God Himself to consider and see how His servant in wholehearted simplicity has chosen God and His standard as their only portion.

We have more than once said that in this wholeheartedness, in the perfect heart, we have the root of all perfection. But it is only the root and beginning: there is another element that may not be lacking. God is to be found in His will; we who would truly find and fully enjoy God, must meet Him in all His will. This is not always understood. We may have our heart intent on serving God perfectly, and yet may be unconscious how very imperfect our knowledge of God's will is. The very earnestness of our purpose and consciousness of integrity towards God, may deceive us. As far as we know, we do God's will. But we forget how much there is of that blessed will that we do not yet know.

We can learn a very blessed lesson from the writer of our psalm. Hear how he speaks: *"I have refrained my feet from every evil way"; "I hate every false way"; "I esteem all Your standards concerning all things to be right."* It is this surrender to a life of entire and perfect obedience that explains at once the need he felt of Divine teaching, and the confidence with which he pleaded for it and expected it: *"Let my heart be perfect in Your testimonies."* The soul that longs for nothing less than to be perfect in the way, and in deep consciousness of its need of a Divine teaching pleads for it, will not be disappointed. …

In the Old Testament, we have the time of preparation, the awakening of the spirit of holy expectancy, waiting God's fulfillment of His promises. In the Old the perfect heart was the receptacle, emptied and cleansed for God's filling. In the New we will find Christ perfected forevermore, perfecting us, and fitting us to walk perfect in Him. In the New the word that looks at the human side, perfect in heart, disappears, to give place to that which reveals the Divine filling that awaits the prepared vessel: Perfect Love; God's love perfected in us.

"Blessed are the perfect in the way!" … Surely now, in the fullness of time, when Jesus our High Priest in the power of an endless life saves completely, and the Holy Spirit has come out of God's Heaven to dwell within us and be our life, surely now there need not be one word of the psalm that is not meant to be literal truth in the mouth of every believer. Let us read it once more. Speaking it word for word before God, as its writer did, we too shall begin to sing, *"Blessed are the perfect in the way that seek Him with their whole heart"; "I will behave myself wisely in a perfect way. Oh! When will You come to me! I will walk within my house with a perfect heart."*

A Perfect Heart Makes a Perfect Man

May 3rd

"The heart of David was perfect with the Lord his God."
—1 KINGS 11: 4, 15: 3);
"Asa's heart was perfect with the Lord all his days."
—1 KINGS 15: 14

We have grouped together four men, of all whom Holy Scripture testifies that they were perfect men, or that their heart was perfect with God. Of each of them Scripture testifies, too, that they were not perfect in the sense of absolute sinlessness. We know how Noah fell. We know how Job had to humble himself before God. We know how sadly David sinned. And of Asa we read that there came a time when he did foolishly, and relied on the Syrians and not on the Lord his God; when in his disease he sought not to the Lord, but to the physicians. And yet the heart of these men was perfect with the Lord their God.

To understand this, there is one thing we must remember. The meaning of the word "perfect" must in each case be decided by that particular stage in God's education of His people in which it is used. What a father or a teacher counts perfection in a child of ten, is very different from what he would call so in one of twenty. As to the disposition or spirit, the perfection would be the same; in its contents, as the proofs by which it was to be judged of, there would be a wide difference. We shall see later on how in the Old Testament nothing was really made perfect; how Christ has come to reveal, and work out, and impart the true perfection; how the perfection, as revealed in the New Testament, is something infinitely higher, more spiritual and efficacious, than under the old economy. And yet at root they are one.

God looks at the heart. A heart that is perfect with Him is an object of complacency and approval. A wholehearted consecration to His will and fellowship, a life that takes as its motto, "Wholly for God," has in all ages, even where the Spirit had not yet been given to dwell in the heart, been accepted by Him as the mark of the perfect.

The lesson which these Scripture testimonies suggest to us is a very simple, but a very searching one. In God's record of the lives of His servants there are some of whom it is written: his heart was perfect with the Lord his God. Is this, let each reader ask, what God sees and says of me? Does my life, in the sight of God, bear the mark of intense, wholehearted consecration to God's will and service? Of a burning desire to be as perfect as it is possible for grace to make me?

Let us yield ourselves to the searching light of this question. Let us believe that with this word, "perfect," God means something very real and true. Let us not evade its force, or hide ourselves from its condemning power, by the vain subterfuge that we do not fully know what it means. We must first accept it, and give up our lives to it, before we can understand it. It cannot be insisted upon too strongly that, whether in the Church at large and its teaching, or in the life of the individual believer, there can be no hope of comprehending what perfection is except as we count all things loss to be apprehended of it, to live for it, to accept of it, to possess it.

But so much we can understand. What I do with a perfect heart I do with love and delight, with a willing mind and all my strength. It implies a fixity of purpose, and a concentration of effort, that makes everything subordinate to the one object of my choice. This is what God asks, what His saints have given, what we must give.

Again I say to everyone who wishes to join me in following through the Word of God its revelation of His will concerning perfection, yield yourself to the searching question: "Can God say of me as of Noah and Job, of David and Asa, that my heart is perfect with the Lord my God; have I given myself up to say that there must be nothing, nothing whatever, to share my heart with God and His will; is a heart perfect with the Lord my God the object of my desire, my prayer, my faith, my hope?" Whether it has been so or not, let it be so today. Make the promise of God's word your own: *"The God of peace Himself perfect you."* The God, who is of power to do above all we ask or think, will open up to you the blessed prospect of a life of which He shall say: *"His heart was perfect with the Lord his God."*

God Himself Will Perfect You

May 4th

"The God of all grace, who called you unto His eternal glory in Christ, after you have suffered awhile, will Himself perfect, establish, and strengthen you."

—1 PETER 5: 10 …

The two aspects of Christ's death: that He suffered for us, and that we are to suffer with Him and like Him, are so clearly and closely linked together. Fellowship with Christ, likeness to Christ, manifested in suffering, is the point of view from which Peter would have us look on life as the path to glory. To be a partaker of the sufferings and the glory of Christ is the Christian's privilege. He was perfected through suffering by God: the same God perfects us for suffering and glorifying Him in it. …

"It suited Him, for whom are all things, and of whom are all things, in leading many sons unto glory, to make the Leader of their salvation perfect through suffering." It was befitting that God should show that He is the God who works out perfection amid the weakness and suffering of a human life. This is what constitutes the very essence of salvation, to be perfected by God….

God has planted deep in our hearts the desire for perfection. … The promise is sure and bright for this our earthly life: *"God will Himself perfect you."* Joined with the words, "*establish, and strengthen you*," the "*Himself perfect you*," can refer to nothing but the present daily life. God shall Himself put you into the right position, and in that position then establish and strengthen you, so as to fit you perfectly for the life you have to live, and the work you have to do.

We find it so hard to believe this, because we do not know what it means. "*You are not under the law, but under grace.*" The law demands what we cannot give or do. Grace never asks what it does not give; and so the Father never asks what we cannot do. He Himself, who raised Jesus from the dead, is always ready, in that same resurrection power, to perfect us to do His will. Let us believe, and be still, until our soul is filled with the blessed truth, and we know that it will be done to us.

O my soul, learn to know this God, and claim Him, in this His character, as yours: "*God will Himself perfect you!*" Worship and adore Him here, until your faith is filled with the assurance: My God Himself is perfecting me. Regard yourself as the clay in the hands of the Great Artist, spending all His thought and time and love to make you perfect. Yield yourself in voluntary, loving obedience to His will and His Spirit. Yield yourself in full confidence into His very hands, and let the word ring through your whole being: "*God shall Himself perfect you*"; perfectly fit you for all He intends you to be or do. Let every perfect bud or flower you see whisper its message: Only let God work; only wait upon God; "*God shall Himself perfect you.*"

Believer! Have you desired this? Oh, claim it, claim it now. Or rather, claim now in very deed this God as your God. Just as the writer to the Hebrews, and Peter in this epistle, gather up all their varied teaching into this one central promise, "*God shall Himself perfect you,*" so there may come in the life of the believer a moment when he gathers up all his desires and efforts, all his knowledge of God's truth, and all his faith in God's promises, concentrates them in one simple act of surrender and trust, and, yielding himself wholly to do His will, dares to claim God as the God that perfects him. And his life becomes one doxology of adoring love: To Him be the dominion for ever and ever.

God Perfects You in Every Good Thing to Do His Will

"Now the God of peace … make you perfect in every good thing to do His will, working in us that which is well pleasing in His sight…" (Hebrews 13: 21). In [this verse] we have another revelation and promise of what this God of redemption will do for us; we again see how God's one aim and desire is to make us perfect. We have said before, the word "perfect" here implies the removal of all that is wrong, and the supply of all that is lacking. This is what God waits to do in us: *"make you perfect in every good thing."*

We need a large faith to claim this promise. So that our faith may be full and strong, we are reminded of what God has done *for* us; this is the assurance of what He will yet do *in* us. Let us look to Him as the God of peace, who has made peace in the entire putting away of sin; who now proclaims peace; who gives perfect peace. Let us look to Jesus Christ, the Great Shepherd of the sheep, our High Priest and King, who loves to care for and keep us. …

And let us believe the message that tells us: *"This God of peace, He will perfect you in every good thing."* … The more we gaze upon Him who has done such wondrous things for us, will we trust Him for this wondrous thing He promises to do in us, to perfect us in every good thing. What God did in Christ is the measure of what He will do in us to make us perfect. The same Omnipotence that worked in Christ to perfect Him, waits for our faith to trust its working in us day by day to perfect us in the doing of God's will. ...

And now hear what this perfection is which this God promises to work in us. It is truly Divine, as Divine as the work of redemption: *the God of peace ... make you perfect in every good thing to do His will.* It is intensely practical: "*in every good thing, to do His will.*" It is universal, with nothing excluded from its operation: in every good thing. It is truly human and personal: God perfects us, "*to do His will.*"

Perfecting Holiness

May 5th

"Having therefore these promises, beloved, let us cleanse ourselves from all defilement of flesh and spirit, perfecting holiness in the fear of God."

—2 CORINTHIANS 7: 1

These words give us an insight into one of the chief aspects of perfection, and an answer to the question, "Wherein is it we are to be perfect?" We must be perfect in holiness. We must be perfectly holy. Such is the exposition of the Father's message, *"Be perfect."*

We know what holiness is. God alone is holy, and holiness is that which God communicates of Himself. Separation and cleansing and consecration are not holiness, but only the preliminary steps on the way to it. The temple was holy because God dwelled in it. Not that which is given to God is holy, but that which God accepts and appropriates, that which He takes possession of, takes up into His own fellowship and use—that is holy. *"I am the Lord who makes you holy,"* was God's promise to His people of old, on which the command was based, *"Be holy."*

God's taking them for His own made them a holy people; their entering into this holiness of God, yielding themselves to His will, and fellowship, and service, was what the command, "*Be holy,*" called them to. Even so it is with us Christians. We are made holy in Christ; we are saints or holy ones. The call comes to us to follow after holiness, to perfect holiness, to yield ourselves to the God who is ready to sanctify us wholly. It is the knowledge of what God has done in making us His holy ones, and has promised to do in sanctifying us wholly, that will give us courage to perfect holiness.

"Having therefore these promises, beloved, let us perfect holiness." Which promises? They had just been mentioned: *"I will dwell in them; I will be their God; I will receive you; I will be to you a Father."* It was God's accepting the temple, and dwelling there Himself, that made it holy. It is God's dwelling in us that makes us holy; that gives us not only the motive, but the courage and the power to perfect holiness, to yield ourselves for Him to possess perfectly and entirely.

It is God's being a Father to us, begetting His own life, His own Son within us, forming Christ in us, until the Son and the Father make their abode in us, that will give us confidence to believe that it is possible to perfect holiness, and will reveal to us the secret of its attainment. *"Having therefore these promises, beloved,"* that is, knowing them, living on them, claiming and obtaining them, let us *"perfect holiness."*

This faith is the secret power of the growth of the inner life of perfect holiness. But there are hindrances that check and prevent this growth. These must be watched against and removed: *"Having these promises, let us cleanse ourselves from all defilement of flesh and spirit, perfecting holiness in the fear of the Lord."*

Every defilement, outward or inward, in conduct or inclination, in the physical or the spiritual life, must be cleansed and cast away. Cleansing in the blood, cleansing by the word, cleansing by the pruning knife or the fire—in any way or by any means—but we must be cleansed. In the fear of the Lord every sin must be cut off and cast out; everything doubtful or defiling must be put away; soul and body and spirit must be preserved entire and blameless. Thus cleansing ourselves from all defilement we will perfect holiness: the spirit of holiness will fill God's temple with His holy presence and power.

"Beloved, having these promises, let us perfect holiness." Perfectly holy! Perfect in holiness; let us yield ourselves to these thoughts, to these wishes, to these promises, of our God. Beginning with the perfect childlike heart, pressing on in the perfect way, clinging to a perfect Savior, living in fellowship with a God whose way and work is perfect, let us not be afraid to come to God with His own command as our prayer: Perfect holiness, O my Lord! He knows what He means by it, and we will know if we follow on to know.

Lord, I am called to perfect holiness: I come to You for it; make me as perfectly holy as a redeemed sinner can be on earth.

Let this be the spirit of our daily prayer. I would walk before God with a perfect heart: perfect in Christ Jesus; in the path of perfect holiness. I would this day come as near perfection as grace can make it possible for me. *"Perfecting holiness"* shall, in the power of His Spirit, be my aim.

The Perfect Selling All to Follow Christ

May 6th

"Jesus said unto him, If you desire to be perfect, go sell everything, and give to the poor, and you will have treasure in Heaven; and come, follow Me."

—MATTHEW 19: 21

To the rich young ruler poverty was to be the path to perfection. "*The disciple is not above his Master, but everyone who is perfected shall be as his Master.*" Poverty was part of the Master's perfection, part of that mysterious discipline of Self-denial and suffering through which it became God to perfect Him: while He was on earth, poverty was to be the mark of all those who would be always with, and wholly as, the Master.

What does this mean? Jesus was Lord of all. He might have lived here on earth in circumstances of comfort and with moderate possessions. He might have taught us how to own, and to use, and to sanctify property. He might in this have become like us, walking in the path in which most men have to walk. But He chose poverty; its life of Self-sacrifice and direct dependence on God, its humiliation, its trials and temptations, were to be elements of that highest perfection He was to exhibit.

In the disciples whom He chose to be with Him, poverty was to be the mark of their fellowship with Him, the training school for perfect conformity to His image, the secret of power for victory over the world, for the full possession of the heavenly treasure, and the full exhibition of the heavenly spirit. And even in him, who, when the humiliation was past, had his calling from the throne, in Paul, poverty was still the chosen and much-prized vehicle of perfect fellowship with his Lord.

What does this mean? The command, *"Be perfect,"* comes to the rich as well as the poor. Scripture has nowhere spoken of the possession of property as a sin. While it warns against the danger riches bring, and denounces their abuse, it has nowhere promulgated a law forbidding riches. And yet it speaks of poverty as having a very high place in the life of perfection.

To understand this we must remember that perfection is a relative term. We are not under a law, with its external commands as to duty and conduct that takes no account of diversity of character or circumstance. In the perfect law of liberty in which we are called to live, there is room for infinite variety in the manifestation of our devotion to God and Christ. According to the diversity of gifts, and circumstances, and calling, the same spirit may be seen in apparently conflicting paths of life. There is a perfection which is sought in the right possession and use of earthly goods as the Master's steward; there is also a perfection which seeks even in external things to be as the Master Himself was, and in poverty to bear its witness to the reality and sufficiency of heavenly things.

In the early ages of the Church this truth, that poverty is for some the path of perfection, exercised a mighty and a blessed influence. Men felt that poverty, as one of the traits of the holy life of Jesus and His apostles, was sacred and blessed. As the inner life of the Church grew feeble, the spiritual truth was lost in external observances, and the fellowship of the poverty of Jesus was scarce to be seen. In its protest against the Self-righteousness and the superficiality of the Romish system, the Protestant Church has not yet been able to give to poverty the place it ought to have either in the portraiture of the Master's image or the disciple's study of perfect conformity to Him.

And yet it is a truth many are seeking after. If our Lord found poverty the best school for His own strengthening in the art of perfection, and the surest way to rise above the world and win hearts for the Unseen, it surely need not surprise us if those who feel drawn to seek the closest possible conformity to their Lord even in external things, and who long for the highest possible power in witnessing for the Invisible, should be irresistibly drawn to count this word as spoken to them too: *"If you desire to be perfect, sell everything, and follow Me."*

When this call is not felt, there is a larger lesson of universal application: No perfection without the sacrifice of all. To be perfected here on earth, Christ gave up all. To become like Him, to be perfected as the Master, means giving up all. The world and Self must be renounced. *"If you desire to be perfect, sell all, and give to the poor; and come, follow Me."*

Christ Made Perfect through Suffering

May 7th

"It was fitting for Him … to make the Captain of their salvation perfect through sufferings."
—HEBREWS 2: 10

We are taught that Jesus Christ Himself, though He was the Son of God, had to be perfected. The first tells us that it was as the Leader of our salvation that He was perfected; that it was God's work to perfect Him; that there was a need-be for it; "it became God" to do it; and that it was through suffering the work was accomplished. The second, what the power of suffering to perfect was, that in it He learned obedience to God's will; and that, being thus perfected, He became the Author of eternal salvation to all who obey Him. …

In Christ there was nothing of sinful defect or shortcoming. He was from His birth the perfect One. And yet He needed to be perfected. There was something in His human nature which needed to grow, to be strengthened and developed, and which could only thus be perfected. He had to follow on, as, step by step, the will of God opened up to Him, and in the midst of temptation and suffering to learn and prove what it was at any cost to do that will alone. It is this Christ who is our Leader and Forerunner, our High Priest and Redeemer. …

We not only take Christ as our example and law in the path of perfection, but as the promise and pledge of what we are to be. All that Christ was and did as Substitute, Representative, Head and Savior, is for us. … This perfection of His is the perfection of His life, His way of living; this life of His, perfected in obedience, is now ours. He gives us His own Spirit to breathe, to work it in us. He is the Vine; we are the branches; the very mind and disposition that was in Him on earth is communicated to us.

Yes, more; it is not only Christ in Heaven who imparts to us somewhat of His Spirit; Christ Himself comes to dwell in our heart: The Christ who was made perfect through learning obedience. It is in this character that He reigns in Heaven: *"He became obedient unto death; therefore God highly exalted Him."* It is in this character that He dwells and rules in the heart. …

Christ Has Perfected Us

"By one offering He has perfected forever them that are sanctified" (Hebrews 10: 14). … He was Himself perfected for our sakes, so that He might perfect us with the same perfection with which God had perfected Him. What is this perfection with which God perfected

Him through suffering, in which He was perfected through obedience, in which as the Son, perfected forevermore, He was made our High Priest? The answer is to be found in what the object was of Christ's redeeming work. The perfection of mankind as created consisted in this: that we had a will with power to will as God willed, and so to enter into inner union with the Divine life and holiness and glory. Our fall was a turning from the will of God to do the will of Self. And so this Self and Self-will became the source and the curse of sin. The work of Christ was to bring man back to that will of God in which alone is life and blessedness. Therefore, "*it was proper and needful...if He was to be the Leader of our salvation, that God should make Him perfect through suffering*" (Hebrews 2: 10).

In His own person He was to conquer sin, to develop and bring to perfection a real human life, sacrificing everything that we hold dear, willing to give up even life itself, in surrender to God's will; proving that it is the meat, the very life of our spirit, to do God's will. This was the perfection with which Christ was perfected as our High Priest, who brings us back to God. This was the meaning and the value of His sacrifice, that "*one sacrifice,*" by which "*He has perfected forever them that are sanctified.*" ...

And how do we become partakers of this perfection with which Christ has perfected us? First of all the conscience is perfected .... The consciousness of a perfect redemption possesses and fills the soul. And then, as we abide in this, God Himself perfects us in every good thing, to do His will, working in us that which is pleasing in His sight, through Jesus Christ. Through Christ, the High Priest in the power of the endless life, there comes to us in a constant stream from on high, the power of the heavenly life. So that day by day we may present ourselves perfect in Christ Jesus. ...

Perfect Love: As He Is, So Are We

May 8th

"Herein is love made perfect in us: ... as He is, even so are we in this world."

—I JOHN 4: 17

Let us look back on the steps in the life of perfected love that have been set before us thus far. The Divine love entering the heart, manifests itself first in loving obedience to Christ. Of that obedience, love to the brethren in active exercise becomes the chief mark and manifestation. In this obedient love and loving obedience, the principle of fellowship with God, God abiding in us, is developed and strengthened. Of this fellowship the Holy Spirit gives the evidence and abiding consciousness. Such is the path in which love is perfected.

Obedience to Christ: love to the brethren; the indwelling of God in us, and us in Him; the communication and revelation of all this by the Holy Spirit: all these are correlated ideas—they imply and condition each other. Together they make up the blessed life of perfect love.

The perfect heart began by seeking God wholly and alone. It found Him in the perfect way, of obedient love to the Lord, ministering and loving to the brethren. ... So it was prepared and opened for that special illumination of the Spirit which revealed God's indwelling: The Father came to take up His abode. What was at first but a little seed—the perfect heart—has grown up and borne fruit; the perfect heart is now a heart in which the love of God is perfected. Love has taken full possession, and reigns throughout the whole being.

Has the apostle now anything more that he can say of perfect love? Yes; two things. He tells what is its highest blessing: *"Herein is love made perfect in us, that we may have boldness in the day of judgment."* And what is its deepest ground or reason? *"Because as He is, even so are we in the world."* It is in Christ we are perfect. It is with the same perfection with which Christ was perfected Himself that He made us perfect, that God now perfects us. Our place in Christ implies perfect unity of life and spirit, of disposition and character. John gathers up all the elements of the perfect love he has mentioned, and in view of the day of judgment, and the boldness perfect love will give us, combines them into this one: *"Because as He is, even so are we in the world."*

"As He is, so are we." In chapter 2 he had said, *"He that says he abides in Him, ought himself also to walk even as He walked."* Likeness to Christ in His walk of obedience on earth is the mark of perfect love.

... In the last night Jesus prayed, *"That they may be one, even as we are one; I in them, and You in Me, that they may be made perfect in one."* Likeness to Christ in His fellowship with the Father, God in us and we in Him, is the mark of perfect love.

God gave Christ to save us, by becoming our life, by taking us up into union with Himself. God could have no higher aim, could bestow no higher blessing than that He should see Christ in us, that we may have boldness in the Day of Judgment. Herein is love made perfect, *"because as He is, even so are we in the world."*

"That we may have boldness in the day of judgment," God has committed judgment unto the Son, as the perfected Son of man. His judgment will be a spiritual one: Himself will be its standard; likeness to Him the fitness to pass in and reign with Him. Perfect love is perfect union and perfect likeness; we have boldness even in the Day of Judgment: because as He is, even so are we in this world. O you seekers after perfection! It is in Christ that it is to be found. In Him is God's love revealed; in Him and His life you enter into it, and it enters into you; in Him love takes possession, and transforms you into His likeness; in Him God comes to make His abode in you; in Him love is perfected. The prayer is fulfilled, *"That the love wherewith You love Me may be in them, and I in them."* The love of God is perfected in us; we are perfected in love; we have boldness in the day of judgment: because as He is, even so are we.

The Love of God, as a fire from the altar before the throne, as the presence of the God of love Himself living in us, makes itself felt in its heavenly power, so that the world may know that God has loved us, as He loved His Son. The Love that flows from God to Christ rests on us also, and makes us one with Him. As He, the Son, is, in Heaven, even so are we, in the world, living in the Father and in His love.

The Perfect Man a Spiritual Man

May 9th

"And I, brethren, could not speak to you as to spiritual, but as to carnal, as to babes in Christ … For whereas there is among you jealousy and strife, are you not yet carnal?"

—1 CORINTHIANS 3: 1, 3

Among the Corinthians there were mighty and abundant operations of the Holy Spirit. Paul could say to them, *"In everything you were enriched in Christ, so that you come behind in no gift."* And yet in the sanctifying grace of the Holy Spirit there was much that was wanting. He had to say, "*There are contentions among you; I beseech you that there be no divisions among you, but that you may be perfected together in the same mind.*" The spirit of humility, and gentleness, and unity was wanting; without these they could not be perfected, either individually or as a body. They needed the injunction, *"Above all these things put on love, which is the bond of perfectness."*

The Corinthians were as yet carnal; the gifts of the Spirit were among them in power; but His grace, renewing, sweetening, sanctifying every temper into the likeness of Jesus, in this they were lacking much. The wisdom Paul preached was a heavenly, spiritual wisdom, God's wisdom in a mystery, even the hidden wisdom, which needed a spiritual, heavenly mind to apprehend it. "*We speak wisdom among the perfect*"; he could not speak to them "*as to spiritual, but as to carnal.*" Spiritual things must be spiritually discerned; the wisdom among the perfect could only be received by those who were not carnal, but spiritual. The perfect of whom Paul speaks are the spiritual.

And who are the spiritual? Those in whom not only the gifts, but the graces of the Spirit have obtained supremacy and are made manifest. God's love is His perfection (Matthew 5: 40–46); Christ's humility is His perfection. The Self-sacrificing love of Christ, His humility, and meekness, and gentleness, manifested in daily life, are the most perfect fruit of the Spirit, the true proof that a man is spiritual. A man may have great zeal in God's service, he may be used to influence many for good, and yet, when weighed in the balance of love, be found sadly wanting. In the heat of controversy, or under unjust criticism, haste of temper, slowness to forgive and forget, quick words and sharp judgments, often reveal an easily wounded sensitiveness, which proves how little the Spirit of Christ has full possession or real mastery. The spiritual man is the man who is clothed with the spirit of the suffering, crucified Jesus.

And it is only the spiritual man who can understand *"the wisdom among the perfect"; "even the mystery which now has been manifested to the holy ones, to whom God was pleased to make known what is the riches of the glory of this mystery, which is Christ in you."* A Christian teacher may be a man of wonderful sagacity and insight, may have the power of opening the truth, of mightily stimulating and helping others, and may yet have so much of the carnal that the deeper mystery of Christ in us remains hidden. It is only as we yield ourselves wholly to the power of God's Holy Spirit, as the question of being made free from all that is carnal, of attaining the utmost possible likeness to Jesus in His humiliation, of being filled with the Spirit, rules heart and life, that the Christian, be he scholar or teacher, can fully enter into the wisdom among the perfect.

To know the mind of God we must have the mind of Christ. And the mind of Christ is this: that "*He emptied and humbled Himself, and became obedient to death.*" This, His humility, was His capacity, His fitness for rising to the throne of God. This mind must be in us if the hidden wisdom of God is to be revealed to us in its power. It is this that is the mark of the spiritual, the perfect. … As the distinction between the carnal and the spiritual, the babes and the perfect, comes to recognition in the Church, the connection between a spiritual life and spiritual insight will become clearer, and the call to perfection will gain new force and meaning. And it will once again be counted just cause of reproof and of shame not to be among the perfect.

Let Us Press on to Perfection

May 10th

"For this reason, let us cease to speak of the first principles of Christ, and press on unto perfection."
—HEBREWS 6: 1

The writer had criticized the Hebrews for being dull of hearing; for having made no progress in the Christian life; for still being as little children who needed milk. They could not bear solid food, the deeper and more spiritual teaching in regard to the heavenly state of life into which Christ had entered, and into which He gives admission to those who are ready for it. Such our writer calls the perfect, mature or full-grown of the house of God.

We must not connect the idea of mature or full-grown with time. In the Christian life it is not as in nature: a believer of three years old may be counted among the mature or perfect, while one of twenty years' standing may be but a babe, unskilled in the word of righteousness. Nor must we connect it with power of intellect or maturity of judgment. These may be found without that insight into spiritual truth, and that longing after the highest attainable perfection in character and fellowship with God, of which the writer is speaking.

We are told what the distinguishing characteristic of the perfect is: "*even those who by reason of use have their senses exercised to discern good and evil.*"

It is the desire after holiness, the tender conscience that longs above everything to discern good and evil, the heart that seeks only, and always, and fully to know and do the will of God, that marks the perfect. Those who have set their heart upon being holy, and in the pursuit after the highest moral and spiritual perfection exercise their senses in everything to discern good and evil, are counted as perfect.

The epistle has spoken of the two stages of the Christian life. It now calls upon the

Hebrews to be no longer babes, no longer to remain content with the first principles, the mere elements of the doctrine of Christ. With the exhortation, *"Let us press on to perfection";* it invites them to come and learn how Jesus is a priest in the power of an endless life, who can save completely; how He is the mediator of a better covenant, lifting us into a better life by writing the law in our heart; how the Holiest of all has been set open for us to enter in, and there to serve the living God. *"Let us go on to perfection"* is the landmark pointing all to that heavenly life in God's presence which can be lived even here on earth, to which the full knowledge of Jesus as our heavenly High Priest leads us.

"Let us press on to Perfection." It is not the first time we have the word in the epistle. We read of God's perfecting Christ through suffering. Perfection is that perfect union with God's will—that blessed meekness and surrender to God's will, which the Father wrought in Christ through His suffering. We read of Christ's learning obedience, and so being made perfect.

This is the true maturity or perfection, the true wisdom among the perfect, the knowing and doing God's will. We read of strong food for the perfect, who by reason of practice, have their senses exercised to discern good and evil. Here again perfection is, even as with Christ, the disposition, the character that is formed when we make conformity to God's will, fellowship with God in His holiness, the one aim of life, to which everything else, even life itself, is to be sacrificed.

It is to this that Jesus, our High Priest, and the further teaching of the Epistle, would lead us on. The knowledge of the mysteries of God, of the highest spiritual truth, cannot profit us, because we have no inward capacity for receiving them, unless our inmost life is given up to receive as ours the perfection with which Jesus was perfected. When this disposition is found, the Holy Spirit will reveal to us how Christ has perfected forever, in the power of an endless life, those who are sanctified. He has prepared a life, a disposition, with which He clothes them. And we will understand that, *"Let us go on to perfection,"* just means this, "Let us go on to know Christ perfectly, to live entirely by His heavenly life now that He is perfected, to follow wholly His earthly life, and the path in which He reached perfection." Union with Christ in Heaven will mean likeness to Christ on earth in that lamb-like meekness and humility in which He suffered, in that Son-like obedience through which He entered into glory.

Not Perfected, Yet Perfect

May 11th

"Not that I have already obtained, or am already perfected; but I press on."

"Let us therefore, as many as be perfect, be thus minded."

PHILIPPIANS 3: 12, 15

In perfection there are degrees. We have perfect, more perfect, most perfect. We have perfect, waiting to be perfected. So it was with our Lord Jesus. In Hebrews we read thrice of Him that He was perfected or made perfect. Of sinful imperfection there was not the faintest shadow in Him. At each moment of His life, He was perfect—just what He should be. And yet [it was God's will] to perfect Him through suffering .... As He conquered temptation, and maintained His allegiance to God, and amid strong crying and tears gave up His will to God's will, His human nature was perfected, and He became High Priest, *"the Son perfected forevermore."* Jesus during His life on earth was perfect, but not yet perfected.

The perfected disciple shall be as his Master. What is true of Him is true, in our measure, of us too. Paul wrote to the Corinthians of speaking wisdom among the perfect, a wisdom carnal Christians could not understand. Here in our text he classes himself with the perfect, and expects and enjoins them to be of the same mind with himself. He sees no difficulty either in speaking of himself and others as perfect, or in regarding the perfect as needing to be yet further and fully perfected.

And what is now this perfection which has yet to be perfected? And who are these perfect ones? The man who has made the highest perfection his choice, and who has given his whole heart and life to attain to it, is counted by God a perfect man.

"The kingdom of Heaven is like a seed." Where God sees in the heart the single purpose to be all that God wills, He sees the Divine seed of all perfection. And as He counts faith for righteousness, so He counts this wholehearted purpose to be perfect as incipient perfection. The one with a perfect heart is accepted by God, amid all imperfection of attainment, as perfect. Paul could look upon the Church and unhesitatingly say, *"As many of us as be perfect, let us be thus minded."*

We know how among the Corinthians he describes two classes. The one, the large majority, carnal and content to live in strife; the other, the spiritual, the perfect. In the Church of our day it is to be feared that the great majority of believers have no conception of their calling to be perfect. They have not the slightest idea that it is their duty not only to be religious, but to be as eminently religious, as full of grace and holiness, as it is possible for God to make them. Even where there is some measure of earnest purpose in the pursuit of holiness, there is such a want of faith in the earnestness of God's purpose when He speaks: "*Be perfect*," and in the sufficiency of His grace to meet the demand, that the appeal meets with no response. In no real sense do they understand or accept Paul's invitation: "*Let us, as many as be perfect, be thus minded.*"

But, thank God! It is not so with all. There is an ever-increasing number who cannot forget that God means what He says when He speaks: "*Be perfect*," and who regard themselves as under the most solemn obligation to obey the command. The words of Christ: "*Be perfect*," are to them a revelation of what Christ is come to give and to work, a promise of the blessing to which His teaching and leading will bring them. They have joined the band of like-minded ones whom Paul would associate with himself; they seek God with their whole heart; they serve Him with a perfect heart; their one aim in life is to be made perfect, even as the Master.

My reader! As in the presence of God, who has said to you: "*Be perfect!*" and of Christ Jesus, who gave Himself that you might obey this command of your God, I charge you that you do not refuse the call God's servant, but enroll yourself among those who accept it: *"Let us, as many as be perfect, be thus minded."*

Fear not to take your place before God with Paul among the perfect in heart. So far will it be from causing Self-complacency, that you will learn from him how the perfect has yet to be perfected, and how the one mark of the perfect is that he counts all things loss as he presses on unto the prize of the high calling of God in Jesus Christ.

We Pray for Your Perfecting; Be Perfected

May 12th

"This we also pray for, even your perfecting."

—2 CORINTHIANS 13: 9

Be perfected, be comforted, be of the same mind, live in peace; and the God of love and peace will be with you."

—2 CORINTHIANS 13: 11

The word here translated "perfect" means to bring a thing into its right condition, so that it is as it should be. It is used of mending nets, restoring them to their right state, or of equipping a ship: fitting it out with all it should have. It implies thus two things: the removal of all that is still wrong; the supply of all that is still lacking.

Within two verses Paul uses the word twice. First, as the expression of the one thing which he asks of God for them, the summary of all grace and blessing: *"This we pray for, even your perfecting."* That you be perfectly free from all that is wrong and carnal, and that you should perfectly possess and exhibit all that God would have you be: we pray for your perfecting. Next as the summing up in a farewell word of what he would have them aim at: *"Finally, brethren, farewell. Be perfected."* And then follow three other verbs, which show how this one, which takes the lead, has reference to the Christian's daily life, and is meant to point to what is to be his daily aim and experience. *"Be perfected, be comforted, be of the same mind, live in peace."* Just as the comfort of the Spirit, and the unity of love, and the life of peace are, if the God of love and peace is to be with us, our duty and our privilege every hour, so, too, the being perfected. The close of the two Epistles gathers up all its teaching in this one injunction: *"Be perfected."*

The two texts together show us what the prayer and the preaching of every minister of the gospel ought to be; what their heart, above everything, ought to be set on. We justly look upon Paul as a model whom every minister ought to copy. Let every Gospel minister copy him in this, so that his people may know as he goes in and out among them that his heart breathes heavenward for them this one wish: *"Your perfecting!"* And may feel that all his teaching has this one aim: *"Be perfected!"*

If ministers are to seek this above everything in their charge of the Church of God, they need themselves to feel deeply and to expose faithfully the low standard that prevails in the Church. Some have said that they have seen perfectionism slay its thousands. All must admit that *imperfectionism* has slain its tens of thousands. Multitudes are soothing themselves in a life of worldliness and sin with the thought that as no one is perfect, imperfection cannot be so dangerous.

Numbers of true Christians are making no progress because they have never known that we can serve God with a perfect heart, that the perfect heart is the secret of a perfect way, of a work going on unto perfection. God's call to us to be perfect, to perfect holiness in His fear, to live perfect in Christ Jesus, to stand perfect in all the will of God, must be preached, until the faith begins to live again in the Church that all teaching is to be summed up in the words, and each day of our life to be spent under their inspiration: *"Be perfected!"*

When once ministers know themselves and are known as the messengers of this God-willed perfection, they will feel the need of nothing less than the teaching of the Holy Spirit to guide men in this path. They will see and preach that religion must indeed be a surrender of all to God. Becoming as conformed to His will, living as entirely to His glory, being as perfectly devoted to His service, as grace can enable us to be, and no less, will be the only rule of duty and measure of expectation.

The message, *"Be perfected!"* will demand the whole heart, the whole life, the whole strength. As the soul learns each day to say, "Father! I desire to be perfect in heart with You today, I desire to walk before You and be perfect," the need and the meaning of abiding in Christ will be better understood, Christ Himself with His power and love will have new preciousness, and God will prove what He can do for souls, for a Church wholly given up to Him.

O you ministers of Christ, you messengers of His salvation, say to the Churches over which the Holy Spirit has made you overseers: This also we pray for—even your perfecting! …

Perfect Love is Keeping Christ's Word

May 13th

"Whosoever keeps His words, in him has the love of God been perfected."

—JOHN 2: 5

Tauler says of the Apostle John: "In three ways, dear children, did the beloved Lord attract to Himself the heart of John."

> First, did the Lord Jesus call him out of the world to make him an apostle. Next, did He grant to him to rest upon His loving breast. Thirdly, and this was the greatest and most perfect nearness, when on the holy day of Pentecost He gave to him the Holy Spirit, and opened to him the door through which he should pass into the heavenly places. Thus, children, does the Lord first call you from the world and make you to be the messengers of God. And next, He draws you close to Himself, that you may learn to know His holy gentleness and lowliness, and His deep and burning love, and His perfect unshrinking obedience. And yet this is not all. Many have been drawn thus far, and are satisfied to go no further. And yet they are far from the perfect

> nearness which the heart of Jesus desires. St. John lay at one moment on the breast of the Lord Jesus, and then he forsook Him and fled. If you have been brought so far as to rest on the breast of Christ, it is well. But, yet there was to John a nearness still to come, one moment of which would be worth a hundred years of all that had gone before. The Holy Spirit was given to him—the door was opened.
>
> There is a nearness in which we lose ourselves, and God is all in all. This may come to us in one swift moment, or we may wait for it with longing hearts, and learn to know it at last. It was of this that St. Paul spoke when he said that the thing which the heart has not conceived, God has now revealed to us by His Holy Spirit. The soul is drawn within the inner chamber, and there are the wonders and the riches revealed." (*Three Friends of God*, by Mrs. Bevan.)

To understand a writer, it is often needful to know his character and history. When John wrote the epistle, he had for fifty years been living in that inmost nearness ... in the inner chamber within the veil. While on earth, Jesus had found in him a congenial spirit, receptive of His highest spiritual teaching, one to whom He felt drawn in special love. Fifty years of communing with the Son in the glory of the Father, and experiencing the power of the Holy Spirit to make the eternal life, the heavenly life of Jesus in fellowship with the Father, an everyday reality! No wonder that when John testifies of it as a life of perfect love, the Church that is not living on this level can only speak of it as an ideal, in this life unattainable.

To one who thinks of what John was and knew of his Lord, and what a Church under his teaching would be, the words are simply descriptive of characters he saw around him; men to whom he could write: *"Beloved, if our hearts condemn us not, we have boldness toward God . . . because we keep His commandments, and do the things that are pleasing in His sight"* (1 John 3: 21). *"Whosoever keeps His word, in him truly has the love of God been perfected"* (1 John 2: 5).

John is the disciple whom Jesus loved! The words Jesus spoke about the love of God had a special attraction for him; the love with which Jesus loved him exercised its mighty influence; the Holy Spirit that came from the heart of the glorified Jesus intensified and spiritualized it all; and John became the Apostle of Love, who, gazing into the very depths of the Divine Glory and Being, found there that "*God is love*."

With this word, "Love," as the sum of his theology, he links to the word he found in the Old Testament and in the writings of his brother apostles, the word "Perfect," and tells us that this is perfection, this the highest type of Christian character, the highest attainment of the Christian life: that we have God's love perfected in us.

The condition and the mark of this being perfected in love Jesus had taught him: *"If a man loves me, he will keep my word, and my Father will love him; and we will come to him, and make our abode with him."* Keeping His word: this is the link between the love of the disciple and the love of the Father, leading to that wondrous union in which the Father's love draws us to come and dwell in the loving heart: "*If you keep my commandments*," Jesus said, "*you shall abide in my love: even as I have kept my Father's commandments, and abide in His love.*" And John confirms from his own experience what the Master spoke: *"Whosoever keeps His word, in him has the love of God been perfected."*

Thank God! This is a life to be found on earth: God's love can be perfected in us.

Let not what we see in the Church around us make us doubt God's word. When John spoke of perfect love, and Paul of the love of God shed abroad in our hearts by the Holy Spirit, they testified from personal experience of what they had received in direct communication from the throne of glory. The words were to them the expression of a life of which we have little conception; to us they convey no more truth than our low experience can put into them. Oh! That our hearts might be roused to believe in their heavenly, supernatural, fullness of meaning, and not to rest until we know that the love that passes knowledge, the love that God is, the love of Christ, dwells within us as a fountain springing up unto everlasting life: "*The love of God perfected in us.*" The prospect is sure to everyone who will allow the love of God in Christ to have the mastery, and to prove what God can do for them that love Him.

Let Patience Have its Perfect Work

May 14th

"And let patience have its perfect work, that you may be perfect and entire, lacking in nothing."

—JAMES 1: 4

The perfection of the perfect heart, a heart wholly yielded to seek God with all its strength, is again a seed, with infinite power of growth and increase. … Perfection is a growth. As we awaken to the consciousness of what God asks and gives, and maintains the vow of a wholehearted surrender, we grow in sense of need and trust in the promise of a Divine life and strength, until all the promises of grace come to a focus in the one assurance: "*The God of all grace will Himself perfect you.*" That faith which was the fruit of previous growth, becomes the new seed of further growth.

Perfection now develops into something riper and mellower. The overshadowing Presence of Him who perfects, rests continually on the spirit, and the whole character bears the impression of heavenliness and fellowship with the Unseen. The soul makes way for God, and gives Him time to do His work; the God of Peace, perfecting in every good thing, gets entire possession. The soul rests in the rest of God.

This is not the work of a day. Perfection is a growth. *"You have need of patience, that having done the will of God, you may inherit the promise"; "Be imitators of them who through faith and patience inherit the promises."* Man is the creature of time, and is under the law of development. In the kingdom of Heaven, it is as in nature, from the seed first the blade, then the ear, then the full corn in the ear. There is nothing at times that appears more mysterious to the believer than the slowness of God. It is as if our prayers are not heard, as if His promises are not fulfilled, as if our faith is vain. And all the time God is hastening on His work with all speed. "*He will avenge His own elect speedily, though He bear long with them.*"

"Let patience have its perfect work." We are so often impatient with ourselves, not content to trust God to do His work, and so hindering just when we want to hurry on His work. We are impatient with God; instead of the adoring trust of Him, the God of peace, who

is perfecting us....

"Rest in the Lord, and wait patiently for Him," is the law of faith, not only in times of well-being, but especially in the path of perfection. Faith is the law of the Christian life to an extent that very few realize. The assurance that rests in the unseen power that is working out its Holy Purpose will never be disappointed. As it has been said of an elderly saint, "She was sure that, however long any soul might have to continue in the path of humiliation, with Self-emptying, the end, with all who were faithful, would one day be a filling to overflowing of all their inward being with the presence of the Holy One."

"Let patience have its perfect work." This is the command. To those who obey it, the potential offered is certain, *"that you may be perfect and entire, lacking in nothing."* ... Such is the Christian character as God's Spirit sets it before us. There is a perfection which the Christian is to regard as his duty and his life. Where patience has its perfect work it will bring forth what the husbandman longs for, fruit unto perfection. ...

But where there is to be this perfect fruit, there must first be the perfect seed. And that seed is the perfect heart. Without this, whence could patience have its perfect work? With this, every trial, every difficulty, every failure even, is accepted as God's training school, and God is trusted as the Faithful One, who is perfecting His own work. Let there be first the perfect heart; that will lead to perfect patience, and that again to the fully perfected man.

Jesus Christ was Himself not perfected in one day: it took time; in Him patience had its perfect work. True faith recognizes the need of time, and rests in God. And time to us means days and years. Let us learn each day to renew the vow: "This day I intend to live for God as perfectly as His grace will enable me. This day I intend, in the patience of hope, to trust the God of all grace, who Himself is perfecting me. This day I intend to be perfect and entire, lacking nothing." With such a vow renewed day by day, with faith in Christ who has perfected us, and God who is perfecting us, patience will do its perfect work. And we will be perfect and entire, lacking nothing.

10

THE HOLIEST OF ALL

An Exposition of the Epistle to the Hebrews

New York: Anson D. F. Randolph & Co., 1894

On Hearing the Voice of God

May 15th

"Wherefore, even as the Holy Spirit said, 'Today, if you shall hear His voice, harden not your hearts, as in the provocation, as in the day of temptation in the wilderness."

—HEBREWS 3: 7–8

The writer has such a deep impression of the low and dangerous state into which the Hebrews had sunk, that, having mentioned the name of Moses, he makes a long digression to warn them against being like their fathers and hardening themselves against Him who is so much more than Moses. From Psalm 45 he quotes what God says of Israel in the wilderness—hardening its heart against Him, so that He swore that they should not enter into His rest. The words of the quotation first point us to what is the great privilege of God's people—they hear His voice—then, to their great danger, hardening the heart against that voice. …

When God spoke to Israel, the first thing he asked of them was for a heart that did not harden itself, but that in meekness and gentleness, in tenderness and docility turned itself to listen to His voice. How much more may He claim this, now that He speaks to us in His Son. As the soil must be broken up by the plough and softened by the rain, so a broken, tender spirit is the first requisite for receiving blessing from God's word, or being in truth made partakers of God's grace. As we read in Isaiah, "*to this man will I look, even to him that is poor and of a contrite heart, and trembles at My word.*" When this disposition exists, and the thirsty heart truly waits for Divine teaching, and the circumcised ear opens to receive it, God's voice will bring real life and blessing, and be the power of living fellowship with Himself. Where it is wanting, the Word remains unfruitful, and we go backward, however much head and mouth be filled with Bible truth. Wherefore, even as the Holy Spirit says, "*Today, if you hear His voice, harden not your hearts.*"

It is not difficult to say what it is that hardens the hearts. ... When we trust too much to the intellect in religion, and very great care is not taken to take each word as from God into the heart, into its life and love, the heart gets closed to the living voice of God. The mind is satisfied with beautiful thoughts and pleasant feelings; but the heart does not hear God. When we are secretly content with our religion, our sound doctrine and Christian life, unconsciously but surely the heart gets hardened. When our life does not seek to keep pace with our knowledge, and we have more pleasure in hearing and knowing than obeying and doing, we utterly lose the meekness to which the promise is given, and, amidst all the pleasing forms of godliness, the heart is too hard to discern the voice of the Spirit. More than all, when unbelief, that walks by sight, and looks at itself and all around in the light of this world, is allowed to have its way, and the soul does not seek in childlike faith to live in the Invisible, as revealed in the Word, the heart gets so hardened that God's word never enters.

Yes, it is an unspeakably solemn thought, that with a mind occupied with religious truth, and feelings stirred at times by the voice and words of men, and a life apparently given to religious works, the heart may be closed to the humble, direct intercourse with God, and a stranger to all the blessing the living word can bring. Wherefore, *even as the Holy Spirit says*, "*Today, if you hear His voice, harden not your hearts.*"

Let all who would seek the blessing to be found in this epistle, beware of studying it simply as an inspired treatise on Divine things. Let it be to us a personal message—the voice of God speaking to us in His Son. Let us, under a sense of the spiritual mystery there is in all Divine truth, and the impotence of the human mind rightly to apprehend spiritual things, open our heart in great meekness and docility to wait on God. The whole of religion, and the whole of salvation, consists in the state of the heart. God can do nothing for us, in the way of imparting the blessings of redemption, but as He does it in the heart.

Our knowledge of the words of God will profit nothing but as the heart is opened to receive Himself to fulfill His words in us. Let our first care be, a meek and lowly heart, that waits on Him. God speaks in His Son, to the heart, and in the heart. It is in the heart that the voice and the Son of God must be received. The voice and the Word have weight according as we esteem the speaker. As we realize the glory and the majesty of God, His holiness and perfection, His love and tenderness, we shall be ready to sacrifice everything to hear what He speaks, and receive what He gives. We shall bid all the world around us, all the world within us, be silent that we may hear aright the voice of the divine Being speaking to us in the Son of His love.

Salvation will be found in these two things—God speaking to me in His Son, and my heart opening to hear His voice. It is not only in order to salvation, as a means to an end that is something different and higher, that He speaks. No, His speaking gives and is salvation, the revelation of Himself to my soul. Let the work of my life be to hearken with a meek and tender spirit. The Lord opened the heart of Lydia to give heed to the things which were spoken. This is what we need. God Himself will draw our heart away from all else, and open it to take heed. Let us ask this very earnestly.

Nothing so effectually hinders hearing God's voice as opening the heart too much to other voices. A heart too deeply interested in the news, the literature, the society of this world, cannot hear the divine voice. It needs stillness, retirement, concentration, to give God the heed that He claims.

The Son More than the Prophets

May 16th

"God, having spoken unto the fathers in the prophets … has at the end of these days spoken unto us in his Son." —HEBREWS 1: 1–2

We all know that there are two Testaments—the Old and the New. These represent two dispensations, two modes of worship, two sorts of religions, two ways in which God has intercourse with man, and man draws nigh to God. The one was provisional, preparatory, and intended to pass away. What it gave and wrought was not meant to satisfy, but only to awaken the expectation of something better that was to come. The other was the fulfillment of what had been promised, and destined to last forever, because it was itself a complete revelation of an everlasting redemption, of a salvation in the power of an endless life.

In both Old and New Testament, it was God who spoke. The prophets in the Old, and the Son in the New, were equally God's messengers. God spoke in the prophets no less truly than in the Son. But in the Old everything was external and through the mediation of men. God Himself could not yet enter and take possession of man and dwell in him. In the New all is more directly and immediately Divine—in an inward power and reality and life, of which the Old had only the shadow and hope. The Son, who is God, brings us into the very presence of God.

And wherefore was it that God did not, could not, from the very beginning, reveal Himself in the Son? What need was there of these two ways of worshiping and serving Him? The answer is twofold: If man were indeed intelligently and voluntarily to appropriate God's love and redemption, he needed to be prepared for it. He needed first of all to know his own utter impotence and hopeless wretchedness. And so his heart had to be wakened up in true desire and expectancy to welcome and value what God had to give.

When God speaks to us in Christ it is as the Father dwelling in the Son. *"The words that I say unto you, I speak not from Myself, but the Father abides in Me does the works."* Just as God's speaking in Christ was an inward thing. So God can still speak to us in no other way. The external words of Christ, just like the words of the prophets, are to prepare us for, and point us to, that inner speaking in the heart by the Holy Spirit, which alone is life and power. This is God's true speaking in His Son.

It is of the utmost consequence for our spiritual life that we should rightly understand these two stages in God's dealing with man. In two ways, not in one: not in more than two; in two ways has God spoken. They indicate what, in substance, is God's way with every Christian. There is, after our conversion, a time of preparation and testing, to see whether we willingly and heartily sacrifices all for the full blessing. If in this stage we persevere in earnest effort and striving, we will be brought to learn the two lessons the Old Testament was meant to teach. We will become more deeply conscious of our own impotence, and the strong desire will be wakened after a better life, to be found in the full revelation of Christ as able to save completely.

When these two lessons are learned—the lesson of despair of Self and hope in God alone—the soul is prepared, if it will yield itself in faith to the leading of the Holy Spirit, to enter truly into the New Testament life within the veil, in the very Holiest of All, as it is set forth in this epistle. Where Christians, through defective instruction, or through neglect and sloth, do not understand God's way for leading them on unto perfection, the Christian life will always remain full of feebleness and failure.

It was thus with the Hebrew Christians. They belonged to the New Testament, but their life was anything but the exhibition of the power and joy Christ came to reveal. They were far behind what many of the Old Testament saints had been; and the reason was this: they knew not the heavenly character of the redemption Christ had brought. They knew not the heavenly place in which He ministers, nor the heavenly blessing He dispenses, nor the heavenly power in which He secures our enjoyment of these blessings. They knew not the difference between the prophets and the Son—what it means that God has now spoken to us in His Son.

The one object of the epistle is to set before us the heavenly priesthood of Christ and the heavenly life to which He in His Divine power gives us access. It is this gives the epistle its inestimable value for all time, that it teaches us the way out of the elementary stage of the Christian life to that of full and perfect access to God.

Let us grasp and hold firmly the difference between the two stages. In the one, the action of man is more prominent: God speaks in the prophets. In the other, the Divine presence and power are more fully revealed: God speaks in the Son, who bears and brings the very life of God, and brings us into living contact with God Himself. In the one, it is the human words that occupy and influence and help us to seek God; in the other, the Divine indwelling Word reveals its power within. In the one, it is multiplicity of thoughts and truths, of ordinances and efforts; in the other, the simplicity and the unity of the one Son of God, and faith in Him alone.

How many have sought by study and meditation and acceptance of the words of the Bible to find God, and yet have failed. They knew not that these were but the finger-posts pointing to the living Son—words coming indeed from God, most needful and profitable, and yet not sufficient; only yielding us their true blessing when they have brought us to hear God Himself speaking in His Son.

In summary: 1. Let none of us rest content with the lower stage. Let us see that personal fellowship with God, through the Holy Spirit, is what Christ gives. God calls us to it: Christ lives in Heaven to work it, through the Spirit He gives from Heaven. 2. One may know much of the Bible and the words of God, and yet remain feeble. What one needs is to know the living Word, in whom God speaks within, in life and power. 3. All the prophets point to the Son, as the true Prophet. Let us take them very definitely as our teachers, to reveal God in us. 4. When I speak a word, I desire all its meaning and force to enter into him whom I address. God has in these last days but one Word. He desires to have all that Word is and means enter in and live in us. Let us open our hearts, and God will speak into it that one Word, *"This is My Son,"* in such a way that He will indeed be all our own.

An Evil Heart of Unbelief

May 17th

"Take heed, lest there shall be in any one of you an evil heart of unbelief, in falling away from the living God."
—HEBREWS 3: 12

The great practical aim of the epistle is to call us to faith. It is with this view that it will show us what a sure ground we have for it in the Word and oath of God, in the person and power of our heavenly High Priest. It will remind us how unbelief has been the cause of all falling away from God, and all failing of entrance into the enjoyment of His promise and His rest, as faith has in all ages been the one power in which God's saints have lived and worked. It has already spoken of "*holding fast our boldness and the glorying of our hope firm to the end*"; it here uses the word "believe" for the first time in the call to beware of an evil heart of unbelief.

An evil heart of unbelief. Think a moment of what the expression means. And note first the place the heart takes in religion. We have heard the warning "*Harden not your hearts*" (Hebrews 3: 7). It is in the heart God speaks, and where He longs to give His blessing. On that there followed God's complaint: "*They do always err in their heart; they did not know my ways.*" It is a heart that goes wrong that cannot know God's ways. And so here again, it is the evil heart that cannot believe, that falls away from the living God. Do let us, in our study of the epistle and in our whole religious life, beware of rejoicing in beautiful thoughts and happy feelings, while the heart, with its desire and will and love, is not wholly given up to God. In our intercourse with God, everything depends on the heart. It is with the heart man believes and receives the salvation of God.

An evil heart of unbelief. Many think and speak of unbelief as a frailty; they wish to believe, but do not feel able; their faith, they say, is too weak. And of course they have no sense of guilt or shame connected with it: not being able to do a thing is counted a sufficient excuse for not doing it. God thinks different! The Holy Spirit speaks of the evil heart of unbelief. The heart is the organ God created in man for holding fellowship with Himself. Faith is its first natural function; by faith and love it lives in God. It is the ear that hears the voice of God, the eye that can ever see Him and the unseen world; the capacity for knowing and receiving all that God can communicate. It begins as trust in the word spoken; it grows into fellowship with the Person who speaks; its fruit is the reception of all God has to bestow.

Sin turned the heart from the unseen to the seen, from God to Self, and faith in God lost the place it was meant to have, and became a faith in the visible world and its good. And now unbelief, whether avowed and definite, or more secret and unconscious, is the great mark of the evil heart, the great proof of sin, the great cause of everlasting darkness and damnation. There is no warning the professing Christian Church needs to have sounded more loudly than this one to the Hebrews: "*Take heed lest there be in any one of you an evil heart of unbelief in falling away from the living God.*"

In falling away from the living God. This is the terrible evil of unbelief; it incapacitates a man for holding fellowship with God as the living One. The expression, "The living God," occurs four times in the Epistle. In the Old Testament it contrasted God with the dead idols, who could not hear or speak or help. Alas, how often professing Christians have, instead of a graven image, the more dangerous idol of a thought-image—a conception of the mind to which they bring their worship. The living God, speaking in His Son, hearing them when they speak, working out in them His mighty salvation—the living God who loves and is loved—Him they know not. With all their Christian profession and religious exercises there is an evil heart of unbelief, in falling away from the living God.

Let us take the warning. Here we come to the deeper truth the Epistle has to teach us, let us learn well our first lesson: the one thing God looks to, the one thing we need to receive, the fullness of blessing our great High Priest has for us and waits to bestow, is a heart of faith—a true heart drawing nigh to God in fullness of faith (Hebrews 10: 23). Take heed—we ought to give more abundant heed, lest there be in any of us, even for a moment, *an evil heart of unbelief.* Let us cast out everything that can cause or can strengthen it, whether it be worldliness or formality, too little knowledge, or too much head-knowledge of God's word, too little looking to the state of our heart or too much occupation with Self; let us "*take heed, lest there be at any time in us an evil heart of unbelief.*"

Let us cast out everything that can cause or can strengthen it, whether it be worldliness or formality, too little knowledge, or too much head-knowledge of God's Word, too little looking to the state of our heart or too much occupation with Self; let us take heed lest there be at any time in us an evil heart of unbelief. Let a tender heart, hearkening to His voice, listening to and trusting His Word, ever be the sacrifice we bring Him. …

Our enjoyment of Christ, our spiritual strength and fruitfulness, our nearness to God, and our experience of His working in us, all depend, not upon single, isolated acts of faith, but upon the state of the heart. … Oh, let us above everything beware of an evil heart of unbelief.

A High Priest Able to Succor

May 18th

"For in that He himself has suffered, being tempted, He is able to succor them that are tempted."
—HEBREWS 2: 18 …

There is no way in which God can take hold of a creature other than by entering into him with His life and spirit, so imparting His own goodness and power, and bringing him into union with Himself. So did Jesus take hold of man. He entered into humanity and became one with it. And so he takes hold of individual souls by entering with each into personal union and fellowship. Wherefore, being thus minded to take hold of man, it behooved Him, it was divinely right and proper, and, in the nature of things, an absolute necessity, as a consequence of His purpose, it behooved Him in all things to be made like unto His brethren. The laying hold implied His identifying Himself with them, and this again was impossible without being made like them in all things. So only could He save them. It was indeed need full, that so He might become a merciful and a faithful High Priest in things pertaining to God, to make propitiation for the sins of the people. …

What it here seeks to press, is that Christ became Man, not merely to die and atone, but that in doing this, He might be a faithful and merciful High Priest. His relation to us was to be a personal one. He must Himself minister to us the salvation He worked out.

Everything would depend upon His winning our confidence, getting possession of our heart and love, and as a living Leader guiding us into the path to God. It is this which makes His human life on earth so precious to us. It proved Him faithful: we dare fully trust Him. It found Him merciful: we need not fear coming to Him. He was made in all things like unto His brethren, that He might become a merciful and faithful High Priest. For in that He Himself hath suffered being tempted, He is able to succor them that are tempted.

The work of our High Priest does not only consist in His atonement, nor even in the advocacy and intercession which is the fruit of that atonement. But above all, as the result of all these, in that personal charge of our spiritual life which He takes, in that never-ceasing succor which He is able to give in every temptation. This is the greatest and most blessed part of His work in bringing us to God, that, as the Leader in the path of suffering and perfection, He inspires us with His own dispositions, and, by the mighty operation of His Spirit within us, gives us His help in every time of need.

The one thing we need is, to know and trust Him fully. To know Him as High Priest who not only has opened a way to God for us to walk in, and not only in Heaven prays for us, but who undertakes to keep us so in fellowship with Himself, and under the covering of His power, and in the experience of His full redemption, that temptation can never conquer us. His divinity secures to us His unfailing and never-ceasing presence. His humanity assures us of His sympathy and compassion. More ever-present and more mighty than the temptation, His unfailing love is always near to give the victory. He can and will do it.

Our High Priest is a living, faithful helper; let us trust Him. Salvation is not a thing He gives us apart from Himself. Full salvation is nothing but Jesus Himself, most compassionately and most faithfully watching over us in daily life, most really and fully giving and living His life in us. The abiding, indwelling presence of Jesus, able to succor, is the true secret of the Christian life. Faith will lead us into the experience that Jesus is and does all that is said of Him.

The Rest in Canaan

May 19th

"And to whom did He swear that they should not enter into His rest, but to them who were disobedient?"
—HEBREWS 4: 18) …

In the opening verses of the epistle [to the Hebrews] we saw that God has two dispensations, or ways of dealing with man, and that these find their counterpart in the Christian life. There are believers who always walk in the twilight and bondage of the Old Testament; there are others, who truly know the joy and the power of the New Testament, and have fellowship with God, not as through the prophets, but truly and directly in the Son Himself. …

Of the people of Israel who came out of Egypt, they did not all enter Canaan. There came a separation among those that God had redeemed out of Egypt; some perished in the wilderness; others did indeed enter and possess the promised land. The cause of this failure to enter Canaan was, we are told, disobedience, arising out of unbelief. When God commanded them to go up and possess the land, they gave way to fear. They believed not God's promise, and were disobedient. Unbelief is ever the cause of disobedience; they could not enter in because of unbelief and disobedience.

The story has a deep spiritual significance, and teaches a lesson of great solemnity. In our chapter we have twice heard already that it is not enough to begin well; we must hold fast to the end. Of the people of Israel, we read, *"By faith they kept the Passover and the sprinkling of the blood; by faith they passed through the Red Sea."* There was the initial faith to go up out of Egypt, but when they were tested to see if they would hold fast the beginning of their confidence firm unto the end, the great majority failed. Their faith was but for a time: they had faith to go out of Egypt; they had not faith to enter Canaan.

Among the Hebrews there were Christians who were in the same state. They had begun well, but had been hindered. Some were standing still; some had already turned back. And even so there are many Christians in our churches who never come farther than the initial faith of conversion. They say they know God has saved them from Egypt. They rest content with the thought of having been converted. There is no hearty desire, no earnest purpose to press on to a life of holiness, no readiness at any sacrifice to go up into the promised land of rest and of victory.

When Israel was about to enter the land of Canaan, Moses used the words: "*He brought us out from thence, that He might bring us in to give us the land.*" It is to be feared that there are many Christians who tear asunder what God has joined together. They would fain be brought out from the land of bondage; they are not ready to go all the length with God, to enter the land and conquer every enemy. They would fain be made happy in being delivered from bondage; they long not to be made holy in a life of separation and service.

To the voice that calls to enter into God's rest they hearken not, but harden their hearts. It was not in Egypt—let us note this well—it was on the very borders of Canaan that the people of God had begun to save hardened their hearts. It is among Christians who profess conversion, who have not only begun the Christian life, but even made some progress in it, that the hardening of the heart is now still found. The call to holiness, the call to cease from the life of wandering and murmuring, and enter into the rest of God, the call to the life of victory over every enemy and to the service of God in the land of promise, is not obeyed. They say it is too high and too hard. They do not believe with Caleb, "*We are well able to possess the land*"; they fear the sacrifice and cling to the carnal life; in not hearkening to God's voice their heart is hardened. God has sworn, they shall not enter into His rest.

I cannot with too much earnestness urge every Christian reader to learn well the two stages of the Christian. There are the carnal, and there are the spiritual; there are those who remain babes, and those who are full-grown men. There are those who come up out of Egypt, but then remain in the wilderness of a worldly life; there are those who follow the Lord fully, and enter the [Canaan] life of rest and victory. Let each of us find out where we stand, and taking earnest heed to God's warnings, with our whole heart press on to go all the length in following Jesus, in seeking to stand perfect and complete in all the will of God.

... No teaching of what Christ is can profit, unless our hearts are longing and ready to follow Him fully. The epistle will sum up all its teachings in its call to enter into the Holiest of All, into the rest of God. But it wants us to feel deeply that there can be no entering in, except in the path of faith and full obedience, except with a heart that is ready to forsake all its own will, to follow Him who bore the cross, a heart that will be content with nothing less than all that God is willing to give.

They were not able to enter in because of unbelief. Take heed, lest there be in any of you an evil heart of unbelief. Everything depends upon faith. At each step in the teaching of our epistle, let faith be exercised. Faith in the God who speaks to us: faith in the blessed Son, in the Divine power and all-pervading nearness in which He works, in His true humanity, and the heavenly life He perfected for us and imparts from heaven; faith in the Holy Spirit who dwells within us, and is God's power working in us. Let faith be the habit of our soul—the every breath of our life. ...

Let us cultivate the deep conviction that the root of all disobedience and failure, of all weariness and trouble in the spiritual life, is unbelief. Let us not think that there is some inexplicable mystery about our prayers not being heard; it is simply unbelief that will not trust God, will not yield itself wholly to God, will not allow God to do what He promises. God save us from unbelief!

Exhort One Another Day by Day

May 20th

"Exhort one another day by day … lest anyone of you be hardened by the deceitfulness of sin.
—HEBREWS 3: 13

In the previous verse we read, "*Take heed lest there be in any one of you an evil heart of unbelief.*" That is not only, let each one look to himself, but let all look to it that there be not in any one of you the evil unbelieving heart. The Church is one body; the sickness of one member is a danger to the whole body. Each one must live to care for those around him. Each member is entrusted by Christ to the love and care of his brethren, and is dependent on their help. Believers who are joined together in one house, in a neighborhood, in a church, are responsible for one another; they must take heed that there be not in anyone the unbelief that falls away from God. They are called to help and encourage each other so that all may at all times continue steadfast in the faith.

We spoke of the painful fact that in so many cases the first boldness and joy of hope is not held fast firm to the end. Here is one cause. There is not the care and help for each other which the Lord intended. In caring only for ourselves, our brothers and sisters not only suffer, but we lose much ourselves. The healthy life of the individual member is dependent on the life around us, and on the part he takes in maintaining that life. The warning has a deeper significance than we think: "*Take heed lest there be in any one of you an evil heart of unbelief.*"

It is this thought our text seeks to enforce: But exhort one another day by day, lest anyone of you be hardened by the deceitfulness of sin. Christians are bound to exhort one another; it is their duty and their right. It is implied in the whole constitution of the body of Christ, that the members care for one another. Its life is entirely dependent on the Spirit of Christ, who pleased not Himself, and that Spirit is a love that seeks not its own, but has its very being in loving and blessing others. As each member humbly yields him or herself to be helped and to help, the safety and the vigor of all will be secured. The communion of saints in all our Church circles must be proved in the cultivation of a practical ministering love and care for each other.

Exhort one another day by day, so long as it is called Today. We saw what solemn meaning there was in the Holy Spirit's call, Today, if you hear His voice. We sought to apply that personally. Mere we are taught that all the urgency that call implies must by each one of us be applied to our neighbor as well as ourselves. We must think of the danger of delay, of the time when it will be no longer Today for those around us, who are forgetting it, and exhort them day by day. … we need. Day by day. The work is slow, and must be done unceasingly, "*so long as it is called Today*." The Spirit of Jesus can give us grace and patience and faith to persevere. "*In due time we shall reap if we faint not.*"

Day by day. This word of the Holy Spirit is the complement of that other, Today. The Today of the Holy Spirit must day by day be afresh accepted and obeyed. It is only as we are ready, every day without one exception, to live fully in the obedience to the voice of God and the faith of Jesus, that our life can grow. What has once, or for a time, been done, will not avail; day by day, our fellowship with Jesus, our consecration to Him, our service for Him, must be renewed. So shall we in our care for others, as much as in our personal walk, hold fast our boldness firm to the end.

"*Exhort one another, lest anyone of you be hardened by the deceitfulness of sin.*" We heard the warning, "*Harden not your hearts.*" Here is its exposition, "*hardened by the deceitfulness of sin.*" All sin is deceit, its promised pleasures are all a lie. But there are some sins that are open and unmistakable. There are others that are especially deceptive. Where the sanction of the Christian world, or the force of habit and custom, or the apparent insignificance of what we do, makes us think little of the sin, it has a terrible power to deceive the professing Christian. And through this deceitfulness of sin, be it worldliness, or unlovingness, or pride, or want of integrity, hearts are hardened, and become incapable of hearing the voice of God.

What a call to all who are awake to their own danger to listen, "*Exhort one another day by day, lest anyone of you be hardened through the deceitfulness of sin.*" Let me press upon everyone who would study this Epistle, the solemn obligation resting upon him to care for those around him—not only the outcast, but those with whom he is associated in church fellowship, very especially any who are in danger of being hardened through the deceitfulness of sin. …

And if we would know where the grace for this work is to be found, the answer is not far to seek. It is in Jesus Christ our Head and in His love shed abroad in our hearts. As in this Epistle we study the compassion of Jesus, as our High Priest and Leader, let us believe that He makes us partakers of His Spirit. He forms us in His own likeness. He leads us in His footsteps. He makes each of us what He was, a Priest with a priestly heart ready to live and die for those around us. Therefore, brethren, exhort one another day by day.

Partakers of Christ

May 21st

"For we are partakers of Christ, if we hold fast the beginning of our confidence firm unto the end."

—HEBREWS 3: 14–15 …

Just as truly as Christ became partaker of flesh and blood we become partakers of Christ. In partaking with us of flesh and blood, Christ entered into perfect fellowship with us in all we were, our life and our death became His. When we become partakers of Christ, we enter into perfect fellowship with Him in all He was and is; His death and His life become ours.

"*We are partakers of Christ!*" What a mystery! What a treasure! What a blessedness! The whole object of the epistle is to show what there is in the Christ of whom we are become partakers, and what He can do for us. But here at the outset, amid needful words of remonstrance against giving way to sloth or unbelief, believers are reminded of what their portion and possession is: they *are partakers of Christ.*

There is often danger, as we listen to the teaching of Scripture about Christ as our High Priest, of regarding Him as an outward person, and His work as something that is done outwardly for us in Heaven. This precious word reminds us that our salvation consists in the possession of Himself, in the being one life with Him, in having Himself as our own. Christ can do nothing for us but as an inward Savior. Himself being our life, personally dwelling and working in us. …

Since Christ became partaker of flesh and blood, He is known, and will be to all eternity, even upon the throne, as the Son of Man. No less will we, when we truly become partakers of Christ, be known, even now and to all eternity, as one with Christ on the throne of glory. Oh, let us know ourselves as God knows us: *partakers of Christ.*

It is the one thing God desires. When God set forth His only begotten Son as the only possible way of access to Himself, it meant that He can delight in or have fellowship with nothing in which the likeness of His Son is not to be seen. We can have no farther entrance into God's favor or good pleasure than He can see Christ in us. If God has called us to the fellowship of His Son, and made us participators of all there is in Christ, the sonship, and the love, and the Spirit of the Father, let us live worthy of our privilege—let us live as men who have— oh the riches of the grace!—have become partakers of Christ!

And how can we know in full assurance that it is so, and ever rejoice in the blessed consciousness of all it implies? Just as it was said before, where our blessed relation to Christ was set forth in another aspect, we are His house, if we hold fast our boldness and the glorying of our hope firm unto the end, so we have the answer here again: "*We are partakers of Christ, if we hold fast the beginning of our confidence firm unto the end.*" The beginning of our confidence must be held fast.

We must not, as many think, begin with faith, and continue with works. No, the confidence with which we began must be held fast firm to the end. We must see that when we are made partakers of Christ, that includes all, and that as at first, so all the way unto the end, we can receive out of Christ only by faith and according to our faith. Apart from faith receiving Christ's strength, our works avail not. God works nothing but through Christ, and it is as by faith we live in our riches in Christ that God can work into us all there is in Him for us. …

For we are … partakers of Christ, if we hold fast to the end. Our perseverance will be the seal of our being partaker of Christ. The faith by which, at conversion, we know at once that we have Christ, grows clearer and brighter, and more mightily effectual in opening up the treasures of Christ, as we hold it fa.st firm unto the end. Persevering faith is the witness that we have Christ, because through it Christ exercises His keeping and perfecting power.

Would you enjoy the full assurance and the full experience that you are a partaker of Christ? It is alone to be found each day in the living fellowship with Christ. Christ is a living person, He can be known and enjoyed only in a living personal intercourse. Christ is my Leader; I must cling to Him, I must follow Him, in His leading. Christ is my High Priest; I must let Him lift me into God's presence. Christ is the living Son of God, our life; I must live Him. I am His house; I can only know Him as Son in His house as I yield myself to His indwelling.

The Rest of God

May 22nd

"Let us fear therefore, lest haply, a promise being left us of entering into His rest, any of you should seem to have come short of it."

—HEBREWS 4:1

It is as faith sees that the creature was destined to find its rest nowhere but in the Creator, and that in the entire surrender to Him, to His will and His working, it may have perfect rest, that it dares to cast itself upon God, and have no care. … Hearkening to the loving offer, it forsakes all to find its dwelling-place in God and His love. Faith sees what the rest of God is; faith believes that it may come and share in it; faith enters in and rests, it yields itself to Jesus to lead it in and make it partaker. Because it honors God and counts Him all, God honors it; He opens the door, and the soul is brought in to His rest. …

It is the finished work of Jesus that is ever set before us in the Epistle as the ground of our faith, the call for us in fullness of faith to draw nigh and enter in and rest. Because Christ has put away sin, has rent the veil, and is set down on the right hand of the throne—because all is finished and perfected, and we have received the Holy Spirit from Heaven in our hearts to make us the partakers of that glorified Christ—we may with confidence, with boldness, rest in Him to maintain and perfect His work in us. And, resting in Him, He becomes our Joshua, perfecting our faith, bringing us in, and giving us a home in the rest of God with Himself, now to go no more out forever.

And if you would know why so few Christians enjoy this rest, it is because they do not know Jesus as their Joshua. … There are two stages in Christian knowledge and experience. All the feebleness of our Christian life is owing to one thing: we do not know Jesus in heaven; we do not know that Jesus has entered in for us (6: 20; 9: 12, 14), and that this secures for us boldness and the power of entrance into a heavenly state of life; that He there sits upon the throne as our High Priest in power, maintaining in us His own heavenly life; keeping us in personal fellowship with the living Father, so that in Him we too enter the rest of God. It is because we do not know Jesus in His heavenly life and power that our life is feeble; if we learn to know Him as He is to be revealed in this epistle, as our heavenly Joshua, actually bringing us and our inmost nature into the rest of God, we cannot but enter into that rest. When Joshua went before, the people followed at once in fellowship with him. Entering the rest of God is a personal practical experience of the soul that receives the Word in living faith, because in it, we receive Jesus on the throne.

Let us do what Israel did in crossing Jordan; they allowed Joshua to bring them in; they followed him. Let us follow Jesus in the path He trod. In Heaven God's will is all. On earth Jesus made that will all. He lived in the will of God, in suffering and doing, in meeting trial, in waiting for the Father's guidance; in giving up everything to it. He proved that God's will was His path. Follow Him. Yield yourself, in the death to Self, to the will of God; have faith in Jesus on the throne, as your Head and life, that He has brought you in and will make it true in your experience; trust Jesus, as being partaker of His nature and life, to work all in you that the Father seeks; and you shall know how blessed it is to enter the rest of God.

Deep restfulness, even amid outward activity, is one of the most beautiful marks and aids of the life of faith. Cultivate that holy stillness that seeks to abide in God's presence, and does not yield too much to things around. This rest is God's rest: it is found in His fellowship. Think of all He sees, of all He feels, and has to bear; think of the Divine peace and patience with which He guides all; and learn to be patient and trustful, and to rest in Him. Believe in Him, as the one God who works all in all, and works in you that which is well-pleasing in His sight, and you shall have perfect rest in letting Him do all for you and in you. God is a supernatural, incomprehensible Being; we must learn to know Him in a way that is above reason and sense. That way is the adoration of faith, and the deep humility of obedience. Through these the Holy Spirit will work the work of God in us.

The Rest of Faith

May 23rd

"Let us fear therefore, lest haply, a promise being left us of entering into His rest, any of you should seem to have come short of it."

—HEBREWS 4: 1

We have seen that with Israel, after its deliverance from Egypt, there were two stages. The one, the life in the wilderness, with its wanderings and its wants, its unbelief and its murmurings, its provocation of God and its exclusion from the promised rest. The other, the land of promise, with rest instead of the desert wanderings, with abundance instead of want, and the victory over every enemy instead of defeat.

These are the symbols of the two stages in the Christian life. The one in which we only know the Lord as the Savior from Egypt, in His work on the cross for atonement and pardon. The other, where He is known and welcomed as the glorified Priest-King in Heaven, who, in the power of the endless life, sanctifies and saves completely, writes

God's laws in the heart, and leads us to find our home in the holiest of God's presence. The aim of the writer in this whole section is to warn us not to rest content with the former, the preparatory stage, but to show all diligence to reach the second, and enter the promised rest of complete deliverance. "*Let us fear, therefore, lest haply, a promise being left of entering into His rest, any of you should come short of it.*"

Some think that the rest of Canaan is the type of Heaven. This cannot be, because the great mark of the Canaan life was that the land had to be conquered and that God gave such glorious victory over enemies. The rest of Canaan was for victory and through victory. And so it is in the life of faith, when a soul learns to trust God for victory over sin, and yields itself entirely, as to its circumstances and duties, to live just where and how He wills, that it enters the rest. It lives in the promise, in the will, in the power of God. This is the rest into which it enters, not through death, but through faith, or rather, not through the death of the body, but the death to Self in the death of Christ through faith.

The one reason why they did not enter Canaan was their unbelief. The land was waiting: the rest was provided; God Himself would bring them in and give them rest. One thing was lacking; they did not believe, and so did not yield themselves to God to do it for them what He had promised. Unbelief closes the heart against God, withdraws the life from God's power; in the very nature of things unbelief renders the Word of promise of none effect. A gospel of rest is preached to us as it was to them. We have in Scripture the most precious assurances of a rest for the soul to be found under the yoke of Jesus, of a peace of God which passes all understanding, of a peace and a joy in the soul which nothing can take away. But when they are not believed they cannot be enjoyed: faith is in its very nature a resting in the promise and the Promiser until He fulfills it in us. Only faith can enter into rest. The fullness of faith enters into the full rest. …

"Today," now and here, we who have believed do enter into rest. It is with the rest of faith here as with what we heard of being partakers of Christ—the blessing is enjoyed, if we hold fast the beginning of our confidence firm unto the end. The initial faith, that passes out of Egypt through the Red Sea, must be held fast firm, then it comes to the fullness of faith that passes through Jordan into the land.

Let every student of this Epistle realize how intensely personal its tone is, and with what urgency it appeals to us for faith, as the one thing needful in our dealings with the Word of God. Without this the Word cannot profit us. We may seek by thought and study to enter into the meaning of the promise: God has sworn that we never shall enter into its possession, or into His rest, but by faith. The one thing God asks in our intercourse with Him and His Word is the habit of faith, that ever keeps the heart open towards God, and longs to enter in and abide in His rest. It is the soul that thirsts for God, for the living God, that will have the spiritual capacity for receiving the revelation of how Jesus, the High Priest, brings us into God's presence.

… Would you enter into the rest? Remember what has been taught us of the two stages. They are represented by Moses and Joshua. Moses the leader, Joshua the perfecter or finisher of the faith of Israel. Moses brought the people out: Joshua brought them in.

Accept Jesus as your Joshua. Let past failure and wandering and sin not cause either despair or contentment with what you are. Trust Jesus who, through the sprinkling of the blood, brought you out of Egypt, to bring you as definitely into the rest. Faith is always repose in what another will do for me. Faith ceases to seek help in itself or its efforts, to be troubled with its need or its weakness; it rests in the sufficiency of the all-sufficient One who has undertaken all. Trust Jesus. Give up and forsake the wilderness. Follow Him fully. *He is the rest.*

Rest from Works

May 24th

"There remains therefore a Sabbath rest for the people of God."
—HEBREWS 4: 9

In God we see, as it were, two distinct stages in His relation to His work. The first was that of creation. … The second, His rest when creation was finished, and He rejoiced in what He had made, now to begin the higher work of watching the development of the life He had entrusted the creature with, and securing its sanctification and perfection. It is a rest from work which is now finished, for higher work now to be carried on.

Even so, there are the two stages in the Christian life. The one in which, after conversion, we seek to work what God would have us do. The second, in which, after many a painful failure, we cease from our works, and enter the rest of God, there to find the power for work in allowing God to work in us.

It is this resting from their own work which many Christians cannot understand. They think of it as a state of passive and Selfish enjoyment, of still contemplation which leads to the neglect of the duties of life, and unfits for that watchfulness and warfare to which Scripture calls. What an entire misunderstanding of God's call to rest. As the Almighty, God is the only source of power: In nature He works all; in grace He waits to work all too, if we will but consent and allow. Truly to rest in God is to yield oneself up to the highest activity. We work, because He works in us to will and to do. As Paul says of himself, "*I labor, striving according to His working who works in me with might.*" … Entering the rest of God is the ceasing from Self-effort, and the yielding up oneself in the full surrender of faith to God's working.

How many Christians are there who need nothing so much as rightly to apprehend this word! Their life is one of earnest effort and ceaseless struggling. They do long to do God's will, and to live to His glory. Continued failure and bitter disappointment is their too frequent experience. Very often as the result they give themselves up to a feeling of hopelessness: it never will be otherwise. Theirs is truly the wilderness life; they have not entered into God's rest. Would that God might open their eyes, and show them Jesus as our Joshua, who has entered into God's presence, who sits upon the throne as High Priest, bringing us in living union with Himself into that place of rest and of love, and, by His

Spirit within us, making that life of Heaven a reality and an experience.

We who have entered into rest, have also rested from our works, as God did from His. And how does one rest and cease from works? It is by ceasing from Self. It is the old Self-life that always insists upon proving its goodness and its strength, and presses forward to do the works of God. It is only in death that we rest from our works. Jesus entered His rest through death; each one whom He leads into it must pass through death. *Reckon yourself to be indeed dead unto sin, and alive unto God in Christ Jesus our Lord."* Believe that the death of Christ, as an accomplished fact, with all that it means and has effected, is working in you in all its power.

You are dead with Him and in Him. Consent to this, and cease from dead works. "*Blessed are the dead that die in the Lord. Yea, says the Spirit, for they do rest from their labors.*" That is as true of spiritual dying with Christ as of the death in the body. To sinful nature there is no rest from work but through death. We who have entered into rest have rested from our works. The ceasing from our works and the entering the rest of God go together. Read the first chapter of Joshua, and hear God's words of strength and encouragement to everyone who would enter. Exchange the wilderness life with your own works for the rest-life in which God works. Fear not to believe that Jesus came to give it, and that it is for you.

Not I, but Christ. This is the rest of faith in which we rest from our works. With the unconverted, it is, *Not Christ, but I.* With the feeble and slothful Christian, *I and Christ*: I first, and Christ to fill up what is wanting. With increasing earnestness it becomes, *Christ and I*: Christ first, but still I second. But, with us who die with Christ it is, *Not I, but Christ*: Christ alone and Christ all. We have ceased from our work: Christ lives in us. This is the rest of faith. …

Give Diligence to Enter into the Rest

May 25th

"Let us therefore give diligence to enter into that rest."

—HEBREWS 4: 11

Let us give diligence. The word means, make haste; be in earnest; put your whole heart into it; see that you do it. The danger is imminent; the loss will be terrible. God has sworn in His wrath that unless we hearken and obey, we shall not enter His rest. Let us give diligence to enter in. All the wonderful teaching the epistle contains farther on, as to the Holiest that is opened for us as the place where God wants to receive us into His rest and live, as to the great High Priest who has opened the way and entered in and lives as our Joshua to bring us in, will profit us nothing, unless there be the earnest desire, the willing readiness, the firm resolve, to enter in. It is this disposition alone that can fit a man spiritually to apprehend the heavenly mysteries the epistle opens up.

And surely it ought not to be needful to press the motives that should urge us to obedience. Ought not the one motive to suffice? The unspeakable privilege God offers me in opening to me the entrance into His own rest. No words can express the inconceivable greatness of the gift. God speaks to me in His Son as one who was created in His image, capable of fellowship with Himself; as one whom He has redeemed out of the awful captivity of sin and death, because He longs to have me living with Him in His love, as one for whom He has made it possible to live the outer life in the flesh, with the inner life in Christ, lifted up, kept safe in the Holiest of All, in God's own rest. Oh, can it be that anyone believes this and does not respond? No, let each heart say: "Blessed be God; into this rest would I enter; here would I dwell."

We are so accustomed to the wilderness life of stumbling and sinning, we have so learned to take the words God speaks of that life—"*They do always err in their heart*"— as description of what must be daily Christian experience, that we hardly count it a practical possibility to enter into the rest. And even when the desire has been awakened, the path appears so dark and unknown. Let me for the sake of such once again gather up what has been said as to the way to enter in: it may be God, of His great mercy, may help some to take the step. First, settle it in your mind, believe with your whole heart that there is such a rest, today. It is God's rest, in which He lives; into which Jesus, as your Joshua, has entered. It is your rest, prepared for you; your land of promise; the spiritual state of life which is as surely yours as Jesus is; into which Jesus will bring you, and where He will keep you. It is the rest in which you can live every hour, free from care and anxiety, free from weariness and wanderings, always resting in the rest that trusts God for all. Believe this.

Then cease from your own works. Not as if you had to attain this perfectly before entering into God's rest. No, but consent, yield, be willing that all Self-working should come to an end. Cease from Self. Where there is life there is action; the Self-life will seek to work, except you give up Self into the death of Christ; with Him you are buried, in Him you live. As Christ said, "*Hate your own life, lose it.*" Cease from your own works, and bow in deep humility and helplessness, as nothing before God.

Trust Jesus as your Joshua, who brings you in, even now. Israel had simply to trust and obey and follow Joshua. Set your heart on Him who has entered the heavens to appear before God for us. Claim Jesus as yours, not only in His cross and death and resurrection, but above all in His heavenliness, in His possession of the rest of heaven. Claim Him, and leave Him to do His blessed work. You need not understand all. Your feelings may not be what you would wish. Trust Him, who has done all for you in earth and heaven, to do all in your heart too.

And then be a follower of them who through faith and patience have inherited the promises. Israel passed in one day through Jordan into Canaan, but did not in one day come to the perfect rest. It is at the end of the life of Joshua we read, "*The Lord gave them rest round about.*" Enter today into the rest. Though all may not be bright at once, look to Jesus, your Joshua, and leave all in His hands. Come away out of Self, and live in Him. Rest in God whatever happens. Think of His Rest, and Jesus who has entered it in your name, and out of it fills you with its Spirit, and fear not. Today, if you hear His voice, enter in.

Jesus said, *"Take My yoke upon you, and learn of Me, for I am meek and lowly in heart, and you shall find rest for your souls."* It was through meekness and lowliness of heart that Jesus found His rest in God. He allowed God to be all, trusted God for all; the rest of God was His abode. He invites us to share His rest, and tells us the secret: In the meekness and lowliness of Jesus is the way to the rest. …

The High Priest: Perfected Through Obedience

May 26th

"Though he was a Son, yet learned obedience by the things which He suffered; And having been made perfect, he became unto all them that obey him, the cause of eternal salvation."

—HEBREWS 5: 8–9

Our Lord Jesus learned obedience by the things which He suffered. Through this obedience He was made perfect, and became the cause of eternal salvation to all that obey Him. So he entered heaven as our High Priest, a Son, perfected for evermore.

The word perfect is one of the keywords of the Epistle. It occurs thirteen times. Four times in regard to the Old Testament, which could make nothing perfect. "*The law made nothing perfect*" (7: 19). "*Sacrifices that cannot, as touching the conscience, make the worshipper perfect*" (9: 9). "*The law can never make perfect them that draw nigh*" (10: 1). "*Apart from us they should not be made perfect*" (11: 40).

As great as is the difference between a promise and its fulfillment, or hope and the thing hoped for, between the shadow and substance, is the difference between the Old and New Testament. The law made nothing perfect: it was only meant to point to something better, to the perfection Jesus Christ was to bring.

With the New Testament perfection would come. Thrice the word is used of our Lord Jesus, who in Himself prepared and wrought out the perfection He came to impart. "*It became God to make the Leader of our salvation perfect through suffering*" (2: 2). "*He learned obedience, and being made perfect, became the cause of salvation*" (5: 9). "*Appointed High Priest; a Son perfected for evermore*" (7: 28).

The perfection brought by Christ was that which was revealed in His own personal life. He came to restore to us the life of God we had lost—a life in the will and love of God. This alone is salvation. God perfected Him through suffering—wrought out in Him a perfect human character, in which the divine life was fully united with the human will. He learned obedience through suffering, and manifested perfectly the humility and submission and surrender to God, which is man's duty and blessedness. So, when He had been perfected, He became the author of eternal salvation to all who obey Him, because He now had that perfected human nature which He could communicate to them. And so "*He was appointed High Priest—a Son, perfected for evermore.*"

As Son of God, He was to take us up into the very life of God; as High Priest, He was to lift us, in actual spiritual reality, into God's fellowship and will and presence; the way in which He was perfected through obedience was the living way in which He was to lead us—as the Son, perfected through obedience, who had found and opened and walked the path of obedience as the path to God, and would animate us with His own Spirit to do it too. He, the perfected One, can alone be our salvation.

Then twice we have the word of what Christ has done for us. "*By one offering He has perfected forever them that are sanctified*" (10:14); "*the Leader and Perfecter of our faith*" (12: 2). Christ's perfecting us forever is nothing but His redeeming us by His one sacrifice into the perfect possession of Himself, the perfected One, as our life. His death is our death to sin, His resurrection as the perfected One is our life, His righteousness is ours, His life ours; we are put in possession of all the perfection which the Father wrought out in Him through suffering and obedience. And once of the spiritual sanctuary opened by Christ: The greater and more perfect tabernacle not made with hands (9: 2). And three times it is used in regard to Christian character: Solid food is for the perfect (5: 14); "*Let us press on to perfection*" (6: 1); "*The God of peace perfect you in every good thing*" (13: 21).

The perfect for whom the solid food is, are those who are not content with the mere beginnings of the Christian life, but have given themselves wholly to accept and follow the perfected Master. These are they who press on to perfection—nothing else than the perfection which Christ revealed, as God's claim on men, and as what He has won and made possible for them.

He learned obedience, and being perfected, became the cause of eternal salvation. The perfection of God is His will. There is no perfection for man but in union with that will. And there is no way for attaining and proving the union with that will but by obedience. Obedience to the good and perfect will of God transforms the whole nature, and makes it capable of union with Him in glory.

Obedience to God's will on earth is the way to the glory of God's will in Heaven. The everlasting perfection of Heaven is nothing but the obedience of earth transfigured and glorified. Obedience is the seed, the power, the life of Christ's perfection and ours. . . . The distinguishing mark of the earthly life of our High Priest; the source of His heavenly glory and His eternal salvation; the power of His atonement of our disobedience; the opening of the living way in which we are to follow Him our Leader; the inner disposition and spirit of the life He bestows—oh, all this, the secret is obedience. Through obedience He was perfected, His sacrifice was perfect, He perfected us forever, He carries us on to perfection.

When the perfect heavenly life of the Lord Jesus comes down from Heaven into our hearts, it can assume no form but that which it had in Him—obedience. God must be obeyed: in that one word you have the key to the life and death of Jesus, His sitting at God's right hand, His priesthood, His dwelling in our hearts, as well as to the whole of the gospel message—God must be obeyed. Christ, the obedient One, who inaugurated for us the new way of obedience unto death as the way to God.

Is this the Christ you love and trust? Is this your delight in Him, that He now has delivered you from thy disobedience, and makes you strong to live only to obey God and Him? Is Christ precious to you because the salvation He gives is a restoration to obedience?

The Danger of Neglecting So Great Salvation

May 27th

"How shall we escape, if we neglect so great salvation?

—HEBREWS 2: 3

Therefore we ought to give more earnest heed to the things that were heard lest haply we drift away. … How shall we escape, if we neglect so great salvation? which having at the first been spoken through the Lord, was confirmed unto us by them that heard; God also bearing witness with them, both by signs and wonders, and by manifold powers, and by gifts of the Holy Spirit, according to his own will (Hebrews 2: 1–4).

The first chapter has set before us the divine glory of Christ the Son, in whom God hath spoken to us in these days. In the second the humanity and the humiliation of Jesus are to be unfolded. Ere the writer proceeds to this; he pauses to sound a note of warning: He reminds his readers of the greater responsibility and greater danger in case of neglect, which greater privileges bring, and to urge them to take more earnest, more abundant heed to what God is speaking in His Son.

Therefore, this is the link between the teaching of chapter 1 with regard to the Godhead and glory of the Son, and the warning that now comes. The everlasting God speaks to us in His Son; we surely ought to give more abundant heed.

"*More abundant heed*"; it is the same word as is used in chapter 6: 17. "*God being minded to shew more abundantly unto the heirs of the promise, the immutability of His counsel.*" In what God speaks and does, it is all with the desire to show to us more abundantly, in full and overflowing measure, what the purpose of His heart is. It is for this He speaks in none less than His own Son. He has a right to claim that we meet Him with a corresponding wholeheartedness, and give more abundant heed to what He speaks. Nothing less will satisfy Him; nothing less, in the very nature of things, will satisfy us, because nothing less than our more abundant heed is capable of receiving God's more abundant grace.

It is the lack of this taking more earnest heed, the lack of intense earnestness, giving God and religion the first place and the best powers of our life, which is at the root of the feebleness and sickliness of the Christian life. God is speaking to us in His Son, therefore we ought to take more abundant heed.

"*Lest haply we drift away—and perish more surely and more terribly than those who sinned under the Old Testament.*" There the word spoken, with its threatening, was steadfast, and every transgression was punished. "*How shall we escape, if we neglect so great salvation?*" The gospel does not, as so many think, lessen—it increases our danger. It does not diminish, but will terribly intensify, the soreness of the punishment in those who neglect it. Oh, let us sound out the warning: it is not only positive enmity or open sin that will be punished. No, simply "not taking earnest heed"; just "drifting away" unconsciously with the current of worldliness and half-hearted religion, "neglecting" to give the great salvation that supremacy, that entire devotion which it claims, it is this which will render escape impossible.

And why? How can we show others that it is right and meet that it should be so? And what is the motive that will stir men to take heed? The answer is in the one word: "*So great salvation.*" The insight into the more abundant glory, the divine, the all-surpassing greatness of this salvation, is what will compel men willingly and joyfully to give up all and buy this pearl of great price.

And wherein does the greatness of this salvation consist? In this that it comes to us from and through the triune God; the Holy Trinity is revealed as combining to work out this salvation for us. Listen: "*So great salvation, which having at the first been spoken by the Lord, was confirmed unto us by them that heard*"; Christ the Son, the brightness of the Father's glory, and the express image of His substance, it was He in whom God spoke to us; it was He, the Redeemer, God and King, who Himself first preached the kingdom which He established when He effected the cleansing of our sins, and sat down on the right hand of the throne. …

"*God also bearing witness, by distributions of the Holy Spirit, according to His own will.*" Not only did God bear witness to the great salvation by signs and wonders and powers, but above all by the Holy Spirit sent down from Heaven. The Holy Spirit is God come to dwell on earth, to strive and plead and testify in the hearts of men. There is no fellowship with the Father but through the Son, and no fellowship with the Son and His salvation, but through the Holy Spirit in us. Let us enter the study of Christ's person and work in the Epistle in this faith. Yes, this is the greatness of the great salvation; in its offer the three-one God comes to us: The Lord preached, the Father bore witness, the Holy Spirit came as the power of God to work. What a salvation! What sin to neglect it! May God reveal to us, as we study this Epistle, the glory of the so great salvation, that we may indeed more abundantly take heed to it.

To know the Son who speaks and reveals the Father; to know the Father to whom, and whose love, the Son brings us in; to know the Holy Spirit with His wonderful gifts of grace and power; to be restored to the image and fellowship of the Holy Trinity: this is salvation. Let every thought of the glory of Christ, and of God, and of the Spirit, and of the great salvation leave this one impression: Take more abundant heed to what you hear! Meet God's abounding grace with abounding desire to listen and believe. …

Once again. This is the greatness of salvation; the everlasting Father in His love speaks to me Himself in the Son. The Son shows and brings and gives me all the Father speaks; and I have the Holy Spirit in me, fitting me to hear and know and possess and enjoy all that the Father in the Son speaks and gives. Let us, above all, hold this fast that there is no divine witness, or assurance, or experience of the salvation Christ effected, except as the Holy Spirit, which came from Heaven, communicates and maintains it within us. Let us, therefore, take more abundant heed to the Holy Spirit in us, in whom the Father and the Son come to us.

The Leader of Our Salvation

May 28th

"For it became Him, for whom are all things, and through whom are all things, in bringing many sons unto glory, to make the author of their salvation perfect through sufferings.'

—HEBREWS 2: 10

We have seen that there is more than one reason for the humiliation of the Lord Jesus, even unto the suffering of death. Here we have the first: that as the Leader of our salvation, through whom God leads His sons to glory, He might open up the path, the way of life, in which we were to go. For this He needed to be made perfect through suffering and death. So only could He become a Leader, in the true and full sense of the word. In suffering, His will was perfected, His character fashioned, His dependence on God and delight in His will was confirmed and made manifest. In suffering, His obedience unto death opened up the living way in which alone the creature can reach the Creator the deepest humility and entire surrender. As Leader He opened up the path of life, a mode of living and acting, in which we are to follow.

It is this that we also spoke of as the second aspect of Christ's death. That death is not only atonement but fellowship. It is only in suffering, in being crucified and dead with Christ, that we know Christ and His salvation. Christ was made perfect through suffering that He might be a Leader, that in conformity to Him, and in partaking of His Spirit and likeness, we might find the path to God and to glory.

The work of a leader supposes three things. The first: He must Himself lead the way, passing through all its difficulties and dangers, knowing and showing it to those who follow. The second: those who follow must yield themselves wholly to His guidance, walking even as He walked. The third: He must take charge of His followers, seeing that all hindrances are removed, and providing for all their needs. Let us see how blessedly all this is fulfilled in Jesus, and what a comfort it brings us to know that Jesus bears this name too: the Leader of our salvation.

The leader must walk in the very path his followers have to go. The path we sought in vain was one that could bring us out from under the dominion of sin, both in its guilt as transgression against God, and its power as death to all that is holy and good. There was no possible way out of this state of sin and guilt and death, but by the submission to the judgment of God, and by giving proof, in bearing that judgment, of entire and willing surrender to God's will. There was no way to come out of fallen nature, with the power of Self and Self-will ruling it, but by entirely dying to it; suffering anything rather than let it have its way. This was the way in which Jesus would have to lead us. And He had to walk in it Himself.

"*It became God, in leading many sons unto glory, to make the Leader of their salvation perfect through suffering.*" Christ was perfect from His birth; every wish and inclination was as it should be; but only as a disposition, as a power, that needed to be tested and developed and strengthened by trial. What the suffering and the death effected in Christ personally, in perfecting His character, is the groundwork of what it effected on our behalf. It was needful that God should make Him perfect through suffering; the perfectness that comes through suffering is meekness and gentleness, patience and perfect resignation to God's will. It was because of the humility and meekness and lowliness of heart, which the Lamb of God showed here upon earth, that He is now the Lamb on the throne. Through suffering He was made perfect, and found worthy to be our High Priest.

A leader must be followed. His followers must walk in the very path in which he walks. Jesus came and was made like us: we must come and be made like Him. His suffering and death is not only substitution and atonement. It is that, thank God! but it is much more too. It calls to fellowship and conformity. The substitution rests on identification: out of that conformity has its growth and strength. The Lamb of God has no salvation and no perfection to give us but His own meek spirit of entire dependence and absolute submission to God. The meekness and humility that it was needful God should perfect in Him are as needful for us. We must suffer and be crucified and die with Him. Death to Self and the world, at the cost of any suffering or Self-denial, this is the only path to glory the Leader of our salvation has opened up to us. ...

My brethren! do you understand what it means that the Father, in leading you to glory, has made Jesus the Leader of our salvation. Jesus is responsible for you. Take Him and trust Him as your Leader. The great need in one who follows a leader is a tender, teachable spirit. Rejoice that you have such a Leader, Himself made perfect in meekness and submission through suffering, that He might lead you in the blessed path that brought Him, and will bring you as surely, to the glory of the Father. And remember who this Leader is the Son of God, the divine Maker and Upholder of all things. Not only the Son of Man as a Leader outside of us, influencing us by example and instruction, by authority and kindness does He guide us. No, but as the Son of God who works in us by His Spirit, yea who Himself dwells within us. Even as it was God who worked in Him and perfected Him, will He, as God, now work in us and perfect us.

Christ came to give us an entirely new conception of what true life is, to show us a new way of thinking and living, to teach us that a heavenly life consists in giving up everything that has the slightest connection with sin for the sake of pleasing the Father perfectly. This is the new and living way He opened up through the rent veil of the flesh. "*It became God to perfect Him*"; All that Christ wrought, and all that was wrought in Him, was wrought by God. He yielded Himself to God: He did nothing of Himself: He allowed God to do all in Him. This is the path of perfection, the path to glory, in which Jesus leads. His divinity is inexpressibly precious to us for what He can be and do in us. But as Inexpressibly precious His humanity, showing us how He was perfected, how God worked in Him, what we must be, what through Him we can most surely be. Seek to get very clear hold of the truth that He is only a Savior as He is a Leader. Salvation is being led by Him.

For Whom and Through Whom Are All Things

May 29th

'For it became Him, for whom are all things, and through whom are all things, in bringing many sons unto glory, to make the author of their salvation perfect through sufferings.'

—HEBREWS 2: 10

When man sinned and fell from God, we lost together the two blessed truths in which his relation to God had stood. Our holy allegiance to God, having all things for Him, our blessed dependence on God, having all things through Him; instead of these came the reign of Self, with its life for Self and through Self.

It was from this life of Self Jesus came to redeem us, to bring us back to God, to know and honor Him as the God and Father, for whom are all things and through whom are all things. In doing this he opened again the only way which could lead to glory. He did it first by showing us in His life, as Man, how we ought to live for God and through God. And then by delivering us through His death from the dominion of sin, and winning for us the power of the heavenly life. For whom are all things, and through whom are all things. It was in this character that God perfected Christ through sufferings. It was in this character that Christ revealed and honored God in His sufferings. It is to win and bring us to know and love and serve God in this character that Jesus is Savior.

For whom are all things. Throughout His whole life there is nothing that Jesus sought to impress more distinctly on His disciples than this, that He was the Father's messenger and servant; that there was no thought of doing His own will or seeking His own honor; that He only sought and did what would be for the Father's pleasure and glory. He gave us the example of a man on earth living absolutely and entirely for God in heaven. His life on earth was the exhibition here in the flesh, the translation into human language, of the divine claim— "*All things for God*"; His allegiance to God was absolute. He proved to us that man's destiny and blessedness and everlasting glory are to be found in this: Living wholly for God.

Through whom are all things. Of this too Christ's life was the exposition. He was not ashamed continually to say that He could do nothing of Himself, and that only as the Father showed Him or spoke to Him, could He work and speak. He counted this His blessedness and His strength not to be able to do anything of Himself, but in continual dependence to wait on God and His working in Him. He knew and taught us that the one who has said in wholehearted devotion to God, "All things *for* God," may confidently say too, "All things *through* God."

"All for God," "All through God." Jesus Christ has made it possible for us to make these our watchwords. In all aspirations after a closer walk with God, in all efforts after a purer, truer, higher life, they are the two poles between which the soul ought to move. They are the sure marks of that true scriptural mysticism, which has such attractions for all hungry souls, who long to know and please God perfectly.

All for God! absolutely, without a moment, a thought, a word, a person, a possession, excepted; wholly for God, this becomes the soul's one desire. It has seen that God is worthy of this, that He claims it, and that in the very nature of things, nothing less can satisfy the heart God made to be filled with Himself.

All through God! The clearer the aim becomes to be all for God, and the deeper the soul sinks into its own emptiness and impotence, under the conviction that with man it is impossible, the sooner does faith rise to see that we can not only say, but that we do dare to say, All for God! because we may also say, All through God! God Himself will work it in us. …

The practice of the presence of God is a most needful and most blessed spiritual exercise. As the soul bows in stillness and lowliness, and worships in silence, it gets into the right spirit for recognizing its own nothingness, and realizing that God is all that all is for Him, and all through Him. All for God: that is consecration. All through God: that is faith. This was the spirit in which Christ yielded Himself to God: consecration and faith. This was the God who perfected Christ. To know and honor God in this character is the secret of perfection, for in such He can do His work. This is the God who is leading many sons to glory; to know and honor Him is the path to glory. To reveal this God and His claims, to show how to give up everything to Him, this was what Christ came for. This is the life He brought us, the path He opened, the salvation He gives.

The High Priest: Saving the Obedient

May 30th

"Though he was a Son, yet learned obedience by the things which He suffered; And having been made perfect, he became unto all them that obey him, the cause of eternal salvation."

—HEBREWS 5: 8–9

The death of Jesus has its value and efficacy in obedience, ours as well as His. With Him obedience was God's great object in His suffering; the root and power of His perfection and His glory; the real efficient cause of our eternal salvation. And with us, the necessity of obedience is no less absolute. With God and with Christ our restoration to obedience was the great aim of redemption. It is the only way to that union with God in which our happiness consists. Through it alone God can reveal His life and power within us. Again I say: The death of Jesus has its value and efficacy in nothing but obedience, ours as well as His. "*He learned obedience, and being perfected became to all them that obey Him the cause of eternal salvation.*" Our obedience is as indispensable as His. As little as He could work out salvation without obedience, can we enjoy it. In us as much as in Him, obedience is the very essence of salvation.

Let us try and grasp this. God is the blessedness of the creature. When God is all to the creature, when He is allowed in humility and dependence to work all, and when all returns to Him in thanksgiving and service, nothing can prevent the fullness of God's love and joy entering and filling the creature. It has but one thing to do—to turn its desire or will toward God, and give Him free scope, and nothing in heaven or earth can prevent the light and the joy of God filling that soul. The living center round which all the perfections of God cluster, the living energy through which they all do their work, is the will of God.

The will of God is the life of the universe; it is what it is because God wills it; His will is the living energy which maintains it in existence. The creature can have no more of God than he has of God's will working in him. He that would meet and find God must seek Him in His will; union with God's will is union with Himself. Therefore, it was that the Lord Jesus, when He came to this world, always spoke of His having come to do one thing—the will of His Father.

This alone could work our salvation. Sin had broken us away from the will of God. In doing the will of God He was to break the power of sin. He was to prove wherein the service of God and true blessedness consist; He was to work out in Himself a new nature to be communicated, a new way of living to be followed; He was to show that the doing of God's will at any cost is blessedness and glory everlasting. It was because He did this, because He was obedient unto death, that God highly exalted Him. It was this disposition. His obedience, that made Him worthy and fit to sit with God on the throne of heaven. Union with the will of God is union with God Himself, and must—it cannot be otherwise—bring to the glory of God. And this is as true of us as of Him.

It is to be feared that there are many Christians who seek salvation, and have no conception in what salvation consists—a being saved from their own will, and being restored to do the will of God alone. They seek after Christ, and trust in Him; but it is not the true Christ, but a Christ of whom they have framed their own image. The true Christ is the incarnate will of God, the incarnate obedience, who works in us what God wrought in Him. Christ came as the Son, to impart to us the very same life and disposition as animated Him on earth. Christ came to be a High Priest, to bring us to God in that very same way of obedience and Self-sacrifice in which He drew nigh to God. As Son and Priest, Christ is our Leader and Forerunner; it is only as we follow Him in His path on earth that we can hope to share His glory in heaven. "*He learned obedience and became the cause of eternal salvation to them that obey Him.*"

Let us beware that no wrong or one-sided views of what salvation by faith means lead us astray. There are some who think that salvation by faith is all, and obedience not so essential. This is a terrible mistake. In our justification, there is indeed no thought of obedience in the past. God justifies the ungodly. But repentance is a return to obedience. And without repentance there can be no true faith. Justification, and the faith by which it comes, are only for the sake of obedience, as means to an end. They point us to Christ, and the salvation which is to be found in union with Him. And He has no salvation but for them that obey Him. Obedience, as the acceptance of His will and life, is our only capacity for salvation.

This is the reason there is so much complaining that we cannot find and do not enjoy a full salvation. We seek it in the wrong way. Jesus Himself said that the Father would give the Holy Spirit, that is, salvation as it is perfected in Christ in Heaven, to them that obey Him. To such would He manifest Himself; with such would the Father and He dwell.

The salvation of Christ was wrought out entirely by obedience; this is its very essence and nature; it cannot be possessed or enjoyed but by obedience. Christ, who was perfected by obedience, is the cause of salvation to none but them who obey Him. God grant that the obedience of Jesus, with the humility in which it roots, may be seen of us to be the crowning beauty of His character, the true power of His redemption, the bond of union and likeness between Him and His followers, the true and real salvation, in the salvation He gives to them that obey Him.

The Son—On the Right Hand of God

May 31st

"But of which of the angels hath he said at any time, 'Sit on My right hand, till I make Your enemies the footstool of Your feet'"?

—PSALM 110

Sit on My right hand, till I make Your enemies the footstool of Your feet. These words we have from Psalm 110. Luther called it the chief of all the Psalms. … It is from this Psalm that the expression, which is become one of the great articles of our faith, "*Sitting on the right hand of God*," has been taken into the New Testament. Our Lord quoted the words when he taught (Matthew 22: 41) how David, when he said, "Jehovah said unto my Lord," had acknowledged that the Messiah who was to be His Son, would also be his Lord. Before Caiaphas (Matthew 26: 64) Christ spoke of Himself as "*the Son of Man, sitting at the right hand of power.*" Mark (26: 19) in the narrative of the ascension, uses the words, "*The Lord Jesus was received up into Heaven, and sat down at the right hand of God.*" At Pentecost (Acts 2: 35), Peter proved from this text that David had prophesied of the Messiah. Paul (1 Corinthians 15: 25) applies the words to the final conquest of all the enemies of the Lord Jesus. And to the Ephesians (1: 20-22) he speaks of the "*working of the strength of God's might, which He wrought in Christ when He raised Him from the dead, and made Him to sit at His right hand in the heavenlies.*" Our Epistle uses the expression five times. The words of David spoken through the Holy Spirit of what he could but very little have apprehended, became, through Jesus and the apostles, the revelation of what is the highest glory of Christ, and the greatest strength of our faith and hope.

The word suggests two thoughts. The one, that as Son of Man, He is admitted to the perfect fellowship and equality with God; the other, that He is now possessor of divine, of universal authority and power. We are so familiar with the truth, that its infinite magnificence hardly strikes us. God is a God who is, and must be, infinitely jealous of His honor: His glory He will not give to another. When Jesus, the crucified Son of Man, takes

His place at the right hand of the Majesty on high, it can only be because He is also the Son of God, because He is God. And it assures us that now the power and dominion of God Himself are in His hands, to carry out the work of redemption to its full consummation, until all His enemies have been put under His feet, and He shall deliver up the Kingdom to the Father.

When the writer quotes the words, it is with the question: "*Of which of the angels has He said at any time*?" And He gives the answer: Are they not all ministering spirits sent forth to do service for them who shall be heirs to salvation? He would impress deep upon us the thought that angels, though they come from God's throne, and are the instruments of His power, are still infinitely distinct from the Son. The redemption from sin, the true fellowship with God. the life and the love of God they cannot communicate.

It is the Son, sitting at the right hand of God, acting in the power of God, to whom we must look for the everlasting redemption, for the true inward deliverance from sin, for a complete salvation. The angels, by contrast, all point us to the Son, seated as Man on the throne, in proof of, and to impart, that perfect restoration to the fellowship of the Most High in the Most Holy Place.

This is the Son in whom God speaks to us. The word, "*Sit on My right hand*," is spoken in our hearing and in our behoof. In that word, we have concentrated all God's speaking. See, He says, how I have exalted Him, your Brother, your Surety, your Head, to my right hand, in token of My perfect acceptance of His work; your perfect admittance to My presence and the enjoyment of all the power of the heavenly life; your full participation, in your inmost being, of what the Kingdom of Heaven is.

"*Sit on My right hand*." Let that word enter and master all our heart and life. I have said that it occurs five times in the Epistle. Compare these passages, and the others having reference to Christ's place in Heaven, and observe how the great truth we are to learn is this: the knowledge of Jesus as having entered Heaven for us, and taken us in union with Himself into a heavenly life, is what will deliver the Christian from all that is low and feeble, and lift him to a life of joy and strength.

To gaze upon the heavenly Christ in the Father's presence, to whom all things are subject, will transform us into heavenly Christians, dwelling all the day in God's presence, and overcoming every enemy. Yes, my Redeemer, seated at God's right hand—if I only know Him aright and trust Him as able to save completely—He will make me more than conqueror.

If we would obtain this blessed knowledge of our Lord, and the blessed life in the experience of His power, Scripture has a prayer for us (Ephesians 1: 17–22), that we will do well to pray often: "*That the God of our Lord Jesus would give us the Spirit of wisdom and revelation, that we may know what is the exceeding greatness of His power to us-ward who believe, according to that working of the strength, of His might which He wrought in Christ, when He made Him to sit at His right hand in the heavenlies*." Let us pray for this Spirit of divine illumination; let us study and adore the strength of God's might that lifted Him to the throne; and let us believe joyfully that that power works in us every day to lift us up and enable us to live as those who are set with Him in the heavenlies. … It was as, during ten days, the disciples worshipped Him that had just sat down on the right hand of God, that they were filled with the Holy Spirit. The Pentecostal gift is ours: here is the place and the posture in which we shall enter into its full experience.

Of the Sin of Not Making Progress in Christ

June 1st

"For when by this time you ought to be teachers, you have need again that someone teach you the rudiments of the first principles of the oracles of God; and are become such as have need of milk, and not of solid food."

—HEBREWS 5: 12

We have here the commencement of the third of the five warnings to be found in the Epistle. The first was against indifference and neglect; the second against unbelief and disobedience; the third deals specially with the sloth that prevents all progress in the Christian life, renders the soul incapable of entering into the full meaning of gospel truth and blessing, and often leads to an entire falling away. In the previous part of the Epistle, the author has been dealing with what he considers more elementary truths, the divinity and humanity of the Savior, and His fitness as a merciful and faithful High Priest for the work He has to do for us. He is about to enter on the higher teaching he has to give us on the heavenly priesthood of Christ, but feels that many of his readers are incapable of following or appreciating such spiritual truth. He feels it needful first to rouse them by words of earnest reproof and exhortation, because no teaching can profit where the heart is not wakened up to hunger for it as its necessary food.

In the Christian Church, there are, alas, too many, of whom we would fain hope that they are believers, who are living in this state. They are content with the thought of pardon and the hope of Heaven; they rest in their orthodoxy, their attachment to the Church and its services, their correct deportment. But as to any strong desire for the deeper truths of God's Word—they have no conception of what is meant, or why they should be needed. When our author speaks of the power of Jesus' blood in Heaven, of the opening of the Holiest of All, of our entering in to dwell there, and then of our going to Him outside the camp, the words find no response, because they meet no need of the soul. Let every reader listen earnestly to what God says of this state.

"*We have many things to say, and hard of interpretation, because you are become dull of hearing*" (Hebrews 5: 11). The writer's complaint is not that they have not sufficient education or mental power to understand what he says. By no means. But spiritual things must be spiritually discerned. Spiritual truth can only be received by the spiritual mind, by a heart that thirsts for God, and sacrifices this world for the knowledge and enjoyment of the unseen One. They were content with their knowledge of the crucified Christ; the heavenly Christ, and His power to draw them up out of the world, and to give Heaven into their hearts, had but little attraction.

He further says, "*By reason of the time you ought to be teachers.*" In the Christian life, everyone who makes real progress feels himself constrained to teach others. Christ's love in the heart must overflow to those around. The Hebrews had been Christians so long that they ought to have been teachers. The very opposite of this, however, was the case. "*You have need again that someone teach you the rudiments of the beginning of the oracles of God.*" So there are numbers of Christians whose Christian life consists very much in always learning. Sermons and books are a delight, but they never get beyond the stage of being fed; they know not what it is to feed others. There is no effort so to appropriate God's Word, as to be strong to impart it to others. Or there is no real longing for deliverance from the power of sin, and the great incentive to the fuller knowledge of Jesus and His heavenly power is wanting.

"*And you are become such as have need of milk, and not of solid food.*" Where there is no hunger for the solid food (the higher truth of Christ's heavenly priesthood), or unwillingness to use what is received in helping others, the spiritual faculties are dwarfed and enfeebled, and the Christian never gets beyond the use of the milk meant for babes. In the Christian life, as in nature, there are two stages, the one of infancy or childhood, the other of manhood. In nature the growth out of the one into the other comes spontaneously. In grace this is not so. It is possible for a Christian to remain in a sickly infancy all his life, always needing help, instead of being a help. The cause of this is sloth, reluctance to make the sacrifice needed for progress, unwillingness to forsake all and follow Jesus. And this again is very much owing to the fatal mistake that in religion our only thought is to be of safety, that we may be content when some assurance of that is attained. Such a soul cares not for the heavenly blessedness of conformity to Jesus, of living fellowship with God, and the Godlike privilege of bringing life and blessing to others.

It is one of the great needs of the teachers in the Church in our day that they should have a clear insight into the feeble and sickly state in which most Christians live, as well as into what constitutes a healthy life that goes on to perfection. As they themselves enter into the full experience of the power of Christ's priesthood, as the Holy Spirit imparts it in the heart, they will be able to reprove with authority, and effectually to help all upright souls into the full salvation Christ has provided. God give His Church such teachers.

Have we not here the reason there is so little earnest pursuit after holiness? so little true consecration to living to bless others? so little of the power of the Holy Spirit in the life of the Church? Let us plead with God to discover the evil and to visit His Church. Let us exhort one another daily, to rest content with nothing less than a whole-hearted enthusiastic devotion to Jesus.

In preparing to go on to the study of the inner sanctuary in all that is to follow, do let us consider it a settled thing, that unless we are really hungering after righteousness, and longing for a very close fellowship with Jesus, our further study of the Epistle will do us very little good. Let us pray God to convince us of our sloth, our contentment with the beginnings of grace, and to stir in us a burning thirst after Himself.

The Heart-Searching Word of God

June 2nd

"The Word of God is living, and active, and sharper than any two-edged sword, and piercing even to the dividing of soul and spirit … and quick to discern the thoughts and intents of the heart.

—HEBREWS 4: 12 …

F*or the Word of God is living and active.* At times it may appear as if the word effects so little. The word is like seed: everything depends on the treatment it receives. Some receive the word with the understanding: there it cannot be quickened.

The Word is meant for the heart, the will, the affections. The Word must be submitted to, must be lived, must be acted out. When this is done it will manifest its living, quickening power. It is not we who have to make the Word alive. When, in faith in the life and power there is in the Word, the heart yields itself in humble submission and honest desire to its action, it will prove itself to be life and power.

"*And sharper than any two-edged sword, and piercing even to the dividing of soul and spirit, of both joints and marrow.*" The first action of God's Word is to wound, to cut, to divide. In the soul the natural life has its seat; in the spirit the spiritual and divine. Sin has brought confusion and disorder; the spirit is under the mastery of the soul, the natural life. God's Word divides and separates; wakens the spirit to a sense of its destiny as the faculty for the unseen and eternal; brings the soul to a knowledge of itself as a captive to the power of sin. It cuts deep and sure, discovering the deep corruption of sin. As the knife of the surgeon, who seeks to heal, pierces even to the dividing of the joints and marrow, where it is needed, so the Word penetrates all; there is no part of the inner being to which it does not pass.

"*And quick to discern the thoughts and intents of the heart.*" It is specially with the heart that God's word deals. In Hebrews 3 we read of the hardened heart, the evil heart of unbelief, the erring heart. When the Word heart occurs later in the Epistle we shall find everything changed; we shall read of a heart in which God's law is written, of a true heart, a heart sprinkled with the blood, a heart stablished by grace (8: 10; 10: 22; 13: 9). We have here the transition from the one to the other. God's appeal was, "*Today, if you hear His voice, harden not your heart.*" The heart that will but yield itself to be searched by God's Word, to have its secret thoughts and intents discerned and judged by it, will be freed from its erring and unbelief, and quickened and cleansed, and made a living table on which the Word is written by God Himself. Oh, to know how needful it is, but also how blessed, to yield our hearts to the judgment of the Word.

"*And there is no creature that is not manifest in His sight.*" God's Word bears the character of God Himself. He is the all-knowing and all-pervading; nothing can hide itself from the judgment of His Word. If we will not have it judge us now, it will condemn us hereafter. For all things are naked and laid open before the eyes of Him with whom we have to do.

Yes, the God with whom we have to do is He of whom we later read: "*It is a fearful thing to fall into the hands of the living God.*" And again: "*Our God is a consuming fire.*" It is this God who now pleads with us to enter into His rest.

Let each of us gladly yield ourselves to have to do with Him. If perhaps there be a secret consciousness that all is not right, that we are not giving diligence to enter into the rest, oh, let us beware of setting such thoughts aside. It is the first swelling of the living seed of the Word within us. Do not regard that thought as coming from yourself, or from man who brings thee God's Word; it is God waking you out of sleep. Have to do with Him. Be willing that the Word should show you what is wrong. Be not afraid of its discovering to you your sin and wretchedness. The knife of the physician wounds to heal. The light that shows you your sin and wrong will surely lead you on. The word is living and will give you life.

God has spoken to us in His Son. This is the keynote of the Epistle. Today, if you hear His voice, harden not your heart: this is the keynote of this long and solemn warning. Let us hearken, let us yield to the Word. … Judge your life not by what thy heart says, or the Church, or the so-called Christian world, but by what the Word says. Let it have its way with you; it will greatly bless you. … The Word is living and active. Have great faith in its power. Be sure that the Holy Spirit, that the living Word, that God Himself works in it. The Word ever points to the living God, who is present in it, and makes it a living Word, in the heart that is seeking for life and for God.

11

ABSOLUTE SURRENDER

And Other Addresses

Chicago: Moody Press, 1895

Absolute Surrender 1

June 3rd

Absolute surrender—let me tell you where I got those words. I used them myself often, and you have heard them numberless times. But in Scotland once I was in a company where we were talking about the condition of Christ's Church, and what the great need of the Church and of believers is; and there was in our company a godly worker who has much to do in training workers, and I asked him what he would say was the great need of the Church, and the message that ought to be preached. He answered very quietly and simply and determinedly: "Absolute surrender to God is the one thing."

The words struck me as never before. And that man began to tell how, in the workers with whom he had to deal, he finds that if they are sound on that point, even though they be backward, they are willing to be taught and helped, and they always improve; whereas others who are not sound there very often go back and leave the work. The condition for obtaining God's full blessing is absolute surrender to Him.

And now, I desire by God's grace to give to you this message—that your God in Heaven answers the prayers which you have offered for blessing on yourselves and for blessing on those around you by this one demand: Are you willing to surrender yourselves absolutely into His hands? What is our answer to be? God knows there are hundreds of hearts who have said it, and there are hundreds more who long to say it but hardly dare to do so. And there are hearts who have said it, but who have yet miserably failed, and who feel themselves condemned because they did not find the secret of the power to live that life. …

God Expects Your Surrender. Let me say, first of all, that God claims it from us. Yes, it has its foundation in the very nature of God. God cannot do otherwise. Who is God? He is the Fountain of life, the only Source of existence and power and goodness, and throughout the universe there is nothing good but what God works. …And God's redeemed children, oh, can you think that God can work His work if there is only half or a part of them surrendered? God cannot do it. God is life, and love, and blessing, and power, and infinite beauty, and God delights to communicate Himself to every child who is prepared to receive Him; but ah! this one lack of absolute surrender is just the thing that hinders God. And now He comes, and as God, He claims it.

You know in daily life what absolute surrender is. You know that everything has to be given up to its special, definite object and service. I have a pen in my pocket, and that pen is absolutely surrendered to the one work of writing, and that pen must be absolutely surrendered to my hand if I am to write properly with it. If another holds it partly, I cannot write properly. … And now, do you expect that in your immortal being, in the Divine nature that you have received by regeneration, God can work His work, every day and every hour, unless you are entirely given up to Him? God cannot. The Temple of Solomon was absolutely surrendered to God when it was dedicated to Him. And every one of us is a temple of God, in which God will dwell and work mightily on one condition: absolute surrender to Him. God claims it, God is worthy of it, and without it God cannot work His blessed work in us. …

God Accomplishes Your Surrender. God not only claims it, but God will work it Himself. God accomplishes your surrender. I am sure there is many a heart that says: "Ah, but that absolute surrender implies so much!" Someone says: "Oh, I have passed through so much trial and suffering, and there is so much of the Self-life still remaining, and I dare not face the entire giving of it up, because I know it will cause so much trouble and agony." Alas! Alas! That God's children have such thoughts of Him, such cruel thoughts.

Oh, I come to you with a message, fearful and anxious one: God does not ask you to give the perfect surrender in your strength, or by the power of your will; God is willing to work it in you. Do we not read: *"It is God that works in us, both to will and to do of his good pleasure?"* (Philippians 2: 13). And that is what we should seek for—to go on our faces before God, until our hearts learn to believe that the everlasting God Himself will come in to turn out what is wrong, to conquer what is evil, and to work what is well-pleasing in His blessed sight. God Himself will work it in you.

Look at the men in the Old Testament, like Abraham. Do you think it was by accident that God found that man, the father of the faithful and the Friend of God, and that it was Abraham himself, apart from God, who had such faith and such obedience and such devotion? You know it is not so. God raised him up and prepared him as an instrument for His glory. Did not God say to Pharaoh: *"For this cause have I raised you up, for to show in you my power"*? (Exodus 9:16). And if God said that of him, will not God say it far more of every child of His? God comes and offers to work this absolute surrender in you. All these searchings and hungerings and longings that are in your heart, I tell you they are the drawings of the Divine magnet, Christ Jesus. He lived a life of absolute surrender, He has possession of you; He is living in your heart by His Holy Spirit. You have hindered and hindered Him terribly, but He desires to help you to get hold of Him entirely. And He comes and draws you now by His message and words. Will you not come and trust God to work in you that absolute surrender to Himself? Yes, blessed be God, He can do it, and He will do it.

God Accepts Your Surrender. God not only claims it and works it, but God accepts it when we bring it to Him. God works it in the secret of our heart, God urges us by the hidden power of His Holy Spirit to come and speak it out, and we have to bring and to yield to Him that absolute surrender. … And when you do yield yourself in absolute surrender, let it be in the faith that God does now accept of it.

I pray you, be occupied with God. We want to get help, every one of us, so that in our daily life God shall be clearer to us, God shall have the right place, and be *"all in all."* And if we are to have that through life, let us begin now and look away from ourselves, and look up to God. Let each believe, while I, a poor worm on earth and a trembling child of God, full of failure and sin, and … in simplicity say, O God, I accept Your terms; … I have accepted Your terms of absolute surrender. While your heart says that in deep silence, remember there is a God present that takes note of it, and writes it down in His book, and there is a God present who at that very moment takes possession of you. …

Absolute Surrender 2

June 4th

God Maintains Your Surrender. In this matter of surrender there are two: God and I—I a worm, God the everlasting and omnipotent Jehovah. Worm, will you be afraid to trust yourself to this mighty God now? God is willing. Do you not believe that He can keep you continually, day by day, and moment by moment? …

A life of absolute surrender has its difficulties. I do not deny that. Yes, it has something far more than difficulties: it is a life that with men is absolutely impossible. But by the grace of God, by the power of God, by the power of the Holy Spirit dwelling in us, it is a life to which we are destined, and a life that is possible for us, praise God! Let us believe that God will maintain it.

Some of you have read the words of that aged saint who, on his ninetieth birthday, told of all God's goodness to him—I mean George Müller. What did he say he believed to be the secret of his happiness, and of all the blessing which God had given him? He said he believed there were two reasons. The one was that he had been enabled by grace to maintain a good conscience before God day by day; the other was, that he was a lover of God's Word. Ah, yes, a good conscience is complete obedience to God day by day, and fellowship with God every day in His Word, and prayer—that is a life of absolute surrender.

Such a life has two sides—on the one side, absolute surrender to work what God wants you to do; on the other side, to let God work what He wants to do.

First, to do what God wants you to do. Give up yourselves absolutely to the will of God. You know something of that will; not enough, far from all. But say absolutely to the Lord God: "By Your grace I desire to do Your will in everything, every moment of every day." Say: "Lord God, not a word upon my tongue but for Your glory, not a movement of my temper but for Your glory, not an affection of love or hate in my heart but for Your glory, and according to Your blessed will."

Someone says: "Do you think that possible?" I ask, What has God promised you, and what can God do to fill a vessel absolutely surrendered to Him? Oh, God wants to bless you in a way beyond what you expect. From the beginning, *"ear has not heard, neither has the eye seen, what God has prepared for them that wait for Him"* (1 Corinthians 2: 9). God has prepared unheard-of things, blessings much more wonderful than you can imagine, more mighty than you can conceive. They are Divine blessings. Oh, say now: "I give myself absolutely to God, to His will, to do only what God wants." It is God who will enable you to carry out the surrender. … God is willing to maintain our life. Only let our absolute surrender be one of simple, childlike, and unbounded trust.

God Blesses When You Surrender. This absolute surrender to God will wonderfully bless. … God wants us to be separate from the world; we are called to come out from the world that hates God. Come out for God, and say: "Lord, anything for You." If you say that with prayer, and speak that into God's ear, He will accept it, and He will teach you what it means.

But do remember, there must be absolute surrender. At every tea-table you see it. Why is tea poured into that cup? Because it is empty, and given up for the tea. But put ink, or vinegar, or wine into it, and will they pour the tea into the vessel? And can God fill you, can God bless you if you are not absolutely surrendered to Him? He cannot. Let us believe God has wonderful blessings for us, if we will but stand up for God, and say, be it with a trembling will, yet with a believing heart: "O God, I accept Your demands. I am yours and all that I have. Absolute surrender is what my soul yields to You by Divine grace."

You may not have such strong and clear feelings of deliverances as you would desire to have, but humble yourselves in His sight, and acknowledge that you have grieved the Holy Spirit by your Self-will, Self-confidence, and Self-effort. Bow humbly before him in the confession of that, and ask him to break the heart and to bring you into the dust before Him. Then, as you bow before Him, just accept God's teaching that in your flesh "*there dwells no good thing*" (Romans 7:18). … You must deny Self once for all … and then Christ will come in and take possession of you. …

Let us bow before God in humility, and in that humility confess before Him the state of the whole Church. No words can tell the sad state of the Church of Christ on earth. I wish I had words to speak what I sometimes feel about it. Just think of the Christians around you. I do not speak of nominal Christians, or of professing Christians, but I speak of hundreds and thousands of honest, earnest Christians who are not living a life in the power of God or to His glory. So little power, so little devotion or consecration to God, so little perception of the truth that a Christian is a man utterly surrendered to God's will! Oh, we want to confess the sins of God's people around us, and to humble ourselves. We are members of that sickly body, and the sickliness of the body will hinder us, and break us down, unless we come to God, and in confession separate ourselves from partnership with worldliness, with coldness toward each other, unless we give up ourselves to be entirely and wholly for God.

How much Christian work is being done in the spirit of the flesh and in the power of Self! How much work, day by day, in which human energy—our will and our thoughts about the work—is continually manifested, and in which there is but little of waiting upon God, and upon the power of the Holy Spirit! Let us make confession. But, as we confess the state of the Church and the feebleness and sinfulness of work for God among us, let us come back to ourselves. Who is there who truly longs to be delivered from the power of the Self-life, who truly acknowledges that it is the power of Self and the flesh, and who is willing to cast all at the feet of Christ? There is deliverance. …

Do you love Christ? Do you long to be in Christ, and not like Him? Let death be to you the most desirable thing on earth—death to Self, and fellowship with Christ. Separation; do you think it a hard thing to be called to be entirely free from the world, and by that separation to be united to God and His love, by separation to become prepared for living and walking with God every day? Surely one ought to say: "Anything to bring me to separation, to death, for a life of full fellowship with God and Christ."

Come and cast this Self-life and flesh-life at the feet of Jesus. Then trust Him. Do not worry yourselves with trying to understand all about it, but come in the living faith that Christ will come into you with the power of His death and the power of His life; and then the Holy Spirit will bring the whole Christ—Christ crucified and risen and living in glory—into your heart.

Peter's Repentance

June 5th

"And the Lord turned, and looked upon Peter. And Peter remembered the word of the Lord, how He had said unto him, Before the cock crows, you will deny me thrice. And Peter went out, and wept bitterly."

—LUKE 22: 61–62

That was the turning-point in the history of Peter. Christ had said to him: "*You cannot not follow Me now*" (John 13: 36). Peter was not in a fit state to follow Christ, because he had not been brought to an end of himself; he did not know himself, and he therefore could not follow Christ. But when he went out and wept bitterly, then came the great change. Christ previously said to him: "*When you are converted, strengthen your brethren.*" Here is the point where Peter was converted from Self to Christ.

I thank God for the story of Peter. I do not know a man in the Bible who gives us greater comfort. When we look at his character, so full of failures, and at what Christ made him by the power of the Holy Spirit, there is hope for every one of us. But remember, before Christ could fill Peter with the Holy Spirit and make a new man of him, he had to go out and weep bitterly; he had to be humbled. If we want to understand this, I think there are four points that we must look at. First, let us look at Peter the devoted disciple of Jesus; next, at Peter as he lived the life of Self; then at Peter in his repentance; and last, at what Christ made of Peter by the Holy Spirit.

Peter the Devoted Disciple of Christ

Christ called Peter to forsake his nets, and follow Him. Peter did it at once, and he afterward could say rightly to the Lord: "*We have forsaken all and followed You*" (Matthew 19: 27). Peter was a man of absolute surrender; he gave up all to follow Jesus. Peter was also a man of ready obedience. You remember Christ said to him, "*Launch out into the deep, and let down the net.*" Peter the fisherman knew there were no fish there, for they had been toiling all night and had caught nothing; but he said: "*At Your word I will let down the net*" (Luke 5: 4–5). He submitted to the word of Jesus. Further, he was a man of great faith.

When he saw Christ walking on the sea, he said: "*Lord, if it be You, bid me come unto You*" (Matthew 14: 28); and at the voice of Christ he stepped out of the boat and walked upon the water. And Peter was a man of spiritual insight. When Christ asked the disciples: "*Whom do you say that I am?*" Peter was able to answer: "*You are the Christ, the Son of the living God.*" And Christ said: "*Blessed are you, Simon Barjona; for flesh and blood has not revealed it unto you, but My Father which is in Heaven.*" And Christ spoke of him as the rock man, and of his having the keys of the kingdom. Peter was a splendid man, a devoted disciple of Jesus, and if he were living nowadays, everyone would say that he was an advanced Christian. And yet how much there was wanting in Peter!

Peter Living the Life of Self

You recollect that just after Christ had said to him: "*Flesh and blood has not revealed it unto You, but my Father who is in Heaven,*" Christ began to speak about His sufferings, and Peter dared to say: "*Be it far from You, Lord; this shall not be unto You.*" Then Christ had to say: "*Get behind me, Satan; for you savor not the things that be of God, but those that be of men*" (Matthew 16: 22–23). There was Peter in his Self-will, trusting his own wisdom, and actually forbidding Christ to go and die. Whence did that come? Peter trusted in himself and his own thoughts about divine things. We see later on, more than once, that among the disciples there was a questioning who should be the greatest, and Peter was one of them, and he thought he had a right to the very first place. He sought his own honor even above the others. It was the life of Self strong in Peter. He had left his boats and his nets, but not his old Self.

When Christ had spoken to him about His sufferings, and said: "*Get behind me, Satan,*" He followed it up by saying: "*If anyone would come after me, let them deny themselves, and take up their cross, and follow me*" (Matthew 16: 24). No one can follow Him unless they do that. Self must be utterly denied. What does that mean? When Peter denied Christ, we read that he said three times: "*I do not know the man*"; in other words: "I have nothing to do with Him; He and I are no friends; I deny having any connection with Him." Christ told Peter that he must deny Self. Self must be ignored, and its every claim rejected. That is the root of true discipleship; but Peter did not understand it, and could not obey it. And what happened? When the last night came, Christ said to him: "*Before the cock crows twice you shall deny me thrice.*" But with what Self-confidence Peter said: "*Though all should forsake You, yet will not I. I am ready to go with You, to prison and to death*" (Mark 14: 29; Luke 22: 33). Peter meant it honestly, and Peter really intended to do it; but Peter did not know himself. He did not believe he was as bad as Jesus said he was.

We perhaps think of individual sins that come between us and God, but what are we to do with that Self-life which is all unclean—our very nature? What are we to do with that flesh that is entirely under the power of sin? Deliverance from that is what we need. Peter knew it not, and therefore it was that in his Self-confidence he went forth and denied his Lord. Notice how Christ uses that word "deny" twice. He said to Peter the first time, "Deny Self"; He said to Peter the second time, "*You will deny Me.*" It is either of the two. There is no choice for us; we must either deny Self or deny Christ. There are two great powers fighting each other—the Self-nature in the power of sin, and Christ in the power of God. Either of these must rule within us. ...

Peter's Repentance

Peter denied his Lord thrice, and then the Lord looked upon him; and that look of Jesus broke the heart of Peter, and all at once there opened up before him the terrible sin that he had committed, the terrible failure that had come, and the depth into which he had fallen, and "*Peter went out and wept bitterly.*" Oh! who can tell what that repentance must have been? During the following hours of that night, and the next day, when he saw Christ crucified and buried, and the next day, the Sabbath—oh, in what hopeless despair and shame he must have spent that day! "My Lord is gone, my hope is gone, and I denied my Lord. After that life of love, after that blessed fellowship of three years, I denied my Lord. God have mercy upon me!"

I do not think we can realize into what a depth of humiliation Peter sank then. But that was the turning point and the change; and on the first day of the week Christ was seen of Peter, and in the evening He met him with the others. Later on at the Lake of Galilee He asked him: "*Do you love Me?*" until Peter was made sad by the thought that the Lord reminded him of having denied Him thrice; and said in sorrow, but in uprightness: "*Lord, You know all things; You know that I love You*" (John 21: 17).

Peter Transformed

Now Peter was prepared for deliverance from Self, and that is my last thought. You know Christ took him with others to the footstool of the throne, and bade them wait there; and then on the day of Pentecost the Holy Spirit came, and Peter was a changed man. I do not want you to think only of the change in Peter, in that boldness, and that power, and that insight into the Scriptures, and that blessing with which he preached that day. Thank God for that. But there was something for Peter deeper and better. Peter's whole nature was changed. The work that Christ began in Peter when He looked upon him, and was perfected when he was filled with the Holy Spirit.

If you want to see that, read the First Epistle of Peter. You know wherein Peter's failings lay. When he said to Christ, in effect: "You never can suffer; it cannot be"—it showed he had not a conception of what it was to pass through death into life. Christ said: "*Deny yourself,*" and in spite of that he denied his Lord. When Christ warned him: "*You shall deny me,*" and he insisted that he never would, Peter showed how little he understood what there was in himself. But when I read his epistle and hear him say: "*If you are reproached for the name of Christ, happy are you, for the Spirit of God and of glory rests upon you*" (1 Peter 4: 14), then I say that it is not the old Peter, but that is the very Spirit of Christ breathing and speaking within him.

I read again how he says: "*Hereunto you are called, to suffer, even as Christ suffered*" (1 Peter 2: 21). I understand what a change had come over Peter. Instead of denying Christ, he found joy and pleasure in having Self denied and crucified and given up to the death. And therefore it is in the Acts we read that, when he was called before the Council, he could boldly say: "*We must obey God rather than men*" (Acts 5: 29), and that he could return with the other disciples and rejoice that they were counted worthy to suffer for Christ's name. You remember his Self-exaltation; but now he has found out that "*the ornament of a meek and quiet spirit is in the sight of God of great price.*" Again he tells us to be "*subject one to another, and be clothed with humility*" (1 Peter 5: 5). …

Look at Peter utterly changed—the Self-pleasing, the Self-trusting, the Self-seeking Peter, full of sin, continually getting into trouble, foolish and impetuous, but now filled with the Spirit and the life of Jesus. Christ had done it for him by the Holy Spirit.

And now, what is my object in having thus very briefly pointed to the story of Peter? That story must be the history of every believer who is really to be made a blessing by God. That story is a prophecy of what everyone can receive from God in Heaven. Now let us just glance hurriedly at what these lessons teach us.

The first lesson is this—You may be a very earnest, godly, devoted believer, in whom the power of the flesh is yet very strong. That is a very solemn truth. Peter, before he denied Christ, had cast out devils and had healed the sick; and yet the flesh had power, and the flesh had room in him. Oh, beloved, we have to realize that it is just because there is so much of that Self-life in us that the power of God cannot work in us as mightily as God is willing that it should work. Do you realize that the great God is longing to double His blessing, to give tenfold blessing through us? But there is something hindering Him, and that something is a proof of nothing but the Self-life. We talk about the pride of Peter, and the impetuosity of Peter, and the Self-confidence of Peter. It all rooted in that one word, Self. Christ had said, "Deny Self," and Peter had never understood, and never obeyed; and every failing came out of that.

What a solemn thought, and what an urgent plea for us to cry: O God, do reveal this to us, that none of us may be living the Self-life! It has happened to many a one who had been a Christian for years, who had perhaps occupied a prominent position, that God found him out and taught him to find himself out, and he became utterly ashamed, falling down broken before God. Oh, the bitter shame and sorrow and pain and agony that came to him, until at last he found that there was deliverance! Peter went out and wept bitterly, and there may be many a godly one in whom the power of the flesh still rules.

And then my second lesson is—It is the work of our blessed Lord Jesus to reveal the power of Self. How was it that Peter, the carnal Peter, Self-willed Peter, Peter with the strong Self-love, ever became a man of Pentecost and the writer of his epistles? It was because Christ had him in charge, and Christ watched over him, and Christ taught and blessed him. The warnings that Christ had given him were part of the training; and last of all there came that look of love. In His suffering Christ did not forget him, but turned round and looked upon him, and "*Peter went out and wept bitterly.*" And the Christ who led Peter to Pentecost is waiting today to take charge of every heart that is willing to surrender itself to Him.

Are there not some saying: "Ah! that is the mischief with me; it is always the Self-life, and Self-comfort, and Self-consciousness, and Self-pleasing, and Self-will; how am I to get rid of it?" My answer is: It is Christ Jesus who can rid you of it; none else but Christ Jesus can give deliverance from the power of Self. And what does He ask you to do? He asks that you should humble yourself before Him.

"O Wretched Man that I Am!"

June 6th

"O wretched man that I am! who shall deliver me from the body of this death? I thank God through Jesus Christ our Lord."

—ROMANS 7: 24–25

In the first sixteen verses of the eighth chapter of Romans the name of the Holy Spirit is found sixteen times; you have there the description and promise of the life that a child of God can live in the power of the Holy Spirit. This begins in the second verse: "*The law of the Spirit of life in Christ Jesus hath made me free from the law of sin and death*" (Romans 8: 12). From that Paul goes on to speak of the great privileges of the child of God, who is to be led by the Spirit of God.

The gateway into all this is in the twenty-fourth verse of the seventh chapter: "*O wretched man that I am!*" There you have the words of a man who has come to the end of himself. He has in the previous verses described how he had struggled and wrestled in his own power to obey the holy law of God, and had failed. But in answer to his own question he now finds the true answer and cries out: "*I thank God through Jesus Christ our Lord.*" From that he goes on to speak of what that deliverance is that he has found.

I want from these words to describe the path by which we can be led out of the spirit of bondage into the spirit of liberty. …We are continually warned that this is the great danger of the Christian life, to go again into bondage; and I want to describe the path by which a man can get out of bondage into the glorious liberty of the children of God. Rather, I want to describe the person.

First, these words are the language of a regenerate man; second, of an impotent man; third, of a wretched man; and fourth, of a man on the borders of complete liberty.

The Regenerate Man. There is much evidence of regeneration from the fourteenth verse of the chapter on to the twenty-third. "*It is no more I that do it, but sin that dwells in me*" (Roman 7: 17): that is the language of a regenerate man, a man who knows that his heart and nature have been renewed, and that sin is now a power in him that is not himself. "*I delight in the law of the Lord after the inward man*" (Romans 7: 22): that again is the language of a regenerate man. He dares to say when he does evil: "*It is no more I that do it, but sin that dwells in me.*" It is of great importance to understand this.

In the first two great sections of the epistle, Paul deals with justification and sanctification. In dealing with justification, he lays the foundation of the doctrine in the teaching about sin, not in the singular, sin, but in the plural, sins—the actual transgressions. In the second part of the fifth chapter he begins to deal with sin, not as actual transgression, but as a power. Just imagine what a loss it would have been to us if we had not this second half of the seventh chapter of the Epistle to the Romans, if Paul had omitted in his teaching this vital question of the sinfulness of the believer. We should have missed the question we all want answered as to sin in the believer. What is the answer? The regenerate man is one in whom the will has been renewed, and who can say: "*I delight in the law of God after the inward man.*"

The Impotent Man. Here is the great mistake made by many Christian people: they think that when there is a renewed will, it is enough; but that is not the case. This regenerate man tells us: "*I will to do what is good, but the power to perform I find not.*" How often people tell us that if you set yourself determinedly, you can perform what you will! But this man was as determined as any man can be, and yet he made the confession: "*To will is present with me; but how to perform that which is good, I find not*" (Romans 7: 18). …

You will find that in this passage (Romans 7: 6–25) the name of the Holy Spirit does not occur once, nor does the name of Christ occur. The man is wrestling and struggling to fulfill God's law. Instead of the Holy Spirit and of Christ, the law is mentioned nearly twenty times. In this chapter, it shows a believer doing his very best to obey the law of God with his regenerate will. Not only this; but you will find the little words, I, me, my, occur more than forty times. It is the regenerate I in its impotence seeking to obey the law without being filled with the Spirit. This is the experience of almost every saint. After conversion, we begin to do our best, and we fail; but if we are brought into the full light, we need fail no longer. … God allows that failure that the regenerate should be taught our own utter impotence. It is in the course of this struggle that there comes to us this sense of our utter sinfulness. It is God's way of dealing with us. He allows us to strive to fulfill the law that, as we strive and wrestle, we may be brought to this: "I am a regenerate child of God, but I am utterly helpless to obey His law."

See what strong words are used all through the chapter to describe this condition: "*I am carnal, sold under sin*" (Romans 7: 14); "*I see another law in my members bringing me into captivity*" (Romans 7: 23); and last of all, "*O wretched man that I am! who shall deliver me from the body of this death*?" (Romans 7: 24). This believer who bows here in deep contrition is utterly unable to obey the law of God.

The Wretched Man. Not only are those who make this confession regenerate and impotent, but they are also wretched. They are utterly unhappy and miserable; and what is it that makes them so utterly miserable? It is because God has given us a nature that loves our Self. We are deeply wretched because we feel we are not obeying our God. We say, with brokenness of heart: "It is not I that do it, but I am under the awful power of sin, which is holding me down. It is I, and yet not I: alas! alas! it is myself; so closely am I bound up with it, and so closely is it intertwined with my very nature." Blessed be God—when we learn to say: "*O wretched man that I am*!" from the depth of our heart; we are on the way to the eighth chapter of Romans. ... But look to the contrast in the second verse of the eighth chapter: "*The law of the Spirit of life in Christ Jesus hath made me free from the law of sin and death.*" That is the deliverance through Jesus Christ our Lord; the liberty to the captive which the Spirit brings. Can you keep captive any longer a man made free by the "*law of the Spirit of life in Christ Jesus*"? ...

God does not work by His Spirit as He works by a blind force in nature. He leads His people on as reasonable, intelligent beings, and therefore when He wants to give us that Holy Spirit whom He has promised, He brings us first to the end of Self, to the conviction that though we have been striving to obey the law, we have failed. When we have come to the end of that, then He shows us that in the Holy Spirit we have the power of obedience, the power of victory, and the power of real holiness.

God works to will, and He is ready to work to do, but, alas! many Christians misunderstand this. They think because they have the will, it is enough, and that now they are able to do. This is not so. The new will is a permanent gift, an attribute of the new nature. The power to do is not a permanent gift, but must be each moment received from the Holy Spirit. It is the man who is conscious of his own impotence as a believer who will learn that by the Holy Spirit he can live a holy life. This man is on the brink of that great deliverance the way has been prepared for the glorious eighth chapter. ...

What the Holy Spirit does is to give the victory. "*If you through the Spirit do mortify the deeds of the flesh, ye shall live*" (Romans 8: 13). It is the Holy Spirit who does this—the third Person of the Godhead. He it is who, when the heart is opened wide to receive Him, comes in and reigns there, and mortifies the deeds of the body, day by day, hour by hour, and moment by moment. ...

There are in Scripture two very different sorts of Christians. The Bible speaks in Romans, Corinthians and Galatians about yielding to the flesh; and that is the life of tens of thousands of believers. All their lack of joy in the Holy Spirit, and their lack of the liberty He gives, is just owing to the flesh. The Spirit is within them, but the flesh rules the life. To be led by the Spirit of God is what they need. Would God that I could make every child of His realize what it means that the everlasting God has given His dear Son, Christ Jesus, to watch over you every day, and that what you have to do is to trust; and that the work of the Holy Spirit is to enable you every moment to remember Jesus, and to trust Him! The Spirit has come to keep the link with Him unbroken every moment.

… What good does it do that we go to church or attend conventions, that we study our Bibles and pray, unless our lives are filled with the Holy Spirit? That is what God wants; and nothing else will enable us to live a life of power and peace. …

"The Fruit of the Spirit is Love" 1

June 7th

"The fruit of the Spirit is love."

—GALATIANS 5: 22

I want to look at the fact of a life filled with the Holy Spirit more from the practical side, and to show how this life will show itself in our daily walk and conduct.

Under the Old Testament you know the Holy Spirit often came upon men as a Divine Spirit of revelation to reveal the mysteries of God, or for power to do the work of God. But He did not then dwell in them. Now, many just want the Old Testament gift of power for work, but know very little of the New Testament gift of the indwelling Spirit, animating and renewing the whole life. When God gives the Holy Spirit, His great object is the formation of a holy character. It is a gift of a holy mind and spiritual disposition, and what we need above everything else, is to say: "I must have the Holy Spirit sanctifying my whole inner life if I am really to live for God's glory."

You might say that when Christ promised the Spirit to the disciples, He did so that they might have power to be witnesses. True, but then they received the Holy Spirit in such heavenly power and reality that He took possession of their whole being at once and so fitted them as holy men for doing the work with power as they had to do it. Christ spoke of power to the disciples, but it was the Spirit filling their whole being that worked the power.

I wish now to dwell upon the passage found in Galatians 5:22: *"The fruit of the Spirit is love."* … Let us try ourselves by this word. Has this been our daily habit, to seek to be filled with the Holy Spirit as the Spirit of love? *"The fruit of the Spirit is love."* Has it been our experience that the more we have of the Holy Spirit the more loving we become? In claiming the Holy Spirit we should make this the first object of our expectation. The Holy Spirit comes as a Spirit of love. Oh, if this were true in the Church of Christ how different her state would be! …

Now, why is it that the fruit of the Spirit is love? Because *God is love* (1 John 4: 8). … God delights to pour His love into us. … The Lord Jesus Christ came down from Heaven as the Son of God's love. *"God so loved the world that He gave His only begotten Son"* (John 3: 16). God's Son came to show what love is, and He lived a life of love here upon earth in fellowship with His disciples, in compassion over the poor and miserable, in love even to

His enemies, and He died the death of love. And when He went to Heaven, whom did He send down? The Spirit of love, to come and banish Selfishness and envy and pride, and bring the love of God into the hearts of men. *"The fruit of the Spirit is love."*

And what was the preparation for the promise of the Holy Spirit? You know that promise as found in the fourteenth chapter of John's Gospel. But remember what precedes in the thirteenth chapter. Before Christ promised the Holy Spirit, He gave a new commandment, and about that new commandment He said wonderful things. One thing was: *"Even as I have loved you, so love you one another."* To them His dying love was to be the only law of their conduct and intercourse with each other. What a message to those fishermen, to those men full of pride and Selfishness! "Learn to love each other," said Christ, *"as I have loved you."* ...

And now He calls us to dwell and to walk in love. He demands that though a man hate you, still you love him. True love cannot be conquered by anything in Heaven or upon the earth. The more hatred there is, the more love triumphs through it all and shows its true nature. This is the love that Christ commanded His disciples to exercise. What more did He say? *"By this shall all men know that you are my disciples, if you have love one to another"* (John 13: 35).

You all know what it is to wear a badge. And Christ said to His disciples in effect: "I give you a badge, and that badge is love. That is to be your mark. It is the only thing in Heaven or on earth by which men can know me." Do we not begin to fear that love has fled from the earth? That if we were to ask the world: "Have you seen us wear the badge of love?" the world would say: "No; what we have heard of the Church of Christ is that there is not a place where there is no quarreling and separation." Let us ask God with one heart that we may wear the badge of Jesus' love. God is able to give it.

Why? Because nothing but love can expel and conquer our Selfishness. Self is the great curse—whether in its relation to God, or to our fellow-men in general, or to fellow Christians—thinking of ourselves and seeking our own. Self is our greatest curse. But, praise God, Christ came to redeem us from Self. We sometimes talk about deliverance from the Self-life—and thank God for every word that can be said about it to help us—but I am afraid some people think deliverance from the Self-life means that now they are going to have no longer any trouble in serving God; and they forget that deliverance from Self-life means to be a vessel overflowing with love to everybody all the day.

And there you have the reason why many people pray for the power of the Holy Spirit, and they get something, but oh, so little! Because they prayed for power for work, and power for blessing, but they have not prayed for power for full deliverance from Self. That means not only the righteous Self in intercourse with God, but the unloving Self in intercourse with men. And there is deliverance. ...

And how can I learn to love? Never until the Spirit of God fills my heart with God's love, and I begin to long for God's love in a very different sense from which I have sought it so Selfishly, as a comfort and a joy and a happiness and a pleasure to myself; never until I begin to learn that *"God is love,"* and to claim it, and receive it as an indwelling power for Self-sacrifice; never until I begin to see that my glory, my blessedness, is to be like God and like Christ, in giving up everything in myself for my fellow-men. …

Oh, just as a mother's love covers her children and delights in them and has the tenderest compassion with their feebleness or failures, so there ought to be in the heart of every believer a motherly love toward every brother and sister in Christ. Have you aimed at that? Have you sought it? Have you ever pleaded for it? Jesus Christ said: *"As I have loved you . . . love one another"* (John 13: 34). And He did not put that among the other commandments, but He said in effect: *"That is a new commandment, the one commandment: Love one another as I have loved you."*

"The Fruit of the Spirit is Love" 2

June 8th

"The fruit of the Spirit is love."

—GALATIANS 5: 22

It is in our daily life and conduct that the fruit of the Spirit is love. From that there comes all the graces and virtues in which love is manifested: joy, peace, longsuffering, gentleness, goodness; no sharpness or hardness in your tone, no unkindness or Selfishness; meekness before God and man. You see that all these are the gentler virtues. I have often thought as I read those words in Colossians, *"Put on therefore as the elect of God, holy and beloved, bowels of mercies, kindness, humbleness of mind, meekness, longsuffering"* (Colossians 3: 12), that if we had written this, we should have put in the foreground the manly virtues, such as zeal, courage, and diligence; but we need to see how the gentler, the most womanly virtues are especially connected with dependence upon the Holy Spirit. These are indeed heavenly graces. They never were found in the heathen world. Christ was needed to come from Heaven to teach us. Your blessedness is longsuffering, meekness, kindness; your glory is humility before God. The fruit of the Spirit that He brought from Heaven out of the heart of the crucified Christ, and that He gives in our heart, is first and foremost—love.

That is, I cannot see God, but as a compensation I can see my brother, and if I love him, God dwells in me. Is that really true? That I cannot see God, but I must love my brother, and God will dwell in me? Loving my brother is the way to real fellowship with God. You know what John further says in that most solemn test, *"If a man say, I love God, and hates his brother, he is a liar; for he that loves not his brother whom he has seen, how can he love God whom he has not seen?"* (1 John 4: 20). There is a brother, a most unlovable man. He worries you every time you meet him. He is of the very opposite disposition to yours. You are a careful businessman, and you have to do with him in your business. He is most untidy, un-businesslike. You say: "I cannot love him."

Oh, friend, you have not learned the lesson that Christ wanted to teach above everything. Let a man be what he will, you are to love him. Love is to be the fruit of the Spirit all the day and every day. Yes, listen! If a man loves not his brother whom he has seen—

if you don't love that unlovable man whom you have seen, how can you love God whom you have not seen? You can deceive yourself with beautiful thoughts about loving God. You must prove your love to God by your love to your brother; that is the one standard by which God will judge your love to Him. If the love of God is in your heart you will love your brother. *The fruit of the Spirit is love.*

And what is the reason that God's Holy Spirit cannot come in power? … We talk about grieving the Spirit of God by worldliness and ritualism and formality and error and indifference, but, I tell you, the one thing above everything that grieves God's Spirit is this lack of love. Let every heart search itself, and ask that God may search it. …

Think of the Church at large. What divisions! … Take the question of holiness, take the question of the cleansing blood; take the question of the baptism of the Spirit—what differences are caused among dear believers by such questions! That there are differences of opinion does not trouble me. We do not have the same constitution and temperament and mind. But how often hate, bitterness, contempt, separation, unlovingness, are caused by the holiest truths of God's Word! Our doctrines, our creeds, have been more important than love. We often think we are valiant for the truth and we forget God's command to speak the truth in love. And it was so in the time of the Reformation between the Lutheran and Calvinistic churches. What bitterness there was then in regard to the Holy Supper, which was meant to be the bond of union among all believers! And so, down the ages, the very dearest truths of God have become mountains that have separated us.

If we want to pray in power, and if we want to expect the Holy Spirit to come down in power, and if we want indeed that God shall pour out His Spirit, we must enter into a covenant with God that we love one another with a heavenly love.

Are you ready for that? Only that is true love that is large enough to take in all God's children, the most unloving and unlovable, and unworthy, and unbearable, and trying. If my vow—absolute surrender to God—was true, then it must mean absolute surrender to the Divine love to fill me; to be a servant of love to love every child of God around me. *"The fruit of the Spirit is love."*

Oh, God did something wonderful when He gave Christ, at His right hand, the Holy Spirit to come down out of the heart of the Father and His everlasting love. And how we have degraded the Holy Spirit into a mere power by which we have to do our work! God forgive us! Oh, that the Holy Spirit might be held in honor as a power to fill us with the very life and nature of God and of Christ!

"The fruit of the Spirit is love." I ask once again, Why is it so? And the answer comes: That is the only power in which Christians really can do their work. Yes, it is that we need. We want not only love that is to bind us to each other, but we want a Divine love in our work for the lost around us. … The baptism of love is what the Church needs, and to get that we must begin at once to get down upon our faces before God in confession, and plead: "Lord, let love from Heaven flow down into my heart. I am giving up my life to pray and live as one who has given himself up for the everlasting love to dwell in and fill him."

The state of Christ's Church is indescribably low. Plead for God's people that He would visit them, plead for each other, plead for all believers who are trying to work for God. Let love fill your heart. Ask Christ to pour it out afresh into you every day. Try to get it into you by the Holy Spirit of God: I am separated unto the Holy Spirit, and the fruit of the Spirit is love. God help us to understand it.

May God grant that we learn day by day to wait more quietly upon Him. Do not wait upon God only for ourselves, or the power to do so will soon be lost; but give ourselves up to the ministry and the love of intercession, and pray more for God's people, for God's people round about us, for the Spirit of love in ourselves and in them, and for the work of God we are connected with; and the answer will surely come, and our waiting upon God will be a source of untold blessing and power. *"The fruit of the Spirit is love."*

"Having Begun in the Spirit"

June 9th

"Having begun in the Spirit, are you now made perfect by the flesh?"
—GALATIANS 3: 3

As we look round about on the Church we see so many indications of feebleness and of failure, and of sin, and of shortcoming, that we are compelled to ask… Why is it, how is it to be accounted for, that God's church as a whole is so feeble, and that the great majority of Christians are not living up to their privileges? …

We find in more than one of the epistles a very solemn answer to that question… especially Paul's epistles to the Corinthians and to the Galatians, where he tells them in many different ways what the one reason was—that they were not living as Christians ought to live; many were under the power of the flesh. My text is one example. He reminds them that by the preaching of faith they had received the Holy Spirit. He had preached Christ to them; they had accepted that Christ and had received the Holy Spirit in power. But what happened? Having begun in the Spirit, they tried to perfect the work that the Spirit had begun in the flesh by their own effort. We find the same teaching in the epistle to the Corinthians.

Now, we have here a solemn discovery of what the great want is in the Church of Christ. God has called the Church of Christ to live in the power of the Holy Spirit, and the Church is living for the most part in the power of human flesh, and of will and energy and effort apart from the Spirit of God. I doubt not that that is the case with many individual believers; and oh, if God will use me to give you a message from Him, my one message will be this: "If the Church will return to acknowledge that the Holy Spirit is her strength and her help, and if the Church will return to give up everything, and wait upon God to be filled with the Spirit, her days of beauty and gladness will return, and we shall see the glory of God revealed among us." This is my message to every individual believer: "Nothing will help you unless you come to understand that you must live every day under the power of the Holy Spirit." God wants you to be a living vessel in whom the power of the Spirit is to be manifested every hour and every moment of your life, and God will enable you to be that. …

Let us try and take hold of this great truth: The beginning of the true Christian life is to receive the Holy Spirit. And the work of every Christian minister is that which was the work of Paul—to remind his people that they received the Holy Spirit, and must live according to His guidance and in His power. And just so God gives Christians the Holy Spirit with this intention—that every day all their life should be lived in the power of the Spirit. …

You sometimes hear the expression used, "religious flesh." What is meant by that? It is simply an expression made to give utterance to this thought: My human nature and my human will and my human effort can be very active in religion, and after being converted, and after receiving the Holy Spirit, I may begin in my own strength to try to serve God. I may be very diligent and doing a great deal, and yet all the time it is more the work of human flesh than of God's Spirit. What a solemn thought, that man can, without noticing it, be shunted off from the line of the Holy Spirit on to the line of the flesh; that he can be most diligent and make great sacrifices, and yet it is all in the power of the human will!

Ah, the great question for us to ask of God in Self-examination is that we may be shown whether our religious life is lived more in the power of the flesh than in the power of the Holy Spirit. A man may be a preacher, he may work most diligently in his ministry, a man may be a Christian worker, and others may tell of him that he makes great sacrifices, and yet you can feel there is a want about it. You feel that he is not a spiritual man; there is no spirituality about his life. How many Christians there are about whom no one would ever think of saying: "What a spiritual man he is!" Ah! There is the weakness of the Church of Christ. It is all in that one word—flesh.

Now, the flesh may manifest itself in many ways. It may be manifested in fleshly wisdom. My mind may be most active about religion. I may preach or write or think or meditate, and delight in being occupied with things in God's Book and in God's Kingdom; and yet the power of the Holy Spirit may be markedly absent. I fear that if you take the preaching throughout the Church of Christ and ask why there is, alas! so little converting power in the preaching of the Word, why there is so much work and often so little result for eternity, why the Word has so little power to build up believers in holiness and in consecration—the answer will come: It is the absence of the power of the Holy Spirit. And why is this? There can be no other reason but that the flesh and human energy have taken the place that the Holy Spirit ought to have. That was true of the Galatians, it was true of the Corinthians. You know Paul said to them: *"I cannot speak to you as to spiritual men; you ought to be spiritual men, but you are carnal."* And you know how often in the course of his epistles he had to reprove and condemn them for strife and for divisions.

What are the proofs or indications that a church like the Galatians, or a Christian, is serving God in the power of the flesh—is perfecting in the flesh what was begun in the Spirit? The answer is very easy. Religious Self-effort always ends in sinful flesh. What was the state of those Galatians? Striving to be justified by the works of the law. And yet they were quarreling and in danger of devouring one another. Count up the expressions that the apostle uses to indicate their want of love, and you will find more than twelve—envy, jealousy, bitterness, strife, and all sorts of expressions.

Many people speak of these things as though they were the natural result of our feebleness and cannot well be helped. … Many people speak of these things in the Church around them, and do not see the least prospect of ever having the things changed. There is no prospect until there comes a radical change, until the Church of God begins to see that every sin in the believer comes from the flesh, from a fleshly life midst our religious activities, from a striving in Self-effort to serve God. …

Oh, are you so foolish? Having begun in the Spirit, are you perfecting in the flesh that which was begun in the Spirit? Let us bow in shame, and confess before God how our fleshly religion, our Self-effort, and Self-confidence, have been the cause of every failure. I have often been asked by young Christians: "Why is it that I fail so? I did so solemnly vow with my whole heart, and did desire to serve God; why have I failed?" To such I always give the one answer: "My dear friend, you are trying to do in your own strength what Christ alone can do in you."

… I ask it of every member of Christ's Church and of every believer: Are you living a life under the power of the Holy Spirit day by day, or are you attempting to live without that? …

Separated unto the Holy Spirit 1

June 10th

"As they ministered to the Lord, and fasted, the Holy Spirit said, Separate Barnabas and Saul for the work whereunto I have called them.

And when they had fasted and prayed, and laid their hands on them, They sent them away.

—ACTS 13: 2–4

In the story of our text we shall find some precious thoughts to guide us as to what God would have of us, and what God would do for us. The great lesson of the verses quoted is this: The Holy Spirit is the director of the work of God upon the earth. And what we should do if we are to work rightly for God, and if God is to bless our work, is to see that we stand in a right relation to the Holy Spirit, that we give Him every day the place of honor that belongs to Him, and that in all our work and (what is more) in all our private inner life, the Holy Spirit shall always have the first place. Let me point out to you some of the precious thoughts our passage suggests.

First of all, we see that God has His own plans with regard to His kingdom. His church at Antioch had been established. God had certain plans and intentions with regard to Asia, and with regard to Europe. He had conceived them; they were His, and He made them known to His servants.

Our great Commander organizes every campaign, and His generals and officers do not always know the great plans. They often receive sealed orders, and they have to wait on Him for what He gives them as orders. God in Heaven has wishes, and a will, in regard to any work that ought to be done, and to the way in which it has to be done. Blessed is the man who gets into God's secrets and works under God.

Some years ago, at Wellington, South Africa, where I live, we opened a Mission Institute—what is counted there a fine large building. At our opening services the principal said something that I have never forgotten. He remarked:

"Last year we gathered here to lay the foundation-stone, and what was there then to be seen? Nothing but rubbish, and stones, and bricks, and ruins of an old building that had been pulled down. There we laid the foundation-stone, and very few knew what the building was that was to rise. No one knew it perfectly in every detail except one man, the architect. In his mind it was all clear, and as the contractor and the mason and the carpenter came to their work they took their orders from him, and the humblest laborer had to be obedient to orders, and the structure rose, and this beautiful building has been completed." "And just so," he added, "this building that we open today is but laying the foundation of a work of which only God knows what is to become."

God has His workers and His plans clearly mapped out, and our position is to wait, that God should communicate to us as much of His will as each time is needful. We have simply to be faithful in obedience, carrying out His orders. God has a plan for His Church upon earth. But alas! we too often make our plan, and we think that we know what ought to be done. We ask God first to bless our feeble efforts, instead of absolutely refusing to go unless God goes before us. God has planned for the work and the extension of His kingdom. The Holy Spirit has had that work given in charge to Him. "*The work whereunto I have called them.*" May God, therefore, help us all to be afraid of touching "*the ark of God*" except as we are led by the Holy Spirit.

Then the second thought—God is willing and able to reveal to His servants what His will is. Yes, blessed be God, communications still come down from Heaven! As we read here what the Holy Spirit said, so the Holy Spirit will still speak to His Church and His people. In these later days He has often done it. He has come to individual men, and by His divine teaching He has led them out into fields of labor that others could not at first understand or approve, into ways and methods that did not recommend themselves to the majority. But the Holy Spirit does still in our time teach His people. Thank God, in our foreign missionary societies and in our home missions, and in a thousand forms of work, the guiding of the Holy Spirit is known, but (we are all ready, I think, to confess) too little known. We have not learned enough to wait upon Him, and so we should make a solemn declaration before God: O God, we want to wait more for You to show us Your will.

Do not ask God only for power. Many a Christian has his own plan of working, but God must send the power. The man works in his own will, and God must give the grace--the one reason why God often gives so little grace and so little success. But let us all take our place before God and say: "What is done in the will of God, the strength of God will not be withheld from it; what is done in the will of God must have the mighty blessing of God."

And so let our first desire be to have the will of God revealed. If you ask me, Is it an easy thing to get these communications from Heaven, and to understand them? I can give you the answer. It is easy to those who are in right fellowship with Heaven, and who understand the art of waiting upon God in prayer.

How often we ask: How can a person know the will of God? And people want, when they are in perplexity, to pray very earnestly that God should answer them at once. But God can only reveal His will to a heart that is humble and tender and empty. God can only reveal His will in perplexities and special difficulties to a heart that has learned to obey and honor Him loyally in little things and in daily life.

That brings me to the third thought—Note the disposition to which the Spirit reveals God's will. What do we read here? There were a number of men ministering to the Lord and fasting, and the Holy Spirit came and spoke to them. Some people understand this passage very much as they would in reference to a missionary committee of our day. We see there is an open field, and we have had our missions in other fields, and we are going to get on to that field. We have virtually settled that, and we pray about it. But the position was a very different one in those former days. I doubt whether any of them thought of Europe, for later on even Paul himself tried to go back into Asia, till the night vision called him by the will of God. Look at those men. God had done wonders. He had extended the Church to Antioch, and He had given rich and large blessing.

Now, here were these men ministering to the Lord, serving Him with prayer and fasting. What a deep conviction they have—"It must all come direct from Heaven. We are in fellowship with the risen Lord; we must have a close union with Him, and somehow He will let us know what He wants." And there they were, empty, ignorant, helpless, glad and joyful, but deeply humbled. "O Lord," they seem to say, "we are Thy servants, and in fasting and prayer we wait upon You. What is Your will for us?" Was it not the same with Peter? He was on the housetop, fasting and praying, and little did he think of the vision and the command to go to Caesarea. He was ignorant of what his work might be.

It is in hearts entirely surrendered to the Lord Jesus, in hearts separating themselves from the world, and even from ordinary religious exercises, and giving themselves up in intense fasting and prayer to look to their Lord—it is in such hearts that the heavenly will of God will be made manifest.

You know that word fasting occurs a second time (in the third verse): "*They fasted and prayed.*" When you pray, you love to go into your closet, according to the command of Jesus, and shut the door. You shut out business and company and pleasure and anything that can distract, and you want to be alone with God. But in one way even the material world follows you there. You must eat. These men wanted to shut themselves out from the influences of the material and the visible, and they fasted. What they ate was simply enough to supply the wants of nature, and in the intensity of their souls they thought to give expression to their letting go of everything on earth in their fasting before God. Oh, may God give us that intensity of desire, that separation from everything, because we want to wait upon God, that the Holy Spirit may reveal to us God's blessed will.

Separated unto the Holy Spirit 2

June 11th

"The Holy Spirit said, Separate Barnabas and Saul for the work whereunto I have called them. And when they had fasted and prayed, and laid their hands on them, they sent them away.

—ACTS 13: 2–4

The fourth thought—What is now the will of God as the Holy Spirit reveals it? It is contained in one phrase: Separation unto the Holy Spirit. That is the keynote of the message from Heaven. "Separate me Barnabas and Saul for the work whereunto I have called them. The work is mine, and I care for it, and I have chosen these men and called them, and I want you who represent the Church of Christ upon earth to set them apart unto me."

Look at this heavenly message in its twofold aspect. The men were to be set apart to the Holy Spirit, and the Church was to do this separating work. The Holy Spirit could trust these men to do it in a right spirit. There they were abiding in fellowship with the heavenly, and the Holy Spirit could say to them, "Do the work of separating these men." And these were the men the Holy Spirit had prepared, and He could say of them, "*Let them be separated unto me.*"

Here we come to the very root, to the very life of the need of Christian workers. The question is: "What is needed that the power of God should rest upon us more mightily, that the blessing of God should be poured out more abundantly among those poor, wretched people and perishing sinners among whom we labor?" And the answer from Heaven is: "I want men separated unto the Holy Spirit."

What does that imply? You know that there are two spirits on earth. Christ said, when He spoke about the Holy Spirit: *"The world cannot receive him"* (John 14:17). Paul said: *"We have received not the spirit of the world, but the Spirit that is of God"* (1 Corinthians 2: 12). That is the great want in every worker—the spirit of the world going out, and the Spirit of God coming in to take possession of the inner life and of the whole being.

I am sure there are workers who often cry to God for the Holy Spirit to come upon them as a Spirit of power for their work, and when they feel that measure of power, and get blessing, they thank God for it. But God wants something more and something higher. God wants us to seek for the Holy Spirit as a Spirit of power in our own heart and life, to conquer Self and cast out sin, and to work the blessed and beautiful image of Jesus into us. There is a difference between the power of the Spirit as a gift, and the power of the Spirit for the grace of a holy life. A man may often have a measure of the power of the Spirit, but if there is not a large measure of the Spirit as the Spirit of grace and holiness, the defect will be manifest in his work. He may be made the means of conversion, but he never will help people on to a higher standard of spiritual life, and when he passes away, a great deal of his work may pass away too. But a man who is separated unto the Holy

Spirit is a man who is given up to say: "Father, let the Holy Spirit have full dominion over me, in my home, in my temper, in every word of my tongue, in every thought of my heart, in every feeling toward my fellow men; let the Holy Spirit have entire possession."

Is that what has been the longing and the covenant of your heart with your God—to be a man or a woman separated and given up unto the Holy Spirit? I pray you listen to the voice of Heaven. "*Separate for me*," said the Holy Spirit. Yes, separated unto the Holy Spirit. May God grant that the Word may enter into the very depths of our being to search us, and if we discover that we have not come out from the world entirely, if God reveals to us that the Self-life, Self-will, Self-exaltation are there, let us humble ourselves before Him.

Man, woman, brother, sister, you are a worker separated unto the Holy Spirit. Is that true? Has that been your longing desire? Has that been your surrender? Has that been what you have expected through faith in the power of our risen and almighty Lord Jesus? If not, here is the call of faith, and here is the key of blessing--separated unto the Holy Spirit. God write the word in our hearts!

I said the Holy Spirit spoke to that church as a church capable of doing that work. The Holy Spirit trusted them. God grant that our churches, our missionary societies, and our workers' unions, that all our directors and councils and committees may be men and women who are fit for the work of separating workers unto the Holy Spirit. We can ask God for that too.

Then comes my fifth thought, and it is this—This holy partnership with the Holy Spirit in this work becomes a matter of consciousness and of action. These men, what did they do? They set apart Paul and Barnabas, and then it is written of the two that they, being sent forth by the Holy Spirit, went down to Seleucia. Oh, what fellowship! The Holy Spirit in Heaven doing part of the work, men on earth doing the other part. After the ordination of the men upon earth, it is written in God's inspired Word that they were sent forth by the Holy Spirit.

And see how this partnership calls to new prayer and fasting. They had for a certain time been ministering to the Lord and fasting, perhaps days; and the Holy Spirit speaks, and they have to do the work and to enter into partnership, and at once they come together for more prayer and fasting. That is the spirit in which they obey the command of their Lord. And that teaches us that it is not only in the beginning of our Christian work, but all along that we need to have our strength in prayer. If there is one thought with regard to the Church of Christ, which at times comes to me with overwhelming sorrow; if there is one thought in regard to my own life of which I am ashamed; if there is one thought of which I feel that the Church of Christ has not accepted it and not grasped it; if there is one thought which makes me pray to God: "Oh, teach us by Your grace, new things"—it is the wonderful power that prayer is meant to have in the kingdom. We have so little availed ourselves of it.

We have all read the expression of Christian in Bunyan's great work, when he found he had the key in his breast that should unlock the dungeon. We have the key that can unlock the dungeon of atheism and of heathendom. But, oh! we are far more occupied with our work than we are with prayer. We believe more in speaking to men than we believe in speaking to God. Learn from these men that the work which the Holy Spirit commands must call us to new fasting and prayer, to new separation from the spirit and the pleasures of the world, to new consecration to God and to His fellowship. Those men gave themselves up to fasting and prayer, and if in all our ordinary Christian work there were more prayer, there would be more blessing in our own inner life.

If we felt and proved and testified to the world that our only strength lay in keeping every minute in contact with Christ, every minute allowing God to work in us—if that were our spirit, would not, by the grace of God, our lives be holier? Would not they be more abundantly fruitful?

I hardly know a more solemn warning in God's Word than that which we find in the third chapter of Galatians, where Paul asked: "Having begun in the Spirit, are ye now made perfect by the flesh?" (Galatians 3: 3).

Do you understand what that means? A terrible danger in Christian work, just as in a Christian life that is begun with much prayer, begun in the Holy Spirit, is that it may be gradually shunted off on to the lines of the flesh; and the word comes: "*Having begun in the Spirit, are you now made perfect by the flesh*?" In the time of our first perplexity and helplessness we prayed much to God, and God answered and God blessed, and our organization became perfected, and our band of workers became large; but gradually the organization and the work and the rush have so taken possession of us that the power of the Spirit, in which we began when we were a small company, has almost been lost.

Oh, I pray you, note it well! It was with new prayer and fasting, with more prayer and fasting, that this company of disciples carried out the command of the Holy Spirit, "*My soul, wait only upon God.*" That is our highest and most important work. The Holy Spirit comes in answer to believing prayer. You know when the exalted Jesus had ascended to the throne, for ten days the footstool of the throne was the place where His waiting disciples cried to Him. And that is the law of the kingdom—the King upon the throne, the servants upon the footstool. May God find us there unceasingly!

Then comes the last thought—What a wonderful blessing comes when the Holy Spirit is allowed to lead and to direct the work, and when it is carried on in obedience to Him!

You know the story of the mission on which Barnabas and Saul were sent out. You know what power there was with them. The Holy Spirit sent them, and they went on from place to place with large blessing. The Holy Spirit was their leader further on. You recollect how it was by the Spirit that Paul was hindered from going again into Asia, and was led away over to Europe. Oh, the blessing that rested upon that little company of men, and upon their ministry unto the Lord! Let us learn to believe that God has a blessing for us. The Holy Spirit, into whose hands God has put the work, has been called "the executive of the Holy Trinity." The Holy Spirit has not only power, but He has the Spirit of love. He is brooding over this dark world and every sphere of work in it, and He is willing to bless.

And why is there not more blessing? There can be but one answer. We have not honored the Holy Spirit as we should have done. Is there one who can say that that is not true? Is not every thoughtful heart ready to cry: "God forgive me that I have not honored the Holy Spirit as I should have done, that I have grieved Him, that I have allowed Self and the flesh and my own will to work where the Holy Spirit should have been honored! May God forgive me that I have allowed Self and the flesh and the will actually to have the place that God wanted the Holy Spirit to have."

Oh, the sin is greater than we know! No wonder that there is so much feebleness and failure in the Church of Christ!

Kept by the Power of God 1

June 12th

"Blessed be the God and Father of our Lord Jesus Christ, who … has begotten us again unto a lively hope by the resurrection of Jesus Christ from the dead, to an inheritance incorruptible … reserved in Heaven for you, who are kept by the power of God through faith unto salvation."

—1 PETER 1: 5

The words of my text are: *"Kept by the power of God through faith."* There we have two wonderful, blessed truths about the keeping by which a believer is kept unto salvation. One truth is, *"Kept by the power of God"*; and the other truth is, kept *"through faith."* We should look at the two sides—at God's side and His almighty power, offered to us to be our Keeper every moment of the day; and at the human side, we having nothing to do but in faith to let God do His keeping work. We are begotten again to an inheritance kept in Heaven for us; and we are kept here on earth by the power of God. We see there is a double keeping—the inheritance kept for me in Heaven, and I on earth kept for the inheritance there.

Now, as to the first part of this keeping, there is no doubt and no question. God keeps the inheritance in Heaven very wonderfully and perfectly, and it is waiting there safely. And the same God keeps *me* for the inheritance. That is what I want to understand. You know it is very foolish of a father to take great trouble to have an inheritance for his children, and to keep it for them, if he does not keep them for it. What would you think of a man spending his whole time and making every sacrifice to amass money, and as he gets his tens of thousands, you ask him why it is that he sacrifices himself so, and his answer is: "I want to leave my children a large inheritance, and I am keeping it for them"—if you were then to hear that that man takes no trouble to educate his children, that he allows them to run upon the street wild, and to go on in paths of sin and ignorance and folly, what would you think of him? Would not you say: "Poor man! He is keeping an inheritance for his children, but he is not keeping or preparing his children for the inheritance"! And there are so many Christians who think: "My God is keeping the inheritance for me"; but they cannot believe: "My God is keeping me for that inheritance." The same power, the same love, the same God doing the double work.

Now, I want to speak about a work God does upon us—keeping us for the inheritance. I have already said that we have two very simple truths: the one the Divine side—we are kept by the power of God; the other, the human side—we are kept through faith.

Look at the Divine side: Christians are kept by the power of God. Some people think that they never can get so far as that every word of their mouth should be to the glory of God. But it is what God wants of them, it is what God expects of them. God is willing to set a watch at the door of their mouth, and if God will do that, cannot He keep their tongue and their lips? He can; and that is what God is going to do for them that trust Him. God's keeping is all-inclusive, and let everyone who longs to live a holy life think out all their needs, and all their weaknesses, and all their shortcomings, and all their sins, and say deliberately: "Is there any sin that my God cannot keep me from?" And the heart will have to answer: "No; God can keep me from every sin." …

Kept by the power of God. I want to get that truth burned into my soul; I want to worship God until my whole heart is filled with the thought of His omnipotence. God is almighty, and the Almighty God offers Himself to work in my heart, to do the work of keeping me; and I want to get linked with Omnipotence, or rather, linked to the Omnipotent One, to the living God, and to have my place in the hollow of His hand. You read the Psalms, and you think of the wonderful thoughts in many of the expressions that David uses; as, for instance, when he speaks about God being our God, our Fortress, our Refuge, our strong Tower, our Strength and our Salvation. David had very wonderful views of how the everlasting God is Himself the hiding place of the believing soul, and of how He takes the believer and keeps him in the very hollow of His hand, in the secret of His pavilion, under the shadow of His wings, under His very feathers. And there David lived. And, oh, we who are the children of Pentecost, we who have known Christ and His blood and the Holy Spirit sent down from Heaven, why is it we know so little of what it is to walk tremblingly step by step with the Almighty God as our Keeper?

Have you ever thought that in every action of grace in your heart you have the whole omnipotence of God engaged to bless you? When I come to a man and he bestows upon me a gift of money, I get it and go away with it. He has given me something of his; the rest he keeps for himself. But that is not the way with the power of God. God can part with nothing of His own power, and therefore I can experience the power and goodness of God only so far as I am in contact and fellowship with Himself; and when I come into contact and fellowship with Himself, I come into contact and fellowship with the whole omnipotence of God, and have the omnipotence of God to help me every day. …

Oh, if you want to grow in grace, do learn to begin here. In all your judgings and meditations and thoughts and deeds and questionings and studies and prayers, learn to be kept by your Almighty God. What is Almighty God not going to do for the child that trusts Him? The Bible says: "*Above all that we can ask or think*" (Ephesians 3: 20). It is Omnipotence you must learn to know and trust, and then you will live as a Christian ought to live. How little we have learned to study God, and to understand that a godly life *is a life full of God*, a life that loves God and waits on Him, and trusts Him, and allows Him to bless it! We cannot do the will of God except by the power of God. God gives us the first experience of His power to prepare us to long for more, and to come and claim all that He can do. God help us to trust Him every day. …

Will our God, in His tenderhearted love toward us, not keep us every moment when He has promised to do so? Oh! If we once got hold of the thought: Our whole spiritual life is to be God's doing. *"It is God that works in us to will and to do of his good pleasure"* (Philippians 2:13). When once we get faith to expect that from God, God will do all for us.

Kept by the Power of God 2

June 13th

And now the other side—Believing: *"Kept by the power of God through faith."* How must we look at this faith? Let me say, first of all, that this faith means utter impotence and helplessness before God.

At the bottom of all faith there is a feeling of helplessness. … We must learn to say: "I give up everything; I have tried and longed and thought and prayed, but failure has come. God has blessed me and helped me, but still, in the long run, there has been so much of sin and sadness." What a change comes when we are thus broken down into utter helplessness and Self-despair, and say: "I can do nothing!"

Remember Paul. He was living a blessed life, and he had been taken up into the third Heaven, and then the thorn in the flesh came, "a messenger of Satan to buffet me." And what happened? Paul could not understand it, and he prayed the Lord three times to take it away; but the Lord said, in effect: "No; it is possible that you might exalt yourself, and therefore I have sent you this trial to keep you weak and humble."

And Paul then learned a lesson that he never forgot, and that was—to rejoice in his infirmities. He said that the weaker he was the better it was for him, for when he was weak, he was strong in his Lord Christ.

Do you want to enter what people call "the higher life"? Then go a step lower down. … Ah, yes, God will have to bring us very low down; there will have to come upon us a sense of emptiness and despair and nothingness. It is when we sink down in utter helplessness that the everlasting God will reveal Himself in His power, and that our hearts will learn to trust God alone.

What is it that keeps us from trusting Him perfectly? … The great hindrance to trust is Self-effort. So long as you have got your own wisdom and thoughts and strength, you cannot fully trust God. But when God breaks you down, when everything begins to grow dim before your eyes, and you see that you understand nothing, then God is coming near, and if you will bow down in nothingness and wait upon God, He will become all. As long as we are something, God cannot be all, and His omnipotence cannot do its full work. That is the beginning of faith—utter despair of Self, a ceasing from man and everything on earth, and finding our hope in God alone.

And then, next, we must understand that faith is rest. In the beginning of the faith-life, faith is struggling; but as long as faith is struggling, faith has not attained its strength. But when faith in its struggling gets to the end of itself, and just throws itself upon God and rests on Him, then comes joy and victory.

Perhaps I can make it plainer if I tell the story of how the Keswick Convention began. Canon Battersby was an evangelical clergyman of the Church of England for more than twenty years, a man of deep and tender godliness, but he had not the consciousness of rest and victory over sin, and often was deeply sad at the thought of stumbling and failure and sin. When he heard about the possibility of victory, he felt it was desirable, but it was as if he could not attain it. On one occasion, he heard an address on "Rest and Faith" from the story of the nobleman who came from Capernaum to Cana to ask Christ to heal his child. In the address it was shown that the nobleman believed that Christ could help him in a general way, but he came to Jesus a good deal by way of an experiment. He hoped Christ would help him, but he had not any assurance of that help. But what happened? When Christ said to him: "Go your way, for your child lives," that man believed the word that Jesus spoke; he rested in that word. He had no proof that his child was well again, and he had to walk back seven hours' journey to Capernaum. He walked back, and on the way met his servant, and got the first news that the child was well, that at one o'clock on the afternoon of the previous day, at the very time that Jesus spoke to him, the fever left the child. That father rested upon the word of Jesus and His work, and he went down to Capernaum and found his child well; and he praised God, and became with his whole house a believer and disciple of Jesus.

Oh, friends, that is faith! When God comes to me with the promise of His keeping, and I have nothing on earth to trust in, I say to God:

"Your Word is enough; kept by the power of God." That is faith, that is rest.

When Canon Battersby heard that address, he went home that night, and in the darkness of the night found rest. He rested on the word of Jesus. And the next morning, in the streets of Oxford, he said to a friend: "I have found it!" Then he went and told others, and asked that the Keswick Convention might be begun, and those at the convention with himself should testify simply what God had done.

It is a great thing when a man comes to rest on God's almighty power for every moment of his life, in prospect of temptations to temper and haste and anger and unlovingness and pride and sin. It is a great thing in prospect of these to enter into a covenant with the omnipotent Jehovah, not on account of anything that any man says, or of anything that my heart feels, but on the strength of the Word of God: "*Kept by the power of God through faith.*"

That brings me to just one more thought in regard to faith—faith implies fellowship with God. … No goodness or power can be received separate from God, and if you want to get into this life of godliness, you must take time for fellowship with God. …

"You Are the Branches"

June 14th

"I am the Vine; you are the branches."

—JOHN 15: 5

Everything depends on our being right ourselves in Christ. If I want good apples, I must have a good apple tree; and if I care for the health of the apple tree, the apple tree will give me good apples. And it is just so with our Christian life and work. If our life with Christ be right, all will come right. There may be the need of instruction and suggestion and help and training in the different departments of the work; all that has value. But in the long run, the greatest essential is to have the full life in Christ--in other words, to have Christ in us, working through us. I know how much there often is to disturb us, or to cause anxious questionings; but the Master has such a blessing for every one of us, and such perfect peace and rest, and such joy and strength, if we can only come into, and be kept in, the right attitude toward Him.

I will take my text from the parable of the Vine and the Branches, in John 15: 5: "*I am the vine, you are the branches.*" Especially these
words: "*You are the branches.*" What a simple thing it is to be a branch, the branch of a tree, or the branch of a vine! The branch grows out of the vine, or out of the tree, and there it lives and grows, and in due time, bears fruit. It has no responsibility except just to receive from the root and stem sap and nourishment. And if we only by the Holy Spirit knew our relationship to Jesus Christ, our work would be changed into the brightest and most heavenly thing upon earth. Instead of there ever being soul-weariness or exhaustion, our work would be like a new experience, linking us to Jesus as nothing else can. For, alas! is it not often true that our work comes between us and Jesus? What folly! The very work that He has to do in me, and I for Him, I take up in such a way that it separates me from Christ.

Many a laborer in the vineyard has complained that they have too much work, and not time for close communion with Jesus, and that their usual work weakens the inclination for prayer, and that too much intercourse with the world darkens the spiritual life. Sad thought, that the bearing of fruit should separate the branch from the vine! That must be because we have looked upon our work as something other than the branch bearing fruit.

Now, just a few thoughts about this blessed branch-life. In the first place, it is a life of absolute dependence. The branch has nothing; it just depends upon the vine for everything. … Christ wants that in all your work, the very foundation should be the simple, blessed consciousness: Christ must care for all. …

Workers, here is your first lesson: learn to be nothing, learn to be helpless. The man who has got something is not absolutely dependent; but the man who has got nothing is absolutely dependent. Absolute dependence upon God is the secret of all power in work.

The branch has nothing but what it gets from the vine, and you and I can have nothing but what we get from Jesus. …

Deep Restfulness

But second, the life of the branch is not only a life of entire dependence, but of deep restfulness. … With all your hurry and effort in Christ's work you never prosper. The first thing you need is to come and rest in your Lord Jesus. … And if you would be a true branch of Christ, the living Vine, just rest on Him. Let Christ bear the responsibility. …

Worker, take your place every day at the feet of Jesus, in the blessed peace and rest that come from the knowledge—"I have no care, my cares are His! I have no fear, He cares for all my fears."

Come, children of God, and understand that it is the Lord Jesus who wants to work through you. You complain of the lack of fervent love. It will come from Jesus. He will give the divine love in your heart with which you can love people. That is the meaning of the assurance: "*The love of God is shed abroad in our hearts by the Holy Spirit*" (Romans 5: 5); and of that other word: "*The love of Christ constrains us*" (2 Corinthians 5: 14). Christ can give you a fountain of love, so that you cannot help loving the most wretched and the most ungrateful, or those who have wearied you hitherto. Rest in Christ, who can give wisdom and strength, and you do not know how that restfulness will often prove to be the very best part of your message. You plead with people and you argue, and they get the idea: "There is a man arguing and striving with me." They only feel: "Here are two men dealing with each other." But if you will let the deep rest of God come over you, the rest in Christ Jesus, the peace and rest and holiness of Heaven, that restfulness will bring a blessing to the heart, even more than the words you speak.

Much Fruitfulness

But third, the branch teaches a lesson of much fruitfulness. The Lord Jesus Christ repeated that word fruit often in that parable. He spoke, first, of fruit, and then of more fruit, and then of much fruit. Yes, you are ordained not only to bear fruit, but to bear much fruit. 'Herein is My Father glorified, that you bear much fruit" (John 15: 8). In the first place, Christ said: 'I am the Vine, and my Father is the Husbandman. My Father is the Husbandman who has charge of me and you." He who will watch over the connection between Christ and the branches is God; and it is in the power of God through Christ we are to bear fruit.

Oh, Christians, you know this world is perishing for the want of workers. And it lacks not only more workers—the workers are saying, some more earnestly than others: "We need not only more workers, but we need our workers to have a new power, a different life; that we workers should be able to bring more blessing." … Except the children of God are filled with the sap of the heavenly Vine, except they are filled with the Holy Spirit and the love of Jesus, they cannot bear much of the real heavenly grape. We all confess there is a great deal of work, a great deal of preaching and teaching and visiting, a great deal of machinery, a great deal of earnest effort of every kind; but there is not much manifestation of the power of God in it.

What is lacking? There is lacking the close connection between the worker and the heavenly Vine. Christ, the heavenly Vine, has blessings that He could pour on tens of thousands who are perishing. Christ, the heavenly Vine, has power to provide the heavenly grapes. But "*You are the branches*," and you cannot bear heavenly fruit unless you are in close connection with Jesus Christ.

Do not confound work and fruit. There may be a good deal of work for Christ that is not the fruit of the heavenly Vine. Do not seek for work only. Oh! Study this question of fruit-bearing. It means the very life and the very power and the very spirit and the very love within the heart of the Son of God; it means the heavenly Vine Himself coming into your heart and mine. …

There is in the heart of Christ Jesus a life, and a love, and a Spirit, and a blessing, and a power for men, that are entirely heavenly and divine, and that will come down into our hearts. Stand in close connection with the heavenly Vine and say: "Lord Jesus, nothing less than the sap that flows through You, nothing less than the Spirit of Your divine life is what we ask. Lord Jesus, I pray, let Your Spirit flow through me in all my work for You."

I tell you again that the sap of the heavenly Vine is nothing but the Holy Spirit. The Holy Spirit is the life of the heavenly Vine, and what you must get from Christ is nothing less than a strong inflow of the Holy Spirit. You need it exceedingly, and you want nothing more than that. Remember that. Do not expect Christ to give a bit of strength here, and a bit of blessing yonder, and a bit of help over there. As the vine does its work in giving its own peculiar sap to the branch, so expect Christ to give His own Holy Spirit into your heart, and then you will bear much fruit. And if you have only begun to bear fruit, and are listening to the word of Christ in the parable, "more fruit," "much fruit," remember that in order that you should bear more fruit you just require more of Jesus in your life and heart.

We ministers of the Gospel, how we are in danger of getting into a condition of work, work, work! And we pray over it, but the freshness and buoyancy and joy of the heavenly life are not always present. Let us seek to understand that the life of the branch is a life of much fruit, because it is a life rooted in Christ, the living, heavenly Vine.

Close Communion

And fourth, the life of the branch is a life of close communion. Let us again ask: What has the branch to do? You know that precious, inexhaustible word that Christ used: Abide. Your life is to be an abiding life. And how is the abiding to be? It is to be just like the branch in the vine, abiding every minute of the day. … You say: "But I am so much occupied with other things." You may have ten hours' hard work daily, during which your brain has to be occupied with temporal things; God orders it so. But the abiding work is the work of the heart, not of the brain, the work of the heart clinging to and resting in Jesus, a work in which the Holy Spirit links us to Christ Jesus. Oh, do believe that deeper down than the brain, deep down in the inner life, you can abide in Christ, so that every moment you are free the consciousness will come. …

What is the application to our life of this abiding communion? What does it mean? It means close fellowship with Christ in secret prayer. I am sure there are Christians who do long for the higher life, and who sometimes have got a great blessing, and have at times found a great inflow of heavenly joy and a great outflow of heavenly gladness; and yet after a time it has passed away. They have not understood that close personal actual communion with Christ is an absolute necessity for daily life. Take time to be alone with Christ. Nothing in Heaven or earth can free you from the necessity for that, if you are to be happy and holy Christians.

Oh! How many Christians look upon it as a burden and a tax, and a duty, and a difficulty to be often alone with God! That is the great hindrance to our Christian life everywhere. We need more quiet fellowship with God, and I tell you in the name of the heavenly Vine that you cannot be healthy branches, branches into which the heavenly sap can flow, unless you take plenty of time for communion with God.

12

THE MASTER'S INDWELLING

Northfield Massachusetts Conference Papers (Rev.), 1895

Carnal Christians 1

June 15th

"I could not speak to you as to spiritual people, but as to those still carnal."
—1 CORINTHIANS 3: 1

The apostle here speaks of two stages of the Christian life, two types of Christians: "*I could not speak to you as to spiritual, but as to carnal, even as unto babes in Christ.*" They were Christians, in Christ, but instead of being spiritual Christians, they were carnal. "*I have fed you with milk, and not with meat, for hitherto you were not able to bear it, neither yet are you able, for you are yet carnal.*" Here is that word a second time. "*For whereas*"—this is the proof—"*there is among you envying, and strife, and divisions, are you not carnal, and walk as men? For while one says, I am of Paul, and another, I am of Apollos, are you not carnal?*" Four times the apostle uses that word carnal. … And so he tells them at the very outset of the epistle what he sees to be their state. In the two previous chapters he had spoken about his ministry being by the Holy Spirit; now he begins to tell them what must be the state of a people in order to accept spiritual truth, and he says: "I have not liberty to speak to you as I would, for you are carnal, and you cannot receive spiritual truth."

That suggests to us the solemn thought, that in the Church of Christ there are two classes of Christians. Some have lived many years as believers, and yet always remain babes; others are spiritual men, because they have given themselves up to the power, the leading and to the entire rule of the Holy Spirit. If we are to obtain a blessing, we must first decide to which of these classes we belong. Are we, by the grace of God, in deep humility living a spiritual life, or are we living a carnal life? Then, let us first try to understand what is meant by the carnal state in which believers may be living.

We notice from what we find in Corinthians, four marks of the carnal state. First: It is simply a condition of protracted infancy. You know what that means. Suppose a beautiful babe, six months old. It cannot speak, it cannot walk, but we do not trouble ourselves about that; it is natural, and ought to be so. But suppose a year later we find the child not grown at all, and three years later still no growth; we would at once say: "There must be some terrible disease"; and the baby that at six months old was the cause of joy to everyone who saw him, has become to the mother and to all a source of anxiety and sorrow. There is something wrong; the child cannot grow. It was quite right at six months old that it should eat nothing but milk; but years have passed by, and it remains in the same weakly state.

Now this is just the condition of many believers. They are converted; they know what it is to have assurance and faith; they believe in pardon for sin; they begin to work for God; and yet, somehow, there is very little growth in spirituality, in the real heavenly life. We come into contact with them, and we feel at once there is something wanting; there is none of the beauty of holiness or of the power of God's Spirit in them. This is the condition of the carnal Corinthians, expressed in what was said to the Hebrews: "*You have had the Gospel so long that by this time you ought to be teachers, and yet you need that men should teach you the very rudiments of the oracles of God.*"

Is it not a sad thing to see a believer who has been converted five, ten, twenty years, and yet no growth, and no strength, and no joy of holiness? What are the marks of a little child? One is, a little child cannot help himself, but is always keeping others occupied to serve him. What a tyrant a baby in a house often is! The mother cannot go out, there must be a servant to nurse it; it needs to be cared for constantly. ... So there are Christians who always want help. Their pastor and their Christian friends must always be teaching and comforting them. They go to church, and to prayer-meetings, and to conventions, always wanting to be helped—a sign of spiritual infancy.

The second mark of the carnal state is this: that there is sin and failure continually. Paul says: "*Whereas there is strife and division among you, and envying, are you not carnal?*" A man gives way to temper. He may be a minister, or a preacher of the Gospel, or a Sunday-school teacher, most earnest at the prayer-meeting, but yet strife or bitterness or envying is often shown by him. Alas! Alas! In Galatians 3:5 we are told that the works of the flesh are specially hatred and envy. How often among Christians, who have to work together, do we see divisions and bitterness! God have mercy upon them, that the fruit of the Spirit, which is love, is so frequently absent from His own people.

You ask, "Why is it, that for twenty years I have been fighting with my temper, and cannot conquer it?" It is because you have been fighting with the temper, and you have not been fighting with the root of the temper. You have not seen that it is all because you are in the carnal state, and not properly given up to the Spirit of God. It may be that you never were taught it; that you never saw it in God's Word; that you never believed it. But there it is; the truth of God remains unchangeable. Jesus Christ can give us the victory over sin, and can keep us from actual transgression. I am not telling you that the root of sin will be eradicated, and that you will have no longer any natural tendency to sin; but when the Holy Spirit comes not only with His power for service as a gift, but when He comes in Divine grace to fill the heart, there is victory over sin; power not to fulfill the lusts of the flesh.

And you see a mark of the carnal state not only in unlovingness, Self-consciousness and bitterness, but in so many other sins. How much worldliness, how much ambition among men, how much seeking for the honor that comes from man—all the fruit of the carnal life—to be found in the midst of Christian activity! Let us remember that the carnal state is a state of continual sinning and failure, and God wants us not only to make confession of individual sins, but to come to the acknowledgment that they are the sign that we are not living a healthy life—we are yet carnal.

A third mark … is that this carnal state may be found in existence in connection with great spiritual gifts. There is a difference between gifts and graces. The graces of the Spirit are humility and love, like the humility and love of Christ. The graces of the Spirit are to make us free from Self; the gifts of the Spirit are to fit us for work. We see this illustrated among the Corinthians. In the first chapter Paul says, "*I thank God that you are enriched unto all utterance, and all knowledge, and all wisdom.*" In the 12th and 14th chapters we see that the gifts of prophecy and of working miracles were in great power among them; but the graces of the Spirit were noticeably absent.

And this may be in our days as well as in the time of the Corinthians. I may be a minister of the Gospel; I may teach God's Word beautifully; I may have influence, and gather a large congregation, and yet, alas! I may be carnal; I may be used by God, and may be a blessing to others, and yet the carnal life may still mark me.

You all know the law that a thing is named according to what is its most prominent characteristic. Now, in these carnal Corinthians there was a little of God's Spirit, but the flesh predominated; the Spirit had not the rule of their whole life. And the spiritual are not called so because there is no flesh in them, but because the Spirit in them has obtained dominance, and when you meet them and have intercourse with them, you feel that the Spirit of God has sanctified them. Ah, let us beware lest the blessing God gives us in our work deceive us and lead us to think that because he has blessed us, we must be spiritual men. God may give us gifts that we use, and yet our lives may not be wholly in the power of the Holy Spirit.

My last mark of the carnal state is that it makes a man unfit for receiving spiritual truths. That is what the apostle writes to the Corinthians: "I could not preach to you as unto spiritual; you are not fit for spiritual truth after being Christians so long; you cannot yet bear it; I have to feed you with milk." I am afraid that in the Church of the nineteenth century we often make a terrible mistake. We have a congregation in which the majority are carnal men. We give these men spiritual teaching, and they admire it, understand it, and rejoice in such ministry; yet their lives are not practically affected. They work for Christ in a certain way, but we can scarce recognize the true sanctification of the Spirit; we dare not say they are spiritual men, full of the Holy Spirit.

Now, let us recognize this with regard to ourselves. A man may become very earnest, may take in all the teaching he hears; he may be able to discern, for discernment is a gift; he may say, "That man helps me in this line, and that man in another direction, and a third man is remarkable for another gift;" yet, all the time, the carnal life may be living strongly in him, and when he gets into trouble with some friend, or Christian worker, or worldly man, the carnal root is bearing its terrible fruit, and the spiritual food has failed to enter his heart. Beware of that. Mark the Corinthians and learn of them. Paul did not say to them, "You cannot bear the truth as I would speak it to you," because they were ignorant or a stupid people. The Corinthians prided themselves on their wisdom, and sought it above everything, and Paul said: "I thank God that you are enriched in utterance, in knowledge, and in wisdom; nevertheless, you are yet carnal, your life is not holy; your life is not sanctified unto the humility of the life of the Lamb of God, you can not yet take in real spiritual truth."

We find the carnal state not only at Corinth, but throughout the Christian world today. Many Christians are asking, "What is the reason there is so much feebleness in the Church?" We cannot ask this question too earnestly, and I trust that God Himself will so impress it upon our hearts that we shall say to Him, "It must be changed. Have mercy upon us." But, ah! that prayer and that change cannot come until we have begun to see that there is a carnal root ruling in believers; they are living more after the flesh than the Spirit; they are yet carnal Christians.

Carnal Christians 2

June 16th

"I could not speak to you as to spiritual people, but as to those still carnal."

—1 CORINTHIANS 3: 1

There is a passage "from carnal to spiritual." Did Paul find any spiritual believers? Undoubtedly he did. Just read the 6th chapter of the Epistle to the Galatians! That was a church where strife, and bitterness, and envy were terrible. But the apostle says in the first verse: "*Brethren, if a man be overtaken in a fault, ye which are spiritual restore such a one in the spirit of meekness.*" There we see that the marks of the spiritual Christian are that he or she will be meek; and will have power, and love to help and restore those that are fallen. The carnal Christian cannot do that.

If there is a true spiritual life that can be lived, the great question is: Is the way open, and how can I enter into the spiritual state? Here, again, I have four short answers.

First, we must know that there is such a spiritual life to be lived by men on earth. Nothing cuts the roots of the Christian life so much as unbelief. People do not believe what God has said about what He is willing to do for His children. They do not believe that when God says, "*Be filled with the Spirit*," He means it for every Christian. And yet Paul wrote to the Ephesians each one: "*Be filled with the Spirit, and do not be drunk with wine.*" Just as little as you may be drunk with wine, so little may you live without being filled with the Spirit. ... God's Word teaches us that God does not expect us to live as we ought for one minute unless the Holy Spirit is in us to enable us to do it. ... That is the mark of the child of God: "*As many as are led by the Spirit of God, they are the sons of God.*" In Romans 5 we read: "*The love of God is shed abroad in our hearts by the Holy Spirit given unto us.*" That is to be the common, every-day experience of the believer, not his life at set times only. …

Oh, let us believe we can be spiritual. Thank God, there is now the blessing waiting us. "*Be filled with the Spirit.*" "*Be led by the Spirit.*" There is the blessing. If you have to say, "Oh, God, I have not this blessing," say it; but say also, "Lord, I know it is my duty, my solemn obligation to have it, for without it I cannot live in perfect peace with You all the day; without it I cannot glorify You, and do the work You would have me do." This is our first step from carnal to spiritual—to recognize a spiritual life, a walk in the Spirit, is within our reach. How can we ask God to guide us into spiritual life, if we have not a clear, confident conviction that there is such a life to be had?

Then comes the second step; we must see the shame and guilt of having lived such a life. … "Alas! it has been our unfaithfulness, our unbelief, our disobedience, that has kept us from giving ourselves utterly to God. We have to blush and to be ashamed before God that we do not live as spiritual Christians."

We do not get converted without having conviction of sin. … But we need a second conviction of sin. … The sins of an unconverted person are different from the sins of a believer. The unconverted, for instance, are not ordinarily convicted of the corruption of their nature. … But the believer is in quite a different condition. Our sins are far more blamable, for we have had the light and the love and the Spirit of God given to us. … We have striven to conquer them and have grown to see that our nature is utterly corrupt, that the carnal mind, the flesh, within, is making our whole state utterly wretched. When a believer is thus convicted by the Holy Spirit, it is specially the life of unbelief that condemns, because he or she sees that the great guilt connected with this has kept them from receiving the full gift of God's Holy Spirit. … God comes near. Job, the righteous man, whom God trusted, saw in himself the deep sin of Self and its righteousness that he had never seen before. Until this conviction of the wrongness of our carnal state as believers comes to each one of us; until we are willing to get this conviction from God, to take time before God to be humbled and convicted, we never can become spiritual.

Then comes the third mark, which is that out of the carnal state into the spiritual is only one step. One step; oh, that is a blessed message I bring to you—it is only one step. I know many people will refuse to admit that it is only one step; they think it too little for such a mighty change. But was not conversion only one step? So it is when a believer passes from carnal to spiritual.

You ask if when I talk of a spiritual man I am not thinking of a man of spiritual maturity, a real saint, and you say: "Does that come in one day? Is there no growth in holiness?" I reply that spiritual maturity cannot come in a day. We cannot expect it. It takes growth, until the whole beauty of the image of Christ is formed in a man. But still I say that it needs but one step for us to get out of the carnal life into the spiritual life. It is when we utterly break with the flesh; when we give up the flesh into the crucifixion death of Christ; when we see that everything about it is accursed and that we cannot deliver ourself from it; and then claims the slaying power of Christ's cross within—it is when we do this and says: "This spiritual life prepared for me is the free gift of my God in Christ Jesus," that we understand how one step can bring him out of the carnal into the spiritual state.

In that spiritual life there will be much still to be learned. There will still be imperfections. Spiritual life is not perfect; but the predominant characteristic will be spiritual. When we have given Self up to the real, living, acting, ruling power of God's Spirit, we have got into the right position in which we can grow. You never think of growing out of sickness into health; you may grow out of feebleness into strength, as the little babe can grow to be a strong man; but where there is disease, there must healing come if there is to be a cure effected. There are Christians who think that they must grow out of the carnal state into the spiritual state. You never can. What could help those carnal Corinthians? To give them milk could not help them, for milk was a proof they were in the wrong state. To give them meat would not help them, for they were unfit to eat it. What they needed was the knife of the surgeon. Paul says that the carnal life must be cut out.

"*They that are Christ's have crucified the flesh.*" When we understand what that means, and accepts it in the faith of what Christ can do, then one step can bring us from carnal to spiritual. One simple act of faith in the power of Christ's death, one act of surrender to the fellowship of Christ's death as the Holy Spirit can make it ours, will make it ours, will bring deliverance from the power of your efforts.

Oh, believers, if any of us who are conscious that the carnal state predominates have to say: "It marks me; I am religious, earnest, a friend of missions; I work for Christ in my church, but, alas! temper and sin and worldliness have still the mastery over my soul," hear the word of God. If any will come and say: "I have struggled, I have prayed, I have wept, and it has not helped me," then you must do one other thing. You must see that the living Christ is God's provision for your holy, spiritual life. You must believe that that Christ who accepted you once, at conversion, in His wonderful love is now waiting to say to you that you may become a spiritual man, entirely given up to God. If you will believe that, your fear will vanish and you will say: "It can be done; if Christ will accept and take charge, it shall be done." …

We go to Christ to take it away, and he does not do it; and we ask, "Why will he not do it? I have prayed very earnestly." It is because you wanted Him to take away the ugly fruits while the poisonous root was to stay in you. You did not ask Him that the flesh should be nailed to His cross, and that you should henceforth give up Self entirely to the power of His Spirit. … But if you will come and give your whole life into His charge, Christ Jesus is mighty to save; Christ Jesus waits to be gracious; Christ Jesus waits to fill you with His Spirit.

Will you not take the step? God grant that we may be led by His Spirit to a yielding up of ourselves to Him as never before. Will you not come in humble confession that, alas! the carnal life has predominated too much, has altogether marked you, and that you have a bitter consciousness that with all the blessing God has bestowed, He has not made you what you want to be—a spiritual man? It is the Holy Spirit alone who by His indwelling can make a spiritual man. Come then and cast yourself at God's feet, with this one thought, "Lord, I give myself an empty vessel to be filled with Your Spirit."

Each one of you sees every day at the tea table an empty cup set there, waiting to be filled with tea when the proper time comes. So with every dish, every plate. They are cleansed and empty, ready to be filled. Emptied and cleansed. Oh, come! and just as a vessel is set apart to receive what it is to contain, say to Christ that you desire from this hour to be a vessel set apart to be filled with His Spirit, given up to be spiritual. Bow down in the deepest emptiness of soul, and say, "O God, I have nothing!" and then surely as you place yourself before Him you have a right to say, "My God will fulfill His promise! I claim from Him the filling of the Holy Spirit to make me, instead of a carnal, a spiritual Christian." If you place yourself at His feet, and tarry there; if you abide in that humble surrender and that childlike trust, as sure as God lives, the blessing will come. …

The Self Life

June 17th

"If anyone will come after Me, let them deny themselves, and take up their cross, and follow Me."
—MATTHEW 16: 24

Let us dwell upon this one word, "Self." It is only as we learn to know what Self is that we really know what is at the root of all our failure, and are prepared to go to Christ for deliverance. Let us consider, first of all, the nature of this Self-life, then denote some of its works and then ask the question: "How may we be delivered from it?" Self is the power with which God has created and endowed every intelligent creature. Self is the very center of a created being. And why did God give the angels or man a Self? The object of this Self was that we might bring it as an empty vessel unto God; that He might put into it His life. God gave me the power of Self-determination, that I might bring this Self every day and say: "Oh, God, work in it; I offer it to you." God wanted a vessel into which He might pour out His Divine fullness of beauty, wisdom and power; and so He created the world, the sun, and the moon, and the stars, the trees, and the flowers, and the grass, which all show forth the riches of His wisdom, and beauty, and goodness. But they do it without knowing what they do. Then God created the angels with a Self and a will, to see whether they would come and voluntarily yield themselves to Him as vessels for Him to fill. …

It was that Self that ruined and brought destruction upon this world, and all that there has been of sin, and of darkness, and of wretchedness, and of misery…. And if we are to understand fully what Christ is to do for us, and are to become partakers of a full salvation, we must learn to know, and to hate, and to give up entirely this cursed Self.

Now what are the works of Self? I might mention many, but let us take the simplest words that we are continually using—self-will, Self-confidence, Self-exaltation. Self-will, pleasing Self, is the great sin of man, and it is at the root of all that compromising with the world which is the ruin of so many. Many cannot understand why they should not please themselves and do their own will. Numbers of Christians have never gotten hold of the idea that a Christian is one who is never to seek one's own will, but is always to seek the will of God, as one in whom the very spirit of Christ lives. "Lo, I come to do Your will, oh, my God!" We find Christians pleasing themselves in a thousand ways, and yet trying to be happy, and good, and useful; and they do not know that at the root of it all is Self-will robbing them of the blessing. . . .

Christians, look at your own lives in the light of the words of Jesus. Do you find there Self-will, Self-pleasing? Remember this: every time you please yourself, you deny Jesus. It is one of the two. You must please Him only, and deny Self, or you must please yourself and deny Him. Then follows Self-confidence, Self-trust, Self-effort, Self-dependence. . . . People have often asked me, "What is the reason that I fail? I desire so earnestly, and pray so fervently, to live in God's will." And my answer generally is, "Simply because you trust yourself." They answer me: "No, I do not; I know I am not good; and I know that God is willing to keep me, and I put my trust in Jesus." But I reply, "No, my brother; no; if you trusted God and Jesus, you could not fall, but you trust yourself." Do let us believe that the cause of every failure in the Christian life is nothing but this. I trust this cursed Self, instead of trusting Jesus. I trust my own strength, instead of the almighty strength of God. And that is why Christ says, "This Self must be denied."

Then there is Self-exaltation, another form of the works of Self. Ah, how much pride and jealousy is there in the Christian world; how much sensitiveness to what men say of us or think of us; how much desire of human praise and pleasing men, instead of always living in the presence of God, with the one thought: "Am I pleasing to Him?" Christ said, "*How can you believe who receive honor one of another*?" Receiving honor of one another renders a life of faith absolutely impossible. . . .

Now comes the third point. What are we to do to get rid of it? Jesus answers us in the words of our text: "*If any man will come after me, let him take up his cross and follow me.*" Note it well—I must deny myself and take Jesus himself as my life—I must choose. There are two lives, the Self life and the Christ life; I must choose one of the two. "Follow me," says our Lord, "make me the law of your existence, the rule of your conduct; give me your whole heart; follow me, and I will care for all." Oh, friends, it is a solemn exchange to have set before us; to come and, seeing the danger of this Self, with its pride and its wickedness, to cast ourselves before the Son of God, and to say, "I deny my own life, I take Your life to be mine."

There is but one way of being delivered from this life of Self. We must follow Christ, set our hearts upon Him, listen to His teachings, give ourselves up every day, that He may be all to us, and by the power of Christ the denial of Self will be a blessed, unceasing reality. Never for one hour do I expect the Christian to reach a stage at which he can say, "I have no Self to deny"; never for one moment in which he can say, "I do not need to deny Self." No, this fellowship with the cross of Christ will be an unceasing denial of Self every hour and every moment by the grace of God. There is no place where there is full deliverance from the power of this sinful Self. We are to be crucified with Christ Jesus.

… And now, what is the use that we are to make of this lesson of the Master? The first lesson will be that we should take time, and that we should humble ourselves before God, at the thought of what this Self is in us; put down to the account of the Self every sin, every shortcoming, all failure, and all that has been dishonoring to God, and then say, "Lord, this is what I am"; and then let us allow the blessed Jesus Christ to take entire control of our life, in the faith that His life can be ours.

Do not think it is an easy thing to get rid of Self. At a consecration meeting, it is easy to make a vow, and to offer a prayer, and to perform an act of surrender, but as solemn as the death of Christ was on Calvary—His giving up of His unsinning Self-life to God—just as solemn must it be between us and our God—the giving up of Self to death. The power of the death of Christ must come to work in us every day. …

We are called upon to live the life of Christ, and Christ comes to live His life in us; but one thing must first take place; we must learn to hate this Self, and to deny it. As Peter said, when he denied Christ, "I have nothing to do with him," so we must say, "I have nothing to do with Self," that Christ Jesus may be all in all. Let us humble ourselves at the thought of what this Self has done to us and how it has dishonored Jesus; and let us pray very fervently: "Lord, by Your light illuminate this Self; we beseech You to reveal it to us. Open our eyes, that we may see what it has done, and that it is the only hindrance that has been keeping us back." …

And then comes the blessed exchange, that a man is made willing and able to say: "Another will live the life for me, another will live with me, another will do all for me." Nothing else will do. Deny Self; take up the cross, to die with Jesus; follow Him only. May He give us the grace to understand, and to receive, and to live the Christ life.

Dead with Christ

June 18th

"I am crucified with Christ."

—GALATIANS 2: 20

Paul says: *"I have been crucified with Christ."* And again: *"God forbid that I should glory, save in the cross of our Lord Jesus Christ, through whom I have been crucified to the world, and the world to me."* … If we want, in very deed, to enjoy fully the rest that there is in Jesus, we can only have it as He comes in, in the power of His death, to slay what is in us of nature, and to take possession, and to live His own life in the fullness of the Holy Spirit.

God's Word takes us to the cross of Christ, and it teaches us about that cross, two things. It tells us that Christ died for sin. We understand what that means, that in His atonement He died as I never die, as I never can die, as I never need die; He died for sin and for me. But what gave His death such power to atone? It was this: the spirit in which He died, not the physical suffering, not the external act of death, but the spirit in which

He died. And what was that spirit? He died unto sin. Sin had tempted Him, and surrounded Him, and had brought Him very nigh to saying, "I cannot die." In Gethsemane, He cried: "*Father, is it not possible that the cup pass from me*?" But God be praised, He gave up His life rather than yield to sin. He died to sin, and in dying He conquered. And now, I cannot die *for* sin like Christ, but I can and I must die *to* sin like Christ. Christ died for me. In that He stands alone. Christ died to sin, and in that I have fellowship with Him. I have been crucified, I am dead.

The great mark of Christ is His death. Even in Heaven, upon the throne, He stands as the Lamb that was slain, and through eternity they ever sing, "*You are worthy, for You was slain*." Beloved, your Boaz, your Christ, your all-sufficient Savior, is a Man of whom the chief mark and the greatest glory is this: He died. And if the Bride is to live with her husband as His wife, then she must enter into His state, and into His spirit, and into His disposition....

If we want to have the real Christ that God has given us, the real Christ that died for us, in the power of His death and resurrection, we must take our stand here. But many Christians do not understand what the 6th chapter of the epistle to the Romans teaches us: ... *"Know not that as many of you as are baptized into Christ Jesus, are baptized into His death?"* How can we who are dead to sin in Christ live any longer therein? ...

It is a command: *"Reckon yourselves dead to sin."* Get hold of your union to Christ; believe in the new nature within you, that spiritual life which you have from Christ, a life that has died and been raised again. ... Praise God, when we begin to see what it is, and begins in obedience to say, "I will do what God's Word says; I am dead; I reckon myself dead," we enter upon a new life. ...

The Holy Spirit came from Heaven, from the glorified Jesus, to bring His death and His life into us. The two are inseparably connected. That Christ died, He died unto sin, and that He lives, He lives unto God. The death and the life in Him are inseparable; and even so in us the life to God in Christ is inseparably connected with the death to sin. And that is what the Holy Spirit will teach us and work in us.

What are the marks of a crucified one? The first is, deep, absolute humility. Christ humbled Himself, and became obedient unto death, even the death of the cross. When the death to sin begins to work mightily, that is one of its chief and most blessed proofs. It breaks us down, down, and the great longing of our heart is, "Oh, that I could get deeper down before my God, and be nothing at all, that the life of Christ might be exalted. I deserve nothing but the cursed cross; I give myself over to it." Humility is one of the great marks of the crucified.

Another mark is impotence, helplessness. ... As long as we Christians are strong, and can work, or struggle, we do not get into the blessed life of Christ; but when we say, "I am crucified; I am utterly helpless, every breath of life and strength must come from my Jesus," then we learn what it is to sink into our own impotence, and say, "I am nothing." ... If you want to live the life of Heaven, there must be death to sin in the power of Jesus. There must be personal entrustment of the soul into His death to sin, personal acceptance of Jesus to do the mighty work. ...

The Kingdom First

June 19th

"Seek first the Kingdom of God."

—MATTHEW 6: 33

A young minister once said to me, "Why is it that I have so much more interest in study than in prayer, and how can you teach me the art of fellowship with God?" My answer was: "Oh, my brother, if we have any true conception of what God is, the art of fellowship with Him will come naturally, and will be a delight."

But, alas! the Kingdom of God looks to many as a burden, and as something unnatural. It looks like a strain, and we seek some relaxation in the world, and God is not our chief joy. I come to you with a message. It is right, on account of what God is as Infinite Love, as Infinite Blessing; it is right and more, it is our highest privilege to listen to Christ's words, and to seek God and His Kingdom first and above everything.

And then look at man again; our nature. What were we created for? To live in the likeness of God, and as His image! Now, if we have been created in the image and likeness of God, we can find our happiness in nothing except that in which God finds His happiness. The more like Him we are the happier.

And in what does God find His happiness? In two things: Everlasting righteousness and everlasting beneficence. God is righteousness everlasting. "He is Light, and in Him is no darkness." The Kingdom, the domination, the rule of God will bring us nothing but righteousness. "Seek the Kingdom of God and His righteousness." If we but knew what sin is, and if we really longed to be free from everything like sin, what a grand message this would be! Jesus comes to lead us to God and His righteousness. We were created to be like God, in His perfect righteousness and holiness. What a prospect! And in His love too.

The Kingdom of God means this: that there is in God a rule of universal love. He loves, and loves, and never ceases to love; and He longs to bless all who will yield to His pleadings. God is Light, and God is Love. And now the message comes to man. Can you think of a higher nobility; can you think of anything grander than to take the position that God takes, and to be one with God in His Kingdom; i.e., to have His Kingdom fill your heart; to have God Himself as your King and portion? …

"The Kingdom of God first!" How am I to reach that blessed life? The answer is: "Give up everything for it." And then a second answer would be this: Live every day and hour of your life in the humble desire to maintain that position. There are people who hear this test, and who say it is true, and that they want to obey it. But if you were to ask them how much time they spend with God day by day, you would be surprised and grieved to hear how little time they give up to Him. And yet they wonder that the blessedness of the Divine life disappears. We prove the value we attach to things by the time we devote to them."

The Kingdom should be first every day, and all the day. Let the Kingdom be first every morning. Begin the day with God, and God Himself will maintain His Kingdom in your heart. Do believe that. Rome did its utmost to maintain the authority of the man who gave himself to live for it. And God, the living God, will He not maintain His authority in your soul if you submit to Him? He will, indeed. Come to Him; only come, and give yourself up to Him in fellowship through Christ Jesus.

Seek to maintain that fellowship with God all the day. Ah, friends, a man cannot have the Kingdom of God first, and at times, by way of relaxation, throw it off and seek his enjoyment in the things of this world. People have a secret idea that such a life will become too solemn, too great a strain—it will be too difficult every moment of the day, from morning to evening, to have the Kingdom of God first. One sees at once how wrong it is to think thus. The presence of the love of God must every moment be our highest joy. Let us say: "By the help of God, it shall ever be the Kingdom of God first."

... Jesus Christ came preaching the Gospel of the Kingdom, and proclaimed "*The Kingdom is at hand.*" "Some," He said, "*are standing here who will not see death until they see the Kingdom come in power.*" He said to the disciples, "*The Kingdom is within you.*" And when did the Kingdom come—that Kingdom of God upon earth? When the Holy Spirit descended. On Ascension Day, the King went and sat down upon the throne at the right hand of God, and the Kingdom of God, in Christ, the Kingdom of Heaven upon earth, was inaugurated. When the Holy Spirit came down He brought God into the heart, and Christ, and established the rule of God in power.

I am afraid sometimes, that in speaking of the Holy Spirit we forget one thing. The Holy Spirit is very much spoken of in connection with power; and it is right that we should seek power. It is not so much spoken of in connection with the graces. And yet these are always more important than the gifts of power—the holiness, the humility, the meekness, the gentleness, and the lovingness; these are the true marks of the Kingdom. We speak rightly of the Holy Spirit as the only one who can breathe all this into us. But I think there is a third thing almost more important, that we forget, and that is: in the Spirit, the Father and the Son themselves come. When Christ first promised the Holy Spirit, and spoke about His approaching coming, He said: "*In that day you shall know that I am in the Father, and you in me, and I in you. He that loves me keeps my commandments; and my Father will love him, and we will come and make our abode with him.*"

Would you have the Kingdom of God first in your life, you must have the Kingdom in your hearts. If my heart be set upon a thing I may be bound with chains, but the moment the chains are loosened I fly towards the object of my affection and desire. And just so the Kingdom must be within us, and then it is easy to say: "The Kingdom first." But to have the Kingdom within us in truth, we must have God the Father, and Christ the Son, by the Holy Spirit within us too. No Kingdom without the King. You are called to likeness with Christ. Oh, how many Christians strive after this part and that part of the likeness of Christ, and forget the root of the whole! What is the root of all? That Christ gave Himself up utterly to God, and His Kingdom and glory. He gave His life, that God's Kingdom might be established. Do you the same to-day and give your life to God to be every moment a living sacrifice, and the Kingdom will come with power into your heart. Give yourself up to Christ. Let Christ the King reign in your heart, and the heavenly Kingdom will come there and the Presence and the Rule of God be known in power. Oh, think of that wonderful thing that is going to happen in the great eternity. We read of it in 1st Corinthians: God has entrusted Christ with the Kingdom, but there is coming a day when Christ shall come Himself again to be subjected unto the Father, and He shall give up the Kingdom to the Father, that God may be all, and in that day Christ shall say before the universe: "This is my glory, I give back the Kingdom to the Father!"

Christians, if your Christ finds His glory here on earth in dying and sacrificing Himself for the Kingdom and then in eternity again in giving the Kingdom to God, shall not you and I come to God to do the same and count anything we have as loss, that the Kingdom of God may be made manifest, and that God may be glorified.

Christ's Humility Our Salvation

June 20th

"Let this mind be in you which was also in Christ Jesus: He humbled Himself and became obedient unto death, even the death of the cross."

—PHILIPPIANS 2: 5–8

If we love Christ above everything, we must love humility above everything, for humility is the very essence of His life and glory, and the salvation He brings. ... He made Himself of no reputation; He emptied Himself; He chose the form of a servant. He said: *"The Son of Man is not come to be ministered unto, to be served, but to serve, and to give His life a ransom for many."* And you know, in the last night, He took the place of a slave, and girded Himself with a towel, and went to wash the feet of Peter and the other disciples.

Beloved, the life of Jesus upon earth was a life of the deepest humility. It was this that gave His life its worth and beauty in God's sight. And then His death ... was an exhibition of unparalleled humility: *"He humbled Himself, and became obedient unto death, even the death of the cross."* My Lord Christ took a low place all the time of His walk upon earth; He took a very low place when He began to wash the disciples' feet; but when He went to Calvary, He took the lowest place there was to be found in the universe of God, the very lowest, and He let sin, and the curse of sin, and the wrath of God, cover Him. ...

We are in danger of thinking about Christ, as God, as man, as the atonement, as the Savior, and as exalted upon the throne, and we form an image of Christ, while the real Christ, that which is the very heart of His character, remains unknown. What is the real Christ? Divine humility, bowed down into the very depths for our salvation. The humility of Jesus is our salvation. We read, "*He humbled Himself, therefore God has highly exalted Him.*"

The secret of His exaltation to the throne is this: He humbled Himself before God and man. Humility is the Christ of God, and now in Heaven, today, that Christ, the Man of humility, is on the throne of God. …

But the salvation that Christ brought is not only a salvation that flows out of humility; it also leads to humility. We must understand that this is not only the salvation which Christ brought; but that it is exactly the salvation which you and I need. What is the cause of all the wretchedness of man? Primarily pride; man seeking his own will and his own glory. Yes, pride is the root of every sin, and so the Lamb of God comes to us in our pride, and brings us salvation from it. We need above everything to be saved from our pride and our Self-will. It is good to be saved from the sins of stealing, murdering, and every other evil; but we need above all to be saved from what is the root of all sin: Self-will and pride. It is not until we begin to feel that this is exactly the salvation we need, that we really can understand what Christ is, and that we can accept Him as his salvation. …

A vessel must be empty if it is to be filled, and if we are to be filled with the life of God we must be utterly empty of Self. This is the glory of God—that He is to fill all things, and more especially His redeemed people. And as this is the glory of the creature, so this is the only redemption, and the only glory of every redeemed soul, to be empty and as nothing before God; to wait upon Him, and to let God be all in all.

Humility has a prominent place in almost every epistle of the New Testament. Paul says: *"Walk with all lowliness and meekness, with longsuffering, forbearing one another in love; endeavoring to keep the unity of the Spirit in the bond of peace."* The nearer you get to God, and the fuller of God, the lowlier you will be; and equally before God and man, you will love to bow very low. We know of Peter's early Self-confidence; but in his epistles what a different language he speaks! He wrote there: *"Let the younger be subject to the elder, and all you be subject one to another; humble yourselves under the mighty hand of God, that He may exalt you in His own time."*

He understood, and he dared to preach, humility to all. It is indeed the salvation we need. What is it that prevents people from coming to that entire surrender that we speak of? Simply that they dare not abandon themselves, and trust themselves, to God; that they are not willing to be nothing, to give up their wishes, and their will, and their honor to Christ. Shall we not accept the salvation that Jesus offers? He gave up His own will; He gave up His own honor; He gave up any confidence in Himself; He lived dependent upon God as a servant whom the Father had sent.

There is the salvation we need, the Spirit of humility that was in Christ. What is it that often disturbs our hearts, and our peace? It is pride seeking to be something. And God's decree is irreversible, *"God resists the proud; He gives grace only to the humble."* How often Jesus had to speak to his disciples about it! You will find repeatedly in the Gospel those simple words: *"He that humbles Himself shall be exalted; he that exalts himself shall be humbled."* He taught His disciples: *"He that would be chief among you, let him be the servant of all."* This should be our one cry before God: "Let the power of the Holy Spirit come upon me, with the humility of Jesus, that I may take the place that He took." …

This is the salvation the Holy Spirit brings. You know what a change took place in those disciples. Let us praise God for it; the Holy Spirit means this: the life, the disposition, the temper, and the inclinations of Jesus, brought down from Heaven into our hearts. That is the Holy Spirit. He has His mighty workings to bestow as gifts; but the fullness of the Holy Spirit is this: Jesus Christ in His humility coming to dwell in us. …

Dear friends, Christ is yours. Christ as He comes in the power of the Holy Spirit is yours. Are you longing to have Him, to have the perfect Christ Jesus? Come, then, and see how, amid the glories of His Godhead—His having been in the form of God, and equal to God; amid the glories of His incarnation—His having become a man; amid the glories of His atonement—His having been obedient to death; and amid the glories of His exaltation, which is the chief and brightest glory, He humbled Himself from Heaven down to earth and on earth down to the cross. He humbled Himself to bear the name and show the meekness, and die the death of the Lamb of God.

And what is it we now need to do? How are we to be saved by this humility of Jesus? It is a solemn question, but, thank God, the answer can be given. First we must desire it above everything. Let us learn to pray God to deliver us from every vestige of pride, for this is a cursed thing. Let us learn to set aside for a time other things in the Christian life, and begin to plead with the Lamb of God day by day, "O Lamb of God, I know Your love, but I know so little of Your meekness." Come day after day, and lay your heart against His heart, and say to Him with strong desire: "Jesus, Lamb of God, give, oh, give me Yourself, with Your meekness and humility," and He will fulfill the desire of them that fear Him. It is not enough to desire it and to pray for it; claim and accept it as yours. This humility is given you in Christ Jesus. …

Joy in the Holy Spirit

June 21st

"For the Kingdom of God is not meat and drink, but righteousness, and peace, and joy in the Holy Spirit."
—ROMANS 14: 17 …

What is this joy? First of all, it is the joy of the presence of Jesus. We are often inclined to speak most of two other things, the power for sanctification, and the power for service. But I find there is a thing more important than either of those two, and that is that the Holy Spirit came from Heaven to be the abiding presence of Christ in His disciples, in the Church, and in the heart of every believer.

The Lord Jesus was going away, and His disciples were very sad; their hearts were sorrowful; but He said to them, *"I will come back again, and I will come to you. Your hearts shall rejoice, and your joy no man shall take from you."* What took place with them, may take place with us too. The Holy Spirit is given to make the presence of Jesus an abiding reality, a continual experience.

And what was that joy that no man could ever touch? It was the joy of Pentecost.

And what was Pentecost? The coming of the Lord Jesus in the Holy Spirit to dwell with His disciples. While Jesus was with His disciples on earth, He could not get into their hearts in the right way. They loved Him, but they could not take in His teaching, they could not partake of His disposition, and they could not receive His very spirit into their being. But when He had ascended to Heaven, He came back in the Spirit to dwell in their hearts. …

With God's people, there seems to be one hindrance: *they do not know their Savior.* … Many Christians are asked as to how one may have the joy unspeakable, the joy that nothing can take away, the joy of the friendship and nearness and love of Jesus filling his heart. We complain that the rush of competition is so terrible that we cannot get time for private prayer. Christian, the Lord Jesus Christ, if He comes to you as a brother and a friend and an abiding guest, can you give your heart the joy of the Holy Spirit, so that business will take its right place under your feet? Your heart is too holy to have it filled with business; let the business be in the head and under the feet, but let Christ have the whole heart, and He will keep the whole life. Our glorious, exalted, almighty, ever present Christ!

We all know what the power of joy is; we know there is nothing so attractive as joy, there is nothing can help us to bear and endure so much as joy; we know that the Lord Jesus Himself "*for the joy that was set before Him endured the cross.*" … Come today and believe the joy of the Holy Spirit is meant for you. …

Let us remember that in the sight of God there is something more than work. There is Christlikeness—the likeness and the life of Christ in us. That is what God wants; that will fit us for work. God asks not that Christ should live in us as separate persons—temples full of filthy, impure, foul creatures, with Christ hidden away somewhere there—that is not the intention of God. But He wants Christ so formed in us that we are one with Christ, and that in our thinking, feeling and living, the image of His blessed Son is manifest…. The Holy Spirit is given to sanctify us. …

The Spirit of God is a holy spirit and His work is to make us free from the power of sin and death. And if you want to live in the joy of the Holy Spirit, the question comes: "Are you willing to surrender everything that is sinful, even what appears good…?" You may be involved in relationships that make your life very difficult. … But is not the blessed Lamb of God worth it all?

What is the Christ worth to you? The question was once asked the disciples, "What think you of Christ?" I ask, "What is Christ worth to you?" And I beseech you, whatever prospective difficulties there may be, and whatever perplexities surround you, take the whole world to-day and cast it at His feet. To have Him is worth any difficulty; to have Him will be the solution of every difficulty. There are not only such external, manifest difficulties and perplexities, there are a thousand little things that come in our life and that often disturb us, temptations to unloving feelings, and sharp words, and hasty judgments.

Oh, come, and believe that the Holy Spirit, the sanctifier, can come in and rule, and give grace to pass through all without sinning, and you shall know what the joy of the Holy Spirit is. Our body, we read in 1st Corinthians, is the temple of the Holy Spirit. It is to be holy in things like eating and drinking. How often a Christian comes to the consciousness that he takes or seeks too much enjoyment in that eating, eating for pleasure, with no Self-denial or Self-sacrifice in his feeding the body! How often we tempt one another to eat, and how often the believer forgets that this body is the very secret temple of the Holy Spirit and that every mouthful we eat and drink must be for the glory of God in such a way as to be perfectly well pleasing to Him!

Beloved, I bring you a message: There is access for you into the rest of God, and the Holy Spirit is given to bring you in, and the Holy Spirit will fill your heart with the unutterable joy of Christ's presence; and with the joy of deliverance from sin, of victory over sin; the unutterable joy of knowing that you are doing God's will and are pleasing in His sight; the unutterable joy of knowing that He is sanctifying and keeping the temple for Christ to dwell in.

Believers, the joy of the Holy Spirit, the joy of that holiness of God, is His blessedness, His purity, His perfection, that nothing can mar or stain or disturb. The Holy Spirit waits to bring and to manifest it in our lives. He wants to come so into our hearts that we shall live, as Holy Spirit men, the sanctified life, with the sanctifying power of Jesus running through our whole beings.

The joy of the Holy Spirit is the joy of the love of the saints. The Holy Spirit was not given to any man on the day of Pentecost separate from the others; He came and filled the whole company. We know how much division and separation and pride there had been among them, but on that day the Holy Spirit so filled their hearts that we find it was afterward said: "*Behold how these men love one another.*" There was a love in the primitive church that the very heathen noticed, and could not understand. ... The Holy Spirit is just the love of God come to dwell in the heart. When He dwells with me and my brother we learn to love each other. ...

Does not the Scripture say, "*If He gave His life for us, we are bound to give our life for the brethren?*" The Holy Spirit comes as a spirit of love, and if you want to know the joy of the Holy Spirit, and want Him to lead you into the rest of God and keep you there, beware above everything on earth or in hell of being unloving. One sharp word to your brother or sister brings a cloud upon you without your knowing it. People are so accustomed to talk just as they like about each other that they say sharp and unkind and unloving things, and when a cloud comes in consequence they cannot understand it. If there is one thing that grieves God, if there is one thing that hinders the Spirit—the fruit of the Spirit is love—it is the want of lovingness. ... And let us say to-day, "I see what the joy is; it is the joy of always loving, it is the joy of losing my own life in love to others." ...

Beloved, are you living in the joy of the Holy Spirit? Come and accept a blessing and give yourself up to live a life of humility in which you are nothing, and a life of love like Christ's in which you only live for your fellow-men, for the kingdom of God is the joy of the Holy Spirit.

My last thought is that the joy of the Holy Spirit is the joy of working for God. The joy of the presence of Jesus, the joy of deliverance from sin, the joy of love for the brethren, and then the joy of working for God. ... The joy of the Holy Spirit comes when a man gives himself up to the Christlike work of carrying the love of God to men. Let us seek the perishing, let us live and die for souls, let us live and die that our fellow men may be reclaimed and brought back to their God. There is no joy like hearing the joy-song of a new-born soul. …

Oh that every fiber of my being may be taken possession of for this great work with God!" The great need is that all Christians should consecrate themselves wholly to God for His work. May God help us to know what is the joy of the Holy Spirit.

That God May Be All in All

June 22nd

"Then comes the end, when He shall have delivered up the Kingdom to God the Father; when He shall have put down all rule, and all authority and power. For He must reign till He has put all enemies under His feet. The last enemy that shall be destroyed is death. For He has put all things under His feet. … And when all things shall be subdued unto him, then shall the Son also Himself be subject unto Him, that God may be all in all."

—1 CORINTHIANS 15: 24–28

This will be the grand conclusion of the great drama of the world's history, and of Christ's redemption. There will come a day—the glory is such we can form no conception of it, the mystery is so deep we cannot realize it, but there is a day coming, when the Son shall deliver up the Kingdom that the Father gave Him, and that He won with His blood, and that He has established and perfected from the throne of His glory. "*He shall deliver up the Kingdom unto the Father.*" The Son Himself shall be subject also unto the Father, "*that God may be all in all.*"

I cannot understand it—the ever blessed Son equal with God, from eternity, and through eternity; the ever blessed Son on the throne shall be subject unto the Father; and in some way utterly beyond our comprehension, it shall then be made manifest, as never before, that God is all in all. It is this that Christ has been working for; it is this that He is working for today in us; it is this that He thought it worthwhile to give His blood for; it is this that His heart is longing for in each of us; this is the very essence and glory of Christianity, "*that God may be all in all.*"

And now, if this is what fills the heart of Christ; if this expresses the one end of the work of Christ, then, if I want to have the spirit of Christ in me, the motto of my life must be: Everything made subject, and swallowed up in Him, "*that God may be all in all.*" What a triumph it would be if the Church were fighting really with that banner floating over her! What a life ours could be if that were really our banner! To serve God fully, wholly, only, to have Him all in all! How it would ennoble, and enlarge, and stimulate our whole being! I am working, I am fighting, "*that God may be all in all*"; that the day of glory may be hastened. I am praying, and the Holy Spirit makes His wrestling in me with unutterable longing, "*that God may be all in all.*" If only we Christians realized in connection with what a grand cause we are working and praying; that we had some conception of what a Kingdom we are partakers of, and what a manifestation of God we are preparing for.

To illustrate what a grand thing it is to belong to the Kingdom of God, and to the glorious Church of Christ on earth, John McNeill tells how when he was a boy twelve years of age, working on a railway line and earning the grand wages of six shillings a week, he used to go home to his mother and sisters, who thought no end of their little Johnnie, and delight them by telling of the position he had. He would say with great pride, "Oh, our company—it has so many thousands of pounds passing through its hands every year; it carries so many hundreds of thousands of passengers every year; and it has so many miles of railway, and so many engines and carriages; and so many thousands in its employ!" And the mother and the sisters had great pride in him, because he was a partner in such an important business. Christians, if we would only rouse ourselves to believe that we belong to the Kingdom that Christ is preparing to deliver up to the Father, that God may be all in all, how the glory would fill our hearts, and expel everything mean, and low, and earthly! How we should be borne along in this blessed faith!

I am living for this: that Christ may have the Kingdom to deliver to the Father. I am living for this, and I will one day see Him made subject to the Father, and then God all in all. I am living for Him, and I shall be there not only as a witness, but I will have a part in it all. The Kingdom delivered up, the Son made subject, and God all in all! I shall have a part in it, and in adoring worship share the glory and the blessedness. Let us take this home to our hearts, that it may rule in our lives—this one thought, this one faith, this one aim, this one joy: Christ lived, and died, and reigns; I live and die and in His power I reign; only for this one thing, "*that God may be all in all.*" Let it possess our whole heart, and life.

. . .

Allow God to take His place in your heart and life. Luther often said to people, when they came troubling him about difficulties, "Do let God be God." Oh, give God His place. And what is that place? "*That God may be all in all.*" Let God be all in all every day, from morning to evening. God to rule and I to obey. Ah, the blessedness of saying, "God and I!" What a privilege that I have such a partner! God first, and then I! And yet there might be secret Self-exaltation in associating God with myself. And I find in the Bible a more precious word still. It is, "God and not I." It is not, "God first, and I second;" God is all, and I am nothing. Paul said, "*I labored more abundantly than they all; though I be nothing.*" Let us try to give God His place—begin in our closet, in our worship, in our prayer. The power of prayer depends almost entirely upon our apprehension of who it is with whom I speak. It is of the greatest consequence, if we have but half an hour in which to pray, that we take time to get a sight of this great God, in His power, in His love, in His nearness, just waiting to bless us. This is of far more consequence than spending the whole half hour in pouring out numberless petitions, and pleading numberless promises. The great thing is to feel that we are putting our supplications into the bosom of omnipotent Love. Before and above everything, let us take time ere we pray to realize the glory and presence of God. Give God His place in every prayer. I say, allow God to have His place. I cannot give God His place upon the throne—in a certain sense I can, and I ought to try. The great thing, however, is for me to feel that I cannot realize what that place is, but God will increasingly reveal Himself and the place He holds. …

"*That God may be all in all*"; I must not only allow Him to take His place, but secondly, I must accept His will in everything. I must accept His will in every providence. Whether it be a Judas that betrays, or whether it be a Pilate in his indifference, who gives me up to the enemy; whatever the trouble, or temptation, or vexation, or worry, that comes, I must see God in it, and accept it as God's will to me. Trouble of any sort that comes to me is God's will for me. It is not God's will that men should do the wrong, but it is God's will that they should be in circumstances of trial. There is never a trial that comes to us but it is God's will for us, and if we learn to see God in it, then we bid it welcome. … Have you learned to say, "There is never a trouble, and never a hurt by which my heart is touched or even pierced, but it comes from Jesus, and brings a message of love?" Will you not learn to say from today, "Welcome every trial, for it comes from God?" If you want God to be all in all, you must see and meet God in every providence. Oh, learn to accept God's will in everything! Come learn to say of every trial, without exception, "It is my Father who sent it. I accept it as His messenger," and nothing in earth or hell can separate you from God.

If God is to be all in all in your heart and life, I say not only, Allow Him to take His place, and accept all His will, but, thirdly, Trust in His power. Dear friends, it is "*God who works to will and to do according to His good pleasure.*" It is "*the God of peace,*" according to another passage, "*who perfects you in every good thing to do His will, working in you what is well-pleasing in His sight.*" You complain of weakness, of feebleness, of emptiness. Never mind; that is what you are made for—to be an emptied vessel, in which God can put His fullness and His strength. Do learn the lesson. I know it is not easy.

Long after Paul had been an apostle, the Lord Jesus had to come in in a very special way to teach him to say, "*I do gladly glory in my infirmities.*" Paul was in danger of being exalted, owing to the revelations from Heaven, and Jesus sent him a thorn in the flesh—yes, Jesus sent it—a messenger of Satan—to buffet him. Paul prayed, and struggled, and wanted to get rid of it. And Jesus came to him, and said, "It is my doing that you may not be free from that. You need it. I will bless you wonderfully in it." Paul's life was changed from that moment in this one respect, and he said, "*I never knew it so before, from henceforth I glory in my infirmities; for when I am weak, then am I strong.*" Do you indeed desire God to be all in all? Learn to glory in your weakness. Take time to say every day as you bow before God, "The almighty power of God that works in the sun, and the moon, and the stars, and the flowers, is working in me. It is as sure as that I live. The almighty power of God is working in me. I only need to get down, and be quiet; I need to be more submissive, and surrendered to His will; I need to be more trustful, and to allow God to do with me what He will." Give God His way with you, and let God work, and He will work mightily. The deepest quietness has often been proved to be the inspiration for the highest action. It has been seen in the experience of many of God's saints, and it is just the experience we need—that in the quietness of surrender and faith, God's working has been made manifest.

Fourthly: If God is to be all in all, sacrifice everything for His Kingdom and glory. "*That God may be all in all.*" This is such a noble, glorious, holy aim that Christ said, "For this I will give my life. For this I will give my all, even to the death of the cross. For this I will give myself." If it was worth that to Christ, is it worth less to you? I pray God that He may give us such a sight of His Kingdom, and His glory, that everything else may disappear. Then, if you had ten-thousand lives, you would say, "This is the beauty and the worth of life, that God may be all in all to me, and that I may prove to men that God is more than everything, that life is only worth living as it is given to God to fill." Do let us sacrifice everything for His Kingdom and glory.

Triumph of Faith

June 23rd

"And the man believed the word that Jesus had spoken to him."

—JOHN 4: 50

Let me point out to you the three aspects of faith which we have here: first, faith seeking; then, faith finding; and then, faith enjoying. Or, still better: faith struggling; faith resting; faith triumphing.

First of all, *faith struggling*. Here is a man, a heathen, a nobleman, who has heard about Christ. He has a dying son at Capernaum, and in his extremity leaves his home, and walks some six or seven hours away to Cana of Galilee. He has heard of the Prophet, possibly, as one who has made water wine; he has heard of His other miracles round Capernaum, and he has a certain trust that Jesus will be able to help him. He goes to Him, and his prayer is that the Lord will come down to Capernaum and heal his son. Christ said to him, "*Except you see signs and wonders, you will not believe.*" …

Many Christians are like the nobleman. They have heard about a better life. They have met certain individuals by whose Christian lives they have been impressed, and consequently have felt that Christ can do wonderful things for a man. Many Christians say in their heart, "I am sure there is a better life for me to live; how I wish I could be brought to that blessed state!" But they have not much hope about it. They have read, and prayed, but they have found everything so difficult. If you ask them, "Do you believe Jesus can help you to live this higher life?" they say, "Yes; He is omnipotent." If you ask, "Do you believe Jesus wishes to do it?" they say, "Yes, I know He is loving." And if you say, "Do you believe that He will do it for you?" they at once say, "I know He is willing, but whether He will actually do it for me I do not know. I am not sure that I am prepared. I do not know if I am advanced enough. I do not know if I have enough grace for that." And so [are many Christians]; they are hungering, struggling, wrestling, and often remain unblessed. … They are just like the Israelites; they limit the Holy One of Israel. …

There is the nobleman, and Christ speaks to him this wonderful word: "*Go your way;*

your son lives"; and the nobleman simply rests upon that word of the living Jesus. He rests on it, and without any proof of what he is to get, and without one man in the world to encourage him. He goes away home with the thought, "I have received the blessing I sought; I have got life from the dead for my son. The living Christ promised it me, and on that I rest." The struggling, seeking faith has become a resting faith. …

Will you not listen and hear Him speak to your soul? "Child, go forward into all the circumstances of life that have tempted you; into all the difficulties that threaten you." Your soul lives with the life of God; your soul lives in the power of God; your soul lives in Christ Jesus. Will you not, like the nobleman, take the simple step of faith, and believe the word Jesus has spoken? Will you not say, "Lord Jesus, You have spoken: I can rest on Your Word. I have seen that Christ is willing to be more to me than I ever knew; I have seen that Christ is willing to be my life in the most actual and intense meaning of the words." All that we know about the Holy Spirit sums itself up in this one thing: The Holy Spirit comes to make Christ an actual, indwelling, always-abiding Savior.

Lastly, comes the triumphant faith. The man went home holding fast the promise. He had only one promise, but he held it fast. … Do not think this is a hard life, to be living upon a promise. It means living upon the everlasting God. …

When God gives me a promise, He is just as near me as when He fulfills it. That is a great comfort. When I have the promise I have also the pledge of the fulfillment. But the whole heart of God is in His promise, just as much as in the fulfillment of it, and sometimes God, the promiser, is more precious because I am compelled to cling more to Him, and to come closer, and to live by simple faith, and to adore His love. Do not think this is a hard life, to be living upon a promise. It means living upon the everlasting God. Who is going to say that is hard? It means living upon the crucified, the loving Christ. Be ashamed to say that is a difficult thing. It is a blessed thing.

13

THE DEEPER CHRISTIAN LIFE

An Aid to Its Attainment

Philadelphia: Fleming H. Revell Co., 1895

Privilege and Experience

June 24th

"And he said to him, Son, you are ever with me, and all that I have is yours."

—LUKE 15: 31

The words of the text are familiar to us all. The elder son had complained and said, that though his father had made a feast, and had killed the fatted calf for the prodigal son, he had never given him even a kid that he might make merry with his friends. The answer of the father was: "*Son, you are ever with me, and all that I have is yours.*"

We cannot have a more wonderful revelation of the heart of our Father in Heaven than this points out to us. We often speak of the wonderful revelation of the father's heart in his welcome to the prodigal son, and in what he did for him. But here we have a revelation of the father's love far more wonderful, in what he says to the elder son. …

We have here two things describing the privilege: First, "*Son, you are ever with Me*"—unbroken fellowship with thy Father is your portion; Second, "*All that I have is yours*"—all that God can bestow upon His children is theirs. …In these promises, we have the rich privilege of God's heritage. We have, in the first place, unbroken fellowship with Him. A father never sends his child away with the thought that he does not care about his child knowing that he loves him. The father longs to have his child believe that he has the light of his father's countenance upon him all the day—that, if he sends the child away to school, or anywhere that necessity compels, it is with a sense of sacrifice of parental feelings. If it be so with an earthly father, what think you of God? Does He not want every child of His to know that he is constantly living in the light of His countenance? This is the meaning of that word: "*Son, you are ever with Me.*"

... Let that thought into your hearts—that the child of God is called to this blessed privilege, to live every moment of his life in fellowship with God; he is called to enjoy the full light of His countenance. There are many Christians—I suppose the majority of Christians—who seem to regard the whole of the Spirit's work as confined to conviction and conversion.... He came not to dwell *near* us, but *in* us—that we might be filled with His indwelling. We are commanded to be "*filled with the Spirit*"; then the Holy Spirit would make God's presence manifest to us. That is the whole teaching of the epistle to the Hebrews—the veil is torn in two; we have access into the holiest of all by the blood of Jesus; we come into the very presence of God, so that we can live all the day with that presence resting upon us. That presence is with us wherever we go; and in all kinds of trouble, we have undisturbed repose and peace: "*Son, you are ever with me.*"

There are some people who seem to think that God, by some unintelligible sovereignty, withdraws His face. But I know that God loves His people too much to withhold His fellowship from them for any such reason. The true reason of the absence of God from us is rather to be found in our sin and unbelief, than in any supposed sovereignty of His. If the child of God is walking in faith and obedience, the Divine presence will be enjoyed in unbroken continuity.

In contrast with this high privilege of believers, look at the low experience of too many of us. The elder son was living with his father and serving him "these many years," and he complains that his father never gave him a kid, while he gave his prodigal brother the fatted calf. Why was this? Simply because he did not ask it. He did not believe that he would get it, and therefore never asked it, and never enjoyed it. He continued thus to live in constant murmuring and dissatisfaction; and the keynote of all this wretched life is furnished in what he said. His father gave him everything, yet he never enjoyed it; and he throws the whole blame on his loving and kind father. O beloved, is not that the life of many a believer? Do not many speak and act in this way? Every believer has the promise of unbroken fellowship with God ....

The elder son thought he was serving his father faithfully "these many years" in his father's house, but it was in the spirit of bondage and not in the spirit of a child, so that his unbelief blinded him to the conception of a father's love and kindness, and he was unable all the time to see that his father was ready, not only to give him a kid, but a hundred, or a thousand kids, if he would have them. He was simply living in unbelief, in ignorance, in blindness, robbing himself of the privileges that the father had for him. So, if there be a discrepancy between our life and the fulfillment and enjoyment of all God's promises, the fault is ours. If our experience be not what God wants it to be, it is because of our unbelief in the love of God, in the power of God, and in the reality of God's promises.

God's word teaches us, in the story of the Israelites, that it was unbelief on their part that was the cause of their troubles, and not any limitation or restriction on God's part. ... They kept distrusting Him from time to time. When they got to Kadesh-Barnea, and God told them to enter the land flowing with milk and honey where there would be rest, abundance, and victory, only two men said, "*Yes; we can take possession, for God can make us conquer.*" But the ten spies, and the six hundred thousand men answered, "*No; we can never take the land; the enemies are too strong for us.*" It was simply unbelief that kept them out of the land of promise.

If there is to be any deepening of the spiritual life in us, we must come to the discovery, and the acknowledgment of the unbelief there is in our hearts. God grant that we may get this spiritual quickening, and that we may come to see that it is by our unbelief that we have prevented God from doing His work in us. Unbelief is the mother of disobedience, and of all my sins and short comings—my temper, my pride, my unlovingness, my worldliness, my sins of every kind. Though these differ in nature and form, yet they all come from the one root, so that we do not believe in the freedom and fullness of the Divine gift of the Holy Spirit to dwell in us and strengthen us, and fill us with the life and grace of God all the day long. …

We all know the parable of the prodigal son and how many sermons have been preached about repentance from that parable. We are told that "*he came to himself and said, I will arise and go to my father, and will say unto him, Father, I have sinned against Heaven and in your sight.*" In preaching, we speak of this as the first step in a changed life—as conversion, as repentance, confession, returning to God. But, as this is the first step for the prodigal, we must remember that this is also the step to be taken by His erring children—by all the ninety-nine "*who need no repentance,*" or think they do not. Those Christians who do not understand how wrong their low religious life is must be taught that this is sin—unbelief—and that it is as necessary that they should be brought to repentance as the prodigal.

You have heard a great deal of preaching repentance to the unconverted; but I want to try to preach it to God's children. We have a picture of so many of God's children in that elder brother. What the father told him, to bring about a consideration of the love that He bore him, just as he loved the prodigal brother, thus does God tell to us in our contentedness with such a low life: "You must repent and believe that I love you, and all that I have is yours." He says, "By your unbelief, you have dishonored me, living for ten, twenty, or thirty years, and never believing what it was to live in the blessedness of My love. You must confess the wrong you have done Me in this, and be broken down in contrition of heart just as truly as the prodigal."

There are many children of God who need to confess, that though they are His children, they have never believed that God's promises are true, that He is willing to fill their hearts all the day long with His blessed presence. Have you believed this? If you have not, all our teaching will be of no profit to you. Will you not say, "By the help of God, I will begin now a new life of faith, and will not rest until I know what such a life means. I will believe that I am every moment in the Father's presence, and all that He has is mine"?

May the Lord God work this conviction in the hearts of all cold believers. Have you ever heard the expression, "a conviction for sanctification?" You know, the unconverted man needs a conviction before conversion. So does the dark-minded Christian need conviction before, and in order for, sanctification—before he comes to a real insight to spiritual blessedness. He must be convicted a second time because of his sinful life of doubt, and temper, and unlovingness. He must be broken down under that conviction; then there is hope for him. May the Father of mercy grant all such that deep contrition, so that they may be led into the blessedness of His presence, and enjoy the fullness of His power and love!

Out of and Into

June 25th

"And He brought us out from thence, that He might bring us in, to give us the land which He promised our fathers."

—DEUTERONOMY 6: 23

I have spoken of the crisis that comes in the life of the man who sees that his Christian experience is low and carnal, and who desires to enter into the full life of God. Some Christians do not understand that there should be such a crisis. They think that they ought, from the day of their conversion, to continue to grow and progress. I have no objections to that, if they have grown as they ought. If their life has been so strong under the power of the Holy Spirit that they have grown as true believers should grow, I certainly have no objection to this.

But I want to deal with those Christians whose life since conversion has been very much a failure, and who feel it to be such because of their not being filled with the Spirit, as is their blessed privilege. I want to say for their encouragement, that by taking one step, they can get out into the life of rest, and victory, and fellowship with God to which the promises of God invite them. …

God's Word brings out the idea of the Christian's entrance into the new and better life by the history of the people of Israel's entrance into the land of Canaan. In our text, we have these words: "*God brought us out from thence (Egypt), that He might bring us in*" into Canaan. There are two steps: one was bringing them out; and the other was bringing them in. So in the life of the believer, there are ordinarily two steps quite separate from each other—the bringing him out of sin and the world; and the bringing him into a state of complete rest afterward.

It was the intention of God that Israel should enter the land of Canaan from Kadesh-Barnea, immediately after He had made His covenant with them at Sinai. But they were not ready to enter at once, on account of their sin and unbelief, and disobedience. They had to wander after that for forty years in the wilderness. Now, look how God led the people. In Egypt, there was a great crisis, where they had first to pass through the Red Sea, which is a figure of conversion; and when they went into Canaan, there was, as it were, a second conversion in passing through the Jordan. At our conversion, we get into liberty, out of the bondage of Egypt; but, when we fail to use our liberty through unbelief and disobedience, we wander in the wilderness for a longer or shorter period before we enter into the Canaan of victory, and rest, and abundance. Thus God did for His Israel two things: He brought them out of Egypt; and He led them into Canaan.

My message, then, is to ask this question of the believer: Since you know you are converted and God has brought you out of Egypt, have you yet come into the land of Canaan? If not, are you willing that he should bring you into the fuller liberty and rest provided for His people? He brought Israel out of Egypt by a mighty hand, and the same mighty hand brought us out of our land of bondage; with the same mighty hand, He brought his ancient people into rest, and by that hand, too, He can bring us into our true rest. The same God who pardoned and regenerated us, is waiting to perfect His love in us, if we but trust Him. …

How glorious was the rest of Canaan after all the wanderings in the wilderness! And so is it with the Christian who reaches the better promised Canaan of rest, when they come to leave all their charge with the Lord Jesus—responsibilities, anxieties, and worry; their only work being to hand the keeping of their soul into the hand of Jesus every day and hour, and the Lord can keep, and give the victory over every enemy. Jesus has undertaken not only to cleanse our sin, and bring us to heaven, but also to keep us in our daily life.

I ask again: Are you hungering to get free from sin and its power? Anyone longing to get complete victory over temper, pride, and all evil inclinations?—Hearts longing for the time when no clouds will come between them and their God?—Longing to walk in the full sunshine of God's loving favor? The very God who brought you from the Egypt of darkness is ready and able to bring you also into the Canaan of rest.

… The first question, then, that I would ask you is, "Are you ready to leave the wilderness"? You know the mark of Israel's life in the wilderness—the cause of all their troubles there—was unbelief. They did not believe that God could take them into the Promised Land. And then followed many sins and failures—lusting, idolatry, murmuring, etc. That has, perhaps, been your life, beloved; you do not believe that God will fulfill His word. You do not believe in the possibility of unbroken fellowship with Him, and unlimited partnership. On account of that, you become disobedient, and did not live like a child doing God's will, because you did not believe that God could give you the victory over sin. Are you willing now to leave that wilderness life? …

Are you now going to give up your whole life to Him? Are you going to approach Him and say, "My God, I do not want to do anything that will be displeasing to You; I want You to keep me from all worldliness, from all Self-pleasure…." Beloved, are you willing to say this? Are you willing to give up your sins, to walk with God continually, to submit yourself wholly to the will of God, and have no will of your own apart from His will? Are you going to live a perfect life? I hope you are, for I believe in such a life—not perhaps in the sense in which you understand "perfection"—entire freedom from wrongdoing and all inclination to it, for while we live in the flesh the flesh will lust against the Spirit and the Spirit against the flesh; but the perfection spoken of in the Old Testament as practiced by some of God's saints, who are said to have "*served the Lord with a perfect heart.*"

What is this perfection? A state in which your hearts will be set on perfect integrity without any reserve, and your will wholly subservient to God's will. Are you willing for such a perfection, with your whole heart turned away from the world and given to God alone? … Oh! I would plead with God's children just to look at the will of God, so full of blessing, of holiness, of love; will you not give up your guilty will for that blessed will of God? … Let us be willing wholly to serve the Lord our God, and "*make no provision for the flesh to fulfil the lusts thereof.*" Let us believe in the love and power of God to keep us day by day, and put "*no confidence in the flesh.*"

Then comes the second step: "I must believe that such a life in the land of Canaan is a possible life." … But we must remember again what it was that kept Israel out of Canaan. When Caleb and Joshua said, "*We are able to overcome the enemy,*" the ten spies, and the six hundred thousand answered, "*We cannot do it; they are too strong for us.*" Take care, dear reader that we do not repeat their sin, and provoke God as these unbelievers did.

He says, it is possible to bring us into the land of rest and peace; and I believe it because He has said so, and because He will do it if I trust Him. …

Looking again at Peter. He had failed again and again, and went from bad to worse until he came to denying Christ with oaths. But what a change came over him! Just study the first epistle of Peter, and you will see that the very life of Christ had entered into him. He shows the spirit of true humility, so different from his former Self-confidence; and glorying in God's will instead of in his own. He had made a full surrender to Christ, and was trusting entirely in Him. Come therefore today and say to God, "You so changed Selfish, proud Peter, and You can change me likewise."

Yes, God is able to bring you into Canaan, the land of rest. You know the first half of the 8th of Romans. Have you noticed the expressions that are to be found there—"*The law of the spirit of life in Christ Jesus has made me free from the law of sin and death.*" To walk after the Spirit; to be after the spirit; to be in the Spirit; to have the Spirit dwelling in us; through the Spirit to mortify the deeds of the body; to be led by the Spirit; to be spiritually minded. These are all blessings which come when we bind ourselves wholly to live in the Spirit. If we live after the Spirit we have the very nature of the Spirit in us. If we live in the Spirit, we shall be led by Him every day and every moment.

What if you were to open your heart today to be filled with the Holy Spirit? Would He not be able to keep you every moment in the sweet rest of God? And would not His mighty arm give you a complete victory over sin and temptation of every kind, and make you able to live in perpetual fellowship with the Father and with His Son, Jesus Christ? Most certainly! This, then, is the second step; this is the blessed life God has provided for us. First, God brought us out of Egypt; secondly, He brings us into Canaan.

How does God bring us in? By leading us in a very definite act, viz, that of committing ourselves wholly to Him—entrusting ourselves to Him, that He may bring us into the land of rest, and keep us in. …

Friend, you have the same God now who brought you out of bondage with a high hand; and can lead you into the place of rest. Look to Him and say, "O God, make an end of my wilderness life—my sinful and unbelieving life—a life of grieving You. Oh, bring me to-day into the land of victory and rest and blessing!" ….

A Word to Workers

June 26th

"He on whom you see the Spirit descend and remain, this is He who baptizes with the Holy Spirit."

—JOHN 1: 33

Some time ago I read this expression in an old author: "The first duty of a clergyman is humbly to ask of God that all that he wants done in his hearers should first be truly and fully done in himself." ...What profit is it to tell men that they may be filled with the Spirit of God, if, when they ask us, "Has God done it for you?" we have to answer, "No, He has not done it." What profit is it for me to tell men that Jesus Christ can dwell within us every moment, and keep us from sin and actual transgression, and that the abiding presence of God can be our portion all the day, if I wait not upon God first to do it truly and fully day by day?

Look at the Lord Jesus Christ; it was of the Christ Himself, when He had received the Holy Spirit from Heaven that John the Baptist said that "He would baptize with the Holy Spirit." I can only communicate to others what God has imparted to me. If my life as a minister be a life in which the flesh still greatly prevails—if my life be a life in which I grieve the Spirit of God, I cannot expect but that my people will receive through me a very mingled kind of life. But if the life of God dwell in me, and I am filled with His power, then I can hope that the life that goes out from me may be infused into my hearers too.

The same writer to whom I alluded, says elsewhere: "The first business of a clergyman, when he sees men awakened and brought to Christ, is to lead them on to know the Holy Spirit." How true! Do not we find this throughout the Word of God?

John the Baptist preached Christ as the "*Lamb of God which takes away the sin of the world.*" We read in Matthew that he also said that Christ would "*baptize with the Holy Spirit and with fire.*" In the gospel by John, we read that the Baptist was told that upon "*Whom he would see the Spirit descending and abiding, He it was who would baptize with the Spirit.*" Thus John the Baptist led the people on from Christ to the expectation of the Holy Spirit for themselves.

And what did Jesus do? For three years, He was with His disciples, teaching and instructing them; but when He was about to go away, in His farewell discourse on the last night, what was His great promise to the disciples? "*I will pray to the Father, and He shall give you another Comforter, even the Spirit of Truth.*" He had previously promised to those who believed on Him that "*rivers of living water*" should flow from them; which the Evangelist explains as meaning the Holy Spirit: "*Thus spoke He of the Spirit.*" But this promise was only to be fulfilled after Christ "*was glorified.*" ...

So in the farewell discourse, Christ leads the disciples to expect the Spirit as the Father's great blessing. Then again, when Christ came and stood at the footstool of His heavenly throne, on the Mount of Olives, ready to ascend, what were His words? "*You shall receive power after that the Holy Spirit is come upon you, and you shall be witnesses unto Me.*" Christ's constant work was to teach His disciples to expect the Holy Spirit.

Look through the Book of Acts; you see the same thing: Peter on the day of Pentecost preached that Christ was exalted, and had received of the Father the promise of the Holy Spirit; and so he told the people: "*Repent and be baptized in the name of Jesus Christ for the remission of sins, and you shall receive the gift of the Holy Spirit.*" So, when I believe in Jesus risen, ascended, and glorified, I shall receive the Holy Spirit.

Look again, after Philip had preached the gospel in Samaria, men and women had been converted, and there was great joy in the city. The Holy Spirit had been working, but something was still wanting; Peter and John came down from Jerusalem, prayed for the converted ones, laid their hands upon them, "and they received the Holy Spirit." Then they had the conscious possession and enjoyment of the Spirit; but till that came they were incomplete.

Paul was converted by the mighty power of Jesus who appeared to Him on the way to Damascus; and yet he had to go to Ananias to receive the Holy Spirit. Then again, we read that when Peter went to preach to Cornelius, as he preached Christ, "*the Holy Spirit fell on all them which heard the word,*" which Peter took as the sign that these Gentiles were one with the Jews in the favor of God, having the same baptism.

And so we might go through many of the Epistles, where we find the same truth taught. Look at that wonderful epistle to the Romans. The doctrine of justification by faith is established in the first five chapters. Then in the sixth and seventh, though the believer is represented as dead to sin and the law, and married to Christ, yet a dreadful struggle goes on in the heart of the regenerate man as long as he has not got the full power of the Holy Spirit. But in the eighth chapter, it is the "*law of the Spirit of life in Christ Jesus*" that makes us free from "*the law of sin and death.*" Then we are "*not in the flesh, but in the Spirit,*" with the Spirit of God dwelling in us. All the teaching leads up to the Holy Spirit.

Look again at the epistle to the Galatians. We always talk of this epistle as the great source of instruction on the doctrine of justification by faith: but have you ever noticed how the doctrine of the Holy Spirit holds a most prominent place there? …

If we look into the epistle to the Ephesians, we find the doctrine of the Holy Spirit mentioned twelve times. It is the Spirit that seals God's people: "*You were sealed with the Holy Spirit of promise.*" He illumines them; "*That God may give the Spirit of wisdom and revelation in the knowledge of Him.*" Through Christ, both Jew and Gentile "*have access by one Spirit unto the Father.*" They "*are built together for a habitation of God through the Spirit.*" They are "*strengthened with might by His Spirit in the inner man.*" …

Just study these epistles carefully, and you will find that what I say is true—that the apostle Paul takes great pains to lead Christians to the Holy Spirit as the consummation of the Christian life. …

Let each one of us ask himself: "Is it my great study to know the Holy Spirit dwelling in me, so that I may help others to yield to the same indwelling of the Holy Spirit; and that He may reveal Christ fully in His Divine saving and keeping power?" Will not everyone have to confess: "Lord, I have all too little understood this; I have all too little manifested this in my work and preaching"?

Beloved, "The first duty of every clergyman is to humbly ask God that all that he wants done in his hearers may be first fully and truly done in himself." And the second thing is his duty towards those who are awakened and brought to Christ, to lead them on to the full knowledge of the presence and indwelling of the Holy Spirit. Now, if we are indeed to come into full harmony with these two great principles, then there come to us some further questions of the very deepest importance. And the first questions is: "Why is it that there is in the Church of Christ so little practical acknowledgment of the power of the Holy Spirit?" I am not speaking to you, as if I thought you were not sound in doctrine on this point. I speak to you as believing in the Holy Spirit as the third person in the ever-blessed Trinity. But I speak to you confidently as to those who will readily admit that the truth of the presence and of the power of the Holy Spirit is not acknowledged in the Church as it ought to be. Then the question is: Why is it not so acknowledged? I answer because of its spirituality. It is one of the most difficult truths in the Bible for the human mind to comprehend.

In the early Pentecostal days of the church, this knowledge was intuitive; they possessed the Spirit in power. But soon after the spirit of the world began to creep into the Church and mastered it. This was followed by the deeper darkness of formality and superstition in the Roman Catholic Church, when the spirit of the world completely triumphed in what was improperly styled the Church of Christ. The Reformation in the days of Luther restored the truth of justification by faith in Christ; but the doctrine of the Holy Spirit did not then obtain its proper place, for God does not reveal all truth at one time. A great deal of the spirit of the world was still left in the reformed churches; but now God is awakening the Church to strive after a fuller scriptural idea of the Holy Spirit's place and power. …

Brethren, sisters, it is our privilege to take part in this great movement; and let us engage in the work more earnestly than ever. Let each of us say my great work is, in preaching Christ, to lead others to the acknowledging of the Holy Spirit, who alone can glorify Christ. I may try to glorify Christ in my preaching, but it will avail nothing without the Spirit of God. I may urge us to the practice of holiness and every Christian virtue, but all my persuasion will avail very little unless I help us to believe that we must have the Holy Spirit dwelling in us every moment enabling to live the life of Christ.

The great reason why the Holy Spirit was given from Heaven was to make Christ Jesus' presence manifest to us. … It was needful, He said, that He should go away, in order that the Spirit might come; and He promised to those who loved Him and kept His commandments, that with the Spirit, He would come, and the Father would also come, and make Their abode with them. It is thus the Holy Spirit's great work to reveal the Father and the Son in the hearts of God's people. If we believe and teach others that the Holy Spirit can make Christ a reality to them every moment, they will learn to believe and accept Christ's presence and power, of which they now know far too little.

I sometimes hear people praying earnestly for a baptism of the Holy Spirit that He may give them power for their work. Beloved brethren, we need this power, not only for work, but for our daily life. Remember, we must have it all the time. In Old Testament times, the Spirit came with power upon the prophets and other inspired men; but He did not dwell permanently in them. In the same way, in the Church of the Corinthians, the Holy Spirit came with power to work miraculous gifts, and yet they had but a small measure of His sanctifying grace. You will remember the carnal strife, envying, and divisions there were. They had gifts of knowledge and wisdom, etc.; but alas! pride, unlovingness, and other sins sadly marred the character of many of them. And what does this teach us? That we may have a great gift of power for work, but very little of the indwelling Spirit. In 1 Corinthians 13 we are reminded that though we may have faith that would remove mountains, if we have not love, we are nothing. We must have the love that brings the humility and Self-sacrifice of Jesus.

Don't let us put in the first place the gifts we may possess; if we do, we shall have very little blessing. But we should seek, in the first place, that the Spirit of God should come as a light and power of holiness from the indwelling Jesus. Let the first work of the Holy Spirit be to humble you deep down in the very dust, so that your whole life shall be a tender, broken-hearted waiting on God, in the consciousness of mercy coming from above.

Do not seek large gifts; there is something deeper you need. It is not enough that a tree shoots its branches to the sky, and be covered thickly with leaves; but we want its roots to strike deeply into the soil. Let the thought of the Holy Spirit's being in us, and our hope of being filled with the Spirit, be always accompanied in us with a broken and contrite heart. Let us bow very low before God, in waiting for His grace to fill and to sanctify us. We do not want a power which God might allow us to use, while our inner part is unsanctified. We want God to give us full possession of Himself. In due time, the special gift may come; but we want first and now, the power of the Holy Spirit working something far mightier and more effectual in us than any such gift. We should seek, therefore, not only a baptism of power, but a baptism of holiness; we should seek that the inner nature be sanctified by the indwelling of Jesus, and then other power will come as needed.

... Give up to God an empty, consecrated vessel that He may fill it with the Holy Spirit. Take that position constantly. It may be that you are not fully prepared. Ask God to cleanse you; to give you grace to separate from everything sinful—from unbelief or whatever hindrance there may be. Then take your position before God and say, "My God, You are faithful; I have entered into covenant with You for Your Holy Spirit to fill me, and I believe You will fulfill it." Brethren, I say for myself, and for every minister of the gospel, and for every fellow worker, man or woman, that if we thus come before God with a full surrender, in a bold, believing attitude, God's promise must be fulfilled.

If you were to ask me of my own experience, I would say this: That there have been times when I hardly knew myself what to think of God's answer to my prayer in this matter; but I have found it my joy and my strength to take and maintain my position, and say: "My God, I have given myself up to You. It was Your own grace that led me to Christ;

and I stand before You in confidence that You will keep Your covenant with me to the end. I am the empty vessel; You are the God that fills all." God is faithful, and He gives the promised blessing in His own time and method.

Beloved, for God's sake, be content with nothing less than full health and full spiritual life. "*Be filled with the Spirit.*"

Consecration

June 27th

All things come of You, and what is Yours have we given back to You."

—1 CHRONICLES 29: 14

To be able to offer anything to God is a perfect mystery. Consecration is a miracle of grace. "*All things come of You, and what is Yours have we given back to You.*" In these words, there are four very precious thoughts I want to try and make clear to you: 1) God is the Owner of all, and gives all to us; 2) We have nothing but what we receive, but everything we need we may receive from God; 3) It is our privilege and honor to give back to God what we receive from Him; and 4) God has a double joy in His possessions when he receives back from us what He gave.

And when I apply this to my life—to my body, to my wealth, property, to my whole being with all its powers—then I understand what Consecration ought to be. It is the glory of God, and His very nature, to be always giving. God is the owner of all. There is no power, no riches, no goodness, no love, outside of God. It is the very nature of God that He does not live for Himself, but for His creatures. His is a love that always delights to give. Here we come to the first step in consecration. I must see that everything I have is given by Him; I must learn to believe in God as the great Owner and Giver of all. Let me hold that fast. I have nothing but what actually and definitely belongs to God. Just as much as people say, "this money in my purse belongs to me," so God is the Proprietor of all. It is His and His only. And it is His life and delight to be always giving. Oh, take that precious thought—there is nothing that God has that He does not want to give. It is His nature, and *therefore when God asks you anything, He must give it first Himself, and He will.* Never be afraid whatever God asks; for God only asks what is His own; what He asks you to give He will first Himself give you. …

Just as it is the nature and glory of God to be always giving, it is the nature and glory of man to be always receiving. What did God make us for? We have been made to be each of us a vessel into which God can pour out His life, His beauty, His happiness, His love. We are created to be each a receptacle and a reservoir of Divine heavenly life and blessing, just as much as God can put into us. Have we understood this, that our great work—the object of our creation—is to be always receiving? If we fully enter into this, it will teach some precious things. One thing—the utter folly of being proud or conceited. What an idea!

Suppose I were to borrow a very beautiful dress, and walk about boasting of it as if it were my own, you might say, "What a fool!" And here it is the Everlasting God owns everything we have; shall we dare to exalt ourselves on account of what is all His? Then what a blessed lesson it will teach us of what our position is! I have to do with a God whose nature is to be always giving, and mine to be always receiving.

If God gives all and I receive all, then the third thought is very simple: *I must give all back again.* What a privilege that for the sake of having me in loving, grateful intercourse with Him, and giving me the happiness of pleasing and serving Him, the Everlasting God should say, "Come now, and bring Me back all that I give." And yet people say, "Oh, but must I give everything back? Brother, don't you know that there is no happiness or blessedness except in giving to God?

Just look at Jesus—God gave Him a wonderful body. He kept it holy and gave it as a sacrifice to God. This is the beauty of having a body. God has given you a soul; this is the beauty of having a soul—you can give it back to God. People talk about the difficulty they meet with in having so strong a will. You never can have too strong a will, but the trouble is we do not give that strong will up to God, to make it a vessel in which God can and will pour His Spirit, so as to fit it to do splendid service for Himself.

We have now had the three thoughts: God gives all; I receive all; I give up all. Will you do this now? Will not every heart say, "My God, teach me to give up everything?" Take your head, your mind with all its power of speaking, your property, your heart with its affections—best and most secret—take gold and silver, everything, and lay it at God's feet and say, "Lord, here is the covenant between me and You. You delight to give all, and I delight to give back all."

God teach us that. If that simple lesson were learned, there would be an end of so much trouble about finding out the Will of God, and an end of all our holding back, for it would be written, not upon our foreheads, but across our hearts, "God can do with me what He pleases; I belong to Him with all I have." Instead of always saying to God, "Give, give, give," we should say, "Yes, Lord; You give; You love to give, and I love to give back." Try that life and find out if it is not the very highest life.

God gives all, I receive all, I give all. Now comes the fourth thought: God does so rejoice in what we give to Him. It is not only I that am the receiver and the giver, but God is the Giver and the Receiver too, and, may I say it with reverence, has more pleasure in the receiving back than even in giving. With our little faith we often think they come back to God again all defiled. God says, "No, they come back beautiful and glorified"; the surrender of the dear child of His, with his aspirations and thanksgivings, brings it to God with a new value and beauty.

Ah! Child of God you do not know how precious the gift that you bring to your Father, is in His sight. Have I not seen a mother give a piece of cake, and the child comes and offers her a piece to share it with her? How she values the gift! And your God, oh, my friends, your God, His heart, His Father's heart of love, longs, longs, longs to have you give Him everything. It is not a demand. It is a demand, but it is not a demand of a hard Master, it is the call of a loving Father, who knows that every gift you bring to God will bind you closer to Himself, and every surrender you make will open your heart wider to get more of his spiritual gifts. …

To be and abide in continual dependence upon God, become nothing—begin to understand that you are nothing but an earthen vessel into which God will shine down the treasure of His love. Blessed is the man who knows what it is to be nothing, to be just an empty vessel meet for God's use. Work, the Apostle says, for it is God who works in you to will and to do. Brethren, come and take tonight the place of deep, deep dependence on God. And then take the place of child-like trust and expectancy. Count upon your God to do for you everything that you can desire of Him. Honor God as a God who gives liberally. Honor God and believe that He asks nothing from you but what he is going first to give. And then come praise and surrender and consecration. Praise Him for it! Let every sacrifice to Him be a thank-offering.

What are we going to consecrate? First of all—our lives. There are perhaps men and women—young men and women—whose hearts are asking, "What do you want me to do—to say I will be a missionary?" No, indeed, I do not ask you to do this. Deal with God, and come to Him and say, "Lord of all, I belong to You, I am absolutely at Your disposal." Yield up yourselves. …

Let us bow down before Him. Let us give Him all our powers—our head to think for His Kingdom, our heart to go out in love for men, and however feeble you may be, come and say: "Lord, here I am, to live and die for Your Kingdom. Some talk and pray about the filling of the Holy Spirit. Let them pray more and believe more. But remember the Holy Spirit came to fit men to be messengers of the Kingdom, and you cannot expect to be filled with the Spirit unless you want to live for Christ's Kingdom. You cannot expect all the love and peace and joy of Heaven to come into your life and be your treasures, unless you give them up absolutely to the Kingdom of God, and possess and use them only for Him.

It is the soul utterly given up to God that will receive in its emptying the fullness of the Holy Spirit. Dear friends we must consecrate not only ourselves—body and soul—but all we have. Some of you may have children; perhaps you have an only child, and you dread the very idea of letting it go. Take care, take care; God deserves your confidence, your love, and your surrender. I plead with you; take your children and say to Jesus: "Anything, Lord, that pleases You." Educate your children for Jesus. God help you to do it. He may not accept all of them, but He will accept of the will, and there will be a rich blessing in your soul for it. …

Oh, friends! Our giving must be in proportion to God's giving. He gives you all. Let us take it up in our Consecration prayer: "Lord, take it all, every penny I possess. It is all Yours." Let us often say "It is all His." You may not know how much you ought to give. Give up all, put everything in His hands, and He will teach you if you will wait.

The Blessing Secured

June 28th

"Be filled with the Spirit."

—EPHESIANS 5: 18

I may have some air, a little air, in my lungs, but not enough to keep up a healthy, vigorous life. But everyone seeks to have his lungs well filled with air, and the benefit of it will be felt in his blood and through his whole being. And just so the Word of God comes to us, and says, "Christians, do not be content with thinking that you have the Spirit, or have a little of the Spirit; but, if you want to have a healthy life, be 'filled with the Spirit.'" …

People often look upon being "filled with the Spirit" as something that comes with a mighty stirring of the emotions, a sort of heavenly glory that comes over them, something that they can feel strongly and mightily; but that is not always the case. I was recently in Niagara Falls. I noticed, and I was told, that the water was unusually low. Suppose the river were doubly full, how would you see that fullness in the Falls? In the increased volume of water pouring over the cataract, and its tremendous noise. But go to another part of the river, or to the lake, where the very same fullness is found, and there is perfect quiet and placidity, the rise of the water is gentle and gradual, and you can hardly notice that there is any disturbance as the lake gets full. And just so it may be with a child of God. To one it comes with mighty emotion and with a blessed consciousness, "God has touched me!" To others it comes in a gentle filling of the whole being with the presence and the power of God by His Spirit. I do not want to lay down the way in which it is to come to you, but I want you simply to take your place before God, and say, "My Father, whatever it may mean, that is what I want." If you come and give yourself up as an empty vessel and trust God to fill you, God will do His own work.

And now, the simple question as to the steps by which we can come to be "filled with the Spirit." I shall note four steps in the way by which a man can attain this wonderful blessing. He must say, "I must have it," then, "I may have it," and, then, "I will have it," and then, last, Thank God, "I shall have it."

The first word a man must begin to say, is, "I must have it." He must feel "It is a command of God, and I cannot live unfilled with the Spirit without disobeying God." It is a command here in this text: … "be filled with the Spirit." Just as much as a man dare not get drunk, if he is a Christian, just as much must a man be filled with the Spirit. God wants it, and, oh, that every one might be brought to say, "I must, if I am to please God, I must be filled with the Spirit!"

I fear there is a terrible, terrible Self satisfaction among many Christians; they are content with their low level of life. They think they have the Spirit because they are converted, but they know very little of the joy of the Holy Spirit, and of the sanctifying power of the Spirit. They know very little of the fellowship of the Spirit linking them to God and to Jesus. They know very little of the power of the Spirit to testify for God, and yet they are content. … Oh, friends, do not be content with that half Christian life that many of you are living, but say, "God wants it, God commands it; I must be filled with the Spirit."

… If you were to send out missionaries full of the Holy Spirit, what a blessing that would be! Why is it that many a missionary complains in the foreign field, "There I learned how weak and how unfit I am?" It is because the churches from which they go are not filled with the Holy Spirit. Someone said to me in England a few weeks ago, "They talk so much about the volunteer movement and more missionaries; but we want something else, we want missionaries filled with the Holy Spirit." If the Church is to come right, and the mission field is to come right, we must each begin with himself. It must begin with you. Begin with yourself and say, "O God, for Your sake; O God, for Your Church's sake; O God, for the sake of the world, help me! I must be filled with the Holy Spirit."

What folly it would be for a man who had lost a lung and a half, and had hardly a quarter of a lung to do the work of two, to expect to be a strong man and to do hard work, and to live in any climate! And what folly for a man to expect to live—God has told him he cannot live—a full Christian life, unless he is full of the Holy Spirit! And what folly for a man who has only got a little drop of the river of the water of life to expect to live and to have power with God and man!

Jesus wants us to come and to receive the fulfillment of the promise, "*He that believes in Me, streams of water shall flow out from him.*" Oh, begin to say, "If I am to live a right life, if I am in every part of my daily life and conduct to glorify my God, I must have the Holy Spirit—I must be filled with the Spirit." Are you going to say that? … Do submit to God, and as an act of submission say, "Lord, I confess it, I ought to be filled, I must be filled; help me!" And God will help you.

And, then comes the second step, I *may* be filled. The first had reference to duty; the second has reference to privilege—I may be filled. Alas! So many have got accustomed to their low state that they do not believe that they may, they can, actually be filled. …

God wants healthy children. I saw today a child of six months old, as beautiful and chubby as you could wish a child to be, and with what delight the eyes of the father and the mother looked upon him, and how glad I was to see a healthy child. And, oh, do you think that God in Heaven does not care for His children, and that God wants some of His children to live a sickly life? I tell you, it is a lie! God wants every child of His to be a healthy Christian; but you cannot be a healthy Christian unless you are filled with God's Spirit. …

My brother, my sister, there is a God in Heaven who has been longing for these past years, while you never thought about it, to fill you with the Holy Spirit. God longs to give the fullness of the Spirit to every child of His. … Do not think that you cannot be filled with the Spirit because God is not willing to give it to you. Did not the Lord Jesus promise the Spirit? Is not the Holy Spirit the best part of His salvation? Do you think He gives half a salvation to any of His redeemed ones? Is not His promise for all, "*He that believes in me, rivers of water shall flow out of him*"? This is more than fullness—this is overflow; and this Jesus has promised to everyone who believes in Him. Oh, cast aside your fears, and your doubts, and your hesitation, and say at once, "I can be filled with the Spirit; I may be filled with the Spirit. There is nothing in Heaven, or earth, or hell, can prevent it, because God has promised and God is waiting to do it for me." …

And then we get to the third step, when a man says, "I *will* have it; … What does that mean? It means, first of all, of course, that you are going to look around into your life, and if you see anything wrong there, it means that you are going to confess it to Jesus and say, "Lord, I cast it at Your feet; it may be rooted in my heart, but I will give it up to You. I cannot take it out, but Jesus, You cleanser of sin, I give it to You." Let it be temper, or pride; let it be money, or lust, or pleasure; let it be the fear of man; let it be anything; but, oh, say to Christ at once, "I will have this blessing at any cost." Oh, give up every sin to Jesus.

And it means not only giving up every sin, but—what is deeper than sin, and more difficult to get at—it means giving up yourself—Self, with your will, and your pleasure, and your honor, and all you have, and saying, "Jesus, I am from this moment going to give myself up, that by Your Holy Spirit You may take possession of me, and that You may by Your Spirit turn out whatever is sinful, and take entire command of me."

14

HUMILITY

The Beauty of Holiness

New York: Anson D. F. Randolph & Co. 1895

The Glory of the Creature

June 29th

"They shall cast their crowns before the throne, so saying: Worthy are You, our Lord and our God, to receive glory, and honor and power: for You created all things, and because of Your will they are, and were created."
—REVELATION 4:11

When God created the universe, it was with the one object of making the creature partaker of His perfection and blessedness, and so showing forth in it the glory of His love and wisdom and power. God wished to reveal Himself in and through created beings by communicating to them as much of His own goodness and glory as they were capable of receiving. But this communication was not a giving to the creature something which it could possess in itself, a certain life or goodness, of which it had the charge and disposal. By no means. But as God is the ever-living, ever-present, ever-acting One, who upholds all things by the word of His power, and in whom all things exist, the relation of the creature to God could only be one of unceasing, absolute, universal dependence.

As truly as God by His power once created, so truly by that same power must God every moment maintain. The creature has not only to look back to the origin and first beginning of existence, and acknowledge that it there owes everything to God; our chief care, our highest virtue, our only happiness—now and through all eternity—is to present our Self an empty vessel, in which God can dwell and manifest His power and goodness. The life God bestows is imparted not once for all, but each moment, continuously, by the unceasing operation of His mighty power.

Humility, the place of entire dependence on God, is—from the very nature of things—the first duty and the highest virtue of the creature, and the root of every virtue. And so pride, or the loss of this humility, is the root of every sin and evil. It was when the now fallen angels began to look upon themselves with Self-complacency that they were led to disobedience, and were cast down from the light of Heaven into outer darkness. Even so it was, when the serpent breathed the poison of his pride, the desire to be as God, into the hearts of our first parents, that they too fell from their high estate into all the wretchedness in which man is now sunk. In Heaven and earth, pride, Self-exaltation, is the gate and the birth, and the curse, of hell.

Hence it follows that nothing can be our redemption, but the restoration of the lost humility, the original and only true relation of the creature to its God. And so Jesus came to bring humility back to earth, to make us partakers of it, and by it to save us. In Heaven, He humbled Himself to become man. The humility we see in Him possessed Him in heaven; it brought Him, He brought it, from there. Here on earth "*He humbled Himself, and became obedient unto death*"; His humility gave His death its value, and so became our redemption. And now the salvation He imparts is nothing less and nothing else than a communication of His own life and death, His own disposition and spirit, His own humility, as the ground and root of His relation to God and His redeeming work. Jesus Christ took the place and fulfilled the destiny of man, as a creature, by His life of perfect humility. His humility is our salvation. His salvation is our humility.

And so the life of the saved ones, of the saints, must needs bear this stamp of deliverance from sin, and full restoration to their original state; their whole relation to God and man marked by an all pervading humility. Without this there can be no true abiding in God's presence, or experience of His favor and the power of His Spirit; without this no abiding faith, or love or joy or strength. Humility is the only soil in which the graces root; the lack of humility is the sufficient explanation of every defect and failure. Humility is not so much a grace or virtue along with others; it is the root of all, because it alone takes the right attitude before God, and allows Him as God to do all.

God has so constituted us as reasonable beings, that the truer the insight into the real nature or the absolute need of a command, the readier and fuller will be our obedience to it. The call to humility has been too little regarded in the Church because its true nature and importance has been too little apprehended. It is not a something which we bring to God, or He bestows; it is simply the sense of entire nothingness, which comes when we see how truly God is all, and in which we make way for God to be all. When the creature realizes that this is the true nobility, and consents to be with his will, his mind, and his affections, the form, the vessel in which the life and glory of God are to work and manifest themselves, he sees that humility is simply acknowledging the truth of his position as creature, and yielding to God His place.

In the life of earnest Christians, of those who pursue and profess holiness, humility ought to be the chief mark of their uprightness. It is often said that it is not so. May not one reason be that in the teaching and example of the Church, it has never had that place of supreme importance which belongs to it? And that this, again, is owing to the neglect of this truth, that strong as sin is as a motive to humility, there is one of still wider and mightier influence, that which makes the angels, that which made Jesus, that which makes the holiest of saints in heaven, so humble; that the first and chief mark of the relation of the creature, the secret of his blessedness, is the humility and nothingness which leaves God free to be all?

I am sure there are many Christians who will confess that their experience has been very much like my own in this, that we had long known the Lord without realizing that meekness and lowliness of heart are to be the distinguishing feature of the disciple as they were of the Master. And further, that this humility is not a thing that will come of itself, but that it must be made the object of special desire and prayer and faith and practice. As we study the word, we shall see what very distinct and oft-repeated instructions Jesus gave His disciples on this point, and how slow they were in understanding Him. Let us, at the very commencement of our meditations, admit that there is nothing so natural to man, nothing so insidious and hidden from our sight, nothing so difficult and dangerous, as pride. Let us feel that nothing but a very determined and persevering waiting on God and Christ will discover how lacking we are in the grace of humility, and how impotent to obtain what we seek.

Let us study the character of Christ until our souls are filled with the love and admiration of His lowliness. And let us believe that, when we are broken down under a sense of our pride, and our impotence to cast it out, Jesus Christ Himself will come in to impart this grace too, as a part of His wondrous life within us.

The Secret of Redemption

June 30th

"Have this mind in you which was also in Christ Jesus: who emptied Himself; taking the form of a servant; and humbled Himself; becoming obedient even unto death. Wherefore, God also highly exalted Him."
—PHILIPPIANS 2: 5–9 …

All the wretchedness of which this world has been the scene, all its wars and bloodshed among the nations, all its Selfishness and suffering, all its ambitions and jealousies, all its broken hearts and embittered lives, with all its daily unhappiness, have their origin in this: hellish pride, either our own, or that of others…. It is from our pride we need above everything to be redeemed. And our insight into the need of redemption will largely depend upon our knowledge of the terrible nature of the power that has entered our being.

… Pride has its root and strength in a terrible spiritual power, outside of us as well as within us; as needful as it is that we confess and deplore it as our very own, is to know it in its Satanic origin. If this leads us to utter despair of ever conquering or casting it out, it will lead us all the sooner to that supernatural power in which alone our deliverance is to be found—the redemption of the Lamb of God. The hopeless struggle against the workings of Self and pride within us may indeed become still more hopeless as we think of the power of darkness behind it all; the utter despair will fit us the better for realizing and accepting a power and a life outside of ourselves, too, the humility of Heaven as brought down and brought nigh by the Lamb of God, to cast out Satan and his pride. .

... In this view it is of inconceivable importance that we should have right thoughts of what Christ is, of what really constitutes Him the Christ, and specially of what may be counted His chief characteristic, the root and essence of all His character as our Redeemer. There can be but one answer: *it is His humility.* What is the incarnation but His heavenly humility, His emptying Himself and becoming man? What is His life on earth but humility—His taking the form of a servant? And what is His atonement but humility? *"He humbled Himself and became obedient unto death."*

Christ is the humility of God embodied in human nature; the Eternal Love humbling itself, clothing itself in the garb of meekness and gentleness, to win and serve and save us. As the love and condescension of God makes Him the benefactor and helper and servant of all, so Jesus of necessity was the Incarnate Humility. And so He is still in the midst of the throne, the meek and lowly Lamb of God. If this be the root of the tree, its nature must be seen in every branch and leaf and fruit. If humility be the first, the all-including grace of the life of Jesus—if humility be the secret of His atonement—then the health and strength of our spiritual life will entirely depend upon our putting this grace first too, and making humility the chief thing we admire in Him, the chief thing we ask of Him, the one thing for which we sacrifice all else.

Is it any wonder that the Christian life is so often feeble and fruitless, when the very root of the Christ life is neglected, is unknown? Is it any wonder that the joy of salvation is so little felt, when that in which Christ found it and brings it, is so little sought? Until a humility which will rest in nothing less than the end and death of Self—which gives up all the honor of men as Jesus did, to seek the honor that comes from God alone—which absolutely makes and counts itself nothing, that God may be all, that the Lord alone may be exalted—until such a humility be what we seek in Christ above our chief joy, and welcome at any price—there is very little hope of a religion that will conquer the world.

I cannot too earnestly plead with my reader, if possibly your attention has never yet been specially directed to the want there is of humility within you or around you, to pause and ask whether you see much of the spirit of the meek and lowly Lamb of God in those who are called by His name. Let us consider how all want of love, all indifference to the needs, the feelings, the weakness of others; all sharp and hasty judgments and utterances, so often excused under the plea of being outright and honest; all manifestations of temper and touchiness and irritation; all feelings of bitterness and estrangement, have their root in nothing but pride, that ever seeks itself, and his eyes will be opened to see how a dark, shall I not say a devilish pride, creeps in almost everywhere, the assemblies of the saints not excepted. Let us begin to ask what would be the effect, if in ourself and around us, if towards fellow-saints and the world, believers were really permanently guided by the humility of Jesus. ... Let us fix our heart on our own lack of the humility which has been revealed in the likeness of Christ's life, and in the whole character of His redemption, and we will begin to feel as if we have never yet really known what Christ and His salvation is.

Study the humility of Jesus. This is the secret, hidden root of your redemption. Sink down into it deeper day by day. Believe with your whole heart that this Christ, whom God has given you, even as His divine humility wrought the work for you, will enter in to dwell and work within you too, and make you what the Father would have you be.

Humility in the Teaching of Jesus

July 1st

"Learn of Me, for I am meek and lowly of heart."
—MATTHEW 11: 29

We have seen humility in the life of Christ, as He laid open His heart to us: let us listen to His teaching. There we shall hear how He speaks of it, and how far He expects us … to be humble as He was. Let us carefully study the passages, which I can scarce do more than quote, to receive the full impression of how often and how earnestly He taught it: it may help us to realize what He asks of us.

1. … In the Beatitudes with which the Sermon on the Mount opens, He speaks: *"Blessed are the poor in spirit; for theirs is the kingdom of Heaven. Blessed are the meek; for they shall inherit the earth."* … The blessings of Heaven and earth are for the lowly. For the heavenly and the earthly life, humility is the secret of blessing.

2. *"Learn of Me; for I am meek and lowly of heart, and you shall find rest for your souls."* Jesus offers Himself as Teacher. He tells what the spirit both is, which we shall find Him as Teacher, and which we can learn and receive from Him. Meekness and lowliness is the one thing He offers us; in it we shall find perfect rest of soul. Humility is to be a salvation.

3. The disciples had been disputing who would be the greatest in the kingdom, and had agreed to ask the Master (Luke 9: 46; Matthew 18: 3). He set a child in their midst and said, *"Whosoever shall humble himself as this little child, shall be exalted."*

"Who the greatest in the Kingdom of Heaven"? What will be the chief distinction in the heavenly kingdom? The answer given was one that no one but Jesus could have given. The chief glory of Heaven, he said—the true heavenly-mindedness, the chief of the graces—*is humility. "He that is least among you, the same shall be great."*

4. The sons of Zebedee had asked Jesus to sit on His right and left, the highest place in the kingdom. Jesus said it was not His to give, but the Father's, who would give it to those for whom it was prepared. They must not look or ask for it. Their thought must be of the cup and the baptism of humiliation. And then He added, *"Whosoever will be chief among you, let him be your servant. Even as the Son of Man came to serve"* (Matthew 10: 27). Humility, as it is the mark of Christ the heavenly, will be the one standard of glory in Heaven: the lowliest is the nearest to God. The primacy in the Church is promised to the humblest.

5. Speaking to the multitude and the disciples, of the Pharisees and their love of the chief seats, Christ said once again, *"He that is greatest among you shall be your servant"* (Matthew

23: 11). Humiliation is the only ladder to honor in God's kingdom.

6. On another occasion, in the house of a Pharisee, He spoke the parable of the guest who would be invited to come up higher, and added, *"For whosoever exalts himself shall be abased; and he that humbles himself shall be exalted"* (Luke 14:1–11). The demand is inexorable; there is no other way. Self-abasement alone will be exalted.

7. After the parable of the Pharisee and the Publican, Christ spoke again, *"Everyone that exalts himself shall be abased; and he that humbles himself shall be exalted"* (Luke18: 14). In the temple and presence and worship of God, everything is worthless that is not pervaded by deep, true humility towards God and men.

8. After washing the disciples' feet, Jesus said, *"If I then, the Lord and Master, have washed your feet, you also ought to wash one another's feet"* (John 13: 14). The authority of command, and example, every thought, either of obedience or conformity, make humility the first and most essential element of discipleship.

9. At the Holy Supper table, the disciples still disputed who should be greatest, Jesus said, *"He that is greatest among you, let him be as the younger; and he that is chief, as he that does serve. I am among you as He who serves"* (Luke 22: 26). The path in which Jesus walked, and which He opened up for us, the power and spirit in which He wrought out salvation, and to which He saves us, is ever the humility that makes me the servant of all.

How little this is preached. How little it is practiced. How little the lack of it is felt or confessed ... How few *ever think of* making it a distinct object of continual desire or prayer. How little the world has seen it. How little has it been seen even in the inner circle of the Church.

"Whosoever will be chief among you, let him be your servant." Would God that it might be given us to believe that Jesus means this! We all know what the character of a faithful servant or slave implies. Devotion to the master's interests, thoughtful study and care to please him, delight in his prosperity and honor and happiness. There are servants on earth in whom these dispositions have been seen, and to whom the name of servant has never been anything but a glory. To how many of us has it not been a new joy in the Christian life to know that we may yield ourselves as servants, as slaves to God, and to find that His service is our highest liberty—the liberty from sin and Self? ... When our own heart is set upon this, the true sanctification, we shall study each word of Jesus on Self-abasement with new zest, and no place will be too low, and no stooping too deep, and no service too mean or too long continued, if we may but share and prove the fellowship with Him who spoke: *"I am among you as He who serves"*.

Brethren, here is the path to the higher life. Down, lower down! This was what Jesus ever said to the disciples who were thinking of being great in the kingdom, and of sitting on His right hand and His left. Seek not, ask not for exaltation; that is God's work. Look to it that you abase and humble yourselves, and take no place before God or man but that of servant; that is your work; let that be your one purpose and prayer. God is faithful. Just as water ever seeks and fills the lowest place, so the moment God finds the creature abased and empty, His glory and power flow in to exalt and to bless. "*He that humbles himself*"—that must be our one care shall be exalted; that is God's care; by His mighty power and in

His great love He will do it. …

Jesus, the meek and lowly One, calls us to learn of Him the path to God. Let us study the words we have been reading, until our heart is filled with the thought: My one need is humility. And let us believe that what He shows, He gives; what He is, He imparts. As the meek and lowly One, He will come in and dwell in the longing heart.

Humility in the Life of Jesus

July 2nd

"I am in the midst of you as He who serves."

—LUKE 22: 27

In the Gospel of John, we have the inner life of our Lord laid open to us. Jesus speaks frequently of His relation to the Father, of the motives by which He is guided, of His consciousness of the power and spirit in which He acts. Though the word humble does not occur, we shall nowhere in Scripture see so clearly wherein His humility consisted.

We have already said that this grace is in truth nothing but that simple consent of the creature to let God be all, in virtue of which it surrenders itself to His working alone. In Jesus we shall see how both as the Son of God in Heaven, and as man upon earth, He took the place of entire subordination, and gave God the honor and the glory which is due to Him. And what He taught so often was made true to Himself: *"He that humbles him: shall be exalted."* As it is written, *"He humbled Himself, therefore God highly exalted Him."*

Listen to the words in which our Lord speaks of His relation to the Father, and how unceasingly He uses the words not, and nothing, of Himself. The not I, in which Paul expresses his relation to Christ, is the very spirit of what Christ says of His relation the Father: *"The Son can do nothing of Himself"* (John 5: 19); *"I can of My own Self do nothing; My judgment is just, because I seek not My own will"* (John 5: 30); *"I receive not glory from men"* (John 5: 41); *"I have come not to do My own will"* (John 6: 38); *"My teaching is not Mine"* (John 7:16); *"I have not come of Myself"* (John 7: 28); *"I do nothing of Myself"* (John 8: 28); *"I have not come of Myself, but He sent Me"* (John 8: 42); *"I seek not My own glory"* (John 8: 50); *"The words that I say, I speak not from Myself"* (John 14: 10); *"The word which you hear is not Mine"* (John 14: 24).

These words open to us the deepest roots of Christ's life and work. They tell us how it was that the Almighty God was able to work His mighty redemptive work through Him. They show what Christ counted the state of heart which became Him as the Son of the Father. They teach us what the essential nature and life is of that redemption which Christ accomplished and now communicates. It is this: He was nothing, that God might be all. He resigned Himself with His will and His powers entirely for the Father to work in Him. Of His own power, His own will, and His own glory, of His whole mission with all His works and His teaching—of all this—He said: "It is not I; I am nothing; I have given Myself to the Father to work; I am nothing, the Father is all."

This life of entire Self-abnegation, of absolute submission and dependence upon the Father's will, Christ found to be one of perfect peace and joy. He lost nothing by giving all to God. God honored His trust, and did all for Him, and then exalted Him to His own right hand in glory. And because Christ had thus humbled Himself before God, and God was ever before Him, He found it possible to humble Himself before men too, and to be the Servant of all. His humility was simply the surrender of Himself to God, to allow Him to do in Him what He pleased, whatever men around might say of Him, or do to Him.

It is in this state of mind, in this spirit and disposition, that the redemption of Christ has its virtue and efficacy. It is to bring us to this disposition that we are made partakers of Christ. This is the true Self-denial to which our Savior calls us, the acknowledgment that Self has nothing good in it, except as an empty vessel which God must fill, and that its claim to be or do anything may not for a moment be allowed. It is in this, above and before everything, in which the conformity to Jesus consists, the being and doing nothing of ourselves, that God may be all.

Here we have the root and nature of true humility. It is because this is not understood or sought after, that our humility is so superficial and so feeble. We must learn of Jesus—how He is meek and lowly of heart. He teaches us where true humility takes its rise and finds its strength—in the knowledge that *"it is God who works all in all"*—that our place is to yield to Him in perfect resignation and dependence, in full consent to be and to do nothing of ourselves. This is the life Christ came to reveal and to impart—a life to God that came through death to sin and Self. If we feel that this life is too high for us and beyond our reach, it must but the more urge us to seek it in Him; it is the indwelling Christ who will live in us this life, meek and lowly. If we long for this, let us, meantime, above everything, seek the holy secret of the knowledge of the nature of God, as He every moment works all in all—the secret, of which all nature and every creature, and above all, every child of God, is to be the witness—that we are nothing but a vessel, a channel, through which the living God can manifest the riches of His wisdom, power, and goodness. The root of all virtue and grace, of all faith and acceptable worship, is that we know that we have nothing but what we receive, and bow in deepest humility to wait upon God for it.

It was because this humility was not only a temporary sentiment, wakened up and brought into exercise when He thought of God, but the very spirit of His whole life, that Jesus was just as humble in His intercourse with men as with God. He felt Himself the Servant of God for those of us whom God made and loved; as a natural consequence, He counted Himself our Servant, that through Him God might do His work of love. He never for a moment thought of seeking His honor, or asserting His power to vindicate Himself. His whole spirit was that of a life yielded to God to work in. It is not until Christians study the humility of Jesus as the very essence of His redemption, as the very blessedness of the life of the Son of God, as the only true relation to the Father, and therefore as that which Jesus must give us, if we are to have any part with Him, that the terrible lack of actual, heavenly, manifest humility will become a burden and a sorrow, and our ordinary religion be set aside to secure this, the first and the chief of the marks of the

Christ within us. …

Humility and Death to Self

July 3rd

"He humbled Himself and became obedient unto death."
—PHILIPPIANS 2: 8

Humility is the path to death, because in death it gives the highest proof of its perfection. Humility is the blossom of which death to Self, is the perfect fruit. Jesus humbled Himself unto death, and opened the path in which we too must walk. As there was no way for Him to prove His surrender to God to the very uttermost, or to give up and rise out of our human nature to the glory of the Father but through death, so with us too.

Humility must lead us to die to Self: so we prove how wholly we have given ourselves up to it and to God; so alone we are freed from fallen nature, and find the path that leads to life in God, to that full birth of the new nature, of which humility is the breath and the joy.

We have spoken of what Jesus did for His disciples when He communicated His resurrection life to them, when in the descent of the Holy Spirit He, the glorified and enthroned Meekness, actually came from Heaven Himself to dwell in them. He won the power to do this through death: in its inmost nature the life He imparted was a life out of death, a life that had been surrendered to death, and been won through death.

He who came to dwell in them was Himself One who had been dead and now lives for evermore. His life, His person, His presence, bears the marks of death, of being a life begotten out of death. That life in His disciples ever bears the death marks too; it is only as the Spirit of the death, of the dying One, dwells and works in the soul, that the power of His life can be known. The first and chief of the marks of the dying of the Lord Jesus, of the death-marks that show the true follower of Jesus, is humility. For these two reasons: only humility leads to perfect death; only death perfects humility. Humility and death are in their very nature one: humility is the bud; in death the fruit is ripened to perfection.

Humility leads to perfect death. Humility means the giving up of Self and the taking of the place of perfect nothingness before God. Jesus humbled Himself, and became obedient unto death. In death He gave the highest, the perfect proof of having given up His will to the will of God. In death He gave up His Self, with its natural reluctance to drink the cup; He gave up the life He had in union with our human nature; He died to Self, and the sin that tempted Him; so, as man, He entered into the perfect life of God. If it had not been for His boundless humility, counting Himself as nothing except as a servant to do and suffer the will of God, He never would have died.

We have spoken of what Jesus did for His disciples when He communicated His resurrection life to them; when in the descent of the Holy Spirit, He—Jesus—*the glorified and enthroned Meekness*, actually came from Heaven to dwell in them. The full manifestation of the power of this death in your disposition and conduct depends upon the measure in which the Holy Spirit imparts the power of the death of Christ. And here it is that the teaching is needed: if you would enter into full fellowship with Christ in His death, and know the full deliverance from Self, humble yourself. This is your one duty.

Place yourself before God in your utter helplessness; ... sink down into your own nothingness, in the spirit of meek and patient and trustful surrender to God. Accept every humiliation, look upon every fellow-man who tries or vexes you, as a means of grace to humble you. Use every opportunity of humbling yourself before your fellow-men as a help to abide humble before God. God will accept such humbling of yourself as the proof that your whole heart desires it as the very best prayer for it, as your preparation for His mighty work of grace, when, by the mighty strengthening of His Holy Spirit, He reveals Christ fully in you, so that He, in His form of a servant, is truly formed in you, and dwells in your heart. It is the path of humility which leads to perfect death, the full and perfect experience that we are dead in Christ.

Humble yourself unto death. It is in the death to Self that humility is perfected. Be sure that at the root of all real experience of more grace, of all true advance in consecration, of all actually increasing conformity to the likeness of Jesus, there must be a deadness to Self that proves itself to God and men in our dispositions and habits. It is sadly possible to speak of the death-life and the Spirit-walk, while even the tenderest love cannot but see how much there is of Self. The death to Self has no surer death-mark than a humility which makes itself of no reputation, which empties out itself, and takes the form of a servant. It is possible to speak much and honestly of fellowship with a despised and rejected Jesus, and of bearing His cross, while the meek and lowly, the kind and gentle humility of the Lamb of God is not seen, is scarcely sought. The Lamb of God means two things—meekness and death. Let us seek to receive Him in both forms. In Him they are inseparable: they must be in us too.

What a hopeless task if we had to do the work! Nature never can overcome nature, not even with the help of grace. Self can never cast out Self, even in the regenerate man. Praise God! the work has been done, and finished and perfected forever. The death of Jesus, once and forever, is our death to Self. And the ascension of Jesus, His entering once and for ever into the Holiest, has given us the Holy Spirit to communicate to us in power, and make our very own, the power of the death-life. As the soul, in the pursuit and practice of humility, follows in the steps of Jesus, its consciousness of the need of something more is awakened, its desire and hope is quickened, its faith is strengthened, and it learns to look up and claim and receive that true fullness of the Spirit of Jesus, which can daily maintain His death to Self and sin in its full power, and make humility the all-pervading spirit of our life.

"*Are you ignorant that all we who were baptized into Jesus Christ were baptized into His death? Reckon yourselves to be dead unto sin, but alive unto God in Christ Jesus. Present yourself unto God, as alive from the dead*" (Romans 6: 13). The whole Self-consciousness of the Christian is to be imbued and characterized by the spirit that animated the death of Christ. He has ever to present himself to God as one who has died in Christ, and in Christ is alive from the dead, bearing about in his body the dying of the Lord Jesus. His life ever bears the two-fold mark: its roots striking in true humility deep into the grave of Jesus, the death to sin and Self; its head lifted up in resurrection power to the heaven where Jesus is.

Believer, claim in faith the death and the life of Jesus as yours. Enter in His grave into the rest from Self and its work—the rest of God. With Christ, who committed His spirit into the Father's hands, humble yourself and descend each day into that perfect, helpless dependence upon God. God will raise you up and exalt you. Sink every morning in deep, deep nothingness into the grave of Jesus; every day the life of Jesus will be manifest in you. Let a willing, loving, restful, happy humility be the mark that you have indeed claimed your birthright—the baptism into the death of Christ. *"By one offering He has perfected forever them that are sanctified."* The souls that enter into His humiliation will find in Him the power to see and count the Self as dead, and, as those who have learned and received of Him, to walk with all lowliness and meekness, forbearing one another in love. The death-life is seen in a meekness and lowliness like that of Christ. …

The one true way of dying to Self is the way of patience, meekness, humility, and resignation to God. This is the truth and perfection of dying to Self. ...

Humility and Holiness

July 4th

"Love vaunts not itself, is not puffed up, seeks not its own."

—1 CORINTHIANS 13: 4

We speak of the Holiness movement in our times, and praise God for it. We hear a great deal of seekers after holiness and professors of holiness, of holiness teaching and holiness meetings. The blessed truths of holiness in Christ, and holiness by faith, are being emphasized as never before. But, the great test of whether the holiness we profess to seek or to attain, in truth and life, will be whether it be manifest in the increasing humility it produces.

In the creature, humility is the one thing needed to allow God's holiness to dwell in us and shine through us. In Jesus, the Holy One of God who makes us holy, a Divine humility was the secret of His life and His death and His exaltation. The one infallible test of *our* holiness will be the humility before God and men which marks us.

Humility is the bloom and the beauty of holiness. The chief mark of counterfeit holiness is its lack of humility. Every seeker after holiness needs to be on his guard, lest unconsciously what was begun in the spirit be perfected in the flesh, and pride creep in where its presence is least expected.

"*Two men went up into the temple to pray: the one a Pharisee, the other a publican*" (Luke 18: 9–14). There is no place or position so sacred but the Pharisee can enter there. Pride can lift its head in the very temple of God, and make His worship the scene of its Self-exaltation. Since the time Christ so exposed his pride, the Pharisee has put on the garb of the publican, and the confessor of deep sinfulness equally with the professor of the highest holiness, must be on the watch. Just when we are most anxious to have our heart the temple of God, we shall find these two men coming up to pray. And the publican will find that his danger is not from the Pharisee beside him, who despises him, but the Pharisee within who commends and exalts.

In God's temple, when we think we are in the holiest of all, in the presence of His holiness, let us beware of pride. *"Now there was a day when the sons of God came to present themselves before the Lord, and Satan came also among them"* (Job 1: 6; 2: 1) …

"*God, I thank you, I am not as the rest of men, or even as this publican.*" It is in that which is just cause for thanksgiving, it is in the very thanksgiving which we render to God, it may be in the very confession that God has done it all, that Self finds its cause of complacency. Yes, even when in the temple the language of penitence and trust in God's mercy alone is heard, the Pharisee may take up the note of praise, and in thanking God be congratulating himself. Pride can clothe itself in the garments of praise or of penitence.

Even though the words, "*I am not as the rest of men*" are rejected and condemned, their spirit may too often be found in our feelings and language towards our fellow worshippers and fellow-men. Would you know if this really is so, just listen to the way in which Churches and Christians often speak of one another. How little of the meekness and gentleness of Jesus is to be seen. It is so little remembered that deep humility must be the keynote of what the servants of Jesus say of themselves or each other.

Is there not many a Church or assembly of the saints—many a mission or convention, many a society or committee, even many a mission away in heathendom—where the harmony has been disturbed and the work of God hindered, because men who are counted saints have proved in touchiness and haste and impatience, in Self-defense and Self-assertion, in sharp judgments and unkind words, that they did not each reckon others better than themselves, and that their holiness has but little in it of the meekness of the saints? In their spiritual history men may have had times of great humbling and brokenness, but what a different thing this is from being clothed with humility, from having a humble spirit, from having that lowliness of mind in which each counts himself the servant of others, and so shows forth the very mind which was also in Jesus Christ. …

Jesus the Holy One is the humble One: the holiest will ever be the humblest. There is none holy but God: we have as much of holiness as we have of God. And according to what we have of God will be our real humility, because humility is nothing but the disappearance of Self in the vision that God is all. The holiest will be the humblest. …

And is there, then, such humility to be found, that men shall indeed still count themselves "*less than the least of all saints*," the servants of all? There is. *"Love vaunts not itself, is not puffed up, seeks not its own"* (1 Corinthians 13: 4). Where the spirit of love is shed abroad in the heart, where the Divine nature comes to a full birth where Christ the meek and lowly Lamb of God is truly formed within, there is given the power of a perfect love that forgets itself and finds its blessedness in blessing others, in bearing with them and honoring them, however feeble they be.

Where this love enters, there God enters. And where God has entered in His power, and reveals Himself as all, there the creature becomes nothing. And where the creature becomes nothing before God; it cannot be anything but humble towards the fellow-creature. The presence of God becomes not a thing of times and seasons, but the covering under which the soul ever dwells, and its deep abasement before God becomes the holy place of His presence whence all its words and works proceed. …

Humility and Happiness

July 5th

"Most gladly will I glory in my weaknesses, that the strength of Christ may rest upon me. Wherefore I take pleasure in weakness: for when I am weak then am I strong."

—2 CORINTHIANS 12: 9–10

Lest Paul should exalt himself, by reason of the exceeding greatness of the revelations, a thorn in the flesh was sent him to keep him humble. Paul's first desire was to have it removed, and he besought the Lord thrice that it might depart. The answer came that the trial was a blessing; that, in the weakness and humiliation it brought, the grace and strength of the Lord could be the better manifested. Paul at once entered upon a new stage in his relation to the trial: instead of simply enduring it, he most gladly gloried in it; instead of asking for deliverance, he took pleasure in it. He had learned that the place of humiliation is the place of blessing, of power, of joy.

Virtually every Christian passes through these two stages in pursuit of humility. In the first we fear and flee and seek deliverance from all that can humble us. We have not yet learned to seek humility at any cost. We have accepted the command to be humble, and seek to obey it, though only to find how utterly we fail. We pray for humility, at times very earnestly; but in secret we pray … to be kept from the very things that will make us humble. We are not yet so in love with humility as the beauty of the Lamb of God, and the joy of Heaven, that we would sell all to procure it. In our pursuit of it, and our prayer for it, there is still somewhat of a sense of burden and of bondage; to humble ourselves has not yet become the spontaneous expression of a life and a nature that is essentially humble. It has not yet become our joy and only pleasure. We cannot yet say, *"Most gladly do I glory in weakness, I take pleasure in whatever humbles me."*

But can we hope to reach the stage in which this will be the case? Undoubtedly. And what will it be that brings us there? That which brought Paul there—a new revelation of the Lord Jesus. Nothing but the presence of God can reveal and expel Self. A clearer insight was to be given to Paul into the deep truth that the presence of Jesus will banish every desire to seek anything in ourselves, and will make us delight in every humiliation that prepares us for His fuller manifestation. Our humiliations lead us, in the experience of the presence and power of Jesus, to choose humility as our highest blessing. Let us try to learn the lessons the story of Paul teaches us. …

The highest lesson a believer has to learn is humility. O that every Christian who seek to advance in holiness may remember this well! There may be intense consecration, and fervent zeal and heavenly experience, and yet, if it is not prevented by very special dealings of the Lord, there may be an unconscious Self-exaltation with it all. Let us learn the lesson: the highest holiness is the deepest humility. And let us remember that comes not of itself, but only as it is made matter of special dealing on the part of our faithful Lord and His faithful servant.

Let us look at our lives in the light of this experience, and see whether we gladly glory in weakness, whether we take pleasure, as Paul did, in injuries, in necessities, in distresses. Yes, let us ask whether we have learnt to regard a reproof, just or unjust, a reproach from friend or enemy, an injury, or trouble, or difficulty into which others bring us, as above all an opportunity of proving Jesus is all to us, how our own pleasure or honor are nothing, and how humiliation is in very truth what we take pleasure in. It is indeed blessed, the deep happiness of heaven, to be so free from Self that whatever is said of us or done to us is lost and swallowed up, in the thought that Jesus is all.

Let us trust Him who took charge of Paul to take charge of us too. Paul needed special discipline, and with it special instruction, to learn, what was more precious than even the unutterable things he had heard in heaven what it is to glory in weakness and lowliness. We need it, too, oh so much. He who cared for him will care for us too. He watches over us with a jealous, loving care, "*lest we exalt ourselves.*"

When we are doing so, He seeks to discover to us the evil, and deliver us from it. In trial and weakness and trouble He seeks to bring us low, until we so learn that His grace is all, as to take pleasure in the very thing that brings us and keeps us low. His strength made perfect in our weakness, His presence filling and satisfying our emptiness, becomes the secret of a humility that need never fail. It can, as Paul, in full sight of what God works in us, and through us, ever say, "*In nothing was I behind the chiefest apostles, though I am nothing*" (2 Corinthians 11: 5). His humiliations had led him to true humility, with its wonderful gladness and glorying and pleasure in all that humbles.

"*Most gladly will I glory in my weaknesses, that the power of Christ may rest upon me; wherefore I take pleasure in weaknesses*" (2 Corinthians 12: 9). The humble have learned the secret of abiding gladness. The weaker we feel, the lower we sink; the greater our humiliations appear, the more the power and the presence of Christ are our portion, until, as we say, "I am nothing," the Word of our Lord brings ever deeper joy: "*My grace is sufficient for you.*"

The danger of pride is greater and nearer than we think, and that especially at the time of our highest experiences. The preacher of spiritual truth with an admiring congregation hanging on his lips, the gifted speaker on a Holiness platform expounding the secrets of the heavenly life, the Christian giving testimony to a blessed experience, the evangelist moving on as in triumph, and made a blessing to rejoicing multitudes, no one knows the hidden, the unconscious danger to which these are exposed. Paul was in danger without knowing it; what Jesus did for him is written for our admonition, that we may know our danger and know our only safety. If ever it has been said of a teacher or professor of holiness, he is so full of Self; or, he does not practice what he preaches; or, his blessing has not made him humbler or gentler, let it be said no more. Jesus, in whom we trust, can make us humble.

Yes, the grace for humility is greater and nearer, too, than we think. The humility of Jesus is our salvation. Jesus Himself is our humility. Our humility is His care and His work. His grace is sufficient for us, to meet the temptation of pride too. His strength will be perfected in our weakness. Let us choose to be weak, to be low, to be nothing. Let humility be to us joy and gladness. Let us gladly glory and take pleasure in weakness, in all that can humble us and keep us low; the power of Christ will rest upon us. …

Humility and Exaltation

July 6th

"God gives grace to the humble. Humble yourself in the sight of the Lord, and He shall exalt you."
—JAMES 4: 10

The command is clear: "*humble yourself.*" That does not mean that it is your work to conquer and cast out the pride of your nature, and to form within yourself the lowliness of the holy Jesus. No, this is God's work; the very essence of that exaltation, wherein He lifts you up into the real likeness of the beloved Son. What the command does mean is this: take every opportunity of humbling yourself before God and man. In the faith of the grace that is already working in you … up to the light that conscience each time flashes upon the pride of the heart and its workings—notwithstanding all there may be of failure and falling—stand persistently as under the unchanging command: "*humble yourself.*" Accept with gratitude everything that God allows from within or without, from friend or enemy, in nature or in grace, to remind you of your need of humbling, and to help you to it. Reckon humility to be indeed the mother-virtue, your very first duty before God, the one perpetual safeguard of the soul, and set your heart upon it as the source of all blessing.

The promise is Divine and sure: *He that humbles himself shall be exalted.* See that you do the one thing God asks: *humble yourself.* God will see that he does the one thing He has promised. He will give more grace; He will exalt you in due time.

All God's dealings with man are characterized by two stages. There is the time of preparation, when command and promise, with the mingled experience of effort and impotence, of failure and partial success, with the holy expectancy of something better which these waken, train and discipline men for a higher stage. Then comes the time of fulfillment, when faith inherits the promise, and enjoys what it had so often struggled for in vain. This law holds good in every part of the Christian life, and in the pursuit of every separate virtue. … It is even thus, too, in the pursuit of humility.

To every Christian the command comes from the throne of God Himself: *humble yourself.* The earnest attempt to listen and obey will be rewarded with the painful discovery of two things. The one, what depth of pride that is of unwillingness to count oneself and to be counted nothing, to submit absolutely to God, there was, that one never knew. The other, what utter impotence there is in all our efforts, and in all our prayers too for God's help, to destroy the hideous monster. Blessed are we who now learn to put our hope in God, and to persevere, notwithstanding all the power of pride within us, in acts of humiliation before God and men.

We know the law of human nature: acts produce habits, habits breed dispositions, dispositions form the will, and the rightly-formed will is character. It is not otherwise in the work of grace. As acts, persistently repeated, beget habits and dispositions, and these strengthened the will, He who works both to will and to do comes with His mighty power and Spirit; and the humbling of the proud heart with which the penitent saint … is rewarded with the "more grace" of the humble heart, in which the Spirit of Jesus has conquered, and brought the new nature to its maturity, and He, the meek and lowly One, now dwells forever.

Humble yourselves in the sight of the Lord, and He will exalt you. And wherein does the exaltation consist? The highest glory of the creature is in being only a vessel, to receive and enjoy and show forth the glory of God. It can do this only as it is willing to be nothing in itself, that God may be all. Water always fills first the lowest places. The lower, the emptier a man lies before God, the speedier and the fuller will be the inflow of the Divine glory. The exaltation God promises is not, cannot be, any external thing apart from Himself: all that He has to give or can give is only more of Himself—Himself to take more complete possession. The exaltation is not, like an earthly prize, something arbitrary, in no necessary connection with the conduct to be rewarded. No, but it is in its very nature the effect and result of the humbling of ourselves. It is nothing but the gift of such *a Divine indwelling* … such a conformity to and possession of the humility of the Lamb of God, as fits us for receiving fully the indwelling of God.

"He that humbles himself shall be exalted." Of the truth of these words Jesus Himself is the proof; of the certainty of their fulfillment to us He is the pledge. Let us take His yoke upon us and learn of Him, for He is meek and lowly of heart. If we are but willing to stoop to Him, as He has stooped to us, He will yet stoop to each one of us again, and we shall find ourselves not unequally yoked with Him. As we enter deeper into the fellowship of His humiliation, and either humble ourselves or bear the humbling of men, we can count upon it that the Spirit of His exaltation, *"the Spirit of God and of glory,"* will rest upon us. The presence and the power of the glorified Christ will come to them who are of a humble spirit.

When God can again have His rightful place in us, He will lift us up. Make His glory your care in humbling yourself; He will make your glory His care in perfecting your humility, and breathing into you, as your abiding life, the very Spirit of His Son. As the all-pervading life of God possesses you, you will be nothing so natural, and nothing so sweet, as to be nothing, with not a thought or wish for Self, because all is occupied with Him who fills all. *"Most gladly will I glory in my weakness that the strength of Christ may rest upon me."*

Brother, sister, have we not here the reason that our consecration and our faith have availed so little in the pursuit of holiness? It was by Self and its strength that the work was done under the name of faith; it was for Self and its happiness that God was called in; it was, unconsciously, but still truly, in Self and its holiness that the soul rejoiced. We never knew that humility, absolute, abiding, Christ-like humility and Self-effacement, pervading and marking our whole life with God and man, was the most essential element of the life of the holiness we sought for.

It is only in the possession of God that I lose myself. As it is in the height and breadth and glory of the sunshine that the littleness of the mote playing in its beams is seen, even so humility is the taking our place in God's presence to be nothing but a mote dwelling in the sunlight of His love. … May God teach us to believe that to be humble, to be nothing in His presence, is the highest attainment, and the fullest blessing of the Christian life. He speaks to us: *"I dwell in the high and holy place, and with him who is of a contrite and humble spirit."* Be this our portion!

Humility in Daily Life

July 7th

"He that loves not his brother whom he has seen, how can he love God whom he has not seen?"

—1 JOHN 4: 20

When, in the presence of God, lowliness of heart has become—not a posture we pray to Him but—the very spirit of our life, it will manifest itself in all our bearing towards our brethren. The lesson is one of deep import: the only humility that is really ours is not that which we try to show before God in prayer, but that which we carry with us, and carry out, in our ordinary conduct; the insignficances of daily life are the importances and the tests of eternity, because they prove what really is the spirit that possesses us. It is in our most unguarded moments that we really show and see what we are. To know the humble man, to know how the humble man behaves, you must follow him in the common course of daily life. …

It is even so in the teaching of Paul. To the Romans He writes: *"In honor preferring one another"*; *"Set not your mind on high things, but condescend to those that are lowly"*; *"Be not wise in your own conceit."* To the Corinthians: *"Love"*—and there is no love without humility as its root—*"vaunts not itself, is not puffed up, seeks not its own, is not provoked."* To the Galatians: *"Through love be servants one of another. Let us not be desirous of vainglory, provoking one another, envying one another."* To the Ephesians, immediately after the three wonderful chapters on the heavenly life: *"Therefore, walk with all lowliness and meekness, with long-suffering, forbearing one another in love"*; *"Giving thanks always, subjecting yourselves one to another in the fear of Christ."* To the Philippians: *"Doing nothing through faction or vainglory, but in lowliness of mind, each counting other better than himself. Have the mind in you which was also in Christ Jesus, who emptied Himself, taking the form of a servant, and humbled Himself."* And to the Colossians: *"Put on a heart of compassion, kindness, humility, meekness, long-suffering, forbearing one another, and forgiving each other, even as the Lord forgave you."* ...

The humble man seeks at all times to act up to the rule: *In honor preferring one another; servants one of another; each counting others better than himself subjecting yourselves one to another.* The question is often asked, how we can count others better than ourselves when we see that they are far below us in wisdom and in holiness, in natural gifts, or in grace received. The question proves at once how little we understand what real lowliness of mind is.

True humility comes when, in the, light of God, we have seen ourselves to be nothing, have consented to part with and cast away Self, to let God be all. The soul that has done this... no longer compares itself with others. It has given up forever every thought of Self in God's presence; it meets its fellow-men as one who is nothing, and seeks nothing for itself; who is a servant of God, and for His sake a servant of all. ... The humble man looks upon every ... child of God, and honors him and prefers him in honor as the son of a King. The spirit of Him who washed the disciples' feet, makes it a joy to us to be indeed the least, to be servants one of another.

The humble man feels no jealousy, or envy. He can praise God when others are preferred and blessed before him. He can bear to hear others praised and himself forgotten, because in God's presence he has learned to say with Paul, *"I am nothing."* He has received the spirit of Jesus, pleased not Himself, and sought not His own honor, as the spirit of his life.

Amid what are considered the temptations to impatience and touchiness, to hard thoughts and sharp words, which come from the failings and sins of fellow-Christians, the humble man carries the oft-repeated injunction in his heart, and shows it in his life, *"Forbearing one another, and forgiving one another, even as the Lord forgave you."* He has learned that in putting on the Lord Jesus he has put on the heart of compassion, kindness, humility, meekness, and long-suffering. Jesus has taken the place of Self, and it is not an impossibility to forgive as Jesus forgave. His humility does not consist merely in thoughts or words of Self-depreciation, but, as Paul puts it, in *"a heart of humility,"* encompassed by compassion and kindness, meekness and longsuffering—the sweet and lowly gentleness recognized as the mark of the Lamb of God.

In striving after the higher experiences of the Christian life, the believer is often in danger of aiming at and rejoicing in what one might call the more human, the manly, virtues, such as boldness, joy, contempt of the world, zeal, Self-sacrifice. Even the old Stoics taught and practiced these, while the deeper and gentler, the Diviner and more heavenly graces—those which Jesus first taught upon earth, because He brought them from Heaven—those which are more distinctly connected with His cross and the death of Self—poverty of spirit, meekness, humility, lowliness—are scarcely thought of or valued. Therefore, let us put on a heart of compassion, kindness, humility, meekness, long-suffering; and let us prove our Christlikeness, not only in our zeal for saving the lost, but before all in our intercourse with the brethren, *forbearing and forgiving one another, even as the Lord forgave us.*

Fellow-Christians, do let us study the Bible portrait of the humble man. And let us ask our brethren, and ask the world, whether they recognize in us the likeness to the original. Let us be content with nothing less than taking each of these texts as the promise of what God will work in us, as the revelation in words of what the Spirit of Jesus will give as a birth within us. And let each failure and shortcoming simply urge us to turn humbly and meekly to the meek and lowly Lamb of God, in the assurance that where He is enthroned in the heart, His humility and gentleness will be one of the streams of living water that flow from within us. …

Humility and Sin

July 8th

"Sinners, of whom I am chief"

—1 TIMOTHY 1: 15

Humility is often identified with penitence and contrition. As a consequence, there appears to be no way of fostering humility but by keeping the soul occupied with its sin. We have learned, I think, that humility is something else and something more. We have seen in the teaching of our Lord Jesus and the Epistles how often the virtue is inculcated without any reference to sin. In the very nature of things, in the whole relation of the creature to the Creator, in the life of Jesus as He lived it and imparts it to us, humility is the very essence of holiness as of blessedness. It is the displacement of Self by the enthronement of God. Where God is all, Self is nothing. …

We have only to look at a man like the Apostle Paul, to see how, through his life as a ransomed and a holy man, the deep consciousness of having been a sinner lives inextinguishably. We all know the passages in which he refers to his life as a persecutor and blasphemer. "*I am the least of the apostles, that am not worthy to be called an apostle, because I persecuted the Church of God ...I labored more abundantly than they all; yet not I, but the grace of God which was with me*" (1 Corinthians 15: 9–10). "*Unto me, who am less than the least of all saints, was this grace given, to preach to the heathen*" (Ephesians 3: 8). "*I was before a blasphemer, and a persecutor, and injurious; howbeit I obtained mercy, because I did it ignorantly in unbelief ...Christ Jesus came into the world to save sinners, of whom I am chief*" (1 Timothy 1: 13, 15). God's grace had saved him; God remembered his sins no more for ever; but never, never could he forget how terribly he had sinned. The more he rejoiced in God's salvation, and the more his experience of God's grace filled him with joy unspeakable, the clearer was his consciousness that he was a saved sinner, and that salvation had no meaning or sweetness except as the sense of his being a sinner made it precious and real to him. Never for a moment could he forget that it was a sinner God had taken up in His arms and crowned with His love.

The texts we have just quoted are often appealed to as Paul's confession of daily sinning. One has only to read them carefully in their connection, to see how little this is the case. They have a far deeper meaning, they refer to that which lasts throughout eternity, and which will give its deep undertone of amazement and adoration to the humility with which the ransomed bow before the throne, as those who have been washed from their sins in the blood of the Lamb. Never, never, even in, glory, can they be other than ransomed sinners; never for a moment in this life can God's child live in the full light of His love, but as he feels that the sin, out of which he has been saved, is his one only right and title to all that grace has promised to do. The humility with which first we came as a sinner, acquires a new meaning when we learn how it becomes us as a creature. And then ever again, the humility, in which we were born as a creature, has its deepest, richest tones of adoration, in the memory of what it is to be a monument of God's wondrous redeeming love.

The true import of what these expressions of St. Paul teach us comes out all the more strongly when we notice the remarkable fact that, through his whole Christian course, we never find from his pen, even in those epistles in which we have the most intensely personal unbosomings, anything like confession of sin. Nowhere is there any mention of shortcoming or defect, nowhere any suggestion to his readers that he has failed in duty, or sinned against the law of perfect love. On the contrary, there are passages not a few in which he vindicates himself in language that means nothing if it does not appeal to a faultless life before God and men. "*You are witnesses, and God also, how holily, and righteously, and unblameably we behaved ourselves toward you*" (1 Thessalonians 2:10); "*Our glorying is this, this testimony of our conscience, that in holiness and sincerity of God we behaved ourselves in the world, and more abundantly to you-ward*" (2 Corinthians 1:12).

This is not an ideal or an aspiration; it is an appeal to what his actual life had been. However we may account for this absence of confession of sin, all will admit that it must point to a life in the power of the Holy Spirit, such as is but seldom realized or expected in these our days.

The point which I wish to emphasize is this—that the very fact of the absence of such confession of sinning only gives the more force to the truth that it is not in daily sinning that the secret of the deeper humility will be found, but in the habitual, never for a moment to be forgotten position, which just the more abundant grace will keep more distinctly alive—that our only place, the only place of blessing, our one abiding position before God, must be that of those whose highest joy it is to confess that they are sinners saved by grace.

With Paul's deep remembrance of having sinned so terribly in the past, ere grace had met him, and the consciousness of being kept from present sinning, there was ever coupled the abiding remembrance of the dark hidden power of sin ever ready to come in, and only kept out by the presence and power of the indwelling Christ. "*In me, that is, in my flesh, dwells no good thing*"—these words of Romans 7 describe the flesh as it is to the end. The glorious deliverance of Romans 8—"*The law of the Spirit of life in Christ Jesus has now made me free from the law of sin, which once led me captive*"—is neither the annihilation nor the sanctification of the flesh, but a continuous victory given by the Spirit as He mortifies the deeds of the body. As health expels disease, and light swallows up darkness, and life conquers death, the indwelling of Christ through the Spirit is the health and light and life of the soul. But with this, the conviction of helplessness and danger ever tempers the faith in the momentary and unbroken action of the Holy Spirit into that chastened sense of dependence which makes the highest faith and joy the handmaids of a humility that only lives by the grace of God. …

It is not sin, but God's grace showing us and ever reminding us what a sinner we were, that, will keep us truly humble. It is not sin, but grace, that will make me indeed know myself a sinner, and make the sinner's place of deepest Self-abasement the place I never leave. I fear that there are not a few who, by strong expressions of Self-condemnation and Self-denunciation, have sought to humble themselves, and have to confess with sorrow that a humble spirit, a "heart of humility," with its accompaniments of kindness and compassion, of meekness and forbearance, is still as far off as ever. Being occupied with Self, even amid the deepest Self-abhorrence, can never free us from Self. It is the revelation of God, not only by the law condemning sin but by His grace delivering from it, that will make us humble. …It is the sinner dwelling in the full light of God's holy, redeeming love, in the experience of that full indwelling of divine love, which comes through Christ and the Holy Spirit, who cannot but be humble. Not to be occupied with your sin, but to be occupied with God, brings deliverance from Self.

15

WITH CHRIST IN THE SCHOOL OF PRAYER

Thoughts on Our Training For the Ministry of Intercession

New York: Fleming H. Revell Co., 1895

Preface

July 9th

"If you abide in Me, and My Word abides in you, ask whatsoever you will, and it shall be done unto you."
—JOHN 15: 7

Of all the promises connected with the command, "*Abide in Me*," there is none higher, and none that sooner brings the confession, "*Not that I have already attained, or am already made perfect*," than this: "*If you abide in Me, ask whatsoever you will, and it shall be done unto you.*" Power with God is the highest attainment of the life of full abiding. And of all the traits of a life *like Christ* there is none higher and more glorious than conformity to Him in the work that now engages Him without ceasing in the Father's presence—His all-prevailing intercession. The more we abide in Him, and grow unto His likeness, will His priestly life work in us mightily, and our life become what His is, a life that ever pleads and prevails for us.

"*You have made us kings and priests unto God.*" Both in the king and the priest the chief thing is power, influence, blessing. In the king it is the power coming downward; in the priest, the power rising upward, prevailing with God. In our blessed Priest King, Jesus Christ, the kingly power is founded on the priestly He is able to save to the uttermost, because "*He ever lives to make intercession.*" In us, His priests and kings, it is no otherwise:

it is in intercession that the Church is to find and wield its highest power, that each member of the Church is to prove his descent from Israel, who as a prince had power with God and with men, and prevailed.

It is under a deep impression that the place and power of prayer in the Christian life is too little understood, that this book has been written. I feel sure that as long as we look on prayer chiefly as the means of maintaining our own Christian life, we shall not know fully what it is meant to be. But when we learn to regard it as the highest part of the work entrusted to us, the root and strength of all other work, we shall see that there is nothing that we so need to study and practice as the art of praying aright. If I have at all succeeded in pointing out the progressive teaching of our Lord in regard to prayer, and the distinct reference the wonderful promises ... John 14: 16 have to the works we are to do in His Name, to the greater works, and to the bearing much fruit, we shall all admit that it is only when the Church gives herself up to this holy work of intercession that we can expect the power of Christ to manifest itself in her behalf. It is my prayer that God may use this little book to make clearer to some of His children the wonderful place of power and influence which He is waiting for them to occupy, and for which a weary world is waiting too.

In connection with this there is another truth that has come to me with wonderful clearness as I studied the teaching of Jesus on prayer. It is this: that the Father waits to hear every prayer of faith, to give us whatsoever we will, and whatsoever we ask in Jesus' name. We have become so accustomed to limit the wonderful love and the large promises of our God, that we cannot read the simplest and clearest statements of our Lord without the qualifying clauses by which we guard and expound them. If there is one thing I think the Church needs to learn, it is that God means prayer to have an answer, and that it hath not into the heart of man to conceive what God will do for His child who gives himself to believe that his prayer will be heard. God hears prayer; this is a truth universally admitted, but of which very few understand the meaning, or experience the power. If what I have written stir my reader to go to the Master's words, and take His wondrous promises simply and literally as they stand, my object has been attained.

And then just one thing more. Thousands have in these last years found an unspeakable blessing in learning how completely Christ is our life, and how He undertakes to be and to do all in us that we need. I know not if we have yet learned to apply this truth to our prayer-life. Many complain that they have not the power to pray in faith, to pray the effectual prayer that avails much. The message I would fain bring them is that the blessed Jesus is waiting, is longing, to teach them this. Christ is our life: In Heaven He ever lives to pray; His life in us is an ever-praying life, if we will but trust Him for it. Christ teaches us to pray not only by example, by instruction, by command, by promises, but by showing us HIMSELF, the ever-living Intercessor, as our Life. It is when we believe this, and go and abide in Him for our prayer-life too, that our fears of not being able to pray aright will vanish, and we shall joyfully and triumphantly trust our Lord to teach us to pray, to be Himself the life and the power of our prayer.

May God open our eyes to see what the holy ministry of intercession is to which, as

His royal priesthood, we have been set apart. May He give us a large and strong heart to believe what mighty influence our prayers can exert. …
—ANDREW MURRAY
Wellington, 28th October, 1895

Christ the Intercessor

July 10th

"Wherefore He is able also to save them to the uttermost that come unto God by him, seeing he ever lives to make intercession for them"
—HEBREWS 7: 25

All growth in the spiritual life is connected with the clearer insight into what Jesus is to us. The more I realize that Christ must be all to me and in me, that all in Christ is indeed for me, the more I learn to live the real life of faith, which, dying to Self, lives wholly in Christ. The Christian life is no longer the vain struggle to live right, but the resting in Christ and finding strength in Him as our life, to fight the fight and gain the victory of faith.

This is specially true of the life of prayer. As it too comes under the law of faith alone, and is seen in the light of the fullness and completeness there is in Jesus, the believer understands that it need no longer be a matter of strain or anxious care, but an experience of what Christ will do for us and in us—a participation in that life of Christ which, as on earth, so in Heaven, ever ascends to the Father as prayer. And we begin to pray, not only trusting in the merits of Jesus, or in the intercession by which our unworthy prayers are made acceptable, but in that near and close union in virtue of which He prays in us and we in Him.

See on the difference between having Christ as an Advocate or Intercessor who stands outside of us, and the having Him within us, we abiding in Him and He in us through the Holy Spirit perfecting our union with Him, so that we ourselves can come directly to the Father in His Name. The whole of salvation is Christ Himself: He has given *Himself* to us; He Himself lives in us. Because He prays, we pray too. As the disciples, when they saw Jesus pray, asked Him to make them partakers of what He knew of prayer, so we, now we see Him as intercessor on the throne, know that He makes us participate with Himself in the life of prayer.

How clearly this comes out in the last night of His life. In His high-priestly prayer (John 17), He shows us how and what He has to pray to the Father, and will pray when once ascended to heaven. And yet He had in His parting address so repeatedly also connected His going to the Father with their new life of prayer. The two would be ultimately connected: His entrance on the work of His eternal intercession would be the commencement and the power of their new prayer-life in His Name. It is the sight of Jesus in His intercession that gives us power to pray in His Name: all right and power of prayer is

Christ's; He makes us share in His intercession.

To understand this, think first of His intercession: "*He ever lives to make intercession for them.*" The work of Christ on earth as Priest was but a beginning. It was as Aaron He shed His blood; it is as Melchizedek that He now lives within the veil to continue His work, after the power of the eternal life. As Melchizedek is more glorious than Aaron, so it is in the work of intercession that the atonement has its true power and glory. It is Christ that died: yea more, who is even at the right hand of God, "*who makes intercession for us.*"

That intercession is an intense reality, a work that is absolutely necessary, and without which the continued application of redemption cannot take place. In the incarnation and resurrection of Jesus the wondrous reconciliation took place, by which we became partakers of the Divine life and blessedness. But the real personal appropriation of this reconciliation in each of His members here below cannot take place without the unceasing exercise of His Divine power by the head in Heaven. In all conversion and sanctification, in every victory over sin and the world, there is a real forth-putting of the power of Him who is mighty to save. And this exercise of His power only takes place through His prayer: He asks of the Father, and receives from the Father.

"*He is able to save to the uttermost, because He ever lives to make intercession on their behalf.*" There is not a need of His people but He receives in intercession what the Godhead has to give: His mediation on the throne is as real and indispensable as on the cross. Nothing takes place without His intercession: it engages all His time and powers, is His unceasing occupation at the right hand of the Father.

And we participate not only in the benefits of this His work, but in the work itself. This because we are His body. Body and members are one: "*The head cannot say to the feet, I have no need of you.*" We share with Jesus in all He is and has: "*The glory which You gave me, I have given them.*" We are partakers of His life, His righteousness, His work: we share with Him in His intercession too; it is not a work He does without us.

We do this because we are partakers of His life: "*Christ is our life*"; "*No longer I, but Christ lives in me.*" The life in Him and in us is identical, one and the same. His life in us is an ever-praying life. When it descends and takes possession of us, it does not lose its character; in us too it is the every-praying life—a life that without ceasing asks and receives from God. And this not as if there were two separate currents of prayer rising upwards, one from Him, and one from His people. No, but the substantial life-union is also prayer-union: what He prays passes through us, what we pray passes through Him. … We live, we abide in Him, the Interceding One. …

As in all other things the fullness dwells in Him, so the true prayer-fullness too; He alone has the power of prayer. And just as the growth of the spiritual life consists in the clearer insight that all the treasures are in Him, and that we too are in Him, to receive each moment what we possess in Him, grace for grace, so with the prayer-life too. Our faith in the intercession of Jesus must not only be that He prays in our stead, when we do not or cannot pray, but that, as the Author of our life and our faith, He draws us on to pray in unison with Himself. Our prayer must be a work of faith in this sense too, that as we know that Jesus communicates His whole life in us, He also out of that prayerfulness which is His alone breathes into us our praying.

To many a believer it was a new epoch in his spiritual life when it was revealed to him how truly and entirely Christ was his life, standing good as surety for his remaining faithful and obedient. It was then first that he really began to life a faith-life. No less blessed will be the discovery that Christ is surety for our prayer-life too, the center and embodiment of all prayer, to be communicated by Him through the Holy Spirit to His people.

"*He ever lives to make intercession*" as the Head of the body, as the Leader in that new and living way which He has opened up, as the Author and the Perfecter of our faith. He provides in everything for the life of His redeemed ones by giving His own life in them: He cares for their life of prayer, by taking them up into His heavenly prayer-life, by giving and maintaining His prayer-life within them. "*I have prayed for you*" not to render your faith needless, but "*that your faith fail not*": our faith and prayer of faith is rooted in His. It is, "*if you abide in Me*," the ever-living Intercessor, and pray with me and in me: "*ask whatsoever ye will, and it shall be done unto you.*"

The thought of our fellowship in the intercession of Jesus reminds us of what He has taught us more than once before, how all these wonderful prayer-promises have as their aim and their justification, the glory of God in the manifestation of His kingdom and the salvation of sinners. As long as we only or chiefly pray for ourselves, the promises of the last night must remain a sealed book to us. It is to the fruit-bearing branches of the Vine; it is to disciples sent into the world as the Father sent Him, to live for perishing men; it is to His faithful servants and intimate friends who take up the work He leaves behind, who have like their Lord become as the seed-corn, losing its life to multiply it manifold; it is to such that the promises are given.

Let us each find out what the work is, and who the souls are entrusted to our special prayers; let us make our intercession for them our life of fellowship with God, and we shall not only find the promises of power in prayer made true to us, but we shall then first begin to realize how our abiding in Christ and His abiding in us makes us share in His own joy of blessing and saving men.

The Model Prayer

July 11th

"After this manner therefore pray: Our Father who is in Heaven."

—MATTHEW 6: 9 …

O*ur Father who is in Heaven!"* To appreciate this word of adoration aright, I must remember that none of the saints had in Scripture ever ventured to address God as their Father. The invocation places us at once in the center of the wonderful revelation the Son came to make of His Father as our Father too. It comprehends the mystery of redemption—Christ delivering us from the curse that we might become the children of God. The mystery of regeneration—the Spirit in the new birth giving us the new life. And the mystery of faith—ere yet the redemption is accomplished or understood, the word is given on the lips of the disciples to prepare them for the blessed experience still to come. The words are the key to the whole prayer….

The knowledge of God's Father-love is the first and simplest, but also the last and highest lesson in the school of prayer. It is in the personal relation to the living God, and the personal conscious fellowship of love with Himself, that prayer begins. It is in the knowledge of God's Fatherliness, revealed by the Holy Spirit, that the power of prayer will be found to root and grow. In the infinite tenderness and pity and patience of the infinite Father, in His loving readiness to hear and to help, the life of prayer has its joy. Oh, let us take time, until the Spirit has made these words to us spirit and truth, filling heart and life: *"Our Father in Heaven."* Then we are indeed within the veil, in the secret place of power where prayer always prevails.

"Hallowed be Your name." There is something here that strikes us at once. While we ordinarily first bring our own needs to God in prayer, and then think of what belongs to God and His interests, the Master reverses the order. First, Your name, Your kingdom, Your will; then, give us, forgive us, lead us, deliver us. The lesson is of more importance than we think. In true worship the Father must be first, must be all. The sooner I learn to forget myself in the desire that He may be glorified, the richer will the blessing be that prayer will bring to myself. No one ever loses by what he sacrifices for the Father.

This must influence all our prayer. There are two sorts of prayer: personal and intercessory. The latter ordinarily occupies the lesser part of our time and energy. This may not be. Christ has opened the school of prayer specially to train intercessors for the great work of bringing down, by their faith and prayer, the blessings of His work and love on the world around. There can be no deep growth in prayer unless this be made our aim. The little child may ask of the father only what it needs for itself; and yet it soon learns to say, Give some for sister too. But the grown-up son, who only lives for the father's interest and takes charge of the father's business, asks more largely, and gets all that is asked. And Jesus would train us to the blessed life of consecration and service, in which our interests are all subordinate to the Name, and the Kingdom, and the Will of the Father. O let us live for this, and let, on each act of adoration, Our Father! there follow in the same breath Thy Name, Thy Kingdom, Thy Will; for this we look up and long.

"Hallowed be Your name." What name? This *new* name of "Father." The word "Holy" was the central word of the Old Testament; the name "Father" of the New. In this name of Love all the holiness and glory of God are now to be revealed. … Our prayer must be that in ourselves, in all God's children, in presence of the world, God Himself would reveal the holiness, the Divine power, the hidden glory of the name of "Father." The Spirit of the Father is the Holy Spirit: it is only when we yield ourselves to be led of Him, that the name will be hallowed in our prayers and our lives. Let us learn to pray: *"Our Father… hallowed be Your name."*

"Your kingdom come." The Father is a King and has a Kingdom. The son and heir of a

king has no higher ambition than the glory of his father's kingdom. … What more natural than that, when they learn to hallow the Father-name, they should long and cry with deep enthusiasm: "*Your kingdom come.*" The coming of the kingdom is the one great event on which the revelation of the Father's glory, the blessedness of His children, and the salvation of the world depends. On our prayers too the coming of the kingdom waits. Shall we not join in the deep longing cry of the redeemed: "*Your kingdom come*"?

"*Your will be done, as in Heaven, so on earth.*" This petition is too frequently applied alone to the suffering of the will of God. In Heaven, God's will is done, and the Master teaches the child to ask that the will may be done on earth just as in Heaven: in the spirit of adoring submission and ready obedience. Because the will of God is the glory of Heaven, the doing of it is the blessedness of Heaven. As the will is done, the kingdom of Heaven comes into the heart. And wherever faith has accepted the Father's love, obedience accepts the Father's will. The surrender to, and the prayer for a life of heaven-like obedience, is the spirit of childlike prayer.

"*Give us this day, our daily bread.* When first the child has yielded himself to the Father in the care for His Name, His Kingdom, and His Will, he has full liberty to ask for his daily bread. A master cares for the food of his servant, a general of his soldiers, a father of his child. And will not the Father in heaven care for the child who has in prayer given himself up to His interests? We may indeed in full confidence say: Father, I live for Your honor and Your work; I know You care for me. Consecration to God and His will gives wonderful liberty in prayer for temporal things: the whole earthly life is given to the Father's loving care.

And forgive us our debts, as we also have forgiven our debtors." As bread is the first need of the body, so forgiveness for the soul. And the provision for the one is as sure as for the other. We are children but sinners too; our right of access to the Father's presence we owe to the precious blood and the forgiveness it has won for us. Let us beware of the prayer for forgiveness becoming a formality: only what is really confessed is really forgiven. Let us in faith accept the forgiveness as promised: as a spiritual reality, an actual transaction between God and us, it is the entrance into all the Father's love and all the privileges of children. Such forgiveness, as a living experience, is impossible without a forgiving spirit to others…. In each prayer to the Father I must be able to say that I know of no one whom I do not heartily love.

"*And lead us not into temptation, but deliver us from the evil one.*" Our daily bread, the pardon of our sins, and then our being kept from all sin and the power of the evil one: in these three petitions all our personal need is comprehended. The prayer for bread and pardon must be accompanied by the surrender to live in all things in holy obedience to the Father's will, and the believing prayer in everything to be kept by the power of the indwelling Spirit from the power of the evil one.

Children of God! it is this way that Jesus would have us to pray to the Father in Heaven. Oh, let His name, and kingdom, and will have the first place in our love; and then His providing, and pardoning, and keeping love will be our sure portion. … Such prayer will, indeed, be the fellowship and interchange of love, always bringing us back in trust and worship to Him who is not only the beginning but the end….

Prayer in Harmony with Our Destiny

July 12th

"And God said, Let us make man in our image, after our likeness."

—GENESIS 1: 26

In accordance with such a destiny was the position we were to occupy, and the power at our disposal. When an earthly sovereign sends a viceroy to a distant province, it is understood that he advises as to the policy to be adopted, and that that advice is acted on—that he is at liberty to apply for troops and the other means needed for carrying out the policy or maintaining the dignity of the empire. If his policy be not approved of, he is recalled to make way for someone who better understands his sovereign's desires. As long as he is trusted, his advice is carried out. As God's representative we were to have ruled; all was to have been done under our will and rule; on our advice and at our request Heaven was to have bestowed its blessing on earth. Our prayer was to have been the wonderful, though simple and most natural channel, in which the intercourse between the King in Heaven and His faithful servant man, as lord of this world, was to have been maintained. The destinies of the world were given into the power of our wishes, our will, our prayer. …

No sooner had God begun in Abraham to form for Himself a people from whom kings, yea the Great King, should come forth, than we see what power the prayer of God's faithful servant has to decide the destinies of those who come into contact with him. In Abraham we see how prayer is not only, or even chiefly, the means of obtaining blessing for ourselves, but is the exercise of his royal prerogative to influence the destinies of men, and the will of God which rules them. We do not once find Abraham praying for himself. His prayer for Sodom and Lot, for Abimelech, for Ishmael, prove what power a man, who is God's friend, has to make the history of those around him.

This had been man's destiny from the first. Scripture not only tells us this, but also teaches us how it was that God could entrust man with such a high calling. It was because He had created him in His own image and likeness. The external rule was not committed to him without the inner fitness: The bearing God's image in having dominion, in being lord of all, had its root in the inner likeness, in his nature.

There was an inner agreement and harmony between God and man, and incipient Godlikeness, which gave man a real fitness for being the mediator between God and His world, for he was to be prophet, priest, and king, to interpret God's will, to represent nature's needs, to receive and dispense God's bounty. It was in bearing God's image that he could bear God's rule. He was indeed so like God, so capable of entering into God's purposes, and carrying out His plans, that God could trust him with the wonderful privilege of asking and obtaining what the world might need. …

Prayer still remains … the proof of our Godlikeness, the vehicle of our intercourse with the Infinite Unseen One, the power that is allowed to hold the hand that holds the destinies of the universe. Prayer is not merely the cry of the suppliant for mercy; it is the highest forth-putting of our will, knowing ourselves to be of Divine origin, created for and capable of being, in king-like liberty, the executor of the counsels of the Eternal.

What sin destroyed, grace has restored. What the first Adam lost, the second has won back. In Christ, we regain our original position, and the Church, abiding in Christ, inherits the promise: *"Ask what you will, and it shall be done unto you."* Such a promise does by no means, in the first place, refer to the grace or blessing we need for ourselves. It has reference to our position as the fruit-bearing branches of the Heavenly Vine, who, like Him, only live for the work and glory of the Father. It is for those who abide in Him, who have forsaken Self to take up their abode in Him with His life of obedience and Self-sacrifice, who have lost their life and found it in Him, who are now entirely given up to the interests of the Father and His Kingdom.

These are they who understand how their new creation has brought them back to their original destiny, has restored God's image and likeness, and with it the power to have dominion. Such have indeed the power, each in their own circle, to obtain and dispense the powers of Heaven here on earth. With holy boldness they may make known what they will: they live as priests in God's presence; as kings the powers of the world to come begin to be at their disposal. They enter upon the fulfillment of the promise: *"Ask whatsoever you will, it shall be done unto you."* …

How Much More the Infinite Fatherliness of God

July 13th

"What man is there of you, who, if his son asks him for a loaf, will give him a stone; or if he shall ask for a fish, will give him a serpent? If you then, being evil, give good gifts unto your children, how much more shall your Father in Heaven give good things to them that ask Him?"

—MATTHEW 7: 9–11

In these words our Lord proceeds further to confirm what He had said of the certainty of an answer to prayer. To remove all doubt, and show us on what sure ground His promise rests, He appeals to what everyone has seen and experienced here on earth. We are all children, and know what we expected of our fathers. We are fathers, or continually see them; and everywhere we look upon it as the most natural thing there can be, for a father to hear his child. And the Lord asks us to look up from earthly parents, of whom the best are but evil, and to calculate "*how much more*" the heavenly Father will *"give good gifts to them that ask Him."*

Jesus would lead us up to see, that as much greater as God is than sinful man, so much greater our assurance ought to be that He will more surely than any earthly father grant our childlike petitions. As much greater as God is than man, so much surer is it that prayer will be heard with the Father in Heaven than with a father on earth.

As simple and intelligible as this parable is, so deep and spiritual is the teaching it contains. The Lord would remind us that the prayer of a child owes its influence entirely to the relation in which he stands to the parent. The prayer can exert that influence only when the child is really living in that relationship, in the home, in the love, in the service of the Father. The power of the promise, "*Ask, and it shall be given you,*" lies in the loving relationship between us as children and the Father in Heaven; when we live and walk in that relationship, the prayer of faith and its answer will be the natural result. And so the lesson we have today in the school of prayer is this: Live as a child of God, then you will be able to pray as a child, and as a child you will most assuredly be heard.

And what is the true child-life? The answer can be found in any home. The child that by preference forsakes the father's house, that finds no pleasure in the presence and love and obedience of the father, and still thinks to ask and obtain what he will, will surely be disappointed. On the contrary, he to whom the intercourse and will and honor and love of the father are the joy of his life, will find that it is the father's joy to grant his requests. Scripture says, "*As many as are led by the Spirit of God, they are the children of God.*" The childlike privilege of asking all is inseparable from the childlike life under the leading of the Spirit. He that gives himself to be led by the Spirit in his life, will be led by Him in his prayers too. And he will find that Father-like giving is the Divine response to childlike living.

To see what this childlike living is, in which childlike asking and believing have their ground, we have only to notice what our Lord teaches in the Sermon on the Mount of the Father and His children. In it the prayer-promises are imbedded in the life-precepts; the two are inseparable. They form one whole; and He alone can count on the fulfilment of the promise, who accepts too all that the Lord has connected with it. It is as if in speaking the word, "*Ask, and you shall receive,*" He says: I give these promises to those whom in the beatitudes I have pictured in their childlike poverty and purity, and of whom I have said, "*They shall be called the children of God*" (Matthew: 5: 3–9); to children, "*who let your light shine before men, so that they may glorify your Father in Heaven*"; to those who "walk in love, *that you may be children of your Father which is in Heaven*"; and to those who seek to "*be perfect even as your Father in Heaven is perfect*" (5: 45); to those whose fasting and praying and almsgiving (6: 1–18) is not before men, but before "*your Father who sees in secret*"; who "*forgive even as your Father forgives you*" (6: 15); who trust the heavenly Father in all earthly need, "*seeking first the kingdom of God and His righteousness*" (6: 26–32); who not only "*say, Lord, Lord, but do the will of my Father which is in heaven*" (7: 21). Such are the children of the Father, and such is the life in the Father's love and service; in such a child-life answered prayers are certain and abundant.

But will not such teaching discourage the feeble one? If we are first to answer to this portrait of a child, must not many give up all hope of answers to prayer? The difficulty is removed if we think again of the blessed name of father and child. A child is weak; there is a great difference among children in age and gift. The Lord does not demand of us a perfect fulfilment of the law; no, but only the childlike and whole-hearted surrender to live as a child with Him in obedience and truth. Nothing more. But also, nothing less. The Father must have the whole heart. When this is given, and He sees the child with honest purpose and steady will seeking in everything to be and live as a child, then our prayer will count with Him as the prayer of a child.

Let anyone simply and honestly begin to study the Sermon on the Mount and take it as his guide in life, and he will find, notwithstanding weakness and failure, an ever-growing liberty to claim the fulfilment of its promises in regard to prayer. In the names of father and child he has the pledge that his petitions will be granted.

This is the one chief thought on which Jesus dwells here, and which He would have all His scholars take in. He would have us see that the secret of effectual prayer is: to have the heart filled with the Father-love of God. It is not enough for us to know that God is a Father: He would have us take time to come under the full impression of what that name implies. We must take the best earthly father we know; we must think of the tenderness and love with which he regards the request of his child, the love and joy with which he grants every reasonable desire; we must then, as we think in adoring worship of the infinite Love and Fatherliness of God, consider with how much more tenderness and joy He sees us come to Him, and gives us what we ask aright.

And then, when we see how much this Divine arithmetic is beyond our comprehension, and feel how impossible it is for us to apprehend God's readiness to hear us, then He would have us come and open our heart for the Holy Spirit to shed abroad God's Father-love there.

Let us do this not only when we want to pray, but let us yield heart and life to dwell in that love. The child who only wants to know the love of the father when he has something to ask, will be disappointed. But he who lets God be Father always and in everything, who would fain live his whole life in the Father's presence and love, who allows God in all the greatness of His love to be a Father to him, oh! he will experience most gloriously that a life in God's infinite Fatherliness and continual answers to prayer are inseparable.

Beloved fellow-disciple! we begin to see what the reason is that we know so little of daily answers to prayer, and what the chief lesson is which the Lord has for us in His school. It is all in the name of Father. We thought of new and deeper insight into some of the mysteries of the prayer-world as what we should get in Christ's school; He tells us the first is the highest lesson; we must learn to say well, "*Abba, Father!*" "*Our Father in Heaven.*" He that can say this, has the key to all prayer.

In all the compassion with which a father listens to his weak or sickly child, in all the joy with which he hears his stammering child, in all the gentle patience with which he bears with a thoughtless child, we must, as in so many mirrors, study the heart of our Father, until every prayer be borne upward on the faith of this Divine word: "*How much more shall your heavenly Father give good gifts to them that ask Him.*" "*Lord, Teach us to pray.*"

The All-Comprehensive Gift

July 14th

"If you, being evil, know how to give good gifts to your children, how much more shall the heavenly Father give the Holy Spirit to them who ask Him?"

—LUKE 11: 13

In the Sermon on the Mount, the Lord had already given utterance to His wonderful "*how much more?*" Here in Luke, where He repeats the question, there is a difference. Instead of speaking, as then, of giving "*good gifts*," He says, How much more shall the heavenly Father give "*the Holy Spirit.*" He thus teaches us that the chief and the best of these gifts is the Holy Spirit, or rather, that in this gift all others are comprised. The Holy Spirit is the first of the Father's gifts, and the one He delights most to bestow. The Holy Spirit is therefore the gift we ought first and chiefly to seek.

The unspeakable worth of this gift we can easily understand. Jesus spoke of the Spirit as "the promise of the Father"; the one promise in which God's Fatherhood revealed itself. The best gift a good and wise father can bestow on a child on earth is his own spirit. This is the great object of a father in education—to reproduce in his child his own disposition and character. If the child is to know and understand his father; if, as he grows up, he is to enter into all his will and plans—if he is to have his highest joy in the father, and the father in him—he must be of one mind and spirit with him. And so it is impossible to conceive of God bestowing any higher gift on His child than this: His own Spirit. God is what He is through His Spirit; the Spirit is the very life of God. Just think what it means—God giving His own Spirit to His child on earth.

Was not this the glory of Jesus as a Son upon earth—that the Spirit of the Father was in Him? At His baptism in Jordan the two things were united—the voice, proclaiming Him the Beloved Son, and the Spirit, descending upon Him. And so the apostle says of us, "*Because you are sons, God sent forth the Spirit of His Son into your hearts, crying, Abba, Father.*" A king seeks in the whole education of his son to call forth in him a kingly spirit. Our Father in Heaven desires to educate us as His children for the holy, heavenly life in which He dwells, and for this gives us, from the depths of His heart, His own Spirit.

This was the whole aim of Jesus when, after having made atonement with His own blood, He entered for us into God's presence, that He might obtain for us, and send down to dwell in us, the Holy Spirit. As the Spirit of the Father, and of the Son, the whole life and love of the Father and the Son are in Him; and, coming down into us, He lifts us up into their fellowship. As Spirit of the Father, He sheds abroad the Father's love, with which He loved the Son, in our hearts, and teaches us to live in it. As Spirit of the Son, He breathes in us the childlike liberty, and devotion, and obedience in which the Son lived upon earth. The Father can bestow no higher or more wonderful gift than this: His own Holy Spirit—the Spirit of sonship.

This truth naturally suggests the thought that this first and chief gift of God must be the first and chief object of all prayer. For every need of the spiritual life this is the one thing needful: The Holy Spirit. All the fullness is in Jesus; the fullness of grace and truth, out of which we receive grace for grace. The Holy Spirit is the appointed conveyancer, whose special work it is to make Jesus and all there is in Him for us ours in personal appropriation, in blessed experience. He is the Spirit of life in Christ Jesus; as wonderful as the life is, so wonderful is the provision by which such an agent is provided to communicate it to us. If we but yield ourselves entirely to the disposal of the Spirit, and let Him have His way with us, He will manifest the life of Christ within us. He will do this with a Divine power, maintaining the life of Christ in us in uninterrupted continuity. Surely, if there is one prayer that should draw us to the Father's throne and keep us there, it is this: for the Holy Spirit, whom we as children have received, to stream into us and out from us in greater fullness.

In the variety of the gifts which the Spirit has to dispense, He meets the believer's every need. Just think of the names He bears. The Spirit of grace, to reveal and impart all of grace there is in Jesus. The Spirit of faith, teaching us to begin and go on and increase in ever believing. The Spirit of adoption and assurance, who witnesses that we are God's children, and inspires the confiding and confident Abba, Father! The Spirit of truth, to lead into all truth, to make each word of God ours in deed and in truth. The Spirit of prayer, through whom we speak with the Father; prayer that must be heard. The Spirit of judgment and burning, to search the heart, and convince of sin. The Spirit of holiness, manifesting and communicating the Father's holy presence within us. The Spirit of power, through whom we are strong to testify boldly and work effectually in the Father's service. The Spirit of glory, the pledge of our inheritance, the preparation and the foretaste of the glory to come. Surely the child of God needs but one thing to be able really to live as a child: it is, to be filled with this Spirit.

And now, the lesson Jesus teaches us today in His school is this: That the Father is just longing to give Him to us if we will but ask in the childlike dependence on what He says: "If ye know to give good gifts unto your children, how much more shall your heavenly Father give the Holy Spirit to them that ask Him."

In the words of God's promise, *"I will pour out my Spirit abundantly"*; and of His command, *"Be you filled with the Spirit,"* we have the measure of what God is ready to give, and what we may obtain. As God's children, we have already received the Spirit. But we still need to ask and pray for His special gifts and operations as we require them. And not only this, but for Himself to take complete and entire possession, and for His unceasing moment-by-moment guidance. Just as the branch, already filled with the sap of the vine, is ever crying for the continued and increasing flow of that sap that it may bring its fruit to perfection, so the believer, rejoicing in the possession of the Spirit, ever thirsts and cries for more. And what the great Teacher would have us learn is: that nothing less than God's promise and God's command may be the measure of our expectation and our prayer; we must be filled abundantly. He would have us ask this in the assurance that the wonderful "how much more" of God's Father-love [in the form of His Spirit] is the pledge that, when we ask, we do most certainly receive. …

Ask, And It Shall Be Given You

July 15th

"Ask, and it shall be given you; seek, and you shall find; knock, and it shall be opened unto you: for every one that asks receives, and he that seeks finds; and to him that knocks it shall be opened."

—MATTHEW 7: 7–8

Our Lord returns here in the Sermon on the Mount a second time to speak of prayer. … Here He wants to teach us what in all Scripture is considered the chief thing in prayer: *the assurance that prayer will be heard and answered.* Observe how He uses words which mean almost the same thing, and each time repeats the promise so distinctly: *You shall receive, you shall find, it shall be opened unto you*; and then gives as ground for such assurance the law of the kingdom: *"He that asks, receives; he that seeks, finds; to him that knocks, it shall be opened."*

We cannot but feel how in this six-fold repetition He wants to impress deep on our minds this one truth: *that we may and must most confidently expect an answer to our prayer.* Next to the revelation of the Father's love, there is, in the whole course of the school of prayer, not a more important lesson than this: *Every one that asks, receives.*

One thing is sure: The Lord does want us to count most certainly on it—that asking, seeking, knocking, cannot be in vain—that receiving an answer, finding God—the opened heart and home of God—are the certain fruit of prayer. That the Lord should have thought it needful in so many forms to repeat the truth, is a lesson of deep import. It proves that He knows our heart, how doubt and distrust toward God are natural to us, and how easily we are inclined to rest in prayer as a religious work without an answer. He knows too how, even when we believe that God is the Hearer of prayer, believing prayer that lays hold of the promise, is something spiritual, too high and difficult for the half-hearted disciple. He therefore at the very outset of His instruction to those who would learn to pray, seeks to lodge this truth deep into their hearts: *prayer does avail much; ask and you shall receive; every one that asks, receives.*

This is the fixed eternal law of the kingdom: if you ask and receive not, it must be because there is something amiss or wanting in the prayer. Hold on; let the Word and the Spirit teach you to pray aright, but do not let go the confidence He seeks to waken: *Every one that asks, receives. "Ask, and it shall be given you."* Christ has no mightier stimulus to persevering prayer in His school than this. As a child has to prove a sum to be correct, so the proof that we have prayed aright is, the answer. If we ask and receive not, it is because we have not learned to pray aright.

Let every learner in the school of Christ take the Master's word in all simplicity: "*Every one that asks, receives.*" He had good reasons for speaking so unconditionally. Let us beware of weakening the Word with our human wisdom. When He tells us heavenly things, let us believe Him: His Word will explain itself to us who believe it fully. If questions and difficulties arise, let us not seek to have them settled before we accept the Word. No; let us entrust them all to Him: it is His to solve them: our work is first and fully to accept and hold fast His promise. Let in our inner chamber, in the inner chamber of our heart too, the Word be inscribed in letters of light: *Every one that asks, receives.*

According to this teaching of the Master, prayer consists of two parts, has two sides, a human and a Divine. The human is the asking, the Divine is the giving. Or, to look at both from the human side, there is the asking and the receiving—the two halves that make up a whole. It is as if He would tell us that we are not to rest without an answer, because it is the will of God, the rule in the Father's family: every childlike believing petition is granted. If no answer comes, we are not to sit down in the sloth that calls itself resignation, and suppose that it is not God's will to give an answer. No; there must be something in the prayer that is not as God would have it—that is, *childlike and believing.* [In this case,] we must seek for grace to pray so that the answer may come. It is far easier to the flesh to submit without the answer than to yield itself to be searched and purified by the Spirit, until it has learned to pray the prayer of faith.

It is one of the terrible marks of the diseased state of Christian life in these days, that there are so many who rest content without the distinct experience of answer to prayer. They pray daily, they ask many things, and trust that some of them will be heard, but know little of direct definite answer to prayer as the rule of daily life. And it is this the Father wills: He seeks daily intercourse with His children in listening to and granting their petitions. He wills that I should come to Him day by day with distinct requests; He wills day by day to do for me what I ask. It was in His answer to prayer that the saints of old learned to know God as the Living One, and were stirred to praise and love. Our Teacher waits to imprint this upon our minds: prayer and its answer, the child asking and the Father giving, belong to each other.

There may be cases in which the answer is a refusal, because the request is not according to God's Word, as when Moses asked to enter Canaan. But still, there was an answer: God did not leave His servant in uncertainty as to His will. ... Our Father lets His child know when He cannot give him what he asks, and he withdraws his petition, even as the Son, Jesus, did in Gethsemane. Both Moses the servant and Christ the Son knew that what they asked was not according to what the Lord had spoken: their prayer was the humble supplication whether it was not possible for the decision to be changed. God will teach those who are teachable and give Him time, by His Word and Spirit, whether their request be according to His will or not. Let us withdraw the request, if it be not according to God's mind, or persevere till the answer come.

Prayer is appointed to obtain the answer. It is in prayer and its answer that the interchange of love between the Father and His child takes place. How deep the estrangement of our heart from God must be, that we find it so difficult to grasp such promises. Even while we accept the words and believe their truth, the faith of the heart, that fully has them and rejoices in them, comes so slowly. It is because our spiritual life is still so weak, and the capacity for taking God's thoughts is so feeble. But let us look to Jesus to teach us as none but He can teach. If we take His words in simplicity, and trust Him by His Spirit to make them within us life and power, they will so enter into our inner being, that the spiritual Divine reality of the truth they contain will indeed take possession of us, and we shall not rest content until every petition we offer is borne heavenward on Jesus' own words: *"Ask, and it shall be given you."*

Believe That You Have Received

July 16th

"Therefore I say unto you, all things whatsoever you pray and ask for, believe that you have received them, and you shall have them."
—MARK 11: 24

If we only see to it that we do the one thing that He asks of us as we pray— *"Believe that you have received"*—He will see to it that He does the thing He has promised: *"You shall have them."* The key-note of Solomon's prayer, "*Blessed be the Lord God of Israel, who has with His hands fulfilled that which He spoke with His mouth to my father David*" (2 Chronicles 6: 4), is the keynote of all true prayer: the joyful adoration of a God whose hand always secures the fulfillment of what His mouth has spoken. Let us in this spirit listen to the promise Jesus gives; each part of it has its Divine message.

"All things whatsoever." At this first word our human wisdom at once begins to doubt and ask: This surely cannot be literally true? But, if it be not, then why did the Master speak it? He even used the very strongest expression He could find: *"All things whatsoever."* And it is not as if this were the only time He spoke thus. Is it not He who also said, *"If you can believe, ALL THINGS are possible to those who believe"* (Mark 9: 23). If you have faith, nothing shall be impossible to you.

Faith is so wholly the work of God's Spirit through His word in the prepared heart of the believing disciple, that it is impossible that the fulfilment should not come; faith is the pledge and forerunner of the coming answer. Yes, "ALL THINGS WHATSOEVER *you shall ask in prayer believing, you receive.*" The tendency of human reason is to interpose here, and with certain qualifying clauses, if expedient, "if according to God's will," to break the force of a statement which appears dangerous. O let us beware of dealing thus with the Master's words. His promise is most literally true.

He wants His oft repeated "*all things*" to enter into our hearts, and reveal to us how mighty the power of faith is—how truly the Head calls the members to share with Him in His power; how wholly our Father places His power at the disposal of the child that wholly trusts Him. In this "*all things*," faith is to have its food and strength; as we weaken it we weaken faith. The "*whatsoever*" is unconditional: the only condition is what is implied: *in the believing.*

Ere we can believe we must find out and know what God's will is; believing is the exercise of a soul surrendered and given up to the influence of the Word and the Spirit; but when once we do believe nothing shall be impossible. God forbid that we should try and bring down His "ALL THINGS" to the level of what we think possible. Let us now simply take Christ's "WHATSOEVER" as the measure and the hope of our faith: it is a seed-word which, if taken just as He gives it, and kept in the heart, will unfold itself and strike root, fill our life with its fullness, and bring forth fruit abundantly.

"*All things whatsoever you pray and ask for.*" It is in prayer that these "*all things*" are to be brought to God, to be asked and received of Him. The faith that receives them is the fruit of the prayer. In one aspect there must be faith before there can be prayer; in another the faith is the outcome and the growth of prayer.

It is in the personal presence of the Savior—in intercourse with Him—that faith rises to grasp what at first appeared too high. It is in prayer that we hold up our desire to the light of God's Holy Will, so that our motives are tested, and proof given whether we ask indeed in the name of Jesus, and only for the glory of God. It is in prayer that we wait for the leading of the Spirit to show us whether we are asking the right thing and in the right spirit.

It is in prayer that we become conscious of our want of faith, that we are led on to say to the Father that we do believe, and that we prove the reality of our faith by the confidence with which we persevere. It is in prayer that Jesus teaches and inspires faith. He that waits to pray, or loses heart in prayer, because he does not yet feel the faith needed to get the answer, will never learn to believe. He who begins to pray and ask will find the Spirit of faith is given nowhere so surely as at the foot of the Throne.

"*Believe that you have received.*" It is clear that what we are to believe is, that we receive the very things we ask. The Savior does not hint that because the Father knows what is best He may give us something else. The very mountain faith bids depart is cast into the sea. There is a prayer in which, in everything, we make known our requests with prayer and supplication, and the reward is the sweet peace of God keeping heart and mind. This is the prayer of trust. It has reference to things of which we cannot find out if God is going to give them. As children we make known our desires in the countless things of daily life, and leave it to the Father to give or not as He thinks best. But the prayer of faith of which Jesus speaks is something different, something higher.

When, whether in the greater interests of the Master's work, or in the lesser concerns of our daily life, the soul is led to see how there is nothing that so honors the Father as the faith that is assured that He will do what He has said in giving us whatsoever we ask for, and takes its stand on the promise as brought home by the Spirit, it may know most certainly that it does receive exactly what it asks. Just see how clearly the Lord sets this before us in verse 23: "*Whosoever shall not doubt in his heart, but shall believe that what he says comes to pass, he shall have it.*" This is the blessing of "*the prayer of faith*" of which Jesus speaks.

"*Believe that you have received.*" This is the word of central importance, of which the meaning is too often misunderstood. Believe that you have received! now, while praying, the thing you ask for. It may only be later that you shall have it in personal experience—that you shall see what you believe. But, now, without seeing, you are to believe that it has been given you of the Father in Heaven. The receiving or accepting of an answer to prayer is just like the receiving or accepting of Jesus or of pardon, a spiritual thing, an act of faith apart from all feeling. When I come as a supplicant for pardon, I believe that Jesus in Heaven is for me, and so I receive or take Him. When I come as a supplicant for any special gift, which is according to God's word, I believe that what I ask is given me: I believe that I have it, I hold it in faith; I thank God that it is mine. *"If we know that He hears us, whatsoever we ask, we know that we have the petitions which we have asked of Him."*

"And you shall have them." That is, the gift which we first hold in faith as bestowed upon us in Heaven will also become ours in personal experience. But, we ask, will it be needful to pray longer if once we know we have been heard and have received what we asked? There are cases in which such prayer will not be needful, in which the blessing is ready to break through at once, if we but hold fast our confidence, and prove our faith by praising for what we have received, in the face of our not yet having it in experience. There are other cases in which the faith that has received needs to be still further tried and strengthened in persevering prayer. God only knows when everything in and around us is fully ripe for the manifestation of the blessing that has been given to faith. Elijah knew for certain that rain would come; God had promised it; and yet he had to pray the seven times. … Faith says most confidently, "I have received it." Patience perseveres in prayer until the gift bestowed in Heaven is seen on earth. …

Have Faith in God

July 17th

"Jesus, answering, said unto them, Have faith in God. Verily I say unto you, Whosoever shall not doubt in their heart, but shall believe that what they pray will come to pass; they shall have it."

—MARK 11: 22

In how many hearts has been raised the question: How ever can I attain the faith that knows that it receives all it asks? It is this question our Lord would answer today. Ere He gave that wonderful promise to His disciples, He spoke another word, in which He points out where the faith in the answer to prayer takes its rise, and ever finds its strength. "*Have faith in God*": this word precedes the other: Have faith in the promise of an answer to prayer. The power to believe a promise depends entirely, but only, on faith in the promiser. Trust in the person begets trust in his word. It is only where we live and associate with God in personal, loving intercourse, where God himself is all to us, where our whole being is continually opened up and exposed to the mighty influences that are at work where His Holy Presence is revealed, that the capacity will be developed for believing that He gives whatsoever we ask.

This connection between faith in God and faith in His promise will become clear to us if we think what faith really is. It is often compared to the hand or the mouth, by which we take and appropriate what is offered to us. But it is of importance that we should understand that faith is also the ear by which I hear what is promised, the eye by which I see what is offered me. On this the power to take depends. I must hear the person who gives me the promise: the very tone of his voice gives me courage to believe. I must see him: in the light of his eye and countenance all fear as to my right to take passes away.

The value of the promise depends on the promiser: it is on my knowledge of what the promiser is that faith in the promise depends. It is for this reason that Jesus, ere He gives that wonderful prayer-promise, first says, "*Have faith in God.*" That is, let your eye be open to the Living God, and gaze on Him, seeing Him who is invisible. It is through the eye that I yield myself to the influence of what is before me; I just allow it to enter, to exert its influence, to leave its impression upon my mind.

So believing God is just looking to God and what He is, allowing Him to reveal His presence, giving Him time and yielding the whole being to take in the full impression of what He is as God, the soul opened up to receive and rejoice in the overshadowing of His love. Yes, faith is the eye to which God shows what He is and does: through faith the light of His presence and the workings of His mighty power stream into the soul. As that which I see lives in me, so by faith God lives in me too.

And even so faith is also the ear through which the voice of God is always heard and intercourse with Him kept up. It is through the Holy Spirit the Father speaks to us; the Son is the Word, the substance of what God says; the Spirit is the living voice. This the child of God needs to lead and guide him; the secret voice from Heaven must teach him, as it taught Jesus, what to say and what to do. An ear opened towards God, that is, a believing heart waiting on Him, to hear what He says, will hear Him speak. The words of God will not only be the words of a Book, but, proceeding from the mouth of God, they will be spirit and truth, life and power. They will bring in deed and living experience what are otherwise only thoughts. Through this opened ear the soul tarries under the influence of the life and power of God Himself. As the words I hear enter the mind and dwell and work there, so through faith God enters the heart, and dwells and works there.

When faith now is in full exercise as eye and ear, as the faculty of the soul by which we see and hear God, then it will be able to exercise its full power as hand and mouth, by which we appropriate God and His blessing. The power of reception will depend entirely on the power of spiritual perception. For this reason Jesus said, ere He gave the promise that God would answer believing prayer: "*Have faith in God.*"

Faith is simply surrender: I yield myself to the impression the tidings I hear make on me. By faith I yield myself to the living God. His glory and love fill my heart, and have the mastery over my life.

Faith is fellowship; I give myself up to the influence of the friend who makes me a promise, and become linked to him by it. And it is when we enter into this living fellowship with God Himself, in a faith that always sees and hears Him, that it becomes easy and natural to believe His promise as to prayer. Faith in the promise is the fruit of faith in the promiser. The prayer of faith is rooted in the life of faith. And in this way the faith that prays effectually is indeed a gift of God—not as something that He bestows or infuses at once, but in a far deeper and truer sense, as the blessed disposition or habit of soul which is wrought and grows up in us in a life of intercourse with Him.

Surely for one who knows his Father well, and lives in constant close intercourse with Him, it is a simple thing to believe the promise that He will do the will of His child who lives in union with Himself. It is because very many of God's children do not understand this connection between the life of faith and the prayer of faith that their experience of the power of prayer is so limited. When they desire earnestly to obtain an answer from God, they fix their whole heart upon the promise, and try their utmost to grasp that promise in faith. When they do not succeed, they are ready to give up hope; the promise is true, but it is beyond their power to take hold of it in faith.

Listen to the lesson Jesus teaches us this day: have faith in God—the *living* God. Let faith look to God more than the thing promised. It is His love, His power, His living presence will waken and work the faith. … Learn to believe in God, to take hold of God, to let God take possession of your life, and it will be easy to take hold of the promise. He that knows and trusts God finds it easy to trust the promise too.

Just note how distinctly this comes out in the saints of old. Every special exhibition of the power of faith was the fruit of a special revelation of God. See it in Abraham: And the word of the Lord came unto Abram, saying, "*Fear not, Abram; I am your shield.*" And He brought him forth abroad, and said … "*and he believed the Lord.*" And later again: "*The Lord appeared unto him, and said unto him, I am God Almighty. And Abram fell on his face, and God talked with him, saying, As for me, behold my covenant is with you.*"

It was the revelation of God Himself that gave the promise its living power to enter the heart and work the faith. Because they knew God, these men of faith could not do anything but trust His promise. God's promise will be to us what God Himself is. It is the man who walks before the Lord, and falls upon his face to listen while the living God speaks to him, who will really receive the promise.

Though we have God's promises in the Bible, with full liberty to take them, the spiritual power is wanting, except as God Himself speaks them to us. And He speaks to those who walk and live with Him. Therefore, "*have faith in God*": let faith be all eye and ear, the surrender to let God make His full impression, and reveal Himself fully in the soul. Count it one of the chief blessings of prayer to exercise faith in God, as the Living Mighty God who waits to fulfil in us all the good pleasure of His will, and the work of faith with power.

See in Him the God of Love, whose delight it is to bless and impart Himself. In such worship of faith in God the power will speedily come to believe the promise too: "*All things whatsoever you ask, believe that you receive.*" Yes! see that you in faith make God your own; the promise will be yours too.

Precious lessons that Jesus has to teach us this day. We seek God's gifts, but God wants to give us *Himself* first.

We think of prayer as the power to draw down good gifts from Heaven; Jesus as the means to draw ourselves up to God. We want to stand at the door and cry; Jesus would have us first enter in and realize that we are friends and children.

Let us accept the teaching. Let every experience of the littleness of our faith in prayer urge us first to have and exercise more faith in the living God, and in such faith to yield ourselves to Him. A heart full of God has power for the prayer of faith. Faith in God begets faith in the promise, in the promise too of an answer to prayer.

Therefore, child of God, take time, take time, to bow before Him, to wait on Him to reveal Himself. Take time, and let thy soul in holy awe and worship exercise and express its faith in the Infinite One, and as He imparts Himself and takes possession of you, the prayer of faith will crown your faith in God. "*Lord, teach us to pray.*"

When You Pray, Forgive … and Love

July 18th

"And whenever you stand praying, forgive, if you have aught against any one; that your Father in Heaven may forgive you your trespasses."

—MARK 11: 25

These words follow immediately on the great prayer-promise: *"All things whatsoever you pray, believe that you have received them, and you shall have them."* We have already seen how the words that preceded that promise—"*Have faith in God*"—taught us that in prayer all depends upon our relation to God being clear. These words that follow on it remind us that our relation with fellow-men must be clear too. Love to God and love to our neighbor are inseparable: the prayer from a heart, that is either not right with God on the one side, or with men on the other, cannot prevail. Faith and love are essential to each other.

We find that this is a thought to which our Lord frequently gave expression. In the Sermon on the Mount (Matthew 5: 23–24), when speaking of the sixth commandment, He taught His disciples how impossible acceptable worship to the Father was if everything were not right with the brother: *"If you are offering your gift at the altar, and there remember that your brother has aught against you, leave there your gift before the altar, and go your way; first be reconciled to your brother, and then come and offer your gift."* And so later, when speaking of prayer to God, after having taught us to pray, *"Forgive us our debts, as we also have forgiven our debtors,"* He added at the close of the prayer: *"If you forgive not trespasses of others, neither will your Father forgive your trespasses."* At the close of the parable of the unmerciful servant He applies His teaching in the words: *"So shall also My Heavenly Father do unto you, if you forgive not your brother from your hearts."*

And so here… He all at once, apparently without connection, introduces the thought: *"Whenever you stand praying, forgive, if you have aught against any one; that your Father also which is in Heaven may forgive you your trespasses."* … Jesus wanted to teach us that disobedience to the law of love to men was the great sin even of praying people, and the great cause of the feebleness of their prayer. And it is as if He wanted to lead us into His own blessed experience that nothing gives such liberty of access and such power in believing as the consciousness that we have given ourselves in love and compassion, for those whom God loves.

The first lesson taught here is that of a forgiving disposition. … *"Forgive one another, even as God also in Christ forgave you."* God's full and free forgiveness is to be the rule of ours with men. Otherwise our reluctant, half-hearted forgiveness—which is not forgiveness at all—will be God's rule with us. Every prayer rests upon our faith in God's pardoning grace. If God dealt with us according to our sins, not one prayer could be heard. Pardon opens the door to all God's love and blessing. Because God has pardoned all our sin, our prayer can prevail to obtain all we need. The deep sure ground of answer to prayer is God's forgiving love. When it has taken possession of the heart, we pray in faith. But also, when it has taken possession of the heart, we live in love. God's forgiving disposition, revealed in His love to us, becomes a disposition in us; as the power of His forgiving love shed abroad and dwelling within us, we forgive even as He forgives. …

My drawing nigh to God is of one piece with my intercourse with men and earth: failure here will cause failure there. And that not only when there is the distinct consciousness of anything wrong between my neighbor and myself; but the ordinary current of my thinking and judging—the unloving thoughts and words that I allow to pass unnoticed—can hinder my prayer. The effectual prayer of faith comes out from a life given up to the will and the love of God. Not according to what I try to be when praying, but what I am when not praying, is my prayer dealt with by God.

We may gather these thoughts into a third lesson: In our life with men the one thing on which everything depends is love. The spirit of forgiveness is the spirit of love. Because God is love, He forgives: it is only when we are dwelling in love that we can forgive as God forgives. In love to the brethren we have the evidence of love to the Father, the ground of confidence before God, and the assurance that our prayer will be heard, (1 John 9: 20; 3: 18–21, 23). *"If our heart condemn us not, we have boldness toward God, and whatever we ask, we receive of Him."*

Neither faith nor work will profit if we have not love; it is love that unites with God, it is love that proves the reality of faith. As essential as in the word that precedes the great prayer-promise in Mark 11: 24, *"Have faith in God,"* is this one that follows it, *"Have love to men."* The right relations to the living God above me, and the living men around me, are the conditions of effectual prayer.

This love is of special consequence when we labor for such and pray for them. We sometimes give ourselves to work for Christ, from zeal for His cause, as we call it, or for our own spiritual health, without giving ourselves in personal Self-sacrificing love for those whose souls we seek. No wonder that our faith is feeble and does not conquer. To look on each wretched one, however unlovable he be, in the light of the tender love of Jesus the Shepherd seeking the lost; to see Jesus Christ in him, and to take him up, for Jesus' sake, in a heart that really loves—this, this is the secret of believing prayer and successful effort. Jesus, in speaking of forgiveness, speaks of love as its root. Just as in the Sermon on the Mount He connected His teaching and promises about prayer with the call to be merciful, as the Father in Heaven is merciful (Matthew 5: 7, 9, 22, 38–48), so we see it here: a loving life is the condition of believing prayer. …

That the Father May be Glorified

July 19th

"I go to the Father. And whatsoever you shall ask in my Name, that will I do, that the Father may be glorified in the Son."

—JOHN 14: 13

That the Father may be glorified in the Son: it is to this end that Jesus on His throne in glory will do all we ask in His name. Every answer to prayer He gives will have this as its object: When there is no prospect of this object being obtained, He will not answer. It follows as a matter of course that this must be with us, as with Jesus, the essential element in our petitions: The glory of the Father must be the aim and end, the very soul and life of our prayer.

It was so with Jesus when He was on earth: *"I seek not My own honor: I seek the honor of Him who sent Me."* In such words we have the keynote of His life. In the first words of the high-priestly prayer He gives utterance to it: *"Father! Glorify Your Son, that Your Son may glorify You. I have glorified You on earth; glorify Me with Yourself."* …

It is as we enter into sympathy with Jesus on this point, and gratify Him by making the Father's glory our chief object in prayer too, that our prayer cannot fail of an answer. There is nothing of which the Beloved Son has said more distinctly that it will glorify the Father than this, His doing what we ask; He will not, therefore, let any opportunity slip of securing this object. Let us make His aim ours: let the glory of the Father be the link between our asking and His doing: such prayer must prevail. …

Jesus in His prayers on earth, in His intercession in Heaven, in His promise of an answer to our prayers from there, makes this His first object—the glory of His Father. Is it so with us too? Or are not, in large measure, Self-interest and Self-will the strongest motives urging us to pray? Or, if we cannot see that this is the case, have we not to acknowledge that the distinct, conscious longing for the glory of the Father is not what animates our prayers? And yet it must be so.

Not as if the believer does not at times desire it. But we have to mourn that we have so little attained. And we know the reason of our failure too. It was, because the separation between the spirit of daily life and the spirit of the hour of prayer was too wide. We begin to see that the desire for the glory of the Father is not something that we can awake and present to our Lord when we prepare ourselves to pray. No! it is only when the whole life, in all its parts, is given up to God's glory, that we can really pray to His glory too. "Do all to the glory of God," and, "Ask all to the glory of God,"—these twin commands are inseparable: obedience to the former is the secret of grace for the latter. A life to the glory of God is the condition of the prayers that Jesus can answer, "*that the Father may be glorified.*" ...

And what motive, what power is there that can urge our slothful hearts to yield themselves to our Lord to work this in us? Surely nothing more is needed than a sight of how glorious, how alone worthy of glory the Father is. Let our faith learn in adoring worship to bow before Him, to ascribe to Him alone the kingdom, and the power, and the glory, to yield ourselves to dwell in His light as the ever-blessed, ever-loving One. Surely we shall be stirred to say, "*To Him alone be glory.*" And we shall look to our Lord Jesus with new intensity of desire for a life that refuses to see or seek ought but the glory of God. When there is but little prayer that can be answered, the Father is not glorified. It is a duty, for the glory of God, to live and pray so that our prayer can be answered. For the sake of God's glory, let us learn to pray well.

What a humbling thought that so often there is earnest prayer ... in which the thought of our joy or our pleasure was far stronger than any yearnings for God's glory. No wonder that there are so many unanswered prayers. Here we have the secret. God would not be glorified when that glory was not our object. We who would pray the prayer of faith, will have to give ourselves to live literally so that the Father in all things may be glorified in us.

This must be our aim: without this there cannot be the prayer of faith. "*How can you believe,*" said Jesus, "*when you receive glory of one another, and the glory that comes from the only God you seek not?*" All seeking of our own glory with others makes faith impossible; it is the deep, intense Self-sacrifice that gives up its own glory, and seeks the glory of God alone, that wakens in the soul that spiritual susceptibility of the Divine, which is faith.

... And how, we ask again, shall we attain to it? Let us begin with confession: How little has the glory of God been an all-absorbing passion; how little our lives and our prayers have been full of it. How little have we lived in the likeness of the Son, and in sympathy with Him—for God and His glory alone. Let us take time, until the Holy Spirit discover it to us, and we see how wanting we have been in this. True knowledge and confession of sin are the sure path to deliverance.

And then let us look to Jesus. In Him we can see by what death we can glorify God. In death He glorified Him; through death He was glorified with Him. It is by dying, being dead to Self and living to God, that we can glorify Him. And this—this death to Self, this life to the glory of God--is what Jesus gives and lives in each one who can trust Him for it. Let nothing less than these—the desire, the decision to live only for the glory of the Father, even as Christ did; the acceptance of Him with His life and strength working it in us; the joyful assurance that we can live to the glory of God, because Christ lives in us—let this be the spirit of our daily life.

Jesus stands surety for our living thus; the Holy Spirit is given, and waiting to make it our experience, if we will only trust and let Him; O let us not hold back through unbelief, but confidently take as our watchword—All to the glory of God! The Father accepts the will, the sacrifice is well-pleasing; the Holy Spirit will seal us within with the consciousness, we are living for God and His glory. And then what quiet peace and power there will be in our prayers, as we know ourselves through His grace, in perfect harmony with Him who says to us, when He promises to do what we ask: That the Father may be glorified in the Son.' With our whole being consciously yielded to the inspiration of the Word and Spirit, our desires will be no longer ours but His; their chief end the glory of God.

According to His Will

July 20th

"And this is the boldness which we have toward Him, that, if we ask anything according to His will, He hears us. And if we know that He hear us, whatsoever we ask, we know that we have the petitions which we have asked of Him."

—1 JOHN 5: 14–15

One of the greatest hindrances to believing prayer is with many undoubtedly this: They know not if what they ask is according to the will of God. As long as they are in doubt on this point, they cannot have the boldness to ask in the assurance that they certainly shall receive. And they soon begin to think that, if once they have made known their requests, and receive no answer, it is best to leave it to God to do according to His good pleasure. …

This is the very opposite of what John aimed at in writing thus. He wished to rouse us to boldness, to confidence, to full assurance of faith in prayer. He says, "*This is the boldness which we have toward Him,*" that we can say: "Father! You know and I know that I ask according to Your will: I know You hear me." This is the boldness, that "*if we ask anything according to His will, He hears us.*" On this account He adds at once: "*If we know that He hears us, whatsoever we ask, we know,*" through this faith, that we have, that we now while we pray receive the petition, the special things, we have asked of Him.

John supposes that when we pray, we first find out if our prayers are according to the will of God. They may be according to God's will, and yet not come at once, or without the persevering prayer of faith. It is to give us courage thus to persevere and to be strong in faith, that He tells us: This gives us boldness or confidence in prayer: *"If we ask anything according to His will, He hears us."* It is evident that if it be a matter of uncertainty to us whether our petitions be according to His will, we cannot have the comfort of what he says: *"We know that we have the petitions which we have asked of Him."*

But just this is the difficulty. More than one believer says: "I do not know if what I desire be according to the will of God. God's will is the purpose of His infinite wisdom; it is impossible for me to know whether He may not count something else better for me than what I desire, or may not have some reasons for withholding what I ask." … With such thoughts the prayer of faith, of which Jesus said, *"Whosoever shall believe that these things which he says shall come to pass, he shall have whatsoever he says,"* becomes an impossibility. There may be the prayer of submission, and of trust in God's wisdom, but there cannot be the prayer of faith. The great mistake here is that God's children do not really believe that it is possible to know God's will [in life's circumstances]. Or if they believe this, they do not take the time and trouble to find it out.

What we need is to see clearly in what way it is that the Father leads His waiting, teachable child to know that his petition is according to His will. It is through God's holy Word, taken up and kept in the heart, the life, the will; and through God's Holy Spirit, accepted in His indwelling and leading, that we shall learn to know that our petitions are according to His will. ... In the Word, the Father has revealed in general promises the great principles of His will with His people. The child has to take the promise and apply it to the special circumstances in life to which it has reference. Whatever we ask within the limits of that revealed will, we can know to be according to the will of God.... In His Word, God has given us the revelation of His will and plans with us, with His people, and with the world, with the most precious promises of the grace and power with which—through His people—He will carry out His plans and do His work. As faith becomes strong and bold enough to claim the fulfillment of the *general* promise in the *special* case, we may have the assurance that our prayers are heard; they are according to God's will.

Take the words of John in the verse following our text as an illustration: "*If anyone sees their brother sinning a sin not unto death, they shall ask and God will give him life.*" Such is the general promise; and the believer who pleads on the ground of this promise, prays according to the will of God, and John would give him boldness to know that he has the petition which he asks. But this apprehension of God's will is something spiritual, and must be spiritually discerned. It is not as a matter of logic that we can argue it out: God has said it; I must have it. Nor has every Christian the same gift or calling.

While the *general* will revealed in the promise is the same for all, there is for each one a *special* different will according to God's purpose. And herein is the wisdom of the saints, to now this special will of God for each of us, according to the measure of grace given us, and so to ask in prayer just what God has prepared and made possible for each. It is to communicate this wisdom that the Holy Spirit dwells in us. The personal application of the general promises of the word to our special personal needs—it is for this that the leading of the Holy Spirit is given us.

It is this union of the teaching of the word and Spirit that many do not understand, and so there is a twofold difficulty in knowing what God's will may be. Some seek the will of God in an inner feeling or conviction, and would have the Spirit lead them without the word. Others seek it in the Word, without the living leading of the Holy Spirit. The two must be united: only in the Word, only in the Spirit... can we know the will of God, and learn to pray according to it. ...

It is only the one who yields entirely in the whole life to the supremacy of the Word and the will of God, who can expect in special cases to discern what that Word and will permit them boldly to ask. And even as with the Word, just so with the Spirit. If I would have the leading of the Spirit in prayer to assure me what God's will is, my whole life must be yielded to that leading... It is he who, through word and Spirit, lives in the will of God *by doing it*, who will know to pray according to that will in the confidence that He hears us.

God's word tells us that the great reason of unanswered prayer is that we do not pray aright: "*You ask and receive not, because you ask amiss.*" In not granting an answer, the Father tells us that there is something wrong in our praying. He wants to teach us to find it out and confess it, and so to educate us to true believing and prevailing prayer. He can only attain His object when He brings us to see that we are to blame for the withholding of the answer; our aim, or our faith, or our life is not what it should be. ... Let that word, "*You receive not because you ask amiss,*" be as the lantern of the Lord, searching heart and life to prove that we are indeed such as those to whom Christ gave His promises of certain answers.

Let us believe that we can know if our prayer be according to God's will. Let us yield our heart to have the Word of the Father dwell richly there, to have Christ's word abiding in us. Let us live day by day with the anointing which teaches us all things.

Let us yield ourselves unreservedly to the Holy Spirit as He teaches us to abide in Christ, to dwell in the Father's presence, and we shall soon understand how the Father's love longs that the child should know His will, and should, in the confidence that that will includes all that His power and love have promised to do, know too that He hears the petitions which we ask of Him. "*This is the boldness which we have—that if we ask anything according to His will, He hears us.*" "*Lord, Teach us to pray!*"

Power for Praying and Working

July 21st

"Verily, I say to you, He that believes on Me, the works that I do shall he do also; and greater works than these shall he do; because I go unto My Father. And whatsoever you shall ask in my Name, that will I do."

—JOHN 14: 12–13

As the Savior opened His public ministry with His disciples by the Sermon on the Mount, so He closes it by the Parting Address preserved for us by John. In both He speaks more than once of prayer. But with a difference. In the Sermon on the Mount it is as to disciples who have only just entered His school, who scarcely know that God is their Father, and whose prayer chiefly has reference to their personal needs. In His closing address He speaks to disciples whose training time is now come to an end, and who are ready as His messengers to take His place and His work. In the former the chief lesson is: Be childlike, pray believingly, and trust the Father that He will give you all good gifts.

Here He points to something higher: They are now His friends to whom He has made known all that He has heard of the Father; they are now His messengers, who have entered into His plans, and into whose hands the care of His work and kingdom on earth is to be entrusted. They are now to go out and do His works, and in the power of His approaching exaltation, even greater works. Prayer is now to be the channel through which that power is to be received for their work. With Christ's ascension to the Father a new epoch commences for their working and praying both.

See how clearly this connection comes out in our text. As His body here on earth, as those who are one with Him in Heaven, they are now to do greater works than He had done; their success and their victories are to be greater than His. He mentions two reasons for this. The one, because He was to go to the Father, to receive all power; the other, because they might now ask and expect all in His Name.

Because "*I go to the Father,*"—and notice this—"*and, whatsoever you shall ask, I will do.*" His going to the Father would thus bring the double blessing: they would ask and receive all in His Name, and as a consequence, would do the greater works. This first mention of prayer in our Savior's parting words thus teaches us two most important lessons. We that would do the works of Jesus must pray in His Name. We that would pray in His Name must work in His Name.

We who would work must pray: It is in prayer that the power for work is obtained. We that in faith would do the works that Jesus did, must pray in His Name. As long as Jesus was here on earth, He Himself did the greatest works: devils the disciples could not cast out, fled at His word. When He went to the Father, He was no longer here in the body to work directly. The disciples were now His body: all His work from the throne in heaven here on earth must and could be done through them.

One might have thought that now He was leaving the scene Himself, and could only work through commissioners, the works might be fewer and weaker. He assures us of the contrary: *"Verily, verily, I say unto you, He that believes on Me, the works that I do shall he do also, and he shall do greater works."* ... With His ascension He was to receive the power to communicate the Holy Spirit so fully to His own; the union, the oneness between Himself on the throne and them on earth, was to be so intensely and Divinely perfect, that He meant it as the literal truth: *"Greater works than these shall he do, because I go to the Father."*

And the issue proved how true it was. While Jesus, during three years of personal labor on earth, gathered little more than five hundred disciples, and the most of them so feeble that they were but little credit to His cause, it was given to men like Peter and Paul manifestly to do greater things than He had done. From the throne He could do through them what He Himself in His humiliation could not yet do. But there is one condition: "*The one who believe in me shall do greater works, because I go to the Father; and whatsoever you shall ask in my Name, that will I do.*" His going to the Father would give Him a new power to hear prayer.

For the doing of the greater works, two things were needed: His going to the Father to receive all power, our prayer in His Name to receive all power from Him again. As He asks the Father, He receives and bestows on us the power of the new dispensation for the greater works; as we believe, and ask in His Name, the power comes and takes possession of us to do the greater works.

Alas! how much working there is in the work of God, in which there is little or nothing to be seen of the power to do anything like Christ's works, not to speak of greater works. There can be but one reason: The believing on Him, the believing prayer in His Name, this is so much wanting. ...

And now the second lesson: He who would pray must work. It is for power to work that prayer has such great promises: it is in working that the power for the effectual prayer of faith will be gained. In these parting words of our blessed Lord we find that He no less than six times (John 14: 13–14; 15: 7, 16; 16: 23–24) repeats those unlimited prayer-promises which have so often awakened our anxious questionings as to their real meaning: *whatsoever, anything, what you will, ask and you shall receive.* How many a believer has read these over with joy and hope, and in deep earnestness of soul has sought to plead them for their own need. And they have come out disappointed. The simple reason was this: they had torn away the promise from its surrounding. The Lord gave the wonderful promise of the free use of His Name with the Father in connection with the doing of His works. It is the disciple who gives themselves wholly to live for Jesus' work and kingdom, for His will and honor, to whom the power will come to appropriate the promise. ...

Bear Fruit

July 22nd

"You did not choose Me, but I chose you, and appointed you, that you should go and bear fruit, and that your fruit should abide: that whatsoever you shall ask the Father in My name, He may give it you."

—JOHN 15: 16

I *"chose you,"* the Master says, *"and appointed you that you should go and bear fruit, and that your fruit should abide"*; and then He adds, *"that whatsoever you"*—the fruit-bearing ones— *"shall ask of the Father in My name, He may give it you."* This is nothing but the fuller expression of what He had spoken in the words, *"If you abide in Me."* He had spoken of the object of this abiding as the "bearing fruit".... In this was God to be glorified, and the mark of discipleship seen. No wonder that He now adds, that where the reality of the abiding is seen in fruit abounding and abiding, this would be the qualification for praying so as to obtain what we ask. Entire consecration to the fulfillment of our calling is the condition of effectual prayer, is the key to the unlimited blessings of Christ's wonderful prayer-promises.

There are Christians who fear that such a statement is at variance with the doctrine of free grace. But surely not of free grace rightly understood, nor with so many express statements of God's blessed word. Take the words of St. John: *"Let us love in deed and truth; hereby shall we assure our heart before Him. And whatsoever we ask, we receive of Him, because we keep His commandments, and do the things that are pleasing in His sight"* (1 John 3: 22). Or take the oft-quoted words of James: *"The fervent effectual prayer of a righteous man avails much"*... Mark the spirit of so many of the Psalms, with their confident appeal to the integrity and righteousness of the supplicant. David says: *"The Lord rewarded me according to my righteousness; according to the cleanness of my hands has He recompensed me. ... I was upright before Him, and I kept myself from mine iniquity: therefore, has the Lord recompensed me according to my righteousness"* (Psalm 18: 20–26). See also Psalm 7: 3–5; 15: 1–2; 18: 3, 6; 16:1–6; 119: 121,153). If we carefully consider such utterances in the light of the New Testament, we shall find them in perfect harmony with the explicit teaching of the Savior's parting words: *"If you keep my commandments, you shall abide in My love"; "You are My friends if you do what I command you."* The word is indeed meant literally: *"I appointed you that you should go and bear fruit, that, then, whatsoever you shall ask of the Father in My name, He may give it you."*

Let us seek to enter into the spirit of what the Savior here teaches us. There is a danger in our evangelical religion of looking too much at what it offers from one side, as a certain experience to be obtained in prayer and faith. There is another side which God's word puts very strongly: that of obedience, as the only path to blessing. What we need is to realize that in our relationship to the Infinite Being whom we call God who has created and redeemed us—the first sentiment that ought to animate us—is that of subjection. The surrender to His supremacy, His glory, His will, His pleasure, ought to be the first and uppermost thought of our life. ...

What this Infinite Being whom we call God in the very nature of things rightfully claims, and is infinitely and unspeakably worthy of, is that His glory and pleasure should be my one object. Surrender to His perfect and blessed will—a life of service and obedience—is the beauty and the charm of Heaven. Service and obedience, these were the thoughts that were uppermost in the mind of the Son, when He dwelled upon earth. Service and obedience, these must become with us the chief objects of desire and aim, more so than rest or light, or joy or strength: in them we shall find the path to all the higher blessedness that awaits us.

Just note what a prominent place the Master gives it, not only in the 15th chapter of John, in connection with the abiding, but in the 14th, where He speaks of the indwelling of the Three-One God. In verse 15 we have it: *"If you love me, keep my commandments, and the Spirit will be given you of the Father."* Then verse 21: *"He that has my commandments and keeps them, he it is that loves me"*; and he shall have the special love of my Father resting on him and the special manifestation of myself. And then again, verse 23, one of the highest of all the exceeding great and precious promises: *"If a man love me he will keep my words, and the Father and I will come and take up our abode with him."* Could words put it more clearly that obedience is the way to the indwelling of the Spirit, to His revealing the Son within us, and to His again preparing us to be the abode, the home of the Father? The indwelling of the Three-One God is the heritage of them that obey.

Obedience and faith are but two aspects of one act—surrender to God and His will. As faith strengthens for obedience, it is in turn strengthened by it: faith is made perfect by works. It is to be feared that often our efforts to believe have been unavailing because we have not taken up the only position in which a large faith is legitimate or possible—that of entire surrender to the honor and the will of God. It is the man who is entirely consecrated to God and His will who will find the power come to claim everything that His God has promised to be for him.

The application of this in the school of prayer is very simple, but very solemn: *"I chose you,"* the Master says, *"and appointed you that you should go and bear fruit,"* much fruit (verses 5, 8), *"and that your fruit should abide,"* that your life might be one of abiding fruit and abiding fruitfulness, that thus, as fruitful branches abiding in me, *"whatsoever you shall ask of the Father in my name, He may give it you."*

O how often we have sought to be able to pray the effectual prayer for much grace to bear fruit, and have wondered that the answer came not. It was because we were reversing the Master's order. We wanted to have the comfort and the joy and the strength first, that we might do the work easily and without any feeling of difficulty or Self-sacrifice. And He wanted us in faith, without asking whether we felt weak or strong, whether the work was hard or easy, in the obedience of faith to do what He said: The path of fruit-bearing [leads] us to the place and the power of prevailing prayer.

Obedience is the only path that leads to the glory of God. Not obedience instead of faith, nor obedience to supply the shortcomings of faith; no, but faith's obedience gives access to all the blessings our God has for us. The baptism of the Spirit (John 14: 16), the manifestation of the Son (14: 21), the indwelling of the Father (14: 23), the abiding in Christ's love (15: 10), the privilege of His holy friendship (15: 14), and the power of all-prevailing prayer (15: 16)—all wait for the obedient. Let us take home the lessons.

Now we know the great reason why we have not had power in faith to pray prevailingly. Our life was not as it should have been: simple downright obedience, abiding fruitfulness, was not its chief mark. And with our whole heart we approve of the Divine appointment: men to whom God is to give such influence in the rule of the world, as at their request to do what otherwise would not have taken place, men whose will is to guide the path in which God's will is to work, must be men who have themselves learned obedience, whose loyalty and submission to authority must be above all suspicion.

Our whole soul approves the law: obedience and fruit-bearing, the path to prevailing prayer. And with shame we acknowledge how little our lives have yet borne this stamp. Let us yield ourselves to take up the appointment the Savior gives us. Let us study His relation to us as Master. Let us seek no more with each new day to think in the first place of comfort, or joy, or blessing. Let the first thought be: I belong to the Master. Every moment and every movement I must act as His property, as a part of Himself, as one who only seeks to know and do His will. A servant, a slave of Jesus Christ; let this be the spirit that animates me. If He says, "*No longer do I call you servants, but I have called you friends,*" let us accept the place of friends: "*You are my friends if ye do the things which I command you.*"

The Power of Persevering Prayer

July 23rd

"And He spoke a parable unto them to the end that they ought always to pray, and not to faint." ...

—LUKE 18: 1–8

Of all the mysteries of the prayer world, the need of persevering prayer is one of the greatest. That the Lord, who is so loving and longing to bless, should have to be supplicated time after time, sometimes year after year, before the answer comes, we cannot easily understand. It is also one of the greatest practical difficulties in the exercise of believing prayer. When, after persevering supplication, our prayer remains unanswered, it is often easiest for our slothful flesh, and it has all the appearance of pious submission, to think that we must now cease praying, because God may have His secret reason for withholding His answer to our request.

It is by faith alone that the difficulty is overcome. When once faith has taken its stand upon God's Word, and the Name of Jesus, and has yielded itself to the leading of the Spirit to seek *God's will and honor alone* in its prayer, it need not be discouraged by delay. It knows from Scripture that the power of believing prayer is simply irresistible; real faith can never be disappointed. It knows how, just as water, to exercise the irresistible power it can have, must be gathered up and accumulated, until the stream can come down in full force, there must often be a heaping up of prayer, until God sees that the measure is full, and the answer comes. It knows how, just as the ploughman has to take his ten thousand steps, and sow his ten thousand seeds, each one a part of the preparation for the final harvest, so there is a need-be for oft-repeated persevering prayer, all working out some desired blessing. It knows for certain that not a single believing prayer can fail of its effect in heaven, but has its influence, and is treasured up to work out an answer in due time to him who perseveres to the end.

Faith knows that it has to do not with human thoughts or possibilities, but with the Word of the living God. And so even as Abraham through so many years in hope believed against hope, *"and then through faith and patience inherited the promise,"* it counts that the long-suffering of the Lord is salvation, waiting and hasting unto the coming of its Lord to fulfil His promise. ...

Why must God's own elect so often, in the midst of suffering and conflict, cry day and night? He is long-suffering over them. *"Behold! the husbandman waits for the precious fruit of the earth, being long-suffering over it, till it receive the early and the latter rain."* The husbandman does indeed long for his harvest, but knows that it must have its full time of sunshine and rain, and has long patience. A child so often wants to pick the half-ripe fruit; the husbandman knows to wait till the proper time. Man, in his spiritual nature too, is under the law of gradual growth that reigns in all created life. It is only in the path of development that we can reach our Divine destiny. And it is the Father, in whose hands are the times and seasons, who alone knows the moment when the soul or the Church is ripened to that fullness of faith in which it can really take and keep the blessing. As a father who longs to have his only child home from school, and yet waits patiently till the time of training is completed, so it is with God and His children: He is the long-suffering One, and answers speedily.

The insight into this truth leads the believer to cultivate the corresponding dispositions: patience and faith, waiting and having—these are the secret of his perseverance. By faith in the promise of God, we know that we have the petitions we have asked of Him. Faith takes and holds the answer in the promise, as an unseen spiritual possession, rejoices in it, and praises for it. But there is a difference between the faith that thus holds the Word and knows that it has the answer, and the clearer, fuller, riper faith that obtains the promise as a present experience. It is in persevering, not unbelieving, but confident and praising prayer, that the soul grows up into that full union with its Lord in which it can enter upon the possession of the blessing in Him. … The faith that has, according to the command, believed that it has received, can allow God to take His time: it knows it has prevailed and must prevail. In quiet, persistent, and determined perseverance it continues in prayer and thanksgiving until the blessing comes. And so we see combined what at first sight appears so contradictory; the faith that rejoices in the answer of the unseen God as a present possession, with the patience that cries day and night until it be revealed. … God's long-suffering is met by the triumphant but patient faith of His waiting child.

Our great danger in this school of the answer delayed, is the temptation to think that, after all, it may not be God's will to give us what we ask. If our prayer be according to God's Word, and under the leading of the Spirit, let us not give way to these fears. Let us learn to give God time. God needs time with us. If we only give Him time; that is, time in the daily fellowship with Himself, for Him to exercise the full influence of His presence on us; and time, day by day, in the course of our being kept waiting, for faith to prove its reality and to fill our whole being, He Himself will lead us from faith to vision; we shall see the glory of God. …

If You Abide in Me

July 24th

"If you abide in Me, and My words abide in you, ask whatsoever you will, and it shall be done unto you."
—JOHN 15: 7

In all God's intercourse with us, the promise and its conditions are inseparable. If we fulfill the conditions, He fulfills the promise. … So in prayer the unlimited promise, *"Ask whatsoever you will,"* has its one simple and natural condition, *"if you abide in Me."* It is Christ whom the Father always hears; God is in Christ, and can only be reached by being in Him; to be in Him is the way to have our prayer heard; fully and wholly abiding in Him, we have the right to ask whatsoever we will, and the promise that it shall be done unto us.

When we compare this promise with the experiences of most believers, we are startled by a terrible discrepancy. Who can number up the countless prayers that rise and bring no answer? The cause must be either that we do not fulfill the condition, or God does not fulfill the promise. Believers are not willing to admit either, and therefore have devised a way of escape from the dilemma. They put into the promise the qualifying clause that our Savior did not put there: *if it be God's will*—and so maintain both God's integrity and their own.

Oh, if they did but accept it and hold it fast as it stands, trusting to Christ to vindicate His truth, how God's Spirit would lead them to see the Divine propriety of such a promise to those who really abide in Christ in the sense in which He means it, and to confess that the failure in the fulfilling the condition is the one sufficient explanation of unanswered prayer. And how the Holy Spirit would then make our feebleness in prayer one of the mightiest motives to urge us on to discover the secret, and obtain the blessing, of full abiding in Christ.

"If you abide in Me." As we grow in grace and in the knowledge of the Lord Jesus, we are often surprised to find how the words of God grow too, in the new and deeper meaning with which they come. We can look back to the day when some word of God was opened up, and we rejoiced in the blessing we had found in it. After a time, some deeper experience gave it a new meaning, and it was as if we never had seen what it contained. And yet once again, as we advanced in the Christian life, the same word stood before us again as a great mystery, until anew the Holy Spirit led us still deeper into its Divine fullness.

One of these ever-growing, never-exhausted words, opening up to us step by step the fullness of the Divine life, is the Master's precious *"Abide in Me."* As the union of the branch with the vine is one of growth, never-ceasing growth and increase, so our abiding in Christ is a life process in which the Divine life takes ever fuller and more complete possession of us. The young and feeble believer may be really abiding in Christ up to the measure of their light; it is we who reaches onward to the full abiding in the sense in which the Master understood the words, who inherits all the promises connected with it.

In the growing life of abiding in Christ, the first stage is that of faith. As we see that, with all our feebleness, the command is really meant for us, our great aim is simply to believe that, as we know we are in Christ, so now, notwithstanding unfaithfulness and failure, abiding in Christ is our immediate duty, and a blessing within reach. We are specially occupied with the love, and power, and faithfulness of the Savior: we feel our one need to be believing.

It is not long before we see something more is needed. Obedience and faith must go together. It is not as if to the faith we have the obedience must be added, but faith must be made manifest in obedience. Faith is obedience at home and looking to the Master: obedience is faith going out to do His will. We see how we have been more occupied with the privilege and the blessings of this abiding than with its duties and its fruit. There has been much of Self and of Self-will that has been unnoticed or tolerated. The peace which, as a young and feeble disciple, we could enjoy in believing goes from us; it is in practical obedience that the abiding must be maintained: *"If you keep my commands, you shall abide in my love."* As before our great aim was through the mind, and the truth it took hold of, to let the heart rest on Christ and His promises; so now, in this stage, the chief effort is to get our will united with the will of the Lord, and the heart and the life brought entirely under His rule.

And yet it is as if there is something wanting. The will and the heart are on Christ's side; we obey and we love our Lord. But still, why is it that the fleshly nature has yet so much power, that the spontaneous motions and emotions of the inmost being are not what they should be? The will does not approve or allow, but here is a region beyond control of the will. And why also, even when there is not so much of positive commission to condemn, why so much of omission, the deficiency of that beauty of holiness, that zeal of love, that conformity to Jesus and His death, in which the life of Self is lost, and which is surely implied in the abiding, as the Master meant it? There must surely be something in our abiding in Christ and Christ in us, which he has not yet experienced.

It is so. Faith and obedience are but the pathway of blessing. Before giving us the parable of the vine and the branches, Jesus had very distinctly told what the full blessing is to which faith and obedience are to lead. Three times over He had said, *"If you love me, keep my commandments,"* and spoken of the threefold blessing with which He would crown such obedient love. The Holy Spirit would come from the Father; the Son would manifest Himself; the Father and the Son would come and make their abode.

It is as our faith grows into obedience, and in obedience and love our whole being goes out and clings itself to Christ, that our inner life becomes opened up, and the capacity is formed within of receiving the life, the spirit, of the glorified Jesus, as a distinct and conscious union with Christ and with the Father. The Word is fulfilled in us: *"In that day you shall know that I am in my Father and you in me, and I in you."* We understand how, just as Christ is in God, and God in Christ, one together not only in will and in love, but in identity of nature and life, because they exist in each other, so we are in Christ and Christ in us, in union not only of will and love, but of life and nature too.

It was after Jesus had spoken thus … that He said: "Abide in Me, and I in you. Accept, consent to receive that Divine life of union with myself, in virtue of which, as you abide in Me, I also abide in you, even as I abide in the Father. So that your life is mine and mine is yours."

To those who thus abide, the promise comes as their rightful heritage: *"Ask whatsoever you will."* It cannot be otherwise. Christ has got full possession of them. Christ dwells in their love, their will, their life. Not only has their will been given up; Christ has entered it, and dwells and breathes in it by His Spirit. He whom the Father always hears, prays in them; they pray in Him: what they ask shall be done unto them.

Beloved fellow believer! let us confess that it is because we do not abide in Christ as He would have us, that the Church is so impotent in presence of the infidelity and world liness and heathendom, in the midst of which the Lord is able to make her more than conqueror. Let us believe that He means what He promises, and accept the condemnation the confession implies.

But let us not be discouraged. The abiding of the branch in the Vine is a life of never-ceasing growth. The abiding, as the Master meant it, is within our reach, for He lives to give it us. Let us but be ready to count all things loss, and to say [with Paul], "*Not as though I had already attained; I follow after, if that I may apprehend that for which I also am apprehended of Christ Jesus.*" Let us not be so much occupied with the abiding, as with Him to whom the abiding links us, and His fullness. Let it be Him, the whole Christ, in His obedience and humiliation, in His exaltation and power, in whom our soul moves and acts; He Himself will fulfil His promise in us.

And then as we abide, and grow evermore into the full abiding, let us exercise our right, the will to enter into all God's will. Obeying what that will commands, let us claim what it promises. Let us yield to the teaching of the Holy Spirit, to show each of us, according to his growth and measure, what the will of God is which we may claim in prayer. And let us rest content with nothing less than the personal experience of what Jesus gave when He said, "*If you abide in Me, ask whatsoever you will, it shall be done unto you.*" Lord, teach us to pray!

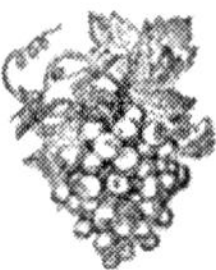

My Words in You

July 25th

"If you abide in Me, and My words abide in you, ask whatsoever you will, and it shall be done unto you."
—JOHN 15: 7

The vital connection between the Word and prayer is one of the simplest and earliest lessons of the Christian life. As that newly-converted heathen put it: I pray—I speak to my Father; I read—my Father speaks to me. Before prayer, it is God's Word that prepares me for it by revealing what the Father has bid me ask. In prayer, it is God's Word strengthens me by giving my faith its warrant and its plea. And after prayer, it is God's Word that brings me the answer when I have prayed, for in it the Spirit gives me to hear the Father's voice.

Prayer is not monologue but dialogue; God's voice in response to mine in its most essential part. Listening to God's voice is the secret of the assurance that He will listen to mine. "*Incline thine ear, and hear; give ear to Me;*" "*Hearken to My voice;*" are words which God speaks to man as well as man to God. His hearkening will depend on ours; the entrance His words find with me, will be the measure of the power of my words with Him. What God's words are to me, is the test of what He Himself is to me, and so of the uprightness of my desire after Him in prayer.

It is this connection between His word and our prayer that Jesus points to when He says, "*If you abide in me, and My words abide in you, ask whatsoever you will, and it shall be done unto you.*"

The deep importance of this truth becomes clear if we notice the other expression of which this one has taken the place. More than once Jesus had said, *"Abide in Me and I in you."* His abiding in us was the complement and the crown of our abiding in Him. But here, instead of *"You in me and I in you,"* He says, *"You in me and my words in you."* His words abiding are the equivalent of Himself abiding.

What a view is here opened up to us of the place the words of God in Christ are to have in our spiritual life, and especially in our prayer. ... When God speaks forth Himself in His words, He does indeed give Himself—His love, and His life, His will and His power—to those who receive these words.... In every promise He puts Himself in our power to lay hold of and possess; in every command He puts Himself in our power for us to share with Him His will, His holiness, His perfection. In God's Word, He gives us HIMSELF; His Word is nothing less than the eternal Son, Christ Jesus. And so all Christ's words are God's words—full of a Divine quickening life and power: *"The words that I speak unto you, they are spirit and they are life."* ...

To offer a prayer—to give utterance to certain wishes and to appeal to certain promises—is an easy thing, and can be learned of man by human wisdom. But to pray in the Spirit, to speak words that reach and touch God, that affect and influence the powers of the unseen world—such praying, such speaking, depends entirely upon our hearing God's voice. Just as far as we listen to the voice and language that God speaks, and in the words of God receive His thoughts, His mind, His life, into our heart, we shall learn to speak in the voice and the language that God hears. It is the ear of the learner, wakened morning by morning, that prepares for the tongue of the learned, to speak to God as well as men....

This hearing the voice of God is something more than the thoughtful study of the Word. There may be a study and knowledge of the Word, in which there is but little real fellowship with the living God. But there is also a reading of the Word, in the very presence of the Father, and under the leading of the Spirit, in which the Word comes to us in living power from God Himself; it is to us the very voice of the Father, a real personal fellowship with Himself. It is the living voice of God that enters the heart, that brings blessing and strength, and awakens the response of a living faith that reaches the heart of God again. ...

"*If you abide in me, and my words abide in you, ask whatsoever you will, and it shall be done unto you.*" We see what this means. In the words the Savior gives Himself. We must have the words in us, taken up into our will and life, reproduced in our disposition and conduct. We must have them abiding in us: our whole life one continued exposition of the words that are within, and filling us; the words revealing Christ within, and our life revealing Him without. It is as the words of Christ enter our very heart, become our life and influence it, that our words will enter His heart and influence Him.

My prayer will depend on my life; what God's words are to me and in me, my words will be to God and in God. If I do what God says, God will do what I say. How well the Old Testament saints understood this connection between God's words and ours, and how really prayer with them was the loving response to what they had heard God speak! If the Word were a promise, they counted on God to do as He had spoken. "*Do as You have said*"; "*For You, Lord, have spoken it*"; "*According to Your promise*"; "*According to Your word*"; in such expressions they showed that what God spoke in promise was the root and the life of what they spoke in prayer.

If the Word was a command, they simply did as the Lord had spoken: "*So Abram departed as the Lord had spoken.*" Their life was fellowship with God—the interchange of word and thought. What God spoke they heard and did; what they spoke God heard and did. In each word He speaks to us, the whole Christ gives Himself to fulfill it for us. For each word He asks no less that we give the whole man to keep that word, and to receive its fulfilment.

"*If my words abide in you*"; the condition is simple and clear. In His words His will is revealed. As the words abide in me, His will rules me; my will becomes the empty vessel which His will fills, the willing instrument which His will wields; He fills my inner being.

In the exercise of obedience and faith my will becomes ever stronger, and is brought into deeper inner harmony with Him. He can fully trust it to will nothing but what He wills; He is not afraid to give the promise, "*If my words abide in you, ask whatsoever ye will, it shall be done unto you.*" To all who believe it, and act upon it, He will make it literally true.

Disciples of Christ! is it not becoming more and more clear to us that while we have been excusing our unanswered prayers, our impotence in prayer, with a fancied submission to God's wisdom and will, the real reason has been that our own feeble life has been the cause of our feeble prayers. Nothing can make strong men but the Word coming to us from God's mouth: by that we must live. It is the Word of Christ, loved, lived in, abiding in us, becoming through obedience and action part of our being, that makes us one with Christ, that fits us spiritually for touching, for taking hold of God. …

If Two Agree: The Power of United Prayer

July 26th

If two of you shall agree as touching anything that they shall ask, it shall be done for them of My Father, who is in Heaven. For where two or three are gathered together in my Name, there am I in the midst of them.

—MATTHEW 18: 19–20

One of the first lessons of our Lord in His school of prayer was: Not to be seen of men; enter your inner chamber; be alone with the Father. When He has thus taught us that the meaning of prayer is personal individual contact with God, He comes with a second lesson: You have need not only of secret solitary, but also of public united prayer. And He gives us a very special promise for the united prayer of two or three who agree in what they ask.

As a tree has its root hidden in the ground and its stem growing up into the sunlight, so prayer needs equally for its full development the hidden secrecy in which the soul meets God alone, and the public fellowship with those who find in the name of Jesus their common meeting-place. The reason why this must be so is plain. The bond that unites a man to his fellow-men is no less real and close than that which unites him to God: he is one with them. Grace renews not alone our relation to God but to man too. We not only learn to say My Father, but "*Our Father.*"

Nothing would be more unnatural than that the children of a family should always meet their father separately, but never in the united expression of their desires or their love. Believers are not only members of one family, but even of one body. Just as each member of the body depends on the other, and the full action of the spirit dwelling in the body depends on the union and cooperation of all, so Christians cannot reach the full blessing God is ready to bestow through His Spirit, but as they seek and receive it in fellowship with each other. It is in the union and fellowship of believers that the Spirit can manifest His full power. It was to the hundred and twenty continuing in one place together, and praying with one accord, that the Spirit came from the throne of the glorified Lord. …

In such agreement it will become very clear to us what exactly we are asking, whether we may confidently ask according to God's will, and whether we are ready to believe that we have received what we ask. … The love and unity of His disciples have to Jesus infinite attraction: "*Where two or three are gathered in my Name, there am I in the midst of them.*" It is the living presence of Jesus, in the fellowship of His loving praying disciples, that gives united prayer its power. … In the unity of faith and of love and of the Spirit, the power of the Name and the Presence of Jesus acts more freely and the answer comes more surely. The mark that there has been true united prayer is the fruit, the answer, the receiving of the thing we have asked: "*I say unto you, It shall be done for them of my Father who is in Heaven.*"

What an unspeakable privilege this of united prayer is, and what a power it might be. If the believing husband and wife knew that they were joined together in the Name of Jesus to experience His presence and power in united prayer (1 Peter); if friends believed what mighty help two or three praying in concert could give each other; if in every prayer meeting the coming together in the Name, the faith in the Presence, and the expectation of the answer, stood in the foreground; if in every Church united effectual prayer were regarded as one of the chief purposes for which they are banded together, the highest exercise of their power as a Church; if in the Church universal the coming of the Kingdom, the coming of the King Himself, first in the mighty outpouring of His Holy Spirit, then in His own glorious person, were really matter of unceasing united crying to God;—Oh, who can say what blessing might come to, and through, those who thus agreed to prove God in the fulfilment of His promise.

In the Apostle Paul, we see very distinctly what a reality his faith in the power of united prayer was. To the Romans he writes: "*I beseech you, brethren, by the love of the Spirit, that you strive together with me in your prayer to God for me.*" He expects in answer to be delivered from his enemies, and to be prospered in his work. To the Corinthians—"*God will still deliver us, you also helping together on our behalf by your supplications*"—their prayer is to have a real share in his deliverance. To the Ephesians he writes: "*With all prayer and supplication praying at all seasons in the Spirit for all the saints and on my behalf, that utterance may be given unto me.*" His power and success in his ministry he makes to depend on their prayers. With the Philippians, he expects that his trials will turn to his salvation—"*through your prayers and the supply of the Spirit of Christ Jesus.*" To the Colossians, he adds to the injunction to continue steadfast in prayer: "*With all praying for us too, that God may open unto us a door for the Word.*" And to the Thessalonians he writes: "*Finally, brethren, pray for us, that the word of the Lord may run and be glorified, and that we may be delivered from unreasonable men.*" …

Who can say what power a Church could develop and exercise, if it gave itself to the work of prayer day and night for the coming of the Kingdom, for God's power on His servants and His Word, for the glorifying of God in the salvation of souls? Most Churches think their members are gathered into one simply to take care of and build up each other. They know not that God rules the world by the prayers of His saints; that prayer is the power by which Satan is conquered; that by prayer the Church on earth has disposal of the powers of the heavenly world. They do not remember that Jesus has, by His promise, consecrated every assembly in His Name to be a gate of Heaven, where His presence is to be felt, and His Power experienced in the Father fulfilling their desires. …

The Holy Spirit and Prayer

July 27th

"In that day you shall ask Me nothing. Verily, verily, I say unto you, Whatsoever you shall ask the Father in My Name, He will give it you."

—JOHN 16: 23

The words of John (1 John 2:12–14) to little children, to young men, and to fathers suggest the thought that there often are in the Christian life three great stages of experience. The first, that of the newborn child, with the assurance and the joy of forgiveness. The second, the transition stage of struggle and growth in knowledge and strength: young men growing strong, God's word doing its work in them and giving them victory over the Evil One. And then the final stage of maturity and ripeness: the Fathers, who have entered deeply into the knowledge and fellowship of the Eternal One.

In Christ's teaching on prayer there appear to be three stages in the prayer-life, somewhat analogous. In the Sermon on the Mount we have the initial stage: His teaching is all comprised in one word, Father. Pray to your Father, your Father sees, hears, knows, and will reward: how much more than any earthly father! Only be childlike and trustful. Then comes later on, something like the transition stage of conflict and conquest, in words like these: "*This sort goes not out but by fasting and prayer*"; "*Shall not God avenge His own elect who cry day and night unto Him?*"

And then we have in the parting words, a higher stage. The children have become men: they are now the Master's friends, from whom He has no secrets, to whom He says, "*All things that I heard from my Father I made known unto you*"; and to whom, in the oft-repeated "*whatsoever you will*," He hands over the keys of the Kingdom. Now the time has come for the power of prayer in His Name to be proved.

The contrast between this final stage and the previous preparatory ones our Savior marks most distinctly in the words we are to meditate on: "*Hitherto you have asked nothing in my Name*"; "*At that day you shall ask in my Name.*" We know what "at that day" means. It is the day of the outpouring of the Holy Spirit. The great work Christ was to do on the cross, the mighty power and the complete victory to be manifested in His resurrection and ascension, were to issue in the coming down from Heaven, as never before, of the glory of God to dwell in men. The Spirit of the glorified Jesus was to come and be the life of His disciples. And one of the marks of that wonderful Spirit-dispensation was to be a power in prayer hitherto unknown—prayer in the Name of Jesus, asking and obtaining whatsoever they would, is to be the manifestation of the reality of the Spirit's indwelling.

To understand how the coming of the Holy Spirit was indeed to commence a new epoch in the prayer-world, we must remember who He is, what His work, and what the significance of His not being given until Jesus was glorified. It is in the Spirit that God exists, for He is Spirit. It is in the Spirit that the Son was begotten of the Father: it is in the fellowship of the Spirit that the Father and the Son are one. The eternal never-ceasing giving to the Son which is the Father's prerogative and the eternal asking and receiving which is the Son's right and blessedness—it is through the Spirit that this communion of life and love is maintained. It has been so from all eternity. It is so specially now, when the Son as Mediator "*ever lives to pray.*" The great work which Jesus began on earth of reconciling in His own body God and man, He carries on in Heaven. To accomplish this He took up into His own person the conflict between God's righteousness and our sin. On the cross He once for all ended the struggle in His own body.

And then He ascended to Heaven, that thence He might in each member of His body carry out the deliverance and manifest the victory He had obtained. It is to do this that "*He ever lives to pray*"; in His unceasing intercession He places Himself in living fellowship with the unceasing prayer of His redeemed ones. Or rather, it is His unceasing intercession which shows itself in their prayers, and gives them a power they never had before.

And He does this through the Holy Spirit. The Holy Spirit, the Spirit of the glorified Jesus, was not (John 7: 39), could not be, until He had been glorified. This gift of the Father was something distinctively new, entirely different from what Old Testament saints had known. The work that the blood effected in Heaven when Christ entered within the veil, was something so true and new, the redemption of our human nature into fellowship with His resurrection-power and His exaltation-glory was so intensely real, the taking up of our humanity in Christ into the life of the Three-One God was an event of such inconceivable significance, that the Holy Spirit, who had to come from Christ's exalted humanity to testify in our hearts of what Christ had accomplished, was indeed no longer only what He had been in the Old Testament.

It was literally true: "*the Holy Spirit was not yet, for Christ was not yet glorified.*" He came now first as the Spirit of the glorified Jesus. Even as the Son, who was from eternity God, had entered upon a new existence as man, and returned to Heaven with what He had not before, so the Blessed Spirit, whom the Son, on His ascension, received from the Father (Acts 2: 33) into His glorified humanity, came to us with a new life, which He had not previously to communicate. Under the Old Testament He was invoked as the Spirit of God: at Pentecost He descended as the Spirit of the glorified Jesus, bringing down and communicating to us the full fruit and power of the accomplished redemption.

It is in the intercession of Christ that the continued efficacy and application of His redemption is maintained. And it is through the Holy Spirit descending from Christ to us that we are drawn up into the great stream of His ever-ascending prayers. The Spirit prays for us without words: in the depths of a heart where even thoughts are at times formless, the Spirit takes us up into the wonderful flow of the life of the Three-One God. Through the Spirit, Christ's prayers become ours, and ours are made His: we ask what we will, and it is given to us. We then understand from experience, "*Hitherto you have not asked in my Name. At that day you shall ask in my Name.*"

Brother! Sister! what we need to pray for in the Name of Christ—to ask that we may receive, that our joy may be full—is the baptism of this Holy Spirit. This is more than the Spirit of God under the Old Testament. This is more than the Spirit of conversion and regeneration the disciples had before Pentecost. This is more than the Spirit with a measure of His influence and working. This is the Holy Spirit—the Spirit of the glorified Jesus in His exaltation-power—coming on us as the Spirit of the indwelling Jesus, revealing the Son and the Father within (John 14: 16–23).

It is when this Spirit is the Spirit not of our hours of prayer, but of our whole life and walk, when this Spirit glorifies Jesus in us by revealing the completeness of His work, and making us wholly one with Him and like Him, that we can pray in His Name, because we are in very deed one with Him. Then it is that we have that immediateness of access to the Father of which Jesus says, "*I say not that I will pray the Father for you.*" Oh! we need to understand and believe that to be filled with this, the Spirit of the glorified One, is the one need of God's believing people. Then shall we realize what it is "*with all prayer and supplication to be praying at all seasons in the Spirit,*" and what it is, "*praying in the Holy Spirit, to keep ourselves in the love of God.*" "*At that day you shall ask in my Name.*"

And so once again the lesson comes: What our prayer avails, depends upon what we are and what our life is. It is living in the Name of Christ that is the secret of praying in the Name of Christ; living in the Spirit that fits for praying in the Spirit. It is abiding in Christ that gives the right and power to ask what we will: the extent of the abiding is the exact measure of the power in prayer. It is the Spirit dwelling within us that prays, not in words and thoughts always, but in a breathing and a being deeper than utterance. Just so much as there is of Christ's Spirit in us, is there real prayer. …

O my God! in holy awe I bow before You, the Three in One. Again I have seen how the mystery of prayer is the mystery of the Holy Trinity. I adore the Father who ever hears, and the Son who ever lives to pray, and the Holy Spirit, proceeding from the Father and the Son, to lift us up into the fellowship of that ever-blessed, never-ceasing asking and receiving. I bow, my God, in adoring worship, before the infinite condescension that thus, through the Holy Spirit, takes us and our prayers into the Divine Life, and its fellowship of love.

O my Blessed Lord Jesus! Teach me to understand Your lesson, that it is the indwelling Spirit, streaming from You, uniting to You, who is the Spirit of prayer. Teach me what it is as an empty, wholly consecrated vessel, to yield myself to His being my life. Teach me to honor and trust Him, as a living Person, to lead my life and my prayer. Teach me specially in prayer to wait in holy silence, and give Him place to breathe within me His unutterable intercession. And teach me that through Him it is possible to pray without ceasing, and to pray without failing, because He makes me partaker of the never-ceasing and never-failing intercession in which You, the Son, appear before the Father. Yea, Lord, fulfill in me Your promise: "*At that day you shall ask in My Name. Verily, verily, I say unto you,*

Whatsoever you shall ask the Father in My Name, that will He give." Amen.

The Ministry of Intercession

July 28th

"A holy priesthood, to offer up spiritual sacrifices acceptable to God in Jesus Christ."

—1 PETER 2: 5

T*he Spirit of the Lord God is upon me: because the Lord has anointed me."* These are the words of Jesus in Isaiah. As the fruit of His work, all redeemed ones are priests, fellow-partakers with Christ and of His anointing with the Spirit as High Priest. … As every son of Aaron, so every member of Jesus' body has a right to the priesthood. But not everyone exercises it and many are still entirely ignorant of it. And yet it is the highest privilege of a child of God, the mark of greatest nearness and likeness to Him, *"whoever lives to pray."*

Do you doubt if this really be so? Think of what constitutes priesthood. There is, first, the work of the priesthood. This has two sides, one Godward, the other manward. "Every priest is ordained for men in things pertaining to God" (Hebrews 5: 1); … On the one hand, the priest had the power to draw nigh to God, to dwell with Him in His house, and to present before Him the blood of the sacrifice or the burning incense. This work he did not do, however, on his own behalf, but for the sake of the people whose representative he was. This is the other side of his work: He received from the people their sacrifices, presented them before God, and then came out to bless in His Name, to give the assurance of His favor and to teach them His law.

A priest is one who does not at all live for Self. He lives *with* God and *for* God; the work is as God's servant to care for His house, His honor, and His worship, to make known His love and His will. He lives with men and for men (Hebrews 5: 2). His work is to find out their sin and need, and to bring it before God, to offer sacrifice and incense in their name, to obtain forgiveness and blessing for them, and then to come out and bless them in His Name. This is the high calling of every believer. Such honor has all His saints. They have been redeemed with the one purpose to be in the midst of the perishing millions around them. God's priests, who in conformity to Jesus, the Great High Priest, are to be the ministers and stewards of the grace of God to all around them.

And then there is the *walk* of the priesthood, in harmony with its work. As God is holy, so the priest was to be especially holy. This means not only separated from everything unclean, but holy unto God, being set apart and given up to God for His disposal. The separation from the world and setting apart unto God was indicated in many ways. … Much that was allowed to an ordinary Israelite was forbidden to them. It was seen in the injunction that the priest must have no bodily defect or blemish; bodily perfection was to be the type of wholeness and holiness in God's service. And it was seen in the arrangement by which the priestly tribes were to have no inheritance with the other tribes; God was to be their inheritance. Their life was to be one of faith: set apart unto God, they were to live on Him as well as for Him. All this is the emblem of what the character of the New Testament priest is to be. Our priestly power with God depends on our personal life and walk. … In the surrender of what may appear lawful to others in our separation from the world, we must prove that our consecration to be holy to the Lord is wholehearted and entire. … And above all, we consent to give up all inheritance on earth; to forsake all, and like Christ to have only God as our portion—to possess as not possessing, and hold all for God alone: it is this marks the true priest, the man who only lives for God and his fellow-men.

And now the way to the priesthood. In Aaron, God had chosen all his sons to be priests: each of them was a priest by birth. And yet he could not enter upon his work without a special act of ordinance—his consecration. Every child of God is priest in light of his birth, his blood relationship to the Great High Priest; but this is not enough: he will exercise his power only as he accepts and realizes his consecration. …

How, for priestly consecration, there was to be closer contact with the blood; ear and hand and foot were by a special act brought under its power, and the whole being taken possession of and sanctified for God. And so, when the believer, who had been content to think chiefly of the blood sprinkled on the mercy-seat as what he needs for pardon, is led to seek full priestly access to God, he feels the need of a fuller and more abiding experience of the power of the blood, as really "sprinkling and cleansing the heart from an evil conscience, so that he has no more conscience of sin" (Hebrews 10: 2) as cleansing from all sin. And it is as he gets to enjoy this, that the consciousness is awakened of his wonderful right of most intimate access to God, and of the full assurance that his intercessions are acceptable.

And as the blood gives the right, the Spirit gives the power, and fits for believing intercession. He breathes into us the priestly spirit—burning love for God's honor and the saving of souls. He makes us so one with Jesus that prayer in His Name is a reality. He strengthens us to believing, importunate prayer. The more the Christian is truly filled with the Spirit of Christ, the more spontaneous will be our giving up ourself to the life of priestly intercession. Beloved fellow Christians! God needs, greatly needs, priests who can draw near to Him, who live in His presence, and by their intercession draw down the blessings of His grace on others. And the world needs, greatly needs, priests who will bear the burden of the perishing ones, and intercede on their behalf.

Are you willing to offer yourself for this holy work? You know the surrender it demands—nothing less than the Christ-like giving up of all, that the saving purposes of God's love may be accomplished among men. Oh, be no longer of those who are content if they have salvation, and just do work enough to keep themselves warm and lively. Oh, let nothing keep you back from giving yourselves to be wholly and only priests—nothing else, nothing less than the priests of the Most-High God. …

Abiding in union with the Great High Priest, you shall *"ask what you will, and it shall be done unto you."* You will have power to pray the effectual prayer of the righteous man that avails much. … Come, brother, come, and be a priest, only priest, all priest. Seek now to walk before the Lord in the full consciousness that you have been set apart for the holy ministry of intercession. This is the true blessedness of conformity to the image of God's Son.

Prayer and Fasting: The Cure of Unbelief

July 29th

"Then the disciples came to Jesus and said, Why could not we cast him out? And Jesus said unto them, Because of your unbelief: for verily I say unto you, If you have faith as a grain of mustard seed, nothing shall be impossible to you. Howbeit this kind goes not out but by prayer and fasting."

—MATTHEW 27: 19–21

When the disciples saw Jesus cast the evil spirit out of the epileptic whom they could not cure, they asked the Master for the cause of their failure. ... Christ's answer was direct and plain: *"Because of your unbelief."* ... He had so often taught them that there is one power—that of faith—to which everything must bow, both in the kingdom of darkness, as in the Kingdom of God. In the spiritual world, failure has but one cause: the want of faith. Faith is the one condition on which all Divine power can enter into and work through us. It is the susceptibility of the unseen: man's will yielded up to, and molded by, the will of God.

The power they had received ... they did not hold in themselves as a permanent gift or possession; the power was in Christ, to be received, and held, and used by faith alone—living faith in Jesus Himself. Had they been full of faith in Him as Lord and Conqueror in the spirit-world ... this faith would have given them the victory.

"Because of your unbelief," was, for all time, the Master's explanation and reproof of impotence and failure in His Church. But such want of faith must have a cause too. ... The Master proceeds to tell them ...: *"This kind goes not out but by fasting and prayer."*

As faith is the simplest, so it is the highest exercise of the spiritual life, where our spirit yields itself in perfect receptivity to God's Spirit and so is strengthened to its highest activity. This faith depends entirely upon the state of the spiritual life. Only when this is strong and in full health—when the Spirit of God has full sway in our life—is there the power of faith to do its mighty deeds. And therefore Jesus adds: *"Howbeit this kind goes not out but by fasting and prayer."* The faith that can overcome such stubborn resistance as you have just seen in this evil spirit, Jesus tells them, is not possible except to those living in very close fellowship with God, and in very special separation from the world—in prayer and fasting.

And so He teaches us two lessons in regard to prayer of deep importance. The one, that faith needs a life of prayer in which to grow and keep strong. The other, that prayer needs fasting for its full and perfect development.

Faith needs a life of prayer for its full growth. ... There can be no true prayer without faith; some measure of faith must precede prayer. And yet prayer is also the way to more faith; there can be no higher degrees of faith except through much prayer. ... If we want to know where and how our faith is to grow, the Master points us to the throne of God. It is in prayer—in the exercise of the faith I have, in fellowship with the living God—that faith can increase. Faith can only live by feeding on what is Divine, on God Himself. It is in the adoring worship of God—the waiting on Him and for Him, the deep silence of soul that yields itself for God to reveal Himself—that the capacity for knowing and trusting God will be developed. It is as we take His word from the Blessed Book, and bring it to Himself, asking him to speak it to us with His living loving voice, that the power will come fully to believe and receive the word as God's own word to us. ...

Many Christians cannot understand what is meant by the much prayer they sometimes hear spoken of; they can form no conception, nor do they feel the need, of spending hours with God. But what the Master says, the experience of His people has confirmed: men of strong faith are men of much prayer. ...

And prayer needs fasting for its full growth.... Prayer is the one hand with which we grasp the invisible; fasting, the other, with which we let loose and cast away the visible. In nothing is man more closely connected with the world of sense than in his need of food, and his enjoyment of it. ... The body has been redeemed to be a temple of the Holy Spirit; it is in body as well as spirit, it is very specially, Scripture says, in eating and drinking, we are to glorify God. It is to be feared that there are many Christians to whom this eating to the glory of God has not yet become a spiritual reality. And the first thought suggested by Jesus' words in regard to fasting and prayer, is, that it is only in a life of moderation and temperance and Self-denial that there will be the heart or the strength to pray much. ... There may come times of intense desire, when it is strongly felt how the body, with its appetites, lawful though they be, still hinder the spirit in its battle with the powers of darkness, and the need is felt of keeping it under.

Our mind is helped by what comes to us embodied in concrete form; and fasting helps to express, to deepen, and to confirm the resolution that we are ready to sacrifice anything—to sacrifice ourselves—to attain what we seek for the Kingdom of God. And He who accepted the fasting and sacrifice of the Son, knows to value and accept and reward with spiritual power the soul that is thus ready to give up all for Christ and His kingdom.

And then follows a still wider application. Prayer is the reaching out after God and the unseen; fasting, the letting go of all that is of the seen and temporal. While ordinary Christians imagine that all that is not positively forbidden and sinful is lawful to them, and seek to retain as much as possible of this world, with its property, its literature, its enjoyments, the truly consecrated soul is as the soldier who carries only what is needed for the warfare. Laying aside every weight, as well as the easily besetting sin, afraid of entangling with the affairs of this life, we seek to lead a life as one specially set apart for the Lord and His service. Without such voluntary separation, even from what is lawful, no one will attain power in prayer: *"this kind goes not out but by fasting and prayer."*

Disciples of Jesus! who have asked the Master to teach you to pray, come now and accept His lessons. He tells you that prayer is the path to faith, strong faith, that can cast out devils. He tells you: "*If you have faith, nothing shall be impossible to you*;" let this glorious promise encourage you to pray much. Is the prize not worth the price? Shall we not give up all to follow Jesus in the path He opens to us here; shall we not, if need be, fast? Shall we not do anything that neither the body nor the world around hinder us in our great life-work, having intercourse with our God in prayer, that we may become people of faith, whom He can use in His work of saving the world? …

Lord! let Your reproof, with its searching, "*Because of your unbelief,*" sink into the very depths of our hearts, and reveal to us how much of the sin and suffering around us is our blame. And then teach us, Blessed Lord, that there is a place where faith can be learned and gained—even in the prayer and fasting that brings into living and abiding fellowship with Yourself and the Father.

O Savior! You are the Author and the Perfector of our faith; teach us what it is to let You live in us by Your Holy Spirit. Lord! our efforts and prayers for grace to believe have been so unavailing. We know why it was: we sought for strength in ourselves to be given from You. Holy Jesus! do at length teach us the mystery of Your life in us, and how You, by Your Spirit, undertake to live in us the life of faith, to see to it that our faith shall not fail. Oh, let us see that our faith will just be a part of that wonderful prayer-life which You give them who expect their training for the ministry of intercession, not in word and thought only, but in the Holy Unction You give— the inflowing of the Spirit of Your own life. And teach us how, in fasting and prayer, we may grow up to the faith to which nothing shall be impossible. Amen.

NOTE:

At the time when Blumhardt was passing through his terrible conflict with the evil spirits in those who were possessed, and seeking to cast them out by prayer, he often wondered what it was that hindered the answer. One day a friend, to whom he had spoken of his trouble, directed his attention to our Lord's words about fasting. Blumhardt resolved to give himself to fasting, sometimes for more than thirty hours. From reflection and experience he gained the conviction that it is of more importance than is generally thought. He says, "Inasmuch as the fasting is before God, a practical proof that the thing we ask is to us a matter of true and pressing interest, and inasmuch as in a high degree it strengthens the intensity and power of the prayer, and becomes the unceasing practical expression of a prayer without words, I could believe that it would not be without efficacy, especially as the Master's words had reference to a case like the present. I tried it, without telling anyone, and in truth the later conflict was extraordinarily lightened by it. I could speak with much greater restfulness and decision. I did not require to be so long present with the sick one; and I felt that I could influence without being present."

16

WAITING ON GOD

London: James Nisbet & Co., 1896

Preface

July 30th

Previous to my leaving home for England last year, I had been much impressed by the thought of how, in all our religion, personal and public, we need more of God. I had felt that we needed to train our people in their worship more to wait on God, and to make the cultivation of a deeper sense of His presence, of more direct contact with Him, of entire dependence on Him, a definite aim of our ministry.

At a "welcome" breakfast in Exeter Hall, I gave very simple expression to this thought in connection with all our religious work. I have already said elsewhere that I was surprised at the response the sentiment met with. I saw that God's Spirit had been working the same desire in many hearts. The experiences of the past year, both personal and public, have greatly deepened the conviction. It is as if I myself am only beginning to see the deepest truth concerning God, and our relation to Him, center in this: *waiting on God.*

Yet, how very little, in our life and work, we have been surrounded by its spirit. The following pages are the outcome of my conviction, and of the desire to direct the attention of all God's people to this one great remedy for all our needs. ...I do not know if it will be possible for me to put into a few words what are the chief things we need to learn. In a note at the close of the book on William Law I have mentioned some. But what I want to say here is this: *The great lack of our religion is, we do not know God.*

The answer to every complaint of feebleness and failure, the message to every congregation or convention seeking instruction on holiness, ought to be simply, What is the matter: Have you not God? If you really believe in God, He will put all right. God is willing and able by His Holy Spirit. Cease from expecting the least good from yourself, or the least help from anything there is in man, and just yield yourself unreservedly to God to work in you: He will do all for you.

How simple this looks! And yet this is the gospel we so little know. … Would God that we might get some right conception of what the influence would be of a life given, not in thought, or imagination, or effort, but in the power of the Holy Spirit, wholly to waiting upon God. …

—ANDREW MURRAY

Wellington, 1896

Extract from Address in Exeter Hall

London, May 31st 1895

I have been surprised at nothing more than at the letters that have come to me from missionaries and others from all parts of the world, devoted men and women, testifying to the need they feel in their work of being helped to a deeper and a clearer insight into all that Christ could be to them. Let us look to God to reveal Himself among His people in a measure very few have realized. Let us expect great things of our God. At all our conventions and assemblies too little time is given to waiting on God. Is He not willing to put things right in His own divine way? Has the life of God's people reached the utmost limit of what God is willing to do for them? Surely not.

We want to wait on Him; to put away our experiences, however blessed they have been; our conceptions of truth, however sound and scriptural we think they seem; our plans, however needful and suitable they appear, and give God time and place to show us what He could do, what He will do. God has new developments and new resources. He can do new things, unheard of things, hidden things. Let us enlarge our hearts and not limit Him. "*When You came down, You did awesome things we looked not for; the mountains flowed down at Your presence.*"

The God of Our Salvation

"My soul waits only upon God; from Him comes my salvation" (Psalm 62: 1). If salvation indeed comes from God, and is entirely His work, just as creation was, it follows, as a matter of course, that our first and highest duty is to wait on Him to do that work as pleases Him. Waiting becomes then the only way to the experience of a full salvation, the only way, truly, to know God as the God of our salvation. All the difficulties that are brought forward as keeping us back from full salvation, have their cause in this one thing: the defective knowledge and practice [related to] waiting upon God.

All that the Church and its members need for the manifestation of the mighty power of God in the world, is the return to our true place, the place that belongs to us, both in creation and redemption, the place of *absolute and unceasing dependence upon God.*

Let us strive to see what the elements are that make up this most blessed and needful waiting upon God: it may help us to discover the reasons why this grace is so little cultivated, and to feel how infinitely desirable it is that the Church, that we ourselves, should at any price learn its blessed secret.

The deep need for this waiting on God lies equally in the nature of man and the nature of God. God, as Creator, formed man, to be a vessel in which He could show forth His power and goodness. Man was not to have in himself a fountain of life, or strength, or happiness; the ever-living and only living One was each moment to be the Communicator to us of all that we needed. Man's glory and blessedness was not to be independent, or dependent upon our Self, but dependent on a God of such infinite riches and love. Man was to have the joy of receiving every moment out of the fullness of God. …

It is God alone who began the work of redemption; it is God alone who continues and carries it on each moment in each individual believer. Even in the regenerate man there is no power of goodness in ourselves: we have and can have nothing that we do not each moment receive; and waiting on God is just as indispensable, and must be just as continuous and unbroken, as the breathing that maintains our natural life.

It is, then, because Christians do not know their relation to God of absolute poverty and helplessness, that they have no sense of the need of absolute and unceasing dependence, or of the unspeakable blessedness of continual waiting on God. But when once a believer begins to see it, and consent to it, that we by the Holy Spirit must each moment receive what God each moment works, waiting on God becomes his brightest hope and joy. As we apprehend how God, as God, as Infinite Love, delights to impart His own nature to His child as fully as He can, how God is not weary of each moment keeping charge of our life and strength, we wonder that we ever thought otherwise of God than as a God to be waited on all the day. God unceasingly giving and working; His child unceasingly waiting and receiving: this is the blessed life.

"*Truly my soul wait upon God; from Him comes my salvation.*" First we wait on God for salvation. Then we learn that salvation is only to bring us to God, and teach us to wait on Him. Then we find what is better still, that waiting on God is itself the highest salvation. It is the ascribing to Him the glory of being All; it is the experiencing that He is All to us. May God teach us the blessedness of waiting on Him. "*My soul, wait only upon God!*"

For the Promise of the Father

July 31st

"*He charged them not to depart from Jerusalem, but to wait for the promise of the Father.*"
—ACTS 1: 4

In speaking of the saints in Jerusalem at Christ's birth, with Simeon and Anna, we saw how, though the redemption they waited for had come. The call to waiting is no less urgent now than it was then; we wait for the full revelation in us of what had come to them, but what they scarce could comprehend. Even so it is with waiting for the promise of the Father. In one sense, the fulfilment can never come again as it came at Pentecost. In another sense—and that in as deep reality as with the first disciples—we daily need to wait for the Father to fulfil His promise in us.

The Holy Spirit is not a person distinct from the Father in the way two persons on earth are distinct. The Father and the Spirit are never without or separate from each other:

The Father is always in the Spirit; the Spirit works nothing but as the Father works in Him. Each moment the same Spirit that is in us, is in God too, and he who is most full of the Spirit will be the first to wait on God most earnestly, further to fulfill His promise, and still "*strengthen him mightily by His Spirit in the inner man*" (Ephesians 3: 16).

The Spirit in us is not a power at our disposal. Nor is the Spirit an independent power, acting apart from the Father and the Son. The Spirit is the real living presence and the power of the Father working in us, and therefore it is just he who knows that the Spirit is in him, who will wait on the Father for the full revelation and experience of what the Spirit's indwelling is, for His increase and abounding more and more.

See this in the apostles. They were filled with the Spirit at Pentecost. When they, not long after, on returning from the Council, where they had been forbidden to preach, prayed afresh for boldness to speak in His name—a fresh coming down of the Holy Spirit was the Father's fresh fulfilment of His promise. At Samaria, by the word and the Spirit, many had been converted, and the whole city filled with joy. At the apostles' prayer the Father once again fulfilled the promise (Acts 8: 14–17). Even so to the waiting company—"*We are all here before God*" (Acts 10: 33)—in Cornelius' house. And so, too, in Acts 13. It was when men, filled with the Spirit, prayed and fasted, that the promise of the Father was afresh fulfilled, and the leading of the Spirit was given from Heaven: "*Separate Me Barnabas and Saul.*" So also we find Paul in Ephesians, praying for those who have been sealed with the Spirit, that God would grant them the spirit of illumination. And later on, that He would grant them, according to the riches of His glory, to *be strengthened with might by the Spirit in the inner man.*

The Spirit given at Pentecost was not a something that God parted with in Heaven, and sent away out of Heaven to earth. God does not, cannot, give away anything in that way. When He gives grace, or strength, or life, He gives it by giving Himself to work it—it is all inseparable from Himself. Much more so the Holy Spirit. He is God, present and working in us: the true position in which we can count upon that working with an unceasing power is as we, praising for what we have, still unceasingly wait for the Father's promise to be still more mightily fulfilled.

What new meaning and promise does this give to our life of waiting! It teaches us ever to keep the place where the disciples tarried at the footstool of the Throne. It reminds us that, as helpless as they were to meet their enemies, or to preach to Christ's enemies, till they were endued with power, we, too, can only be strong in the life of faith, or the work of love, as we are in direct communication with God and Christ, and they maintain the life of the Spirit in us. It assures us that the Omnipotent God will, through the glorified Christ, work in us a power that can bring to pass things unexpected, things impossible.

Oh! what will not the Church be able to do when her individual members learn to live their lives waiting on God, and when together, with all Self and the world sacrificed in the fire of love, they unite in waiting with one accord for the promise of the Father, once so gloriously fulfilled, but still unexhausted.

Come and let each of us be still in the presence of the inconceivable grandeur of this prospect: the Father waiting to fill the Church with the Holy Spirit. And willing to fill me, let each one say. With this faith let there come over the soul a hush and a holy fear, as it waits in stillness to take it all in. And let life increasingly become a deep joy in the hope of the ever-fuller fulfilment of the Father's promise. "*My soul, wait only upon God*!"

The Keynote of Life

August 1st

"I have waited for Your salvation, O Lord!."

—GENESIS 49: 18

It is not easy to say exactly in what sense Jacob used these words, in the midst of his prophecies in regard to the future of his sons. But they do certainly indicate that both for himself and for them his expectation was from God alone. It was God's salvation he waited for; a salvation which God had promised and which God Himself alone could work out. He knew himself and his sons to be under God's charge. Jehovah the Everlasting God would show in them what His saving power is and does. The words point forward to that wonderful history of redemption which is not yet finished, and to the glorious future in eternity. They suggest to us how there is no salvation but God's salvation, and how waiting on God for that, whether for our personal experience, or in wider circles, is our first duty, our true blessedness.

Let us think of ourselves, and the inconceivably glorious salvation God has wrought for us in Christ, and is now purposing to work out and to perfect in us by His Spirit. Let us meditate until we somewhat realize that *every participation of this great salvation, from moment to moment, must be the work of God Himself.* God cannot part with His grace, or goodness, or strength, as an external thing that He gives us, as He gives the raindrops from Heaven. No; He can only give it, and we can only enjoy it, as He works it Himself directly and unceasingly [in us]. And the only reason that He does not work it more effectually and continuously is, that we do not let Him. We hinder Him either by our indifference or by our Self-effort, so that He cannot do what He would.

What He asks of us, in the way of surrender, and obedience, and desire, and trust, is all comprised in this one word: *waiting* on Him, waiting for His salvation. It combines the deep sense of our entire helplessness of ourselves to work what is Divinely good, and the perfect assurance that our God will work it all in His Divine power. …

Again, I say, let us meditate on the divine glory of the salvation God purposes to work out in us, until we know the truth it implies. Our heart is the scene of a Divine operation more wonderful than Creation. We can do as little towards the work as towards creating the world, except as God works in us to will and to do. God only asks of us to yield, to consent, to wait upon Him, and He will do it all. Let us meditate and be still, until we see how meet and right and blessed it is that God alone do all, and our soul will of itself sink down in deep humility to say: "*I have waited for Your salvation, O Lord.*" And the deep blessed background of all our praying and working will be: "*Truly my soul waits upon God.*"

The application of the truth to wider circles, to those we labor among or intercede for, to the Church of Christ around us, or throughout the world, is not difficult. There can be no good but what God works; to wait upon God, and have the heart filled with faith in His working, and in that faith to pray for His mighty power to come down, is our only wisdom. Oh for the eyes of our heart to be opened to see God working in ourselves and in others, and to see how blessed it is to worship and just to wait for His salvation!

Our private and public prayer are our chief expression of our relation to God: it is in them chiefly that our waiting upon God must be exercised. If our waiting begins by quieting the activities of nature, and being still before God; if it bows and seeks to see God in His universal and almighty operation, alone able and always ready to work all good; if it yields itself to Him in the assurance that He is working and will work in us; if it maintains the place of humility and stillness, and surrender, until God's Spirit has quickened the faith that He will perfect His work: it will indeed become the strength and the joy of the soul. Life will become one deep blessed cry: "*I have waited for Your salvation, O Lord.*"

Patiently

August 2nd

"*Rest in the lord, and wait patiently for Him.*"

—PSALM 37: 7

"*Let patience have its perfect work, that ye may be perfect and entire.*" Such words of the Holy Spirit show us what an important element in the Christian life and character patience is. And nowhere is there a better place for cultivating or displaying it than in waiting on God. There we discover how impatient we are, and what our impatience means. We confess at times that we are impatient with men and circumstances that hinder us, or with ourselves and our slow progress in the Christian life. If we truly set ourselves to wait upon God, we shall find that it is with Him we are impatient, because He does not at once, or as soon as we could wish, do our bidding. It is in waiting upon God that our eyes are opened to believe in His wise and sovereign will, and to see that the sooner and the more completely we yield absolutely to it, the more surely His blessing can come to us.

"*It is not of him that wills, nor of him that runs, but of God that shows mercy.*" We have as little power to increase or strengthen our spiritual life, as we had to originate it. We "*were born not of the will of the flesh, nor of the will of man, but of the will of God.*" Even so, our willing and running, our desire and effort, avail nought; all is "of God that shows mercy." All the exercises of the spiritual life, our reading and praying, our willing and doing, have their very great value. But they can go no farther than this, that they point the way and prepare us in humility to look to and to depend alone upon God Himself, and in patience to await His good time and mercy. The waiting is to teach us our absolute dependence upon God's mighty working, and to make us in perfect patience place ourselves at His disposal. They that wait on the Lord shall inherit the land; the promised land and its blessing. The heirs must wait; they can afford to wait.

"*Rest in the Lord, and wait patiently for Him.*" ... It is resting in the Lord, in His will, His promise, His faithfulness, and His love, that makes patience easy. And the resting in Him is nothing but being silent unto Him, still before Him. Having our thoughts and wishes, our fears and hopes, hushed into calm and quiet in that great peace of God which passes all understanding. That peace keeps the heart and mind when we are anxious for anything, because we have made our request known to Him. The rest, the silence, the stillness, and the patient waiting, all find their strength and joy in God Himself.

The needs be, and the reasonableness, and the blessedness of patience will be opened up to the waiting soul. Our patience will be seen to be the counterpart of God's patience. He longs far more to bless us fully than we can desire it. But, as the husbandman has long patience until the fruit be ripe, so God bows Himself to our slowness and bears long with us. Let us remember this, and wait patiently: of each promise and every answer to prayer the word is true: "*I the Lord will hasten it in its time.*"

"*Rest in the Lord, and wait patiently for Him.*" Yes, for Him. Seek not only the help, the gift, you need; seek Himself; wait for Him. Give God His glory by resting in Him, by trusting him fully, by waiting patiently for Him. This patience honors Him greatly; it leaves Him, as God on the throne, to do His work; it yields Self wholly into His hands. It lets God be God. If your waiting be for some special request, wait patiently. If your waiting be more the exercise of the spiritual life seeking to know and have more of God, wait patiently. Whether it be in the shorter specific periods of waiting, or as the continuous habit of the soul; rest in the Lord, be still before the Lord, and wait patiently. "*They that wait on the Lord shall inherit the land.*" "*My soul, wait only upon God!*"

The Way to the New Song

"*I waited patiently for the Lord, and He inclined unto me, and heard my cry... And He hath put a new song in my mouth, even praise unto our God*" (Psalm 40:1–3. Come and listen to the testimony of one who can speak from experience of the sure and blessed outcome of patient waiting upon God. True patience is so foreign to our Self-confident nature, it is so indispensable in our waiting upon God, it is such an essential element of true faith, that we may well once again meditate on what the word has to teach us.

The word *patience* is derived from the Latin word for suffering. It suggests the thought of being under the constraint of some power from which we want to be free. At first we submit against our will; experience teaches us that when it is vain to resist, patient endurance is our wisest course. In waiting on God it is of infinite consequence that we not only submit, because we are compelled to, but because we lovingly and joyfully consent to be in the hands of our blessed Father.

Patience then becomes our highest blessedness and our highest grace. It honors God, and gives Him time to have His way with us. It is the highest expression of our faith in His goodness and faithfulness. It brings the soul perfect rest in the assurance that God is carrying on His work. It is the token of our full consent that God should deal with us in such a way and time as He thinks best.

True patience is the losing of our Self-will in His perfect will. Such patience is needed for the true and full waiting on God. Such patience is the growth and fruit of our first lessons in the school of waiting.

To many a one it will appear strange how difficult it is truly to wait upon God. The great stillness of soul before God that sinks into its own helplessness and waits for Him to reveal Himself; the deep humility that is afraid to let own will or own strength work aught except as God works to will and to do; the meekness that is content to be and to know nothing except as God gives His light; the entire resignation of the will that only wants to be a vessel in which His holy will can move and mould: all these elements of perfect patience are not found at once. But they will come in measure as the soul maintains its position, and ever again says: "*Truly my soul waits upon God; from HIM comes my salvation: He only is my rock and my salvation.*"

Have you ever noticed what proof we have that patience is a grace for which very special grace is given, in these words of Paul: "Strengthened with all might, according to His glorious power, unto all"—what? "*patience and longsuffering with joyfulness.*" Yes, we need to be strengthened with all God's might, and that according to the measure of His glorious power, if we are to wait on God in all patience. It is God revealing Himself in us as our life and strength, that will enable us with perfect patience to leave all in His hands. If any are inclined to despond, because they have not such patience, let them be of good courage; it is in the course of our feeble and very imperfect waiting that God Himself by His hidden power strengthens us and works out in us the patience of the saints, the patience of Christ Himself.

Listen to the voice of one who was deeply tried: "*I waited patiently for the Lord, and He inclined unto me, and heard my cry.*" Hear what he passed through: "*He brought me up also out of a horrible pit, out of the miry clay, and set my feet upon a rock, and established my goings. And He has put a new song in my mouth, even praise unto our God.*" …

For More Than We Know

August 3rd

"And now, Lord, what wait I for? My hope is in You."

—PSALM 39: 7

There may be times when we feel as if we knew not what we are waiting for. There may be other times when we think we do know, and when it would just be so good for us to realize that we do not know what to ask as we ought. God is able to do for us exceeding abundantly above what we ask or think, and we are in danger of limiting Him, when we confine our desires and prayers to our own thoughts of them. It is a great thing at times to say, as our psalm says: "*And now, Lord, what wait I for?*" I scarce know or can tell; this only I can say: "*My hope is in You.*"

How we see this limiting of God in the case of Israel! When Moses promised them meat in the wilderness, they doubted, saying, "Can God furnish a table in the wilderness? He smote the rock that the water gushed out; can He give bread also? Can He provide flesh for His people?" If they had been asked whether God could provide streams in the desert, they would have answered, Yes. God had done it: He could do it again. But when the thought came of God doing something new, they limited Him.

Their expectation could not rise beyond their past experience, their own thoughts of what was possible. Even so we may be limiting God by our conceptions of what He has promised or is able to do. Do let us beware of limiting the Holy One of Israel in our very prayer. Let us believe that every promise of God we plead has a Divine meaning, infinitely beyond our thoughts of them. Let us believe that His fulfillment of them can be, in a power and an abundance of grace, beyond our largest grasp of thought. And let us therefore cultivate the habit of waiting on God, not only for what we think we need, but for all His grace and power are ready to do for us.

In every true prayer there are two hearts in exercise. The one is your heart, with its little, dark, human thoughts of what you need and God can do. The other is God's great heart, with its infinite, its Divine purposes of blessing. What think you? To which of these two ought the larger place to be given in your approach to Him? Undoubtedly, to the heart of God: everything depends upon knowing and being occupied with that. But how little this is done. This is what waiting on God is meant to teach you. Just think of God's wonderful "love" and "redemption," in the meaning that these words must have to Him.

Confess how little you understand what God is willing to do for you, and say each time as you pray with the Psalmist: "*And now, what do I wait for?*" My heart cannot say. God's heart knows and waits to give. "*My hope is in You.*" Wait on God to do for you more than you can ask or think.

Apply this to the prayer that follows: "Deliver me from all my transgressions." You have prayed to be delivered from temper, or pride, or Self-will. It is as if it is in vain. May it not be that you have had your own thoughts about the way or the extent of God's doing it, and have never waited on the God of glory, according to the riches of His glory, to do for you what has not entered the heart of man to conceive? Learn to worship God as the God who does wonders, who wishes to prove in you that He can do something supernatural and Divine. Bow before Him, wait upon Him, until your soul realizes that you are in the hands of a Divine and almighty worker. Consent not to know what and how He will work; expect it to be something altogether godlike, something to be waited for in deep humility, and received only by His Divine power.

Let the, "*And now, Lord, what do I wait for? My hope is in You*" become the spirit of every longing and every prayer. He will in His time do His work. Dear soul, in waiting on God you may often be ready to be weary because you hardly know what you have to expect. I pray you, be of good courage—this ignorance is often one of the best signs. He is teaching you to leave all in His hands, and to wait on Him alone. "*Wait on the Lord! Be strong, and let your heart take courage. Yea, wait on the Lord.*"

In Times of Darkness

August 4th

"I will wait upon the Lord, who hides His face from the house of Jacob."

—ISAIAH 8: 17

Here we have a servant of God, waiting upon Him, not on behalf of himself, but of his people, from whom God was hiding his face from His people around us. We may be walking in the full light of God's countenance, and God yet be hiding His face from His people around us; far from our being content to think that this is nothing but the just punishment of their sin, or the consequence of their indifference, we are called with tender hearts to think of their sad estate, and to wait on God on their behalf. The privilege of waiting upon God is one that brings great responsibility.

Even as Christ, when He entered God's presence, at once used His place of privilege and honor as intercessor, so we, no less, if we know what it is really to enter in and wait upon God, must use our access for our less favored brethren. *"I will wait upon the Lord, who hides His face from the house of Jacob."*

You worship with a certain congregation. Possibly there is not the spiritual life or joy either in the preaching or in the fellowship that you could desire. You belong to a Church, with its many congregations. There is so much of error or worldliness, of seeking after human wisdom and culture, of trust in ordinances and observances, that you do not wonder that God hides His face, in many cases, and that there is but little power for conversion or true edification. Then there are branches of Christian work with which you are connected—a Sunday school, a gospel hall, a young men's association, a mission work abroad—in which the feebleness of the Spirit's working appears to indicate that God is hiding His face. You think, too, you know the reason. There is too much trust in men and money; there is too much formality and Self-indulgence; there is too little faith and prayer; too little love and humility; too little of the spirit of the crucified Jesus. At times, you feel as if things are hopeless; nothing will help.

Do believe that God can help and will help. Let the spirit of the prophet come into you, as you take his words, and set yourself to wait on God, on behalf of His erring children. Instead of the tone of judgment or condemnation, of despondency or despair, realize your calling to wait upon God. If others fail in doing it, give yourself doubly to it. The deeper the darkness, the greater the need of appealing to the one only Deliverer. The greater the Self-confidence around you, that knows not that it is poor and wretched and blind, the more urgent the call on you who profess to see the evil and to have access to

Him who alone can help, to be at your post, waiting upon God. As often as you are tempted to complain, or to sigh and say ever afresh: "*I will wait on the Lord, who hides His face from the house of Jacob.*"

There is a still larger circle—the Christian Church throughout the world. Think of Greek, Roman Catholic, and Protestant churches, and the state of the millions that belong to them. Or think only of the Protestant churches with their open Bible and orthodox creeds. How much nominal profession and formality! how much of the rule of the flesh and of man in the very temple of God! And what abundant proof that God does hide His face!

What are those to do who see and mourn this? The first thing to be done is this: *"I will wait on the Lord, who hides His face from the house of Jacob."* Let us wait on God, in the humble confession of the sins of His people. Let us take time and wait on Him in this exercise. Let us wait on God in tender, loving intercession for all saints, our beloved brethren, however wrong their lives or their teaching may appear. Let us wait on God in faith and expectation, until He shows us that He will hear. Let us wait on God, with the simple offering of ourselves to Himself, and the earnest prayer that He would send us to our brethren.

Let us wait on God, and give Him no rest until He make Zion a joy in the earth. Yes, let us rest in the Lord, and wait patiently for Him who now hides His face from so many of His children. And let us say of the lifting up of the light of His countenance we desire for all His people, *"I wait for the Lord, my soul does wait, and my hope is in His word. My soul waits for the Lord, more than the watchers for the morning, the watchers for the morning." "My soul, wait only upon God!"*

17

EAGLE WINGS

Three Talks on Prayer at London's Exeter Hall, 1895

London: Marshall Brothers, c1896

With Wings as Eagles 1

August 5th

"But they that wait upon the Lord shall renew their strength; they shall mount up with wings as eagles; they shall run, and not be weary; and they shall walk, and not faint."

—ISAIAH 40: 31

The subject announced for this evening is *Working and Waiting*. All that we have been asking God to do must manifest itself in new work. Those who have never worked cannot have been in earnest this morning when asking God to honor them with the indwelling of His heavenly love— not if they are going to live Selfish lives. They cannot have been honest when they prayed the prayer: "O God, let your own, blessed love fill me, and then I will spend it, give it out; and scatter the blessing." And those who have been working—oh, how conscious they are of the feebleness of their work! And as some may work less with great advantage, it is not always more work that is needed. The main thing is the quality of the work that is done. This afternoon we prayed for God's mercy upon London, the workers in London, and for grace that every one of us might go out to live in the power of God's strength and love. It is hardly needful that I should speak much to you about the secret of strength for work. That is what we all need. As God's children, a divine strength is promised and prepared for us. But how many are conscious of it? They do not know the way to receive it. And just as that one word work means so much earthward and manward, so the word wait means everything Godward. And if your work towards men is to bring blessing, it will depend entirely upon your waiting upon God.

Listen to the words of my text: "*They that wait upon the Lord will renew their strength*" every day; "*they shall run and*" never "*be weary; they shall walk and not faint.*" Blessed life! To work, work, work, sometimes in weariness of body and of mind, sometimes in despair and failure, and yet never to be weary in spirit, and always to be carried on in the joy of God—what a kind Master! You can see that He cares for His servants, and that they are children and heirs of God. And will God allow them to be weary in spirit? Never! Especially, if they will come and dwell with Him as He is ready to have them. They that wait upon the Lord will renew their faith and shall always be strong for work.

Would God, that I had known that when I was a young minister! Would God, that I knew it even fully tonight! I thank Him for what He has shown me of it. But Oh, that He might reveal fully to my soul— and to every soul here— that they that wait upon the Lord, their strength shall always be new: "*they shall run and not be weary; they shall walk, and not faint*"! How many are fainthearted in their work, and stop working, or work wearily, or work very little, or work with effort and struggle? And all because they do not know the joy of the Lord. May God teach us tonight how to work.

Let me take this one expression first: "*They that wait upon the Lord shall renew their strength; they shall mount up with wings as eagles.*" I'm sure most of you have heard sermons preached on that text or read expositions of it. But just let me give you two or three very simple thoughts about the mounting up on eagle wings. You know the eagle is called the king of the birds, and it is said to fly the highest of all the birds, and to go straight towards the sun. And this king of birds is taken to be the image of God's children. Why? What are eagles' wings for? To carry the king of birds high up into the heavens. Dear Christian! You are a heavenly man or woman, and are to lead a heavenly life. Your place is in the heavenlies. And how can you rise to heaven unless you have eagle wings to mount with? But, thank God! If He created the eagles with their wings to rise heavenward, He can give me eagle wings so that I too can rise upward. Yes, the believer is to live a heavenly life. His home is within the veil, in the Holist of All. He is to walk on "high places." He is to live in the love of God unclouded. He is to live with the joy of Heaven in his heart. He is to live a life in which the will of God is done as in Heaven, so on earth. The Christian needs eagle wings. But, alas! How many Christians are bound and weighed down here below!

Once when I was in Switzerland, I saw an eagle— a splendid bird— but it was chained to a rock. It had some twenty or thirty feet of chain attached to its legs and to an iron bolt in the rock. And there was the king of birds—who was meant to soar up to heaven—chained down to earth.

That is a picture of multitudes of believers. Is that your life? Are you just dragging along in the Christian life? Are you a child of God?

That eagle was a king of birds, a noble king, but something kept it down. Are you allowing business, the cares of the world, the flesh to chain you down so that you cannot rise up? God forbid it should be so. I invite every believer to say tonight, "God help me to mount up on eagle wings. I want to live the heavenly life." God help us!

And then you ask me: "How can I get these eagle wings?" I answer: "How did the eagle get its wings? By its birth. It was born a royal eagle. It had a royal descent."

Every child of God is born with eagle wings. But, alas! They do not know it. And, alas! It is not sufficiently preached. And, alas! The realization of it is not sufficiently sought from God. We are all born with eagle wings and have within us a divine nature and the very Spirit of Christ Jesus to draw us heavenward. But there are many believers who do not know they have the Spirit of Heaven within them, and many who barely know it. There are many who have an inkling of it, but are unfaithful and turn away to the world again.

Oh, Christian! I tell everyone of you tonight: You have a divine nature, you have a heavenly nature, and God means you to live a heavenly life. …

How does God teach His eaglet children to use their wings? He comes and stirs up their nest. How does He do that? Sometimes with a trying providence, with a death, with sickness, with loss, with some tribulation, and with temptation. And why? Just as those eaglets, ready to sink, find the mother coming under them and carrying them, so the Everlasting Arms are stretched out underneath the soul that feels ready to perish. God calls upon the soul to trust Him. And just as the eaglet trusts the mother to carry it, so my God asks me to trust Him to bear me. …

With Wings as Eagles 2

August 6th

"But they that wait upon the Lord shall renew their strength; they shall mount up with wings as eagles; they shall run, and not be weary; and they shall walk, and not faint."

—ISAIAH 40: 31

Yes, God often comes to the Christian worker and stirs up his nest, because He sees the eagle wings are not being used. God finds a worker very earnest, and perhaps for a time there has been blessing, but somehow Self-will and the power of the flesh have come in. He has trusted in himself, so God comes and stirs up his nest.

The question now comes to the Christian worker. "What is this? Have I served my God as I might have done, or have I sinned against Him?" Then His blessed Word comes with a message, to this effect, "No, your Father loves you, but there is one thing He misses about you. You are not heavenly enough. You have worked hard, and you have worked well, and you have worked successfully, but the tenderness and the beauty of the heavenly love of Jesus are too little seen in you. The Father wants you to mount up on eagle wings. Your fellowship with your God is not as tender as it ought to be, and God has stirred and broken up your nest."

The worker is now all dark and anxious, and fears that everything will perish. He no longer finds the power he once had. Praise God! If you just learn to see that God wants you to trust Him more— to come into close union with himself.

Beloved Christian! Listen to God's Word: "*They that wait upon the Lord shall renew their strength.*" They shall go on from strength to strength. They shall get stronger month by month and year by year. They shall renew their strength and mount up with eagle wings. God help us to believe it and say tonight, "That is going to be my lot—a life mounting up on eagle wings." Does everyone dare to say that? Yes, if you dare say, "My life shall be one of waiting upon God."

To be able to mount up to the heavens, the wings of the eagle must have greater strength than the wings of any other bird. And God wants His children to be strong enough that they can live above the world, so they can show the men of the world: "I am living in another world." The great mark of a disciple that Christ spoke of in His prayer to the Father was: "*They are not of the world even as I am not of the world*" (John 17: 16). They belong to Heaven as their life and heart are there.

Oh, Christian! Do believe that in your business in the city of London, in a house full of care and anxiety, you can live a heavenly life in the peace and love and joy of God. The eagle's wings are strong wings that can resist the gravitation and attraction of earth. They can rise heavenward. Praise God! We can live heavenly lives.

Just look how this idea of strength is the great idea of our text, and how you have it in the words that precede it: "*Have you not known? Have you not heard, that the everlasting God, the Lord, the Creator of the ends of the earth, faints not, neither is weary? There is no searching of his understanding. He gives power to the faint; and to them that have no might he increases strength" (Isaiah 40: 28-29).*

Let me ask you weary worker: Have you heard it? Have you known that the everlasting God is never weary? You tell me, "Of course I have known it." Then believe it in the application God makes. You ask me: "What is this application?" The application is that if the everlasting God is never weary, you need never be weary, because your God is your strength. That is what the Bible teaches. You have no strength but what God gives. And you can have all the strength that God can give.

... If there is one lesson we need to learn, it is the lesson of our impotence. When I was studying and learning to be a Christian as a young man, I was told a great deal about my want of righteousness, and about my absolute worthlessness. And I believed it, and believe it still. I have no righteousness before God in myself. But I was never taught that just as little righteousness as I have, so just as little strength I have. That just as much as I am dependent on the righteousness of Christ alone for salvation, so I am also dependent on the strength of God alone for sanctification. I was not taught that, and that is the truth of God. At least, it was not taught clearly enough so as to enter my heart. It may have been my fault, but since that time, I have found so many who have not been taught it. If you are to live holy lives and work for God, you must learn that your only hope for being holy and working in the proper way is through the everlasting God in Heaven.

Then follows the promise: "He gives power to the faint; and to them that have not might he increases strength" (Isaiah 40: 29). God offers himself to be the power and the strength and the might of every one of His children, Oh! Is that not what we need in all our religious work—to get to that secret place of God's power, so that it can work in us?

You ask: "How can I get that power?" Listen to the glorious answer: "*They that wait upon the Lord shall renew their strength; they shall mount up with wings as eagles.*"

Where do I get the power to use eagle wings, to mount and soar and rise higher and higher? *In waiting upon God.*

Are there any of you who have not yet found the secret of a life in the full joy of Jesus' countenance and love all the day? Come tonight, and claim His omnipotence to work it in you. Let the exchange be clear. God has given you all things in Christ—all spiritual blessing, all strength, all wisdom, everything in Him. You have been holding back; you have been afraid; you have perhaps been ignorant, and have never understood it. Come tonight and say: "Absolute surrender! Lord Jesus, you shall have everything." Then trust in Him. Trust in His omnipotence to work in you all that God would have. "*They that wait upon the Lord shall renew their strength.*"

Count upon the fact that as you go out tonight and tomorrow, you need never maintain by effort what you have got, or what has been given to you. Rather, in childlike abandonment and simple faith, say, "I am counting upon God to work it all in me." Take this word tonight: "*They that wait upon the Lord shall renew their strength.*" That is the life of power and joy!

18

THE KINGDOM OF HEAVEN IS WITHIN YOU

London: Service and Paton, 1897

The Kingdom of God 1

August 7th

"Verily I say unto you, whosoever shall not receive the Kingdom of God as a little child, shall not enter therein."
—MARK 10: 15 …

I think this word of the Lord Jesus will guide us exactly where we ought to be. It will tell us what God asks of us if we are even now to enter His Kingdom and live in it: that each of us receive it into our hearts as a little child. These are the things we need to know to enter into the enjoyment of full salvation. With these two things all our Convention teaching will be occupied: the wonderful blessing God has for us, the wonderful way in which we are to become possessors of it. …

First: *What is the Kingdom of God?* You know how John the Baptist preached that the Kingdom of God or of Heaven had come nigh. During the Old Testament times it had been spoken of, and promised, and hoped for, but it had not come. During the life of Christ on earth there were mighty tokens of its coming and its nearness, but it had not yet come in power. What it would be Christ foretold when He once said, *"the Kingdom of God is within you"*; and another time, *"There be some standing here who shall not see death, till they see the Kingdom of God come in power."* On the day of Pentecost that word was fulfilled. The Holy Spirit brought down out of Heaven the Kingdom of God into the hearts of the disciples, and they went forth and preached the Gospel of the Kingdom not as at hand or coming, but as come. …

What is the Kingdom of God? It is that spiritual state in which the life of God and of Heaven is made accessible to men, and they enter into its enjoyment here on earth. If we ask what its marks are, we find the answer in the wondrous change that we see in the life of the disciples. The mark of a kingdom is the presence of the king. With the Holy Spirit, Christ came down to be with His disciples as really, and more nearly, than when He was with them in the flesh. The abiding nearness and fellowship of Christ, and in Him of God the Father, is the very central blessing of the Kingdom. This experience was what the Holy Spirit at Pentecost made real. The disciples had their Lord with them as consciously as the angels in heaven. His presence made heaven all around and in them. A believer to whom a full entrance into the Kingdom is given, has the Presence of God and Christ as the good part that cannot be taken away.

The mark of the kingdom is the rule of the king. We read, "His Kingdom rules over all." Before Pentecost the disciples could not love or be humble, could not trust or be bold. But when the kingdom came the dominion of God prevailed, God's Presence through the Holy Spirit gained the victory, sin was overcome, and the will of God done in them to pray, *"Your Kingdom come, Your will be done on earth as in Heaven."* He promised this. As the Kingdom came down with the Holy Spirit the promise was fulfilled. And our entering into the kingdom means our being brought into a life in which God rules over all, His will is truly and joyfully done, and all the blessedness that reigns in Heaven finds its counterpart here below. As it is written, *"The Kingdom of God is righteousness, and peace, and joy in the Holy Spirit."*

The mark of a kingdom is power. *"The Kingdom of God is not in word but in power."* Just think of the work these simple fishermen dared to undertake, and were able to accomplish. Think of the weapon with which they had to do their work—the despised Gospel of the crucified Nazarene. Think of all that God wrought through them, and see how the coming of the Kingdom brought a new power from Heaven by which feeble men were made mighty through God, and the slaves of Satan were made God's holy children.

Believers! it is this Kingdom of God come from Heaven that we preach. We come to tell you that a life in the presence and the will and the power of God, has been opened up, that souls have been brought to enter into it and live in it, and that you too can enter in. There are some of you who are confessing the feebleness of your Christian life, and the failure of all your efforts to make it better. You have believed in Jesus as your Savior, but of an entrance into the Kingdom as it came in power you know nothing. I beseech you begin at once to believe that there is such a life in the kingdom here on earth. Believe that Christ's death wrought such a wonderful and complete redemption, and that the coming down of the Holy Spirit, nothing else but the glorified Christ coming in the Spirit, brought down the heavenly life in such reality, that, even as the first disciples, we can be endued with power on high. If you will believe that, if you hold fast, there is a Kingdom of Heaven on earth, your desire will be stirred to become partakers of its blessedness, and as we point out the way how, your hope will begin to see that this life is even for you too.

... *What is it to enter the Kingdom?* This is our second question. You know the meaning of the word enter. It is most commonly used in Scripture of the entrance of the children of Israel into the land of promise, and of the believer's entrance by faith into the rest of God. ... The word does not refer to Heaven, and our entering that when we die. It speaks of the Kingdom of Heaven come to earth, and our entering into it in power, as the disciples did at Pentecost. There are many Christians who are content with a Heaven after death. The promise of living in a Kingdom of Heaven here on earth has not attraction, and wakens no response. They cannot understand what we mean. But there are hearts in whom the longing has been wakened for something better, and who would fain know what it is to enter the Kingdom. … Just think of the blessings of the Kingdom we mentioned. God's manifested presence with us without ceasing; God's blessed rule and dominion over us established, so that His heavenly will is done in us and by us; God's mighty power descending upon us, so that through us Christ can do His word of saving souls. Into a life in which these blessings are your daily experience, you can enter even now. That life has been prepared for you, and is promised; it is waiting for you. … As Joshua brought Israel into the land of promise, and Jericho fell without a blow being struck, our Lord Jesus waits to bring us into the good land. It was He who from Heaven gave the disciples their abundant entrance into the Kingdom; it is He who still by His Holy Spirit will lead each one of us in. By faith in Him He brings us in.

The Kingdom of God 2

August 8th

"Verily I say unto you, whosoever shall not receive the Kingdom of God as a little child, shall not enter therein."
—MARK 10: 15 …

What is it to receive the Kingdom? Receive the Kingdom: the word is very simple. It implies two things: there is one who gives, and another who accepts. How many there are who have heard of the blessed life in the Kingdom, and the wonderful joy it gives, and who have never thought that it must be received from the living God Himself.

What we need is to be brought to such consciousness of our utter ignorance and impotence, that we feel we cannot grasp or apprehend this wonderful salvation that is offered, but that we are to come into contact with the Father in Heaven, as a heavenly bestowal, receive from Him the Kingdom in power. And that not as something that we have to persuade Him to give us, but as the child's portion that actually belongs to us, and that He yearns to see us enjoy. It is as we believe this, and look up to the everlasting God, infinitely ready and able to give the Kingdom in its power into our very heart, that our hearts will take courage to expect that the Kingdom with its blessings can, indeed, enter into us.

Then our accepting will become so simple. When we see the God who has promised, in His infinite love, just as the sun seeks to enter with its light and life into every little flower and every blade of grass, longing to enter into us, and be all that as God He can be, we shall understand how our place is simply to rest in what He will do, to claim His great gift of the Spirit who brings the Kingdom into us, and to wait in patient dependence for Him to do His mighty work. Our position day by day will be as of those who, having accepted, now count upon God to reveal and work in us all that He has for us.

You may be inclined to ask, If the receiving be so simple, how is it that it is still so difficult, and that so few really find what they seek? The answer is, the whole thing is so simple, but we are not simple. The simplicity of the thing is its difficulty, because we have lost our simplicity. It is this Jesus teaches us in the words He adds, and which we must still speak of.

What is it to receive the Kingdom as a little child? Have we any illustration of this nature? Yes. How did the Prince of Wales become heir to the throne of England? By his birth as a little child he received the kingdom. He was born to it. And so we must be born by the Holy Spirit into that disposition of heart or childlike simplicity which will receive the Kingdom as a little child. When a little child receives a kingdom, it does so as a feeble, helpless little thing. As it grows up and hears of what is coming to it, does so in simple trustfulness and gladness. Even so Jesus calls us to become little children and as such receive the Kingdom.

Oh! how hard it is for men and women, with all their will and their strength and their wisdom, will all the power of Self and the old man, to become as little children. It is impossible. And yet without this we cannot enter the Kingdom and its heavenly life. We can know about the Kingdom, we may taste some of its powers, we may work for it and often rejoice in it – but we cannot enter in fully and entirely, until we become as a little child. And with men this is impossible. But with God all things are possible.

There are some things we can do towards it. We can yield to the teaching of God's Spirit when He convinces us of our pride and Self-confidence. We can confess our Self-will and Self-effort. We can pray and long and strive after the childlike spirit. We can go as far as Peter and the disciples did before Pentecost. But the little-child nature that enters into the Kingdom, the Holy Spirit, the Spirit of God's Son, who cries Abba, Father, the Spirit that claims and expects and receives all from God alone, alone can give. He is within you, as the Spirit of Christ, to work this; He gives the grace to become a little child, and so He fits the heart for receiving from heaven His fullness, as He brings the Kingdom in heavenly power.

How to become a little child? How to lose all our strength and wisdom, our will and life, and be as little new-born children? Oh that I knew the way hither, you cry. Look to Jesus! As a babe in Bethlehem, He was born heir to the Kingdom of David. He grew up to manhood, and then giving up His will in Gethsemane when He cried Abba, Father, He gave up His life, and was laid in the dark grave in the helplessness of death. Thence He arose, as the first-begotten of the dead, born again out of the dead to the Throne of Glory. In the feebleness of the grave He gained His throne. We need to die with Christ—that is the way to get delivered from the old man and Self, the way to receive the heavenly life as a little child, and so to enter the Kingdom. The feebleness of Bethlehem and the manger, of Calvary and the grave, was Christ's way to enter the Kingdom— for us there is no other way. …

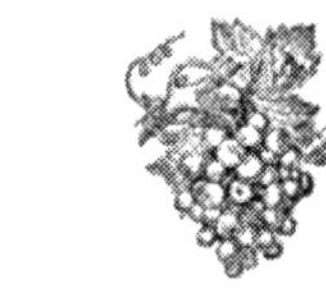

Jesus Christ in You 1

August 9th

"Examine yourselves to see whether you are in the faith; prove yourselves. Do you not know that Jesus Christ is in you?"

—2 CORINTHIANS 13: 5 …

How is it that so many Christians fail? To this the answer comes: We do not know aright that Jesus Christ is in us. Not one of us could live a worldly life, could give way to pride and Selfishness and temper, could so grieve the Holy Spirit of God, if we knew, indeed, that Jesus Christ was in us. The effect of this knowledge would be simply wonderful. On the one hand, it would solemnize and humble, and draw us to say: I cannot bear the thought of grieving the Christ within me. On the other hand, it would encourage and strengthen us to say: Praise God I have Jesus Christ within me, He will live my life for me. May God bring us to the confession of how much we have lost because we lacked this faith, and teach us to pray much that from moment to moment our life may be: Jesus Christ in us.

Then comes the other question. If I find that I have not known and lived this life, am I ready to say: Henceforth, by the grace of God, I will. I can rest content with nothing less than the full experience, Jesus Christ is in me? Let us but come in deep poverty and emptiness: He who did the work for us so perfectly on Calvary undertakes to do it in our hearts too. May God by the Holy Spirit, reveal to each of us all the He means us to enjoy. …

If you would know the power of this life: Believe in and accept the indwelling Christ. Let me ask you the question: Do you fully and truly believe in the indwelling Christ? You do believe in an incarnate Christ. When the name of Christ is mentioned, you at once think of One who was born a little babe at Bethlehem, who took our nature upon Him and lived as a man upon the earth. That thought is inseparable from your faith in Him. You believe, too, in the crucified Christ, dying on Calvary for our sins. You believe, too, in the risen Savior, one who lives for evermore. And you believe in the glorified Lord, now sitting on the throne of Heaven. But do you believe as definitely—as naturally—in the indwelling Christ? Have you made that one of the articles of your faith, as really as you believe in Christ incarnate or Christ crucified?

It is only as the truth is accepted and held that the others can really profit. The experience of the love and the saving power of our incarnate, crucified, glorified Lord depends entirely upon His indwelling in us to reveal His presence and to do His work. If you find your life feeble or sickly, you may be assured that it is because you do not know that Jesus Christ is in you. Do come to-night and begin at once to say: I want with my whole heart to get possessed of this wonderful knowledge, not as a doctrine, but as an experience;

Jesus Christ is in me. Begin to believe it at once. Accept of Him, even now, as an indwelling Savior. Day by day be content with nothing less than the blessed consciousness of His indwelling presence.

He loves to reveal Himself. … The Lord Jesus brings the heart which accepts and trusts Him to dwell within, into sympathy and harmony with Himself. And if you ask what the influence is He will exert, the answer is not difficult: He becomes your life, all your thoughts and tempers and dispositions and actions—will have His life and spirit breathing in them. Oh, Christians who have never yet known yourselves that Jesus Christ is in you, believe in Him, accept Him even now as the indwelling Christ.

A second thought: When you accept Christ to dwell in you, be sure and accept the whole Christ. There are some people who long for the indwelling Christ, but think of Him chiefly as one who comes to comfort and make glad, to bring peace and joy, but who do not accept of him in all his characters and offices. Beware of being content with only half of Christ; see to it that you have the whole Christ. There are people who accept of Christ as a priest to atone for their sins, but do not yield to His rule as King; they never think of giving up their own will wholly and entirely to Him. They come to Christ for happiness but not for holiness. They trust in the work He has done for them; they do not surrender themselves to Him for the work He is to do in them. They speak of the forgiveness of sins, but of the cleansing from all unrighteousness they know little. They have not accepted a whole Christ, the Savior from the power as much as from the guilt of sin.

Let me urge you to make a study of this. As you read of the life of Christ on earth, take every trait of that holy character, as the will of God concerning you. Study His holy humility and meekness, and say, "This is the Christ who dwells in me." Look upon His deep dependence upon the Father, and the perfect surrender of His will to do only what pleased the Father, and say, "I have yielded myself that my indwelling Lord may work this in me too." As you gaze upon Him as the crucified One, think not only of the cross in its atonement, as the means of propitiation for your sin, but of its fellowship, as the means of victory over sin. Beware of only saying, "Christ crucified *for me*," ever say too, "I am crucified *with Christ*." The one thing for which He lives in you is to breathe His own likeness into your nature, to impart to you His own crucifixion spirit, that blessed disposition that made His sacrifice so well pleasing to the Father. Do accept the whole Christ as dwelling in you.

Accept the whole Christ as dwelling in you. Especially, do not forget that the Christ who is in you is the loving One, the Servant and the Savior of the lost. This is the chief mark and glory of the Son of God: that He lived and died, not for Himself, but for others. When He comes to dwell in you, He cannot change His nature; it is the crucified, redeeming Love of God has taken possession of you. Yield yourself to Him that He may breathe into you His own love for souls, His own willingness to give up all, that they may be saved, His own faith in God's almighty conquering grace. Do accept a whole Christ, a Savior from all sin and Selfishness, a Savior, not only for yourself, but for all around you.

If you accept the whole Christ, accept Him *with the whole heart.* Nothing less than this can satisfy God, can secure Christ's full indwelling, can give our heart rest. This was what even the Old Testament demanded: *"You shall love the Lord your God with all your heart and with all your strength."* To it alone the promise is given: Blessed are they which seek Him with their whole heart.

Jesus Christ in You 2

August 10th

"You shall love the Lord your God with all your heart and with all your strength."

—DEUTERONOMY 6: 5

The old saints made confession: I have sought You with *my whole heart*. How can we think that this wondrous New Testament blessing, Jesus Christ, the whole Christ, in us, can be known in power, unless the whole heart be given to Him.

With the whole heart—what does that mean? First of all, the heart means love and affection. Our relationship to Christ must not only be that of trust in His help and devotion to His service, but one of intense personal attachment. His heart toward us is all love; His work was and is nothing but the revelation of infinite love and tenderness; and nothing but love on our part can be the proof that we have really accepted and known His love. When Peter had denied Christ, his restoration to Christ's favor and to his place as the shepherd of Christ's flock, all hinged on his answer to the thrice-repeated question, *"Do you love Me?"* Do not let us think that it is only for women and children, or for mystics and saints, to speak the language of tender, fervent love to the Savior. If we accept him with the whole heart, let us cultivate an intense personal love. Let us not hesitate to say often, "You know that I love You." The heart means love, and the whole heart means love with all our strength.

Then the heart also means the will. Accept Christ with the whole heart—that is to say, give up your will entirely and absolutely to Him. Say to yourself that it is a settled thing that never in anything are you to seek your own will. In things great and small, in decisions of supreme importance, in the most apparently insignificant questions of daily life, live as one who only exists that the will of God and of Christ may be carried out. It was to do God's will that Christ came from Heaven. It is to do God's will in you that He has entered your heart. Beware of hindering or grieving Him in this His blessed work.

People sometimes ask: Did not God give us a will for us to use? Is it not this man's nobility that he has a will? How can you ask us to give up that will so entirely and absolutely to God? What misunderstanding the question implies.

God gave us a will that with it we might intelligently will what He wills. It is no degradation to a child to give up his will to be guided by that of a wise and loving father. So it is man's highest dignity to find out and accept and delight in the perfect will of God. Accept Christ with the whole heart and a perfect will; count it your true and only blessedness to let Him breathe and work all God's will in you. The whole heart means the whole will given up. Never my own will in anything; let that be the decision with which you bow to let His will rule.

And let every sense of difficulty and feebleness only urge you afresh to believe that there is but one way of having your desire fulfilled—accepting Jesus Christ within you as an indwelling Savior, the living, inspiring power that breathes through all your will. You can have just as much of Christ as you give of yourself to Him: the whole heart can have the whole Christ.

At a meeting of the speakers this afternoon the conversation and prayer, we were asking what is needed to make our Convention a blessing. One said that there seldom was much blessing until there had first come a great breaking down and Christians had been brought to feel how much there is wanting in their life. In England, at Keswick, last year, I heard tell of Conventions where Christians were so convicted of the evil and the shame of their Christian life, that as they left the meeting they hardly dared to speak, and felt driven to go to God and make confession. This is what we need; what we cannot give ourselves; what God can work in us. When once we begin to see that, just as it is a matter of shame and humiliation when a husband or wife has been unfaithful to the husband to whom they had pledged their whole heart, the thought that we have been guilty of withholding from God that undivided love to which, as the all-glorious One, our Creator, and our Redeemer, He had such perfect right, ought to bow us in the very dust, then the sense of not having given the whole heart to Christ will become unbearable.

As we make confession that we have not given God His glory, that we have sought our own will and honor and pleasure, that we have given Self and the world a place in the heart where Christ wanted to dwell alone, God's Holy Spirit can so show us the sinfulness of our Christian life, as to leave us no rest until we have said with full purpose, and the assurance of Divine approval: I accept the whole Christ with my whole heart.

Now comes the fourth thought: Count upon the indwelling Christ to do all in your heart that needs to be done. In a verse just preceding our text, Paul says: "You seek for a proof of Christ speaking in me." It was not only Christ living in him, but Christ acting and speaking through him, they looked for. The Corinthians were justified in that expectation. And so when Christ comes in to take possession, He will by His Spirit, do within us what we cannot do.

He will make you what God would have you be—conformable to the image of His Son. It is utterly vain for us to think of following Christ's steps or imitating His example, or copying His life, by any effort of ours. Jesus lived upon earth a human life that He might show us what the life is we are to live. But what folly for us to think now we are Christians, that we can or shall approach to anything like His life. It is impossible. We are, indeed, called to it. It is our first duty. But it can only be if we let Himself live that life in us.

The life of Christ is altogether too high and too divine for us to reproduce. It is His own life, and only His. But He will live it out in us. You would fain be humble, or patient or gentle. How often have you prayed and struggled, but all in vain. You sought for a humility here on earth, in yourself, something like that which He, as God, brought from heaven. What folly. Oh, learn to cease from Self and its efforts. Turn inwards; let faith be occupied with and rest in the Almighty indwelling One, who has become your life, for the very purpose of filling it with His own. Count upon Him who dwells within you to do the work He has undertaken. … Then comes the time to heed His command: only believe. Trust in Him with an unmeasured confidence, that He will do His work within you in His own way and time. However slow and hidden and all unlikely things seem to be within, hold fast your confidence that He is there, and that He is working, and that in due time He will reveal Himself.

Dear Christians, when you believe in the incarnate or the crucified Christ, it means that you believe that He did the work perfectly, for which He came to live and die upon earth. When you believe in the risen and glorified Lord, it means that you have no shadow of doubt but that He is now living and reigning at God's right hand, in divine power. Let your faith in the indwelling One be as simple and clear. The work for which He entered your heart, the great work of possessing and renewing and glorifying your whole inner life, He will do in wondrous power and love. Trust Him for it; the Christ of Bethlehem, the Christ of Calvary, the Christ of the Throne in Heaven, is the Christ in you. Do begin to believe: Jesus Christ is in me; Jesus Christ will do the work perfectly in me.

Just listen to that wonderful promise in Hebrews: "*The God of peace perfect you in every good work, that ye may do His will, working in you that which is pleasing in His sight, through Jesus Christ.*" Yes, through Jesus Christ! If it is through Jesus Christ that God Himself works in you, how can this be in any other way but Jesus Christ Himself being in you? God fits you to do His will through Jesus Christ dwelling in you. Doubt no longer, but rejoice. Know … that Jesus Christ is in you. …

Blessed Lord! even now we give ourselves, and know You accept, that You are within, and that You will fill us with Yourself.

Daily Fellowship with God

August 11th

The first and chief need of our Christian life is fellowship with God. The Divine life within us comes from God, and is entirely dependent upon Him. As I need every moment afresh the air to breathe … so it is only in direct living communication with God that my soul can be strong. The manna of one day was corrupt when the next day came. I must every day have fresh grace from Heaven; and I obtain it only in direct waiting upon God Himself.

Begin each day by tarrying before God, and letting Him touch you. Take time to meet God. To this end let the first act in your devotions be setting yourself still before God. In prayer or worship everything depends upon God taking the chief place. I must bow quietly before Him in humble faith and adoration. God is. God is near. God is love, longing to communicate Himself to me. God the Almighty One, who works all in all, is even now waiting to work in me, and make Himself known.

Take time, till you know God is very near. When you have given God His place, of honor, glory and power, take your place of deepest lowliness, and seek to be filled with the spirit of humility. As a creature it is your blessedness to be nothing that God may be all in you. As a sinner you are not worthy to look up to God; bow in Self-abasement. As a saint, let God's love overwhelm you, and bow you down before Him in humility, meekness, patience, and surrender to His goodness and mercy. He will exalt you. Oh take time, to get very low before God. Then accept and value your place in Christ Jesus. God delights in nothing but His beloved Son, and can be satisfied with nothing less in those who draw nigh to Him.

Enter deep into God's holy presence in the boldness which the blood gives, and in the assurance that in Christ you are most well-pleasing. In Christ you are within the veil. You have access into the very heart and love of the Father. This is the great object of fellowship with God that I may have more of God in my life, and that God may see Christ formed in me. Be silent before God, and let Him bless you.

This Christ is a living Person. He loves you with a personal love, and He looks every day for the personal response of your love. Look into His face with trust, till His love really shines into your heart. Make His heart glad by telling Him that you do love Him. He offers Himself to you as a personal Savior and Keeper from the power of sin. … We have not only Christ's life in us as a power, and His presence with us a person, but we have His likeness to be wrought unto us. His is to be formed in us, so that His form or figure, His image can be seen in us. Bow before God until you get some sense of the greatness and blessedness of the work to be carried on by God in you this day.

Say to God, "Father, here I am for You to give as much in me of Christ's likeness as I can receive." And wait to hear Him say, "My child, I give you as much of Christ as your heart is open to receive." The God who revealed Jesus in the flesh and perfected Him, will reveal Him in you and perfect yourself in Him. The Father loves the Son, and delights to work out His image and likeness in you. Count upon it that this blessed work will be done in you as you wait on your God, and hold fellowship with Him.

The likeness to Christ consists chiefly in two things: the likeness of His death and resurrection (Romans 6: 5). The death of Christ was the consummation of His humility and obedience, the entire giving up of His life to God. In Him we are dead to sin. As we sink down in humility and dependence and entire surrender to God, the power of His death works in us, and we are made conformable to His death. And [through this death] do we know Him in the power of His resurrection, in the victory over sin, and all the joy and power of the risen life. Therefore, every morning, present yourselves unto God as those that are alive from the dead. He will maintain the life He gave, and bestow the grace to live as the risen ones. All this can only be in the power of the Holy Spirit, who dwells in you. Count upon Him to glorify Christ in you. Count upon Christ to increase in you the inflowing of His Spirit.

As you wait before God to realize His presence, remember that the Spirit is in you to reveal the things of God. Seek in God's presence to have the anointing of the Spirit of Christ so truly that your whole life may every moment be spiritual.

As you meditate on this wondrous salvation, and seek full fellowship with the great and holy God, and wait on Him to reveal Christ in you, you will feel how needful is the giving up of all to receive Him. Seek grace to know what it means to live as wholly for God as Jesus did. Only the Holy Spirit Himself can teach you what an entire yielding of the whole life to God can mean. Wait upon God, and every request for fellowship with Him, be accompanied by a new, very definite, and entire surrender to Him to work in you.

"By faith." Here, as through all Scripture and all the spiritual life this must be the keynote. As you tarry before God, let it be in a deep quiet faith in Him, the Invisible One, who is so near, so holy, so mighty, so loving. In a deep, restful faith, too, that all the blessings and powers of the heavenly life are around you, and in you. Just yield yourself in the faith of a perfect trust to the ever-blessed Holy Trinity, to work out all God's purpose in you. Begin each day thus in fellowship with God, and God will be all in all to you.

The Indwelling of God 1

August 12th

"For you are the temple of the living God; as God has said, I will dwell in them and walk in them; and I will be their God, and they shall be my people."

—2 CORINTHIANS 6: 16

We have here an answer to the question, "How is God going to be my God? Am I to regard Him as a great and Almighty and distant God, outside of me and separate from me in the Heaven above, from whom I am from time to time to have a little help?" That is what many Christians think, and it is owing to this thought of God that they experience so little of His real presence and power. No, this thought of God is only the beginning of true faith in Him. As we learn to know Scripture better, and the deep need of our heart, and the wonderful love of God that longs to enter completely into us, we learn that there is something better. The question, "How is God going to be my God?" finds its answer in the words I have just read. "*God has said, I will dwell in them, and I will be their God.*" That is God's answer to your question.

And what a wonderful answer it is. You know what a difference there is between the things that surround us and force themselves on our notice and occupy us, but which we never give place in our heart, and others that enter into us and take possession of our very life. A mother has a place for the child in her heart—it lives there. The gold of a miser has his heart, with all its love and hope. How little we think that our heart was actually created that God might dwell there, that He might show forth His life and love there, and that there our love and joy might be in Him alone. How little we know that just as naturally we have the love of parents or children filling our heart and making us happy, we can have the living God, for whom the heart was made, dwelling there and filling it with His own goodness and blessedness. This is my message this evening: God wants your heart; if you give it Him, He will dwell in it.

You heard what was said this afternoon about God, and what He was to the Psalmist, in Psalm 42 and 43, as he calls Him, "*the end of my life, the God of my strength, end of my exceeding joy, and my end.*" But how is God to be the strength of my life and my God? In no other way but by coming into my life with His divine life, and so filling it with His Almighty strength- then He is the strength of my life. With His holy life and love. He comes into my heart, the very seat and center of my life, and acts within me as my God, working out my life for me. He makes Divinely and blessedly true what is written here: "*God has said, I will dwell in them, and so I will be their God.*"

Do you think it would make a wonderful difference in our life if we really believe this, and in believing received the blessing it speaks of? What a holy awe there would be in us. And what tender fear lest we should hurt or grieve this holy, loving God. What a longing would be awakened: "I want to know how to walk with this God and have full communion with Him." And what a bright confidence: "Now my God has come to dwell in me, I need fear no more that I shall not have His presence, or that He will not do for me and in all that I need."

I want to speak to you very simply about this wonderful indwelling, and to give a few thoughts that may help you to see how it is the very essence of true Christianity—the very thing man as a sinner needed to have restored to him, and the very thing Christ Jesus came to give. And let me say in the first place, that it was for nothing less, and nothing else, than this indwelling that man was created by God. Have you ever wondered why God created man at all? The reason was this: God brought creatures into existence that He might show forth and impart His own Divine goodness and glory to them in a creaturely fashion, so that they, as far as they were capable of it, might share with Him His Divine perfections and blessings.

And He specially created man in His own image and likeness, that in him He might show how the Life of God could dwell in the human creature, and gradually fit him and lift him up for dwelling with God and in God through eternity. God's love said: "In his measure, I want man to be as holy and as good and as blessed as I am. I cannot give him the holiness or blessedness apart from Myself, but I can and will dwell in him, in the inmost depths of his life, and be to him his goodness and his strength." Yes, this was the glory of the Divine Creating Love—God wanted to give man all He had: Himself. God gave Himself to be our life and joy.

In no other possible way could God do this but by dwelling in him. Just as an oil lamp has its light inside, and through the globe gives light all around, so the God of love created us, that He might be within us the light of his life. This was to be our dignity and our blessedness, that in and through us all the glories of the blessed God should ever be shining out before the universe. Our whole nature, will and affections, and powers, were all to be the vessel to receive and hold and overflow with the blessed fullness of the life of God in us.

And it was to be our high prerogative and privilege just to offer and yield our Self to

God in the consciousness of this holy partnership. What God was in Himself in Heaven, living out His own life there, that He was to be on earth in and through us, living out His own life and truly in Heaven. Oh! the glory and the bliss of being a man! Glory to God for our creation. …

God had made man to be His home, His temple, where His presence, His will would be all in all. It is of this indwelling that sin has robbed both God and us. The temptation with which Satan came to man in Paradise really meant this—would he with his whole heart yield to God as Father and doing His will alone? Or would he not do his own will, and let Self rule as master in his own house? Alas! that fatal choice. God was dethroned and cast out of His temple, and Self sat upon the throne. Just as really as in later days the image of an idol was set up in the very home that God had caused to be built for us Himself, so Self was enthroned in the seat of God.

The description of the man of sin, when he is fully revealed come to full maturity, "*who opposes and exalts himself about all that is called God, or that is worshipped, so that he as God sits in the temple of God and shows himself that he is God,*" is the true Self at every stage and in every state: Self sits in the temple of God as God.

All the sin of heathendom—and how awful it is—and all the sin of Christendom—no less terrible!—is but the outgrowth of that one root—God dethroned, Self enthroned, in the heart of man. All the sin and sorrow of the life of each one of us has been nothing but this: you were not what you were created to be—you had not God dwelling in your heart to fill it with His life and peace and love.

I can with confidence ask any man here, Would you be content to have all filthy reptiles and animals occupy your houses along with yourselves? Would you allow other people to be masters of your home you dwell in? You never would. And yet, alas! you allow so much else to occupy the heart and have the place God alone is meant to have. And so many are quite unconscious of it. We come today with the message: let there be an end of all this desecration of God's temple. God asks your whole heart for Himself—oh! let it be given to Him.

The Indwelling of God 2

August 13th

"As You, Father, are in Me, and I in You, that they may be one with us."

—JOHN 17: 21

In the light of this indwelling of God, look at Christ's work of redemption. What was the object of Christ's coming from Heaven? It was to show us the possibility and blessedness of being a man with God living His life in Him. We teach children by means of pictures and models. When God's Son became man, He lived a perfect human life—"*made like us in all things*"—and told us it was by the power of the Father dwelling in Him. "*I do nothing of Myself – the Father in Me doeth the work.*" Here is no question of abstract thought or deep theology – here is a true man, sleeping, hungering, wearied, tempted, weeping, suffering like ourselves, telling us that the Father dwells in Him, and that this is the secret of His perfect blessed life. He felt it all just as we feel it, but He could do and bear all because the Father was in Him. He showed us how a man can live, and how He would enable us to live.

When He had done this in His life, He died that He might deliver us from the power of sin, and open up the way for us to return to God. On the cross He proved that a man in whom God dwells will be ready to suffer anything and to give his life even to the death, that he may enter into the fullness of the life of God. When sin entered, man lost the life of God dwelling in him, and became dead to it. There was no way for man to be freed from the life of sin but by dying to it. Christ died to sin, that He might take up into His fellowship and that we too might be dead to sin, and live unto God and His own life. And so, Jesus won back for us the life that man had been created for, with God dwelling in us, by giving to us His life, the very life He had lived. As He spoke, *"As You, Father, are in Me, and I in You, that they may be one with us"* (John 17: 21).

Oh! My beloved fellow Christians, this is the salvation Christ has won for us: a deliverance from Self by a death to it in the death of the cross; a restoration to the life we were created for, with our heart a home for God.

And how now are we to become partakers of this salvation? Look once again in the light of this blessed truth of the Divine indwelling at Pentecost and the coming of the Holy Spirit. Have you realized what the meaning is of God's sending the Holy Spirit into our hearts? It is nothing less than this: Christ who had been with the disciples on earth, but not in them, came back to them in the Spirit, now to dwell in them just as He had before dwelled with them. All that we read of the wondrous change that came over the disciples—their Selfishness changed into love, their pride into humility, their fear of suffering into boldness and joy, their unbelief into fullness of faith, their feebleness into power—was owing to this one thing: the glorified Christ had come to dwell within them as their life. That was the joy of Pentecost in Heaven: God regained possession of His temple, and could now again dwell in us....

When we look at the great promise—"*I will dwell in them*"—and its fulfillment at Pentecost, we are reminded of the great difference between the preparatory working of the Spirit in conversion and regeneration, and His Pentecostal indwelling. The former every Christian must have: without that there is no life. The life may be feeble and sickly, still where there is life, it is the Spirit's working. But that is only to prepare the temple. Pentecost is the glory of God filling the temple, God coming to abide. Let us believe that the promise can and will be fulfilled.

One more thought. In the light of our text, look at the state of the Church of Christ. How many believers there are of whom one would never say that their hearts are a temple that God has cleansed, and where He dwells. How much there is of coldness and worldliness, and Selfishness and sin, and inconsistency of profession, that makes one sometimes doubt whether there are Christians at all.

The state of Christ's Church is sad indeed. How little zeal for God's honor, delight in His fellowship, devotion to His service and kingdom, how little of a life in the power of the Holy Spirit. It surely manifests that promise "*I will dwell in them*" has never been understood, or believed, or claimed by a large majority of Christians.

Let me ask: Have you claimed it? Do you seek to live it out? If not, the one great object of our Convention is to set before you this blessed life to which God has redeemed you, to urge and to help you to enter upon it and walk in it.

Think of how it must have grieved the love of your Father, that after all He had done through His Son and the Spirit to get His abode again, you have cared so little to know about it or seek for it. Confess, too, your helplessness. You have tried to be better than you are, and you have failed. You must fail, until you receive His word that nothing less is needed, nothing less is offered, than that God Himself become the strength of your life.

Set your heart upon the blessing. You know how desire is the great moving power of the world. Fix your desire upon this Divine, this wondrous grace: *"I will dwell in them."* Let no thought of your unworthiness or feebleness discourage you. …He can and will fulfill His promise. Let it become the one desire of your heart. Understand that this is the salvation the Holy Spirit brings you as soon as you are ready to give up all for it. As soon as the heart is ready to lose all, to be emptied of all, to be cleansed of all that is of Self or nature, the promise will surely be fulfilled: *"I will dwell in them, and I will be their God."*…

"Wherefore come out from among them and be separate, says the Lord, and touch not the unclean thing, and I will receive you" (Isaiah 53: 11; 2 Corinthians 6: 17). Come out from all that is of the world and a worldly religion, from all that is inconsistent with the holy privilege of being God's holy temple and dwelling. Come out and be separate, take your stand as one who is going to live a life different from the crowd around you, be separate unto God and His will. "*And touch no unclean thing*"—be as a cleansed temple where nothing that defiles in the very least may enter—be wholly for God and holy to God—and He will make His word good: "*I will dwell in you.*" He Himself will reveal and impart and maintain within you all that the promise means.

Believer! will you accept of this full salvation? Will you do it now? I pray you, reject not this wonderful love. Oh! let your God have you, to satisfy His love and yours by dwelling in you. …

19

THE MYSTERY OF THE TRUE VINE

Chicago: Moody Press, 1897

The Vine

August 14th

"I am the Vine; you are the branches."

—JOHN 15: 5

In the opening words of the parable He had already spoken: "*I am the Vine.*" He now repeats the words. He would have us understand—note well the lesson, simple as it appears, it is the key of the abiding life—that the only way to obey the command, "*Abide in Me,*" is to have eye and heart fixed *upon Himself.* "*Abide in Me ... I am the true Vine.*" Yea, study this holy mystery until you see *Christ* as the true Vine, bearing, strengthening, supplying, inspiring all His branches, being and doing in each branch all it needs, and the abiding will come of itself. Yes, gaze upon Him as the true Vine, until you feel what a heavenly Mystery it is, and are compelled to ask the Father to reveal it to you by His Holy Spirit. The one to whom God reveals the glory of the true Vine, the one who sees what Jesus is and waits to do every moment, they cannot but abide. The vision of Christ is an irresistible attraction; it draws and holds us like a magnet. Listen ever to the living Christ still speaking to you, and waiting to show you the meaning and power of His Word: "*I am the vine.*"

Do notice how Christ said, "Abide in Me; I am the Vine that brings forth, and holds, and strengthens, and makes fruitful the branches. Abide in Me, rest *in Me,* and *let Me* do *My work.* I am the true Vine, all I am, and speak, and do is divine truth, giving the actual reality of what is said. I am the Vine, only consent and yield your all *to Me; I will do all* in you." ...

Not that the word "abide" is not needful; Christ used it so often, because it is the very key to the Christian life. But He would have us understand it in its true sense—"Come out of every other place, and every other trust and occupation, come out of Self with its reasonings and efforts, come and rest in what I shall do. Live out of yourself; abide in Me. Know that you are in Me; you need no more; remain in Me." ...

"*I am the Vine.*" Christ did not keep this mystery hidden from His disciples. He revealed it, first in words here, then in power when the Holy Spirit came down. He will reveal it to us too, first in the thoughts and confessions and desires these words awaken, then in power by the Spirit. Do let us wait on Him to show us all the heavenly meaning of the mystery. Let each day, in our quiet time, in the inner chamber with Him and His Word, our chief thought and aim be to get the heart fixed on Him, in the assurance: All that a vine ever can do for its branches, my Lord Jesus will do, is doing, for me. Give Him time, give Him your ear, that He may whisper and explain the Divine secret: "*I am the Vine.*"

Above all, remember, Christ is the Vine of God's planting, and you are a branch of God's grafting. Ever stand before God, in Christ; ever wait for all grace from God, in Christ; ever yield yourself to bear the more fruit the Husbandman asks, in Christ. And pray much for the revelation of the mystery that all the love and power of God that rested on Christ is working in you too. "I am God's Vine," Jesus says; "all I am I have from Him; all I am is for you; God will work it in you."

"*I am the Vine.*" Blessed Lord, speak You that word into my soul. Then shall I know that *all Your fullness is for me.* And that I can count upon You to stream it *into me*, and that my abiding is so easy and so sure when I forget and lose myself in the adoring faith that the Vine holds the branch *and supplies its every need.*

You, The Branches

"*I am the Vine; you are the branches*" (John 15: 5). Christ had already said much of the branch; here He comes to the personal application: "You are the branches of whom I have been speaking. As I am the Vine, engaged to be and do all the branches need, so I now ask you, in the new dispensation of the Holy Spirit whom I have been promising you, to accept the place I give you, and to be My branches on earth." The relationship He seeks to establish is an intensely personal one: it all hinges on the two little words I and You. And it is for us as intensely personal as for the first disciples. Let us present ourselves before our Lord, until He speak to each of us in power, and our whole soul feels it: "*I am the Vine; you are the branch.*"

Dear disciple of Jesus, however young or feeble, hear the voice. "*You are the branches.*" You must *be nothing less.* Let no false humility, no carnal fear of sacrifice, no unbelieving doubts as to what you feel able for, keep you back from saying: "I will be a branch, with all that may mean—a branch, very feeble, but yet as like the Vine as can be, for I am of the same nature, and receive of the same spirit. A branch, utterly helpless, and yet just as manifestly set apart before God and men, as wholly given up to the work of bearing fruit, as the Vine itself. A branch, nothing in myself, and yet resting and rejoicing in the faith that knows that He will provide for all. Yes, by His grace, I will be nothing less than a branch, and all He means it to be, that through me, He may bring forth His fruit."

"You are the branch"; you need be *nothing more*. You need not for one single moment of the day take upon you the responsibility of the Vine. You need not leave the place of entire dependence and unbounded confidence. … The Vine will give all and work all. The Father, the Husbandman, watches over your union with and growth in the Vine. You need be nothing more than a branch. Only a branch! Let that be your watchword; it will lead in the path of continual surrender to Christ's working, of true obedience to His every command, of joyful expectancy of all His grace.

Is there anyone who now asks: "How can I learn to say this aright, 'Only be a branch!' and to live it out?" Dear soul, the character of a branch, its strength, and the fruit it bears, depend entirely upon the Vine. And your life as branch depends entirely upon your apprehension of what our Lord Jesus is. Therefore, never separate the two words: "I the Vine—you the branch." Your life and strength and fruit depend upon what and who your Lord Jesus is!

Therefore, worship and trust Him; let Him be your one desire and the one occupation of your heart. And when you feel that you do not and cannot know Him aright, then just remember it is part of His responsibility as Vine to make Himself known to you. He does this not in thoughts and conceptions—no—but in a hidden growth within the life that is humbly and restfully and entirely given up to wait on Him.

The Vine reveals itself within the branch; then comes the growth and fruit, Christ dwells and works within His branch; only be a branch, waiting on Him to do all; He will be to you the true Vine. The Father Himself, the divine Husbandman, is able to make you a branch worthy of the heavenly Vine. You shall not be disappointed. …

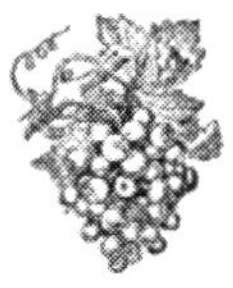

Abide in My Love

August 15th

"Even as the Father has loved Me, I also have loved you: Abide in My Love"."

—JOHN 15: 9

A*bide in My love.* We speak of a man's home as his abode. Our abode, the home of our soul, is to be the love of Christ. We are to live our life there, to be at home there all the day: this is what Christ means our life to be, and really can make it. Our continuous abiding in the Vine is to be an abiding in His love.

You have probably heard or read of what is called the higher, or the deeper life, of the richer or the fuller life, of the life abundant. And you possibly know that some have told of a wonderful change, by which their life of continual failure and stumbling had been changed into a very blessed experience of being kept and strengthened and made exceeding glad. If you asked them how it was this great blessing came to them, many would tell you it was simply this, that they were led to believe that this abiding in Christ's love was meant to be a reality, and that they were made willing to give up everything for it, and then enabled to trust Christ to make it true to them.

The love of the Father to the Son is not a sentiment; it is a divine life, an infinite energy, an irresistible power. It carried Christ through life and death and the grave. The Father loved Him and dwelled in Him, and did all for Him. So the love of Christ to us too is an infinite living power that will work in us all He delights to give us. The feebleness of our Christian life is that we do not take time to believe that this divine love does really delight in us, and will possess and work all in us. We do not take time to look at the Vine bearing the branch so entirely, working all in it so completely. We strive to do for ourselves what Christ alone can, what Christ, oh, so lovingly, longs to do for us.

And this now is the secret of the change we spoke of, and the beginning of a new life, when the soul sees this infinite love willing to do all, and gives itself up to it.

"*Abide in my love*": To believe that it is possible so to live moment by moment; to believe that everything that makes it difficult or impossible will be overcome by Christ Himself; to believe that Love really means an infinite longing to give itself wholly to us and never leave us; and in this faith to cast ourselves on Christ to work it in us; this is the secret of the true Christian life.

And how to come to this faith? Turn away from the visible if you would see and possess the invisible. Take more time with Jesus, gazing on Him as the heavenly Vine, living in the love of the Father, wanting you to live in His love. Turn away from yourself and your efforts and your faith, if you would have the heart filled with Him and the certainty of His love. Abiding means going out from everything else, to occupy one place and stay there. Come away from all else, and set your heart on Jesus, and His love, that love will waken your faith and strengthen it. Occupy yourself with that love, worship it, wait for it. You may be sure it will reach out to you, and by its power take you up into itself as your abode and your home.

"*Abide in My love*": Lord Jesus, I see it, it was Your abiding in Your Father's love that made You the True Vine, with Your Divine fullness of love and blessing for us. Oh, that I may even so, as a branch, abide in Your love, for its fullness to fill me and overflow on all around.

Abide

"*Abide in Me, and I in you.*" (John 15: 4). When a new graft is placed in a vine and it abides there, there is a twofold process that takes place. The first is in the wood. The graft shoots its little roots and fibers down into the stem, and the stem grows up into the graft, and what has been called the structural union occurs. The graft abides and becomes one with the vine, and even though the vine were to die, would still be one wood with it.

Then there is the second process, in which the sap of the vine enters the new structure, and uses it as a passage through which sap can flow up to show itself in young shoots and leaves and fruit. Here is the vital union. Into the graft which abides in the stock, the stock enters with sap to abide in it.

When our Lord says: "*Abide in Me, and I in you,*" He points to something analogous to this. "*Abide in Me*"; that refers more to that which *we* have to do. *We* have to trust and obey, to detach ourselves from all else, to reach out after Him and cling to Him, to sink ourselves into Him. As we do this, through the grace He gives, a character is formed, and a heart prepared for the fuller experience: "*I in you*," God strengthens us with might by the Spirit in the inner man, and Christ dwells in the heart by faith.

Many believers pray and long very earnestly for the filling of the Spirit and the indwelling of Christ, and wonder that they do not make more progress. The reason is often this, the "I in you" cannot come because the "abide in Me" is not maintained. … Before the Spirit can fill, there must be a body prepared. The graft must have grown into the stem, and be abiding in it before the sap can flow through to bring forth fruit.

It is as in lowly obedience that we follow Christ—even in external things, denying ourselves, forsaking the world, and even in the body seeking to be conformable to Him, as we thus seek to abide in Him, that we shall be able to receive and enjoy the "I in you." The work enjoined on us: "Abide in Me," will prepare us for the work undertaken by Him: "I in you."

"*In*." The two parts of the injunction have their unity in that central deep-meaning word "in." There is no deeper word in Scripture. God is *in* all. God dwells *in* Christ. Christ lives *in* God. We are *in* Christ. Christ is in us: our life taken up into His; His life received into ours; in a Divine reality that words cannot express, we are in Him and He in us. And the words, "Abide in Me and I in you," just tell us to believe it, this Divine mystery, and to count upon our God the Husbandman, and Christ the Vine, to make it Divinely true.

No thinking or teaching or praying can grasp it; it is a divine mystery of love. As little as we can effect the union can we understand it. Let us just look upon this infinite, divine, omnipotent Vine loving us, holding us, working in us. Let us in the faith of His working abide and rest in Him, ever turning heart and hope to Him alone. And let us count upon Him to fulfill in us the mystery: "You in Me, and I in you." …

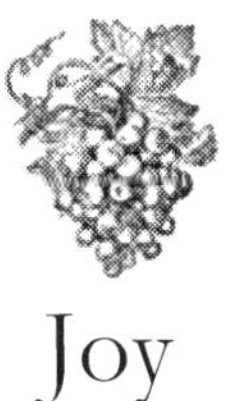

Joy

August 16th

"These things have I spoken unto you, that My joy may be in you, and that your joy may be full."

—JOHN 15: 11

If anyone asks the question, "How can I be a happy Christian?" our Lord's answer is very simple: "These things," about the Vine and the branches, "*I have spoken to you, that my joy may be in you, and that your joy may be full*." "You cannot have My joy without My life. Abide in Me, and let Me abide in you, and My joy will be in you." All healthy life is a thing of joy and beauty; live undividedly the branch life; you will have His joy in full measure.

To many Christians the thought of a life wholly abiding in Christ is one of strain and painful effort. They cannot see that the strain and effort only come, as long as we do not yield ourselves unreservedly to the life of Christ in us. The very first words of the parable are not yet opened up to them: "I am the true Vine; I undertake all and provide for all; I ask nothing of the branch but that it yields wholly to Me, and allows Me to do all. I engage to make and keep the branch all that it ought to be." Ought it not to be an infinite and unceasing joy to have the Vine thus work all, and to know that it is none less than the blessed Son of God in His love who is each moment bearing us and maintaining our life?

That My joy may be in you—We are to have Christ's own joy in us. And what is Christ's own joy? There is no joy like love. There is no joy but love. Christ had just spoken of the Father's love and His own abiding in it, and of His having loved us with that same love. His joy is nothing but the joy of love, of being loved and of loving. It was the joy of receiving His Father's love and abiding in it, and then the joy of passing on that love and pouring it out on sinners. It is this joy He wants us to share: the joy of being loved of the Father and of Him; the joy of in our turn loving and living for those around us. This is just the joy of being truly branches: abiding in His love, and then giving up ourselves in love to bear fruit for others. Let us accept His life, as He gives it in us as the Vine, His joy will be ours: the joy of abiding in His love, the joy of loving like Him, of loving with His love.

"*And that your joy may be full*"—That it may be complete; that you may be filled with it. How sad that we should so need to be reminded that as God alone is the fountain of all joy, "*God our exceeding joy*," the only way to be perfectly happy is to have as much of God, as much of His will and fellowship, as possible!

Religion is meant to be in everyday life a thing of unspeakable joy. And why do so many complain that it is not so? Because they do not believe that there is no joy like the joy of abiding in Christ and in His love, and being branches through whom He can pour out His love on a dying world.

Oh, that Christ's voice might reach the heart of every Christian, and persuade us to believe that His joy is the only true joy, that His joy can become ours and truly fill us, and that the sure and simple way of living in it is—only this—to abide as branches in Him our heavenly Vine. Let the truth enter deep into us—as long as our joy is not full, it is a sign that we do not yet know our heavenly Vine aright; every desire for a fuller joy must only urge us to abide more simply and more fully in His love.

My joy—your joy. In this too it is: as the Vine, so the branch; all the Vine in the branch. Your joy is our joy—Your joy in us, and our joy fulfilled. Blessed Lord, fill me with Your joy—the joy of being loved and blessed with a divine love; the joy of loving and blessing others.

Love One Another

"*This is My commandment, that you love one another*" (John 15: 12). God is love. His whole nature and perfection is love, living not for Himself, but to dispense life and blessing. In His love He begat the Son, that He might give all to Him. In His love He brought forth creatures that He might make them partakers of His blessedness. Christ is the Son of God's love, the bearer, the revealer, the communicator of that love. His life and death were all love. Love is His life, and the life He gives. He only lives to love, to live out His life of love in us, to give Himself in all who will receive Him. The very first thought of the true Vine is love—living only to impart His life to the branches.

The Holy Spirit is the Spirit of love. He cannot impart Christ's life without imparting His love. Salvation is nothing but love conquering and entering into us; we have just as much of salvation as we have of love. Full salvation is perfect love.

No wonder that Christ said: "*A new commandment I give unto you*"; "*This is my commandment*"—the one all-inclusive commandment—"*that you love one another.*" The branch is not only one with the vine, but with all its other branches; they drink one spirit, they form one body, they bear one fruit. Nothing can be more unnatural than that Christians should not love one another, even as Christ loved them.

The life they received from their heavenly Vine is nothing but love. This is the one thing He asks above all others. "*By this shall all know that you are my disciples: if you have love for one another.*" As the special sort of vine is known by the fruit it bears, the nature of the heavenly Vine is to be judged of by the love His disciples have to one another.

See that you obey this commandment. Let your "obey and abide" be seen in this. Love your brothers and sisters as the way to abide in the love of your Lord. Let your vow of obedience begin here. Love one another. Let your intercourse with the Christians in your own family be holy, tender, Christlike love. Let your thoughts of the Christians round you be, before everything, in the spirit of Christ's love. Let your life and conduct be the sacrifice of love—give yourself up to think of their sins or their needs, to intercede for them, to help and to serve them.

Be in your church or circle the embodiment of Christ's love. The life Christ lives in you is love; let the life in which you live it out be all love. … Christ commands it: you must obey. Christ means it: you must obey, or you cannot abide in His love.

But I have tried and failed. … Ah! that is because you have failed to take in the first word of the parable—"I am the true Vine: I give all you need as a branch, I give all I myself have." I pray you, let the sense of past failure and present feebleness drive you to the Vine. He is all love. He loves to give. He gives love. He will teach you to love, even as He loved. Love one another.

Whatsoever You Will

August 17th

"If you abide in Me, and My Words abide in you, ask whatsoever you will, and it shall be done unto you."
—JOHN 15: 7

The whole place of the branch in the vine is one of unceasing prayer. Without intermission it is ever calling: "O my vine, send the sap I need to bear Your fruit." And its prayers are never unanswered: it asks what it needs, what it will, and it is done.

The healthy life of the believer in Christ is equally one of unceasing prayer. Consciously or unconsciously, he lives in continual dependence. The Word of our Lord, "*You can do nothing,*" has taught us that not more unbroken than the continuance of the branch in the vine, must be our asking and receiving.

The promise of our text gives us infinite boldness: "*Ask whatsoever you will, and it shall be done unto you.*" The promise is given in direct connection with fruit-bearing. Limit it to yourself and your own needs, and you rob it of its power; you rob yourself of the power of appropriating it. Christ was sending these disciples out, and they were ready to give their life for the world; to them He gave the disposal of the treasures of Heaven. Their prayers would bring the Spirit and the power they needed for their work.

The promise is given in direct connection with the coming of the Spirit. The Spirit is not mentioned in the parable, just as little as the sap of the vine is mentioned. But both are meant all through. In the chapter preceding the parable, our Lord had spoken of the Holy Spirit, in connection with their inner life, being in them, and revealing Himself within them (John 14:15–23). In the next chapter He speaks of the Holy Spirit in connection with their work, coming to them, convincing the world, and glorifying Him (John 16: 7–14). To avail ourselves of the unlimited prayer promises, we must be filled with the Spirit, and wholly given up to the work and glory of Jesus. The Spirit will lead us into the truth of its meaning and the certainty of its fulfillment.

Let us realize that we can only fulfill our calling to bear much fruit, by praying much. In Christ are hid all the treasures men around us need; in Him all God's children are blessed with all spiritual blessings. He is full of grace and truth. But it needs prayer, much prayer, strong believing prayer, to bring these blessings down. And let us equally remember that we cannot appropriate the promise without a life given up for others. Many try to take the promise, and then look round for what they can ask. This is not the way; but the very opposite. Get the heart burdened with the need of souls, and the command to save them, and the power will come to claim the promise.

Let us claim it as one of the revelations of our wonderful life in the Vine: He tells us that if we ask in His name, in virtue of our union with Him, whatsoever it be, it will be done to us. Souls are perishing because there is too little prayer. God's children are feeble because there is too little prayer. We bear so little fruit because there is so little prayer. The faith of this promise would make us strong to pray; let us not rest till it has entered into our very heart, and drawn us in the power of Christ to continue and labor and strive in prayer until the blessing comes in power. To be a branch means not only bearing fruit on earth, but power in prayer to bring down blessing from Heaven. Abiding fully means praying much.

Prevailing Prayer

"I appointed you that you should go and bear fruit, that whatever you shall ask of the Father in My Name, He may give it to you." (John 15: 16). In the first verse of our parable, Christ revealed Himself as the true Vine, and the Father as the Husbandman, and asked for Himself and the Father a place in the heart. Here, in the closing verse, He sums up all His teaching

concerning Himself and the Father in the twofold purpose for which He had chosen them.

With reference to Himself, the Vine, the purpose was, that they should bear fruit. With reference to the Father, it was, that whatsoever they should ask in His name, should be done of the Father in Heaven. As fruit is the great proof of the true relation to Christ, so prayer is of our relation to the Father. A fruitful abiding in the Son, and prevailing prayer to the Father, are the two great factors in the true Christian life.

"That whatsoever you shall ask of the Father in my name, he may give it to you." These are the closing words of the parable of the Vine. The whole mystery of the Vine and its branches leads up to the other mystery—that whatsoever we ask in His name the Father gives! See here the reason of the lack of prayer, and of the lack of power in prayer.
It is because we so little live the true branch life, because we so little lose ourselves in the Vine, abiding in Him entirely, that we feel so little constrained to much prayer, so little confident that we shall be heard, and so do not know how to use His name as the key to God's storehouse.

The Vine planted on earth has reached up into Heaven; it is only the soul wholly and intensely abiding in it, can reach into Heaven with power to prevail much. Our faith in the teaching and the truth of the parable, in the truth and the life of the Vine, must prove itself by power in prayer. The life of abiding and obedience, of love and joy, of cleansing and fruit-bearing, will surely lead to the power of prevailing prayer.

"*Whatsoever you shall ask.*" The promise was given to disciples who were ready to give themselves, in the likeness of the true Vine, for their fellow man. This promise was all their provision for their work; they took it literally, they believed it, they used it, and they found it true. Let us give ourselves, as branches of the true Vine, and in His likeness, to the work of saving others, of bringing forth fruit to the glory of God, and we shall find a new urgency and power to pray and to claim the "*whatsoever you ask.*" We shall waken to our wonderful responsibility of having in such a promise the keys to the King's store-houses given us, and we shall not rest till we have received bread and blessing for the perishing.

"I chose you, that you may bring forth fruit, and that your fruit may abide; that whatsoever you shall ask of the Father in my name, he may give it to you." Beloved disciple, seek above everything to be a man or woman of prayer. Here is the highest exercise of your privilege as a branch of the Vine; here is the full proof of your being renewed in the image of God and His Son; here is your power to show how you, like Christ, live not for yourself, but for others; here you enter Heaven to receive gifts for others; here your abiding in Christ has led to His abiding in you, to use you as the channel and instrument of His grace. The power to bear fruit for others has been crowned by power to prevail with God.

"I am the Vine; my Father is the Husbandman." Christ's work in you is to bring you so to the Father that His Word may be fulfilled in you: *"At that day you shall ask in My name; and I say not that I will pray the Father for you; for the Father himself loves you."*

The power of direct access to the Father for others, the liberty of intercession—claiming and receiving blessing for them in faith—is the highest exercise of our union with Christ. Let all who would truly and fully be branches give themselves to the work of intercession. It is the one great work of Christ the Vine in Heaven, the source of power for all His work. Make it your one great work as branch: it will be the power of all your work.

More Fruit

August 18th

"Every branch that bears fruit, He cleanses it, that it may bear more fruit."
—JOHN 15: 2

The thought of fruit is so prominent in the eye of Him who sees things as they are, fruit is so truly the one thing God has set His heart upon, that our Lord, after having said that the branch that bears no fruit is taken away, at once adds: and where there is fruit, the one desire of the Husbandman is more fruit. As the gift of His grace, as the token of spiritual vigor, as the showing forth of the glory of God and of Christ, as the only way for satisfying the need of the world, God longs and fits for, more fruit.

More Fruit: This is a very searching word. As churches and individuals, we are in danger of nothing so much as Self-contentment. The secret spirit of Laodicea—that "*we are rich and increased in goods and have need of nothing*"—may prevail where it is not suspected. The Divine warning—that we may be "*poor and wretched and miserable*"—finds little response just where it is most needed.

Let us not rest content with the thought that we are taking an equal share with others in the work that is being done, or that men are satisfied with our efforts in Christ's service, or even point to us as examples. Let our only desire be to know whether we are bearing all the fruit Christ is willing to give through us as living branches, in close and living union with Himself, whether we are satisfying the loving heart of the great Husbandman, our Father in Heaven, in His desire for more fruit.

More Fruit: The word comes with divine authority to search and test our life: the true disciple will heartily surrender himself to its holy light, and will earnestly ask that God Himself may show what there may be lacking in the measure or the character of the fruit he bears. Do let us believe that the Word is meant to lead us on to a fuller experience of the Father's purpose of love, of Christ's fullness, and of the wonderful privilege of bearing much fruit in the salvation of men.

More Fruit: The word is a most encouraging one. Let us listen to it. It is just to the branch that is bearing fruit that the message comes: *more fruit.* God does not demand this as Pharaoh the task-master, or as Moses the lawgiver, without providing the means. He comes as a Father, who gives what He asks, and works what He commands. He comes to us as the living branches of the living Vine, and offers to work the more fruit in us, if we but yield ourselves into His hands. Shall we not admit the claim, accept the offer, and look to Him to work it in us?

"*That it may bear more fruit*": do let us believe that as the owner of a vine does everything to make the fruitage as rich and large as possible, the Divine Husbandman will do all that is needed to make us bear more fruit. All He asks is, that we set our heart's desire on it, entrust ourselves to His working and care, and joyfully look to Him to do His perfect work in us. God has set His heart on more fruit; Christ waits to work it in us; let us joyfully look up to our Divine Husbandman and our heavenly Vine, to ensure our bearing more fruit.

The Cleansing

"*Every branch that bears fruit, He cleanses it, that it may bear more fruit*" (John 15: 2). Our Lord tells us, here at the very outset of the parable, that the one work the Father does to the branch that bears fruit is: *He cleanses it, that it may bear more fruit.*

Consider a moment what this pruning or cleansing is. It is not the removal of weeds or thorns, or anything from without that may hinder the growth. No; it is the cutting off of the long shoots of the previous year, the removal of something that comes from within, that has been produced by the life of the vine itself. It is the removal of something that is a proof of the vigor of its life; the more vigorous the growth has been, the greater the need for the pruning.

It is the honest, healthy wood of the vine that has to be cut away. And why? Because it would consume too much of the sap to fill all the long shoots of last year's growth: the sap must be saved up and used for fruit alone. The branches, sometimes eight and ten feet long, are cut down close to the stem, and nothing is left but just one or two inches of wood, enough to bear the grapes. It is when everything that is not needful for fruit-bearing has been relentlessly cut down, and just as little of the branches as possible has been left, that full, rich fruit may be expected.

What a solemn, precious lesson! It is not to sin only that the cleansing of the Husbandman here refers. It is to our own religious activity, as it is developed in the very act of bearing fruit. It is this that must be cut down and cleansed away. We have, in working for God, to use our natural gifts of wisdom, or eloquence, or influence, or zeal.

And yet they are ever in danger of being unduly developed, and then trusted in. And so, after each season of work, God has to bring us to the end of ourselves, to the consciousness of the helplessness and the danger of all that is of man, to feel that we are nothing. All that is to be left of us is just enough to receive the power of the life-giving sap of the Holy Spirit. What is of man must be reduced to its very lowest measure.

All that is inconsistent with the most entire devotion to Christ's service must be removed. The more perfect the cleansing and cutting away of all that is of Self, the less of surface over which the Holy Spirit is to be spread, so much the more intense can be the concentration of our whole being, to be entirely at the disposal of the Spirit. This is the true circumcision of the heart, the circumcision of Christ. This is the true crucifixion with Christ, bearing about the dying of the Lord Jesus in the body. …

Obey and Abide

August 19th

"If you keep My commandments, you shall abide in My love, even as I have kept my Father's commandments, and abide in His love."

—JOHN 15:10

In our former meditation reference was made to the entrance into a life of rest and strength which has often come through a true insight into the personal love of Christ, and the assurance that that love indeed meant that He would keep the soul. In connection with that transition, and the faith that sees and accepts it, the word surrender or consecration is frequently used. The soul sees that it cannot claim the keeping of this wonderful love unless it yields itself to a life of entire obedience. It sees too that the faith that can trust Christ for keeping from sinning must prove its sincerity by venturing at once to trust Him for strength to obey. In that faith it dares to give up and cut off everything that has hitherto hindered it, and to promise and expect to live a life that is well pleasing to God.

This is the thought we have here now in our Savior's teaching. After having in the words, "*Abide in my love*," spoken of a life in His love as a necessity, because it is at once a possibility and an obligation, He states what its one condition is: "*If you keep my commandments, you shall abide in my love.*" This is surely not meant to close the door to the abode of His love which he had just opened up. Not in the most distant way does it suggest the thought which some are too ready to entertain, that as we cannot keep His commandments, we cannot abide in His love. No; the precept is a promise: "*Abide in my love*," could not be a precept if it were not a promise.

And so, the instruction as to the way through this open door points to no unattainable ideal; the love that invites to her blessed abode reaches out the hand, and enables us to keep the commandments. Let us not fear, in the strength of our ascended Lord, to take the vow of obedience, and give ourselves to the keeping of His commandments. Through His will, loved and done, lies the path to His love.

Only let us understand well what it means. It refers to our performance of all that we know to be God's will. … Obedience has reference to the positive keeping of the commandments of our Lord, and the performance of His will in everything in which we know it. This is a possible degree of grace, and it is the acceptance in Christ's strength of such obedience as the purpose of our heart, of which our Savior speaks here. Faith in Christ as our Vine, in His enabling and sanctifying power, fits us for this obedience of faith, and secures a life of abiding in His love.

"*If you keep My commandments, you shall abide in My love*": It is the heavenly Vine unfolding the mystery of the life He gives. It is to those abiding in Him to whom He opens up the secret of the full abiding in His love. It is the wholehearted surrender in everything to do His will, that gives access to a life in the abiding enjoyment of His love.

Obey and abide. Gracious Lord, teach me this lesson, that it is only through knowing Your will one can know Your heart, and only through doing that will one can abide in Your love. Lord, teach me that as worthless as is the doing in my own strength, so essential and absolutely indispensable is the doing of faith in Your strength, if I would abide in Your love.

You, Even as I

"*If you keep My commandments, you shall abide in My love, even as I have kept My Father's commandments, and abide in His love*" (John 15: 10). We have had occasion more than once to speak of the perfect similarity of the vine and the branch in nature, and therefore in aim. Here Christ speaks no longer in a parable, but tells us plainly out of how His own life is the exact model of ours. He had said that it is alone by obedience we can abide in His love. He now tells that this was the way in which He abode in the Father's love.

As the Vine, so the branch. His life and strength and joy had been in the love of the Father: it was only by obedience He abode in it. We may find our life and strength and joy in His love all the day, but it is only by an obedience like His we can abide in it. Perfect conformity to the Vine is one of the most precious of the lessons of the branch. It was by obedience Christ as Vine honored the Father as Husbandman; it is by obedience the believer as branch honors Christ as Vine.

Obey and abide: That was the law of Christ's life as much as it is to be that of ours. He was made like us in all things that we might be like Him in all things. He opened up a path in which we may walk even as He walked. He took our human nature to teach us how to wear it, and show us how obedience, as it is the first duty of the creature, is the only way to abide in the favor of God and enter into His glory. And now He comes to instruct and encourage us, and asks us to keep His commandments, even as He kept His Father's commandments and abides in His love.

The Divine fitness of this connection between obeying and abiding, between God's commandments and His love, is easily seen. God's will is the very center of His Divine perfection. As revealed in His commandments, it opens up the way for the creature to grow into the likeness of the Creator. In accepting and doing His will, I rise into fellowship with Him. Therefore, it was that the Son, when coming into the world, spoke: "*I come to do your will, O God*"! This was the place and this would be the blessedness of the creature.

... "*You, even as I*"—The branch cannot bear fruit except as it has exactly the same life as the Vine. Our life is to be the exact counterpart of Christ's life. It can be, just in such measure as we believe in Him as the Vine, imparting Himself and His life to His branches. "*You, even as I*," the Vine says: one law, one nature, one fruit. Do let us take from our Lord the lesson of obedience as the secret of abiding. Let us confess that simple, implicit, universal obedience has taken too little the place it should have. Christ died for us as enemies, when we were disobedient. He took us up into His love; now that we are in Him, His Word is: "*Obey and abide; you, even as I.*" Let us give ourselves to a willing and loving obedience. He will keep us abiding in His love.

20

THE SPIRITUAL LIFE

A Series of Lectures Delivered Before the Students of the Moody Bible Institute, Chicago, 1895

Philadelphia: George W. Jacobs & Co., 1897

Carnal or Spiritual 1

August 20th

"I could not speak to you as unto spiritual, but as to carnal, even as to babes in Christ."

—1 CORINTHIANS 3: 4

Throughout the Church of Christ there is a universal complaint of the feebleness of the Christian life, and there are tens of thousands of souls longing to know how to lead a better life. They find in God's word promises of perfect peace, of a faith that overcomes the world, of a joy that is unspeakable, of a life of ever abiding-communion with Christ, hidden in the hollow of God's hand, and in the secret of his pavilion. But alas, thousands say they know not how to obtain it. Our meetings have just this object: To try and find out what are the possibilities of the Christian life as God has revealed them in His word, what are the hindrances that keep the majority of believers out of that life, and what are the steps by which to come in and take possession.

There are two stages in the Christian life: the lower stage under the power of the flesh, and the stage of the true life in the power of the Spirit.

Let me direct your attention to a passage in 1 Corinthians 3: 1–4. There you have the first sorted Christians; some are spiritual and some are carnal. And Paul says… *"I could not speak to you as unto spiritual, but as to carnal, even as to babes in Christ."* You are in Christ, you are real Christians, but alas, you are feeble Christians, just like infants. He added, *"I have fed you with milk and not with meat."*

In other words, there are some truths that are just like milk, suitable for carnal Christians; other truths of God's word, deep spiritual truths, are for spiritual people. *"For hitherto, you were not able to bear it, neither yet now are you able for you are yet carnal."* There you have the word "carnal" again. He says plainly, I want you to know that you are carnal, believers, but carnal believers, "For," here comes the proof, *"For whereas there is among you envying and strife, and divisions, are ye not carnal, and walk as men?"* He asks them to answer the question. The word "carnal" comes from the Latin word meaning "flesh." If you do the works of the flesh this proves you are carnal, you walk as men do, not as children of God do, who lead a heavenly life. …

I think if we look carefully at this passage we shall find principal marks of the carnal state.

First, it is a state of protracted infancy. If I had here today a beautiful little child six months old with its chubby hands and feet, you would say "What a perfect child," but if in three years' time we found that the child had not grown an inch we should conclude that something was the matter. If in another three years we again found no growth, we should at once say there is some terrible disease in that child that prevents its growth, for where there is health there is growth.

That is now what Paul says to the Corinthians. You are young Christians, babes in Christ. At first a Christian may be carnal for he is young and does not know what sin is, but when someone has been a Christian for some time—say after six months, a year or three years, or even ten years—and they do not grow, but remain at the same place where they started from as a babe, there is something the matter; there is some terrible disease. That disease is the carnal mind.

A Christian when under the power of the flesh is in a state of protracted infancy. You find it said in the epistle to the Hebrews that when after they had been so long Christians they ought to be teachers, helping others, they still had to be fed with milk and were not able to take the meat of the full-grown man. This is a state of protracted infancy and it is the state of the greater part of the Christian church. How many there are who will testify that the best time was the first three months after conversion; and after that they began to go back; they lost their joy and alas, they have never had such joy since then. They have lost their first love. At that time, they used to conquer sin, but now it has the mastery. …

Second, the carnal state is a state of sin and failure; no victory over sin. Paul writing to the Corinthians says, *"There is among you envying, and strife, and divisions."* That was the work of the flesh and this was the great reason that he had to write to them the thirteenth chapter, because of their quarrelling. One exalted Paul, another thought Apollos was the more eloquent; another thought that Peter was older than either and better; they were divided into religious parties. They were just squabbling among themselves and got excited, and had strifes, divisions and envy. In Galatians, 5th chapter, you have envyings, strifes, etc., as the works of the flesh.

Do we not find Christians who in some respects have a good measure of the grace of God and yet have never really conquered their temper, and so when another says a sharp thing to them they give a sharp reply? How many Christians there are who have never learned to love as God wants them to love—to love the unlovable. What is this but that they are yet in the carnal state? In them the flesh has more power than the Spirit. Friends, until we confess with shame, I am carnal, we will not get into the life of the spiritual man.

Two powers are striving for mastery over you, Spirit and flesh; and if the Spirit is not ruling you it is because the flesh is ruling. This is why we give way to pride, Self-conceit, worldliness, the lust of the eyes, the lust of the flesh, and the pride of life. It is nothing but that we are still in the carnal state. You know a thing always gets its name from what is its most prominent characteristic. A spiritual man gets his name from the fact that the Spirit triumphs, rules in his life, even though there may still be somewhat of the flesh. You cannot be in intercourse with him without feeling that the Spirit is leading, guiding and controlling. He is called spiritual because spirituality is his chief characteristic.

Paul writes to the Corinthians, *"Know you not that you are the temple of the Holy Spirit that dwells in you."* There was somewhat of the Spirit in them, but they had allowed the flesh to rule. The question comes to us, as a voice from Heaven, *"Are you not carnal?"* That worldliness, that unfaithfulness, that neglect of God's word. It is but the mark of one thing—you are carnal, you have not given yourself over wholly to live the spiritual life.

Along with this carnal state there may be found a great deal of spiritual gift. This is a very solemn thought. You know how this is illustrated in the case of the Corinthians. In the 1st chapter Paul says, "*I thank God that in everything you are enriched by him in all utterance and in all knowledge.*" There were spiritual gifts among the Corinthians: gifts of prophecy, tongues, and many other gifts most remarkable. … And yet Paul writes the whole epistle with the one idea—that they were full of quarrelling, pride, Selfishness, etc. A man may have a spiritual gift of preaching or be able to speak with power, and yet his private life may be filled with pride until the world says, "we don't believe in that man." Where is his humility? A man may be an evangelist and lead hundreds to Christ and yet you will hear it said, "How full of Self." The world says, "I don't believe in that man he is too full of himself."

Can it be that someone who is powerful in the service of God can be carnal? It can be. That is what we want to make plain. We may claim the baptism of the Holy Spirit and get it as a Spirit of power and a Spirit of zeal, and yet be terribly lacking in the graces of a holy life—in humility, gentleness, tenderness, before God and man, in that meekness of the Lamb of God which is the chief grace of the Christian life. Look at the Corinthians; they had spiritual gifts of prophecy, tongues, etc., yet they were unwilling to be subject one to the other, there was strife as to who should speak first.

Don't think that the carnal state is the state in whom there is no good. We may be a preacher, evangelist, Sabbath school teacher, organizer, and yet, alas, God may say to us, "Are you not carnal?" Does such a person not do as much good in the end? No. They may help another to the Christian life but the Christian life they help them to is such a mixed one that it is feeble and does not stand. Those whose inner life is under the rule of the Spirit, who are spiritual, will beget really spiritual children; they will impart the life of God in power. Being able to exercise spiritual gifts is no necessary proof that we are not carnal. …

Carnal or Spiritual 2

August 21st

"I could not speak to you as unto spiritual, but as to carnal, even as to babes in Christ."
—1 CORINTHIANS 3: 4

And the question comes, how are we to get from the one to the other? Note four of the principal steps.

The first step is that the believer must be convicted, and brought to the confession of his being in the carnal state. You know that before sinners can be converted they must be convicted of sin; we must know and confess our transgressions, and our lost estate. Just so, believers [who want to move from the carnal to the spiritual life] must see that we are in a wrong state; before they can get into the spiritual life we must be brought under conviction of the shame and evil of this carnal state.

There is a great difference between conviction before conversion and this. [After conversion], there were two things that we were not convicted of: first, that our nature is utterly sinful, the other, that there are many hidden heart sins that we have never known. This is the reason God brings a believer into what might be termed a second conviction. … The flesh is ruling us. We have the Spirit of God in us, and why does we yet do these things? It is just the seventh of Romans, "*I am struggling to do right and I cannot.*" Oh friends, it is when we are brought under conviction of the utter impotence of the flesh to do good, its helplessness, that we will understand why we lost our temper, and why pride comes up, and why we speak wrong words. The flesh takes us captive; the law of sin in us binds us hand and foot.

Then comes those great hidden sins that the world counts very little, which are seen to be works of the flesh. The Holy Spirit convicts of pride …, unloving thoughts towards [others], Self-pleasing before God and others; and so we need an entire deliverance, different from that at conversion. Then we were delivered from the *curse* of sin; now we want deliverance from the *power* of sin. Many in the Church of Christ will have to cry, "*Woe is me, O wretched man that I am, in my flesh dwells no good thing.*"…

The second step is that a we must be made to see and believe that the spiritual life is a possibility. A great many people will say in a creed that they believe in the Holy Spirit. They have no doubt about the existence of the Holy Spirit and that He is the Third Person of the Blessed God-Head. They are orthodox on all these points; but, it is an intellectual belief. They practically do not believe in what the Holy Spirit can do in a believer every day of his life. We must be brought to see that there is … a spiritual life we are in need of and may claim; that there is a spiritual life which it is our duty to live.

There is a life in the Spirit. Note such expressions as "*Walk in the Spirit*," "*Live in the Spirit*," "By the Spirit, mortify the deeds of the body." Just take the sixteen verses of the eighth chapter of Romans in which the Holy Spirit is mentioned, and we begin to see that God wants us to be spiritual; He cannot bear to have us carnal. God commands us to be spiritual and by the grace of God, just as certainly as Christ's blood flowed for our sins, so Christ's Spirit can lead us down into the place of absolute helplessness where He will live in us in His Divine power, and renew our whole nature into spiritual.

Oh, take this step before I go further. Reach out at once and begin in a simple act of faith to obey God's call. Say, "O God, a spiritual life is possible, I can become a spiritual man." Let us begin and believe that the God who gave the Holy Spirit delights in nothing more than to give the Holy Spirit in each of us to live this life.

The third step [is this]: … Are you willing to give up everything to get the spiritual life? … A great many delight to read about the spiritual life, but that is not enough. I must buy. At what price? *Give up all. You must sell all* to buy the pearl of great price. Come with every sin and every folly, all temper, everything you love, your whole life, and place it in the possession of Christ. Die to everything and be fully given up to God. It is only in the vessel that is fully cleansed that the Holy Spirit can do His work. …

The fourth and last step is when someone says "I am willing"; then they must come in faith and claim it. … When a person gives up all, they must look up at the Lord Jesus to whom the Father has given the Holy Spirit, claim the promise and believe that they receive it. Bow before God, the Holy One, in deep humility and submission; with faith in His promise. His power. His great love. His near providence. God, who is a spirit and gives the Spirit, will, in the fellowship with Himself, make you a spiritual Christian. …

The Self Life

August 22nd

"Then said Jesus unto His disciples, if any man will come after me, let him deny himself and take up his cross and follow me."

—MATTHEW 16: 24

Many Christians feel that their life is not right. They long to have their life put right, and ask the question, "Is it possible to live as God would have us do?" We desire to come and show them exactly what it is that is wrong, and exactly what it is that God is willing and able to do for them, and then to bring them to take the step by which they pass out of the wrong state into the life that is well pleasing to God. ….

If love be the fruit of the Holy Spirit and I have the Holy Spirit given me in conversion, why is it I do not live such a life of perfect love, and that so few live it? There must be some terrible hindrance. And so there is. The hindrance is just one word, one little word of four letters, "S-E-L-F." The life of God and the life of Christ and the life of the Holy Spirit are all waiting to come into you. But on one condition: you must lose your own life. Give it up and God will give you the new life. But if you allow Self to live in you and have its way even partially, it hinders the work of the Holy Spirit and though you have the Holy Spirit in you as a child of God He cannot do His work in power.

Now I want to tell you how you can get rid of this hindrance. My text is Matthew 16:24: *"Then said Jesus unto His disciples, if any man will come after me, let him deny himself and take up his cross and follow me."* What must we do? We must deny our Self; we must deny Self. We all, by nature, follow Self. Every man does it. It is natural. Christ says we must give up Self, must forever give up listening to Self, and listen to Him alone. Take Him in the place of Self, give up the life of Self and take Him to be your life. ...

There are so many Christians who believe in a thousand wonderful and beautiful things about Christ but they do not believe the chief thing of all, that of taking their cross and being crucified with Jesus. Did not God create that Self in me? Of course He did. Every man and angel has got a Self that comes from God's hands. God gave me a Self-determining power by which I can say what I want to do with myself, and what for? That every day I may come to God and bring myself for him to fill, and find my blessedness in waiting upon Him and receiving of His fullness.

But what a ruin sin has wrought. Listen for a moment while I speak to you of something that was before ever man came on this world. The throne of God was surrounded by bright spirits, all pure and perfect. One of the brightest of these pure spirits began to look at himself and wonder at all the beauty and glory God had given him. He admired himself and pride came into his heart. ... He turned his desire from God to Self....

We know too little what an evil nature we have within. We have an evil nature that exalts itself against God and over our fellowmen. The whole history of the human race is nothing but one great struggle, man against man, each trying to exalt himself higher than the other. One wants more power, another more learning, another more culture, another more pleasure than anyone else around. Alas! Self is the God that rules the world. There is not one exception. Oh, if we were but conscious that we have this evil Self within us how we would cry, "Deliver me from this monster, O, my God."

If there were to come creeping along here a poisonous snake and making straight for someone, how we would jump away and say, "Kill that beast, deliver me from its poison." But alas, we are blind and run into our danger. ... What do we not do to please Self and nourish Self, and we make the devil within us strong. This is the reason why Christ calls us entirely to deny Self. To deny Self means that you must have nothing to do with him. If you did not steal that watch you must deny it, you reject with indignation the charge, the statement, that you stole it. So you must reject Self.

Look in your own life. What are the works of Self? They are chiefly these three. Self-will, Self-trust and Self-exaltation.

First let us look at Self-will. God created me with a will, and there is nothing in man more noble than a will. ...It is the great power with which a man can serve God. ... Self-will rules in the life of every natural man. He says, "I do what I like and I have a right to do what I like." But I find among Christians that there are hundreds, who, if you ask, "Did ever you understand that when you became a Christian it was on the condition that you promise never to seek your own will?" They will all tell you they never understood that. But that is just what Christ demands. You are to do nothing but what God wills. You are to give up your will; Self is to have no say in your life. That is the whole secret of salvation, to give up your will, yourself, to God.

His will is the manifestation of what is in His heart, and if I take my will like an empty cup and say, "Fill my will with Your will," then I live a blessed life. Many say, "I think I am a Christian and I must of course do the will of God in important things, but in the little things I cannot help following my own will." No. Self is the cause of all our sin against God, and all our wretchedness.

Self-pleasing is another of the works of Self. The whole life of man and nature has the pleasing of Self as its moving principle. And even Christians seek far more to please themselves than to please God. No wonder that Self becomes strong and that for its sake we sin unceasingly against the law of love to God and man.

Another work of Self is Self-confidence. … A young person often says, "Six months ago I gave myself to the Lord and I had such a bright and happy time serving Jesus, but some way or other I got cold and went back and what is the reason?" My answer always is, "Only one thing, you trusted yourself." … You trusted in your earnestness, in your integrity or something in yourself, and then came all the trouble." …

The third form of Self is Self-exaltation, pride. Jesus said, *"How can you believe, who take honor one from another."* I am not speaking now of the people of the world. All the wretched history of the world is owing to pride. But I am speaking about Christians. How much of touchiness there is about our position. If a man does not give me the honor I think I ought to have; if he puts me down to a lower place than I expect, how sensitive I am. How much envy and jealousy there is. Where does this come from? Self-exaltation. …

How can Self be conquered? Christ tells us: *"Let a man deny himself and take up his cross and follow me."* … You can come and quietly condemn it at the feet of Jesus as an accursed thing. You can cast it down there and say, "Son of God, I follow You with my whole heart to the very uttermost. I desire to follow You to the very depths of death. I desire to give myself up utterly and wholly to You. I desire to take You and let You fill my whole being." Believer, Christ can do it.

Seven Blessings 1

August 23rd

"As many as are led by the Spirit of God they are the sons of God."

—ROMANS 8: 14

We learned from God's Word to the Corinthians that there are two classes of Christians. Paul speaks of some who are carnal and of others who are spiritual. I tried to point out what the life of the carnal Christian is, what a wrong and wretched state it is; and on the other hand what the steps are by which we can get out of the carnal state into the spiritual. Among these steps I mentioned first of all that we must be fully convicted of the wrongness of the carnal state, and of the possibilities and blessedness of the spiritual state. I want to speak of the latter and to set before you what God's Word teaches of a life in the Spirit.

You know when the Children of Israel got to Kadesh-Barnea they sent out spies to see what the land was like. God expected that when they saw the grapes and heard of the beauty of that land they would all enter in; so [this is how] God wants us to look at the spiritual life… to believe that it is indeed to be divided and within our reach. I want, by God's help, just to set before you what the life is in the fullness of the Spirit, as God expects His children to live it day by day. I want to take you to a chapter in God's Word where it is set before us more plainly than in any other chapter: Romans, the eighth chapter. Let us read the first sixteen verses. You will find in these seven blessings—seven of the blessed fruits of the Spirit in us. I shall point them out as we read.

1. "*Who walk not after the flesh but after the Spirit.*" The whole of our conduct is under the rule of the Spirit.

2. "*For the law of the Spirit of life in Christ Jesus has made me free from the law of sin and death.*" The Spirit brings us into liberties.

3. "*They that are after the Spirit … you are in the Spirit … the Spirit dwells in you.*" The Christian has a new nature; God's Spirit is in us.

4. "*Do mind the things of the Spirit.*" To be spiritually minded is life and peace. Mind means disposition; to mind the things of the Spirit, to have a spiritual disposition.

5. "*If you through the Spirit do mortify the deeds of the body, you shall live.*" The Spirit makes the death to sin an actual reality in our body.

6. "*As many as are led by the Spirit of God they are the sons of God.*" Divine guidance.

7. "*You have not received the spirit of bondage again to fear, but you have received the Spirit of adoption.*" The Spirit bears witness with our spirit.

What I want to put before you is this—that all we have in this chapter is simply the description of the *normal* Christian life. This is a life for *every* believer. We are sometimes in danger of talking about the baptism of the Spirit, of being filled with the Spirit for service, as though that were all, but it is possible, as I pointed out, to have a baptism of the Holy Spirit for special service and yet be carnal. …

Let me point you to seven principal thoughts in the passage.

1. The Christian is someone who walks after the Spirit. In Galatians it is said, "*If we live in the Spirit let us also walk in the Spirit.*" "*Walk in the Spirit and you shall not fulfill the lusts of the flesh.*" My walk is my conduct, what the Bible calls my conversation, my course of life, my external manner of life. Here I am told as a Christian, God will enable me to walk after the Spirit, with the Spirit as my inspiration. Unconverted men walk after the flesh; the flesh leads them and tells them what to do. The Christian can come into the life of the Spirit; in it we act, in it we walk, we have the continual hidden guidance of the Spirit of God molding and shaping our will and walk. … I need the Spirit so that when I sit down

at my table, when my temper might be tempted to rise; in my business, in trials of any kind I may feel the power of the Holy Spirit working in me, and moving me. All my walk is to be according to the Spirit. How can I get to that?

2. Paul says in the second verse, *"For the law of the Spirit of life in Christ Jesus has made me free from the law of sin and death."* In the seventh chapter he speaks of a believer, a regenerated man, who delights in the law of God after the inward man but who finds another law in his members that leads him into captivity to the law of sin and death. I am a prisoner, I am a captive, I want to do good but I cannot. … Why? Because he is bound with the chains of the flesh, in captivity to the law of sin and death in his members. But the Spirit sets a man free out of this captivity. *"The law of the Spirit of life has made me free from the law of sin and death."*

Let us believe there are two powers—the power of the Spirit and the power of sin. Which is stronger? Many Christians tell me the power of the flesh is stronger. It is very sad that so many think thus. Paul tells me, God tells me, that the power of the Holy Spirit is stronger and that the power of the Holy Spirit can make me free from the law of sin and death if I trust Him. It is not here a question of the last root of sin being exterminated. We believe the tendency to evil remains to the end, but, we believe this word, too, is literal truth, that the Spirit of life in Christ makes me free from the law of sin to such extent that it has no power over me. My enemy is there, but he cannot touch me. After the close of your civil war those who had been slaves could dwell in the presence of their former masters; the masters were not dead and yet they could not touch them. Just so the Holy Spirit can take possession, and in presence of the power of sin the Holy Spirit can fill the believer and make sin powerless. …

If you believed it, if you trusted God's word for it; you would begin to long for the fullness of the Holy Spirit and you would understand that nothing less than this being made free by the Holy Spirit dwelling in His fullness in you can enable you to live an inwardly holy life.

3. *"You are not in the flesh but in the Spirit if the Spirit of God dwells in you." "Of the Spirit," "After the Spirit," "In the Spirit," "The Spirit of God in you."* All these expressions are used [in this chapter of Romans 8] to express the one thought of the closeness and the reality of the blessed union by which the Holy Spirit takes possession of me. I am in Him and He is in me just as a man is in the air and the air is in him. The air is in my lungs and I am in the air that surrounds me. The two things go together; I go into the fresh air and the fresh air comes into me. Even so the child of God is taken out of the life of the flesh and taken into the life of the Spirit. The Spirit surrounds us on every side with a Divine power that is breathed into us and that constitutes our life. … We are after the Spirit and the very nature, the Divine nature of the Spirit is in us.

Have you ever thought about it, how wonderful the Spirit of God becomes the very spirit of our life? Many people think of the Holy Spirit dwelling in us as a man dwells in a house, the man and the house remain separate existences all the time. There is no organic union, no participation of life or nature between the two. That is not the way with the Holy Spirit. He comes into my very being and just as my thinking and willing and feeling is my very nature, so by the Holy Spirit, I become partaker of the Divine nature; He enters deep, deep, into me and pervades my whole inner life.

Seven Blessings 2

August 24th

"If you through the Spirit do mortify the deeds of the body you shall live."

—ROMANS 8: 13

The Spirit of God is in me and I am in the Spirit of God. Ought that not to fill us with a holy fear and a holy joy? fear lest we should remain ignorant of the truth; joy in the expectation of all we will do. The Spirit who came out from the Father and the Son brings and reveals them to me. And the three persons in the one God-Head through Him come into my heart and so I live in the Spirit. Oh believers who do not think it possible to live this blessed life. I will tell you the simple reason. Because you do not believe God, do not believe that Almighty God will dwell in you. Will you not begin and say, if it be true I may be in the Spirit just as I am in the air, thank God, I think I can lead a holy and blessed life.

4. "*They that are after the Spirit do mind the things of the Spirit.*" What does that word "mind" mean? Generally, it is used of the intellect, but here it means something else. You know when I speak of a high-minded man, by mind I mean disposition. A large-hearted man is one of a large-hearted disposition. To be a spiritual minded man is to have the disposition of the Holy Spirit; heavenly minded is a mind that has the spirit and disposition of Heaven. To be spiritually minded is life and peace. The Holy Spirit is ready to breathe within me the very mind and disposition of Christ; that is what Paul meant in writing to the Philippians, "*Let this mind be in you that was in Christ Jesus,*" etc. If the Holy Spirit comes in and takes possession of my disposition, I shall have the mind of Christ.

God's word says, *"Love your neighbor as yourself";* you have tried hard but failed because it is not natural. But it is no difficulty to a mother to be gentle and loving because it is her natural disposition to be so. Just so the Holy Spirit will make my disposition spiritual minded. He lives within me, and breathes into me everything that is gentle and Christ-like and humble. He puts it so into me that it becomes my very nature. I can love him whom I hated. The love of God is indeed a wonderful mystery; when it becomes ours the more unlovable a man is the more we love him, the more unworthy a man is the more love is magnified in loving him. …

The Spirit of God must come and fill you. You may have had Him in some measure but He must fill you deeper and deeper. He must fill you with the disposition of Jesus so that you become spiritually minded. Christians! Would you not long to have such a disposition that everything about you might be spiritual. The Spirit who dwells in you can and will give if you yield to Him.

5. *"If you through the Spirit do mortify the deeds of the body you shall live."* The word "mortify"

simply means to die. "*If you make dead the deeds of the body you shall live.*" The one who has not given the body over to the Spirit to do His work, what a trouble the body gives that person. How much sin comes out of the body! Many Christians never understand that it is the deeds of the body that must be made dead. But it is very hard, and in fact impossible, until we begin to see that it is through the Holy Spirit who is the mighty power of God. It is a very simple thing eating and drinking a little too much. And is that such a great sin? Ask the Bible. "*Whether you eat or drink do all to the glory of God.*" … When you think you are only feeding the body you are feeding the flesh, you are strengthening it by gratifying its appetite. That cannot please God.

If you want to have the deeds of the body mortified, beware of the lust of the flesh and the lust of the eyes. Ah, Christians, remember if you want to have your body the temple of the Holy Spirit, if you want to live a holy life, you must be filled with the Spirit; your body, too, must be under the power. You might know the mysteries of the heavens, like the apostle Paul, but this could give you no help to live a holy life. God's word has no help for you except as it tells you that you must be filled with the Spirit.

6. "*As many as are led by the Spirit of God they are the sons of God.*" … Dear Christians, would you not be willing to sacrifice everything for that, that you might be led by the Spirit? You know God cannot abate His requirements. I must give up having any will of my own, I must desire above everything to lead a holy life like Jesus, in dependent, humble, waiting upon God. You say that is hard. It is not hard. It is the most blessed life. It is exactly the life that Jesus lived. Is it not a privilege to have the blessed God lead and guide me all along, in everything? He has promised to do that.

Oh, beloved let us realize what this life is. If you speak about the baptism of the Holy Spirit, for service—and I want you to speak about it. I want you to be filled with the Holy Spirit for your work—remember there is something of far deeper importance. It is that your whole life, from moment to moment, bear the mark of being led by the Spirit, of being spiritually minded. The Spirit of Jesus makes you like Jesus.

7. "*You have not received the spirit of bondage again to fear, but you have received the spirit of adoption whereby we cry Abba, Father.*" "*The Spirit dwells with our spirit.*" … "Abba, Father," I do not have to try and feel, or claim, or struggle for the relationship, but the Everlasting God reveals Himself to me as a Father. So the Living Father makes us to know what it means to be dwelling in love and dwelling in God, and what all the promises about the Holy Spirit mean, "The Father shall send the Comforter that He may abide with you forever."

Beloved Christians there is a wonderful life, which the Holy Spirit makes intensely true. It is a real Canaan life. It is indeed a solemn, precious thought. God's Holy Spirit can make all God's promises and provisions in Christ our experience. Who are ready to come into this life today, and claim the heritage as the child of God? Who will cry: I am going to ask that Romans 8:1–16 shall be literally fulfilled in my life. Let me suggest four simple steps. Say today!:

1. I must be filled with the Spirit. God commands it. My soul needs it. The Spirit longs for it. Christ will do it. The world needs it. I cannot live aright without it. I must be

filled with the Spirit.

2. I may be filled with the Spirit. God does not give a "must" without a "may." God does not say, you must live holy, without saying you may, you can live holy. Say, "I may." God has promised it; Christ has purchased it; the Word reveals it; thousands have experienced it. I may be filled with the Spirit.

3. I would be filled with the Spirit. Say, Lord, my heart longs for it. Begin to say, I give up everything O, God: Self, sin, Self-will, Self-confidence, the flesh; I give up everything. I would be filled with the Holy Spirit. Lord God, set Your mark upon me; I am an empty vessel waiting to be filled. I would be filled with the Holy Spirit. I am ready.

4. I shall be filled with the Holy Spirit. God has promised it to me. I have a right to say, I shall be filled with the Spirit. Say that tremblingly and very, very humbly. I confess I am carnal, I have felt my sinfulness, I confess my sin. My heart is willing for it; I am going to trust God for it. …

Be Filled with the Spirit 1

August 25th

"Be filled with the Spirit."

— EPHESIANS 5: 18

You will find the words of my text in the Acts of the Apostles, second chapter, fourth verse: *"And they were all filled with the Holy Spirit."* Along with that look at Ephesians 5:18: *"Be filled with the Spirit."* The first of these words is history; the 120 disciples were filled with the Holy Spirit. The second is a command— *"Be filled with the Holy Spirit."*

There are often very difficult questions suggested in connection with the question, "How can we be filled with the Spirit?" I do not think there is any better way to answer these than by looking at the disciples and seeing how they were prepared for receiving the Spirit and being filled with Him.… Christ does not give the Spirit to an unprepared soul. He could not.…

They were men who had forsaken all for Christ. It was three years before this time that Christ had taken them into His school of preparation for Pentecost. … What was their condition on entering the baptism class? They had given up all for Christ. They had to give up their fishing nets; Matthew had to leave the receipt of the custom; they had to forsake all. Christ often repeated the truth, *"Except a man hate father and mother, except a man forsake houses and lands, he is not worthy of Me."* On one occasion Peter said, "Lord, we have forsaken all and followed You." My dear friends, it was this that was the first step in their preparation for the Baptism of the Spirit at Pentecost. Christ could not impart His own heavenly life and Spirit except to men who gave up all to receive Him. … Jesus Christ comes to us with the same demand *"Except a man forsake all he cannot be My disciple."* …

I must let go the world; I must let go family and friends so far as the supreme place in my heart is concerned; I must be prepared to let go possessions, honor of men and opinions of men; I must be prepared to let go everything I have; I must be prepared to let go Self, my intellect, my heart's affections, everything must be sacrificed and made subordinate to this wonderful blessing—the Holy Spirit to come and dwell in me.

The Holy Spirit is not something I can merely own or have at my disposal, but in Him Christ is a Divine Master, coming to take charge of me, and He wants every breath of my life, every word of my tongue; He wants the whole of the Self-life deposed to make room for His life. Christ comes and tells me that the most important, the only thing on earth worth living for is to *"be filled with the Spirit."* ...

But if there is anything in which your heart condemns you, beware! If your secret conviction is, I have not forsaken all, there are little sins I have never given up, there is my temper, my own will, which I dare not forsake, then, I ask you, how can you expect to be filled with the Spirit? It cannot be. Oh, come tonight! do not hesitate any longer! There is the Everlasting God in Heaven waiting to fill you with His holy, blessed, Divine Spirit. And, will you, for the sake of something in the world, or for the sake of the flesh and its pleasure, or for the sake of your own will, hold back and say, "No, I cannot be filled with the Spirit, I must give up too much?" I wish I could plead with you to come. Come! For God's sake let us all say, "I forsake all to follow Jesus. I long to be filled with the Holy Spirit; I want the heavenly life to live in me fully every moment. I want to pray that I may have this "*pearl of great price*." The first condition of receiving the Holy Spirit, then, was that these men had forsaken all.

And the second condition [for being filled with the Holy Spirit]: They had been brought to utter Self-despair. It was at the very beginning of Christ's teaching that He taught them to forsake their boats and fishing nets; but later on they found they had a very difficult lesson to learn—to forsake Self. We had that in the words to Peter, last night, "Let a man deny himself." They did not know how terrible the power of Self within them was. ...

The Holy Spirit must come to take the place of Self-life; so consuming it that a man can say, "The life that I now live in the flesh, I live by the faith of the Son of God." It is only out of the grave of Self that the Spirit life can rise. ...

Be Filled with the Spirit 2

August 26th

"Be filled with the Spirit."

— EPHESIANS 5: 18

Perhaps many of you have asked and received what you thought was a baptism of the Holy Spirit, but you did not know the dangers. You have said, "Well, that is a wonderful thing I have got, a wonderful blessing; God has done a great thing in me"; and there was a secret Self-satisfaction, and a great want of humility, and a great want of utter nothingness before God. Come and say, I want to be forever done with Self; I will deny Self; I have asked God to cast it out, and that my heart may be empty and broken.

That is the second step to be filled with the Holy Spirit. Get down, lower down! Do not be in a hurry to get up. My brother, get lower down, and become nothing, and let Self be cast into the depths. The lowly, truly humble, Self-despairing one is prepared for the baptism of the Spirit.

Your Father longs to have, as children, a church of believers filled with the Holy Spirit, and He has got the residue of the Spirit in great abundance. He has purposed to give it to you as He gives the water and air, freely and abundantly. The river of the water of life is flowing full from the throne of God. He wants you to say, I long to have my whole being saturated, fully dominated, ruled, possessed by the Holy Spirit of God. Brother, if you have despaired of yourself, thank God that it is so! If you have not, are you willing here to cast Self at the feet of Jesus, and to fall in utter helplessness and say, "Lord, I cannot conquer Self; I have been fighting but I have failed; have mercy upon me! Let it henceforth be. None of Self but all You?" …

Here is our third step in the preparation for the baptism of the Holy Spirit. It is when the heart of a believer clings to Jesus with an intense and continual love. There are some Christians in whom there is very little personal attachment to the Lord Jesus. A man may preach sermons about Christ, talk about Him, work for Him, and give liberally, but this is not what I am speaking about. What was the charge of Christ against the Church at Ephesus? "You have left your first love." There was no personal tender love to Jesus. There are some people who talk about being filled with the Spirit, and pray for it, but I am afraid they will not get it. They do not know what it is to be clinging to Jesus as a personal friend.

… You can get it [this infilling of the Holy Spirit] tonight if you see your sin and shame, and confess the want of this personal, clinging love, and say, Lord, let my love now be a tender, intimate fellowship; I want my whole being to be filled with the love of God. Say it in humility and say it in faith. He accepts that, when the soul has pledged itself to begin loving Him wholly. He will accept it, and will send down His Holy Spirit upon you. Sister, brother, are you ready? Jesus wants to fill us with His Holy Spirit. …

Oh, take care! Don't let unbelief tell you that this is too high for a man on earth, that a man in the flesh cannot live filled with the Spirit. That is unbelief. Beloved children of God, take care of unbelief, and come now to-night and say, "I do believe what Jesus says: that the Father delights to fill a child of His with the Holy Spirit. I do believe that the life of the Holy Spirit is meant to be lived by me every day in the week and every moment of my life. I do believe what the Scriptures say, that "the Holy Spirit is able to fill me with God's love, so that my life shall be one of humility and tenderness, giving glory to God and the Lord Jesus." … If you believe there is a God in Heaven, and there is a blessing waiting, and God is willing to give it, will you say that? …

Would you be ready to say, "God, fill me with the Holy Spirit; I am ready"? … What is it? It is to have my whole being placed at His disposal, and then in faith to receive the gift of God, the Holy Spirit taking possession of me as an empty vessel to separate myself….

Some people think it must come as a great emotion, stirring their whole being. It does not always come that way. It may come as the night dew on the grass, quiet and gentle. They think people must talk and shout. No! …

You know, a river can be filled in two ways. In South Africa we have terrible valleys, which might be called dry rivers, and then high up the course of the river there come immense thunder storms and the water comes pouring down with such a rush that it causes the stream in these lower reaches to rise eight or ten feet high at once, and it keeps on rising until it overflows its banks. … But sometimes rivers get full in quite a different way. There are great snow mountains, and the snow melts gently, and the water flows and fills the river. There is very little commotion. The stream rises slowly, and gradually the river gets full, until its banks overflow. How different from the former!

… Oh, are you ready for it? Remember, the Holy Spirit is the heritage of God's church. It is not meant for something extraordinary. Each of us may say. The fullness of the Holy Spirit is mine. It is mine for my daily life, to enable me to live a holy life every day. Are you ready?

The Fruit of the Spirit is Love

August 27th

"The fruit of the Spirit is love…"

—GALATIANS 5: 22

I tried to put before you what a life filled with the Holy Spirit may be, but more from the doctrinal side. These expressions were found in Romans, 8th chapter: *"Walk in the Spirit," "Being made free by the Spirit from the law of sin and death." "Being in the Spirit," "Having the Spirit dwelling in us," "Through the Spirit mortifying the deeds of the body," "Being led by the Spirit," "Having the Spirit of adoption."* …

Under the Old Testament you know the Holy Spirit often came upon men as a Divine Spirit of revelation, to reveal the mysteries of God, or for power to do the work of God. *But he did not then dwell in them.* Now, as I said, many just want the Old Testament gift of power for work, but know very little of the New Testament gift of the indwelling Spirit, animating and renewing the whole life. We saw last night that when God gives the Holy Spirit His great object is the formation of holy character. We saw that it was a gift of a holy mind and spiritual disposition, and that we need above everything else to say, "I must have the Holy Spirit sanctifying my whole inner life if I am really to live for God's glory."

… I wish to speak upon the passage found in Galatians 5: 22: *"The fruit of the Spirit is love."* We read that *"Love is the fulfilling of the whole law,"* and my desire is to speak to you this morning on love as a fruit of the Spirit with a two-fold object. One is that this word may be a searchlight in our hearts and give us a test by which to try all our thoughts about the Holy Spirit and all our experience of the holy life. Let us try ourselves by this word. Has this been your daily habit, to seek the being filled with the Holy Spirit as the Spirit of love?

"The fruit of the Spirit is love." Has it been your experience that the more you have of the Holy Spirit the more loving you become? In claiming the Holy Spirit, you should make this the first object of your expectation, the Holy Spirit comes as a Spirit of love. Oh, if this were true in the Church of Christ how different her state would be. May God help us this morning to just get hold of this simple heavenly truth, that the fruit of the Spirit is a love which appears in the life, and that just as the Holy Spirit gets real possession of the life, the heart will be filled with real, Divine, universal love.

To understand this fully let us remember that God from whom the Spirit comes is love. Love is not a mere attribute of God, but God is love, and because this Holy Spirit comes as the Spirit of God, He comes as the Spirit of love. What does it mean that God is love? You have in the 13th chapter of 1 Corinthians the most perfect definition of love. *"Love seeks not its own."* It goes out of itself and lives in its object, etc. Love longs to commend itself to and bless the object of its love. Therefore, it was an absolute necessity in the idea of a perfect God that He should have a Son to whom He could communicate Himself. We cannot conceive of God, who is love, alone, He must have a Son to whom He can communicate Himself and with whom we can have fellowship.

So God is love. And in the everlasting intercourse of the Trinity the Spirit is the bond of fellowship between the Father and Son. The Holy Spirit is the overflowing and interchange of the love between Father and Son. He is the very life of Deity; if that Spirit comes to us He comes in no other way than as the Spirit of love. ...

God is love. God created angels and men that they might enjoy fellowship with Him—His love permeating and filling their whole being. When man had fallen, when sin had darkened this love of God in man, what did He do? He gave His own Son to the death to restore it. To that fallen world God gave His Son in a new way, in the flesh to prove to man the power of His love. And with His Son He gave His life. His joy. His glory, His holiness, His power. His blessedness; in Christ He gives it all. God is love, ever delighting to give and communicate Himself.

Love is the essential nature of God; with the Holy Spirit coming from this God, must we not expect that He will fill us with love?

Sin has robbed us of love. You know that God created man, male and female, that they might live a life of love even as God lives in love, and they might be happy in love. ... The worst thing sin ever did was, it made men Selfish and Selfishness cannot love. Selfishness can do something that is called love; it can lead me to love someone who pleases me or makes me happier, but that is not real love. The true unselfish love, that loves the unworthy or unlovable, sin destroyed.

To bring this love back to us Jesus came. He came as the manifestation of Divine love. ... In the 17th chapter [of John] He prayed, *"That they may be one as we are one, that the world may know You have loved me and have sent me and have loved them as You have loved me."* The world is to know the love of God through Christ by our love to one another. So we are taught that the great mark of the believer is that he is to be a man of love. Dear friends, how little the world understands that; how little the Church understands that; how little it is preached, or proved in practice, that love [the kind of love that Jesus exemplified] is actually the chief thing for every believer to set his heart upon. …

The Lord Jesus came to bring love back to the world. He did so when He died on Calvary, it was the triumph and the revelation of love. And now He calls us to dwell and to walk in love. He demands that though a man hate you still you love him. …

John in his epistle says that Christ laid down His life for us, therefore we ought to lay down our life for the brethren. How little we understand that. Look at the disciples. How often there were dissensions among them; more than once they disputed as to who should be chief in the kingdom; there was pride because of their want of love. Love is humility. Love says, I only exist to be a blessing to others. Love cannot be Selfish; it loves as Jesus loved. The disciples whom Christ had chosen had to be taught many things, but one chief object was to let us see what human nature is and how incapable it is of the higher life, of love like Christ's, until the Holy Spirit comes. …

If we wait upon the Holy Spirit and yield ourselves to Him He will fill us with the love of God. Look at this as we have it here in our text. It is in our daily life and conduct that the fruit of the Spirit is love; from that there comes all the graces and virtues in which love is manifested: joy, peace, longsuffering, gentleness, goodness; no sharpness or hardness in your tone, no unkindness or Selfishness; meekness before God and man. You see that all these are the gentler virtues. I have often thought as I read those words in Colossians, "*Put on therefore as the elect of God, holy and beloved, bowels of mercies, kindness, humbleness of mind, meekness, longsuffering,*" that if we had written this, we should have put in the foreground the manly virtues, zeal, courage and diligence; but we need to see how the gentler, the most womanly, virtues are specially connected with dependence upon the Holy Spirit.

These are indeed heavenly graces. They never were found in the heathen world. Christ was needed to come from Heaven to teach us. Your blessedness is longsuffering, meekness, kindness; your glory is humility before God. The fruit of the Spirit, that He brought from Heaven, out of the heart of the crucified Christ and that He gives in our heart, is first and foremost, love.

Don't you see that if this is really true, our great desire in asking to be filled with the Holy Spirit, our great study now that we are talking about, the filling of the Spirit, and how to be filled with power by the Spirit, our great aim and study must be to get hold of this thought, if we are to have the Holy Spirit we must give up ourselves, give up Self to live the life of love. How sadly has this been wanting?

Our doctrines, our creeds hare been more important than love. In these later times, even the baptism of the Holy Spirit is a cause of separation. Let us learn not to expect that everyone should think the same or express themselves in the same way; let our first care be to exercise love, gentleness, kindness. … Because of differences of temperament or opinion, estrangements and jealousies come in and love waxes cold.

What a sad thing in the Church that earnest Christians who have given up all for Christ have never learned the mystery of love. Is it any different at home? Is there not often, in the circles where we meet together, in church councils, and committees, in missions and associations, a want of that love among fellow workers, which is the true mark of the presence of the Holy Spirit? Is there not often harsh judgment, evil-speaking, etc., all because the love of Christ has not been allowed to take complete possession? Is there not often even in the family the outburst of temper and haste? Alas! we have not learned to love, have not even learned to count love the chief fruit of the Spirit.

We must learn to take this word as the true test of life in the Spirit. All our desire to be filled with the Spirit must center here, to have Self sunk down in willingness and humility, and to have the love of God and Jesus become the life of our life. I want to lead you to the life in which love is supreme, in which love shall bow you down in such deep humility that go where you will and let man do what they will, you shall say, by the help of God I must love. …

Let us think of the Church and Christians around us. When you have looked around well then look at yourself and say, "Oh God, I ask You so often to fill Your church with the Holy Spirit. Have I been filled with the Spirit of love?" You know what John says… "*If we love one another, God dwells in us.*" That is, I cannot see God, but as a compensation I can see my brother and if I love him God dwells in me. … Loving my brother is the way to real fellowship with God. … You must prove your love to God by your love to your brother; that is the one standard God will judge your love to Him by. If the love of God is in your heart you will love your brother.

The fruit of the Spirit is love. … Nothing can enable you to live such a life of love but the fullness of the Holy Spirit. The two texts are inseparably connected—*"Be filled with the Spirit," "The fruit of the Spirit is love."* …

You must come with the humble confession of how little you have loved, or even desired to be full of love. You have sought for the power of the Holy Spirit in your work in pride and Selfishness you have not given up yourself to Him to be filled, first of all, with love, with gentleness and humility and meekness. Oh! Come and make confession, and let Christ cleanse you from the Selfishness and pride and unlovingness. Seek to be filled with the Spirit for a daily life of humility and love, and the power of the Spirit for service will come.

Brother, do you want to be filled with the Spirit of God? Is it true? Do you really want to be filled with love that you may be the humblest, gentlest of men, so that everyone may know that you are a disciple by the love you have? Brethren, if we love one another God dwells in us and we in God, and then we can be perfected in love. …

Let us even now absolutely and entirely give ourselves to be just vessels filled with the love of God. Let us even now say to God that we accept the lesson, that the Spirit comes to fill us with the love of Heaven, with a love that makes loving others the one joy of our life; that we yield ourselves to it, and that by His grace we will make this our one object and desire. May God write it in our hearts. The Holy Spirit's fruit and chief work is to give Christ and the love of God in us for our everyday life. By His grace we can live lives of unceasing love.

Praying in the Power of the Holy Spirit

August 28th

"Praying always with all prayer and supplication in the Spirit, and watching thereunto with all perseverance and supplication for all saints...."

—EPHESIANS 6: 18

You need before everything in prayer a deep consciousness of your ignorance. What a wonderful blessing if I come into this ignorance. The Holy Spirit will be my helper in prayer. This blessed ignorance is one of the most remarkable elements of faith. Abraham went out not knowing whither he went. It was a beautiful ignorance, it taught him to trust God. ... Oh, listen, the Holy Spirit cannot teach you until all your Self-conceit and Self-confidence is taken away and you get broken down into a nothingness that says, "Lord, I know nothing." Thus will you learn to be quiet before God, and in your ignorance to wait on God to teach you.

What a blessed thought that the Holy Spirit is given to help our infirmities, and that He prays in us. What a blessed thought! You are believers in the Holy Trinity—Father, Son and Holy Spirit. The Father—He sits upon the throne as God. The Son sits on His right hand as Mediator and Intercessor—He lives ever to pray. Think of that. The Son in His glory has got no other work but praying; His whole being. His presence before God as the Lamb that was slain, is one unceasing prayer, and we read that that is the reason He can save completely, because *"He ever lives to pray."* He is the King in glory, but His highest work is prayer, and continually there goes up to the Father from Him a stream of intercession: Father, bless Your children, bless My people on earth. And unceasingly there comes from the Father in answer a stream of blessing. And unceasingly from the Son there streams out the flow of the Holy Spirit to bring the blessing to us. And the Spirit is in the heart of the believer to teach what this blessing is that Christ has for them; to teach them all that is prepared for them.

But when we are Self-satisfied, and imagine that we know how to pray, then we cannot wait for the Holy Spirit to teach us and we lose all the wonderful gifts He could reveal to us. Just think what it means. The Father on the throne to give; the Son at His right hand to bless, and down in your heart and mine the Holy Spirit, the third Person of the Blessed Trinity, proceeding from the Father. It is God giving, Christ praying, and the Holy Spirit receiving and imparting; teaching you to pray in perfect harmony with God and Christ. ...

When you pray so glibly and easily it is very much human feeling and human words, and the power of the Holy Spirit is not there. ... To this Holy Spirit, if He is to be my helper, I must give way, I must stand aside. ... If you are to get the help of the Spirit let me give you one lesson, and let me urge this upon you: When you are in your closet to pray alone you should always take plenty of silent time before your prayers and in between your prayers.

It is a solemn thing to think that I am going to exercise power on Heaven and bring down here heavenly blessings upon myself and others, and I ought to be very quiet before God. Think of God, the Three-One God, as engaged in your prayer. Let us always spend a few minutes, at least, in worship, until our faith realizes. "Here is the Almighty God, waiting to bless me; He is longing to fill me with His Holy Spirit." This faith will not come unless we take time to think about it: "The Everlasting God is waiting to bless me. Let me believe God will bless." Just be quiet and sink down into nothingness and let the Holy Spirit pray in you. The Holy Spirit will do it. The Father has given you His Spirit on purpose to do it. He will pray in you. Again when you have prayed, be quiet a little and just sit still until your heart gets fully into the faith that the Holy Spirit is doing His work in you just now. …

When you have no inclination to pray, when your heart is very cold, just go to Jesus and say, You have appointed prayer as the means to come to You, and my heart is cold. Your heart is full of love, here I come in my feebleness. If you will abide in His presence He will meet you, and the Spirit will teach you to trust and to pray. *"The Holy Spirit is given to help our infirmities."*

We must take care of making a mistake. Some think that when the Holy Spirit comes and teaches them to pray there will be a great, burning rush of feeling and they will pray such beautiful prayers. Feeling may indeed stir and help us, but many times it is superficial. Let me read the words of the text again, *"But the Spirit makes intercession for us with groanings that cannot be uttered!"* … He goes deeper than our thoughts and minds into the heart and He prays there with groanings, with longings that cannot be expressed in words. He gives us a deep, an inexpressible yearning, a deep thirst for God and for God's glory.

The Spirit makes intercession in us for all saints. It is your highest privilege as priests of God to be intercessors. Oh, the value of the intercession! When I pray for other people who may be at a distance, or when we gather in a small prayer meeting, I sometimes say, what utter folly this would be if God's word did not teach it. Here are 50 people praying for something in China, or Africa, or England, and these so feeble ones believe that they can actually stir the Almighty Everlasting God to action by their prayers, and that in answer to their prayers He would do something that He would not have done if they had not prayed. …

Children of God! yield yourselves up to the Holy Spirit as the Spirit of intercession; study your work of intercession. If all believers were only to give an hour a day for interceding for the Church of God! Oh, pray for the Church of God. If you would have your eyes opened, think of the state of Christendom. Take London with its five million, only one million of these go to church, four million who practically are not Christians. Think of Chicago with one million and a half and you have only 200,000 people going to church. Just imagine.

Think of those who do go to church. Out of these how many go through mere formality; how many who are living in sin; how many who are not converted, and how many who are worldly. Think that this is not only true of London and Chicago, but of all the world. Upon you and me God has left the responsibility of praying and taking hold of Him. He has told us not to let Him go and has given us wonderful promises. Take time to pray.

If we will give up ourselves to intercession God will bless. I would like to ask everyone here, "Do you pray for the Church of Christ in the United States?" You talk about its worldliness, so much higher criticism and error, you talk about these, but, do you go to God and cry, Lord, visit Your church? Oh, do cry to Him, Lord strengthen all Your people who are trying to live true to You. It is one Spirit and one body and if you will give way to the Holy Spirit He will teach you to pray for the church. Paul says to the Ephesians, *"Praying always with all prayer and supplication in the Spirit, and watching thereunto with all perseverance and supplication for all saints...."* The Holy Spirit is not a Selfish Spirit. The fruit of the Spirit is love and it is one Spirit and one body.

May God make you young men and women, may God make all us, men and women of intercession, filled with the power of the Holy Spirit, for this our highest and holiest work, to intercede for all saints.

If your inmost being is humbly and patiently made subject to Him, He can take and make you, not a prayer machine, but a vessel in which He lives and in which He works His prayers down into your desires and will, so that you pray in the Spirit and the Spirit prays in you. May all us learn the blessed privilege of intercession in the power of the Holy Spirit. May all us know the joy of having God search our hearts and answering us abundantly according to what He finds there of the need of the Spirit. May all us know what it is to cry to God with unutterable and unceasing longings "for all saints," that He might indeed visit and revive His people.

The Holy Spirit in Galatians 1

August 29th

"That we might receive the promise of the Spirit, through faith."
—GALATIANS 3: 14

You know that the Galatians had been converted under the preaching of Paul. There had been very blessed times and the Holy Spirit had been among them in great power, and yet, strange to say, they had very shortly afterwards gone back. They had been led away by Jewish teachers and had fallen away from the simple life of faith. Paul writes the Epistle to reprove and instruct them. From what I have said you will see the state of the Church was very low. The works of the flesh were very manifest. There was a great deal of bitterness, jealousy and clamor; consequently, the teaching of the Epistle is one of warning.

I wish to point out specially, how, in connection with the mention of the Holy Spirit there are certain dangers against which we need to be warned. There are many people who think that when someone is filled with the Spirit, they are in a state of perfection. They will very soon find out that they are wrong. I want to impress this very much upon you, that when someone gets the fullness of the Spirit, the life of the Spirit, it is a thing that makes them very gentle, very humble, very much afraid of sinning against God and very tender lest they should be led to walk astray. They have a spirit of deep, deep humility and fear of pride.

Let us find out what God's word tells us and warns us to beware of.

1st Warning. The first mention of the Spirit is Galatians 3: 2. *"This only would I learn of you: Did you receive the Spirit by the works of the law, or by the hearing of faith?"* There we see plainly that there are two ways in which men often think they can get the Holy Spirit. One is by the works of the law. That is the religion of human nature. We think we must work. We have been doing wrong, of course we must do right; we have been sinning, of course we must give up sin, and the more we give up sin and obey God the more we get of the Holy Spirit. The Epistle teaches us that this is wrong. …

As a condition, you have to confess sin, and to give up sin; but the more earnest and intense your desire the more you fail, until you see that you cannot conquer sin yourself. It is as you come to Jesus and confess you are not strong enough to cast out sin, and say, "Lord, in Your power I will live a holy life," that you will obtain the Holy Spirit—you receive the Spirit by faith.

As we read in the 14th verse of the same chapter, *"That we might receive the promise of the Spirit, through faith."* Now remember, everyone who is beginning to long for the filling of the Holy Spirit, that here is the great truth you need: you must get it by faith. Faith always means this: there is something I cannot do myself, I trust another to do it for me. Faith is always a confession of helplessness. Faith, if it means anything, means this: Lord, I cannot make myself worthy, but I can trust in Your love. You can and will give me the Holy Spirit. I want you to say that without any doubt. And it is not only by faith once for all, but it is by faith every morning, that the action of the Holy Spirit may be received fresh from Heaven.

Many people have a precious experience and live on that for forty years. We need the Holy Spirit fresh from Heaven every day. I don't know of a more solemn lesson than that of the manna that came from Heaven. It became corrupt twenty-four hours after it fell. Water you want every day fresh from the spring; stagnant water corrupts. If you want to live the life of the Holy Spirit it must be a life continually renewed from Heaven. I must come every day to be filled fresh with the Holy Spirit. This must be the holy habit of my life. As you began so continue, by faith. You must learn to get hold of God's promises, to believe in the Divine, God-given power working in you and then your walk will be a humble one, from hour to hour. … As I need the sunshine every minute of the day, the sunshine of five minutes ago does not help me now. Every minute the Sun must shine on me from above; so every moment the Holy Spirit must come to my heart fresh from God. …

2nd Warning. In the fourth verse: *"Are you so foolish, having begun in the Spirit are you now made perfect in the flesh?"* This is a most important and instructive lesson, conveying the solemn warning, that we can begin in the Spirit and then get off the line and go on to perfect in the flesh what was begun in the Spirit. … In Romans, eighth chapter, we saw the great contrast between the Spirit and the flesh. *"Not in the flesh but in the Spirit," "Not after the flesh but after the Spirit."* So, too, in Galatians the contrast is pressed. We can begin with the Holy Spirit and unconsciously be led to perfect, to seek our religious progress, in the flesh. Thousands have done it. We have, for a time, been under the power of the Spirit, and yet been led to seek the maintenance of our life and work in what is human and carnal. You may have the Holy Spirit in you and yet you have the flesh in you too, and the flesh is always active and ready to live the religious life.

I have seen those in whom the power of the Holy Spirit is manifest, and yet there is just a little of Self. God uses such a one, and yet Self-confidence may corrupt all. That person perfects in the flesh what was begun in the Spirit. This is a danger to which you and I are exposed and therefore we must take the warning. … Oh, that we might have a real sense of our danger, a sense of our utter inability to keep away the secret, insidious power of the flesh … conscious that all the time we are in the enemy's territory, and may be led to allow the flesh to assert itself in our religion.

You want to be brought to such a sense of your helplessness and dependence upon God as shall lead you really to yield yourself to the Holy Spirit alone. Dear Christians, you have a great many enemies, but watch specially against one. That one, how hard to be overthrown. It is Self. Self is the flesh and the flesh is Self. … Beware!

The Holy Spirit in Galatians 2

August 30th

"That we might receive the promise of the Spirit, through faith."

—GALATIANS 3: 14

Third warning. In the fourth chapter, sixth and seventh verses: *"And because you are sons God has sent forth the Spirit of His Son into your hearts, crying, Abba, Father. Wherefore you are no more a servant, but a son; and if a son, then an heir of God through Christ."* In the previous verse there was a warning against the spirit of bondage, here we are taught that the Spirit that comes in us is the Spirit of adoption; we are the heirs of God in His Son. The whole teaching of the epistle is this, not to go to God as servants but as sons. You have the Spirit of sonship. You all know the parable of the prodigal son and the elder son. How the elder son said to the father, "I have served you these many years, yet you never gave me a kid." The father replied, *"Son, you are ever with me and all I have is yours."* You have free access to my presence and all my possessions. What was wrong with that young man? He had the spirit of a servant and not of a son. Instead of trusting his father he was living the life of a slave.

The spirit of bondage is so natural to us. Therefore God's word says, do remember you are sons. Let us show it in our whole lives, in our intercourse with God and our walk before men, that the spirit of a son is in us, the Spirit of God's own Son. God holds back no good thing from His sons. Our whole life ought to be in the faith, I am always a son of God. I have always everything I need. Most Christians do not enjoy that because they do not live in the spirit of sonship.

The object of the Holy Spirit is to give you a full child-like heart toward God. Here in Galatians we are warned to take care that we don't live before God as servants in the spirit of bondage. God gave the Spirit of His Son; He sent Him forth into our hearts. Oh that we might realize the simplicity of being a child of God all the day long. My father loves me so. See the little child's actions toward his father. He loves him and jumps on his knee and says, Won't you give me this? The heart of the child is full of confidence in the father. How blessed if we allowed this Spirit of sonship to possess us.

… *Fourth Warning.* In Chapter 5:1–5, you see here that there were many of the Galatians, who had been justified by faith in Christ, who had taken to works again. They were seeking for obedience in an external religion, a religion of works. Beware of that. A true believer waits through the Spirit for the hope of righteousness through faith. Everything that is promised to the righteous I am to hope for. Everything I hope for the Holy Spirit teaches me to expect by faith.

Do you not see our whole life is to be believing? Some people ask, have you not told us to work very hard? Yes, but it is a very different thing to work under the law and to work by grace. … We are always in danger of thinking we ought to be doing something, instead of going to Christ, in faith, and saying, I can do nothing, work You in me.

… Let there, every day of your lives, every morning, especially, be a time set apart for acting faith, for exercising yourself in believing, before you pray. There are Christians who study their Bibles so earnestly for half an hour, they have read and thought on God's word, have prayed and told God what they want, but they have done no believing. … Am I sure that God hears me and can I trust Him fully that He is going to bless me. ...

Let your heart go up in confession and tell God you are willing to give up everything; you will learn to see the teaching about the Holy Spirit and to believe in the reality of the work in you. The Holy Spirit is not merely for speaking or preaching, but for every hour of the day. … I need to have the Holy Spirit to rule my disposition and keep me gentle, heavenly, Christ-like, devoted to God. … What did God give the Holy Spirit for? That we might live like Jesus. That our life, like His, might be the exhibition of what the power of God's Spirit can work. If we would but live the life of faith how wonderfully God would meet and bless us.

Fifth Warning. Our next warning is found in the 25th verse of the 5th chapter. *"If we live in the Spirit, let us walk in the Spirit."* Let me press upon you the great difference between the two things. Paul says you may have received the Holy Spirit when you believed, but that is not enough. You must also walk in the Spirit. It is possible for a man to separate the two things, one from the other. Men may be very anxious to get pardoned and become God's children, and yet think that after that they must be content to walk in the flesh. Look at pride, temper, worldliness, jealousy, coldness toward Christ, so little personal love. These are all the works of the flesh, and may be found in a man living in the Spirit and yet not walking in the Spirit. Now Paul comes to us and says that if we live in the Spirit we must also walk in the Spirit.

What does that mean? Walk includes all our intercourse in daily life, our contact with people, our conversation with the world. All this must be in fellowship with the Spirit of God. Paul meant this Spirit to be in my home life, my church life, money making, money giving, money spending, every part of my life. Paul says that if you live in the Spirit, you should walk in the Spirit. Every step must be in the Spirit.

Am I preaching an impossible thing? Verily no. The message is the very mind of God and God's Word. What did He send the Holy Spirit for, if it was not to enable His children to live a holy and a heavenly life? It was to sanctify us, to bring Christ into our lives and to make us one with Christ. In this chapter it is stated the fruit of the Spirit is love, joy, peace, long-suffering, gentleness, goodness, faith, meekness, temperance. How am I to live that? Paul did not mean that for people who are better than we are. No, it is for each of us. … If we yield our lives entirely with child-like faith, God will lead us into that life.

Sixth warning. In the last chapter: "*Be not deceived, God is not mocked, for whatsoever a man sows that shall he also reap. For he that sows to his flesh shall the flesh reap corruption; but he that sows to the Spirit shall the Spirit reap life everlasting.*" The Galatians had gone back to the life of the flesh. They worshipped God very earnestly but they were Self-righteous. They thought to do a great deal to please God but all sorts of bitter jealousies and envyings broke out among them. Paul said they were in danger of devouring one another. … Religious flesh, with its Self-effort, is still sinful flesh. The man who is trying to conquer sin and serve God, without the filling of the Holy Spirit, finds sin stronger in Him every day, because he is trying to serve God in the power of the flesh. It is Self, Self-effort and Self-confidence.… There is no getting over this, we must not sow in the flesh; we must sow in the Spirit if we would reap the fruit of the Spirit. …

"Be Filled with the Spirit" 1

August 31st

"*Be filled with the Spirit.*"

—EPHESIANS 5: 18

I want to conclude these addresses on the Holy Spirit and His work in us, by a short summary of what that work is, showing the great and wonderful blessedness that the Holy Spirit brings to them that yield to Him. As my text I mean to take again the words that we have had before, Ephesians 5:18. "*Be filled with the Spirit.*" I think we have said that we are in very great danger when we read that text, of thinking of the Holy Spirit coming in great power, under a conscious sense of His presence, with a great stir of the emotions, with a great revelation of the glory of God, with a great quickening of our power for work, and yet very often this is not the case. I used the illustration of a river being filled up at once by heavy storms of rain, or a river being filled very gradually. … Sometimes it is filled by the rain coming down in torrents, causing great noise and turmoil, and that same river might be filled with the water running down from the melted snow on the mountains, so that there will be a calm-like, steady rising, silently, without any noise or disturbance, and so the Holy Spirit may come with noise as of the sound of a rushing wind and with a wonderful thrilling throughout the whole being, yet, many times, He may come on the ordinary level of the daily life and a man can live filled with the Holy Spirit just while he is walking along quietly in his daily duties.

Then the great thing to know and understand is, what is it that the Holy Spirit will work in such a man? I want to give you three very simple answers. The Holy Spirit brings the presence of Christ; He gives the likeness of Christ, and the Holy Spirit works the power of Christ.

The Holy Spirit is meant to give the presence of Christ. You know, dear friends, that during the three years of Christ's work on earth, to the disciples, His presence was everything. … Everything depended upon having Christ with them. … But now, Christ was to go away to Heaven and the hearts of the disciples were very sad, but listen, before He went away He said, *"I am coming again." "I will not leave you comfortless."* He told them that it was by the Holy Spirit He was coming to them. He promised them that He would pray the Father and that He would send the Comforter, He told them that if they loved Him they would keep His commandments and then He promised to come and manifest Himself unto them, and that both He and the Father would come and take up their abode with them. … He promised in the first place, above everything else this—His abiding presence….

We don't know what it is to walk with Jesus as a little child walks with his father, and I want to press this upon you, the Lord Jesus is longing and willing to come so close to us and to stay so near to us that we can have His presence always. This is not impossible, don't think it. Jesus is able to give us the consciousness of His abiding presence, and how does He do it? He does it by filling us with the Holy Spirit. This is the great work of the Holy Spirit, to glorify Christ.

Remember the words John wrote when Christ said, *"He that believes on Me as the Scripture has said, out of his belly shall flow rivers of living water. But this spoke He of the Spirit which they that believe on Him should receive; for the Holy Spirit was not yet given; because that Christ was not yet glorified."* When Christ was glorified, when He had died and glorified the Father, and the Father had glorified Him in Heaven, then the Holy Spirit came as the Spirit of Christ to show us Christ's heavenly glory, and that is why Christ says, *"He shall glorify Me; He shall receive of mine, and shall shew it unto you."* The Holy Spirit is able to fill me with a real deep sense of the presence of Jesus Christ and of His glory. This is one of the essential roots of the Christian life, the presence of Jesus.

You have heard of what is called, in England, the Keswick Movement. Keswick is in the north of England. The friends who are at the head of this movement stand for what they call the beginning of the spiritual life. Their great object is to show Christians how wrong and feeble their life is, sometimes light and sometimes dark, sometimes strong and sometimes weak, and to point out a better way. Many admit that they ought to live a different life. They are brought to the acknowledgment of what is wrong, to earnest Self-searching, to give themselves up to God to be searched, and when the consciousness becomes strong and deep of what is wrong, then there is pointed out to them from God's Word what the true life is. They don't talk so much about the baptism of the Holy Spirit at those conventions, but the most prominent thought is, Jesus Christ is the Savior from sin and He is able to keep you always. They bring, by God's help, many to see that Jesus requires one step. This step only takes a moment. You don't have to wrestle, but just throw yourself in the arms of Christ and let that living Christ take hold of you, never letting Him go but having Him with you all the day.

Out at the Cape I met a young missionary, just returned from Keswick, where he had been greatly blessed. I asked him what was the difference between his former life and now. He said it was just the personal friendship of Jesus. This is it: you know the Lord Jesus is such a dear friend. He is such a heavenly friend, and such a fountain of love, that is, if you get into the right relationship. Oh, then you must do it. The presence of Jesus must be like the sunlight, for the presence of Jesus makes everything bright. How can I get this, so that I have the Lord Jesus always with me, and I always know it, and I never get out of the realization of it for a minute? That is what Christ longs for.

Don't think He is content with the way most Christians live. He is such a lover. He longs to be very near to us and have us wholly for Himself. Listen friends, the way by which we can always have the presence of Christ, is by the power of the Holy Spirit, and what is that way? Why, very simple; we must confess, "I have not been living as I should, in close fellowship with Jesus. Sometimes I have met Him, but just as often I have forgotten and forsaken Him, living after my own heart, and although I have been kept from open sin, there has not been that holy warmth of one whose walk is with his Lord. The Lord wants to have me always with Him, and the power of my Lord is to keep me always with Him, and the presence of my Lord is the only secret of a spiritual life." Believe this, say it, accept Him thus, in the fullness of His presence.

"Be Filled with the Spirit" 2

September 1st

"Be filled with the Spirit."

—EPHESIANS 5: 18

Let me say that it is the wonderful purpose of God to make Jesus present with me every day and hour. … Oh, that God might work a deep desire in our hearts and make us all ready to say, I want a life of unbroken communion with Jesus. I want Jesus to do the utmost He can for me. I want His love to rule and work through me all day. Is it possible? The answer comes: "Have I not given the Holy Spirit, have I not sent the Holy Spirit into your heart for this one purpose: that He should always glorify Jesus in you"?

Oh come, believers, you have the Holy Spirit within you now, come and bow with shame and say, "Oh God, how little have I let the Holy Spirit manifest the presence of Jesus. Forgive me. Father, my heart responds and I want to open my whole being to Him; I want to yield entirely to Him; I want to be filled completely with the Holy Spirit that my whole being may be under His control, so that He may have power to reveal Christ always within me." …

Dear friends, the first work of the Holy Spirit is to reveal the presence of Jesus. The Holy Spirit not only reveals the presence of Jesus but He gives the likeness of Jesus. This is something additional. When a young Christian comes to understand what the presence of Jesus is, he or she finds how much there is of sin and flesh, Self and failure…. The disciples had the presence of Jesus though they did not have His likeness. He was humble, they were proud. He was unselfish, they were Selfish.

Many want to have the presence of Jesus to keep them up, but they do not want to be entirely like Him. You cannot have that. They will say, "I cannot expect to be too holy. I want the presence of Jesus very near of course, but I don't expect to be very much like Jesus." The Holy Spirit comes to reveal the presence of Jesus in you, not as a separate person, but as dwelling in your life and heart and disposition and character. The Holy Spirit wants to reveal the very likeness of Christ in you. The characteristics and disposition of Christ should all come to you.

What are these characteristics, and what was His disposition? I cannot mention all, but it is a great thing, when looking on Christ's character, to find out what is His chief virtue? What is His chief characteristic? The answer is very simple, humility. Did He not say; "*Take my yoke upon you and learn of Me, for I am meek and lowly in heart, and you shall find rest to your souls.*" Did He not continually speak about the Father, saying, "*The Father has sent Me.*" He wanted people to know that He was a servant. He said, in substance, "I am not my own master, the words I speak are not mine; I don't speak of myself, I dare not speak one word of myself, but what I hear I speak. The works that I do I do not of myself, but the Father has shown Me the works. I can do nothing of myself." Christ's life was a life of absolute dependence upon the Father, to do nothing of Himself, but just to let the Father teach Him, and let the Father work in Him, and let the Father carry out His will. "*I seek not my honor, but the honor of Him who sent Me.*" … "I came not to do my own will, I have a will, but I gave it up, I came to do the will of the Father." There was with Him a certain Self-abnegation. He wanted to be nothing and God to be all. His chief virtue was humility. …

We must humble ourselves and become nothing before God if we wish to return to Him. The Lord Jesus came from Heaven and took that name—the Lamb of God—that He might prove to us that He was the Lamb of God in littleness, meekness, gentleness and humility, and this is why Paul said, "*He humbled Himself, and became obedient unto death, even the death of the cross.*" …

Deep humility was the Spirit of Christ, and now when the Holy Spirit comes to us does He come to bring us a very different disposition? You know the answer. The Holy Spirit wants to bring the likeness of Jesus in us—deep dependence upon God. This is what is wanted in the Church of Christ. There is so much pride, Selfishness, unloving and Self-seeking. May God help us to see the beauty of Christ, just to be in love with His humility and to believe that the Holy Spirit will breathe the humility of Christ into us.

Let me say something to you who are in earnest in seeking the filling of the Holy Spirit. … Take a very earnest young man. He hears about this higher life. He says, "I want to get it"; he struggles, feels, and wills and cannot get it. Why? Because there is a great deal of Self-will and Self-trust in all that fighting. That is not the way to get it. How did Christ get the throne of glory? By going" down into the grave, and God lifted Him up to the throne There is the place to get glory. You must sink down into death.

… Remember, as often as you read, "The likeness of Jesus," this is what the Holy Spirit is going to put into my heart, whether it be Self-sacrifice or whether it be humility, gentleness, or poverty before God. Oh, do believe that the Holy Spirit is come to bring the likeness of Christ in you. …

Heavenly Treasure in Earthen Vessels

September 2nd

"But we have this treasure in earthen vessels, that the excellency of the power may be of God and not of us."
—2 CORINTHIANS 4: 7

We may be making a great mistake when we seek for the baptism of the Spirit for power for work and service… and not realizing that the Holy Spirit waits to come as a life, renewing our whole being into the likeness of Christ. … But I would be very sorry if anyone should think that I count work of little value. All that God wants to do for you has this object: *"That you may bring forth much fruit."* Therefore, beware of misunderstanding me, and thinking that I would have you seek only for the higher life. That might be a Selfish thing, and therefore I want to speak about work, the work every one of us has to do. …

A good while before I came away from South Africa, I read, in an old author, a sentence that impressed me deeply ... It was this: "The first duty of every clergyman is to beg of God, very humbly, that all that he wants to be done in his hearers, may first be fully and truly done in himself." I cannot say what power there appears to be in this sentence. Brother minister and brother worker, the first duty of one who works for Christ and speaks for Him, is to humbly come to God and ask that everything he wants done in his hearers may first be thoroughly and fully done in himself. … You and I need to have God do the thing in ourselves, and the more earnestly we seek that, the more there will be a hidden power of the Holy Spirit to pass through from us. … Paul writes about his ministry, in the first five verses, and then he says, when he had spoken the wonderful words, "*God has shined into our hearts, to give us, and through us to give others, the light of the knowledge of the glory of God in the face of Jesus Christ.*"

Christ wants to bring us to God, and in the face of Christ, our one great study, our one great object and desire should be, that the glory of God may be revealed in us .... God shines into our hearts by the Holy Spirit, and by the Holy Spirit He reveals the light of the knowledge of the glory of God. It is not an intellectual knowledge, but in the heart. A man may have beautiful thoughts, he may be a splendid preacher, he may be a most edifying instructor, yet, there may be very much more of intellect in him than of God's Spirit. It must be a religion of the heart. God is love. ....

... Believer, if you get the consciousness, I am a rich man, I am a millionaire, I have heavenly treasures, I have the key of the treasures of my God. Oh! What joy and confidence and power you will have to make others believe there is a heavenly blessing to get. ... How different, if our hearts were burning with the heavenly life of God. If the life of God burns in us, in the deepest regions of our being, what a life of blessing. Just think of a life, with the light of the face of the glory of God shining into us all the day. What a heavenly treasure to carry about with us! That light would shine through us, and would be reflected from us. I pray you, get the light of the glory of God into your souls. Oh! Workers, the heavenly treasure is not human knowledge, it is not thought, it is not a little experience, but it is the very sunshine of God's glory in the soul. ...

Young man and young woman, students of this Bible Institute, I pray you remember, a man has as much real power for eternity as he has of God shining into his heart. And while I pray you to be faithful in your study and use your time well, and while I would urge you use every opportunity for getting acquainted with that precious word, yet I say, first and last, everything depends upon a man living in the light of God's presence, in the light of God's love, and waiting until he has the heavenly treasure in his heart, God shining there the light of the knowledge of the glory of God in the face of Jesus Christ. ... Let there be a holy hunger and thirst of the heart after God and after a life like that of Christ's, living every hour in fellowship with the Father, and in dependence upon Him. ...

We are, by nature, so full of pride and Self in the most spiritual believer there is always danger of Self-exaltation. Remember, in 2 Corinthians 12, Paul writes, "*Lest I should be exalted by the revelations I had received, God sent a thorn in the flesh to humble me,*" and you know how Christ taught him that when he was weak he would be strongest, because Christ's power would rest upon his weakness. And even so God comes to us. When the Lord sent that messenger of Satan to buffet him he said, three times, "Lord, do take it away." The Lord came to Paul and said, "You do not know that the messenger of Satan is your greatest blessing." "Why, Lord?" "Because he will teach you to be absolutely dependent upon Me every moment." Paul got a sight of it; he said, "*I will glory, will rejoice in my infirmities, in the weakness of the earthen vessel.*" That is a higher attainment, not only to endure but to rejoice in being an earthen vessel.

Remember, no matter how full God may fill your heart with His salvation, the consciousness will always have to grow deeper, I am an earthen vessel. That is why Paul says, in the same chapter, "*In nothing am I behind the chief of the Apostles, though I am nothing.*"

God made the creature originally to be a vessel, in which to show forth His Divine glory. This is your highest honor, to be a vessel to carry the power and light of God. That is what angels were created for, to be vessels in which the glory of God could be shown forth. That is what the child of God should be content to be, a vessel, empty, low and broken, if need be, to be filled with Christ, the treasure of God.

My last thought. The abiding union between the two; the living union. … The treasure of God enters into a man; though I remain an earthen vessel, the heavenly treasure becomes mine in such a way that it enters my life and becomes myself. All the life of God, and the Holy Spirit of God, and the Holy love of God and Holy Son of God, and the Holy glory of God, they all, all pass down into my very being in such an infinite, Divine reality, that they are my very own and they make up myself.

God teaches me a double lesson. First of all, to understand the everlasting difference, that I as a creature, ever am nothing but a vessel. If I begin to know the glory of God I don't want to be anything else; I become jealous of the honor and glory of God and my highest desire is to get lower and deeper down that God may be all. But with this abiding difference there comes what appears a contradiction, and yet is a blessed reality. I know that the treasure is not in me and that all my being is only emptiness that holds it; yet this living treasure becomes my very Self. … Let my one aim be to be nothing. No being can tell how God will give the heavenly treasure into the heart that is thoroughly empty. …

Christ Bringing Us to God 1

September 3rd

"Christ, also, has suffered for sins, the just for the unjust, that He might bring us to God."

—1 PETER 3: 18

The words I wish to speak on you find in 1 Peter 3:18: *"Christ, also, has suffered for sins, the just for the unjust, that He might bring us to God."* They went into the great object of Christ's work. What was it for that He came? "*That He might bring us to God.*" … Christ is the way; what is the end of the way? The end is God. Christ wants to bring us to God.

You often find Christians so occupied with Christ that they never get time for God. You ask me, is there any difference between going to Christ and going to God? A very great difference. In Christ I have the gracious and merciful side of God's character. But that is not the only side of the Divine character I need to know. In Christ I have the condescension of God coming near to me, but the object of that condescension is to bring me back to righteousness and holiness. You can never have true strength and an all-round Christian experience unless you learn the lesson that Christ is going to win your heart that He may bring you back to God.

Just think, Christ was not, in Himself, Self-sufficient when He was on earth. He lived every day with the thought within Him: There is one greater than I, and my blessedness is to live in dependence upon Him, with a will given up to His will and in a trust that counts upon His working. And if I am to be in Christ and Christ in me, what was His life must become my life; fellowship with God and dependence upon God. There are aspects of the Divine character that are more fully revealed in God the Father than in God the Son. Take, for instance, the fear of God. I never, in the New Testament, read of the fear of Christ. He came to reveal the other side, the love and the attractiveness and the trustworthiness of God. The element of fear and holy reverence was an element in Christ's own character. …

He had godly fear towards the Father, and if my Christian character is to be perfect and all-around, I must have the fear of God as it is revealed in the Old Testament, working into the very foundations of my life, with this most child-like confidence there must ever be a deep, deep fear of God before the throne. I read that the four living creatures and twenty-four elders cast their crowns before the throne. I read that angels and seraphim veil their faces with their wings; if my Christian character is to be perfect there must be in it that deep consciousness of the inconceivable greatness of God above me that makes me bow in the very dust before Him. …

Before I am brought to God I must know who God is, and as I bow before Him, I must say, "He is the Almighty One, the All Holy One. He cannot bear sin or the shadow of sin. He wants to take it away. He is the All Loving One, He wants to communicate Himself to me. The Everywhere Present One, who is with me and able to make Himself known to my soul." If I want to be brought nigh to God I must first say, "He is God, and my soul must bow in lowly stillness and in an attitude of faith, and just exercise the belief: God is here. He, the Creator of all things on the earth, the Incomprehensible One; He is a consuming fire; He is love and wants to impart Himself wholly to me. That God is near. But I do not know Him; I know so little of Him, how can I come nigh to Him?"

Then next I begin to think, Who am I, and I say, If I give God His place I must take the right place for myself. I am a creature and I have nothing holy. I have nothing good except what God gives me. I am nothing except a vessel in which God can show forth His glory, and therefore I want to take my place before God as nothing. If Christ is to bring me to God I must sink down into my nothingness. I am not only a creature but I am a sinner. That ought to make me take a still lower place. …

There are certain rules if I am to meet God. I must come in deep Self-abnegation. And then I am a redeemed sinner; this humbles me still more. I take the lowest place. There is God waiting for me to hear my cry.

How can I have intercourse with this God? Jesus Christ brings me to God. Take the third step. The first was: give God His place and let Him be seated on His throne of glory; the second: take your place before God. The third: take your place in Christ Jesus. I am speaking to believers. You understand what the atonement is; that we have been brought nigh by the blood. You have believed that for yourself personally, that your sins are pardoned and you have had access to God's favor.

You want to be brought into a life always near to God. You need Christ to do it. How can He do it? Take your place in Christ Jesus and by an act of faith and by the light of the Holy Spirit see and believe that you are one with Christ. Christ is before the Father and you are in Him and He is in you. No branch was ever so really in the vine, no finger of my hand was ever so truly in my body, as I am in Christ by a vital union, and as Christ is in me. And when I want to come to God I am told that the place I am to occupy is the place of the most intimate nearness. The writer of the Hebrews teaches it. The efficacy of the blood is our boldness; the living High Priest waits to bring us in. It is not that I am down here while He does a little work in and for me. No! As the High Priest who says, "You in Me, and I in you," He brings me to God. In the power of my union with Him, in living fellowship with Himself, He presents me, and I, by faith, have a real, abiding access within the veil, into the very life, into the very heart and love of God.

Christ came to bring us unto God. I am not only in Him but Christ is in me as a living person. Christ takes charge of me, Christ introduces me to the Father, and as I am before the Father, Christ gives the working of the Holy Spirit, and He teaches me what my work is when I am brought nigh to God. It was that God might get His children in a life of fellowship to understand and realize who He is. Some, when they get within the veil, when they are brought nigh into the holiest of all, look upon it as a grand attainment. It is only the beginning of the blessed life. For, when I am there, then God is able to let His light shine into my whole being. Then God is able to let His holiness come upon me. When I am there God is able to make me bow and sink down into a nothingness and into humility that I never thought possible to attain to, that I may be there receiving the inflowing of God's Holy Spirit in a freshness and a fullness inconceivable.

Christ Bringing Us to God 2

September 4th

"Christ, also, has suffered for sins, the just for the unjust, that He might bring us to God."

—1 PETER 3: 18

Oh! beloved, Christ came to bring us very nigh to God. It is not only nearness of acceptance but nearness of love, the consciousness that He loves me and I love Him. It is the nearness of that union of love which consists in the closest possible fellowship. Give up all in emptiness for Him to fill, and God waits to come down and pour His fullness into me. Christ died that He might bring us unto God, and in that place, in God's presence, oh, there it is, that not only God's work in me is to be done, but there it is I am to learn how to do my work for God.

In that nearness to God is the place of intercession. Throughout the Church of Christ there is a universal complaint that we pray too little. Some work much but pray little. We pay far more attention to what we have to do with men than to what we have to do with God. Beloved, the fountains of the Christian life, the fountains of the outflow of the Holy Spirit, the fountains of love and power to be broken up in our hearts and to be poured out to men, these fountains rise from the throne of God, and it is only as we tarry before

God in fellowship with the Most High, that God's love can flow through us. …

And where am I to receive this inflowing love? It is when I am brought nigh to God. There it is I learn what intercession is; there I become strong to bear the burden of the Church and of the world in quiet pleading with God. I have such access to Him, I am so really His friend. He gives me such power with Him that I know I have only to plead and an answer will come. Dear friends, is there not a great deal of our living of which we might confess it bears but little mark of Christ having brought us nigh to God.

There is another step. I say Christ brings us thus nigh to God in Himself that we may act out and live our lives in the world in that nearness to God. You occasionally find men, when they speak in public, they have a sense of God upon them. I have been told that at the great International Convention in London there was more than one speaker of great eloquence, but there was one man, whose very presence, when he rose to speak, hushed the audience. The very presence of God was with him. So, with a man like George Müller, who has spent his whole life in prayer, the presence of God is on him. But how seldom one finds this. Of George Bowen, of India, it is told, that he had said that the nearness of God was nearer unto him than any man upon earth. A friend asked him about it, and his answer was: "Yes, God is nearer to me, consciously, than anyone in this room." Is it not that presence we want? That presence of God to go out and meet men, to go out and do work, to go out and engage in business, to go out and be tempted and tried, the presence of the Everlasting God to be with us from morning to night, moment by moment. …

We need not be in the dark, without the light of the sun, twelve hours of the day, and would God not be able and make provision that you should every moment abide in the light of His presence and the joy of His immediate nearness. Christ came and died to bring us unto God. Listen to what we read in the Hebrews, about the better hope of the New Testament "*by which we draw nigh unto God.*" Listen to what we read in the same chapter, "*He is able to save completely them that come to God by Him.*" If you will learn, not only to ask this blessing among other blessings, but if you will, indeed, believe that Christ will fulfill this work in you and bring you nigh unto God, so that every moment of your life is spent in His presence, Christ will work it out in your life.

Christ suffered that "*He might bring us to God.*" Dear friends, as surely as we are God's children our life can be full of God. In Ephesians, Paul tells us that God is willing to strengthen us with might by His Spirit in the inner man, until we are filled with the fullness of God or unto the fullness of God. I long thought that meant some high experience, but it means simply that God wants to be present with us with such conscious ness that our heart is all the time full of His blessed presence, His holy will and His divine inworking. Christ wants to bring us nigh to God.

One more thought. When Christ brings us nigh to God He brings our will in perfect harmony to the will of God. I cannot have my will at variance with God's will, or mourning its inability to do God's will, and all the time have the enjoyment of the blessing of God's light and God's presence, Christ came to bring me to God.

I not only need faith to realize that He is in me and I in Him, but by faith I need to give myself up to His working, that as a living person He shall reveal the will of God perfectly in me, and so breathe into me His own disposition and His own life. Christ is to dwell and live in me. I am not to count Christ as a separate being, dwelling in my heart as a locality, but Christ is to be in my heart, in my life, in my thinking, living and willing, as the very life of all I do, so that He lives Himself out through me. So, Christ is formed in me, and God sees the very figure, the very form of Christ within me. And as Christ is thus manifested within me in His disposition and Spirit, the nearness of God becomes more intimate and the fellowship with God becomes more close.

Oh! beloved, God wants us to come nigh to Him in Christ. Are there not many Christians who live far from God? … We talked, last week, about the baptism of the Holy Spirit, and the baptism of power, and the life of the Spirit, but I do pray you, young men and women, who are going to devote yourselves to service, and you believers who are longing to live holy lives, remember one thing, you want more of God in your life. A man has just as much religion as he has of God, and if a man wants more religion he must have more of God. We have a great deal of seeking of more religion, more power, and yet we do not think of having more of God.

God created you for Himself to fill you with Himself. Christ redeemed you to be filled with your God. Oh, come and let Christ do His work ….

When you pray, two minutes spent in quietly giving yourself to be brought near to God by Christ would be better than twenty minutes in prayer in the ordinary way. We often pour out our petitions, praise and confessions to a distant God. If you want your life changed, if you want God to come into your life, if you want God to take possession of your life, in prayer always make your first desire: "Son of the Father, bring me near to God." Bow in the very deepest adoration and reverence, and wait, wait before Him. It is God's own work to reveal Himself. Bow in an act of faith; the Everlasting God is here, longing to take possession of me, willing to make Himself known. I wait upon God. Bow in deep lowliness, and beseech God, for His great mercy's sake, to come near and make Himself known to you. …

Christ Lives in Me

September 5th

"Christ lives in me. I am crucified with Christ, nevertheless I live, yet not I, but Christ lives in me."

—GALATIANS 2: 20

I want to speak about the life that Christ lives in us. You have it here in the parable of the vine. What can be closer or more intimate than the union between the vine and the branch? How the very same sap that is in the vine is to be found in the branch. We have very many kinds of grapes, but in each case the juice that is in the vine is the very same juice that is in the branch. And so the very same life and Spirit which is in Christ is to be in us. This is the great lesson we want to learn tonight. Read John 15: 1–12: Our life is to be a life of perfect union with Jesus. …

I said that we too often think of Christ as an outward person here on earth, who hears and helps us. A man may come and give me $10,000, and so be my helper, but there is no further union between him and me. The man may be a great benefactor, but there is no organic union between him and me. … Many people look upon Christ as such a separate, outward Savior. They never can fully enjoy His salvation. I must believe that even as Christ is in Heaven, so He is here *in* me, His branch. He comes into my inmost life. He occupies that life. He lives there, and by living there He enables me to live as a child of God.

Some think that when Christ dwells within us He comes somewhere in the region of the heart, and He lives there. We are two separate persons, Christ one and I one, and somehow He works in me at times. No! That is not the way. Christ comes into me and becomes my very life. He comes into the very root of my heart and being. He comes into my willing and thinking and feeling and living, and lives in me in the power which the Omnipresent God, alone, can exercise. … I live in the flesh, the life of flesh and blood, but Christ dwelling in me is the true life of my life.

The words which I want to speak are very simple and well-known; Galatians 2: 20: *"Christ lives in me. I am crucified with Christ, nevertheless I live, yet not I, but Christ lives in me."* Now, the point to which I want to direct attention, is that if Christ is to live in me, He does not live in me by a blind force, nor without my knowing it. He calls me to come and see what His life is, and so, if I desire His life, I must give up mine. I must also give up all wrong ideas about what the life of Christ really is. I cannot have the life of Christ, in power, in me, unless I seek to know truly what the life is that He lived.

Oh! Come, and let the *living* Christ live in you. And to that end, seek to know the life He has set before you in His example. Not that we are able to imitate Christ [on our own]. But because Christ lived His life for us, and imparts it to us, therefore we can do it. … The Bible tells me I must do it. The Bible also tells me I can do it, because "*Christ lives in me*." If I allow the *living* Christ to take possession of my will and desires, I can walk even as He walked. Let us come to the life of Christ, and try and find out what is that life that He lived on earth, with His Father. That is exactly the Christ who lives in us. There are not two Christs, only one, the Christ that lived on earth is the Christ that lives in my heart.

The great mark of Christ is that He lived in the deepest humility and dependence upon the Father. He said, *"I can do nothing of Myself."* In everything He had His life from God. … And that is what we want Christ to come into us for, to breathe in us that very disposition, and that is what I speak of. The very highest virtues of any Christian life is only to let God have His way. Only to give God the opportunity of doing His work in us, and coming day by day, hour by hour, to the place of absolute dependence upon God, and to learn one lesson. "Oh! God, I have nothing. I do not know anything, I am nothing, nothing, and I can only do what God makes me."

And now, how is Christ to bring me near to God? He cannot bring me near to God in any other way than the way He came Himself. What was that way? The way of the deepest Self-abnegation, the way of the most entire surrender to God. He was forever expecting God to work in Him, to look to God for strength. He prayed to God for guidance. He cried to God in His trouble. God was everything, everything to Him, and Christ was content to be nothing.

Are you willing to have this Christ to come into your life? Dear friends, I cannot speak it out plain enough in words. The great reason why our Christian life does not advance more, is: we try to do too much ourselves. We are far too Self-active and Self-confident. We, perhaps, never learned the simple elementary lesson that the only place for me before God is just to be nothing—and God will work in me. …

And why was Christ so perfect, and why did Christ gain such victory, and why did Christ please God so? It is this one reason. He allowed God to work in Him from morning until night, and every step was just in dependence upon God. He said, "Father, guide me," "Father, I wait upon You," "Father, work in me," and when Christ comes to live in us, do believe me and God's word, the first and chief thing He wants to work in you, is an absolute dependence upon your God. …

That teaches me this: That if I am willing to lay down my evil life, my evil will, my heart and its affections, all my power in this world, to give it all up to God, to die to it, and to give up myself wholly to trust and wait upon God, God will give the new and resurrection life of Christ, in my heart, here on earth. …

Willing and Doing 1

September 6th

"To will is present with me, but how to do that which is good, I know not."

—ROMANS 7: 18

"For it is God who works in you, both to will and to do of His good pleasure."

—PHILIPPIANS 2: 12

You see how these two texts appear to contradict one another. The first text gives us the experience of the one who says, "*To will is present with me.*" My will is right; I am willing to do God's will; I am willing to do what is good. "But," he says, "I have not the power. How to perform I find not." It is the one with whom there is a great gulf between willing and doing. That is just the state of a great many Christians. They will what is good, and somehow they have not the strength to perform. … *"To will is present with me, but how to perform I find not."*

In the second text you have the very opposite. There Paul says, *"Work out your own salvation with fear and trembling, for it is God which works in you, both to will and to do according to His good pleasure."* Here is the one in whom Paul says that God does both the things—not only the willing, but the doing also.

Now in these two texts we have just the exact description of the two stages of the Christian life that I have been speaking about so repeatedly. You know when we began to speak about the carnal and spiritual, I pointed out that there are two styles of Christian living. The one is that of the carnal Christians, who try to be good but can't succeed. They always fail; temper and strife and sin get the better of them. The other is the spiritual Christians, who get the victory … Christians, to whom Paul's words to the Philippians come as a reality. God works, not only to will, but He also works to do in them. Let us try to find out what the difference is between these two states; what the reason is that so many continue in the former state; what the way is to get out of it into the second.

I spoke, in one of the addresses, about there being needed two convictions of sin; a conviction of sin for the unconverted to bring them to repentance and faith, and for the believers a conviction of sin and sinfulness to prepare them for full salvation. That is the apostle's teaching here in the second half of the seventh chapter. Dear friends, if you read it carefully, you will see that Paul is speaking there about those Christians who are regenerate, who delight in the law of God, long to do what is right and good, and yet are not able. And why not? The answer is, simply because they have not yielded to the Holy Spirit to work all in them.

Notice in chapter seven, from the seventh verse, the name of Christ is not once mentioned except down at the very verse before the last.... Notice, the Holy Spirit is not mentioned. Notice, Paul is speaking always about the law. The word law occurs from twenty to thirty times. The speaker is always speaking about I and me. It is a regenerate person, doing his very best to keep the law of God, but he or she fails utterly. That is just the life of the multitude of believers. They are sometimes doing their very best, trying hard, praying and crying to God, Lord help me! But it does not help.

What a change comes in the eighth chapter. Paul begins in the second verse: *the law, the dominion of the Spirit, of the life in Christ has set me free from the dominion of sin and death.* That is it. A new power comes in. The power of the Holy Spirit, to enable a man, not only to will, but to do the will of God. That is the transition from the first state to the second state. This second state you find described in Philippians second, verses twelve and thirteen … *for it is God which works in you both to will and to do."* …

Willing and Doing 2

September 7th

"For it is God who works in you, both to will and to do His good pleasure."

—PHILIPPIANS 2: 12

Regeneration gives us a new will, but the regenerate, after we have gotten the new will, are still impotent things. And the great mischief in our churches and among our Christians is that they don't know that. People think, Well, I am regenerate and I have the grace of God in me and I have got somewhat of God's Spirit in me and I ought to be able to do God's will. And they try and do their very best, and they fail. But here comes now the important lesson about the second blessing and the higher life, or the spiritual life, or whatever name you call it by: that God comes and tells the regenerate one, "My son, I have given you a new will, but that new will, alone, cannot help you." Many think, "If I were only fixed and firm in my will, I would be able to obey God." They groan and cry to God about it. They delight in the law of God and yet cannot do what they want to do.

Does that not teach me clearly that the regenerate are still impotent? Do I not see it every day of my life? And are there not a hundred witnesses in this building now who can say it is so? There are some things that we can't do; there are some things that we can't forsake. When you come to the daily temptations of the inner life, the regenerate are still impotent ones. There are those who, for thirty or forty years, have fought against their temper and never conquered it, and they have admitted it with grief. There are those who have fought for thirty or forty years against Self-will and unlovingness and they have never conquered it. Why? Because the regenerate are still impotent as long as we try, in virtue of our regeneration, to serve God. …

The regenerate, if we are actually to do God's will, need a new blessing. Need a new blessing? Yes, that is the great truth which the eighth chapter of Romans teaches us. Paul, in the seventh chapter, is silent about the Spirit—not a word about Him. All about the law and the regenerate one who is under the law, still, trying to obey the law. But then he comes in the eighth chapter and says, "Not the law, but the power of the Spirit of life in Christ has set me free from that law which took me captive and which prevented my doing what I really willed to do." He says, "*The Spirit of Christ does set me free.*" In chapter seven I have a man who is a captive; in chapter eight, a man who has been set at liberty by God's Spirit. He goes on to tell me that the Spirit of Christ enables me to walk after the Spirit; by the Spirit I can mortify the deeds of the body, so that I do not do any longer what I do not want to.

Oh, the blessedness of knowing there is a second step! That second step need not be long after conversion. It sometimes comes with conversion, when the Holy Spirit comes very mightily down upon someone and they at once begins to will and to do. But in the Church as it is now, in most cases it does not come at once, and therefore we must preach to you, beloved brethren, that there is a different stage from that, on which most of us live. And what is that stage? That stage is when the Holy Spirit comes and fills the heart and one believes, not only God does work in me to will, but God will work in me to do.

You ask me, perhaps, why has God arranged it so that there are to be two separate stages—the willing and the doing? … Israel, at Mount Sinai, said, "*All that the Lord has spoken, we will do*," but they did not know what they were saying. Just so, when the unconverted come to conversion, they do not know what the will of God is. But after they are converted, then God gives them time—a year, or two years, or three years—and, as regenerate, they begin earnestly to try and do God's will. As a rule, they fail utterly. Then God comes and deals with each of them a second time, and He says, My child, I gave you a new will to love My will and you thought you were able to do it; I want to cure you now entirely of Self and Self-confidence; I have allowed you to try your best and you have seen how you have utterly failed in the doing of my will. Come now, a second time, and let me give you a new blessing. And if they ask, Father, what is this blessing? Have You not given me the Holy Spirit? God answers: "Yes, you are a temple of the Spirit and the Spirit is in you, but you have never understood what it is to have your whole being entirely filled with the Spirit. You have never understood what it is, all the day and every day to be entirely dependent upon the Holy Spirit. You have never understood how fully and entirely I want you, in everything, to glorify Me. Come, my child, and I will have a second transaction with you. And, if you will come and transact with Me, as you did at conversion, and with a new meaning and a new depth and with new intensity of purpose, will yield yourself [fully] to Me, … I will give the Holy Spirit fully in you." …

Wherein consists the secret of entering into this second blessing? My answer is simply, entire dependence upon God. … Don't you begin to see that God must take a much larger and higher place in our life? If I want, not only to will, but also to do, then the Holy Spirit must teach me to come and wait upon God with a dependence and with a helplessness and with a patience that I never exercised before. …

Dear Christian friends, I ask myself, sometimes, "Is not the reason of all the weakness in the Church of Christ just this: people do not know their God?" In the prophet Daniel we read that people who know their God shall be strong and do exploits. You must know your God. Your God is the great power in the universe that works everything. … God is everywhere present in nature; and God wants to be much more distinctly and really, practically present in the heart of the believer. …

Yield Yourselves unto God 1

September 8th

"Present yourselves unto God as alive from the dead, and present your members as instruments of righteousness unto God."

—PHILIPPIANS 2: 12

If the believer wants to know what is the position he has to take before God to know whether he can conquer sin, he will find it in these words: Present yourselves unto God. How often have I to do it? It must be every moment. It must become a habit of my life. I have to do it every day, until the consciousness takes possession of me, I have a Divine life from God; I bring it to God because God does not give me life in myself that I can have as a possession, that I have as my own, but as His life working in me only so far as I yield to Him and abide in communion with Him.

You who are alive from the dead, present yourselves unto God; do it every day until your whole soul is filled with the living faith of your true position. The everlasting God has begun a life in me, and is carrying it on every moment of the day; every moment I can count that God will maintain it.

Don't you see that we have been too much guilty of breaking off the connection with God, and our life is in broken communion? If I can learn to walk all the day in God's presence, presenting myself unto Him as alive from the dead, God will make the resurrection life of Christ to work in me day and night, secretly, quietly, gently, and effectively. …

What are the marks of those that are alive? God's life is no mere imagination, thought, conception; it is a great reality. Remember that this life must bear two marks. It is a life that has been dead and a life that is now alive from the dead. These are the marks of Christ's life in Heaven. In Revelation He says, "*I am He that live and was dead, and am alive for evermore.*" The life of Christ in glory is ever a life from the dead. In Heaven they ever sing the song of the Lamb and the praise of His blood. If the death and the life are linked together there, it must be so too in the believer here. There must be the mark of death and the mark of life.

What are the marks of death? The death marks of Jesus, the disposition which took Him to death, we know—humility. He humbled Himself and gave Himself up to death. Humility is one of the death marks in the believer. Death to sin, separation from all sin, is another mark. Another death mark is separation from the world, to be crucified to the world. Then there is deep impotence, helplessness. … And this is perfect restfulness.

… In the believer who is really dead in Christ you will find these marks. You will find very deep humility. I am nothing but a redeemed sinner, nothing but a creature in whom God can work His glory. It was humility that led Christ to the death, and humility will be the death mark in every one that has died in Christ Jesus.

Separation from all sin. Christ died to sin; died rather than yield to sin. An intense desire to be free from every sin; the readiness to give up life rather than sin; counting all things but loss to be made conformable to His death, are the marks of a life that roots in the death of Christ.

Separation from the world. A man feels, I belong to another sphere, I am living in eternity. I am living with God. I am separate from the world. I may have to do my work because I am in the world, but I am not of the world as Christ was not of the world.

Along with that, another mark is impotence; nothing of Self-effort. We ever try to do something of ourselves instead of taking our place at the foot of the throne so that God can work in us. The deeper the Spirit of Christ's death enters us, the more we shall be willing to be nothing, that God may be and may work all.

The last mark is restfulness. … The death mark of the believer is deep restfulness. Jesus knew God would fulfill His work. As the believer advances he learns to rest perfectly in his God.

On the other side, let us look at the life marks. The first life mark is victory. Jesus has conquered death and hell, and we are more than conquerors through Him that loved us. Another life mark is joy. It was for the joy that was set before Him He endured the cross. Deliverance gives joy. …

Another mark is the power of blessing. The Lord Jesus rose from the dead and began to bless. The first night He breathed His Spirit upon the disciples. On the day of His resurrection there was blessing, and in the outpouring of His Spirit this dispensation became one of Divine, infinite blessing. If you are living in Christ, your resurrection life will be one of blessing to others.

Present yourselves unto God, all that are alive from the dead. Present yourself by the Holy Spirit and ask God to make the death marks clearer and the life marks more beautiful, and your whole life will be from God and before God as of those alive from the dead. … The more intensely you present yourselves to God in that life, the more intensely will it manifest itself in your daily life. A life out of death, a life to victory, the resurrection life in Christ will be yours in truth; you will begin to walk before God as one alive from the dead.

With Christ I go down into the grave, give up myself as lost; God raises me up in Christ and makes me alive from the dead. Yield up yourselves, believers, to know Christ. You are alive from the dead; accept it in faith. Yield yourselves, present yourselves unto God!

Yield Yourselves unto God 2

September 9th

"Present yourselves unto God as alive from the dead,
and present your members as instruments of righteousness unto God."
—PHILIPPIANS 2: 12

Paul speaks of the center of his life as the renewed "I." The "I" has been regenerated. The "I" is alive now in Christ. It is that "I" of which he says: *"I have died to sin, I am alive to God. It is not I but sin."* That new "I" dwells in the body with its members. Sin is in my flesh, so I find the law of sin in my members that leads me into captivity to the law of sin and death. It is a saved man who says, *"I delight in the law of God after the inward man."* It is not I who sins; my will utterly loathes the sin, but this body of death is full of sin. I am impotent and am taken captive. And then Paul says the reason is that he was trying to obey the law in his own strength, but failed.

This leads me on to chapter 8, where you get at once the deliverance of the Holy Spirit, who personally works in you what Christ has done, and sets you free from the law of sin and death in your members, and enables you through the Spirit, to mortify the deeds of the body. It is in this sense he says, *"Yield yourself unto God as alive from the dead, and your members as instruments of righteousness unto God."* He does not say that the members are alive from the dead. You as the living one are to present them to God. You ask how you are to bring your members into subjection, to yield them as instruments of righteousness unto God. I must not only try as a spiritual man to say: "Lord, here is my Self, my inmost heart and love"; but I must take my members, my flesh, my body, in which is the power of sin, and I must say, "Lord, these members I give up to You as instruments of righteousness." …

Righteousness. You have been declared righteous by God that you may live in practical righteousness upon earth. Be careful. If you are going to live as alive from the dead, do not sin. … Take simply what God says, "Sin not." Say, I am going to live for the highest righteousness. Righteousness is the very foundation of God's throne; it must be so too in the Christian life. Do not seek beautiful spiritual thoughts and experiences when you speak of being dead and alive in Christ, but come at once and yield every member to be nothing but an instrument of righteousness.

You are to be the servant of righteousness. … We need the deep conviction, I have been delivered from the service of sin to become a servant of God and His righteousness. As we yield ourselves to God daily it must be with the one desire: to keep the place of servants before Him. Our Jesus took the form of a servant; that was His life, and made Him the Father's delight. That must be our Spirit. …

Remember, you are not only to live as a servant but as one who obeys, who waits daily upon God to find out His will…. Yield yourselves, your inmost being, as renewed in Christ, as alive from the dead unto God, and bring your members each time and present each one of them, each power and movement of your being to God, as an instrument of righteousness. And your inner life with God will be manifested in your conversation among men. …

Every time you think of it, "I am alive from the dead," let your heart rise up with wonderful thanksgiving. Present yourself unto God, yield your body, soul, and spirit a living sacrifice. Is that not a privilege, an unspeakable honor? You may walk in the sunshine of God's love with God, in the gladness that says, "I offer myself just out of deep gratitude for the life of Christ. I am alive from the dead."

O beloved, if you would have the joy of God's Heaven in your heart, praise Him for the wonderful mystery of the resurrection of Christ in you. You dead with Christ and alive with Christ, present yourselves to God in praise.

Present yourself in surrender. I am not my own, I have been bought with the blood. I have been paid for. I present myself as belonging to God. Christ suffered that He might bring us to God. Christ died; we died with Him; God made us alive with Him, that we might serve God. Give yourself up in absolute surrender. Have nothing in your members, your conduct, and your temper that is not entirely subjected to the life of God. Bring all, every day, to God that by His Holy Spirit the death in Christ may be fully manifested in you. Bring everything you have, dear friends, your mind, your power of thought, your heart, your love, your joy; bring everything and lay it before God.

He waits for you every day to present yourself as alive from the dead; to bring every member as an instrument of righteousness, and to have large expectations of what your God will do for you. Do believe with your whole heart, my brother, that God is able and willing to lead you to live upon earth as a living Lazarus, raised from the dead by the mighty power and to the glory of God. He can enable you every day to live the resurrection life. Do believe that. Only remember this, you must in Christ present yourself every day to God in holy expectancy, waiting for Him to work in you, waiting on Him in faith to answer prayer in which you express your surrender to God. … Christ suffered that He might bring us unto God. Let this be your one object, as you reckon yourselves as alive from the dead, dead to Self and alive with Jesus; let it be your one object to get near to God. We want more time in secret prayer if the resurrection life is to work in power; more time alone with God for God to perfect His work in me.

Believer, yield yourself unto God. Let your life bear the stamp; ask God to write it in your heart, a God-yielded man or woman, a God-devoted one, that God may perfect the life that He began in Christ. It will be a life of victory, of joy, of blessing, to live as a God-yielded one, waiting continually upon God to work His work perfectly in you. …

The Life of Rest

September 10th

"Be anxious for nothing, but in everything by prayer and supplication, with thanksgiving, let your requests be made known unto God."

—PHILIPPIANS 4: 5–6

We have been speaking for two weeks about the spiritual life, but you know where the spiritual life is to be put into practice—in the everyday life. And today, therefore, I want to come down very low, to the level of our everyday Christianity. It is in the rush of daily life that the presence of God is to be experienced, and His power to be proved. We began last week by speaking about the work of the Holy Spirit. I tried to point out to you what God intends that Spirit to be in your daily life, in your walk as holy and spiritually minded people, in a walk in love and humility. I tried to point what the great hindrances are to a spiritual life, especially Self. I tried to point out what the blessedness is, that will come if we give ourselves to the leading of the Spirit and what the object is for which we are to seek it.

Then we came, this week, to speak about the work of Christ. I began by pointing out that His great work is just to bring us very near to God, and how I believe that this is a great want in the Church of Christ; we need more of God, more humble waiting upon God in our private prayer and worship, and in public services. God must take the first place in everything; we must take time to wait upon God for God to take that place in our souls. I then spoke about how Christ came to exhibit just this one thing: a life of absolute dependence upon God. He came to reveal to us that God was everything to Him.

We spoke of other parts of His work, and last night we closed by speaking about Jesus Christ in His blessed work as an Almighty Keeper, and ended by a consecration meeting in which we gave up ourselves to Him; God grant that many souls may know what it is that the Everlasting God is keeping them. And now we have to go away to our daily life, our homes, our business, our studies, our duties, and all of you know by experience that it is just there that the failure comes in.

It is all right in my closet and it is all right in my worship and all right in my work when I am speaking for Christ, but oh, the times of relaxation, the times when I am off my guard and times when I am in the duties of this life, these are the times when failures come; and the great question now arises: How can I live so that not only on the mount of worship, but down low in the valley of the most ordinary everyday life I may have unbroken the sense of the presence of God?

Dear friends, if you want the revelation of God, I have told you more than once you must take more time in prayer and have daily fellowship with God. You must take more time in your secret hour of prayer just quietly to realize God and adore Him. But the fullest revelation of God cannot satisfy unless it is carried out in the daily life. The value of contact with God every day, and the value of the power of the Holy Spirit daily, and the value of Christ as a keeper must be proved in daily life.

Listen to the word I have for you this morning; it is one of the simplest descriptions of the life of faith: "*Be anxious for nothing, but in everything by prayer and supplication with thanksgiving let your requests be made known unto God*" (Philippians 4: 5–6). Here we have a restful life. It is the life of continual trust, continual prayer, continual praise, continual peace, continual safety. …

The restful life is a life of continual trust. That is where it begins. You notice that we have the name of God in these two verses twice. In the first verse it is, bring your needs, your requests, unto God. That is to say let God be the one object of your trust and then comes in the second verse and God will be a fountain of blessing to you, "*The peace of God will keep you.*" These are the two sides. My love must be turned to God and God's love and blessing will be turned to me. Be anxious for nothing. …

"*Be anxious for nothing.*" And why? Because you have a God that cares for you. Oh I wish I could say to my friends and myself what I see sometimes. Is God going to do everything so perfectly in nature all around me, and is the only place He is going to fail here in my life? … I cannot believe it. I believe that the God who works so gloriously in the universe is willing to work more gloriously in your heart, so that your heart shall be the scene where His glory is fully revealed. But why does He not do it? Because you won't let Him. Because you don't trust Him. Because you allow circumstances to come between you and God. Because you in your heart believe circumstances are stronger than God. You think, God cannot deliver me from their power. You have not got fully under the power of the promises and love of God. …

How can that be? In this way alone—that you carry all the care and the trouble and the circumstances to the living God, and that you wait upon Him until you get sight of God undertaking and taking complete charge. When the soul gets sight of that the anxiety goes away and we rest in the perfect trust, God cares; God has charge, and God will guide us right. … A God is meant to have charge of the creatures He has made and to fill their life with His blessedness. Look at your God. Never did a mother care for a little child with such watchful tenderness from morning to night as your God is willing to take charge of your life. Do you know this God? Have you learned to say, "I do trust You. I have no anxiety, for my God provides. He is God Almighty and His promises are so wonderful and He is so loving and tender. I will trust my God." …

Children of God, "Do not worry about your life" (Matthew 6: 25). You know the 6th chapter of Matthew, with those precious words of the Lord Jesus. They are not only for poor people who have no clothes, but they are meant for every one of us. If God clothe

the lilies with His beauty how much more will He clothe you? Just think of that. How does God clothe the lilies? Not from without. He puts within the life that grows up into them and with most beautiful freshness there comes up a lily. A lily has the life of God, the Spirit of nature that comes from God working in it. God clothed that lily and will God not much more clothe you and me with the beauty of holiness and of humility. Oh Christian, take this word, "Be anxious for nothing." The restful life is a life of continual trust.

… The next mark of a restful life. "*In everything, by prayer and supplication, let your requests be known unto God.*" Continual prayer. It is in prayer that you will learn the secret of trusting. If you take but little time to pray you will have but little power to trust.

Trust toward God is not natural to us. Trust is very natural to us toward a fellowman. When a man tells me a thing I do not take a moment to believe. We are on the platform of nature. When my God speaks, we are on another platform. God is the Invisible One, a Spirit of holiness, and I can trust Him only by the Holy Spirit coming into me. If I live under the leading of the Holy Spirit my heart grows larger, my capacity of trust is increased, my eyes are opened and I see the glory and limitless promises of God and the treasures of His grace. …

Jesus Able to Keep

September 11th

"I am persuaded that He is able to keep."

—2 TIMOTHY 1: 12

This morning, I got a request from some twelve or fifteen brethren in the ministry, or in the work of God, asking me to give a testimony as to my own personal experience in the Christian life. ... What God has done to me is not mine but His own. …

If I speak of my life, my Christian life, the first fifteen years, perhaps, I call a time of darkness and of struggling after the light. I could divide my Christian life into three periods: The time of darkness, the time of the vision of the light, and then the time of the richer experience. I was, as a young minister, most earnest. I was counted a most faithful gospel preacher, and I was diligent in the enormous parish that was entrusted to me. I loved my work and yet all the time my spiritual life was one of deep unhappiness. I was bound in the chains of misapprehension and prejudice.

One thing that I thought was that a Christian must go on sinning every day. I really thought that this was a must. As a result of that, I had no definite expectation that God would keep me from it. I am sorry to say that that was my belief, and then along with that I had no conception that obedience was a possible thing. I look back with shame when, in later years, I began to see the place that obedience ought to take in a Christian life. I remember how little I understood that—that Christianity is to give up yourself to entire obedience to God. I never saw it.

And then, along with that, I had no real faith in the keeping, sanctifying power of

God's Holy Spirit or of Jesus Christ. Yet I was most earnest, studying the matter of sanctification, praying about it, but I got very little light. But it was a time on which God looked with mercy, for it was a time of great desire and often of crying to God, and God hears cries. …

Well, as I said, I suppose for fifteen years after my conversion, I went on, and then came the time when, in England, there was a great stir about the higher life, and I got some of these books and they helped me wonderfully, and I then began to say, "Yes, there is a better life." It was at that time, now thirty years ago, in a time of revival in my Dutch parish in Worcester, South Africa, that I wrote "Abide in Christ" in Dutch. It was not, perhaps, exactly the same as now, but the substance. It was at that time that my heart was feeling after the truth and beginning to find it, beginning to get hold of something—a little of the blessed experience of better knowledge of God and of more trust in Him.

And yet I have to confess with shame that, at that time, I often stumbled. One thing was, I had never been taught the absolute necessity, the supreme importance of literal, immediate, actual obedience to God. …

So it went on, year after year. I enjoyed more of God, I enjoyed more rest, I enjoyed more peace, I got more victory, and I learned to trust God more. The path God led me in was not that of one decisive crisis, but step by step. Mind, I have great faith that God is willing to take a man in by a sudden step, by a crisis in his life, and I count it a very blessed thing, and I think the reason that God did not take me in that way was simply that I was not properly instructed. …

I can see that when I contrast the last fifteen years of my life with the first fifteen, I praise God for a very great difference. And what I praise God for is this: the rest of faith. I can see that He has taught me to rest in Him and to trust Him and to believe, even if my faith does not always rise to its fullest height, but yet to continue in the abiding belief that my God is working in me; that my God loves me, with a wonderful love, and that as I yield entirely to Him He will do a perfect work in me.

… I feel, very deeply, how little I am able to speak aright about the sin and the low state of God's people. I feel how little I am able to show them what the unbelief and the want of righteousness and the fruitlessness of that mixed life which so many live. I feel what a solemn thing it is, that I am not able to sound the trumpet as I ought to and to awaken them out of sleep and to call them and to make them feel, "Man, you can't live one day longer in this low carnal life, you must come out undividedly, for Christ." …

Are you willing to come and to say, "Lord Jesus, I want to be someone utterly given up to God, so that everybody can see it. I want to be someone with nothing for myself, walking just in the deepest humility and dependence, and letting God glorify Himself in me. I want to be someone sacrificing everything for the sake of God's Son and God's love. I want to be someone wholly and unreservedly given to God, that God may do His very best with me." Is that your desire? Then I invite you to come, however feeble and however unworthy. Christ is waiting. You never can honor and glorify God in the way you are living now, but come and commit yourself to the keeping of Jesus, and will He not prove faithful? Will He not gloriously and wondrously keep you and bless you?

And now, secondly: Look at the mighty keeper. Paul said, "*I am persuaded that He is able to keep.*" Oh, the mighty keeping of Jesus! May God open our eyes to see that. Dear friends, there was a time, when I was a young minister—I remember it very well—that when I read of the omnipotence of God that I thought, well that is not one of the principal attributes of God that I have to do with. We make a difference, in theology, between the natural attributes of God and the moral attributes. The moral attributes are holiness, goodness, righteousness, truth and faithfulness. They have to do with character. And I thought that that is what a Christian has to do with, but the natural attributes that can be seen in creation—wisdom, omnipotence and such like—I thought of minor importance.

After a time I began to find out how wrong I was, for I began to find out in reading the Bible that at the bottom of all faith is [belief in God's] omnipotence—the mighty power of God. I read about Abraham, how God met him and said, "I am God Almighty," and I saw that thought was the rock upon which Abraham stood. I found so often, in the history of Israel, that God came and appealed to His own mighty power in His promises; I came down to the New Testament and I found how Jesus said that the things that are impossible with men are possible with God, and I began to see that one of the attributes that I need most in my spiritual life is the omnipotence of God.... And I think I am learning every day more that that [omnipotence of God] is what I need to rest in, because the whole work that is to be done in me, in keeping, sanctifying and teaching me, is all a work of God's omnipotence.

And then, dear friends, there is the Lord Jesus Christ. I used to preach upon His miracles with great pleasure, and I always spoke of His mighty power, but it was only later on that I began to see that that that almighty power must not only be exercised when a man is pardoned and made a child of God, but that almighty power must be exercised every moment in my life. Every moment. There is not five minutes in the day that I do not need the Almighty Keeper to keep charge of me. ... Oh, that I could get souls to trust the almightiness of God for their daily life. You need it, my brother, my sister, for your daily life. You do not need it now and then, on great occasions, but you need it for every hour of your life, the Almighty Christ to keep you right every day. ...

Let us all come to our God in Christ. Come and look at your life; then gaze at Christ and His keeping, and come and trust Him to do it. Old men and old women, I call upon every Christian, and if there are unconverted people here, who have never done it, they can come with us, and they can begin and say, "Christ, You would have me holy; if You will make me holy, and if You will keep me day by day; today, I will give up my soul into the hands of my Creator." ...

21

THE SCHOOL OF OBEDIENCE

New York: Fleming H. Revell Company, 1898

Obedience: Its Place in Scripture 1

September 12th

"Blessed are they that do His commandments, that they may have a right to the tree of life."
—REVELATION 22: 14

In undertaking the study of a Bible word, or of a truth of the Christian life, it is a great help to take a survey of the place it takes in Scripture. …

We begin with Paradise. In Genesis 2:16, we read: *"And the Lord God commanded the man, saying…."* And, later (3:11), *"Have you eaten of the tree, whereof I commanded you that you should not eat?"* Note how obedience to the command is the one virtue of Paradise, the one condition of man's abiding there, the one thing his Creator asks of him. Nothing is said of faith, or humility, or love: *obedience includes all.* … In the life of man, to obey is the one thing needful.

Turn … to the close of the Bible. In its last chapter you read *"Blessed are they that do His commandments, that they may have a right to the tree of life"* (Revelation 22:14). … We have the same thought in chapters 12 and 14, where we read of the seed of the woman (12:17), *"which keep the commandments of God, and hold the testimony of Jesus"*; and of the patience of the saints (14:12), *"Here are they that keep the commandments of God, and the faith of Jesus."* From beginning to end, from Paradise lost to Paradise regained, the law is unchangeable—it is only obedience that gives access to the tree of life and the favor of God.

And if you ask how the change was effected—out of the disobedience at the beginning that closed the way to the tree of life, to the obedience at the end that again gained entrance to it—turn to that which stands midway between the beginning and the end, the cross of Christ. Read a passage like Romans 5:19, *"Through the obedience of the One shall the many be made righteous";* or Philippians 2:8, *"He became obedient unto death, therefore God has highly exalted Him"*; or Hebrews 5:8, 9, *"He learned obedience and became the Author of salvation to those who obey Him,"* and you see how the whole redemption of Christ consists in restoring obedience to its place. The beauty of His salvation consists in this, that He brings us back to the life of obedience, through which alone the creature can give the Creator the glory due to Him, or receive the glory of which our Creator desires to make us partakers.

Paradise, Calvary, Heaven, all proclaim with one voice: "Child of God! the first and the last thing your God asks of you is simple, universal, unchanging obedience."

Let us turn to the Old Testament. Here let us specially notice how, with any new beginning in the history of God's kingdom, obedience always comes into special prominence. Take Noah, the new father of the human race, and you will find four times written (Genesis 6:22; 7:5, 9, 16), "*According to all that God commanded Noah, so did he.*" It is the one who does what God commands, to whom God can entrust His work, whom God can use to be a savior of others.

Think of Abraham, the father of the chosen race. "By faith Abraham obeyed" (Hebrews 11:7). When he had been forty years in this school of faith-obedience, God came to perfect his faith, and to crown it with His fullest blessing. Nothing could fit him for this but a crowning act of obedience. When he had bound his son on the altar, God came and said (Genesis 22:12, 18), "*By Myself have I sworn, in blessing I will bless you, and in multiplying I will multiply you; and in your seed shall all nations be blessed, because you have obeyed My voice.*" And to Isaac He spoke (26: 3, 5), "*I will perform the oath which I swore to Abraham, because that Abraham obeyed my voice.*" Oh, when shall we learn how unspeakably pleasing obedience is in God's sight, and how unspeakable is the reward He bestows upon it! The way to be a blessing to the world is to be people of obedience; known by God and the world by this one mark—a will utterly given up to God's will. Let all who profess to walk in Abraham's footsteps walk thus.

Go on to Moses. At Sinai, God gave him the message to the people (Exodus 19:4), "*If you will obey My voice indeed, you shall be a peculiar treasure to Me above all people.*" In the very nature of things, it cannot be otherwise. God's holy will is His glory and perfection; it is only by an entrance into His will, by obedience, that it is possible to be His people. Take the building of the sanctuary in which God was to dwell. In the last three chapters of Exodus you have the expression nineteen times, "*According to all the Lord commanded Moses, so did he,*" And then, "*The glory of the Lord filled the tabernacle.*" Just so again in Leviticus 8 and 9, you have, with reference to the consecration of the priests and the tabernacle, the same expression twelve times. And then, "*The glory of the Lord appeared before all the people, and fire came out from before the Lord, and consumed the burnt-offering.*" Words cannot make it plainer, that it is amid what the obedience of His people has wrought that God delights to dwell, that it is the obedient whom He crowns with His favor and presence.

After the forty years wandering in the wilderness, and its terrible revelation of the fruit of disobedience, there was again a new beginning when the people were about to enter Canaan. Read Deuteronomy, with all Moses spoke in sight of the land, and you will find there is no book of the Bible which uses the word obey' so frequently, or speaks so much of the blessing obedience will assuredly bring. The whole is summed up in the words (11: 27), *"I set before you a blessing if you obey, a curse if you will not obey."*

Yes, a Blessing if you Obey! that is the key-note of the blessed life. Canaan, just like Paradise and Heaven, can be the place of blessing as it is the place of obedience. Would God we might take it in! Do beware only of praying only for a blessing. Let us care for the obedience, God will care for the blessing. Let my one thought as a Christian be, how I can obey and please my God perfectly.

The next new beginning we have is in the appointment of kings in Israel. In the story of Saul we have the most solemn warning as to the need of exact and entire obedience in a man whom God is to trust as ruler of His people. Samuel had commanded Saul (1 Samuel 10: 8) to wait seven days for him to come and sacrifice, and to show him what to do. When Samuel delayed (13: 8–14) Saul took it upon himself to sacrifice. When Samuel came, he said: "*You have not kept the commandment of the Lord your God, which He commanded you; your kingdom shall not continue, because you have not kept that which the Lord commanded you.*"

God will not honor the one who is not obedient. … God speaks to Samuel, "*It grieves Me that I have set up Saul to be king, for he has not performed My commandment.*" When Samuel comes, Saul twice over says, "*I have performed the commandment of the Lord*"; "*I have obeyed the voice of the Lord.*" And so he had, as many would think. But his obedience had not been entire. God claims exact, full obedience. Sad type of so much obedience, which in part performs God's commandment, and yet is not the obedience God asks! God says of all sin and all disobedience: "Utterly destroy all! spare not!" May God reveal to us whether we are indeed going all lengths with Him, seeking utterly to destroy all and spare nothing that is not in perfect harmony with His will. It is only a whole-hearted obedience, down to the minutest details, that can satisfy God. …

Next to Deuteronomy, Jeremiah is the book most full of the word obey, though—alas!—mostly in connection with the complaint that the people had not obeyed. God sums up all His dealings with the fathers in the one word, "*I spoke not with them concerning sacrifices, but this thing I commanded them, Obey My voice and I will be your God.*" … Into all the inconceivable meaning of the word, "I will be your God," there is no gateway but this, "*Obey My voice.*"

Obedience: Its Place in Scripture 2

September 13th

"Here I am; I come to do Your will, O God."

—HEBREWS 10: 7

We come to the New Testament. Here we think at once of our blessed Lord, and the prominence He gives to obedience as the one thing for which He was come into the world. He who entered it with His *"I come to do Your will, O God,"* ever confessed, *"I seek not My own will, but the will of Him that sent Me."* Of all He did and of all He suffered, even to the death, He said, *"This commandment have I received of My Father."* If we turn to His teaching, we find everywhere, that the obedience He rendered is what He claims from everyone who would be His disciple. During His whole ministry, from beginning to end, obedience is the very essence of salvation.

In the Sermon on the Mount He began with it: *"No one could enter the kingdom, but he that does the will of My Father which is in Heaven."* And in the farewell discourse, how wonderfully He reveals the spiritual character of true obedience as it is born of love and inspired by it, and as it also opens the way into the love of God. Do take into your heart the wonderful words, (John 14:15, 16, 21, 23), "*If you love Me, you will keep my commandments. And the Father will send forth the Spirit.*" "*He has My commandments and keeps them, he it is that loves Me; he shall be loved of My Father, and I will love him, and will manifest Myself unto him.*" "*If a man loves Me, he will keep My words, and My Father will love him, and We will come unto him, and make Our abode with him.*"

No words could express more simply or more powerfully the inconceivably glorious place Christ gives to obedience, with its twofold possibility, (1) as only possible to a loving heart, (2) as making possible all that God has to give of His Holy Spirit, of His wonderful love, of His indwelling in Christ Jesus. …

We have thought of more study of the Word, more faith, more prayer, more communion with God, and we have overlooked the simple truth that Jesus teaches so clearly, "*If you keep My commandments, you shall abide in My love,*" with its Divine sanction, "*Even as I kept My Father's commandments, and abide in His love.*" For Him as for us, the only way under Heaven to abide in Divine love is to keep the commandments. Do let me ask, have you known it, have you heard it preached, have you believed it and proved it true in your experience: obedience on earth is the key to a place in God's love in Heaven? Unless there be some correspondence between God's wholehearted love in Heaven, and our wholehearted, loving obedience on earth, Christ cannot manifest Himself to us, God cannot abide in us, we cannot abide in His love.

If we go on from our Lord Jesus to His apostles, we find in the Acts two words of Peter's which show how our Lord's teaching had entered into him. In the one, "*God has given His Holy Spirit to them that obey Him*"—he proves how he knew what had been the preparation for Pentecost, the surrender to Christ. In the other, "*We must obey God rather than man*"—we have the man-ward side: obedience is to be unto death; nothing on earth dare or can hinder it in the man who has given himself to God.

In Paul's Epistle to the Romans, we have, in the opening and closing verses the expression, "*the obedience of faith among all nations*" (1:5; 16:26), as that for which he was made an apostle. He speaks of what God had wrought "*to make the Gentiles obedient.*" He teaches that, as the obedience of Christ makes us righteous, we become the servants of obedience unto righteousness.

We all know how James warns us not to be hearers of the Word only but doers, and expounds how Abraham was justified, and his faith perfected, by his works.

In Peter's First Epistle we have only to look at the first chapter, to see the place obedience has in his system. In verse 2 he speaks to the Elect, in sanctification of the

Spirit, unto obedience....and so points us to obedience as the eternal purpose of the Father, as the great object of the work of the Spirit, and a chief part of the salvation of Christ. In verse 13 he writes, "As children of obedience," born of it, marked by it, subject to it, "be you holy in all manner of conversation." Obedience is the very starting point of true holiness. In verse 22 we read, "*Seeing you have purified your souls in your obedience to the truth*,"—the whole acceptance of the truth of God was not merely a matter of intellectual assent or strong emotion: it was a subjection of the life to the dominion of the truth of God: the Christian life was in the first place obedience.

Of John, we know how strong his statements are. "*He that says, I know Him, and keeps not His Commandments, is a liar.*" Obedience is the one certificate of Christian character. ... "*And whatsoever we ask we receive of Him, because we keep His commandments, and do the things that are pleasing in His sight.*" Obedience is the secret of good conscience, and of the confidence that God hears us. "*This is the love of God, that we keep His Commandments.*" The obedience that keeps His commandments: this is the garment in which the hidden, invisible love reveals itself, and whereby it is known.

Such is the place obedience has in Holy Scripture, in the mind of God, in the hearts of His servants. We may well ask, "Does it take that place in my heart and life?" Have we indeed given obedience that supreme place of authority over us that God means it to have, as the inspiration of every action, and of every approach to Him? If we yield ourselves to the searching of God's Spirit, we may find that we never gave it its true proportion in our scheme of life, and that this lack is the cause of all our failure in prayer and in work. We may see that the deeper blessings of God's grace, and the full enjoyment of God's love and nearness, have been beyond our reach, simply because obedience was never made what God would have it be—the starting-point and the goal of our Christian life.

The Morning Watch 1

September 14th

"If the root is holy, so are the branches."

—ROMANS 11: 16

It is in the closet, in the morning watch, that our spiritual life is both tested and strengthened. There is the battlefield where it is to be decided every day whether God is to have all, whether our life is to be absolute obedience. If we truly conquer there, getting rid of ourselves into the hands of our Almighty Lord, the victory during the day is sure. It is there, in the inner chamber, proof is to be given whether we really delight in God, and make it our aim to love Him with our whole heart. Let this, then, be our first lesson: the presence of God is the chief thing, in our devotions. To meet God, to give ourselves into His holy will, to know that we are pleasing to Him, to have Him give us our orders, and lay His hand upon us, and bless us, and say to us, "Go in this your strength"—it is when the soul learns that this is what is to be found in the morning watch, day by day, that we shall learn to long for it and delight in it.

Let us next speak of the reading of God's Word, as part of what occupies us there. With regard to this I have more than one thing I wish to say.

One is that unless we beware, the Word, which is meant to point us away to God, may actually intervene and hide Him from us. The mind may be occupied and interested and delighted at what it finds, and yet, because this is more head knowledge than anything else, it may bring little good to us. If it does not lead us to wait on God, to glorify Him, to receive His grace and power for sweetening and sanctifying our lives, it becomes a hindrance instead of a help.

Another lesson that cannot be repeated too often, or pressed too urgently, is that it is only by the teaching of the Holy Spirit that we can get at the real meaning of what God means by His Word, and that the Word will really reach into our inner life, and work in us. The Father in Heaven, who gave us His Word from Heaven, with its Divine mysteries and message, has given us His Holy Spirit in us, to explain and internally appropriate that Word. The Father wants us each time to ask that He teach us by His Spirit. He wants us to bow in a meek, teachable frame of mind, and believe that the Spirit will, in the hidden depth of our heart, make His Word live and work. He wants us to remember that the Spirit is given us that we should be led by Him, should walk after Him, should have our whole life under His rule, and that therefore He cannot teach us in the morning unless we honestly give up ourselves to His leading. But if we do this and patiently wait on Him, not to get new thoughts but to get the power of the Word in our heart, we can count upon His teaching. …

A third remark I want to make, in confirmation of what was said above, is this: ever study in God's Word in the spirit of an unreserved surrender to obey. You know how often Christ, and His apostles in their Epistles, speak of hearing and not doing. If you accustom yourself to study the Bible without an earnest and very definite purpose to obey, you are getting hardened in disobedience. Never read God's will concerning you without honestly giving up yourself to do it at once, and asking grace to do so. God has given us His Word, to tell us what He wants us to do and what grace He has provided to enable us to do it: how sad to think it a pious thing just to read that Word without any earnest effort to obey it! May God keep us from this terrible sin! Let us make it a sacred habit to say to God, "Lord, whatever I know to be Your will, I will at once obey." Ever read with a heart yielded up in willing obedience. … It is only as we are willing to know all God's will that, He will from time to time reveal more of it to us, and that we, will be able to do it all.

It is in the light of these thoughts I want now to say a few words on what prayer is to be in the morning watch.

First of all, see that you secure the presence of God. Do not be content with anything less than seeing the face of God, having the assurance that He is looking on you in love, and listening and working in you. If our daily life is to be full of God, how much more the morning hour, where the life of the day alone can have God's seal stamped upon it.

In our religion we want nothing so much as more of God—His love, His will, His holiness, His Spirit living in us, His power working in us for men. Under Heaven there is no way of getting this but by close personal communion. And there is no time so good for securing and practicing it, as the morning watch.

The superficiality and feebleness of our religion and religious work all come from having so little real contact with God. If it be true that God alone is the fountain of all love and good and happiness, and that to have as much as possible of His presence and His fellowship, of His will and His service, is our truest and highest happiness, surely then to meet Himself alone in the morning watch ought to be our first care. To have had God appear to them, and speak to them, was with all the Old Testament saints the secret of their obedience and their strength. Do give God time in secret so to reveal Himself, that your soul may call the name of the place Peniel—*"for I have seen Him face to face."*

The Morning Watch 2

September 15th

"If the root is holy, so are the branches."

—ROMANS 11: 16

Let the renewal of your surrender to absolute obedience for that day be a chief part of your morning sacrifice. Let any confession of sin be very definite—a plucking out and cutting off of everything that has been grieving to God. Let any prayer for grace for a holy walk be as definite—an asking and accepting in faith of the very grace and strength you are specially in need of. Let your outlook on the day you are entering on be a very determined resolve that obedience to God shall be its controlling principle.

Do understand that there is no surer way, rather, that there is no other possible way, of getting into God's love and blessing in prayer, than by getting into His will. In prayer, give up yourself most absolutely to the blessed will of God: this will avail more than much asking. Beseech God to show you this great mercy, that He allows you, that He will enable you, to enter into His will, and abide there—that will make the knowing and doing His will in your life a blessed certainty. Let your prayer indeed be a morning sacrifice, a placing yourself as a whole burnt-offering on the altar of the Lord.

Then remember that true prayer and fellowship with God cannot be all from one side. We need to be still, to wait and hear what response God gives. This is the office of the Holy Spirit, to be the voice of God to us. In the hidden depths of the heart, He can give a secret but most certain assurance that we are heard, that we are well-pleasing, that the Father engages to do for us what we have asked.

What we need, to hear the Voice, to receive this assurance, is the quiet stillness that waits on God, the quiet faith that trusts in God, the quiet heart that bows in nothingness and humility before God, and allows Him to be all in all. It is when God *is waited on to take*

His part in our prayer that the confidence will come to us that we receive what we ask, that our surrender of ourselves in the sacrifice of obedience is accepted, and that therefore we can count upon the Holy Spirit to guide us into all the will of God, as He means us to know and do it.

And now comes the last and the best of all: Let your prayer be intercessional, on behalf of others. In the obedience of our Lord Jesus, as in all His fellowship with the Father, the essential element was [self-sacrifice]—it was [giving our] *all for others.* … The highest form of prayer is intercession. The chief object for which God chose Abraham and Israel and us was to make us a blessing to the world. We are a royal priesthood—a priestly people. As long as prayer is only a means of personal improvement and happiness, we cannot know its full power. Let intercession be a real longing for the souls of those around us, a real bearing of the burden of their sin and need, a real pleading for the extension of God's kingdom, real labor in prayer for definite purposes to be realized--let such intercession be what the morning watch is consecrated to, and see what new interest and attraction it will have.

Intercession! Oh, to realize what it means! To take the name, and the righteousness, and the worthiness of Christ—to put them on, and in them to appear before God! In Christ's stead, now that He is no longer in the world, to beseech God, by name, for the individual men and needs, where His grace can do its work! In the faith of our own acceptance, and of the anointing with the Spirit to fit us for the work, to know that our prayer can avail to save a soul from death, can bring down and dispense the blessing of Heaven upon earth! To think that in the hour of the morning watch this work can be renewed and carried on day by day, each inner chamber maintaining its own separate communication with Heaven, and helping together in bringing down its share of the blessing. It is in intercession—more than in the zeal that works in its own strength with little prayer—that the highest type of piety, the true Christlikeness is cultivated. It is in intercession that a believer rises to his true nobility in the power of imparting life and blessing. It is to intercession we must look for any large increase of the power of God in the Church and its work for men. …

The Obedience of Christ 1

September 16th

"Through the obedience of the One shall all the many be made righteous."

"Know you not that you are servants of obedience unto righteousness?"

—ROMANS 5:19; 6:16

It is evident that the one work a Christ was needed for was to remove this disobedience its curse, its dominion, its evil nature and workings. Disobedience was the root of all sin and misery. The first object of His salvation was to cut away the evil root, and restore us to our original destiny—a life in obedience to our God.

How did Christ do this?

First of all, by coming as the Second Adam, to undo what the first had done. Sin had made us believe that it was a humiliation always to be seeking to know and do God's will. Christ came to show us the nobility, the blessedness, the heavenliness of obedience. When God gave us the robe of creaturehood to wear, we knew not that its beauty, its unspotted purity, was obedience to God. Christ came and put on that robe that He might show us how to wear it, and how with it we could enter into the presence and glory of God. Christ came to overcome, and so bear away our disobedience, and to replace it by His own obedience on us and in us. As universal, as mighty, as all-pervading as was the disobedience of Adam, yea, far more so, was to be the power of the obedience of Christ. …

The disobedience of Adam, in all its possible bearings, was to be put away and replaced by the obedience of Christ. Judicially, by that obedience we are made righteous. Just as we were made sinners by Adam's disobedience, we are at once and completely justified and delivered from the power of sin and death: we stand before God as righteous. Vitally, for the judicial and the vital are as inseparable as in the case of Adam—we are made one plant with Christ in His death and resurrection, so that we are as truly dead to sin and alive to God, as He is. And the life we receive in Him is no other than a life of obedience.

Let every one of us who would know what obedience is, consider well: It is the obedience of Christ that is the secret of the righteousness and salvation I find in Him. The obedience is the very essence of that righteousness: obedience is salvation. …

The more carefully we trace the parallel between the first and Second Adam, and see how in the former the death and disobedience reigned in his seed equally with himself, and how both were equally transmitted, through union with him, the more will the conviction be forced upon us that the obedience of Christ is equally to be ours, not only by imputation, but by personal possession. It is so inseparable from Him that to receive Him and His life is to receive His obedience. When we receive the righteousness which God offers us so freely, it at once points us to the obedience out of which it was born, with which it is inseparably one, in which alone it can live and flourish.

See how this connection comes out in the next chapter. After having spoken of our life—union to Christ, Paul, for the first time in the epistle (6:12), gives an injunction, *"Let not sin reign; ... present yourselves unto God"*; and then immediately proceeds to teach how this means nothing but obedience: *"Know you not, that you are servants of sin unto death, or of obedience unto righteousness?"* Your relation to obedience is a practical one; you have been delivered from disobedience (Adam's and your own), and now have become "*servants of obedience—and that unto righteousness.*" Christ's obedience was unto righteousness—the righteousness which is God's gift to you. Your subjection to obedience is the one way in which your relation to God and to righteousness can be maintained.

Christ's obedience unto righteousness is the only beginning of life for you; your obedience unto righteousness, its only continuance. There is but one law for the head and the members. As surely as it was with Adam and his seed, disobedience and death, it is with Christ and his seed, obedience and life. The one bond of union, the one mark of likeness, between Adam and his seed was disobedience. The one bond of union between Christ and His seed, the one mark of resemblance, is obedience.

It was obedience made Christ the object of the Father's love (John 10:17, 18) and our Redeemer; it is obedience alone can lead us in the way to dwell in that love (John 14:21, 23) and enjoy that redemption.

The Obedience of Christ 2

September 17th

"Through the obedience of the One shall all the many be made righteous."
"Know you not that you are servants of obedience unto righteousness?"
—ROMANS 5:19; 6:16

Everything depends upon our knowledge of and participation in the obedience, as the gateway and path to the full enjoyment of the righteousness. At conversion the righteousness is given to faith, once for all, completely and forever, with but little or no knowledge of the obedience. But as the righteousness is indeed believed in and submitted to, and its full dominion over us, *"as servants of righteousness,"* sought after, it will open to us its blessed nature, as born out of obedience, and therefore ever leading us back to its Divine origin. The truer our hold of the righteousness of Christ, in the power of the Spirit, the more intense will be our desire to share in the obedience out of which it sprang. In this light let us study the obedience of Christ, that like Him we may live as servants of obedience unto righteousness.

1. In Christ this obedience was a life principle. Obedience with Him did not mean a single act of obedience now and then, not even a series of acts, but the spirit of His whole life. "*I came, not to do My own will*"; "*I come, to do Your will, O God.*" He had come into the world for one purpose. He only lived to carry out God's will. The one supreme, all-controlling power of His life was obedience. He is willing to make it so in us. This was what He promised when He said, "*Whosoever shall do the will of My Father which is in Heaven*, the same is My brother and sister and mother." The link in a family is a common life shared by all and a family likeness. The bond between Christ and us is that He and we together do the will of God.

2. In Christ this obedience was a joy. "*I delight to do Your will, O God.*" "*My meat is to do the will of Him that sent Me.*" ... And so, doing the will of God was the food that Christ hungered after and without which He could not live, the one thing that satisfied His hunger, the one thing that refreshed and strengthened Him and made Him glad.

3. In Christ this obedience led to a waiting on God's will. God did not reveal all His will to Christ at once, but day by day, according to the circumstances of the hour. In His life of obedience there was growth and progress; the most difficult lesson came the last. Each act of obedience fitted Him for the new discovery of the Father's further command. He spoke, "*My ears have You opened; I delight to do Your will, O God.*" It is as obedience

becomes the passion of our life that the ears will be opened by God's Spirit to wait for His teaching, and we be content with nothing less than a Divine guidance into the Divine will for us.

4. In Christ this obedience was unto death. When He spoke, *"I came not to do My own will, but the will of Him that sent Me,"* He was ready to go all lengths in denying His own will and doing the Father's. He meant it. In nothing My will; at all costs God's will. This is the obedience to which He invites and for which He empowers us. This whole-hearted surrender to obedience in everything is the only true obedience, is the only power that will avail to carry us through. Would God that Christians could understand that nothing less than this is what brings the soul gladness and strength!

As long as there is a doubt about universal obedience, and with that a lurking sense of the possibility of failure, we lose the confidence that secures the victory. But when once we set God before us, as really asking full obedience, and engaging to work it, and see that we dare offer Him nothing less, we give up ourselves to the working of the Divine power, which by the Holy Spirit can master our whole life.

5. In Christ this obedience sprang from the deepest humility. "*Have this mind in you, which was also in Christ Jesus, who emptied Himself—who took the form of a servant—who humbled Himself, becoming obedient to death.*" It is the one who is willing for entire, Self-emptying, is willing to be and live as the servant, "a servant of obedience"; is willing to be humbled very low before God and man, to whom the obedience of Jesus will unfold its heavenly beauty and its constraining power. There may be a strong will, that secretly trusts in Self, that strives for the obedience, and fails. It is as we sink low before God in humility, meekness, patience, and entire resignation to His will, and are willing to bow in an absolute helplessness and dependence on Him, as we turn away wholly from Self, that it will be revealed to us how it is the one only duty and blessing of a creature to obey this glorious God!

6. In Christ this obedience was of faith—in entire dependence upon God's strength. "*I can do nothing of Myself; The Father that dwells in Me does the works.*" The Son's unreserved surrender to the Father's will was met by the Father's unceasing and undeserved bestowment of His power working in Him. Even so it will be with us. If we learn that our giving up our will to God is ever the measure of His giving His power in us, we shall see that a surrender to full obedience is nothing but a full faith that God will work all in us. God's promises of the New Covenant all rest on this: "*The Lord Your God will circumcise your heart to love the Lord your God with all your heart, and you shall obey the Lord your God*"; "*I will put My Spirit within you, and cause you to walk in My statutes, and you shall keep My judgments.*"

Let us, like the Son, believe that God works all in us, and we shall have the courage to yield ourselves to an unreserved obedience—an obedience unto death. That yielding ourselves up to God will become the entrance into the blessed experience of conformity to the Son of God in His doing the Father's will, because He counted on the Father's power. Let us give our all to God. He will work His all in us. …

The Entrance to the Life of Full Obedience 1

September 18th

"He became obedient unto death."

—PHILIPPIANS 2: 8

He became obedient unto death. There is no other Christ for any of us; no other obedience that pleases God; no other example for us to copy; no other Teacher from whom to learn to obey. Christians suffer inconceivably because they do not at once and heartily accept this as the only obedience they are to aim at. The youngest Christian will find it a strength in the school of Christ to make nothing less from the commencement his prayer and his vow: Obedient unto Death. It is at once the beauty and the glory of Christ. A share in it is the highest blessing He has to give. The desire for and the surrender to it is possible to the youngest believer. …

It is such obedience God wants. It is such obedience Christ gave. It is such obedience He teaches. Be it such obedience and nothing less we seek to learn. From the very outset of the Christian life let this be our aim, that we may avoid the fatal mistake of calling Christ Master and yet not doing what He says.

In Jeremiah, the prophet who more than any other speaks of the disobedience of God's people, God says, *"Return, you backsliding Israel, says the Lord; for I am merciful. Only acknowledge your iniquity that you have not obeyed My voice, says the Lord God. Turn, O backsliding children, says the Lord."* As little as there can be pardon at conversion without confession can there be, after conversion, deliverance from the overcoming power of sin and the disobedience it brings, without a new and deeper conviction and confession.

The thought of our disobedience must not be a vague generality. The special things in which we actually disobey must be definitely found out, and in confession given up and placed in the hands of Christ, and by Him cleansed away. … Let us search our life by the light of the teaching of our Lord.

Let us take a single sin—such as that of lying. … How much there is in ordinary society … that will not stand the test of strict truthfulness! And so, there are other commandments, up to the very last, with its condemnation of all coveting and lusting after what is not ours, in which too frequently the Christian gives way to disobedience.

To be merciful as the Father in Heaven, to forgive just as He does, to love enemies and to do good to them that hate us, and to live lives of Self-sacrifice and beneficence—this was the religion Jesus taught on earth. Let us look upon an unforgiving spirit when we are provoked or ill-used, upon unloving thoughts and sharp or unkind words, upon the neglect of the call to show mercy and do good and bless, all as so much disobedience, which must be felt and mourned over ….

Christ spoke much of Self-denial. Self is the root of all lack of love and obedience. Our Lord called His disciples to deny themselves and to take up their cross; to forsake all, to hate and lose their own life, to humble themselves and become the servants of all [Matthew 16: 24]. He did so, because Self—self-will, Self-pleasing, Self-seeking—is simply the source of all sin. When we indulge the flesh in such a simple thing as eating and drinking; when we gratify Self by seeking or accepting or rejoicing in what indulges our pride; when Self-will is allowed to assert itself, and we make provision for the fulfillment of its desire, we are guilty of disobedience to His command. This gradually clouds the soul and makes the full enjoyment of His light and peace an impossibility.

When the call is heard to come and now begin anew a true life of obedience, there are many who feel the desire to do so, and try quietly to slip into it. They think that by more prayer and Bible study they will grow into it—it will gradually come. They are greatly mistaken. The word God uses in Jeremiah might teach them their mistake: "*Turn, you backsliding children, turn to Me.*" … There is no growing out of disobedience into obedience. A turning back, a turning away, a decision, a crisis, is needed. And that only comes by the very definite insight into what has been wrong, and its confession with shame and penitence. Then alone will the soul seek for that Divine and mighty cleansing from all its filthiness which prepares for the consciousness of the gift of the new heart, and God's Spirit in it causing us to walk in His statutes.

If you would hope to lead a different life, to become a man or a woman of a Christ-like obedience unto death, do begin by beseeching God for the Holy Spirit of conviction, to show you all your disobedience and to lead you in humble confession to the cleansing God has provided. Rest not till you have received it.

The Entrance to the Life of Full Obedience 2

September 19th

"He became obedient unto death."

—PHILIPPIANS 2: 8

We must attend carefully to the difference between voluntary and involuntary sin. It is with the former alone that obedience deals. We know that the new heart which God gives His child is placed in the midst of the flesh with its sinfulness. Out of this there often arises, even in one who is walking in true obedience, evil suggestions of pride, unlovingness, impurity, over which we have no direct control. They are in their nature utterly sinful and vile; but they are not imputed to us as acts of transgression. They are not acts of disobedience, which we can break off and cast out, as we can the disobedience of which we have spoken. The deliverance from them comes in another way—not through the will of the regenerate man, by which obedience always comes, *but through the cleansing power of the blood and the indwelling Christ.* …

It is of great consequence to note the distinction. It keeps the Christian from thinking obedience impossible. It encourages us to seek and offer our obedience in the sphere where it can avail. And it is just in proportion as in its own sphere the power of the will for obedience is maintained, that the power of the Spirit can be trusted and obtained to do the cleansing work in what is beyond the reach of the will. …

[Our Father in Heaven] asks of us only the obedience of each day, or rather, each hour at a time. He sees whether I have indeed chosen and given myself up to the whole-hearted performance of every known command. He sees whether I am really longing and learning to know and do all His will. And when His child does this, in simple faith and love, the obedience is acceptable. The Spirit gives us the sweet assurance that we are well-pleasing to Him, and enables us to have confidence before God, because we know that *"we keep His commandments, and do the things that are pleasing in His sight"* (1 John 3: 22). This obedience is indeed an attainable degree of grace. The faith that it is [possible], is indispensable to the obedient walk. You ask for the ground of that faith in God's Word? You find it in God's New Covenant promise, *"I will write My law in their heart. I will put My fear in their heart, and they shall not depart from Me."*

The great defect of the Old Covenant was that it demanded, but did not provide, the power for obedience. This the New Covenant did. The heart means the love, the life. The law put into, written into the heart, means that it has taken possession of the inmost life and love of the renewed man. The new heart delights in the law of God, it is willing and able to obey it.

You doubt this; your experience does not confirm it. No wonder! A promise of God is a thing of faith; you do not believe it, and so cannot experience it. … Christian! Do believe that the law lives in your inmost being! Speak in faith the words of David and of Christ, *"I delight to do Your will O God! Yea, Your law is written on my heart."*

"Turn to Me, you backsliding children, and I will heal your backsliding," God said to Israel. They were His people, but had turned from Him; the return must be immediate and entire. To turn our back upon the divided life of disobedience, and in the faith of God's grace to say I will obey, may be the work of a moment.

The power for it, to take the vow and to maintain it, comes from the living Christ. We have said before, the power of obedience lies in the mighty influence of a living personal Presence. … If we take Jesus, in His unchanging nearness, as at once our Lord and our Strength, we can obey. … Christ becomes all in all to us; the Master who commands the Example who teaches, the Helper who strengthens. Turn from your life of disobedience to Christ; give up yourself to Him in surrender and faith. In surrender, let Him have all. Give up your life to be as full of Him, of His presence, His will, His service, as He can make it. Give up yourself to Him… that He may have you wholly for Himself, as a vessel, as a channel, which He can fill with Himself, with His life and love for fellow man … in His blessed service. …

God sent Christ into the world to restore obedience to its place in our heart and life, to restore man to His place in the obedience to God. … The Christ who loves us, who leads and teaches and strengthens us, who lives in us, is the Christ who was obedient unto death. *"Obedient unto death"* is the very essence of the life He imparts. Shall we not accept it and trust Him to manifest it in us?

We begin to see it; all our disobedience was owing to our not knowing Christ aright. We see it; obedience is only possible in a life of unceasing fellowship with Himself. The inspiration of His voice, the light of His eyes, the grasp of His hand make it possible, make it certain.

The Secret of True Obedience

September 20th

"He learned obedience from the things He suffered."

—HEBREWS 5: 8

The secret of true obedience—let me say at once what I believe it to be—is the clear and close personal relationship to God. All our attempts after full obedience will be failures until we get access to His abiding fellowship. It is God's holy presence, consciously abiding with us, that keeps us from disobeying Him.

Defective obedience is always the result of a defective life. To rouse and spur on that defective life by arguments and motives has its use, but their chief blessing must be that they make us feel the need of a different life, a life so entirely under the power of God that obedience will be its natural outcome. The defective life, the life of broken and irregular fellowship with God, must be healed, and make way for a full and healthy life; then full obedience will become possible. The secret of a true obedience is the return to close and continual fellowship with God.

"He learned obedience" (Hebrews 5: 8). And why was this needful? And what is the blessing He brings us? Listen, *"He learned obedience by the things which He suffered,"* and *"became the author of eternal salvation to all them that obey Him."* Suffering is unnatural to us, and therefore calls for the surrender of our will. ... The very essence of salvation is obedience to God. Christ as the obedient One saves us as His obedient ones. Whether in His suffering on earth, or in His glory in Heaven, whether in Himself or in us, obedience is what the heart of Christ is set upon. On earth Christ was a learner in the school of obedience; in Heaven He teaches it to His disciples here on earth. In a world where disobedience reigns unto death, the restoration of obedience is in Christ's hands. As in His own life, so in us, He has undertaken to maintain it. He teaches and works it in us.

... Day by day, each moment as He taught and worked, He lived, as man, in continual communication with the Father, and received the Father's instructions just as He needed them. Does He not say, *"The Son can do nothing of Himself but what He sees the Father do; for the Father shows the Son all things that Himself does; and He will show Him greater things"*; *"As I hear, I judge"*; *"I am not alone, but I and the Father that sent Me..."*; *"The words that I speak, I speak not of Myself, but the Father that dwells in Me"*? It is everywhere a dependence upon a *present fellowship* and operation of God, a hearing and a seeing of what God speaks and does and shows.

Our Lord ever spoke of His relation to the Father as the type and the promise of our relation to Him, and to the Father through Him. With us as with Him, the life of continual obedience is impossible without continual fellowship and continual teaching. It is only when God comes into our lives, in a degree and a power which many never consider possible, when His presence as the Eternal and Ever-present One is believed and received, even as the Son believed and received it, that there can be any hope of a life in which every thought is brought into captivity to the obedience of Christ. …

The Obedience of Faith

September 21st

"By faith Abraham, when he was called to go out into a place; which he should after receive as an inheritance, obeyed."
—HEBREWS 11: 8

Abraham believed that there was a land of Canaan, of which God had spoken. He believed in it as a land of promise, secured to him as an inheritance. He believed that God would bring him there, would show it him, and give it him. In that faith he dared go out, not knowing where he went. In the blessed ignorance of faith, he trusted God, and obeyed, and received the inheritance.

The land of promise that has been set before us is the blessed life of obedience. We have heard God's call to go out and dwell there…. We have heard the promise of Christ to bring us there, and to give us possession of the land…. Our desire now is that all our life and work in it may be lifted up to the level of a holy and joyful obedience: and that through us God may make obedience the key-note of the Christian life we aim at promoting in others. Our aim is high: we can only reach it by a new inflow of the power that comes from above. It is only by a faith that gets a *new* vision and hold of the powers of the heavenly world, secured to us in Christ, that we can obey and obtain the promise.

… Come and prove what He can work in you. Come and experience what the nobility is of a Christlike obedience unto death. Come and see what blessing God will give to him who, with Christ, gives himself the uttermost unto the ever-blessed and most holy will of God. Only believe in the glory of this good land of whole-hearted obedience….

Faith Sees It. Is there really such a land of promise, in which continuous obedience is certainly, is Divinely possible? As long as there is any doubt on this point, it is out of the question to go up and possess the land. Just think of Abraham's faith. It rested in God, in His omnipotence and His faithfulness. We have put before you the promises of God. Hear another of them: *"I will give you a new heart, and I will put My Spirit within you, and I will cause you to walk in my judgments, and you shall keep them."* Here is God's covenant engagement. He adds, *I the Lord have spoken, and I will do it.* He undertakes to cause and enable you to obey. In Christ and the Holy Spirit, He has made the most wonderful provision for fulfilling His engagement.

Just do what Abraham did—fix your heart upon God. He was strong in faith, giving glory to God, *"being fully persuaded that what He had promised He was able to perform."* God's omnipotence was Abraham's stay. Let it be yours. Look out on all the promises God's Word gives of a clean heart, a heart established blameless in holiness, of a life in righteousness and holiness, of a walk in all the commandments of the Lord blameless and well-pleasing to Him.... Let the assurance that a life of full obedience is possible, possess you. Faith can see the invisible and the impossible. Gaze on the vision until your heart says: "It must be true. It is true. There is a life promised that I have never yet known."

Faith Desires It. When I read the gospel story and see how ready the sick and the blind and the needy were to believe Christ's word, I often ask myself what it was that made them so much more ready to believe than we are. The answer I get in the Word is this: that one great difference lies in the honesty and intensity of the desire. They did indeed desire deliverance with their whole heart. There was no need of pleading with them to make them willing to take His blessing.

Alas, that it should be so different with us! All indeed wish, in a sort of way, to be better than they are. But how few there are who really *"hunger and thirst after righteousness"*; how few who intensely long and cry after a life of close obedience, and the continual consciousness of being pleasing to God. ... It is alone the desire for salvation that brings a sinner to Christ. It is the desire for God, and the closest possible fellowship with Him, the desire to be just what He would have us be, and to have as much of His will as possible, that will make the promised land attractive to us.

Shame on us...that the most desirable of all things—likeness to God in the union with His will and doing it—has so little attraction for us! Let us take it as a sign of our blindness and dullness, and beseech God to give us by His Spirit enlightened eyes of the heart, *"that we may see and know the riches of the glory of our inheritance"* waiting upon the life of true obedience. Let us turn and gaze, in this light of God's Spirit, and gaze again on the life as possible, as certain, as Divinely secured and Divinely blessed, until our faith begins to burn with desire, and to say: "I do long to have it. With my whole heart will I seek it."

Saint Teresa [of Ávila, the Spanish mystic] writes that after her conversion she spent more than eighteen years of her life in that miserable attempt to reconcile God and her life of sin. But at last she was able to write: "I have made a vow never to offend God in the very least matter. I have vowed that I would rather die a thousand deaths than do anything of that kind, knowing I was doing it—this was obedience unto death. I am resolved never to leave anything whatever undone that I consider still to be more perfect, and more for the honor of my Lord." ... Set your heart upon it, and expect it. The same God lives still. Set your hope on Him; He will do it.

Faith Accepts It. To all who say they do expect, we urgently say, "accept." Faith has the wondrous God-given power of saying, "I accept, I take, I have." It is for the lack of this definite faith, that claims and appropriates the spiritual blessing we desire, that so many prayers appear to be fruitless. For such an act of faith all are not ready. Where there is no true conviction of the sin of disobedience, and alas! no true sorrow for it—where there is no strong longing or purpose really in everything to obey God; where there is no deep interest in the message of Holy Scripture, that God wants to perfect us to do His will, *"by Himself working in us that which is pleasing in His sight"*—there is not the spiritual capacity to accept the blessing. That Christian is content to be a babe…not able to bear the strong meat of which Jesus ate—*doing, the will of His Father.*

And yet we come to all with the entreaty, Accept it—the grace for this wondrous new life of obedience—accept it now. Without this your act of consecration will come to little. Without this your purpose to try and be more obedient must fail. Has not God shown you that there is an entirely new position for you to take—a possible position of simple childlike obedience, day by day, to every command His voice speaks to you through the Spirit: a possible position of simple childlike dependence on and experience of His all-sufficient grace, day by day, for every command He gives? …

Take that position, make that surrender, take that grace. Accept and enter on the true life of faith, and the unceasing obedience of faith. As unlimited and as sure as God's promise and power are, may your faith be. As unlimited as your faith is, will your simple childlike obedience be. Oh! Ask God for His aid, and accept all He has offered you.

Faith Trusts Christ for All. All the promises of God are in Christ Jesus…. We have seen more than once how His whole redemption, as He effected it, is nothing but obedience. … He gives us the spirit of obedience as the spirit of our life. This spirit comes to us each moment through Him. He Himself keeps charge of our obedience. … He offers Himself to us as surety for its maintenance, and asks us to trust Him for it. It is in Jesus Himself all our fears are removed, all our needs supplied, all our desires met. As He the righteous One is your righteousness; He the obedient One is your obedience.

Will you not trust Him for it? What faith sees and desires and expects and accepts, surely it dare trust Christ to give and to work. Will you not to-day take the opportunity of giving glory to God and His Son, by trusting Jesus now to lead you into the promised land? Look up to your glorified Lord in Heaven, and in His strength renew, with new meaning, your vow of allegiance, your vow never to do anything knowingly or willingly that would offend Him. Trust Him for the faith to make the vow, for the heart to keep it, for the strength to carry it out. Trust Him, the loving One, by His living presence, to secure both your faith and obedience. …

The School of Obedience 1

September 22nd

"If any man wills to do His Will, he shall know of the teaching, whether it be of God."

—JOHN 7: 17

The unreserved surrender to obey, as it is the first condition of entering Christ's school, is the only fitness for receiving instruction as to the will of God for us.

There is a general will of God for all His children, which we can, in some measure, learn out of the Bible. But there is a special individual application of these commands—God's will concerning each of us personally, which only the Holy Spirit can teach. And He will not teach it, except to those who have taken the vow of obedience.

This is the reason why there are so many unanswered prayers for God to make known His will. Jesus said, "*If any man wills to do His Will, he shall know of the teaching, whether it be of God.*" If our will is really set on doing God's will, that is, if our heart is given up to do, and we as a consequence do it as far as we know it, we shall know what God has further to teach us. It is simply what is true of every scholar with the art he studies, of every apprentice with his trade, of every man in business doing is the one condition of truly knowing. And so obedience, the doing of God's will as far as we know, and the will and the vow to do it all as He reveals it, is the spiritual organ, the capacity for receiving the true knowledge of what is God's will for each of us.

In connection with this let me press upon you three things.

1. Seek to have a deep sense of your very great ignorance of God's will, and of your impotence by any effort to know it aright. The consciousness of ignorance lies at the root of true teachableness. The meek will He guide in the way—those who humbly confess their need of teaching. Head-knowledge only gives human thoughts without power. God by His Spirit gives a living knowledge that enters the love of the heart, and works effectually.

2. Cultivate a strong faith that God will make you know wisdom in the hidden part, in the heart. You may have known so little of this in your Christian life hitherto that the thought appears strange. Learn that God's working, the place where He gives His life and light, is in the heart, deeper than all our thoughts. Any uncertainty about God's will makes a joyful obedience impossible. Believe most confidently that the Father is willing to make known what He wants you to do. Count upon Him for this. Expect it certainly.

3. In view of the darkness and deceitfulness of the flesh and fleshly mind, ask God very earnestly for the searching and convincing light of the Holy Spirit. There may be many things which you have been accustomed to think lawful or allowable, which your Father wants different. To consider it settled that they are the will of God because others and you think so, may effectually shut you out from knowing God's will in other things. Bring everything, without reserve, to the judgment of the Word, explained and applied by the Holy Spirit. Wait on God to lead you to know that everything you are and do is pleasing in His sight.

On Obedience unto Death

There is one of the deeper and more spiritual aspects of this truth to which I have not alluded. It is something that as a rule does not come up in the early stages of the Christian life, and yet it is needful that every believer know what the privileges are that await him. There is an experience into which whole-hearted obedience will bring the believer, in which he will know that, as surely as with his Lord, obedience leads to death.

Let us see what this means. During our Lord's life, His resistance to sin and the world was perfect and complete. And yet His final deliverance from their temptations and His victory over their power, His obedience, was not complete until He had died to the earthly life and to sin. In that death He gave up His life in perfect helplessness into the Father's hands, waiting for Him to raise Him up. It was through death that He received the fullness of His life and glory. Through death alone, the giving up of the life He had, could obedience lead Him into the glory of God.

The believer shares with Christ in this death to sin. In regeneration he is baptized by the Holy Spirit into it. Owing to ignorance and unbelief he may know little experimentally of this entire death to sin. When the Holy Spirit reveals to him what he possesses in Christ, and he appropriates it in faith, the Spirit works in him the very same disposition which animated Christ in His death. With Christ it was an entire ceasing from His own life, a helpless committal of His spirit into the Father's hands. This was the complete fulfillment of the Father's command: Lay down Your life in My hands. Out of the perfect Self-oblivion of the grave He entered the glory of the Father.

It is into the fellowship of this a believer is brought. We find that in the most unreserved obedience for which God's Spirit fits us, there is still a secret element of Self and Self-will. We long to be delivered from it. We are taught in God's Word that this can only be by death. The Spirit helps us to claim more fully that we are indeed dead to sin in Christ, and that the power of that death can work mightily in us. We are made willing to be obedient unto death, this entire death to Self, which makes us truly nothing. In this we find a full entrance into the life of Christ.

The School of Obedience 2

September 23rd

"If any man wills to do His Will, he shall know of the teaching, whether it be of God."

—JOHN 7: 17

In regard to the knowledge of God's will, we must see and give conscience its place, and submit to its authority.

There are a thousand little things in which the law of nature or education teaches us what is right and good, and in regard to which even earnest Christians do not hold themselves bound to obey. Now, remember, if you are unfaithful in that which is least, who will entrust you with the greater? Not God. If the voice of conscience tells you of some course of action that is the nobler or the better, and you choose another because it is easier or pleasing to Self, you unfit yourself for the teaching of the Spirit, by disobeying the voice of God in nature.

A strong will always to do the right, to do the very best, as conscience points it out, is a will to do God's will. Paul writes, "*I lie not, my conscience bearing me witness in the Holy Spirit.*" The Holy Spirit speaks through conscience: if you disobey and hurt conscience, you make it impossible for God to speak to you.

Obedience to God's will shows itself in tender regard for the voice of conscience.

This holds good with regard to eating and drinking, sleeping and resting, pending money and seeking pleasure—let everything be brought into subjection to the will of God.

This leads to another thing of great importance in this connection. If you would live the life of true obedience, see that you maintain a good conscience before God, and never knowingly indulge in anything which is contrary to His mind. George Muller attributed all his happiness during seventy years to this, along with his love of God's Word. He had maintained a good conscience in all things, not going on in a course he knew to be contrary to the will of God. Conscience is the guardian or monitor God has given you, to give warning when anything goes wrong. Up to the light you have, give heed to conscience. Ask God, by the teaching of His will, to give it more light. Seek the witness of conscience that you are acting up to that light. Conscience will become your encouragement and your helper, and give you the confidence, both that your obedience is accepted, and that your prayer for ever-increasing, knowledge of the will is heard.

What the law demands from us, grace promises and performs for us. The law deals with what we ought to do, whether we can or not, and by the appeal to motives of fear and love stirs us to do our utmost. But it gives no real strength, and so only leads to failure and condemnation. Grace points to what we cannot do, and offers to do it for us and in us. The law comes with commands on stone or in a book. Grace comes in a living, gracious Person, who gives His presence and His power. The law promises life, if we obey. Grace gives life, even the Holy Spirit with the assurance that we can obey.

Human nature is ever prone to slip back out of grace into the law, and secretly to trust to trying and doing its utmost. The promises of grace are so Divine, the gift of the Holy Spirit to do all in us is so wonderful, that few believe it. This is the reason they never dare take the vow of obedience, or, having taken it, turn back again. I beseech you, study well what gospel obedience is. The gospel is good tidings. Its obedience is part of that good tidings—that grace, by the Holy Spirit, will do all in you. Believe that, and let every undertaking to obey be in the joyous hopefulness that comes from faith in the exceeding abundance of grace, in the mighty indwelling of the Holy Spirit, in the blessed love of Jesus whose abiding presence makes obedience possible and certain.

Of the Obedience of Love

This is one of the special and most beautiful aspects of gospel obedience. The grace which promises to work all through the Holy Spirit is the gift of eternal love. The Lord Jesus (who takes charge of our obedience, teaches it, and by His presence secures it to us) is He who loved us unto the death, who loves us with a love that passes knowledge. Nothing can receive or know love but a loving heart. And it is this loving heart that enables us to obey. Obedience is the loving response to the Divine love resting on us, and the only access to a fuller enjoyment of that love.

How our Lord insisted upon that in His farewell discourse! Thrice He repeats it in John 14—"*If you love Me, you will keep My commandments*"; "*He that keeps My commandments, he it is that loves Me*"; "*If a man love Me, he will keep My word.*" Is it not clear that love alone can give the obedience Jesus asks, and receive the blessing Jesus gives to obedience? The gift of the Spirit, the Father's love and His own, with the manifestation of Himself; the Father's love and His own making their abode with us: into these, loving obedience gives the assured access.

In the next chapter He puts it from the other side, and shows how obedience leads to the enjoyment of God's love—He kept His Father's commandments, and abides in His love. If we keep His commandments, we shall abide in His love. He proved His love by giving His life for us; we are His friends, we shall enjoy His love, if we do what He commands us. Between His first love and our love in response to it, between our love and His fuller love in response to ours, obedience is the one indispensable link. True and full obedience is impossible, except as we live and love. "*This is the love of God, that we keep His commandments.*"

Do beware of a legal obedience, striving after a life of true obedience under a sense of duty. Ask God to show you the "newness of life" which is needed for a new and full obedience. Claim the promise, "*I will circumcise your heart, to love the Lord your God with all your heart; and you shall obey the Lord your God.*" Believe in the love of God and the grace of our Lord Jesus. Believe in the Spirit given in you, enabling you to love, and so causing you to walk in God's statutes. In the strength of this faith, in the assurance of sufficient grace, made perfect in weakness, enter into God's love, and the life of living obedience it works. For it is nothing but the continual presence of Jesus in His love can fit you for continual obedience. Beware of seeking just religion enough to give ease to the conscience, and then not desiring to do and be and give God all He is worthy of.

And beware, above all, of limiting God, of making Him a liar, by refusing to believe what He has said He can and will do. If our study in the school of obedience is to be of any profit, rest not till you have written it down: Daily obedience to all that God wills of me is possible, is possible to me. In His strength I yield myself to Him for it. …

Obedience to the Last Command

September 24th

"You shall receive power, when the Holy Spirit is come upon you: and you shall be My witnesses unto the uttermost parts of the earth."

—ACTS 1:8

All these words breathe nothing less than the spirit of world conquest. "All the nations," "all the world," "every creature," "the uttermost parts of the earth,"—each expression indicates that the heart of Christ was set on claiming His rightful dominion over the world He had redeemed and won for Himself. He counts on His disciples to undertake and carry out the work. As He stands at the foot of the throne, ready to ascend and reign, He tells them, "*All authority has been given unto Me in Heaven and on earth,*" and points them at once to "*all the world,*" to the "*uttermost parts of the earth,*" as the object of His and their desire and efforts. … They are to be the advance guard of His conquering hosts even to the end of the world. He Himself will carry on the war. He seeks to inspire them with His own assurance of victory, with His own purpose to make this the only thing to be thought of as worth living or dying for--the winning back of the world to its God.

Christ does not teach or argue, ask or plead: He simply commands. … Formerly, during His life on earth, they had more than once expressed their doubt about the possibility of fulfilling His commands. But here, as quietly and simply as He speaks these Divine words, they accept them. And no sooner has He ascended than they go to the appointed place, to wait for the equipment of a heavenly power from their Lord in Heaven, for the heavenly work of making all the nations His disciples. …

The command is for us, too, for each one of us. … The life Christ imparts is His own life, the spirit He breathes is His very own Spirit, the one disposition He works is His own Self-sacrificing love. It lies in the very nature of His salvation that every member of His body, in full and healthy access with Him feels himself urged to impart what he has received. The command is no arbitrary law from without. It is simply the revelation, for our intelligent and voluntary consent, of the wonderful truth that we are His body, that we now occupy His place on earth, and that His will and love now carry out through us the work He began, and that now in His stead we live to seek the Father's glory, in winning a lost world back to Him. …

The last great command has been so prominently urged in connection with Foreign Missions that many are inclined exclusively to confine it to them. This is a great mistake. Our Lord's words, *"Make disciples of all nations; teaching them to observe all things whatsoever I have commanded you,"* tell us what our aim is to be—nothing less than to make every man a true disciple, living in holy obedience to all Christ's will. …

And what a need that the whole Church, with every believer in it, realize that to do this work is the sole object of its existence! The gospel brought fully, perseveringly, savingly to every creature: this is the mission, this ought to be the passion, of every redeemed soul. For this alone is the Spirit and likeness and life of Christ formed in you. … And therefore I say to every reader who has taken the vow of full obedience—and dare we count ourselves true Christians if we have not done so?—place yourself at once and wholly at Christ's disposal.

22

THE MINISTRY OF INTERCESSION

A Plea for More Prayer

London: James Nisbet & Co., 1898

Introduction

September 25th

"If you abide in Me, and My words abide in you, you shall ask whatsoever you will, and it shall be done for you."
—JOHN 15: 7

Our Lord continually spoke of prayer as a means of obtaining what we desire, and how He seeks in every possible way to waken in us the confident expectation of an answer. … The blessing of prayer is that you can ask and receive what you will; the highest exercise and the glory of prayer is that persevering importunity can prevail and obtain what God at first could not and would not give. …

But, why, if the answer to prayer is so positively promised, why are there such numberless unanswered prayers? … Christ taught us that the answer depended upon certain conditions. He spoke of faith, of perseverance, of praying in His Name, of praying in the will of God. But all these conditions were summed up in the one central one: *"If you abide in Me, ask whatsoever you will and it shall be done unto you."* … The power to pray the effectual prayer of faith depends upon the life. It is only to a man given up to live as entirely in Christ and for Christ as the branch in the vine and for the vine, that these promises can come true. *"In that day"* Christ said, the day of Pentecost, "*You shall ask in My Name.*" It is only in a life full of the Holy Spirit that the true power to ask in Christ's Name can be known. ... The ordinary Christian life cannot appropriate these promises; it needs a spiritual life, altogether sound and vigorous, to pray in power. The teaching naturally led to press the need of a life of entire consecration. ... Beloved fellow-Christian, [let us have] some right impression of the reality and the glory of our privilege as God's children: *"Ask whatsoever you will, and it shall be done unto you."* ...

Christ actually meant prayer to be the great power by which His Church should do its work, and that the neglect of prayer is the great reason the Church has not greater power over the masses in Christian and in heathen countries. In the first chapter I have stated how my convictions in regard to this have been strengthened, and what gave occasion to the writing of the book. It is meant to be, on behalf of myself and my brethren in the ministry and all God's people, a confession of shortcoming and of sin, and, at the same time, a call to believe that things can be different, and that Christ waits to fit us by His Spirit to pray as He would have us. This call, of course, brings me back to what I spoke of in connection with the former volume [*With Christ in the School of Prayer*]: that there is a life in the Spirit, a life of abiding in Christ, within our reach, in which the power of prayer both the power to pray and the power to obtain the answer can be realized in a measure which we could not have thought possible before. ... It is only by a full surrender to the life of abiding, by the yielding to the fullness of the Spirit's leading and quickening, that the prayer-life can be restored to a truly healthy state. ...

We have far too little conception of the place that intercession, *as distinguished from prayer for ourselves*, ought to have in the Church and the Christian life. In intercession our King upon the throne finds His highest glory; in it we shall find our highest glory too. Through it He continues His saving work, and can do nothing without it; through it alone we can do our work, and nothing avails without it. In it He ever receives from the Father the Holy Spirit and all spiritual blessings to impart; in it we too are called to receive in ourselves the fullness of Gods Spirit, with the power to impart spiritual blessing to others. The power of the Church truly to bless rests on intercession: asking and receiving heavenly gifts to carry to men. Because this is so, it is no wonder that where, owing to lack of teaching or spiritual insight, we trust in our own diligence and effort, to the influence of the world and the flesh, and work more than we pray....

There are tens of thousands of workers who have known and are proving wonder fully what prayer can do. But there are tens of thousands who work with but little prayer... —and as many more who do not work because they do not know how or where to pray— who might all be won to swell the host of intercessors who are to bring down the blessings of Heaven to earth. ...

It is in doing that we learn to do; it is as we take hold and begin that the help of God's Spirit will come. It is as we daily hear God's call, and at once put it into practice, that the consciousness will begin to live in us—"I too am an intercessor"—and that we shall feel the need of living in Christ and being full of the Spirit if we are to do this work aright.

Nothing will so test and stimulate the Christian life as the honest attempt to be an intercessor. It is difficult to conceive how much we ourselves and the Church will be the gainers, if with our whole heart we accept the post of honor God is offering us. With regard to the school of intercession, I am confident that the result of the first month's course will be to awake the feeling of how little we know how to intercede. … This will be an unspeakable blessing. The confession, "*We know not how to pray as we ought,*" is the introduction to the experience, "*The Spirit makes intercession for us*" our sense of ignorance will lead us to depend upon the Spirit praying in us, to feel the need of living in the Spirit.

The faith in God's Word can nowhere be so exercised and perfected as in the intercession that asks and expects and looks out for the answer. Throughout Scripture, in the life of every saint, of God's own Son, throughout the history of God's Church, God is, first of all, a prayer-hearing God. Let us try and help God's children to know their God, and encourage all God's servants to labor with the assurance: the chief and most blessed part of my work is to ask and receive from my Father *what I can bring to others.*

The Ministration of the Spirit and Prayer

September 26th

"If you, being evil, know how to give good gifts to your children;
how much more shall your Heavenly Father give the Holy Spirit to those who ask Him?"
—LUKE 11: 13

Christ had just said, "*Ask, and it shall be given*" (Luke 11: 9). God's giving is inseparably connected with our asking. He applies this especially to the Holy Spirit. As surely as a father on earth gives bread to his child, so God gives the Holy Spirit to those who ask Him. The whole ministration of the Spirit is ruled by the one great law: God must give; we must ask. When the Holy Spirit was poured out at Pentecost with a flow that never ceases, it was in answer to prayer. The inflow into the believer's heart, and His outflow in the rivers of living water, ever still depend upon the law: "*Ask, and it shall be given.*"

In connection with our confession of the lack of prayer, we have said that what we need is some due apprehension of the place it occupies in God's plan of redemption; we shall perhaps nowhere see this more clearly than in the first half of the Acts of the Apostles. The story of the birth of the Church in the outpouring of the Holy Spirit, and of the first freshness of its heavenly life in the power of that Spirit, will teach us how prayer on earth, whether as cause or effect, is the true measure of the presence of the Spirit of Heaven.

We begin with the well-known words: "*They all continued with one accord in prayer and supplication*" (Acts 1: 13). And then there follows: "*And when the day of Pentecost was fully come, they were all with one accord in one place. And they were all filled with the Holy Spirit. And the same day there were added to them about three thousand souls.*" The great work of redemption had been accomplished. The Holy Spirit had been promised by Christ "*not many days hence.*" He had sat down on His throne and received the Spirit from the Father. But all this was not enough. One thing more was needed: the ten days united continued supplication of the disciples. It was intense, continued prayer that prepared the disciples hearts that opened the windows of Heaven that brought down the promised gift.

As little as the power of the Spirit could be given without Christ sitting on the throne, could it descend without the disciples on the footstool of the throne. For all the ages the law is laid down here, at the birth of the Church, that whatever else may be found on earth, the power of the Spirit must be prayed down from Heaven. The measure of believing, continued prayer will be the measure of the Spirit's working in the Church. Direct, definite, determined prayer is what we need.

See how this is confirmed in the Book of Acts chapter four, where Peter and John had been brought before the Council and threatened with punishment. When they returned to their brethren, and reported what had been said to them, they *"all lifted up their voice to God with one accord,"* and prayed for boldness to speak the Word. *"And when they had prayed, the place was shaken, and they were all filled with the Holy Spirit, and they spoke the word of God with boldness. And the multitude of them that believed were one heart and one soul. And with great power gave the apostles witness of the resurrection of the Lord Jesus; and great grace was upon them all."* It is as if the story of Pentecost is repeated a second time over, with the prayer, the shaking of the house, the filling with the Spirit, the speaking God's word with boldness and power, the great grace upon all, the manifestation of unity and love to imprint it ineffaceably on the heart of the Church: it is prayer that lies at the root of the spiritual life and power of the Church. The measure of God's giving the Spirit is our asking. …

Go on to the sixth chapter. There we find that when murmurings arose as to the neglect of the Grecian Jews in the distribution of alms, the apostles proposed the appointment of deacons to serve the tables. We, they said, *"will give ourselves to prayer and the ministry of the Word."* …

What does this teach? That the maintenance of the spirit of prayer, such as is consistent with the claims of much work, is not enough for those who are the leaders of the Church—to keep up the communication with the King on the throne and the heavenly world clear and fresh; to draw down the power and blessing of that world, not only for the maintenance of our own spiritual life, but for those around us; and continually to receive instruction and empowerment for the great work to be done. The apostles, as the ministers of the Word, felt the need of being free from other duties, that they might give themselves to much prayer. …

In chapter eight of Acts we have the intimate connection between the Pentecostal gift and prayer, from another point of view. At Samaria, Philip had preached with great blessing, and many had believed. But the Holy Spirit was, as yet, fallen on none of them. The apostles sent down Peter and John to pray for them, that they might receive the Holy Spirit. The power for such prayer was a higher gift than preaching the work of the men who had been in closest contact with the Lord in glory, the work that was essential to the perfection of the life that preaching and baptism, faith and conversion had only begun. Surely of all the gifts of the early Church for which we should long there is none more needed than the gift of prayer. Prayer that brings down the Holy Spirit on believers. This power is given to those who say: *"We will give ourselves to prayer."*

In the outpouring of the Holy Spirit, in the house of Cornelius at Cesarea, we have another testimony to the wondrous interdependence of the action of prayer and the Spirit, and another proof of what will come to those who have given ourselves to prayer. Peter went up at midday to pray on the housetop. And what happened? He saw Heaven opened, and there came the vision that revealed to him the cleansing of the Gentiles; with that came the message of the three men from Cornelius, a man who *"prayed always,"* and had heard from an angel, "*Your prayers have come up before God.*" ...

Our next reference will show us faith in the power that the Church's prayer has with its glorified King, as it is found, not only in the apostles, but in the Christian community. In Acts chapter twelve we have the story of Peter in prison on the eve of execution. The death of James had aroused the Church to a sense of real danger, and the thought of losing Peter too, wakened up all its energies. It betook itself to prayer. *"Prayer was made for him by the Church without ceasing."* That prayer availed much; Peter was delivered. When he came to the house of Mary, he found *"many gathered together praying."* Stone walls and double chains, soldiers and keepers, and the iron gate, all gave way before the power from Heaven that prayer brought down to his rescue. The whole power of the Roman Empire, as represented by Herod, was impotent in presence of the power the Church of the Holy Spirit wielded in prayer.

... Just one more illustration of the place and the blessing of prayer among men filled with the Holy Spirit. In chapter thirteen of the Book of Acts we have the names of five men at Antioch who had given themselves specially to ministering to the Lord with prayer and fasting. Their giving themselves to prayer was not in vain. As they ministered to the Lord, the Holy Spirit met them, and gave them new insight into God's plans. He called them to be fellow-workers with Himself. There was a work to which He had called Barnabas and Saul. Their part and privilege would be to separate these men with renewed fasting and prayer, and to let them go, *"sent forth of the Holy Spirit."* God in Heaven would not send forth His chosen servants without the cooperation of His Church; those on earth were to have a real partnership in the work of God. It was prayer that fitted and prepared them for this; it was to praying souls that the Holy Spirit gave authority to do His work and use His name. It was for prayer that the Holy Spirit was given. It is still prayer that is the only secret of true Church. ...

As one looks back upon these chapters in the history of the Pentecostal Church, how clear the two great truths stand out: where there is much prayer there will be much of the Spirit; where there is much of the Spirit there will be ever-increasing prayer. So clear is the living connection between the two, that when the Spirit is given in answer to prayer it ever wakens more prayer to prepare for the fuller revelation and communication of His Divine power and grace. ...

Let us learn what ought to be counted axioms in our Church work: Heaven is still as full of stores of spiritual blessing as it was then. God still delights to give the Holy Spirit to them that ask Him. Our life and work are still as dependent on the direct impartation of Divine power as they were in Pentecostal times. Prayer is still the appointed means for drawing down these heavenly blessings in power on ourselves and those around us. God still seeks for men and women who will, with all their other work of ministering, specially give themselves to persevering prayer. …

The Lack of Prayer

September 27th

"You have not, because you ask not."

—JAMES 4: 2

"And He … wondered that there was no intercessor."

—ISAIAH 59:16

We all know the difference between a man whose profits are just enough to maintain his family and keep up his business, and another whose income enables him to extend the business and to help others. There may be an earnest Christian life in which there is prayer enough to keep us from going back, and just maintain the position we have attained to, without much of growth in spirituality or Christ-likeness. The attitude is more defensive, seeking to ward off temptation, than aggressive, reaching out after higher attainment. If there is indeed to be a going from strength to strength, with some large experience of God's power to sanctify ourselves and to bring down real blessing on others, then there must be more definite and persevering prayer. The scripture teaching about crying day and night, continuing steadfastly in prayer, watching unto prayer, being heard for our importunity, must in some degree become our experience if we are really to be intercessors. …

Do let us believe that God's call to much prayer need not be a burden and cause of continual Self-condemnation. He means it to be a joy. He can make it an inspiration, giving us strength for all our work, and bringing down His power to work through us in our fellowmen. Let us not fear to admit to the full the sin that shames us, and then to face it in the name of our Mighty Redeemer. The light that shows us our sin and condemns us for it, will show us the way out of it, into the life of liberty that is well-pleasing to God.

If we allow this one matter—unfaithfulness in prayer—to convict us of the lack in our Christian life which lies at the root of it, God will use the discovery to bring us not only the power to pray that we long for, but the joy of a new and healthy life, of which prayer is the spontaneous expression. …

A fresh sight of what prayer is according to the will of God, of what our prayers can be, through the grace of God, will free us from those feeble defective views, in regard to the absolute necessity of continual prayer, which lie at the root of our failure. As we get an insight into the reasonableness and rightness of this Divine appointment, and come under the full conviction of how wonderfully it fits in with God's love and our own happiness, we shall be freed from the false impression of its being an arbitrary demand. We shall with our whole heart and soul consent to it and rejoice in it, as the one only possible way for the blessing of Heaven to come to earth. All thought of task and burden, of Self-effort and strain, will pass away in the blessed faith that as simple as breathing is in the healthy natural life, will praying be in the Christian life that is led and filled by the Spirit of God. …

Our failure in the prayer-life is owing to failure in the Spirit-life. Prayer is one of the most heavenly and spiritual of the functions of the Spirit-life. … The insight into the place God means prayer to take, and which it only can take, in a full Christian life, will show us that we have not been living the true, the abundant life, and that any thought of praying more and effectually will be vain, except as we are brought into a closer relation to our Blessed Lord Jesus. Christ is our life—Christ lives in us—in such reality that His life of prayer on earth, and of intercession in Heaven, is breathed into us in just such measure as our surrender and our faith allow and accept it. …

Let us all unite in praying God that He would visit our souls and fit us for that work of intercession, which is at this moment the greatest need of the Church and the world. It is only by intercession that that power can be brought down from Heaven which will enable the Church to conquer the world. … Nothing but intense believing prayer can meet the intense spirit of worldliness, of which complaint is everywhere made.

The Life that Can Pray 1

September 28th

"Beloved, if our heart condemns us not, we have boldness toward God;
and whatsoever we ask, we receive of Him, because we keep His commandments,
and do the things that are pleasing in His sight."
—1 JOHN 3: 21–22

Here on earth the influence of one who asks a favor for others depends entirely on their own character, and the relationship they have with the one to whom they are interceding. It is what that person is that gives weight to what they ask. It is not otherwise with God. Our power in prayer depends upon our life. Where our life is right we shall know how to pray so as to please God, and prayer will secure the answer.

The texts quoted above all point in this direction. *"If you abide in Me" our Lord says, "You shall ask, and it shall be done unto you."* It is *"the prayer of a righteous man,"* according to James, *"that avails much." "We receive whatsoever we ask,"* John says, because we obey and please God. All lack of power to pray aright and perseveringly, all lack of power in prayer with God, points to some lack in the Christian life. It is as we learn to live the life that pleases God that God will give what we ask.

Let us learn from our Lord Jesus, in the parable of the vine, what the healthy, vigorous life is that may ask and receive what it will. Hear His voice, *"If you abide in Me, and My words abide in you, you shall ask what you will, and it shall be done unto you."* And again at the close of the parable: *"You did not choose Me, but I chose you, and appointed you, that you should go and bear fruit, and that your fruit should abide: that whatsoever you shall ask the Father in My name, He may give it you."*

And what is now, according to the parable, the life that one must lead to bear fruit, and then ask and receive what we will? What is it we are to be or do, that will enable us to pray as we should, and to receive what we ask? The answer is in one word: it is *the branch life* that gives power for prayer. We are branches of Christ, the Living Vine. We must simply live like branches, and abide in Christ, then we shall ask what we will, and it shall be done unto us.

We all know what a branch is, and what its essential characteristic. It is simply a growth of the vine, produced by it and appointed to bear fruit. It has only one reason of existence; it is there at the bidding of the vine, that through it the vine may bear and ripen its precious fruit. Just as the vine only and solely and wholly lives to produce the sap that makes the grape, so the branch has no other aim and object but this alone, to receive that sap and bear the grape. Its only work is to serve the vine, that through it the vine may do its work. … It is to such that the unlimited prayer promises of the parable are given. It is the branch-life, existing solely for the Vine that will have the power to pray aright. With our life abiding in Him, and His words abiding, kept and obeyed, in our heart and life, transmuted into our very being, there will be the grace to pray aright, and the faith to receive whatsoever we will.

Do let us connect the two things, and take them both in their simple, literal truth, and their infinite, divine grandeur. The promises of our Lord's farewell discourse, with their wonderful six-fold repetition of the unlimited, "*anything*," "*whatsoever*" (John 14: 13–14; 15: 7, 16; 16: 23–24), appear to us altogether too large to be taken literally, and they are qualified down to meet our human ideas of what appears seemly. It is because we separate them from that life of absolute and unlimited devotion to Christ's service to which they were given.

God's covenant is ever: Give all and take all. We who are willing to be wholly branch, and nothing but branch, who are ready to place ourselves absolutely at the disposal of Jesus the Vine of God—to bear His fruit through us, and to live every moment only for Him—will receive a Divine liberty to claim Christ's "whatsoever" in all its fullness, and a Divine wisdom and humility to use it aright. We will live and pray, and claim the Father's promises, even as Christ did, only for God's glory in the salvation of men. We will use boldness in prayer only with a view to power in intercession, and getting others blessed.

The unlimited devotion of the branch life to fruit-bearing, and the unlimited access to the treasures of the Vine life, are inseparable. It is the life abiding wholly in Christ that can pray the effectual prayer in the name of Christ. Just think for a moment of the men of prayer in Scripture, and see in them what the life was that could pray in such power. We spoke of Abraham as intercessor. What gave Him such boldness? He knew that God had chosen and called him away from his home and people to walk before Him, that all nations might be blessed in him. He knew that he had obeyed, and forsaken all for God. Implicit obedience, to the very sacrifice of his son, was the law of his life. He did what God asked: he dared trust God to do what he asked.

We spoke of Moses as intercessor. He, too, had forsaken all for God, "*counting the reproach of Christ greater riches than all the treasures of Egypt.*" He lived at God's disposal: "*as a servant he was faithful in all His house."* How often it is written of him, *"According to all that the Lord commanded Moses, so did he."* No wonder that he was very bold: his heart was right with God: he knew God would hear him. No less true is this of Elijah, the man who stood up to plead for the Lord God of Israel. The man who is ready to risk all for God can count upon God to do all for him.

It is as we live that we pray. It is the life that prays. It is the life that, with whole hearted devotion, gives up all for God and to God that can claim all from God. Our God longs exceedingly to prove Himself the Faithful God and Mighty Helper of His people. He only waits for hearts wholly turned from the world to Himself, and open to receive His gifts. Those who lose all will find all; we dare to ask and take it. The branch that only and truly lives abiding in Christ, the Heavenly Vine, entirely given up, like Christ, to bear fruit in the salvation of others, and has His words taken up into and abiding in its life may and dare ask what it will it shall be done. …

The Life that Can Pray 2

September 29th

"Beloved, if our heart condemns us not, we have boldness toward God; and whatsoever we ask, we receive of Him, because we keep His commandments, and do the things that are pleasing in His sight."

—1 JOHN 3: 21–22

And if any are asking, with somewhat of a despair of attainment, what the reason may be of the failure in this blessed branch life, so simple and yet so mighty, and how they can come to it, let me point them to one of the most precious lessons of the parable of the Vine. It is one that is all too little noticed. Jesus said, *"I am the true Vine, and my Father is the Husbandman."* We have not only Himself, the glorified Son of God, in His divine fullness, out of whose fullness of life and grace we can draw, this is very wonderful, but there is something more blessed still. We have the Father, as the Husbandman, watching over our abiding in the Vine, over our growth and fruitbearing. It is not left to our faith or our faithfulness to maintain our union with Christ: The God, who is the Father of Christ, and who united us with Him, God Himself will see to it that the branch is what it should be, will enable us to bring forth just the fruit we were appointed to bear.

Hear what Christ said of this, *"Every branch that bears fruit, He cleanses it, that it may bear more fruit."* More fruit is what the Father seeks; more fruit is what the Father will Himself provide. It is for this that He, as the Vinedresser, cleanses the branches.

Just think a moment what this means. It is said that of all fruitbearing plants on earth there is none that produces fruit so full of spirit, from which spirit can be so abundantly distilled, as the vine. And of all fruitbearing plants there is none that is so ready to run into wild wood, and for which pruning arid cleansing are so indispensable. The one great work that a vinedresser has to do for the branch every year is to prune it. Other plants can for a time dispense with it, and yet bear fruit: the vine must have it. And so the one thing the branch that desires to abide in Christ and bring forth much fruit, and to be able to ask whatsoever it will, must do, is to trust in and yield itself to this Divine cleansing. What is it that the vinedresser cuts away with his pruning-knife? Nothing but the wood that the branch has produced true, honest wood, with the true vine nature in it. This must be cut away. And why? Because it draws away the strength and life of the vine, and hinders the flow of the juice to the grape.

The more it is cut down, the less wood there is in the branch, the more all the sap can go to the grape. The wood of the branch must decrease, that the fruit for the vine may increase; in obedience to the law of all nature, that death is the way to life, that gain comes through sacrifice, the rich and luxuriant growth of wood must be cut off and cast away, that the life more abundant may be seen in the cluster.

Even so, child of God, branch of the Heavenly Vine, there is in you that which appears perfectly innocent and legitimate, and which yet so draws out thy interest and thy strength, that it must be pruned and cleansed away. We saw what power in prayer men like Abraham and Moses and Elijah had, and we know what fruit they bore. But we also know what it cost them; how God had to separate them from their surroundings, and ever again to draw them from any trust in themselves, to seek their life in Him alone.

It is only as our own will, and strength and effort and pleasure, even where these appear perfectly natural and sinless, are cut down, so that the whole energies of our being are free and open to receive the sap of the Heavenly Vine, the Holy Spirit, that we shall bear much fruit. It is in the surrender of what nature holds fast, it is in the full and willing submission to God's holy pruning-knife, that we shall come to what Christ chose and appointed us for to bear fruit, that whatsoever we ask the Father in Christ's name, He may give to us.

What the pruning-knife is, Christ tells us in the next verse. "*You are clean through the word which I have spoken to you*"; As He says later, "*Sanctify them through Your truth; Your Word is truth*"; "*The Word of God is sharper than any two-edged sword, piercing even to the dividing of soul and spirit.*" What heart-searching words Christ had spoken to His disciples on love and humility, on being the least, and, like Himself, the servant of all, on denying Self, and taking the cross, and losing the life. Through His word the Father had cleansed them, cut away all confidence in themselves or the world, and prepared them for the inflowing and filling of the Spirit of the Heavenly Vine. It is not we who can cleanse ourselves: God is the Vinedresser: we may confidently entrust ourselves to His care. ... Oh! Come and listen to your beloved Lord as He tells you, "only be a branch, united to, identified with, the Heavenly Vine, and your prayers will be effectual and much availing." ... Oh! Come and listen again. "*More fruit*"; is not only your desire, but the Father's too. He is the Husbandman who cleanses the fruitful branch, that it may bear more fruit.

Cast yourself upon God, to do in you what is impossible to man. Count upon a Divine cleansing, to cut down and take away all that Self-confidence and Self-effort, that has been the cause of your failure. The God who gave you His beloved Son to be your Vine, who made you His branch, will He not do His work of cleansing to make you fruitful in every good work, in the work of prayer and intercession too?

Here is the life that can pray: A branch entirely given up to the Vine and its aims, with all responsibility for its cleansing cast on the Vine dresser; a branch abiding in Christ, trusting and yielding to God for His cleansing, can bear much fruit. In the power of such a life we shall love prayer, we shall know how to pray, we shall pray, and receive whatsoever we ask.

Restraining Prayer: Is it Sin?

September 30th

"God forbid that I should sin against the Lord in ceasing to pray for you."

—1 SAMUEL 12: 23

Any deep quickening of the spiritual life of the Church will always be accompanied by a deeper sense of sin. This will not begin with theology; that can only give expression to what God works in the life of His people. Nor does it mean that that deeper sense of sin will only be seen in stronger expressions of Self-reproach or penitence: that is sometimes found to consist with a harboring of sin, and unbelief as to deliverance. But the true sense of the hatefulness of sin, the hatred

of it, will be proved by the intensity of desire for deliverance, and the struggle to know to the very utmost what God can do in saving from it a holy jealousy, in nothing to sin against God.

If we are to deal effectually with the lack of prayer we must look at it from this point of view and ask: Restraining prayer, is it sin? And if it be, how is it to be dealt with, to be discovered, and confessed, and cast out by us, and cleansed away by God? Jesus is a Savior from sin. It is only as we know sin truly that we can truly know the power that saves from sin. The life that can pray effectually is the life of the cleansed branch the life that knows deliverance from the power of Self. To see that our prayer-sins are indeed sins, is the first step to a true and Divine deliverance from them.

In the story of Achan we have one of the strongest proofs in Scripture that it is sin that robs God's people of His blessing, and that God will not tolerate it; and at the same time the clearest indication of the principles under which God deals with it, and removes it. Let us see in the light of the story if we can learn how to look at the sin of prayerlessness, and at the sinfulness that lies at the root of it. The words …

"Neither will I be with you any more, except you put away the accursed thing from among you" (Joshua 7: 12) take us into the very heart of the story, suggest a series of the most precious lessons around the truth that the presence of sin makes the presence of God impossible.

1. The presence of God is the great privilege of God's people, and their only power against the enemy. God had promised to Moses, *"I will bring you in into the land."* Moses proved that he understood this when God, after the sin of the golden calf, spoke of withdrawing His presence and sending an angel. He refused to accept anything less than God's

presence. *"For whereby shall it be known that I and Your people have found grace in Your sight? Is it not that You go with me?"* It was this gave Caleb and Joshua their confidence: The Lord is with us. It was this that gave Israel their victory over Jericho: the presence of God. This is throughout Scripture the great central promise: *I am with you.* This marks off the whole-hearted believer from the worldling and worldly Christians around him: we live consciously hidden in the secret of God's presence.

2. Defeat and failure are always owing to the loss of God's presence. It was thus at Ai. God had brought His people into Canaan with the promise to give them the land. When the defeat at Ai took place Joshua felt at once that the cause must be in the withdrawal of God's power. He had not fought for them. His presence had been withheld. In the Christian life and the work of the Church, defeat is ever a sign of the loss of God's presence. If we apply this to our failure in the prayer-life, and as a result of that to our failure in work for God, we are led to see that all is simply owing to our not standing in clear and full fellowship with God. His nearness, His immediate presence, has not been the chief thing sought after and trusted in. He could not work in us as He would. Loss of blessing and power is ever caused by the loss of God's presence.

3. The loss of God's presence is always owing to some hidden sin. Just as pain is ordered in nature to warn of some hidden evil in the system, defeat is God's voice telling us there is something wrong. He has given Himself so wholly to His people, He delights so in being with them, and would so fain reveal in them His love and power, that He never withdraws Himself unless they compel Him by sin.

Throughout the Church there is a complaint of defeat. The Church has so little power over the masses, or the educated classes. Powerful conversions are comparatively rare. The fewness of holy, consecrated, spiritual Christians, devoted to the service of God and their fellowmen, is felt everywhere. The power of the Church for the preaching of the gospel to the heathen is paralyzed by the scarcity of money and men; and all owing to the lack of the effectual prayer which brings the Holy Spirit in power, first on ministers and believers, then on missionaries and the heathen. Can we deny it that the lack of prayer is the sin on account of which God's presence and power are not more manifestly seen among us?

4. God Himself will discover the hidden sin. We may think we know what the sin is; it is only God who can discover its real deep meaning. When He spoke to Joshua, before naming the sin of Achan, God first said, "*They have transgressed My covenant which I commanded them.*" God had commanded that all the booty of Jericho—gold and silver and all that was in it—was to be a devoted thing, consecrated unto the Lord, and to come into His treasury. And Israel had broken this consecration vow: it had not given God His due; it had robbed God.

It is this we need: God must reveal to us how the lack of prayer is the indication of unfaithfulness to our consecration vow, that God should have all our heart and life. We must see that this restraining prayer, with the excuses we make for it, is greater sin than we have thought. For, what does it mean?—that we have little taste or relish for fellowship with God; that our faith rests more on our own work and efforts than on the power of

God; that we have little sense of the heavenly blessing God waits to shower down; that we are not ready to sacrifice the ease and confidence of the flesh for persevering waiting on God; that the spirituality of our life, and our abiding in Christ, is altogether too feeble to make us prevail in prayer.

When the pressure of work for Christ is allowed to be the excuse for our not finding time to seek and secure His own presence and power in it, as our chief need, it surely proves that there is no right sense of our absolute dependence upon God; no deep apprehension of the Divine and supernatural work of God in which we are only His instruments, no true entrance into the heavenly, altogether other-worldly, character of our mission and aims, no full surrender to and delight in Christ Jesus Himself.

If we were to yield to God's Spirit to show us that all this is in very deed the meaning of remissness in prayer, and of our allowing other things to crowd it out, all our excuses would fall away, and we should fall down and cry, "We have sinned! we have sinned!" Samuel once said, "*As for me, God forbid that I should sin against the Lord in ceasing to pray for you.*" Ceasing from prayer is sin against God. …

The Secret of Effectual Prayer

October 1st

"Whatsoever you desire, when you pray, believe that you have received them, and you shall have them."
—MARK 11: 24

Here we have a summary of the teaching of our Lord Jesus on prayer. Nothing will so much help to convince us of the sin of our remissness in prayer, to discover its causes, and to give us courage to expect entire deliverance, as the careful study and then the believing acceptance of that teaching. The more heartily we enter into the mind of our blessed Lord, and set ourselves simply just to think about prayer as He thought, the more surely will His words be as living seeds. They will grow and produce in us their fruit, a life and practice exactly corresponding to the Divine truth they contain. Do let us believe this: Christ, the living "Word of God," gives in His words a Divine quickening power which brings what they say, which works in us what He asks, which actually fits and enables for all He demands.

Learn to look upon His teaching on prayer as a definite promise of what He, by His Holy Spirit dwelling in you, is going to work into your very being and character. Our Lord gives us the five marks, or essential elements, of true prayer. There must be, first, the heart's desire; then the expression of that desire in prayer; with that, the faith that carries the prayer to God; in that faith, the acceptance of God's answer; then comes the experience of the desired blessing. … Let us meditate on our Lord's words, in the confidence that He will teach us how to pray for this blessing.

1. *"Whatsoever you desire."* Desire is the secret power that moves the whole world of

living men, and directs the course of each. And so desire is the soul of prayer, and the cause of insufficient or unsuccessful prayer is very much to be found in the lack or feebleness of desire.

Some may doubt this: they are sure that they have very earnestly desired what they ask. But if they consider whether their desire has indeed been as whole hearted as God would have it, as the heavenly worth of these blessings demands, they may come to see that it was indeed the lack of desire that was the cause of failure. What is true of God is true of each of His blessings, and is the more true the more spiritual the blessing: *"You shall seek Me, and shall find, when you shall search for Me with all your heart"* (Jeremiah 29: 13).

Of Judah in the days of Asa it is written, *"They sought Him with their whole desire"* (2 Chronicles 15: 15). A Christian may often have very earnest desires for spiritual blessings. But alongside of these there are other desires in his daily life occupying a large place in his interests and affections. The spiritual desires are not all-absorbing. He wonders that his prayer is not heard. It is simply that God wants the whole heart. *"The Lord your God is one Lord, therefore you shall love the Lord your God with all your heart."*

The law is unchangeable: God offers Himself, gives Himself away, to the wholehearted who give themselves wholly away to Him. He always gives us according to our heart's desire. But not as we think it, but as He sees it. If there be other desires which are more at home with us, which have our heart more than Himself and His presence, He allows these to be fulfilled, and the desires that engage us at the hour of prayer cannot be granted.

We desire the gift of intercession, grace and power to pray aright. Our hearts must be drawn away from other desires: we must give ourselves wholly to this one. We must be willing to live wholly in intercession for the Kingdom. By fixing our eye on the blessedness and the need of this grace, by thinking of the certainty that God will give it us, by giving ourselves up to it, for the sake of the perishing world, desire may be strengthened, and the first step taken towards the possession of the coveted blessing. Let us seek the grace of prayer, as we seek the God with whom it will link us "with our whole desire"; we may depend upon the promise, *"He will fulfill the desire of them that fear Him."* Let us not fear to say to Him, "I desire it with my whole heart."

2. *"Whatsoever you desire, when you pray."* The desire of the heart must become the expression of the lips. Our Lord Jesus more than once asked those who cried to Him for mercy, "*What do you want?*" He wanted them to say what they wanted. To speak it out roused their whole being into action, brought them into contact with Him, and wakened their expectation. To pray is to enter into God's presence, to claim and secure His attention, to have distinct dealing with Him in regard to some request, to commit our need to His faithfulness and to leave it there ....

3. "*Whatsoever you desire, when you pray, believe.*" As it is only by faith that we can know God, or receive Jesus Christ, or live the Christian life, so faith is the life and power of prayer. If we are to enter upon a life of intercession, in which there is to be joy and power and blessing, if we are to have our prayer for the grace of prayer answered, we must learn anew what faith is, and begin to live and pray in faith as never before.

Faith is the opposite of sight, and the two are contrary the one to the other. *"We walk by faith, and not by sight."* If the unseen is to get full possession of us, and heart and life and prayer are to be full of faith, there must be a withdrawal from, a denial of, the visible. … *"We look not at the things that are seen"*—the negative side—needs to be emphasized if the positive—"but at the things which are not seen"—is to become natural to us. In praying, faith depends upon our living in the invisible world. …

The great reason of our lack of faith is our lack of knowledge of God and intercourse with Him. *"Have faith in God,"* Jesus said when He spoke of removing mountains. It is as a soul knows God, is occupied with His power, love, and faithfulness, comes away out of Self and the world, and allows the light of God to shine on it, that unbelief will become impossible. All the mysteries and difficulties connected with answers to prayer will, however little we may be able to solve them intellectually, be swallowed up in the adoring assurance: "This God is our God. He will bless us. He does indeed answer prayer. And the grace to pray I am asking for He will delight to give."

A soul that not only seeks an answer, but seeks first the God who gives the answer, receives the power to know that it has what it has asked of Him. If it knows that it has asked according to His will and promises, and that it has come to and found Himself to give it, it does believe that it has received. *"We know that He hears us."* … Here comes in the real need for per severing and ever-importunate prayer that will not rest, or go away, or give up, till it knows it is heard, and believes that it has received. …

Beloved! Do you truly desire that God should enable you so to pray that your life may be free from continual Self-condemnation, and that the power of His Spirit may come down in answer to your petition? Come and ask it of God. Kneel down and pray for it in a single definite sentence. When you have done so, kneel still in faith, believing in God who answers. Believe that you do now receive what you have prayed: believe that you have received. If you find it difficult to do this, kneel still, and say that you do it on the strength of His own Word. If it cost time, and struggle, and doubt, fear not; at His feet, looking up into His face, faith will come. *"Believe that you have received."* …

Who Shall Deliver? 1

October 2nd

"Is there no balm in Gilead; is there no physician there?
Why then is not the health of my people recovered?"
—JEREMIAH 8: 22 …

Law demands; grace bestows. Law commands, but gives no strength to obey; grace promises, and performs, does all we need to do. Law burdens, and casts down and condemns; grace comforts, and makes strong and glad. Law appeals to Self, to do its utmost; grace points to Christ to do all. Law calls to effort and strain, and urges us towards a goal we never can reach; grace works in us all God's blessed will. … We must come out from under law and Self and effort, and take his place under grace, allowing God to do all. …

We have so often resolved to pray more and better, and have failed. We have not the strength of will some have, with one resolve to turn round and change our habits. The press of duty is as great as ever it was; it is so difficult to find time for more prayer; real enjoyment in prayer, which would enable us to persevere, is what we do not feel; we do not possess the power to supplicate and to plead, as we should; our prayers, instead of being a joy and a strength, are a source of continual Self-condemnation and doubt. We have at times mourned and confessed and resolved; but, to tell the honest truth, we do not expect, for we do not see the way to, any great change. It is evident that as long as this spirit prevails, there can be very little prospect of improvement. …

One of the first objects of a physician is ever to waken hope; without this he knows his medicines will often profit little. No teaching from God's Word as to the duty, the urgent need, the blessed privilege of more prayer, of effectual prayer, will avail, while the secret whisper is heard: There is no hope. Our first care must be to find out the hidden cause of the failure and despair, and then to show how divinely sure deliverance is. We must, unless we are to rest content with our state, listen to and join in the question, "*Is there no balm in Gilead; is there no physician there? why then is not the health of the daughter of my people restored?*"; We must listen, and receive into our heart, the Divine promise with the response it met with: "*Return, you backsliding children, and I will heal your backslidings. Behold, we come unto You, for You are the Lord our God.*" We must come with the personal prayer, and the faith that there will be a personal answer. Shall we not even now begin to claim it in regard to the lack of prayer, and believe that God will help us: "*Heal me, Lord, and I shall be healed.*"

It is always of consequence to distinguish between the symptoms of a disease and the disease itself. Feebleness and failure in prayer is a sign of feebleness in the spiritual life. If a patient were to ask a physician to give him something to stimulate his feeble pulse, he would be told that this would do him little good. The pulse is the index of the state of the heart and the whole system: the physician strives to have health restored.

What everyone who would fain pray more faithfully and effectually must learn is this, that his whole spiritual life is in a sickly state, and needs restoration. It is as he comes to look, not only at his shortcomings in prayer, but at the lack in the life of faith, of which this is the symptom, that he will become fully alive to the serious nature of the disease. He will then see the need of a radical change in his whole life and walk, if his prayer life, which is simply the pulse of the spiritual system, is to indicate health and vigor. God has so created us that the exercise of every healthy function causes joy. Prayer is meant to be as simple and natural as breathing or working to a healthy man. The reluctance we feel, and the failure we confess, are God's own voice calling us to acknowledge our disease, and to come to Him for the healing He has promised.

And what is now the disease of which the lack of prayer is the symptom? We cannot find a better answer than is pointed out in the words, "*You are not under the law, but under grace.*" Here we have suggested the possibility of two types of Christian life. There may be a life partly under the law and partly under grace; or, a life entirely under grace, in the full liberty from Self-effort, and the full experience of the Divine strength which it can give. A true believer may still be living partly under the law, in the power of Self-effort, striving to do what we cannot accomplish.

The continued failure in our Christian life to which we confess is owing to this one thing: we trust in our Self, and try to do our best. We do, indeed, pray and look to God for help, but still it is we in our strength, helped by God, who is to do the work. In the Epistles to the Romans, and Corinthians, and Galatians, we know how Paul tells them that they have not received the spirit of bondage again, that they are free from the law, that they are no more servants but sons; that they must beware of nothing so much as to be entangled again with the yoke of bondage. Everywhere it is the contrast between the law and grace, between the flesh, which is under the law, and the Spirit, who is the gift of grace, and through whom grace does all its work.

In our days, just as in those first ages, the great danger is living under the law, and serving God in the strength of the flesh. With the great majority of Christians, this appears to be the state in which they remain all their lives. Hence the lack to such a large extent of true holy living and power in prayer. They do not know that all failure can have but one cause: Men seek to do themselves what grace alone can do in them, what grace most certainly will do. …

Who Shall Deliver? 2

October 3rd

"Wretched man that I am! Who shall deliver me out of the body of this death? I thank God through Jesus Christ our Lord. The law of the Spirit of life in Christ Jesus made me free from the law of sin and death."

—ROMANS 7: 24; 8: 2

We know how often we may be suffering from a disease without knowing it. What we count a slight ailment turns out to be a dangerous complaint. Do not let us be too sure that we are not, to a large extent, still living "under the law," while considering ourselves to be living wholly "*under grace.*" Very frequently the reason of this mistake is the limited meaning attached to the word "grace." …

Has not the very term, "grace abounding," from Bunyan's book downward, been confined to the one great blessed truth of free justification with ever renewed pardon and eternal glory for the vilest of sinners, while the other equally blessed truth of "*grace abounding*" in sanctification is not fully known. Paul writes: "*Much more shall they which receive the abundance of grace reign in life through Jesus Christ.*" That reigning in life, as conqueror over sin, is even here on earth.

"*Where sin abounded*" in the heart and life, "*grace did abound more exceedingly, that grace might reign through righteousness,*" in the whole life and being of the believer. It is of this reign of grace in the soul that Paul asks, "*Shall we sin because we are under grace?*" and answers, "*God forbid.*"

Grace is not only pardon of, but power over, sin; grace takes the place sin had in the life, and undertakes, as sin had reigned within in the power of death, to reign in the power of Christ's life. It is of this grace that Christ spoke, "*My grace is sufficient for you,*" and Paul answered, "*I will glory in my weakness; for, when I am weak, then am I strong.*" It is of this grace, which, when we are willing to confess ourselves utterly impotent and helpless, comes in to work all in us, that Paul elsewhere teaches, "*God is able to make all grace abound unto you, that ye, always having all sufficiency in all things, may abound unto all good works.*"

It has often happened that a seeker after God and salvation has read his Bible long, and yet never seen the truth of a free and full and immediate justification by faith. When once his eyes were opened, and he accepted it, he was amazed to find it everywhere. Even so many believers, who hold the doctrines of free grace as applied to pardon, have never seen its wondrous meaning as it undertakes to work our whole life in us, and actually give us strength every moment for whatever the Father would have us be and do.

When God's light shines into our heart with this blessed truth, we know what Paul means, "*Not I, but the grace of God.*" There again you have the twofold Christian life. The one, in which that "Not I"—I am nothing, I can do nothing—has not yet become a reality. The other, when the wondrous exchange has been made, and grace has taken the place of our effort, and we say and know, "*I live, yet no longer I, but Christ lives in me.*" It may then become a lifelong experience: "The grace of our Lord was exceeding abundant, with faith and love which is in Christ Jesus."

Beloved child of God! what think you, is it not possible that this has been the want in your life, the cause of your failure in prayer? You knew not how grace would enable you to pray, if once the whole life were under its power. You sought by earnest effort to conquer your reluctance or deadness in prayer, but failed. You strove by every motive of shame or love you could think of to stir yourself to it, but it would not help. Is it not worthwhile asking the Lord whether the message I bring you as His servant may not be more true for you than you think? Your lack of prayer is owing to a diseased state of life, and the disease is nothing but this you have not accepted, for daily life and every duty, the full salvation which the word brings: "You are not under the law, but under grace."

As universal and deep-reaching as the demand of the law and the reign of sin, yea, more exceeding abundant, is the provision of grace and the power by which it makes us reign in life. In the chapter that follows that in which Paul wrote, "You are not under the law, but under grace," he gives us a picture of a *believer's life under law*, with the bitter experience in which it ends: "*wretched man that I am! who shall deliver me from the body of this death?*" His answer to the question, "*I thank God through Jesus Christ our Lord,*" shows that there is deliverance from a life held captive under evil habits that have been struggled against in vain.

That deliverance is by the Holy Spirit giving the full experience of what the life of Christ can work in us: "*The law of the Spirit of life in Christ Jesus hath made me free from the law of sin and death.*" The law of God could only deliver us into the power of the law of sin and death. The grace of God can bring us into, and keep us in, the liberty of the Spirit. We can be made free from the sad life under the power that led us captive, so that we did not what we would.

The Spirit of life in Christ can free us from our continual failure in prayer, and enable us in this, too, to walk worthy of the Lord unto all well pleasing. Oh! be not hopeless, be not despondent; there is a balm in Gilead; there is a Physician there; there is healing for our sickness. What is impossible with man is possible with God. What you see no possibility of doing, grace will do. Confess the disease; trust the Physician; claim the healing; pray the prayer of faith, "Heal me, and I shall be healed." You too can become a man of prayer, and pray the effectual prayer that avails much.

The Spirit of Supplication 1

October 4th

"With all prayer and supplication praying at all seasons in the Spirit, watching thereunto in all perseverance and supplication for all the saints."

—EPHESIANS 6: 18

The Holy Spirit has been given to every child of God to be his life. He dwells in him, not as a separate Being in one part of his nature, but as his very life. He is the Divine power or energy by which his life is maintained and strengthened. All that a believer is called to be or to do, the Holy Spirit can and will work in him. If he does not know or yield to the Holy Guest, the Blessed Spirit cannot work, and his life is a sickly one, full of failure and of sin. As he yields, and waits, and obeys the leading of the Spirit, God works in him all that is pleasing in His sight.

This Holy Spirit is, in the first place, a Spirit of prayer. He was promised as a *"Spirit of grace and supplication,"* the grace *for* supplication. He was sent forth into our hearts as *"the Spirit of adoption, whereby we cry, Abba, Father."* He enables us to say, in true faith and growing apprehension of its meaning, *"Our Father which are in Heaven." "He makes intercession for the saints according to God."* And as we pray in the Spirit, our worship is as God seeks it to be, *"in spirit and in truth."* Prayer is just the breathing of the Spirit in us; power in prayer comes from the power of the Spirit in us, waited on and trusted in.

Failure in prayer comes from feebleness of the Spirit's work in us. Our prayer is the index of the measure of the Spirit's work in us. To pray aright, the life of the Spirit must be right in us. For praying the effectual, much-availing prayer of the righteous man everything depends on being full of the Spirit.

There are three very simple lessons that the believer, who would enjoy the blessing of being taught to pray by the Spirit of prayer, must know: The first is: *"Believe that the Spirit dwells in you"* (Ephesians 1: 13). Deep in the inmost recesses of his being, hidden and unfelt, every child of God has the Holy, Mighty Spirit of God dwelling in him. He knows it by faith, the faith that, accepting God's word, realizes that of which he sees as yet no sign.

"We receive the promise of the Spirit by faith." As long as we measure our power, for praying aright and perseveringly, by what we feel, or think we can accomplish, we shall be discouraged when we hear of how much we ought to pray. But when we quietly believe that, in the midst of all our conscious weakness, the Holy Spirit as a Spirit of supplication is dwelling within us, for the very purpose of enabling us to pray in such manner and measure as God would have us, our hearts will be filled with hope.

The second lesson is: *"Beware ... of grieving the Holy Spirit"* (Ephesians 4: 30). If you do, how can He work in you the quiet, trustful, and blessed sense of that union with Christ which makes your prayers well pleasing to the Father? Beware of grieving Him by sin, by unbelief, by Selfishness, by unfaithfulness to His voice in conscience. ... Do not consider it impossible to obey the command, *"Grieve not the Holy Spirit."* He Himself is the very power of God to make you obedient. The sin that comes up in you against your will, the tendency to sloth, or pride, or Self-will, or passion that rises in the flesh, your will can, in the power of the Spirit, at once reject, and cast upon Christ and His blood, and your communion with God is immediately restored.

Accept each day the Holy Spirit as your leader and life and strength; you can count upon Him to do in your heart all that ought to be done there. He, the unseen and unfelt One, but known by faith, gives there, unseen and unfelt, the love and the faith and the power of obedience you need, because He reveals Christ unseen within you, as actually your life and strength. Grieve not the Holy Spirit by distrusting Him, because you do not feel His presence in you. ...

"We know not what to pray as we ought"; ignorance, difficulty, struggle, marks our prayer all along. But, *"the Spirit helps our infirmities."* How? *"The Spirit Himself,"* deeper down than our thoughts or feelings, *"makes intercession for us with groanings which cannot be uttered."* When you cannot find words, when your words appear cold and feeble, just believe: *The Holy Spirit is praying in me.* Be quiet before God, and give Him time and opportunity; in due season you will learn to pray. Beware of grieving the Spirit of prayer, by not honoring Him in patient, trustful surrender to His intercession in you.

The third lesson: *"Be filled with the Spirit"* (Ephesians 5: 18). I think that we have seen the meaning of the great truth: It is only the healthy spiritual life that can pray aright. The command comes to each of us: *"Be filled with the Spirit."* That implies that while some rest content with the beginning, with a small measure of the Spirit's working, it is God's will that we should be filled with the Spirit. That means, from our side, that our whole being ought to be entirely yielded up to the Holy Spirit, to be possessed and controlled by Him alone. And, from God's side, that we may count upon and expect the Holy Spirit to take possession and fill us.

Has not our failure in prayer evidently been owing to our not having accepted the Spirit of prayer to be our life; to our not having yielded wholly to Him, whom the Father gave as the Spirit of His Son, to work the life of the Son in us? Let us, to say the very least, be willing to receive Him, to yield ourselves to God and trust Him for it.

Let us not again willfully grieve the Holy Spirit by declining, by neglecting, by hesitating to seek to have Him as fully as He is willing to give Himself to us. If we have at all seen that prayer is the great need of our work and of the Church, if we have at all desired or resolved to pray more, let us turn to the very source of all power and blessing let us believe that the Spirit of prayer, even in His fullness, is for us.

We all admit the place the Father and the Son have in our prayer. It is to the Father we pray, and from whom we expect the answer. It is in the merit, and name, and life of the Son, abiding in Him and He in us, that we trust to be heard. But have we understood that in the Holy Trinity all the Three Persons have an equal place in prayer, and that the faith in the Holy Spirit of intercession as praying in us is as indispensable as the faith in the Father and the Son? How clearly we have this in the words, *"Through Christ we have access by one Spirit to the Father."* As much as prayer must be to the Father, and through the Son, it must be by the Spirit. And the Spirit can pray in no other way in us than as He lives in us. It is only as we give ourselves to the Spirit living and praying in us, that the glory of the prayer-hearing God, and the ever-blessed and most effectual mediation of the Son, can be known by us in their power.

The Spirit of Supplication 2

October 5th

Our last lesson: *"Pray in the Spirit for all saints"* (Ephesians 6: 18). The Spirit, who is called *"the Spirit of supplication,"* is also and very the Spirit of intercession. It is said of Him… *"He makes intercession for the saints."* It is the same word as is used of Christ, *"who also makes intercession for us."* The thought is essentially that of mediation one pleading for another. When the Spirit of intercession takes full possession of us, all Selfishness …is banished, and we begin to avail ourselves of our wonderful privilege to plead for others. We long to live the Christ-life of Self-consuming sacrifice for others, as our heart unceasingly yields itself to God to obtain His blessing for those around us.

Intercession then becomes, not an incident or an occasional part of our prayers, but their one great object. Prayer for ourselves then takes its true place, simply as a means for fitting us better for exercising our ministry of intercession more effectually.

May I be allowed to speak a very personal word to each of my readers? I have humbly besought God to give me what I may give them Divine light and help truly to forsake the life of failure in prayer, and to enter, even now, and at once, upon the life of intercession which the Holy Spirit can enable them to lead. It can be done by a simple act of faith, claiming the fullness of the Spirit, that is, the full measure of the Spirit which you are capable in God's sight of receiving, and He is therefore willing to bestow. Will you not, even now, accept of this by faith?

Let me remind you of what takes place at conversion. Most of us, you probably too, for a time sought peace in efforts and struggles to give up sin and please God. But you did not find it thus. The peace of God's pardon came by faith, trusting God's word concerning Christ and His salvation. You had heard of Christ as the gift of His love, you knew that He was for you too, you had felt the movings and drawings of His grace; but never till in faith in God's word did you accept Him as God's gift to you, and did you know the peace and joy that He can give. Believing in Him and His saving love made all the difference, and changed your relation from one who had ever grieved Him, to one who loved and served Him. And yet, after a time, you have a thousand times wondered why you love and serve Him so ill.

At the time of your conversion you knew little about the Holy Spirit. Later on you heard of His dwelling in you, and His being the power of God in you for all the Father intends you to be, and yet His indwelling and inworking have been something vague and indefinite, and hardly a source of joy or strength. At conversion you did not yet know your need of Him, and still less what you might expect of Him. But your failures have taught it you. And now you begin to see how you have been grieving Him, by not trusting and not following Him, by not allowing Him to work in you all God's pleasure.

All this can be changed. Just as you, after seeking Christ, and praying to Him, and trying without success to serve Him, found rest in accepting Him by faith, just so you may even now yield yourself to the full guidance of the Holy Spirit, and claim and accept Him to work in you what God would have. Will you not do it? Just accept Him in faith as Christ's gift, to be the Spirit of your whole life, of your prayer-life too, and you can count upon Him to take charge. …

My dear friend, as you consciously by faith accepted Christ, to pardon, you can consciously now in the like faith accept of Christ who gives the Holy Spirit to do His work in you. *"Christ redeemed us that we might receive the promise of the Spirit by faith."* Kneel down, and simply believe that the Lord Christ, who baptizes with the Holy Spirit, does now, in response to your faith, begin in you the blessed life of a full experience of the power of the indwelling Spirit.

Depend most confidently upon Him, apart from all feeling or experience, as the Spirit of supplication and intercession to do His work. Renew that act of faith each morning, each time you pray; trust Him, against all appearances, to work in you. Be sure He is working, and He will give you to know what the joy of the Holy Spirit is as the power of your life.

"I will pour out the Spirit of supplication." Do you not begin to see that the mystery of prayer is the mystery of the Divine indwelling. God in Heaven gives His Spirit in our hearts to be there—the Divine power praying in us, and drawing us upward to our God. God is a Spirit, and nothing but a like life and Spirit within us can hold communion with Him. It was for this man was created, that God might dwell and work in Him, and be the life of his life. It was this Divine indwelling that sin lost. It was this that Christ came to exhibit in His life, to win back for us in His death, and then to impart to us by coming again from Heaven in the Spirit to live in His disciples. It is this, the indwelling of God through the Spirit that alone can explain and enable us to appropriate the wonderful

promises given to prayer. God gives the Spirit as a Spirit of Supplication, too, to maintain His Divine life within us as a life out of which prayer ever rises upward. …

My God Will Hear Me

October 6th

"The Lord will hear when I call upon Him."

—PSALM 4: 3

The power of prayer rests in the faith that God hears it. In more than one sense this is true. It is this faith that gives a man courage to pray. It is this faith that gives him power to prevail with God. The moment I am assured that God hears me too, I feel drawn to pray and to persevere in prayer. I feel strong to claim and to take in faith the answer God gives.

One great reason of lack of prayer is the want of the living, joyous assurance: *"My God will hear me."* If once God's servants got a vision of the living God waiting to grant their request, and to bestow all the heavenly gifts of the Spirit they are in need of, for themselves or those they are serving, how everything would be set aside to make time and room for this one only power that can ensure heavenly blessing: *the prayer of faith!*

When we can, and do say, in living faith, "*My God will hear me*!" surely nothing can keep us from prayer. We know that what we cannot do or get done on earth, can and will be done for us from Heaven. Let each one of us bow in stillness before God, and wait on Him to reveal Himself as the prayer-hearing God. In His presence the wondrous thoughts gathering round the central truth will unfold themselves to us.

"My God will hear me." What a blessed certainty! We have God's word for it in numberless promises. We have thousands of witnesses to the fact that they have found it true. We have had experience of it in our lives. We have had the Son of God come from Heaven with the message that if we ask, the Father will give. We have had Himself praying on earth, and being heard. And we have Him in Heaven now, sitting at the right hand of God and making intercession for us. God hears prayer God delights to hear prayer. He has allowed His people a thousand times over to be tried, that they might be compelled to cry to Him, and learn to know Him as the Hearer of Prayer.

Let us confess with shame how little we have believed this wondrous truth, in the sense of receiving it into our heart, and allowing it to possess and control our whole being. That we accept a truth is not enough; the living God, of whom the truth speaks, must in its light so be revealed, that our whole life is spent in His presence, with the consciousness as clear as in a little child towards its earthly parent: "I know for certain my father hears me." …

Beseech God to reveal Himself to you. If you want to live a different prayer-life, bow each time ere you pray in silence to worship this God; to wait till there rests on you some right sense of His nearness and readiness to answer. So will you begin to pray with the words, *"My God will hear me!"*

"*My God will hear me.*" What a wondrous grace! Think of God in His infinite majesty, His altogether incomprehensible glory, His unapproachable holiness, sitting on a throne of grace, waiting to be gracious, inviting, encouraging you to pray with His promise: *"Call upon Me, and I will answer you."* Think of yourself, in your nothingness and helplessness as a creature; in your wretchedness and transgressions as a sinner; in your feebleness and unworthiness as a saint; and praise the glory of that grace which allows you to say boldly of your prayer for yourself and others, *"My God will hear me."*

Think of how you are not left to yourself, and what you can accomplish, in this wonderful intercourse with God. God has united you with Christ; in Him and His Name you have your confidence; on the throne He prays with you and for you; on the footstool of the throne you pray with Him and in Him. His worth, and the Father's delight in hearing Him, are the measure of your confidence, your assurance of being heard.

Think of the Holy Spirit, the Spirit of God's own Son, sent into your heart to cry, Abba, Father, and to be in you a Spirit of Supplication, when you know not what to pray as you ought. Think, in all your insignificance and unworthiness, of your being as acceptable as Christ Himself. Think in all your ignorance and feebleness, of the Spirit making intercession according to God within you, and cry out, "What wondrous grace! Through Christ I have access to the Father, by the Spirit. I can, I do believe it: My God will hear me."

"My God will hear me." What a deep mystery! There are difficulties that cannot but at times arise and perplex even the honest heart… the multitude of apparently vain and unanswered prayers. How many have pleaded for loved ones, and they die unsaved. How many cry for years for spiritual blessing, and no answer comes. To think of all this tries our faith, and makes us hesitate as we say, *"My God will hear me."*

Beloved! prayer, in its power with God, and His faithfulness to His promise to hear it, is a deep spiritual mystery. To the questions put above answers can be given that remove some of the difficulty. But, after all, the first and the last that must be said is this: As little as we can comprehend God can we comprehend this, one of the most blessed of His attributes, that He hears prayer.

It is a spiritual mystery nothing less than the mystery of the Holy Trinity. God hears because we pray in His Son, because the Holy Spirit prays in us. If we have believed and claimed the life of Christ as our health, and the fullness of the Spirit as our strength, let us not hesitate to believe in the power of our prayer too. The Holy Spirit can enable us to believe and rejoice in it, even where every question is not yet answered. He will do this, as we lay our questionings in God's bosom, trust His faithfulness, and give ourselves humbly to obey His command to pray without ceasing.

Every are unfolds its secrets and its beauty only to the man who practices it. To the humble soul who prays in the obedience of faith, who practices prayer and intercession diligently, because God asks it, the secret of the Lord will be revealed, and the thought of the deep mystery of prayer, instead of being a weary problem, will be a source of rejoicing, adoration, and faith, in which the unceasing refrain is ever heard: *"My God will hear me!"*

"My God will hear me." What a solemn responsibility! How often we complain of darkness, of feebleness, of failure, as if there was no help for it. And God has promised in answer to our prayer to supply our every need, and give us His light and strength and peace. Only had we realized the responsibility of having such a God, and such promises, with the sin … of not availing ourselves of them to the utmost. …

There is more. This access to a prayer-hearing God is specially meant to make us intercessors for our fellow-men. Even as Christ obtained His right of prevailing intercession by His giving Himself a sacrifice to God for us, and through it receives the blessings He dispenses, so, if we have truly with Christ given ourselves to God for others, we share His right of intercession, and are able to obtain the powers of the heavenly world for them too. The power of life and death is in our hands (1 John 5: 16). In answer to prayer the Spirit can be poured out, souls can be converted, believers can be established. In prayer the kingdom of darkness can be conquered, souls brought out of prison into the liberty of Christ, and the glory of God be revealed. Through prayer, the sword of the Spirit, which is the Word of God, can be wielded in power, and, in public preaching as in private speaking, the most rebellious made to bow at Jesus feet. …

"My God will hear me." What a blessed prospect! I see it all the failures of my past life have been owing to the lack of this faith. My failure, especially in the work of intercession, has had its deepest root in this I did not live in the full faith of the blessed assurance, *"My God will hear me!"*

Praise God! I begin to see it I believe it. All can be different. Or, rather, I see Him, I believe Him. "My God will hear me!" Yes, me, even me! Commonplace and insignificant though I be—filling but a very little place, so that I will scarce be missed when I go—*even I* have access to this Infinite God, with the confidence that He hears me. One with Christ, led by the Holy Spirit, I dare to say: "I will pray for others, for I am sure my God will listen to me: *"My God will hear me."* …

In the Name of Christ 1

October 7th

"Whatsoever you shall ask in My Name, that will I do; If you shall ask anything in My Name, I will do it."
—JOHN 14: 13–14

In "*my name*," repeated six times over. Our Lord knew how slow our hearts would be to take it in, and He so longed that we should really believe that His Name is the power in which every knee should bow, and in which every prayer could be heard, that He did not weary of saying it over and over: *"In My Name!"* Between the wonderful *"whatsoever you shall ask,"* and the Divine *"I will do it,"* the Father will give it, this one word is the simple link: *In My Name*. Our asking and the Father's giving are to be equally in the name of Christ. Everything in prayer depends upon our apprehending this *"In My Name."* …

To ask in the name of Christ is to pray in union with Him. When first as sinners we believe in Christ, we only know and think of His merit and intercession. And to the very end that is the one foundation of our confidence. And yet, as we grow in grace and enter more deeply and truly into union with Christ—that is, as we abide in Him—we learn that to pray in the Name of Christ also means in His Spirit, and in the possession of His nature, as the Holy Spirit imparts it to us. As we grasp the meaning of the Words, *"At that day you shall ask in My Name"*—the day when in the Holy Spirit Christ came to live in His disciples—we shall no longer be staggered at the greatness of the promise: *"Whatsoever you shall ask in My Name, I will do it."* We shall get some insight into the unchangeable necessity and certainty of the law: what is asked in the name of Christ, in union with Him, out of His nature and Spirit, must be given. As Christ's prayer-nature lives in us, His prayer-power becomes ours too. Not that the measure of our attainment or experience is the ground of our confidence, but the honesty and whole-heartedness of our surrender to all that we see that Christ seeks to be in us, will be the measure of our spiritual fitness and power to pray in His Name.

"If you abide in Me," He says, *"You shall ask what you will."* As we live in Him, we get the spiritual power to avail ourselves of His Name. As the branch wholly given up to the life and service of the Vine can count upon all its sap and strength for its fruit, so believers, who in faith have accepted the fullness of the Spirit to possess our whole life, can indeed avail ourselves of all the power of Christ's Name.

Here on earth Christ as man came to reveal what prayer is. To pray in the name of Christ we must pray as He prayed on earth; as He taught us to pray; in union with Him, as He now prays in Heaven. We must in love study, and in faith accept, Him as our Example, our Teacher, our Intercessor.

Christ our Example. Prayer in Christ on earth and in us cannot be two different things. Just as there is but one God, who is a Spirit, who hears prayer, there is but spirit of acceptable prayer. When we realize what time Christ spent in prayer, and how the great events of His life were all connected with special prayer, we learn the necessity of absolute dependence on and unceasing direct communication with the heavenly world, if we are to live a heavenly life, or to exercise heavenly power around us. We see how foolish and fruitless the attempt must be to do work for God and Heaven, without in the first place in prayer getting the life and the power of Heaven to possess us. Unless this truth lives in us, we cannot avail ourselves aright of the mighty power of the name of Christ. His example must teach us the meaning of His Name.

Of His baptism we read, *"Jesus having been baptized, and praying, the Heaven was opened."* It was in prayer Heaven was opened to Him, that Heaven came down to Him with the Spirit and the voice of the Father. In the power of these He was led into the wilderness, in fasting and prayer to have them tested and fully appropriated. Early in His ministry Mark records *"And in the morning, a great while before day, He rose and departed into a desert place, and there prayed."* And somewhat later Luke tells *"Multitudes came together to hear and to be healed. But He withdrew Himself into the desert, and prayed."* He knew how the holiest service, preaching and healing, can exhaust the spirit; how too much intercourse with the world could cloud the fellowship with God; how time, time, full time, is needed if the spirit is to rest and root in Him; how no pressure of duty among others can free from the absolute need of much prayer. If anyone could have been satisfied with always living and working in the spirit of prayer, it would have been our Master. But He could not; He needed to have His supplies replenished by continual and long-continued seasons of prayer.

To use Christ's Name in prayer surely includes this, to follow His example and to pray as He did. Of the night before choosing His apostles we read, *"He went out into the mountain to pray, and continued all night in prayer to God"* (Luke 6: 12). The first step towards the constitution of the Church, and the separation of men to be His witnesses and successors, called Him to special long-continued prayer. *"All had to be done according to the pattern on the mount." "The Son can do nothing of Himself: The Father shows Him all things that Himself does."* It was in the night of prayer it was shown Him.

In the night between the feeding of the five thousand, when Jesus knew that they wanted to take Him by force and make Him King, and the walking on the sea, *"He withdrew again into the mountain, alone, to pray"* (Matthew 14: 2 –3; Mark 6: 46; John 6:15). It was God's will that He was come to do, and God's power that He was to show forth. He had it not as a possession of His own; it had to be prayed for and received from above. The first announcement of His approaching death, after He had elicited from Peter the confession that He was the Christ, is introduced by the words, *"And it came to pass that He was praying alone"* (Luke 9: 15). The introduction to the story of the Transfiguration is *"He went up into the mountain to pray"* (Luke 9: 28). The request of the disciples, "*Lord, teach us to pray*" (Luke 11: 1), follows on, *"It came to pass as He was praying in a certain place."*

In His own personal life, in His intercourse with the Father, in all He is and does for men, the Christ whose name we are to use is a Man of prayer. It is prayer gives Him His power of blessing, and transfigures His very body with the glory of Heaven. It is His own prayer-life makes Him the teacher of others how to pray. How much more must it be prayer, prayer alone, much prayer, that can fit us to share His glory of a transfigured life, or make us the channel of heavenly blessing and teaching to others. To pray in the name of Christ is to pray as He prays.

As the end approaches, it is still more prayer. When the Greeks asked to see Him, and He spoke of His approaching death, He prayed. At Lazarus grave He prayed. In the last night He prayed His prayer as our High Priest, that we might know what His sacrifice would win, and what His everlasting intercession on the throne would be. In Gethsemane He prayed His prayer as Victim, the Lamb giving itself to the slaughter. On the cross it is still all prayer the prayer of compassion for His murderers; the prayer of atoning suffering in the thick darkness; the prayer in death of confiding resignation of His spirit to the Father.

Christ's life and work, His suffering and death: it was all prayer, all dependence on God, trust in God, receiving from God, surrender to God. Your redemption, believer, is a redemption wrought out by prayer and intercession. Your Christ is a praying Christ; the life He lived for you, the life He lives in you, is a praying life, that delights to wait on God and receive all from Him. ... Christ is only our example because He is our Head, our

Savior, and our Life. In virtue of His Deity and of His Spirit He can live in us: we can pray in His Name, because we abide in Him and He in us.

In the Name of Christ 2

October 8th

"You have not chosen me, but I have chosen you, and ordained you, that you should go and bring forth fruit, and that your fruit should remain: that whatsoever you shall ask of the Father in my name, he may give it you"
—JOHN 15: 16

Christ our teacher. Christ was what He taught. All His teaching was just the revelation of how He lived, and praise God of the life He was to live in us. His teaching of the disciples was first to awaken desire, and so prepare them for what He would by the Holy Spirit be and work in them. Let us believe very confidently: all He was in prayer, and all He taught, He Himself will give. He came to fulfill the law; much more will He fulfill the gospel in all He taught us, as to what to pray, and how.

What to pray. … If we carefully study all that our Lord spoke of prayer, we shall see that this is not His teaching. In the Lord's Prayer, in the parables on prayer, in the illustration of a child asking bread, of our seeking and knocking, in the central thought of the prayer of faith, *"Whatsoever you pray, believe that you have received,"* in the oft-repeated "whatsoever" of the last evening—everywhere our Lord urges and encourages us to offer definite petitions, and to expect definite answers.

It is only because we have too much confined prayer to our own needs, that it has been thought needful to free it from the appearance of Selfishness, by giving the petitions a subordinate place. If once believers were to awake to the glory of the work of intercession, and to see that in it, and the definite pleading for definite gifts on definite spheres and persons, lie our highest fellowship with our glorified Lord, and our only real power to bless men, it would be seen that there can be no truer fellowship with God than these definite petitions and their answers, by which we become the channel of His grace and life to the world. Then our fellowship with the Father is even such as the Son has in His intercession.

How to pray. Our Lord taught us to pray in secret, in simplicity, with the eye on God alone, in humility, in the spirit of forgiving love. But the chief truth He reiterated was ever this: to pray in faith. And He defined that faith, not only as a trust in God's goodness or power, but as the definite assurance that we have received the very thing we ask. And then, in view of the delay in the answer, He insisted on perseverance and urgency. We must be followers of those *"who through faith and patience inherit the promises"*—the faith that accepts the promise, and knows it has what it has asked; the patience that obtains the promise and inherits the blessing. We shall then learn to understand why God, who promises to avenge His elect speedily, bears with them in seeming delay. It is that their faith may be purified from all that is of the flesh, and tested and strengthened to become that spiritual power that can do all things can even cast mountains into the heart of the sea.

Christ Our Intercessor. We have gazed on Christ in His prayers; we have listened to His teaching as to how we must pray; to know fully what it is to pray in His Name, we must know Him too in His heavenly intercession. Just think what it means: that all His saving work wrought from Heaven is still carried on, just as on earth, in unceasing communication with, and direct intercession to the Father, who works all in all, who is All in All. Every act of grace in Christ has been preceded by, and owes its power to, intercession. God has been honored and acknowledged as its Author. On the throne of God, Christ's highest fellowship with the Father, and His partnership in His rule of the world, is in intercession. Every blessing that comes down to us from above bears upon it the stamp from God: through Christ's intercession. His intercession is nothing but the fruit and the glory of His atonement. When He gave Himself a sacrifice to God for men, He proved that His whole heart had the one object: the glory of God, in the salvation of men. In His intercession this great purpose is realized: He glorifies the Father by asking and receiving all Him; He saves men by bestowing what He has obtained from the Father. Christ's intercession is the Father's glory, His own glory, our glory.

And now, this Christ, the Intercessor, is our life; He is our Head, and we are His body; His Spirit and life breathe in us. As in Heaven so on earth, intercession is God's chosen, God's only channel of blessing. Let us learn from Christ what glory there is in it; what the way to exercise this wondrous power; what the part it is to take in work for God.

The glory of it. By it, beyond anything, we glorify God. By it we glorify Christ. By it we bring blessing to the Church and the world. By it we obtain our highest nobility the Godlike power of saving others.

The way to it. Paul writes, *"Walk in love, even as Christ loved us, and gave Himself a sacrifice to God for us."* If we live as Christ lived, we will, as He did, give ourselves, for our whole life, to God, to be used by Him for men. When once we have done this, given ourselves, no more to seek anything for ourselves, but for others, and that to God, for Him to use us, and to impart to us what we can bestow on others, intercession will become to us, as it is in Christ in Heaven, the great work of our life. And if ever the thought comes that the call is too high, or the work too great, the faith in Christ, the Interceding Christ, who lives in us, will give us the victory.

We will listen to Him who said, *"The works that I do, shall you do; and greater works shall you do."* We shall remember that we are not under the law, with its impotence, but under grace with its omnipotence, working all in us. We shall believe again in Him who said to us, *"Rise and walk,"* and gave us—and we received it—His life as our strength. We shall claim afresh the fullness of God's Spirit as His sufficient provision for our need, and count Him to be in us the Spirit of Intercession, who makes us one with Christ in His. Oh! let us only keep our place giving up ourselves, like Him, in Him, to God for men.

Then we shall understand the part intercession is to take in God's work through us. We shall no longer try to work for God, and ask Him to follow it with His blessing. We shall do what the friend at midnight did, what Christ did on earth, and ever does in Heaven we shall first get from God, and then turn to men to give what He gave us. As with Christ, we shall make our chief work, we shall count no time or trouble too great, to receive from the Father; giving to others will then be in power.

Servants of Christ! children of God! be of good courage. Let no fear of feebleness or poverty make you afraid ask in the Name of Christ. His Name is Himself, in all His perfection and power. He is the living Christ, and will Himself make His Name a power in you. Fear not to plead the Name; His promise is a threefold cord that cannot be broken: "*Whatsoever you ask in My Name it shall be done for you.*"

NOTE:

There is a question, the deepest of all, on which I have not entered in this book. I have spoken of the lack of prayer in the individual Christian as a symptom of a disease. But what shall we say of it, that there is such a widespread prevalence of this failure to give a due proportion of time and strength to prayer. Do we not need to inquire, How comes it that the Church of Christ, endued with the Holy Spirit, cannot train its ministers and workers and members to place first what is first? How comes it that the confession of too little prayer, and the call for more prayer, is so frequently heard, and yet the evil continues?

The Spirit of God, the Spirit of supplication and intercession, is in the Church and in every believer. There must surely be some other spirit of great power resisting and hindering this Spirit of God. It is indeed so. The *spirit of the world*, which under all its beautiful and even religious activities is the spirit of the god of this world, is the great hindrance. Everything that is done on earth, whether within or without the Church, is done by either of these two spirits. What is in the individual the flesh, is in mankind as a whole the spirit of the world; and all the power the flesh has in the individual is owing to the place given to the spirit of this world in the Church and in Christian life. It is the spirit of the world is the great hindrance to the spirit of prayer. All our most earnest calls to men to pray more will be vain except this evil be acknowledged and combated and overcome.

The believer and the Church must be entirely freed from the spirit of the world. And how is this to be done? There is but one way the Cross of Christ, by which, as Paul says, "*the world is crucified unto me, and I unto the world.*" It is only through death to the world that we can be freed from its spirit. The separation must be vital and entire. It is only through the acceptance of our crucifixion with Christ that we can live out this confession, and, as crucified to the world, maintain the position of irreconcilable hostility to whatever is of its spirit and not of the Spirit of God; and it is only God Himself who, by His Divine power, can lead us into and keep us daily dead to sin, and alive unto God in Christ Jesus.

The cross, with its shame and its separation from the world, and its death to all that is of flesh and of Self, is the only power that can conquer the spirit of the world. … Christ prayed on the way to the cross. He prayed Himself to the cross. He prayed on the cross. He prays ever as the fruit of the cross. As the Church lives on the cross, and the cross lives in the Church, the spirit of prayer will be given. In Christ it was the crucifixion spirit and death that was the source of the Intercession Spirit and Power. With us it cannot be otherwise.

Paul: A Pattern for Prayer

October 9th

"For this cause I obtained mercy, that in me, Jesus Christ might show forth all long-suffering, as a pattern to those who would hereafter believe on Him to life everlasting."

—1 TIMOTHY 1: 16

Our Lord took Paul, a man of like passions with ourselves, and made him a pattern of what he could do for one who was "*the chief of sinners.*" And Paul, the man who, more than any other, has set his mark on the Church, has ever been appealed to as a pattern man. In his mastery of Divine truth, and his teaching of it; in his devotion to his Lord, and his Self-consuming zeal in His service; in his deep experience of the power of the indwelling Christ and the fellowship of His cross; in the sincerity of his humility, and the simplicity and boldness of his faith; in his missionary enthusiasm and endurance in all this, and so much more, *"the grace of our Lord Jesus was exceeding abundant in him."*

Christ gave him, and the Church has accepted him, as a pattern of what Christ would have, of what Christ would work. Seven times Paul speaks of believers following him: *"Wherefore I beseech you, be you followers of me"* (1 Corinthians 4: 16); *"Be you followers of me, even as I am of Christ"* (1 Corinthians 11: 1; Philippians 3: 17, 4: 9; 1 Thessalonians 1: 6; 2 Thessalonians 3: 7–9). …

The heavenly vision which brought him to his knees ever after ruled his life. Christ at the right hand of God, in whom we are blessed with all spiritual blessings, was everything to him; to pray and expect the heavenly power in his work and on his work, from Heaven direct by prayer, was the simple outcome of his faith in the Glorified One. In this, too, Christ meant him to be a pattern, that we might learn that, just in the measure in which the heavenliness of Christ and His gifts, the unworldliness of the powers that work for salvation, are known and believed, will prayer become the spontaneous rising of the heart to the only source of its life. Let us see what we know of Paul.

Paul's Habits of Prayer

These are revealed almost unconsciously. He writes: *"God is my witness, that without ceasing I make mention of you always in my prayers. For I long to see you, that I may impart unto you some spiritual gift, to the end you may be established"* (Ephesians 1: 9). *"My heart's desire and prayer to God for Israel is, that they may be saved"*; *"I have great heaviness and continual sorrow of heart; for I could wish that myself were accursed from Christ for my brethren"* (Ephesians 10: 1; 9: 2, 3). *"I thank my God always on your behalf, for the grace of God which is given you by Jesus Christ"* (1 Corinthians 1: 4). *"Approving ourselves as the ministers of Christ, in watchings, in fastings"* (2 Corinthians 6: 4; 6). *"My little children, of whom I travail in birth again till Christ be formed in you"* (Galatians 4: 19). *"I cease not to give thanks for you, making mention of you in my prayers"* (Ephesians 1: 16). *"I bow my knees to the Father, that He would grant you to be strengthened with might by His Spirit in the inner man"* (Ephesians 3: 14). *"I thank my God upon every remembrance of you, always in every prayer of mine making request for you all with joy. For God is my record, how greatly I long after you all in the bowels of Jesus Christ. And this I pray"* (Philippians 1: 3, 4, 8, 9); *"We give thanks to God, praying always for you. For this cause also, since the day we heard it, we do not cease to pray for you"* (Colossians 1: 3, 9). *"We are bound to thank God always for you. Wherefore also we always pray for you"* (2 Thessalonians 1: 3). *"I thank God, that without ceasing I have remembrance of you night and day"* (2 Timothy 1: 3). *"I thank my God, making mention of you always in my prayers"* (Philemon 4).

These passages taken together give us the picture of a man whose words, *"Pray without ceasing,"* were simply the expression of his daily life. He had such a sense of the insufficiency of simple conversion—of the need of the grace and the power of Heaven being brought down for the young converts in prayer; of the need of much and unceasing prayer, day and night, to bring it down; of the certainty that prayer would bring it down—that his life was continual and most definite prayer.

He had such a sense that everything must come from above, and such a faith that it would come in answer to prayer, that prayer was neither a duty nor a burden, but the natural turning of the heart to the only place whence it could possibly obtain what it sought for others.

It is of as much importance to know what Paul prayed, as how frequently and earnestly he did so. … Much as he praised God when he heard of conversion, he knew how feeble the young converts were, and how for their establishing nothing would avail without the grace of the Spirit prayed down. If we notice some of the principal of these prayers, we shall see what he asked and obtained.

Take the two prayers in Ephesians the one for light, the other for strength. In the former (Ephesians 1: 15), he prays for the Spirit of wisdom to enlighten them to know what their calling was, what their inheritance was, what the mighty power of God working in them. Spiritual enlightenment and knowledge was their great need, to be obtained for them by prayer. In the latter (3:15), he asks that the power they had been led to see in Christ might work in them, and they be strengthened with Divine might, so as to have the indwelling Christ, and the love that passes knowledge, and the fullness of God actually come on them. These were things that could only come direct from Heaven; these were things he asked and expected. …

Look at the prayer in Philippians (1: 9–11); there, too, it is first for spiritual knowledge; then comes a blameless life, and then a fruitful life to the glory of God. So also in the beautiful prayer in Colossians (1: 9–11); first, spiritual knowledge and understanding of God's will, then the strengthening with all might to all patience and joy.

Or take the two prayers in 1 Thessalonians (3: 2, 13, 23); the one, *"God so increase your love to one another, that He may establish your hearts unblameable in holiness"*; the other, *"God sanctify you wholly, and preserve you blameless."* The very words are so high that we hardly understand, still less believe, still less experience what they mean. Paul so lived in the heavenly world, he was so at home in the holiness and omnipotence of God and His love, that such prayers were the natural expression of what he knew God could and would do.

"God establish your hearts unblameable in holiness"; *"God sanctify you wholly."* Those who

believe in these things and desire them, will pray for them for others. The prayers are all a proof that we seek for them the very life of Heaven upon earth. …

Because of His Importunity

October 10th

"Because of his importunity he will arise and give him as much as he needs."

—LUKE 11: 8

In our intercourse with God, the difficulty is not on His side, but on ours. In connection with the first parable He tells us that our Father is more willing to give good things to those who ask Him than any earthly father to give his child bread. In the second, He assures us that God longs to avenge His elect speedily. The need of urgent prayer cannot be because God must be made willing or disposed to bless; the need lies altogether in ourselves. But because it was not possible to find any earthly illustration of a loving father or a willing friend from whom the needed lesson of importunity could be taught, He takes the unwilling friend and the unjust judge to encourage in us the faith that perseverance can overcome every obstacle.

The difficulty is not in God's love or power, but in ourselves and our own incapacity to receive the blessing. And yet, because there is this difficulty with us, this lack of spiritual preparedness, there is a difficulty with God too. His wisdom, His righteousness, yea His love, dare not give us what would do us harm, if we received it too soon or too easily. The sin, or the consequence of sin, that makes it impossible for God to give at once, is a barrier on God's side as well as ours; to break through this power of sin in ourselves, or those for whom we pray, is what makes the striving and the conflict of prayer such a reality. And so in all ages men have prayed, and that rightly too, under a sense that there were difficulties in the heavenly world to overcome. As they pleaded with God for the removal of the unknown obstacles, and in that persevering supplication were brought into a state of utter brokenness and helplessness, of entire resignation to Him, of union with His will, and of faith that could take hold of Him, the hindrances in themselves and in Heaven were together overcome. As God conquered them, they conquered God. As God prevails over us, we prevail with God.

God has so constituted us that the clearer our insight is into the reasonableness of a demand, the more hearty will be our surrender to it. One great cause of our remissness in prayer is that there appears to be something arbitrary, or at least some thing incomprehensible, in the call to such continued prayer. If we could be brought to see that this apparent difficulty is a Divine necessity, and in the very nature of things the source of unspeakable blessing, we should be more ready with gladness of heart to give ourselves to continue in prayer. Let us see if we cannot understand how the difficulty that the call to importunity throws in our way is one of our greatest privileges.

I do not know whether you have ever noticed what a part difficulties play in our natural life. They call out our powers as nothing else can. They strengthen and ennoble character. We are told that one reason of the superiority of the Northern nations, like Holland and Scotland, in strength of will and purpose, over those of the sunny South, as Italy and Spain, is that the climate of the latter has been too beautiful, and the life it encourages too easy and relaxing the difficulties the former had to contend with have been their greatest boon; how all nature has been so arranged by God that in sowing and reaping, as in seeking coal or gold, nothing is found without labor and effort. …

It is even so in our intercourse with God. Just imagine what the result would be if the child of God had only to kneel down and ask, and get, and go away. What unspeakable loss to the spiritual life would ensue. It is in the difficulty and delay that calls for persevering prayer, that the true blessing and blessedness of the heavenly life will be found. We there learn how little we delight in fellowship with God, and how little we have of living faith in Him. We discover how earthly and unspiritual our heart still is, how little we have of God's Holy Spirit. We there are brought to know our own weakness and unworthiness, and to yield to God's Spirit to pray in us, to take our place in Christ Jesus, and abide in Him as our only plea with the Father. There our own will and strength and goodness are crucified. There we rise in Christ to newness of life, with our whole will dependent on God and set upon His glory.

Do let us begin to praise God for the need and the difficulty of importunate prayer, as one of His choicest means of grace.

Just think what our Lord Jesus owed to the difficulties in His path. In Gethsemane it was as if the Father would not hear: He prayed yet more earnestly, until "*He was heard.*" In the way He opened up for us: "*He learned obedience by the things He suffered, and so was made perfect*" (Hebrews 5: 8–9). His will was given up to God; His faith in God was proved and strengthened; the prince of this world, with all his temptation, was overcome. This is the new and living way He consecrated for us; it is in persevering prayer we walk with and are made partakers of His very Spirit.

Prayer is one form of crucifixion, of our fellowship with Christ's cross, of our giving up our flesh to the death. O Christians! Shall we not be ashamed of our reluctance to sacrifice the flesh and our own will and the world, as it is seen in our reluctance to pray much? Shall we not learn the lesson which nature and Christ alike teach? The difficulty of importunate prayer is our highest privilege; the difficulties to be overcome in it bring is our richest blessings.

In importunity there are various elements; of these, the chief are perseverance, determination, intensity. It begins with the refusal to at once accept a denial. It grows to the determination to persevere, to spare no time or trouble, till an answer comes. It rises to the intensity in which the whole being is given to God in supplication, and the boldness comes to lay hold of God's strength. At one time it is quiet and restful; at another passionate and bold. Now it takes time and is patient; then again it claims at once what it desires. In whatever different shape, it always means and knows God hears prayer: I must be heard.

Remember the wonderful instances we have of it in the Old Testament saints. Think of Abraham, as he pleads for Sodom. Time after time he renews his prayer until the sixth time he has to say, *"Let not my Lord be angry."* He does not cease until he has learned to know God's condescension in each time consenting to his petition—until he has learned how far he can go, has entered into God's mind, and now rests in God's will. And for his sake Lot was saved. …

Think of Jacob, when he feared to meet Esau. The angel of the Lord met him in the dark, and wrestled with him. And when the angel saw that he prevailed not, he said, *"Let me go."* And Jacob said, *"I will not let you go."* And the angel blessed him there. And that boldness that said, "I will not," and forced from the reluctant angel the blessing, was so pleasing in God's sight, that a new name was there given to him: *"Israel, he who strives with God, for you have striven with God and with men, and have prevailed."*

And through all the ages God's children have understood, what Christ's parables teach—that God holds Himself back, and seeks to get away from us, until what is of flesh and Self and sloth in us is overcome, and we so prevail with Him that He can and must bless us. Oh! Why is it that so many of God's children have no desire for this honor being princes of God, strivers with God, and prevailing?

What our Lord taught us, *"Whatsoever you desire, believe that you have received,"* is nothing but His putting of Jacob's words, *"I will not let You go except you bless me."* This is the importunity He teaches, and we must learn: to claim and take the blessing.

Think of Moses when Israel had made the golden calf. Moses returned to the Lord and said, *"Oh, this people have sinned a great sin. Yet now, if You will forgive their sin; and if not, blot me, I pray You, out of Your book which You have written."* That was importunity that would rather die than not have his people given him. … As an intercessor Moses used importunity with God, and prevailed. He proves that those who truly live near to God, and with whom God speaks face to face, become partakers of that same power of intercession which there is in Him who is at God's right hand and ever lives to pray.

Think of Elijah in his prayer, first for fire, and then for rain. In the former you have the importunity that claims and receives an immediate answer. In the latter, bowing himself down to the earth, his face between his knees, his answer to the servant who had gone to look toward the sea, and come with the message, *"There is nothing,"* was *"Go again seven times."* Here was the importunity of perseverance. He had told Ahab there would be rain; he knew it was coming; and yet he prayed till the seven times were fulfilled. And it is of this Elijah and this prayer we are taught, *"Pray for one another. Elijah was a man of like passions with ourselves. The effectual fervent prayer of a righteous man avails much."*

Will there not be some who feel constrained to cry out, "Where is the Lord God of Elijah—this God who draws forth such effectual prayer, and hears it so wonderfully?" His name be praised; He is still the same. Let His people but believe that He still waits to be inquired of! Faith in a prayer-hearing God will make a prayer-loving Christian.

Let each servant of Christ learn to know his calling. His King ever lives to pray. The Spirit of the King ever lives in us to pray. It is from Heaven the blessings, which the world needs, must be called down in persevering, importunate, believing prayer. It is from

Heaven, in answer to prayer, the Holy Spirit will take complete possession of us to do His work through us. Let us acknowledge how vain our much work has been owing to our little prayer. Let us change our method, and let henceforth more prayer, much prayer, unceasing prayer, be the proof that we look for all to God, and that we believe that He hears us.

The Coming Revival

October 11th

"Come, and let us return to the Lord, for He has sworn, and He will heal us. He will revive us"

—HOSEA 6: 1–2

The coming revival: one frequently hears the word. There are teachers not a few who see the tokens of its approach, and confidently herald its speedy appearance. … There are others who, while admitting the truth of some of these facts, yet fear that the conclusions drawn from them are one-sided and premature. … They remind us of the power of worldliness and formality, of the increase of the money-making and pleasure-loving spirit among professing Christians, to the lack of spirituality in so many, many of our churches, and the continuing and apparently increasing estrangement of multitudes from God's Word, as proof that the great revival has certainly not begun, and is hardly thought of by the most. They say that they do not see the deep humiliation, the intense desire, the fervent prayer which appear as the forerunners of every true revival.

There are right-hand and left-hand errors which are equally dangerous. We must seek as much to be kept from the superficial optimism, which never is able to gauge the extent of the evil, as from the hopeless pessimism which can neither praise God for what He has done, nor trust Him for what He is ready to do. The former will lose itself in a happy Self-gratulation, as it rejoices in its zeal and diligence and apparent success, and never see the need of confession and great striving in prayer, ere we are prepared to meet and conquer the hosts of darkness. The latter virtually gives over the world to Satan, and almost prays and rejoices to see things get worse, to hasten the coming of Him who is to put all right. May God keep us from either error….

Let us listen to the lessons suggested by the passages we have, quoted; they may help us to pray the prayer aright: "*Revive Your work, Lord!*" "*Revive Your work, Lord.*" Read again the passages of Scripture, and see how they all contain the one thought: Revival is God's work; He alone can give it; it must come from above. We are frequently in danger of looking to what God has done and is doing, and to count on that as the pledge that He will at once do more.

And all the time it may be true that He is blessing us up to the measure of our faith or Self-sacrifice, and cannot give larger measure, until there has been a new discovery and confession of what is hindering Him. Or we may be looking to all the signs of life and good around us, and congratulating ourselves on all the organizations and agencies that are being created, while the need of God's mighty and direct interposition is not rightly felt, and the entire dependence upon Him not cultivated. Regeneration, the giving of Divine life, we all acknowledge to be God's act, a miracle of His power. The restoring or reviving of the Divine life, in a soul or a Church, is as much a supernatural work.

To have the spiritual discernment that can understand the signs of the heavens, and prognosticate the coming revival, we need to enter deep into God's mind and will as to its conditions, and the preparedness of those who pray for it or are to be used to bring it about. ... It is God who gives the revival; it is God who reveals His secret; it is the spirit of absolute dependence upon God, giving Him the honor and the glory, that will prepare for it.

A second lesson suggested is, that the revival God is to give will be given in answer to prayer. It must be asked and received direct from God Himself. Those who know anything of the history of revivals will remember how often this has been proved both larger and more local revivals have been distinctly traced to special prayer. In our own day there are numbers of congregations and missions where special or permanent revivals are all—glory be to God— connected with systematic, believing prayer. The coming revival will be no exception. An extraordinary spirit of prayer, urging believers to much secret and united prayer, pressing them to labor fervently in their supplications, will be one of the surest signs of approaching showers and floods of blessing.

Let all who are burdened with the lack of spirituality, with the low state of the life of God in believers, listen to the call that comes to all. If there is to be revival, a mighty, Divine revival, it will need, on our part, corresponding whole-heartedness in prayer and faith. ... And let us have the truth graven deep in our hearts: every revival comes, as Pentecost came, as the fruit of united, continued prayer. The coming revival must begin with a great prayer revival. It is in the closet, with the door shut, that the sound of abundance of rain will be first heard. An increase of secret prayer with ministers and members, will be the sure harbinger of blessing.

It is to the humble and contrite that the revival is promised. We want the revival to come upon the proud and the Self-satisfied, to break them down and save them. God will give this, but only on the condition that those who see and feel the sin of others take their burden of confession and bear it, and that all who pray for and claim in faith God's reviving power for His Church, shall humble themselves with the confession of its sins. The need of revival always points to previous decline; and decline was always caused by sin. Humiliation and contrition have, therefore, ever been the conditions of revival.

In all intercession, confession of sin and God's righteous judgment is ever an essential element. Throughout the history of Israel, we continually see this. It comes out in the reformations under the pious Kings of Judah. We hear it in the prayer of men like Ezra and Nehemiah and Daniel. In Isaiah and Jeremiah and Ezekiel, as well as in the minor prophets, it is the keynote of all the warning as of all the promise. If there be no humiliation and forsaking of sin, then there can be no revival or deliverance: "*To this man will I look, even to him that is poor and of a contrite spirit, and that trembles at My word.*" ...

We find the same in the New Testament. The Sermon on the Mount promises the

Kingdom to the poor and them that mourn. In the epistles to the Corinthians and Galatians, the religion of man—of worldly wisdom and confidence in the flesh—is exposed and denounced. Without its being confessed and forsaken, all the promises of grace and the Spirit will be vain. In the epistles to the seven churches we find five of which He, out of whose mouth goes the sharp, two-edged sword, says, that He has something against them. In each of these the keyword of His message is not to the unconverted, but to the Church: Repent! …

And if there is to be a revival, not among the unsaved, but in our churches, to give a holy, spiritual membership, will not that trumpet sound need to be heard: Repent? … Is there not in the Church of our days an idolatry of money and talent and culture, a worldly spirit, making it unfaithful to its one only Husband and Lord, a confidence in the flesh which grieves and resists God's Holy Spirit? Is there not almost everywhere a confession of the lack of spirituality and spiritual power? Let all who long for the coming revival, and seek to hasten it by their prayers, pray this above everything, that the Lord may prepare His prophets to go before Him at His bidding: "*Cry aloud and spare not, lift up your voice like a trumpet, and show My people their transgression.*"

Every deep revival among God's people must have its roots in a deep sense and confession of sin. Until those who would lead the Church in the path of revival bear faithful testimony against the sins of the Church, it is to feared that it will find people unprepared. Men would fain have a revival as the outgrowth of their agencies and progress. God's way is the opposite: it is out of death, acknowledged as the desert of sin, confessed as utter helplessness, that He revives. He revives the heart of the contrite one.

There is a last thought, suggested by the text from Hosea. It is as we return to the Lord that revival will come; for if we had not wandered from Him, His life would be among us in power. "*Come and let us return to the Lord: for He has sworn, He will heal us … He will revive us….*" As we have said, there can be no return to the Lord, where there is no sense or confession of wandering. "*Let us return to the Lord*" must be the keynote of the revival. Let us return, acknowledging and forsaking whatever there has been in the Church that is not entirely according to His mind and spirit. Let us return, yielding up and casting out whatever there has been in our religion or along with it of the power of God's two great enemies: confidence in the flesh, or the spirit of the world. …Let us return to the Lord with our whole heart, that He may make and keep us wholly His. …

23

THE TWO COVENANTS AND THE SECOND BLESSING

London: James Nisbet & Co., 1899

The First Covenant

October 12th

"Now therefore, if you will obey My voice, and keep My covenant, you shall be a peculiar treasure unto Me."
—EXODUS 19: 5

To understand the Old Covenant aright we must ever remember its two great characteristics—the one, that it was of Divine appointment, fraught with much true blessing, and absolutely indispensable for the working out of God's purposes; the other, that it was only provisional and preparatory to something higher, and therefore absolutely insufficient for giving that full salvation which man needs if his heart or the heart of God is to be satisfied.

Note now the terms of this first Covenant: *"If you will obey My voice and keep My covenant, you shall be unto Me a holy nation."* Or, as it is expressed in Jeremiah (7: 23, 11: 4), *"Obey My voice, and I will be your God."* Obedience everywhere, especially in the Book of Deuteronomy, appears as the condition of blessing. *"A blessing if you obey"* (11: 27).

... In taking Israel into His training, God dealt with them as a people in whom, with all the ruin sin had brought, there still was a conscience to judge of good and evil, a heart capable of being stirred to long after God, and a will to choose the good and to choose Himself. Before Christ and His salvation could be revealed and understood and truly appreciated, these faculties of man had to be stirred and wakened. ... Under the law, administered by the grace that ever accompanied it, there was trained up a number whose great mark was the fear of God, and a desire to walk blameless in all His commandments.

And yet, as a whole, Scripture represents the Old Covenant as a failure. The law had promised life; but it could not give it (Deuteronomy 4: 1; Galatians 3: 21). The real purpose for which God had given it was the very opposite: it was meant by Him as "a ministration of death." He gave it that it might convince us of our sin, and might so waken the confession of our impotence, and of our need of a New Covenant and a true redemption. It is in this view that Scripture uses such strong expressions, [such as]: "The law entered, that the offence might abound"; "That sin by the commandment might appear exceeding sinful" … The great work of the law was to [help us] discover what sin was: its hatefulness as accursed of God; its misery, working temporal and eternal ruin; its power, binding man down in hopeless slavery; and the need of a Divine interposition as the only hope of deliverance.…

The two great lessons God would teach us by it are very simple. The one is the lesson of SIN, the other the lesson of HOLINESS. The Old Covenant attains its object only as it brings us to a sense of our utter sinfulness and our hopeless impotence to deliver ourselves. As long as we have not learned this, no offer of the New Covenant life can lay hold of us. As long as an intense longing for deliverance from sinning has not been wrought, we will naturally fall back into the power of the law and the flesh. …

The other is the lesson of Holiness. In the New Covenant the Triune God engages to do all. He undertakes to give and keep the new heart, to give His own Spirit in it, to give the will and the power to obey and do His will. As the one demand of the first Covenant was the sense of sin, the one great demand of the New is faith that that need, created by the discipline of God's law, will be met in a Divine and supernatural way. The law cannot work out its purpose, except as it brings a man to lie guilty and helpless before the holiness of God. There the New finds him, and reveals that same God, in His grace accepting him and making him partaker of His holiness. …

The practical lesson taught us by the fact that there was a first Covenant that its one special work was to convince of sin, and that without it the New Covenant could not come, is just what many Christians need. At conversion they were convinced of sin by the Holy Spirit. But this had chiefly reference to the guilt of sin and, in some degree, to its hatefulness. But a real knowledge of the power of sin, of their entire and utter impotence to cast it out, or to work in themselves what is good, is what they did not learn at once. And until they have learned this, they cannot possibly enter fully into the blessing of the New Covenant.

The New Covenant

October 13th

"This is the covenant that I will make with the house of Israel. … I will put My law in their inward parts, and write it in their hearts."

—JEREMIAH 31: 33. …

In words which the New Testament (Hebrews 8) takes as the Divinely inspired revelation of what the New Covenant is—of which Christ is the Mediator—God's plan is revealed and we are shown what it is that He will do in us, to make us fit and worthy of being the people of which He is the God. Through the whole of the Old Covenant there was always one trouble: man's heart was not right with God. In the New Covenant the evil is to be remedied. Its central promise is a heart delighting in God's law and capable of knowing and holding fellowship with Him. …

Nothing can be put into the heart, and especially by God, without entering and taking possession of it, without securing its affection and controlling its whole being. And this is what God undertakes to do in the power of His Divine life and operation, to breathe the very spirit of His law into and through the whole inward being. *"I will put it into their inward parts, and write it in their hearts."* … And so the heart in which God gets His way, and writes His law in power, lives only and wholly to carry that writing, and is unchangeably identified with it. So alone can God realize His purpose in creation, and have His child of one mind and one spirit with Himself, delighting in doing His will.

When the Old Covenant with the law graven on stone had done its work in the discovering and condemning of sin, the New Covenant would give in its stead the life of obedience and true holiness of heart. The whole of the Covenant blessing centers in this—the heart being put right and fitted to know God: *"I will give them a heart to know Me, that I am the Lord; and they shall be My people, and I will be their God; for they shall return unto Me with their whole heart"* (Jeremiah 24: 7).

"And I will be their God, and they shall be My people" (Jeremiah 31: 34). Do not pass these next words lightly. They occur chiefly in Jeremiah and Ezekiel in connection with the promise of the everlasting Covenant. They express the very highest experience of the Covenant relationship. It is only when His people learn to love and obey His law, when their heart and life are together wholly devoted to Him and His will, that He can be to them the altogether inconceivable blessing which these words express, "*I will be your God*":

"All I am and have as God shall be yours. All you can need or wish for in a God, I will be to you. In the fullest meaning of the word, I, the Omnipresent, will be ever present with you, in all My grace and love. I, the Almighty One, will each moment work all in you by My mighty power. I, the Thrice-Holy One, will reveal My sanctifying life within you. I will be your God. And you shall be My people, saved and blessed, ruled and guided and provided for by Me, known and seen to be indeed the people of the Holy One, the God of glory."

Only let us give our hearts time to meditate and wait for the Holy Spirit to work in us all that these words mean. … Perfect harmony with God's will, holiness in heart and life, is the only thing that can satisfy God's heart or ours. And it is this the New Covenant gives in Divine power: *"I will give them a heart to know Me; and I will be their God, and they shall be My people; for they shall turn to Me with their whole heart."* It is on the state of the heart, it is on the new heart as given by God, that the New Covenant life hinges.

But why, if all this is meant to be literally and exactly true of God's people, why do we see so little of this life, experience so little in ourselves? There is but one answer: Because of your unbelief! … He can only fulfill His purpose as the heart is willing and accepts His offer. In the New Covenant all is of faith. Let us turn away from what human wisdom and human experience may say, and ask God Himself to teach us what His Covenant means.

If we persevere in this prayer in a humble and teachable spirit, we can count most certainly on its promise: *"They shall no more every man teach his neighbor: Know the Lord, for they shall all know Me."* The teaching of God Himself, by the Holy Spirit, to make us understand what He says to us in His Word, is our Covenant right. Let us count upon it. It is only by a God-given faith that we can appropriate these God-given promises. And it is only by a God-given teaching and inward illumination that we can see their meaning, so as to believe them. When God teaches us the meaning of His promises in a heart yielded to His Holy Spirit, then alone we can believe and receive them in a power which makes them a reality in our life.

But is it really possible, amid the wear and tear of daily life, to walk in the experience of these blessings? Are they really meant for all God's children? Let us rather ask the question, Is it possible for God to do what He has promised? The one part of the promise we believe—the complete and perfect pardon of sin. Why should we not believe the other part—the law written in the heart, and the direct Divine fellowship and teaching? We have been so accustomed to separate what God has joined together, the objective, outward work of His Son, and the subjective, inward work of His Spirit, that we consider the glory of the New Covenant above the Old to consist chiefly in the redeeming work of Christ for us, and not equally in the sanctifying work of the Spirit in us. It is owing to this ignorance and unbelief of the indwelling of the Holy Spirit, as the power through whom God fulfills the New Covenant promises, that we do not really expect them to be made true to us.

Do let us turn our hearts away from all past experience of failure, as caused by nothing but unbelief; do let us admit fully and heartily, what failure has taught us, the absolute impossibility of even a regenerate man walking in God's law in his own strength, and then turn our hearts quietly and trustfully to our own Covenant God. Let us hear what He says He will do for us, and believe Him; let us rest on His unchangeable faithfulness and the surety of the Covenant, on His Almighty power and the Holy Spirit working in us; and let us give up ourselves to Him as our God. He will prove that what He has done for us in Christ is not one whit more wonderful than what He will do in us every day by the Spirit of Christ.

Jesus, the Mediator of the Better Covenant

October 14th

"He is the mediator of the better covenant, established upon better promises"

—HEBREWS 8: 6

We have already seen, in studying the New Covenant, how all these blessings culminate in the one thing—that the heart of man is to be put right, as the only possible way of his living in the favor of God, and God's love finding its satisfaction in him. That he is to receive a heart to fear God, to love God with all his strength, to obey God, and to keep all His statutes. All that Christ did and does has this for its aim; all the higher blessings of peace and fellowship flow from this. In this God's saving power and love find the highest proof of their triumph over sin. Nothing so reveals the grace of God, the power of Jesus Christ, the reality of salvation, the blessedness of the New Covenant, as the heart of a believer, where sin once abounded, with grace now abounding more exceedingly within it.

I do not know how I can better set forth the glory of our Blessed Lord Jesus as He accomplishes this, the real object of His redeeming work, and as He takes entire possession of the heart He has bought and won and cleansed as a dwelling for His Father, than by pointing out the place He takes, and the work He does, in the case of a soul who is being led out of the Old Covenant bondage with its failure, into the real experience of the promise and power of the New Covenant. …

The first step towards it, in one who has been truly converted and assured of his acceptance with God, is the sense of sin. He sees that the New Covenant promises are not made true in his experience. There is not only indwelling sin, but he finds that he gives way to temper, and Self-will, and worldliness, and other known transgressions of God's law. The obedience to which God calls and will fit him, the life of abiding in Christ's love which is his privilege, the power for a holy walk, well-pleasing to God—in all this his conscience condemns him.

It is in this conviction of sin that any thought or desire of the full New Covenant blessing must have its rise. Where the thought that obedience is an impossibility, and that nothing but a life of failure and Self-condemnation is to be looked for, has wrought a secret despair of deliverance, or contentment with our present state, it is vain to speak of God's promise or power. … The New Covenant is meant to be the deliverance from the power of sin; a keen longing for this is the indispensable preparation for entering fully into the Covenant.

Now comes the second step. As the mind is directed to the literal meaning of the terms of the New Covenant, in its promises of cleansing from sin, and a heart filled with God's fear and God's law, and a power to keep God's commands and never to depart from Him; as the eye is fixed on Jesus the Surety of the Covenant, who will Himself make it all true; and as the voice is heard of witnesses who can declare how, after years of bondage, all this has been fulfilled in them—the longing begins to grow into a hope, and the inquiry is made, as to what is needed to enter this blessed life.

Then follows another step. The heart-searching question comes whether we are willing to give up every evil habit, all our own Self-will, all that is of the spirit of the world, and surrender ourselves to be wholly and exclusively for Jesus. God cannot take so complete possession of a man, and bless him so wonderfully, and work in him so mightily, unless He has him very completely, yea, wholly for Himself.

Now comes the last, the simplest, and yet often the most difficult step. … I am willing, but have I the power to make, and what is more, to maintain this full surrender? Have

I the power, the strong faith, so to grasp and hold this offered blessing that it shall indeed be and continue mine? How such questions perplex the soul until it finds the answer to them in the one word: *Jesus!* It is He who will bestow the power to make the surrender and to believe. This is as surely and as exclusively His work, as atonement and intercession are His alone. As sure as it was His to win and ascend the throne, it is His to prove His dominion in the individual soul. It is He, the Living One, who is in Divine power to work and maintain the life of communion and victory within us. He is the Mediator and Surety of the Covenant—He, the God-man, who has undertaken not only for all that God requires, but for all that we need too.

When this is seen, the believer learns that here, just as at conversion, it is all faith. The one thing needed now is, with the eye definitely fixed on some promise of the New Covenant, to turn from Self and anything it could or need do, to let go Self, and fall into the arms of Jesus. …

The Two Covenants in Christian Experience

October 15th

"Are you so foolish? Having begun in the Spirit, are you made perfect in the flesh?"
—GALATIANS 3: 3

The house of Abraham was the Church of God of that age. The division in his house, one son, his own son, but born after the flesh, the other after the promise, was a divinely-ordained manifestation of the division there would be in all ages between the children of the bondwoman, those who served God in the spirit of bondage, and those who were children of the free, and served Him in the Spirit of His Son. The passage teaches us what the whole epistle confirms: that the Galatians had become entangled with a yoke of bondage, and were not standing fast in the freedom with which Christ makes free indeed. Instead of living in the New Covenant, in the Jerusalem which is from above, in the liberty which the Holy Spirit gives, their whole walk proved that, though Christians, they were of the Old Covenant, which brings forth children unto bondage. The passage teaches us the great truth, which it is of the utmost consequence for us to apprehend thoroughly, that a man, with a measure of the knowledge and experience of the grace of God, may prove, by a legal spirit, that he is yet practically, to a large extent, under the Old Covenant. And it will show us, with wonderful clearness; what the proofs are of the absence of the true New Covenant life.

A careful study of the Epistle shows us that the difference between the two Covenants is seen in three things. The law and its works is contrasted with the hearing of faith, the flesh and its religion with the flesh crucified, the impotence to good with a walk in the liberty and the power of the Spirit. May the Holy Spirit reveal to us this twofold life. …

Almost every believer makes the same mistake as the Galatian Christians. Paul asks: *"Are you so foolish? Having begun in the Spirit, are you made perfect in the flesh?"* Flesh means our sinful human nature. At conversion, Christians have generally no conception of the terrible evil of our nature, and the subtlety with which it offers itself to take part in the service of God. It may be most willing and diligent in God's service for a time; it may devise numberless observances for making His worship pleasing and attractive; and yet this may be all only what Paul calls *"making a fair show in the flesh," "glorying in the flesh,"* in human will and human efforts. This power of the religious flesh is one of the great marks of the Old Covenant religion; it misses the deep humility and spirituality of the true worship of God—a heart and life entirely dependent upon Him.

"They that are Christ's have crucified the flesh, with its desires and affections." Scripture speaks of the will of the flesh, the mind of the flesh, the lust of the flesh; all this the true believer has seen to be condemned and crucified in Christ: he has given it over to the death. He not only accepts the cross, with its bearing of the curse, and its redemption from it, as his entrance into life; he glories in it as his only power day by day to overcome the flesh and the world. *"I am crucified with Christ." "God forbid that I should glory save in the cross of my Lord Jesus Christ, by which I am crucified to the world."* Even as nothing less than the death of Christ was needed to inaugurate the New Covenant, and the resurrection life that animates it, there is no entrance into the true New Covenant life other than by a partaking of that death.

"Fallen from grace." This is a third word that describes the condition of these Galatians in that bondage in which they were really impotent to all true good. Paul is not speaking of a final falling away here, for he still addresses them as Christians, but of their having wandered from that walk in the way of enabling and sanctifying grace, in which a Christian can get the victory over sin. As long as grace is principally connected with pardon and the entrance to the Christian life, the flesh is the only power in which to serve and work. ...

The contrast to this life of impotence and failure is found in the one word, "the Spirit." *"If you be led of the Spirit, you are not under the law,"* with its demand on your own strength. *"Walk in the Spirit, and you shall not"*—a definite, certain promise—*"You shall not fulfill the lusts of the flesh."* The Spirit gives liberty from the law, from the flesh, from sin. *"The fruit of the Spirit is love, peace, joy."* Of the New Covenant promise, *"I will put My Spirit within you, and I will cause you to walk in My statutes, and you shall keep My judgments,"* the Spirit is the center and the sum. He is the power of the supernatural life of true obedience and holiness.

And what would have been the course that the Galatians would have taken if they had accepted this teaching of St. Paul? As they hear his question, "*Now that ye have come to know God, why turn back again into the weak and beggarly rudiments, whereunto you desire to be in bondage again*?" they would have felt that there was but one course. Nothing else could help them but at once to turn back again to the path they had left. At the point where they had left it, they could enter again. With any one of them who wished to do so, this turning away from the Old Covenant legal spirit, and the renewed surrender to the Mediator of the New Covenant, could be the act of a moment—one single step. As the light of the New Covenant promise dawned upon him, and he saw how Christ was to be all, and faith all, and the Holy Spirit in the heart all, and the faithfulness of a Covenant-keeping God all in all, he would feel that he had but one thing to do—in utter impotence to yield himself to God, and in simple faith to count upon Him to perform what He had spoken.

In Christian experience there [either] may be still the Old Covenant life of bondage and failure, [or] … a life that gives way entirely to the New Covenant grace and spirit … when the true vision has been received of what the New Covenant means, a faith that rests fully on the Mediator of the New Covenant can enter at once into the life which the Covenant secures. I cannot too earnestly beg all believers who long to know to the utmost what the grace of God can work in them, to study carefully the question as to whether the acknowledgment that our being in the bondage of the Old Covenant is the reason of our failure, and whether a clear insight into the possibility of an entire change in our relation to God, is not what is needed to give us the help we seek. … There is a secret root of evil which must be removed. That root is the spirit of bondage, the legal spirit of Self-effort, which hinders that humble faith that knows that God will work all, and yields to Him to do it. …

The New Covenant; A Covenant of Grace

October 16th

"Sin shall not have dominion over you: for you are not under the law, but under grace."
—ROMANS 6: 14

The word, covenant of grace, though not found in Scripture, is the correct expression of the truth it abundantly teaches—that the contrast between the two covenants is none other than that of law and grace. Of the New Covenant, grace is the great characteristic: *"The law came in, that the offence might abound; but where sin abounded, grace did abound more exceedingly."* It is to bring the Romans away entirely from under the Old Covenant, and to teach them their place in the New, that Paul writes: *"You are not under the law, but under grace."* …

The word *grace* is used in two senses. It is first the gracious disposition in God which moves Him to love us freely without our merit, and to bestow all His blessings upon us. Then it also means that power through which this grace does its work in us. The redeeming work of Christ, and the righteousness He won for us; equally with the work of the Spirit in us, as the power of the new life, are spoken of as grace. It includes all that Christ has done and still does, all He has and gives, all He is for us and in us. … What the law demands, grace supplies.

The contrast which John pointed out is expounded by Paul: "*The law came in, that the offence might abound*," and the way be prepared for the abounding of grace more exceedingly. The law points the way, but gives no strength to walk in it. The law demands, but makes no provision for its demands being met. The law burdens and condemns and slays. It can waken desire, but not satisfy it. It can rouse to effort, but not secure success. It can appeal to motives, but gives no inward power beyond what man himself has. And so, while warring against sin, it became its very ally in giving the sinner over to a hopeless condemnation. *"The strength of sin is the law."*

To deliver us from the bondage and the dominion of sin, grace came by Jesus Christ. Its work is twofold. Its exceeding abundance is seen in the free and full pardon there is of all transgression, in the bestowal of a perfect righteousness, and in the acceptance into God's favor and friendship. …

The exceeding abundance of grace is equally seen in the work which the Holy Spirit every moment maintains within us. We have found that the central blessing of the New Covenant, flowing from Christ's redemption and the pardon of our sins, is the new heart in which God's law and fear and love have been put. It is in the fulfillment of this promise, in the maintenance of the heart in a state of meetness for God's indwelling, that the glory of grace is specially seen.

All the sin in earth and hell could not harm me, were it not for its presence in my heart. It is there it has exercised its terrible dominion. And it is there the exceeding abundance of grace must be proved, if it is to benefit me. All grace in earth and Heaven could not help me; it is only in the heart it can be received, and known, and enjoyed. … Grace is not only the power that moves the heart of God in its compassion towards us, when He acquits and accepts the sinner and makes him a child, but is equally the power that moves the heart of the saint, and provides it each moment with just the disposition and the power which it needs to love God and do His will. …

The Two Covenants: Their Relation

October 17th

"Abraham had two sons, one by the bondmaid, and one by the freewoman. Howbeit, the one by the bondmaid is born after the flesh; but the son by the freewoman is born through promise. Which things contain an allegory: for these women are two covenants."

—GALATIANS 4: 22–24

There are two covenants, one called the Old, the other the New. God speaks of this very distinctly in Jeremiah, where He says: *"The days come, that I will make a new covenant with the house of Israel, not after the covenant I made with their fathers"* (Jeremiah 31). This is quoted in Hebrews, with the addition: *"In that He gives a new covenant, He has made the first obsolete."*

… They indicate two stages in God's dealing with man; two ways of serving God, a lower or elementary one of preparation and promise, a higher or more advanced one of fulfillment and possession. … In the Old Covenant, man had the opportunity given us to prove what we could do, with the aid of all the means of grace God could bestow. That Covenant ended in our proving our unfaithfulness and failure. In the New Covenant, God is to prove what He can do with us—all unfaithful and feeble as we are, when He is allowed and trusted to do all the work. The Old Covenant was one dependent on our obedience, one which we could break, and did break (Jeremiah 31: 32). The New Covenant was one which God has engaged shall never be broken; He Himself keeps it and ensures our keeping it: so He makes it an Everlasting Covenant. …

God proposed to make a man in His own image and likeness. The chief glory of God is that He has life in Himself; that He is independent of all else, and owes what He is to Himself alone. If the image and likeness of God was not to be a mere name, and man was really to be like God in the power to make ourselves what we were to be, we must have the power of free will and Self-determination. This was the problem God had to solve in our creation in His image. Man was to be a creature made by God, and yet we were to be, as far as creatures could be, like God, Self-made. In all God's treatment of man these two factors were ever to be taken into account. God was ever to take the initiative, and be to man the source of life. Man was ever to be the recipient, and yet at the same time the disposer of the life God bestowed.

When man had fallen through sin, and God entered into a covenant of salvation, these two sides of the relationship had still to be maintained intact. God was ever to be the first, and man the second. And yet man, as made in God's image, was ever, as second, to have full time and opportunity to appropriate or reject what God gave, to prove how far he could help himself, and indeed be Self-made. His absolute dependence upon God was not to be forced upon him; if it was really to be a thing of moral worth and true blessedness, it must be his deliberate and voluntary choice.

And this now is the reason why there was a first and a second covenant, that in the first, man's desires and efforts might be fully awakened, and time given for us to make full proof of what our human nature, with the aid of outward instruction and miracles and means of grace, could accomplish. When our utter impotence, our hopeless captivity under the power of sin had been discovered, there came the New Covenant, in which God was to reveal how our true liberty from sin and Self and the creature, our true nobility and God-likeness, was to be found in the most entire and absolute dependence, in God's being and doing all within us. In the very nature of things there was no other way possible to God than this in dealing with a being whom He had endowed with the Godlike power of a will. And all the weight this reason for the Divine procedure has in God's dealing with His people as a whole, it equally has in dealing with the individual.

The two covenants represent two stages of God's education of man and of man's seeking after God. The progress and transition from the one to the other is not merely chronological or historical; it is organic and spiritual. In greater or lesser degree, it is seen in every member of the body, as well as in the body as a whole. … The New Testament proves, in some of its most important epistles—especially those to the Galatians, Romans, and Hebrews—how possible it is within the New Covenant still to be held fast in the bondage of the Old.

This is the teaching of the passage from which our text is taken. In the home of Abraham, the father of the faithful, Ishmael and Isaac are both found—the one born of a slave, the other of a free woman; the one after the flesh and the will of man, the other through the promise and the power of God; the one only for a time, then to be cast out, the other to be heir of all. A picture held up to the Galatians of the life they were leading, as they trusted to the flesh and its religion, making a fair show, and yet proved, by their being led captive to sin, to be, not of the free but of the bond woman. Only through faith in the promise and the mighty quickening power of God could they, could any of them, be made truly and fully free, and stand in the freedom with which Christ has made us free.

As we proceed to study the two covenants in the light of this and other scriptures, we shall see how they are indeed the Divine revelation of two systems of religious worship, each with its spirit or life-principle ruling every man who professes to be a Christian. We shall see how the one great cause of the feebleness of so many Christians is just this, that the Old Covenant spirit of bondage still has the mastery. And we shall see that nothing but a spiritual insight, with a whole-hearted acceptance, and a living experience, of all the New Covenant engages that God will work in us, can possibly fit for walking as God would have us do.

This truth of there being two stages in our service of God, two degrees of nearness in our worship, is typified in many things in the Old Covenant worship; perhaps nowhere more clearly than in the difference between the Holy Place and the Most Holy Place in the temple, with the veil separating them. Into the former the priests might always enter to draw near to God. And yet they might not come too near; the veil kept them at a distance. To enter within that, was death. Once a year the High Priest might enter, as a promise of the time when the veil should be taken away and the full access to dwell in God's presence be given to His people. In Christ's death the veil of the temple was rent, and His blood gives us boldness and power to enter into the Holiest of all and live there day by day in the immediate presence of God. It is by the Holy Spirit, who issued forth from that Holiest of all, where Christ had entered, to bring its life to us, and make us one with it, that we can have the power to live and walk always with *the consciousness of God's presence in us.*

The Everlasting Covenant of the Spirit

October 18th

A new heart also will I give you, and a new spirit will I put within you: and I will take the stony heart out of your flesh…And I will put my Spirit within you, and cause you to walk in My statutes."

—EZEKIEL 36: 26–27

If a New Covenant were to be made, and if that was to be better than the Old, obedience was the one thing to be provided for. No New Covenant could be of any profit unless provision were made for securing obedience. Obedience there must be. God as Creator could never take His creatures into His favor and fellowship, except they obeyed Him. The thing would have been an impossibility. If the New Covenant is to be better than the Old, if it is to be an everlasting Covenant, never to be broken, it must make some sufficient provision for securing the obedience of the Covenant people. And this is indeed the glory of the New Covenant … that this provision has been made. …

By an undertaking in which God's infinite condescension and power and faithfulness are to be most wonderfully exhibited, by a supernatural mystery of Divine wisdom and grace, the New Covenant provides a guarantee, not only for God's faithfulness, but for ours too! And this in no other way than by God Himself undertaking to secure our part as well as His own. Do try and get hold of this. … Christians, from the Galatians downwards, have not been able to see and believe what the New Covenant really brings. They have thought that human unfaithfulness was a factor permanently to be reckoned with as something utterly unconquerable and incurable, and that the possibility of a life of obedience, with the witness from within of a good conscience, and from above of God's pleasure, was not to be expected. …

Listen to what God says in Jeremiah of the two parts of His everlasting Covenant…. The central thought of that—that the heart is to be put right—is here reiterated and confirmed: *"I will make an everlasting covenant with them, that I will not turn away from them, to do them good."* That is, God will be unchangeably faithful. He will not turn from us. *"But I will put My fear into their heart, that they shall not depart from Me."* This is the second half: Israel will be unchangeably faithful too. … As faithfully as He undertakes for the fulfillment of His part, will He undertake for the fulfillment of their part, that they shall not depart from Him!

Listen to God's word in Ezekiel, in regard to one of the terms of His Covenant of peace, His everlasting Covenant: *"I will put My Spirit within you, and cause you to walk in My statutes, and you shall keep My judgments, and do them"* (Ezekiel 36: 25, 27; 37: 26). In the Old Covenant we have nothing of this sort. You have, on the contrary, from the story of the golden calf and the breaking of the Tables of the Covenant onward, the sad fact of continual departure from God. We find God longing for what He would so fain have seen, but was not to be found. *"Oh, that there was such a heart in them, that they would fear Me, and keep all My commandments always"* (Deuteronomy 5: 29). …

It is only at the close of his threatenings (Deuteronomy 30: 6) that he gives the promise of the new time that would come: *"The Lord your God will circumcise your heart, to love the Lord your God with all your heart, and with all your soul, and you shall obey the voice of the Lord your God."* The whole Old Covenant was dependent on our faithfulness: *"The Lord your God keeps covenant with them that keep His commandments."* God's keeping the Covenant availed little, if we did not keep it.

Nothing could help us until the *"If you shall diligently keep"* of the law, was replaced by the Word of promise, *"I will put My Spirit in you, and you shall keep My judgments, and do them."* The one supreme difference of the New Covenant; the one thing for which the Mediator, and the Blood, and the Spirit were given; the one fruit God sought and Himself engaged to bring forth was this: a heart filled with His fear and love, a heart to cleave unto Him and not depart from Him, a heart in which His Spirit and His law dwells, a heart that delights to do His will.

Here is the inmost secret of the New Covenant. It deals with the heart of man in a way of Divine power. It … reveals God Himself, cleansing our heart and making it new

… making the promise true, *"I will cause you to walk in My statutes, and you shall keep My judgments."* A heart in perfect harmony with Himself, a life and walk in His way—God has engaged in Covenant to work this in us. He undertakes for our part in the Covenant as much as for His own.

This is nothing but the restoration of the original relation between God and the man He had made in His likeness. We are on earth to be the very image of God, because God was to live and to work all in him, and he to find his glory and blessedness in thus owing all to God. This is the exceeding glory of the New Covenant, of the Pentecostal dispensation, that by the Holy Spirit God could now again be the indwelling life of His people, and so make the promise a reality: *"I will cause you to walk in My statutes."* With God's presence secured to us every moment of the day… and our heart thus responding to His holy presence, … we can, we shall walk in His statutes, and keep His judgments.

The great sin of Israel under the Old Covenant, that by which they greatly grieved Him, was this: *"they limited the Holy One of Israel."* Under the New Covenant there is no less danger of this sin. It makes it impossible for God to fulfill His promises. Let us seek, above everything, for the Holy Spirit's teaching, to show us exactly what God has established the New Covenant for, that we may honor Him by believing all that His love has prepared for us. …

The subtle unbelief, that thinks it impossible to be kept from sinning, cuts away the power of accepting the provision of the everlasting Covenant. God's Word, *"I will put My fear in their heart, that they shall not depart from Me"; "I will put My Spirit within you, and you shall keep My judgment,"* is understood in some feeble sense, according to our experience, and not according to what the Word and what God means. And the soul settles down into a despair, or a Self-contentment, that says it can never be otherwise, and makes true conviction for sin impossible.

The New Covenant: A Ministration of the Spirit

October 19th

"You are an epistle of Christ, ministered by us, written not with ink,
but with the Spirit of the living God; not on tables of stone, but on tables that are hearts of flesh."
—2 CORINTHIANS 3: 3

In this wonderful chapter Paul reminds the Corinthians, in speaking of his ministry among them, of what its chief characteristics were. As a ministry of the New Covenant he contrasts it, and the whole dispensation of which it is part, with that of the Old. … With the Old there was the veil on the heart; in the New, the veil is taken away from the face and the heart, the Spirit of the Lord gives liberty, and, reflecting with unveiled face the glory of the Lord, we are changed from glory to glory, into the same image, as by the Spirit of the Lord. … Instead of a law graven in stone, the law written in the heart, worked into the heart's affection and powers, making it one with them. Instead of the vain attempt to work from without inward, the Spirit and the law are put into the inward parts, thence to work outward in life and walk. …

In working out our salvation God bestowed upon us two wonderful gifts. We read: "*God sent forth His Son, that He might redeem them that were under the law, that we might receive the adoption of sons. And because you are sons, God sent forth the Spirit of His Son into your hearts, crying, Abba, Father.*" Here we have the two parts of God's work in salvation. The one, the more objective, what He did that we might become His children—He sent forth His Son. The second, the more subjective, what He did that we might live like His children—He sent forth the Spirit of His Son into our hearts. In the former we have the external manifestation of the work of redemption; in the other, its inward appropriation; the former for the sake of the latter. These two halves form one great whole, and may not be separated.

In the promises of the New Covenant, as we find them in Jeremiah and Ezekiel, as well as in our text and many other passages of Scripture, it is manifest that God's great object in salvation is to get possession of the heart. The heart is the real life; with the heart a man loves, and wills, and acts; the heart makes the man. God made man's heart for His own dwelling, that in it He might reveal His love and His glory. God sent Christ to accomplish a redemption by which man's heart could be won back to Him; nothing but that could satisfy God. And that is what is accomplished when the Holy Spirit makes the heart of God's child what it should be. The whole work of Christ's redemption—His Atonement and Victory, His Exaltation and Intercession, His glory at the right hand of God—all these are only preparatory to what is the chief triumph of His grace: the renewal of the heart to be the temple of God. Through Christ God gives the Holy Spirit to glorify Him in the heart, by working there all that He has done and is doing for the soul.

In a great deal of our religious teaching, [we have been] giving Christ's work for us on the cross or in Heaven a greater prominence than His work in our heart by the Holy Spirit. The result has been that the indwelling of the Holy Spirit, and His mighty work as the life of the heart, as very little known in true power. If we look carefully at what the New Covenant promises mean, we shall see how the "sending forth of the Spirit of His Son into our hearts" is indeed the consummation and crown of Christ's redeeming work.

… In the Old Covenant man had failed in what he had to do. In the New, God is to do everything in him. The Old could only convict of sin. The New is to put it away and cleanse the heart from its filthiness. In the Old it was the heart that was wrong; for the New a new heart is provided, into which God puts His fear and His law and His love. The Old demanded, but failed to secure obedience; in the New, God causes us to walk in His judgments. The New is to fit man for a true holiness, a true fulfillment of the law of loving God with the whole heart, and our neighbors as ourselves, a walk truly well-pleasing to God. The New changes a man from glory to glory after the image of Christ. All because the Spirit of God's Son is given into the heart. The Old gave no power: in the New all is by the Spirit, the mighty power of God. As complete as the reign and power of Christ on the throne of Heaven, is His dominion on the throne of the heart by His Holy Spirit given to us.

It is as we bring all these traits of the New Covenant life together into one focus, and look at the heart of God's child as the object of this mighty redemption, that we shall begin to understand what is secured to us, and what it is that we are to expect from our Covenant God. We shall see wherein the glory of the ministration of the Spirit consists, even in this, that God can fill our heart with His love, and make it His abode. … We shall see how the glory of the ministration of the Spirit is no other than the glory of the Lord, as it is not only in Heaven, but resting upon us and dwelling in us, and changing us into the same image from glory to glory. The inconceivable glory of our exalted Lord in Heaven has its counterpart here on earth in the exceeding glory of the Holy Spirit who glorifies Him in us, who lays His glory on us, as He changes us into His likeness.

A Covenant God

October 20th

"Know therefore that the Lord your God, He is God, the faithful God, who keeps covenant and mercy with those who love Him and keep His commandments."
—DEUTERONOMY 7: 9 …

In His infinite condescension to our human weakness and need, there is no possible way in which we pledge their faithfulness, that God has not sought to make use of, to give us perfect confidence in Him, and the full assurance of all that He, in His infinite riches and power as God, has promised to do to us. It is with this view He has consented to bind Himself by covenant, as if He could not be trusted. Blessed is the one who truly knows God as their Covenant God; who knows what the Covenant promises; what unwavering confidence of expectation it secures, that all its terms will be fulfilled to them; what a claim and hold it gives them on the Covenant-keeping God Himself.

To many who have never thought much of the Covenant, a true and living faith in it would mean the transformation of the whole life. The full knowledge of what God wants to do for us the assurance that it will be done by an Almighty Power; the being drawn to God Himself in personal surrender, and dependence, and waiting to have it done; all this would make the Covenant the very gate of Heaven. …

Of the many devices of which God's patient and condescending grace made use to stir up and strengthen faith, one of the chief was—the Covenant. … His Covenant was always a revelation of His purposes, holding out, in definite promise, what God was willing to work in those with whom the Covenant was made. It was a Divine pattern of the work God intended to do in their behalf, that they might know what to desire and expect, that their faith might nourish itself with the very things, though as yet unseen, which God was working out.

Then, the Covenant was meant to be a security and guarantee, as simple and plain and humanlike as the Divine glory could make it, that the very things which God had promised would indeed be brought to pass and wrought out in those with whom He had entered into covenant. Amid all delay and disappointment, and apparent failure of the Divine promises, the Covenant was to be the anchor of the soul, pledging the Divine veracity and faithfulness and unchangeableness for the certain performance of what had been promised. And so, the Covenant was, above all, to give us a hold upon God, as the Covenant-keeping God, to link us to God Himself in expectation and hope, to bring us to make God Himself alone the portion and the strength of our soul.

Oh, that we knew how God longs that we should trust Him, and how surely His every promise must be fulfilled to those who do so! Oh, that we knew how it is owing to nothing but our unbelief that we cannot enter into the possession of God's promises.... No wonder that, where that Covenant, with its wonderful promises, is so little thought of, its plea for an abounding and unhesitating confidence in God so little understood, its claim upon the faithfulness of the Omnipotent God so little tested; no wonder that Christian life should miss the joy and the strength, the holiness and the heavenliness which God meant and so clearly promised that it should have.

Let us listen to the words in which God's Word calls us to know, and worship, and trust our Covenant-keeping God. It may be we shall find what we have been looking for: the deeper, the full experience of all God's grace can do in us. In our text, Moses says: *"Know therefore that the Lord your God, He is God, the faithful God, which keeps covenant with them that love Him."* Hear what God says in Isaiah: *"The mountains shall depart, and the hills be removed; but My kindness shall not depart from you, neither shall My covenant of peace be removed, says the Lord that has mercy on you."* More sure than any mountain is the fulfillment of every Covenant promise.

Of the New Covenant, in Jeremiah, God speaks: *"I will make an everlasting covenant with them, that I will not turn away from them, to do them good; but I will put My fear in their hearts, that they shall not depart from Me."* The Covenant secures alike that God will not turn from us, nor we depart from Him. ... Let us ask very earnestly whether the lack in our Christian life, and specially in our faith, is not owing to the neglect of the Covenant. We have not worshipped nor trusted the Covenant-keeping God. Our soul has not done what God called us to: *"to take hold of His Covenant,"* *"to remember the Covenant."* Is it wonder that our faith has failed and come short of the blessing? ...

The great lack of our religion is this: *we need more of God.* We accept salvation as His gift, and we do not know that the only object of salvation, its chief blessing, is to fit us for, and bring us back to, that close intercourse with God for which we were created, and in which our glory in eternity will be found. All that God has ever done for His people in making a covenant was always to bring them to Himself as their chief, their only good, to teach them to trust in Him, to delight in Him, to be one with Him. It cannot be otherwise. If God indeed be nothing but a very fountain of goodness and glory, of beauty and blessedness, the more we can have of His presence, the more we conform to His will, the more we are engaged in His service, the more we have Him ruling and working all in us, the more truly happy shall we be.

If God indeed be thereby Owner and Author of life and strength, of holiness and happiness, and can alone give and work it in us, the more we trust Him, and depend and wait on Him, the stronger and the holier and the happier we shall be. And that only is a true and good religious life, which brings us every day nearer to this God, which makes us give up everything to have more of Him. No obedience can be too strict, no dependence too absolute, no submission too complete …to a soul that is learning to count God Himself as its chief good, its exceeding joy.

In entering into covenant with us, God's one object is to draw us to Himself, to render us entirely dependent upon Himself, and so to bring us into the right position and disposition in which He can fill us with Himself, His love, and His blessedness.

His Holy Covenant

October 21st

"To remember His Holy Covenant; to grant unto us that we, being delivered out of the hands of our enemies, should serve Him without fear, in holiness and righteousness before Him, all our days."

—LUKE 1: 68–75

When Zacharias was filled with the Holy Spirit and prophesied, he spoke of God's visiting and redeeming His people, as a remembering of His Holy Covenant. He speaks of what the blessings of that Covenant would be, not in words that had been used before, but in what is manifestly a Divine revelation to him by the Holy Spirit; and gathers up all the former promises in these words: *"That we should serve Him without fear, in holiness and righteousness before Him all the days of our life."* Holiness in life and service is to be the great gift of the Covenant of God's Holiness. As we have seen before, the Old Covenant proclaimed and demanded holiness; the New provides it; holiness of heart and life is its great blessing.

There is no attribute of God so difficult to define, so peculiarly a matter of Divine revelation, so mysterious, incomprehensible, and inconceivably glorious, as His Holiness. It is that by which He is specially worshipped in His majesty on the throne of Heaven (Isaiah 6: 2; Revelation 4: 8, 15: 4). It unites His righteousness that judges and condemns with His love that saves and blesses. As the Holy One He is a consuming fire (Isaiah 10: 17); as the Holy One He loves to dwell among His people (Isaiah 12: 6). As the Holy One He is at an infinite distance from us; as the Holy One He comes inconceivably near, and makes us one with, makes us like Himself. The one purpose of His holy Covenant is to make us holy as He is holy.

As the Holy One He says: *"I am holy; be you holy; I am the Lord who hallows you, who makes you holy."* The highest conceivable summit of blessedness is our being partakers of the Divine nature, of the Divine holiness. This is the great blessing that Christ, the Mediator of the New Covenant, brings. He has been made unto us *"both righteousness and sanctification"*—righteousness in order to, as a preparation for, sanctification or holiness. He prayed to the Father: *"Sanctify them; for their sakes I sanctify Myself, that they themselves may also be sanctified in truth."* In Him we are sanctified, saints, holy ones (Romans 1: 7; 1 Corinthians 1: 2). We have put on the new man which after God is created in righteousness and holiness. Holiness is our very nature.

We are holy *in Christ.* As we believe it, as we receive it, as we yield ourselves to the truth, and draw nigh to God to have the holiness drawn forth and revealed in fellowship with Him, its fountain, we shall know how Divinely true it is. It is for this the Holy Spirit has been given in our hearts. He is the *"Spirit of Holiness."* His every working is in the power of holiness. Paul says: *"God has chosen us unto salvation, in sanctification of the Spirit and belief of the truth."* As simple and entire as is our dependence on the word of truth, as the external means, must our confidence be in the hidden power for holiness which the working of the Spirit brings. The connection between God's electing purpose, and the work of the Spirit, with the word we obey, comes out with equal clearness in Peter: *"Elect, in sanctification of the Spirit, unto obedience."* ...

The Church believes so little in the mighty power of God, and the truth of His Holy Covenant, that the grace of such heart-holiness is hardly spoken of. ... Remember that the words sanctify, sanctity, saint are the same as make holy, holiness, holy one. Listen: "*The God of peace Himself...sanctify you wholly*"; this you may ask and expect, "*and may your spirit and soul and body be preserved entire, unblameable at the coming of our Lord Jesus Christ.*" ...

The Whole Heart

October 22nd

Let me give the principal passages in which the words "*the whole heart,*" "*all the heart,*" are used. A careful study of them will show how wholehearted love and service is what God has always asked, because He can, in the very nature of things, ask nothing less. The prayerful and believing acceptance of the words will waken the assurance that such wholehearted love and service is exactly the blessing the New Covenant was meant to make possible. That assurance will prepare us for turning to the Omnipotence of God to work in us what may have hitherto appeared beyond our reach.

Hear, first, God's word in Deuteronomy: 4: 29: *"If you seek the Lord your God, you shall find Him, if you seek Him with all your heart and all your soul."* 6: 4, 5: *"Hear, O Israel, the Lord our God is one Lord; and you shall love the Lord your God with all your heart, and with all your soul, and with all your might."* 10: 12: *"What does the Lord your God require of you but to fear the Lord your God, to walk in all His ways, and to love Him, and to serve Him with all your heart and all your soul."* 11: 13: *"Hearken diligently unto My commandments, to love the Lord your God, and to serve Him with all your heart and all your soul."* 13: 3: *"The Lord your God proves you, whether you love the Lord your God with all your heart and all your soul."* 26: 16: *"You shall therefore keep these statutes and do them with all your heart and all your soul."* 30: 2: *"You shall obey His voice with all your heart and with all soul."* 30: 6: *"The Lord your God will circumcise your heart, to love the Lord your God with all your heart and with all your soul."*

Take these oft-repeated words as the expression of God's will concerning His people, and concerning yourself; ask if you could wish to give God anything less. Take the last-cited verse as the Divine promise of the New Covenant—that He will circumcise, will so cleanse the heart to love Him with a wholehearted love, that obedience is within your reach; and say whether you will not vow afresh to keep this His first and great commandment. Listen to Joshua (22: 5): *"Take diligent heed to love the Lord your God, and to walk in all His ways, and to keep His commandments, and to cleave unto Him, and to serve Him, with all your heart and with all your soul."* Listen to Samuel (1 Samuel 12: 20, 24): *"Turn not aside from following the Lord, but serve the Lord with all your heart. Only fear the Lord, and serve Him in truth with all your heart."* Hear David repeating God's promise to Solomon (1 Kings 2: 4): *"If your children take heed to their way, to walk before Me in truth with all their heart and all their soul."*

Hear God's word concerning David (1 Kings 14: 8): *"My servant David, who followed Me with all his heart, to do that only which was right in My eyes."* Hear Solomon in his temple prayer (1 Kings 8: 48): *"If they return to You with all their heart and all their soul, hear You their prayer."* Listen to what is said of Jehu (2 Kings 10: 31): *"The Lord said unto Jehu, You have done well in executing that which is right in My eyes. But Jehu took no heed to walk in the law of the Lord with all his heart."*

Of Josiah we read (2 Kings 23: 3, 25): *"The king and all the men of Judah made a covenant with the Lord, to walk after the Lord, with all their heart and with all their soul, to perform the words of this covenant ... There was no king like him, that turned to the Lord with all his heart, and all his soul, and all his might."* Of Jehoshaphat, men said (2 Chronicles 22: 9): *"He sought the Lord with all his heart."* And of Hezekiah it is written (2 Chronicles 31: 21): *"In every work that he began, to seek his God, he did it with all his heart…."* Oh that all would ask God to give us, by the Holy Spirit, a simple vision of Himself!—claiming, giving, accepting, blessing, delighting in, the love and service of the whole heart….

Turn to the Psalms. Hear David (9: 1, 111; 1, 138: 1): *"I will praise You with my whole heart."* And in Psalm 119, the Psalm of the way of blessedness: *"Blessed who seek Him with the whole heart. With my whole heart have I sought You. I shall keep Your law, yea I shall observe it with my whole heart. I entreated Your favor with my whole heart. I will keep Your precepts with my whole heart. I cried with my whole heart."* Praise and prayer; seeking God and keeping His precepts; all equally with the whole heart.

Shall we not begin asking more earnestly than ever, as often as we see men engaged in their earthly pursuits in search of money, or pleasure, or fame, or power, with their whole heart: Is this the spirit in which Christians consider that God must be served? Is this the spirit in which I serve Him? Is not this the one thing needful in our religion? Lord, reveal unto us Your will!

Now, just a few words more from the Prophets about the new time, the great change that can come into our lives. Jeremiah

24: 7: *"I will give them a new heart to know Me that I am the Lord; and they shall be My people and I will be their God; for they shall return to Me with their whole heart."*

29: 13: *"You shall seek Me, and find Me, when you shall search for Me with all your heart. And I will be found of you, says the Lord."*

32: 39–41: Let my reader not be weary of reading carefully these Divine words: they contain the secret, the seed, the living power of a complete transition out of a life in the bondage of half-hearted service, to the glorious liberty of the children of God. *"I will make an everlasting covenant with them, that I will not turn away from them to do them good; but I will put my fear in their heart, that they shall not depart from Me. Yea, I will rejoice over them to do them good, with My whole heart and My whole Soul!"*

It is to be all God's doing. And He is to do it with His whole heart and His whole soul. It is the vision of this God with His whole heart loving us, longing and delighting to fulfill His promise, and make us wholly His own, that we need. This vision makes it impossible not to love Him with our whole heart. Lord, open our eyes that we may see!

Joel 2:12: *"Therefore also now, says the Lord, turn to Me with all your heart."* …

Now, one word from our Lord Jesus (Matthew 22: 37): "*Jesus said, You shall love the Lord your God with all your heart.*" This is the first and great commandment. This is the sum of that law He came to fulfill for us and in us, came to enable us to fulfil. "*For what the law could not do, in that it was weak through the flesh, God, sending His own Son, condemned sin in the flesh, that the righteousness of the law might be fulfilled in us who walk after the Spirit.*"…

The Ministry of The New Covenant

October 23rd

"You are our epistle, written in our hearts, known and read of all; being made manifest that you are an epistle of Christ, … written not with ink, but with the Spirit of the living God: not in tables of stone, but in tables that are hearts of flesh. And such confidence have we through Christ Godward… who also made us sufficient as ministers of a new covenant; not of the letter, but of the Spirit; for the letter kills, but the Spirit gives life."

—2 CORINTHIANS 3: 2–6

We have seen that the New Covenant is a ministration of the Spirit. The Holy Spirit ministers all its grace and blessing in Divine power and life. He does this through us, who are called ministers of a New Covenant, ministers of the Spirit. The Divine ministration of the Covenant to men, and the earthly ministry of God's servants, are equally to be in the power of the Holy Spirit. The ministry of the New Covenant has its glory and its fruit in this—that it is all to be a demonstration of the Spirit and of power. …

God has made us ministers of the Spirit. The first thought is that a minister of the New Covenant must be one personally possessed of the Holy Spirit. There is a twofold work of the Spirit: one in giving a holy disposition and character, the other in qualifying and empowering us for work. The former must always come first. The promise of Christ to His disciples, that they should receive the Holy Spirit for their service, was very definitely given to those who had followed and loved Him, and kept His commandments. It is by no means enough that we have been born of the Spirit. If we are to be "sufficient ministers" of the New Covenant, we must know what it is to be led by the Spirit, to walk in the Spirit, and to say, "*The law of the Spirit of life in Christ Jesus has made me free from the law of sin and death.*"

Who that wants to learn Greek or Hebrew would accept a professor who hardly knows the elements of these languages? And how can we be ministers of the New Covenant, which is so entirely "a ministration of the Spirit," a ministration of heavenly life and power, unless we know by experience what it is to live in the Spirit? The minister must, before everything, be a personal proof and witness of the truth and power of God in the fulfillment of what the New Covenant promises. Ministers are to be picked—the best specimens and examples of what the Holy Spirit can do to sanctify us—and by the working of God's power in us to fit us for His service.

Next to this thought, of being personally possessed by the Spirit, comes the truth that all their work in the ministry can be done in the power of the Spirit. What an unspeakably precious assurance—Christ sends them to do a heavenly work, to do His work, to be the instruments in His hands, by which He works: He clothes them with a heavenly power. Their calling is "*to preach the gospel with the Holy Spirit sent down from Heaven.*" As far as feelings are concerned, they may have to say as Paul: "*I was with you in weakness, and in fear, and in much trembling.*" That does not prevent their adding, nay rather, that may just be the secret of their being able to add: "*My preaching was in demonstration of the Spirit and of power.*" If we are to be a minister of the New Covenant, a messenger and a teacher of its true blessing, so as to lead God's children to live in it, nothing less will do than a full experience of its power in our Self, as the Spirit ministers it. … This is his sufficiency for the work. We may every day afresh claim and receive the anointing with fresh oil, the new inbreathing from Christ of His own Spirit and life. …

The minister of the Spirit, very definitely and perseveringly, points away from him or herself to the Spirit. This is what John the Baptist did. He was filled with the Holy Spirit from his birth, but sent others away from himself to Christ, to be by Him baptized with the Spirit. Christ did the same. In His farewell discourse He called His disciples to turn from His personal instruction to the inward teaching of the Holy Spirit, who should dwell in them, and guide them into the truth and power of all He had taught them.

There is nothing so needed in the Church today. All its feebleness and formalities and worldliness, the lack of holiness, of personal devotion to Christ, of enthusiasm for His cause and kingdom, is owing to one thing—the Holy Spirit is not known and honored and yielded to, as the one only, as the one all-sufficient source of a holy life. The New Covenant is not known as a ministration of the Spirit in the heart of every believer. The one thing needful for the Church is—the Holy Spirit in His power dwelling and ruling in the lives of God's saints.

And as one of the chief means to this there are needed ministers of the Spirit, themselves living in the enjoyment and power of this great gift, who persistently labor to bring their brethren into the possession of their birthright: the Holy Spirit in the heart, maintaining, in Divine power, an unceasing communion with the Son and with the Father. …

Entering the Covenant with All the Heart

October 24th

"And I will give them a heart to know Me … for they shall turn to Me with their whole heart."
—JEREMIAH 34: 7

In the days of Asa, Hezekiah, and Josiah, we read of Israel entering into "the Covenant" with their whole heart, "*to perform the words of the Covenant which are written in the book.*" Of Asa's day, we read: *"They swore unto the Lord; and all Judah rejoiced at the oath, for they had sworn with their whole heart, and sought Him with their whole desire; and He was found of them."* Wholeheartedness is the secret of entering the Covenant, and God being found of us in it.

Wholeheartedness is the secret of joy in religion—a full entrance into all the blessedness the Covenant brings. God rejoices over His people to do them good, with His whole heart and His whole soul: it needs, on our part, our whole heart and our whole soul to enter into and enjoy this joy of God in doing us good with His whole heart and His whole soul. With what measure we mete, it shall be measured unto us again.

If we have at all understood the teaching of God's Word in regard to the New Covenant, we know what it reveals in regard to the two parties who meet in it. On God's side there is the promise to do for us and in us all that we need to serve and enjoy Him. He will rejoice in doing us good, with His whole heart. He will be our God, doing for us all that a God can do, giving Himself as God to be wholly ours. And on our side there is the prospect held out of our being able, in the power of what He engages to do, to *"turn to Him with our whole heart," "to love Him with all our heart and all our strength."* The first and great commandment—the only possible terms on which God can fully reveal Himself, or give Himself to His creature to enjoy—is, *"You shall love the Lord your God with all your heart."* …

Wholeheartedness in the love and the service of God! how shall I speak of it? Of its imperative necessity? It is the one unalterable condition of true communion with God. … Surely there cannot for a moment be a thought of anything else being His due, or of our consenting to offer Him anything less, than the love of the whole heart. To love Him with the whole heart, this is the only possible way of receiving His great love into our heart and rejoicing in it—yielding oneself to that mighty love, and allowing God Himself, just as an earthly love enters into us and makes us glad, to give us the taste and the joy of the heavenliness of that love. …

God has planted the new heart in the midst of the flesh, which, with its animating principle, Self, has to be denied, to be kept crucified, and by the Holy Spirit to be mortified. God has placed you in the midst of a world, from which, with all that is of it and its spirit, you are to come out and be entirely separate. God has given you your work in His kingdom, for which He asks all your interest, and time, and strength. In all these three respects you need wholeheartedness, to enable you to make the sacrifices that may be required. If you take the ordinary standard of Christian life around you, you will find that wholeheartedness, intense devotion to God and His service, is hardly thought of. How to make the best of both worlds, innocently to enjoy as much as possible of this present life, is the ruling principle, and, as a natural consequence, the present world secures the larger share of interest. To please Self is considered legitimate, and the Christlike life of not pleasing Self has little place.

Wholeheartedness will lead you, and enable you too, to accept Christ's command and sell all for the pearl of great price. Though at first afraid of what it may involve, do not hesitate to speak the word frequently in the ear of your Father: *with my whole heart.* You may count on the Holy Spirit to open up its meaning, to show you to what service or what sacrifice God calls you in it, to increase its power, to reveal its blessedness, to make it the very spirit of your life of devotion to your Covenant God. …

Let us close and part with this one thought. A redeeming God, rejoicing with His whole heart and whole soul to do us good, and to work in us all that is well-pleasing in His sight: this is the one side. Such is the God of the Covenant. Gaze upon Him. Believe Him. Worship Him. Wait upon Him, until the fire begin to burn, and your heart be drawn out with all its might to love this God. Then the other side. A redeemed soul, rejoicing with all its heart and all its soul in the love of this God, entering into the covenant of wholehearted love, and venturing, ere it knows, to say to Him: With my whole heart I do love You, God, my exceeding joy. Such are the children of the Covenant.

New Covenant Obedience

October 25th

"I will put My Spirit within you, and cause you to walk in My statutes, and you shall keep My judgments."
—EZEKIEL 36: 27

In making the New Covenant, God said very definitely, *"Not after the covenant I made with your fathers."* We have learned what the fault was with that Covenant: it made God's favor dependent upon the obedience of the people. *"If you obey, I will be your God."* We have learned how the New Covenant remedied the defect: God Himself provided for the obedience. It changes *"If you keep My judgments"* into *"I will put My Spirit within you, and you shall keep."* Instead of the Covenant and its fulfillment depending on man's obedience, God undertakes to ensure the obedience. The Old Covenant proved the need, and pointed out the path of holiness; the New inspires the love, and gives the power of holiness.

In connection with this change, a serious and most dangerous mistake is often made. Because in the New Covenant obedience no longer occupies the place it had in the Old, as the condition of the Covenant, and free grace has taken its place, justifying the ungodly, and bestowing gifts on the rebellious, many are under the impression that obedience is now no longer as indispensable as it was then. The error is a terrible one. The whole Old Covenant was meant to teach the lesson of the absolute and indispensable necessity of obedience for a life in God's favor. The New Covenant comes, not to provide a substitute for that obedience in faith, but through faith to secure the obedience, by giving a heart that delights in it and has the power for it.

And we abuse the free grace … when we rest content with the grace, without the obedience it is meant for. We boast of our higher privileges of the New Covenant, while its chief blessing—the power of a holy life, a heart delighting in God's law, and a life in which God causes and enables us, by his indwelling Spirit, to keep His commandments—is neglected. If there is one thing we need to know well, it is the place obedience takes in the New Covenant.

Let our first thought be: Obedience is essential. At the very root of the relation of a creature to his God, and of God admitting the creature to His fellowship, lies the thought of obedience. … In Christ's great salvation it is the power that redeemed us: "*By the obedience of one shall many be made righteous*." In the promise of the New Covenant it takes the first place. God engages to circumcise the hearts of His people—in the putting off of the body of the flesh, in the circumcision of Christ—to love God with all their heart, and to obey His commandments. The crowning gift of Christ's exaltation was the Holy Spirit, to bring salvation to us as an inward thing. The first Covenant demanded obedience, and failed because it could not find it. The New Covenant was expressly made to provide for obedience. To a life in the full experience of the New Covenant blessing, obedience is essential.

It is this indispensable necessity of obedience that explains why so often the entrance into the full enjoyment of the New Covenant has depended upon some single act of surrender. There was something in the life, some evil or doubtful habit, in regard to which conscience had often said that it was not in perfect accord with God's perfect will. Attempts were made to push aside the troublesome suggestion. Or unbelief said it would be impossible to overcome the habit, and maintain the promise of obedience to the Voice within. Meantime, all our prayer appeared of no avail. It was as if faith could not lay hold of the blessing which was full in sight, until at last the soul consented to regard this little thing as the test of its surrender to obey in everything, and of its faith that in everything the Surety of the Covenant would give power to maintain the obedience. With the evil or doubtful thing given up, with a good conscience restored, and the heart's confidence before God assured, the soul could receive and possess what it sought. Obedience is essential.

Second, obedience is possible. When the law is written in the heart; when the heart is circumcised to love the Lord with all our heart, and to obey Him; when the love of God is shed abroad in the heart; it means that the love of God's law and of Himself has now become the moving power of our life. This love is no vague sentiment, in our imagination of something that exists in Heaven, but a living, mighty power of God in the heart, working effectually according to His working, which works in us mightily. A life of obedience is possible. ... Christ and His wonderful redemption need not remain at a distance from us in Heaven, but can become our continual experience. …

And last of all, let us understand: Obedience is blessedness. Do not regard it only as the way to the joy and blessings of the New Covenant, but as itself, in its very nature, joy and happiness. To have the voice of God teaching and guiding you, to be united to God in willing what He wills, in working out what He works in you by His Spirit, in doing His Holy Will, and pleasing Him—surely all this is joy unspeakable and full of glory.

To [the heir and the son] it is a delight to walk or work, to put forth strength and conquer difficulties. To a slave or a hireling it is bondage and weariness. The Old Covenant demanded obedience with an inexorable must, and the threat that followed it. The New Covenant changes the must to can and may. Do ask God, by the Holy Spirit, to show you how *"you have been created in Christ Jesus unto good works,"* and how, as fitted as a vine is for bearing grapes, your new nature is perfectly prepared for every good work. Ask Him to show you that He means obedience, not only to be a possible thing, but the most delightful and attractive gift He has to bestow, the entrance into His love and all its blessedness.... For this man was created, for this He was redeemed again, for this, that it maybe our actual experience, the Holy Spirit has been given and is dwelling in us. ...

Nothing of Myself

October 26th

The one difference between Old and New is, that in the latter everything is to be done by God Himself. And yet believers and even teachers do not take it in. And even those who do, find it hard to live it out. Our whole being is so blinded to the true relation to God, His inconceivable Omnipresent Omnipotence working every moment in us is so far beyond the reach of human conception, our little hearts cannot rise to the reality of His Infinite Love making itself one with us, and delighting to dwell in us, and to work all in us that has to be done there—that, when we think we have accepted the truth, we find it is only a thought. We are such strangers to the knowledge of what a God really is, as the actual life by which His creatures live. "*In Him we live and move and have our being.*" And specially is the knowledge of the Triune God too high for us, in that wonderful, most real, and most practical indwelling, to make which possible the Son became Incarnate, and the Holy Spirit was sent forth into our hearts. Only they who confess their ignorance, and wait very humbly and persistently on our Blessed God to teach us by His Holy Spirit what that all-working indwelling is, can hope to have it revealed to them. ...

The deepest secret of [Jesus'] life on earth, [is] His dependence on the Father. [In just the Gospel of John], some twelve times and more He uses the word "not" and "nothing of Himself." *Not My will. Not My words. Not My honor. Not Mine own glory. I can do nothing of Myself. I speak not of Myself. I came not of Myself. I do nothing of Myself ... "The Son can do nothing of Himself, but what He sees the Father do."* The chief mark of this Divine life He has in Himself is evidently unceasing dependence, receiving from the Father, by the moment, what He bad to speak or do. Nothing of Myself is manifestly as true of Him as it ever could be of the weakest or most sinful man. The life of the Father dwelling in Christ, and Christ in the Father, meant that just as truly as when He was begotten of the Father, He received Divine life and glory from Him, so the continuation of that life came only by an eternal process of giving and receiving, as absolute as is the eternal generation itself.

The more closely we study this truth, and Christ's life in the light of it, the more we are compelled to say, the deepest root of Christ's relationship to the Father, the true reason why He was so well-pleasing, the secret of His glorifying the Father, was this: He allowed God to do all in Him. ...His whole attitude was that of the open ear, the servant spirit, the childlike dependence that waited for all on God.

The infinite importance of this truth in the Christian life is easily felt. The life Christ lived in the Father is the life He imparts to us. We are to abide in Him and He in us, even as He in the Father and the Father in Him. And if the secret of His abiding in the Father be this unceasing Self-abnegation—"*I can do nothing of Myself*"—this life of most entire and absolute dependence and waiting upon God—must it not far more be the most marked feature of our Christian life, the first and all-pervading disposition we seek to maintain?

In a little book of William Law's, that has just been issued, he specially insists upon this in his so striking repetition of the call, if we would die to Self in order to have the birth of Divine love in our souls, to sink down in humility, meekness, patience, and resignation to God. I think that no one who at all enters into this advice, but will feel what new point is given to it by the remembrance of how this entire Self-renunciation was not only one of the many virtues in the character of Christ, but, indeed, that first essential one without which God could have wrought nothing in Him, through which God did work all.

Let us make Christ's words our own: "*I can do nothing of Myself.*" Take it as the keynote of a single day. Look up and see the Infinite God waiting to do everything as soon as we are ready to give up all to Him, and receive all from Him. Bow down in lowly worship, and wait for the Holy Spirit to work some measure of the mind of Christ in you. Do not be disconcerted if you do not learn the lesson at once: there is the God of love waiting to do everything in us who are willing to be nothing. At moments the teaching appears dangerous, at other times terribly difficult. The Blessed Son of God teaches us—this was His whole life—*I can do nothing of Myself.* He is our life; He will work it in us. And when as the Lamb of God He begets this His disposition in us, we shall be prepared for Him to rise on us and shine in us in His heavenly glory.

"*Nothing of Myself*"—that word spoken eighteen hundred years ago, coming out of the inmost depths of the heart of the Son of God—is a seed in which the power of the eternal life is hidden. Take it straight from the heart of Christ, and hide it in your heart. Meditate on it till it reveals the beauty of His Divine meekness and humility, and explains how all the power and glory of God could work in Him. Believe in it as containing the very life and disposition which you need, and believe in Christ, whose Spirit dwells in the seed to make it true in you. Begin, in single acts of Self-emptying, to offer it to God as the one desire of your heart. Count upon God accepting them, and meeting them with His grace, to make the acts into habits, and the habits into dispositions. And you may depend upon it, there is nothing that will lift you so near to God, nothing that will unite you closer to Christ, nothing that will prepare you for the abiding presence and power of God working in you, as the death to Self which is found in the simple word—*nothing of myself.*

The Second Blessing

October 27th

In the life of the believer there sometimes comes a crisis, as clearly marked as his conversion, in which he passes out of a life of continual feebleness and failure to one of strength, and victory, and abiding rest. The transition has been called the Second Blessing. Many have objected to the phrase, as being unscriptural, or as tending to make a rule for all, what was only a mode of experience in some. Others have used it as helping to express clearly in human words what ought to be taught to believers as a possible deliverance from the ordinary life of the Christian, to one of abiding fellowship with God, and entire devotion to His service. In introducing it into the title of this book, I have indicated my belief that, rightly understood, the words express a scriptural truth, and may be a help to believers in putting clearly before them what they may expect from God. Let me try and make clear how I think we ought to understand it. …

Conversion makes of a sinner a child of God, full of ignorance and weakness, without any conception of what the whole-hearted devotion is that God asks of him, or the full possession God is ready to take of him. In some cases the transition from the elementary stage is by a gradual growth and enlightenment. But experience teaches, that in the great majority of cases this healthy growth is not found. To those who have never found the secret of a healthy growth, of victory over sin and perfect rest in God, and have possibly despaired of ever finding it, because all their efforts have been failures, it has often been a wonderful help to learn that it is possible by a single decisive step, bringing them into a right relationship to Christ, His Spirit, and His strength, to enter upon an entirely new life.

… Confessing and giving up all that is of Self and sin, yielding our Self wholly to Christ and His service, we believe and receive a new power to live our life by the faith of the Son of God. The change is in many cases as clear, as marked, as wonderful, as conversion. For lack of a better name, that of "A Second Blessing" came most naturally. When once it is seen how greatly this change is needed in the life of most Christians, and how entirely it rests on faith in Christ and His power, as revealed in the Word, all doubt as to its scripturalness will be removed. And when once its truth is seen, we shall be surprised to find how, throughout Scripture, in history and teaching, we find what illustrates and confirms it.

Take the twofold passage of Israel through water, first out of Egypt, then into Canaan. The wilderness journey was the result of unbelief and disobedience, allowed by God to humble them, and prove them, and show what was in their heart. When this purpose had been accomplished, a second blessing led them through Jordan as mightily into Canaan, as the first had brought them through the Red Sea out of Egypt.

Or take the Holy Place and the Holiest of All, as types of the life in the two covenants, and equally in the two stages of Christian experience. In the former, very real access to God and fellowship with Him, but always with a veil between. In the latter, the full access, through a rent veil, into the immediate presence of God, and the full experience of the power of the heavenly life. As the eyes are opened to see how terribly the average Christian life comes short of God's purpose, and how truly the mingled life can be expelled by the power of a new revelation of what God waits to do, the types of Scripture will shine with a new meaning.

Or look to the teachings of the New Testament. In Romans, Paul contrasts the life of the Christian under the law with that under grace, the spirit of bondage with the Spirit of adoption. What does this mean but that Christians may still be living under the law and its bondage, that they need to come out of this into the full life of grace and liberty through the Holy Spirit, and that, when first they see the difference, nothing is needed but the surrender of faith, to accept and experience what grace will do by the Holy Spirit.

To the Corinthians, Paul writes of some being carnal, and still babes, walking as men after the flesh; others being spiritual, with spiritual discernment and character. To the Galatians, he speaks of the liberty with which Christ, by the Spirit, makes free from the law, in contrast to those who sought to perfect in the flesh, what was begun in the Spirit, and who gloried in the flesh—all to call them to recognize the danger of the carnal, divided life, and to come at once to the life of faith, the life in the Spirit, which alone is according to God's will.

Everywhere we see in Scripture, what the state of the Church at the present day confirms, that conversion is only the gate that leads into the path of life, and that within that gate there is still great danger of mistaking the path, of turning aside, or turning back, and that where this has taken place we are called at once, and with our whole heart, to turn and give ourselves to nothing less than all that Christ is willing to work in us. Just as there are many who have always thought that conversion must be slow, and gradual, and uncertain, and cannot understand how it can be sudden and final, because they only take man's powers into account, so many cannot see how the revelation of the true life of holiness, and the entrance on it by faith out of a life of Self-effort and failure, may be immediate and permanent. They look too much to man's efforts, and know not how the second blessing is nothing more nor less than a new vision of what Christ is willing to work in us, and the surrender of faith that yields all to Him.

I would fain hope that what I have written in this book may help some to see that the second blessing is just what they need, is what God by His Spirit will work in them, is nothing but the acceptance of Christ in all His saving power as our strength and life, and is what will bring them into, and fit them for, that full life in the New Covenant, in which God works all in all.

Canon Battersby

October 28th

I do not know that I can find a better case by which to illustrate the place Christ, the Mediator of the Covenant, takes in leading into its full blessing than that of the founder of the Keswick Convention, the late Canon Battersby. It was at the Oxford Convention in 1873 that he witnessed to having "received a new and distinct blessing to which he had been a stranger before." For more than twenty-five years he had been most diligent as a minister of the gospel, and, as appears from his journals, most faithful in seeking to maintain a close walk with God. But he was ever disturbed by the consciousness of being overcome by sin. So far back as 1853 he had written, "I feel again how very far I am from enjoying habitually that peace and love and joy which Christ promises. I must confess that I have it not; and that very ungentle and unchristian tempers often strive within me for the mastery."

When in 1873 he read what was being published of the Higher Life, the effect was to render him utterly dissatisfied with himself and his state. There were indeed difficulties he could not quite understand in that teaching, but he felt that he must either reach forward to better things, nothing less than redemption from all iniquities, or fall back more and more into worldliness and sin.

At Oxford, he heard an address on the rest of faith. It opened his eyes to the truth that a believer who really longs for deliverance from sinning must simply take Christ at His word, and reckon, without feeling, on Him to do His work of cleansing and keeping the soul. "I thought of the sufficiency of Jesus, and said, I will rest in Him, and I did rest in Him. I was afraid lest it should be a passing emotion; but I found that a presence of Jesus was graciously manifested to me in a way I knew not before, and that I did abide in Him. I do not want to rest in these emotions, but just to believe, and to cling to Christ as my all." He was a man of very reserved nature, but felt it a duty ere the close of the Conference to confess publicly his past shortcoming, and testify openly to his having entered upon a new and definite experience.

In a paper written not long after this he pointed out what the steps are leading to this experience. First, a clear view of the possibilities of Christian attainment—a life in word and action, habitually governed by the Spirit, in constant communion with God, and continual victory over sin through abiding in Christ. Then, the deliberate purpose of the will for a full renunciation of all the idols of the flesh or spirit, and a will-surrender to Christ. And then this last and important step: We must look up to, and wait upon our ascended Lord for all that we need to enable us to do this.

A careful perusal of this very brief statement will prove how everything centered here in Christ. The surrender for a life of continual communion and victory is to be to Christ. The strength for that life is to be in Him and from Him, by faith in Him. And the power to make the full surrender and rest in Him was to be waited for from Him alone.

In June 1875, the first Keswick Convention was held. In the circular calling it, we read: "Many are everywhere thirsting that they may be brought to enjoy more of the Divine presence in their daily life, and a fuller manifestation of the Holy Spirit's power, whether in subduing the lusts of the flesh, or in enabling them to offer more effective service to God. It is certainly God's will that His children should be satisfied in regard to these longings, and there are those who can testify that He has satisfied them, and does satisfy them with daily fresh manifestations of His grace and power."

The results of the very first Convention were most blessed, so that after its close he wrote: "There is a very remarkable resemblance in the testimonies I have since received as to the nature of the blessing obtained, viz., the ability given to make a full surrender to the Lord, and the consequent experience of an abiding peace, far exceeding anything previously experienced." Through all the chief thought, was Christ, first drawing and enabling the soul to rest in Him, and then meeting it with the fulfillment of its desire, the abiding experience of His power to keep it in victory over sin, and communion with God.

George Müller

October 29th

In the life of George Müller of Bristol there was an epoch, four years after his conversion, to which he ever after looked back, and of which he often spoke, as his entrance into the true Christian life. In an address given to ministers and workers after his ninetieth birthday, he spoke thus of it himself:

> That leads to another thought—the full surrender of the heart to God. I was converted in November 1825, but I only came, into the full surrender of the heart four years later, in July 1829. The love of money was gone, the love of place was gone, the love of position was gone, the love of worldly pleasures and engagements was gone. God, God, God alone became my portion. I found my all in Him; I wanted nothing else. And by the grace of God this has remained, and has made me a happy man, an exceedingly happy man, and it led me to care only about the things of God.

... The account he gives of this change in his journal is as follows. He speaks of one whom he had heard preach at Teignmouth, where he had gone for the sake of his health:

> Though I did not like all he said, yet I saw a gravity and solemnity in him different from the rest. Through the instrumentality of this brother the Lord bestowed a great blessing upon me, for which I shall have cause to thank Him throughout eternity. God then began to show me that the Word of God alone is to be our standard of judgment in spiritual things; that it can only be explained by the Holy Spirit, and that in our day, as well as in former times, He is the Teacher of His people. ...
>
> It was my beginning to understand this point in particular which had a great

effect on me; for the Lord enabled me to put it to the test of experience by laying aside commentaries and almost every other book, and simply reading the Word of God and studying it. The result of this was that the first evening that I shut myself into my room to give myself to prayer and meditation over the Scriptures, I learned more in a few hours than I had done during a period of several months previously. But the particular difference was that I received real strength in my soul in doing so.

> In addition to this, it pleased the Lord to lead me to see a higher standard of devotedness than I had seen before. He led me, in a measure, to see what is my glory in this world, even to be despised, to be poor and mean with Christ. … I returned to London much better in body. And as to my soul, the change was so great that it was like a second conversion.

In another passage, he speaks thus:

> "I fell into the snare into which so many young believers fall, the reading of religious books is preferred to the Scriptures. Now the scriptural way of reasoning would have been: God Himself has condescended to become an author, and I am ignorant of that precious Book which His Holy Spirit has caused to be written; therefore I ought to read again this Book of books most earnestly, most prayerfully, and with much meditation. Instead of acting thus, and being led by my ignorance of the Word to study it more, my difficulty of understanding it made me careless of reading it, and then, like many believers, I practically preferred for the first four years of my Christian life, the works of uninspired men to the oracles of the Living God. The consequence was that I remained a babe, both in knowledge and grace. In knowledge, I say, for all true knowledge must be derived by the Spirit from the Word.

> This lack of knowledge most sadly kept me back from walking steadily in the ways of God. For it is the truth makes us free, by delivering us from the slavery of the lusts of the flesh, the lusts of the eyes, and the pride of life. The Word proves it, the experience of the saints proves it, and also my own experience most decidedly proves it. For when it pleased the Lord, in August 1829, to bring me really to the Scriptures, my life and walk became very different.

> "If anyone would ask me how he may read the Scriptures most profitably, I would answer him:

> "1. Above all he must seek to have it settled in his own mind that God alone, by the Holy Spirit, can teach him, and that, therefore, as God will be inquired for all blessings, it becomes him to seek for God's blessing previous to reading, and also while reading.

> "2. He should also have it settled in his mind that though the Holy spirit is the best and sufficient Teacher, yet that He does not always teach immediately when we desire it, and that, therefore, we may have to entreat Him again and again for the explanation of certain passages; but that He will surely teach us at last, if we will seek for light prayerfully, patiently, and for the glory of God."

For sixty-nine years and ten months, Müller said that he had been a very happy man. That he attributed to two things. He had maintained a good conscience, not willfully going on in a course he knew to be contrary to the mind of God. …

In connection with what has been said about the New Covenant being a ministration of the Spirit this narrative is most instructing. It shows us how George Muller's power lay in God's revealing to him the work of the Holy Spirit. He writes that up to the time of that change he had "not experimentally understood the office of the Holy Spirit."

We speak much of George Muller's power in prayer; it is of importance to remember that that power was entirely owing to his love of, and faith in, God's Word. But it is of still more importance to notice that his power to believe God's Word so fully was entirely owing to his having learned to know the Holy Spirit as his Teacher. When the words of God are explained to us, and made living within us by the Holy Spirit, they have a power to awaken faith which they otherwise have not. The Word then brings us into contact with God, comes to us as from God direct, and binds our whole life to Him.

When the Holy Spirit thus feeds us on the Word, our whole life comes under His power, and the fruit is seen, not only in the power of prayer, but as much in the power of obedience. Notice how Mr. Muller tells us this, that the two secrets of his great happiness were, his great love for God's Word, and his ever maintaining a good conscience, not knowingly doing anything against the will of God. In giving himself to the teaching of the Holy Spirit, as he tells us in his birthday address, he made a full surrender of the entire heart to God, to be ruled by the Word. He gave himself to obey that Word in everything, he believed that the Holy Spirit gave the grace to obey, and so he was able to maintain a walk free from knowingly transgressing God's law.

This is a point he always insisted on. So he writes, in regard to a life of dependence upon God: "It will not do—it is not possible—to live in sin, and at the same time, by communion with God, to draw down from Heaven everything one needs for the life that now is." Again, speaking of the strengthening of faith: "It is of the utmost importance that we seek to maintain an upright heart and a good conscience, and therefore do not knowingly and habitually indulge in those things which are contrary to the mind of God. All my confidence in God, all my leaning upon Him in the hour of trial, will be gone if I have a guilty conscience, and do not seek to put away this guilty conscience, but still continue to do things which are contrary to His mind."

A careful perusal of this testimony will show us how the chief points usually insisted upon in connection with the second blessing are all found here. There is the full surrender of the heart to be taught and led alone by the Spirit of God. There is the higher standard of holiness which is at once set up. There is the tender desire in nothing to offend God, but to have at all times a good conscience, that testifies that we are pleasing to God. And there is the faith that where the Holy Spirit reveals to us in the Word the will of God, He gives the sufficient strength for the doing of it. "The particular difference," he says of reading with faith of the Holy Spirit's teaching, "was that I received real strength in my soul in doing so." No wonder that he said: The change was so great, that it was like a second conversion.

All centers in this, that we believe in the New Covenant and its promises as a ministration of the Spirit. That belief may come to some suddenly, as to George Muller; or it may dawn upon others by degrees. Let all say to God that they are ready to put their whole heart and life under the rule of the Holy Spirit dwelling in them, teaching them by the Word, and strengthening them by His grace. He enables us to live pleasing to God.

24

WORKING FOR GOD

A Sequel to Waiting on God

New York: Fleming H. Revell, 1901

Introduction

October 30th

The object of this little book is first of all to remind all Christian workers of the greatness and the glory of the work in which God gives a share. It is nothing less than that work of bringing men back to their God, at which God finds His highest glory and blessedness. As we see that it is God's own work we have to work out, that He works it through us, that in our doing it His glory rests on us and we glorify Him, we shall count it our joy to give ourselves to live only and wholly for it.

The aim of the book at the same time is to help those who complain, and perhaps do not even know to complain, that they are apparently laboring in vain, to find out what may be the cause of so much failure. God's work must be done in God's way, and in God's power. It is spiritual work, to be done by spiritual men, in the power of the Spirit. The clearer our insight into, and the more complete our submission to, God's laws of work, the surer and the richer will be our joy and our reward in it.

Along with this I have had in view the great number of Christians who practically take no real part in the service of their Lord. They have never understood that the chief characteristic of the Divine life in God and Christ is love and its work of blessing men. The Divine life in us can show itself in no other way. I have tried to show that it is God's will that every believer without exception, whatever be his position in life, gives himself wholly to live and work for God.

I have also written in the hope that some, who have the training of others in Christian

life and work, may find thoughts that will be of use to them in teaching the imperative duty, the urgent need, the Divine blessedness of a life given to God's service, and to waken within the consciousness of the power that works in them, even the Spirit and power of Christ Himself.
—ANDREW MURRAY
Wellington, 1901

Waiting and Working

"They that wait upon the Lord shall renew their strength" (Isaiah 40: 31); "*From of old no one has heard or perceived by the ear, no eye has seen a God besides You, who works for those who wait for Him*" (Isaiah 64: 4). Here we have two texts in which the connection between waiting and working is made clear. In the first we see that waiting brings the needed strength for working—that it fits for joyful and unwearied work. "*They that wait on the Lord shall renew their strength; they shall mount up on eagles' wings; they shall run, and not be weary; they shall walk, and not faint.*" Waiting on God has its value in this: it makes us strong in work for God. The second reveals the secret of this strength. "*God works for Him who wait for Him.*" The waiting on God secures the working of God for us and in us, out of which our work must spring. The two passages teach the great lesson, that as waiting on God lies at the root of all true working for God, so working for God must be the fruit of all true waiting on Him. Our great need is to hold the two sides of the truth in perfect conjunction and harmony.

… There are some, there are many, who work for God, but know little of what it is to wait on Him. They have been led to take up Christian work, under the impulse of natural or religious feeling, at the bidding of a pastor or a society, with but very little sense of what a holy thing it is to work for God. They do not know that God's work can only be done in God's strength, by God Himself working in us. They have never learned that, just as the Son of God could do nothing of Himself, but that the Father in Him did the work, as He lived in continual dependence before Him, so, and much more, the believer can do nothing but as God works in him. They do not understand that it is only as in utter weakness we depend upon Him, His power can rest on us.

And so they have no conception of a continual waiting on God as being one of the first and essential conditions of successful work. And Christ's Church and the world are sufferers today—oh, so terribly—not only because so many of its members are not working for God, but because so much working for God is done without waiting on God. …

Let us pray that…the Holy Spirit may show us how sacred and how urgent our calling is to work, how absolute our dependence is upon God's strength to work in us, how sure it is that those who wait on Him shall renew their strength, and how we shall find waiting on God and working for God to be indeed inseparably one. It is only as God works for me, and in me, that I can work for Him. All His work for me is through His life in me. He will most surely work, if I wait on Him. All His working for me, and my waiting on Him, has but one aim, to fit me for His work of saving men.

Abounding Grace for Abounding Work

October 31st

"And God is able to make all grace abound unto you, that you may abound unto every good work."
—2 CORINTHIANS 9: 8

Our text today assures us that for abounding work we have the ability provided: *"God is able to make all grace abound, that we may abound to all good works."* Every thought of abounding grace is to be connected with the abounding in good works for which it is given. And every thought of abounding work is to be connected with the abounding grace that fits for it.

Abounding grace has abounding work for its aim. It is often thought that grace and good works are at variance with each other. This is not so. What Scripture calls the works of the law—our own works, the works of righteousness which we have done, dead works—works by which we seek to merit or to be made fit for God's favor—these are indeed the very opposite of grace. But they are also the very opposite of the good works which spring from grace, and for which alone grace is bestowed.

As irreconcilable as are the works of the law with the freedom of grace, so essential and indispensable are the works of faith, good works, to the true Christian life. God makes grace to abound, that good works may abound. The measure of true grace is tested and proved by the measure of good works. God's grace abounds in us that we may abound in good works. We need to have the truth deeply rooted in us: Abounding grace has abounding work for its aim. …

There often is abounding work without abounding grace. Just as any man may be very diligent in an earthly pursuit, or a heathen in his religious service of an idol, so men may be very diligent in doing religious work in their own strength, with but little thought of that grace which alone can do true, spiritual effective work. For all work that is to be really acceptable to God, and truly fruitful, not only for some visible result here on earth, but for eternity, the grace of God is indispensable. Paul continually speaks of his own work as owing everything to the grace of God working in him: *"I labored more abundantly than they all: yet not I, but the grace of God which was with me"* (1 Corinthians 15: 10). *"According to the gift of that grace of God which was given me according to the working of His power"* (Ephesians 3: 7). And he as frequently calls upon Christians to exercise their gifts "*according to the grace that was given us*" (Romans 12: 6). The grace given "*according to the measure of the gift of Christ*" (Ephesians 4:7). It is only by the grace of God working in us that we can do what are truly good works. It is only as we seek and receive abounding grace that we can abound in every good work. …

Child of God! do take time to study and truly apprehend God's purpose with you, that you abound in every good work! He means it! He has provided for it! Make the measure of your consecration to Him nothing less than His purpose for you. And claim, then, nothing less than the abounding grace He is able to bestow. Make His omnipotence and His faithfulness your confidence. And live ever in the practice of continual prayer and dependence upon His power working in you. This will make you abound in every good work. "*According to your faith be it unto you.*"

Christian worker, learn here the secret of all failure and all success. Work in our own strength, with little prayer and waiting on God for His spirit, is the cause of failure. The cultivation of the spirit of waiting, and of absolute impotence and unceasing dependence, will open the heart for the workings of the abounding grace. We shall learn to ascribe all we do to God's grace. We shall learn to measure all we have to do by God's grace. And our life will increasingly be in the joy of God's making His grace to abound in us, and our abounding in every good work.

The Father Abiding in Me Does the Work

November 1st

The words that I speak I speak not of Myself: but the Father abiding in Me does the work."

—JOHN 14: 10

Jesus Christ became man that He might show us what a true man is, how God meant to live and work in man, and how man may find his life and do his work in God. In words like those above, our Lord opens up the inner mystery of His life, and discovers to us the nature and the deepest secret of His working. He did not come to the world to work instead of the Father; the Father was ever working—"*works even until now.*"

Christ's work was the fruit, the earthly reflection of the Heavenly Father working. And it was not as if Christ merely saw and copied what the Father willed or did: *"the Father abiding in Me does the work."* Christ did all His work in the power of the Father dwelling and working in Him. So complete and real was His dependence on the Father, that, in expounding it to the Jews, He used the strong expression: *"The Son can do nothing of Himself, but what He sees the Father doing,"* and *"I can do nothing of Myself"* (John 5:19, 30). As literally as what He said is true of us, "*Apart from Me you can do nothing,*" is it true of Him too. *"The Father abiding in Me does the work."*

Jesus Christ became man that He might show us what true man is, what the true relation between man and God, what the true way of serving God and doing His work. When we are made new creatures in Christ Jesus, the life we receive is the very life that was and is in Christ, and it is only by studying His life on earth that we know how we are to live. "*As I live because of the Father, so he that partakes of Me shall live because of Me.*" His dependence on the Father is the law of our dependence on Him and on the Father through Him. Christ counted it no humiliation to be able to do nothing of Himself, to be always and absolutely dependent on the Father. He counted it His highest glory, because so all His works were the works of the all glorious God in Him. When shall we understand that to wait on God, to bow before Him in perfect helplessness, and let Him work all in us, is our true nobility, and the secret of the highest activity? This alone is the true Son-life, the true life of every child of God. As this life is known and maintained, the power for work will grow, because the soul is in the attitude in which God can work in us as the God who "*works for those that wait on Him.*"

It is the ignorance or neglect of the great truths—that there can be no true work for God but as God works it in us, and that God cannot work in us fully but as we live in absolute dependence on Him, that is the explanation of the universal complaint of so much Christian activity with so little real result. The revival which many are longing and praying for must begin with this: the return of Christian ministers and workers to their true place before God—in Christ and like Christ, one of complete dependence and continual waiting on God to work in them.

Let me invite all workers, young and old, successful or disappointed, full of hope or full of fear, to come and learn from our Lord Jesus the secret of true work for God. *"My Father works, and I work"; "The Father abiding in Me does the works."* Divine Fatherhood means that God is all, and gives all, and works all. Divine Sonship means continual dependence on the Father, and the reception, moment by moment, of all the strength needed for His Work. Try to grasp the great truth that because it is "*God who works all in all,*" your one need is, in deep humility and weakness, to wait for and to trust in His working.

Learn from this that God can only work in us as He dwells in us. *"The Father abiding in Me does the works."* Cultivate the holy sense of God's continual nearness and presence—of you being His temple, and of His dwelling in you. Offer yourself for Him to work in you all His good pleasure. You will find that work, instead of being a hindrance, can become your greatest incentive to a life of fellowship and childlike dependence. At first it may appear as if the waiting for God to work will keep you back from your work. It may indeed--but only to bring the greater blessing, when you have learned the lesson of faith, that counts on His working even when you do not feel it. You may have to do your work in weakness and fear and much trembling. You will know that it is all, that the excellency of the power may be of God and not of us. As you know yourself better and God better, you will be content that it should ever be *"His strength made perfect in our weakness."*

1. *"The Father abiding in Me does the work."* There is the same law for the Head and the member, for Christ and the believer. It is the same God *"that works all in all."* 2. The Father not only worked in the Son when He was on earth, but now, too, that He is in Heaven. It is as we believe in Christ in the Father's working in Him, that we shall do the greater works. See John 14:10–12. 3. It is as the indwelling God, the Father abiding in us, that God works in us. Let the life of God in the soul be clear, the work will be sure. 4. Pray much for grace to say, in the name of Jesus, *"The Father abiding in me does the work."*

Work, for God Works in You

"Work out your own salvation with fear and trembling; for it is God who works in you both to will and to work, for His good pleasure" (Philippians 2: 12, 13). … One great cause of the failure of believers in their work is that, when they think that God has given them to will, they undertake to work in the strength of that will. They have never learned the lesson, that

because God has created us in Christ Jesus for good works, and has afore prepared the good works in which we are to walk, that He will most certainly Himself work them all in us. They have never listened long to the voice speaking, *"It is God which works in you."*

We have here to do with one of the deepest, most spiritual, and most precious truths of Scripture—the unceasing operation of Almighty God in our heart and life. In virtue of the very nature of God, as a Spiritual Being not confined to any place, but everywhere present, there can be no spiritual life but as it is upheld by His personal indwelling.

Not without the deepest reason does Scripture say, He works all in all. Not only of Him are all things as their first beginning, and to Him as their end, but also through Him, who alone maintains them.

In the man Christ Jesus the working of the Father in Him was the source of all He did. In the new man, created in Christ Jesus, the unceasing dependence on the Father is our highest privilege, our true nobility. This is indeed fellowship with God: God Himself working in us to will and to do.

Let us seek to learn the true secret of working for God. It is not, as many think, that we do our best, and then leave God to do the rest. By no means. But it is this, that we know that God's working His salvation in us is the secret of our working it out. That salvation includes every work we have to do. The faith of God's working in us is the measure of our fitness to work effectively. The promises, "*According to your faith be it unto you,*" "*All things are possible to those that believe,*" have their full application here. The deeper our faith in God's working in us, the more freely will the power of God's work in us, the more true and fruitful will our work be. …

Let me ask, Have you really believed that your only power to do God's work is as one who has been created in Christ Jesus for good works, as one in whom God Himself works to will and to work? Have you yielded yourself to wait for that working? Do you work because you know God works in you? Say not that these thoughts are too high. The work of leading young souls to Christ is too high for us indeed, but if we live as little children, in believing that God will work all in us, we shall do His work in His strength. Pray much to learn and practice the lesson in all you do: Work, *for God works in you.*

According to the Working of His Power

November 2nd

I also labor, striving according to His working, which works in me mightily."

—COLOSSIANS 1:29

It is only by God's working in us that we can do true work. In our texts we have Paul's testimony as to his own experience. His whole ministry was to be according to the grace which was given him according to the working of God's power. And of his labor he says that it was a striving according to the power of Him who worked mightily in him.

We find here the same principle we found in our Lord—the Father doing the works in Him. Let every worker who reads this pause, and say: If the ever-blessed Son, if the Apostle Paul, could only do their work according to the working of His power who worked in them mightily, how much more do I need this working of God in me, to fit me for doing His work aright. This is one of the deepest spiritual truths of God's word; let us look to the Holy Spirit within us to give it such a hold of our inmost life, that it may become the deepest inspiration of all our work. I can only do true work as I yield myself to God to work in me.

We know the ground on which this truth rests: *"There is none good but God"; "There is none holy but the Lord"; "Power belongs unto God."* All goodness and holiness and power are only to be found in God, and where He gives them. And He can only give them in the creature, not as something He parts with, but by His own actual presence and dwelling and working. And so God can only work in His people in as far as He is allowed to have complete possession of the heart and life. As our will and life and love are yielded up in dependence and faith, and God is waited on to keep possession and to abide, even as Christ waited on Him, God can work in us.

This is true of all our spiritual life, but specially of our work for God. The work of saving souls is God's own work: none but He can do it. The gift of His Son is the proof of how great and precious He counts the work, and how His heart is set upon it. His love never for one moment ceases working for the salvation of men. And when He calls His children to be partners in His work, He shares with them the joy and the glory of the work of saving and blessing men. He promises to work His work through them, inspiring and energizing them by His power working in them. To him who can say with Paul: *"I labor, striving according to His power who works in me mightily,"* his whole relation to God becomes the counterpart and the continuation of Christ's, a blessed, unceasing, momentary, and most absolute dependence on the Father for every word He spoke and every work He did.

Christ is our pattern. Christ's life is our law and works in us. Christ lived in Paul his life of dependence on God. Why should any of us hesitate to believe that the grace given to Paul of laboring and striving "*according to the working of the power*" will be given to us too. Let every worker learn to say, As the power that worked in Christ worked in Paul too, that power works no less in me. There is no possible way of working God's work aright, but by God working it in us.

How I wish that I could take every worker who reads this by the hand, and say: Come, let us quiet our minds, and hush every thought in God's presence, as I whisper in your ears the wonderful secret: God is working in you. All the work you have to do for Him, God will work in you. Take time and think it over. It is a deep spiritual truth which the mind cannot grasp nor the heart realize. Accept it as a Divine truth from Heaven; believe that this Word is a seed out of which can grow the very spiritual blessing of which it speaks. And in the faith of the Holy Spirit's making it live within you, say ever again: God works in me. All the work I have to work for Him, God will work in me. The faith of this truth, and the desire to have it made true in you, will constrain you to live very humbly and closely with God. You will see how work for God must be the most spiritual thing in a spiritual life. And you will ever anew bow in holy stillness: God is working; God will work in me; I will work for Him according to the power which works in me mightily.

In the Work of Ministering

November 3rd

"And he gave some to be apostles; and some, prophets; and some, evangelists; and some, pastors and teachers; for the perfecting of the saints, unto the work of ministering, unto the building up of the body of Christ."
—EPHESIANS 4: 11–12

The object of Christ when He ascended to Heaven and bestowed on His servants the various gifts that are mentioned is threefold: Their first aim is *"for the perfecting of the saints."* Believers as saints are to be *"led on in the pursuit of holiness until they stand perfect and complete in all the will of God."* It was for this that Epaphras labored in prayer. It is of this Paul writes, *"teaching everyone in all wisdom, that we may present them perfect in Christ"* (Colossians 4:12; 1: 28).

This perfecting of the saints is, however, only a means to a higher end: unto the work of ministering—to fit all the saints to take their part in the service to which every believer is called. … And this, again, is also a means to a still higher end: "*unto the building up of the body of Christ.*" As every member of our body takes its part in working for the health and growth and maintenance of the whole, so every member of the body of Christ is to consider it his first great duty to take part in all that can help to build up the body of Christ. And this, whether by the helping and strengthening of those who are already members, or the ingathering of those who are to belong to it. And the great work of the Church is, through its pastors and teachers, so to labor for the perfecting of the saints in holiness and love and fitness for service, that every one may take his part in the work of ministering, that so, the body of Christ may be built up and perfected.

Of the three great objects with which Christ has given His Church apostles and teachers, the work of ministering stands in the middle. On the one hand, it is preceded by that on which it absolutely depends: *"the perfecting of the saints."* On the other, it is followed by that which it is meant to accomplish: *"the building up of the body of Christ."* Every believer without exception—every member of Christ's body—is called to take part in this work of ministering. Let every reader try and realize the sacredness of his holy calling.

Let us learn what the qualification is for our work. *"The perfecting of the saints" "prepares them for the work of ministering."* It is the lack of true sainthood, of true holiness, that causes such lack and feebleness of service. As Christ's saints are taught and truly learn what conformity to Christ means, a life like his, given up in Self-sacrifice for the service and salvation of men, as His humility and love, His separation from the world and devotion to the fallen, are seen to be the very essence and blessedness of the life He gives, the work of ministering, the ministry of love, will become the one thing we live for. Humility and love—these are the two great virtues of the saint; they are the two great powers for the work of ministering. Humility makes us willing to serve; love makes us wise to know how to do it. Love is inventive; it seeks patiently, and suffers long, until it finds a way to reach its object. Humility and love are equally turned away from Self and its claims. Let us pray, let the Church labor for "*the perfecting of the saints*" in humility and love, and the Holy Spirit will teach us to minister.

Let us look at what the great work is the members of Christ have to do. It is to minister to each other. Place yourself at Christ's disposal for service to your fellow Christians. Count yourself their servant. Study their interest. Set yourself actively to promote the welfare of the Christians round you. Selfishness may hesitate, the feeling of feebleness may discourage, sloth and ease may raise difficulties. Ask your Lord to reveal to you His will, and give yourself up to it. Round about you there are Christians who are cold and worldly and wandering from their Lord. Begin to think what you can do for them. Accept as the will of the Head that you as a member should care for them. Pray for the Spirit of love. Begin somewhere—only begin.... Begin the work of ministering *"according to the measure of the grace you have."* He will give more grace.

Let us believe in the power that works in us as sufficient for all we have to do. As I think of the thumb and finger holding the pen with which I write this, I ask, How is it that during all these seventy years of my life they have always known just to do my will? It was because the life of the head passed into and worked itself out in them.

"*He who believes in Me*," as his Head working in him, "*the works that I do shall he do also.*" Faith in Christ, whose "*strength is made perfect in our weakness*" will give the power for all we are called to do. Let us cry to God that all believers may waken up to the power of this great truth: Every member of the body is to live wholly for the building up of the body.

Laboring More Abundantly

November 4th

I labored more abundantly than they all: yet not I, but the grace of God which was with me"

—1 CORINTHIANS 15: 10

And He has said unto me, My grace is sufficient for you: for My power is made perfect in weakness."

—2 CORINTHIANS 12: 9

In both of these passages Paul speaks of how he had abounded in the work of the Lord. ... In both he tells how entirely it was all God, who worked in Him, and not of himself. In the first he says: *"Not I, but the grace of God which was with me."* And then in the second, showing how this grace is Christ's strength working in us, while we are nothing, he tells us: *"He said unto me: My grace is sufficient for you: My power is made perfect in weakness."*

May God give us the Spirit of revelation, enlightened eyes of the heart, to see this wonderful vision—those who knows ourself to be nothing, glorying in our weakness, that the power of Christ may rest on us, and work through us, and who so labors more abundantly than all. What does this teach us as workers for God.

God's work can only be done in God's strength. It is only by God's power, that is, by God Himself working in us, that we can do effective work. Throughout this little book this truth has been frequently repeated. It is easy to accept of it; it is far from easy to see its full meaning, to give it the mastery over our whole being, to live it out. This will need stillness of soul, and meditation, strong faith and fervent prayer. As it is God alone who can work in us, it is equally God who alone can reveal Himself as the God who works in us. Wait on Him, and the truth that ever appears to be beyond your reach will be opened up to you, through the knowledge of who and what God is. When God reveals Himself as *"God who works all in all,"* you will learn to believe and work *"according to the power of Him who works in you mightily."*

God's strength can only work in weakness. It is only when we truly Say [with Paul], *"Not I!"* that we can fully say, *"but the grace of God with me."* ... He could say: *"I take pleasure in weaknesses, for when I am weak then am I strong."* This is the true relation between the Creator and the creature, between the Divine Father and His child, between God and His servant. Christian worker! learn the lesson of your own weakness, as the indispensable condition of God's power working in you. Do believe that to take time and in God's presence to realize your weakness and nothingness is the sure way to be clothed with God's strength. Accept every experience by which God teaches you your weakness as His grace preparing you to receive His strength. Take pleasure in weaknesses!

God's strength comes in our fellowship with Christ and His service. Paul says: *"I will glory in my weakness, that the strength of Christ may rest upon me." "I take pleasure in weaknesses for Christ's sake."* And he tells how it was when he had besought the Lord that the messenger of Satan might depart from him, that He answered: *"My grace is sufficient for you." "Christ is the wisdom and the power of God."*

We do not receive the wisdom to know, or the power to do God's will as something that we can possess and use at discretion. It is in the personal attachment to Christ, in a life of continual communication with Him, that His power rests on us. It is in taking pleasure in weaknesses for Christ's sake that Christ's strength is known.

God's strength is given to faith, and the work that is done in faith. It needs a living faith to take pleasure in weaknesses, and in weakness to do our work, knowing that God is working in us. Without seeing or feeling anything, to go on in the confidence of a hidden power working in us—this is the highest exercise of a life of faith.

To do God's own work in saving souls—in persevering prayer and labor; amid outwardly unfavorable circumstances and appearances still to labor more abundantly—this faith alone can do. Let us be strong in faith, giving glory to God. God will show Himself strong towards him whose heart is perfect with Him.

My beloved! Be willing to yield yourself to the very utmost to God, that His power may rest upon you, may work in you. Do let God work through you. Offer yourself to Him for His work as the one object of your life. Count upon His working all in you, to fit you for His service, to strengthen and bless you in it. Let the faith and love of your Lord

Jesus, whose strength is going to be made perfect in your weakness, lead you to live even as He did, to do the Father's will and finish His work. …

Greater Works

November 5th

"He that believes on Me, the works that I do shall he do also, and greater works shall he do; because I go unto the Father. And whatsoever you ask in My name, that will I do, that the Father may be glorified in the Son."
—JOHN 14: 12–14

In the words, *"The Father abiding in Me does the works"* (John 14: 10), Christ had revealed the secret of His and of all Divine service: *man yielding himself for God to dwell and to work in him.* When Christ now promises, *"He that believes on Me, the works that I do shall he do also,"* the law of the Divine in-working remains unchanged. In us, as much as in Him—one might even say a thousand times more than with Him—it must still ever be: *"The Father in me does the works."* With Christ and with us, it is the same God *"who works all in all."*

How this is to be, is taught us in the words, *"He that believes on Me."* That does not only mean, for salvation, as a Savior from sin; but much more. Christ had just said (verses 10, 11), *"Believe Me that I am in the Father, and the Father in Me: the Father abiding in Me does the works."* We need to believe in Christ as Him in and through whom the Father unceasingly works. To believe in Christ is to receive Him into the heart. When we see the Father's working inseparably connected with Christ, we know that to believe in Christ, and receive Him into the heart, is to receive the Father dwelling in Him and working through Him. The works His disciples are to do cannot possibly be done in any other way than His own are done.

This becomes still more clear from what our Lord adds: "*And greater works shall he do; because I go unto the Father.*" What the greater works are, is evident. The disciples at Pentecost with three thousand baptized, and multitudes added to the Lord; Philip at Samaria, with the whole city filled with joy; the men of Cyprus and Cyrene, and, later on, Barnabas at Antioch, with much people added to the Lord; Paul in his travels, and a countless host of Christ's servants down to our day, have in the ingathering of souls, done what the Master condescendingly calls greater works than He did in the days of His humiliation and weakness.

The reason why it should be so our Lord makes plain, *"Because I go to the Father."* When He entered the glory of the Father, all power in Heaven and on earth was given to Him as our Redeemer. In a way more glorious than ever the Father was to work through Him; and He then to work through His disciples. Even as His own work on earth in the days of the weakness of the flesh, had been in a power received from the Father in Heaven, so His people, in their weakness, would do works like His, and greater works in the same way, through a power received from Heaven. The law of the Divine working is unchangeable: God's work can only be done by God Himself. It is as we see this in Christ, and receive Him in this capacity, as the One in and through whom God works all, and so yield ourselves wholly to the Father working "in Him and in us," that we shall do greater works than He did.

The words that follow bring out still more strongly the great truths we have been learning, that it is our Lord Himself who will work all in us, even as the Father did in Him, and that our posture is to be exactly what His was, one of entire receptivity and dependence. *"Greater works shall he do, because I go to the Father, and whatsoever you shall ask in My name, that will I do."* Christ connects the greater works the believer is to do, with the promise that He will do whatever the believer asks. Prayer in the name of Jesus will be the expression of that dependence that waits on Him for His working, to which He gives the promise: *"Whatsoever you ask, I will do, in you and through you."*

And when He adds, *"that the Father may be glorified in the Son,"* He reminds us how He had glorified the Father, by yielding to Him as Father, to work all His work in Himself as Son. In Heaven Christ would still glorify the Father, by receiving from the Father the power, and working in His disciples what the Father would.

The creature, as the Son Himself, can give the Father no higher glory than yielding to Him to work all. The believer can glorify the Father in no other way than the Son, by an absolute and unceasing dependence on the Son, in whom the Father works, to communicate and work in us all the Father's work. "*If you shall ask anything in My name, that will I do*," and so "*you shall do greater works.*" The creature, as the Son Himself can give the Father no higher glory than yielding to Him to work all. The believer can glorify the Father in no other way than the Son, by an absolute and unceasing dependence on the Son, in whom the Father works, to communicate and work in us all the Father's work. *"If you shall ask anything in My name, that will I do, and so you shall do greater works."*

I Know Your Works

November 6th

"To the angel of the Church in Ephesus—in Thyatira—in Sardis—in Philadelphia—in Laodicea write: "I know your works."

—REVELATION 2: 3

These are the words of Him who walks in the midst of the seven golden candlesticks, and whose eyes are like a flame of fire. As He looks upon the churches, the first thing He sees and judges is—the works. The works are the revelation of the life and character. If we are willing to bring our works into His holy presence, His words can teach us what our work ought to be.

To Ephesus He says: *"I know your works, and your toil and patience, and that you cannot bear evil men, and you have patience and did bear for My name's sake, and have not grown weary. But I have this against you, that you have left your first love. Repent, and do the first works."* There was here much to praise—toil, and patience, and zeal that had never grown weary. But there was one thing lacking—the tenderness of the first love.

In His work for us Christ gave us before and above everything His love, the personal tender affection of His heart. In our work for Him He asks us nothing less. There is such a danger of work being carried on, and our even bearing much for Christ's sake, while the freshness of our love has passed away. And that is what Christ seeks. And that is what gives power. And that is what nothing can compensate for. Christ looks for the warm loving heart, the personal affection which ever keeps Him the center of our love and joy. Christian workers, see that all your work be the work of love, of tender personal devotion to Christ Jesus.

"To Thyatira: I know your works, and your love and faith and ministry and patience, and that the last works are more than the first. But I have this against you, that you suffers the woman Jezebel, and she teaches and seduces My servants." Here again the works are enumerated and praised: the last had even been more than the first. But then there is one failure: a false toleration of what led to impurity and idolatry. And then He adds of His judgments: *"the churches shall know that I am He which searches [the intents] and hearts; and I will give to each one of you according to your works."*

Along with much of good works there may be some one form of error or evil tolerated which endangers the whole church. In Ephesus, there was zeal for orthodoxy, but a lack of love; here love and faith, but a lack of faithfulness against error. If good works are to please our Lord, if our whole life must be in harmony with them—in entire separation from the world and its allurements— we must seek to be what He promised to make us: established in every good word and work. ...

"To Sardis: I know your works, that you have a name [or reputation for being alive], and you are dead. Be watchful and establish the things that are ready to die: for I have found no works of yours fulfilled before My God." There may be all the forms of godliness without the power; all the activities of religious organization without the life. There may be many works, and yet He may say: I have found no work of yours fulfilled before My God, none that can stand the test and be really acceptable to God as a spiritual sacrifice. In Ephesus, it was works lacking in love, in Thyatira works lacking in purity, in Sardis works lacking in life.

"To Philadelphia: I know your works, that you have a little power, and did keep My word and did not deny My name. Because you did keep My word, I also will keep you."

On earth Jesus had said: *"He that has My commandments and keeps them, he it is that loves Me." "If a man love Me, he will keep My word, and My Father will love him."* Philadelphia, the Church for which there is no reproof, had this mark: its chief work, and the law of all its work, was, it kept Christ's word, not in an orthodox creed only, but in practical obedience. Let nothing less, let this truly, be the mark and spirit of all our work: a keeping of the word of Christ.

"To Laodicea: I know your works, that you are neither cold nor hot. You say, I am rich and have gotten riches, and have need of nothing." There is not a church without its works, its religious

activities. And yet the two great marks of Laodicean religion—lukewarmness, and its natural accompaniment, Self-complacence—may rob them of their worth. It not only, like Ephesus, teaches us the need of a fresh and fervent love, but also the need of that poverty of spirit, that conscious weakness out of which the absolute dependence on Christ's strength for all our work will grow, and which will no longer leave Christ standing at the door, but enthrone Him in the Heart.

"I know your works." He who tested the works of the seven churches still lives and watches over us. He is ready in His love to discover what is lacking, to give timely warning and help, and to teach us the path in which our works can be fulfilled before His God. Let us learn from Ephesus the lesson of fervent love to Christ, from Thyatira that of purity and separation from all evil, from Sardis that of the need of true life to give worth to work, from Philadelphia that of keeping His word, and from Laodicea that of the poverty of spirit which possesses the Kingdom of Heaven, and gives Christ the throne of all! Workers! Let us live and work in Christ's presence. He will teach and correct and help us, and one day give the full reward of all our works because they were *His own works in us.*

25

THY WILL BE DONE

The Blessedness of a Life in the Will of God

London: James Nisbet & Co. Ltd, 1901

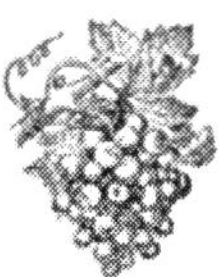

The Will of God, The Glory of Heaven

November 7th

"Thy will be done, as in Heaven, so on earth."

—MATTHEW 6: 10

In the will of God, we have the perfect expression of His Divine perfection. Because He is a fountain of all beauty and blessedness, His will is inconceivably beautiful and blessed. In it His Divine wisdom and goodness make themselves known. Through it alone the creature can know God; in accepting and doing that will we find the only and the sure way to fellowship and union with God.

The glory and the blessedness of Heaven consist in nothing but this, that God's will is done there in and by all. There is nothing to hinder God's working freely and fully all His blessed will in Heaven's countless hosts. To all that He wills for them of goodness and blessedness and service, the whole being [of each host of Heaven] is surrendered in submission and adoration. God lives in them and they in God; they are filled with the fullness of God.

In the Lord's Prayer our Blessed Master teaches us to come to the Father with the wonderful petition—that His will may be done on earth, even as in Heaven! He calls us to open our hearts, to think and lift them heavenwards in real desire and prayer. He bids us count upon an answer, and, according to the power that works in us, expect the experience in such measure as we are fitted for: God's will done in us and by us, on earth, as it is in Heaven. The God who works it in Heaven is our Father who delights to work it on earth. The blessedness of earth cannot possibly be other than that of Heaven: let our hearts desire and delight to have the will of God done.

Thy will be done, as in Heaven, so on earth! ... Come and meditate on this petition, if so be the Father may, by His Holy Spirit, show you the Divine beauty of His will, and the altogether heavenly blessedness of living in it. Let us begin by considering what God's will includes, that we may know aright what our Lord means and what we are to expect, when we pray: *Thy will be done*!

There is, first, the will of God's holy Providence. Everything that happens on earth comes to the child of God as the will of His Father. In His infinite wisdom God so overrules all the evil of men and devils, that in permitting it, He can take it up into His will, and make it work out His purposes. Joseph says of the sin of his brethren: "*You thought evil against me, but God meant it unto good.*" Jesus said to Pilate: "*You could have no power against Me except it were given you from above.*" In everything that came on Him, Jesus saw God's will: it was all the cup the Father gave Him. It is when the Christian learns to see God's will in everything that comes—grievous or pleasing, great or small—that the prayer, *Your will be done*, will become the unceasing expression of adoring submission and praise. The whole world, with its dark mysteries, and life, with all its difficulties, will be illumined with the light of God's presence and rule. And the soul will taste the rest and the bliss of knowing that it is every moment encircled and watched over by God's will, that nothing can separate it from the Love of which the will is the expression. Happy the Christian who receives everything in Providence as the will of His Father.

There is, next, the will of God's righteous Precepts. Every command of our Father in Heaven is a ray of the Divine will, radiant, to the eye that can see it, with all the perfection of the Divine nature. It comes as a proof of the Divine condescension, tenderly accommodating itself to our feebleness, as it puts the Divine will into human words, suited to our special capacity and circumstances. We all naturally connect the rays of light on earth with the sun from which they come. The more the Christian learns to link every precept with the Infinite Will of Love whence it comes, the more will he see the nobility and the joy of a life of entire obedience, the privilege and the honor of carrying out in human forms the perfect will of the Father in heaven. We then learn to say of God's precepts what first appeared too high: They are the rejoicing of my heart. And, *Your will be done*, as in Heaven, becomes the secret inspiration of a glad fulfilment of all God's commands.

Then comes—the will of God's precious Promises. We often fail in the power of grasping or holding some promise, of which we fain would have the comfort, because we deal with it as a fragment, and do not connect it with the great whole of God's blessed will for us. Let every believer seek earnestly to realize what God's will in His promises is. It is His determination to do a certain thing, His engagement to do it for or in me, if I will trust Him. Behind the promise there is the faithful Almighty God waiting to fulfil it. What a strength it would give in prayer, what a confidence in expectation, to be quiet, and trace the promise to the Living Will, the Loving Heart, that wills to make it true to everyone that yields himself in trust and dependence. As, Your will be done, in view of God's Providence, was the language of a glad submission, in view of His Precepts, the surrender to a full obedience, so here, in relation to the Promises, it becomes the song of an assured hope: Your Will will indeed be done, by You in us, O our Father in Heaven.

One thought more: There is the will of God's Eternal Purpose. Our view of God's will in His Providence, His Precepts, His Promises, is often very much confined to ourselves. The believer, who through these longs to enter fully into all the will of God, will be led on into a wider and a deeper insight into the glory of its counsels. We will learn something of that Great Purpose which filled the heart of God from Eternity, which reveals nothing less than the triumph of God's redeeming love in a world of sin. As we are led by the Holy Spirit into the great counsels of redemption—into the meaning of the sacrifice by which God has sought to accomplish them, of the patience with which He is working out His plans, and the final triumph which is so sure and so glorious—we feel how little we have realized our position or the meaning of this prayer. *Thy will be done, as in Heaven, so on earth*! becomes the expression of our fellowship with God in His wondrous carrying out of His everlasting counsel of grace, of our intercession on behalf of a perishing world, of our joyful anticipation of all flesh seeing the glory of God. We feel our Self as a mote floating in the sunlight of God's presence. We know our Self as an instrument—a vessel, a member of the body of Christ—through which God's glory is working out His perfect will.

Believer, come and listen. This prayer needs your whole heart. It needs the teaching, yea, the indwelling of Jesus Christ in the heart, to be able to pray it aright. It calls for a heart, a will, a life, entirely given up to the Father in Heaven, by His Spirit dwelling in us, to understand it aright. Let the glory of God doing His will in us and through us be met by nothing less than a will wholly given up to do His will on earth as it is done in Heaven. Study how God's will is done in Heaven. Yield yourself to do it even so on earth.

Standing Perfect, In All the Will of God

November 8th

"Epaphras, always striving for you in his prayers,
that you may stand perfect and fully assured in all the will of God."
—COLOSSIANS 4: 12.

In the first chapter of the epistle, we had Paul praying, here we have Epaphras. The prayers of both had reference to this one thing—of such supreme consequence is it in the Christian life— the will of God. Paul prayed that their hearts might be filled with the spiritual knowledge of God's will; then they would walk worthy of the Lord to all pleasing. Epaphras prays that their lives may be so filled with that will, that they may stand complete in all the will of God. Paul says that he does not cease to pray thus. Of Epaphras, he says that he always strives for them in his prayers. In both cases the relation to God's will is to be no partial or divided one—but whole and entire, as expressed by the word all. Paul asks that they may be filled with the knowledge of His will in all spiritual wisdom, to walk worthy of the Lord unto all pleasing. Epaphras strives for them in his prayers that they may stand complete in all the will of God. Nothing less than all God's will is to be the standard, the desire, the prayer, the hope of the believer.

To stand perfect in all the, will of God—the believer's only standard. How can it be otherwise? The will of God is one whole, all equally Divine, and beautiful, and blessed. All, all equal obligation, equally needful for our peace and perfection, with equal provision made for its performance in the grace that is in Christ Jesus. The will of God is so entirely one with the nature, the perfection, and the love of God, that to neglect or refuse any part of it is making it impossible for God fully to reveal Himself to us and to bless us. As perfect and complete as the will of God is as a whole, ought to be the believer's acceptance of and surrender to it as his only standard.

Paul and Epaphras regarded this as an attainable measure of perfection among the Colossians. There are many Christians who admit that the words express the Scripture standard of duty, but rob that admission of all its power by counting it impossible. The standard is only an ideal one, not really practicable or practical. They regard it very much as the law of Moses, with its demands that never can be fulfilled. They do not understand the words, "*You are not under law*," which demands what you cannot do, and gives no power to do, "*but under grace*," which demands only what it will give and work in you, and so enables you to do all it demands All His will is God's standard for us actually asked and provided for; let it be ours too. Your Father asks nothing less; let nothing less be what you ask of Him and offer Him.

To stand complete in all the will of God—the believer's one desire. Desire is the one great power in the world that urges and enables men to undertake and accomplish what at first sight appears impossible.

When we have set our heart upon a thing, difficulties only rouse our energy and increase our power. Oh, that Christians might be taught and trained to set their heart upon "*all the will of God*" as their highest and only blessedness, upon "*standing perfect in it*" as the one hope of their calling! It is to be feared that the preaching of the will of God has not had the same place as the preaching of the grace of God. …

To stand perfect in all the will of God—the believer's continual prayer. The teaching about the knowledge of God's will, and the standing complete in God's will, comes in connection with the telling of Paul's unceasing prayer and Epaphras' striving always. It is not earnest thought, or clear apprehension, or strong desire, that will bring us what we need—but unceasing prayer. Doing the will of God is the life of Heaven, because God is there, and works His will without hindrance in all the holy spirits who are wholly yielded up to Him and ever wait upon Him. It is from God in Heaven that this heavenly life of doing His will must come down. And it will come down and be carried on and maintained in us just in proportion as we too wait upon God, yield ourselves to Him, and continue offered up to His Holy Spirit to work in us. Whether it be in the quiet, steady perseverance of our daily prayer, or in the fervent striving in seasons when the need and the desire are specially felt, or in the inward supplication of the heart that prays without ceasing—it is only the life that is continually looking upward, and depending alone upon God's working His own will in us, that will feel that God's standard is not too high, because what the word of His mouth demands, the power of His hand performs.

To stand complete in all the will of God—the believer's sure hope. Paul and Epaphras were praying out of their blessed experience. We, alas! have grown so accustomed to use words in prayer for things we never expect. They lived so under the power of the Holy Spirit, they saw, notwithstanding so much to grieve and disappoint them, some whom they could call spiritual, and they knew that in answer to their prayer it would be given—Christians "*filled with the knowledge of God's will, in all spiritual wisdom,*" believers "*standing complete in all the will of God.*"

Let us pray without ceasing, let us strive always, for the churches or the saints with whom we are connected, that these two prayers may be fulfilled in them. Let us to that end ask God to reveal in ourselves and our experience their full truth and meaning. Amid all disappointment let us say: "*My soul, hope in God! I shall yet praise Him for the help of His countenance!*" Let us set our hope upon God, who works all things after the purpose of His will. … God alone can work His will in us. In a heart that prays and waits without ceasing in dependence upon Him, He can and will do it. Oh, let us believe that these precious words of Epaphras' prayer are not vain! in them the Holy Spirit reveals the sure hope of every believer who will trust God. Let us not doubt, but "*stand complete and fully assured in all the will of God.*"

Doing God's Will: The Secret of Abiding

November 9th

"*The world passes away, and the lust thereof: but the one that does the will of God abides forever.*"
—1 JOHN 2: 15, 17

Here we have once again the contrast between the two great powers that contend for mastery over us. We saw, in Romans 12: 2, how the great danger that threatens the consecrated man, and makes a life in God's will impossible, comes from the side of worldly conformity. And, in Galatians 1: 4, how the one great aim of God's will in the death of Christ was to deliver us from this present evil world. The irreconcilable hostility of the two principles is brought out here with equal force. "*If anyone loves the world, the love of the Father is not in them.*" Freedom from the love of the world, by the love of the Father utterly expelling it, is the law of the normal Christian life. And the exercise and discipline by which the true position is to be maintained, with the love of the Father and not the love of the world filling the heart and life, is the doing the will of God: "*The one that does the will of God abides forever*"— abides unchangeably in God and an unchangeable love.

What sacred associations there are connected with that word abiding! Abiding in

Christ and in His love (John 15); abiding in the Son and in the Father (1 John 2: 24, 28); God and Christ, the truth and the anointing abiding in us (1 John 2: 14, 27; 3: 24). The chief thought is permanent, steadfast, immovable continuance in the place and the blessing secured to us in Christ and God. The great secret of the world is its transitoriness—it passes away with all its glory. And all who are of it partake of its vanity and uncertainty. And just as far as the Christian breathes its spirit, and allows its love a place in his heart, he loses the power of abiding. All failure in abiding, all lack of permanence and perseverance in the Christian life, can have no other cause than that the spirit and life of the world are robbing the soul of its real and only strength. The Word and Will of God are unchangeable and eternal: *the one that does the will of God abides forever.* As a man does the will of God, and in doing appropriates it, feeds upon and assimilates it, its very essence enters into his being, and he becomes partaker of its Divine strength and unchangeableness. As the life of God is, so is His will, without variableness and shadow of turning. And as the will of God is taken up into the life of the believer, it too is changed into the likeness of the Divine life, and becomes freed from all the variableness and every shadow of turning which is the mark of this world. "*This world passes away*; *the one that does the will of God abides forever.*"

"*The one that does the will of God.*" It is by doing that the will of God enters into us, and communicates its own Divine unchangeableness. The revelation by the Spirit, the knowledge and contemplation of the love and adoration of the will of God—all these have their place and value. But it is not until we have really done, and are continually doing, the will of God, that it has really mastered us, conquered every enemy, and transformed us into the perfect likeness to itself. It is as the doing of the Father's will becomes our meat, that is, the satisfaction of our soul's hunger, and our nourishment, that God Himself becomes the strength of our life. It is only then that we are brought back to our original glory. We were created with a will, that into it we might receive the will of God, that God might work His will into us, and so we, in working that will out again, might become the partner and fellow-worker with God in all His works.

Jesus Christ, as man, restored human nature to its ideal destiny, and proved what blessedness and glory it is to live only to do the will of God. And the redeemed receive the Spirit of Jesus Christ that they, even as He, might find their life in accepting and living and doing nothing but the will of God. As God's will is the only power that upholds and secures the existence of the universe, so that will, done by the believer, is the one security that we never shall be moved. The whole of redemption, all that it reveals of pardoning and sanctifying and preserving grace, has this as its aim and its crown—that we should find our blessedness and our fellowship with God, our likeness to Him, in doing His will. "*The one that does the will of God abides forever.*"

Blessed abiding! How often believers have mourned and wondered that there was so little abiding peace and joy in their life—that the abiding in Christ and His love was so fluctuating and uncertain. They knew not how near the answer lay as to the cause: "*The one that does the will of God abides forever.*" They never noticed how distinctly our Lord had laid down this as the one condition of abiding in Him: "*If you keep My commandments, you shall abide in My love, even as I kept the commandments of My Father, and abide in His love.*" Could words make it plainer that obedience, doing His will, is the secret of abiding? And that if, instead of occupying ourselves with the abiding as the object of direct desire and faith and prayer, and effort, we were to give up ourselves wholly to keep the commandments and do the will, the abiding would come of itself, because it would be given us by a secret power from on High. "*The one that does the will of God abides forever,*" and will always and unceasingly abide.

It is to be feared that in the teaching of the Church of Christ, and in the life of the great majority of believers, the doing of the will of the Father has not that overwhelming prominence which it had in the life and teaching of Christ, as in the purpose of the Father. Any revival that is really to affect the spiritual life and elevate the standard of Christian living, must be a revival of holy living, with the vindication of God's claim that every child of His should give Himself to do God's will on earth as it is done in Heaven. … Everything depends upon the simple and whole-hearted acceptance of the great truth, that to be brought back to do the will of God is the one thing we have been redeemed for, and that doing that will is, on earth as in Heaven, with us, as with our Lord Jesus, the one secret of abiding in the love of God.

The Will of God, Your Sanctification

November 10th

"*For this is the will of God, even your sanctification.*"

— 1 THESSALONIANS 4: 3

The Apostle had closed the third chapter of this epistle with the wondrous prayer for the Thessalonian believers that the Lord might "*establish their hearts unblameable in holiness before our God and Father.*" … Just as he had pleaded with God to establish them unblameable in holiness, so he pleads with them to remember and yield to the blessed truth: "*This is the will of God, your sanctification.*" "*God has not called us for uncleanness, but for sanctification.*" The great plea against sin is that we are called to be holy. And the great power of holiness is that it is God's will for us.

And what is holiness? God alone is the Holy One. There is none holy but the Lord. There is no holiness but His. And nothing can be holy except as He makes it holy. "*Be holy, for I am holy.*" "*I am the Lord who sanctifies you.*" Holiness is the very nature of God, inseparable from His being, and can only be communicated by His communicating Himself and His own life. We are in Christ, *who is made of God unto us sanctification.* The Spirit of God is the Spirit of Holiness. We are God's "*elect in sanctification of the Spirit,*" "*chosen to salvation through sanctification of the Spirit.*" The Three-One God is the Thrice Holy One, and Father, Son, and Spirit each share in making us holy. Our part in sanctification consists in our recognizing how God makes us holy.

We have been sanctified in Christ Jesus. The new nature we have derived from Him has been created in true holiness. Our holy calling is in the power of the new, Divine, holy nature, to act out its impulses and principles. Our justification and our sanctification are equally in Christ, by union with Him, and therefore equally of faith. It is as we believe in God working in us, through Christ and the Spirit, that the inflow of the holy life from above is renewed, and that we have the courage and the power to live out the precepts that reveal the way in which it is to act. Like the whole of salvation, sanctification, or the life of holiness, is the result of man's co-operating with God. That means first of all his entire dependence on, and surrender to, the Divine operation, as the only source of goodness or strength. And then the acting out in life and conduct all that God has worked within us.

And what is now the help we can get from the words—*This is the will of God, your sanctification*? The first thought is that of the Divine obligation of holiness. God wills it. It is not enough to regard it in the other aspects in which it can be presented. It is indeed an essential element of the Christian life, the great proof of our gratitude for our deliverance from the guilt of sin, indispensable to true peace and happiness, our only preparation for Heaven. All this is of great importance.

But at the back of all this there is something of still greater force. We need to realize that God wills it. In eternity God predestinated us to be holy, "*we are elect according to the foreknowledge of God in sanctification of the Spirit*" (Ephesians 1: 4; 1 Peter 1: 2). God's whole purpose as a holy God, was to make us holy, as He is holy. The whole of redemption was ordered with a view to this. It is not only one of His commands, among many, it is the command which includes all. The whole being and character of God proclaim it; the whole nature and aim of redemption insist upon it; believers, God wills your sanctification! Worship God in His holiness, until every thought of God in His glory and grace is connected with the deep conviction: This blessed God wills my holiness. Rest not until your will has surrendered unconditionally to the will of God, and found its true destiny in receiving that Divine will and working it out.

A second thought that suggests itself is that of the Divine possibility of holiness. The will of God is not only a Divine purpose of what God is to do, or a Divine precept as to what we are to do, but a Divine power that works out its own purpose. All that God wills He works. Not, indeed, in those who refuse to accept or submit to that will. They have the power to resist it. But in those who yield their consent, who love that will and long that it should be done on earth as in Heaven, God Himself works out all things after the purpose of His will. In every one with a sound, strong will, it seeks at once to embody itself in action, and to effect what had been counted an object of desire. God works in us both to will and to do. When He has worked the willing, He delights, if He be waited on and yielded to, to work the doing.

When, by His grace, the believer wills as God wills, when we have accepted God's will for sanctification as our own will, we can count upon God's working it. God wills it with all the energy of His Divine being. God can as little cease working holiness as He can cease being holy or being God. He wills our sanctification; and if we will but will it too, in the faith of the new nature in which the Holy Spirit works, and yield ourselves to the will of Omnipotent Love in the assurance of His working in us, we shall experience how true and blessed the message is: God wills, and therefore most certainly works your sanctification.

The third lesson suggested by our text is—the Divine means of holiness. The will of God is your sanctification—that is, all that God wills has this one object, will secure this one result. ...This gives a new meaning, and its true glory, to every command of Scripture. The commands of God have unspeakable value, as marking out for us the path of safety and of life, as guiding us to all that is lovely and of good report. But here is their highest glory: through them the Holy One seeks to make us partakers of His own holiness. Do let us learn to regard every indication of God's will, in Scripture or in Nature, in things great or little, as the will of the Holy One coming to make us holy. Let every thought of God's will fill us with the longing and the hope to be holy.

And let every thought of holiness lead us to the study of, and the delight in, and the faithful doing of, God's will. Let every sin that God's Word forbids, such as those Paul mentions of uncleanness and fraud, be put far from us. Let everything that is of the earthly, carnal, Selfish nature be put off, that the whole spirit, soul, and body may be sanctified. Let every command that points to the true Christ-like life—humility, and love, and Self-sacrifice—be welcomed as the channel of God's holiness. The desire after, and delight and faith in, God's holiness and God's will become inseparably one. .... As we know Him as the Living God, and have intercourse with Him as the Holy, Loving, Almighty, ever-present and ever-working One, His will and His holiness will become to us heavenly realities, and we shall know how certainly, how blessedly, His will is our sanctification.

The Salvation of All; The Will of God

November 11th

"The Lord is longsuffering, not wishing that any should perish, but that all should come to repentance."
—2 PETER 3: 9

After Paul had urged that supplications, prayers, and intercessions should be made for all, he reminds us that we may do so in confident assurance that it is good and acceptable to God, because He wills that all should be saved. The knowledge and faith of God's will for all is to be the motive and the measure of our prayer for all. What God in Heaven wills and works for His children on earth, we are to will and work for too. As we enter into His will for all, we shall know what we are to do to fulfill that will. And as we pray and labor for all, the faith in His will for all will inspire us with confidence and love.

Perhaps the question arises, If God wills the salvation of all, how is it that it is not effected? What of the doctrine of election, as Scripture teaches it us? And what of the Omnipotence of God, which is surely equal to the Love that wills the salvation of all?

As to election, let us remember that there are mysteries in God and in Scripture which are beyond our reach. If there are apparently conflicting truths which we cannot reconcile, we know that Scripture was not written, like a book of science, to satisfy the intellect, but as the revelation of the hidden wisdom of God, to test and strengthen faith and submission, to waken love and childlike teachableness. If we cannot understand why His power does not work what His will has purposed, we shall find that, as the endowment of the creature with a free will is an act by which the will of God has limited itself.

All that God does or does not do is decided by conditions far beyond our ken, and which it needs a Divine wisdom to grasp and to order. We shall learn that God's will is as much beyond our comprehension as God's being, and that it is our wisdom and safety and happiness to accept every revealed truth with the simplicity and the faith of little children, and yield ourselves to it to prove its living power within our hearts. Let us not fear to yield ourselves to the uttermost to this blessed word: *God wills that all should be saved.*

God is love. His will is love. As He makes His sun to shine on the good and the evil, so His love rests upon all. However little we can understand why His love is so longsuffering and patient, and does not take its power and reign, we believe and know the love that God has for us—a love whose measure in Heaven is the gift of His Son, and on earth every child. His love is nothing but His will in its Divine energy doing its very utmost, in accordance with the Divine law by which His relation to His creature is regulated, to make us partakers of its blessedness. His will is nothing but His love in its infinite patience and tenderness delighting to win and bless every heart into which it can gain access.

If we only knew God and His love, how we should look upon every one we see as one upon whom that love rests and for whom it longs. We should begin to wonder at the mystery of grace that has taken up the Church, as the body of Christ, as a partner in the great work of making that love known, and rendered itself dependent upon its faithfulness. And we should see that all living to do God's will must lead up to this as its central glory: our doing the will that wills that all should be saved.

God wills that all should be saved. This truth is a supernatural mystery, not to be apprehended but by a spiritual mind through the teaching of the Holy Spirit. It is in itself so Divine and beyond our apprehension, the difficulties that surround it are so many and so real, it needs so much of time and of the sacrifice of the humble loving heart to master its teaching, that to very many the words carry but little meaning. To the believer, who in very deed seeks to know and do all God's will, they give a new meaning to life. We begin to see that this call to love and to save others is not something accidental or additional that, along with other things, goes up to make our life, and to which we can devote as much of time and thought as we see fit. We learn that just as this loving, saving will of God is the secret source of all His will, and rules it all, so this loving, saving will is to be the chief thing we live for too. I have been redeemed and organically united to and made a member of the saving Christ, who came to do this will of the Father. I have been chosen and set apart and fitted for this as the one object of my being in the world. I begin to see faintly that the prayer, *Thy will be done*! means above everything that I give myself for this loving, saving will of God to possess, to inspire, to use, if need be to consume me. And I feel the need of spelling out the words of the sentence till my heart can call them its own:

God —my God, who lives in me—wills, with His whole heart, in that will which He has revealed to His people that they may carry it into effect, that all—here around me, and to the ends of the earth—should be saved, should have everlasting life.

Paul wrote these words in connection with a call to prayer for all men. Our faith in the truth of God's loving, saving will must be put into practice. It must stir us to prayer. And prayer will most certainly stir us to work. We must not only seek to believe and feel the truth of these words, but must act. This will of God must be done. Let us look upon those around us as the objects of God's love, whom His saving will is seeking to reach. Let us, as we yield ourselves to this will, go and speak to those around us of God's love in Christ. It is possible that we are not succeeding in doing God's will in our personal life because we neglect the chief thing.

As we pray to be possessed and filled with the knowledge of this will of God, let us, in our Sunday-school class, or Gospel work, in our efforts for young or old, for poor or rich, seek to have hearts filled with this love, tongues that speak of Jesus and His salvation, and a will that finds its strength in God's own will—that all men should be saved. So will our life, and our love, and our work, and our will in some measure be like that of Jesus Christ—a doing of the Father's will, that none of these little ones should perish.

Praying According to God's Will

November 12th

"And this is the boldness which we have in Him, that, if we ask anything according to His will, He hears us. And if we know that He hears us, whatsoever we ask, we know that we have what have asked of Him."

—1 JOHN 5: 14–15

God works out His will through the willing and doing of His people. He works in them, all unconsciously to them, to will and to do. While they study His will in His Word, and take it up into their wills and lives and work it out, He is all the while working it out through them. It is a heart and life filled with the love of God's will that becomes the prepared instrument through which God can do His work.

It is with prayer as with work. As God has taken up into His eternal purpose the co-operation and the labor of His people, so their prayers too. These have their human origin in our desires as wakened by our need or by God's promises, and are yet God's own working in us. They cannot effect any change in the will of God, for they are God's will realizing itself through us, and their first condition is that they must be according to God's will They may indeed, and do, effect a change to what appears to be God's will, in what is His will for a time, or as a preliminary to something higher; their real power consists in their being according to God's will, because God works out His will as much through our prayers as our works.

The question has often caused much difficulty: How can I know that my prayers are according to the will of God? The question lies at the very root of our prayer life, as well as of a life in the will of God. It is not easy to give an exhaustive answer. And yet it may be possible to give suggestions that will enable thoughtful Christians to find the answer that meets their own case. The Holy Spirit, where He is to reveal the will of God, where He is too to help us in prayer, must be our Teacher.

Let us, first of all, see that we understand the words, "*According to His will*," correctly. Many connect them exclusively with "*anything*": the thing asked must be according to His will. But there is something more important than this—not only the thing asked for, but the disposition and character of the asker must be according to God's will. In this last lies the real secret of power in prayer. Two Christians both ask for something according to the will of God. He gives it to one and not to another. And why? Because the asking of the one was different from the other. We must connect the words, "According to His will," with asking. That will include both that the thing asked and the spirit of the asking be in harmony with God's will.

That the latter is of primary importance is evident from our Lord's teaching of His disciples. He continually connected the answer to prayer with their state. They must forgive, they must be merciful, they must be humble, they must be believing, they must ask in His name, they must abide in Him in keeping His commandments, and His words abide in them; their life must be according to God's will. If they loved Him, and kept His commandments, He would pray the Father for them. Only the man whose life and conduct, whose heart and disposition, is according to God's will, can ask according to His will. So James speaks of the fervent, effectual prayer of the righteous man. And John says, "*Whatever we ask we receive, because we kept His commandment.*" It is the life that prays; the prayer has power according to the life; a life according to God's will can ask according to God's will.

One great reason of this is that the man who lives according to God's will is able spiritually to discern what he may ask for. A Christian may take some promise of God's word, say for the conversion of sinners, and begin and pray for someone in the mere power of human love, and without seeking at all to be led by the Spirit into the faith that enables him to pray successfully. It is simply a matter of human will; I would like the conversion of this friend. God wills that all should be saved; I will ask it. While there is no thought of that abiding in Christ through obedience to which the promise of an answer has been given. This is not asking according to the will of God, in the deep consciousness of dependence on the Holy Spirit, in that true obedient abiding in Christ Jesus which alone is truly asking in His Name. Doing is the only way to knowing the will of God, and therefore the only way of asking according to His will.

As long as I only desire to know God's will with regard to certain things I desire or need, I may find it difficult to know it. A life yielded to and molded by the will of God will know what and how to pray. A heart seeking to be "*filled with the knowledge of His will in all wisdom and spiritual understanding*," and striving fervently "*to stand perfect and complete in all the will of God*," will be able joyfully to appropriate the promise, "*This is the boldness we have toward Him, that if we ask anything according to His will, He hears us.*"

Let us try and learn the lessons: Boldness in prayer comes from the assurance that both the spirit of asking and the thing we ask are according to the will of God. ... In all our prayers that we have learnt from His Word, let us take time to realize that they are indeed according to God's loving, mighty will, and therefore sure to be heard. … Let us remember how essentially one our lives and our prayers are, and live wholly to God's will—that will ensure our praying according to His will. … Let us pray first and wait for the things that God has clearly revealed to be His will, things that concern His love and kingdom and glory—that will give us liberty with the lesser things that concern our interests. … Only the Holy Spirit in the spirit of prayer can lead us into the will of God, as we wait on Him even in the things we know to be according to God's will. He can give us Divine assurance in regard to things that no human reason could believe beforehand to be God's will. … Let our first desire in regard to every petition ever be: Lord, teach me how to pray only according to Your will.

God's will is at first a deep hidden mystery. He that lives to that will as far as he knows it, may count upon being led deeper into it as the manifestation of a holy, mighty, infinite goodness. Let me give myself to it as to Infinite Love. God works out His will equally by the works and the prayers of His people. Yield yourself equally without reserve to that will, in working as in praying, in praying as in working. The absolute joyful surrender of our life to that will, in full obedience and in perfect truth, gives boldness in doing and in asking. And this text, instead of being a stumbling-block, will give us new joy and confidence in prayer, because the prayer according to the will of God must prevail.

Doing God's Will: The Way to Heaven

November 13th

"Not everyone who says to Me, Lord, Lord, shall enter into the kingdom of Heaven; but the one that does the will of My Father…."

—MATTHEW 7: 21.

We have seen that the will of God constitutes the glory of Heaven. Heaven is nothing but the unhindered manifestation of the working of God's will, the outshining of His hidden glory in what He does. … The petition in the Lord's Prayer teaches us to long and ask that earth may become like Heaven, and that His will may be done here even as there. From this truth that of our text follows naturally: The only way to be fit to enter Heaven must be to do the will of God here on earth. Every thought of Heaven that does not lead us to do the will of God is a vain imagination.

There are multitudes of Christians who have never seen this. They think that the way to heaven is found in pious desires and religious duties, in trusting Christ for mercy, and seeking to be kept from gross sin. But the thought that Christ puts here—that only those who love to do the will of God can enter Heaven—has never taken possession of their mind or heart. And yet our Lord makes the difference between the religion of prayer and profession, and the religion of obedience and performance, as plain as words can make it: Not everyone that says unto Me, Lord, Lord—that prays to Me and professes to acknowledge and honor Me as Savior; but those that does the will of My Father in Heaven—they alone shall enter the kingdom of Heaven.

It is the Father's presence and the Father's will in Heaven that makes Heaven what it is: doing the Father's will on earth is the only conceivable way of entering heaven: nothing else can give the capacity for enjoying it. There must always be harmony between a life and its environment. To enter the heaven of God's will, without a nature that loves and does God's will, is an impossibility.

But, how then comes the terrible mistake that so many make, who think that they are honestly longing and striving to get to Heaven? Let us try and answer this question. In everything that exists there is an outward form or shape in which it manifests itself and an inward power or life which constitutes its true nature or being. It is thus with Heaven and our thought of it. We regard it as a place full of brightness and glory and happiness—free from all sorry or pain, full of all that can give rest and joy. And who would not wish to enter there? The most worldly hope to find a place in it when compelled to leave the present life. But they never think that what attracts them is only an external image they form of Heaven. And they know not what constitutes the actual, essential glory of Heaven—what really gives Heaven and its inhabitants their rest and joy and everlasting song—is the Presence of the Father who is in Heaven, and the undisturbed supremacy of His Holy Will. Because in Heaven God's will does everything, and is done by everyone, God's own blessedness fills all. Oh, the folly of thinking of entering Heaven while they are utterly incapable of enjoying Heaven! The Father in Heaven, and His will on earth as in Heaven, are not the desire or joy of their heart.

The same error, in mistaking the outward for the inward, is made in regard to religion. God's Word calls us to seek and to strive, to listen to God's truth, to pray and believe, to forsake sin and follow after that which is good. And so we seek to put our trust in Christ, to confess Him, and do many things in His name, and think that this is religion. And all the while we forget that the inner spiritual reality of true religion is this—the knowing, and loving, and doing of the Father's will as our one desire and delight.

Did not Christ just come for those who had sinned, and had not done God's will? He did indeed, blessed be God! But not for those who continue in sin, and do not make the will of God the object of their life. Our sin and misery was that we had fallen out of the will of God into our own will and the will of Satan. Christ came with the one object of redeeming us from the power of our own will, and giving us a new nature and His Holy Spirit, to enable us here on earth to love and do God's will. Without this, our Lord assures us, there can be no thought of our entering Heaven.

The same righteous grace that in Justification receives the ungodly into favor without works, through faith alone, for the sake of Christ and His work, will in the great day take the works and the life into account as the proof of the reality of faith and union to Christ, and of the fitness for entering Heaven. As we are saved without works, "*we are created in Christ Jesus for good works, which God afore prepared that we should walk in them.*" Without these there can be no entrance into heaven; they are indispensable. The Master's words are plain and decisive: They that do the will of My Father in Heaven, will enter into the Kingdom of Heaven (Study carefully Matthew 16: 27; 25: 31–46; Romans 2: 6–7; 2 Corinthians 5: 10).

Christ came from Heaven to show us that doing the will of the Father is the one mark of a son of God, and to save us into doing that will. True conversion is turning away from our Self-will and giving ourselves to the will of God as our duty and our only blessedness. I ask every believer who reads this to inquire, and say whether he thinks that the doing of the Father's will, as the one object of Christ's salvation, and the one preparation for entering heaven, has taken the place in his life and faith and conduct, that it had in the life and conduct and teaching of Jesus Christ. ...

All salvation on earth or in Heaven is—doing the will of God. If we find that this blessed truth has never shone with its full heavenly light into our souls, let us at once turn to our Lord Jesus and ask Him to teach us. Let us give ourselves up to it, to study, to believe, to practice, to rejoice in it. Let us each day choose the will of God, His whole will, and nothing but His will, to have rule over us and dwell within us. The living Father, whose love can make it our blessedness, through the living Christ, who loves to teach it us and work it in us, will enable us to do His will.

26

KEY TO THE MISSIONARY PROBLEM

Thoughts on the Report of the Ecumenical Missionary Conference New York, April 1900

New York: Fleming H. Revell Co., 1902

Foreign Missions: A Test of the State of the Church

November 14th

"If the root be holy, so are the branches."

—ROMANS 11: 16

I was glad to read, on the first page of our program, those dying words of Simeon Calhoun: "It is my deep conviction, and I say it again and again, that IF the Church of Christ were what she ought to be, twenty years would not pass away till the story of the cross would be uttered in the ears of every living man." And to quote only one more instance Rev. W. Perkins, Secretary of the Wesleyan Missionary Society, London, said "Great as are the results of Foreign Missions, over which we rejoice and give thanks, they would have been a hundredfold greater, IF the Church had been what she ought to be in the two great matters of prayer and beneficence."

We all know the force of the word IF. It suggests the cause from which certain effects follow. It points to the conditions needed to ensure the results we desire. In the passages we have quoted, and in different forms of expression frequently recurring in missionary literature, we find the same thought incessantly repeated: It tells us how certainly and speedily the evangelization of the world would be accomplished, were it not for the failure of the Church in doing the part that has been assigned her by God. …

1. These IFs all indicate something wrong in the Church in reference to Christ's command to evangelize the world. … Here is the solemn fact: a Church, purchased by the blood of the Son of God to be His messenger to a dying world, for the greater part failing entirely in understanding or fulfilling its calling. …

2. And let us not think that it is owing to some fatal necessity, some natural impossibility, that it is so. … These IFs suggest what is certainly and divinely possible. They point us to the Church of Pentecost. "To evangelize the world in this generation is possible," they say, "in view of the achievements of the Christians of the first generation. They did more to accomplish the work than has any succeeding generation. In studying the secret of what they accomplished, one. is led to the conclusion that they employed no vitally important method which, cannot be used today, and that they availed themselves of no power which we cannot utilize." The mighty power of God and His Holy Spirit are ours as theirs. The power of His dying love in the heart; of a triumphant faith in Christ; of simple, bold, personal testimony; of patient suffering; of absolute passionate consecration; the heavenly power that overcomes the world and makes us more than conquerors through Him that loved us all these belong to us as much as to them. …

3. These IFs invite us to an inquiry as to the causes of the terrible failure. How comes it that the Church of Christ has been so utterly unfaithful? Does not our Protestant Christendom profess, and that honestly, to acknowledge Christ its Lord, and God's holy Word as the law of its life? … Is it not our boast that we are in the true succession of the Pentecostal Church, the heir of all its promises and powers? … And is it not the very sum and center of our profession, that we acknowledge Jesus as Master and Lord, and have given ourselves to do what He says? And how comes it that, in the very thing on which Christ's glory most depends, on which His heart of love is most set, the Church should have failed to realize or fulfill its destiny?

It would be easy to mention many causes that co-operate in producing this unfaithfulness. But they may all be summed up in the one answer: The low spiritual state of the Church as a whole. The control of the Holy Spirit in power and fullness over the life of believers is essential to the health and strength of the Church. Scripture teaches us how easy it is for a Church and its members to have a sound creed, a faithful observance of religious services and duties, a zeal for the extension of the Church and for works of philanthropy, which are within the range of human nature, while that which is definitely spiritual, supernatural, and Divine is to a large extent lacking.

The spirit of the world, the wisdom and the will of man in the teaching of the Word and the guidance of the Church, make it very much like any human institution, with little of the power of the heavenly world and the endless life to be seen in it. In such a Church, missions may have a place, though not the place nor the power which is needed for fulfilling the command of Christ. The passion of love to Christ and to souls, the enthusiasm of sacrifice for men, and of faith in the omnipotent Power that can quicken the dead, is wanting.

Among the chief symptoms of this sickly state are worldliness and lack of prayer. If there is one thing that Christ and Scripture insist on, it is that His kingdom is not of this world, that the spirit of the world cannot understand the things of God, that separation from the world in fellowship and conduct, and surrender to the Spirit which is from Heaven, is essential to the faithful following of the Lord Jesus.

The one universally admitted fact that the majority of Christians care and give nothing for missions, that a large number give but little and not from the highest motives, is simply a proof of the worldliness in which most Christians live, and which the Church either does not seek, or is not able, to cast out. It needed Christ to come from Heaven to save men out of the world: it needs nothing less than the Spirit of Heaven in Christ's disciples to free them from the spirit of the world, to make them willing to sacrifice all to win the world for Christ. It needs the same Spirit, through which Christ gave His life for the world, to revive His Church to win the world for God.

Lack of prayer is another symptom of this sickly state. A worldly spirit in the Christian hinders our praying much. We look at things in the light of the world; we are not at home in the heavenly places; we do not realize the dark power of sin in those around us, or the urgent need of a direct Divine interposition. We have little faith in the efficacy of prayer, in the need of much and unceasing prayer, in the power there is in him to pray in Christ's name and prevail. True beneficence, the giving from devotion to Christ and for Him, and true prayer, the asking and counting upon Him to bless the gift and bestow His Spirit in His work, are the proof that the worldly spirit is being overcome, and that the soul is being restored to spiritual health.

The Church of Pentecost and the Holy Spirit 1

November 15th

We have looked at three cases in which we have seen how wonderfully God has led His servants in modern times into the secret of power and blessing in the mission field. Let us now go back to Pentecost, and there see how, in the birth of the Christian Church, are revealed the great root-principles in which, through all ages, it will find the law of its service and its triumph over the powers of darkness. …

The words in which Mr. Mott appealed to the example of the pentecostal Church:

> It is possible to evangelize the world in this generation in view of the achievements of the Christians of the first generation. They did more to accomplish the evangelization of the world than any succeeding generation. The persecutions of the first and second centuries attest how vigorously the faith of Christ must have been propagated by the first disciples. … In studying the secret of what they accomplished, one is led to the conclusion that they employed no vitally important method which cannot be used today, and that they availed themselves of no power which we also cannot

utilize. …

If this statement be true, and it is true, it is a terrible condemnation to the Church of our day. And if the admission of the truth is to have any real influence to stimulate or to guide, it is needful that we take time to come to the deep conviction of wherein the difference between us and them consists, and what it is that can enable us truly to walk in their footsteps, and do our work as they did theirs. Our ascended Lord has not only given us His Holy Spirit, but in the men in whom He first came to dwell, the living embodiment of what He is able to do for us too.

It has been well said that men become interested not so much in abstract ideas, as in individuals who represent these ideas. The Church of the first generation is given us by God as an example and a pledge of what the Holy Spirit can do in men wholly possessed by Him. If the Church of our day is really to be and do what God desires it to be and do, pastors and congregations must be led to study the pentecostal pattern, and to be content with nothing less than an equal devotion to the work of making Christ everywhere known. A tree can only thrive and grow strong by abiding in the root from which it was born. The missionary revival we need and pray for within the Church, ere it is fitted to do its work aright, can only come by a return to Pentecost. The end is ever contained in the beginning, and returns to the beginning. To know what Pentecost means, to have its faith and its Spirit, is the only power to evangelize the world in this generation.

Let us strive to realize our position. The great commission was given in connection with Pentecost, and its fulfilment was made entirely dependent on it. "*It behoved … that repentance and remission of sins should be preached in His name among all nations; but tarry at Jerusalem, until you be endued with power from on high.*" "*You shall receive power, when the Holy Spirit is come upon you, and you shall be My witnesses unto the ends of the earth.*" The pentecostal commission can only be carried out by a pentecostal Church, in pentecostal power.

The charge has been laid against the Church of our day, and admitted, that she is not what she ought to be. It is vain to think of this generation accomplishing the pentecostal commission without a return to the pentecostal state.

The great and burning question of the missionary problem is, How can the Church be brought back to the place where the disciples and the early Church were, when, in the power of the Holy Spirit, they did what no other generation since their time has done? The Church of Pentecost was not merely an example and pledge of what God could do, leaving it to us to choose if we would enjoy the same blessing. Nay, it is much more a revelation of God's will as to what His Church ought to be, and of what is absolutely indispensable if there is to be any real hope of securing obedience to the command to bring the gospel to every creature. The pentecostal state is the only one that satisfies God, the only one that ought to satisfy us.

Like all seed, Pentecost was a fruit too. The fruit not only of Christ's work for us on the cross and in Heaven, but the fruit also of His work in the disciples in preparing them for the reception of the Spirit. The pastor who would learn what the missionary enthusiasm of his ministry ought to be, and how he can communicate it to his people; the leader of a mission circle who would fain find for his band the full equipment for the service of the Kingdom; every believer who would personally learn from his Lord the secret of entire devotion to His work, of being filled with His Spirit, and of winning souls to the knowledge of His love must become a learner in the school in which Christ trained His disciples. There we find how they were fitted to be the vessels and channels of the Spirit on earth, when He should have gone to Heaven.

The first coming of the Holy Spirit in power was to a prepared people. For the Church in our day to receive the Spirit in pentecostal power there is a need of the same preparation, a giving up and forsaking of all that hinders, an emptying and a cleansing, a thirsting and waiting and entire surrender, to which the blessing of the Spirit's power surely comes. Let us consider what were the chief elements of that training:

1. There was, first of all, a calling out and separation from the ordinary interests and claims of daily life. The principle that underlies the life of all God's great servants in the previous ages Abraham and Joseph, Moses and Joshua, David and Elijah is a taking out of and setting apart of them from their ordinary environment, often by persecution and suffering, that they might be brought into solitude with God alone, and be free and disengaged, from what is otherwise innocent or lawful on earth, to listen to the Divine voice, to receive the Divine revelation, to be changed and fitted by the Divine power for the work they had to do. Even so Christ called His disciples to forsake all, to deny themselves what to others might be perfectly legitimate, and to share with Him His cross and all it would entail. For three years He had them in His training by His intercourse, by the sight of what He did, by His reproofs and instructions, preparing them to be the recipients and the channels of that Holy Spirit from Heaven, who should come to take the place of His earthly presence, and open within them His abiding indwelling.

In a sinful world, sacrifice is the law of life and of love. The men whom Christ had fitted to become the leaders of the pentecostal Church, and to embody in their lives His own, with the mind and the life of the Spirit, had learned to give up everything for Christ. As their Lord could not give Himself for us without sacrificing all, they too had learned, in giving themselves, to part with all for the sake of His service and Kingdom. In that entire Self-abandonment of their Lord to one purpose the pentecostal Church had struck its roots deep.

In a time when there is no persecution, when money and comfort and Christian civilization surround us on every side, when it appears to cost little to be a Christian, many find it difficult to know where the forsaking all to become a disciple comes in, or what shape it will assume. We shall find the answer if we think of the second great element in Christ's training of His disciples.

2. This was an intense personal attachment to Christ, as the chief fruit of their three years intercourse. When Christ first called them, there was something in Him that attracted them and made that call irresistible. As Christ drew them without their knowing how and why, so He led them by a way and to a goal they knew not. They began by believing in Him as the Messiah: He led them on to know Him as the Son of God, as a Friend, as a Master, as a Redeemer. Of His love to them, or theirs to Him, He said little or nothing till the last night of His life.

Then He opened up to them the mystery of His loving them with a Divine love of His giving His life for them, of the Father's love resting on them, of their loving Him and keeping His commandments. It was not the disciples who had followed Him with any thought of such an aim: it was Christ who had, by His Divine love, thus, in the course of His three years training, attached them to Himself. It is this intense personal living attachment to Christ that prepares for receiving the Holy Spirit, and brings that pentecostal power without which the Church cannot hope to conquer the world. …

Detachment comes only through a new and stronger attachment. As Christians see that, though we know so little of our Lord's love, the Lord is ready to lead us on to it in a way we know not, we become willing to turn away from everything that can occupy the heart, and to yield our Self, in patient obedient discipleship, to the influences of intercourse with our Lord. We learn to believe that that love can master us. The love of Christ asks and claims the whole heart and life.

If we are really to appeal to our Churches to follow in the footsteps of the pentecostal Church, and to claim its power and blessing, do let us encourage them to enter the school in which Christ trained His disciples. When the love of Christ becomes everything to any of us, and we yield ourselves to His love, dying for sinners, to take possession of us and use us, that love will teach us, it will constrain us, to part with all for this pearl of great price. Detachment from the world, attachment to Christ, are the secrets of pentecostal blessing.

3. Closely connected with this love, as another element of preparation for Pentecost, was the brotherly love which Christ had taught them and wrought in them. He had bound them to Himself, but also to each other. Christ ever dealt with individual men. He calls His sheep by name. He knows and meets the needs of each. But His work does not end there. He makes them members of His body. The Divine life is a life of love. He leads us into a life of love; He calls us, His Spirit enables us, to love each other as He loved us. His own love is to dwell in us, and bind the body into a living whole.

In this is to be the Church's power to convince the world of its Divine origin: a love that is supernatural and Divine. The union this love gives brings strength to each member, multiplying the strength of all by the aid derived from the whole body. It was this love that often made men say, See how they love one another. It was this love, in the unity of the body, that made feeble men and women strong to conquer.

… When we begin to seek Christ's Spirit in earnest for our mission work, or when we think that His first movings are felt, do let us remember that there is no place where the Spirit works so surely as when we are gathered together with our brethren into the Name of Jesus.

To speak together of that name and love has more to do with our spiritual life than we think. To give ourselves to encourage the feeble, to instruct the ignorant, to warn the erring, by telling what Christ is to us, is one of the sure means of drawing down the presence of the Lord, of building the separate members into one body, of rousing the hope of all and preparing them for that blessed outpouring of the Spirit which is indispensable if we are to witness for Christ in power.

The Church of Pentecost and the Holy Spirit 2

November 16th

Is it necessary to speak of faith as one of the chief lessons that was needed for the pentecostal mission work of the first century and of ours?

4. It was not only in His direct teaching of the disciples, but in all He said to others in their hearing, and in all the proofs He gave in their presence of the indispensable need, of the conditions, of the power of faith, that He trained them into the apprehension of the place it must have in their life and work,

We know what faith is. From the first simple faith that hears a promise and believes God's Word, to the faith that enters into full and conscious union with our Lord, and abides in Him and does the "greater works," faith is ever one of the first conditions of the power of the Spirit's working. The pentecostal Church received and maintained its blessing and power, did its work, endured its sufferings, and gained its conquests, all through faith.

Faith is such a simple thing that many think it an easy thing. As the power to overcome the world, and cast out Satan, and bring men out of darkness into God's light, it is no easy thing. It implies the renunciation of Self, the crucifixion to the world, the ceasing from man with his wisdom and his power, and dependence on God alone. We speak of faith missions, in which faith, in some one of its special aspects is specially prominent. We need to emphasize the great truth that all mission work is to be faith work. And that, if this is to be, we want to begin at the beginning, and seek not only to have the word mixed with faith in them that hear, but to have all our work and prayer mixed with faith too. "*By faith Abel offered a better sacrifice.*"

When the offering of money in a collection is as sacred a thing as the offering of prayer, when the faith which is essential to make a prayer effectual is seen to be just as indispensable to make a gift effectual, we shall find the point of contact in dealing with individual believers, and our missionary meetings and collections will become as helpful to the life of faith as the preaching of the gospel. From the individuals we shall then rise to the various societies or congregations to which they belong, and through these on to leaders and directors and missionaries, until all unite in the one deep and overmastering conviction: Mission work is faith work. When the faith which comes from knowing Christ, in His saving power in ourselves, in His saving power over all, from knowing Him as the Triumphant and Almighty One who Himself will work in them that believe in Him, is acknowledged as indispensable for all our workers at home and abroad, we shall be approaching the new pentecostal era.

5. One more thought. When Christ ascended the throne, one would say the preparation was complete. It was not so. One thing more was needed to finish the work. Even

with the three years training, the mysterious influence of the fellowship with Christ in the death they had seen Him die, the mighty power of the resurrection-life He breathed into them, the wonderful revelations of the forty days all in the power of the New Life, the ascension to the throne and the sitting down at the right hand of the Father, and Christ's receiving from Him of the Holy Ghost, there is still something needed. It was the ten days of continued, united prayer and supplication. I hardly know a passage in Scripture which presents prayer in such a wondrous light. God in heaven has done all that was needed; Christ has finished His work for His disciples and in them: Pentecost has still to wait ten days for their prayers. Prayer is to put the finishing touch to the work of preparation. In it is to be found that complete and continuous turning away from earth, that opening of the whole being to God, that rising into heaven, and that abiding in Christ there, which is to prove that these men are indeed prepared vessels for God's Holy Spirit. When Jesus had been glorified, when the Lamb had taken His place in the midst of the throne, the stream of the river of the water of life broke forth from the throne of God and the Lamb, and flowed as streams of living water into and out of these praying disciples.

It is even as it is written of Christ: "*And it came to pass that, Jesus also being baptized, and praying, the heaven was opened, and the Holy Spirit descended upon Him.*" When every other condition has been fulfilled, prayer, continued prayer, is needed to bring down the blessing. If the pentecostal Church is to be an example, and that cannot be without the pentecostal era being repeated, prayer must again be the key that opens the windows of Heaven. Prayer must be preached and practiced as the first and the last duty of a Church that hopes to have the power of God seen in its work. The ten days continued prayer must teach the lesson that is so simple, and yet so difficult to master, that what little prayer does not obtain, much prayer, earnest believing prayer, prayer continued long enough, will bring down.

It was said in the words we quoted at the beginning of this chapter: "They availed themselves of no power which we cannot also utilize." We have seen what some of these powers are. The power of separation from the world and true Self-sacrifice, of intense attachment and devotion to Jesus, of love and fellowship making us one with the saints around us, of faith, of continued prayer these were the things that fitted the disciples to receive the promise of the Father, and be the fit instruments for the Holy Spirit's mighty work in witnessing for Christ to the uttermost parts of the earth.

We have seen the preparation, the wonderful forming of men to have, in human nature, as Jesus had, the Spirit of God dwelling in them. Think, now, how wonderful this blessing was in itself the fruit and the crown of Christ's redeeming work. These men, prepared by Christ, were all filled with the Holy Spirit. On earth Christ's body had been the home of the Spirit and the instrument of His work. They now are His body; they take His place; the Spirit dwells in them as the instruments for His work, the continuance of Christ's own work. The Spirit, through whom God is God, and Father and Son each is what He is, and both are One, the Spirit, the very life of God, fills them.

In the threefold operation of His quickening grace, He enlightens, He sanctifies, He strengthens. That is, He reveals Divine truth, He makes partaker of the holy life and disposition of Christ, and He endues with the Divine power that, in the midst of weakness, labors and suffers and triumphs. As Christ's training was to prepare them, so this enduement was actually to fit them for His work. "*You shall receive power when the Holy Spirit is come upon you.*" God's power for God's work was to be the one condition of success in their undertaking to bring the gospel to every creature, in being Christ's witnesses to the ends of the earth.

"That pentecostal generation did more to accomplish the evangelization of the world than any succeeding generation." If we are to do as much as they did, considering the increase in the population of the world and the increase of the Church, we ought to do tenfold more than they did, we need this one thing: To be filled with the Holy Spirit, as the Power of God to do the work of God! It is not enough that the river of the water of life is still flowing from under the throne of God and the Lamb; it is not enough that we are the temple of God, and the Spirit of God dwells in us. The Spirit may be in us, and yet be grieved, or quenched, or resisted, or neglected. Where He is to work in power, He asks the whole being, to fill it. He claims control of the whole life, for it to be led and ruled by Him in everything. He asks that the man shall be a living sacrifice, a whole burnt-offering, to be consumed by the fire of God. If there is to be any hope of our working like the Church of Pentecost, we must have a new era in our missions.

There must be a real restoration of the pentecostal life and power in the Church at home. The *power* of God for the *work* of God must be the watch word of every worker. Then alone will our mission work, both in its extent and its intensity, be able to overtake the thousand millions who are still without the knowledge of Christ.

If the appeal that has been made to the Church, to believe that there is nothing which the pentecostal Church did that we cannot and ought not to do, is to be taken seriously, what are we to do with it? We are confessedly, in an overwhelming majority of our Church members, very far from Pentecost. What is to be done to get all our leaders in churches and boards, hi societies and committees, to take up the watchword: Back to Pentecost. Without this the work cannot be done?

Is there no way of reaching our pastors and congregations, and gathering all who feel that God's work is not being done as it should be, into one holy bond of union until the watchword has rung through the Church: Back to Pentecost; God's Power for God's work? Without this the work cannot be done.

The missionary problem is a personal one. Every believer, in receiving the love of Christ into his heart, has taken in a love that reaches out to the whole world. On every member of the Church the great commission rests: The gospel to every creature. Let each of us begin with himself in seeking for the Church the restoration of her pentecostal power for the work of conquering the world for her King. It was prayer brought Pentecost intense, continued, united prayer; prayer that did not cease till it was answered. Such prayer is not an easy thing. As Hudson Taylor said at the Conference:

> Not only must the missionaries suffer in going forth, but the Church must go forward in Self-denial to the point of suffering. Redemptive work, soul-saving work cannot

be carried on without suffering. If we are simply to pray to the extent of a simple, pleasant, and enjoyable exercise, and know nothing of watching in prayer, and weariness in prayer, we shall not draw down the blessing we may. We shall not sustain our missionaries, who are overwhelmed with the appalling darkness of heathenism; we shall not even sufficiently maintain the spiritual life of our own souls. We must serve God even to the point of suffering, and each one ask himself, In what degree, in what point, am I extending, by personal suffering, by personal Self-denial even to the point of pain, the kingdom of Christ?"

Let us give ourselves anew to prayer, that the Church may be restored to her pentecostal state. Let us by faith yield ourselves wholly to the Spirit, and receive Him by faith to fill us. Let us give ourselves to prayer for the power of the Spirit in the life and work of the Church at home and abroad. The pentecostal command to preach the gospel to every creature is urgent, all the more from having been neglected so long. The need of the pentecostal power is urgent beyond all thought. Yet prayer brought it. Prayer still brings it. And few feel how feeble our power of prayer and our power in prayer is. Let us go back and study what it was that fitted these humble fishermen and women to pray so. It was this one thing: Jesus Christ had their whole heart. They had forsaken everything for Him. His love filled them and made them one with Him, and with each other. The fellowship of love strengthened them. Their ascended Lord was everything to them: they could not but pray. Let us pray in secret. Let us unite in love with others, and pray without ceasing, and watch unto prayer that, for the sake of His Son and a perishing world, God would restore His people to their first estate in the devotion and power and joy of Pentecost.

But let us ever again remember: The Missionary Problem is a personal one. A passionate love to Jesus Christ, born out of His love, truly possessing each of us personally, will teach us to pray, and to labor, and to suffer. Let us pray for such a love.

A Missionary Ministry

November 17th

We need not seek to apportion exactly the measure of responsibility as between the ministry and the membership of the Church; that on the ministry a holy and heavy responsibility rests in this matter, all are agreed. Let all ministers heartily admit and accept it, and prepare themselves to live up to it. Let us try, first of all, to find the ground on which that responsibility rests. The principles out of which it grows are simple, and yet of inconceivable importance. They are these four: That missions are the chief end of the Church. That the chief end of the ministry is to guide the Church in this work, and fit her for it. That the chief end of the preaching in a congregation ought to be to train it to take its part in helping the Church to fulfil her destiny. And that the chief end of every minister in this connection ought to be to seek grace to fit himself thoroughly for this work.

Let no one think these statements exaggerated. They appear so because we have been so accustomed to give missions a very subordinate place in our thoughts of the Church and its ministry. We need ever to be brought back to the great central truth, "the mystery of God," that the Church is the body of Christ, as absolutely and exclusively ordained by God to carry out the purpose of His redeeming love in the world as Christ the Head Himself. The Church has, even as Christ, but one object of being to be the light of the world. As Christ died for every man, as God wills that all men should be saved, so the Spirit of God in the Church knows no object but this that the gospel be brought to every creature. Missions are the chief end of the Church. All the work of the Holy Spirit in converting sinners and sanctifying believers, has this for its one aim to fit them for the part that each must at once take in winning back the world to God. Nothing less than what God's eternal purpose, and Christ's dying love, aimed at, can be the aim of the Church. As we see this to be true, we shall see that the chief end of the ministry ought to be to fit the Church for this. Paul writes, "*God gave pastors and teachers for the perfecting of the saints unto (as what these saints have to do) the work of ministering, or serving, unto (as the final aim of this work of the saints) the building up of the body of Christ*" (Ephesians 4: 11–16). It is through the ministering, the loving service of the saints that the body of Christ is to be gathered and built up. And the pastors and teachers are given to perfect the saints for this work of ministering. …

Each congregation is meant to be a training class. Every believer, without exception, is to be "perfected," to be thoroughly fitted for the work of ministering and taking his part in labor and prayer for those near and far off. In all the pastor's teaching of repentance and conversion, of obedience and holiness, this ought definitely to be his supreme aim to call men to come and serve God in the noble, holy, Christlike work of saving the lost and restoring God's kingdom on earth. The chief end of the Church is of necessity the chief end of the ministry.

Out of this follows, naturally, the statement that the chief end of preaching ought to be to train every individual believer and every congregation to take its part in helping the Church to fulfill her destiny. … At times, again, it may be that while there is no direct preaching on missions, yet all the teaching on love and faith, on obedience and service, on holiness and conformity to Christ, may be inspired by this one truth that we are to be "*imitators of God, and walk in love, even as Christ loved and gave Himself a sacrifice for us.*" Missions are the chief end of the Church, and therefore of the ministry, and therefore of all its preaching. All this now leads up to what, in view of the responsibility of the minister, is the main point that must be pressed, that the chief aim of every minister ought to be to fit himself for this great work.

… If the question be asked how the minister is thus to fit himself for carrying out his responsibility, the first answer will usually be, and we may take it first, "By study." In regard to this, many pointed things were said, at the Conference, of the members of the Church, which are specially applicable to the pastor, as the representative and guide of his people in this. … And what is it a pastor will need specially to study? In the missionary problem, there are three great factors. The world in its sin and misery; Christ in His dying love; the Church as the link between the two.

The first thing is: Study the world. … God to give you an eye to see and a heart to feel that misery. … That man is your brother. He has, like you, a nature formed for worship. He does not, like you, know the true God. Will you not sacrifice everything, sacrifice yourself, to save him? Study, sometimes in its great whole, sometimes in its detail, the state of the world, until you begin to feel that God has placed you in this dark world with the one object of studying that darkness, and living and helping those who are dying in it. And if at times you feel that it is more than you can bear, cry to God to help you to look again, and yet again, until you know that the need of the world makes it the very place where you choose to dwell. But remember always: The strongest intellect, the most vivid imagination, the most earnest study, cannot give you the right sense of these things; nothing but the Spirit and Love of Jesus, waited on to make you feel what He feels, and love as He loves.

Then comes the second great lesson: Christ's love, dying for these sinners, and now longing to have them won for Him. Oh, do not think you know that dying love, that love resting on and thirsting for every creature on earth! If it takes time, and a humble, reverent, loving spirit, to enter into the meaning and spirit of nature and its beauty, what think you, my brother minister, is it an easy thing to enter into the Holiest of All, the sanctuary of God's love, and in very deed have it possess our hearts? Love is needed in the poet who would woo the secrets of nature. The Divine love, Christ's love to every creature, can only be known and felt by the loving heart that gives itself up to it, that reverently waits for it as it pleases to make itself known. If you would study the missionary problem, study it in the heart of Jesus.

The missionary problem is a personal one that is meant of every believer. But it is specially true of the minister, who is to be the pattern, the teacher, of believers. Study, experience, prove the power of the personal relationship, that you may be able to teach well this, the deepest secret of true mission work.

And then with Christ's love there is His power. Study this until the vision of a triumphant Christ, with every enemy at His feet, has cast its light upon the whole earth. The whole work of saving men is Christ's work, as much to-day as on Calvary, as much with each individual conversion as in the propitiation for the sins of all. His Divine power carries on the work in and through His servants.

In studying the possible solution of the problem, in any case of special difficulty, beware of leaving out the omnipotence of Jesus. Humbly, reverently, patiently worship Him, until Christ's love and power become the inspiration of your life.

And the third great lesson to study is the Church the connecting link between the two, between the dying Savior and the dying world. And here some of the deepest mysteries of the missionary problem will be found. That the Church should really be the Body on earth of Christ, the Head in Heaven, as indispensable to Him as He is to it! That His omnipotence and His infinite redeeming love should have linked themselves, for the fulfilment of His desires, to the weakness of His Church! That the Church should now these hundred years have heard the preaching, Missions the supreme end of the Church! and yet be so content with a state in which that end is not counted the supreme thing!

And that the Lord should yet be waiting to prove most wonderfully how really He counts His Church one with Himself, and be ready to fill her with His Spirit and power and glory! And that there is abundant ground for a confident faith that the Lord is able and waiting to restore the Church to its pentecostal state, and so fit it for carrying out its pentecostal commission! In the midst of such study there will grow up the clearer conviction of how really the Church is His Body, endued with the power of His Spirit, true partaker of His Divine love, the blessed partner of His life and His glory. And the faith will be awakened that if the Church in her members, who see the evil and believe in the Divine possibility of deliverance, will but arise and give themselves, in true renunciation of all, to their Lord, the pentecostal glory can still return.

The world in its Sin and Woe, Christ in His Love and Power, the Church as the Link between the two these are the three great magnitudes the minister must know if he is to master the missionary problem. In his study he may have to go to Scripture, and to missionary literature, and to books on theology or the spiritual life; but in the long run he will ever have to come back to the truth: the problem is a personal one. It demands a most complete and unreserved giving up of the whole being to live for that world, for that Christ, for that Church. And it demands, as we have already shown, that that personal surrender shall not merely be that of a student who is determined to master some human problem, but of one who, like a true observer of nature, gives himself humbly, reverently, lovingly, to wait, and gaze, and listen till the spirit-world unlocks its secrets.

The Living Christ can manifest Himself; He can, to the penitent, patient supplicant, impart His love in its power. He can make His love ours, that we may feel as He does. He can let the light of His love fall on the world, to reveal at once its need and its hope. He can give the experience in the soul of how close and how real is His union with the believer, and how divinely He can dwell and work in us. The missionary problem is a personal one, to be solved by the power of Christ's love. Let the minister thus study it, and he will learn to preach in new power Missions, the great work, the supreme end, of Christ, of the Church, of every congregation, of every believer, and, specially, of every minister.

We have said that the first need of the ministry, if it is to fulfil its calling in regard to missions, is to study them. But when light begins to come, and the mind is convinced and the emotions are stirred, these must at once be translated into action, if the knowledge and sentiment are not to remain barren.

And where shall this action begin? Undoubtedly in prayer, more definite prayer, for missions. It may be for the awakening of the mission spirit in the Church at large, or in his own church, or in special congregations. It may be for some special field or station. It may be for God's leading in regard to his own people or the Church around him. It may be, it must be, for himself very specially, that God would give and ever renew the mission fire from Heaven. Whatever the prayer be the study must lead at once to more prayer, or the fruit will be comparatively small. Without this, there may be more interest in missions, more work for them, better success in organization and collections, while the real growth of the spiritual life, and of the love of Christ in the soul, is but very small.

Let us turn aside a moment to think of this. In all religions, there are two factors—God and man. Religion ever has its character from the degree of prominence which either of these receives. When man's will and work are in the foreground, the spiritual life is feeble; God's presence and power are little known. It is very markedly so in missions. You may have people who read missionary books and faithfully give liberal subscriptions as part of their religion, while there is but little love to Christ or prayer for His Kingdom. You may, on the contrary, have humble, simple people, who can give but little, but with that little give their whole heart's love and prayer. The one is the religion in which man is prominent; the other is on a higher and more spiritual level, in which the love of God is the supreme aim. No one needs to watch more earnestly than the minister to see that the missionary enthusiasm he fosters in himself and others is, in very deed, the fire that comes from Heaven in answer to believing prayer to consume the sacrifice.

The missionary problem is a personal one. The minister who has solved it for himself will find grace to lead others to find its solution too in the constraining power of Christ's love.

27

THE INNER CHAMBER

And the Inner Life

New York: Fleming H. Revell Co., 1905

Preface

November 18th

"If the root be holy, so are the branches."

—ROMANS 11: 16

The Inner Chamber suggests thoughts of the utmost importance. The daily need of retirement and quiet; the true Spirit of prayer; the devotional reading of God's Word; the fellowship with God for which these are meant and by which alone they bring a blessing; the spiritual life which they are meant to strengthen and fit for daily duty in intercourse with the world; the service for the Kingdom of God in soul-winning and intercession—all these truths have their share in making our devotions a source of joy and of strength. In this little book I have not attempted to take them up systematically, but I hope that the fragments I have given may bring help to some in the cultivation of the hidden life and its intercourse with God.

In this South African country, there are various diseases that affect our orange trees. One of them is popularly known by the name of the root-disease. A tree may still be bearing, and an ordinary observer may not notice anything wrong, while an expert sees the beginning of a slow death. The phylloxera in the vineyards is nothing but a root disease, and it has been found that there is no radical cure but by taking out the old roots and providing new ones. The old sort of grape is grafted on an American root, and in course of time you have the same stem and branches and fruit as before; But the roots are new and able to resist the disease.

It is in the part of the plant that is Hid from sight, that the disease comes, and where healing must be sought. How the Church of Christ, and the spiritual life of thousands of its members, suffers from the root disease—the neglect of secret intercourse with God.

It is the lack of secret prayer, the neglect of the maintenance of that hidden life "*rooted in Christ*," "*rooted and grounded in love*," that explains the feebleness of the Christian life to resist the world, and its failure to bring forth fruit abundantly. Nothing can change this but the restoration, in the life of the believer, of the inner chamber to the place which Christ meant it to have. As Christians learn, instead of trusting their own efforts, what it is daily to strike their roots deeper into Christ, and to make the secret personal fellowship with God their chief care, true godliness will flourish. "*If the root be holy, so are the branches.*"

If the morning hour be holy to the Lord, the day with its duties will be so too. *If the root be healthy, so are the branches.*

The most of these chapters have already appeared in *The South African Pioneer*; it is at the request of some who read them that I have consented to these now being republished. I pray that God may bless them to some of His children in the pursuit of the deeper and more fruitful life, the life hid with Christ in God.

—ANDREW MURRAY

The Morning Hour

"*My voice shall you hear in the morning, O Lord; in the morning will I direct my prayer unto You, and will look up*" (Psalm 5: 3). From the earliest ages God's servants have thought of the morning as the time specially fitted for the worship of God. … Many Christians, and specially the Student's Christian Association, observe The Morning Watch; the Y. P. C. E. Society speaks of it as the Quiet Hour; others use the name of the Still Hour or the Quiet Time. All these, whether they think of a whole hour or half an hour, or a quarter of an hour, unite with the Psalmist in what he says, "*My voice shall you hear in the morning, Lord.*" In speaking of the extreme importance of this daily time of quiet for prayer and meditation on God's Word, Dr. John. R. Mott [founder of Foreign Missions Conference of North America (1893)] has said: "Next to receiving Christ as Savior, and claiming the Baptism of the Holy Spirit, we know of no act attended with larger good to ourselves or others, than the formation of an undiscourageable resolution to keep the morning watch, and spend the first half hour of the day alone with God."

At first sight the statement appears too strong. The act of receiving Christ as Savior is one of such infinite consequences for eternity the act of claiming the Holy Spirit is one that works such a revolution in the Christian life, that such a simple thing as the firm determination to keep the morning watch hardly appears sufficiently important to be placed next to them. If, however, we think how impossible it is to live out our daily life in Christ as our Savior from sin, or to maintain a walk in the leading and power of the Holy Spirit, without daily, close fellowship with God, we soon shall see the truth of the sentiment. Because it simply means the fixed determination that Christ shall have the whole life, that the Holy Spirit shall in everything be fully obeyed. The morning watch is the key to the position in which the surrender to Christ and the Holy Spirit can be unceasingly and fully maintained.

To realize this, let us look first at what ought to be the object of the morning watch. The morning watch must not be regarded as an end in itself. It is not sufficient that it gives us a blessed time for prayer and Bible study, and so brings us a certain measure of refreshment and help. It is to serve as a means to an end. And that end is: to secure the presence of Christ for the whole day.

Personal devotion to a friend or a pursuit means that that friend or pursuit shall always hold their place in the heart, even when other engagements occupy the attention. Personal devotion to Jesus means that we allow nothing to separate us from Him for a moment. To abide in Him and His love, to be kept by Him and His grace, to be doing His will and pleasing Him—this cannot possibly be an intermittent thing to one who is truly devoted to Him. …

The believer cannot stand for one moment without Christ. The personal devotion to Him refuses to be content with anything less than to abide always in His love and His will. Nothing less is the true scriptural Christian life. And the importance and blessedness and true aim of the morning watch can only be seen as nothing less than this is its first object. The clearer the object of our pursuit is, the better we shall be able to adapt the means to its attainment. Consider the morning watch now as the means to this great end: I want to secure absolutely the presence of Christ all the day, to do nothing that can interfere with it. I feel at once that my success for the day will depend upon the clearness and the strength of the faith that seeks and finds and holds Him in the closet. Meditation and prayer and the word will all be used as subordinate and auxiliary to this: the link for the day between Christ and me must be renewed and firmly fastened in the morning hour. …

True religion aims at having the character of Christ so formed in us, that in our most common acts His temper and disposition shall show themselves. The spirit and the will of Christ are meant so to possess us that in our intercourse with others, in our relaxation, in our business, it shall be a second nature to us to act according to them. All this can be, because Christ Himself, as the Living One, lives in us.

Be not disturbed if at first the aim appears too high or difficult, and occupies too much of your time in the hour of private prayer. The time you give it will be richly rewarded. You will return to prayer and scripture with new purpose and new faith. As the morning watch begins to have its effect on the day, the day will react on its first half hour, and fellowship with Christ have a new meaning and a new power.

It will specially have its influence on the Spirit in which you keep the morning watch. As the grandeur of the aim—unbroken fellowship with God in Christ through the day—and the true nature of the means to secure it—a definite conscious meeting with Christ and a securing His presence for the day—possesses us, it will be seen that the one essential thing is, wholehearted purpose: the fixed determination, whatever effort or Self-denial it may cost, to win the prize. In study or on the sport field every student knows what need there is of vigorous will and determined purpose if we are to succeed.

Religion needs, and indeed deserves, not less but more of intense devotion. If anything, surely the love of Christ needs the whole heart. It is this fixed determination before everything to secure Christ's presence, that will overcome every temptation to be unfaithful or superficial in the keeping of our pledges. It is this will make the morning watch itself a mighty means of grace in strengthening character, and serving us to say no to every call for Self-indulgence. It is this will enable us at once, when we enter the inner chamber and shut the door, to be there with our whole heart, ready at once for our intercourse with Christ. And it is this determination that, from the morning watch on, will become the keynote of our daily life.

In the world it is often said: Great things are possible to anyone who knows what they will, and wills it with all their heart. The student who has made personal devotion to Christ his watchword, will find in the morning hour the place where day by day the insight into their holy calling is renewed; where his will is braced up to walk worthy of it; and his faith rewarded by the presence of Christ waiting to meet him, and take charge of him for the day. We are more than conquerors through Him who loves us. A living Christ waits to meet us.

Life and Knowledge

November 19th

"And out of the ground made the Lord God to grow the tree of life in the midst of the garden, and the tree of knowledge of good and evil."

—GENESIS 2: 9

There are two ways of knowing things. The one is in the mind by notion or conception; I know about a thing. The other is in the life; I know by inward experience. A blind man, who is clever, may know all that science teaches about the light, by having books read to him. A child, or a savage, who has never thought what light is, yet knows it far better than the blind scholar. The latter knows all about it by thinking; the former knows it in reality by seeing and enjoying it.

It is even so in religion. The mind can form thoughts about God from the Bible, and know all the doctrines of salvation, while the inner life does not know the power of God to save. This is why we read: "*Those who love not, know not God; for God is love.*" We may know all about God and about love; we may be able to utter beautiful thoughts about it; but unless we love, we do not know God. Only love can know God.

The knowledge of God is life eternal. God's Word is the word of life. Out of the heart are the issues of life. The life may be strong, even where knowledge in the mind is feeble. And the knowledge may be the object of most diligent pursuit and of great delight, while the life is not affected by it. …

And so the inner divine life in a man is something quite different from the intellect with which he knows about it. That intellect is indeed most needful, to offer to the heart the Word of God which the Holy Spirit can quicken. And yet it is absolutely impotent, either to impart, or quicken, the true life. It is but a servant that carries the food; it is the heart that must feed, and be nourished and live.

The two trees in Paradise are God's revelation of the same truth. If Adam had eaten of the tree of life, he would have received and known all the good God had for him in living power as an experience. And he would have known evil only by being absolutely free from it. But Eve was led astray by the desire for knowledge —"*the fruit was to be desired to make one wise*," and man got a knowledge of good without possessing it—a knowledge of it only from the evil that was its opposite. And since that day man has ever sought his religion more in knowledge than in life.

It is only life, experience, possession, of God and His goodness that gives true knowledge. The knowledge of the intellect cannot quicken. "*Though I ... understand all mysteries and all knowledge ... and have not love, I am nothing*" (1 Corinthians 13: 2). It is in our daily Bible reading that this danger meets us; it is there it must be met and conquered. We need the intellect to hear and understand God's Word in its human meaning. But we need to know that the possession of the truth by the intellect cannot profit but as the Holy Spirit makes it life and truth in the heart. We need to yield our heart, and wait on God in quiet submission and faith to work in us by that Spirit.

As this becomes a holy habit, we shall learn the art of intellect and heart working in perfect harmony, and each movement of the mind being ever accompanied by the corresponding movement of the heart, waiting on and listening for the teaching of the Spirit.

The Heart and the Understanding

"*Trust in the Lord with all your heart, and lean not on your own understanding*" (Proverbs 3: 5). The chief object of the Book of Proverbs is to teach knowledge and discretion, and to guide in the path of wisdom and understanding. To understand righteousness, to understand the fear of the Lord, to find good understanding— it is to this the Proverbs offer to guide us. But it gives the warning in the pursuit of this, to distinguish between trusting to our own understanding, and intellect, and seeking spiritual understanding, which God gives—an understanding heart.

"*Trust in the Lord with all your heart, and lean not to your own understanding.*" In all our seeking after knowledge and wisdom, in all our planning our life, or studying of the "Word," we have these two powers: the understanding or intellect, which knows things from without, by nature and the conceptions we form, and the heart, which knows them by experience as it takes them up into the will and affection.

I am deeply persuaded that one of the chief reasons why so much Bible teaching and Bible knowledge is comparatively fruitless, one of the chief causes of the lack of holiness, and devotion, and power in the Church, is to be found here: *the trusting to our own understanding in religion.*

I beseech my readers to give me a patient hearing here. Many argue: But surely God gave us our intellect, and without it there is no possibility of knowing God's "Word." Most true; but listen. By the fall our whole human nature was disordered. The will became enslaved, the affections were perverted, the understanding was darkened.

All admit the ruin of the fall in the two former, but practically deny it in the latter.

We admit that even as believers we have not in our Self the power of a holy will, and need the daily renewing of the grace of Jesus Christ. We admit that we have not the power of holy affection, loving God and our neighbor, except as it is wrought in us unceasingly by the Holy Spirit. But we do not notice that the intellect is just as much spiritually ruined and impotent, and incapable of apprehending spiritual truth. …

To think that we can take the knowledge of God's truth for ourselves out of His word as we will, is still our greatest danger. We need a deep conviction of the impotence of our understanding really to know the truth, and of the terrible danger of Self-confidence and Self-deception in doing so, to see the need of the word, "*Trust in the Lord with all of your heart, and lean not on your own understanding.*"

It is with the heart man believes. It is with all the heart we are to seek, and serve, and love God. It is only with the heart we can know God, or worship God, in spirit and truth. It is in the heart, therefore, that the Divine Word does the work. It is into our heart God hath sent forth the Spirit of His Son. It is the heart, the inward life of desire and love and will and surrender, that the Holy Spirit guides into all the truth.

In Bible study, "*Trust in the Lord with all of your heart, and lean not on your own understanding.*" Trust not, wholly distrust, your own understanding. It can only give thee thoughts and conceptions of Divine things without the reality. It will deceive you with the thought that the truth, if received into the mind, will somehow surely enter the heart. And so it will blind you to the terrible experience which is universal, that men daily read, and every Sunday delight to hear God's Word, and yet are made neither humble, nor holy, nor heavenly minded by it. Instead of trusting the understanding, come with the heart to the Bible. Instead of trusting the understanding, trust in the Lord, and that with all of your heart. Let not the understanding, but the whole heart set upon the living God as the Teacher, be the chief thing, when you enter your prayer closet. Then shall you find good understanding. God will give you an understanding heart, a spiritual understanding.

You may ask me, as I have been often asked, "But what am I to do? How am I to study my Bible? I see no way of doing so, but by using the understanding." Perfectly right. But do not use it for what it cannot do. Remember two things. One is, that it can only give you a picture or thought of spiritual things. The moment it has done this, go with your heart to the Lord to make His Word life and truth in you. The other is, remember that pride of intellect, the danger of leaning to your own understanding is unceasing, and that nothing, not even the most determined purpose, can save you from this, but only the continual dependence of the heart on the Holy Spirit's teaching. It is alone through the Holy Spirit quickening the Word in the heart, in the disposition and affections, that He can guide the intellect. "*The meek will He guide in judgment; the meek will He show His way.*" "*The fear of the Lord,*"—a disposition—"*is the beginning of wisdom.*"

With every thought from the Word the understanding grasps, bow before God in dependence and trust. Believe with the whole heart that God can and will make it true. Ask for the Holy Spirit to make it work effectually in the heart. So the Word becomes the strength of our life. Persevere in this, and the time will come when the Holy Spirit, dwelling in the heart and life, will hold the understanding in subjection, and let His holy light shine through it.

Revealed unto Babes

November 20th

"I thank You, Father … that You have hidden these things from the wise and prudent, and revealed them unto babes."

—MATTHEW 11: 25

The wise and prudent are the men who are conscious and confident of their power of mind and reason to aid them in their pursuit of Divine Knowledge. The babes are those whose chief work is not the mind and its power, but the heart and its disposition. Ignorance, helplessness, dependence, meekness, teachableness, trust and love—these are the tempers God seeks in those whom He teaches (Psalm 25: 9, 12, 14, 17, 20).

One of the most important parts of our devotions is the study of God's Word. Of what deep importance that we should ever receive the Word in the Spirit that waits for the Father to reveal its truth in us. And of what importance that we should have the child-like, yea the babe-like disposition to which the Father loves to impart the secrets of His love. With the wise and prudent head-knowledge is the first thing; from them God hides the spiritual meaning of the very thing they *think they understand*. With the babes, not the head and its knowledge but the heart and Feeling, the sense of humility, love and trust, is the first thing, and to them God reveals, in their inner life and experience, the very thing they *know they cannot understand*.

Education tells us that there are two styles of teaching. The ordinary teacher makes the communication of knowledge his chief object, and cultivates the powers of the child as far as they help him to attain his object. The true teacher considers the amount of knowledge a secondary thing. His first aim is to develop the power of mind and spirit, and to aid the pupil, both men tally and morally, in using his powers aright in the pursuit and the application of knowledge.

Even so there are two classes of preachers. Some pour forth instruction and argument and appeal unceasingly, leaving it to the hearers to make the best use they can of what is brought them. The true preacher knows how much depends upon the state of heart, and seeks, even as our Lord Jesus did, to subordinate the teaching of objective truth or doctrine to the cultivation of those dispositions without which teaching profits little.

A hundred sermons, eloquent and earnest, to the wise and prudent, to Christians who listen with the thought that they can understand, and that what they hear will somehow profit them, will bring less real blessing, than one sermon to hearers in whom the preacher has awakened a consciousness of spiritual ignorance, a babe-like docile spirit that waits for and depends on, that truly accepts and obeys, the Father's teaching.

In the secret chamber everyone is, as far as human aid is concerned, his or her own teacher and preacher. We are to train ourselves in the blessed habit of babe-like simplicity and teachableness. Remembering that it was not only needful that Divine Truth should be revealed in the world, but that there must be an individual revelation to each, by the Holy Spirit, our first care is to wait on the Father to reveal to us, and within us, the hidden mystery in its power in the inner life.

In this posture, we exercise the babe-like spirit, and receive the Kingdom as a little child. All Evangelical Christians believe in regeneration. How few believe that when we are born of God, A babe-like dependence on God for all teaching and strength ought to be our chief characteristic. It was the one thing our Lord Jesus insisted on above all. When He pronounced the poor in heart, the meek, the hungry, "blessed," when He called us to learn of Him that He was meek and lowly in heart, when He spoke so often of our humbling ourselves and becoming as little children, it was because the first and chief mark of being a child of God, of being like Jesus Christ, is *an absolute dependence upon God for every blessing and specially* for any real knowledge of spiritual things.

Let each ask himself: Have I counted the babe-like spirit the first essential in my Bible study? Of what use is Bible study without the babe-like spirit? It is the real and only key to God's school. Would it not be well to set aside everything to secure this? Then alone will God reveal His hidden wisdom. The new birth, being begotten of God, by which we become God's children, is meant to make us babes. It will give us the child-spirit as well as the child-teaching. It cannot do the second without the first. Let us believe and yield ourselves to the new life in us, to the leading of the Spirit; He will breathe in us the spirit of little children.

The first object of Bible study is to learn the hidden wisdom of God. The first condition of obtaining this knowledge, is to accept the fact that God Himself reveals it to us. The first disposition needed for receiving that revelation is a babe-like spirit. We all know how the first thing a wise workman does is to see that he has the proper tools, and that they are in proper order. He does not count it lost time to stop his work and sharpen the tools. It is not lost time to let the Bible study wait, till you see whether you are in the right position—waiting for the Father's revelation in the meek and babe-like spirit. If you feel that you have not read your Bible in this spirit, confess and forsake at once the Self-confident spirit of the wise and prudent.

Not only pray for the babe-like spirit, but believe for it. It is in you, though neglected and suppressed; you may begin at once as a child of God to experience it.

Seek not by reflection or argument to bring this babe-like spirit into your heart. "Work from within outwards. It is in you, as a seed, in the new life, born of the Spirit. It must rise and grow in you as a birth of the indwelling Spirit. In this faith you must not only pray, but pray also very specially for this grace of the Spirit, and exercise it. Live as a babe before God. As a new-born babe desire the milk of the Word.

And beware of trying to assume this state of mind only when you want to study Scripture. It must be the permanent habit of your mind, the state of your heart. Then alone can you enjoy the continual guidance of the Holy Spirit.

The Will of God

November 21st

"Your will be done on earth as it is in Heaven."

—MATTHEW 6: 10

The will of God is the living power to which the world owes its existence. Through that will, and according to that will, it is what it is. It is the expression or manifestation or embodiment of that Divine Will in its wisdom, power and goodness. It has, in beauty and glory, but what it owes to God's having willed it. As that Will formed it, so it upholds it every day. Creation thus does what it was destined for, it shows forth the glory of God. "*They gave glory to Him who lives for ever and ever, saying, You are worthy to receive glory, for You have created all things, and because of Your will they are, and were created.*"

This is true of inanimate nature. It is still more true of intelligent creatures. The Divine Will undertook the creation of a creature will in its own image and likeness, with the living power to know and accept and co-operate with that Will to which it owed its being. The blessedness of the unfallen angels, consists in counting it their highest honor and happiness to be able to will and do exactly what God wills and does. The glory of Heaven is that God's will is done there. The signal misery of fallen angels and men, consists simply in their having turned away from, and refused to abide in, and to do, the will of God.

Redemption is nothing but the restoration of God's will to its place in the world. To this end Christ came and showed in a human life, how man has but one thing to live for: the doing of God's will. He showed us how there was one way of conquering Self-will—by a death to it, in obeying God's will even to death. So He atoned for our Self-will and conquered it for us, and opened a path through death and resurrection into a life entirely united with, and devoted to, the will of God.

God's redeeming will is now able to do in fallen man what His creating will had wrought and ever works in nature, or in unfallen beings. In Christ and His example, God has revealed the devotion to and the delight in His will which He asks and expects of us. In Christ and, His Spirit He renews and takes possession of our will—works in it both to will and to do, making us able and willing to do all His will. He Himself works all things after the counsel of His will. "*He makes us perfect in every good thing to do His will, working in us that which is pleasing in His sight.*" As this is revealed by the Holy Spirit, and believed, and received into the heart, we begin to get an insight into the prayer, "*Your will be done on earth as it is in Heaven,*" and the true desire is awakened for the life it promises.

How essential it is to believers that we realize our relations to God's will, and its claim on us. Many, many, believers have no conception of what their faith or their feeling ought to be in regard to the will of God. How few who say: "My whole thought of blessedness is in nothing but the most complete harmony with the will of God. I feel my one need to be, the ever maintained surrender, not, in the very least thing, ever to do other than what

God wills me to do." By God's grace every hour of my life may be a living in the will of God, and doing it as it is done in Heaven.

It is only as a living faith in the Divine Will, working out its purposes increasingly in us, masters the heart, that we shall have the courage to believe in the answer to the prayer our Lord taught us. It is only as we see, that it is through Jesus Christ, that this working of God's will in us is carried out, that we shall understand how it is the close union to Him that gives the confidence that God will work all in us. And it is only this confidence in God, through Jesus Christ, that will assure us, that we too can do our part, and that our feeble will on earth can truly ever correspond and cooperate with the will of God. Let us but accept our destiny and our obligation as the one thing our heart desires, that in everything the will of God be done in us and by us, as it is done in Heaven; that Faith will overcome the world.

The will may not be disconnected from its living union with the Father here, nor the living presence of the Blessed Son. It is only by a divine guidance given through the Holy Spirit, that the will of God in its beauty, in its application to daily life, in its ever-growing revelation, can be truly known. This teaching will be given not to the wise and prudent, but to the babes, those of childlike disposition, who are willing to wait for and depend on what is given them. The Divine guidance will lead in the path of God's will.

Our secret intercourse with God is the place where we repeat and learn the great lessons. … The God whom I worship asks of me perfect union with His will. … My worship means "*I delight to do Your will, God.*" The morning hour, the inner chamber, the secret intercourse with God, as in these the knowledge of God's will, the power to perform it, the entire and joyful surrender to do all God wills, are sought and cultivated, our study of God's Word and our prayer will bring their true and full blessing.

Doing and Knowing

November 22nd

"But Jesus said, "blessed are they that hear the word of God, and keep it."

"If any man wills to do His will, he shall know."

—LUKE 2: 28; JOHN 7:17

In your Bible study everything will depend upon the spirit in which you come to it, upon the Object or End you propose to yourself. In worldly things, we are ruled and urged on by the End or Aim we set before ourself. It is not otherwise with the Bible. If your aim be simply to know the Bible well, you will be disappointed. If you think that the thorough knowledge of the Bible will necessarily be a blessing, you are mistaken. To some it is a curse. To others it is powerless, it does not make them either holy or happy. To some it is a burden, it depresses them instead of quickening them or lifting them up.

And what ought then to be the Aim or End, the real disposition of the Bible student?

God's Word is food, bread from Heaven; the first need for Bible study is: a great hunger after righteousness—a great desire to do all God's will. The Bible is a light: the first condition to its enjoyment is—a hearty longing to walk in God's ways. Is not this what the texts I have placed above teach us? "*Blessed are they that hear the Word of God and keep it*" There is no blessedness in hearing or knowing God's word apart from keeping it. The Word is nothing if it be not kept, obeyed, done. "*If any one wills to do His will, they shall know....*"

According to this saying of our Lord, all true knowledge of God's word depends upon there being first the will to do it. Is this not the very lesson we are enforcing? God will refuse to unlock the real meaning and blessing of His word to any but those whose will is definitely set upon doing it. I must read my Bible with one purpose: "*Whatsoever He says unto you, do it.*"

Why this should be so, is easily ascertained when we think of what Words are meant for. They stand between the will and the deed. A man wills to do something for you; before he does it, he expresses his thought or purpose in words; then he fulfils the words by doing what he has promised. Even so with God. His words have their value from what He does. In creation, His word was with power: He spoke and it was done. In grace, He does what He says. David prays, "*Do as You have spoken*" (2 Samuel 7: 25); Solomon says at the consecration of the temple, "*Who has with His hand fulfilled that which He spoke with His mouth*"; "*who has performed His Word that He spoke*"; "*who has kept that which You promised*"; "*who spoke it with Your mouth, and has fulfilled with Your hand*"; "*let Your Word be verified, which You have spoken*" (2 Chronicles 6: 4, 10, 15, 16).

In the prophets, God says, "*I the Lord have spoken it; I Will Do It.*" And they say, "*What You have spoken, is done.*" The truth and the worth of what God promises consists in this, that He does it. His word of promise is meant to be done. This is no less true of His word of command, of things which He meant us to do. If we do not do them, if we seek to know them, if we admire their beauty and praise their wisdom, but do not do them we delude ourselves. They are meant to be done; it is only as we do them that their real meaning and blessing can be unfolded to us. It is only as we do them, that we really can grow in the Divine life. "*Walk worthy of the Lord unto all pleasing, bearing fruit unto every good work and increasing in the knowledge of God.*" It is only when we approach God's words with the same object which God had in view—that they should be done—that we can have any hope of blessing.

Is this not what we see all around us in the pursuit of knowledge, or in any branch of trade? The apprentice or pupil is expected to put the lessons he receives into practice; only then is he prepared for further teaching. And even so in the Christian life, Bible study is mere theory, a pleasing exercise of mind and imagination, worth little or nothing for a life of true holiness or Christlikeness, until the student be ready never to open or close his Bible without making God's purpose His very own, and hearkening when He says, "*Do all that I speak.*"

This was the mark of the saints of old. "*So Abram went, as the Lord had spoken to him.*" "*As the Lord had commanded Moses, so did he,*" is the description of the man who as a servant was faithful in all his house. And of David we read: "*I have found a man after mine own heart, who shall do all my will.*" In Psalm 119 we hear him speaking with God about His word, and praying for Divine light and teaching, but ever accompanied by the vow of obedience, or some other expression of love and delight. It is the doing of God's will, that even with God's own Son, is the one secret of entrance into the favor and the mind of God. …

Young Christian! I beseech you by the mercies of God, when you ask God to lead you into the treasures of His word, into the palace where Christ dwells, do it as one who presents himself a living sacrifice, ready to do whatever God shall speak. Do not think this a matter of course. It is of deeper importance than you know. This is more frequently absent from Bible study than you think. Seek for it with deep humility. The first need for enjoying your food is hunger. The first requirement for the Bible study is a simple, determined longing to find out what God wants you to do, and a dead-in-earnest resolve to do it. "*If any man wills to do His will, he shall know of the teaching*"—to him the Word of God will be opened up.

The Blessedness of the Doer

November 23rd

"Be doers of the Word, and not hearers only, deluding yourselves.
But . . . being not a hearer that forgets, but a doer that works, this man shall be blessed in his doing."
—JAMES 1: 22–25

What a terrible delusion to be content with, to delight in hearing the word, and yet not to do it. And how terribly common, the sight of multitudes of Christians listening to the word of God most regularly and earnestly, and yet not doing it. If their own servant were to do so, hearing but not doing, how summary the judgment would be. And yet, so complete is the delusion, they never know that they are not living good Christian lives. What can it be that thus deludes us?

There is more than one thing. One is that people mistake the pleasure they have in hearing, for religion and worship. The mind delights in having the truth put clearly before it; the imagination is gratified by its illustration; the feelings are stirred by its application. To an active mind knowledge gives pleasure. We may study some branch of science—say electricity—for the enjoyment the knowledge gives us, without the least intention of applying it practically. And so people go to church, and enjoy the preaching, and yet do not do what God asks.

Another cause of this delusion is the terrible perversion of the doctrine of our impotence to good. The grace of Christ to enable us to obey, to keep from sinning and really to make us holy, is so little believed, that men practically think that there is a necessity of sinning on them—that God cannot expect an exact obedience of them, for He knows they cannot render it. This error cuts away the very root of a determined purpose to do all God has said. It closes the heart to any earnest desire to believe and experience all God's grace can do in us, and keeps men Self-contented in the midst of sin. Hearing and not doing—what terrible Self-delusion.

There is a third reason for it, having special reference to private Bible reading. For us, the hearing or reading is regarded as a duty, the performance of which is considered to be a religious service. We have spent our five or ten minutes in the morning reading; we have read thoughtfully and attentively; we have tried to take in what was read: a duty faithfully performed eases the conscience, and gives a sense of satisfaction. And there is hardly any conception of the worthlessness, and more than that, of the hardening influence of a duty performed or of knowledge acquired, unless we go out with our whole heart set upon literally doing and being what God's Word says He would have us and can make us. Terrible delusion! "*Be doers of the word, and not hearers only, deluding yourselves.*" It is in the closet, in the morning watch, that this delusion must be fought and conquered. … Everything depends on this. Our Lord Jesus said: "*If any man wills to do His will, he shall know of the teaching whether it be of God.*" It is only the heart that delights in God's law, and has set its will determinedly on doing it that can receive the Divine illumination, which spiritually knows the teaching of Christ in its Divine origin and power. Without this will to do, our knowledge will not profit: it is mere head knowledge.

In life, in science and are, in business, the only way of truly knowing, is doing. What a man cannot do he does not thoroughly know. The only way to know God, to taste his blessedness, is through the doing of His will. That proves whether it is a God of my own sentiment and imagination that I confess, or the true and living God who rules and works all. It is only in doing His will that I prove I love it and accept it, and make myself one with it. And there is no possible way under Heaven of being united to God but by being united to His will in the doing of it. It is the quiet of the inner chamber, in the spirit in which I do my private Bible reading, in the determination with which I seek to have this point absolutely and finally settled: I am going to do whatever God says, that the awful Self-delusion of hearing and not doing must be conquered.

It may help us if we take some portion of God's Word and see how we are to deal with it. Suppose it to be the Sermon on the Mount. I begin with the first Beatitude: "*Blessed are the poor in spirit.*" I ask, what does this mean? Am I obeying this injunction? Am I at least thoroughly in earnest in seeking day by day to maintain this disposition? As I feel how far my proud, Self-confident nature is from it, am I willing to wait, and plead with Christ, and believe that He can work it in me? Am I going to do this—to be poor in spirit? Or shall I again be a hearer and not a doer?

And so I may go through the Beatitudes, and through the whole Sermon, with its teaching on meekness and mercy, on love and righteousness, on doing everything as unto the Father, and in everything trusting Him, on doing His will and Christ's words, and verse by verse ask—Do I know what this means? Am I living it out? Am I doing it? Am I what He speaks? … And I shall ask whether the vow—Whatever He says I am going to do—has ever taken the place, either in my Bible reading or inn my life, which He demands that it should have. …

Holiness: The Chief Aim of Bible Study

November 24th

"Sanctify them in Your truth; Your word is truth."

—JOHN 17:17

In his great intercessory prayer our Lord spoke of the words which the Father had given Him, of His own giving them to His disciples, and of their having received and believed them. It was this that made them disciples. It was their keeping these words that would really enable them to live the life and do the work of true disciples. Receiving the words of God from Christ AND keeping them, is the mark and power of true discipleship.

In praying the Father to keep them in the world when He had left it, our Lord asks that He would sanctify them in the truth, as it dwells and works in His Word. Christ had said of Himself, "*I am the truth.*" He was the only begotten of the Father, full of grace and truth. His teaching was not like that of the law which came by Moses, giving a knowledge, a promise of good things to come which was but an image or a shadow.

"*The words I speak unto you are spirit and life,*" giving the very substance and power and Divine possession of what they speak of. Christ had spoken of the Spirit as the Spirit of truth who would lead into all the truth that there was in Himself, not as a matter of knowledge or doctrine, but into its actual experience and enjoyment.

And then He prays that in this living truth, as it dwells in the Word, and is revealed in Him by the Spirit, and the Father would sanctify them. "*For their sakes,*" He says, "*I sanctify Myself that they themselves may also be sanctified in truth.*" And He asks the Father in His power and love to take charge of them, that His object—to sanctify them in the truth, through His Word which is truth—may be realized, that they, like Himself, may be sanctified in truth. Let us study the wonderful lessons here given in regard to God's Word.

"*Sanctify them in Your truth; Your Word is truth.*" The great object of God's Word is to make us Holy. No diligence or success in Bible study will really profit us unless it makes us humbler, holier men. In all our use of Holy Scripture this must be definitely our main object. The reason there is often so much Bible reading with so little real result in a Christ-like character, is that "*salvation, through sanctification of the Spirit and belief of the truth,*" is not truly sought. People imagine that if they study the Word and accept its truths, this will in some way, of itself, benefit them. But experience teaches that it does not. The fruit of holy character, of consecrated life, of power to bless others, does not come, for the simple and most natural reason that we only get what we seek.

Christ gave us God's Word to make us holy; it is only when we make this our definite aim in all Bible study, that the truth, not the doctrinal truth, but its Divine quickening power, imparting the very life of God, that it contains as a seed, can open and impart itself to us.

"*Sanctify them in Your truth. Your word is truth.*" It is God Himself who alone can make us Holy by His Word. The Word, separate from God and His direct operation, cannot avail. The Word is an instrument: God Himself must use it. God is the alone Holy One. He alone can make holy.

The unspeakable value of God's word is that it is God's means of holiness. The terrible mistake of many is that they forget that God alone can use it or make it effectual. It is not enough that I have access to the dispensary of a physician. I need him to prescribe. Without him my use of his medicines might be fatal. It was so with the scribes. They made their boast of God's law; they delighted in their study of Scripture and yet remained unsanctified. The Word did not sanctify them, because they did not seek for this in the Word, and did not yield to God to do it for them.

"*Sanctify them in Your truth. Your Word is truth.*" This Holiness through the Word must be sought and waited for from God in prayer. Our Lord not only taught His disciples that they must be holy; He not only sanctified Himself for them, that they might "*be sanctified in truth*," but He brought His words and His work to the Father with the prayer that He would sanctify them. It is most needful to know God's word and meditate on it.

It is most needful to set our heart upon being holy, as our first and chief object in studying the Word. But all this is not enough; everything depends upon our following Christ in asking the Father to sanctify us through the Word. It is God the holy Father who makes us holy by the Spirit of holiness who dwells in us. He works in us the very mind and disposition of Christ who is our sanctification. "*There is none holy but the Lord*"; all holiness is His and what He gives by His holy presence. The tabernacle and temple were not holy in virtue of cleansing, or separation or consecration. They became holy by the incoming and indwelling God. His taking possession made them holy. God even so makes us holy through His word bringing Christ and the Holy Spirit into us.

And the Father cannot do this except as we tarry before Him, and are still, and in deep dependence and full surrender give ourselves up to Him. It is in the prayer offered in the Name, and the fellowship, and the faith of the Great Intercessor—"*Sanctify Me through Your truth, Your word is truth*"— that the Father's sanctifying power will be found, and our knowledge of God's Word truly make us holy.

Keeping Christ's Commandments

November 25th

"If you know these things, blessed are you if you do them."

—JOHN 8: 17

The blessedness and the blessing of God's Word is only to be known by *doing* it. The subject is of such supreme importance in the Christian life, and therefore in our Bible study, that I must ask you to return to it once more. And let us this time just take the one expression, Keeping the Word, or keeping the commandments.

Let us take it first in the farewell discourse. You may be familiar with the passages, but it will be of use to look at them together.

"If you love Me, keep my commandments, and the Father will send you the Comforter" (John 14: 15–16); *"He that has My commandments, and keeps them, he it is that loves Me: and he that loves Me shall be loved of My Father, and I will love him, and will manifest Myself to him"* (John 14: 21); *If a man loves Me, he will keep My words: and My Father will love him, and We will come unto him, and make Our abode with him"* (John 14: 23). … *"If you keep My commandments, you shall abide in My love"* (John 15: 10); "*You are My friends, if you do whatsoever I command you*" (John 5: 10).

Study and compare these passages, until the words enter the heart and work the deep conviction that keeping Christ's commandments is *the* indispensable condition of all true spiritual blessing. For the coming of God the Holy Spirit, and His actual indwelling, for the enjoyment of the Father's love, the inward manifestation of Christ, the abode of the Father and the Son in the heart, the power of prayer, the abiding in Christ's love, and the enjoyment of His friendship, the keeping of the commandments is the one requisite.

And for the power to claim and enjoy these blessings in faith day by day, the childlike consciousness that we do keep them is indispensable too. And no less indispensable is, for fruitful Bible study, the quiet assurance that dare expect Divine light and strength with every word of God because He knows that we are ready to obey to the very utmost.

Through the will of God, delighted in, and done, lies our only way to the heart of the Father, and His only way to our heart. Keep the commandments: this is the way to every blessing. See how strikingly all this is confirmed by what we find in John's first epistle: *"Hereby do we know that we know Him, if we keep his commandments. He that says, I know Him, and keeps not His commandments, is a liar. But whosoever keeps His word, in him verily is the love of God perfected"* (1 John 2: 3–5). The only proof of true, living, saving knowledge of God; the only proof of not being Self-deceived in our religion; of God's love not being an imagination, but a possession, is, keeping His word.

"If our heart does not condemn us, we have boldness toward God; and whatsoever we ask we receive, because we keep His commandments… (1 John 3: 21–22). *And He that keeps His commandments, abides in Him"* (1 John 3: 24). Keeping the commandments is the secret of confidence toward God, and true intimate fellowship with Him.

"*By this we know that we love the children of God, when we love God, and keep His commandments. For this is the love of God, that we keep His commandments: and His commandments are not grievous*" (1 John 5: 2–3). Our profession of love is worthless, except as it is proved to be true by the keeping of His commandments in the power of a life begotten of God. Knowing God, having the love of God perfected in us, having boldness with God, and abiding in Him, being begotten of Him and loving Him—all, all, is dependent on the one thing: keeping the commandments.

It is only as we realize the prominence Christ and Scripture give to this truth, that we shall learn to give it the same prominence in our life. It will become to us one of the keys to true Bible study.

Those who read the Bible with the longing and determined purpose to search out and to obey every commandment of God and of Christ are on the right track to receiving all the blessing the Word was ever meant to bring. … We will find how all daily life is elevated, when we say as Christ did: "*This commandment received I of My Father.*" The Word will become the light and guide by which all our steps are ordered. And our life will become the training school in which the sanctifying power of the Word is proved, and the mind ever prepared anew for its teaching and encouragement. And so the keeping of the commandments will be the key to every spiritual blessing.

Make a determined effort to grasp what this life of full obedience means. Take some of Christ's clearest commands—"*Love one another even as I have loved you*"; "*you ought to wash one another's feet*"; "*you should do as I have done to you*"—and accept a Christ-like love and humility as the law of the supernatural life that you are to live. …

Once again, our one aim must be perfect harmony between conscience and conduct. Every conviction must be carried out into action. Christ's commands were meant to be obeyed. If this be not done, the accumulation of Scripture knowledge only darkens and hardens, and works that satisfaction with the pleasure which the acquisition of knowledge brings, which unfits us for the Spirit's teaching.

I pray you, do not weary of my repeating so often the blessed, solemn message. In your inner chamber the question is to be decided whether you will through the day keep the commandments of Christ. And there too will be decided whether in future life you are to bear the character of a man wholly given up to know and do the will of God.

28

THE FULL BLESSING OF PENTECOST

The One Thing Needful

London: James Nisbet & Co., 1908

Introduction

November 26th

The message which this little book brings is simple but most solemn. It is to the effect that the one thing needful for the Church, and the thing which, above all others, Christians ought everywhere to seek for with one accord and with their whole heart, is to be filled with the Spirit of God. In order to secure attention to this message and attract the hearts of my readers to the blessing of which it speaks, I have laid particular emphasis on certain main points. These I briefly state here:

1) It is the will of God that every one of His children should live entirely and unceasingly under the control of the Holy Spirit.

2) Without being filled with the Spirit, it is utterly impossible that an individual Christian or a church can ever live or work as God desires.

3) Everywhere and in everything we see the proofs, in the life and experience of Christians, that this blessing is but little enjoyed in the Church, and, alas! is but little sought for.

4) This blessing is prepared for us and God waits to bestow it. Our faith may expect it with the greatest confidence.

5) The great hindrance in the way is that the Self-life, and the world, which it uses for its own service and pleasure, usurp the place that Christ ought to occupy.

6) We cannot be filled with the Spirit until we are prepared to yield ourselves to be led by the Lord Jesus to forsake and sacrifice everything for this pearl of great price. …

We have such a feeble conception of the unspiritual and sinful state which prevails in the Church, that, unless we take time to devote our heart and our thoughts to the real facts of the case, the promise of God can make no deep impression upon us. I hope that the attempt I have made to exhibit the subject in various aspects will help to prepare the way for the conviction that this blessing is in truth the one thing needful, and that to get possession of this one thing we ought to bid farewell to everything else we hold dear. …

Owing to the prevailing lack of the presence and operation of the Spirit, it takes a long time ere these spiritual truths concerning the need, and the fullness, and the reality of the Spirit's power can obtain entire mastery over us. It is only by the exercise of Self-sacrifice and persisting in keeping our minds occupied with these thoughts, that we can ever obtain what might otherwise come to us at once. …

On reviewing what I have written, I am inclined to think that there is one point on which I ought to have spoken more definitely. I refer to the place which persevering prayer must occupy in connection with this blessing. This little book was not exclusively written for prayer at the season of Pentecost. Every day ought to be a Pentecostal season in the Church of Christ. For just as little as a man can remain in sound health without the fresh air of heaven, can Christians or the Church live according to the will of God without this blessing.

The book is designed to point to what must prevail throughout all the year; and it seems to me now that, perhaps under the impression that in the season of Pentecost prayer for the blessing is practically unanimous, I have not strongly enough exhorted my readers to ceaseless calling upon God in the confidence that He will answer. Let me advert again to this point in a few sentences.

When we read the Book of the Acts, we see that the filling with the Spirit and His mighty operation was always obtained by prayer. Recall, for example, what took place at Antioch. It was when the Christians there were engaged in fasting and prayer that God regarded them as prepared to receive the revelation that they must separate Barnabas and Saul; and it was only after they had once more fasted and prayed that these two men went forth, sent by the Holy Spirit.

These servants of God felt that the boon they needed must come only from above. To obtain the blessing we so much need, from Heaven and out of the hands of the living God Himself, we in like manner, even with fasting, must liberate ourselves as far as possible from the demands of the earthly life, even in that which otherwise appears quite lawful; and no less must we betake ourselves wholly to God in prayer. Let us therefore never become weary or dispirited, but in union with God's own elect, who call upon Him day and night, entreat Him and even weary Him by our incessant entreaties that the Holy Spirit may again assume His rightful place and exercise full dominion in ourselves and the Church as a whole: yea, more, that He may again have His true place in the Church, be held in honor by all, and in everything reveal the glory of our Lord Jesus.

To the soul that in sincerity prays according to His Word, God's answer will surely come. There is nothing so fitted to search and to cleanse the heart as true prayer. It teaches one to put to himself such questions as these: Do I really desire what above everything I pray for? Am I willing to cast out everything to make room for what God is prepared to give me? Is the prayer of my lips really the prayer of my life? Do I really continue in intercourse with God, waiting upon Him, in quiet trust, until He gives me this great, heavenly, super natural gift, His own Spirit, to be my spirit, the spirit of my life every hour?

Let us "*pray always and not faint*," setting ourselves before God with supplications and strong crying as His priests and the representatives of His Church. We may reckon upon it that He will hear us. "*In my distress I called upon the Lord, And cried unto my God: He heard my voice out of His temple, And my cry before Him came into His ears. He delivered me from my strong enemy, He brought me forth also into a large place*" (Psalm 28: 6, 17, 19). Brother, sister, you know that the Lord is a God that often hides Himself. He desires to be trusted. He is oftentimes very near to us without our knowing it. He is a God who knows His own time. Yet, "*though He tarry, wait for Him. He will surely come. He will not tarry*" (2 Habakuk 2).

How It Was Bestowed from Heaven 1

November 27th

"If you love Me, you will keep My commandments. And I will pray to the Father, and He shall give you another Comforter—the Spirit of Truth."

—JOHN 14: 15–16

A tree lives always according to the nature of the seed from which it sprang. Every living being is always guided and governed by the nature which it received at its birth. Thus the Church of Christ received the promise and the law of her existence and her growth in that which was bestowed upon her in the Holy Spirit on the day of her birth. This is the reason why it is of such importance for us to turn back often to the day of Pentecost and not to rest until we thoroughly understand, and receive, and experience what God did for His people on that day. When we see how the blessing was then for the first time given from Heaven, and what the disposition of heart was that fitted the disciples for receiving the Spirit, then we know for all coming time what remains to be done by ourselves to enjoy the same blessing.

The first disciples serve us as examples and forerunners on the way to the fullness of the Spirit. What, then, was there in them which enabled them to become the recipients of these heavenly gifts and made them fit objects of the unspeakable grace that in them first of all the Three-One God came to take up His abode? The right answer to this question will help us not a little on the way to be filled with the Holy Spirit. …

I

In the first place, there is the fact that they were deeply attached to the Lord Jesus. The Son of God came into the world in order to unite the divine life which He had with the Father with the life of man, and thus to secure that the life of God should penetrate into the life of the creature. When He had completed the work in His own person by His obedience, and death, and resurrection, He was exalted to the throne of God on high in order that in spiritual power, and not only apart from the limitations of earthly life but in the might of the all-penetrating sovereign presence of God, His disciples and His Church might participate in His own very life.

We read that the Holy Spirit "*was not yet,*" because Jesus was not yet glorified (John 7: 39). It is the Spirit of the glorified Jesus that the disciples received on the day of Pentecost, the Spirit of the Head, penetrating all the members of His body. It is evident without proof that, if the fullness of the Spirit thus dwells in Jesus, a personal relationship to Him is the first condition for the reception of the full gift of the Comforter.

It was to attain this end that the Lord Jesus throughout all His three years' work on earth kept the disciples in such close converse with Himself. He desired to attach them to Himself. He wanted them to feel themselves truly one with Him. He wanted them to identify themselves with Him, as far as this was possible. By knowledge and intercourse, by love and obedience, they became inwardly knit to Him. This was the preparation for participating in the Spirit ....

The lesson that is here taught us is indeed extremely simple, but it is one of profound significance. There are not a few Christians who believe in the Lord and are very zealous in His service, who eagerly desire to become holy, and who yet do not succeed in their endeavor. It seems oftentimes as if they could not understand the promise of the Spirit. The thought of being filled with the Spirit exercises but little influence upon them. The reason is obvious. There is lacking in their religion that personal relationship to the Lord Jesus, that inward attachment to Him, that perfectly natural reference to Him as the best and nearest Friend, as the beloved Lord.... This, however, is absolutely indispensable. It is a heart that is entirely occupied with the Lord Jesus, and depends only upon Him, that can alone hope for the fullness of the Spirit.

II

They had left all for Jesus. "Nothing for nothing." This proverb contains a deep truth. A thing that costs me nothing may nevertheless cost me much. It may bring me under an obligation to the giver, and so cost me more than it is worth. I may have so much trouble in appropriating it and keeping it that I may pay much more for it than the price which should be asked for it. "Nothing for nothing": the maxim holds good also in the life of the Kingdom of Heaven. The parables of the Pearl of great price and the Treasure hid in a field teach us that, in order to obtain possession of the kingdom within us, we must sell all that we have. This is the very renunciation that Jesus literally demanded of the disciples who had to follow Him. This is the requirement He so often repeated in His preaching: *"He that forsakes not all that he has cannot be My disciple"* (Luke 14: 33).

The two worlds betwixt which we stand are in such direct conflict with one another, and the world in which we by nature live exercises such a mighty influence over us, that it is often necessary for us, even by external and visible sacrifice, to with draw from it. It was thus that Jesus trained His disciples to long for that which is heavenly. Only thus could He prepare them to desire and receive the heavenly gift with an undivided heart.

The Lord has left us no outward directions as to how much of the world we are to abandon or in what manner. But by His whole Word He teaches us that without sacrifice, without a deliberate separation from the world and forsaking of it, we shall never make much progress in grace. The spirit of this world has penetrated so deeply into us that we do not observe it. We share in its desire for comfort and enjoyment, for Self-pleasing and Self-exaltation, without our knowing how impossible these things make it for us to be filled with the Spirit.

Let us learn from the early disciples that to be filled from the heavenly world with the Spirit that dwells there, we must be entirely separate from the children of this world or from worldly Christians. We must be ready and eager to live as entirely different men, who literally represent Heaven upon earth, because we have received the Spirit of the King of Heaven.

How It Was Bestowed from Heaven 2

November 28th

"If you love Me, you will keep My commandments. And I will pray to the Father, and He shall give you another Comforter—the Spirit of Truth."

—JOHN 14: 15–16

The disciples had despaired utterly of themselves and all that is of man. We have two great enemies by which the devil tempts us and with which we have to contend: The one is the world without, the other is the Self-life within. This last, the Selfish Ego, is much more dangerous and stronger than the first. It is quite possible for us to have made much progress in forsaking the world while the Self-life retains full dominion within us. You see this fact illustrated in the case of the disciples. Peter could say with truth: *"Lo! we have left all and followed You."* Yet how manifestly did the Selfish Ego, with its Self-pleasing and its Self-confidence, still retain its full sway over him.

As the Lord at their first calling led them up to the point of forsaking their outward possessions and following Him, so shortly afterwards He began to teach them that a disciple must deny the Self and lose our own life if we would be worthy of receiving His. … It was love for this Self-life, more than [anything] that hindered the Lord Jesus from doing His work in the heart. It was to cost them more to be redeemed from the Selfish Ego within them than to get quit of the world around them. The Self-life is the natural life of sinful man. He can be liberated from it by nothing save by death that is, by first dying to it and then living in the strength of the new life that comes from God.

The forsaking of the world began at the outset of the three years' discipleship. It was at the end of that period, at the cross of Jesus, that dying to the Self-life first took place. When they saw Him die, they learned to despair of themselves and of everything on which they had hitherto based their hope. Whether they thought of their Lord and the redemption which they had expected, or whether they thought of themselves and their shameful unfaithfulness towards Him, everything tended to fill them with despair. Little did they know that it was just this despair which was to prove the breaking up of their hard hearts the mortification of the Self-life and of confidence in themselves which would enable them to receive something entirely new namely, a divine life through the Spirit of the glorified Jesus in the innermost depths of their souls.

That we understood better that there is nothing which so hampers us as secret reliance on something in ourselves or in the Church around us, which we imagine can help us! On the other hand, there is nothing that brings so much blessing as entire despair of ourselves and of all that is upon the earth, in the way of teaching us to turn our hearts only and wholly to heaven and to partake of the heavenly gift which comes thence.

IV

They received and held fast the promise of the Spirit given by the Lord Jesus. We know how, in His farewell address on the last night of His sojourn on earth, Jesus comforted His disciples in their sorrow over His departure with one great promise: namely, the mission of the Holy Spirit from Heaven. This was to be better than His own bodily presence among them. It would be to them the full fruit and power of His redemption. The Divine Life yea, He Himself, with the Father was to make abode within them. The unheard-of wonder, the mystery of the ages, was to be their portion. They were to know that they were in Him and He in them. …

Now it is just the same disposition that we have so much need of now. To us also, even as to them, has the word of the Lord come concerning the Spirit who is to descend from the throne in the power of His glorified life. "*They that believe in Me, out of their hearts shall flow rivers of living water.*" For us also it is the one thing needful to hold fast that word; to set our whole desire upon the fulfilment of it; to lay aside all else, until we inherit the promise. The word from the mouth of Jesus concerning the reception of the Spirit in such measure that we shall be endued with power from on high must animate and fill us with strong desire, with firm and joyful assurance.

V

They waited upon the Father until the performance of the promise came and they were filled with the Spirit. The ten days of waiting were for them days in which they were continually in the Temple *"praising and blessing God"* and *"continuing instant in prayer and supplication."* … The principal thing is to set ourselves in close and abiding contact with God. … What we desire is the personal occupancy and indwelling of God the Holy Spirit.

God Himself must bestow this personally upon us. A man gives another a piece of bread or a piece of money. He gives it away from himself and has nothing further to do with it. It is not thus with God's gift of the Holy Spirit. No; the Spirit *is* God. God is in the Spirit who comes to us, even as He was in the Son. The gift of the Spirit is the most personal act of the Godhead: it is the gift of Himself unto us. We have to receive it in the very closest personal contact with God. …

It is the Goodness of God alone that must give it; it is His Omnipotence that must work it in us. Our disposition must be one of silent assurance that the Father desires to give it to us; that He will not keep us waiting one moment longer than is absolutely necessary; and that there shall not be a single soul which persists in waiting in the pathway of Self-abnegation and dependence that shall not be filled with the glory of God.

... The day of Pentecost was the planting of the Christian Church, and the Holy Spirit became the power of its life. Let us turn back to that experience. There is our power still. We learn from the disciples what is really necessary. Attachment to Jesus, the abandonment of everything in the world for Him, despair of Self and of all help from man, holding on to the word of promise, and then waiting on God, "the living God," this is the sure way of living in the joy and the power of the Holy Spirit.

How Fully It Is Assured to Us

November 29th

"If you then, being evil, know how to give good gifts to your children, how much more shall your Heavenly Father give the Holy Spirit to them that ask Him?"

—LUKE 11: 13

There are many preliminary questions which arise at once in connection with this subject, and which tempt us to resolve that we shall first take in and understand everything about it before we expect the blessing. Two of these questions I shall venture to mention now.

The first is: whence must this blessing come, from within or from above? Some earnest Christians will say at once that "it must come from within." The Holy Spirit descended upon the earth on the day of Pentecost and was given to the Christian community. At the moment of conversion He comes into our heart. We have therefore no longer to pray that He may be given to us: we have simply to recognize and use what we already have. It is not as if we had to seek to have more of the Spirit: we have Him in the fullness of the gift as it is. It is rather the Holy Spirit who must have more of us. As we yield ourselves entirely to Him He will entirely fill us. It is from within that the blessing must come: the fountain of living water is already there; the fountain has only to be opened and every obstruction cleared out of the way and the water shall stream forth. It must spring from within.

On the other hand, there are not a few that say, "No; it must come from above." When, on the arrival of the day of Pentecost, the Father bestowed the Spirit, He did not give Him away beyond His own control. The fullness of the Spirit still remains in God. God bestows nothing apart from Himself, to work without or independently of His will. He Himself works only through the Spirit, and every new and greater manifestation of the Spirit's power comes directly from above. Long after the day of Pentecost the Spirit came down again from heaven at Samaria and Cesarea. In His fullness He is in Heaven still; and it is from God in heaven that the fullness of the Spirit is to be ever waited for.

Brother Christian, pray, do not linger till by reasonings of your own you have decided which of these representations is the right one. God can bless men in both ways. When the flood came all the fountains of the abyss were broken up and the sluices of heaven were opened. It came simultaneously from beneath and from above. God is prepared to bless men in both of these methods. He desires to teach us to know and honor the Spirit who is already within us. He would fain also bring us to wait upon Himself in a spirit of utter dependence, and to beseech Him that He as our Father would give us our daily bread, the new, the fuller influx of His Spirit. I entreat you not to suffer yourself to be held back by such a question as this. God understands your petition. He knows what you would have. Believe that God is prepared to fill you with His Spirit; let that faith look up to Him with unceasing prayer and confidence. He will give the blessing.

Does this blessing come gradually or at once? Will it manifest itself in the shape of a silent, unobserved increase of the grace of the Spirit or as a momentary, immediate outpouring of His power? It must suffice for me to say here again that God has already sent this blessing in both modes, and will continue to do so still. What must take place at once is this: there must be a definite resolve to place the whole life unreservedly under the control of the Spirit, and a conviction of faith that God has accepted this surrender. In the majority of cases this is done at once. It must at last come to this, perhaps after a long course of seeking and praying, that the soul shall present itself to God for this blessing in one definite, irrevocable act, and shall believe that the offering is then sanctified and accepted upon the altar. Thenceforth, whether the experience of the blessing comes at once and with power, or comes quietly and gradually, the soul must maintain its act of Self-dedication and simply look to God to do His own work.

Thus in dealing with all such questions, the chief concern is this: "only believe" and rest in the faithfulness of God. Hold fast this one principle: God has given us a promise that He will fill us with His Spirit. It is His work to make His promise an accomplished fact. Thank God for the promise even as you would thank Him for the fulfillment of it. In the promise, God has already pledged Himself to you. Rejoice in Him and in His faithfulness. Be not held back by any questions whatever. Set your heart on what God will do, and on Himself from whom the blessing must come. The result will be certain and glorious.

It is one of the saddest tokens of the unspiritual condition of the Church that so many are content with things just as they are, and have no desire to know more of this seeking for the reality of the Spirit's power. … Such people would condemn the language of Laodicea, and would refuse to say that they were rich and increased in goods and had need of nothing (Revelation 3: 17), and yet there are some traces of this spirit in what they say. They do not consider the injunction to be "*filled with the Spirit.*" … When you speak of these things you will receive little encouragement from them. They do not understand what you mean. They believe indeed in the Holy Spirit, but their eyes have not been opened to the fact that more of the Spirit, the fullness of the Spirit, is the one thing needful for the Church. …

Pray to the Father that He would grant unto you to be strengthened with might by His Spirit. Adore Him who is able to do for us exceeding abundantly above all that we ask and think, and give Him the glory. Let faith in the Omnipotence of God fill your soul and you will be full of the assurance that, however difficult, however improbable, however impossible it may seem, God can fill us with His Spirit. "Only believe."

… Cast yourself into the arms of your Father who gives His children the Holy Spirit much more readily than an earthly father gives bread. Only believe, and count upon the love of God. All your Self-dedication and surrender—all your faith and integrity—is not a work by which you have to move God or make Him willing to bless you. Far from it. It is God that desires to bless you, and that will Himself work everything in you. God loves you as a father and sees that, to be able to live in perfect health and happiness as His child, you have need of nothing but this one thing to be full of His Spirit. Jesus has by His blood opened up the way to the full enjoyment of this love.

You must learn to enter into this love, to abide in this love, and by faith to acknowledge that it shines upon you and surrounds you, even as the light of the Sun illumines and animates your body. Begin to trust this love. … It is your Father, whose love waits to make you full of His Spirit. He Himself will do it for you.

And what does He crave at your hands? Simply this—that you yield yourself to Him in utter unworthiness, nothingness, and impotence, to let Him do this work in you. He is prepared to take charge of all the preparatory work. You may be sure that He will help you by His Spirit. He will strengthen you with might in the inner man, silently and hiddenly, yet none the less surely, to abandon everything that has to be given up and to receive this treasure. He will help you in the faith of appropriation to rest in His word and to wait for Him; and He will hold Himself responsible for all the future. He will make provision that you shall be able to walk in the fullness of this blessing. …

In His promise of the blessing and the power of the Spirit the Lord Jesus always pointed to God the Father. He called it "*the promise of the Father*" (Luke 24: 49). He directed us to the faithfulness of God: "*The One who calls you is faithful, and He will do it*" (1 Thessalonians 5: 24). He directed us to the power of God: The Spirit was, as power from on high, to come from God Himself (Acts 1: 4, 8). He directed us to the love of God; it is as a Father that God is to give this boon to His children. Let every thought of this blessing and every desire for it only lead us to God. Here is something that HE must do, that He must give, that HE, HE ALONE, must work. Let us in silent adoration set our heart upon God: He will do something for us. Let us joyfully trust in Him: He is able to do above all praying and thinking. His love will, so willingly, bestow upon us a full blessing.

Therefore, "*only believe*": God will make me full of the Spirit. And say humbly: Behold the servant of the Lord. Let Him do to me what is good in His sight. Be it unto me according to Your word. "*The One who calls you is faithful, and He will do it.*"

How Glorious It Is 1

November 30th

"They were all filled with the Holy Spirit"

—ACTS 2: 4

Whenever we speak of being filled with the Holy Spirit, and desire to know what it precisely is, our thoughts always turn back to the day of Pentecost. There we see as in a mirror how glorious the blessing is that is brought from heaven by the Holy Spirit and with which He can fill the hearts of men.

There is one fact which makes the great event of the day of Pentecost doubly instructive: this namely, that we have learned to know very intimately the men who were then filled with the Spirit, by their fellowship for three years with the Lord Jesus. Their infirmities and defects, their sins and perversities, all stand open to our view.

But the blessing of Pentecost wrought a complete transformation. They became entirely new men, so that one might say of them with truth: "*Old things have passed away; behold, all things have become new*" (2 Corinthians 5: 17). Close study of them and their example helps us in more than one way. It shows us to what weak and sinful men the Spirit will come. It teaches us how they were prepared for the blessing.

It teaches us also—and this is the principal thing—how mighty and complete the revolution is that is brought to pass when the Holy Spirit is received in His fullness. It lets us see how glorious the grace that awaits us is if we press on to the full blessing of Pentecost.

The ever-abiding presence and indwelling of the Lord Jesus.

In this we have the first and principal blessing of the Pentecostal life. In the course of our Lord's dealings with His disciples on earth He spared no pains to teach and train them, to renew and sanctify them. In most respects, however, they remained just what they were. The reason was that up to this point He was nothing more than an external Christ who stood outside of them and from without sought to work upon them by His word and His personal influence. With the advent of Pentecost this condition was entirely changed.

In the Holy Spirit, He came down as the inward, indwelling Christ, to become in the very innermost recesses of their being the life of their life. This is what He Himself had promised in the words: "*I will not leave you comfortless: I will come to you.*" "*At that day, you shall know that I am in My Father, and you in Me, and I in you*" (John 14: 18, 20).

This was the source of all the other blessings that came with Pentecost. Jesus Christ, the crucified, the glorified, the Lord from heaven, came in spiritual power, by the Spirit, to impart to them that ever-abiding presence of their Lord that had been promised to them. And that was in a way that was most intimate, all-powerful, and wholly divine: by the indwelling which makes Him in truth their life. Him whom they had had in the flesh, living with them on earth, they now received by the Spirit in His heavenly glory within them! Instead of an outward Jesus near them, they now obtained the inward Jesus within them.

The Spirit of Jesus came into them as the life and the power of sanctification.

This springs from the first and principal blessing. Here I shall allude at the outset to only one feature in this change. We know how often the Lord had to rebuke them for their pride and exhort them to humility. It was all no avail. Even on the last night of His earthly life, at the table of the holy supper, there was a strife amongst them as to which of them should be the greatest (Luke 22: 24).

The outward teaching of the outward Christ, whatever other influences it may have exercised, was not sufficient to redeem them from the power of indwelling sin. This could be achieved only by the indwelling Christ. Only when Jesus descended into them by the Holy Spirit did they undergo a complete change. They received Him in His heavenly humility and subjection to the Father, and in His Self-sacrifice for others, as their life. Henceforth all was changed. From that moment onwards they were animated by the spirit of the meek and lowly Jesus.

This in very truth is still the only way to a real sanctification, to a life that actually overcomes sin. Many preachers and many Christians keep their minds occupied only with the external Christ on the cross or in heaven, and wait for the blessing of His teaching and His working without understanding that the blessing of Pentecost brings Him into us, to work Himself all in us. Because of this, they make little progress in sanctification. Christ Himself is of God made unto us sanctification: and that in no other way than by our living and being moved and existing in Him, because He lives and abides in our heart and works all there (1 Corinthians 1: 30).

An overflowing of the heart with the love of God.

This also is a part of the blessing of Pentecost. Next to pride, lack of love—or as we may put it in one word, lovelessness—was the sin for which the Lord had so often to rebuke His disciples. These two sins have in truth one and the same root: the Self-seeking I, the desire for Self pleasing. The new commandment that He gave them, the token whereby all men should know that they were His disciples, was love to one another (John 13: 35). How gloriously was it manifested on the day of Pentecost that the Spirit of the Lord shed abroad His love in the hearts of His own. The multitude of them that believed were as one heart, one soul. All things they possessed were held in common. No one said that anything of that which he had was his own. The Kingdom of Heaven with its life of love had come down to them. The spirit, the disposition, the wonderful love of Jesus, filled them, because He Himself had come into them.

How closely the mighty working of the Spirit and the indwelling of the Lord Jesus are bound up with a life in love appears from the prayer of Paul in behalf of the Ephesians. He asks that they might be strengthened with power by the Spirit, in order that Christ might dwell in their hearts. Then he forthwith makes this addition: "*that you, being rooted and grounded in love, may be strong to apprehend the love of Christ which passes knowledge*" (Ephesians

3:1 7–19).

The filling with the Spirit and the indwelling of Christ bring of themselves a life that has its root, its joy, its power, its evidence in love, because the indwelling Christ Himself is Love. Oh, how would the love of God fill the Church and convince the world that she has received a heavenly element into her life, if the filling with the Spirit and the indwelling of Christ in the heart were recognized as the blessing which the Father has promised us!

How Glorious It Is 2

December 1st

We all know how, from fear rising in his heart at the word of a woman, Peter denied his Lord, and how that same night all the disciples fled and forsook Him. Their hearts were really attached to Him, and they were sincerely willing to do what they had promised and go to die with Him. But when it came to the crisis, they had neither courage nor power. They had to say: "*To will is present with me, but to perform that which is good I find not*" (Romans 7: 18).

The coming of the Spirit changed weakness and fear into courage and power.

After the blessing of the Spirit of Pentecost, there was no more question of merely willing apart from performing. By Christ dwelling in us God works both the willing and the doing (Philippians 2: 13). With what confidence of spirit did Peter on the day of Pentecost dare to preach the Crucified One to thousands of hostile Jews. With what boldness was he able in opposition to the leaders of the people, to say, "*We ought to obey God rather than men*" (Acts 5: 29).

With what courage and joy were Stephen and Paul and so many others enabled to encounter threatening and suffering and death. They did this even triumphantly. It was because the Spirit of Christ, the Victor—yes, the Christ Himself, who had been glorified—dwelled within them. It is the joy of the blessing of Pentecost that gives courage and power to speak for Jesus, because by it the whole heart is filled with Him.

The blessing of Pentecost makes the whole Word of God new.

How distinctly do we see this fact in the case of the disciples. As with all the Jews of that age, their ideas of the Messiah and the Kingdom of God were utterly external and carnal. All the instruction of the Lord Jesus throughout three long years could not detach their minds from them. They were utterly unable to comprehend the doctrine of a suffering and dying Messiah or the hope of His invisible spiritual dominion. Even after His resurrection He had to rebuke them for their unbelieving spirit and their backwardness in understanding the Scriptures

With the coming of the day of Pentecost an entire change took place. The whole of their ancient Scriptures opened up before them. The light of the Holy Spirit in them illumined the Word. In the preaching of Peter and Stephen, in the addresses of Paul and James, we see how a divine light had shone upon the Word of the Old Testament. They saw everything through the Spirit of this Jesus who had made His abode with them. So will it be also with ourselves. It is as necessary as it is helpful that we should study the Scriptures and meditate upon them, and keep the Word of God alike in head and heart and daily walk. Let us, however, constantly remember that it is only when we are filled with the Spirit that we can rightly and fully experience the spiritual power and truth of the Word. He is "*the Spirit of truth.*" He alone guides into all truth when He dwells in us (John 14: 17; 16: 13).

It is the blessing of Pentecost that gives power to bless others.

The divine power of the exalted Jesus to grant repentance and the forgiveness of sins is exercised by Him through His servants whom He sends forth to proclaim these blessings. The minister of the Gospel who desires to preach repentance and forgiveness through Jesus with success in winning souls, must do the work in the power of the Spirit of this Jesus.

The chief reason why so much preaching of conversion and pardon is fruitless lies in the fact that these elements of truth are presented only as a doctrine. Preachers endeavor to secure a way to the hearts of their audience in the power of merely human earnestness and reasoning and eloquence. But little blessing is won by these means.

It is the man that makes it his chief desire to be filled with the Spirit of God, and then by faith in the indwelling of Christ comes to be assured that the glorified Lord will speak and work in him, who will obtain blessing. It is true, indeed, that this blessing will not always be given in the very same measure or in the very same manner, but it will always certainly come, just because the preacher permits the Lord to work in and through him. Alike in preaching and in the daily life of a servant of Christ, the full blessing of Pentecost is the sure way of becoming a blessing to others. "He that believeth in Me," said Jesus, "out of his belly shall flow rivers of living water" (John 7: 38). This He said of the Holy Spirit. A heart filled with the Spirit will overflow with the Spirit.

It is the blessing of Pentecost that will make the Church of Christ what God would have her be.

We have spoken of what the Spirit will do in individual believers. We have also to think of what the blessing will be when the Church as a whole shall apprehend her calling to be filled with the Spirit, and then to exhibit the life and the power—yes, and the very presence—of her Lord to the world. ... To this end, let us simply recall the morning of the day of Pentecost. At that juncture the Christian Church in Jerusalem consisted only of one hundred and twenty disciples, most of them unlearned fishermen, publicans and humble women, an insignificant and despised gathering (Acts 1:15). Yet it was just by these believers that the Kingdom of God had to be proclaimed and extended, and they did it. By them, and those who were added to them, the power of Jewish prejudice and of pagan hardness of heart was overcome, and the Church of Christ won glorious triumphs.

This grand result was achieved simply and only because the first Christian Church was filled with the Spirit. The members of it gave themselves wholly to their Lord. They allowed themselves to be filled and consecrated, governed and used only by Him. They yielded themselves to Him as instruments of His power. He dwelt in them and wrought in them all His wondrous deeds. It is to this same experience that the Church of Christ in our age must be brought back. This is the only thing that will help her in the conflict with mere civilization or paganism, with sin or the world. She must be filled with the Spirit.

One Thing Needful

Beloved fellow Christians, this summons comes to you. "*One thing is needful*" (Luke 10: 42). Alike for yourselves and the whole Church of the Lord, this is the one thing that is needful: we have to be filled with the Spirit. Please do not imagine that you must comprehend or understand it all before you seek and find it. For those who wait upon Him, God will do even that which has not yet entered into their heart to conceive. If you would taste the happiness, if you would know by personal experience the unutterable blessedness of having Jesus in the heart, of having in you His Spirit of holiness and humility, of love and Self-sacrifice, of courage and power, as naturally and continuously as you have your own spirit; if you would have the Word of God in you as light and power, and be enabled to carry it about as a blessing for others; if you would see the Church of Christ stand forth arrayed in her first splendor—then separate yourselves from everything that is evil. Cast evil utterly out of your heart, and fix your desire on this one thing: to be filled with the Spirit of God. Reckon upon receiving this as your rightful heritage. Appropriate it and hold it fast by faith. It shall certainly be given you.

How It is Obtained by Us

December 2nd

"Be not drunken with wine, wherein is riot, but be filled with the Spirit."
—EPHESIANS 5: 18

The command to be filled with the Spirit is just as peremptory as the prohibition not to be drunken with wine. As truly as we are not at liberty to be guilty of the vice are we bound not to be disobedient to the positive injunction. The same God who calls upon, us to live in sobriety urges us with equal earnestness to be filled with the Spirit. ...I desire now to suggest to those who really long for this blessing some directions whereby they may obtain what is prepared for them.

I

The full blessing of Pentecost is the inheritance of all the children of God. This is the first principle we have to enunciate. There are many of God's children who do not fully believe this. They imagine that the day of Pentecost was only the birthday feast of the Church, and that it was thus a time of blessing and of power which was not destined to endure. They do not reflect on the command to be filled with the Spirit. The result is that they never with earnestness seek to receive the full blessing. They take their ease and remain content with the weak and defective life in which the Church of the day exists.

Is not this the case with you, my reader? Far be it from us. In order to carry on her work in the world, the Church requires the full blessing. To please your Lord and to live a life of holiness, and joy, and power, you too have need of it. To manifest His presence, and indwelling, and glory in you, Jesus counts it necessary that you should be filled with the Spirit. Believe firmly that the full blessing of Pentecost is a sacred reality. A child of God may and must have it. Take time to contemplate it and to suffer yourself to be fully possessed by the thought of its glorious significance and power. A firm confidence that the blessing is actually within our reach is the first step towards obtaining it and a powerful impulse in the pursuit.

II

I do not as yet have this blessing. This is the second step towards it. You may perhaps put the question why it should be necessary to cherish this conviction. I will tell you briefly the reasons why I consider it of importance. The first is that there are many Christians who think that they already have the Holy Spirit, and that all they require is to be more faithful in the endeavor to know and to obey Him. They think that they are already standing in God's grace, and that they only need to make a better use of the life they possess. …

Just as the first condition of any recovery from disease is the knowledge that I am sick, so it is absolutely necessary for them to discover and acknowledge that they do not live the life of Pentecost, that they do not walk in the fullness and the joy of the Spirit, that they do not possess the full blessing which is indispensable for them if they are to please God in everything. Once this first conviction is made thoroughly clear to them, they will be prepared for another consideration namely, that they ought to acknowledge the guiltiness of their condition. They ought to see that if they have not yet rendered obedience to the command to *"be filled with the Spirit,"* this defect is to be ascribed to sluggishness, and Self-satisfaction, and unbelief. … When once the confession that they have not yet received the full blessing is deeply rooted in them, there will spring from it a stronger impulse to attain to it. …

III

The thought that will come next in succession is: This blessing is for me. I have spoken of those who suppose that the full blessing of Pentecost was only for the first Christian community. There are others who are willing enough to acknowledge that it was intended also for the Church of later times but still think that all are not entitled to expect it.

Soul, do not permit yourself to be deceived by such shallow views. All the members of a body, even to the very least, must be healthy before the body as a whole can be healthy. The indwelling, the fullness of the Spirit, is nothing but the entire healthfulness of the body of Christ. Be assured that, even though you are actually the most insignificant member of it, the blessing is for you. In your own little measure you can at least be full. In this respect the Father makes no exceptions.

A great distinction doubtless prevails in point of gifts, and calling, and circumstances; but there can be no distinction in the love of the Father and His desire to see every one of His children in full health and in the full enjoyment of the Spirit of adoption. Learn, then, to express and to repeat over again the conviction: "This blessing is for me. My Father desires to have me that He may fill me with His Spirit. The blessing lies before me, to be taken with my full consent. I will no longer despise by unbelief what falls to me as my birthright. With my whole heart I will say: This blessing is for me."

IV

I cannot grasp this blessing in my own power. Whenever a Christian begins to strive for this blessing, we generally make a variety of efforts to reach after the faith, and obedience, and humility, and submission which are the conditions of obtaining it. Then, when we do not succeed, we are tempted to blame ourself, and if we do not become utterly discouraged, we rouse ourself to still stronger effort and greater zeal. All this struggling is not without its value and its use. It has its use, however, in other ways than are commonly anticipated. It does the very work that the law does that is to say, it brings us to the knowledge of our entire impotence; it leads us to that despair of ourselves in which we become willing to give to God the place that belongs to Him.

This lesson is entirely indispensable: "I can neither bestow this blessing on myself nor take it. It is God alone that must work it in me." The blessing of Pentecost is a supernatural gift, a wonderful act of God in the soul. The life of God in every soul is just as truly a work of God as when that life was first manifested in Jesus Christ. … The impartation of this heavenly blessing is as entirely an act of God as the resurrection of Christ from the dead was His Divine work. As Christ Jesus had wholly and entirely to go down unto death, and lay aside utterly the life He had, in order to receive a new life from God, so must the believer abandon all power and hope of his own to receive this full blessing as a free gift of Divine Omnipotence. This acknowledgment of our utter impotence, this descent into true Self-despair, is indispensable if we would enjoy this supreme blessing.

V

I must have this blessing at any cost. To get possession of the pearl of great price, the merchant man had to sell all that he had. The full blessing of Pentecost is to be obtained at no smaller price. He that would have it must sell all, must forsake all: sin to its smallest item, the love of the world in its most innocent forms, Self-will in its simplest and most natural expressions, every faculty of our nature, every moment of our life, every pleasure that feeds our Self-complacency, every exercise of our body, soul, and spirit all must be surrendered to the power of the Spirit of God. In nothing can independent control or in dependent force have a place: everything I say must be under the leading of the Spirit. One must indeed say: "Cost what it may, I am determined to have this blessing." Only the vessel that is utterly empty of everything can be filled and overflow with this living water. …

This, accordingly, is what must be done by the soul who intends to be sincerely ready to part with everything, even though he feels that he has no power to accomplish it. The selling price is not always paid at the moment; nevertheless, the purchaser may become the possessor as soon as the sale is concluded and security is given for the payment. My brother, this very day speak the word: "Cost what it may, I will have this blessing." Jesus is surety that you will have power to abandon everything. Express your decision in the presence of God with confidence and perseverance. Repeat it before your own conscience and say: "I am a purchaser of the pearl of great price: I have offered everything to obtain the full blessing of Pentecost. I have said to God that I must, I will have it.

VI

In faith that God accepts my surrender and bestows this blessing upon me, I appropriate it for myself. There is a great difference betwixt the appropriation of a blessing by faith and the actual experience of it. It is because Christians do not understand this that they often become discouraged, when they do not at once experience the feeling and the enjoyment of what is promised them. Whenever in response to the offer of Christ you have said that you forsake all, and count it but loss for the full blessing of Pentecost, then from that moment you have to believe that He receives your offer and that He bestows upon you the fullness of the Spirit.

Yet it may easily be that you cannot at that crisis trace any marked change in your experience. It is as if everything in you remained in its old condition. Now, however, is just the very time to persevere in faith. Learn by faith to be as sure as if you had seen it written in Heaven that God has accepted your surrender of everything as a certain and completed transaction. In this faith look upon yourself as one who is known to God as having sold everything to obtain this heavenly treasure. Believe that God has in Heaven bestowed upon you the fullness of the Spirit. In this faith regard yourself as on the way to know the full blessing also in feeling and experience. Believe that God will order this blessing to break forth and be revealed in you. In this faith let your life be a life of joyful thanksgiving and expectation. God will not disappoint you.

… God desires to make you full of the Holy Spirit. He would fain have your whole nature and life under the power of the Holy Spirit. He asks if you on your part are willing, if you really desire to have it. Pray let there be in your answer no uncertain sound, but let all that is within you cry out: "Yea, Lord, with all my heart." Let this promise of your God become the chief element in your life, the most precious, the chief, the only thing you seek. Do not be content to think and pray over it, but this very day enter into a transaction and a compact with God that will admit of no doubt concerning the choice you have made.

How It Is to be Found by All 1

December 3rd

"And I will sprinkle clean water upon you, and you shall be clean: from all your filthiness, and from all your idols, will I cleanse you. And I will put My Spirit within you, and cause you to walk in My statutes, and you shall keep My judgments, and do them."

—EZEKIEL 36: 25, 27

The full Pentecostal blessing is for all the children of God. *"As many as are led by the Spirit of God, they are the children of God"* (Romans 8: 14). God does not give a half portion to any one of His children. To everyone He says: *"Son, you are ever with Me, and all that I have is yours"* (Luke 15: 31). Christ is not divided; the one who receives Him receives Him in all His fullness. Every Christian is destined by God, and is actually called, to be filled with the Spirit. …

Amongst those who read this book there may be Christians who have heard but little of the full Pentecostal blessing, and in whose hearts the desire has arisen to obtain a share in it. There is, however, so much that they do not as yet understand, that they are willing indeed to have pointed out to them in the simplest possible fashion, where they are to begin, and what they have to do, in order to succeed in their desire. They are prepared to acknowledge that their life is full of sin, and that it seems to them as if they would have to strive long and earnestly, ere they can become full of the Spirit. I should like much to inspire them with fresh courage and to direct them to the God who has said: *"I the Lord will hasten it in its time."* I should like to take them and guide them to the place where God will bless them, and to point to them out of His Word what the disposition and the attitude must be in which they can receive this blessing.

I

First of all, there must be a new discovery and confession and casting away of sin. In the message of Ezekiel, God first promised: *"I will cleanse you,"* and then: *"I will put My Spirit within you."* A vessel into which anything precious is to be poured must always first be cleansed. So, if the Lord is to give you a new and full blessing, a new cleansing must also take place. In your conversion, it is true, there was a confession and putting away of sin. Yet this separation was but superficial and external. The soul was still half enveloped in darkness: it thought more of its heinous sins and the punishment they might entail. After conversion it did indeed endeavor to overcome sin, but the effort did not succeed. It did not know in what holiness the Lord desires His people to live: it did not know how pure and holy the Lord would have it be and would make it be.

This new cleansing must come through new confession and discovery of sin. The old leaven cannot be purged away unless it be first searched for and found. Do not say that you already know sufficiently well that your Christian life is full of sin. Sit down in silent meditation and with the express purpose of seeing of what sort your life as a Christian has been. How much pride, Self-seeking, worldliness, Self-will, and impurity has been in it. Can such a heart receive the fullness of the Spirit? It is impossible. Look into your home life. In your intercourse with wife and children … do not hastiness of temper, anxiety about yourself, bitterness, idle or harsh or unbecoming words testify how little you have been cleansed? Look into the current life of the Church. How much religion is there that is merely intellectual, or formal, or pleasing to men, without that real humiliation of spirit, that real desire for the living God, that real love for Jesus, that real subjection to the word, which constitute worship in spirit and in truth. Look into your general course of conduct. Consider whether the people amongst whom you mingle can testify that they have observed, by your honorable spirit and disinterestedness and freedom from worldly-mindedness, that you are one who has been cleansed from sin by God.

Contemplate all this in the light of what God expects from you and has offered to work in you, and take your place as a guilty, helpless soul that must be cleansed before God can bestow the full blessing upon you. On the back of this discovery follows the actual putting away and casting out of what is impure. This is something that you are simply bound to do. You must come with these sins, and especially with those that are most strictly your own besetting sins, and acknowledge them before God in confession, and there and then make renunciation of them. You must be brought to the conviction that your life is a guilty and shameful life. You are not at liberty to take comfort from the consideration that you are so weak, or that the majority of Christians live no higher life. It must become a matter of earnest resolve with you that your life is to undergo a complete transformation. The sins that still cleave to you are to be cast off and done away with.

Perhaps you may say in reply that you find yourself unable to do away with them or cast them off. I tell you that you are quite able to do this; and in this way. … You can give up to God those sins of yours, against which you feel yourself utterly impotent. You can give them up to Him to be dealt with as He desires and He will fulfill His promise: *"I will cleanse you from all your filthiness."* There is nothing so needful as that there should be a very definite understanding between you and the Lord, that you on your part really confess your sin and bid it everlasting farewell and give it up, and that you wait on Him until He assures you that He has taken it, or rather has taken your heart and life, into His own hands to give you a complete victory.

II

In this way you come to a new discovery, and reception, and experience of what Christ is and is prepared to do for you. If the knowledge of sin at conversion is superficial, so also is the faith in Jesus. Our faith, our reception of Jesus never goes further or deeper than our insight into sin. If since your conversion you have learned to know the inward invincible power of sin in you, you are now prepared to receive from God a discovery of the inward invincible power of the Lord Jesus in your heart, such as you have hitherto had no idea of.

If you really long for a complete deliverance from sin, so as to be able to live in obedience to God, God will reveal the Lord Jesus to you as a complete Savior. He will make you to know that, although the flesh always remains in you, with its inclination to evil, the Lord Jesus will so dwell in your heart that the power of the flesh shall be kept in subjection by Him, in order that you may no longer do the will of the flesh. Through Jesus Christ, God will cleanse you from all unrighteousness, so that day by day you may walk before God with a pure heart.

What you really need is the discovery that He is prepared to work this change in you, and that you may receive it by faith, here and now. Yes, this is what Jesus Christ desires to work in you by the Holy Spirit. He came to put away sin; not the guilt and punishment of it only, but sin itself. He has not only mastered the power and dominion of the law and its curse over you, but has also completely broken and taken away the power and dominion of sin. He has completely rescued you as a newborn soul from beneath the power of sin; and He lives in His heavenly authority and all-pervading presence in order to work out this deliverance in you. In this power He will live in you and Himself carry out His work in you. As the indwelling Christ, He is bent on maintaining and manifesting His redemption in you. The sins which you have confessed, the pride and the lovelessness, the worldly-mindedness and vanity and all uncleanness, He will by His power take out of your heart; so that, although the flesh may tempt you, the choice and the joy of your heart abide in Him and in His obedience to God's will. Yes: you may indeed become *"more than conquerors through Him that loved you"* (Romans 8: 37). As the indwelling Christ, He will overcome sin in you.

How It is to Be Found by All 2

December 4th

What then is required on our side? Only this, a thing that can be done at once, namely, that when the soul sees it to be true that Jesus will carry out this work, it shall then open the door before Him and receive Him into the heart as Lord and King. Yes: that can be done at once. A house that has remained closely shut for twenty years can be penetrated by the light in a moment, if the doors and windows are thrown open. In like manner, a heart that has remained enveloped in darkness and impotence for twenty years, because it knew not that Jesus was willing to take the victory over sin into His own hands, can have its whole experience changed in a moment. When it acknowledges its sinful condition and yields itself to God, and believes that the Son of God is prepared to assume the responsibility of the inner life and its purification from sin; when it ventures to trust the Lord that He will do this work at the very moment; then it may firmly believe that it is done, and that Jesus takes all that is in me into His own hands.

This is indeed an act of faith, that must be held fast in faith. When doors and windows are thrown open, and the light streaming in drives out the darkness, we discover at once how much dust and impurity there is in the house. But the light shines just in order that we may see how to take it away. When we receive Christ into the heart everything is not yet perfected: light and gladness are not seen and experienced at once; but by faith the soul knows that He who is faithful will keep His word and will surely do His work. The faith that has up to this moment only sought and wrestled, now rests in the Lord and His word. It knows that what was begun by faith must be carried forward only by faith. It says: "I abide in Jesus; I know that He abides in me and that He will manifest Himself unto me." As Jesus cleansed the lepers with a word, and it was only when they were on their way to the priest that they found out they were clean, so He cleanses us by His Word. He that firmly holds that fact in faith will see the proofs of it.

III

So the soul is prepared to receive the full blessing of the Spirit. The Lord gave first the promise, I will cleanse you; and then the second promise, I will put My Spirit within you. The Holy Spirit cannot come with power or fill the heart and continue to dwell in it, unless a special and complete cleansing first takes place within it. The Spirit and sin are engaged in a mortal combat. The only reason why the Spirit works so feebly in the Church is sin, which is all too little known or dreaded or cast out. We do not believe in the power of Christ to cleanse; and therefore He cannot do His work of baptizing with the Spirit. ... Cleave to Jesus, who cleanses you: let Him be all within you; God will see to it that you are filled with the Spirit.

Only keep in view these two truths: First, that the gift and the blessing and the fullness of the Spirit do not always come, as on the day of Pentecost, with external observation. God is often a God that hides Himself. Do not be surprised, therefore, if your heart does not at once feel, as you should like it to feel, immediately after your act of surrender or appropriation. Best assured that, if you fully trust Christ to do everything for you, He there and then begins to do it in secret by His Spirit. Count upon it that, if you present yourself to God as a pure vessel, cleansed by Christ, to be filled with the Spirit, God will take you at your word and say unto you: "*Receive the Holy Spirit; be it unto you according to your faith*" (John 20: 22).

At that moment bow down before Him, more and more silently, more and more deeply, in holy adoration and expectation, in the blessed assurance that the unseen God has now begun to carry on His work more mightily in you, and that He will also manifest it to you more gloriously than ever before.

The other thing you must keep in view is the purpose for which the Spirit is given. "*I will put My Spirit within you, and I will cause you to walk in My statutes and to keep My judgments and do them*" (Ezekiel 36: 27). The fullness of the Spirit must be sought and received and kept with the direct aim that you shall now simply and wholly live to do God's will and work upon the earth, yes: only to be able to live like the Lord Jesus, and to say with Him: "*Lo! I come to do Your will*" (Psalm 40: 7; Hebrews 10: 7) If you cherish this disposition, the fullness of the Spirit may be positively expected. Be full of courage and yield yourself to walk in God's statutes and to keep His judgments and do them, and you may trust God to keep His word that He will cause you to keep and do them. He, the living God, will work in you. Even before you are aware how the Spirit is in you, He will enable you to experience the full blessing.

Christian! Have you never yet known the fullness of the Spirit, or have you perhaps been really seeking it for a long while without finding it? Here you have at last the sure method of winning it. Acknowledge the sinfulness of your condition as a Christian and make renunciation of it, once and for all, by yielding it up to God. Acknowledge that the Lord Jesus is ready and able to cleanse your heart from its sin; to conquer these sins by His entrance into it, and to set you free; and that His purpose is to do this at once. Take Him now as your Lord, at once and for ever. Then you may be assured that God will put His Spirit within you in a way and a measure and a power of which you have hitherto had no idea. Be assured that He will do it. Permit Him to begin; let Him do it in you now.

How Everything Must be Given Up for It 1

December 5th

"Then shall the Son also Himself be subjected to Him who subjected all things unto Him, that God may be all in all."

—1 CORINTHIANS 15: 28

If then we speak of entire consecration, we are frequently asked what the precise distinction is betwixt the ordinary doctrine of sanctification, and the preaching of that gracious work which has begun to prevail in the Church in recent years. One answer that may be given is that the distinction lies solely in the little word, *all.* That word is the key of the secret. The ordinary method of proclaiming the necessity of holiness is true so far as it goes; but sufficient emphasis is not laid on this one point of the "All."

So is it also with the question as to the reasons why the fullness of the Spirit is not more widely enjoyed. That little word "All" suggests the explanation. So long as the "All" of God, of sin, of Christ, of surrender, of the Spirit, and of faith, is not fully understood, the soul cannot enjoy all that God desires to give and be, all that God would have it be. In this our last meditation let us consider the full Pentecostal blessing from this standpoint. We would fain do this in a spirit of humble waiting on God, and with the prayer that He would make us by His Spirit feel so deeply where the evil lies and what the remedy is, that we shall be ready to give up everything in order to receive nothing less than everything.

I

The all of God. It lies in the very being and nature of God that He must be all. From Him and through Him and to Him are all things. As God He is the life of everything: all life is only the effect of His direct and continuous operation. It is because all is thus through Him and from Him that it is also to Him. Everything that exists serves only as a means for the manifestation of the goodness and wisdom and power of God.

Sin consists in nothing but this, that man determined to be something and would not suffer God to be everything; and the redemption of Jesus has no other aim than that God should again become everything in our heart and life. At the end, even the Son shall be subjected to the Father, that God may be all in all. Nothing less than this is what redemption is to secure. Christ Himself has shown in His life what it means to be nothing, and to suffer God to be everything; and as He once lived upon the earth, so does He still live in the hearts of His people. According to the measure in which they receive and rejoice in the truth that God is all, will the fullness of the blessing be able to find its way into their life.

The All of God: that is what we must seek. In His will, His honor, His power must He be everything for us. No moment of our time, no word of our lips, no movement of our heart, no satisfying of the needs of our physical life, should there be that is not the expression of the will, the glory, the power of God. Only the one who discerns this and consents to it, who desires and seeks after it, who believes and appropriates it, can rightly understand what the fullness of the Spirit must effect, and why it is necessary that we should forsake everything if we desire to obtain it. God must be not merely something, not merely much, but literally, *All.*

II

The All of sin. What is sin? It is the absence of God; separation from God. Where man is guided by his own will, his own honor, his own power; where the will, the honor, the operation of God are not manifested, there sin must be at work. Sin is death and misery, only because it is a turning away from God to the creature.

Sin is in no sense a thing that may exist in man along with other things that are good. No: as God was once everything, so has sin in fallen man become everything. It now dominates and penetrates our whole being, even as God should have been allowed to do. Our nature in every part of it is corrupt. We still have our natural existence in God, and doubtless with not a few good inclinations in nature and character, just as these are to be found in the lower creatures. But of what is good in the spiritual and heavenly sense of the word, of what is done out of inward harmony with God or the direction of His Spirit of all this there is nothing that has its origin in His nature. All is in sin, and under the influence of sin.

The All of sin: some small measure of the knowledge of this fact was necessary even at the time of conversion. This, however, was still very imperfect. If Christians are to make progress and become fully convinced of the necessity of being filled with the Spirit, our eyes must be opened to the extent in which sin dominates over everything within.
Everything in us is tainted with sin—our will, our power, our heart; and therefore the omnipotence of God must take in hand the renewal of everything by the Holy Spirit. Man is utterly impotent to that which is good in the highest sense: we can do no more of what is good than what the Spirit actually works in us at any moment. We learn also to see the *all of sin* just as distinctly in the world around him; for the fairest, the most useful, and the most legitimate possessions or enjoyments are all under the power of sin.

Everything must be sacrificed and given over to death: The All of God must expel the All of sin. God must live wholly and entirely within us, and take inwardly and continuously the place which sin usurped. The one who desires this change will rightly understand and desire the fullness of the Spirit, and as we believe will certainly receive it.

III

The All of Christ. The Son is the revelation of the Father: the All of God is exhibited to our view and made accessible to us in the Son. On this account the All of Christ is just as necessary and infinite as that of God. Christ is God come upon the earth to undo the All of sin, to win back and restore in man the lost All of God. To this end we must know thoroughly the All of Christ.

The idea which most believing disciples have of the All of Christ is that He alone does everything in the atonement and the forgiveness of sin. This is indeed the glorious beginning of His redemptive work, but still only the beginning. God has given in Him all that we have need of: life and all grace. Christ Himself desires to be our life and strength, the Indweller of our heart, who animates that heart and makes it what it ought to be before God. To know the All of Christ, and to understand how intensely and how completely and how really Christ is prepared to be everything in us, is the secret of true sanctification. He that discerns the will of God in this principle and from the heart yields himself to its operation has found the pathway to the full blessing of Pentecost. …

How Everything Must be Given Up for It 2

December 6th

The All of Surrender. Leave all, sell all, forsake all: that was the Lord's requirement when He was here on earth: the requirement is in force still. The discernment of the fact that Christ is all leads of itself to the acknowledgment that He must have all. The chief hindrance of the Christian life is that, because men do not believe that Christ is all, they consequently never think of the necessity of giving Him all.

Everything must be given to Him, because everything is under sin. He cannot cleanse and keep a thing when it is not so yielded up to Him that He can take full possession of it and fill it. All must be given up to Him, because He alone can bring the all of God to its rightful supremacy within us. Even what appears useful or lawful or innocent becomes defiled by the stain of our Selfishness when it is held fast in our own possession and for our own enjoyment. We must surrender it into the hands and the power of Christ: only there can it be sanctified.

The All of surrender: It is because Christians are so ignorant of the requirement that all their praying and hearing avail so little. If then, Soul, you are really prepared to turn to God for the fullness of the Spirit; if you have turned to Christ to have your heart purified and kept pure; then be assured that it is your blessed privilege to regard and deal with everything—everything—that you have to strive for or do as given up to Him.

The All of surrender will be the measure of your experience of the All of Christ. … We have seen that surrender may be carried out at once and as a whole: let us not merely read and think of this, but actually do it. Yes; this very day, let the All of Christ be the power of a surrender on our part that shall be immediate, complete, and everlasting.

V

The All of the Spirit. The All of God and the All of Christ demand is a necessary consequence the All of the Spirit. It is the work of the Spirit to glorify the Son as dwelling in us, and by Him to reveal the Father. How can He do this if He Himself is not All and has not All and does not possess and penetrate All with His own power? To be filled with the Spirit, to let the Spirit have All, is indispensable to a true, healthful Christian life.

It is a source of great loss in the life of Christendom today that the truth is not discerned, that the Three–One God must have All. Even the professing Christian oftentimes makes it his very first aim to find out what he is and what he desires, what pleases him and makes him happy. Then he brings in God in the second place to secure this happiness. The claim of God is not the primary or main consideration. He does not discern that God must have him at His disposal even in the most trivial details of his life to manifest His divine glory in him. He is not aware that this entire filling with the will and the operation of God would prove to be his highest happiness. He does not know that the very same Christ who once lived upon the earth as the obedient, lowly Servant of God, entirely surrendered to the will of the Father, is prepared to abide and work in like manner in his heart and life now. It is on this account that he can never fully comprehend how necessary it is that the Spirit must be all and must fill him completely.

My brother, if these thoughts hare had any influence with you, surfer yourself to be brought without delay to the acknowledgment that the Spirit must be all in you. Say from the heart: "*I am not at liberty to make any, even the least, exception: the Spirit must have all.*" Then add to this confession the simple thought that Christ has come to restore the All of God; that the Spirit is given to reveal the All of Christ within us, so that God may again be all; that the love of the Father is eagerly longing to secure again His own supreme place with us; and then your heart will be filled with the sure confidence that the Father actually gives you the fullness of the Spirit.

VI

The All of Faith. "*All things are possible to them who believe.*" "*All things whatsoever you pray and ask for, believe that ye have received them, and you shall have them*" (Mark 11: 24). The preceding sections of this chapter have taught us to understand why it is that faith is all. It is because God is all. It is because man is nothing, and thus has nothing good in him except the capacity for receiving God. When he becomes a believer, that which God reveals becomes of itself a heavenly light that illumines him. He sees then what God is prepared to be for him; he keeps his soul silent before God and open to God, and gives God the opportunity of working all by the Spirit. The more unceasingly and undividedly he believes, the more fully can the All of God and Christ prevail and work in him.

The All of Faith. How little is it understood in the Church that the one and only thing I have to do is without ceasing to keep my soul in its nothingness and dependence silent and open before God, that He may be free to work in me; that faith as the willing acceptance and expectation of God's working, receives all and can achieve all. Every glance at my own impotence or sin, every glance at the promise of God and His power to fulfill it, must rouse me to the gladness of faith, to the willing, cheerful acknowledgment that God is able to work all, to the assurance that He will do it.

Let such a faith, as the act of a moment, look upon Christ even today and move you on the one hand to make renunciation of every known sin, and on the other to receive Him as One who purifies you, who keeps you, who dwells in your heart. that faith might receive the All of Christ and take Him with All that He is! that your faith might then see that the All of the Spirit is your rightful heritage, and that your hope is sure that the full blessing has been bestowed upon you by God Himself, and will be revealed in you!

Soul, if the All of God, the All of Christ, the All of the Spirit be so immeasurable, if the dominion and power of the terrible All of sin be so unlimited, if the All of your surrender to God and your decision to live wholly for Him be also so real, then let your faith in what God will do for you be also unlimited. "*The one who believes in Me, out of the heart shall flow rivers of living water.*" ...

Let me press on your heart one thing. There is something that can be done today. As the Holy Spirit says: "*Today, if you hear His voice, harden not your heart*" (Hebrews 3: 15). I cannot promise that you shall immediately overflow with the light and joy of the Holy Spirit. I do not promise you that you shall today feel very holy and truly blessed. But what can take place is this: to day you may receive Christ as One who purifies you, and baptizes, and fills with the Spirit. Yes: to-day you may surrender your whole being to Him to be henceforth wholly under the mastery of the Spirit. Today you may acknowledge and appropriate the All of the Spirit as your personal possession. Today you may submit to the requirement of the All of faith and begin to live only and wholly in the faith of what Christ will do in you through the Spirit. This you may do; this you ought to do. Kneel down at the mercy- seat and do it. Read once more the earlier chapter with its directions as to what Christ is prepared to do, and surrender yourself this very hour as an empty vessel to be filled with the Spirit, that your whole life may be carried out under the leading of the Spirit. In His own time God will certainly accomplish it in you.

There is also something, however, that He on His part is prepared to do. Today He is ready to give you the assurance that He accepts your surrender and to seal on your heart the conviction that the fullness of the Spirit belongs to you. Wait upon Him to give you this today! ...

How It Is to be Taught 1

December 7th

"And it came to pass that Paul came to Ephesus and found certain disciples: and he said unto them, Did you receive the Holy Spirit when you believed?"

—ACTS 19: 1–2

It was about twenty years after the outpouring of the Holy Spirit that the incident which is referred to in the beginning of this chapter of the Acts took place. In the course of his journey Paul came to Ephesus, and found in the Christian church there some disciples in whom he observed that there was something lacking in their belief or experience. Accordingly, he put to them the question: "*Did you receive the Holy Spirit when you believed?*" Their reply was that they had not yet heard of the Holy Spirit. They had been baptized by disciples of John the Baptist with the baptism of repentance with a view to faith in Jesus as One who was to come; but with the great event of the outpouring of the Spirit or the significance of it they were still unacquainted.

They came from a region of the country into which the full Pentecostal preaching of the exalted Savior had not yet penetrated. Accordingly, Paul took them at once under his care, made them conversant with the full gospel of the glorified Lord, who had received the Spirit from the Father and had sent Him down to this world, that every one of His believing disciples might also receive Him. Hearing this glad tiding and consenting to it, they were baptized into the name of this Savior, who baptizes with the Holy Spirit. Thereupon Paul prayed for them and laid his hands upon them, and they received the Holy Spirit; and then, in token of the fact that this whole transaction was a heavenly reality, they obtained a share in the Pentecostal miracle, and spoke "*with other tongues.*" …

There is a twofold Christian life. The one is that in which we experience something of the operations of the Holy Spirit, just as many did under the old covenant, but do not yet receive Him as the Pentecostal Spirit, as the personal indwelling Guest…. On the other hand, there is a more abundant life, in which the indwelling just referred to is known and the full joy and power of redemption are facts of personal experience. It will be only when Christians come to understand fully the distinction betwixt these two conditions, and discern that the second of these is in very deed the will of God concerning them, and therefore a possible experience for each believer; when with shame and confusion of face they shall confess the sinful and inconsistent elements that still mark their life: that we shall dare to hope that the Christian community will once more be restored to its Pentecostal power. It is with our eye fixed on this distinction that we desire to ponder the lessons presented to us in the record of this incident at Ephesus.

I

For a healthful Christian life, it is indispensable that we should be fully conscious that we have received the Holy Spirit to dwell in us. Had it been otherwise, Paul would never have put the question [to the disciples at Ephesus]: *"Did you receive the Holy Spirit when you believed?"* These disciples were recognized as believers. This position, however, was not enough for them. The disciples who walked with the Lord Jesus on earth were also true believers, yet He commanded them not to rest satisfied until they had received the Holy Spirit from Himself in Heaven. Paul too had seen the Lord in His heavenly glory and was by that vision led to conversion; yet even in his case the spiritual work he required to have done in him was not thereby completed. Ananias had to go to him and lay his hands upon him that he might receive the Holy Spirit. Only then could he become a witness for Christ.

All these facts teach us that there are two ways in which the Holy Spirit works in us. The first is the preparatory operation in which He simply acts on us but does not yet take up His abode within us, though leading us to conversion and faith and ever urging us to all that is good and holy. The second is the higher and more advanced phase of His working when we receive Him as an abiding gift, as an indwelling Person, concerning whom we know that He assumes responsibility for our whole inner being, working in it both to will and to do. This is the ideal of the full Christian life.

II

There are disciples of Christ who know little or nothing of this conscious indwelling of the Holy Spirit. It is of the utmost importance to understand and hold fast this statement. ... Consider what took place at Samaria. Philip the evangelist had preached there; many had been led to believe in Jesus and were baptized into His name; and there was great joy in that city. When the apostles heard this news, they sent down Peter and John, who, when they came to Samaria, prayed that these new converts might receive the Holy Spirit (Acts 8: 16–17). This gift was thus something quite different from the working of the Spirit that led them to conversion and faith and joy in Jesus as a Savior. It was something higher; for now from Heaven, and by the glorified Lord Himself, the Holy Spirit was imparted in power with His abiding indwelling, to consecrate and fill their hearts.

If this new experience had not been bestowed, the Samaritan disciples would still indeed have been Christians, but they would have remained weak, defective, and sickly; and thus it is that in our own days there is still many a Christian life that knows nothing of this bestowment of the Holy Spirit. Amidst much that is good and amiable, with even much earnestness and zeal, the life of such Christians is still hampered by weakness and stumbling and disappointment, simply because it has never been brought into vitalizing contact with power from on high, because such souls have not received the Holy Spirit as the Pentecostal gift, to be possessed, and kept, and filled by Him.

III

It is the great work of the gospel ministry to lead believers to the Holy Spirit. Was it not the great aim of the Lord Jesus, after He had educated and trained His disciples for three years by His intercourse with them, to lead them up to the point of waiting for the promise of the Father and receiving the Holy Spirit sent down from heaven? Was not this the chief object of Peter on the day of Pentecost, when, after summoning those who were pricked in their hearts to repent and be baptized for the forgiveness of sins, he assured them that they should then "*receive the Holy Spirit*"? (Acts 2: 38).

Was it not this also that Paul aimed at when in his Epistles he asked his fellow Christians if they did not know that they were each one "*a temple of the Holy Spirit,*" or reminded them that they had to be "*filled with the Holy Spirit*" (1 Corinthians 6: 19; Ephesians 5: 18)? Yes: the supreme need of the Christian life is to receive the Holy Spirit, and when we have it, to be conscious of the fact and live in harmony with it. An evangelical minister must not merely preach about the Holy Spirit from time to time or even oftentimes, but also direct all his efforts towards teaching his congregation that there can be no true worship save through the indwelling and unceasing operation of the Holy Spirit.

How It Is to be Taught 2

December 8th

To lead believers to the Holy Spirit, the great lack in their life must be pointed out to them. This was manifestly the intention in Paul's question: *"Did you receive the Holy Spirit when you believed?"* Just as only those that are thirsty will drink water with eagerness and only those that are sick will desire a physician, so it is only when believers are prepared to acknowledge the defective and sinful character of their spiritual condition, that the preaching of the full blessing of Pentecost will find an entrance into their hearts.

So long as Christians imagine that the only thing lacking in their life is more earnestness, or more importunity, or more strength, and that if they only obtain these benefits they themselves will become all they ought to be, the preaching of a full salvation will be of little avail. It is only when the discovery is made that they are not standing in a right attitude towards the Holy Spirit, that they have only His preparatory operations, but do not yet know and honor Him in His indwelling, that the way to something higher will ever be open or even be desired. For this discovery, it is indispensable that the question should be put to each, man by man, as pointedly and as personally as may be: "*Did you receive the Holy Spirit when ye believed?*" When the answer shall take the shape of a deeply felt and utterly sincere Alas! the time of revival is not far off.

V

Believers must receive help to appropriate this blessing in faith. In the Acts of the Apostles we read often about laying on of hands and prayer. Even a man like Paul whose conversion was due to the direct interposition of the Lord, and was therefore so effectual had to receive the Spirit through laying on of hands and prayer on the part of Ananias (Acts 9: 17). This implies that there must be amongst ministers of the gospel and believers generally a power of the Spirit which makes them the channel of faith and courage to others. Those who are weak must be helped to appropriate the blessing for themselves. But those who have and bring this blessing, as well as those who desire to have it, must realize and acknowledge their absolute dependence on the Lord and expect all from Him.

The gift of the Spirit is imparted only by God Himself. Every fresh bestowment of the Spirit comes from above. There must be frequent personal dealing with God. The minister of the Spirit whom God is to use for communicating the blessing, as well as the believer who is to receive it, must meet with God in immediate and closest intercourse. Every good gift comes from above: it is faith in this truth that will give us courage to expect with confidence and gladness that the full Pentecostal blessing may confidently be looked for, and that a life under the continual leading of the Holy Spirit is within our reach.

VI

The proclamation and appropriation of this blessing will restore the Christian community to the primary Pentecostal power. On the day of Pentecost the speaking "*with other tongues*" and the prophesying was the result of being filled with the Spirit. Here at Ephesus, twenty years later, the very same miracle is again witnessed, as the visible token and pledge of the other glorious gifts of the Spirit. We may reckon upon it that where the reception of the Holy Spirit and the possibility of being filled with Him are proclaimed and appropriated, the blessed life of the Pentecostal community will be restored in all its pristine power.

In our days there is an increasing acknowledgment of the lack of power in the Church of the Lord. In spite of all the multiplication of the means of grace, there is neither the power of the divine salvation in believers, nor the power for conversion in preaching, nor the power in the conflict of the Church with worldliness and unbelief and unrighteousness that, according to God's Word, we are bound to look for. ... Would that the expression of it became so strong that the children of God, driven by a keen sense of need, might be led to cast themselves upon the great truth which the Word of God teaches namely, that it is only when faith in the full Pentecostal blessing and the full enjoyment of it are found in the Christian Church that the members of it shall again find their strength and be able to do their first works.

VII

The most urgent need of the Church is that of people who shall be able to bear testimony to this blessing. Whether it be of teachers like Peter and Paul, of deacons like Philip, or of ordinary believers like Ananias who came to Paul, this is our first need. It furnishes abundant reason why teachers and members of congregations should unitedly call upon God, that alike in preaching and pastoral intercourse there may be more manifest proof that those who preach Christ Jesus may preach Him as John the Baptist did, as the "*One who baptizes with the Holy Spirit.*" It is only the minister that stands forth as a personal witness and living proof of the ministry of the Spirit whose word will have full entrance into the hearts of the people and exercise full sway over them. The first disciples obtained the baptism on their knees; on their knees they obtained it for others. It will be on our knees also that the full blessing will be won to-day. On our knees: let this be the attitude in which we await the full blessing of our God, alike in our individual and collective life.

"*Have you received the Holy Spirit since you believed?*" Let every reader submit himself to this heart-searching question. To be filled with the Holy Spirit of God, to have the full enjoyment of the Pentecostal blessing, is the will of God concerning us. Let us judge our life and our work before the Lord in the light of this question, and return the answer to God. Do not be afraid to confess before your Lord what is still lacking in you. Do not keep back, although you do not as yet fully understand what the blessing is or how it comes. The early disciples did not know that, yet they called upon their Lord and waited for it with prayer....

Be filled with a deep conviction of what you lack—a desire for what God offers, a willingness to sacrifice everything for it—and you may rest assured that the marvel of Jerusalem and of Samaria, of Cesarea and Ephesus, will once again be repeated. We may, we shall, be filled with the Spirit.

How It May Be Increased 1

December 9th

"*He who believes in Me, out of him shall flow rivers of living water.*"
—JOHN 7: 38

Can the full blessing of Pentecost be still further increased? Can anything that is full become still fuller? Yes: undoubtedly. It can become so full that it always overflows. This is especially the characteristic and law of the blessing of Pentecost.

The words of our blessed Lord Jesus which have been quoted, point us to a double blessing. First, Jesus says that we who believe in Him shall never thirst: we shall always have life in our Self that is to say, the satisfaction of all our needs. Then He speaks of something that is grander and more glorious: we who believe in Him, out of our heart shall flow rivers of living water to quench the thirst of others. It is the distinction betwixt full and overflowing. A vessel may be full and yet have nothing over for others. When it continues full, and yet has something over for others, there must be in it an over-brimming, ever-flowing supply. This is what our Lord promises to His believing disciples. At the outset, faith in Him gives us the blessing that we shall never thirst. But as we advance and become stronger in faith, it makes us a fountain of water out of which streams flow to others. The Spirit who at first only fills us will overflow out of us to souls around us. ...

See to it that you do not misunderstand the blessing which God has given you. Be sure that you do not form any wrong conceptions of what the full blessing is. Do not imagine that the animation, and joy, and power of Pentecost must be felt and seen immediately. No: The Church at present is in a dead-and-alive condition, and the restoration often comes slowly. At first, indeed, one receives the full blessing only as a seed: the full life is wrapped up in a little invisible capsule. The quickened soul has longed for it—has surrendered unreservedly for it; has believed in silence that God has accepted consecration and fulfilled His promise. In that faith we went on our way, silent and happy, saying to our Self: "The blessing of the fullness of the Spirit is for me."

But the actual experiences of the blessing did not come as we had anticipated; or they did come, but lasted only for a short time. The result was that we began to fear that our surrender was not a reality; that he had been rejoicing in what was only a transient emotion. …

The cause of this condition is simply lack of faith. We are bent on judging God and His work in us by sight and feeling. We forget that the whole process is the work of faith. Even in its highest revelations in Christians that have made the greatest progress, faith rests not on what is to be seen of the work of God or on the experiences of it, but on the work of God as spiritual, invisible, deeply hidden, and inconceivable. To you, therefore, my brother, who desire in this time of discouragement to return to the true life according to the promise, my counsel is not to be greatly surprised if it comes to you slowly….

If you know that you have given yourself to God with a perfect heart, and if you know that God, really and with His whole heart, waits to fulfill His promise in you with Divine power, then rest in silence before His face and hold fast your integrity. Although the cold of winter appears to bury everything in death, say with the prophet Habakkuk: "*Though the fig tree shall not blossom, neither shall fruit be in the vines, yet I will rejoice in the Lord, I will joy in the God of my salvation.*" Do this, and you shall know God, and God will know you. If you are sure that you have set yourself before God as an empty, separated, purified vessel, to become full of His Spirit, then continue still to regard yourself so and keep silence before Him. If you have believed that God has received you to fill you as a purified vessel purified through Jesus Christ and by your entire surrender to Him then abide in this attitude day by day, and you may reckon upon it that the blessing will grow and begin to flow. "*He who believes shall not be ashamed*" (Isaiah 28: 16; 1 Peter 2: 11). Persevere in the entire denial of yourself and the sacrifice of everything.

If I wish to have a reservoir of water, the greater the excavation I make for it, the wider the space I occupy with it, the greater is the quantity of water I can collect, and the stronger is the stream that flows from it when the sluices are opened. In your surrender for sanctification, or for the full blessing of the Spirit, you have said in truth and uprightness that you are prepared to sacrifice and forsake all in order to win this pearl of the Kingdom of Heaven; and this consecration was acceptable to God. But you have not yet fully understood the full import of the words you have used. The Lord has still much to teach you concerning what the individual Self is, how deeply rooted in your nature, how utterly corrupt as well as deeply hidden it is, as the secret source of many things you both say and do.

Be willing to make room for the Spirit by a constant, daily, and entire denial of the Self-life, and you may be sure that He will always be willing to come and fill the empty place. You have forsaken and sacrificed everything so far as you know; but keep your mind open to the teaching of the Spirit, and He will lead you farther on, and let you see that only when the entire sacrifice of everything after the example of Christ comes again to be the rule in His Church, shall the full blessing again break forth like an overflowing stream.

How It May Be Increased 2

December 10th

It is surprising how sometimes a very little thing may hinder the continuance in the increase of the blessing. It may, for example, be a little variance betwixt friends, in which they show that they are not willing to forgive and to forbear at once according to the law of Christ. Or it may be some unobserved yielding to undue sensitiveness or to the ambition which is not prepared to take the lowest place. Or it may be the possession or use of earthly property as if it were our own. Or it may be some providing for the flesh in the enjoyment of eating and drinking without the Self-denial which Christ always expects at our hands every day. Or it may be in connection with things that are lawful and in themselves innocent, which, however, do not befit us in our profession of being led by the Spirit of God. For here, like the Lord Jesus in His poverty, we are bound to show that the heavenly portion we possess is itself sufficient to satisfy all our desires. …

Christians, do you really desire to enjoy the full measure of the blessing of the Spirit? Then, before temptation comes, train yourself to understand the fundamental law of the imitation of Jesus and of full discipleship namely, Forsake all. Suffer yourself also to be strengthened and drawn into the observance of it by the sure promise of the "hundredfold in this life." A full blessing will be given you, a measure shaken together and running over.

Regard yourself as living only to make others happy. God is Love. His whole being is nothing but a surrender of Himself in love to be the life of the creature, to make the creature participate in His holiness and blessedness. He blesses and serves all that lives. His glory as God is that He puts all that He has at the disposal of His creatures. Jesus Christ is the Son of God's love, the Bearer, the Bringer, the Dispenser of the love. What God is as invisible in Heaven, He was as visible on earth. He came, He lived, He suffered and died only to glorify the Father that is, to let it be seen how glorious the Father in His love is, and to show that in the Godhead there is no other purpose than to bless men and make them happy; to make it manifest that the highest honor and blessedness of any being is to give and to sacrifice.

The Holy Spirit came as the Spirit of the Father and the Son to make us partakers of this Divine nature, to shed abroad the love of God in our hearts, to secure the indwelling of the Son and His love in our hearts to such an extent that Christ may verily be formed within us, and that our whole "inner man" shall bear the impress of His disposition and His likeness. Hence, when any soul seeks and receives the fullness of the Spirit, and desires to have it increased, is it not perfectly evident that he can enjoy this blessing only according as he is prepared to give himself to a life in the service of love? The Spirit comes to expel the life of Self and Self-seeking. The fullness of the Spirit presupposes a willingness to consecrate ourselves to the blessing of others and as the servants of all, and that in a constantly increasing and unreserved measure. The Spirit is the outflowing of the life of God. If we will but yield ourselves to Him, He will become rivers of living water, flowing from the depths of our heart.

Christian! If you will have the blessing increased, begin to live as one who is left here on earth only in order that the love of God may work by you. Love all around you with the love of God which is in you through the Spirit. Love the children of God cordially, even the weakest and most perverse. Exercise and exhibit your love in every possible way.

… When the Lord spoke of "rivers of living water," He connected the promise with faith in Himself: "*The one who believes in Me, out of their heart shall flow rivers.*" If we only understood that word "believe" rightly, we should require no other answer than this to the question as to how the blessing may be increased. …Then it is an embracing of the promise, an appropriation of the blessing as it is provided in Christ, a resting in the certainty of it, and a thanking of God for what He is yet to do. Thereafter, faith is keeping open the soul, so that Christ can come in with the blessing, take possession and fill all. …

If you believe, you shall see the glory of God. Let every doubt, every weakness, every temptation find you trusting, rejoicing in Jesus, and reckoning upon Him always to work all in you. You know that there are two ways in which a believer can encounter and strive against sin. One is to endeavor to ward it off with all our might, seeking our strength in the Word and in prayer. In this form of the conflict we use the power of the will. The other is to turn at the very moment of the temptation to the Lord Jesus in the silent exercise of faith and say to Him: "Lord, I have no strength. You are my Keeper." This is the method of faith. "*This is the victory that overcomes the world, even your faith*" (1 John 5: 4). Yes; this is indeed "*the one thing needful,*" because it is the only way in which Jesus, who is in Himself "*The One Thing Needful,*" can maintain the work of His Spirit in us. It is by the exercise of faith without ceasing that the blessing will flow without ceasing.

Christ must be all to us every moment. It is of no avail to me that I have life on earth unless that life is renewed every moment by my inbreathing of fresh air. Even so must God actually renew, and uphold, and strengthen the divine life in me every moment. He does this for me in my union with Christ. Christ is simply the fullness of God, the life of God, the love of God prepared for us and communicating itself to us. The Spirit is simply the fullness of Christ, the life of Christ, the Self- communicating love of Christ, surrounding us as the air surrounds the body.

Let us believe that we are in Christ, who surrounds us in His heavenly power, longing to make the rivers of His Spirit flow forth by us! Let us endeavor to obtain a heart filled with the joyful assurance that the Almighty Lord will fulfil His word with power, and that our only choice is to see Him, to rejoice in Him, and sacrifice all for Him. Then shall His word become true: "*The one who believes in Me, out of the heart shall flow rivers of living water.*"

How It Comes to Its Full Manifestation 1

December 11th

"That He would grant you that you may be strengthened with power through His Spirit in the inward man; that Christ may dwell in your hearts through faith; That you, being rooted and grounded in love, may be strong to know the love of Christ which passes knowledge; that you may be filled unto all the fullness of God."

—EPHESIANS 3: 14–19

Every blessing which God gives is like a seed with the power of an indissoluble life hidden in it. Let no one therefore imagine that to be filled with the Spirit is a condition of perfectness which leaves nothing more to be desired. In no sense can this be true. It was after the Lord Jesus was filled with the Spirit at His baptism He had to go forth to be still further perfected by temptations and the learning of obedience. When the disciples were filled with the Spirit on the day of Pentecost, this equipment with power from on high was given to them that they might carry out the victory over sin in their own lives and all around them. The Spirit is the Spirit of truth, and He must guide us into it. It will only be by slow degrees that He will lead us into the eternal purpose of God, into the knowledge of Christ, into true holiness, into full fellowship with God. The fullness of the Spirit is simply the full preparation for living and working as a child of God.

When we consider the matter from this point of view, we see at a glance how entirely indispensable it is for every child of God to aim at obtaining this blessing. … And Paul's request was that by the special, powerful, and ever-deepening work of the Spirit, God would bring them to what was their true destiny namely, to be filled unto all the fullness of God. This prayer of Paul is everywhere regarded as one of the most glorious representations that the Word of God gives of what the life of a Christian ought to be. Let us then endeavor to learn what the full revelation and manifestation of this blessing of the Spirit may become.

"*That the Father would grant you that you may be strengthened with power through the Spirit.*" That these Christians had received the Spirit when they believed in Christ is clear from a previous statement of the Epistle. But he sees that they do not yet know or have all that the Spirit can do for them, and that there is a danger that, by their ignorance, they may make no further progress. Hence he bows his knees and prays without ceasing in their behalf that the Father would strengthen them with might by His Spirit in the inner man. This powerful strengthening with the Spirit is equivalent to being filled with the Spirit, is indeed this same blessing under another aspect. It is the indispensable condition of a healthful, growing, and fruitful life.

Paul … asks for a new, definite operation of God. He entreats that God would do this according to the riches of His glory. It is surely not any trilling thing, anything very common, that he thus craves. He desires that God would remember and bring into play all the riches of His grace and, in a fashion commensurate with the divine glory of His power, do a heavenly wonder and as the living God strengthen these believers with might by His Spirit in the inner man. …

Just as no creature in the natural world can exist for a moment if God does not work in it to sustain its life, so the gift of the Holy Spirit is the pledge that God Himself is to work everything in us from moment to moment. Learn to know your entire, your blessed dependence on God, and the claim which you have on Him as your Heavenly Father to begin in you a life in the mighty strengthening of the Spirit and to maintain it without the interruption of a single moment.

Paul tells these believers what he prays for in their behalf, in order that they may know what they have need of and ask for it for themselves. Do you also learn to offer up this petition? Expect everything from God alone. Bow your knees, and ask and expect from the Father that He would manifest to you yes, in you the riches of His glory. Ask and expect that He would strengthen you with might by His Spirit— that Spirit who in fact is already in you, but only as an unknown, hidden, and slumbering seed. Let this become the one desire, the strong confidence of your soul: "God will fill me with the Spirit: God will strengthen me through the Spirit with His Almighty energy." Let your whole life every day be permeated by this prayer and this expectation.

"*That Christ may dwell in your hearts by faith.*" This is the glorious fruit of the Divine strengthening with might in the inner man by the Spirit. The great work of the Father in eternity is to bring forth the Son. In Him alone is the good pleasure of God realized. The Father can have no fellowship with the creature except through the Son. He can have no joy in it except in so far as He beholds His Son in it. Hence it is His great work in redemption to reveal His Son in us, and so to obtain an abode for Him in us, that our life shall be a visible expression of the life of Jesus.

That is the aim He has in view in "*strengthening us with might by the Spirit in the inner man.*" It is "*that Christ may dwell in our hearts by faith.*" This indwelling of Christ in us is not like that of a man who abides in a house, but is nevertheless in no sense identified with it. No: His indwelling is a possession of our hearts that is truly divine, quickening and penetrating their inmost being with His life. The Father strengthens us inwardly with might by His Spirit, so that the Spirit animates our will and brings it, like the will of Jesus, into entire sympathy with His own. The result is that our heart then, like the heart of Jesus, bows before Him in humility and surrender; our life seeks only His honor; and our whole soul thrills with desire and love for Jesus. This inward renewal makes the heart fit to be a dwelling- place of the Lord. By the Spirit He is revealed within us and we come to know that He is actually in us as our life, in a deep, divine unity, One with us.

Brother, sister, God longs to see Jesus in you. He is prepared to work mightily in you that Christ may dwell in you. The Spirit has come, and the Father is willing to work mightily by Him that the living presence of His Son may always abide in you. Jesus loves you so dearly and longs so intensely for you that He cannot rest until He makes His abode in your heart. This is the supreme blessing that the fullness of the Spirit brings you.

How It Comes to Its Full Manifestation 2

December 12th

"That you, being rooted and grounded in love,
may be strong to know the love of Christ which passes knowledge."
—EPHESIANS 3: 19

T*hat Christ may dwell in your heart by faith.*" It is by faith that you receive and know the indwelling of the Spirit and the operation of the Father by Him. By faith, which discerns things invisible as clearly as the sun, you receive and know the living Jesus in your heart. As constantly as He was with His disciples on earth, yea, more constantly than with them, because more inwardly and more really He will be in you and will grant you to enjoy His presence and His love. Soul, pray that the Father would strengthen you with might by the Spirit, would open your heart for the fullness of the Spirit, and enable you trustfully to appropriate it. Then at last shall you know what it means to have Christ dwelling in your heart by faith.

Here is the glorious fruit of the indwelling of Christ in the heart. By the Spirit the love of God is shed abroad in the heart. By Christ who dwells in the heart the love wherewith God loved Him comes into us; and we learn that just as life in God, between Father, Son, and Spirit, is only infinite love, so the life of Christ in us is nothing but love. Thus we become rooted and grounded in love. We are implanted in the soil of love: we strike our roots into heavenly love; henceforth we have our being in it and draw our strength from it. Love is the supreme element in our spiritual life. The Spirit in us and the Son in us bring us nothing but the love of God. Love is the first and the chief among the streams of living water that are to flow from us.

It is thus that we come to discover the truths that love is the fulfilling of the law—that love does no ill to one's neighbor; love seeks not its own; that love lays down its life for the brethren. Our heart becomes ever larger and larger; our friends, our enemies, the children of God and the children of the world, those that are worthy to be loved and those that are hateful, the ransomed and the lost, the world as a whole and every individual creature in particular are all embraced in the love of God. We find, then, our happiness lies in the sacrifice of our own honor, our own advantage and comfort, in favor of others. Love takes no account of sacrifice: it is its blessedness to love: it cannot do otherwise; actual loving is its nature and its life. We are able so to love, because the Father with His Spirit works mightily within us; because the Son, "*who loved me and gave Himself for me*," dwells in us, and He, who is crucified Love, has filled the heart completely with Himself. We are rooted in love, and in accordance with the nature of the root in God is the fruit from God love.

"*That you may be strong to know the love which passes knowledge*"; that is, to know love not with the knowledge of the understanding and its thoughts alone, but in the conscious blessedness of a heart in which Jesus dwells … to be strong to know it fully, so far as this is possible before God, in order that He may fill you, an earthen vessel, with His own love to overflowing.

Souls, pray, listen to the word: "*God is Love*"; and He has provided everything to the end that you may know love fully. It is for this object that the Spirit is in you, and that the Father will work mightily in you: it is with this aim that Christ desires to have your whole heart. let us begin to pray, as never before, that the Father would strengthen us with might by the Spirit; that the Father would grant unto us to be filled with the Spirit; that ye may be strong to know the love of Christ.

"*That you may be filled unto all the fullness of God.*" What an expression! what an impenetrable mystery! what a divine blessedness! Filled unto all the fullness of God: this is the experience to which the fullness of the Spirit is intended to bring us, and will bring us.

"*Filled unto all the fullness of God*": Who shall ever unfold the meaning of this expression to us? How shall we ever reach any definite idea of what it signifies? God has made provision for our enlightenment. In Christ Jesus we see a man full of God, a man who was perfected by suffering and obedience, filled unto all the fullness of God: yea, a man who in the solitariness and poverty of an ordinary human life, with all its needs and infirmities, has nevertheless let us see on earth the life enjoyed by the inhabitants of heaven, as they are there filled unto all the fullness of God. The will and the honor, the love and the service of God were always visible in Him. God was all to Him. …

When God created man after His image, it was in order that He Himself might be seen in man, that man should simply serve as a reflection of His likeness. The image of a man never serves any other purpose than to represent the man. As the image of God man was destined simply to receive the glory of God in his own life, to bear it and make it visible. God was to be all to him; to be all in him: he was to be full of God.

By sin this divine purpose has been frustrated. Instead of being full of God, man became full of himself and the world; and to such an extent has sin blinded us that it appears an impossibility ever to become full of God again. Alas! even many Christians see nothing desirable in this fullness. Yet it is back to this blessing that Jesus came to redeem and bring us; and this is the end for which God is prepared to work mightily within us by His Spirit. This is no less the result for which the Son of God desires to dwell in our heart, and which He will bring to accomplishment: it is all that we may be filled unto the fullness of God.

Yes; this is the highest aim of the Pentecostal blessing. To attain this, we can count upon the Spirit to make sure of our reaching it. He will open the way for us and guide us in it. He will work in us the deep humility of Jesus, who always said: "*I can of Myself do nothing*;" "*I do not My own will*;" "*The words I speak, I speak not of Myself.*" Amidst this Self-emptying and sense of dependence He will work in us the assurance and the experience that for the soul which is *nothing*, God is surely *all*. By our faith He will reveal to us Jesus, who was full of God, as our life. He will cause us to be rooted in the love in which God gives all, and we shall take God as all. Thus it will be with us as with Jesus: man nothing, and God's honor, God's will, God's love, God's power, *everything*. Yes; the issue will be that we shall be "*filled unto all the fullness of God.*" …

He is bent on fulfilling His promise: He Himself will work it out. Today, then, in humility and faith take this word, "filled unto all the fullness of God," as the purpose and the watchword of your life, and see what it will do for you. It will become to you a mighty lever to raise you out of the Self-seeking which is quite content with only being prepared for blessing. It will urge you to enter into and become firmly rooted in the love of God which gives everything to you, and thereby in the love which gives everything back to Him. It will convince you, that nothing less than Christ Himself dwelling in your heart can. keep such a love abiding in you, or actually make the fullness of God a reality within you. It will train you to fix your only hope of all this blessing on the mighty operation of God Himself by the Spirit. It will also move you to go down upon your knees and summon to your aid the wealth of God's glory, that it may itself prepare you for this great wonder. This it will continue to do until your heart is enabled to utter the response: "Yes: filled unto all the fullness of God is what my God has prepared for me."

With this glorious prospect before us, come and let us join with the apostle in the doxology: "*Unto Him that is able to do exceeding abundantly above all that we ask or think, according to the power that works in us (the power of His might), unto Him be the glory for ever and ever.*" Let us desire nothing less than these riches of the glory of God. Today, if we have never done it before, let us make a beginning and appropriate to ourselves the full blessing of the Spirit as the power which is sure to lead us to be "*filled unto all the fullness of God.*"

How the Blessing is Hindered 1

December 13th

"If any man would come after Me, let him deny himself, and take up his cross, and follow Me. For whosoever would save his life shall lose it, and whosoever shall lose his life for My sake shall find it."

—MATTHEW 16: 24–25

There are many who seek the full blessing of Pentecost long and earnestly and yet do not find it. Often the question is put as to what may be the cause of this failure. To this inquiry more than one answer may be given. Sometimes the solution of the problem points in the direction of one or another sin which is still permitted. Worldliness, lovelessness, lack of humility, ignorance of the secret of walking in the way of faith these, and indeed many more causes, may also be often mentioned with justice.

There are, however, many people who think that they have come to the Lord with what of these sources of failure still remains in them, and have sincerely confessed them and put them away, and yet complain that the blessing does not come. For all such it is particularly necessary to point out that there remains still one great hindrance namely, the root from which all other hindrances have their beginning. This root is nothing else than our individual Self, the hidden life of Self with its varied forms of Self-seeking, Self-pleasing, Self-confidence, and Self-satisfaction. The more earnestly anyone strives to obtain the blessing and would fain know what prevents him, the more certainly will he be led to the discovery that it is here the great evil lies. We our Self are our worst foe: we must be liberated from our Self; the Self-life to which we cling must be utterly lost. Only then can the life of God entirely fill us.

… Every disciple "*must deny himself and take up his cross*" in order that we may be crucified and put to death on it. We that would fain save our life will lose it; and we who are prepared to lose our life for Christ's sake will find it.

You see, then, what the Lord here teaches and requires. Peter had learned through the Father to know Christ as the Son of God, but he did not yet know Him as the Crucified One. Of the absolute necessity of the cross, and death on the cross, he as yet knew nothing. It may be so with Christians. We know the Lord Jesus as Savior; we desire to know Him better, yea, fully; but we do not yet understand that for this end it is necessary that we must have a deeper discernment of the death of the cross as a death which we must die; that we must actually deny, and hate, and lose this life—our whole life and being in the world—ere we can receive the full life of God. …

Why should Christians be called upon always to deny our Self, our own feeling, and will, and pleasure? Why must we part with this life … why should we hate and lose our life? The answer is very simple: It is because that life is so completely under the power of sin end death that it has to be utterly denied and sacrificed. The Self-life must be wholly taken away to make room for the life of God. We who would have the full, the overflowing life of God, must utterly deny and lose our own life.

You see it now, do you not? There is only one great stumbling-block in the way of the full blessing of Pentecost. It lies in the fact that two diverse things cannot at one and the same time occupy the very same place. Your own life and the life of God cannot fill the heart at the same time. Your life hinders the entrance of the life of God. When your own life is cast out, the life of God will fill you. So long as I myself am still something, Jesus Himself cannot be everything. My life must be expelled; then the Spirit of Jesus will flow in. Let every seeker of the full blessing of Pentecost accept this principle and hold it fast. …

Our life, our individual Self, is entirely and completely under the power of sin. When God created the angels and man, He gave them a separate personality, a power over themselves, with the intention that they should of their own free will present and offer up that life, that individual Self, to Him, in order that He in turn might fill them with His life and His glory. This was to be the highest blessed ness of the creature. It was to be a vessel filled with the life and the perfection of God.

The whole Fall … consisted of nothing but the perversion of their life, their will, their personality, away from God, in order to please themselves. This Self-exaltation was the pride that changed the angels into demons and cast them out of Heaven into hell. … It was no wonder that Jesus said: "*You must hate—you must utterly lose that life—ere the full life of the Spirit of God can be yours.*"

To the minutest details, always and in everything, you must deny that Self-life; otherwise the life of God cannot possibly fill you. *"He that will come after Me, let him deny himself, and take up his cross, and follow Me"* (Matthew 16: 24). A deep conviction of the entire corruption of our nature, manifesting itself in the fact that even the Christian still pleases himself in many things, is an experience that is still lacking in many people. It appears to them both strange and harsh, when we say that in nothing is the Christian free to follow his own feeling, that Self-denial is a requirement that must prevail in every sphere of life and without any exceptions. The Lord has never withdrawn His words: *"He that forsakes not all that he has cannot be My disciple, cannot walk with Me, cannot be as I"* (Luke 14: 33).

Our own life must be utterly cast aside to make full room for the life of God. At the time of his conversion the young Christian has but little understanding of this requirement. He receives the seed of the new life into his heart while the natural life is still strong. … This, accordingly, is the point to which we must all in the long-run come. So long as Christians imagine that in some things—for example, in eating and drinking, in the spending of time or money, in thinking and speaking about others—we have still the right and the liberty to follow our wishes, to please our Self, to maintain our own life, we cannot possibly attain to the full blessing of Pentecost.

How the Blessing is Hindered 2

December 14th

"He that forsakes not all that he has cannot be My disciple, cannot walk with Me, cannot be as I."
—LUKE 14: 33

It is an unspeakably holy and glorious thing that we can be filled with the Spirit of God. It demands inevitably that the present occupant and governor of the heart, our individual Self, shall be cast out, and that everything within it, everything wholly and entirely, shall be surrendered into the hands of the new Inhabitant, the Spirit of God. Would that we could understand that the joy and power of being filled with the Spirit will come of themselves when once we comply with the first and principal condition namely, that He alone shall be acknowledged as our Life and our Leader.

It is once for all impossible for the Christian to bring about this great transformation in himself. At no stage of our spiritual career are the power and the deceitfulness of our individual Self and the Self-life more manifest than in the attempt to grasp the full blessing of Pentecost. Many people endeavor to appropriate this blessing, and that by a great variety of efforts. They do not succeed, and they are not able to discover the reason why. They forget that Self-will can never cast out Self-will: that Self can never really mortify itself.

Happy is the man who is brought up to the point of acknowledging his helplessness and impotence. He will here specially need to deny himself, and so cease to expect anything from his own life and strength, but will rather lay himself down in the presence of the Lord as one who is alike impotent and dead, that he may really receive the blessing from Him. It was not Peter that prepared himself for the day of Pentecost or brought down the Pentecostal blessing from heaven; it was his Lord that did all this for him. His part was to despair of himself and yield himself to his Lord to accomplish in him what He had promised. Hence also it is your part, believer, while yielding obedience to this call, to deny yourself, and to lose your own life, and in presence of the Lord to sink down in your nothingness and impotence.

Accustom yourself to set your heart before Him in deep humility, and silent patience, and childlike submission. The humility that is prepared to be nothing, the patience that will wait for Him and His time, the submission that will yield itself wholly that He may do what seems Him good, is all that you can do to show that you are ready to lose your life. Jesus summons you to follow Him. Remember how He first sacrificed His will, and when He had laid down His life into the hands of the Father, and went down into the grave, waited till God raised Him again to life. Be you in like manner ready to lay down your life in weakness, and be assured that God will raise it up again in power with the fullness of the Spirit. Be done with the strength of mere personal efforts; abandon the dominion of your own power of apprehension. *"Not by might, nor by power, but by My Spirit, says the Lord"* (Zechariah 4: 6).

It is the surrender of faith to Jesus in His Self-humiliation and death that opens the way to the full blessing of Pentecost. You of course say at once: "Who is sufficient for these things? Who can sacrifice everything and die and lay down his life utterly as Jesus did? To man such a surrender is impossible." My reply is that it is indeed so. But "*with God all things are possible.*" You cannot literally follow Jesus, and like Him go down into death and the grave. That ever remains beyond your power. Never will our individual Self yield itself up to death or rest quietly in the grave. But hear the glad tidings. In Christ you have died and have been buried. The power of His dying, of His willing surrender of His spirit into the hands of the Father, of His silent resting in the grave, works in you. In faith in this working, however little you may understand it in faith—in this working in you of the spirit and the power of the death and the life of the Lord Jesus—give up yourself willingly to lose your life.

For this end, begin to regard the denying of yourself as the first and most necessary work of every day. Accept the message I bring you: The great hindrance in the way of the life of Pentecost is the Self-life. Believe in the sinfulness, the detestableness, of that life: not on account of its gross external sins, but because it sets itself in the place of God; seeks, and pleases, and honors itself more than God. Exercise yourself in what Jesus lays upon you, and hate your own life as your own worst foe and as the foe of God. Begin to see what the full blessing is that Jesus has prepared for you and which He bestowed at Pentecost namely, His own life, His own indwelling; and count nothing too precious or too costly to give as an exchange for this pearl of great price.

Christian, are you really in earnest about having the full blessing of Pentecost and being filled with the Spirit of God? Is it your great desire to be made to know what hinders you from obtaining it? Take the word of our Lord and keep it in your heart. Take it and go with it to Himself. He is able to make you understand, and consider, and experience it. It is He who baptizes with the Holy Spirit. Let everything in you that belongs to Self be sacrificed to Him, and be counted as loss, and cast away to give place to Himself. He who by His death obtained the Spirit, who prepared Peter for Pentecost in the fellowship of His suffering, has your guidance in His hands. Trust, trust Him, your own Jesus. He baptizes with the Spirit, beyond doubt or question: deny yourself, and follow Him; lose your own life and find His. Let Him impart Himself in the place you have hitherto retained for yourself. From Him there will flow rivers of living water.

How It May Be Kept 1

December 15th

"But you, praying in the Holy Spirit, keep yourselves in the love of God...

—JUDE 21

Can anyone who has the full blessing of Pentecost lose it again? Yes: undoubtedly. God does not bestow this boon with such constraint that a man retains it whether he will or not. No: this blessing also is entrusted to him as a talent which must be used; and only by use does it become secure and win success. Just as the Lord Jesus after He was baptized with the Holy Spirit had to be perfected by obedience and submission to the leading of the Spirit, so the Christian who has received the blessing of Pentecost has to see to it that he guards safely the deposit that has been entrusted to him.

When we inquire how we can keep it, Scripture points us to the fact that our keeping of it consists in our entrusting it to the Lord to be kept by Him. Paul places these two ideas alongside one another in his second letter to Timothy: *"He is able to keep my deposit"*; *"That good thing which was committed unto you, guard through the Holy Spirit which dwells in us"* (Timothy 1: 12, 14). Jude also, after saying, *"Keep yourselves in the love of God,"* adds the doxology: *"Unto Him that is able to keep us be glory"* (Jude 21, 24).

The main secret of success in the preservation of the blessing is the exercise of a humble dependence on the Lord who keeps us and on the Spirit by whom we ourselves are kept in close fellowship with Him. It is with this blessing as with the manna that fell in the wilderness: it must be renewed from Heaven every day. It is with the new heavenly life as with the life we live on earth: the fresh air that sustains it must be drawn in every moment from without and from above.

Jesus will keep the blessing, as He gave it, by faith. The law that prevails at every stage in the progress of the kingdom of God is: *"Be it unto you according to your faith."* The faith that in the first reception of the Lord Jesus was as small as a grain of mustard seed must, in the course of the Christian life, become always so enlarged that it shall see more and receive and enjoy more of the fullness that is in the Lord.

Paul wrote to the Galatians: *"I live, yet no longer I, but Christ lives in me: and that life which I now live in the flesh I live in faith"* (Galatians 2: 20). His faith was as broad and boundless and unceasing as were the needs of his life and work. In everything and at all times, without ceasing, he trusted in Jesus to do all. His faith was as wide and abundant as the energy that flows from Jesus for the enrichment of His people is mighty and glorious. He had given up his whole life to Jesus: he himself lived no longer. By a continuous and unrestricted faith that he gave to Jesus the liberty of energizing his life without ceasing and without limitation.

The fullness of the Spirit is not a gift that is bestowed once for all as a part of the heavenly life. No: it is not so. It is rather a constantly flowing stream of the river of the water of life that issues from beneath the throne of God and of the Lamb. It is an uninterrupted communication of the life and the love of Jesus, the most personal and intimate association of the Lord with His own upon the earth. It is by the faith which discerns this truth, and assents to it, and cleaves to it with joy, that Jesus will certainly do His work of keeping.

Jesus keeps this blessing in fellowship with Himself. The single aim of the blessing of Pentecost is to reveal Jesus as a Savior, so that He may exhibit His power to redeem souls in us and by us here in the world. The Spirit did not come merely to occupy the place of Jesus, but only and wholly to unite the disciples with their Lord more closely, and deeply, and completely than when He was on earth. The power from on high did not come as a power which they were thenceforth to reckon as their own: the power was inseparably bound up with the Lord Jesus and the Holy Spirit. Every operation of the power was a direct working of God in them. The intercourse which the disciples had with Jesus on earth, the following of Him, the reception of His teaching, the doing of His will, the participation in His suffering all this was to be still their experience, only in greater measure.

Not otherwise, accordingly, is it with us. The Spirit in us will always glorify Jesus, will always make it manifest that He alone is to be Lord, that all which is glorious comes only from Him. Close communion with God in the inner chamber, faithfulness in searching His Word and seeking to know His will in the Scriptures, sacrifice of time and business and intercourse with the world, to bring us into touch with the Savior all this is indispensable for the keeping of the blessing. …

How It May Be Kept 2

December 16th

Jesus keeps the blessing in the pathway of obedience. When the Lord Jesus promised the Holy Spirit, He said three times over that the blessing was for the obedient. *"If you love*

Me, you will keep My commandments: and I will pray to the Father, and He shall give you another Comforter" (John 14: 15–16). Peter speaks of *"the Holy Spirit whom God has given to them who obey Him"* (Acts 5: 32). Of our Lord Himself we read that *"He became obedient unto death. Wherefore also God highly exalted Him."* Obedience is what God cannot but demand. It is the only true relation and blessedness of the creature. It is obedience that attains what was lost by the Fall. It is the power of obedience Jesus came to restore. It is His own life. Apart from obedience the blessing of Pentecost can neither come nor abide.

There are two kinds of obedience. There is one that is very defective, like that of the disciples previously to Pentecost. They desired from the heart to do what the Lord said, but they had not the power. Yet the Lord accounted their desire and purpose as obedience. On the other hand, there is a more abundant life, which comes with the fullness of the Spirit, where new power is given for full obedience. The characteristic of the full blessing of Pentecost, and the way to keep it, is a surrender to obedience in the minutest details. To listen to the voice of Jesus Himself, to the voice of the Spirit, to the voice of Conscience, this is the way in which Jesus leads us. The method of making the life of Pentecost within us sure and strong is to know Jesus and to love Him, and receive Him in that aspect which made Him well-pleasing to the Father namely, as the Obedient One. The whole Jesus becomes the life of the soul.

It is the exercise of this obedience that gives to the soul a wonderful firmness and confidence and power to trust God and to expect all from Him. A strong will is necessary for a strong faith, and it is in obedience that the will is strengthened to trust God to the uttermost. This is the only way in which the Lord can lead us to ever richer blessing.

Jesus keeps the blessing in fellowship with His people. At the outset of His seeking for the full blessing a Christian thinks for the most part only of himself. Even after he receives the blessing as a new experience, he is still rather disposed to see merely how he can keep it safely for himself. But very speedily the Spirit will teach him that a member of the body cannot enjoy the flow of healthful life in a state of separation from others. He begins to understand that "there is one body and one Spirit." The unity of the body must be realized to enjoy the fullness of the Spirit.

This principle teaches us some very important lessons about the condition on which the blessing received can be maintained. All that you have belongs to others, and must be employed for their service. All that they have belongs to you, and is in turn indispensable for you. The Spirit of the body of the Lord can work effectively only when the members of it work in unison. You should confess to others what the Lord has done for you, ask their intercession, seek their fellowship, and help them with what the Lord has given you. You should lay to heart the unhappy condition of the enfeebled Christian Church in our days, yet not in the spirit of judgment or bitterness, but rather in the spirit of humility and prayer, of gentleness and willingness to serve. Jesus will teach you what is meant by Paul's saying [of the greatest gifts of the Spirit] that "*the greatest of these is love*" (1 Corinthians 13: 13); and by the very intensity of your surrender to the welfare of His Church He will both keep and increase the blessing in you.

Jesus keeps the blessing in the service of His kingdom. We have said more than once that the Spirit came as the power for work. The very name of Jesus Christ involves entire consecration to God's work, utter devotion to the rescue of souls. It was for this end alone that He lived: it is only for this cause that He lives in Heaven. How can anyone ever dream of having the Spirit of Christ otherwise than as a Spirit which aims at the work of God and the salvation of souls? It is an impossibility. Hence from the outset we must keep these two aspects of the Spirit's operation closely knit together. What the Spirit works in us is for the sake of what He works by us. Our seeking for the blessing will miscarry, our initial possession of the blessing will be lost, if we do not as the dominant feature of our life present ourselves to be used by the Spirit in the doing of His work.

The blessing of Pentecost does not always come with equal power and not always at once. God often gives preparatory experiences and awakenings that must lead to the full blessing. Every attempt to keep such gracious gifts for ourselves will entail loss. He that does not follow his own inclination, either in being silent or in speaking, but presents himself to the Lord and waits upon Him with an undivided spirit, will experience that work, so far from exhausting or weakening, is the sure way to keep the treasure.

It is as the indwelling Lord that Jesus keeps the blessing of Pentecost in us. Whenever mention is made of Jesus as our Keeper, it is oftentimes difficult to believe that we who are upon the earth can really know ourselves to be always, without interruption, in His hands and under His power. How much clearer and more glorious does the truth become when the Spirit discovers to us that Christ is in us; and that, not only as a tenant in a house, or water in a glass, in such a fashion that they continue quite distinct, but rather as the soul is in the body animating and moving every part of it, and never to be separated from each other except by a violent death. Yes: it is thus that Christ dwells in us, penetrating our whole nature with His nature.

The Holy Spirit came for the purpose of making Him thus deeply present within us. As the Sun is high in the firmament above me, and yet by his heat penetrates my bones and marrow and quickens my whole life, so the Lord Jesus, who is exalted high in Heaven, penetrates my whole nature by His Spirit in such a way, that all my willing, and thinking, and feeling are animated by Him. Once this fact is fully grasped, we no longer think of an external keeping through a person outside of us in Heaven, but rather become convinced that our whole individual life is itself quickened and possessed by One who, not in a human but in a Divine, all-penetrating manner, occupies and fills the heart.

29

THE STATE OF THE CHURCH

London: James Nisbet & Co., 1912

Repent!

December 17th

"Remember therefore from whence you have fallen, and repent and do the works you did at first; or else I will come quickly and will remove your candlestick out of his place, unless you repent."

—REVELATION 2: 5

In the epistles to the seven churches of Asia Minor… one of the central words is "repent." … To Ephesus, after mentioning eight things in which they had proved their discipleship, He says: *"I have this against you, that you left your first love."* In all the highest relationships of life, love is everything; between a mother and a child, a husband and a wife, a king and his people, love is the chief thing. And so with Christ too. There may be diligence in His service, there may be zeal for the honor of His name, there may be patient endurance of suffering for Him, and yet Christ's heart can be satisfied with nothing less than the first love, the constraining love which delights in His fellowship, yielding itself wholly to His personal influence, and giving a living testimony to Himself. Amid all her activities the true tender love to Christ was wanting. It is of this that Christ says: *"Remember therefore from whence you have fallen, and repent, and do the first works."*

As we think of the failure of the Church of our day in regard to making Christ known, and her utter unfitness for taking up the work to which she is now being led, do we not here find the secret cause of it all—the lack of personal love to Christ? And does not the word of the Lord come to us too, *"repent, or else I come and remove your candlestick out of its place, except you repent!"*

To Pergamos: *"I have a few things against you."* Their sin was: they tolerated false teachers. "*Repent therefore.*" It is often said that the Higher Criticism and its advanced teaching has much to do with the loss of power in the preaching and the lack of an earnest Christian life among the people. … We quoted a writer who said: "In many of our churches the great underlying doctrines and facts of the Gospel are scarcely ever referred to in preaching; the note of personal appeal to the conscience and direct effort for conversion is seldom heard."

And one has had more than one public testimony in regard to the lack of the full and fearless preaching of Christ and His cross. And even those who are sound themselves are only too ready to be silent in regard to a preaching of which they know that it cannot satisfy the need or exercise Divine power to salvation. Christ's "*repent*" is a summons to see whether our teaching is truly the proclamation of the message of God's inspired Word, or seeks to impress others by its excellency of speech and persuasive words of human wisdom.

To Sardis: *"I know your works, that you have a name that you live, and are dead, for I have found no works of yours fulfilled before My God. Remember how you have received, and repent."* ...

To Laodicea: *"I know your works, that you are neither cold nor hot. You say, I am rich, and have gotten riches and have need of nothing, and know not that you are the wretched one, and miserable, and poor, and blind, and naked."* Have we not here a true picture of a great many of our Churches and our Christians—neither cold nor hot, but lukewarm, with a form of godliness, without the power, seeking and succeeding to their own minds, to unite the friendship of God with the friendship of the world? And as the result of this, the spirit of Self-satisfaction and mutual Self-congratulation is everywhere heard, with its deep undertone, *"We are rich, and increased in goods, and have need of nothing."* And Christ comes solemnly: *"And you know not that you are the wretched one."*

How does Christ meet these lukewarm Self-satisfied Christians? He has again just that same solemn word: *"repent."* Whatever the evil is, there is but one gate out of it—that hard, stern, but blessed word, repent. Just think for a moment of the four Churches that have been mentioned. In Ephesus it was a lack of LOVE—the constraining love of Christ was no longer found. In Pergamos it was a lack of TRUTH—they had forsaken the inspired Word, they tolerated the teaching of error. In Sardis it was a lack of LIFE—they had a name to live, but were dead. In Laodicea it was a lack of FIRE—the baptism of the Spirit and of fire was no longer known. Whatever the state of a Church may be, however closely minister and people may be bound together, Christ in Heaven has one message: *"REPENT!"*

Think of what that means from Him Who gave His life to win the hearts for Himself. He is now seated on the throne to give repentance. He pleads by His cross and blood, and seeks to touch the heart and break it with that love of His. With a voice of infinite holiness and tenderest compassion, He pleads with those whom His heart-searching words have warned and roused—just that one word: "*repent.*"

That is the word which He commissions the angels of the Churches to sound in the ears of His people, to bring nigh and to open up to them, and to plead with them till they bow before it: "*repent.*" He had spoken the word first of all to the Angel of the Church himself, and whether he had been found wanting in Love to Christ, or in the Truth of Christ, or in the Life of Christ, or in the Fire of Christ, He had called him to come and as a penitent to receive His pardon and the new experience of His blessing and power. He then sends him forth with his whole heart to sound out the note of warning and of welcome: *"Repent, O my people, repent."*

We are accustomed to use the word, "*repent*" in our evangelistic missions or in our ordinary conversion preaching. The … ministers to whom Christ has committed the charge of a whole Church, in which the decline of membership proves what a lack of power there was in the preaching and in the spiritual life, are here called to take up this word, "*repent*," in its deeper meaning.

The Church has been on the down-grade. In Ephesus the defection began amid great zeal for the truth, with the loss of the first love. In Pergamos comes a step lower: God's Holy Word is no longer taken as the only standard of teaching. In Sardis the evil becomes still more manifest: with a name to live, they are dead. In Laodicea it reaches its full growth: men are so utterly unconscious of anything wrong, so satisfied with themselves and with each other, so blind to what Christ calls their wretchedness and nakedness, that they proudly boast in their meetings and reports: *"Rich and increased in goods, and having need of nothing."*

What a work for the angels of the Churches to take that word, "*repent*" on their knees from Christ's own lips, to bow to it with their whole heart, and then in the power of His Spirit to carry it throughout the Church as the one great means of revival and restoration!

Let no one think that this message is too hard who can bear it. Listen to what Christ says of it: *"As many as I love, I reprove and chasten; be zealous therefore and repent."* … *"Behold I stand at the door and knock, if any man hears My voice, and open the door, I will come in."* Be not afraid, O man of God, to sound the word, "repent," loud and clear; it is Christ's infinite love that speaks the word that will give the blessing with it that will reveal Himself to His penitent people. Out of the fullness of a living faith in the love of Christ, call men to repent in the assurance of His welcome and His blessing.

Christ closes each of these seven Epistles with the word: *"He that has an ear, let him hear what the Spirit says to the churches."* Let the minister of Christ take that word into the depth of his heart; let him pray and believe till he is sure the blessed Spirit is speaking through him; let him tell the Church that the power of the Spirit is working to reveal Christ and His love; and let him henceforth carry on His work as never before, in the assurance that, in answer to much prayer, the mighty power of the Spirit will secretly work, will restore God's children in the path of repentance to a new and more abundant life. …

A Holiness Revival

December 18th

In answer to the question how the Church is to be lifted up to the abundant life in Christ, to that expanded vitality which will fit her for the work that God is putting before her, many will without hesitation say: Nothing will help but a revival. That alone will be that something which must happen to the Church. … It is a new and living apprehension of God and of His purpose for the world, that we seem most of all to need, if there is to be that irresistible spiritual movement which is the only thing adequate to the needs of the situation. Great tides of spiritual energy must be set in motion, if the work is to be accomplished.

Yes, all will answer, nothing less than a mighty revival is needed to rouse and fit the Church for the work to which God calls her. And yet there may be a great difference in what we understand by revival. Many will think of the power of God as it has been manifested in the work of evangelists like Moody and Torrey, and they feel sure that what God has done in the past He can do again.

They will perhaps hardly be able to understand us when we say that we need a different and a mightier revival than those were. In them the chief object was the conversion of sinners and, in connection with that, incidentally the quickening of believers. But the revival that we need calls for a deeper and more entire upheaval of the Church. The great defect of those revivals was that the converts were received into a Church that was not living on a high level of consecration and holiness, and speedily they sank down to the average standard of ordinary religious life. Even the believers who had taken part in the work and had been roused by it, also gradually returned to their former life of clouded fellowship and lack of power to testify for Christ.

The revival we need is the revival of holiness, in which the consecration of the whole being to the service of Christ, and that for the whole life, shall be counted possible. And for this there will be needed a new style of preaching, in which the promises of God to dwell in His people, and to sanctify them for Himself, will take a place which they do not now have.

Let me try and make this plain by an illustration from the history of Israel. When God redeemed His people from Egypt, by the blood of the Passover, and the deliverance at the Red Sea, this was but a beginning of what He intended to do. He had a higher purpose and a fuller blessing. He meant to dwell among them as the Holy One, and to be their God, and to hallow them to be His people. We find this twofold aim in the song of Moses: "*You in Your mercy have led forth the people which You have redeemed*" (Exodus 15:13–17).

… Just as God had said to Moses, "*I am the Lord, who brings you out from Egypt, and I will bring you into the land,*" the redemption from Egypt was but the foundation; the house to be built upon it was the sanctuary in which God dwelled in the midst of His people as the Holy One to make them holy too. And yet how many of Israel there were who were brought out from bondage, but never were brought in into the rest; they perished in the wilderness through unbelief.

When our Lord Jesus, in His farewell discourse, gave the promise of the Holy Spirit, He spoke of the great New Covenant blessing that would then be experienced: God dwelling in His people. "*If a man loves Me, he will keep My words; and My Father will love him, and I will love him, and we will make our abode with him.*" So Paul also writes, "*that Christ may dwell in your hearts by faith, that you might be filled with all the fullness of God.*" Dr. Maclaren has said that it seems as if the thought of Christ dwelling in the heart has been lost in the Church.

With the Reformation the great truth of Justification—the bringing out from the bondage of Egypt—was restored to its place. But the other great truth of Sanctification—the bringing in into the land with its rest and victory—has never yet taken the place in the preaching and practice of the Church which God's Word claims for it. It is for this we need a revival, that the Holy Spirit may so take possession of us that the Father and the Son can live in us, and that fellowship with them, and devotion to their will and service, shall be our chief joy. This will be in very deed a Holiness Revival.

A Holiness Revival! Has there ever been such a thing? There have been movements in the Church, sometimes more or less local, which, though they have not been known by that name, have resulted in definite and intense consecration to God and His will. But there have also been fuller manifestations of the Spirit which have left their marks in history. …

A Holiness Revival! What was the great Evangelical Revival in England through Whitefield and Wesley, but this? They had together at Oxford been members of "The Holy Club." With their whole heart they had sought to live for God, to keep themselves separate from the world, to devote their life to the welfare of their fellow-men. They had not only sought deliverance from the guilt, but also from the power, of sin. When their eyes were opened to see how faith can claim the whole Christ in all His fullness, they found the key to that preaching which was so mightily effectual for the salvation of men.

There may be great differences of doctrine, but no one can be blind to the seal God has set upon the intense desire to preach a full salvation and an entire consecration.

A Revival of Holiness is what we need. Such a preaching of the claim that Christ has on us as shall lead us to live entirely for Him and His Kingdom; such an attachment of love to Him as shall make His fellowship our highest joy; such a faith in His freeing us from the dominion of sin as shall enable us in all things to obey His commandments; such a yielding to the Holy Spirit as to be led by Him in all our daily walk—these will be some of the elements of the revival of true holiness for which the Church must learn to seek as for the Pearl of great price.

And how is it to be found? It will cost much prayer. It will cost more than that—much sacrifice of Self and of the world. It will need a surrender to Christ Jesus to follow Him as closely as God is able to work it in us. We must learn to look upon religion, upon a life like Christ's, having the very same mind that was in Him, as the supreme object of daily life.

The Promise of the Father

December 19th

The Holy Spirit is the promise of the Father. That includes everything. If we are to know God aright—if we are to enjoy and experience all that Christ is and has for us, if we are to enter into possession of the heritage of the true and full life which a child of God may expect even here on earth—everything depends on our being possessed and filled with the Holy Spirit of God. Above all, if we are not only individually, but as a corporate body, to exercise the rule and dominion over our fellow-men in the power of the eternal redemption, we are absolutely dependent on that abundant measure of the Spirit, which God is so willing to give.

The Spirit is the promise of the Father. Everything that reminds us of the fallen state of the Church, of her unfaithfulness and lack of loyalty to Christ, of the terrible power that the world has over her, of her impotence to carry out her mission here on earth, is just another call: *"Return you at My reproof; I will pour out My Spirit abundantly."*

Listen now to the promise of the Father: *"If you, being evil, know how to give good gifts unto your children; how much more shall your heavenly Father give the Holy Spirit to them that ask Him?"* In these words, we find four deep and unfathomable mysteries. The first, the mystery of the Holy Spirit whom God offers to give us. Next, the mystery of the Father's infinite willingness to bestow that gift. Third, the mystery of the Son of God who came from Heaven to bring the promise, to open the way for its fulfillment, and then from Heaven to be the channel through whom the Father bestows it. And fourth, the mystery of prayer by which that great gift can be drawn down upon ourselves and others. If it were to please God to open our eyes fully to see the glory of these mysteries, we could not for a moment hesitate to give up everything to have the promise fulfilled in us.

1. The inconceivable mystery of the gift of the Holy Spirit—Who is He? The Spirit of God, in Whom ...the whole life and glory of Deity is comprehended. The Spirit is the bond of union between the Father and the Son. He is the Spirit of the Father and of the Son too. And this very same Spirit is to be the Spirit of our life, dwelling in us as the hidden God, doing His work to reveal the Son and the Father within us—*the Spirit of God dwelling in us.* The thought is so overwhelming that it constrains us to worship and adore.

And of this blessed Spirit God has said that He will be the life of our life. He is given with the express purpose of working out in us all that God wants us to be and to do. He is given with the understanding that we never need, in our own strength, to do what God commands: *"the Spirit will work it in us."* He comes as the whole God to take possession of the whole man; He will be responsible for our whole being, if we will yield ourselves to Him in faith. He will glorify Christ in us, and as we look up to Christ, and through Him to the Father, the blessed Spirit will work in the depth of our hearts the likeness of God and His Christ.

2. And now the second mystery—the mystery of the Father's inconceivable willingness to bestow this infinite gift. *"How much more will your heavenly Father give the Holy Spirit to them that ask Him?"* Christ takes an illustration from the deepest experience of our daily life. Have we not as children learned to know and trust and rejoice in the willingness of a father to give us the bread we need? How natural, how easy, what joy it was, to live in that confiding assurance of what a father would do! And now just think of what that word means, *"How much more will your heavenly Father."* Think of His greatness. Think of His holiness. Think of His love and His tender compassion, and say: Have we not reason for the

most unbounded confidence; the Father is just longing to fill us with His Holy Spirit. Oh the mystery of this inconceivable longing of God to give us His Holy Spirit! Take time to take it in.

But why then, if He is so willing, do *we* so often pray and have to wait long for the answer? It is simply that we are not willing. We hinder Him, we do not yield our whole heart and soul, our whole being. … We are not ready to sacrifice everything and only seek what the Father longs to give. Do let us believe in the mystery of this Divine willingness to give the Spirit. It will draw us to come closer to Him and under the power of His love to lay ourselves at His feet.

3. The third mystery. Who is this who brings this wonderful message? None less than the Son of God. As if to make unbelief impossible, God sends His only begotten Son as the bearer of the good tidings. He came to prepare the way to deliver us from the power of sin, to yield His own body to the Holy Spirit as a living sacrifice on the cross, that He might then receive the Spirit from the Father to impart to us. Sin had so separated us and our whole being from God, that it was only by death to the old nature, death to sin, that a new body could be formed in which the Holy Spirit could dwell.

And here we have the reason why, with the infinite willingness of God to bestow the Spirit, we find it so difficult to receive Him. As Christ could not receive the Spirit in His fullness of power to impart to us until He had died the death of the cross, so it is alone in the full fellowship of that death like Him that we are made partakers of the fullness of the Spirit. It is when we are with Him crucified to the world, and in Him live as those who are dead to sin, that He can do His blessed work in us.

4. The fourth mystery—the inconceivable power of my feeble prayer to draw down the Holy Spirit from Heaven, to work where and what I ask in the name of Jesus. It is not only that the Father will give me the Spirit, but He will send at my request the Spirit on other souls around me, sometimes in far-distant lands. Yes, this is what prayer has done and is doing today, and will do far more abundantly when God's children learn to believe the promise and to take hold of His strength.

It is high time for the Church not to look only at prayer in the light of our feebleness or our limited desires. We must begin to believe that God, in the mystery of prayer, has entrusted us with a force that can move the heavenly world and bring its power down to this earth. The prayer of one hundred and twenty at Pentecost brought down the power of the promised Spirit. When the Church continues with one accord in prayer and supplication, it will again be seen, to an extent of which we have no conception at the present time, that the Kingdom of Heaven will come down in power into our hearts and lives.

Oh, take time, you children of God, and fall down in adoration in view of these four great mysteries—the gift of the Holy Spirit, the infinite willingness of the Father to bestow Him, the blessed Son who is the channel, and the inconceivable power of the prayer of faith! Let each of us for himself ask and receive. Let us believe with our whole heart, God gives, God gives every day afresh, God gives in increasing power, His blessed Spirit to every child that asks aright.

Let each of us believe in the power of prayer to bring the blessing to others, and without ceasing cry to God that His children may learn to believe in His blessed promise, and to live in the power of it.

Let us very specially, as we think of what has been called "this Spiritless age," and the low state of spiritual life in the Church, and the terrible need of the world, yield ourselves to the work of intercession, and allow the Holy Spirit to make us of those who cry to God day and night until He pour out His blessed Spirit that there be not room to receive it. And let every prayer breathe the confident assurance, *"How much more will your Father give the Spirit to them that ask Him."*

Christ's Last Words

December 20th

"But you shall receive power when the Holy Spirit comes on you;
and you will be my witnesses in Jerusalem, and in all Judea and Samaria, and to the ends of the earth."
—ACTS 1: 8

When our Lord ascended to Heaven He left behind Him three last words. The very last was, *"My witnesses ... to the ends of the earth."* We read, "When He had said this, He ascended to Heaven." He left this world and His disciples with that one word, *"My witnesses... to the ends of the earth."* ... With that one word in His heart, He sat down upon the throne—expecting, longing, that every child of man should learn to know Him and His love.

The second word, that had just preceded it, was, *"You shall receive power."* As He sent them forth for the conquest of the world, He bade them not think of their own impotence or their own strength, but of all the power in Heaven and on earth that He was now to receive from the Father, and that through the Holy Spirit would work in them and give them the victory.

And then we have the first of the three last words, *"Wait"*—*"Wait for the promise of the Father"*—*"Tarry in the city, until you be clothed with power from on high."* Those words, *"Wait," "Tarry until"*, they understood so simply that they at once returned to the city and for ten days continued with one accord in prayer and supplication, until on the Day of Pentecost they were indeed baptized with the heavenly fire and all filled with the Holy Spirit and with power.

These three words still express the relation in which Christ on the throne stands to His people. Just suppose for a moment that it were given you to be caught up into paradise, and to see and to hear what men may not know. You would in the light and the power of that Spirit life, where words are eternally existing realities, be permitted to see the risen Lord on the throne, living with this one thought—*"The ends of the earth"*—ever in His heart, and ever listening to the song of the redeemed from every people and nation and tongue. The world God loved, the world for which Christ gave His blood and His life, how He waits and longs for the time when His love can reach every soul.

And you would see what a reality that second word was too, as you saw a *"Lamb standing as it had been slain, having seven eyes which are the seven Spirits of God sent forth unto all the earth."* That holy symbol would show you how the Lamb on the Throne lives to send forth God's Spirit wherever God's servants go, to enable them to make known His love and win souls for His Kingdom.

And then, that first of the three last words—*"Wait, Tarry"*—translated by the disciples into much prayer and supplication. You will find [in Jesus' revelation to John] that *"the four-and-twenty elders fall down before the Lamb, having each one a harp, and golden bowls full of incense which are the prayers of the saints."* The prayers of men here upon earth have their place and their part before the throne of God. You would see the smoke of the incense in the golden censer with the prayers of the saints going up before God. And you would understand, what it is so hard for us to realize, that the prayers on earth are in very deed the condition for the power from Heaven for the extension of the Kingdom on earth. *"The four-and-twenty elders fall down before the Lamb, having each one a harp, and golden bowls full of incense which are the prayers of the saints"* (Revelation 8: 4).

And if in that vision you saw that it was passing, you felt bold to say to the blessed One, "Have You no message to give me to Your people on earth?" You would not be surprised if the answer came: "Tell them in My name to remember My last three words. I carry the ends of the earth, for which I gave My blood and My love, in My heart. Let them do so too. I live on the throne to send forth the Spirit into all the earth. Let them believe My promise, yield wholly to My Spirit, and victory will assuredly come. I am waiting to hear how much they are willing to have and to use; I am longing for more intercession and supplication, for more faith and prayer. Tell them to wait and tarry in prayer, and not to rest till they are clothed with power from on high. Oh, tell them the kingdom, their Lord and King, waits for their prayer."

Shall we not take these last words of Christ afresh into our hearts?

Have not other testimonies as to the state of the Church, its ignorance and its neglect and its rejection of the cross, its lack of the sense of holiness and crucifixion to the world, its neglect of the blessed truth of the Holy Spirit, its lack of loyalty to the Lord Jesus, its terrible feebleness in prayer—have not these testimonies become to some of us a burden that we cannot bear? And shall we not turn away from all our devices and efforts and give heed, with new, wholehearted devotion, to the great charter the Church has too long neglected, the last words of the ascending Lord? To take the words that live in Christ's heart and let them live in ours, will be the secret of wonderful happiness and irresistible power.

"The ends of the earth"; "All the world"; "Every creature": Is it possible for the ordinary Christian in everyday life to be so possessed by these words that, without effort or strain, they shall be the spontaneous expression of his inmost life? Thank God, it is possible, where the love of God and of Christ is shed abroad in the heart. Poor simple men and women have proved it by the intense devotion with which they could sacrifice everything to make the love of Jesus known to their fellow-men. The love with which Christ loves us is a love that takes in the whole world. Of that love we cannot take just enough for

ourselves, and be indifferent to all the others who share in it. Such is the feeble, Selfish, and unhappy life which so many Christians seek to live. Truly to possess Christ, and fully to enjoy Him, it is essential that we take in His love in all its fullness, that we yield ourselves to the service of that love, and find our happiness in making that love known to those who are still ignorant of it.

When the Church is quickened into some measure of the experience of the abundant life that there is in Christ Jesus, *"the ends of the earth"* will become its watchword, and men will begin to understand that what fills and satisfies the heart of Christ in Heaven is enough and more than enough to fill our hearts with the blessedness and the beauty of likeness to Him.

Remember, He says, My very last word, as I ascended the throne: *"You shall be My witnesses unto the ends of the earth."*

The word that preceded this very last was, *"You shall receive power when the Holy Spirit is come upon you."* Yes, that is one of the last words: *"The Holy Spirit."* That was to be the Divine empowerment which would carry them on irresistibly to universal conquest. It would be through suffering and death, through long and patient labor, through many disappointments and trials. But the victory was sure.

The Spirit is inseparably linked to the cross. In the fellowship of the cross they could always count upon the fellowship of the Spirit and His almighty power. But alas, how soon the Church began to shrink from the cross, and without knowing it began to lose that power of the Spirit without which it was impotent to resist the power of the world. Oh that God would raise up men who could, as with a trumpet voice, sound out this last word of Christ, *"You shall receive power when the Holy Spirit is come upon you,"* and might lead the Church to return to the cross, with its Crucifixion to the world, and yield itself to the glorious task of carrying the cross in triumph to the ends of the earth.

Let us beseech our blessed Lord to write in our heart this precious last word too: The Holy Spirit.

And then comes the first of the three last words, *"Wait, Pray."* ... Jesus Christ in Heaven waits for our prayers. The world conquest waits for our prayers. It has been said —the essential task of evangelizing the world is the lifting up of the Church into "a fuller spiritual life." This lifting up of the Church waits for our prayer. Let us above everything beseech God for the Spirit of prayer. Does not the Holy Spirit of God here take the central place in these last instructions of Christ? Without faith in the promise of the Spirit, the Church will fail of her duty, and lose both the courage to pray and to testify through all the earth. Ought not everyone who desires to live for Christ and His Kingdom, to beseech God to remove that terrible blindness which hinders men from seeing that there is just one thing lacking in her work—the power of the Spirit, and just one thing required, that she fall down in intense fervent prayer to wait till she be endued with power from on high?

"Why Could We Not Cast Him Out?"

December 21st

"Then came the disciples to Jesus, and said, Why could not we cast him out? And Jesus said to them, Because of your unbelief: for truly I say to you, If you have faith as a grain of mustard seed, you shall say to this mountain, Remove hence to yonder place; and it shall remove; and nothing shall be impossible to you. However, this kind goes not out but by prayer and fasting."

—MATTHEW 17: 19 –21

The disciples felt ashamed at their not being able to cast out the evil spirit. When Christ had sent them out to do the work, they had come back rejoicing that the evil spirits were subject to them. And here, in presence of the Pharisees, they had been brought to confusion by their impotence. They felt it deeply, and asked the Master to tell them what the cause of failure was. He answered with one word: *"unbelief"*; they had not been living in communion with God and separation from the world; they had neglected prayer and fasting.

It is when the Church begins to feel the shame of the decline in membership as the loss of a power that she had in time past, and confesses that it is beyond her reach to find the cause and the cure, that she will learn to bow in penitent prayer for the Master to reveal to her the depth of the trouble, and the only way out of it.

In this chapter I want to call up three witnesses among the servants of Christ, to give evidence as to what they think of the state of affairs. Let the first be D. L. Moody. In the *Christian* of 24th December 1897, there appeared a letter to the *New York Independent* on the subject. He refers to a statement in a previous issue of that paper: that "there were over three thousand churches in the Congregational and Presbyterian bodies in the United States that did not report a single member added by profession of faith during the year." Mr. Moody then adds, "Can this be true? The thought has taken such hold of me that I cannot get it out of my mind. It is enough almost to send a thrill of horror through the soul of every true Christian. Are we all going to sit still and let this thing continue? Shall we not lift up our voice like a trumpet about this matter? What must the Son of God think of such a result of our labor as this?"

In answer to Mr. Moody, the *Independent* explains that some allowance must be made for the new churches founded within the year, for small churches without a pastor, and for others that have failed to send up any report. The editor expresses his disagreement with what Mr. Moody had said in his letter about modern criticism and other causes of the evil. And then he proceeds: "But with all this true, Mr. Moody does well to be astonished and pained at the thousands of churches which reported not a single member added by profession of the faith last year. It is enough to send a thrill of pain through the soul of every true Christian."

What ought all this to mean to the Church? Let Dr. Forsyth be the second witness. In his book, *The Cruciality of the Cross,* he writes:

> It is reported from most quarters in England that there is a serious decline in Church membership. For this several explanations are given. But it is well to face the situation, and to avoid extenuation, and if we do we may discover that the real cause is the decay, not in religious interests or sympathies, but in personal religion of a positive and experienced kind, and often in the pulpit.
>
> Religious sympathies or energies are not Christian faith. We have become familiar with the statement that there is as good Christianity outside the Churches as in. This is not quite false, but it is much more false than true. It would be true enough if Christianity meant decent living, nice ways, precious kindness, business honor, ardent philanthropy and public righteousness.
>
> But all these fine and worthy things are quite compatible with the absence of personal communion with God, personal faith as Christ claims it; in the sense of personal experience of God in Jesus Christ, personal repentance, and personal peace in Christ as our eternal life. Yet that is God's first charge on us, if Christianity be true. And it is this kind of Christianity which alone makes for a Church and its membership. Decay in membership of the Church is due to a decay of membership in Christ. Even among those who remain in active membership of our Churches, the type of religion has changed, the sense of sin can hardly be appealed to by preachers now, and to preach grace is in many (even orthodox quarters) regarded as theological obsession, and the wrong language for the hour, while justification by faith is practically obsolete.
>
> The grace of God cannot return to our preaching, or to our faith, till we recover from what has almost clean gone from our general, familiar, and current religion, what liberalism has quite lost—I mean a due sense of the holiness of God. This holiness of God is the real foundation—it is certainly the ruling interest of the Christian religion. Have our Churches lost that seal? Are we producing reform, social or theological, faster than we are producing faith? We are not seeking first the Kingdom of God and His holiness, but only carrying on with very expensive and noisy machinery a "kingdom-of-God industry." We are merely running the kingdom, and running it without the cross. We have the old trademark, but what does that matter in a dry and thirsty land where no water is, if the artesian well on our premises is growing dry?

Let us take to heart the lesson: It is the lack of positive personal religion, sometimes even in the pulpit, that explains the decline of membership.

Our third witness is the Rev. F. B. Meyer. In an address on Acts 19 and the anointing power of the Holy Spirit, he says: "There are four different planes of power—the lowest is the physical, above that is the mental, above that is the moral, and above all is the spiritual. … It is because too many ministers and too many Christian workers today are content to live upon the intellectual level, or upon the moral plane, that their work is impotent to touch the mighty stronghold of Satan."

He then tells the story of how the sons of Sceva had tried to cast out evil spirits in the name of Jesus whom Paul preached, of the answer that the evil spirit gave, "*Jesus I know, and Paul I know, but who are you?*" … and then proceeds:

> Oh, where are we? We have been praying that God would send converts to the Churches, and stop this awful ebb; still the people are leaving our Churches, and the pews are empty. We have no additions, or few, to our Churches, and, pray as we may, we cannot avert it. Why? why? Because the devil does not fear us. We have no power.

The devil masters the Church and masters the world, and here are all we powerless, and he says, "*Jesus I know, and Paul I know; who are you?*"

You remember the words of our Lord: How can you enter into a strong man's house until you have bound the strong man? We cannot spoil the house, because we have not bound the strong man. We have not bound the strong man in our own house. We do not know what it is to master the power of evil in our own hearts. How then can we rescue the men who are led captive at his will? It seems to me we have got to get back to prayer. O God, forgive us for our prayerlessness! God knows what a prayerless people we are. I do not wonder at things being as they are.

Let us learn the lesson. The decline in membership is nothing but what may be most naturally expected where the work is not done in the power of the Spirit and in prayer. The spirit of darkness that rules in the world, and with its mighty attraction draws people from Christ and His Church, is too strong for us. Nothing and none can give the victory but the Spirit of God working in us.

Would not one imagine that God's servants would be delighted to think that they have such a Divine power working in them, and with their whole heart yield to its influence? Oh, let us turn to the Master to give us, into the very depth of our hearts, the answer to the question, "*Why could we not cast this evil spirit out?*" "Because of your unbelief. You did not believe in Me and in the power of My Spirit, and with prayer and fasting seek for it."

The Supernatural

December 22nd

Christianity is nothing if it be not supernatural. It is only where that is fully realized and acted on that the true Church can flourish. Let us try and understand what the word teaches us in connection with our study of the state of the Church.

It teaches us, first of all, that Christianity is a religion that came down from Heaven and has still unceasingly to be received from there. It is ever dependent on the extent to which its believers yield themselves to the immediate operation of the Divine power. It points to God the Father and that unceasing action by which He works out everything according to the counsel of His will even to its minutest detail. He is the God Who works all in all. It points to Christ the Lord to Whom all power has been given that, just as He wrought his mighty works on earth, He may now live out and may live over again in His people the life that He lived on earth, and in the power of His resurrection do even greater works than He then did. It points to the Holy Spirit, proceeding unceasingly from the Father and the Son, and continuously working out in us God's plan according to the exceeding greatness of His power in us who believe.

Just as Israel was brought out of Egypt by a mighty hand and an outstretched arm amid great and mighty wonders, so now still the Church is upheld and guided by the omnipotent action of the Three-One God. And that not only in regard to the great events of her history or special interpositions in her experience, but in the care for every individual life, for all the work that is done from hour to hour by the feeblest of His servants.

Christianity is nothing if it be not from the beginning to the end, through all and in all, the hidden but direct and mighty energy of the living God continuing and working out the great redemption which He accomplished in His Son. Beyond all that He has given in Creation and Providence, is that special exercise of the power of the Divine life in its infinite holiness which ever works in us that likeness to Himself which is pleasing in His sight.

The Word teaches us more. We learn from it what the disposition and attitude ought to be of man towards God His Redeemer—absolute and unceasing dependence. The more faith in the revelation of the supernatural, as we have it in God's Word, is brought into exercise, the more we shall learn that the first of our virtues is to be a deep fear of God, a holy reverence in the presence of His glory, a consciousness of our impotence under the sinful accursed state which marks everything that is of nature. Humility and a sense of nothingness is the posture that becomes us. Faith in what God can do, will do, is always doing, and is waiting to do still more abundantly, becomes the unceasing habit of the soul, as unbroken in its continuity as the breathing of our lungs. What at first appeared a difficulty becomes a deep joy, the spontaneous surrender of the heart to the mighty working of God and His life within us.

To some the supernatural may appear unnatural. It is simply because they have never understood how the supernatural may become in the true sense most natural. As natural and joyous as our breathing, can be the movements of our spiritual life when God is allowed to take perfect possession. But for this there is needed the consciousness of how little our natural mind or heart can take in this Divine working. We need to learn that to know what the Divine power can work in us is beyond the reach of human wisdom. As supernatural as is the redemption and its almighty action in our life, must be the revelation of that redemption. From beginning to end, the work of grace is all, and always, and in all things, the presence of God working and dwelling in us.

The Word teaches us still more. The more fully we yield ourselves to it, the clearer will be the discovery that all the defects in our Christian life and in the Church around us are owing to this one thing—*that we have not taken our true place before this glorious God to work out in us what He has promised.* In the Church the question is evermore coming up, "What can be the reason that Christianity has so little true power and so little fulfills all the wonderful promises that it makes?" Read all the discussions that are going on, notice carefully all the plans and efforts that are suggested for enabling the Church to exercise the power it ought to have, and to influence men, either the masses of nominal Christians, or the millions of the heathen, and you will everywhere find how the thoughts and plans center in what man's wisdom can devise and his zeal and energy can accomplish. Everywhere there is the thought that if we will only keep up our courage and do our work faithfully, all must come right.

How seldom the great truth is insisted on, or pressed home, that the Holy Spirit is our only power. An entire and absolute surrender to Him is our only hope. How seldom one hears from the leaders, to whom the Church looks for its guidance, the clear and unceasing summons: Brethren, pray. We must pray more; we must pray without ceasing; Prayer will bring blessing. The measure of prayer is the measure of power. Every deeper insight into what Christianity is, into what our daily life ought to be, into what the ministry is and needs, will all lead us to the one deep conviction: *Christianity is nothing except it be supernatural.* Our Christian life and work must be a failure, except as we live deeply rooted in the power of God's inspired Word, in the power of the Holy Spirit, and in the importunate prayer to which the promise of the Father will most surely be given.

All this brings us to the last lesson our word is going to teach us: There is no hope for the restoration of the Church, no hope of its being lifted up into the abundant life that there is in Christ, and so to be fitted in holiness and strength for the work that is so urgently calling, of making Christ known to every living creature, except in our return to God. Church of Christ! GIVE GOD HIS PLACE. And take your place of absolute dependence, of unbroken fellowship, of unceasing prayer, of living, confident faith, and see if He will not turn and bless us above all that we can ask or think.

The one real lack today is a lack of spiritual life; the one great need, the realization of the constant presence and power of the Holy Spirit. Back to Divine wisdom, to the living power of Jesus Christ, back through prayer to the source of all power, must be our watchword.

How strange that what God meant to be an inconceivable privilege and honor, and the secret of all our strength for the work He has given us, absolute dependence upon Himself. Just as His Son lived in it, and went to the grave to prove how surely God will work mightily for one that gives himself up wholly to His will. How strange that this should cost us such trouble to understand and believe! Let the thought teach us the impotence and the incapacity for spiritual things which is natural to us, and bring us in a new surrender to accept of the birthright that belongs to us as His children—*the power of a Divine life in Christ through the Spirit.*

What we have seen of the state of the Church, as revealed in its neglect and indifference to Missions and its decline in membership, leads us to the inquiry as to the real cause and the true cure of the evil condition. It is all comprised in the one word. Let us hold it fast in our further study. We are naturally so inclined to listen to anything that calls forth our activities, and so ready to undertake the fulfillment of Divine commands in our own strength, that unless we are very watchful we may be deceived into the putting our hope on what will turn out to be nothing but human devices.

Supernatural! Give the word its full force. Let us cultivate with our whole heart such a sense of God's power going to work in us, such an attitude of dependence and prayer and waiting upon God, such a deep consciousness that God will work in us and the Church around us above what we can ask or think, that the deeper we enter into the grievous need of the Church and the world, the stronger may become the assurance that God is preparing us for deliverance. But remember the one condition: a habitual, unceasing, absolute dependence upon Him. He must do all. He will do all for them who wait on Him.

Fear Not, Only Believe

December 23rd

There is an easy optimism that imagines that it is faith in God, and has a right and is able to claim every promise in God's Word. It does not understand how inseparably the words "Repent" and "Believe" are bound together. It has never learned how throughout Scripture a chief element in faith in God is a sense of impotence and utter helplessness. We want to speak here, as our book closes, on the place faith must have if we are indeed to go forward in the certain hope that in our own life, in the Church around us, and specially in its ministry, God's mighty power will be manifested, in working that deep, intense, living vitality which we are longing for. If we are to appropriate the words, *"Fear not, only believe,"* as really spoken by our Lord to ourselves, we must note well the attitude of the man to whom they were first given.

We find here Jairus in great trouble; his little daughter is at the point of death. He falls at Christ's feet, and beseeches Him much to come and lay His hand on her. Jesus went with him. But all at once there was an interruption, with the woman who touched the hem of Christ's garment, and Jairus fears lest they may come too late. His worst fears are realized. There come messengers to say: "Your daughter is dead; why trouble the Master any further?" It was to such a one in deep distress, beseeching Him greatly to come, and now brought to utter hopelessness by the tidings of death, that Christ spoke the word: *"Fear not, only believe."* The soil had been broken up deep; the heart was prepared to believe; Christ's precious Word entered in and took possession.

If we are bearing the burden of a dead or a dying Church, if we are going to take part in the work of rousing her and lifting her up into the abundant life that there is in Christ, we need nothing so much as a word like this. It will bring us the joyous assurance, day by day, that Christ is with us, that He will work through us and that we can count upon Him to give the blessing.

But we must take the place that Jairus did, falling at His feet, beseeching Him greatly, graciously; and mightily to interpose. Even when the tidings come, "There is no hope, death reigns, all our efforts are in vain," we are still to be of good cheer and hold on to His word. *"Fear not, only believe,"* must be our watchword. But only—I say it once again—only to the one who tarries at Christ's feet in prayer, and looks to Him alone. There we shall learn that— throughout all Scripture—it is faith, in the midst of seeming impossibility, that waits and claims the fulfillment of the promise.

Think of Abraham, *"who waxed strong through faith, giving glory to God, being fully assured that what He had promised, He was able also to perform."* It is as we persevere in prayer, and take hold of definite promises, and beseech Him greatly to fulfill them, that we shall through every obstacle hold fast our confidence to the end. We may find that as time goes on, as the insight into the deadly state of the Church grows deeper, and as experience teaches us how very hard it is to rouse Christians to the full meaning of, and the full surrender to, the claims of Christ, our hearts will often fail us for fear and grow faint. But if we have made our covenant with Christ that we dare not go back, but are determined to hold on, we shall find that just one word from our Lord hidden in the heart, and lived on day by day, will give strength in time of greatest darkness.

Just think of the words of Christ in regard to what appears to man to be impossible. He had said of the young ruler, *"How hard it is for the rich to enter Heaven."* The disciples had said, *"Who then can be saved?"* Christ's answer was, *"With men it is impossible,"* but, He added, *"with God all things are possible."* And elsewhere He said, *"All things are possible to those who believe."* These words are a threefold cord that cannot be broken.

First, *"With men it is impossible."* It seems easy to say, and yet how difficult to realize it, and act it out. What is it that hinders the Church in this day from falling on its knees and beseeching God by His Holy Spirit to give revival? Nothing but this: we do not consider that the work that we have got to do is impossible with man. We consult, and organize, and labor, oh, so diligently, and yet the members decline by the thousands. And we cannot see that the work of winning others to become members of Christ and His Church is a work that God alone can do through us who have yielded ourselves to the Holy Spirit. What a day that would be if the Church were to fall down before God, and bow in the dust with the cry: O God, it is impossible with man.

We should then be prepared for the second lesson, *"all things are possible with God."* At first sight this word also appears easy to accept. We are so sure that there is nothing impossible with such a God. And yet when we ask whether God's servants really believe it, and in the joyful confidence that He is going to do it, wait upon Him and expect His working, we soon find out how hard it is to get such an impression of God's power and His readiness to work out in us what He has bidden us to do. God is so little of a reality to us. How few the men are who take time with God that the blessed sense of His holy presence can fill their hearts and strengthen them in their work.

Oh, all you who are beginning to take the state of the Church to heart, and to bear it as a burden before the Lord, be not surprised if you have found it a hard thing. Fully to grasp the truth in regard to the objects of your labor and your prayer, *"With God all things are possible."* Learn the lesson of bringing that blessed truth into contact with your daily prayer and your daily work. Let its light shine into your heart, on your sphere of labor, on the Church around you, on the feeblest and most hopeless part of the Church, until all your thoughts have this as their keynote, *"All things are possible with God."* He is able to rouse the Church out of her apathy, and lift Christians into the abundant life.

But now comes the third and most difficult lesson: *"All things are possible to those who believe."* It is something great to really believe that all things are possible with God. And yet the soul may be troubled as to how and when it may come. This Word of Christ throws the responsibility on ourselves. It is to us who believe that God makes all things possible. When Christ spoke that word to the father of the lunatic, the man felt so deeply his responsibility, if he should not have the needful faith, that he cried out, *"Lord, I believe; help my unbelief."* And Christ heard that prayer. ... He Who helped the father of the lunatic child, He Who said to Peter, *"I have prayed for you, that your faith fail not"*—Jesus Christ, who became man to bring us into fellowship with the omnipotent God—He will give us the confidence to believe that it is God's will: *"If you abide in Me, and My words abide in you, you shall ask what you will."* Let us live in fellowship with Christ, who spoke these words; He will enable us to receive them until they become the joy and the strength of our heart. …

As we look out upon a Church so feeble and faithless as we have seen, do let us listen to the voice of Jesus as He says, *"Fear not, only believe."* What I have already said, I say again: The Church around you may be in a dying state, with no possibility of being reached by human effort. I beseech you: look up to God; tarry before Him in prayer until stronger desire is stirred, and faith rises to link itself to His omnipotence. Believe in the power of our Lord Jesus, and in His tender relationship to you, watching over your faith. Believe in the power of the Holy Spirit, the promise of the Father, the birthright of the Church, surrounding you on every side, and longing to get possession of you and those for whom you are praying. And so let the study of the state of the Church give you a knowledge of God and a trust in Him, beyond what you have ever known or thought.

30

THE PRAYER LIFE

Chicago: Moody Press, 1912

Foreword

December 24th

A few words with regard to the origin of this book and the object with which it was written will help to put the reader into the right position for understanding its teaching. It was the outcome of a conference of ministers at Stellenbosch, South Africa, April 11–14,1912. The occasion of the conference was as follows: Professor de Vos, of our Theological Seminary, had written a letter to the ministers of our church (Dutch Reformed Church) concerning the low state of spiritual life which marked the Church (universal) generally, which, (he said), ought to lead to the inquiry as to how far that statement included our church too.

What had been said in the book, *The State of the Church*, called for deep searching of heart. He thought there could be no doubt about the truth of the statement in regard to the lack of spiritual power. He asked whether it was not time for us to come together and in God's presence to find out what might be the cause of the evil. He wrote: "If only we study the conditions in all sincerity, we shall have to acknowledge that our unbelief and sin are the cause of the lack of spiritual power; that this condition is one of sin and guilt before God, and nothing less than a direct grieving of God's Holy Spirit." His invitation met with a hearty response. Our four theological professors, with more than two hundred ministers, missionaries, and theological students, came together with the above words as the keynote of our meeting. From the very first, in the addresses there was the tone of confession as the only way to repentance and restoration.

At a subsequent meeting the opportunity was given for testimony as to what might be the sins which made the life of the Church so feeble. Some began to mention failings that they had seen in other ministers, either in conduct, or in doctrine, or in service. It was soon felt that this was not the right way; each must acknowledge that in which he himself was guilty. The Lord graciously so ordered it that we were gradually led to the sin of prayerlessness as one of the deepest roots of the evil. No one could plead himself free from this.

Nothing so reveals the defective spiritual life in minister and congregation as the lack of believing and unceasing prayer. Prayer is in very deed the pulse of the spiritual life. It is the great means of bringing to minister and people the blessing and power of Heaven. Persevering and believing prayer means a strong and an abundant life.

When once the spirit of confession began to prevail, the question arose as to whether it would be indeed possible to expect to gain the victory over all that had in the past hindered our prayer life. In smaller conferences held previously, it had been found that many were most anxious to make a new beginning and yet had not the courage to expect that they would be able to maintain that prayer life which they saw to be in accordance with the Word of God. They had often made the attempt but had failed. They did not dare to make any promise to the Lord to live and pray as he would have them; they felt it impossible.

Such confessions gradually led to the great truth, that the only power for a new prayer life is to be found in an entirely new relation to our blessed Savior. It is as we see in him the Lord who saves us from sin—the sin of prayerlessness too—and our faith yields itself to a life of closer intercourse with Him, that a life in His love and fellowship will make prayer to Him the natural expression of our soul's life.

Before we parted, many were able to testify that they were returning with new light and new hope to find in Jesus Christ strength for a new prayer life.

The Sin and Cause of Prayerlessness 1

December 25th

If conscience is to do its work, and the contrite heart is to feel its misery, it is necessary that each individual should mention his sin by name. The confession must be severely personal. In a meeting of ministers there is probably no single sin which each one of us ought to acknowledge with deeper shame—"Guilty, verily guilty"—than the sin of prayerlessness. What is it, then, that makes prayerlessness such a great sin? At first it is looked upon merely as a weakness.

There is so much talk about lack of time and all sorts of distractions that the deep guilt of the situation is not recognized. Let it be our honest desire that, for the future, the sin of prayerlessness may be to us truly sinful.

Consider, 1: *What a reproach it is to God.* There is the holy and most glorious God who invites us to come to him, to hold converse with him, to ask from him such things as we need, and to experience what a blessing there is in fellowship with him. He has created him we might find our highest glory and salvation. What use do we make of this heavenly privilege? How many there are who take only five minutes for prayer! They say that they have no time and that the heart desire for prayer is lacking; they do not know how to spend half an hour with God! It is not that they absolutely do not pray; they pray every day; but they have no joy in prayer, as a token of communion with God which shows that God is everything to them.

If a friend comes to visit them, they have time, they make time, even at the cost of sacrifice, for the sake of enjoying converse with him. Yes, they have time for everything that really interests them, but no time to practice fellowship with God and delight themselves in him! They find time for a creature who can be of service to them; but day after day, month after month passes, and there is no time to spend one hour with God. Do not our hearts begin to acknowledge what a dishonor, what a despite of God this is, that I dare to say I cannot find time for fellowship with him?

If this sin begins to appear plain to us, shall we not with deep shame cry out: "Woe is me, for I am undone, O God; be merciful to me, and forgive this awful sin of prayerlessness."

Consider further, 2: *It is the cause of a deficient spiritual life.* It is a proof that, for the most part, our life is still under the power of "the flesh". Prayer is the pulse of life; by it the doctor can tell what is the condition of the heart. The sin of prayerlessness is a proof for the ordinary Christian or minister that the life of God in the soul is in deadly sickness and weakness. Much is said and many complaints are made about the feebleness of the Church to fulfill her calling, to exercise an influence over her members, to deliver them from the power of the world, and to bring them to a life of holy consecration to God. Much is also spoken about her indifference to the millions of heathen whom Christ entrusted to her that she might make known to them His love and salvation.

What is the reason that many thousands of Christian workers in the world have not a greater influence? Nothing save this—the prayerlessness of their service. In the midst of all their zeal in the study and in the work of the Church, of all their faithfulness in preaching and conversation with the people, they lack that ceaseless prayer which has attached to it the sure promise of the Spirit and the power from on high. It is nothing but the sin of prayerlessness which is the cause of the lack of a powerful spiritual life!

Consider further, 3: *The dreadful loss which the Church suffers as a result of the prayerlessness of the minister.* It is the business of a minister to train believers up to a life of prayer; but how can a leader do this if he himself understands little the art of conversing with God and of receiving from the Holy Spirit, every day, out of heaven, abundant grace for himself and for his work? A minister cannot lead a congregation higher than he is himself. He cannot with enthusiasm point out a way, or explain a work, in which he is not himself walking or living. How many thousands of Christians there are who know next to nothing of the blessedness of prayer fellowship with God!

How many there are who know something of it and long for a further increase of this knowledge, but in the preaching of the Word they are not persistently urged to keep on till they obtain the blessing! The reason is simply and only that the minister understands so little about the secret of powerful prayer and does not give prayer the place in his service which, in the nature of the case and in the will of God, is indispensably necessary. Oh, what a difference we should notice in our congregations if ministers could be brought to see in its right light the sin of prayerlessness and were delivered from it!

Once more consider, 4: *The impossibility of preaching the gospel to all men—as we are commanded by Christ to do—so long as this sin is not overcome and cast out.* Many feel that the great need of missions is the obtaining of men and women who will give themselves to the Lord to strive in prayer for the salvation of souls. It has also been said that God is eager and able to deliver and bless the world he has redeemed, if his people were but willing, if they were but ready, to cry to him day and night But how can congregations be brought to that unless there comes first an entire change in ministers and that they begin to see that the indispensable thing is not preaching, not pastoral visitation, not church work, but fellowship with God in prayer till they are clothed with power from on high?

Oh, that all thought and work and expectation concerning the kingdom might drive us to the acknowledgement of the sin of prayerlessness! God help us to root it out! God deliver us from it through the blood and power of Christ Jesus! God teach every minister of the Word to see what a glorious place he may occupy if he first of all is delivered from this root of evils; so that with courage and joy, in faith and perseverance, he can go on with his God! The sin of prayerlessness! The Lord lay the burden of it so heavy on our hearts that we may not rest till it is taken far from us through the name and power of Jesus He will make this possible for us. …

The Sin and Cause of Prayerlessness 2

December 26th

In an elder's prayer meeting, a brother put the question: "What, then, is the cause of so much prayerlessness? Is it not unbelief?" The answer was: "Certainly; but then comes the question what is the cause of that unbelief?"

When the disciples asked the Lord Jesus: "*Why could not we cast the devil out?*" His answer was: "*Because of your unbelief.*" He went further and said: "*Howbeit this kind goes not out but by prayer and fasting*" (Matthew 17:19-21). If the life is not one of Self-denial—of fasting—that is, letting the world go; of prayer—that is, laying hold of Heaven, faith cannot be exercised.

A life lived according to the flesh and not according to the Spirit—it is in this that we find the origin of the prayerlessness of which we complain. As we came out of the meeting a brother said to me: "That is the whole difficulty; we wish to pray in the Spirit and at the same time walk after the flesh, and this is impossible."

If one is sick and desires healing, it is of prime importance that the true cause of the sickness be discovered. This is always the first step toward recovery. If the particular cause is not recognized, and attention is directed to subordinate causes, or to supposed but not real causes, healing is out of the question.

In like manner, it is of the utmost importance for us to obtain a correct insight into the cause of the sad condition of deadness and failure in prayer in the inner chamber, which should be such a blessed place for us. Let us seek to realize fully what is the root of this evil.

Scripture teaches us that there are but two conditions possible for the Christian. One is a walk according to the Spirit, the other a walk according to "the flesh". These two powers are in irreconcilable conflict with each other. So it comes to pass, in the case of the majority of Christians, that, while we thank God that they are born again through the Spirit and have received the life of God—yet their ordinary daily life is not lived according to the Spirit but according to "the flesh".

Paul writes to the Galatians: "*Are you so foolish? having begun in the Spirit, are you now made perfect by the flesh?*" (Galatians 3: 3). Their service lay in fleshly outward performances. They did not understand that where "the flesh" is permitted to influence their service of God, it soon results in open sin. So he mentions not only grave sins as the work of the flesh, such as adultery, murder, drunkenness; but also the more ordinary sins of daily life—wrath, strife, variance; and he gives the exhortation: "*Walk in the Spirit, and you shall not fulfill the lust of the flesh... If we live in the Spirit, let us also walk in the Spirit*" (Galatians 5: 16, 25). The Spirit must be honored not only as the author of a new life but also as the leader and director of our entire walk. Otherwise we are what the apostle calls "carnal'.

The majority of Christians have little understanding of this matter. They have no real knowledge of the deep sinfulness and godlessness of that carnal nature which belongs to them and to which unconsciously they yield. "God... condemned sin in the flesh" (Romans 8: 3)—in the cross of Christ. "*They that are Christ's have crucified the flesh with the affections and lusts*" (Galatians 5: 24).

The flesh cannot be improved or sanctified. "*The carnal mind is enmity against God; for it is not subject to the law of God, neither indeed can be*" (Romans 8: 7). There is no means of dealing with the flesh, save as Christ dealt with it: bearing it to the cross. "*Our old man is crucified with him*" (Romans 6: 6); so we by faith also crucify it, and regard and treat it daily as an accursed thing that finds its rightful place on the accursed cross.

It is saddening to consider how many Christians there are who seldom think or speak earnestly about the deep and immeasurable sinfulness of the flesh—"*In me (that is, in my flesh) dwells no good thing*" (Romans 7: 18). The one who truly believes this may well cry out: "*I see another law in my members ... bringing me into captivity to the law of sin... O wretched man that I am! who shall deliver me from the body of this death?*" (Romans 7: 23, 24). Happy are they who can go further and say: "*I thank God, through Jesus Christ our Lord... For the law of the Spirit of life in Christ Jesus hath made me free from the law of sin and death*" (Romans 7: 25; 8: 2). Would that we might understand God's counsels of grace for us! The flesh on the cross—the Spirit in the heart and controlling the life.

This spiritual life is too little understood or sought after; yet it is literally what God has promised and will accomplish in those who unconditionally surrender themselves to him for this purpose. Here then we have the deep root of evil as the cause of a prayerless life. The flesh can say prayers well enough, calling itself religious for so doing and thus satisfying conscience. But the flesh has no desire or strength for the prayer that strives after an intimate knowledge of God; that rejoices in fellowship with him; and that continues to lay hold of his strength.

So, finally, it comes to this, the flesh must be denied and crucified. The Christian who is still carnal has neither disposition nor strength to follow after God. He rests satisfied with the prayer of habit or custom; but the glory, the blessedness of secret prayer is a hidden thing to him, till someday his eyes are opened, and he begins to see that the flesh, in its disposition to turn away from God, is the archenemy which makes powerful prayer impossible for him.

I had once, at a conference, spoken on the subject of prayer and made use of strong expressions about the enmity of the flesh as a cause of prayerlessness. After the address, the minister's wife said that she thought I had spoken too strongly. She also had to mourn over too little desire for prayer, but she knew her heart was sincerely set on seeking God. I showed her what the Word of God said about the flesh, and that everything which prevents the reception of the Spirit is nothing else than a secret work of the flesh.

Adam was created to have fellowship with God and enjoyed it before his fall. After the fall, however, there came immediately, a deep- seated aversion to God, and he fled from him. This incurable aversion is the characteristic of the unregenerate nature and the chief cause of our unwillingness to surrender ourselves to fellowship with God in prayer. The following day she told me that God had opened her eyes; she confessed that the enmity and unwillingness of the flesh was the hidden hindrance in her defective prayer life.

O my brethren, my sisters, do not seek to find in circumstances the explanation of this prayerlessness over which we mourn; seek it where God's Word declares it to be, in the hidden aversion of the heart to a holy God. When a Christian does not yield entirely to the leading of the Spirit—and this is certainly the will of God and the work of His grace—we live, without knowing it, under the power of the flesh.

This life of the flesh manifests itself in many different ways. It appears in the hastiness of spirit, or the anger which so unexpectedly arises in you, in the lack of love for which you have so often blamed yourself; in the pleasure found in eating and drinking, about which at times your conscience has chidden you; in that seeking for your own will and honor, that confidence in your own wisdom and power, that pleasure in the world, of which you are sometimes ashamed before God. All this is life after the flesh: "*You are yet carnal*" (1 Corinthians 3: 3). That text, perhaps, disturbs you at times; you have not full peace and joy in God. I pray you take time and give an answer to the question: Have I not found here the cause of my prayerlessness, of my powerlessness to effect any change in the matter? I live in the Spirit, I have been born again, but I do not walk after the Spirit; the flesh lords it over me.

The carnal life cannot possibly pray in the spirit and power. God forgive me. The carnal life is evidently the cause of my sad and shameful prayerlessness. …

Mention was made in conference of the expression "strategic position"—used so often in reference to the great strife between the Kingdom of Heaven and the powers of darkness. When a general chooses the place from which he intends to strike the enemy, he pays most attention to those points which he thinks most important in the fight. … It is the same in the conflict between the believer and the powers of darkness. The inner chamber is the place where the decisive victory is obtained. The enemy uses all his power to lead the Christian and above all the minister, to neglect prayer. He knows that however admirable the sermon may be, however attractive the service, however faithful the pastoral visitation, none of these things can damage him or his kingdom if prayer is neglected.

When the Church shuts herself up to the power of the inner chamber, and the soldiers of the Lord have received on their knees "power from on high," then the powers of darkness will be shaken and souls will be delivered. In the Church, on the mission field, with the minister and his congregation, everything depends on the faithful exercise of the power of prayer.

I found the following in *The Christian*: Two persons quarrel over a certain point. We call them Christian and Apollyon. Apollyon notices that Christian has a certain weapon which would give him a sure victory. They meet in deadly strife, and Apollyon resolves to take away the weapon from his opponent and destroy it. For the moment the main cause of the strife has become subordinate; the great point now is who shall get possession of the weapon on which everything depends? It is of vital importance to get hold of that.

So it is in the conflict between Satan and the believer. God's child can conquer everything by prayer. Is it any wonder that Satan does his utmost to snatch that weapon from the Christian, or to hinder him in the use of it? How now does Satan hinder prayer? By temptation to postpone or curtail it, by bringing in wandering thoughts and all sorts of distractions; through unbelief and hopelessness. Happy is the prayer hero who, through it all, takes care to hold fast and use his weapon. Like our Lord in Gethsemane, the more violently the enemy attacked the more earnestly he prayed and ceased not till he had obtained the victory. …

The Fight Against Prayerlessness

December 27th

As soon as the Christian becomes convinced of his sin in this matter, his first thought is that we must begin to strive, with God's help, to gain the victory over it. But alas, we soon experience that our striving is worth little, and the discouraging thought comes over us like a wave, that such a life is not for us—we cannot continue faithful!

At conferences on the subject of prayer, held during the past years, many a minister has openly said that it seemed impossible for him to attain such a strict life. Recently I received a letter from a minister, well known for his ability and devotion, in which he writes:

As far as I am concerned, it does not seem to help me to hear too much about the life of prayer, about the strenuous exertion for which we must prepare ourselves, and about all the time and trouble and endless effort it will cost us. These things discourage me; I have so often heard them. I have time after time put them to the test, and the result has always been sadly disappointing. It does not help me to be told: "You must pray more, and hold a closer watch over yourself, and become altogether a more earnest Christian."

My reply to him was as follows: "I think in all I spoke at the conference or elsewhere, I have never mentioned exertion or struggle, because I am so entirely convinced that our efforts are futile unless we first learn how to abide in Christ by a simple faith." My correspondent said further: "The message I need is this: 'See that your relationship to your living Savior is what it ought to be. Live in His presence, rejoice in his love, rest in Him."

A better message could not be given, if it is only rightly understood. "See that your relationship to the living Savior is what it ought to be." But this is just what will certainly make it possible for one to live the life of prayer. We must not comfort ourselves with the thought of standing in a right relationship to the Lord Jesus while the sin of prayerlessness has power over us, and while we, along with the whole Church, have to complain about our feeble life which makes us unfit to pray for ourselves, for the Church, or for missions, as we ought.

But if we recognize, in the first place, that a right relationship to the Lord Jesus, above all else, includes prayer, with both the desire and power to pray according to God's will, then we have something which gives us the right to rejoice in Him and to rest in Him.

I have related this incident to point out how naturally discouragement will be the result of Self-effort and will so shut out all hope of improvement or victory. And this indeed is the condition of many Christians when called on to persevere in prayer as intercessors. They feel it is certainly something entirely beyond their reach; they have not the power for the Self-sacrifice and consecration necessary for such prayer; they shrink from the effort and struggle which will, as they suppose, make them unhappy. They have tried in the power of the flesh to conquer the flesh—a wholly impossible thing. They have endeavored by Beelzebub to cast out Beelzebub and this can never happen. It is Jesus alone who can subdue the flesh and the devil. We have spoken of a struggle which will certainly result in disappointment and discouragement. This is the effort made in our own strength.

But there is another struggle which will certainly lead to victory. The Scripture speaks of "the good fight of faith"; that is to say, a fight which springs from and is carried on by faith. We must get right conceptions about faith and stand fast in our faith. Jesus Christ is ever the author and finisher of faith. It is when we come into right relationship with him that we can be sure of the help and power he bestows. Just, then, as earnestly as we must, in the first place. say: "Do not strive in your own strength; cast yourself at the feet of the Lord Jesus, and wait upon him in the sure confidence that he is with you, and works in you"; so do we, in the second place, say: "Strive in prayer; let faith fill your heart—so will you be strong in the Lord, and in the power of his might."

An illustration will help us to understand this. A devoted Christian woman who conducted a large Bible class with zeal and success once came in trouble to her minister. In her earlier years she had enjoyed much blessing in the inner chamber, in fellowship with the Lord and His Word. But this had gradually been lost and, do what she would, she could not get right. The Lord had blessed her work, but the joy had gone out of her life. The minister asked what she had done to regain the lost blessedness. "I have done everything," said she, "that I can think of, but all in vain." He then questioned her about her experience in connection with her conversion. She gave an immediate and clear answer: "At first I spared no pains in my attempt to become better, and to free myself from sin, but it was all useless. At last I began to understand that I must lay aside all my efforts, and simply trust the Lord Jesus to bestow on me his life and peace, and he did it." "Why then," said the minister, "do you not try this again? As you go to your inner chamber, however cold and dark your heart may be, do not try in your own might to force yourself into the right attitude. Bow before him, and tell him that he sees in what a sad state you are that your only hope is in him. Trust him with a childlike trust to have mercy upon you, and wait upon him. In such a trust you are in a right relationship to him. You have nothing he has everything." Sometime later, she told the minister that his advice had helped her; she had learned that faith in the love of the Lord Jesus is the only method of getting into fellowship with God in prayer.

Do you not begin to see, my reader, that there are two kinds of warfare: The first, when we seek to conquer prayerlessness in our own strength. In that case, my advice to you is: "Give over your restlessness and effort; fall helpless at the feet of the Lord Jesus; He will speak the Word, and your soul will live." If you have done this, then, second, comes the message: "This is but the beginning of everything. It will require deep earnestness, and the exercise of all your power, and a watchfulness of the entire heart—eager to detect the least backsliding. Above all, it will require a surrender to a life of Self-sacrifice that God really desires to see in us and which he will work out for us."

31

BACK TO PENTECOST

The Fulfillment of "the Promise of the Father," Acts 1:4

London: Oliphants, ca1930

The only work of Rev. Murray published after his death.

In the School of Christ: A Forward

December 28th

In studying the conditions of Pentecost the question naturally arises what there was in the disciples that made them fit to be the chosen recipients of the wonderful gift from Heaven. It needs but little reflection, when once the question has been seriously put, to find the answer. The school through which our Lord has passed when "*He, through the eternal Spirit, offered Himself to God,*" and proved Himself worthy of receiving from the Father in glory the fullness of the Spirit to men, was the school through which they had passed too. To Him it meant that death to sin and the world was the one condition for His being made partaker of the glory of Heaven, and the fullness of the Spirit to impart to His disciples on earth.

Christ had, though they knew it not, undertaken to fit them for the gift. When they forsook all and followed Him, when they accepted His teaching to hate and even lose their own life, to deny themselves and take up their cross, to follow Him even to the shame and utter darkness of Calvary, they were in reality being prepared to sacrifice the whole world and their own life, as the one thing that would prepare them for being filled with the Spirit of their crucified and glorified Lord. When once we strive to take in the full meaning of this preparation, the entire emptying of Self, and of everything that this world can offer, we begin to understand how it is that there is often much prayer for the power of the Holy Spirit without any apparent answer. It is because the Holy Spirit claims nothing less than absolute and entire surrender, for the life of Heaven to take complete possession and exercise full mastery.

Is it not because in the Church there is so much prevailing of the spirit of the world, with its lust of the flesh, and lust of the eyes, and the pride of life, that the Holy Spirit is so little known in His blessed presence and power?

In a little book that has just been published, *When God Came*, we have some account of three of the great revivals that there have been in the Church, in which we have discovered what an extent the enjoyment of whatever pleasure this world can give has to be completely sacrificed and put away, ere the presence and the power of God can be revealed in full measure.

The first revival alluded to was that in which Francis of Assis was the leader. After struggling for two years in the dark, he cried in his heart: "Great and glorious God, and Lord Jesus, I pray, shed abroad Your light in the darkness of my mind. Be found by me, Lord, so that in all things I may act only in accordance with Your holy will." As he knelt in silence, he heard the voice of Christ speaking to him.

At once he knew what was required of him—to give up everything and follow the Crucified. He resolved to sell all his remaining possessions and leave his home for good. He spent much time in quiet contemplation and in ministering to the lepers, until one day he heard the Gospel read: "Wherever you go, preach, saying, The Kingdom of Heaven is at hand. Heal the sick, cleanse the lepers, cast out devils; freely you have received, freely give."

This is what he longed for. And his life proved most wonderfully how his surrender of all to Christ was owned and blessed by God. In the midst of a Church in which wealth and the world with its sins held rule, God used Francis to help tens of thousands of hungry, seeking souls, to bring to them the knowledge of Christ as a personal Savior, and the service of God as the one object of life.

The question arises: In how far this devotion of all his possessions, this sacrifice of everything that the world counts pleasure, was needed, to rouse others to an interest in heavenly things, and to give him that wonderful power of the Holy Spirit to carry the life and the love of Christ into the hearts of those who knew Him not? It is only as we seek an answer to this question that we shall be able to find light in regard to that other question so important to all us: What is it that hinders the power of the Spirit in the Church? What is it that will fit us as clean vessels, wholly given to Christ, for the power of the Spirit to have free course through us, to bring light to the millions that are waiting for some power to life them out of darkness into the light and joy of God.

In the second sketch we have the story of the "Friends of God" in the fourteenth century, and specially of their influence on Tauler of Strasburg. When this great preacher was at the height of his popularity, one of the friends asked him to preach a sermon—the way to attain the highest spiritual life. When he had done this, speaking of Self-surrender and renunciation as the only path to true inward holiness, the friend, after they had partaken together of the Holy Communion, told him that though his sermon contained much that was good, he himself did not live according to it. He trusted his learning and the letter of Scripture, but as yet knew nothing of the power of the Holy Spirit. Tauler's answer was: "Dear Son, I would have you know that, old as I am, I have never been spoken to in such a fashion in all my life."

The layman quietly persisted: "If you look into yourself you will, for one thing, find it out by the love of vanity and carnal ease, whereby your vessel is spoiled and made unclean. And so it comes to pass that your teaching is without savor and brings no grace. And whereas I further said that you were still in darkness, this is also true, and may be seen hereby that so few receive the grace of the Holy Spirit through your teaching."

After further talk, and hearing the layman's experience, the preacher was convinced that he had indeed been living the life of a Pharisee before God, speaking of things of which he had no experience, and binding upon others teachings of perfections which he did not follow himself. The layman counselled him to cease from preaching for a time, and retire from the world, setting before him the sufferings of our Lord.

Acting on the layman's advice, Tauler retired into his convent, and betook himself to the life of discipline and trial. For two years he struggled on, suffering terrible inward conflicts. At last one day, as he was thinking of the sufferings of Christ and how poor his life had been compared with the love of God, he was overwhelmed with contrition and exclaimed: "O merciful God, have mercy upon me, a poor sinner, for Your boundless mercy's sake, for I am not worthy that the earth should bear me." At this moment of utter breaking down, he was filled with a great trust in God, and knew that Christ had indeed power to heal his sinful soul.

When the layman came again, he told Tauler that now that he had received the light of the Holy Spirit, he could communicate it to others. When he did preach, he spoke of the love of the soul for the heavenly Bridegroom, and of the joy and rapture of union with the Beloved, with such a passionate conviction that the sermon brought light and the power of the Spirit to many, and was the beginning of a great revival which spread through the neighboring country. He had trodden the path of Self-surrender about which he had formerly merely talked, and his life was filled with the power of the Spirit as it never could have been before.

Like Francis, Tauler laid great emphasis on the need of detachment and freedom from the things of the world, the putting aside of everything that might stand between the soul and God, [for example]:

> If God is to shine in on your soul brightly without a cloud, and accomplish His noble and glorious will in you, you must be free and unencumbered by all that affords you comfort that is out of God.
>
> It is not a pitiful thing that a religious man should spend his whole industry and sole effort, and have his thoughts turned day and night on his own little doings, and should be so full of them that he can hardly properly hold converse with God?

Tauler lived eight years after this time and was the center of a great revival. And what was the reason? Simply this. He had found that his preaching was without power, that he was not converting men to God, because his own sinful Self stood between those whom he fain would help and the power of the Spirit's working. His long spiritual travail was needed because it was so hard for him to get rid of himself and to become a clear channel of God's power.

What would be the effect upon the Church today if every preacher, every Sunday school teacher, were to prove in their own experience that to be baptized with the power of the Spirit, is the right, nay more, is the bounden duty of every Christian soul.

"This is God's righteousness," said Tauler, "that He will give us to find His Kingdom by treading in Christ's footsteps in true Self-surrender and willing poorness of spirit."

The Promise of the Father

December 29th

"Wait for the promise of the Father, you shall be baptized with the Holy Spirit not many days hence."

—ACTS 1: 4, 5

When Christ came to this world to work out our redemption He received from the Father the Promise, when His work had been accomplished, of a rich reward. This was nothing less than that the Father would give to Him as Man the whole fullness of the Divine spirit to bestow on all who believed in Him. It was in the last night, on His way to the cross that He communicated to the disciples the wonderful promise, with a revelation of all the glory that the Holy Spirit would work in them. We are accustomed to think of the work of the Spirit as something that is easily understood, while we have very little apprehension of the super-natural and inconceivable blessedness of having the Spirit of God's own Son to dwell in us as our Life, our Teacher, and our Strength. Let us with holy reverence pause and consider what it implies.

Who is the Holy Spirit? He is a Person. He is the Spirit of God, He is God. He is the Third Person in the Godhead, the living bond of union between the Father and the Son. And no tongue can express the inconceivable privilege it is that this Spirit, Who searches the deep things of God, and knows all the secrets of the Trinity, should come in to us, dwell in us as in the temple of God, and pour all the love of God into our hearts. We often think of the Spirit as something that God gives us, a power or operation of the Divine Being. But no, He is much more—He is the spirit of the Father and of the son, in Whom They have Their life and love, and as such He will also be the Spirit of our life.

And what is to be His special work? The first thing that He does is, according to the teaching of our Lord in the last night, to reveal Christ Jesus in us in His indwelling and abiding presence. It was for this reason that He was called THE COMFORTER. The disciples were troubled, and their hearts filled with deep sorrow at the thought that they would lose His presence.

For the space of three years they had lived in His fellowship. It had been to them an unspeakable privilege and happiness to be His friends and companions, and enjoy the blessedness of His teaching and holy intimacy. Their hearts were in sore anguish at the very thought of losing Him, and here our Lord comes to tell them that the Holy Spirit, the very life of Godhead, would come from heaven and make Christ's presence such a reality within them that they would have Him, their beloved Lord, more near to them, more intimately and powerfully present with them than they had ever know Him upon earth.

And so, it actually happened. When the Spirit came, their hearts overflowed with the love and the joy and the abiding consciousness of Christ with them and Christ in them. And this was not to be for those alone who had lived with Him on earth, but for all who would yield themselves in undivided surrender to Him, their Master.

The second work of the Holy Spirit of which our Lord speaks is that He, as THE SPIRIT OF TRUTH, would reveal God's truth, not only be enlightening the understanding, but by making the truth a reality as life and power in their inmost being. He would, as the Spirit of wisdom and revelation, give such a Divine enlightening of the eyes that heavenly things would in very truth form a heavenly life within them.

He would especially remind them of the words Christ had spoken upon earth, so that they might have the heavenly instruction Christ had given them but with this difference, that while Christ was upon earth they were not capable of accepting and carrying out what He taught them, whereas now the Spirit would work in them in the power of the unseen world.

A third name given to the Spirit is "THE HOLY SPIRIT." He is the Spirit of God's holiness, to Whom the work is entrusted of bringing that holiness into our heart and life. The word, "holy," is only thrice used in the Old Testament in regard to the Spirit, but in the New it is almost exclusively used in regard to Him. We think of Him as the One who imparts the Divine life and holiness to all who are willing to receive Him.

It is He for Whom all souls unconsciously long to satisfy their spiritual need. It is He Who offers Himself to every living soul as a fountain of life and blessing. Unsearchable in the glory of His Divine being, He reveals Himself to all who truly long for His presence. He fills Heaven and earth with God's glory, and is yet present in very single soul, as if this were the only one. He leads God's children into their blessed heritage—the Father's love and abiding presence, and the likeness to His image. It is to the sanctification of this Spirit of holiness that we have been called.

Now comes the fourth operation of the Spirit. "*HE SHALL TESTIFY OF ME, and you shall also bear witness.*" The Spirit would first of all give witness to their being in Christ, and Christ in them (Romans 8:16). And the Spirit would then through them testify as to what Christ was for them and in them. This would be the great mark of their preaching, that they did not speak of what they had not experienced, but of what Christ had done for them. They could boldly say: "Christ has done it for me, He will do it for you."

And that would not only be true of the Apostles and teachers, but of every Christian as he told of what Christ had done for him. It was the testimony of a heavenly love filling the heart that gave such power to the message of simple and unlearned men. Heathen writers have left on record the power that such lives exercised. It was all the fulfillment of Christ's words: "*You shall receive power when the Holy Spirit comes upon you, and be My witnesses to the ends of the earth.*"

The last work of the Holy Spirit in Christ's disciples of which He spoke was—"*THE SPIRIT SHALL GLORIFY ME; He shall take of Mine, and show it unto you.*" Christ was to ascend to heaven and to be seated on the throne in the glory of the Father. The disciples could form no conception of what that glory was.

The Spirit would come forth out of that glory, and bring it, with the very joy and power of heaven, into their hearts. It was as the Conqueror over every enemy, the conqueror of all sin, that Christ was seated upon the throne. The Holy Spirit would so reveal this conquering Christ in their hearts that they themselves would be more than conquerors through Him that loved them. Their life would then indeed be what Christ had promised: "*If you love Me, keep My commandments, and My Father will love you, and I will love you, and we will come and make our abode with you.*" It is Jesus the crucified, Jesus the glorified, Whom the Spirit will glorify in us, taking of the things that are Christ's and declaring and imparting them to us.

Here we have the five-fold office of the Holy Spirit in the work He does in believers. Our Lord spoke also of the work of the Spirit on the world, in convincing men of their sin in not believing in Christ. It was this that gave the disciples the assurance that their testimony would indeed have power to break the hardest heart, and to convince of sin and of righteousness and of judgement. And if ever, as alas is so universally the case now, the Church were to allow the spirit of the world to have the mastery, then the Holy Spirit would have to perform the work which was meant for the world on God's own people, and bring them to a new conviction of sin and of righteousness and of judgment.

A careful study of the teaching of our Lord in regard to the work of the blessed Spirit will show us that there is a double relation between the Spirit and the believer. First of all, He works in all that is needed for a life of abiding in Christ and His love—a life of unceasing trust and dependence, and of absolute, unconditional obedience. And then He works further, in those who are filled with the Spirit, what is needed to make Christ know to others and to win men for Him. These are the two things that must go inseparably together: "*The one who abides in Me bears much fruit.*" The Spirit reveals Christ in His abiding presence and love as the joy and the strength of my life. And from this, flows most naturally and blessedly the power of bearing much fruit.

Let us seek, by a thoughtful and prayerful study of Christ's teaching in the last night, to realize fully the wonderful mystery of this heavenly life of love and power which the Holy Spirit is given to maintain in us. And as we feel how little the Church experiences of that power, let us in singleness of heart seek nothing less than to have the promise of the Father fulfilled to us in all its power and blessing.

The One Thing Needful

December 30th

The same Lord Who had given the great commission, "*Preach the Gospel to every creature,*" had also given as His last injunction the command: "*Tarry; go not; preach not; wait until you receive the power of the Holy Spirit coming on you.*"

The Church has, during this last century, with ever increasing seriousness of purpose sounded the Great Commission: "*Preach the Gospel to every creature,*" until it has gradually become with all earnest Christians an article of faith. Every Christian is bound to take his part in making Christ known throughout the world. That command was not meant for the disciples alone: they would within a few years all have passed away. The command was meant for all disciples, all believers, to the end of the world.

Christ meant the gift of the Spirit to be for all who believe in Him; and He counted upon it that everyone who had tasted His love would help to make that love known to others. And just as it was with this command, so it was with the promise that the Father should give the Spirit in answer to prayer. That promise is meant for every believer, and the command to wait for the promise of the Father and to yield to the Holy Spirit for the power to witness for Christ is also for everyone.

The promise of the Spirit, and the command to wait in prayer for his filling and fitting for service are meant for every child of God. And there thus rests upon every member of the Church the double responsibility; first of all, to be ready to obey the command of making Christ know to every creature, and then to wait and strive together in prayer until the fullness of the Spirit has come to us too.

But see what has happened; there are many who admit that the calling to obey the first half of the command, and to help to make the Gospel known to every creature, rests upon them, and who are willing to give their money or their aid in making that Gospel known. But they are not willing to obey the second half of the command, and to unite in fervent and unceasing prayer for the power of the Holy Spirit to enable them and the Church around them to testify in power for Christ.

Everyone can understand that it profits but little to help in making the Gospel know unless we are ready also to pray every day for the demonstration of the Spirit and of power. Everyone can understand that just as the one thing needful from God's side is the continual renewal of the gift of the Spirit, so the one thing needful on our side must be the willingness and the surrender in very deed to ask and to wait for and to expect the Spirit as the power for service.

The important question now arises: Can anything be done to rouse the Church to a right sense of the indispensable need of much, of continual, of believing prayer for the powerful manifestation of God's Spirit, first in all His children, then specially in all ministers and workers, and then in the souls that as yet do not know God? We may be sure that there is no fate ruling over us, condemning us to continue content with the present conditions. We know for certain that as God is an ocean of infinite love and compassion which He longs to pour out over us, He is as able as He is eager to work in us the great things for which His Spirit was promised.

Will it not be the beginning of the change, if each Christian will offer themselves personally to the Lord to wait upon Him, to be taught and trained as an intercessor, to plead for the great gift from Heaven? If this is indeed to come, then we need to give ourselves the time for fellowship with God, that He may sanctify us and inspire us with the desire and the courage of the first disciples….

The Great Hindrance

December 31st

We find the first answer in the words of our Lord Jesus, when His disciples asked him, "*Why could we not?*"—"*BECAUSE OF YOUR UNBELIEF.*" God's promises concerning the power of the Holy spirit, with which His servants should be endued for their work in the world, are so clear and definite that if we only had the necessary faith, the promise would assuredly be fulfilled: "*He that believes in Me, out of him shall flow rivers of living water.*"

God waits for the believing prayers of His people to give the power of the Holy Spirit in full measure. But we often lack the faith and the child-like confidence that can claim the promise. Even those who pray most earnestly acknowledge that it is hard to attain to the full assurance of faith that the blessing will come.

This brings us to the second question, a word of still deeper meaning: Why were the disciples, who had formerly cast out devils, now lacking the in the necessary faith? Christ gives us the answer: "*This kind goes not out, BUT BY PRAYER AND FASTING.*" That is to say: "You have prayed, but your prayer was not the prayer of Self-sacrifice that is so essential in the fight with the power of the Evil One." Fasting signified the sacrifice, not only of what was lawful, but of whatever tended to the gratification of the senses and occupied the mind with that which was seen and temporal. And the prayer that avails much demands Self-denial and the giving up of all that would hinder the soul in its approach to God.

David said of such prayer: "*Let my prayer be set forth before You as incense, and the lifting up of my hands as the evening sacrifice.*" The evening sacrifice was the lamb that was laid on the altar each evening as a burnt offering, to be wholly consumed by the fire. David's longing desire was that his prayer should be such a sacrifice.

Such was the prayer of our Lord when "*in the days of His flesh He offered up prayers and supplications with strong crying and tears.*" That prayer was the full surrender of His will to God. Such was the prayer of which Isaiah says: "*There is none that calls upon Your Name, that stirs up himself to take hold of You.*" The disciples too had lacked the prayer of Self-sacrifice, and so their faith had failed. Many a one who would fain pray in faith finds that he has not the power to do so, because he has not surrendered his will unreservedly to God, and he lacks the Self-denial and Self-control which are essential.

Is there not something wrong with our Christianity that God's children know so little experimentally what the prayer of faith is as a result of God's grace in the heart? We read this solemn word in Isaiah: "*When ye make many prayers I will not hear.*" Are our prayers not too often a form of words alone? God has graciously granted us blessing in the past in the conversion of souls. God's children, feel deeply that a victorious life of prayer in the Church is not more visibly manifest, or the power from on high to win souls for the Kingdom. We must ask ourselves if there is not something fundamentally wrong in the state of the Church all over the world to account for its feeble condition. May we not find an explanation in these words of Paul: "*My preaching was not in persuasive words of man's wisdom, but in the demonstration of the Spirit and of power; that your faith should not stand in the wisdom of men, but in the power of God.*"

The Reformation—as even the Reformers themselves acknowledged—was more a reformation in doctrine than in life. On the Day of Pentecost there was a complete change in the spiritual life of the disciples; the joy and the love and the holiness of Heaven came down to earth through the power of the Holy Spirit. And the preaching of the Word was manifestly "*in demonstration of the Spirit and of power.*" After the Reformation the doctrines of justification by faith and the forgiveness of sins by God alone were taught by the Church, but too often "*in persuasive words of human wisdom.*" Unfortunately, this is still the case. "*The demonstration of the Spirit and of power*" is lacking in much of our present-day preaching.

We put our trust in man's wisdom rather than in the almighty power of God. The whole education of our ministers tends to teach them to regard the preaching a good sermon as the test of a good minister. Our Lord's command was: "Tarry"—wait—do not preach—"until you are clothed with power from on high." With Him the first great need of the preacher was the baptism of the Spirit. Is this no the reason of the feebleness of the Church, that our faith is in man's wisdom more than in the power of God?

Is this not the reason that with all our efforts to believe and to pray aright we are powerless to take God's Word and hold on to it in faith? Is this not the reason why many of God's children are discouraged and deeply convinced of their own inability to pray the effectual fervent prayer that prevails with God? But there is more. Shall we not go a step further and ask: What is the teaching of God's Word by which we may regain the first joy and power of the Church of Christ? We must first learn how impossible it is for us to attain to a life of faith in our own strength or by efforts of our own. We must acknowledge our impotence, and expect God by the continual inspiration of His Holy Spirit to work in us a full and strong faith in the promises of His Word.

Notes

[1] J. Du Plessis, *The Life of Andrew Murray of South Africa* (London: Marshall, Morgan & Scott, 1919), 464–468, 499.
[2] W.M. Douglas, *Andrew Murray and His Message: One of God's Choice Saints* (Oliphants: London, 1925), 7.
[3] Augustus Warner Williams, *Life and Work of Dwight L. Moody: The Great Evangelist of the XIXth Century* (D.W. Caskey), 257–258.
[4] D. L. Pierson, ed., *Northfield Echoes, Vol II. A Report of the Northfield Conferences for 1895* (East Northfield MA: Rastall & McKinley, 1895), 619-620.
[5] Du Plessis 1919, 474.
[6] Andrew Murray, *The Spiritual Life: A Series of Lectures Delivered Before the Students of the Moody Bible Institute, Chicago* [1895] (Philadelphia: George W. Jacobs & Co., 1897).
[7] Du Plessis 1919, 64.
[8] Douglas 1925, 165-6.
[9] Douglas 1925, 166.
[10] Douglas 1925, 67.
[11] Du Plessis 1919, 448.
[12] Douglas 1925, 166.
[13] Olea Nel, *South Africa's Forgotten Revival: The Story of the Cape's Great Awakening in 1860* (Xulon: 2008), 149.
[14] Du Plessis 1919, 194-95.
[15] Nel 2008, xiv.
[16] Nel 2008, 149.
[17] Du Plessis 1919, 194.
[18] Du Plessis 1919, 448.
[19] Du Plessis 1919, 448.
[20] Andrew Murray, *The Two Covenants and the Second Blessing* (London: James Nisbet & Co., 1899).
[21] Murray 1899.
[22] Murray 1899.
[23] Du Plessis 1919, 332.
[24] Douglas 1925, 184.
[25] [Charles Cullis] *Dorothea Trudel: Or The Prayer of Faith* (London. Morgan & Scott, 1865).
[26] William Boardman, *Faith Work Under Dr. Cullis in Boston* (Boston: Willard Tract Repository, 1874).
[27] Du Plessis 1919, 338.
[28] Du Plessis 1919, 340.
[29] Du Plessis 1919, 341.
[30] Du Plessis 1919, 337
[31] Du Plessis 1919, 448.
[32] Douglas 1925, 303.
[33] William E. Boardman, *"The Lord that Healeth Thee" (Jehovah-Rophi)* (London: Morgan and Scott, 1881).
[34] Murray 1899.
[35] Douglas 1925, 304-305.
[36] Murray 1899.
[37] Du Plessis 1919, 448.
[38] Douglas 1925, 200.
[39] Du Plessis 1919, 352.
[40] Du Plessis 1919, 442-443.
[41] Du Plessis 1919, 443-444.
[42] Du Plessis 1919, 458.
[43] Du Plessis 1919, 472–473.
[44] Du Plessis 1919, 440-441.
[45] Douglas 1925, 145–6.
[46] Du Plessis 1919, 512.
[47] Du Plessis 1919, 518.

78184400R10449

Made in the USA
Columbia, SC
13 October 2017